READINGS IN LINGUISTICS I

READINGS IN LINGUISTICS I

The Development of Descriptive Linguistics in America 1925–56

FOURTH EDITION

Edited by Martin Joos

THE UNIVERSITY OF CHICAGO PRESS

CHICAGO AND LONDON

Prepared for the Committee on Language Programs of the American Council of Learned Societies

Library of Congress Catalog Card Number: 58-13036

The University of Chicago Press, Chicago & London
The University of Toronto Press, Toronto 5, Canada

Fourth Edition published 1966. Printed in the United States of America

PREFACE

The reissue of this volume by a second publisher, after three printings with progressive removal of misprints but unchanged content, comes in radically altered circumstances. In 1957 a great deal was taken for granted in American linguistics which has been called into question since. This book was first prepared simply because too much was being taken for granted. The tradition which these papers define was three decades old and still growing as rapidly as ever. Hardly anyone who counted on the American linguistic scene seemed to be outside this tradition. It is easy to name important scholars of the same tradition who are not represented in this volume; but there are other reasons for that, especially the limitations of its size.

Descriptive linguistics, as defined by these papers, seemed in 1956 to be without a serious competitor on our scene, with the natural result that too many students were accepting the current techniques without inquiring into what lay behind them. There were even beginning to be teachers of linguistic science who had missed reading some of the basic papers, now that the teachers were being recruited from among the recent students and new departments of linguistics were being set up. Today the Ph.D. in linguistics is granted on more than thirty American campuses, on roughly half of them in departments of that name; in 1940 only a handful of persons held that degree, nearly all the teachers having earned their doctorates in either anthropology or a language and having learned linguistics of the modern kind in the midst of its first strong growth. By the early 1950's, however, linguistics was an autonomous discipline. Textbooks were beginning to appear; students were becoming oriented to the deadening route of using "the book" as if books grew on trees or had been handed down from Mount Sinai. The better teachers could not always send their pupils to the original papers, because some of these were inaccessible outside the largest libraries.

In 1946 it was thought that a volume containing only the least accessible papers would serve the need; page 267 of *Language* (Vol. 22) named eight of them and promised that the Linguistic Society of America would soon issue such a volume. The plan was dropped for lack of response to the invitation to nominate other papers. The Committee on the Language Program of the American Council of Learned Societies (since renamed the Committee on Language Programs) remained aware of the problem and frequently discussed what could be done. By 1954, when I had been a member of the Committee for several years, had developed techniques for preparing such book-pages as the present volume contains, and had edited several books for the teaching of English as a foreign language for the ACLS, the Committee had arrived at a new plan for the content of the needed volume of *Readings in Linguistics*. I was directed to circulate a list of papers for possible inclusion and to ask for the help of scholars in defining the scope and purpose.

From the three dozen useful responses, it appeared that about eight hundred pages would have satisfied the sum of the well-argued demands. The impossibility of that size of book seemed evident. From the responses and the Committee's deliberations, however, a practical solution emerged quite clearly. The theme of the book would have to be the *development* rather than the exemplification of descriptive theory. One consequence was that it would have to exclude any article which reported on a single language without at the same time going beyond adequate statement into restatement via some at least partly new theoretical development. Also, the size limit forbade any further pursuit of the branches that keep leaving the main stem during the development of descriptive linguistics. Examples of such exclusion are acoustic phonetics, perception theory, semantic theory, information theory, the discourse analysis of Zellig Harris—and, since that time, the whole new trend in modern American linguistics which began as ancillary to that work and was known at first as transformational grammar. Finally, the size limit, together with the impossibility of securing permission to reprint certain crucial papers, forced omission of all papers devoted specifically to the phonology of English. This omission does no serious harm, for the lines of theoretical development from the 1920's to 1956 are still clear in the present volume.

During 1955 and 1956, I retyped most of the papers and supplied pedagogical notes to three fourths of them, added the front and back matter, and assembled the volume for the printer's cameras. What I added to the original papers is my personal responsibility; but the selection of them was done by the Committee as a whole, except that from their selection I omitted one paper of my own. All revenues from sales of the volume have gone into the linguistic funds of the American Council of Learned Societies (see page 108).

In 1957 we supposed that such a book would not remain in demand for as much as a decade with unchanged content, and postponed all decisions as to whether to let it go out of print in five years or so or to proceed to successive editions with deletion of some papers and addition of others each time. The pressure of increasing demand has forced unchanged reprinting. Additions and deletions have not been called for by the market, conceivably to some extent because of inertia, but in my belief principally because of an unforeseen factor. Both for intrinsic and for extrinsic reasons, the development of this tradition in descriptive linguistics happened to slacken just at the time when the volume first appeared.

The intrinsic reason is named in the last line of page 418, where the word *reached* was ill-advised: it should have been *touched*. The extrinsic reason is that most of the young men in the profession have turned to a new trend, what is now called generative-transformational grammar, and some of them think of it as a surely victorious competitor to our tradition. At the beginning of page 97 here, Hockett called descriptive linguistics a *classificatory* science; an excellent synonym for this is *taxonomic* linguistics, which certain proponents of the new trend use as a derogatory term. Now when anyone holds that the existence of two kinds of linguistics—taxonomic and, for example, generative-transformational—strictly implies the inferiority or even nullity of one of them, that opinion can only be pernicious no matter which of the two is denigrated. Both extreme views will fade out in due course, especially as each side reads more of what has been published by the other.

Both in such new trends and in the older ones represented in this volume, linguistics has been preeminently a young man's pursuit ever since the 1920's. Only two of our twenty-six authors had died in the thirty years before 1957. A third, Bernard Bloch, died in 1965 at the age of fifty-eight; he had published his crucial contributions by the age of forty-three. Meanwhile, he had been in the middle of it all from the age of about thirty; directly, or in a few cases indirectly, he had strongly influenced some thirty of the thirty-three papers following his first one included in this volume.

It is convenient to take Bloch as the central point for a statement of this sort, but the phenomenon was general: nearly all those same authors strongly influenced him, and they all influenced each other. To this, one detail must be added, and it is of far greater importance than I can hope to make clear. The most significant interactions among all these men were not by way of publication, but characteristically face to face: partly by letter, but mostly in each summer's Linguistic Institute, in local clubs, within working groups (see page 108 again), in social clusters and tête-à-têtes, only partly in annual meetings of the Linguistic Society of America.

Frequently an acute ear can detect all this, when the style of some paper betrays the sociable thinking that gave rise to its publication. But for the most part the origins of the papers in this volume are concealed from us in their printed form. Those origins await historical research; meanwhile, readers of this volume, and especially the younger readers, will be well advised to participate in just such conversations assiduously for several years and thus to gain an understanding of the process. That is likely to be more significant to them than the sum and sequence of the theses presented in the papers.

Here I can do no more than offer a few notes, both long notes at the ends of the majority of the papers and short insertions along the way. These are enclosed in double square brackets resembling the printer's outline-brackets here: ⟦ ⟧. There are also a good many cross-references to other pages within this volume; these are enclosed in doubled round parentheses: (( )).

Martin Joos

CONTENTS

CONTENTS

DE SAUSSURE'S SYSTEM OF LINGUISTICS

RULON S. WELLS

Word 3.1–31—1947

1. Though the Cours de linguistique générale[1] is justly credited with providing 'a theoretic foundation to the newer trend of linguistics study,'[2] it strikes the reader as very often obscure in intention, not seldom inconsistent with itself, and in the main too barren of detail to be satisfying. In short, it needs exegesis. The present study takes a cue from de Saussure's treatment of language, by treating his thought as a synchronic self-contained system.[3] It is our thesis that the solutions to most of the unclarities in the Cours can be resolved by careful internal collation of the Cours itself. Often a problem presented by a certain statement is cleared up by one or more slightly different expressions of the same idea to be found elsewhere in the book. Much of our work consists in bringing such scattered passages together. Beyond this, analysis shows how the various doctrines that de Saussure maintains are related to fundamental principles. In stating his ideas as sharply as possible, we bring to bear insights that have been gained since his day. Occasionally our interpretation leads us to venture a guess about how de Saussure would have dealt with facts or viewpoints that do not come up in the Cours.

Naturally, many of the ambiguities and inadequacies of exposition in the Cours must be attributed to the circumstances under which the work was prepared. The editors' task of integrating students' notes (not their own) on courses given in the three years 1906–7, 1908–9, and 1910–11 must have called for a good deal of adjustment in the wording and the manner of exposition. However, the main theses are expressed over and over, giving confidence that they are amply attested in the notes. Moreover, the editors occasionally indicate in footnotes points which they do not understand, or feel impelled to comment upon. This suggests that most of what they wrote had a clear basis in the notes or in their memory of discussions with de Saussure.

After the difficulties due to de Saussure's or his editors' exposition have been resolved there remain the ones inherent in the thought itself. Two evidently untenable notions we probe into at some length: the idea that the formal systematic properties of phonemes are independent of their specific quality, and the idea that a change suffered by a system (a particular language at a particular time) is never engendered by that system itself.

Our treatment falls into six sections, as follows: Phonetics, Phonemics, Historical Phonetics; Language as a Synchronic System; Langue and Parole; Linguistic Change; Critique; de Saussure as Methodologist.

Phonetics, Phonemics, Historical Phonetics

2. De Saussure distinguishes three different points of view from which speech may be studied. First, it may be studied as a set of physical-physiological events with correlated psychic events: phonation, sound-waves, audition. Second, it may be studied from the point of view of native speakers and hearers of the language to which it belongs. And third, one may study the sound-changes which a language undergoes in the course of time. Since 'bien loin que l'objet précède le point de vue, on dirait que c'est le point de vue qui crée l'objet' (23b), we may recognize three sciences, each of which studies speech in its own way: phonetics, phonemics (see §5), historical phonetics.

3. The phonational act (acte phonatoire 69a, c, 83b, 103c; cf. 65b) gives rise, in the hearer, to an acoustic image which is distinct from the physical sound (29a). Viewed as physical sounds, many words, phrases, and even whole sentences are continuous; but the acoustic images to which they give rise are not continuous but beaded, segmented, sequences of units (32b, 64a).

La délimitation des sons de la chaîne parlée ne peut donc reposer que sur l'impression acoustique; mais pour leur description, il en va autrement. Elle ne saurait être faite que sur le base de l'acte articulatoire; car les unités acoustiques prises dans leur propre chaîne sont inanalysables. Il faut recourir à la chaîne des mouvements de phonation; on remarque alors qu'au même son correspond le même acte: b (temps acoustique) = b′ (temps articulatoire). Les

[1] By Ferdinand de Saussure (1857–1913), edited posthumously by two disciples, Charles Bally and Albert Sechehaye, first edition 1916, second 1922. Our page references are to the second edition. A letter after a page number indicates the paragraph, the letter a being assigned to the beginning of the page even when the paragraph is continued from the preceding page. — A study and research fellowship from the American Council of Learned Societies has greatly encouraged and aided our work. We thank two eminent admirers of de Saussure, Professors Leonard Bloomfield and Roman Jakobson, for reading and commenting upon an earlier version of this article.

[2] L. Bloomfield, review of Sapir's Language in the Classical Weekly 15.142–3 (1922).

[3] A historical study of de Saussure's thought is in preparation.

premières unités qu'on obtient en découpant la chaîne parlée seront composées de b et b'; on les appelle phonèmes; le phonème est la somme des impressions acoustiques et des mouvements articulatoires, de l'unité entendue et de l'unité parlée, l'une conditionnant l'autre: ainsi c'est déjà une unité complexe, qui a un pied dans chaque chaîne (65b).

As for the length of these phonèmes, 'la chaîne acoustique ne se divise pas en temps égaux, mais en temps homogènes, charactérisés par l'unité d'impression' (64a).

To paraphrase: phonetics (phonologie[4]) does not treat sounds in the raw, but as broken up into segments. It must consider acoustic images as well as phonation (63b), and the reason is that only the images can yield the segments. But (and de Saussure's doctrine presumably reflects the conspicuous failure on the part of phoneticians to produce a workable analysis of sounds as such) it must return to phonation for a means of distinguishing one sound from another. This procedure will work because 'un phonème est identifié quand on a déterminé l'acte phonatoire' (69c).

4. 'La phonologie [phonetics] est en dehors du temps [cf. 135, 194b end, 202c–3c], puisque le mécanisme de l'articulation reste toujours semblable à lui-même' (56a). This differentiates it from historical phonetics, which 'se meut dans le temps' (ibid.). Moreover, 'il peut être intéressant de rechercher les causes de ces changements, et l'étude des sons nous y aidera; mais cela n'est pas essentiel: pour la science de la langue, il suffira toujours de constater les transformations de sons et de calculer leurs effets' (37a).

5. The third science that deals with sound is linguistics in the narrow sense, that is, linguistics of langue.[5] It is distinct from phonetics. 'Quand on a expliqué tous les mouvements de l'appareil vocal nécessaires pour produire chaque impression acoustique, on n'a éclairé en rien le problème de la langue. Celle-ci est un système basé sur l'opposition psychique de ces impressions acoustiques' (56b).

De Saussure nowhere differentiates a specific sub-branch of linguistics dealing with phonemes, as is usual nowadays. However, he shows (see §§20, 23, 27) that langue is made up of phonemes and morphemes, both of which form systems. Hence, it is easy to abstract the materials in the Cours which fall under phonemics, and it is convenient to do so for the purposes of exposition and comparison. But it is necessary to warn the reader that no such concept and no such term are to be found in de Saussure.

6. The trichotomy of speech-sciences into phonetics, phonemics, and historical phonetics fits neatly into the structure of de Saussure's classification. Phonetics has to do with parole (56b), phonemics with langue, and historical phonetics with the diachronic aspect. The how and why will be shown in §§23, 36, 37. Let it suffice for now to remark that according to de Saussure, phonemics is irrelevant to historical studies.

7. Before comparing de Saussure's conception of phonemes with that of the present day, we must eliminate from consideration the superficially similar notion of phonetic species (espèce phonologique).

The Appendix to the Introduction (63–95), Principes de phonologie, is an excursus dealing, not with langue like the rest of the book, but with phonetics. It incorporates material not only from the lectures of 1906–7 and 1910–11, but also from three lectures of 1897 on the theory of the syllable (63a). Regardless of what de Saussure may have said about the independence of linguistics from phonetics, he devised an original phonetic theory with the aim of making intelligible the Indo-European semivowels (79b); the excursus expounds this theory of what constitutes a syllabic, the core of a syllable.

The fundamental classification of speech-sounds is by their degree of aperture (70c); this yields seven classes: stops; spirants; nasals; liquids; i, u, ü (the semivowels 75b); e, o, ö; a. (Only the main sounds are reckoned with, 71c, 73fn., 80d, 85b.) Sounds of all classes except the a-class (80a, 81b) exist in pairs: an implosive or fermant (symbolized $\overset{>}{p}$, $\overset{>}{i}$, etc.) and an explosive or ouvrant variety ($\overset{<}{p}$, $\overset{<}{i}$, etc.) (80b, 81c; 93a). A syllabic (point vocalique) is now very simply defined as an implosion not immediately preceded by another implosion (87c; cf. the ed. note of 94b); when a second implosion follows immediately without interruption, the two implosions together form a diphthong (92b). It follows that every sound except a is capable of functioning either as syllabic or as non-syllabic; in practice, the ambivalence is mainly limited to nasals, liquids and semivowels (88a).

8. Now when we consider any minimal segment of speech, e.g. t, 'Le fragment irréductible t, pris à part, peut être considéré in abstracto, en dehors du temps. On peut parler de t en général, comme de l'espèce T (nous désignerons les espèces par des majuscules), de i comme de l'espèce I, en ne s'attachant qu'au caractère distinctif, sans se préoccuper de tout ce qui dépend de la succession dans le temps' (66a). This sounds as if species were phonemes, whose allophones we are being invited to neglect. The impression seems to be supported by the statement: 'on parle de P [the species of p-sounds] comme on parlerait d'une espèce zoologique; il y

[4] 'La physiologie des sons (all. Laut- ou Sprachphysiologie) est souvent appelée "phonétique" (all. Phonetik, angl. phonetics). Ce terme nous semble impropre; nous le remplaçons par celui de phonologie. Car phonétique a d'abord désigné et doit continuer à designer l'étude des évolutions des sons...' (55–6). This argument has not prevailed; and standard English terminology will be best preserved by translating phonologie as phonetics and phonétique as historical phonetics.

[5] We adopt langue and parole as technical terms in English.

a des exemplaires mâles et femelles, mais pas d'exemplaire idéal de l'espèce' (82b). But what can we make of it, then, when he (ibid.) calls species abstractions? We shall see (§56) how strongly he insists that phonemes are not abstract but concrete.

9. The answer is that 'phonetic species' is primarily a phonetic, not a phonemic notion. For instance, i and y are of the same phonetic species (presumably regardless of the language where they occur), and so are u and w (87d–8a, 88d–9, 92a, 93). The whole point of de Saussure's theory of the syllable is that one cannot tell just from knowing the phonetic species of a sound whether it will be syllabic or not (89c). Another matter on which the theory throws light is length by position: only an implosive consonant, not an explosive one, can make length by position (91a, b). So for phonetic purposes it is vital to distinguish implosive and explosive; and hence 'on peut dire que P n'était rien sinon une unité abstraite réunissant les caractères communs de $\overset{>}{p}$ et de $\overset{<}{p}$, qui seuls se rencontrent dans la réalité (82b)'. The great mistake of phonetics was to consider only these abstractions (82c), that is, not to consider separately implosive allophones and explosive allophones. Otherwise put, its mistake was to neglect what Sweet calls synthesis, the fact 'qu'il y a dans la langue non seulement des sons, mais des étendues de sons parlés' (77c): Therefore, 'à côté de la phonologie des espèces, il y a donc place pour une science qui prend pour point de départ les groupes binaires et les consécutions de phonèmes, et c'est tout autre chose' (78b; cf. 79). We hereinafter call these two studies analytic and synthetic phonetics respectively.

10. Several unclarities remain. If phonetic species are purely phonetic, what does de Saussure mean by their 'caractère distinctif'? Actually, de Saussure's term refers only to the kind of units that phoneticians have hitherto talked about. Now phoneticians do not distinguish sounds to the limit of discriminability; they deal with types of sounds that they call 'the s-sound', 'the front unrounded a-sound', etc. Each type includes a range of sounds, whose limits are left vague. In practice the limits are often decided by the phonemics of the languages best known to the phoneticians, particularly their native tongues. This practice accounts for many a resemblance between phonetic species and phonemes, in respect of their range of membership. De Saussure does not say this, but we, having hindsight, can see that 'phonetic species' was a mixture of phonetics and phonemics; and de Saussure does say in effect that in limiting their attention to phonetic species, phoneticians do a halfway job. Qua phonetician, de Saussure has no interest in making precise the notion of species, but only in distinguishing between implosives and explosives. And hence, pursuant to his policy of simplification (see references in §7), he does not raise such questions as 'In a language where i and y contrast and so are phonemically distinct, do they belong to the same species?' and, conversely, 'In a language where a stop and a spirant or a voiced and a voiceless stop belong to the same phoneme, do they belong to the same species?' The implication (see 71b, 84d; 87c is carelessly worded) is that one species falls wholly within one degree of aperture. But the fact that languages differ markedly in the phonetic varieties of sounds that they unite under one phoneme is not brought out by de Saussure. Occasional individual examples (e.g. 72b) may illustrate it, but the reader of the Cours would not emerge with an appreciation of it as a sweeping, general truth. Pointing it out was Franz Boas's contribution; de Saussure approached phonemics by a different route, namely by drawing the parallel between morphemic and phonemic systems.

11. De Saussure does speak (68–9) of the distinctive character of species: 'énumérer ces facteurs de production du son, ce n'est pas encore déterminer les éléments différentiels des phonèmes. Pour classer ces derniers, il importe bien moins de savoir en quoi ils consistent que ce qui les distingue les uns des autres.' But the context shows that the viewpoint is not specifically phonemic; he means merely that 'par exemple l'expiration, élément positif, mais qui intervient dans toute acte phonatoire, n'a pas de valeur différentiatrice; tandis que l'absence de résonance nasale, facteur négatif, servira, aussi bien que sa présence, à caractériser des phonèmes' (ibid.). It would do so in any language. The English *a* is as much characterized by the absence of nasalization as the French *a*, although in French but not in English there is an opposing *ã*. French š, ž, ɲ are phonetically differentiated from the other French sounds not merely by being 'back' (which is their phonemic position), but by being palatal. At least there is no denial in de Saussure, explicit or implicit, of the above interpretation; and it is sounder method to lean over backward than to read too much into him.

Outside of the Appendix, there is just one other passage where de Saussure speaks of species; this is apropos of sound-changes: 'Les exemples précédents montrent déjà que les phénomènes phonétiques, loin d'être toujours absolus, sont le plus souvent liés à des conditions déterminées; autrement dit, ce n'est pas l'espèce phonologique qui se transforme, mais le phonème tel qu'il se présente dans certaines conditions d'entourage, d'accentuation, etc.' (199b). Not analytic but only synthetic phonetics (see §9 end) can help historical phonetics.

12. It has been necessary to devote a very elaborate discussion to de Saussure's notion of phonetic species, in order to disentangle it from his genuine contribution to phonemics. *Phonème*, in the passages where we have encountered it so far, has meant simply an acoustically minimal and homogeneous segment of speech. Now de Saussure never lays down the necessary and sufficient conditions under which

two sounds are the same phoneme; therefore we cannot ascertain in what degree his sense of phoneme is similar to ours, except by squeezing what information we can from his few examples.

In the first place, the number of phonemes, unlike the number of sounds, is sharply definite (32b, 164c). In the second place, we are invited (83b, 84c) to disregard, even in phonetics, 'furtive' transitional sounds which are not perceivable by the ear [of native speakers? of trained phoneticians?]. In the third place, the existence of voiceless m and l is noted in French (72e, 74 D 1), 'mais les sujets parlants n'y voient pas un élément différentiel'—differential, presumably, from the voiced varieties. In other words, we are told to consider voiceless m, l as belonging in French to the m and l phonemes respectively. In the fourth place, the existence of free and individual variations is noted, apropos of French 'r grasseyé' and 'r roulé' (164d-5a). In the fifth place, speaking about synthetic phonetics (see §9 end), de Saussure says (78-9): 'Dès qu'il s'agit de prononcer deux sons combinés,...on est obligé de tenir compte de la discordance possible entre l'effet cherché et l'effet produit; il n'est pas toujours en notre pouvoir de prononcer ce que nous avons voulu. La liberté de lier des espèces phonologiques est limitée par la possibilité de lier les mouvements articulatoires.'

All these stray hints do not tell us the necessary and sufficient conditions for two distinguishable sounds to be assigned to the same phoneme. The concept of complementary distribution is nowhere stated, and only remotely implied. The drift of de Saussure's remarks is that two sounds (of the same dialect, let us add) belong to one phoneme if they do not convey to native hearers distinct acoustic impressions. But this means that an implosive and its corresponding explosive, being acoustically different (65 fn, 79c-80), are different phonemes, a conclusion proclaimed by de Saussure (81c). But perhaps we ought to regard the following amazing statement as a lapse: When the early Greeks distinguished between kappa and koppa, 'Il s'agissait de noter deux nuances réelles de la prononciation, le k étant tantôt palatal, tantôt vélaire; <u>d'ailleurs le koppa a disparu dans la suite</u>' (65 fn; emphasis ours).

13. If de Saussure has not told us definitely whether and when two segments belong to one phoneme, at least he plainly answers the converse question: one segment can never belong to two phonemes at once. Thus the accent of a syllabic can not be considered a separate phoneme. His stated reason is that 'la syllabe [rather <u>le point vocalique</u>, since a syllable may be more than one segment, 65a, 66a] et son accent ne constituent qu'un acte phonatoire; il n'y a pas dualité à l'intérieur de cet acte, mais seulement des oppositions diverses avec ce qui est à côté' (103c). It is surprising to find unity ascribed here to the phonational act rather than to the acoustic image (65b, 'l'unité parlée,' is not to be taken seriously, since de Saussure has told us that la chaîne parlée is broken up into units only by its correspondence with the acoustic image); but the import is the same.

14. The upshot of all the previous discussion is that a number of passages which might seem, to a hindsighted reader, adumbrations of phonemics cannot be so regarded after careful study. Yet de Saussure does make a major contribution to phonemics, greater than any of his predecessors. For his whole system is the contribution. In this system, phonemics occupies a clear place; it belongs to the system only because of its analogies with grammar. The discussion of phonemics is generally a simple transfer, mutatis mutandis, of principles of grammar proper, that is, of the relations between morphemes, and this schematizing and abstract theory, rather than any specific and particular analysis, is de Saussure's contribution to phonemics. We are thus led to an abrégé of his entire system.

<u>Language as Synchronic System</u>

15. Speech (la parole) is made up (146c; cf. 167a) of two linear sequences, each of which is articulated (26b, 156c), that is discrete. The members of the one sequence are <u>tranches de sonorité</u> (146a, 150b) which are in turn sequences of one or more phonemes (180b); and (103, 170c) two phonemes cannot occur at once (cf. §13). Now phonemes are defined as sums of acoustic images and articulatory movements; but in the synchronic study of langue (see §§33, 37), the acoustic image alone is relevant (98c). So much so that in one place de Saussure proposes, on etymological grounds, to discard the term 'phoneme'. 'C'est parce que les mots de la langue sont pour nous des images acoustiques qu'il faut éviter de parler des "phonèmes" dont ils sont composés. Ce terme, impliquant une idée d'action vocale, ne peut convenir qu'au mot parlé, à la réalisation de l'image intérieur dans le discours. En parlant des <u>sons</u> et des <u>syllabes</u> d'un mot, on évite ce malentendu, pourvu qu'on se souvienne qu'il s'agit de l'image acoustique' (98d). In practice he retains the term; but we must remember that in the passages quoted from now on, it has a more limited sense; the phoneme no longer 'has a foot in each chain' (cf. §3).

16. The other sequence composing speech is a sequence of meanings. A meaning is not a physical thing but a concept (98c). The boundaries of a <u>tranche de sonorité</u> are not marked phonemically, but only by the fact that just this much of the stream of speech is correlated with a certain meaning and the next <u>tranche</u> is correlated with another meaning (145d-6a; cf. 135a).

A <u>tranche de sonorité</u> consisting of one (180b) or more phonemes which is associated with a concept de Saussure calls a <u>signifiant</u>; the concept with which it is correlated, a <u>signifié</u>; and 'nous appelons <u>signe</u> la combinaison du concept et de l'image acoustique', (99c), 'le total résultant de l'association d'un signifiant à un signifié' (100c; cf. 32a, 99d, 144c–5). However, de Saussure does not always adhere strictly to this definition. Now and then (e.g. 159b) he applies the term sign to 'le rapport qui relie ses deux éléments'; more often (e.g. 26b, 33c, 109d twice; 208c; also 98d, 99c, 160a, 162b, where mots, which are elsewhere called signs, are treated as signifiants) he lapses into 'l'usage courant' according to which 'ce terme désigne généralement l'image acoustique seule' (99c). But a definition that conforms better to de Saussure's regular usage in practice is that a sign is neither a relation nor a combination of signifiant and of signifié, but the signifiant itself qua signifiant. In adding 'qua signifiant' we are taking note of the caution that 'si arbor est appelé signe, ce n'est qu'en tant qu'il porte le concept "arbre"' (99c), which means two facts: 1) every sign is a tranche de sonorité but not vice versa (135, 146–7); 2) if one tranche de sonorité is associated with two distinct signifiés, it constitutes two distinct, though homonymous, signs (147a, 255c; cf. 150b–1). Needless to say, the converse is also true: if one signifié is expressed by two (therefore synonymous) signifiants, these signifiants are still different signs (147c–8); this applies even to what would nowadays be regarded as morpheme alternants. See also §23. The signifié is also, for its part, sometimes called 'la signification' (158e, 159c, 160a, 162b). Our proposed emendation harmonizes with the definition (146a) of a linguistic unit (which is a linguistic entity 145c, this in turn being, 144a, a sign): 'une tranche de sonorité qui est, à l'exclusion de ce qui précède et de ce qui suit dans la chaîne parlée, le signifiant d'un certain concept' (italicized in the text).

17. Signs are the primary objects of linguistic study. Words, word-groups, and sentences are all signs—signifiants linked with signifiés (177c); but they are, in general, further analyzable into component signs. Those that are simple (not further analyzable) are the units par excellence of linguistics (145 ff.).

The term 'units' (unités) is de Saussure's own; it is obvious from their definition that the simple units are essentially the same as the morphemes of Baudouin de Courtenay and of modern linguistics, except that what we today regard as morpheme alternants, de Saussure subsumes under his broader concept of alternance (cf. §§22, 45). The term morphème was current in de Saussure's day, but with a specialized significance: the 'formative' elements of a word (affixes, endings, etc.) as opposed to the root. For clarity's sake, let us define a simple unit (=simple sign) more rigorously than he did but probably in accord with his intentions, as a sign meeting the following conditions: 1) it is an uninterrupted linear sequence of phonemes; 2) it has a meaning; 3) it is not divisible into two sequences meeting conditions 1) and 2) and such that its meaning is derived from their meanings. Thus there are two signs haiə in Southern British English: one, spelled higher, is composed of hai and -ə; the other, spelled hire, cannot be divided into parts which meet the required conditions and it is therefore a simple sign. A compound sign, i.e. an uninterrupted sequence of morphemes (no two of which occur simultaneously) is called a syntagm (170c).

18. De Saussure ascribes (100b, 103b) to linguistic signs two fundamental properties; they are arbitrary and they are arranged in a line. But he neglects to mention in this place another essential trait which figures far more prominently in his theory than linearity, to wit that linguistic signs are systematic. The characterization of langue as a deposit of signs 'passivement enregistrés' (see §31) does not mean that these signs are disordered, and simply a nomenclature (34c, 97a, 158d; cf. 162b); on the contrary, they form a very tightly knit system (26b, 29g, 32a, 43b, 107c, 124c, 149d, 154a, 157e). 'Arbitrary' and 'systematic' are the two fundamental properties of signs. A further discussion of the arbitrariness of the sign will be deferred to §§28, 44; it will suffice here to say that signs are arbitrary, according to de Saussure, in the sense that they are unmotivated (101c, 102b, 180–4): there is no natural, inherent connection between a signifiant and its signifié; any signifié could be expressed by any signifiant. This is proved a posteriori by the existence of different languages and by the fact that languages change. The same concept is equally well expressed by bœuf (which in turn came from a former bov-em) and by Ochs (100). The element of onomatopy in language is too slight to invalidate the general principle (101–2). Linguistic signs are not aptly called symbols, since 'symbol' ordinarily connotes a more or less natural non-arbitrary sign (101b).

19. Simple signs (e.g. Fr. neuf, dix, vingt) are wholly arbitrary (unmotivated), but syntagms (e.g. dix-neuf) are relatively motivated (180–4). Their motivation consists in the fact that each is related syntagmatically to its components and associatively to the other syntagms having the same pattern (182b). But this is a poor explanation of what de Saussure is driving at, since simple signs also stand both in syntagmatic and in associative relations. A better statement, we suggest, would be as follows. Let us call a class of similar syntagms a pattern. Given a syntagm S_1 consisting of morphemes M_1, M_2,...M_n, then any syntagm belongs to the same pattern as S_1 if its first morpheme belongs to the same morpheme-class as M_1, its second to the same class as M_2, and so on to M_n. Now patterns have meanings, and the meaning of a syntagm is a function of the meaning of the morphemes contained in it and of the pattern to which it belongs. From a small number of morphemes and a smaller number of patterns a very large number of sentences can be constructed; this is how we understand sentences that we have never heard before. (Cf. Bertrand Russell, An Inquiry into Meaning and

Truth 1940, pp. 11a, 34a, 238b, 306f, 386c–7). French deux-cents and cent-deux contain the same morphemes, but the pattern-meanings are different: since deux-cents means 'two hundred', the meaning of the pattern is 'multiplied by', and since cent-deux means 'one hundred and two', the meaning of its pattern is 'added to'. The meaning of a pattern is not determined simply by the order of the morphemes, because one pattern (as defined above) may have very different meanings—e.g. old men and women means either 'old men and old women' or 'women and old men'. It is important to realize that the meaning of a pattern is as arbitrary, as unmotivated as the meaning of a morpheme; the meaning of a syntagm on the other hand is motivated in that it is a function of the meanings of the morphemes and the patterns entering into it. Moreover, not every mathematically possible combination of morphemes occurs; there is the syntagm désireux but no eux-désir (190c). For these two reasons, although 'une unité telle que désireux se décompose en deux sous-unités (désir-eux),... ce ne sont pas deux parties indépendentes ajoutées simplement l'une à l'autre (désir + eux). C'est un produit, une combinaison de deux éléments solidaires, qui n'ont de valeur que par leur action réciproque dans une unité supérieure (désir × eux)' (176c; cf. 182a).

20. As we have shown (§18), a fundamental property of linguistic signs is that they are systematic. Now, de Saussure does not hold that every linguistic fact fits into a system. He holds that, as we narrow our attention from language as a whole (langage) to that part of it which is a socially acquired and passive repository in the minds of native speakers (langue), we find that langue, thus defined, is a system. What de Saussure calls parole embraces the nonsystematic elements of language. Precisely what is the difference between langue and parole, and why langue should engage the primary attention of the linguist, are points dealt with in §§30–2, 36, 37, 56.

De Saussure says, 'En déterminant...les éléments qu'elle manie, notre science remplirait sa tâche tout entière (154c). By continued and very clear implication, the elements of langue are of two kinds: signs, divided into morphemes and syntagms, and tranches de sonorité—phonemes and sequences of phonemes. In order to understand de Saussure's views about the properties and relations of phonemes, it is well to examine first his notions on the relations of signs.

21. In linguistics, 'comme en économie politique, on est en face de la notion de valeur; dans les deux sciences, il s'agit d'un système d'équivalences entre des choses d'ordres différents: dans l'une un travail et un salaire, dans l'autre un signifié et un signifiant' (115a; cf. 116b, 160a, and 164b). The linguistic analogue of economic value consists (158–60) in the relations of a sign (1) to its signifié, and (2) to other signs. (160a weighed against 159b and the diagram of 159c proves again the conclusion of §16 that in practice signe means for de Saussure 'signifiant qua signifiant.') Since value includes relations to other signs, it can change without either the sign itself changing or its relation to its signifié (166b, 179d), and different languages can have signs that have the same signifié but different values (160b–c).

Relations of a sign to other signs are again of two types (170–5): associative and syntagmatic. The relations of a sign to signs that may precede, follow or include it, and also to those included in it if it is a syntagm, are its syntagmatic relations. All these result from the fact that the signs constituting an utterance are arranged in a line; and it may be that de Saussure's insistence upon the linearity both of phonemes and of signs was for the sake of preserving the picture of language as articulated (§15). Of an entirely different type are the associative relations; a sign can recall other signs which are grammatically like it, or semantically affiliated with it, or even connected by nothing more than similarity of sound (e.g. enseignement, justement). 'Le rapport syntagmatique est in praesentia: il repose sur deux ou plusieurs termes également présents dans une série effective. Au contraire le rapport associatif unit des termes in absentia dans une série mnémonique virtuelle' (171). The two types of relation support each other (177–80); de Saussure's meaning, restated in modern terms, is that each syntagm (e.g. French défaire, Latin quadruplex) is capable of associatively recalling all the other syntagms that have the same pattern (e.g. Fr. décoller, déplacer,...; refaire, contrefaire), and that each morpheme is associatively connected with all the other signs which may replace it to form syntagms having the same pattern.

22. The want of detail in de Saussure's classification is deliberate; it is scarcely necessary to point out that a sign stands in much more intimate relations with some signs than with others. For example, there is the special kind of associative relation called by de Saussure (as also in his Mémoire of 1878, and by Baudouin de Courtenay as a borrowing therefrom) alternance (215–20; cf. §45). Again (174b–5) a sign stands in associative relations sometimes with a definite, sometimes with an indefinite number of other signs. But quite apart from this lack of detail, it would seem that there is no room in de Saussure's scheme for frequency relations, much emphasized nowadays. Perhaps he would have held that relative frequency pertains to parole, not to langue. But the bearing of frequency on linguistic change (§50) seems to oppose such an explanation.

23. The crux of de Saussure's theory, for the statement of which all the preceding exposition has been preparatory, is the role of relations in a system: Signs are constituted partly, and phonemes wholly, by their relations, that is by belonging to a system. (But cf. §53.) For them, to be is to be related.

A langue is a system of signs. Signs, therefore, are its elements. And yet, in some sense phonemes and their sequences are also elements (cf. §20. 27).

How so? 'Une suite de sons,' we are told in 144c, 'n'est linguistique que si elle est le support d'une idée; prise en elle-même, elle n'est plus que la matière d'une étude physiologique.' Ambiguous passage; for it might mean that a phonetic sequence is the object of linguistics only if it is a signifiant; or it might mean that only psychic sounds (phonemes) and their sequences (including signifiants) are linguistic because only they are supports of ideas: signifiants directly, and phonemes indirectly in that signifiants are built out of them. The former interpretation seems to be borne out by the context; yet cf. 180b: 'Un phonème joue par lui-même un rôle dans le système d'un état de langue.'

24. The important concept of opposition is treated by de Saussure in several passages:

(i) [le] signifiant linguistique ... n'est aucunement phonique, il est incorporel, constitué, non par sa substance matérielle, mais uniquement par les différences qui séparent son image acoustique de toutes les autres (164b; cf. 163a-b).

(ii) Ce principe est si essentiel qu'il s'applique à tous les éléments matériels de la langue, y compris les phonèmes.... Ce qui les caractérise, ce n'est pas, comme on pourrait le croire, leur qualité propre et positive, mais simplement le fait qu'ils ne se confondent pas entre eux. Les phonèmes sont avant tout des entités oppositives, relatives et négatives (164c).

(iii) The same is true of signifiés considered in themselves: concepts 'sont purement différentiels, définis non pas positivement par leur contenu, mais négativement par leurs rapports avec les autres termes du système. Leur plus exacte caractéristique est d'être ce que les autres ne sont pas' (162a). Trubetzkoy, La phonologie actuelle, Jour. de Psych. 1933, 233 fn 1, quotes this passage as though it applies to phonemes, but since de Saussure's view of signifiants and signifiés was the same in this respect, no misrepresentation results.

(iv) Tout ce qui précède revient à dire que dans la langue il n'y a que des différences ... sans termes positifs' (166b).

(v) But this is true only of signifiés and signifiants considered apart from each other; 'bien que le signifié et le signifiant soient, chacun pris à part, purement différentiels et négatifs, leur combinaison est un fait positif; c'est même la seule espèce de faits que comporte la langue, puisque le propre de l'institution linguistique est justement de maintenir le parallélisme entre ces deux ordres de différences' (166-7; cf. 146c, cited in §15).

(vi) In short, 'Dès que l'on compare entre eux les signes—termes positifs—on ne peut plus parler de différence; l'expression serait impropre ...; deux signes ... ne sont pas différents, ils sont seulement distincts. Entre eux il n'y a qu'opposition' (167c).

25. Let us try to find out exactly what de Saussure means by opposition. 'En grec éphēn est un imparfait et éstēn un aoriste, bien qu'ils soient formés de façon identique; c'est que le premier appartient au système de l'indicatif présent phēmi 'je dis,' tandis qu'il n'y a point de présent *stḗmi; or c'est justement le rapport phēmi-éphēn qui correspond au rapport entre le présent et l'imparfait (cf. deíknūmi -edeíknūn), etc. Ces signes agissent donc, non par leur valeur intrinsèque, mais par leur position rélative' (163-4). To quote an example from Bally, Ferdinand de Saussure et l'état actuel des études linguistiques (Lecture delivered 27 October 1913), p. 14: 'Dans chevaux la finale -ô ... a la valeur d'un pluriel parce que notre esprit l'oppose au signe -al du singulier cheval, tandis que dans tuyaux [phonemically the same as the singular tuyau] le même son -ô est dépourvu de valeur, parce que notre esprit ne l'oppose à rien.' Similarly, in the Cours, 'Le fait de synchronie est toujours significatif; il fait toujours appel à deux termes simultanés; ce n'est pas Gäste qui exprime le pluriel, mais l'opposition Gast:Gäste' (122b). And so, since 'la valeur de l'un [terme] ne résulte que de la présence simultanée des autres' (159c), ce qu'on appelle communément un "fait de grammaire" répond en dernière analyse à la définition de l'unité, car il exprime toujours une opposition de termes; seulement cette opposition se trouve être particulièrement significative, par exemple la formation du pluriel allemand du type Nacht: Nächte. Chacun des termes mis en présence dans le fait grammatical (le singulier sans umlaut et sans e final, opposé au pluriel avec umlaut et -e) est constitué lui-même par tout un jeu d'oppositions au sein du système; pris isolément, ni Nacht ni Nächte ne sont rien... Cela est si vrai qu'on pourrait fort bien aborder le problème des unités en commençant par les faits de grammaire. Posant une opposition telle que Nacht: Nächte, on se demanderait quelles sont les unités mises en jeu dans cette opposition (168b).

The oppositions of a sign are its relations, syntagmatic and associative, with other signs (180b, apropos of phonemes), and are therefore part of its value.

De Saussure goes so far as to say (vii) 'les caractères de l'unité se confondent avec l'unité elle-même. Dans la langue, comme dans tout système sémiologique, ce qui distingue un signe, voilà tout ce qui le constitue. C'est la différence qui fait le caractère, comme elle fait la valeur et l'unité' (168a).

26. We have now come to the genuine crux of de Saussure's theory.

Passage i tells us that signifiants are characterized by their differences. Now what is the difference between, say, English hit and hits, hid, hot, bit, etc.? That they are composed of different phonemes, no doubt. But ii tells us that phonemes are characterized—not by their differences—but by the fact that they are different, 'le fait qu'ils ne se confondent entre eux.' If phonemes are characterized only by being different, it does not matter how they differ; pushed to its extreme this means that only the number of distinct phonemes matters. If any or all of the elements should be respectively replaced by materially different ones, provided that the same number be preserved, the system would be the same (43b, 153d–4). There could not be two distinct systems of phonemes whose number of phonemes was the same, for if so they could differ only in some property or relation of the phonemes other than that of being different, which violates the hypothesis. On the other hand if the phonemes are characterized by their differences, then they are like signifiants as described in passage i. It is yet a third thing to say as de Saussure says of signs (vii) that they are characterized by those of their properties that are distinct, i.e. not common to all the signs, phonemes, or whatever one makes the statement about. A distinctive feature or property, a difference or distinction, and the property of being different or distinct are all three entirely distinct properties, and it is far from hyper-subtle to say this. It is not clear, even from the larger context of the whole Cours, whether ii is meant simply as a restatement of i (a rather careless one, if so), or whether it is intended to say something different about phonemes than has been said about signifiants. In 163b, we read (viii) that 'puisqu'il n'y a point d'image vocale qui réponde plus qu'une autre à ce qu'elle est chargée de dire, il est évident, même *a priori*, que jamais un fragment de langue ne pourra être fondé, en dernière analyse, sur autre chose que sur sa non-coïncidence avec le reste. *Arbitraire* et *différentiel* sont deux qualités corrélatives.' This lends color to the view that ii is meant to apply to signifiants as well as to phonemes, and that i is simply a preliminary version of it. The next paragraph says: 'la conscience ... n'aperçoit perpétuellement que la différence a/b' (163c); but the following example and comment show that 'la différence a/b' means 'the fact that a differs from b.' The total impression conveyed by all the statements is that de Saussure means to say that phonemes, signifiants and signifiés are all alike in being characterized not by their differential properties—nor by their differences—, but by their being different; but that to be different is only part of the characterization of signs. This is what he means in saying that signs are distinct, not merely different.

27. De Saussure does not consistently maintain the terminological separation between difference and distinction, nor his restriction of opposition to signs (to the exclusion of phonemes and signifiants); phonemes as well as signs enter into oppositions, and of the same two types:

Un phonème joue par lui-même un rôle dans le système d'un état de langue. Si par exemple en grec m, p, t, etc., ne peuvent jamais figurer à la fin d'un mot, cela revient à dire que leur présence ou leur absence à telle place compte dans la structure du mot et dans celle de la phrase. [For other anticipations of Trubetzkoy's concept of Grenzsignale, cf. 256c, 316b.] Or dans tous les cas de ce genre, le son isolé, comme toutes les autres unités, sera choisi à la suite d'une opposition mentale double: ainsi dans la groupe imaginaire *anma*, le son m est en opposition syntagmatique avec ceux qui l'entourent et en opposition associative avec tous ceux que l'esprit peut suggérer, soit a n m a (180b).
v
d

Let the reader thoroughly absorb this passage, for it is all that de Saussure has to say about the system of phonemes. And with this quotation we have concluded our exposition of de Saussure's direct contribution to phonemics. His greater contribution is indirect, his linguistic theory in general and his concept of synchronic systems in particular. All he has to say about phonemes is that what is true of morphemes is true mutatis mutandis of them also; but he does not indicate what the mutanda are. From the standpoint of present-day phonemics, we can see the analogues: the syntagmatic relations of phonemes are what we call their positions of occurrence, and the phonemes with which a given phoneme is associatively related are the phonemes involved in the same morphophonemes as it, and the phonemes which occur in the same position; also those which undergo similar morphophonemic changes. But of all this there is no hint in de Saussure.

28. What are the relations between the two fundamental properties of signs, their arbitrary and their systematic nature (see §18)?

'Une langue constitue un système. ... C'est le côté par lequel elle n'est pas complètement arbitraire et où il règne une raison relative' (107c, cf. 180–4, esp. 182b). We have discussed this contrast between the absolutely arbitrary and the relatively motivated in §19.

A sentence of 157c, 'Les valeurs restent entièrement relatives, et voilà pourquoi le lien de l'idée et du son est radicalement arbitraire,' makes it sound as if arbitrariness resulted from the nature of value; but this contravenes de Saussure's whole teaching, and is merely careless wording. His basic teaching may be stated as follows: (1) Signs stand in systematic relations to one another. (2) Simple signs are completely arbitrary; all that matters is that they be distinct from one another. (3) Therefore, *only* the relations of signs, i.e. their values, are relevant to the system; the systematic (relational) properties and the non-relational properties are independent of each other, they do not involve or affect each other. Signs are distinct, not merely different; this means, we take it, that not only their relations to each other but their relations to their respective signifiés are relevant and in fact essential. And all that is relevant to signifiants and to the phonemes of which they are composed is that they are different from each other. This follows from the arbitrariness of the sign (cf. 165e).

This framework of ideas is strikingly similar to the doctrine known in anthropology as functionalism, to which de Saussure comes closest in his discussion

(150–4) of synchronic identity: two materially different entities are the same as far as the system goes if and only if they have the same value (154a), that is, are characterized by the same relations.

29. By the comparative method linguists have reconstructed large parts of the vocabulary of Proto-Indo-European. This method lets us ascertain the number of phonetic elements and their combinations. Its validity, according to de Saussure, is not contingent upon our demonstration of the precise or even the rough phonetic properties, articulatory or acoustic, of these elements, though we are often in a position to do so; it is sufficient to establish the number and distinctness of these elements (302–3).

Offhand one might think that this example shows the relevance of phonemics to historical linguistics. But actually it is not part of history in the strict sense, according to de Saussure's conception. For, though no doubt linguists have ascribed to PIE features that were not in fact contemporaneous, so that our reconstruction of it does not represent a language spoken by one particular community in one particular year or even decade or century, still PIE is roughly and in the main a single language-state.

And in fact, de Saussure does not apply phonemics to problems of historical change. This is no accidentally omitted detail; it reflects his general doctrine of linguistic change: every linguistic change is isolated. A system does not engender changes within itself.

By Sapir, Bloomfield, and the Prague School, phonemics is thought to be just as relevant to problems of linguistic change as to the descriptions of languages in their momentary states. It is part of our job, therefore, to show why de Saussure holds the opposite view. This requires that we penetrate still more deeply into the groundwork of his system of thought.

Langue and Parole

30. Language (le langage), like any social phenomenon, is subject to perpetual change, and so may be analyzed at any one time into an inherited or institutional element and an element of innovation. The institutional element de Saussure calls la langue, and the innovational element la parole; by definition the two together exhaust le langage (36a, 37c, 112c).

31. Langue is (30f, 32b; cf. §18) a deposit of signs that each individual has received from other members of the same speech-community, l'ensemble des habitudes linguistiques qui permettent à un sujet de comprendre et de se faire comprendre (112c; cf 100f); in other words, it is a passively accumulated repository in relation to which each person is a hearer, not a speaker (30f, 31d). Parole, by contrast, is both active and individual (30–1); it consists of particular speech-utterances. It is (24, 30e) le côté individuel as opposed to le côté social of language. A sentence is the typical unit of parole (148c, 172c), for 'le propre de la parole, c'est la liberté des combinaisons.' More comprehensively stated (38c; 30g–1a), 'la parole ... est la somme de ce que les gens disent, et elle comprend: a) des combinaisons individuelles, dépendant de la volonté de ceux qui parlent, b) des actes de phonation également volontaires, nécessaires pour l'exécution de ces combinaisons.'

32. Langue, though described as a repository, is not to be thought of simply as a pile of words (cf. §18); the previous sections have shown clearly how it is essentially a system, to which belong not only the signs with their values but what we defined as patterns. Native speakers (excluding scholars) are ignorant of the history of their own language, which means that the history is irrelevant to the system as they know it: 'La parole n'opère jamais que sur un état de langue, et les changements qui interviennent entre les états n'y ont eux-mêmes aucune place' (127a). And 'la première chose qui frappe quand on étudie les faits de langue, c'est que pour le sujet parlant leur succession dans le temps est inexistante: il est devant un état' (117c). It follows (ibid.) that 'aussi le linguiste qui veut comprendre cet état doit-il faire table rase de tout ce qui l'a produit.' It is the business of the linguist, in describing a system, to describe just those relations of which the native speakers are aware (128c, 136a, 140c, 189b, 251b–2), though in precision and explicitness the linguist's comprehension of the system will far exceed the speaker's. There are syntagms of whose analysis the speakers are doubtful (234a, 258c), and even signs such that the speakers are doubtful whether to regard them as syntagms or as simple signs (181c). 'Autre chose est de sentir ce jeu rapide et délicat des unités, autre chose d'en rendre compte par une analyse méthodique' (148b; cf. 106b, d, 107c, 256b). This methodical analysis is grammar (141).

33. The point of view so far described is what de Saussure calls (117, 12c) synchronic linguistics, whose essence is that it considers langues one by one. In discussing it, de Saussure speaks as though it were opposed only to historical or diachronic linguistics, but actually the Cours recognizes two or possibly three non-synchronic studies, each of which considers langues two or more at a time.

34. The first such study is diachronic linguistics, which differs from the synchronic branch in taking change into account. But an immediate elucidation is needed. On the one hand, synchronic lingustics abstracts from time and change not by treating facts of different times as though they were simultaneous—doing so has been a common mistake (137b–8, 202a), sometimes deliberate (251a, 252b); but by considering a langue during a span of time too short to show any appreciable change (142b). In short, synchronic linguistics describes language-states (117a). And on the other hand, diachronic linguistics does not directly capture the process of change. De Saussure seems to have adopted the physicists' conception that change may be described as a succession of states (117a only

apparently contradicts this); diachronic linguistics, taking as its data synchronic descriptions of different states of cognate languages, infers the changes that led from the earlier states to the later ones (128a, 140d). To do this one must have ascertained the diachronic identities (249; cf. §53)—e.g. that Latin *passum* is diachronically identical with French *pas*. Diachronic identity does not imply synchronic identity, nor vice versa; *pas* 'step' and *pas* 'not' are diachronically but not synchronically identical (129b, 150b, 250a); whereas *décrépi* < Latin *de* + *crispus* and *décrépit* < Latin *decrepitus* are synchronically identical (119d; 160c; 167b, 136a). Thus diachronic linguistics arrives inferentially at the phenomena which are its special province, viz. events (117a, 129b).

35. Diachronic linguistics is achieved by two different techniques (128c, 291–4), according to the character of the data on which it operates. The *prospective* method requires as data records of two or more states of the same language, that is, such that each state is either an ancestor or a descendant of each other state; this is the method mainly used in Romance linguistics. The *regressive* (better known as the comparative) method is primarily inferential, and requires—to continue the metaphor of family-terms—that they be brothers, cousins, uncles and nephews etc. of each other; in other words, that they be only collaterally, not linearly, related. From these data it infers so far as possible the state which was the last common ancestor of all these known states. In practice, the data are usually such as to admit and require the application of both prospective and retrospective methods.

36. The langue-parole distinction entails (37c, 38e) a corresponding dichotomy of linguistics (cf. §§37, 56). Of the two branches, linguistics of langue is primary, and the main object of the Cours (39b, 317c); as we have seen, it is in turn bifurcated into synchronic and diachronic linguistics. Now by definition, langue and parole stand in a chicken-and-egg relation to each other. On the one hand, parole is based on langue (227a–b); we might restate de Saussure's idea in Aristotelian terms and say that langue is the active potentiality of producing parole. And on the other hand 'c'est la parole qui fait évoluer la langue' (37d; cf. 127a, 138c–9, 231a). More specifically, 'un fait d'évolution est toujours précédé d'un fait, ou plutôt d'une multitude de faits similaires dans la sphère de la parole; cela n'infirme en rien la distinction établie ci-dessus, elle s'en trouve même confirmée, puisque dans l'histoire de toute innovation on rencontre toujours deux moments distincts: 1° celui où elle surgit chez les individus; 2° celui où elle est devenue un fait de langue, identique extérieurement, mais adopté par la collectivité' (139a). Now since parole is the source, the *situs* of linguistic change, how does linguistics of parole differ from diachronic linguistics (of langue)? Are they not the same province under different names? De Saussure does not anticipate this question, but the answer is clearly implied. There is no necessary passage from the first of the two moments mentioned above to the second; 'toutes les innovations de la parole n'ont pas le même succès' (138c, cf. 232b). Diachronic linguistics does not take parole as its subject matter; by a comparison of earlier and later states it ascertains the changes from one to the other; and though these changes arose in parole, its concern is with the changes and not with their source. We have already (§§4, 6) pointed out how historical phonetics (which is part of diachronic linguistics) is wholly separate from the study of 'la parole y compris la phonation' (37c), which includes phonetics.

37. From the characterization of diachronic linguistics, it is clear that it rests upon synchronic descriptions (128a)—a doctrine which is the polar reversal of Hermann Paul.[6] And yet diachronic and synchronic linguistics are two radically separate enterprises.

According to de Saussure, synchronic linguistics is grammar (cf. §32 end), and (as we shall see in §§43, 44), diachronic linguistics is historical phonetics (137a, 194c, 209c, 226c, 228a, 317a). 'Qui dit grammatical dit synchronique et significatif, et comme aucun système n'est à cheval sur plusiers époques à la fois [cf. 140d, 122b], il n'y a pour nous de "grammair historique"...' (185b). What, then, says Jespersen (Linguistica 109–15; originally written 1916) have people like myself been writing about all these years, if not historical grammar? De Saussure has anticipated the question: 'Il faut s'en souvenir pour ne pas affirmer à la légère qu'on fait de la grammaire historique quand, en réalité, on se meut successivement dans la domaine diachronique, en étudiant le changement phonétique, et dans le domaine synchronique, en examinant les conséquences qui en découlent' (195d; cf. §62).

38. So much for the delineation of diachronic linguistics. There is a second non-synchronic study which may belong with it, and that is dialect-geography. De Saussure distinguishes (40–3) between internal and external linguistics, by the latter term understanding in particular (40a, 41d, cf. Bally, L'état actuel 21b) the type of studies upon 'words and things' undertaken by Meringer. The significance of the distinction is evidently methodological: 'La séparation des deux points de vue s'impose... La meilleure preuve en est que chacun d'eux crée une méthode distincte' (42–3). The following formulation, we think, expresses de Saussure's basic thought more incisively than his own characterizations do: That is internal which lets systems be studied autonomously, whether one by one or two or more at a time, without reference to anything except other linguistic systems; in short, internal linguistics of langue is *pure* linguistics of langue (cf. 143a).

6 'Es ist eingewendet, dass es noch eine andere wissenschaftliche Betrachtung der Sprache gäbe, als die geschichtliche. Ich muss das in Abrede stellen' (Prinzipien 3te Aufl., Einl. §10).

Now de Saussure relegates dialect geography to external linguistics (41c, 261a), presumably on the ground that it studies correlations between langues and something else. However, could we not consider that dialect geography is the spatial analogue of diachronic linguistics in that it considers contemporaneous cognate systems as they are arrayed in space rather than in time? There would be two significant differences: the array would have to be two-dimensional rather than one-dimensional (because isoglosses cross over each other), and there would be no direction to the array—nothing corresponding to the earlier and later of time. Of two contemporaneous dialects, one could not be singled out as cause and the other as effect. Still, inter-dialect identities could be established; this is done in phonemics by Daniel Jones's notion of diaphone. It is true that dialect geography as ordinarily conceived includes more than the pure comparison of the spatial relations of linguistic states; these other topics are truly external and would have to be separated in order that dialect geography might be regarded as part of the internal linguistics of langue. There would of course be combinations of the dialectal and the diachronic mode of comparison. We are content to have suggested this viewpoint without insisting upon it.

39. The third non-synchronic study of language is the comparison of two or more non-cognate languages (263-4; cf. 183-4), a branch of study to which de Saussure barely alludes.

Linguistic Change

40. According to the neo-grammarian picture, linguistic change consists of (1) sound-change, (2) analogy, (3) borrowing, and (4) miscellaneous minor processes, such as coinage, blending, folk-etymology, syncope, obsolescence (or, as we would put it today in more general terms, change of frequency), semantic change, syntactic change (distribution of morphemes), and perhaps sundry others. De Saussure's discussion leaves out of account the third and fourth groups of changes except for brief examples and adventitious chapters, and states (194b) that linguistic change is, in the main, phonetic change. Moreover (198a), that every linguistic change is isolated.

By the latter statement de Saussure appears to mean two things: (1) linguistic changes are not general, and (2) they are not systematic.

41. The Cours says:

Les faits diachroniques sont particuliers; le déplacement d'un système se fait sous l'action d'événements qui non seulement lui sont étrangers ..., mais qui sont isolés et ne forment pas système entre eux' (134b). [This is as true when the change is semantic as when it is phonetic.] A une certaine époque presque toutes les formes de l'ancien cas sujet ont disparu en français; n'y a-t-il pas là un ensemble de faits obéissant à la même loi? Non, car tous ne sont que les manifestations multiples d'un seul et même fait isolé. C'est la notion particulière de cas sujet qui a été atteinte et sa disparition a entraîné naturellement celle de toute une série de formes (132c).

Clearly, insofar as it applies to phonetic change, this is simply the neo-grammarian proposition 'sound-changes have no exceptions.'

When a certain phoneme or cluster of phonemes in a certain environment undergoes a certain change no matter in what words it is contained, it is easy to say that the change in the words is secondary, stemming from the primary change of the phoneme. When all the words having a certain meaning become obsolete, it is easy to say that it is primarily the meaning and only secondarily the individual words which have perished. But certain apparent embarrassments come to mind.

The Cours (130) mentions four phonetic laws concerning the passage from Indo-European to Greek: (1) voiced aspirates become voiceless aspirates; (2) initial prevocalic s becomes h; (3) final m becomes n; (4) final stops are dropped. Now (2) and (3) concern one phoneme each; but (1) concerns bh, dh, ĝh, gh, g^wh, and (4) concerns p, t, k̂ and q. Are not then (1) and (4) general? De Saussure's only answer seems to squarely avoid the issue (133b; cf. 248c):

La vraie question est de savoir si les changements phonétiques atteignent les mots ou seulement les sons; la réponse n'est pas douteuse: dans néphos, méthu, ánkhō, etc. [instances of (1)], c'est un certain phonème, une sonore aspirée indo-européenne qui se change en sourde aspirée, c'est l's initial du grec primitif qui se change en h, etc. et chacun de ces faits est isolé, indépendant des autres événements du même ordre, indépendant aussi des mots où il se produit.

But (1) and (4) are not isolated in the same sense as (2) and (3), since each of them concerns not one phoneme but a class—of five and of four phonemes respectively. One could of course go a step further and, seeking a property common to all the voiced aspirates or all the stops, say it is this which has changed. This obvious suggestion is made by the editors, 133 fn, and seems to be implicit in 203c also. Another response, in the vein of the dismissal (102) of onomatopy, would be that even though whole classes of phonemes sometimes undergo a common change, such cases are the exceptions, or at least are not the only kind, and that it is the existence of changes like (2) and (3), rather than like (1) and (4), that is noteworthy. But de Saussure's own answer is right in the quotation above. He would not have hesitated to admit that (1) and (4) are general in a sense —only not in the sense which he had in mind. In his sense, to ask whether phonetic changes are general or particular is to ask whether they 'atteignent les mots ou seulement les sons.' Phonetic changes are specific in that 'le déplacement d'un système se fait sous l'action d'événements qui ... lui sont étrangers.' (134b; cf. 133c). The point would have been much clearer if de Saussure had given some examples of what he would be prepared to call a general change, but we shall undertake to construct one. A change is particular if there is common to all the entities which exhibit this change some part or else some property which changes. But if all members of a certain class change, not by change of their common part or common property but by changes in their respectively peculiar features, the change is called general. Thus suppose that in a certain language all nouns are single morphemes and that they end in a consonant, and that the names of plants have no common feature of phonemic structure that differentiates them from other nouns; in particular that for every consonant in the language there is at least one plant-name and also at least one other noun ending in that consonant. Now suppose that in the course of time every plant-name loses its final consonant, but every other morpheme retains it. The change cannot be ascribed to the common feature of plant-names, which is semantic only; it is therefore general, and if our interpretation is correct it is this sort of change whose occurrence de Saussure denies. On the other hand, if all feminine nouns become neuter, this could be regarded as a particular (even though not a phonetic) change like the French loss of the Latin nominative or (122–3) the loss of the post-tonic syllables of Latin words.

42. De Saussure's meaning is clear when he says that linguistic changes are non-systematic, for we know what it is that he is denying. Changes do not depend on each other, they do not have value; they are brute facts. The change of bh to ph would in nowise have been affected had dh and the others remained as they were. Nor does a later change depend directly on an earlier one; the earlier one results in a certain state, and the later one then affects this state. 'La parole n'opère jamais que sur un état de langue, et les changements qui interviennent entre les états n'y ont eux-mêmes aucune place' (127a).

In 125b, de Saussure compares synchronic description with the description of a transverse cross-section of a plant-stalk, and diachronic description with the description of an axial (longitudinal) section. He tells us that the study of the transverse section 'fait constater entre les fibres certains rapports qu'on ne pourrait jamais saisir sur un plan longitudinal.' True; but the converse is also true: the tissues are as 'solidaire' in the longitudinal section as in the transverse. The analogy of the plant-section is ill-chosen to illustrate de Saussure's teaching that in studying the 'axis of successivities' 'on ne peut jamais considérer qu'une chose à la fois, mais où sont situées toutes les choses du premier axe [the 'axis of simultaneities'] avec leurs changements' (115b).

43. De Saussure admits difficulties in his thesis that all linguistic change is phonetic. Quite apart from the tremendous role of analogy (of which more anon, §§47–51), there are purely syntactical changes like the one mentioned on p. 247: the Indo-European verbal modifiers, still fairly freely placed in early Greek (e.g. óreos baínō káta 'I descend from the mountain'), came to be fastened to the verb (katabaínō óreos). 'Si donc la phonétique intervient le plus souvent par un côté quelconque dans l'évolution, elle ne peut pas l'expliquer tout entière; le facteur phonétique une fois éliminé, on trouve un résidu qui semble justifier l'idée d'une 'histoire de la grammaire"; c'est là qu'est la véritable difficulté; la distinction—qui doit être maintenue—entre le diachronique et le synchronique demanderait des explications délicates, incompatibles avec le cadre de ce cours (196–7; cf. 194c–d and 248a).

44. The concession does not imperil de Saussure's argument; for the important point is that every linguistic change is external to the synchronic system which it affects. In the first place, it is not deliberate, not motivated by the system; the arbitrariness of the sign excludes deliberateness (106b–d, 107c, 110d, 116b). 'La langue ne prémédite rien' (127b; cf. 30f). Though one sometimes speaks of langue as a convention (25c) or a contract (31d), it is not really either of these, because 'à tout instant, la solidarité avec le passé met en échec la liberté de choisir' (108b). Thus 'on arrive au principe de continuité, qui annule la liberté' (113c; cf. 34e, 101c, 102b, 104, 110d, 113c). The question about the origin of langue is meaningless, because (111c):

aucune sociéte ne connait et n'a jamais connue la langue autrement que comme un produit hérité des générations précédentes et à prendre tel quel' (105b).

Langue is not only social but bound to time (108b, 112f–3). On the other hand, when a change arises from without, 'une langue est radicalement impuissante à se défendre contre les facteurs qui déplacent d'instant en instant le rapport du signifié et du signifiant. C'est une des conséquences de l'arbitraire du signe' (110c). And such factors are constantly arising (111e–2); hence 'la continuité du signe dans le temps, liée à l'altération dans le temps, est un principe de la sémiologie générale.

45. In the second place, a linguistic change is not telic: it does not work for the benefit of the system (121c); on the contrary it disrupts it (211–13, 219d, 221a). Or, at best, by creating alternances, it merely supports a grammatical difference which already existed (219d–20). Thus, there is a French alternance eu/ou; but neuv- comes from L. nóv (accented, of novum) and nouv- from nov (accentless, of novellum); there was already a phonetic difference in Latin and it expressed a grammatical relation (216–7; cf. 215a). (By alternance de Saussure means (216c) a regular alternation, that is, one occurring in may pairs of morphemes of a certain category, not one confined to isolated pairs like French moi/me. So 'la langue est un mécanisme qui continue à fonctionner malgré les détériorations qu'on lui fait subir' (124a).

46. In the third place, a linguistic system is never modified all at once; 'ce qui domine dans toute altération, c'est la persistence de la matière ancienne; l'infidélité au passé n'est que relative. Voilà pourquoi le principe d'altération se fonde sur le principe de continuité' (109a). Specifically, only certain units, certain signs of a system are violently changed; and, by definition of value and system, their change involves a change in the values of all the other signs.

Jamais le système n'est modifié directement; en lui-même il est immuable; seuls certains éléments sont altérés sans égard à la solidarité qui les lie au tout. C'est comme si une des planètes qui gravitent autour du soleil changeait de dimensions et de poids: ce fait isolé entraînerait des conséquences générales et déplacerait l'équilibre du système solaire tout entier (121e; cf. 37a, 124d, 126c–d, 134b).

Critique

47. Of the varieties of linguistic change, only phonetic change receives extended consideration. Although de Saussure regards semantic change as being fundamentally like it in that each is 'un déplacement du rapport entre le signifié et le signifiant' (109c), it is dealt with only in passing (cf. 33 fn. 1), perhaps for that very reason.

But analogy cannot be neglected so easily. Does it not contradict everything that de Saussure has said about linguistic change? He has taught that system limits the arbitrariness of signs, and also (226c, 227b) that speakers manifest their understanding of the system by analogical creation. Then isn't analogy a change of the system which is inspired by the system itself?

48. De Saussure undercuts all these objections with one bold sweep. Analogy is not change at all, but a synchronic fact. 'L'analogie est d'ordre grammatical: elle suppose la conscience et la compréhension d'un rapport unissant les formes entre elles' (226c; cf. 226e, 227d–8). But how can he say this, especially when he notes explicitly that 'la création qui en est l'aboutissement ne peut appartenir d'abord qu'à la parole' (227a; cf. §36)? The answer is short. 'Il faut y distinguer deux choses: 1° la compréhension du rapport qui relie entre elles les formes génératrices; 2° le résultat suggéré par la comparaison, la forme improvisée par le sujet parlant pour l'expression de sa pensée. Seul ce résultat appartient à la parole' (ibid.). This result of analogy is never a simple sign, but always a syntagm which is, most often, nothing but a new arrangement of old simple signs (235c–6); 'et sa réalisation dans la parole est un fait insignifiant en comparaison de la possibilité de le former' (227c).

49. Here is another reason why analogy is not regarded as a change. When rhotacism had changed Latin honōsem to honōrem but left honōs untouched, and when honor had come into general currency alongside of honōs, on the pattern ōrātor : ōrātōrem, etc., 'au moment où naît honor, rien n'est changé puisqu'il ne remplace rien; la disparition de honōs n'est pas davantage un changement, puisque ce phénomène est indépendant du premier. Partout où l'on peut suivre la marche des événements linguistiques, on voit que l'innovation analogique et l'élimination de la forme ancienne sont deux choses distinctes et que nulle part on ne surprend une transformation' (224d–5). It is in this sense that the disappearance of the older syntagm is independent of the instituting of the new one; 'tandis que le changement phonétique n'introduit rien de nouveau sans annuler ce qui a précédé (honōrem remplace honōsem), la forme analogique n'entraîne pas nécessairement la disparition de celle qu'elle vient doubler' (224d).

50. It is true that neither honōs nor honor has been 'changed' if one declines to call generation and obsolescence change (cf. 225b–6a); the fact remains that the system has been changed, once when honor entered it and again when honōs left it (cf. 232c, 235a). Moreover, the patterns have been changed (cf. 235c, also 227b). And we see how de Saussure neglects change of frequency, just as he neglected relative frequency as a synchronic relation (cf. §22). An analogical creation, like the other innovations of parole, more often than not fails to take hold (231–2); but whether it or its older rival wins, the loser is likely to disappear (unless it is saved in a special meaning), since 'la langue répugne à maintenir deux signifiants pour une seule idée' (224d; a concomitant principle is stated 167b). Thus casually is mentioned one of the fundamental principles governing changes in relative frequency.

51. Even if analogy is synchronic, it is nevertheless clear that the system itself inspires certain innovations of parole, some of which succeed in changing the system by leading to the currency of some new terms and the obsolescence of some old ones. One can readily grant that analogical change is different in the ways named by de Saussure from phonetic change, and still contend that it is a type of change whose ultimate cause may be external to the system, but whose immediate cause is the system itself.

The fact is that de Saussure's idea of system is radically vitiated by an ambiguity. In his parlance, 'système' has two meanings: (1) state and (2) stable state, that is, equilibrium. His argument that linguistic changes always arise externally is wholly dependent upon the switch from one of these senses to another. Every language during a sufficiently short span of time is necessarily a system in the first sense; but when de Saussure says that a system never originates a change, he can only mean an equilibrium, as he himself calls it (126c, f, 154a, 169a). In a passage already quoted, he compares a language with the solar system, but as usual he does not follow his simile through. At each instant the solar system is a state, but at no time is it an equilibrium. It is at all times changing, but the changes from any prior state to a following state are caused immediately by the prior state, and can even be computed if one knows three data: the general laws of dynamics, the prior state, and either the direction of change or a sufficient number of earlier states. The original impetus was doubtless external (one of the fundamental ideas of science is that all change may be ultimately traced to an external cause), yet one change inaugurates a chain of others lasting for a shorter or longer time. Another way of expressing de Saussure's ambiguity is that in effect he assumed the effects of every linguistic change to be instantaneous. His idea seems to have been that linguistic change is like a car going uphill: it stops as soon as it is no longer actively propelled. It is quite true that he declares linguistic change to be unlimited (126e, 208–10; cf. 121c, 124d); but he simply means that one diachronically identical sign may become vastly changed by a series of phonetic changes (e.g. German je stemming from PIE aiwom), and also that phonetic change of certain signs indirectly affects other signs.

52. Can one, by an inductive study of antecedent and consequent states, establish that given states lead to given changes, regardless of the external buffets or supports to which they are subjected? Or can one make such predictions by taking into account the prior history of the system? If so, one will have founded, alongside of retrospective and of what de Saussure inaptly calls prospective linguistics, a third branch of diachronics, a truly prospective branch—predictive, let us call it, for it would enable one, given a set of linguistic states as data, to infer another state which is later than all of them. When it becomes predictive not only of the past but also of the future, linguistics will have attained the inner circle of science. In admitting that 'on ne peut pas dire d'avance jusqu'où s'étendra l'imitation d'un modèle, ni quels sont les types destinés à la provoquer' (222d), de Saussure shows that linguistics has not yet achieved this triumph. The Prague school believes that it has been able to make the beginning steps; and it is mainly because their efforts were formulated as a refutation of de Saussure's opposite view that we have analyzed the latter so carefully.

53. De Saussure teaches in effect that signs have two independent sets of properties: their values or relations (with their signifiés and with other signs) and their content or 'material envelope.' This thesis is true in a sense and in another sense not, and calls for some remarks of elucidation.

The distinction between synchronic and diachronic linguistics is methodological (115b): '[La] différence de nature entre termes successifs et termes coexistants, entre faits partiels et faits touchant le système, interdit de faire des uns et des autres la matière d'une seule science' (124d). But diachronic linguistics cannot ignore synchronic relations, for a diachronic identity (cf. §34) between a sign of state S_1 and a sign of a later state S_2 can be established only by considering both the phonemic makeup of the signs and their relations to other contemporary signs.

Furthermore, as de Saussure has pointed out at great length, a change in the content of a sign generally entails a change in its synchronic relations. This could not be so if the relations were completely independent of the 'material envelope.' However, de Saussure has nowhere implied that the independence is complete. He has only implied, by his doctrine that phonemes and signifiants are differential in function, that if one were to replace the material envelopes of all the signs of a system by any others whatsoever which would keep all those same signs phonemically distinct from each other, the relations of the signs and therefore the system would be preserved intact (see esp. 43b and 153d–4, and cf. §26).

Finally, the material envelope is relevant to the synchronic system in yet another respect. Though de Saussure points out 'la latitude dont les sujets jouissent pour la prononciation dans la limite où les sons restent distincts les uns des autres,' (164d; cf. all of 164b–6a), there are limits to this latitude, much narrower limits than mere preservation of the system would require. This is because of the continuity with the past which de Saussure has pointed out. In short, his own discussion (104–8) of the 'immutability' of the sign indicates a sense in which material envelopes as well as relations constitute the system.

De Saussure as Methodologist

54. If there is one feature of the Cours de linguistique générale which is more striking than all others, it is that it holds true to its name by dealing strictly with principles. It is clear that de Saussure was a meticulous thinker. He reexamined methodically and painstakingly the doctrines which lay at the basis of current thinking, ferreting out the tacit and hidden ones as well as testing the propositions which were daily mouthed by everyone. His conclusions he sought to weave into a coherent and almost deductive system.

55. The propositions involved in any field of inquiry are of three sorts: First, delimitations of the aims of the inquiry, characterizing the objects which it studies. Second, the description of methods. And third, the results, the statements of fact which emerge from the inquiry.

Those ideas of the Cours which we have discussed up to this point, as well as the contributions of the Mémoire and the other papers which de Saussure published in his lifetime, deal with the results of linguistics, the matters of fact. But these do not begin to exhaust the content of the Cours. For an appraisal of de Saussure's thought, the keen interest which he manifests in aims and methods has a twofold importance. In the first place, the discussions of aims and the strictures about methods that are dispersed throughout the Cours add up to a considerable portion of it; they are not intrusive, but integral, and they have influenced other thinkers. In the second place, de Saussure's method of thinking was systematic. He did not merely track down premises and consequences; he did not merely try to segregate truths of linguistics into basic principles and derived propositions. He strove to contract the group of basic principles still more and exhibit the relations between those that remained irreducible. We do not mean to say that he anticipated modern logistic method or that, like Newton and Spinoza, he emulated Euclid by casting his treatise into axioms, theorems, corollaries and lemmas. But in 100e, 103b, 104c, and other passages he signalizes propositions (that signs are arbitrary, linearly arrayed, and independent of individual volition) from which many consequences follow; and it is a good guess—though one which the pitiful meagerness of biographical data prevents us from testing—that this patient weaving of the general facts of linguistics into a fabric of premises and consequences was for de Saussure an actual method of discovery which led to many of his aperçus and to his grappling with problems not faced, and for the most part not even sensed, by previous thinkers (see Bally, L'état actuel 8d–9 and 12b).

56. De Saussure lists (20) three tasks for linguistics: to describe all languages and their histories as far as possible; to seek universal laws and forces; and 'de se délimiter et de se définir elle-même.' The brand of linguistics pursued by his predecessors from Bopp onward, he says, 'ne sait pas exactement vers quel but elle tend' (118c; cf. 16c, 18c, 20e item c, and all of 118–9b). The reason for this confusion is that the phenomena of language can be studied from different points of view. Dozens of sciences can study linguistic phenomena (20–1, 24e–5, 40–3) from as many points of view—each one putting these phenomena into relation with phenomena of some other sort. What aspect of the phenomena, if any, is left to linguistics as its exclusive property? How can language be studied not in relation to other phenomena but as the self-contained object of an autonomous science? As de Saussure himself puts it, 'Quel est l'objet à la fois intégral et concret de la linguistique?' (23). The sequel makes it clear that signs are the integral and concrete objects of linguistic study; and that by concentrating first on the synchronic systems which they form (langues), then on the diachronic relations between these systems, and lastly upon parole, linguistics will have found a rational and unifying order (23–30, esp. 25b, d; 36a, 37b; 38e, 139b), an ideal order, whether or not it prove practicable (139c–40).

Now what is the methodological significance of the quest for objects that are both integral and concrete?

57. By calling a class of phenomena or of objects 'integral' (though the word itself is not used after 24e), de Saussure means that the phenomena are all of one kind and are sufficiently unified that they may be studied by one science, that they are 'classable parmi les faits humains' (33a, 25c). Now 'tandis que le langage est hétérogène [cf. 24e, 25c, 31d, 38e], la langue ainsi délimitée est de nature homogène: c'est un système de signes où il n'y a d'essentiel que l'union du sens et de l'image acoustique, et où les deux parties du signe sont également psychiques' (32d; cf. 29a, 37c, 98b–c). It is true that the study of langue is subdivided into synchronic and diachronic linguistics; moreover, within the class of psychic entities, images are different from concepts (98c, 115a). But these diversities are nothing like the diversity within la parole 'y compris la phonation' (37c), the study of which is, therefore, psychophysical (ibid.).

58. De Saussure's idea of concreteness is less easy to establish. He uses the term 'concret' in several senses.

(1) Phonetic species are abstract whereas allophones are concrete (82b); words (e.g. the word mois 'month') are abstract whereas their alternant forms (e.g. the two liaison forms, phonetically mwa and mwaz) are concrete (147c–8; cf. 188b); form-classes, such as the genitive case, are abstract (190b, 191b) whereas the forms that belong to them are concrete. The sense in question is explicitly stated in 148c–9 of sentences: the class of sentences is abstract because there is no property common to all sentences. Consonantly, the sign is so defined that the signifiant must be just one sequence of phonemes, just as the signifié must be just one concept, one meaning. Slight variation in the shades of meaning is allowed (151a, 152b), but (255c) if one signifiant is correlated with two distinct signifiés, we must consider that there are two distinct signs. This saves the concreteness of the sign.

(2) An entity is concrete in the second sense insofar as it has instances (173b), a material realization (151b–2b). This implies, though de Saussure does not point it out, that there is a gradation from greatest concreteness to greatest abstractness. Thus, the 8:45 train from Geneva is a concrete entity, even though the material realization of it on different days need not be the same train in the physical sense. The analogs in linguistics are obvious: a phoneme is concrete because many sounds are instances of it; a signifiant is concrete because many tranches de sonorité belong to it, and so on. Langue and the signs that compose it are concrete in the second sense; '[ils] ont leur siège dans le cerveau' (32b). People sometimes use 'abstract' as synonymous with 'universal' and 'concrete' as synonymous with 'particular,' but in the present usage both abstractness and concreteness are predicated only of universals.

(3) Signs are concrete, whereas signifiants and signifiés are abstract (144; 153c, 157a), it is presumably in this sense that words are said to be concrete (158b), implying no contradiction of the other sense, in which some words are abstract. To emphasize his

point, de Saussure compares the sign to a chemical compound, such as of water out of hydrogen and oxygen (145), an inapt analogy since both hydrogen and oxygen can exist separately with properties distinct from the compound. The point seems to be that wholes are concrete whereas each of their parts, considered by itself, is abstract, and apparently de Saussure's intention is the same as when he says (162a, 166b–7) that both signifiants and signifiés are, by themselves, purely negative, differential entities whose positive qualities do not matter in the least whereas (167c; though cf. 168a) signs are positive entities which are not merely different but distinct. If one carried out this viewpoint fully, one would expect that a whole system would be concrete but its parts, the component signs, would not.

59. It is plain that in these different passages de Saussure speaks of 'concreteness' in different senses. When he says (32b) that 'la langue n'est pas moins que la parole un objet de nature concrète,' I think he means simply that it admits of being studied by itself: that is concrete (to put it paradoxically) which can be successfully studied in abstracto. His insistence that the objects of study must be concrete is in effect a critique of the neo-grammarians, as is evident from the following passage. Remarking that 'l'ancienne école [Bopp etc.] partageait les mots en racines, thèmes, suffixes, etc. et donnait à ces distinctions une valeur absolue,' he continues:

> On devait nécessairement réagir contre ces aberrations, et le mot d'ordre, très juste, fut: observez ce qui se passe dans les langues d'aujourd'hui, dans le langage de tous les jours, et n'attribuez aux périodes anciennes de la langue aucun processus, aucun phénomène qui ne soit pas constatable actuellement. [Lyell's principle of uniformitarianism, enunciated 1830 in his Principles of Geology, which had a great influence upon Darwin and others.] Et comme le plus souvent la langue vivante ne permet pas de surprendre des analyses comme en faisait Bopp, les néogrammariens, forts de leur principe, déclarent que racines, thèmes, suffixes, etc. sont de pures abstractions de notre esprit et que, si l'on en fait usage, c'est uniquement pour la commodité de l'exposition. Mais s'il n'y a pas de justification à l'établissement de ces catégories, pourquoi les établir? Et quand on le fait, au nom de quoi déclare-t-on qu'une coupure comme hípp-o-s, par exemple, est préférable à une autre comme hípp-os?
>
> L'école nouvelle, après avoir reconnu les défauts de l'ancienne doctrine, ce qui était facile, s'est contentée de la rejeter en théorie, tandis qu'en pratique elle restait comme embarrassée dans un appareil scientifique dont, malgré tout, elle ne pouvait se passer. Dès qu'on raisonne ces 'abstractions,' on voit la part de réalité qu'elles représentent, et un correctif très simple suffit pour donner à ces artifices du grammarien un sens légitime et exact. (252)

In short, roots etc. are concrete after all, not abstract: but they are relevant units primarily in diachronic, and only occasionally and accidentally in synchronic descriptions.

60. Whichever sense of concreteness he meant, there remains the task of deciding which of the various entities (morphemes, syntagms, words, phrases, sentences) are concrete. De Saussure puzzles over this task (148a–b, 149d–e, 153c, 154c, 158b) without making the ground of his perplexity clear. Is it because there are signs of which we are uncertain whether they are morphemes or syntagms (181c)? Only in part; but mainly, I think, because of difficulties in accurately defining the 'word.' On the one hand, 'le mot, malgré la difficulté qu'on a à le définir, est une unité qui s'impose à l'esprit, quelque chose de central dans le mécanisme de la langue' (154c); on the other, it does not exactly fit the definition of linguistic unit (158b)—presumably because of the existence (147c–8) of alternant forms of what we want to call one word and which, not differing in a regular manner, cannot be subsumed under de Saussure's concept (215–20) of alternation. However, he makes an attempt to characterize words: 'Un mot représente toujours une idée relativement déterminée, ou moins au point de vue grammatical' (255c); and moreover, 'tout mot qui n'est pas une unité simple et irréductible ne se distingue pas essentiellement d'un membre de phrase, d'un fait de syntaxe; l'agencement des sous-unités qui le composent obéit aux mêmes principes fondamentaux que la formation des groupes de mots' (187b; cf. 172a). This is perhaps why 'en matière de langue on s'est toujours contenté d'opérer sur des unités mal définies' (154c).

There is another problem of concreteness. Language is a social phenomenon which requires 'une masse parlante' (112–3). 'C'est un trésor déposé par la pratique de la parole dans les sujets appartenant à une même communauté, un système grammatical existant virtuellement dans chaque cerveau, ou plus exactement dans les cerveaux d'un ensemble d'individus; car la langue n'est complète dans aucun, elle n'existe parfaitement que dans la masse' (30d, emphasis ours). More specifically: 'Tous les individus ainsi reliés par le langage ... reproduiront,—non exactement sans doute, mais approximativement—les mêmes signes unis aux mêmes concepts' (29 bottom, emphasis ours). Can langue be concrete when it does not repose complete in any one individual?

Speaking of linguistic change de Saussure says it is incessant and gradual, and (296a) for this very reason there is no sense in speaking of 'mother-languages' and 'daughter-languages.' 'D'ailleurs la délimitation dans le temps n'est pas la seule difficulté que nous rencontrons dans la définition d'un état de langue; le même problème se pose à propos de l'espace' (143). That many dialects shade off into one another is set forth (275–80), but the most striking fact is not mentioned: there can be an area divided into a series of sub-areas such that people of any two adjacent sub-areas understand each other readily, but people from the two extreme sub-areas scarcely understand each other at all. What this proves is that the concept of langue is an idealized one. There are degrees of intelligibility; every one can understand some speakers better than others. Can a langue be concrete when it does not even have fixed limits? It is a montage, a composite photograph. It is not enough to admit the indefinite subdivisibility of a language into distinguishable dialects (128d; cf. 264b, 278–80). The only real solution is to admit that 'one language,' like a perfectly pure chemical or a cause without any interfering complications whatsoever, is nowhere to be met with in experience, but is an idealized construct designed to make explanation practicable; and to boldly embrace what seems to be, for de Saussure, a reluctantly wrung admission: 'La notion d'état de langue ne peut être qu'approximative. En linguistique statique, comme dans la plupart des sciences, aucune démonstration n'est possible sans une simplification conventionelle des données' (143, emphasis ours).

61. The notion of langue is the first step in making linguistics a science. It not only orders the problems of language among themselves, but it gives linguistics a place among the sciences (33d–4a): there is a science of semiology, hitherto unrecognized, (34b) 'qui étudie la vie des signes au sein de la vie sociale; elle formerait une partie de la psychologie sociale, et par conséquent de la psychologie générale.... Elle nous apprendrait en quoi consistent les signes, quelles lois les régissent' (33d). This semiology is differentiated by definition from semantics, 'qui étudie les changements de la signification' (33 fn. 1, editorial note). Sign-systems are necessarily social (34d; 112d–3, 157d), but they have their own differentia: 'la signe échappe toujours en une certaine mesure à la volonté individuelle ou sociale, c'est là son caractère essentiel' (34e). The reason is that a system of signs is strictly bound to the past (104–8, 113), as a heritage. There are constant laws of semiology (135 lines 4–5, referring to 126b); one of these is (111c) 'la continuité du signe dans le temps, liée à l'altération dans le temps.' According to de Saussure (34), semiology has never been recognized as a science, first because langue has rarely been treated as a self-contained object of study, second because people think of langue as a nomenclature, third because they study it in relation to the individual, and fourth because even when it is studied as social, the distinctive feature of sign-systems—their arbitrariness—is not sufficiently recognized.

Even if semiology includes the study of symbols, 'les signes entièrement arbitraires réalisent mieux que les autres l'idéal du procédé sémiologique; c'est pourquoi la langue, le plus complexe et le plus répandu des systèmes d'expression, est aussi le plus caractéristique de tous' (101a). To differentiate langue from other sign-systems is the business of the linguist (33e).

62. The second step in making linguistics a science is the clear-cut discrimination in principle, even when it is difficult in practice (139c) between the synchronic and diachronic branches. In attaining to this discrimination, linguistics has passed through an interesting triad of stages (118–9. Grammaire raisonnée was synchronic but normative. The nineteenth century inaugurated a phase that abandoned the prescription of norms (a last shred of prescription was the temptation to brand analogy as 'false'), but was preponderantly historical. The latest phase is to study both synchronic and diachronic linguistics, but to study both of them factually and in conscious contrast with each other.

63. Nevertheless, neither synchronic nor diachronic linguistics is able to arrive at true laws, says de Saussure. The word law is commonly used in two senses: juridical and natural (134e). A juridical or social law is imperative and general (130a); by contrast (134c) 'les faits synchroniques, quels qu'ils soient, présentent une certain régularité, mais ils n'ont aucun caractère impératif; les faits diachroniques, au contraire, s'imposent à la langue, mais ils n'ont rien de général.' Are there natural, i.e. panchronic laws 'qui se vérifient partout et toujours' (134e)? 'En linguistique comme dans le jeu d'échecs ..., il y a des règles qui survivent à tous les événements [the constant laws of semiology are instances, see §61]. Mais ce sont là des principes généraux existant indépendemment des faits concrets; dès qu'on parle de faits particuliers et tangibles, il n'y a pas de point de vue panchronique' (135).

This critique is remarkable in its oversights. We have seen de Saussure's reason for saying that diachronic facts are particular, not general. Now 'on pourra objecter que dans le fonctionnement de la parole, la loi synchronique est obligatoire, en ce sens qu'elle s'impose aux individus par la contrainte de l'usage collectif ...; sans doute; mais [emphasis ours] nous n'entendons pas le mot d'impératif dans le sens d'une obligation relative aux sujets parlants; il signifie que [emphasis de Saussure's] dans la langue aucune force ne garantit le maintien de la régularité quand elle règne sur quelque point' (131d). It is curious that de Saussure failed to think of a very simple retort which renders his critique nugatory: a juridical law itself is not imperative in this sense, for dictators, legislators, and even common consent may change laws and statutes. And as for natural laws, in no empirical science do they exist strictly 'indépendemment des faits concrets.' It is true that the statement 'intervocalic s is replaced by r' differs from the chemical proposition 'vaporized hydrochloric acid and vaporized ammonia mixed together produce a white cloud' in not being panchronic. But the other sciences of life and mind (or behavior) are in pretty much the same state. Moreover, de Saussure has said nothing to show that this deficiency is inherent in linguistics; he has adduced no reason to believe that no possible future progress will ever be able, by specifying the conditions more fully, to state panchronic laws of sound-change or of other linguistic phenomena.

64. De Saussure's critique of law brings out a general trait of his methodological viewpoint that is worth noting because it lets us draw an inference about his background. He habitually exaggerates the unique features of linguistic phenomena and the concomitant peculiar difficulties of linguistics. For example, he tells us that 'en zoologie, c'est l'animal qui s'offre dès le premier instant' whereas 'la langue présente donc ce caractère étrange et frappant de ne pas offrir d'entités perceptibles de prime abord' (149). But if the linguist is offered a multiplicity of objects—languages, utterances, words, morphemes, sounds—equally the zoologist has to contend with species, individuals, systems (the vascular system), organs (the heart), tissues, cells, and the parts of cells. The Cours (114) tells us that astronomy, geology and even political history (cf. 116d–7) do not need to be divided into a synchronic and a diachronic part, and presumably de Saussure would have said the same of zoology; but in fact zoology is divided into a synchronic and a diachronic part; indeed, into two parts each. Each species can be studied synchronically, as a fixed type, and diachronically, as a product of evolution. The diachronic study is called phylogeny. Then again, anatomy studies the members of each species in one stage of their lives (e.g. the mature adult stage), embryology their development from inception onward.

Further, de Saussure approves (25, 110e) Whitney's conception of language as a social institution, but insists upon a differentia: language is purely conventional and traditional, unlike manners, ethical institutions, economic set-ups and so on; there is no rational norm to regulate its changes either by arresting or by hastening and guiding them (105d, 106d, 110d, 116b). Later, to be sure, this broadly sweeping statement is, if not retracted, at least reinterpreted: there is no rational norm to stay or encourage the changes of simple signs (morphemes), nor the concomitant changes in syntagms, but there is a norm which can lead to further changes. And analogical remodeling is precisely the result of applying this norm.

So language is not so different from other institutions after all. And it may be asked whether de Saussure has not exaggerated the extent to which institutions other than sign systems are shaped by rational criticism, and subject to the deliberate volition of the community; and whether on the other hand, quite apart from analogy, he has not underplayed the element of natural symbolism, i.e. of onomatopy, in language.

In fine, language (le langage), the immediately given object of linguistics, is as complex as the immediately given object of zoology or of any other science, but no more so. Its complexity begets the problem of finding an object at once integral and concrete, but at the same time it also furnishes the solution. For language is an assemblage of facts some of which can be considered apart from others; this is why langue, although in one sense an abstraction, is also concrete. For it is self-contained. And it is in this sense that, to repeat a passage that we have already quoted at the beginning of our paper (§2), 'bien loin que l'objet précède le point de vue, on dirait que c'est le point de vue qui crée l'objet.'

⟦The position of de Saussure in linguistics today is very much like that of Ibsen in the drama. Only now and then is he spoken of, and then in a ritualistic way. The innocent bystander or the neophyte gets the impression that this or that detail derives from him and that all else, for which he is customarily not cited, is independent of him. Actually the inverse of this would be nearer the truth. His contribution is rather a whole mode of thought, a whole structure of interests and values, within which all the central discussions of linguistics today remain—only the marginal interests, such as glottochronology or information theory, escape this thought-world. On the other hand, most details of his doctrine have been replaced by others. Thus it is in general possible to say, of any single paragraph of a modern linguistic treatise, both 'This is de Saussure' and 'This is not de Saussure' with reference to the same doctrine.

He is most often cited for two ideas. One is the positing of two realms of being to which language belongs: 'langue' and 'parole'. The other is his key principle for the structure of 'langue': that it consists basically of contrasts, so that 'constituents' (if anyone insists upon talking of such things) are to be considered as essentially secondary, derived, in relation to the primary autonomous contrasts. But though the survival of these ideas of his has been continuous down to today, their content is now quite other than when he formulated them. Still, this much at least remains: a cardinal distinction between the institution 'langue' and the act 'parole', and a working principle that the structure of the institution is accessible only through the contrasts. De Saussure would very likely disown my 'institution' versus 'act' (whatever I mean thereby) or any other modern version of the distinction, and there is certainly a huge difference between saying that structure 'is' contrast and saying that structure 'is accessible only through contrast'; and yet these more modern formulations derive from de Saussure's by continuous modulation —a gradual metamorphosis which becomes evident upon careful reading of the papers in this collection.

At least half of these authors had read the Cours. The others got it second-hand: in an atmosphere so saturated with those ideas, it has been impossible to escape that. The difference is hard to detect, and it is generally unsafe to accuse a contemporary linguist of not having read the Cours, as has happened to me.⟧

SOUND PATTERNS IN LANGUAGE

EDWARD SAPIR

Language 1.37–51—1925

There used to be and to some extent still is a feeling among linguists that the psychology of a language is more particularly concerned with its grammatical features, but that its sounds and its phonetic processes belong to a grosser physiological substratum. Thus, we sometimes hear it said that such phonetic processes as the palatalizing of a vowel by a following i or other front vowel ('umlaut') or the series of shifts in the manner of articulating the old Indo-European stopped consonants which have become celebrated under the name of 'Grimm's Law' are merely mechanical processes, consummated by the organs of speech and by the nerves that control them as a set of shifts in relatively simple sensorimotor habits. It is my purpose in this paper, as briefly as may be, to indicate that the sounds and sound processes of speech cannot be properly understood in such simple, mechanical terms.

Perhaps the best way to pose the problem of the psychology of speech sounds is to compare an actual speech sound with an identical or similar one not used in a linguistic context. It will become evident almost at once that it is a great fallacy to think of the articulation of a speech sound as a motor habit that is merely intended to bring about a directly significant result. A good example of superficially similar sounds is the wh of such a word as when, as generally pronounced in America (i.e., voiceless w or, perhaps more accurately analyzed, aspiration plus voiceless w plus voiced w-glide), and the sound made in blowing out a candle, with which it has often been compared. We are not at the present moment greatly interested in whether these two articulations are really identical or, at the least, very similar. Let us assume that a typically pronounced wh is identical with the sound that results from the expulsion of breath through pursed lips when a candle is blown out. We shall assume identity of both articulation and quality of perception. Does this identity amount to a psychological identity of the two processes? Obviously not. It is worth pointing out, in what may seem pedantic detail, wherein they differ.

1. The candle-blowing sound is a physical by-product of a directly functional act, the extinguishing of the candle by means of a peculiar method of producing a current of air. So far as normal human interest is concerned, this sound serves merely as a sign of the blowing out, or attempted blowing out, itself. We can abbreviate our record of the facts a little and say that the production of the candle-blowing sound is a directly functional act. On the other hand, the articulation of the wh-sound in such a word as when has no direct functional value; it is merely a link in the construction of a symbol, the articulated or perceived word when, which in turn assumes a function, symbolic at that, only when it is experienced in certain linguistic contexts, such as the saying or hearing of a sentence like When are you coming? In brief, the candle-blowing wh means business; the speech sound wh is stored-up play which can eventually fall in line in a game that merely refers to business. Still more briefly, the former is practice; the latter, art.

2. Each act of blowing out a candle is functionally equivalent, more or less, to every other such act; hence the candle-blowing wh is, in the first instance, a sign for an act of single function. The speech sound wh has no singleness, or rather primary singleness, of reference. It is a counter in a considerable variety of functional symbols, e.g. when, whiskey, wheel. A series of candle-blowing sounds has a natural function and contextual coherence. A series of wh-sounds as employed in actual speech has no such coherence; e.g., the series wh(en), wh(iskey), wh(eel) is non-significant.

3. Every typical human reaction has a certain range of variation and, properly speaking, no such reaction can be understood except as a series of variants distributed about a norm or type. Now the candle-blowing wh and the speech sound wh are norms or types of entirely distinct series of variants.

First, as to acoustic quality. Owing to the fact that the blowing out of a candle is a purely functional act, its variability is limited by the function alone. But, obviously, it is possible to blow out a candle in a great number of ways. One may purse the lips greatly or only a little; the lower lip, or the upper lip, or neither may protrude; the articulation may be quite impure and accompanied by synchronous articulations, such as a x-like (velar spirant) or sh-like sound. None of these and other variations reaches over into a class of reactions that differs at all materially from the typical candle-blowing wh. The variation of wh as speech sound is very much more restricted. A when pronounced, for instance, with a wh in which the lower lip protruded or with a wh that was contaminated with a sh-sound would be felt as distinctly 'off color.' It could be tolerated only as a joke or a personal speech defect. But the variability of wh in language is not only less wide than in candle-blowing, it is also different in tendency. The latter sound varies chiefly along the line of exact place (or places) of articulation, the former chiefly along the line of voicing. Psychologically wh of when and similar words is related to the w of well and similar words. There is a strong tendency to minimize the aspiration and to voice the labial. The gamut of variations, therefore, runs roughly from hW (I use W for voiceless w) to w. Needless to say, there is no tendency to voicing in the candle-blowing wh, for such a tendency would contradict the very purpose of the reaction, which is to release a strong and unhampered current of air.

Second, as to intensity. It is clear that in this respect the two series of variations differ markedly. The normal intensity of the candle-blowing sound is greater than that of the linguistic wh; this intensity, moreover, is very much more variable, depending as it does on the muscular tone of the blower, the size of the flame to be extinguished, and other factors. All in all, it is clear that the resemblance of the two wh-sounds is really due to an intercrossing of two absolutely independent series, as of two independent lines in space that have one point in common.

4. The speech sound wh has a larger number of associations with other sounds in symbolically significant sound-groups, e.g. wh-e-n, wh-i-s-k-ey, wh-ee-l. The candle-blowing sound has no sound associations with which it habitually coheres.

5. We now come to the most essential point of difference. The speech sound wh is one of a definitely limited number of sounds (e.g. wh, s, t, l, i, and so on) which, while differing qualitatively from one another rather more than does wh from its candle-blowing counterpart, nevertheless belong together in a definite system of symbolically utilizable counters. Each member of this system is not only characterized by a distinctive and slightly variable articulation and a corresponding acoustic image, but also—and this is crucial—by a psychological aloofness from all other members of the system. The relational gaps between the sounds of a language are just as necessary to the psychological definition of these sounds as the articulations and acoustic images which are customarily used to define them. A sound that is not unconsciously felt as 'placed'[1] with reference to other sounds is no more a true element of speech than a lifting of the foot is a dance step unless it can be 'placed' with reference to other movements that help to define the dance. Needless to say, the candle-blowing sound forms no part of any such system of sounds. It is not spaced off from nor related to other sounds—say the sound of humming and the sound of clearing one's throat—which form with it a set of mutually necessary indices.

It should be sufficiently clear from this one example—and there are of course plenty of analogous ones, such as m versus the sound of humming or an indefinite series of timbre-varying groans versus a set of vowels—how little the notion of speech sound is explicable in simple sensorimotor terms and how truly a complex psychology of association and pattern is implicit in the utterance of the simplest consonant or vowel. It follows at once that the psychology of phonetic processes is unintelligible unless the general patterning of speech sounds is recognized. This patterning has two phases. We have been at particular pains to see that the sounds used by a language form a self-contained system which makes it impossible to identify any of them with a non-linguistic sound produced by the 'organs of speech,' no matter how great is the articulatory and acoustic resemblance between the two. In view of the utterly distinct psychological backgrounds of the two classes of sound production it may even be seriously doubted whether the innervation of speech-sound articulation is ever actually the same type of physiological fact as the innervation of 'identical' articulations that have no linguistic context. But it is not enough to pattern off all speech sounds as such against other sounds produced by the 'organs of speech.' There is a second phase of sound patterning which is more elusive and of correspondingly greater significance for the linguist. This is the inner configuration of the sound system of a language, the intuitive 'placing' of the sounds with reference to one another. To this we must now turn.

Mechanical and other detached methods of studying the phonetic elements of speech are, of course, of considerable value, but they have sometimes the undesirable effect of obscuring the essential facts of speech-sound psychology. Too often an undue importance is attached to minute sound discriminations as such; and too often phoneticians do not realize that it is not enough to know that a certain sound occurs in a language, but that one must ascertain if the sound is a typical form or one of the points in its sound pattern, or is merely a variant of such a form. There are two types of variation that tend to obscure the distinctiveness of the different points in the phonetic pattern of a language. One of this is individual variation. It is true that no two individuals have precisely the same pronunciation of a language, but it is equally true that they aim to make the same sound discriminations, so that, if the qualitative differences of the sounds that make up A's pattern from those that make up B's are perceptible to a minute analysis, the relations that obtain between the elements in the two patterns are the same. In other words, the patterns are the same pattern. A's s, for instance, may differ markedly from B's s, but if each individual keeps his s equally distinct from such points in the pattern as th (of think) and sh and if there is a one-to-one correspondence between the distribution of

[1] This word has, of course, nothing to do here with 'place of articulation.' One may feel, for instance, that sound A is to sound B as sound X is to sound Y without having the remotest idea how and where any of them is produced.

A's s and that of B's, then the difference of pronunciation is of little or no interest for the phonetic psychology of the language. We may go a step further. Let us symbolize A's and B's pronunciation of s, th, and sh as follows:

A: th s sh
B: th_1 s_1 sh_1

This diagram is intended to convey the fact that B's s is a lisped s which is not identical with his interdental th, but stands nearer objectively to this sound than to A's s; similarly, B's sh is acoustically somewhat closer to A's s than to his sh. Obviously we cannot discover B's phonetic pattern by identifying his sounds with their nearest analogues in A's pronunciation, i.e. by setting th_1 = th, s_1 = variant of th, sh_1 = s. If we do this, as we are quite likely to do if we are obsessed, like so many linguists, by the desire to apply an absolute and universal phonetic system to all languages, we get the following pattern analysis:

A: th s sh
/\
B: th_1 s_1 sh_1 —

which is as psychologically perverse as it is 'objectively' accurate. Of course the true pattern analysis is:

A: th s sh
B: th_1 s_1 sh_1

for the objective relations between sounds are only a first approximation to the psychological relations which constitute the true phonetic pattern. The size of the objective differences th—s, s—sh, th_1—s_1, s_1—sh_1, th—s_1, s_1—s, s—sh_1, and sh_1—sh does not correspond to the psychological 'spacing' of the phonemes th, s, and sh in the phonetic pattern which is common to A and B.

The second type of variation is common to all normal speakers of the language and is dependent on the phonetic conditions in which the fundamental sound ('point of the pattern') occurs. In most languages, what is felt by the speakers to be the 'same' sound has perceptibly different forms as these conditions vary. Thus, in (American) English there is a perceptible difference in the length of the vowel a of bad and bat, the a-vowel illustrated by these words being long or half-long before voiced consonants and all continuants, whether voiced or unvoiced, but short before voiceless stops. In fact, the vocalic alternation of bad and bat is quantitatively parallel to such alternations as bead and beat, fade and fate. The alternations are governed by mechanical considerations that have only a subsidiary relevance for the phonetic pattern. They take care of themselves, as it were, and it is not always easy to convince natives of their objective reality, however sensitive they may be to violations of the unconscious rule in the speech of foreigners. It is very necessary to understand that it is not because the objective difference is too slight to be readily perceptible that such variations as the quantitative alternations in bad and bat, bead and beat, fade and fate stand outside of the proper phonetic pattern of the language (e.g., are not psychologically parallel to such qualitative-quantitative alternations as bid and bead, fed and fade, or to such quantitative alternations as German Schlaf and schlaff, Latin āra and ārā), but that the objective difference is felt to be slight precisely because it corresponds to nothing significant in the inner structure of the phonetic pattern. In matters of this kind, objective estimates of similarity and difference, based either on specific linguistic habits or on a generalized phonetic system, are utterly fallacious. As a matter of fact, the mechanical English vocalic relation bad: bat would in many languages be quite marked enough to indicate a relation of distinct points of the pattern, while the English pattern relation -t : -d, which seems so self-evidently real to us, has in not a few other languages either no reality at all or only a mechanical, conditional one. In Upper Chinook, for instance, t : d exists objectively but not psychologically; one says, e.g. inat 'across,' but inad before words beginning with a vowel, and the two forms of the final consonant are undoubtedly felt to be the 'same' sound in exactly the same sense in which the English vowels of bad and bat are felt by us to be identical phonetic elements. The Upper Chinook d exists only as a mechanical variant of t; hence this alternation is not the same psychologically as the Sanskrit sandhi variation -t : -d.

Individual variations and such conditional variations as we have discussed once cleared out of the way, we arrive at the genuine pattern of speech sounds. After what we have said, it almost goes without saying that two languages, A and B, may have identical sounds but utterly distinct phonetic patterns; or they may have mutually incompatible phonetic systems, from the articulatory and acoustic standpoint, but identical or similar patterns. The following schematic examples and subjoined comments will make this clear. Sounds which do not properly belong to the pattern or, rather, are variants within points of the pattern are put in parentheses. Long vowels are designated as a·; ŋ is ng of sing; θ and δ are voiceless and voiced interdental spirants; x and γ are voiceless and voiced guttural spirants; ' is glottal stop; ' denotes aspirated release; ɛ and ɔ are open e and o.

A:	a	(ɛ)	(e)	i	u	(o)	(ɔ)	
	a·	(ɛ·)	(e·)	i·	u·	(o·)	(ɔ·)	
	’	h	w	y	l	m	n	(ŋ)
	p	t	k					
	p‘	t‘	k‘					
	(b)	(d)	(g)					
	f	θ	s	x				
	(v)	(δ)	(z)	(γ)				
But B:	a	ɛ	e	i	u	o	ɔ	
	(a·)	(ɛ·)	(e·)	(i·)	(u·)	(o·)	(ɔ·)	
	(’)	h	(w)	(y)	(l)	m	n	ŋ
	p	t	k					
	(p‘)	(t‘)	(k‘)					
	b	d	g					
	(f)	(θ)	s	(x)				
	v	δ	z	γ				

We will assume for A and B certain conditional variants which are all of types that may be abundantly illustrated from actual languages. For A:

1. ɛ occurs only as palatalized form of a when following y or i. In many Indian languages, e.g., yɛ = ya.

2. e is dropped from i-position when this vowel is final. Cf. such mechanical alternations as Eskimo -e : -i-t.

3. o is dropped from u-position when this vowel is final. Cf. 2.

4. ɔ occurs only as labialized form of a after w or u. Cf. 1. (In Yahi, e.g., wɔwi ‘house’ is objectively correct, but psychologically wrong. It can easily be shown that this word is really wawi and ‘feels’ like a rhyme to such phonetic groups as lawi and bawi; short ɔ in an open syllable is an anomaly, but ɔ· is typical for all Yana dialects, including Yahi.)

5. ŋ is merely n assimilated to following k, as in Indo-European.

6. b, d, g, v, z, δ, γ are voiced forms of p, t, k, f, s, θ, x respectively when these consonants occur between vowels before the accent (cf. Upper Chinook wa´pul ‘night’ : wabu´lmax ‘nights’). As the voiced consonants can arise in no other way, they are not felt by the speakers of A as specifically distinct from the voiceless consonants. They feel sharply the difference between p and p‘, as do Chinese, Takelma, Yana, and a host of other languages, but are not aware of the alternation p : b.

And for B:

1. Long vowels can arise only when the syllable is open and stressed. Such alternations as ma·´la : u·´-mala are not felt as involving any but stress differences. In A, ma·la and mala are as distinct as Latin ‘apples’ and ‘bad’ (fem.).

2. ’ is not an organic consonant, but, as in North German, an attack of initial vowels, hence ’a- is felt to be merely a-. In A, however, as in Semitic, Nootka, Kwakiutl, Haida, and a great many other languages, such initials as ’a- are felt to be equivalent to such consonant + vowel groups as ma- or sa-. Here is a type of pattern difference which even experienced linguists do not always succeed in making clear.

3. w and y are merely semi-vocalic developments of u and i. Cf. French oui and hier. In A, w and y are organically distinct consonants. Here again linguists often blindly follow the phonetic feeling of their own language instead of clearly ascertaining the behavior of the language investigated. The difference, e.g., between aua and awa is a real one for some languages, a phantom for others.

4. l arises merely as dissimilated variant of n.

5. p‘, t‘, k‘ are merely p, t, k with breath release, characteristic of B at the end of a word, e.g. ap-a : ap‘. This sort of alternation is common in aboriginal America. It is the reverse of the English habit: <u>tame</u> with aspirated t (t‘e·im) but <u>hate</u> with unaspirated, or very weakly aspirated, release (he^{i}t).

6. f, θ, and x similarly arise from the unvoicing of final v, δ, and γ; e.g., av-a : af. z and s also alternate in this way, but there is a true s besides. From the point of view of B, s in such phonemes as sa and asa is an utterly distinct sound, or rather point in the phonetic pattern, from the objectively identical as which alternates with az-a.[2]

The true or intuitively felt phonetic systems (patterns) of A and B, therefore, are:

A:	a			i	u			
	a·			i·	u·			
	’	h	w	y	l	m	n	
	p	t	k					
	p‘	t‘	k‘					
	f	θ	x	s				
B:	a	ɛ	e	i	u	o	ɔ	
	h	m	n	ŋ				
	p	t	k					
	b	d	g					
	s							
	v	δ	z	γ				

which shows the two languages to be very much more different phonetically than they at first seemed to be.

[2] If B ever develops an orthography, it is likely to fall into the habit of writing <u>az</u> for the pronounced <u>as</u> in cases of type <u>az-a</u> : <u>as</u>, but <u>as</u> in cases of type <u>as-a</u> : <u>as</u>. Philologists not convinced of the reality of phonetic patterns as here conceived will then be able to ‘prove’ from internal evidence that the change of etymological v, z, δ, γ to -f, -s, -θ, -x did not take place until after the language was reduced to writing, because otherwise it would be ‘impossible’ to explain why -s should be written -z when there was a sign for s ready to hand and why signs should not have

The converse case is worth plotting too. C and D are languages which have hardly any sounds in common, but their patterns show a remarkable one-to-one correspondence. Thus:

C:	a	ɛ	i	u		
	a·	ɛ·				
	h	w	y	l	m	n
	p	t	k	q (velar k)		
	b	d	g	g̣ (velar g)		
	f	s	x	x̣ (velar x)		
D:	ä	e	i	ü		
	ä·	e·				
	h	v	j[3]	r	m	ŋ
	p‘	t‘	k‘	q‘		
	β[4]	δ	γ	γ̣ (velar γ)		
	f	š	x̯[5]	ḥ (laryngeal h)		

Languages C and D have far less superficial similarity in their sound systems than have A and B, but it is obvious at a glance that their patterns are built on very much more similar lines. If we allowed ourselves to speculate genetically, we might suspect, on general principles, that the phonetic similarities between A and B, which we will suppose to be contiguous languages, are due to historical contact, but that the deeper pattern resemblance between C and D is an index of genetic relationship. It goes without saying that in the complex world of actual linguistic history we do not often find the phonetic facts working out along such neatly schematic lines, but it seemed expedient to schematize here so that the pattern concept might emerge with greater clarity.

An examination of the patterns of C and D shows that there is still a crucial point that we have touched on only by implication. We must now make this clear. We have arranged the sounds of C and D in such a way as to suggest an equivalence of ‘orientation’ of any one sound of one system with some sound of the other. In comparing the systems of A and B we did not commit ourselves to specific equivalences. We did not wish to imply, for instance, that A’s s was or was not ‘oriented’ in the same way as B’s, did or did not occupy the same relative place in A’s pattern as in B’s. But here we do wish to imply not merely that, e.g., C’s p corresponds to D’s p‘ or C’s h to D’s h, which one would be inclined to grant on general phonetic grounds, but also that, e.g., C’s w corresponds to D’s v while C’s b corresponds to D’s β. On general principles such pattern alignments as the latter are unexpected, to say the least, for bilabial β resembles w rather more than dentilabial v does. Why, then, not allow β to occupy the position we have assigned to v? Again, why should D’s j be supposed to correspond to C’s y when it is merely the voiced form of š? Should it not rather be placed under š precisely as, in C’s system, b is placed under p? Naturally, there is no reason why the intuitive pattern alignment of sounds in a given language should not be identical with their natural phonetic arrangement, and, one need hardly say, it is almost universally true that, e.g., the vowels form both a natural and a pattern group as against the consonants, that such stopped sounds as p, t, k form both a natural and a pattern group as opposed to the equally coherent group b, d, g (provided, of course, the language possesses these two series of stopped consonants). And yet it is most important to emphasize the fact, strange but indubitable, that a pattern alignment does not need to correspond exactly to the more obvious phonetic one. It is most certainly true that, however likely it is that at last analysis patternings of sounds are based on natural classifications, the pattern feeling, once established, may come to have a linguistic reality over and above, though perhaps never entirely at variance with, such classifications. We are not here concerned with the historical reasons for such phonetic vagaries. The fact is that, even from a purely descriptive standpoint, it is not nonsense to say that, e.g., the s or w of one linguistic pattern is not necessarily the same thing as the s or w of another.

It is time to escape from a possible charge of phonetic metaphysics and to face the question, “How can a sound be assigned a ‘place’ in a phonetic pattern over and above its natural classification on organic and acoustic grounds?” The answer is simple.

come into use for f, θ, and x. As soon as one realizes, however, that ‘ideal sounds,’ which are constructed from one’s intuitive feeling of the significant relations between the objective sounds, are more ‘real’ to a naive speaker than the objective sounds themselves, such internal evidence loses much of its force. The example of s in B was purposely chosen to illustrate an interesting phenomenon, the crossing in a single objective phoneme of a true element of the phonetic pattern with a secondary form of another such element. In B, e.g., objective s is a pool of cases of ‘true s’ and ‘pseudo-s’. Many interesting and subtle examples could be given of psychological difference where there is objective identity, or similarity so close as to be interpreted by the recorder as identity. In Sarcee, an Athabaskan language with significant pitch differences, there is a true middle tone and a pseudo-middle tone which results from the lowering of a high tone to the middle position because of certain mechanical rules of tone sandhi. I doubt very much if the intuitive psychology of these two middle tones is the same. There are, of course, analogous traps for the unwary in Chinese. Had not the Chinese kindly formalized for us their intuitive feeling about the essential tone analysis of their language, it is exceedingly doubtful if our Occidental ears and kymographs would have succeeded in discovering the exact patterning of Chinese tone.

[3] As in French <u>jour</u>.

[4] Bilabial <u>v</u>, as in Spanish.

[5] As in German <u>ich</u>.

"A 'place' is intuitively found for a sound (which is here thought of as a true 'point in the pattern,' not a mere conditional variant) in such a system because of a general feeling of its phonetic relationship resulting from all the specific phonetic relationships (such as parallelism, contrast, combination, imperviousness to combination, and so on) to all other sounds." These relationships may, or may not, involve morphological processes (e.g., the fact that in English we have morphological alternations like wife : wives, sheath : to sheathe, breath : to breathe, mouse : to mouse helps to give the sounds f, θ, s an intuitive pattern relation to their voiced correlates v, δ, z which is specifically different from the theoretically analogous relation p, t, k : b, d, g; in English, f is nearer to v than p is to b, but in German this is certainly not true).

An example or two of English sound-patterning will help us to fix our thoughts. P, t, k belong together in a coherent set because, among other reasons: 1, they may occur initially, medially, or finally; 2, they may be preceded by s in all positions (e.g. spoon : cusp, star : hoist, scum : ask); 3, they may be followed by r initially and medially; 4, they may be preceded by s and followed by r initially and medially; 5, each has a voiced correspondent (b, d, g); 6, unlike such sounds as f and θ, they cannot alternate significantly with their voiced correspondents; 7, they have no tendency to be closely associated, either phonetically or morphologically, with corresponding spirants (p : f and t : θ are not intuitively correct for English; contrast Old Irish and Hebrew t : θ, k : x, which were intuitively felt relations—Old Irish and Hebrew θ and x were absolutely different types of sounds, psychologically, from English θ and German x. These are merely a few of the relations which help to give p, t, k their pattern place in English.

A second example is ŋ of sing. In spite of what phoneticians tell us about this sound (b : m as d : n as g : ŋ), no naïve English-speaking person can be made to feel in his bones that it belongs to a single series with m and n. Psychologically it cannot be grouped with them because, unlike them, it is not a freely movable consonant (there are no words beginning with ŋ). It still feels like ŋg, however little it sounds like it. The relation ant : and = sink : sing is psychologically as well as historically correct. Orthography is by no means solely responsible for the 'ng feeling' of ŋ. Cases like -ŋ- in finger and anger do not disprove the reality of this feeling, for there is in English a pattern equivalence of -ŋg- : -ŋ and -nd- : -nd. What cases like singer with -ŋ- indicate is not so much a pattern difference of -ŋg- : -ŋ-, which is not to be construed as analogous to -nd- : -n- (e.g. window : winnow), as an analogous treatment of medial elements in terms of their final form (singer : sing like cutter : cut).[6]

To return to our phonetic patterns for C and D, we can now better understand why it is possible to consider a sibilant like j as less closely related in pattern to its voiceless form š than to such a set of voiced continuants as v, r, m, ŋ. We might find, for instance, that š never alternates with j, but that there are cases of š : δ analogous to cases of f : β and x : γ; that ava, aja, ara alternate with au, ai, ar; that combinations like -aβd, -aδg, -aγd are possible, but that combinations of type -ajd and -avd are unthinkable; that v- and j- are possible initials, like r-, m-, and ŋ-, but that β-, δ-, γ-, χ- are not allowed. The product of such and possibly other sound relations would induce a feeling that j belongs with v, r, m, ŋ; that it is related to i; and that it has nothing to do with such spirants as š and δ. In other words, it 'feels' like the y of many other languages, and, as y itself is absent in D, we can go so far as to say that j occupies a 'place in the pattern' that belongs to y elsewhere.

In this paper I do not wish to go into the complex and tangled problems of the nature and generality of sound changes in language. All that I wish to point out here is that it is obviously not immaterial to understand how a sound patterns if we are to understand its history. Of course, it is true that mechanical sound changes may bring about serious readjustments of phonetic pattern and may even create new configurations within the pattern (in Modern Central Tibetan, e.g., we have b-, d-, g- : B'-, D'-, G'-,[7] while in Classical Tibetan we have, as correspondents, mb-, nd-, ŋg- : b-, d-, g-; here mb-, nd-, ŋg- are to be morphologically analyzed as nasal prefix + b-, d-, g-). But it is equally true that the pattern feeling acts as a hindrance of, or stimulus to, certain sound changes

[6] Incidentally, if our theory is correct, such a form as singer betrays an unconscious analysis into a word of absolute significance sing and a semi-independent agentive element -er, which is appended not to a stem, an abstracted radical element, but to a true word. Hence sing : singer is not psychologically analogous to such Latin forms as can- : cantor. It would almost seem that the English insistence on the absoluteness of its significant words tended at the same time to give many of its derivative suffixes a secondary, revitalized reality. -er, for instance, might almost be construed as a 'word' which occurs only as the second element of a compound, cf. -man in words like longshoreman. As Prof. L. Bloomfield points out to me, the agentive -er contrasts with the comparative -er, which allows the adjective to keep its radical form in -ŋg- (e.g., long with -ŋ : longer with -ŋg-).

[7] B, D, G represent intermediate stops, 'tonlose Medien.' In this series they are followed by aspiration.

[8] The slight objective differences between English and Spanish θ and δ are of course not great enough to force a different patterning. Such a view would be putting the cart before the horse.

and that it is not permissible to look for universally valid sound changes under like articulatory conditions. Certain typical mechanical tendencies there are (e.g. nb > mb or -az > -as or tya > tša), but a complete theory of sound change has to take constant account of the orientation of sounds in our sense. Let one example do for many. We do not in English feel that θ is to be found in the neighborhood, as it were, of s, but that it is very close to δ. In Spanish, θ is not far from s, but is not at all close to δ.[8] Is it not therefore more than an accident that nowhere in Germanic does θ become s or proceed from s, while in certain Spanish dialects, as so frequently elsewhere, θ passes into s (in Athabaskan θ often proceeds from s)? In English θ tends to be vulgarized to t as δ tends to be vulgarized to d, never to s; similarly, Old Norse θ has become t in Swedish and Danish. Such facts are impressive. They cannot be explained on simple mechanical principles.

Phonetic patterning helps also to explain why people find it difficult to pronounce certain foreign sounds which they possess in their own language. Thus, a Nootka Indian in pronouncing English words with ŋ or l invariably substitutes n for each of these sounds. Yet he is able to pronounce both ŋ and l. He does not use these sounds in prose discourse, but ŋ is very common in the chants and l is often substituted for n in songs. His feeling for the stylistic character of ŋ and for the n–l equivalence prevents him from 'hearing' English ŋ and l correctly. Here again we see that a speech sound is not merely an articulation or an acoustic image, but material for symbolic expression in an appropriate linguistic context. Very instructive is our attitude towards the English sounds j, ŋ, and ts. All three of these sounds are familiar to us (e.g. azure, sing, hats). None occurs initially. For all that, the attempt to pronounce them initially in foreign words is not reacted to in the same way. ŋa- and tsa- are naïvely felt to be incredible, not so ja-, which is easily acquired without replacement by dja- or ša-. Why is this? ŋa- is incredible because there is no mba-, nda-, ŋ(g)a- series in English. tsa- is incredible because there is no psa-, tsa-, ksa- series in English; -ts is always morphologically analyzable into -t + -s, hence no feeling develops for ts as a simple phoneme despite the fact that its phonetic parallel tš (ch of church) is found in all positions.[9] But ja- is not difficult, say in learning French, because its articulation and perception have been mastered by implication in the daily use of our phonetic pattern. This is obvious from a glance at the formula:

-j-	-z-	-δ-	-v-
—	z-	δ-	v-

which is buttressed by:

-š-	-s-	-θ-	-f-
š-	s-	θ-	f-

Is it not evident that the English speaker's pattern has all but taught him j- before he himself has ever used or heard an actual j-?

There are those who are so convinced of the adequacy of purely objective methods of studying speech sounds that they do not hesitate to insert phonetic graphs into the body of their descriptive grammars. This is to confuse linguistic structure with a particular method of studying linguistic phenomena. If it is justifiable in a grammatical work to describe the vocalic system of a language in terms of kymograph records,[10] it is also proper to insert anecdotes into the morphology to show how certain modes or cases happened to come in handy. And a painter might as well be allowed to transfer to his canvas his unrevised palette! The whole aim and spirit of this paper has been to show that phonetic phenomena are not physical phenomena per se, however necessary it may be to get at the phonetic facts by way of their physical embodiment. The present discussion is really a special illustration of the necessity of getting behind the sense data of any type of expression in order to grasp the intuitively felt and communicated forms which alone give significance to such expression.

9 Obviously we need not expect -ts and -tš to develop analogously even if s and š do.

10 Needless to say, such records are in place in studies explicitly devoted to experimental phonetics.

⟦Besides his book Language, which is read with pleasure and profit by all sorts and conditions of men and is not likely to go out of print in our time, the easiest way to get more of Sapir is in the Selected Writings, U. of California Press, 1949; analysis of his way of thinking will be found in Zellig Harris's review of this volume, Lang. 27.288 (1951).

There was a brillance about Edward Sapir which fascinated and awed all who encountered him, and which is not only evident in his own writings but even lends an extra phosphorescent glow to certain of his pupils' works. But there are others who sometimes sound like it who actually never were pupils of his: for his contribution was not the developing of any method, but rather the establishing of a charter for the free intellectual play of personalities more or less akin to his own. If their wits happen to be dimmer (and here he had few equals), their blunders may betray the essential irresponsibility of what has been called Sapir's 'method'. We welcome the insights of his genius, which allowed no scrap of evidence to escape at least subconscious weighing; where it is possible to check up, we normally find him right; thus we seem captious when we point out that he also said many things which are essentially uncheckable ('invulnerable') and thus not science.⟧

A SET OF POSTULATES FOR THE SCIENCE OF LANGUAGE

LEONARD BLOOMFIELD

Language 2.153-64—1926

I. Introductory

The method of postulates (that is, assumptions or axioms) and definitions[1] is fully adequate to mathematics; as for other sciences, the more complex their subject-matter, the less amenable they are to this method, since, under it, every descriptive or historical fact becomes the subject of a new postulate.

Nevertheless, the postulational method can further the study of language, because it forces us to state explicitly whatever we assume, to define our terms, and to decide what things may exist independently and what things are interdependent.[2]

Certain errors can be avoided or corrected by examining and formulating our (at present tacit) assumptions and defining our (often undefined) terms.[3]

Also, the postulational method saves discussion, because it limits our statements to a defined terminology; in particular, it cuts us off from psychological dispute.[4] Discussion of the fundamentals of our science seems to consist one half of obvious truisms, and one half of metaphysics; this is characteristic of matters which form no real part of a subject: they should properly be disposed of by merely naming certain concepts as belonging to the domain of other sciences.

Thus, the physiologic and acoustic description of acts of speech belongs to other sciences than ours. The existence and interaction of social groups held together by language is granted by psychology and anthropology.[5]

Psychology, in particular, gives us this series: to certain stimuli (A) a person reacts by speaking; his speech (B) in turn stimulates his hearers to certain reactions (C).[6] By a social habit which every person acquires in infancy from his elders, A-B-C are closely correlated. Within this correlation, the stimuli (A) which cause an act of speech and the reactions (C) which result from it, are very closely linked, because every person acts indifferently as speaker or as hearer. We are free, therefore, without further discussion, to speak of vocal features or sounds (B) and of stimulus-reaction features (A-C) of speech.

II. Form and Meaning

1. Definition. An act of speech is an utterance.

2. Assumption 1. Within certain communities successive utterances are alike or partly alike.

A needy stranger at the door says I'm hungry. A child who has eaten and merely wants to put off going to bed says I'm hungry. Linguistics considers only those vocal features which are alike in the two utterances, and only those stimulus-reaction features which are alike in the two utterances. Similarly, The book is interesting and Put the book away, are partly alike (the book). Outside of our science these similarities are only relative; within it they are absolute. This fiction is only in part suspended in historical linguistics.

3. Def. Any such community is a speech-community.

4. Def. The totality of utterances that can be made in a speech-community is the language of that speech-community.

We are obliged to predict; hence the words 'can

[1] For a clear exposition of this method, see J. W. Young, Lectures on the Fundamental Concepts of Algebra and Geometry, New York 1911.

[2] Cf. A. P. Weiss's set of postulates for psychology, Psychological Review 32.83.

[3] Examples are many. Bopp took for granted that the formative elements of Indo-European were once independent words; this is a needless and unwarranted assumption. The last descendant of his error is the assumption that IE compound words are historically derived from phrases (Jacobi, Compositum und Nebensatz, Bonn 1897; this even in Brugmann, Grundriss II[2], 1, pp. 37-78; cf. TAPA 45.73 ff.). The notion is gaining ground that some forms have less meaning than others and are therefore more subject to phonetic change (Horn, Sprachkörper und Sprachfunktion, Palaestra 135, Berlin 1921); I, for one, can discover no workable definition of the terms 'meaning' and 'phonetic change' under which this notion can be upheld. The whole dispute, perhaps today as unstilled as fifty years ago, about the regularity of phonetic change, is at bottom a question of terminology.

[4] Recall the difficulties and obscurities in the writings of Humboldt and Steinthal, and the psychological dispute of Paul, Wundt, Delbrueck. From our point of view, the last-named was wrong in denying the value of descriptive data, but right in saying that it is indifferent what system of psychology a linguist believes in (Grundfragen der Sprachforschung, Strassburg 1901). The trouble over the nature of the sentence is largely non-linguistic; contrast the simplicity and usefulness of Meillet's definition (adopted below), Introduction à l'étude comparative des langues indo-européennes[3], Paris 1912, p. 339. I am indebted also to Sapir's book on Language, New York 1921, and to de Saussure's Cours de linguistique générale[2], Paris 1922; both authors take steps toward a delimitation of linguistics.

[5] Cf. Weiss, l. c., p. 86: 'The language responses establish the ... social type of organization ...'

[6] Cf. Weiss, Journal of Philosophy, Psychology and Scientific Methods 15.636: 'The significant thing about the speech reaction is that it may be either the adequate reaction to a situation, or it may be the adequate stimulus for either another speech reaction or some bodily reaction.'

be made'. We say that under certain stimuli a Frenchman (or Zulu, etc.) will say so-and-so and other Frenchmen (or Zulus, etc.) will react appropriately to his speech. Where good informants are available, or for the investigator's own language, the prediction is easy; elsewhere it constitutes the greatest difficulty of descriptive linguistics.

5. Def. That which is alike will be called same. That which is not same is different.

This enables us to use these words without reference to non-linguistic shades of sound and meaning.

6. Def. The vocal features common to same or partly same utterances are forms; the corresponding stimulus-reaction features are meanings.

Thus a form is a recurrent vocal feature which has meaning, and a meaning is a recurrent stimulus-reaction feature which corresponds to a form.

7. Assumption 2. Every utterance is made up wholly of forms.

III. Morpheme, Word, Phrase

8. Def. A minimum X is an X which does not consist entirely of lesser X's.

Thus, if X_1 consists of $X_2X_3X_4$, then X_1 is not a minimum X. But if X_1 consists of X_2X_3A, or of X_2A, or of A_1A_2, or is unanalyzable, then X_1 is a minimum X.

9. Def. A minimum form is a morpheme; its meaning a sememe.

Thus a morpheme is a recurrent (meaningful) form which cannot in turn be analyzed into smaller recurrent (meaningful) forms. Hence any unanalysable word or formative is a morpheme.

10. Def. A form which may be an utterance is free. A form which is not free is bound.

Thus, book, the man are free forms; -ing (as in writing), -er (as in writer) are bound forms, the last-named differing in meaning from the free form err.

11. Def. A minimum free form is a word.

A word is thus a form which may be uttered alone (with meaning) but cannot be analyzed into parts that may (all of them) be uttered alone (with meaning). Thus the word quick cannot be analyzed; the word quickly can be analyzed into quick and -ly, but the latter part cannot be uttered alone; the word writer can be analyzed into write and -er, but the latter cannot be uttered alone (the word err being, by virtue of different meaning, a different form); the word blackbird can be analyzed into the words black and bird and the word-stress ⸗ –, which last cannot be uttered alone (i.e., it differs in form and meaning from the phrase black bird).

12. Def. A non-minimum free form is a phrase.

E.g., the book, or The man beat the dog; but not, e.g., book on (as in Lay the book on the table), for this is meaningless, hence not a form; and not blackbird, which is a minimum free form.

13. Def. A bound form which is part of a word is a formative.*

A formative may be complex, as, Latin verb-endings -abat, -abant, -abit, -abunt, etc., or minimum (and hence a morpheme), as Latin -t of third person.

14. Assumption 3. The forms of a language are finite in number.

IV. Example of a Special Assumption

The phenomena of specific languages will no doubt necessitate further assumptions of form; and these will sometimes modify the general assumptions. The following is an example of such a special assumption.

Assumption Sl. A phrase may contain a bound form which is not part of a word.

For example, the possessive [z] in the man I saw yesterday's daughter.

Def. Such a bound form is a phrase-formative.*

This assumption disturbs the definition of phrase above given. Strictly speaking, our assumptions and definitions would demand that we take the-man-I-saw-yesterday's daughter as two words. Convenience of analysis makes an assumption like the present one preferable for English. A similar assumption might be convenient for the Philippine 'ligatures'.

V. Phonemes

15. Assumption 4. Different morphemes may be alike or partly alike as to vocal features.

Thus book : table [b]; stay : west [st]; -er (agent) : -er (comparative). The assumption imples that the meanings are different.

16. Def. A minimum same of vocal feature is a phoneme or distinctive sound.

As, for instance, English [b, s, t], the English normal word-stress, the Chinese tones.

17. Assumption 5. The number of different phonemes in a language is a small sub-multiple of the number of forms.

18. Assumption 6. Every form is made up wholly of phonemes.

These two assumptions are empiric facts for every language that has been observed, and outside of our science are theoretical necessities (Boas, Handbook of American Indian Languages, Bureau of American Ethnology, Bulletin 40, vol. 1, pp. 24 ff.).

*Letter from Bloomfield to John Kepke, April 17, 1934: You are right about the term formative, which in 1926 I used in the value 'a bound form which is part of a word.' At that time I had not the courage to call the-King-of-England's and the like 'one word'. Hence the possessive -'s was here a bound form which was not part of a word. And so for the usual kind of bound forms I needed a special name, and chose 'formative.' Today I call the-King-of-England's and the like 'one word'; hence every bound form will now be part of a word, and the term 'formative' is no longer needed.

Such a thing as a 'small difference of sound' does not exist in a language. Linguists who believe that certain forms resist phonetic change, implicitly reject these assumptions, though, so far as I can see, we could not work without them.

The morphemes of a language can thus be analyzed into a small number of meaningless phonemes. The sememes, on the other hand, which stand in one-to-one correspondence with the morphemes, cannot be further analyzed by linguistic methods. This is no doubt why linguists, confronted with the parallelism of form and meaning, choose form as the basis of classification.

19. Assumption 7. The number of orders of phonemes in the morphemes and words of a language is a sub-multiple of the number of possible orders.

20. Def. The orders which occur are the sound-patterns of the language.

As, English word-initial [st-] but never [ts-].

21. Def. Different forms which are alike as to phonemes are homonymous.

VI. Construction, Categories, Parts of Speech

22. Assumption 8. Different non-minimum forms may be alike or partly alike as to the order of the constituent forms and as to stimulus-reaction features corresponding to this order.

The order may be successive, simultaneous (stress and pitch with other phonemes), substitutive (French au [o] for à le), and so on.

23. Def. Such recurrent sames of order are constructions; the corresponding stimulus-reaction features are constructional meanings.

This expands the use of the term meaning.

24. Def. The construction of formatives in a word is a morphologic construction.

Thus, book-s, ox-en have the construction of formative plus formative and the meaning 'object in number'.

25. Def. The construction of free forms (and phrase formatives) in a phrase is a syntactic construction.

Thus, Richard saw John, The man is beating the dog show the construction of free form plus free form plus free form meaning 'actor acting on goal'.

26. Def. A maximum X is an X which is not part of a larger X.

27. Def. A maximum form* in any utterance is a sentence.

Thus, a sentence is a form* which, in the given utterance, is not part of a larger construction.

*Bloomfield in his review of Ries, Was ist ein Satz? (Lang. 7.209 fn. 6 [1931]): E. A. Esper calls my attention to an error in my English wording of Meillet's definition, Lang. 2.158 [1926]: 'A maximum construction in any utterance is a sentence.' For 'construction' one must, of course, read 'form', since otherwise, the definition, if it meant anything at all, would exclude largest-forms that happened to contain only a single morpheme; e.g. Come! Ouch! Yes.

Every utterance therefore consists of one or more sentences, and even such utterances as Latin pluit, English Fire! or Ouch! are sentences.

28. Assumption 9. The number of constructions in a language is a small sub-multiple of the number of forms.

29. Def. Each of the ordered units in a construction is a position.

Thus the English construction of formative plus formative meaning 'object in number' has two positions; and that of free form plus free form plus free form meaning 'actor acting on goal' has three.

30. Assumption 10. Each position in a construction can be filled only by certain forms.

Thus, in the English construction of formative plus formative meaning 'object in number' the first position can be filled only by certain formatives (noun-stems), and the second only be certain other formatives (affixes of number, such as the plural-sign -s). And in the English construction of free form plus free form plus free form meaning 'actor acting on goal' the first and third positions can be filled only be certain free forms (object expressions) and the second only by certain other free forms (finite verb expressions). This assumption implies the converse, namely, that a given form will appear only in certain positions of certain constructions. Thus, an English noun-stem will appear only in the first position of the construction 'object in number', in the second position of the construction formative plus formative meaning 'object having such an object' (long-nose), and in certain positions of a certain few other constructions. Similarly, an object expression, such as John, the man will appear in the first position of the construction 'actor acting on goal', or in the third, or in certain positions of a certain few other constructions.

31. Def. The meaning of a position is a functional meaning.

That is, the constructional meaning of a construction may be divided into parts, one for each position; these parts are functional meanings. It would be more concrete, but perhaps less useful, if we said: the meaning common to all forms that can fill a given position, when they are in that position, is a functional meaning. Thus, in the English construction of 'object in number' the first position has the functional meaning 'object', or, more concretely, all the formatives (noun-stems) which can occur in this position, have in common, when they so appear, the functional meaning 'object'. And in the English construction of 'actor acting on goal' the first position has the functional meaning 'actor', or, more concretely, all the free forms (object-expressions, such as nouns, noun-phrases, pronouns, etc.) which can occur in this position, have in common, when they so appear, the functional meaning 'actor'. And in this same construction, the third position has the meaning 'goal', or, more concretely, all the free forms (largely the same as those just mentioned) which can appear in this position, have in common, when they so appear, the meaning 'goal'.

32. Def. The positions in which a form occurs are its functions.

Thus, the word John and the phrase the man have the functions of 'actor', 'goal', 'predicate noun', 'goal of preposition', and so on.

33. Def. All forms having the same functions constitute a form-class.

Examples of English form-classes are: noun-stems, number-affixes, object expressions, finite verb expressions.

34. Def. The functional meanings in which the forms of a form-class appear constitute the class-meaning.

Thus, the meanings found in all the functions of the form-class of English object expressions, namely 'actor', 'goal', etc. (§32) together constitute the class-meaning of these forms, which may be summed up as 'numbered object' or in the name 'object expression'.

35. Def. The functional meanings and class-meanings of a language are the categories of the language.

Thus, the above examples enable us to determine the following categories of the English language: from functional meanings: object, number, actor, action, goal; from class-meanings: object, number, numbered object (object expression), predicative action (finite verb expression).

36. Def. If a form-class contains relatively few forms, the meanings of these forms may be called sub-categories.

Thus, the English category of number contains only two meanings, singular-indefinite (egg) and plural (eggs). Hence one may speak of the sub-categories of singular and plural; it is convenient to do so when, as in this case, the sub-categories play a part in the alternation of other forms (see VII).

37. Def. A form-class of words is a word-class.

38. Def. The maximum word-classes of a language are the parts of speech of that language.

VII. Alternation

39. Assumption 11. In a construction a phoneme may alternate with another phoneme according to accompanying phonemes.

As in Sanskrit sandhi: tat pacati, tad bharati.

40. Def. Such alternation is phonetic alternation.

41. Assumption 12. In a construction a form may alternate with another form according to accompanying forms.

As, in English, the plural affixes book-s [s], boy-s [z], ox-en, f-ee-t. Or, verbs: He skates, They skate, according to number of actor.

42. Def. Such alternation is formal alternation.

43. Assumption 13. Absence of sound may be a phonetic or formal alternant.

44. Def. Such an alternant is a zero element.

The postulation of zero elements is necessary for Sanskrit (Pāṇini 1, 1, 61), for Primitive Indo-European (Meillet, Introduction à l'étude comparative des langues indo-européennes[3], Paris 1912, p. 127 f.), and probably economical for English (singular book with affix zero, as opposed to book-s, cf. f-oo-t : f-ee-t).

45. Def. If a formal alternation is determined by the phonemes of the accompanying forms, it is an automatic alternation.

Thus, the alternation of [-s, -z, -ez] in the regular English plural suffix of nouns is automatic, being determined by the final phoneme of the noun-stem. This differs from phonetic alternation since not every [s] in English is subject to this alternation, but only the (four) morphemes of this form. Similarly, Sanskrit tat pacati : tan nayati, since the alternation takes place only in wordfinal (contrast, e.g., ratnam).

The phonetic alternations and the automatic formal alternations of a language allow of a classification of the phonemes, to which the sound-patterns (§20) may contribute. Thus, the regular English plural suffix implies a classification of those English phonemes (the great majority) which may occur at the end of a noun-stem into the classes (1) sibilant, (2) non-sibilant (a, unvoiced; b, voiced). Ordinary phonetics can go no farther than this; phonetics which goes farther is either a personal skill or a science for the laboratory.

46. Def. The classification of phonemes implied in the sound-patterns [§20], phonetic alternations [§40], and automatic formal alternations [§45] of a language is the phonetic pattern.

For the sound-patterns and phonetic pattern see Sapir, Lang. 1.37 ((19)), and cf. Baudouin de Courtenay, Versuch einer Theorie Phonetischer Alternationen, Strassburg, 1895.

47. Def. If formal alternation is otherwise determined, it is grammatical alternation.

As, English plural suffix -en in ox-en alternating with the regular suffix above described; the verb-forms in he skates : they skate.

48. Def. If the accompanying forms which determine one grammatical variant predominate as to number, this variant is said to be regular; the others are irregular.

Thus, -en is an irregular plural suffix.

49. Def. If in a construction all the component forms are irregular, the whole form is suppletive.

If go be taken as the stem of the verb, then the past went is suppletive. Under this definition better as comparative of good would not be suppletive, since the ending -er is regular; a definition that will include such forms can be made only within English (or Indo-European) grammar, after 'stem' and 'affix' have been defined for this language.

50. Def. Whatever has meaning is a glosseme. The meaning of a glosseme is a noeme.

Thus the term glosseme includes (1) forms, (2) constructions, (3) zero elements.

The assumptions and definitions so far made will probably make it easy to define the grammatical phenomena of any language, both morphologic (affixation, reduplication, composition) and syntactic (cross-reference, concord, government, word-order), though I cannot say whether any such further definitions would apply to all languages. Other notions, such as subject, predicate, verb, noun, will apply only to some languages, and may have to be defined differently for different ones,—unless, indeed, we prefer to invent new terms for divergent phenomena.

VIII. Historical Linguistics

The following assumptions and definitions for historical linguistics are added for the sake of completeness. Insofar as they are correctly formulated, they will merely restate the working method of the great majority of linguists.

51. Assumption H1. Every language changes at a rate which leaves contemporary persons free to communicate without disturbance.

The ways in which it changes are described in Assumptions H3 and following.

52. Assumption H2. Among persons, linguistic change is uniform in ratio with the amount of communication between them.

These two assumptions and the assumptions and definitions based on them are necessarily loose, not because the process is too slow for any methods of direct observation that have been used—assumptions could ignore this—but because in historical linguistics it is our purpose to envisage the phenomena as relative. Ultimately no two speakers, and indeed no two utterances, have the same dialect: our assumptions must leave us free to examine the historical process with any desired degree of detail.

53. Def. If linguistic change results in groups of persons between which communication is disturbed, these groups speak dialects of the language.

54. Def. A relatively uniform auxiliary dialect used by such groups is a standard language.

55. Def. If linguistic change results in groups of persons between which communication is impossible, these groups speak related languages.

56. Assumption H3. Phonemes or classes of phonemes may gradually change.

For 'classes of phonemes' see §§45, 46.

57. Def. Such change is sound-change.

This assumption, by naming phonemes, implies that meaning is not involved. Owing to the assumptions that limit the number of phonemes (Assumptions 5 and 6), the change must affect the phonemes at every occurrence and do away with the older form of any phoneme that is changed.

58. Assumption H4. Sound-change may affect phonemes or classes of phonemes in the environment of certain other phonemes or classes of phonemes.

59. Def. This change is conditioned sound-change.

60. Assumption H5. Sound-change preponderantly favors shorter forms.[7]

61. Assumption H6. Linguistic change may substitute sames for differents.

62. Def. This change is analogic change.

63. Def. Analogic change which creates or enlarges a glosseme is contamination.

For example, creation (of a morpheme), pre-Germanic *hweð̌wōrez 'four', *fimfe 'five' > *f-eð̌wōrez, *f-imfe. Increase in size (of a morpheme), late Latin gra-ve, le-ve > gr-eve, l-eve (Italian).

64. Def. Analogic change which extends the use of a glosseme is adaptation.

Late Latin reddere > rendere, extending to a new word the morpheme -end- of pr-endere, p-endere, att-endere (v-endere?).

65. Def. Adaptation which replaces one alternant by another is proportional analogy.

English bēc > book-s; the plural affixes vary according to the accompanying noun-stem (grammatical alternation, §41), and now one alternant replaces another. The diagram showing the proportional character is familiar.

66. Def. Analogic change of formatives is formal analogy.

It may of course be contamination, adaptation, or proportional analogy. In a language in which stems and affixes are definable, it is customary to distinguish between 'material' formal analogy (affecting stems) and 'grammatical' formal analogy (affecting affixes).

67. Def. Analogic change of words is semantic change.

It may of course be contaminative, adaptive, or proportional. E.g., English meat 'pabulum' > 'caro'; or home 'Heim' > 'Haus'. Probably proportional:

He left the bones and took the flesh : He left the bones and took the meat :: She cooked the beans with the flesh : She cooked the beans with the meat.

They have a lovely house : They have a lovely home (intensive) :: A fine new house for sale : A fine new home for sale (intensive).[8]

68. Assumption H7. Analogic change predominantly disfavors irregular glossemes and those which diverge from their fellows; it tends to disfavor them in inverse ratio to their frequency of occurrence.

This is necessarily vague, because we know little about replacement and obsolescence through such factors as unusual homonymy, word-tabu, and other deviations of glossemes, that is, about inadequacy of glossemes and its effects. Cf. Gilliéron, Pathologie et thérapeutique verbales, Collection linguistique,

[7] Assumptions H5 and H7 try to embody the results of Jespersen's Progress in Language, New York 1894.

[8] The word 'intensive' is meant merely to describe the meaning of home in its new use (intensive of house), and is not meant as a technical term. Cf. also Kroesch, Lang. 2.35–45 (1926).

vol. 11, Paris 1921.

69. Assumption H8. Whoever speaks a foreign language or dialect may in it substitute resemblant features of his native speech.

70. Def. This is linguistic substitution.

71. Def. Linguistic substitution of phonemes is sound-substitution.

72. Assumption H9. Whoever hears a foreign language or dialect may adopt features of it into his own speech.

73. Def. Such adoption is linguistic borrowing.

74. Def. Borrowed words are loan-words.

75. Assumption H10. The phonemes of analogic forms and loan-words may be changed so as to fit the sound patterns of the language.

Western European peregrinus > pilgrim; German klüppel > knüppel.

76. Def. Such change is sudden sound-change.

77. Assumption H11. Glossemes may go out of use. Compare the comment on Assumption H7, §68.

[[Just as 'genius' is the word that first comes to mind on turning to Edward Sapir, so the word for Leonard Bloomfield's work is 'classic'. Here it seems most natural to speak of the work rather than the man. He was well liked as well as respected. But his modesty was infectious in two senses: after meeting him, one was apt to value one's self less and one's work more and to value Bloomfield's work so high that the man himself was apt to be left unmentioned: just what he preferred. His direct personal influence, then, is in a sense correctly said to have been small; and he certainly avoided occasions for exerting any. But in so far as he had any, it seems to have been mostly in this one direction: that he infected people with a high and serious respect for the evidence and for responsible statement about it.

He must have taken pleasure in his work: nothing done so well can have been done without pleasure. It was not that pleasure in random activity which, when coupled with intelligence, produces a mixture of a few valuable things and many worthless ones (so that good luck and some critical talent are both needed to avoid making a fool of oneself in print). Rather, his pleasure lay in deliberately constructing something without weak spots, a coherent whole that coheres with a uniform tenacity.

He would have taken no pleasure in such hollow victories as others have gained (temporarily) by convincing with specious wordings, or by making statements that have been allowed to stand for lack of any evident way to refute them. I don't know that he ever put it in these or similar words, but his practice was in accord with the principle that a scientific statement is a statement that can be disproved, by which we mean, of course, a statement worded in such a way as to make it clear what sort of data would be adequate to overthrow it; in other words, a scientific statement is a vulnerable statement. It takes a large-scale talent with words to find the adequately vulnerable wording, and Bloomfield had that. Still, not content with that, and as if to emphasize the point, he often indulged in deliberately shocking formulations, especially formulations that at first seem too naive to be scholarly and then turn out to be gems of ingenious simplicity. Possibly he did not entirely understand this point about himself; he once said to me, apropos of the number of symbols in a phonetic alphabet (I think it was when I said that he seemed to be making a virtue out of using the fewest possible symbols) 'Of course; that's what I mean by a scientific description,' as if to say that simplicity (not that he could have meant that it was that easy to measure simplicity) was the measure of science. I prefer to think that simplicity was not his aim for its own sake, or simply as a measure of being scientific, but rather because the simple statement can be checked by its author to make sure that it is vulnerable throughout, and checked by its critic throughout to make sure that he has overlooked no point of attack. I prefer to think this because Bloomfield did not hesitate to elaborate a series of statements as far as necessary to cover any expanse of data, but on the other hand seldom or never (I can find no instance in a hurry) gave the reader a brief and loosely simple advance statement of what he was about to present rigorously in detail. And in those detailed developments he did not hesitate to introduce new technical terms and require them to be read strictly according to his definitions of them, a behavior which was often misinterpreted as an unnecessary complication.

A good workman is known by his tools; for he not only chooses good ones, and sharpens them himself, but must even shape them. Bloomfield's Postulates, as well as his other more scattered methodological statements, thus naturally represent a central part of his work. A complete bibliography was published with his obituary, Lang. 25.87 ff. (1949), but the titles naturally seldom indicate where the methodological materials are included. For comments supplementary to these (and which might well have replaced much of these) see that obituary.

The Postulates have been called the Charter of contemporary descriptive linguistics. Nothing in them has been truly superseded, though much of Bloomfield's other work has been, a fate which he regarded as perfectly natural and indeed inevitable.]]

THE PHONEMIC PRINCIPLE

MORRIS SWADESH

Language 10.117-29—1934

As basic as the phonemic principle is to linguistic science, it is only quite recently that it has had the serious attention of linguists. In studying the phonemes of Chitimacha (an Indian language of Louisiana) I knew of no single source from which I could learn to understand all the phenomena that I observed. There seemed to be a need for an adequate and complete exposition of the phonemic principle including, especially, an account of how it applies to the more marginal and difficult types of phenomena. I at first intended to include this discussion in my paper on the Chitimacha phonemes, but the wider interest of the general discussion makes it more appropriate that it be published separately. The specific treatment of Chitimacha, which can now appear without theoretical digressions, will serve to illustrate many of the points discussed here. I do not attempt to cite previous authors[1] on all of the points treated in this paper, though I recognize fully my dependence on them. On a few points my treatment attempts to avoid weaknesses in previous treatments, and a point or two are perhaps introduced here for the first time. However, the chief ideals of this paper are theoretical comprehensiveness, consistency of treatment, and brevity.

The phonemic principle is that there are in each language a limited number of elemental types of speech sounds, called phonemes, peculiar to that language; that all sounds produced in the employment of the given language are referable to its set of phonemes; that only its own phonemes are at all significant in the given language.

The phonemes of a language are, in a sense, percepts to the native speakers of the given language, who ordinarily hear speech entirely in terms of these percepts. If they hear a foreign tongue spoken, they still tend to hear in terms of their native phonemes. Bilinguals and phonetically schooled individuals hear speech in a language native to them now in terms of the native phonemic system, now in terms of other percepts. If linguists occasionally have difficulty in discovering the phonemes of a language, it is usually when the language is not native to them, unless, indeed, in dealing with their own language, they be confused by some irrelevant or only partly relevant insight (as, for example, the knowledge of etymology or phonetics). At any rate, it is well to realize that one can learn nothing about the phonemes of one language by knowledge of those of another.

If the phonemes are percepts to the native speakers of the language, they are not necessarily percepts that he experiences in isolation. They occur ordinarily as the elements of words or sentences. Phonemes are perceptive units in the sense that the native can recognize as different, words different as to one of the component phonemes, e.g., bid and hid or bid and bed or bid and bit. The phoneme is the smallest potential unit of difference between similar words recognizable as different to the native. Given a correct native word, the replacement of one or more phonemes by other phonemes (capable of occurring in the same position) results in a native word other than that intended, or a native-like nonsense word. Other possible or conceivable differences are either not perceived, or are perceived as distortions of proper phonemes, or are chance oral sounds that are not classed as speech sounds at all.

The word sometimes has regular variant forms; in this event, two forms may differ as to one or more phonemes though they are in a sense the same word. Since variants sometimes confuse the phonemic problem, it may be well to point out some of the types of variants:

[1] The principal works consulted were:
Bloomfield, Language, Chapters 5-8. New York, Henry Holt, 1933.
Jones, On Phonemes, Travaux du cercle linguistique de Prague 4.74-9; Projet de terminologie phonologique standardisé, op.cit. 4.309-22.
Sapir, Sound Patterns in Language, Lang. 1.37-51 ⟨⟨19⟩⟩; La réalité psychologique du phonème, Journal de psychologie 30.247-55 [[58, fn. 13]].
Troubetzkoy, Zur allgemeinen Theorie der phonologischen Vokalsysteme, Travaux du cercle linguistique de Prague 1.39-66; Die phonologischen Systeme, op.cit. 96-115.
Ułaszyn, Laut, Phonema, Morphonema, op.cit. 4.53-61.

I am most directly indebted to Professor Sapir, as my teacher, for my understanding of the phonemic principle. The present paper has benefited by discussion with him and with my colleagues Dr. Stanley Newman, Dr. George Herzog, and Mrs. Mary Haas Swadesh.

I Free Variants (either variant is equally correct in any position)
  A Particular (applying to a single word or a limited number of isolated words), e.g., Nootka ʔapw'inqis, ʔapw'inʔis 'in the middle of the beach'; Eng. economics beginning like eke or like echo
  B General (applying to all words of a given class), e.g., Chitimacha words of three or more syllables ending in -VʔV vary with -V as k'ahtiʔi, k'ahti 'he bites'

II Conditional variants (determined by position in the sentence)
  A Particular, e.g. Eng. a, an
  B General
    (a) Phonetically conditioned, e.g., Sanskrit punar, punaḥ 'back, again'
    (b) Structurally conditioned, e.g., Tunica disyllabic words of the form CVʔV have that form only when spoken in isolation; in context they become CV as: riʔi 'house', context form ri.[2]

Conditional variants may be regular, as the examples given, or may be optional, as the Eng. sandhi type of as you [az yu, až(y)u], both of which are sometimes interchangeably employed by the same speakers.

Characteristics of the Phoneme

A phoneme, as a speech sound type, is defined by the separate instances of the type. If I say 'Peter Piper', I have produced three instances of the English phoneme p and every time any one pronounces these words or others like dip, pit, speed, supply, further instances of the phoneme are produced. On the basis of the separate occurrences (or a proper sampling of them) it is possible to define the type in terms of a norm and of deviation from the norm. Each individual has his own norm and range of deviation, the social norm being a summation of the individual norms. The description of the phoneme in terms of norm and deviation belongs to the science of phonetics.

The norm of the phoneme may be a multiple one. That is, instead of one norm, there may be two or more. Such variant norms are ordinarily conditional, depending on the phonetic surroundings in which the phoneme occurs. Thus one may distinguish at least three norms for English p:

(1) Relatively fortis, aspirated: e.g., in initial position, as in pit
(2) Fortis unaspirated: e.g., medially between vowels, as in upper
(3) Lenis unaspirated: e.g., after s, as in spill.

Positional variants may be even more strikingly different, as, for example the two variants of German x (ch) in, e.g. Macht, Licht. Positional variants are unlike phonemes in that to substitute one positional variant for the other distorts the word, sometimes beyond recognition, but never changes it into another native word.

Occasionally one finds free variants, that is, non-conditional or optional variants. Thus, there are many people in the Connecticut valley who interchangeably use either an r or a mid-mixed vowel with or without retroflexion in words like board and far.[3] It sometimes happens that one of a pair of free variants coincides with some other phoneme. Thus, Chitimacha w', y', m', n' may be pronounced with or without a glottal stricture, coinciding in the latter instance with the phonemes w, y, m, n. Another instance of this phenomenon, which may be called phonemic interchange, is the interchange of initial ð with d in words like the and they in Edgecombe County (near Rocky Mount), North Carolina.[4] Optional employment or omission of a phoneme occurs, for example, in the case of postvocalic r (e.g., barn) in certain sections of New England.[5]

Distribution

In a given language, some phonemes are frequent, some are infrequent. Sometimes the disparity in relative frequencies is great indeed, as that between English s and θ. Sometimes, a phoneme occurs in only one or a few isolated words; thus g occurs in Tunica only in the stem -gatci 'mother'.

All phonemes, as a general thing, are limited as to the positions in which they may occur. Two stops may not occur together at the beginning of an English word; yet such clusters do occur in certain other languages, as Sahaptin (e.g., tkwalwípt 'evening meal')[6] or ancient Greek. Again, English l does not occur after d or t at the beginning of a word. Every phoneme has its positional limitations, so that range of distribution constitutes a definite characteristic of each phoneme.

If a phoneme is much more limited as to positions of occurrence than other comparable phonemes of the same language, one may refer to it as a defective phoneme. Such a phoneme is ŋ in English, since it occurs only after and between vowels and never at the beginning of a word.

[2] Data on Tunica (an Indian language of Louisiana) were supplied by Mary Haas Swadesh.

[3] I have this information from Professor Hans Kurath, director of the Linguistic Atlas of the United States and Canada.

[4] Observed by Dr. Lowman for the Linguistic Atlas, and mentioned in his paper Regional Differences in Virginian Speech, read at the tenth annual meeting of the Linguistic Society of America.

[5] I owe this information to Dr. Lowman. The interchange was observed, for example, in one of his informants at Rockport, Massachusetts.

[6] See Jacobs, A Sketch of Northwest Sahaptin Grammar, Univ. of Washington Publications in Anthropology 4.85–292.

Phoneme Classes

English p, t, and k have common phonetic characteristics, relatively analogous positional variants, and relatively similar ranges of distribution; they are relatively different in these three respects from all other phonemes of the language. They therefore constitute a special class of English phonemes. English t, d, and θ have roughly the same articulating position and have distributional features in common, for example, that they occur initially before r but never initially before l. They constitute a class intercrossing with the p, t, k set. On the basis of similarities, all the sounds of a language may be thus classified, sub-classified, and cross-classified. The principal classes are those whose members have the most significant features in common, the sub-classes those that have less significant features in common. The bases of classification are common phonetic, variational, and distributional features. Classes are significant because of the general tendency of these features to occur in correlation.

But even in the absence of variational and distributional similarities, phonetic analogies are significant when they are recurrent. Whenever the phonetic relation of two sounds like English b and p is found to be the same as that of another pair like d and t, it is evident that the relation is not haphazard but systematic. Phonemes tend to occur in more or less consistent patterns.[7]

It is important to distinguish between the phonetic differentiae of phoneme classes and psychologically separable synchronous features. Thus nasalization is the phonetic differentia which in French distinguishes the nasalized vowel phonemes from their non-nasalized parallels; the tone upon which vowels are pronounced in French belongs to the prosody of the sentence and the occurrence of this or that phoneme on this or that pitch does not change its phonemic identity. In addition to patterns of sentence prosody, psychologically separable synchronous phonemes include tonemes in tone languages and tasemes (phonemes of stress) in stress languages, for these features apply to the syllables rather than to any of the phonemes in particular. Syllabic phenomena are necessarily most evident in connection with the vowel, but also apply, where possible, to the consonants. In Navaho ǹs-nèʔz 'I am tall', the tone of the first syllable is actualized in the syllabic consonant n and not with the consonant s, the tone of the second syllable is carried by the vowel and both consonants.

But prosodic features, often psychologically separable from the sounds with which they occur, do sometimes constitute mere differentiae of phonemes. In Chitimacha ə is distinguished from the other vowels by quality, quantity, and force of enunciation. Thus stress constitutes one of its differentiae.

[7] See the papers of Sapir and Troubetzkoy (fn. 1).

Considerations mentioned above give rise to three fundamental kinds of phonemes, as follows:

1. Sentence phonemes (patterns of sentence prosody)
2. Syllable phonemes (tonemes, tasemes)
3. Self-contained phonemes, phonemes proper

All languages have phonemes of type 3, but may or may not have phonemes of types 1 and 2. English has all three types; French has 1 and 3; Navaho has 2 and 3; Nitinat has only type 3. Of course, it is impossible to speak without prosody, but unless a prosodic feature has some contrastive significance, it is not phonemic. Thus, Nitinat has a very noticeable melody, but there is generally speaking only one melody which then is a concomitant of the sentence. In Navaho, the succession of syllable tones gives the effect of a sentence melody, but this melody has no significance of its own.

Word Structure

Each language has a characteristic word and syllable structure. Some of the limitations of occurrence of phonemes are best accounted for as connected with principles of word structure. Thus in Chitimacha all words begin in a single consonant followed immediately by a vowel. In Nootka a monosyllabic word may end in a consonant or a long vowel, but never in a short vowel. Any language will be found to have a whole set of such rules.

The limits of the word are often marked in special ways. Phonemes may have a special variant for the beginning or end of words. Thus the aspirate stops of Chitimacha are unaspirated at the end of the word; at the beginning of the word they are more fully aspirated than at the beginning of a medial or final syllable. Again, the limits of the word may be indicated by some non-phonemic element like the word accent of Latin or Polish, the initial glottal stop in German, or the aspiration that follows a final vowel in Nitinat. Such elements are not phonemes, but mechanical signs of the limits of the word units.

The sentence too may have characterizing phonetic features. A common mark of the sentence is the pause.

Method

The phonemes of a language can be discovered only by inductive procedure. This going from particular instances to general conception is as characteristic of the unconscious process of a native acquiring his language as it must be of conscious scientific study. But the scientist studying an alien language will make more rapid progress if he understands the essential details of the inductive process involved. A useful set of criteria, which follow from the nature of the phoneme, is given below. It should be remembered that they apply to any single given language, not to all languages taken together.

1. The criterion of consistency of words. Except for word variants (see above, second page) different occurrences of the same word have the same phonemic make-up. If differences are observed in different pronunciations of the same word, these are to be taken as showing the range of deviation of the component phonemes.
2. The criterion of partial identities. By a thoroughgoing comparison of all sets of words having a phonetic resemblance (e.g., pit–bit, late–latent, etc.), one arrives at a notion of the significant elemental sound types. But in the application of this criterion one must bear in mind the one given next.
3. The criterion of constant association. If a set of phonetic elements only occur together, they constitute a phonemically unitary complex; thus, the stop and the aspiration in English initial p. One or both of the phonetic elements may recur in other complexes without affecting the unitary nature of the complexes; in this event, all the phonemes that involve a given phonetic element constitute a phonemic class.
4. The criterion of complementary distribution. If it is true of two similar types of sounds that only one of them normally occurs in certain phonetic surroundings and that only the other normally occurs in certain other phonetic surroundings, the two may be sub-types of the same phoneme. If the distribution of one type of sound is complementary to that of more than one other, it is to be identified with one rather than the other if there is a more definite phonetic similarity in that direction; an example is the p of English speech whose distribution is complementary to that of the voiced labial b as well as to that of the voiceless labial stop sounds of peak, keep, happen, but goes with the latter rather than the former because of the phonetic similarity. If a sound in a relation of complementary distribution to two sounds is not particularly similar to either of them, it has to be reckoned as phonemically independent.
5. The criterion of pattern congruity. Particular formulations must be congruous with the general phonemic pattern of the given language. Thus, although Navaho i (occurring only after consonants) and y (occurring only before vowels) are complementary in distribution, they are nevertheless independent phonemes because of the fact that Navaho is generally characterized by a sharp distinction between vowel and consonant. (As a matter of fact, any vowel would be found to be in complementary distribution to almost any consonant.) In another language, non-syllabic and syllabic i might be positional variants of the same phoneme.

Throughout the phonemic study of a language, one may frequently employ with profit:

6. The test of substitution. This consists in pronouncing a word with some modification in one of the phonemes. If the modification cannot be perceived by a native, it is within the range of normal deviation. If the modification seems to trouble the native, it is an extreme deviation from the norm, a distortion. If the native definitely hears some other word or feels that one has the word wrong, one may conclude that the modification has amounted to the substitution of one phoneme for another.

Since the phonemic facts may be dependent on position in the word and the sentence, it is necessary always to determine the limits of the word and the sentence and the phonetic and phonemic peculiarities of the word and the sentence as units.

Discovering the phonemes is the first step in the phonemic study of a language. The second step consists in defining the nature of each phoneme in terms of 1) its norm and range of deviation for each position in which it may occur; 2) its positional distribution. One may also study its frequency, though this is somewhat less essential. Finally, it is necessary to study the phonemic system in its totality to find the significant classes, sub-classes, and cross-classes into which the phonemes fall.

Orthography

A phonemic orthography provides the most adequate, economical, and effective method of writing a language. Morphological and grammatical study of a language and the recording of its conclusions looks to orthography as an instrument of fundamental importance. A phonemic alphabet is the only kind that is truly adequate, for it alone represents all the pertinent facts and only the pertinent facts. Each sign in a phonemic alphabet represents one phoneme, and the implicit or explicit definition of each sign is an account of the norms (and deviations) of the phoneme in the various positions in which it may occur. If the writing is entirely in keeping with the phonemics of the language, a mechanical substitution of the values of the signs for the signs will reproduce the recorded forms correctly and completely.

Even in the problem of phonemics itself, orthography is a valuable technique. Indeed, the problem of ascertaining the phonemes of a language may be stated in large part in terms of the devising and defining of a set of symbols that will represent the sounds of the language most adequately and most economically. The test of an adequate phonemic writing is that it be possible for one who does not know the meaning of the words to read them off correctly and without serious distortions (it is assumed in this that the reader has made himself familiar with the key to the system and that he has learned to produce the required sounds). The test of an economical phonemic writing is that it employ as few and as simple signs as possible. However, these tests are insufficient in some details of the choice of signs for sound-types of complementary distribution; this matter is explained above (criterion 4).

Where convenient, the phonemic symbols should be made to reflect the phonemic pattern by having some point of resemblance in the signs for the members of each class of phonemes;[8] such a situation is attained in part when some diacritical mark is used to represent a given feature of differentiation, e.g., Hungarian í, ű, ú, é, ő, ó, á (long vowels),[9] Chitimacha p', t', k', č', c', w', y', m', n', ŋ' (glottalized consonants). Finally, it is important that the symbols be in general accord with those generally in use, except that this consideration is secondary to the two essentials of accuracy and simplicity.

Since the phonemes of different languages are different as to their norms and even more strikingly so as to their positional variants, one might argue that it is necessary to have different symbols for each new language, that the English voiceless labial stop, for example, be written differently from that of French. It is obvious that such a treatment would make linguistic science extremely difficult. It has therefore become conventional to use the same or similar signs in different languages to represent roughly similar phonemes. This method works out perfectly as long as one does not carelessly assume standard or familiar values for given signs wherever they occur.

Normalization

When two or more forms of a word are both correct, two courses are possible, namely, to record the form employed at each given time, or to always write one of the variants. The latter treatment is called normalization. In the case of particular word-variants,[10] normalization would have to be entirely arbitrary and is therefore to be avoided. In the case of optional general variants,[10] it is usually possible to normalize without obscuring the fact of variation. This is possible when one can so define one's symbols that the affected phonemes in such a variation are readable in two ways. For example, one may write äz yu for English 'as you', and indicate as part of the definition of the symbol z that before y it may have the value ž, the y being sometimes then lost; to be complete one may indicate that the variation is usually a function of speed and care of speech, the series being äz yu, äž yu, äžu (not to speak of äžə). Similarly, in the case of phonemic interchange, one may write the distinctive form and mention the interchange in the definition of the phonemic symbol.

[8] An ideal working out of this principle would give us a phonemic 'visible speech' in which each phonemic sign would be a composite of elements each of which would represent one of the class, sub-class, and cross-class differentiae or sets of differentiae of the phoneme. However, such an orthography might prove impractical for other reasons.

[9] ű and ő represent long ü and ö respectively.

[10] See the second page of this paper.

Phonetics

Phonetics (the science of the study of speech sounds) benefits the student of phonemics in two ways. First, it is valuable in the discovery of the phonemes of a foreign language. Secondly, it provides the technique for study and description of the phonemes once they are known.

At the outset of one's study of a foreign language, it is convenient to make a phonetic record based on aural observation and written in terms of a general phonetic alphabet which provides symbols for selected characteristic points in the total range of possible speech sounds. As one continues to work with a language, one replaces the strict phonetic alphabet with a tentative phonemic alphabet which is then corrected from time to time until one arrives at a final, adequate phonemic orthography. A certain number of linguists feel that a phonetic orthography is in itself sufficient, and some even hold that a phonemic orthography is incorrect. However, as I have shown, a phonemic writing (together with its key giving the value of the signs employed) records all the pertinent phonetic facts. A phonetic writing, on the other hand, is lacking in the following ways:

1. It does not indicate the phonetic units that are significant for the given language.
2. It is overly microscopic, complex, and hard to handle.
3. It does not distinguish errors and distortions from normal forms.
4. It is likely to be phonetically inaccurate.

On the last point, I quote Bloomfield (Language 84–5):

> Practical phoneticians sometimes acquire great virtuosity in discriminating and reproducing all manner of strange sounds. In this, to be sure, there lies some danger for linguistic work. Having learned to discriminate many kinds of sounds, the phonetician may turn to some language, new or familiar, and insist on recording all the distinctions he has learned to discriminate, even when in this language they are non-distinctive and have no bearing whatever ... The chief objection to this procedure is its inconsistency. The phonetician's equipment is personal and accidental; he hears those acoustic features which are discriminated in the languages he has observed. Even his most 'exact' record is bound to ignore innumerable non-distinctive features of sound; the ones that appear in it are selected by accidental and personal factors. There is no objection to a linguist's describing all the acoustic features that he can hear, provided he does not confuse these with the phonemic features. He should remember that his hearing of non-distinctive features depends upon the accident of his personal equipment, and that his most elaborate account cannot remotely approach the value of a mechanical record.

Furthermore, in the extreme concentration required for minute discrimination of certain features of sound, the phonetician may easily overlook other features that may be of prime importance in the given language.

Some linguists employ a normative phonetic writing in preference to either phonemic or strict phonetic writing. If the interpretation of actual sounds in terms of the norms of the language is correct and if the correction of errors is made without error, a normative phonetic orthography shares some of the advantage of a phonemic orthography. Simplification of the phonetic writing of a given language is also an improvement in the general direction of phonemic writing. As a matter of fact a phonemic orthography is the inevitable result if normalization and simplification are carried out thoroughly, consistently, and correctly.

Historical Phonology

In determining the phonemic system of a language, only phonetic data are relevant. Historical phonology is not relevant. To base one's spelling of a word on the form of the word in a known or reconstructed parent language neither benefits historical study of language nor provides a dependable method of accurate phonemic analysis. Historical etymology in a matter of phonemics is an acceptable aid only when one is dealing with an inadequately recorded noncontemporary language. Of course, phonemes are a historical product and a step in a historical development, but to argue from phonetic law to descriptive fact is discovering the arguments from the conclusion when the procedure should always be the opposite.

The fact that a phonemic system is a step in historical development suggests that one way to understand historical change is to understand phonemics more fully.[11] On the basis of facts pointed out in this paper and on the basis of some simple truths about historical phonetic change, one may make the following suggestions. Phonetic change must consist in the change of the norm of a sound or one of its positional variants. Change in a phonemic norm does not affect the actual phonemic pattern unless the phoneme thereby comes to coincide with some other phoneme or splits up into more than one phoneme. The intermediate step in coalescence of phonemes is the condition of phonemic interchange. The intermediate step in the split-up of a phoneme is the presence of markedly different positional variants; in this situation, if, through analogy or borrowing of foreign words one of the variants comes to be employed in positions other than within its original limits, it takes on the character of an independent phoneme. I shall not illustrate these processes, since the matter is only incidental to my subject; instances are to be found everywhere where we have an actual record of a historical change.

[11] This important incidental value of phonemics was called to my attention by Professor Sapir.

Morpho-phonology

Morpho-phonology includes, in addition to the study of the phonemic structure of morphemes, the study of interchange between phonemes as a morphological process. If a given morphologic interchange is sufficiently regular and characteristic, the interchanging phonemes may be regarded as a morphologically unitary set. Examples are Indo-European e/o/ē/ō/zero, English f/v (in, e.g., <u>leaf</u>, <u>leaves</u>). Whether it is a convenient fiction or a true reflection of linguistic psychology, morphological processes are usually described as having a definite order. <u>Leaves</u> is taken to be a secondary formation from <u>leaf</u>, and in consequence v is the mutation of f and not f that of v. But f does not always change to v in the morphological process of plural formation; thus, we have <u>cuff</u>, <u>cuffs</u>. The f of <u>cuff</u> is therefore morphologically different from the f of <u>leaf</u>, though phonemically it is the same entity. Morphologically, we have two f's so that $f_1 : v :: f_2 : f$. Morphologically distinct phonemes are called morpho-phonemes.

A morpho-phoneme is one of a class of like phonemes considered as components of actual morphemes which behave alike morphologically, i.e., have a like place in the same mutation series. The morpho-phoneme is never to be confused with the phoneme as such, even in the event that all instances of a given phoneme are members of the same morpho-phonemic class. One may devise a morphologic writing for use in morphological discussion or in a dictionary, but such a writing is not to be employed in ordinary linguistic records.[12]

The phonemic principle when properly understood provides the only completely consistent and adequate method of understanding the nature of the phonetics of a given language. Phonetics provides the technique of discovering and defining the phonemes. Morphology includes a study of the phonemic structure of morphemes and of morphological interrelations among phonemes as components of morphemes. Historical phonology studies the evolution of phonemes. In these ways phonemics interrelates with other phases of linguistic science, but it does not compete with these other phases. In developing the phonemic principle, its proponents are only bringing into plain view a hitherto imperfectly lighted area in which there has always been a certain amount of stumbling.

[12] Of course there are instances where it is desirable to use non-phonemic diacritical marks as a special aid to non-native students.

⟦At this time the only Americans who had a fair chance to learn linguistic method were apprentices under one of the few leaders in anthropological linguistics: there were no textbooks. The appearance of this paper by one of Sapir's most noted pupils therefore meant a very great advance in public knowledge of its subject.⟧

THE NON-UNIQUENESS OF PHONEMIC SOLUTIONS OF PHONETIC SYSTEMS

YUEN-REN CHAO

Bulletin of the Institute of History and Philology
Academia Sinica, Vol. IV, Part 4, 363–97—1934

In reading current discussions on the transcription* of sounds by phonemes, one gets the impression of a tacit assumption that given the sounds of one language, there will be one and only one way of reducing them to a system of phonemes which represent the sound-system correctly. Since different writers do not in fact agree in the phonemic treatment of the same language, there arise then frequent controversies over the 'correctness' or 'incorrectness' in the use of phonemes.

The main purpose of the present paper is to show that given the sounds of a language, there are usually more than one possible way of reducing them to a system of phonemes, and that these different systems or solutions are not simply correct or incorrect, but may be regarded only as being good or bad for various purposes.

I. DEFINITIONS OF A PHONEME

The most comprehensive discussion of the phoneme and related ideas seems to be that by H. E. Palmer,[1] of which we shall now give a brief summary. Palmer begins by quoting at length Jimbo's writing on 'The Concrete and Abstract Nature of Sounds:' 'One concrete sound has one definite quality, one definite pitch, one definite loudness, one definite length,' in other words, it corresponds to one particular oscillograph curve or stretch of the groove of a faithful phonograph record, which is therefore not the usual object of study for phonetics. By collecting examples of actual utterances of what is considered the same word with the same meaning by speakers of the same language of concrete sounds, one arrives at 'an abstract sound of the first degree', such as the first sound in the word army. By comparing different words such as army, archer, art, argue, one concludes, after due examination, that the first sound in these words are 'the same', which is then 'an abstract sound of the second degree'.

Taking Palmer's own system, we note that he finds it more convenient to replace the term abstract speech-sound by the term phone. His system of phones is then as follows:

*Since this was written at a time when the differences between transcription and phonemicization and between phonemes and morphophonemes were not as clear as they are today, the article would have to be reworded in many places if these differences were to be taken into account. In this reprint no attempt was made to make such changes, except to correct minor errors of fact.—Y. R. C.

[1] H. E. Palmer, The Principles of Romanization, 1931, Tokyo, pp. 52 ff.

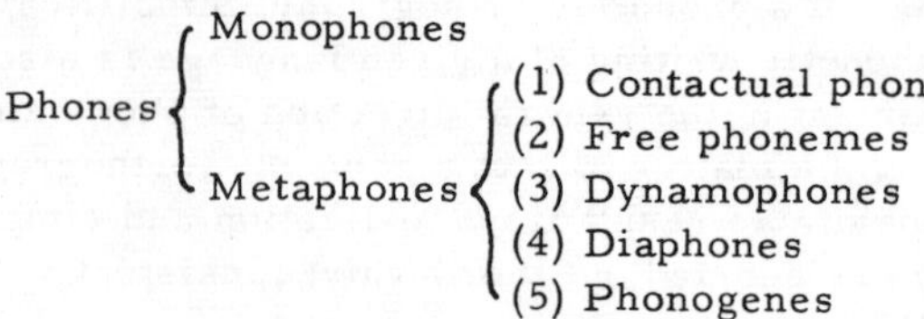

A Monophone is 'any phone of the first or second degree of abstraction of which the concrete members are so similar in point of production and of acoustic effect even when observed by a competent observer, that it may be regarded as a minimal unit of pronunciation (i.e. practically insusceptible of subdivision).' (We may add: 'or of further differentiation'.) 'Contrasted with monophones we have metaphones, which we may define as two or more phones which serve jointly as units of meaning within the limits of a given linguistic community.'

(1) Palmer goes on to identify Jones's definition of a phoneme with his idea of a contactual phoneme: 'A phoneme is a group of sounds consisting of an important sound of the language (i.e. the most frequently used member of that group) together with others which take its place in particular sound-groups.... The use of subsidiary members of phonemes is, in most languages, determined by simple principles which can be stated once for all, and which can be taken for granted in reading phonetic texts.'

(2) A free phoneme is like a contactual phoneme except that it is impossible to say in what phonetic circumstances one or another of its members will be actually used. We can give the apparently random[2] use of the tip or back of the tongue in the nasal ending of words like 林 [lin ∼ liŋ], 明 [min ∼ miŋ] in Nanking as an example of free phonemes. This is the same as Jones's variphone.

(3) A dynamophone is a metaphone which contains two or more phones differing not only in quality, but also in regard to the intensity or force of the articulation that produces them. Palmer cites the first phone in the word as as an example which shades from the first phone of act to the obscure sound of the first phone of about, and even to zero value.

It would seem convenient also to include under this heading those metaphones whose members differ according to conditions of length and intonation (in which case a term wider than dynamophone will have to be used). Thus, the vowel in French bette and bête is a metaphone whose members differ slightly in quality according to the conditions of length.

[2] That is, determined by psychological or physiological conditions other than those which usually are considered to be phonetic.

Those who transcribe eat, it as [i:t], [it] are also considering the vowel in these words as forming one metaphone whose members differ in quality according to conditions of length. Again, the vowel in the Foochow words 哥 [kɔ55:] and 個 [kɔ˅12:] is a metaphone whose members differ in quality according as the intonation belongs to one or the other of two sets of tones.

Before taking up the next two terms, it will be well to examine a later definition of a phoneme given by Jones: 'Definition of a phoneme: a family of sounds in a given language which are related in character and are such that no one of them ever occurs in the same surroundings as any other in words.' (The term 'language' here means the pronunciation of one individual speaking in a definite style. 'In the same surroundings' means surrounded by the same sounds and in the same condition as regards length, stress and intonation.'[3]) This definition differs from the earlier one quoted above in that it no longer mentions a 'principal member', but specifies that the different members should be 'related in character' and that no two of them should occur 'in the same surroundings as regards length, stress and intonation'. It seems therefore that Jones's conception of a phoneme includes not only Palmer's contactual phonemes, but also some at least of his dynamophones.

(4) The term diaphone is used by Palmer following the usage of Jones: 'The diaphone is a family of sounds heard when we compare the speech of one person with that of another.' Jones cites [o:], [ou], [əu], [ʌu] as members of the diaphone occurring in words like coat, road, home. Similarly, we can cite [ɑu], [ou], [əu], [ɤ], [ɯ], [øy], [ei], [ɪ] as members of the diaphone occurring in words like 歐'Europe', 狗'dog', 後'after'.

(5) The phonogene, a term also proposed by Jones, is 'a given phone together with its ancestral forms,' thus the vowel [ou] in stone, together with [o], [ɔ], [ɑ] form a phonogene. Similarly, [ɚ], [əɹ], [ɹ̩], [ɹi], [ʑi], [ɲʑi], [ɲi], [ni] form one phonogene in words like 兒'child', 耳 'ear', 二 'two'.

Bloomfield gives no formal definition of a phoneme. He begins by distinguishing the 'gross acoustic features' of language (Jimbo's 'concrete sounds' or sounds of low degrees of abstraction) and 'distinctive' or 'significant features'. By comparing the partial identities and differences between words like pin, tin, tan, tack, he succeeds in analyzing the distinctive features of words like pin into indivisible units which cannot be analyzed any further (from the standpoint of the language under investigation): each of these units is 'a minimum unit of distinctive sound-feature, a phoneme,'[4] which phrase is the nearest Bloomfield comes to a formal definition of a phoneme.

Differences of quality conditioned by length are grouped by Bloomfield under the same phoneme, as German Beet [be:t], Bett [bet]. He also writes hatte ['hate], where the stress on the first syllable indicates sufficiently the weakened and obscure value of the second vowel. Bloomfield's phoneme therefore also includes Palmer's dynamophones.

Bloomfield makes no explicit mention of free phonemes or variphones. In cases like the apparently random use of final [n] and [ŋ] in some Chinese dialects for the same word in the same phonetic surroundings, he would probably consider simple nasality as being the distinctive feature and the place of articulation as among the gross acoustic features. In other words, variphones are also phonemes, except that the choice of the exact shade of the sound used is determined by psychological and physiological factors other than those of phonetic environment. Since, however, whether variation of sounds determined by non-phonetic conditions are wide enough to be called two or more 'different' sounds or simply inevitable small 'accidental' variations depends upon the degree of narrowness of the phonetician's scale of division, Bloomfield is within his rights in neglecting the existence of variphones.[5]

From the preceding, it may seem that Bloomfield has a different conception of the phoneme from that of Jones and Palmer. For Jones and Palmer, a phoneme is a group of sounds, while for Bloomfield it is a sound-feature. If, however, we examine the two ideas more closely, we shall find that they amount to the same thing. Take for example the English phoneme [h]. From one point of view, we may say that it is a group of different sounds [h_i], [h_e], [h_a], [h_u], etc., where the subscripts are an indication of the tongue and lip positions during the pronunciation of the consonant. But from the other point of view we may just as well say that the phoneme [h] is simply the feature of voiceless glottal friction and leave the other non-significant features unspecified. There is therefore no real difference in the use of the term phoneme by those writers, so far as this point is concerned.

For the present discussion, we shall group together Palmer's contactual phoneme, free phoneme, and dynamophone, all under the term phoneme, to be defined as follows:

A phoneme is one of an exhaustive list of classes of sounds in a language,[6] such that every word in the language can be given as an ordered series of one or more of these classes and such that two different

3 Proceedings of the International Congress of Phonetic Sciences, 1932, Amsterdam, p. 23.

4 Leonard Bloomfield, Language, 1933, New York, p. 79.

5 See however III below on the finiteness of the number of distinguishable speech sounds.

6 Taken in the sense of the pronunciation of a homogeneous speech community, such that members of the same community will find absolutely no 'accent' in one another's speech.

words which are not considered as having the same pronunciation differ in the order or in the constituency of the classes which make up the word.

Observations:

(1) This definition presupposes that it is possible to enumerate exhaustively the total number of phonemes for any given language.

(2) It does not exclude the possibility of the same sound belonging to more than one class (Cf. II 2 (f), (g) below).

(3) It is non-committal as to whether given a language, there is one unique way for grouping its sounds into phonemes or there are other possible ways.

(4) It leaves unspecified the scope of the word 'sound' as regards size and kind, i.e. the degree of analysis into successive elements and the degree of differentiation into kinds.

(5) It includes both the cases where, given the phonemes in a word and its phonetic environment, it is possible to determine the actual pronunciation of the word by a set of 'rules of pronunciation' (i.e. to know which member-sounds of sound-classes will actually be used) and those cases where a given word in a given phonetic environment may still contain a phoneme of which one or another member may be used. The former will be a contactual phoneme or a dynamophone and the latter a free phoneme. (This remark, however, would be superfluous if we repudiate the validity of descriptive phonetics, with its narrow transcriptions.)

(6) The clause that every word consists of a series of 'classes' may sound a little strange. But if, as is convenient in the study of languages, we speak of recognizable words consisting of recognizable phonemes, then such phonemes are usually classes of sounds, which a trained ear would distinguish as different sounds. The statement sounds no more strange than that 1, 2, 3, 4 are a series of classes, which is what mathematicians define numbers as.

(7) If each phoneme is written with one definite symbol, then every word will have a definite form of transcription. Homophones, or different words having the same pronunciation, will be transcribed alike. It should be noted, however, that the boundary between a homophone and a word with variations in meaning is often hard to determine.

(8) A phonemic transcription is pronounceable without reference to grammatical or lexical consideration. Thus, the Chinese National Phonetic Script and the National Romanization are phonemic transcriptions in a sense in which English or even German orthography is not.

II. FACTORS WHICH INFLUENCE THE PHONEMIC SOLUTIONS OF PHONETIC SYSTEMS

As the grouping of sounds in a language into phonemes as defined above does not necessarily lead to one unique solution, we shall now consider the various factors which influence the form of the solutions.

1. Size of Unit in Time.

(a) Under-analysis. In the early days of phonetic transcription, the slogan was 'one sound, one symbol'. In these days of phonemic transcription, this has been changed to 'one phoneme, one symbol', so that it is now permissible to represent more than one sound by one symbol.

But there are two aspects to the idea of 'one sound'. From the point of view of differentiation of quality, 'one sound' is one kind of sound, which is what one usually has in mind when using the phrase in discussions about phonemes. But from the point of view of analysis in time, 'one sound' is one piece of sound, such that its quality is homogeneous throughout its duration. Discussions about phonemes do not seem to have been very explicit about the change of quality in time which may be included within the scope of one phoneme. We recall that Palmer defines a monophone 'as a minimal unit of pronunciation (i. e. practically insusceptible of further subdivision)'. All the preceding discussions in the passage quoted have to do with the question of differentiation, but as the words 'minimal' and 'subdivision' can also be taken in the temporal sense, it would seem that a monophone should be both one kind of sound and one piece of sound.

Now if it is convenient to group into classes and call phonemes different kinds of sounds in a language which go together in a certain way, it would also be convenient to join into compounds successive pieces of sounds which act as units in a language. This is by no means new practice. Our point here is only to make it explicit and put it on a par with the differential aspect of phonemes.

All kinetic speech-sounds, diphthongs, affricates, aspirates, and other sounds with their usual glides are compounds which act as units and can be treated as phonemes. Thus, Bloomfield considers the English affricates [č] and [ǰ] as independent phonemes. The English plosives [p], [t], [k] are treated by all writers as single phonemes, although in initial stressed positions they have a slight aspiration and have a larger size than in unstressed positions or after [s] (in [sp-], [st-], [sk-]). In the former case, the inclusion of [č] and [ǰ] is optional, for these could be resolved into the phonemes [tʃ] and [dʒ] respectively. In cases like he cheats [hi: 'tʃi:ts], heat sheets [hi:t 'ʃi:ts]; What can each add? [...i:tʃ 'æd], What can eat shad? [...i:t 'ʃæd], the distinction may either be made by considering [č] and [tš] as different phonemes, as with Bloomfield, or simply by the difference in the position of the minimum point, as with most other writers; that is to say, since the [č] in each add and the [tʃ] in eat shad never occur under the same conditions as regards stress, [č] need not be considered as a separate phoneme. In many Chinese dialects, the initial [k] always occurs before low front vowels or central or back vowels, and initials of the [tɕ] type always occur before high front vowels. The two may therefore be taken as the same phoneme, although the latter is an affricate. Similarly, the [t] in [ta] タ, the [tɕ] in [tɕi] チ and the [ts] in [tsɯ] ツ in Japanese may be taken as belonging to one phoneme.

Kinetic sounds of the diphthong type need special consideration. While affricates, aspirates and sounds with characteristic glides can usually be analyzed, if desired, into two or three recognizable elements, kinetic vowels and quasi-vowels are sounds with even more gradual change in quality. The usual method of representing these sounds is simply to indicate the two end-positions of the whole movement, as [ei], or to indicate the open position and the extreme close position even though never actually reached, as [ai] for what is actually never wider than [ae]. In the case of movement not by the most direct line, the turning point is indicated by inserting an additional symbol, as [uei], but not [ɑou], as [ɑu] means [ɑou] or [ɑɔou].

Now by our definition of a phoneme, there is nothing to prevent us from regarding characteristic kinetic open sounds in a language as independent phonemes, which is in fact the practice of the designers of the Chinese National Phonetic Script, who represent [ai], [ei], [ɑu], [ou] by the single symbols ㄞㄟㄠㄡ, and even [an], [ən], [ɑŋ], [əŋ] by ㄢㄣㄤㄥ. It may seem unorthodox to take the National Phonetic Script as serious phonemic transcription, but we should be less sure of ourselves when we come to cases of narrow-range kinetic sounds. There is a real difference in practice, if not of opinion, between Bloomfield's use of [ij] and [uw] for English and other writers' use of [i:] and [u:], as contrasted with [i] and [u]; or of [i] and [u] (with implied relative length) as contrasted with [ɪ] and [ʊ]. Again, in many American dialects, it is a toss-up whether to write bet, bait as [bet], [beit] or as [bet], [be:t], or [bɛt], [b̄et] (with implied length). The most interesting case of the size-of-unit question is that of the Foochow dialect, where a whole series of vowels in the same words are static or kinetic according to the tone in which each is pronounced. Thus, 氣 [k'ei 12:] 'air', 竹 [tøyk 23:] 'bamboo', 護 [hou 242:] 'protect', take on the following sounds when they are pronounced in the following combinations of tonal environment: 氣壓 [k'i 53: ɑk 23:] 'air pressure', 竹節 [ty 5: ʒaik 23:] 'bamboo section', and 護兵 [hu 55: ʋiŋ 55:] 'guards' (protecting soldiers), respectively. We have therefore on our hands the question of choice between (1) admitting phonemes of which some members are static and other members kinetic vowels, or diphthongs, and (2) regarding the static members as forming one phoneme and the corresponding kinetic vowels as two phonemes in succession, thus allowing the same word to have two forms. The presence and absence of the aspiration in English [p], [t], [k] mentioned above is also a similar case, though not so striking.

Another very peculiar case is that of a vowel in a concave circumflex tone in a number of Chinese dialects, such as the yangshaang tone of Hwangyan, Chekiang, where the valley is so low or simply so narrow that the voice is lost into a glottal stop in the middle of the syllable, so that [ɔ 313:] actually becomes [ɔ31: ʔɔ3:]. Phonetically, it sounds like three sounds forming two syllables. But phonemically, it is much more natural to consider it as a form of [ɔ] in a certain tone.

On the whole, the usual practice allows a great deal of latitude in taking kinetic consonants as single phonemes, but is not so free in giving single symbols for kinetic vowels. Bloomfield gives a list of eight diphthongs and one triphthong for English, and calls them 'compound primary phonemes', all their elements occurring also as single primary phonemes. [1955 note: The word 'primary' does not affect this discussion; it was simply Bloomfield's word for our 'segmental' phonemes—the vowels and consonants.]

The chief point we wish to emphasize here is that it is not always advisable or convenient to take the smallest static unit of sound analyzable by the trained ear as the unit of phonemic members ('one piece sound, one symbol'), and that according as we take a smaller or a larger unit for our phonemic members, we sometimes arrive at different forms of phonemic pattern for the same language, which are equally valid, though they may not be equally suitable for this or that purpose.

(b) Over-analysis. The principle of 'one piece sound, one symbol' has yet to allow a class of exceptions in the opposite direction, namely, one piece sound, two or three piece symbols. Jones and Camilli give the following cases where combinations of letters are permitted to represent single phonemes:[7]

a) The affricates [pf], [bv], [ts], [dz], [tʃ], [dʒ], [tɕ], etc.

b) The aspirates [ph], [th], [kh], [tlh], [tʃh], etc., and weak aspirates [p'], [t'], etc.

c) The aspirated [s] or [sh].

d) [t], [d] with lateral explosions: [tl], [dl].

e) The voiceless nasals, [hm], [hn], [hɲ], [hŋ], when these are distinct phonemes.

f) Retroflex vowels, as American [əɹ], or Peiping [ɨɹ]. ⟦Chao quoted Jones's '[uɹ]'.⟧

g) Labiovelar consonants: [kp], [gb].

[7] Fondamenti di Grafia Fonetica, by Daniel Jones and Amerindo Camilli, 1933, Aube and London, 11–12.

Of these cases, a) and b) are recognizably compound sounds, which we should consider as two or three piece sounds, for which the use of [tʃ], [dʒ], [ph], [th], etc. would be considered as normal and the use of [č], [ǰ], (or [c], [ɟ]), [p], [t], etc. would be considered as cases of under-analysis. c) and d) may be regarded as borderline cases. e), f), and g) are clear cases of over-analysis, that is, cases of one homogeneous sound represented by two or three piece symbols, each of which represents some aspect or aspects of the sound.[8] Thus, [hm̥] is a [m]-sound which is breathed (i.e. [h]-ized) or a [h]-sound with labio-nasal articulation (i.e. [m]-ized). It is meaningless to ask which is the substantive and which the adjective, as they are all constituting attributes which together form the sound in question and could be represented by Jespersen's over-analytical analphabetic symbols. Similarly, American [əɹ] is a single vowel formed by the middle of the tongue in the [ə] position with the apex curled back (sometimes transcribed as [ɚ]). The representation of voiceless [w] or [ʍ] by [hw] is another case, which is mentioned by Jones and Camilli under an earlier section in the same pamphlet quoted.[9]

Among the uses of diacritical marks, Jones and Camilli[10] mention 'the saving of a series of new letters,' such as adding ˜ to [ɑ], [ɔ], [œ], [ɛ], to form [ɑ̃], [ɔ̃], [œ̃], [ɛ̃] in transcribing French. The reader will recall the great furore which was aroused by Passy's proposal to use [ɑŋ], [ɔŋ], [œŋ], [ɛŋ] for these French vowels in the first post-war issues of Le maître phonétique. He modestly called it orthographic transcription; but if [əɹ] can represent [ɚ], there is no reason why [ɑŋ] cannot represent [ɑ̃]. To object that other French dialects or German actually has [ɑŋ] as two successive sounds is beside the point, as we are talking about phonemic transcriptions and our universe of discourse is limited to one dialect or one language, otherwise we should have to go back to narrow phonetic transcriptions. Not that [ɑŋ] is the only right way or even a good way of representing French [ɑ̃], but there seems to be nothing wrong, so far as usage in other cases goes, with representing one piece sound by two piece symbols.

Jones and Camilli do another thing along the same line. Without mentioning the saving of a series of modified letters under any of the principles, they also use the device of representing one piece sound by two piece symbols in transcribing the Russian palatalized consonants, where the explanatory note says, 'j is used as the sign of palatalization, that is, tj = ƫ, nj = ɲ, lj = ȴ, snj = sɲ, tnj = tɲ, lnj = lɲ, etc.'[11] This [j] is therefore a significant feature, but it does not necessarily occupy any time of its own.

Another important case is that of the 'voiced h', which plays a very important part in the Wu-dialects in China. These dialects usually have an ordinary [h], which has different values according to the vowel following and may therefore be taken as one phoneme, just as in the case of English or German, so that instead of having 2n symbols for h_1a_1, h_2a_2, ... h_na_n (where a_1, a_2, ... a_n are the vowels which may follow the h in the language), we need only n+1 symbols for ha_1, ha_2, ... ha_n. But in the case of the voiced h, not only the vowel quality (or the vowel articulation) begins at the very beginning of the breathing, but the breathiness also lasts till the very last moment of the vowel, so as to form one homogeneous breathy vowel, and there is neither question of order of succession nor question of substantive and adjective. If we must have one piece symbol for one piece sound, we should have to have either a series of different voiced h symbols for different vowels, or an extra series of breathy vowels have to be recognized. The only practical thing to do here is to consider voiced h as one phoneme and write the vowel symbols after it as [ɦɑ], [ɦe], [ɦo], etc., although we know that these digraphs represent perfectly homogeneous sounds.

There are also borderline cases where it is open to question whether certain sound-elements are simultaneous or successive. According to ordinary transcriptions, the English word sway is transcribed as [swei] while the Chinese word 歲 'year' is transcribed as [suei], from which it would seem that the first two elements in Chinese 歲 would be separated more clearly than in English sway. As a matter of fact, the contrary is the case. While the [s] in English sway is not at all labialized for most of its duration, the [s] in Chinese 歲 is completely labialized. Moreover, the diphthong [ei] starts almost as soon as the tongue leaves the [s]-position without leaving any appreciable duration for the [u] or [w] to stand alone, so that a narrow transcription might give 歲 as [s̰ei] or, as the velar element is rather weak in this type of word, as [σei]. But in similar syllables in other tones or with other initial consonants, there is more independence in the [u]-element. It would be contrary to the spirit of phonemic transcription to write 歲 as [σei] and 對 as [tuei]. Consequently, we must allow as a possible phonemic 'solution' the over-analysis of [σ] into two phonemes [su] or [sw], and so long as our universe of discourse is Chinese (Mandarin) phonemes, we should not be disturbed by the fact that [sw] in English is a succession of two sounds in which [s] is little or not at all [w]-ized.

From the consideration of these cases of under-analysis and over-analysis, we see the great advan-

8 G. M. Bolling must have overlooked such cases when he said, 'At least I can recall no example of... a digraph for a non-compound phoneme,' in an editorial note on R. G. Kent's review of Bloomfield's Language in the journal Language, X, 1, 1934, pp. 51–52.

9 Fondamenti, p. 11, section 15.

10 Fondamenti, p. 4, section 3.

11 Fondamenti, p. 17.

tage of Bloomfield's speaking of sound-features instead of sounds. If we consider a sound as made of a number of features, then a phoneme is a combination of certain (simultaneous and/or successive) features, leaving other features unspecified. The English [t]-phoneme, for instance, consists of the features of voicelessness, apico-alveolar articulation of a certain range (eighth, tea, tray), and complete stop of breath, while the exact position of articulation, the force of stopping, the nature of on-glides (heat, hoot) and off-glides (tar, star, tea, two, little, button, but) are left unspecified. The Chinese [u]-phoneme consists of the features of lip-narrowing, a slight velar action, and voice, and as the position of the tip of the tongue is left unspecified, it is perfectly free to form the [s]-articulation while the [u]-articulation is being held, so that we can entertain the idea of two phonemes [s] and [u] being telescoped into one single sound [σ] without necessarily considering the sound [σ] as one new phoneme or as one member of a new phoneme. Similarly, the [ɦ]-phoneme in the Wu-dialects consists of the feature of emitting more air than usual in producing voice, and as it does not specify anything about the oral or nasal features of articulation, the speaker is free to do all kinds of articulatory tricks at the same time with [ɦ],[12] so that there is an [ɑ] type of [ɦ], an [e] type of [ɦ], etc., and even an [m] type of [ɦ], as [ɦm̩] 'have not', as contrasted with [m̩] in [m̩-mɑ] 'mother', and yet all this does not prevent us from considering the [ɦ] and [ɑ] in [ɦɑ] as two theoretically separate phonemes.

(c) Zero Symbols.[13] As limiting cases of the variation in size of unit, we have the possibility of using zero symbol for sounds or sound-features and of counting absence of sound as a phoneme or as one member of a phoneme.

Where there are several degrees of significant stress, significant length, or kinds of significant intonation, it is the usual practice to represent one of them by zero symbol. Thus, unmarked syllables in polysyllabic English words are understood to have the low degrees of stress. Vowels without length marks are understood to be short. In most systems of tone-marking, the first tone in Chinese is 'marked' by not marking it.

In the Chinese syllables [tʂʅ], [tʂ'ʅ], [ʂʅ], [ʐʅ], [tsɿ], [ts'ɿ], [sɿ],[14] there is a vowel which is a vocalized prolongation of the preceding consonant, and it is understood to be present when these syllables are written in the standard way, that is with the consonantal symbols standing alone: ㄓ, ㄔ, ㄕ, ㄖ, ㄗ, ㄘ, ㄙ, in the National Phonetic Script. This is therefore a way of representing actual sounds by zero symbol.

In German stressed syllables beginning orthographically with a vowel, there is normally a glottal stop. Some writers give the symbol [ʔ] for this sound, but others omit the symbol, and in internal positions, as in Verein, a stress mark suffices to indicate the presence of the [ʔ], as [fer'ain]. It would be perfectly possible, though hardly conventional, for us to favor some other phoneme with the saving of a symbol, say [h], and transcribe Hauch as [ɑux] and auch as [ʔɑux].

Readers of Bloomfield's Language who are used to ordinary types of transcriptions of English must have been impressed by forms like these on pages 111, 112, 121, 122:

gentleman ['ǰentl̩mn̩]
atom ['ɛtm̩]
maintenance ['mejntn̩n̩s]
maintain [mn̩'tejn]
stirring ['str̩iŋ] vs. string [striŋ]
pattern ['pɛtr̩n] vs. patron ['pejtrn̩]
erring ['r̩iŋ] vs. ring [riŋ]
error ['err̩]
butter ['botr̩] on a par with bottle ['bɑtl̩]
bottom ['bɑtm̩] on a par with button ['botn̩]
anatomy [e'nɛtm̩ij] vs. met me [met mij]

Now Bloomfield systematically avoids the use of the obscure vowel letter [ə], and plays his game admirably well. The e in French le he considers as a short variety of [œ] (p. 106), which agrees more or less with the idea of the French themselves. For German, he lets the difference in stress take care of the difference between [e] and [ə]. For American English, he uses the strong forms where there is no following consonant or where the following consonant is not usually considered to be a syllable-carrier in English, but leaves out the symbol entirely in other cases. Now from the point of view of actual sound, weakened orthographically written vowels either become [ə] or disappear entirely. If we take ordinary deliberate conversation as the style of 'language' to consider, we can say, according to the writer's own observation of Middle Western American speech, that the presence or absence of a vocalized [ə] is about as follows:

12 There is a trick recitation in one of the dialects near Nanking in the form of a story consisting mostly of phrases like 鵝對鴨[ŋɔ tuei ŋɑʔ] 'goose versus duck', in which a flapped click is made with the front of the tongue each time [ŋ] is pronounced. The effect is that of beating a pair of clapping boards as an independent rhythmic accompaniment to the recitation. In other words, the [ŋ]-phoneme consists of the features of voice, nasality, and articulation with the back of the tongue. The front of the tongue can do as it pleases.

13 Under this heading, we are not including cases like ancient Hebrew, in which the vowels were not written. For in this system of writing, the vowels cannot be deduced from the phonetic environment alone by any set of phonetic rules. The writing is therefore an orthography and not a transcription.

14 The symbols ʅ and ɿ are Karlgren's.

[ə] compulsory or preferred	[ə] optional	Absence of [ə] compulsory or preferred
arbor [-bər] vs. club rate	happen [-p(ə)n]	able [-bl̩]
upper [-pər] vs. upright	often [-f(ə)n]	simple [-pl̩]
gentleman [-mən] vs. autumnal	even [-v(ə)n]	dismal [-ml̩]
humor [-mər] vs. am ready	bacon [-k(ə)n]	careful [-fl̩]
kingdom [-dəm] vs. bed-mate	Winkum [-k(ə)m]	devil [-vl̩]
London [-ndən] vs. kindness	Beauchamp [-č(ə)m]	sudden [-dn̩]
under [-dər] vs. shad roe	Gresham [-š(ə)m]	middle [-dl̩]
atom [-təm] vs. met me	patron [-tr(ə)n]	colonel [-nl̩]
pattern [-tərn] vs. outright	Durham [-r(ə)m]	wiggle [-gl̩]
maintenance [-nəns] vs. main news	coral [-r(ə)l]	engine [-ǰn̩]
Barnum [-nəm] vs. on me	handsome [-s(ə)m]	cordial [-ǰl̩]
corner [-nər] vs. Henry	bosom [-z(ə)m]	luncheon [-čn̩]
Helen [-lən] vs. hell no	Bentham [θ(ə)m]	celestial [-čl̩]
alum [-ləm] vs. elm (but also [eləm])	fathom [-ð(ə)m]	nation [-šn̩]
Keller [-lər] vs. all right	lengthen [-θ(ə)n]	special [-šl̩]
finger [-gər] vs. big row	heathen [-ð(ə)n]	vision [-žn̩]
teacher [-čər] vs. teach right		listen [-sn̩]
pleasure [-žər] vs. rouge-red		tassel [-sl̩]
error [-rər] vs. her right		dozen [-zn̩]
tracer [-sər] vs. viceroy		hazel [-zl̩]
Caesar [-zər] vs. phase-rule		Ethel [-θl̩]
ether [-θər] vs. Ruth ran		brothel [-ðl̩]
father [-ðər] vs. with rum		

Opinions may differ as to the placing of particular cases under each heading, but there seems to be no doubt as to the presence of [ə] in gentleman [-mən] or its absence in able [-bl̩]. Historically, as the orthography indicates, many of these words had clear vowels. Now some of them have an obscure vowel even in deliberate speech, which does not however entirely disappear in some cases. Since the presence, option, or absence of the [ə]-sound are more or less determined by the nature of the sounds preceding and following, and sometimes by conditions of syllabication, we can regard this as one phoneme of which one member is the obscure vowel [ə], a second member is a variphone (or dynamophone) consisting of [ə] and zero, and a third member is zero. Bloomfield has therefore as much right to represent this phoneme by zero symbol as one has to represent German [ʔ] by zero symbol. Apparent ambiguities as in the case of string and stirring may be avoided by marking the syllabication: ['str̩iŋ], which will remind us to explode the [t] before the [r], as it is a case of the first member of the phoneme.

It should be noted that our discussion here is to find a methodological justification for Bloomfield's used of zero symbol for an actual sound. There are other considerations from which this avoidance of the symbol [ə] seems rather inconvenient. Thus, when there is no final consonant like [l], [n], etc., to act as a syllable carrier, as in America, suppose, jealous, he is obliged to use exclusively strong forms like [e'merike] or [ɛ'merika], [so'powz], ['ǰelos], which are rarely heard even in deliberate speech (understanding of course that [o] is the 'short u'). The definite article the will have to be either [ðij] or [ð], with no middle ground. Those who favor Bloomfield's system for English will find that he is simply carrying the omission of [ə] to its logical conclusion. Those who do not will consider forms like ['str̩iŋ], ['mejntn̩n̩s], [e'merika] a reductio ad absurdum.

Under cases of under-analysis, we considered the representation of affricates, aspirates, and narrow-range diphthongs by single symbols. Now if the symbol used is obviously one of the elements in the compound, as [p] for [p'], [c] (instead of [č]) for [cɕ], [ɟ] (instead of [ǰ]) for [ɟʑ], or [o] for [ou], then we can regard that element which is understood but not represented as having zero symbol. For instance, in the Soochow dialect, labials go with [ʉ], velars and dentals go with [əu], and alveolars go with an apical vowel with protruding lips, for which the writer has proposed the symbol [ʮ],[15] as 布 [pʉ], 故 [kəu], 註 [tɕʮ]. All these can be considered as members of one phoneme [u], in which case the [ə] in [əu] would be a sound with zero symbol. Again, in the Foochow vowels [u] ∼ [ou], [i] ∼ [ei], [y] ∼ [øy] according to tone, as cited above, it is common practice to consider the first tone, which goes with [i], [u], [y], as basic, so that it is convenient to write these phonemes as [i], [u], [y], in which case a tone mark would suffice to remind one of the addition of [e-], [o-], [ø-] (by no means weak and parasitic), though these elements still have no symbol to themselves except as implied by the tone.

[15] A combination of Karlgren's [ɿ] and [ɥ].

(d) Zero Sound. In the cases of over-analysis, as in [ɦɑ], we had two features representing separate phonemes which together make one single sound. But if we take the series [ʉ], [əu], [ɥ] in Soochow and consider them as varieties of [əu], of which the [ə] is absent after labials and alveolars, then under the latter conditions the phoneme [ə] will have zero as a member. Similarly, if we write in the symbol [ə] for maintenance [-nəns], happen [-pən], button [-tən], all alike, then the [ə] will be a symbol for a phoneme, of which one member (in words of the type in the third column in the preceding table) has the value zero. Again, Bloomfield's use of [ij] and [ow] in unstressed positions may be regarded as cases of [j] and [w] with zero sound. In Passy's 'orthographic' notation referred to above, he spelt out the 'mute e' as [ə] in all cases, letting the 'rule of three consonants' take care of the presence or absence of the actual sound. From our point of view, [ə] would then be a phoneme with zero as a possible member. In the system of Ancient Chinese initials, there are two called yiing (影) and yuh (喻) which have been reconstructed by Karlgren as [ʔ] and smooth vowel respectively. Those are of course only the names of the initials. But Jang Tayyan (章太炎) has devised an alphabet with a symbol for each of the 36 initials, so that his symbol for yuh would be a symbol with zero value, very much like the ʼ symbol for the smooth ingress of vowels in Greek.

In the theory of sheh (攝) or 'rim-emes' in traditional Chinese phonology, the use of a symbol for zero is extremely useful. Taking again the National Phonetic Script, which is constructed very much in the spirit of traditional phonology, we have the rimemes ㄟ, ㄡ, ㄣ, ㄥ which, like the other rimemes, may be preceded by the medials ㄧ, ㄨ, or ㄩ so as to form the following complete finals (i. e. syllables minus initial consonant, if any) which actually occur in words:

without medial :	ㄟ	ㄡ	ㄣ	ㄥ
with medial ㄧ :		ㄧㄡ	ㄧㄣ	ㄧㄥ
with medial ㄨ :	ㄨㄟ		ㄨㄣ	ㄨㄥ
with medial ㄩ :			ㄩㄣ	ㄩㄥ

A simple phonemic transcription in the IPA would be

əi	əu	ən	əŋ
	iəu	iən	iəŋ
uəi		uən	uəŋ
		yən	yəŋ

In these twelve finals, the [ə] in [iən], [iəŋ], and [yəŋ] always has zero value (in [yəŋ], the [y] is broken up into an intermediate value between [iu] and [yu]), just like the [ə] in [ba:dən] for German baden.[15a] In the case of [uəi] and [iəu], the [ə] has zero sound in the first and second tones and has some sound in the third and fourth tones, except that in [uəi] not preceded by an initial consonant, [ə] does not entirely disappear in any tone. In [uən] the [ə] has zero sound in the first and second tones when there is an initial consonant, is fully sounded when there is no initial, and is very weak in other cases. With [uəŋ], the [ə] is sounded only when there is no initial consonant. With [yən], the [ə] is sounded (with the value [ɩ]) when there is a palatal initial or no initial, but has zero sound with other initials. With such a complicated group of facts, where each case is a law unto itself, we should still fail to attain perfect phonetic accuracy by writing something like:

ei	ou	ən	ʌŋ
	iu	in	iŋ
uei		un	uŋ
		yn	iuŋ,

although this may be a useful form of transcription for certain purposes. The paradoxical appearance of a symbol with widely different values, including zero, would disappear if we stuck to the National Phonetic Script or used some non-committal symbol such as 'ɸ' for the phoneme in question, thus:

ɸi	ɸu	ɸn	ɸŋ
	iɸu	iɸn	iɸŋ
uɸi		uɸn	uɸŋ
		yɸn	yɸŋ.

This is of course not the only or even the best phonemic treatment of these finals, but by allowing the possibility of zero members of phonemes, we do gain a number of advantages.[16]

(e) Phonemic Treatment of Conditional End-consonants. In ordinary transcription of French, cases of liaison and elision are spelt as they sound. The word pas then has two forms [pɑ] and [pɑz], le has [lə] and [l], and by the 'rule of three consonants' the word demander has the two forms (vous) [dmɑ̃de] and (pour) [dəmɑ̃de]. Similarly, Southern English sore has the two forms [sɔ:][17] (throat) and [sɔ:r] (eyes). The presence or absence of the sound in question is not distinctive, so that it and zero may be considered as members of the same phoneme. But the difference between saw [sɔ:] and sore [sɔ:] is distinctive, and for the phoneme with the conditional [r], the symbol '*' has been used in dictionaries, though the writer has never seen it used in texts, probably because ordinary transcriptions are not phonemic. From arguments with unsophisticated Frenchmen, who insisted that point did not have the same pronunciation as poing, the writer would think that a special phonemic symbol for these optional sounds would be welcomed by the French, say something like [pɑz̤], [pwɛ̃t̤], so as to avoid the pitfalls of

15a Bloomfield, Language, p. 113.

16 In this article, we are limiting ourselves to the discussion of phonemes of single languages. If we extend our universe of discourse to diaphones, say about 100 miles south of Peiping, the advantage of the above form will be enormously increased.

17 One type of Southern British English.

the '[patakɛs]' business.[18] Better symbols than these may be devised. Our interest here is in the obvious phonemic nature of these groups [z] ∿ zero, [t] ∿ zero, etc. It may not be necessary to outlaw the writing of two alternate forms for one word. But it would be an advantage not to have to do so.[19]

In this connection, we may mention the so-called 'aspirated h' in French as a consonant phoneme which always has zero sound, but has a very definite 'feature' of its own, and may be conveniently symbolized as [h̲]. The great advantage in regarding this as a consonant phoneme lies in that it greatly simplifies the description of the behavior of other phonemes. We can then say that [-t̲] (liaison t) has the sound [t] before vowels, and zero sound before consonants or in end-position. If we refuse existential status to [h̲], we have to say that [-t̲] has the sound [t] before vowels, except before the following exhaustive list of words: [aza:r], [ɔ̃:z], etc., which is no way of stating the 'rule of pronunciation' for phonemes.

In many Chinese dialects, final consonants like [-n], [-k], [-ʔ] are pronounced very clearly at the end of phrases, but become weakened or disappear entirely when followed immediately by another word. The [ʔ] in Foochow or the Wu-dialects is a phoneme which has zero value before another word. Thus, Soochow 八 [poʔ] 'eight', 八百 [popɑʔ] 'eight hundred', 八百八 [popɑpoʔ] 'eight hundred eight(y)'. The vowel is not even lengthened (as it is in Soochow under certain conditions) to make up for the time of the original [ʔ]. If we write phonemically, we can represent this phoneme with [ʔ] and zero sound as its two members either by (1) zero symbol (and let the symbol for the entering tone, with which it is always associated in these dialects, indicate its presence), or (2) the symbol [-ʔ] or [-ʔ̲] in all cases, whether the glottal stop is articulated or not.

It is not our purpose here to propose purely for the pleasure of perversity either to under-analyze two or more piece sounds and treat them as single phonemes or to over-analyze one piece sounds and treat them as successions of phonemes, nor purposely to write something where there is nothing to write, or to write nothing where there is something to write. We wish only to indicate that all such tricks are actually being done in current transcriptions, and that according to the way in which we treat the time unit of phonemes in a language we may arrive at one or another of various possible solutions for that language.

18 'Puisque ce n'est pat à moi et n'est poins à vous, je ne sais pat à qu'est-ce.' From Passy's Chrestomathie.

19 The case of English a : an is somewhat doubtful. If English never had a system of writing, or if its orthography had come to writing for uncle : fo mother, just like an uncle : a mother, we might then be inclined to treat the indefinite article as one word (as it was) and provide a special phoneme [-n̲] as its second element, a phoneme which occurs only in one word. Cf. II(e) below on word identity.

2. The Grouping of Sounds into Phonemes.

So long as we confine ourselves to the consideration of stock examples like keep, call, cool, our construction of phonemic systems is smooth-sailing. We need only to disregard slight variations of what is generally regarded as 'the same sound' and call it a phoneme. But on many questions of the identification of sounds in a language, we are not favored with such general consensus of opinion. Is the second element of the English 'long i' to be identified with the first element in yes (Bloomfield's [aj]), or with the first element in it ([aɪ] by many writers), or with the final element in very (Palmer's [aɩ]), or with the undistinguished [i] in it [it], eat [i:t], very ['veri] ([ai] by many writers), or with the first element in eight ([ae] in certain 'narrow' transcriptions)? Is the palatal series [tɕ], [tɕ'], [ɕ] in words like 家, 青, 下 (occurring only before high front vowels) to be identified with the velar series [k], [k'], [x] or with the retroflex series [tʂ], [tʂ'], [ʂ] (none of either series ever occurring before high front vowels)? According as we emphasize this or that motive, we should arrive at a different system of organization of elements into phonemes. We may desire to have (a) phonetic accuracy, or smallness of range of phonemes, (b) simplicity or symmetry of phonetic pattern for the whole language, (c) parsimony in the total number of phonemes, (d) regard for the feeling of the native speaker, (e) regard for etymology, (f) mutual exclusiveness between phonemes, (g) symbolic reversibility, and these motives are often conflicting.

(a) A minimum degree of phonetic accuracy is provided for by the 'similar in character' clause contained in Jones's later definition. By our purely logical definition, we should have the possibility of regarding English [h] and [ŋ] as members of one phoneme, which never occur in the same phonetic environment, and we could write forms like [ɧæt], [bi'ɧeiv], [sɔɧ], ['siɧə*] for hat, behave, song, singer, and learn very quickly when to say [h] and when to say [ŋ]. Such practice, however, would not be favored by either the phonetician or the philologist. Now the automaticity of variation within a phoneme has two senses. (1) The variation of [h] of the shades [h_e], [h_a], [$h_ə$], [h_o],[20] etc., according to the following vowel is automatic practically in all languages which have these sounds. So is the variation of the [t] in [ts] and [tʃ] in all languages which have these affricates, that is, if we take affricates as successions of two phonemes. But such cases are much rarer than we are inclined to think. (2) In most cases, the automaticity of variation holds only for the particular language in question, although familiarity with the language may give one the impression of its universality. Thus, speakers of one

20 Not to include cases of high vowels, which involve other questions.

language, e.g. Japanese, would find the change of [h] into [ç] before [i] so natural as to be something inherent in the nature of speech sounds, while in another language, e.g. German, [h] can be followed by [i] without becoming [ç], which belongs to another phoneme. The variation of Foochow [a] and [ɛ] [illegible], 'to be able to', according to tonal environment, is so natural to the native speaker that he refuses to admit that he is not pronouncing it always in one and the same way, while in many languages these are widely different phonemes. Since, therefore, the automaticity of variation is mostly of conditional nature, we shall have to allow a good deal of latitude in the interpretation of the 'similar in character' clause. For the sake of phonetic accuracy, it would be an advantage to construct our phonemes with as narrow ranges of variation as possible (though it is never desirable to limit ourselves to universally automatic groups of the type (1) mentioned above), but this one desideratum may have to be sacrificed to some extent for other motives.

(b) Simplicity or symmetry of phonetic pattern is a factor which greatly influences our organization of phonemes. Bloomfield wishes to say that there are no long vowels in English, a statement which, from our standpoint, is neither true nor false, but may be estimated as methodologically desirable or not desirable. He has eight vowels:

i	u
e	o
ɛ	ɔ
a	ɑ

and eight diphthongs or triphthongs:

aj	ɔj[21]	ej	ij	juw
aw	ow		uw	

It would seem that he could gain phonetic accuracy by writing [ai], [ɔi], [ou], even without the addition of special symbols like [ɪ] and [ʊ], but then he could not very well go on and write [ii], [uu], and if he indicated the diphthongal character of these vowels by [ij], [uw], the system would look much less symmetrical. The table would also look less symmetrical if he wrote [iː], [uː], with the American narrow-range [eː] and [oː] lurking around for recognition, while [aj], [aw], and [ɔj] must still remain as diphthongs. The use of the nonce phoneme 'ɸ' for Chinese (see I (d) above) with zero as a possible member of the phoneme, gives great symmetry to the system. Again, the series ㄢ, ㄧㄢ, ㄨㄢ, ㄩㄢ may be symmetrically rendered as [an], [ian], [uan], [yan] instead of the usual [an], [iɛn],[22] [uan], [yan], which is phonetically more accurate but by no means necessary. When symmetry runs parallel to structural or etymological considerations, so that the phonemes also agree with diaphones or phonogenes, its claim for consideration will of course be greatly increased.

(c) Parsimony of entities in the spirit of 'Occam's razor' is of course the hobby of symbologists. We have already noted the admission of digraphs for single sounds for the saving of a whole series of new letters. The use of [ij] and [uw] or introduction of length saves the use of the letters [ɪ], [ʊ], and [ɒ] for English. Palmer deplores this 'exaggerated compliance with the principle of symbol economy,'[23] because, among other reasons, the symbol for length, e.g. in although [ɔːlˈðou] does not necessarily indicate length. The writer can recognize the usefulness of the letters [ɪ], [ʊ], and [ɒ] from motives of phonetic accuracy, but the objection to the length mark does not seem to be fatal, for the symbol [ɔː] may also be taken phonemically in such a way that it is long in stressed positions, less long before voiceless consonants, and short (without change of quality) in unstressed positions, while [ɔ] can still be considered a separate phoneme. Bloomfield's avoidance of [ə] and his identification of the vowel in son with the first vowel in own (instead of writing the former [ʌ] or [ɤ]) also effects a saving of 'queer symbols'.

The extent to which one could go in the parsimony of symbols can best be illustrated by Liu Fu's numerical code for the Peiping syllables.[24] He used only six symbols in six positions (or 'plus' six positions, if we count positions as part of the set of symbols) as shown by the table on the next page. Thus 光 [kuaŋ] would be 312241, where 31 stands for [k], 224 is [uaŋ] and the last figure '1' means the first tone. 000042 would be the nasal interjection meaning 'What did you say?' This system is extremely symmetrical in structure, economical in the number of kinds of symbols used, and very illuminating as to the phonetic pattern of the language, but it can hardly be used as a system of transcription and was never intended to be. It may be noted here that his 'Abdomen No. 1' includes [ɤ], [ʌ], [ɛ], [ɔ], [ɪ], [ə], and zero as members, and corresponds to our 'ɸ'. In the body of the table, he gave also a somewhat narrow transcription of all the syllables.

21 Regard for 'similarity in character' probably prompted him to identify the first element of oil with the first element of or, rather than the first element of up. He would gain still greater symmetry if he wrote [oj], [ow], or still better [ɔj], [ɔw], as the first element in own is much nearer the first element in or [ɔr] than the first element in up [op] in American English.

22 Considering ㄧㄢ as the nasal ending counterpart of ㄧㄝ [iɛ].

23 H. E. Palmer, Principles of Romanization, pp. 68–69.

24 'A Table of the Analytical Numbers of the Beeipyng Dialect,' The Kwoshyue Jihkan, III, 3, 1932, pp. 533 ff.

Position / Figure	I. HEAD Place of articulation	II. FACE Manner of articulation	III. NECK 'Medial'	IV. ABDOMEN Principal vowel	V. TAIL Final vowel or consonant	VI. EXPRESSION Tone
0	zero		zero	zero	zero	——
1	labial	unaspirated	i	ə	i	1st
2	dental	aspirated	u	ɑ	u	2nd
3	velar or palatal	nasal	y		n	3rd
4	retroflex	voiceless continuant			ŋ	4th
5	dental advanced	voiced continuant				

(d) The feeling of the native speaker is a factor which is greatly emphasized by Sapir. Where the feeling comes from obvious misconceptions, arising often from orthographic considerations, such as the idea that principal and principle have different pronunciations,[25] or that ng = n + g,[26] we need not take it very seriously. But when there is no question of misconception, but one of preference of choice between alternate manners of organization of phonemes, then the feeling of the native should be given due consideration, though it need not be taken as the deciding factor. Thus, while the phonetician would write Chinese ㄢ, ㄧㄢ, ㄨㄢ, ㄩㄢ as [an], [iɛn], [uan], [yan], the speaker of the dialect of Peiping feels that they all belong to the same rimeme with different medials. This is further supported by the fact that when the [-n] is dropped when the syllable is amalgamated with a following retroflex vowel, [iɛn] does not become [iɛr], but [iar], as in 一點兒 [i tiɛn ər] > [itiar] 'a little'. Most speakers of the Foochow dialect feel that among the vowels in the following words,

音	iŋ55:	詠	eiŋ242:
鶯	eiŋ55:	限	aiŋ242:
溫	uŋ55:	問	ouŋ242:
恩	ouŋ55:	鈗	əuŋ242:

those in the same row are tonal variations of the same vowel, while refusing to recognize that the vowels in 詠 [eiŋ242:] and 鶯 [eiŋ55:] or those in 問 [ouŋ242:] and 恩 [ouŋ55:] are the same. As there are very definite rules for the diphthongization of single vowels (or opening of close vowels, as [ɛ] ∾ [a]), it is quite possible to arrange the Foochow vowel phonemes according to the native conception as an alternate and for some reasons a better way of grouping the phonemes. On the ambiguity of the phonemic membership of Peiping ㄐ, ㄑ, ㄒ, the native speaker will also have something to say.

The distribution or patterning of these sounds and related sounds is as follows:

1	ㄐㄑㄒ	tɕ	tɕ'	ɕ	always before [i] or [y]
2	ㄍㄎㄏ	k	k'	x	never before [i] or [y]
3	ㄗㄘㄙ	ts	ts'	s	
4	ㄓㄔㄕ	tʂ	tʂ'	ʂ	

It is therefore possible to identify the series '1' phonemically with any one of the other three series. Wade identifies it partially with '4': he writes ch, ch', hs for '1', and ch, ch', sh for '4'. The National Romanization identifies '1' with '4' completely by writing j, ch, sh for both. The French system of romanization for Chinese has '2' or '3' according to etymology, which was what '1' came from, and overzealous adopters of the French system identify '1' with '3' completely, and write forms like Sien Sien for 獻縣, although both belonged to series '2'. Now as to the feeling of the native, the favored series is '2'. For he feels [kə, tɕi, ku, tɕy] or [xə, ɕi, xu, ɕy] to be alliterative series with only different vowels. Moreover, in the system of a secret language which breaks every syllable with initial-final I+F into Iai + kF, (e.g. 北 [pei] > [pai-kei]),[27] the [k] becomes [tɕ] when the final begins with a high front vowel, as 米 [mi] > [mei-tɕi].

(e) Regard for etymology is properly not within the scope of our present study, which is concerned only with the descriptive study of one language of one period. But in the very frequent case of possibility of alternate phonemic treatment, we should certainly be allowed to steal a squint towards extrinsic factors. As a matter of fact, consideration of etymology does have a great weight with many writers. The identification of [tɕ], [tɕ'], [ɕ] with [k], [k'], [x] is etymologically preferable, if only partially, to identifying them with [tʂ], [tʂ'], [ʂ]. It would, however, cease to be strictly phonemic transcription of the Peiping dialect if we split [tɕ], [tɕ'], [ɕ] into a velar and a dental series according to derivation, as [xi] for 希 and [si] for 西, for

25 Except when the former is pronounced [prinsi'pæl], which is merely an abbreviated way of saying, 'the word which ends in -p-a-l.'

26 Even this is open to question, if we take a broader linguistic (as contrasted with phonetic or phonemic) point of view. Cf. Sapir's discussion on this point in 'Sound patterns in language,' Lang. 1.49 (1925) ((25)).

27 Y. R. Chao, 'Eight varieties of Secret Language Based on the Principle of Faanchieh,' Bulletin of the Institute of History and Philology, Academia Sinica, II, No. 3, 1931, pp. 320 ff.

then no rule of phonemic membership short of lexical enumeration could tell us when it is [xi] and when it is [si].

It is also of etymological interest to try to secure identity of words by giving them constant phonemic forms. Thus, we can write [sɜ:*] or [sɜ:r̲] for sir and let the phonetic environment decide when it is to be pronounced [sɜ:r], [sɜ:], [sər], or [sə]. Again, by writing [ɛ:trə] for être, instead of [ɛ:tr] before vowels, [ɛ:trə] before consonants, and [ɛ:tr̥] at the end of phrases, Passy gives the word a constant form, the value of the phoneme [ə], which may be written in italics if desired, to be determined by the 'rule of three consonants', etc. The Foochow word [illegible] 'to be able to' may be given the constant form [a], or a compromise form [æ], and the choice of values between [ɛ] and [a] may be determined by a very simple tonal rule. The identity-of-word interest, however, must not go so far as to cover grammatical considerations, where the rule of pronunciation would have to contain other than purely phonetic conditions. Thus, while we can write French en as [an], understanding that it is to be pronounced [ɑ̃] before consonants (s'en va) and [an] before vowels (s'en aller), we cannot write fin as [fin] in order to provide for the pronunciation of the feminine form [fin]. In such cases, we shall have to consider fin [fɛ̃] (or [fɛn]) and fine [fin] as two separate words, as much as fils and fille.[28]

(f) Mutual exclusiveness between phonemes is another desideratum we wish to consider; that is, the list of phonemes shall not only be exhaustive for the language, but, other things being equal, we should try to make the membership of the classes mutually exclusive. Other things, however, are never equal, and we have in fact already allowed the possibility of over-lapping of membership between phonemes in cases like the Foochow:

one phoneme	[i]	[ei]
another phoneme	[ei]	[ai]
one phoneme	[u]	[ou]
another phoneme	[ou]	[əu],

and in cases of different phonemes each of which contain zero as a member. The treatment of affricates as independent phonemes where their occlusive and fricative element can easily be identified with other phonemes in the same language, such as Bloomfield's [ǰ] and [č] for what many other writers give as [dʒ] and [tʃ], may also be considered as a case of over-lapping of membership. Palmer calls this 'multiple identity',[29] under which he cites a number of examples from Japanese and English. We should note, however, that the 'same sound' which belongs to two or more phonemes may be taken in two senses. In a conditional sense, 'the same sound' never occurs under the same conditions as to contiguous sounds or as to conditions of stress, length, and tone. The [ei] in the Foochow [i]∿[ei] phoneme occurs always in the tones [12:], [242:], [23:], while the [ei] in the [ei]∿[ai] phoneme occurs always in the tones [55:], [53:], [22:], [5:].[30] The English [č] and [ǰ] also occur under different conditions of stress from combinations like heat sheets and and Jeanne. In an absolute sense, on the other hand, Palmer's 'multiple identity' implies that two phonemes will have in common one member identical in all respects. Thus, there is absolutely no difference between the initial in 希 [ɕi] and the initial in 西 [ɕi], discussed above under (e). We could, if we like, put both into the [x] phoneme or both under the [s] phoneme, but if we write 希 [xi] and 西 [si], then the identical [ɕ] would belong to two phonemes under the same conditions. This treatment brings up the question of

(g) Symbolic Reversibility. The use of symbols has two aspects, the aspect of reading, or the determination of the object from the given symbol, and the aspect of writing, or the determination of the symbol from the object. The reading aspect of phonemic symbols is always determinate with respect to the language in question. Given a phonemic symbol, the range of sounds is determined, and the choice within the range is usually further determined by phonetic conditions. It would also be a desirable thing to make this reversible, so as to include the aspect of writing; that is, given any sound in the language, its phonemic symbol is also determined. If phonemes do not overlap, this is obvious. If they overlap, and the common members occur under different phonetic conditions, the reversibility still obtains. For instance, although 電報 is normally pronounced [tiɛmpɑu], so that the m sounds exactly like the m in 門 [mən], yet we can tell that it is only a member of the phoneme n, as the phoneme m never occurs in this position in standard Chinese. Again, in the dialect of Foochow, if we had the symbol A for the [i]∿[ei] phoneme and the symbol B for the [ei]∿[ai] phoneme, we could still tell whether a given case of the sound [ei] is to be written A or B from the tone.[31] But if the identity of a common member between phonemes is unconditional, as the distinction of 希 [xi] and 西 [si] for the Peiping dialect, then it would be impossible to go from the sound to the symbol even for the native speaker. Strictly, a non-reversible symbolization of sounds based on etymological or other considerations becomes an

28 Cf. Bloomfield's distinction between phonetic alternation and formal alternation, 'A set of postulates for the science of language,' Lang. 3.160 (1926) ((29)).

29 The Principles of Romanization, p. 151.

30 A pure phonetician would therefore prefer to take [ei] as one phoneme (or succession of two phonemes) in seven tones, although this would be against the 'feeling of the native'.

31 This is not as complicated as the description looks on paper. The native speaker is not even aware of the vocalic identity or similarity of the [ei] in the two sets of tones.

orthography and ceases to be a transcription, and the French system of romanization of Chinese, which distinguishes 基, 欺, 希 ki, k'i, hi from 躋, 妻, 西 tsi, ts'i, si (also favored by Bernhard Karlgren) is a case of this kind. In other words, homonyms should not have different transcriptions. There is, however, a class of intermediate cases, where the common member between two phonemes occurs sometimes under exactly the same phonetic conditions, but at other times becomes differentiated in some way under other sets of identical conditions. Thus, the same [ə] which occurs in mica [ˈmaikə] and in poker [ˈpoukə] before consonants becomes differentiated, for some speakers of English, into [ə] and [ər] respectively before vowels. If we write the former as [ə] and the latter as [ə*] or as [əṛ], then it will be possible to go from sound to symbol only when the sound in question is followed by a vowel, but not when followed by a consonant. The reversibility is therefore only partial. Usage is by no means uniform in such cases. Sometimes, symbolic reversibility is secured at the expense of word identity, the same word poker appearing in two forms [ˈpoukə] and [ˈpoukər], considered as different sets of phonemes. At other times, identity of word form is secured at the expense of reversibility, the same word Fr. espèce always appearing as [ɛspɛs], where the final [s] is pronounced [z] when followed by a voiced consonant, so that given the final sound [z], one cannot tell whether it is a member of the [s]-phoneme or a member of the [z]-phoneme.

3. Choice of Symbols.

It is one problem to group the sounds of a language into such and such phonemes and another thing to assign such and such symbols or letters to these phonemes. As a phonemic transcription has reference to one language, there is a great degree of freedom in our use of symbols. The freedom, however, is not so unlimited as in the case of mathematics, where the same symbol changes value not only from problem to problem, but also within the same problem. From purely logical considerations, it would seem that once the phonemes themselves are agreed upon, it is only a 'matter of form' as to the symbols used for them, 'What's in a letter?' Who ever heard of one mathematician writing l, m, n and another insisting that the same items shall be written as p, q, r? In phonetic symbols, however, there is tradition, or rather, what is more unfortunate, a number of conflicting traditions in the use of symbols. Consequently, there arise frequent controversies with as much vehemence as about the use of words. We shall feel the importance of the use of symbols when we realize that it often has an influence on our actual organization of phonemes. Some of the factors which influence our choice of symbols run parallel to those which influence the organization of phonemes. Thus, symmetry and simplicity of phonetic pattern corresponds to a certain degree of symmetry and simplicity in the symbols. Parsimony in the number of phonemes implies also parsimony in the number of symbols. The feeling of the native as to sound will also apply to the choice of the symbol if the language already has an alphabet, although this is often less dependable than his feeling for the pattern in the abstract. In addition to these, we have following questions especially concerned with the choice of symbols.

(a) The desire to keep within the limits of the ordinary 26 letters of the roman alphabet is such a powerful one that transcribers yield to it at great cost to other considerations. Thus, if a language has [ɑ], [ɔ], or [ɛ] but no [a], [o], or [e], then the latter symbols will be used as a rule.[32] If a language has only [ʀ], but no [r], then [r] would be used, although phonetically it would be taking as much liberty as writing [t] for [ĸ]. Bloomfield's use of [o] in the phoneme [o] and the diphthong [ow] avowedly comes from the desire to avoid 'queer symbols'. So far as parsimony of number of phonemes and symbols is concerned, [ɤ] would do just as well as [o], but would be even more appropriate, as it is more natural to say that the [ɤ]-phoneme is rounded in the diphthong [ɤw], on account of the labial [w], than to say that the vowel [o] in American English is an unrounded vowel except in the diphthong [ow]. This avoidance of queer letters means that while theoretical phonetics tells us that there are such and such sounds, or at least advises us to recognize conveniently such and such distinguishable sounds in the main, yet we feel inclined to identify the phonemes of a language with those sounds which happen to be favored with 'lower case' letters.

(b) Of those symbols which are not the ordinary letters of the alphabet some are considered less 'queer' than others, either on account of old standing or on account of the importance of their position in the scheme of general phonetics. Thus, [ŋ], [ʃ], [ð], [ø], [ɔ] are usually considered much less queer, and less effort is usually made to avoid them than in the case of symbols like [ʂ], [β], [ɯ], [ɤ]. Again, in the abstract scheme of cardinal vowels, a special symbol for the part between [ɛ] and [a] would be of less importance than the eight main positions. And since it is possible to group all the [e]–[ɛ]-region sounds in English under the phoneme [e], the symbol [ɛ] is left free for indicating the phoneme between cardinal [ɛ] and [a], which is what Bloomfield does: using the less queer symbol [ɛ] instead of the symbol [æ], which is 'queer' in that it occupies a less strategic position.

32 Jones and Camilli, Fondamenti, p. 3.

(c) The scale of division into which a variable range of sounds is supposed to be divided will have a great influence on the choice of the symbols. Thus, the traditional triangular scale

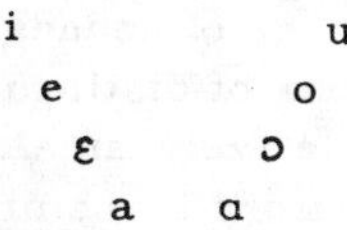

and the cardinal scale

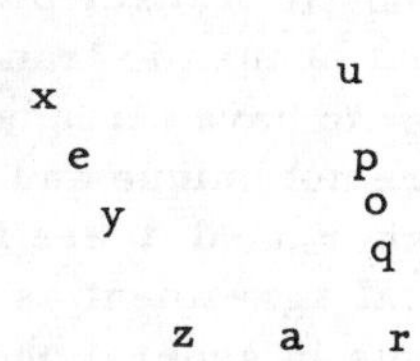

differ in the number of intervals into which the vowels are divided. The difference would be less confusing if we had non-conflicting symbols in the new scale, something like:

i
x u
e p
y o
q
z a r

As a matter of fact, one does find a partiality for using [e] for [ɛ] and [o] for [ɔ] (Cf. (a) above), and, less frequently, [a] for [ɑ], which shows the influence of the prestige of the i-e-a-o-u system. Every transcriber feels that somehow [ɛ] is a variety of [e] and not a variety of [a], [ɔ] is a variety of [o] and not a variety of [ɑ]. If we took our scheme of cardinal vowels seriously, we ought not to have such feelings.[33]

In Karlgren's scheme of vowels, using Lundell's dialect alphabet, the 3-point 2-interval high vowel scale of [i(y) — ɨ(ʉ) — ɯ(u)] of the IPA is given as a 2-point 1-interval scale of i(y) —— ɯ(u). (More accurately speaking, ɯ is placed in Karlgren a little to the front of u.)[34] The Russian ы, which on the 3-point scale is nearest to [ɨ], is therefore given as [ɨ] in the IPA,[35] but as ɯ by Karlgren, as it is nearer to the back vowel than to the front i on his 2-point scale.

(d) The avoidance of diacritical marks, which are now reserved for modifiers, also influences our choice of letters. We have already noted that rather than writing [s] for the single sound in Chinese 歲, we allowed the modifier to be written separately, thus: [suei]. Again, if a language has only two series of voiceless plosives, one unaspirated and one aspirated, but no voiced plosives, then either [p, t, k; ph, th, kh] or [b, d, g; p, t, k] would be preferable to [p, t, k; p', t', k'] or [b̥, d̥, g̊; p, t, k].

(e) Consistency with phonemic transcriptions of other languages is a thing that one may keep in mind, but which one must not go out of one's way to obtain. Where our phonemes are of narrow ranges and the symbols given them are the nearest phonetic letter we happen to have, the resulting transcription is not likely to conflict seriously with other transcriptions. But if for one reason or another our phonemes vary within very wide ranges, and if, further, we wish to secure certain symbolic advantages by departing somewhat from the usual range of values of the letters, then the chance of conflict with other transcriptions will be greater.

III. PHONETIC AND PHONEMIC TRANSCRIPTIONS

It is the usual practice to distinguish between phonetic, or narrow, transcriptions and phonemic, or broad, transcriptions. The former express the actual sounds [ɹaɩt], [tɹaɩ], ['veɾɩ], [eɩt], [geᵛt], [ðɛə], [æt], while the latter only indicate the distinctive classes of sounds [rait], [trai], ['veri], [eit], [get], [ðeə], [æt] (or [ɛt]). From the previous discussions, however, we have seen that there is no such thing as the correct phonemic transcription for any given language. According as we emphasize one or another factor in the size of the unit, method of phonemic grouping, and choice of symbols, we arrive at one or another form of phonemic solution. There is nothing in our definition of a phoneme or any other of the definitions quoted that can decide for us, for example, whether the Chinese [ɕ] shall be a member of [x] or [ʂ] or [s], or how the [ɩ] in [aɩ], the [j] in [ij], the [ɪ] in [ɪt], and the [j] in [jes] should be grouped into phonemic classes. The definition permits us to devise ways and means of grouping together distinguishable sounds that are not distinctive with respect to the particular system of phonemic grouping. It also implies that certain sounds in a language are never distinctive in that language by any reasonable manner of symbolic juggling, e.g. the difference between the [k]'s in keep, call, coo, etc., or the [h]'s in heap, hall, who, etc., can never be considered as being distinctive, unless we should do the very unnatural thing of considering all the vowels [iː], [ɔː], [uː], etc. as non-distinctive members of one vowel phoneme X, the value to be determined by the nature of the preceding consonant k_1, k_2, k_3, etc., h_1, h_2, h_1, etc., or $zero_1$, $zero_2$, $zero_3$, etc. (i.e. in words like eat, all, ooze). But many sounds in a language are neither distinctive nor non-distinctive per se, but depend upon our particular manner of phonemic treatment. Thus, by writing up, owe, oil as [op], [ow], [ɔjl], Bloomfield considers the difference between the first elements in up and owe as non-dis-

33 The writer once heard a piece of music and interpreted it as being here in major and there in minor and its notes as being do, re, mi, etc., only slightly 'off', but subsequently learned to his surprise that it was a scale of seven equal steps in the octave. The illusion persisted even after he was told. He had forced his own intervals into the new scale, just as we all tend to force the 4-step i-e-a-o-u scale into the 7-step cardinal scale.

34 Bernhard Karlgren, Études sur la phonologie chinoise, p. 316.

35 As for instance by Daniel Jones.

tinctive and the difference between elements in owe and oil as distinctive. But precisely the reverse thing will have to be said if we treat the same sounds as [o], [ɔw], [ɔj], a modification which would do no damage to Bloomfield's system as a whole either by way of compromising the parsimony of letters, or by way of introducing queer symbols. Again, in most of the Wu-dialects, in words of the type [tɕ^{i}ɑ], [ɕ^{i}ɑ], [ɲ^{i}ɑ], etc., as against [kɑ], [xɑ], [ŋɑ], the [^{i}] is so short that it can be considered as a glide of the preceding consonant and can be left out of the transcription, in which case the difference between [k], [x], [ŋ] and [tɕ], [ɕ], [ɲ] would be considered distinctive. On the other hand, if we write the [^{i}] on the line then we could consider the [tɕ]-series as members of the [k]-series phonemes: [ki], [xi], [ŋi], and it is now the difference between [ɑ] and [iɑ] that is distinctive. In practice, no phonetic transcription is so narrow and concrete as to distinguish between the [h]'s in [he], [hɛ], [hə] in any language, and no phonemic transcription is so broad and so purely abstract as to group English [h] and [ŋ] under the same phoneme [ꜧ]. Between these extremes, there are all intermediate proportions of phoneticity and phonemicity. On the whole, we may say that a phonetic transcription is one which makes use of all the usual distinctions which the majority of phoneticians are expected to be familiar with, irrespective of their distinctiveness in the language, and that a phonemic transcription is one which, given a particular set of directions of approach, makes only such distinctions as are necessary in distinguishing words from that particular set of directions.

The reader will notice the unsatisfactory nature of the phrase 'the usual distinctions which the majority of phoneticians are expected to be familiar with.' This comes from the unsatisfactory nature of the actual state of affairs. In the field of descriptive phonetics, there is nothing like the near unanimity of opinion which exists among physicists, either as to the organization of facts or as to the use of symbols for referring to them. Thus, Bloomfield says, 'The phonetician's equipment is personal and accidental; he hears those acoustic features which are discriminated in the languages he has observed... He should remember that his hearing of non-distinctive features depends upon the accident of his personal equipment, and that the most elaborate account cannot remotely approach the value of a mechanical record.'[36] This is all true to a great extent, but in the opinion of the writer, Bloomfield is going too far in saying further: 'Only two kinds of linguistic records are scientifically relevant. One is a mechanical record of the gross acoustic features, such as is produced in the phonetic laboratory. The other is a record in terms of phonemes, ignoring all features that are not distinctive in the language. Until our knowledge of acoustics has progressed far beyond its present state, only the latter kind of record can be used for any study that takes into consideration the meaning of what is spoken.' We need not, however, be worried if we cannot read or copy the grooves of a phonograph record. The phonograph record is at best an icon, or a picture, not a symbol in the usual sense of something that we can 'read' and 'write'. Nor need we be worried that the number of sounds in human speech is infinite. The number of distinguishable sounds in human speech is relatively small, limited by the condition of oral-auditory transmission of phonemic distinctions from one generation to the next. When the average actual difference falls below a certain finite limen, the distinction becomes unstable, and the two phonemes soon coalesce into one later phonogenic member. We cannot say, as Bloomfield seems to imply, that phonetic transcriptions are mostly subjective and that phonemic transcriptions are mostly objective. We have already seen how phonemic transcriptions are not unique and to that extent subjective. On the other hand, there is also a certain degree of practical agreement as to the non-phonemic use of symbols in general phonetics. For purpose of (1) citation of forms where a feature which is non-distinctive in the language cited is relevant to the point under discussion, (2) giving forms of words or sounds in comparative dialectology, (3) noting incipient or vestigial traces of sound-change, (4) impartial consideration of the gross features of a language before a good phonemic system has been worked out for it, and (5) as a less worthy purpose, for pedagogical use—for all these a narrow phonetic transcription is sometimes very useful and sometimes quite indispensible. One should not do the worst of narrow transcriptions all the time, but one should be prepared for the worst at any time. The dialect alphabet of Lundell, used by Karlgren in his Phonologie Chinoise, both in his main discussions and in the appended dialect dictionary, is a very narrow and non-phonemic transcription. The writer has nevertheless found the system thoroughly usable and understandable, and although for typographical reasons he has changed it into the IPA form in the Chinese translation,[37] he has been able to equate the symbols of the systems with relatively few additions and few doubtful points of classification arising from the number-of-scale-steps problem. In the writer's own experience in the recording of Chinese dialects, he found that besides the matching and comparison of words with related sounds, a very important procedure is to give a reasonably narrow phonetic transcription at the start, so that we have materials to base our decisions upon when we come to questions of choice among alternate treatments.

36 Bloomfield, Language, pp. 84–85.

37 中國音韻學研究, 趙元任, 羅常培, 李方桂合譯 Changsha, 1940.

Bloomfield observes rightly that phonetic transcriptions are often inconsistent as to what features to include and what features to neglect. This difficulty can be met in two ways. In the first place, we can lay down as a principle of symbolology that the position of a symbol in its context may be considered to be one constituent of the symbol. Thus, there is no inconsistency in the figure 1 meaning 1 X 10 and 7 meaning 7 X 1 in the form '17', as the symbol 1 is not just '1', but '1 in the second position'. Similarly, there is no inconsistency in the symbol '>' meaning 'greater than' in 19 > 17 and meaning 'changes into' in p > f, or even between the two uses of '>' in a > o according as the formula occurs in an article on phonetics or in one on mathematics.[38] So in discussions on diphthongs, we may need to mention forms like [čaj], [čae], [čææ], etc., while in discussions on affricates, we may refer to [tʂai], [tšai], [tɕai], [tɹ̣ai], etc., just as Bolling finds it perfectly in order to write Enroughity is coming : The Enroughities are coming, so long as the discussion is about the forms of the plural.[39] But if our discussion should turn on the forms of the indefinite article, it would then be necessary to write [ɛn ˈeg], but [ej ˈda:bi] (the correct pronunciation of the name Enroughity according to Bolling), as it would not bring out the point at all if we wrote an egg but a Enroughity.

For avoiding too much inconsistency in the citation of forms, both Karlgren and users of the IPA have resorted to the distinction between broad and narrow transcriptions apart from considerations of significant distinction. Karlgren's practice, as carried out in his Phonologie (pp. 260 ff.), is very consistent. He has a set of bold-faced letters for a broad transcription, under each of which he puts a number of the Lundell letters, which are always in italics. Thus, what corresponds to the [ɛ] and [æ] in the IPA are grouped under **ă**, what corresponds to [ʂ], [ɕ], [ʃ] in the IPA are grouped under **š**, and so on. There are a few cases of overlapping groups, but on the whole the groups are mutually exclusive. The relation between the two sets is therefore very much like that between phonemes and members except that no reference is made to word distinction. A similar tendency is noticeable among users of the IPA, but no systematic division has ever been made between a narrow and a broad transcription. Nevertheless, there are certain unsystematic traditions among phoneticians which are based, on the whole, on the identity of the letters in the roman alphabet. Thus, r is somehow recognized as a broad form covering [r] and [ʀ], whereas [t] and [ĸ] are not covered by any broad form. Similarly [e] and [ɛ] are felt as members of a group of the e-type in a way that [i] and [e] do not seem to be. All this points to a conception which no one consciously recognizes, but which seems to be assumed by many, that there are such things as phonemes in general, apart from reference to any particular language, and that all we need to do either for the study of one language or for comparative work is to use one consistent phonemic transcription for all languages. This would of course be recognized by anyone as an impossible illusion as soon as the situation is thus made explicit, as we may be called upon at any time to make phonemic distinctions between shades of sounds whose differentiation we never anticipated in either our narrow or broad system of phonetic symbols. The existence of the tradition of usage, however, is real. It is true that the existence of only one common letter r for [r] and [ʀ] but two common letters t and k for [t] and [k] (or [ĸ]) is a matter of historical accident. But we shall see the significance of this accident when we note that as a matter of fact most of the languages which phoneticians, or at least European phoneticians, have studied, do take [t] and [k] as separate phonemes, while [r] and [ʀ] rarely, if ever, occur as separate phonemes. The idea of general phonemes, which we have just proposed and condemned in the same breath, is therefore not entirely baseless. Without entertaining the idea of general phonemes as such, the writer wishes to propose the term typical phoneme, to be defined as those groups of sounds which very often go together to form phonemes in many of the major languages studied by phoneticians. This definition of course makes the idea of a typical phoneme depend again on historical accident, the fact that most contemporary phoneticians are speakers of the Germanic and Romance languages. Thus, for a broad transcription using typical phonemes, a European would group [p] and [pʻ] under one typical phoneme, as against [b],[40] while an unsophisticated Chinese phonetician would most likely group [p] and [b] under one typical phoneme as against [pʻ].

The troublesome part of the transcription problem comes from the inconsistency in using the same symbol sometimes in a general and sometimes in a particular sense. In the citations in this article, the writer has found it hard to do better, and has tried to manipulate the context (taken as part of the symbolic system) in such a way as to eliminate ambiguity. But there is always the danger of slips. When we refer to the English [i], one may not know whether it is narrow [i] or [ɪ] that is meant.[41] This is very similar to the old practice of referring to the ancient

[38] In discussions like the present, where there may be a call for 'narrow symbols', one could use '→' for 'changes into' and '>' for 'greater than', thus making peace among mathematics, phonetics, and chemistry.

[39] From an editorial note on R. G. Kent's review of Bloomfield's Language, Lang. 10.50 (1934)

[40] Except speakers of certain German dialects.

[41] On the principle of non-uniqueness of phonemic transcriptions, we cannot prohibit the writing of the vowels in eat, it as [i], [ɪ], and insist on the writing of [i:], [i] or of [ij], [i].

Chinese initials 照, 穿, 牀, 審 in this way:

General names: 照穿牀審

For the apical series: 莊初牀山 [tʂ][tʂ‘][dʐ‘][ʂ]

For the dorsal series: 照穿乘審 [tɕ][tɕ‘][dʑ‘][ɕ]

so that when 照 is mentioned, one is at a loss as to whether it is the 照 in general (including both [tʂ] and [tɕ]) that is meant, or only 照 [tɕ] as against 莊 [tʂ]. He has therefore proposed the following names for the differentiated series, reserving the traditional names for the general sense, incidentally also using an inclusive broad transcription for the general series, thus:

General names: 照穿牀審 [č] [č‘] [ǰ‘] [š]

For the apical series: 莊初崇生 [tʂ][tʂ‘][dʐ‘][ʂ]

For the dorsal series: 章昌乘書 [tɕ][tɕ‘][dʑ‘][ɕ]

Karlgren's use of a special series of boldfaced types is based on the same principle. Symbols may be as general and inclusive as we may have use for, but must not be vague and ambiguous. An approach to this method of having both general and particular use of symbols is made in connection with the usage of a few symbols in the IPA. Thus, the symbol [ə] is usually understood to be a general form for [ɜ] (half-close) and [ɐ] (half-open). [ʃ] and [ʒ] may be used either for [ʂ] and [ʐ] or for [ɕ] and [ʑ] respectively. This latter, however, is less satisfactory, as in the dialect of Lintzy (臨淄), Shandong, [ʂ], [ʃ], [ɕ], all three exist as separate phonemes, in which the [ʃ] series is intermediate between apical and dorsal articulations of the tongue and is identical with English [ʃ] except that there is no protrusion of the lips. [š] and [ž] would be better general symbols, though they are not properly IPA letters.

SUMMARY

We have proposed a new definition of a phoneme and have endeavored to show that given a language, there is not necessarily one unique solution for the problem of reducing its sounds into elements. We have considered what factors can influence, and have influenced, the phonemic treatment of languages: the variability of the size of the phonemic unit, including the admission of zero symbols and zero sounds, the grouping of phonemic membership, and the choice of actual symbols. Because phonemic solutions are not unique, it is necessary, before arriving at solutions, to have recourse to considerations of descriptive phonetics and the use of phonetic transcriptions. These are also necessary for other purposes, such as the comparative study of dialects. We have also noted that there is a tendency among phoneticians to group together sounds under broad symbols, which form phonemes in a number of languages, and we have called them 'typical phonemes', although there is no consistency in the use of symbols for these. It is hoped that a more consistent system of symbols be devised for indicating both narrow shades of sounds and typical phonemes for the purpose of phonetic and phonemic transcriptions, but for the time being, we have to let the context serve as part of the symbol to inform us as to shade (if particular) or scope (if general). It is not necessary to take serious exception to anyone's transcription so long as it is self-consistent and its interpretation is clear to the extent it is meant for, and so long as it does not claim unique correctness to the exclusion of other possible treatments. Usage may in time become unified, but problems will always vary. Our motto must be: Write, and let write!

⟦It would be hard to imagine a better single guide to early phonemics than Chao's paper. Bloomfield's book Language had just appeared, and the public was reacting to its transcription with mixed emotions, mostly within the range from benevolent scepticism to dismay and here and there even outraged horror. Most responsible of all linguists in his formulations, Bloomfield was being accused of irresponsibility. To an apprentice linguist in 1957 who has at least noted the dates of de Saussure and the Sapir and Bloomfield papers here, this may well be puzzling. But only a tiny fraction of the readers of Bloomfield's new book were properly prepared for it. The largest single group of its more or less professional readers had been brought up on the International Phonetic Alphabet, especially as used in Le Maître Phonétique. To transcribe ten as [tɛn], omitting all indication of the customary aspiration of its [t‘], occasional nasality of its vowel or a personal diphthongization [ɛə], and of the specifically English dark [n$_ə$] compared to a bright German [n$_e$], was to them a matter of simple common sense requiring no more justification than convenience. A standard argument was to call all diacritics 'dust in the eyes'. That we now speak of 'description' where the 1920's spoke of 'transcription' may seem inconsequential; but this choice of terms is symptomatic of a deep philosophical difference, and Bloomfield's first readers were mostly on the other side of the gulf from us today. It is one of the most interesting things about Chao and his paper that it can be read either way; I take it as a proof of his very great intellectual talent and freedom from prejudice; I have also heard it explained by the simple formula 'Chao can do nothing badly', as if to say that his work always pleases everybody, which to my knowledge is either true or nearly so.⟧

ON DEFINING THE PHONEME

W. FREEMAN TWADDELL

Language Monograph No. 16—1935

I. INTRODUCTION

For many years, now, and particularly within the last decade, there has been increasing use of the term 'phoneme',[1] 'wenn man sich auch nicht immer über seine definition einig ist'.[2] Parallel to this increased use of the term, there has been the re-emergence of a concept of some unit of the spoken language, a unit which is not the same as a 'sound of speech'. It has long been known to phoneticians and linguists in general that the sounds of speech, even within the narrowest restrictions of time and place, even within the usage of a single individual, present an almost infinite variety. Scarcely any two speakers of a given dialect pronounce the same word exactly alike, either as to their articulatory movements or as to the sound-waves which those movements set up in the atmosphere. And yet, within the communicative and expressive medium, those (articulatorily and acoustically) slightly different processes are still the same word; and the 'sounds' which comprise this same word are in some way the same sounds, within the frame of that communicative and expressive medium which is the language of the community. It is the recognition of this sameness, this effective unity, which has found expression in the term 'phoneme' as a unit of spoken language.

In many ways, this concept of unity is not recent; its apparent newness is a product of the increased accuracy of phonetic observation which has accumulated evidence of almost infinite variety in the actual 'sounds' of speech (as articulations and sound-waves). It was only after the recognition of actual measurable variety that the recognition of effective structural unity could appear as a contrast, and hence as needing a new technical term: the term which most students of language now use to indicate such an effective structural unit is 'phoneme'. Before accurate phonetic observation had established the objective variety of the sounds of speech, there was obviously no necessity for such a distinction; earlier students could say 'sound' and mean both the objective articulatory and acoustic phenomenon on the one hand, and the structural unit on the other. Jakob Grimm was in some ways a 'phonologist' (in the sense of the Cercle Linguistique de Prague) precisely because he was not a phonetician; it is regrettable that some contemporary students of language also find it necessary to achieve 'phonological' insight through a resolute disregard of phonetic procedure.

With the increased use of the term 'phoneme' have naturally come attempts by thoughtful linguists to define the term precisely and usefully. It is the purpose of this study to examine the principal definitions of the phoneme, and to propose a new procedure of definition. To some linguists, an examination of fundamental terms and concepts may appear a waste of time. Thus N. S. Trubetzkoy:[3] 'En s'attachant aux formules générales, aux définitions provisoires, qui sont souvent automatiquement répétées même après que l'emploi du terme a changé, on risque de perdre son temps à une critique superficielle et stérile.' And Daniel Jones[4] is 'inclined to think that the terminology usually employed in referring to phonetic phenomena is sufficiently near the mark for all ordinary practical purposes.' But beside this point of view, which is perfectly appropriate for a pioneer, there is certainly justification for a careful examination of the significance of fundamental

1 In the preparation of this study I have drawn heavily upon several of my friends. The discussions with Mr. Martin Joos have been especially fruitful in numerous invaluable suggestions and criticisms. My colleagues Professor A. Senn, Professor E. I. Haugen, and Mr. David Sheldon have been most helpful. I am indebted to Professor Leonard Bloomfield for his patience and kindness in discussing the phoneme and our views on it personally and by correspondence.

2 Jespersen, Linguistica 214.

3 Journal de Psychologie 30.229.

4 Le Maître Phonétique (1933) 29.

terms, especially when the significance appears to be far from fixed, in the usage of different linguists. That this is the case with the phoneme will appear in later sections of this study; here it suffices to quote Mr. J. R. Firth:[5] 'The meaning of any ordinary word is subject to change without notice, but technical terms must not be handled in that way. Notice must be given. A word of warning would appear to be necessary with regard to the word "phoneme". What does it mean?' Professor Leonard Bloomfield, whose work exemplifies the value of precise terminology and consistent logic, has briefly stated that value:[6] 'Certain errors can be avoided or corrected by examining and formulating our (at present tacit) assumptions and defining our (often undefined) terms.' Professor Bloomfield has further pointed out[7] the serious consequences of a failure to define clearly and to state assumptions.

The confusion of usage with the term 'phoneme' is unfortunately not unique in linguistic terminology.[8] But in the case of the phoneme this confusion is particularly distressing because of the relatively recent introduction of the term.

To me, at any rate, it has appeared worth while to subject the various definitions and uses of the term 'phoneme' to analytic scrutiny. It has further appeared to me that as between the converse vices of hair-splitting and methodological chaos, the former is preferable.

It will be agreed, I take it, that a satisfactory definition of a fundamental term should meet these criteria: (1) It must be distinctive, i. e. not overlap any other definition of the same order within the frame of study; (2) It must not contain any unstated assumption or ambiguous term; (3) It must be methodologically feasible, i. e. not define an entity which is inaccessible to methods within the frame of study.

The definitions of the phoneme which have been proposed fall into two general groups: definitions in terms of a mental reality, and definitions in terms of a physical reality.[9]

5 Le Maître Phonétique (1934) 46; cf. also H. Pedersen in Litteris 5.154.

6 Lang. 2.153 ⟪26⟫.

7 Lang. 8.220 ff.; 10.32 ff.; see also Modern Philology 25.211 ff.

8 Cf. L. Weisgerber, Vorwort zur Probe eines Wörterbuchs der sprachwissenschaftlichen Terminologie 5 ff.; Beiheft IF 51.

9 The definition to be found in The Cyclopedia of Medicine 6.149 f. (F. A. Davis Company, Philadelphia, 1933) appears to have little bearing on linguistic methodology: 'A phoneme is an auditory hallucination consisting of spoken words'.

II. THE PHONEME AS A MENTAL OR PSYCHOLOGICAL REALITY

I have above loosely characterized the difference between sounds and phonemes: 'Within the communicative and expressive medium, those (articulatorily and acoustically) slightly different processes are still the same word, and the "sounds" which comprise this same word are in some way the same sounds.' Another, and even looser, way of formulating the contrast would be this: Although the speakers produce and the hearers experience objectively different sounds, they are not aware of that difference; the speaker intends to produce the same sound, and the hearer has the impression of hearing the same sound. It is in terms of some such formulation that many linguists, particularly those of the school of Baudouin de Courtenay and the members of the Cercle Linguistique de Prague and others with related views, have attempted to define the phoneme as a mental reality, as the intention of the speaker or the impression of the hearer, or both.

An anthology of such definitions in terms of mental reality, taken from recent publications, will serve to characterize all essential aspects of this procedure. A. Sommerfelt, Sur la nature du phonème:[1] 'Les phonèmes sont des modèles que les sujets parlants cherchent à imiter' (23). 'L'image articulatoire et auditive d'un phonème donné est toujours le même' (25). 'On ne pourra insister assez sur le caractère psychique des phonèmes' (25).[2] Tytus Benni, Zur neueren Entwicklung des Phonembegriffs:[3] 'Ein Phonem, eine Lautvorstellung, ein gedachter Laut.' N. S. Trubetzkoy, Zur allgemeinen Theorie der phonologischen Vokalsysteme:[4] 'die einzelnen Lautvorstellungen oder Phoneme.' The Cercle Linguistique de Prague, Thèses:[5] 'Images acoustico-motrices les plus simples et significatives dans une langue donnée (phonèmes).' H. Ułaszyn, Laut, Phonema, Morphonema:[6] 'Diese akustisch-artikulatorischen Vorstellungen sind als solche nicht weiter teilbar. Ich nenne sie "Phonemata"' (54). 'Das Phonema ist also die Vorstellung von einem aus Lautkomplexen abstrahierten selbständigen Laut, der seines semasiologisch-morphologsichen Wertes entkleidet ist' (56). 'Für mich ist ein Phonema ein psychisches Äquivalent eines "empirischen Lautes" und zwar eines Lautes, der als Typus empfunden wird, der sich aber unter gewissen Bedingungen ändert' (61).

1 Norsk Tidsskrift for Sprogvidenskap 1.22 ff.

2 Cf. Trubetzkoy, in Actes du deuxième congrès international de linguistes 109: 'Die Phonologie befasst sich ... mit den Phonemen, d. i. mit den sich in den Sprachlauten realisierenden, im Sprachbewusstsein lebenden Lautabsichten.'

3 Donum Natalicium Schrijnen (1929) 36.

4 Travaux du Cercle Linguistique de Prague (hereafter referred to as TCLP) 1.39.

5 TCLP 1.10 f.

6 TCLP 4.53 ff.

All these definitions agree in the ascription of mental reality to the phoneme, and for me thus fail to meet the requirement of methodological feasibility, i. e. they identify an entity which is inaccessible to scientific methods within the frame of linguistic study. The objections to mentalistic procedure in linguistics have been put by Bloomfield[7] in a form which appears unanswerable and has thus far, at least, been unanswered. It is a work of supererogation to try to restate what Bloomfield has so well stated. For the sake of completeness, though, it may be justifiable to recapitulate the general principles which invalidate any 'mental' definition of the phoneme.

Such a definition is invalid because (1) we have no right to guess about the linguistic workings of an inaccessible 'mind', and (2) we can secure no advantage from such guesses. The linguistic processes of the 'mind' as such are quite simply unobservable; and introspection about linguistic processes is notoriously a fire in a wooden stove. Our only information about the 'mind' is derived from the behavior of the individual whom it inhabits. To interpret that behavior in terms of 'mind' is to commit the logical fallacy of 'explaining' a fact of unknown cause by giving that unknown cause a name, and then citing the name x as the cause of the fact. 'Mind' is indeed a summation of such x's, unknown causes of human behavior.[8]

These logical objections to mentalistic explanation might be suspended (under properly defined assumptions) if there were any pragmatic utility in operating with 'mind' as a linguistic-scientific fiction. But the actual result of mentalistic assumptions is not progress, but obstruction, in scientific work. For the operation with mental 'causes' produces, in Bloomfield's phrase, 'a short-circuit of inquiry'. The procedure of pretending to explain phenomena by giving mentalistic names to their previously unnamed and still unknown causes 'short-circuits inquiry' until some investigator perceives the fraud and returns to the study of phenomena and their correlations. Any correlation of phenomena which can be established on the basis of mental entities or events can also, and more economically, be established on the basis of the phenomena themselves. Such remarks as Trubetzkoy's[9] 'In allen diesen Fällen hat die Akzentbewegung einen Sinn, der auch vom Sprachbewusstsein bis zu einem gewissen Grade empfunden wird' or Baudouin de Courtenay's 'Wörter mit psychisch auslautenden Konsonanten'[10] are meaningless unless accompanied by phenomenological evidence, and unnecessary if so accompanied.

The application of these principles to the definition of the phoneme is obvious. We can investigate 'mental phonemes' ('psychophones' in the terminology of Tytus Benni[11]) only through our observations of the sounds a speaker produces and the reaction of a hearer to those sounds. Any correlations of those 'mental phonemes' must be established on the basis of sounds produced and reacted to. Any classification in terms of 'intention' or 'impression' is therefore either a needless incursion into the unobservable or an evasion of the task of classifying the sounds as sounds produced and reacted to, or the task of classifying the production of and reaction to the sounds.

E. Sapir is the only 'phonologist', so far as I know, who has perceived the necessity of justifying the ascription of reality to mental sounds and sound-patterns. In his important essay on Sound patterns in language,[12] he is aware of 'a possible charge of phonetic metaphysics.' ⟪23⟫ He gives illustrations of the mental reality of certain phonetic patterns. Thus ⟪25⟫ he adduces the difficulty which speakers of English experience in pronouncing initially certain consonants which they pronounced readily in other positions. 'ŋa- is incredible because there is no mba-, nda-, ŋ(g)a- series in English.' One may be surprised at finding [ŋ] placed in a series with [mb] and [nd] rather than with the simple nasals [m] and [n]. Sapir has prepared for this surprise; he has said ⟪24⟫: 'in spite of what phoneticians tell us about this sound (b : m as d : n as g : ŋ), no naive English-speaking person can be made to feel in his bones that it belongs to a single series with m and n. Psychologically it cannot be grouped with them because, unlike them, it is not a freely movable consonant (there are no words beginning with ŋ). It still feels like ŋg, however little it sounds like it.' In other words, [ŋ] is difficult to pronounce initially because it forms a mental series with the initially non-occurrent [mb, nd] rather than with the initially occurrent [m, n]. It belongs with the former group rather than the latter because it does not occur initially. . . . In still other words, [ŋ] is difficult to pronounce initially because it does not occur initially.

7 Modern Philology 25.211 ff.; his Language 32 ff.; and reviews in Lang. 8.220 ff.; 10.32 ff.

8 The principles presented in this section are limited strictly to applications of scientific methodology, and accordingly do not involve a discussion with those to whom behaviorism is unacceptable as a psychological assumption or (irrelevantly) as a 'philosophy'. Whatever our attitude toward mind, spirit, soul, etc. as realities, we must agree that the scientist proceeds as though there were no such things, as though all his information were acquired through processes of his physiological nervous system. In so far as he occupies himself with psychical, non-material forces, the scientist is not a scientist. The scientific method is quite simply the convention that mind does not exist: science adopts the nominalistic attitude toward the problem of the universals, in matters of procedure.

9 Das morphonologische System der russischen Sprache (TCLP 5.2) 35.

10 Fakultative Sprachlaute, in Donum Natalicium Schrijnen 38.

11 Donum Natalicium Schrijnen 35.

12 Lang. 1.37 ff. ⟪19⟫.

A rather more valid procedure to suggest the mental reality of a series [mb, nd, ŋ(g)] would be to try to elicit a positive response from a phonetically naive subject. Teach him to pronounce [ŋɑ]; secure from him the statement that it sounds queer; and then ask him to produce some other similar queer sound. When he fails to respond (or responds with [mɑ, nɑ]), suggest [mbɑ], and ask for still another similar queer syllable. If the hypothecated mental series is a reality, he should certainly respond with [ndɑ]. I have made this experiment with several phonetically naive friends, with uniformly negative results.

Sapir has subsequently returned to the problem of demonstrating the mental reality of quasi-phonetic units. His article, The psychological reality of phonemes,[13] proceeds on the principle that 'if the phonemic attitude is more basic, psychologically speaking, than the more strictly phonetic one, it should be possible to detect it in the unguarded speech judgments of naive speakers who have a complete control of their language in a practical sense but have no rationalized or consciously systematic knowledge of it.' To examine in detail each of the incidents which Sapir narrates would take us too far afield; it must suffice here to consider those features which are essential to a determination of the psychological reality of phonemes.

In all these 'tests', Sapir is obliged to present negative evidence of the real mental existence of a phoneme: i.e., the constant failure of his subjects to record differently sounds which are objectively different. His Paiute guide, in the first case, responds to various kinds of labial consonants with a single symbol [p]. Sapir's procedure is thus to elicit a uniform response to different stimuli. This uniformity of response appears comparable to that of the small child who responds to the sight of various trouser-wearing individuals with a uniform 'Papa'. This response can scarcely be adduced as evidence of the reality of a concept of paternal achievement or potentiality, or of a concept of adult human male, or even a concept of trouser-wearing individual. It might be interpreted as positive evidence of the mental reality of a concept if, to a uniform stimulus, different responses were made. If Sapir's Paiute guide had been trained to record one variety of labial consonant as [p]; if he had been requested to pronounce all other varieties of 'the same sound'; if he had then without hesitation and without duplication responded with examples of all those other varieties—we might then concede that he appeared to have some mental concept of a unified [p]-phoneme which was variously actualized in his speech. But even this demonstration would be a convenience rather than a necessity for linguistic study; it would represent a summary of the behavior of native speakers, a behavior which is already available for the student of language, though in less concentrated form. In each of his experiments, Sapir has to demonstrate the 'correctness' of his guide's uniform responses by a sketch of the pertinent linguistic data, data which he has assembled and interpreted as a trained, accurate, objective linguist, not as an intuitive native speaker.

(1) In Southern Paiute, objectively different labial consonants occur postvocalically—fricatives, voiced and voiceless; stops, aspirated and unaspirated, long and short, nasalized and oral. These differences are apparently not primarily or inherently distinctive, but may be regarded as 'largely determined by the nature of the element (stem or suffix) which precedes them and which may be said to have an inherently spirantizing, nasalizing, or geminating force' (49). Initially, only a voiceless stop occurs as unnasalized labial. Sapir's guide, whom he describes as 'a young man of average intelligence',[14] surprised him by writing a voiced labial fricative as [p], although objectively of course this [β] differs more from the initial [p] than does the postvocalic long or short stop [p·, p]. We are not told how Tony wrote these latter sounds; if he wrote them, too, as [p], then his procedure is a simple case of uniform response to different stimuli. If Tony wrote the postvocalic stops with a different symbol, then there might be some basis for stating 'that the postvocalic -β- is more closely related functionally to a simple initial p- than is the postvocalic -p- (after unvoiced vowel), which must always be interpreted as a secondary form of -p·-' (50). But this statement would be strictly inconsistent with Sapir's report:[15] 'The tendency to use geminated consonants in composition is probably due to the greater phonetic similarity thus brought about between a simplex and its compound'.

(2) John Whitney, another native interpreter, assured Sapir that the two Sarsi words, dìní 'this' and dìní 'it makes a sound', apparently homonyms, 'were totally different'. John insisted that the second of these words ended in [t]. As Sapir tells us, both final vowels are aspirated; the increment of aspiration to a vowel may be a positional variant of [t], or it may a feature of utterance-conclusion. In the one case, John analyzed the aspiration as a [t]-variant,

[13] Selected Writings of Edward Sapir, University of California Press 1949, 46ff. ⟦Here this original English version replaces the French translation that was Twaddell's source, in Journal de Psychologie 30.247 ff. (1933); nothing is lost by this, since the translation was reliable, and Sapir's wording is what Twaddell would certainly have quoted if possible.⟧

[14] We learn from the Proceedings of the American Academy of Arts and Sciences 65.2.299, that he was Tony Tillohash, who at that time was 'just about to complete his course at the Carlisle Indian School in Pennsylvania'.

[15] Proc. Amer. Acad. 65.1.70.

in the other as a finality-feature. The reason for the native speaker's choice of mode of analysis is, Sapir indicates, the occurrence of morphological variants of dìní 'it makes a sound' which contain an unambiguous [t]. In so far as this incident may be interpreted as evidence of any mental reality, it would appear to be rather a morphological class or lexical unit than any phonetic or quasi-phonetic class or unit.

(3) Similarly, Alex Thomas's transcription of his native Nootka distinguished between long consonants as positional variants of short consonants and as the product of combination of similar final and initial consonants of separate lexical elements. This practice, too, appears more appropriately referred to lexical than to quasi-phonetic consciousness, in terms of mental reality.

(4) Alex Thomas used the same diacritic modifier to identify the glotticized plosives (plosives followed by glottal stop) and the glotticized nasals (nasals preceded by glottal stop). By disregarding the factor of sequence, according to Sapir, Alex has given us 'valuable evidence ... for the phonologic reality [sic] of a glottalized class of consonants.' Whether this procedure is the product of phonetic analysis or of phonological intuition would appear to depend in part, at least, upon the question whether the glottal stop occurs in Nootka as an autonomous distinctive speech-sound or only as an incremental feature of some oral occlusion. If the latter, then Alex's disregarding the sequential factory is obviously less significant. In my ignorance of Nootka, I can only affirm that the hypothesis of phonetic analysis is tenable: Sapir describes Alex as 'the most successful American Indian pupil that I have had in practical phonetics'; and phonetic innocence can be rapidly lost.

(5) Sapir's final bit of evidence, the tendency of English-speaking students, taking nonsense-dictation, to indicate an unpronounced glottal stop after short accented final vowels, involves an auditory hallucination of a non-native speech-sound, and is accordingly only negatively and inferentially admissible, at best.

The first and fourth incidents thus represent simple cases of uniform response to different stimuli. The second and third are compound; in these, variants of two different 'phonemes' are objectively very similar (at any rate, elicit a uniform response from the trained phonetician Sapir); the native speaker distinguishes these variants from each other, or better, fails to distinguish each from other forms of its own 'phoneme'. The basis is, as Sapir indicates, a morphological, syntactical, or lexical correlation with other forms. The fifth case involves a positive response, to be sure, but one which must be interpreted negatively with respect to the mental reality which Sapir wishes to demonstrate.

In short, until positive and unambiguous evidence of the mental reality of phonemes can be adduced, it appears methodologically dangerous to define the phoneme in terms of mental reality. Sapir himself defines the phoneme[16] as 'a functionally significant unit in the rigidly defined pattern or configuration of sounds peculiar to a language'. He quotes[17] with apparent approval Bloomfield's non-mentalistic definition, 'a minimum same of vocal feature'. In 1921, Sapir wrote:[18] 'In watching my Nootka interpreter write his language, I often had the curious feeling that he was transcribing an ideal flow of phonetic elements which he heard, inadequately from a purely objective standpoint, as the intention of the actual rumble of speech.' That 'curious feeling' has apparently become a conviction; but it is, I believe, safe to say (and rejoice) that his linguistic methodology has not undergone any comparable metamorphosis. I believe it is fair to say that that methodology does not exemplify, and the unrelated quasi-experimental theorizings do not establish, either the justification or the necessity for making guesses about linguistic mental processes.

It must be emphasized that these criticisms of Sapir's doctrines are not due to any opinion that his position is more vulnerable than that of other mentalistic definers of the phoneme. It is precisely Sapir's acuteness and conscience which appear in his realization of the necessity of justifying the ascription of mental reality to phonemes and phonemic patterns. It is precisely his merit to have avoided the care-free irresponsibility of the others who also consider the phoneme a mental reality, without taking the trouble to give their reasons.[19]

There are some definitions which appear to ascribe both mental and physical reality to the phoneme. Thus in W. L. Graff's definition:[20] 'A speech sound represented by a number of unimportant varieties but interpreted as a unit in a given language at a given time', the constituents of a phoneme are physical, but the constitution is mental. The compromise proposal of Otto Jespersen at the Copenhagen Conference belongs here: 'A family of sounds which from an objective point of view may be regarded as distinct, but which are felt naturally by the speakers of a certain language as identical, because they are not used to keep words apart.'

Similarly the definitions of J. Marouzeau:[21] 'Phonème (Laut, Sprechlaut): Élément auquel conduit l'analyse du langage articulé, défini d'une part par la disposition des organes vocaux et les mouvements

16 Selected Writings of Edward Sapir 46.

17 In S. A. Rice, Methods in Social Science (1931), 305.

18 In his Language 58.

19 For a presentation of other grounds of objection to the definition of the phoneme in terms of mental reality, see (TCLP 4): D. Čyževśkyj (3 ff.); K. Bühler (22 ff.); and W. Doroszewski (61 ff.).

20 In his Language (1932) xl.

21 Lexique de la terminologie linguistique, Paris, 1933.

qui accompagnent ou provoquent le courant d'air expiré ou inspiré, d'autre part par l'impression auditive qui en résulte' (141 f). S. v. Phonologie: '... des phonèmes, c'est-à-dire des sons réalisés dans la langue et propres à exprimer des notions (école linguistique de Prague)' (143).

Finally, there are definitions on the basis of the phoneme's function, i.e. its utilization in distinguishing words and sentences. This utilization is usually, either explicitly or by implication, related to the intention of the speaker. Thus J. Vachek, in What is Phonology?,[22] refers to the phoneme as 'a functional unit and later (83) states: 'The immense, practically unlimited number of sounds and sound variations in every language appears to be a manifestation (or, perhaps, realization) of a definite and strictly limited number of phonemes.' Vilém Mathesius defines phonemes as 'Laute, die in dem analysierten System funktionelle Geltung haben';[23] as 'sounds endowed with functional values';[24] and as 'des éléments phonologiques fondamentaux appelés phonèmes, c.-à-d. des sons (simples ou composites) qui ont une valeur fonctionnelle.'[25] And in his article Ziele und Aufgaben der vergleichenden Phonologie,[26] he salutes Sapir as one of the founders of 'phonology'. The Cercle Linguistique de Prague, which in 1929 defined phonemes as 'images acoustico-motrices',[27] in 1931 shifts the emphasis to a functional characterization: 'Phonème: Unité phonologique non susceptible d'être dissociée en unités phonologiques plus petites et plus simples. (Unité phonologique: Terme d'une opposition phonologique quelconque. Opposition phonologique: Différence phonique susceptible de servir, dans une langue donnée, à la différenciation des significations intellectuelles.)'[28]

22 English Studies 15.82.
23 Xenia Pragensia (1929) 435.
24 Donum Natalicium Schrijnen 47.
25 TCLP 1.68. 26 Xenia Pragensia 432 ff.
27 TCLP 1.10. 28 TCLP 4.311.

III. THE PHONEME AS A PHYSICAL REALITY

Nearly all students of language who use the term 'phoneme' as in contrast with 'speech-sound' apply the term 'phoneme' to some larger unit. The speech-sounds are, objectively, of an almost infinite variety; the phonemes of a given language are constant. It follows that each larger unit, each phoneme, may correspond to a number of actual speech-sounds. This correspondence may be of two kinds: (1) The phoneme may correspond to some peculiarity or peculiarities, characteristic of all the speech-sounds in question and characteristic of only these speech-sounds; the phoneme is then a feature[1] of the actual speech-sounds. (2) The phoneme may correspond to the sum of all the speech-sounds in question; the phoneme is then a group of speech-sounds. Those who define the phoneme in terms of physical realities follow one of these procedures: Bloomfield, I believe, the first;[2] and Daniel Jones the second.[3]

Bloomfield has defined the phoneme on several occasions; each definition requires consideration.

In A set of postulates for the science of language, (Lang. 2.157 ((27))) he writes: 'Assumption: Different morphemes may be alike or partly alike as to vocal features. Thus book : table [b]; stay : west [st]; -er (agent): -er (comparative). Definition: A minimum same of vocal feature is a phoneme or distinctive sound.'

It must first be observed that the assumption ('different morphemes may be alike or partly alike as to vocal features') is itself based upon another assumption of a different order. For we all know that in any occurrences of the events book and table, those sections which we call [b] are not objectively alike; and this would be even more prominently the case if Bloomfield had found [t] as the "minimum same of vocal feature" in ten : stay : writing : bottle : hat. He means, of course, that the [b] of book and the [b] of table are not significantly different within the frame of the American English language. But the equivalence 'not significantly different' : 'alike' implies an assumption that some differences of vocal feature are not significant. This assumption Bloomfield formulates (154 f. ((26))) as follows: 'Within certain communities successive utterances are alike or partly alike.... Linguistics considers only those vocal features which are alike in the two utterances, and only those stimulus-reaction features which are alike in the two utterances.... Outside of our science these similarities are only relative; within it they are absolute.'

This statement is obviously of prime methodological importance. Bloomfield has defined an utterance as 'an act of speech' and this, in turn, as 'vocal features or sounds'. An utterance, for him, is accordingly an event in a space-time continuum, an event which is correlated to a (potentially) substantially recurrent social situation. Now, the important aspect of successive utterances, as events in a space-time continuum, is that no two of them are alike. It is only linguistically, i. e. as correlated to a recurrent social situation, that two utterances may be alike. Of the practically infinite objective variations between utterances as physical events, not all are lin-

1 The definition of this term will be discussed later.

2 The definitions of K. Bühler appear to belong here: '(Jene) lautlichen Besonderheiten, ... die von den einzelnen Sprachen zum Range von diakritischer Zeichen erhoben worden sind' (TCLP 4.44). 'Une invariante qui sert de marque diacritique en vue de distinguer les significations intellectuelles' (TCLP 4.295).

3 W. Doroszewski's definition may belong here: 'Mais je pense qu'il est plus simple de considérer comme "phonème" le son tel qu'il est réalisé en position isolée, en traitant de "variantes" les produits combinatoires' (TCLP 4.73).

guistically significant. Those physical events are the material of linguistic study, however, and accordingly the first step in linguistic study must be the establishing of criteria for determining which of the innumerable physical differences are also significant linguistic differences. Until those criteria have been established, the use of the terms 'linguistically same' and 'linguistically different' is unjustified. Every one of the succeeding definitions in Bloomfield's Set of postulates, accordingly, appears conditional upon the assumption of the application of correct criteria to determine the linguistic significance of the objective variations in successive utterances. Those criteria can be applied, I believe; otherwise linguistic study is a sheer impossibility. By the failure to expound the criteria whereby linguistic differences are distinguished from physical differences, Bloomfield's definition of the phoneme does not (for me) fulfill the requirements of methodological practicability. It characterizes the difference between a phoneme and a morpheme and a taxeme, etc.; but it is as though a meter were defined as 'the standard unit of linear measurement'. That would suffice to characterize the difference between a meter and a sonnet, or a cumulus cloud; but it would not furnish a basis for application of the unit within the frame of scientific study.

It might be objected that Bloomfield, in his Set of postulates, is merely concerned with setting up a theoretical frame-work of terminology, not with indications of practical procedure. In that case, it would of course be unreasonable to expect his definitions to meet requirements of working technique; but the methodological value of the Set of postulates for the science of language is thereby seriously impaired.

The foregoing observations apply to the logical procedure in Bloomfield's definition of the phoneme in his Set of postulates. In a later definition of the phoneme (in his book Language 77 ff.), he mentions a criterion whereby significant linguistic differences are to be distinguished from the objective physical differences in successive speech-events. The criterion is 'our every-day knowledge', which is a generalization from a large number of experiments. This knowledge can be trusted to 'tell us whether speech-forms are "the same" or "different".' By experimenting with such a speech-form, pin, Bloomfield finds certain relationships between this and other forms. Thus: 'pin ends with the same sound as fin, sin, tin, but begins differently; ... pin begins with the same sound as pig, pill, pit; etc.' 'In this way, we can find forms which partially resemble pin, by altering any one of three parts of the word . . . we conclude that the distinctive features of the word are three indivisible units. Each of these units occurs also in other combinations, but cannot be further analyzed by partial resemblances: each of the three is a minimum unit of distinctive sound-feature, a phoneme.'

Bloomfield summarizes: 'Among the gross acoustic features of any utterance, then, certain ones are distinctive, recurring in recognizable and relatively constant shape in successive utterances. These distinctive features occur in lumps or bundles, each one of which we call a phoneme. The speaker has been trained to make sound-producing movements in such a way that the phoneme features will be present in the sound-waves, and he has been trained to respond only to these features and to ignore the rest of the gross acoustic mass that reaches his ears. ... The phonemes of a language are not sounds, but merely features of sound which the speakers have been trained to produce and recognize in the current of actual speech-sound—just as motorists are trained to stop before a red signal, be it an electric signal-light, a lamp, a flag, or what not, although there is no disembodied redness apart from these actual signals.'

In connection with this analogy, it is pertinent to remark that 'although there is no disembodied redness', all these signals do possess a characteristic peculiarity which is constantly associated with their 'redness', viz. the property of emitting or reflecting to the eye of the motorist photo-magnetic impulses in which wave-lengths around 670 $\mu\mu$ predominate. It appears fair to read into Bloomfield's discussion, accordingly, the opinion that a corresponding constant characteristic is a property of every occurrence of a phoneme; this appears to be supported by his reference to 'phoneme-features' as 'present in the sound-waves.'

It must be noted that Bloomfield makes use of the terms 'feature' and 'features' in what appear to be at least two different senses, none of them explicitly defined. In his Set of postulates (154 ((26))), he introduces the linguistic discussion thus: 'Psychology, in particular, gives us this series: to certain stimuli (A) a person reacts by speaking; his speech (B) in turn stimulates his hearers to certain reactions (C). By a social habit which every person acquires in infancy from his elders, A-B-C are closely correlated. Within this correlation, the stimuli (A) which cause an act of speech and the reactions (C) which result from it, are very closely linked, because every person acts indifferently as speaker or as hearer. We are free, therefore, without further discussion to speak of vocal features or sounds (B) and of stimulus-reaction features (A-C) of speech. Definition. An act of speech is an utterance.' Here the 'vocal features' are equated to 'sounds' (B); they are also 'speech' (B), defined as a sound-continuum which is a reaction to speaker's stimuli (A) and a stimulus to hearer's reactions (C). 'Vocal features' are an interval-fraction of a social situation; 'vocal features' are a sound-continuum, an utterance, a total act of speech. The plurality of the expression 'vocal features' is essentially meaningless, for all we know about them (or it) is the equivalence to 'an act of speech'.

In the same Set of postulates (157 ((27))), Bloomfield characterizes the phoneme as 'a minimum same of vocal feature'. This shift from plural to singular is bewildering; it implies a transformation of a continuous 'act of speech' into hitherto unmentioned parts, for we have had no clue as to the procedure whereby the continuum 'vocal features' is to be split up into minimum units. All that Bloomfield has previously said about 'vocal features' describes them as an utterance-totality, a continuous event, a coherent, autonomous, and integral fraction of a social event (B in the series A-B-C). Now we are confronted with that continuous event as composed of units; those units are declared to be minimum, and some of them even declared to be 'same'. The term 'vocal features' as synonymous with 'utterance' is potentially confusing; the behind-stage analysis of the otherwise wholly undefined 'vocal features' into a sequence of precisely separated and somehow similar 'minimum sames of vocal feature' definitely is confusing. The mere description of a totality by a plural noun does not justify the claim that by using that noun in the singular the totality is automatically analyzed into its components.

The definition 'minimum same of vocal feature', by this pregnant inflectional shift from 'features' to 'feature' involves, as I see it, two assumptions: (1) that the speech-event has been correctly analyzed into minimum interval-fractions, (2) that some of these minimum fractions are alike in various utterances. The second of these, that 'some morphemes may be alike or partly alike as to vocal features', has already been touched upon. The first assumption is nowhere explicitly stated.

It must be assumed that a substantially similar reasoning is to be followed with the later definition (Language 79): 'a minimum unit of distinctive sound-feature'. It is difficult to associate any meaning with the expression 'unit of ... feature'; if a 'sound-feature' is understood as a 'sound-continuum', as an event, as a fraction of a social situation, then the expression 'minimum distinctive unit of sound-continuum' may have a meaning.

In the definitions, then, Bloomfield uses a singular form of a term used previously only in the plural, and in its plural use equated to a coherent, autonomous, integral event. That shift involves considerable difficulties.

But new difficulties, involving perhaps another sense of the term 'feature', appear in the course of the discussion of the phoneme in Bloomfield's Language (79 ff.). In that passage, as we have seen, he has defined the phoneme as 'a minimum unit of distinctive sound-feature'. Then he adds: 'The phonemes of a language are not sounds, but merely features of sound which the speakers have been trained to produce and recognize in the current of actual speech-sound. ...' A phoneme is thus a 'feature of sound' which the speaker produces. A phoneme must therefore be a part of the sound produced by the speaker. A phoneme must therefore be a fraction of the sound; it must be a fraction of an acoustic event. In so far as acoustic fractions of different utterances are occurrences of the same phoneme, those fractions must be some constant fraction, common to all the utterances. A phoneme thus appears to be some constant fraction, common to all the utterances. Since the 'phoneme-features' are distinctive, a phoneme must be a distinctive or characteristic fraction of each acoustic event. A phoneme thus appears to be a constant, characteristic fraction of phonetic events; a phoneme-feature is then a constant, characteristic acoustic fraction which is present in the sound-waves at each occurrence of that phoneme.[4] Whether a 'phoneme-feature' is a feature <u>of</u> a phoneme, or a feature <u>which is</u> a phoneme, we are not told: presumably the former. But that Bloomfield appears to accept the existence of some kind of 'phoneme-features', we have already seen.

He describes these features further (Language 79): 'Among the gross acoustic features of any utterance, then, certain ones are distinctive, recurring in recognizable and relatively constant shape in successive utterances.[5] These distinctive features occur in lumps or bundles, each one of which we call a phoneme.' By 'lump or bundle' of features, we are apparently to understand the simultaneous or immediately sequential occurrences of certain acoustic fractions. In so far as a phoneme is a 'lump or bundle' of 'distinctive features', it must be a combination

4 These complexities connected with the use of the terms 'feature' and 'features' represent for me the greatest difficulty in determing precisely the meaning of Bloomfield's definitions of the phoneme. That difficulty is due not only to the lack of any preliminary definition of the terms as applied to events, but also to the unannounced introduction of different usages for the terms. At all events, it is hard to see how any definition of 'phoneme' or 'feature' could warrant the optimism with which Bloomfield writes (Modern Philology 25.217): 'The logical demand that a science speak in quantitative terms is met by linguistics because it speaks in terms of phonemes'. The phoneme as a quantitative unit (even of feature) is a difficult enough concept. But these units are by no means quantitatively comparable; one [r]-phoneme is not equal to 3.76 [p]-phonemes; and unless quantitative units are quantitatively comparable, it appears unjustified to claim that 'we speak in quantitative terms'.

5 In so far as the 'constant shape in successive utterances' is only 'relative', the recurrence of the phonemes is only relative. But if the phoneme is 'a minimum same'; if 'the distinctive features of the word (pin) are three indivisible units', and 'each of these units occurs also in other combinations' (Language 79), then the recurrence must in some sense be absolute; and in that same sense the 'shape in successive utterances' must be absolutely constant. If that 'shape' is only relatively constant, then the recurrence is only relative, the sameness of phonemes in successive utterances is only relative; and the entire procedure is necessarily invalid.

of acoustic fractions (the time correlation not being stated). It is worth noting that if a phoneme is a combination of distinctive features, it can scarcely be defined as 'a minimum same of distinctive sound-feature'.

Despite the difficulty of arriving at any clear formulation of these uses of 'feature', it appears that as Bloomfield defines the phoneme, it is a constant, characteristic fraction or combination of fractions of acoustic events; it is (or is accompanied by) 'phoneme-features in the sound-waves'.

If such features existed, the determination of the phonemes of a given language, and the definition of the phoneme, would be achieved. We should ask Bloomfield to write out a text in his admirably practicable phonemic transcription and read it into a high-quality oscillograph hook-up. We should then examine the record of his total acoustic production. We should, to be sure, find much in the 'gross acoustic mass' which was non-distinctive; but we should also find the 'phoneme-features'. On every occasion which corresponded to a [t] in his transcription, we should find in the acoustic record some constant, characteristic fraction of sound-waves.

That we do not find any such constant, characteristic fraction is of course a commonplace of experimental phonetics. If Bloomfield is right, the only explanation for our failure to find 'phoneme-features' in an acoustic record is the inadequacy of our recording apparatus. Such appears to be the explanation Bloomfield would advance; in an outline of an address on The Phoneme to the Language and Literature Club of the University of Wisconsin, 13 April 1934, he states: 'The physical (acoustic) definition of each phoneme of any given dialect can be expected to come from the laboratory within the next decades.'

Two queries suggest themselves here. The first is the question as to the propriety of basing a definition (for it is the recurrence of the 'phoneme-features' which Bloomfield adduces as evidence of the sameness of these minimum units) upon a discovery which is envisaged only as a future possibility. The more serious question is this: What is the basis for the belief that future laboratory research will possess more adequate apparatus? Granted that our present acoustic records are far from perfect; granted that considerable technical improvements are to be expected: it remains, however, extremely doubtful whether these improvements will be of a sort to reveal what Bloomfield hopes to find, a set of records which will enable an observer to determine a constant, characteristic fraction of sound-wave, common to all occurrences of 'the same phoneme'. For whatever that (hypothecated) fraction may be, we have no reason to believe that it is beyond the range of our present recording apparatus.

The researches of C. Stumpf, reported in the Handbuch der Physik (Berlin 1927) 8.456, indicate that with an upper transmission limit of 6020 cycles, the only acoustic disturbance was a slight 'blunting' of [s]. Even with so low an upper limit as 2460 cycles, the act of speech is reported as being 'noch ganz gut verständlich', though certain distortions of front vowels and voiceless fricatives are noted. It appears justifiable, then, to assert that the frequencies up to 6500 cycles contain all the distinctive acoustic 'features' of speech. As a matter of fact, many phonograph records and radio loud-speakers transmit speech with a much lower limit (not to speak of the telephone); yet the distinctive sound-features must be present, for it is a matter of 'our every-day knowledge' that we 'understand' that speech.

But our present recording apparatus has a fairly uniform response up to at least 8000 cycles.[6] All those 'phoneme-features' which are associated with pitch and timbre (frequency and wave-form) must therefore be present in our records. The factors of duration and intensity (amplitude) are of course very precisely determinable.

The laboratory situation appears, then, to be as follows: We know the range within which the distinctive features must lie; we have records covering that range. Yet those records do not reveal any constant characteristic of sound-waves (an acoustic feature) for each phoneme; even with the acoustically relatively simple vowels the so-called 'formants' are only proximately determinable, and within very wide ranges.

The only legitimate conclusion at present appears to be that the presence of 'phoneme-features' as positive, additive entities in the sound-waves is not demonstrable, and there is no reason to believe that it will be.

It has been necessary to consider at some length this question of the existence of 'phoneme-features in the sound-waves', for this existence appears to be an indispensable part of Bloomfield's definition. He is justified in calling various sections of utterance-events occurrences of the *same* phoneme only if he can establish some recurrent fraction, some sameness in all such occurrences. By the discovery that '*pin* ends with the same sound as *fin*, *sin*, *tin*, but begins differently', he is justified in saying that the [p] of *pin* is a different phoneme from the [f, s, t] of *fin*, *sin*, *tin*. But before he may 'recognize a phoneme even when it appears in different parts of words, as *pin*, *apple*, *mop*', he will need more than 'a little practice'. He must establish some constant characteristic fraction.

By setting up the groups (1) pin : fin, sin, tin; (2) apple : addle; (3) mop : moll, we obtain the following relations: (1) [p] which is different from [f, s, t]; (2) [p] which is different from [d]; (3) [p] which is different from [l]. But the grouping together of these various [p]s is legitimate only when there is

[6] Cf. Hdb. d. Phys. 8.559 ff., 603; H. Fletcher, Speech and Hearing 27.

positive evidence of their constituting a positive entity. As K. Jimbo, quite soundly, says:[7] 'We cannot assert from this without dogmatism that the [a] of ame and the [a] of aka are exactly the same. They may be the same, but we cannot prove the identity until due examination, investigation and experiment be made.' The evidence of identity which Bloomfield appears to regard as appropriate is the presence of 'phoneme-features in the sound-wave'. That evidence cannot yet be adduced, and the expectation that it will be forthcoming is itself in need of justification.[8]

Daniel Jones has given definitions of the phoneme in three significant passages: (1) in Trofimov and Jones, The Pronunciation of Russian (1923) 49 ff.; (2) in his notes On Phonemes (TCLP 4.74); (3) in the course of the proceedings of the International Congress of Phonetic Sciences at Amsterdam, 1932. The definitions are: (1) 'A phoneme is a group of sounds consisting of an important sound of the language (i.e. the most frequently used member of that group) together with others which take its place in particular sound-groups.' (2) 'A Phoneme may be defined as a family of sounds in a given language, consisting of an important sound of the language together with other related sounds, which take its place in particular sound-sequences.' (3) 'Definition of a phoneme: a family of sounds in a given language, which are related in character and are such that no one of them ever occurs in the same surroundings as any other in words.'

It will be observed that these definitions represent a progress toward precision. The elimination of the ambiguous uses of the term 'group' in the first definition is of course desirable. The addition of the term 'related' in the second and third definitions appears to make difficult the connection of the English sounds [h] and [ŋ] in a single phoneme; under the first formulation, such a combination would be possible: For [h] occurs only before stressed vowels and [w, j], and might thus be said to 'take the place of' [ŋ], which never occurs in these positions. Presumably the use of the somewhat fanciful term 'family' in the second and third definitions is to be understood as emphasizing the necessity of an organogenitic relationship of the various sounds which are to be grouped together in a phoneme. The second and third definitions differ in the elimination of the distinction between 'important' and 'unimportant' members of a phoneme.

Essentially, it is fair to say, the three definitions agree. A phoneme is for Jones a 'group or family of sounds'. It is clear from his use of terms that by 'sound' he understands an abstraction of a large number of separate sound-events differing so little from one another that the difference is imperceptible. The different sounds which compose a phoneme are related sounds; i.e. they possess or are marked by similarities in the organogenetic processes which produce them. Finally, these different but organogenetically similar sounds alternate with one another in an absolute correlation to particular (preceding and succeeding) sound-sequences.

Sounds which alternate otherwise than in correlation to particular sound-sequences are called 'variphones' by Jones. 'It occasionally happens that a speaker uses one of two or more sounds absolutely indifferently and apparently at random. The Japanese r furnishes a good illustration. A single speaker will sometimes pronounce it very much like an English r and sometimes as a sound resembling l. But he does not do this according to a definite system as in the case of members of the same phoneme; when he says any particular word (say miru 'to see') he sometimes says it with English r and sometimes with this l-like sound and sometimes with an actual l. He is unaware that his pronunciation varies. These three sounds may be said to constitute a variphone.'[9] In Jones's terminology, the expressions 'sound, phoneme, variphone' appear to correspond respectively to 'phone, contactual phoneme, free phoneme' in the terminology which H. E. Palmer had made use of in The Principles of Romanization.[10]

Both the phoneme and the variphone, then, are groups of related sounds which alternate, the members of the phoneme systematically, the members of the variphone unsystematically. The organization of these different sounds into a group depends upon their being related; the organization within the group depends upon the nature of their alternation. It is the organization into groups which concerns us here; therein the Jones phoneme and variphone need not be distinguished.

A phoneme or a variphone is a group of sounds which are related, i.e. which are, as a group, organogenetically similar to each other, and, as a group, organogenetically different from the sounds of all other groups within the language.[11] There is a

[7] In H. E. Palmer, The Principles of Romanization (Tokyo 1931) 44.

[8] Further, quite apart from technical considerations, it is difficult to see what reason there should be for expecting to find any common acoustic characteristic of the [p]s and [t]s, respectively, in pit and tip, especially if the final stops are pronounced without explosion.

[9] In Proceedings of the International Congress of Phonetic Sciences, reprint distributed with Le Maître Phonétique (1933).

[10] It should be noted that Palmer explicitly describes the 'phone' as an abstraction.

[11] Cf. Definition of a phoneme (Le Maître Phonétique [1929] 43 f.): 'Two sounds of a language are said to belong to the same phoneme when they are related in character and it so happens that one of them never occurs in exactly the same situation as the other in connected sentences of that language. ... It would indeed be possible to group the sounds of a language into phonemes without knowing the meanings of any words.' Query: without knowing that they are words and different words? Cf. Jones's discussion (Le Maître Phonétique [1933] 30) of Palmer's principle of 'multiple identity'.

minimum of organogenetic similarity without which two sounds cannot be considered members of the same phoneme or variphone. There must, accordingly, be a hiatus of similarity between the members of one group and the members of another. For 'the same sound' obviously cannot be a member of two different phonemes or variphones, since it would then be more similar to itself than to the other members of its respective phonemes or variphones. Thus, if a sound x could belong to both phonemes A and B, then Ax would have greater similarity to one member of the B phoneme (namely Bx) than to the other members of the A phoneme. Further, such a various distribution of the 'same sound' would be possible only on the basis of a principle of autonomy on the part of the phoneme or variphone itself; since those units are described as 'groups of sounds', the grouping must be in terms of the nature of the sounds themselves.

It appears that Jones's task in determining a phoneme is in a way the converse of Bloomfield's. Whereas Bloomfield has to determine some constant characteristic (acoustic) fraction which marks all members of the group, Jones has to determine the hiatus of organogenetic similarity which sets off all members of the group as distinguished from the members of all other groups.

The difficulty of establishing such a hiatus of similarity between the sounds of two groups can be indicated by an example from the usage of many speakers of General American English. If we examine the vowels of the two lists of words (1) den, ell, mess, bet and (2) Dane, ale, mace, bait, it is not hard to find that the vowels of each list do constitute such groups of related organogenetically similar sounds. We can establish a hiatus of similarity between the members of the two groups. But when we consider the vowels of such words as dare, air, mare, bear, we discover a sound which lies squarely across our hiatus. The situation is complicated by our failure to find in any monosyllable ending with -r a vowel which falls entirely within the similarity-boundaries previously set up for either of our two phonemes.[12] To assign the sound of dare, air, etc. to one or the other phoneme appears arbitrary;[13] to assign it to both is illogical; to assign it to neither (by calling it, in connection with the -r, a diphthong) is to set a precedent which will involve the creation of a large number of such phonemes, and thus disturb the numerical strict limitation which most definers of the phoneme impose. Further, such a procedure would lead to difficulty in classifying the vowels of many a speaker of General American, who sometimes pronounces Mary and merry as homophones, with the sound of mare, at other times pronounces them differently. (We should then have two variphones, the constituent members of which would be organogenetically related to the members of two or three different phonemes!)

To be sure, consistent and comprehensible transcriptions of General American can be written by assigning the vowel of dare, air, etc., to either of the phonemes in question. Thus Bloomfield assigns it to the same phoneme as Dane, ale; C. K. Thomas, for example, assigns it to the same phoneme as den, ell. These two transcribers are not necessarily indicating a difference of phonemic usage in their speech; they may be simply adopting different conventions. That both conventions are transcriptionally practicable does not alter the arbitrary nature of either.

If Jones's definition of the phoneme (and variphone) appears inadequate as a theoretical basis for the study of phonetic relations within a language, it is probably because he had so such aim in view. He would probably agree with J. Vachek:[14] 'The phoneme of Professor Jones is a unit the establishing of which was due to purposes of phonetic transcription, not to the study of language as a functioning system.' Certainly Jones has always professed himself satisfied with a definition of a unit for purposes of transcription. In his paper On Phonemes (TCLP 4.78) he writes: 'The main object of grouping the sounds of a language together into phonemes is to establish a simple and adequate way of writing the language.' And at Amsterdam in 1932, under the heading 'Practical importance of the phoneme', he observed: 'The grouping of sounds into phonemes enables us to construct the simplest systems of phonetic transcription for every language.'

The purposes of transcription and of the study of phonetic relations within a language are not the same. It is not surprising that a unit defined for the one purpose should not be wholly applicable to the other. After all, a perfectly consistent and unambiguous transcription of English is possible with the use of a single symbol in the place of [h] and [ŋ]; but no phonetician or phonologist could consent to regarding these two 'sounds' as variants of the same phoneme.

The units with which Harold E. Palmer operates, in The Principles of Romanization, appear to be basically similar to those of Jones. Palmer's generic term for 'group of sounds', the metaphone, is to be sure defined as 'two or more phones which serve jointly as units of meaning within the limits of a given linguistic community' (thereby giving rise to cases of 'multiple identity'); and the introduction of considerations of meaning is quite properly avoided by Jones. But the various kinds of metaphones appear to be legitimately equated with various of the Jones units. Thus, the Palmer contactual phoneme corresponds to the Jones phoneme, and the Palmer

[12] Cf. Bloomfield, Language 124 ff.

[13] Particularly since it could fit equally well into the 'internal organization' within either group.

[14] English Studies 15.89. Cf. also Vachek's Daniel Jones and the Phoneme, in Charisteria Guilelmo Mathesio (Prague 1932) 25 ff.

free phoneme to the Jones variphone What Palmer calls dynamophones (e. g., the phones or 'sounds' of the vowel of at in 'He wasn't at home' and 'He's always at it'), may be properly regarded as contactual phonemes, if we follow Bloomfield in admitting stress as a phoneme. (The only objection raised by Jones[15] to Bloomfield's procedure in considering stress a phoneme is on the basis of the traditional use of the term 'phoneme'; it should be clear by now that the tradition is scarcely consistent.) The two other kinds of metaphones, the diaphone and the phonogene, involve more than one dialect or more than one chronological stage, and accordingly fall outside the scope of this study.

The units of Palmer thus appear to be strictly comparable to those of Jones, and the observations above therefore equally applicable to them. It is fair to note that although Palmer proceeds with much more cautious and explicit logic, his purpose is essentially the same as Jones's: the establishing of sanctions for the graphical representation of a language.

It appears proper to include this mention of Palmer's units in a section dealing with definitions of the phoneme in terms of physical reality, despite his rather frequent references to 'Lautvorstellungen', 'the feeling that native language-users have towards the phonetic units', etc. For he quotes[16] with apparent approval Jimbo's note: 'The treating of "abstract" sounds does not mean the treating of empty, psychical, non-existing, chimerical notions or ideas. What we are treating are concrete sounds, but only those parts of concrete sounds that have been "abstracted" or "picked out".'

The most comprehensive and methodologically lucid treatment of the phoneme with which I am acquainted is The phonemic principle, by Morris Swadesh.[17] Swadesh has recognized and avoided many of the palpable weaknesses of earlier writings on the subject. The dangers of a treatment which is at once comprehensive and concise are eclecticism and circularity; and it is possible that Swadesh's treatment is not invulnerable on these counts. Thus, a phoneme is defined as one of 'a limited number of elemental types of speech sounds' (the term 'type' is not defined); and yet 'the phonemes of a language are, in a sense, percepts to the native speakers of the given language'. Can 'type' be so defined that 'a type of speech sound' is in any sense 'a percept to the native speakers'? And it appears circular to apply pattern congruity', which is certainly an attribute of the group-totality of phonemes, as a criterion in the determination of any particular phoneme.

But these objections would be minor and probably relate more to details of phrasing than to any fundamental procedures. A much more important objection is that Swadesh, too, leaves open the possibility of arbitrary procedure in the application of his method. One of his tests for the discovery of the phonemes of a language is (123): 'The criterion of complementary distribution. If it is true of two similar types of sounds that only one of them normally occurs in certain phonetic surroundings and that only the other normally occurs in certain other phonetic surroundings, the two may be sub-types of the same phoneme. If the distribution of one type of sound is complementary to that of more than one other, it is to be identified with one rather than the other if there is a more definite phonetic similarity in that direction; an example is the p of English speech whose distribution is complementary to that of the voiced labial b as well as to that of the voiceless labial stop sounds of peak, keep, happen, but goes with the latter rather than the former because of the phonetic similarity.' The case may not be so troublesome as the disposition of, say, the vowel in sing, but it may be taken as an example of what Swadesh calls multiple 'complementary distribution'.

Swadesh has said (119): 'The norm of the phoneme may be a multiple one. That is, instead of one norm, there may be two or more. Such variant norms are ordinarily conditional, depending on the phonetic surroundings in which the phoneme occurs. Thus one may distinguish at least three norms for English p:

(1) Relatively fortis, aspirated: e.g., in initial position, as in pit.
(2) Fortis unaspirated: e.g., medially between vowels, as in upper.
(3) Lenis unaspirated: e.g., after s, as in spill.'

Let us consider, on the basis of these descriptions, the bilabial stops in the words pill, upper, spill, bill.

1. pill: fortis, aspirated, voiceless.
2. upper: fortis, unaspirated, voiceless.
3. spill: lenis, unaspirated, voiceless.
4. bill: lenis, unaspirated, voiced.

The first and fourth sound-types obviously represent the maximal differentiation of the two phonemes. In the position in which the two phonemes are most decisively differentiated, p is fortis, aspirated, voiceless; and b is lenis, unaspirated, voiced. Taking, for a moment, those factors as characteristic, we may describe our four sounds thus:

1. pill: tension, p; aspiration, p; voice, p. (p p p)
2. upper: tension, p; aspiration, b; voice, p. (p b p)
3. spill: tension, b; aspiration, b; voice, p. (b b p)
4. bill: tension, b; aspiration, b; voice, b. (b b b)

The third sound, which is complementary distribution to each of the others, differs from the second and fourth in one articulatory factor, from the first in two. What, except the conventional spelling, justifies the inclusion of the stop of spill in a [p]-phoneme? Is it any more arbitrary to regard this stop as a conditional variant of [b] (voiceless after a voiceless fricative)? It must further be remembered that the arbitrary ascription of any decisive potency

15 Le Maître Phonétique (1933) 53; (1934) 54.
16 Page 45, footnote 2.
17 Lang. 10.117 ff. ((32)).

to the factor of voice will lead to insoluble difficulties in the disposition of the 'voiced t' in latter and writing as compared with ladder and riding, in General American.

It appears arbitrary, in the absence of more decisive 'phonetic similarity', to assign the stop of spill to [p] or to [b]. Arbitrary, from the point of view of the study of phonetic relations within the language, where a [b]-phoneme without a post-sibilant member is just as defective as a similarly defective [p]-phoneme; arbitrary, even, from the relatively trivial point of view of phonetic transcription, for an equally consistent and unambiguous transcription could be written with sb- instead of sp- in such words.

The inevitability of such an arbitrary procedure in phoneme-determination could be removed only by that discovery of positive phoneme-features which Bloomfield expects. The dilemma appears to be absolute, if the phoneme is defined in terms of observable phenomena. In cases of multiple complementary distribution, a 'sound' must be assigned to one of several phonemes arbitrarily. The only way out is the hypothesis of a positive observable phoneme-feature; Bloomfield, in electing this procedure, achieves coherent structure in his treatment of the phoneme, but must accept the onus of discovering and determining those features. Pending that discovery and determination, the numerous instances of multiple complementary distribution will furnish difficulties which can often be solved only on grounds of arbitrary preference or convention—especially since it is very often precisely in such cases of multiple complementary distribution that the speakers of a language grieve us by their malignant perversity in producing sounds which are not unambiguous as to 'phonetic similarity'.

IV. THE PHONEME AS A FICTION

All attempts to associate the term 'phoneme' with either a mental or a physical reality appear open to serious if not unanswerable objection. And although the wide and increasing use of the term by linguistic students indicates that it is an eminently useful term (for that use cannot be explained by any pleasure in using esoteric or complicated terminology), it is obviously undesirable to have that term questionably defined. The stature of the scholars who have presented definitions is such that it would be difficult if not impertinent to hope that any one else could avoid the difficulties they encountered. Where Bloomfield, Sapir, Daniel Jones, Trubetzkoy, and the others have not been completely successful, it appears improbable that their methods of definition could lead to better results in other hands.

Is a different procedure possible? Although these two procedures of definition for the phoneme—regarding it as a physical reality of some order or as a mental (or psychological) reality—appear to represent the two possibilities, perhaps they are only subalternatives of one of two possible procedures. It may be that before it is appropriate to answer or even to ask the question as to the nature of the reality associated with the term 'phoneme', we should first ask and answer the question whether the term can be profitably associated with any reality at all. It is what might be called the thesis of this paper that it is inexpedient and probably impossible (at present) to associate the term with a reality: probably impossible, because the attempts by competent and conscientious linguists to define the phoneme in terms of reality have not been wholly satisfactory; inexpedient, because the purposes to which the term may be put in our discipline are served equally well or better by regarding the phoneme as an abstractional, fictitious unit.

If a satisfactory procedure of definition of the phoneme as an abstractional fiction can be worked out, that definition would have two advantages: (1) we could use the phoneme as a terminological convenience just as well as at present; (2) we should not have to use as legal currency in our study the promissory notes of the laboratory, which are liable to a heavy discount. Then, if the next decades should bring a satisfactory physical definition of the phoneme from the laboratory, we could discard the abstractional and substitute the physical definition, without disturbing the products of earlier linguistic study. If advances in psychological methods, at present unimaginable, should justify the use of psychological units in linguistic study, we could substitute a psychological definition without the necessity of reappraising all preceding phonological research. We could simply say: 'The phoneme, which we have been cautiously regarding as a convenient fiction, appears to be an objectively determinable reality. How nice!' In the happy event that the phoneme should prove determinable both physically and psychologically, the abstractional fiction definition might prove the method of rapprochement between the two determinations, a rapprochement of significance far beyond the field of linguistics. But pending those physical or psychological determinations, we should be able to use the term 'phoneme' without being subjected to the embarassment of having in our discipline a fundamental unit which is undetermined and the nature of which is a matter of wide disagreement among linguists.

The reluctance to attribute reality or even linguistic autonomy to the phoneme is nothing new. Otto Jespersen could with comfort reprint in 1933[1] some remarks he had made on this subject almost half a century earlier. He summarizes the basic Junggrammatiker postulate: 'denn das organgefühl wird ja nicht für das einzelne wort, sondern für den einzelnen laut gebildet; die aussprache wird nicht für jedes einzelne wort gelernt.' He goes on to say:

[1] Linguistica 180 f.

'Gegen diese letzte kategorische behauptung wäre man versucht die gerade entgegengesetzte zu stellen: die aussprache muss immer für jedes einzelne wort gelernt werden, denn die aussprache ist ja nichts als das wort selbst, oder besser die eine, die nach aussen gekehrte seite des wortes im gegensatz zu der innern der bedeutung.' Jespersen does not of course maintain this extreme statement in all literalness; but as between the two formulations of the relation of 'sound' (or phoneme) and 'word' (or free form), his is incomparably the more clear-headed and linguistically valid.

Bloomfield goes at least part of the way with Jespersen: he observes:[2] 'The phoneme is an abstraction obtained from series of utterances, e. g., the English phoneme [t] from [tin, win, pin], etc., and [tin, tuk, it], etc. An ear trained to other languages will hear differences between the [t]'s of [tik, stik, botr, bit] which are not distinctive, that is, in English non-linguistic.' This characterization of the phoneme as an abstraction is not necessarily inconsistent, of course, with Bloomfield's definitions of the phoneme in terms of acoustic reality. He means, I take it, that the determination of a phoneme is a process of abstracting from the utterance (or 'word') as a gross acoustic event certain constant characteristic phoneme-features and disregarding the variable non-distinctive features. But when he uses (217) such a formula as 'This word consists of such and such of the basic phonemes of my language arranged in such and such sequence', it is apparent that he is following essentially the Junggrammatiker procedure and regards the phonemes as positive additive entities.

The theoretical objections to regarding the phonemes as positive additive entities, advanced by Jespersen in terms of learning, can be supported by the evidence of actual linguistic behavior. We respond differently to 'pen' and 'pin'. But it cannot be demonstrated that this difference is conditioned by any psychic isolation of the second phoneme in each word; it is even questionable whether the response to the isolated acoustic complexes [ɛ] and [ɪ] may properly be called linguistic. If I ask for a pen and you bring me a pin, I correct you by saying 'No; I wanted a PEN.' Only if I were speaking to another student of phonetics—that is, in an abnormal social situation—would I say anything like '[ɛ], not [ɪ]'; or 'the half-open front vowel, not the close lax one'. Even when longer words are involved (say illusion and allusion), the correction is made not by isolating the 'misheard phoneme' but by emphasizing it in its phonetic context through an unconventional incidence of accent.

⟦Omission: Laboratory data on understandability of continuous speech in spite of its having lost most of the phoneme-identifying evidence by distortion.⟧ That is to say, the utterance was still at least minimally distinctive ('understandable') even though the 'phoneme-features' as such were not 'present in the sound-waves'.

[2] Modern Philology 25.216 f.

In the following section, a procedure is proposed for defining the phoneme as an abstractional fiction. It is suggested that the phoneme so defined is to be regarded as a heuristic or pragmatic fiction, a mere terminological convenience in describing the phonological relations which obtain among the elements of a language. Those elements are, for me, the (minimum) free forms, as defined by Bloomfield in his Language 158 ff., and in his Set of postulates.

The minimum free forms are themselves, of course, abstractions, in that each occurrence of any of them is a fraction (approaching totality) of an acoustico-articulatory continuum which accompanies a social situation. It is a basic convention of all the social sciences that some social situations may be regarded as substantially recurrent, i. e., that certain objective differences can be disregarded. In so far as we demonstrate or assume a one-to-one correspondence between recurrent features of social situations and recurrent fractions of acoustico-articulatory continua, these latter may be regarded as linguistically recurrent. It is only a convention of linguistic science to regard these (by convention) recurrent fractions as 'elements' of a language which can be compared and from which an abstraction can be made, as a 'form'. But these conventionally or assumptionally determined abstractions appear to be as close to linguistic reality as we can at present arrive;[5] operations with them as basic elements appear to involve a minimum of undemonstrable assumption.

[5] Cf. Bloomfield, Language 21 ff.

V. DEFINITION OF THE PHONEME AS AN ABSTRACTIONAL FICTITIOUS UNIT

In addition to those of the preceding paragraph, the following are the assumptions and conventions which are, I believe, necessary for this procedure of defining the phoneme. The basic assumption of all human study: Within limits knowledge is possible and communicable, and our material is within those limits. The basic concessive assumption of science: No two things and no two events[1] are exactly alike. The basic convention of science: In terms of definite criteria, if an overwhelming majority of observers agree in recognizing qualitative differentiations, the phenomena observed are different; if not, the phenomena observed are the same, in terms of those criteria. A corollary, the basic convention of linguistics:

[1] By regarding 'things' as entities of more than molecular magnitude, and 'events' as changes in position of such things, we avoid discussions of the identical nature of such abstractions as atoms and quanta.

Utterances are acoustico-articulatory events accompanying social situations and correlated to them. In terms of that accompaniment and correlation, some utterances are alike and some are different in a given community.[2] We thus set up as a criterion the observable responses of members of the community as hearers. By defining 'phonetic' as subsuming all observable phenomena associated with an utterance, we deduce that, as events, all utterances must be phonetically different. But in a given community, in terms of hearers' responses in recurrent social situations, all utterances which are the same are phonetically significantly alike; and all utterances which are different are phonetically significantly different. Laboratory phonetics furnishes a generalization developed inductively from an adequate body of qualitative pointer-readings: Corresponding to significant phonetic differences are specifically articulatory differences.

With these conventions established, we can, I believe, proceed to define an abstractional fiction and apply to it a name which might as well be 'phoneme' as anything else. The procedure here given, first in consecutive development, later expanded and illustrated.

1. In a given community there are like utterances and different utterances. Utterances are phonetic events.

2. The forms abstracted from utterances which are the same are the same forms. Forms which are the same correspond to phonetically significantly like events. Such forms are called phonologically alike.

3. Some of the forms abstracted from utterances which are different are different forms. Excepting homonyms, forms which are different correspond to phonetically significantly different events. Such forms are called phonologically different.

4. Corresponding to phonologically different forms are significantly different phonetic events. Each of these phonetic events is composed of phonetic fractions.

5. A minimum phonological difference (greater than zero) among forms corresponds to a consistently recurring difference of one fraction of each of the phonetic events which correspond to the forms.

6. A group of forms which are minimally phonologically different constitutes an ordered class of forms.

7. This group is determined as a class by the fractional similarities of the phonetic events which correspond to the several forms.

8. This group is an ordered class, its ordering being determined by the nature of the consistently recurring phonetic differences among the fractions of the phonetic events which correspond to the several forms.

[2] Cf. Bloomfield, Language 78,144.

9. The relations among the members of a class of phonologically minimally different forms are minimum phonological differences. The term of any minimum phonological difference among forms is called a micro-phoneme.

10. Corresponding to every phonetic difference, there is a specifically articulatory difference. That articulatory difference can be observed and recorded as a consistently recurring qualitative difference among successive phonetic events which correspond to phonologically different forms.

11. In a class of minimally phonologically different forms, the ordering (see paragraph 8) corresponds to the qualitative articulatory differences of the corresponding phonetic events.

12. Two or more such classes of minimally phonologically different forms are similarly ordered, if the qualitative articulatory differences among the corresponding phonetic events are similar and in a one-to-one relation.

13. In articulatorily similarly ordered classes of forms, the differences (i. e. ordering) of the several classes are respectively similar. The micro-phonemes, as terms of these similar and one-to-one differences, are similarly ordered in classes. The sum of all similarly ordered terms (micro-phonemes) of similar minimum phonological differences among forms is called a macro-phoneme.

Before an expanded and illustrated exposition of this technique of defining the phoneme is in order, it may be proper to state certain preliminary definitions.

A 'class' is used in the logician's sense of 'group', usually a group the members of which share some common peculiarity. Thus the fingers of a hand may be considered as constituting a class, sharing as they do the common peculiarity of being part of the same hand, or attached to the same palm. A class is an 'ordered class', and the members of the class are 'ordered terms', when the class may be regarded as displaying some principle of organization within the class. The five fingers of a given hand are thus an ordered class, the organization of which is determined by (let us say) the relative spatial positions of the various fingers to each other with reference to the wrist, or to a given point on the palm. The finger-classes of two individuals are similarly ordered classes, for two unmutilated hands display similar relative spatial positions of the various fingers to each other with reference to the wrists, or to a given point on the palms. A's middle finger may, in and of itself, resemble B's ring finger as to length; but those two fingers are not similarly ordered in their respective classes. A's middle finger and B's middle finger, though perhaps objectively quite dissimilar, are similarly ordered in their respective classes; they are similarly ordered terms of similarly ordered classes.

We may set up an abstraction: the sum of all middle fingers of unmutilated human hands. Those various middle fingers will unquestionably present fairly wide variations in size, shape, and color. But despite the wide objective variations, all those middle fingers are recognized as similarly ordered terms of similarly ordered classes. We may go further, and speak of a 'set' of similarly ordered terms—say, all right middle fingers. In that case, we have a fraction of the sum-abstraction earlier set up.

Within the frame of this procedure of definition, a term of an ordered class of minimum phonological differences among forms is a micro-phoneme; the sum of all similarly ordered terms of similarly ordered classes is the abstraction called a macro-phoneme; a fraction of that sum-abstraction is a set of micro-phonemes.

(In the expanded exposition which follows, the numbering of the various sections is retained to correspond to that of the earlier condensed version.)

1. In a given community there are like utterances and different utterances. Utterances are phonetic events.

2. The forms abstracted from utterances which are the same are the same forms. Forms which are the same correspond to phonetically significantly like events. Such forms are called phonologically alike.

3. Some of the forms abstracted from utterances which are different are different forms. Excepting homonyms, forms which are different correspond to phonetically significantly different events. Such forms are called phonologically different.

It cannot be too strongly emphasized that a form is not a part of any specific utterance. An utterance is an event; a form is an abstraction from a large number of utterances. If I say "That's a fine lamp", "Won't you light the lamp?", "Where's your old lamp?", each of these acts of speech constitutes an utterance. As a human being, I make utterances and respond to them. As a physicist, I may record and study, as physical events, the sound-waves which occur. As a physiologist, I may observe, record, and study the muscular movements which occur. As a student of language, I abstract from utterance-events certain fractions which I assume to be substantially recurrent, and (in the example above) I call that abstraction the form lamp. The utterance occurs, it is speech, 'parole'; the form exists, so to say, it is a part of the language, 'langue'.

Throughout the rest of this discussion, these two levels must be borne in mind. We must operate with the abstracted forms and their relations; but these forms are not themselves susceptible of observation. Accordingly, we observe the utterance-fractions which correspond to a form; we study the abstracted form which corresponds to utterance-fractions. By way of emphasizing the distinction between forms and utterance-fractions, the form (abstraction) is underlined; the utterance-fraction (event) is put in quotation marks. This distinction is further reinforced by the use of 'phonetic' to characterize the relations of events, of 'phonological' to characterize the relations of the abstracted forms. The inconvenience of operating on these two levels must be conceded; but the distinctions involved are indispensable.

The form lamp is an abstraction of a large number of utterance-fractions; it is all that is similar and nothing that is different in those utterance-fractions. When we speak of the form lamp, we ignore some objective differences between the corresponding fractions of various utterances, such as the differences between an act of speech by a feeble old woman and by a vigorous young man.

Forms, therefore, are either alike or different; they are also phonologically alike or phonologically different. The events which correspond to forms are all phonetically different (for no two events are exactly alike). The events which correspond to the 'same' form are phonetically significantly alike, for by 'significant' we indicate the correlation of an utterance to a social situation. The phonetic events "Light the lamp" as produced by two different individuals are objectively very different; in so far as those events evoke similar responses in similar social situations, the two events are phonetically significantly alike. In speaking of utterances as phonetic events, we use the terms 'phonetically significantly alike or different'. In speaking of the forms which correspond to events, the terms 'phonologically alike or different' suffice. For the form is all that is similar and nothing that is different in the various events; thus only significant differences are phonologically relevant.

If two forms are phonologically different, there must be a consistently recurring phonetic significant difference between the two sets of events from which the forms are abstracted. If we say that lamp and limp are phonologically different forms, we must assert (and should demonstrate) that in any pair of phonetic events corresponding to these forms, a phonetic significant difference recurs consistently. Although A's "lamp"s are not like B's "lamp"s, nor A's "limp"s like B's "limp"s, if we can find that in A's utterances his "limp"s are characterized by a more forward and higher tongue position during some intervals than his "lamp"s, and similarly in B's utterances, then the difference recurs consistently, and there is a corresponding phonological difference between the forms which are abstracted from the utterances of both speakers taken together. The various objective variations in A's successive "limp"s or in B's successive "limp"s do not recur consistently, and therefore do not correspond to any differentiation of the form limp. In so far as A's "limp"s differ consistently from B's "limp"s, that difference is a personal peculiarity, of no linguistic relevance. It is only the significant differences between "limp" and "lamp" in everybody's utterances that concern us here; and corresponding to those consistently recurring differences of everybody's utterances is the phonological difference between the abstracted forms limp and lamp.

4. Corresponding to phonologically different forms are significantly different phonetic events. Each of these phonetic events is composed of phonetic fractions. These fractions are usually reckoned in terms of intervals during which the articulatory organs are substantially at rest, or are leaving such a position; intervals during which some articulatory organs are making a unidirectional movement; or intervals during which some articulatory organs are moving toward a position, maintain it substantially, and leave it. These fractions are, in short, what we call 'speech-sounds', i.e. time-intervals of the actual utterance-events. In theory, these intervals might be reckoned in terms of either acoustic event (sound-waves) or articulatory event (behavior of the vocal organ muscles); in practice, the considerations of greater accessibility and susceptibility of analysis dictate the choice of the articulatory procedure.

5. A minimum phonological difference (greater than zero) among forms corresponds to a consistently recurring difference of one fraction of each of the phonetic events which correspond to the forms. A phonological difference among forms has been defined as corresponding to a consistently recurring phonetic difference among fractions of utterance-events. If we have properly reckoned the phonetic fractions, the minimum difference which can recur consistently as between two phonetically significantly different events is a difference of one of the fractions of each event. Corresponding to such a consistently recurring difference of one fraction of the various phonetic events is a minimum phonological difference among the forms which are abstracted from the phonetic events. Thus, in American English, the forms beet : bit : bait : bet : bat are minimally phonologically different. If we consider any pair of these forms, we find that a pair of the corresponding phonetic events will be characterized by a consistently recurring phonetic difference of their second fractions.

6. A group of forms which are minimally phonologically different constitutes an ordered class of forms. Before we can conveniently operate with the group of forms beet, bit, bait, bet, bat, we must indicate wherein the group constitutes a class, and wherein the terms of that class are ordered.

7. This group is determined as a class by the fractional similarities of the phonetic events which correspond to the several forms. In the group of forms beet, bit, bait, bet, bat, the significant similarity of the beginnings and ends of the corresponding phonetic events corresponds to a phonological sameness which can be represented by the symbols [b] and [t]. [b] corresponds to all that which is similar in the beginnings of the events, i.e. closure of the lips with simultaneous vibration of the vocal cords. And [t] corresponds to all that which is similar in the ends of the events, i.e. presence of the tongue tip and blade in contact with the alveolar ridge with simultaneous non-vibration of the vocal cords. We do not assume that the beginnings of all the events are absolutely identical; we merely assert that objective observation of the events reveals some similarity. Corresponding to that similarity, to whatever degree it can be determined, is a phonological sameness, which we indicate with the symbol [b]. We dare not operate with this phonological sameness as anything positive; all that we can assert is that these forms beet, bit, bait, bet, bat are not phonologically different as to their beginnings and endings. We discover from observation that the corresponding events display some objective similarity; we discover from experiment and observation that within the range of this similarity (voiced bilabial stop, voiceless alveolar stop), no differences in response can be correlated to differences in the initial and final fractions of these utterance-events. We can thus assert that our group is a phonological class of forms beet : bit : bait : bet : bat, the class [b–t].

8. This group is an ordered class, its ordering being determined by the nature of the consistently recurring phonetic differences among the fractions of the phonetic events which correspond to the several forms. The forms which are members of the class beet : bit : bait : bet : bat are abstractions from phonetic events. Any pair or any class of forms are phonologically different if there is a consistently recurring phonetic difference among the events which correspond to the forms. The phonological relations thus correspond to the consistently recurrent phonetic differences among utterance-fractions. The nature of the consistently recurring phonetic differences is determined by observation. In so far as this observation can be tabulated and classified, the nature of the phonetic differences can be determined. The phonological differences of the abstracted forms are thereby correspondingly determined. In our class, we may indicate the terms of the phonological differences by the symbols [i, ɪ, e, ɛ, æ]. The difference between any pair of symbols indicates the phonological difference between the forms involved; and that phonological difference corresponds to a consistently recurring phonetic difference of the utterance-fractions. Thus, the relation [i : æ] indicates a phonological difference which corresponds to the consistently recurrent difference between A's "beet"s, B's "beet"s, C's "beet"s,...N's "beet"s as compared with A's "bat"s, B's "bat"s, C's "bat"s,...N's "bat"s. Those phonetic differences can be determined, and the nature of the various phonetic differences in any speaker's "beet : bit : bait : bet : bat" can be classified; those phonetic differences constitute an ordered class of relations. Correspondingly, the phonological differences abstracted from the utterance-fractions uttered by A, B, C,...N constitute an ordered class of relations; and the various terms of those relations are the terms of minimum phonological differences.

9. The relations among the members of a class of phonologically minimally different forms are minimum phonological differences. The term of any minimum phonological difference is called a micro-phoneme.

The differences obtaining in the series of micro-phonemes [i : ɪ : e : ɛ : æ] are abstracted from the phonological differences of the forms beet : bit : bait : bet : bat. This series of forms constitutes a phonologically ordered class, in American English. It is determined as a class by the constant phonological sameness of the beginnings and ends of the forms, [b–t]. Its ordering is determined by the nature of the consistently recurring phonetic differences of the corresponding phonetic events "beet" : : "bit" : "bait" : "bet" : "bat". We indicate the abstractional phonological differences which correspond to these consistently recurring phonetic differences with the symbolical relations [i:ɪ:e:ɛ:æ]. The terms of these phonological minimum differences are micro-phonemes, as compared with each other and with reference to the class. Thus the [i] of the form beet is not a micro-phoneme per se; it is a micro-phoneme only in comparison with the [ɪ] of the form bit, etc. Further, neither of these micro-phonemes can thus far be brought into any relation with any portion or characteristic of such forms as seek, sick, pier. The micro-phonemes we have so far determined are the terms of the abstracted phonological differences of the forms of the class [b–t]. The [i] of beet, as a micro-phoneme, corresponds to everything in all the utterances "beet" which is consistently and recurringly different from the utterances "bit", "bait", etc. If the nature of the labial closures in utterances "beet" and "bat" differs consistently, then that difference is included in the corresponding phonological difference which is represented symbolically as [i : æ].

10. Corresponding to every phonetic difference, there is a specifically articulatory difference. That articulatory difference can be observed and recorded as a consistently recurring qualitative difference among successive phonetic events which correspond to phonologically different forms.

From the preceding developments, we can make the following summaries: A phonological difference among forms corresponds to a consistently recurring phonetic difference among utterance-events. A minimum phonological difference corresponds to a difference of one phonetic fraction. A micro-phoneme corresponds to a term of a consistently recurring phonetic difference in one fraction of various utterance-events.

Laboratory phonetics furnishes us with the generalization that corresponding to every phonetic difference there is a specifically articulatory difference. The facts of articulation are accessible to observation; we can observe and tabulate the consistently recurring articulatory differences which correspond to phonetic differences. We may therefore set up a new and more practicable set of correspondences: a phonological difference corresponds to a consistently recurring articulatory difference among utterance-events. A micro-phoneme corresponds to a term of a consistently recurring articulatory difference in one fraction of various utterance-events.

11. In a class of minimally phonologically different forms, the ordering (see paragraph 8) corresponds to the qualitative articulatory differences of the corresponding phonetic events.

Let us consider, for example, the classes of forms: I. pill : till : kill : bill; II. fin: thin: sin: shin; III. nap : gnat : knack : nab. On the basis of articulatory observation of utterance-events which correspond to these forms, we may describe the consistently recurring articulatory differences among the events. We may represent the various component terms of those articulatory differences as follows: 1 bilabial, 2 aspirated, 3 voiceless, 4 exploded stop, 5 alveolar, 6 palato-velar, 7 voiced, 8 unaspirated, 9 unexploded stop, 10 labio-dental, 11 interdental, 12 dental-alveolar, 13 alveolar-palatal, 14 fricative, 15 slit narrowing, 16 groove narrowing.[3] Then we may represent our classes as being articulatorily ordered as follows:

I		II		III	
pill	1-2-3-4	fin	10-3-14-15	nap	1-8-3-9
till	5-2-3-4	thin	11-3-14-15	gnat	5-8-3-9
kill	6-2-3-4	sin	12-3-14-16	knack	6-8-3-9
bill	1-8-7-4	shin	13-3-14-16	nab	1-8-7-9

It is obvious that the same procedure is valid if the final stops of phonetic events corresponding to the forms of class III are exploded; the choice of the unexploded form is merely in the interests of reducing the similarity and rendering the connection less immediately apparent.

It is understood that these descriptions have to do only with relations. For laboratory phonetics does not tell us that the initial fraction of each event corresponding to the form pill is an absolutely identical articulatory complex. Laboratory phonetics merely tells us that as between the initial fractions of events corresponding to pill, till, etc., a consistently recurring articulatory difference has been observed, and that that difference is therefore a qualitatively constant differential relation. When we write 'pill 1-2-3-4 (=bilabial aspirated voiceless exploded stop)', we indicate that the initial fraction of any event "pill" is marked by closure of the lips as compared with any "till"; by a following aspiration and by openness of the glottis as compared with any "bill"; by an exploded stop mode of articulation as compared with any "fill". Since the forms in each class are minimally phonologically different, the consis-

3 This list of certain articulatory components is very sketchy, of course, omitting as it does factors of muscular tension and the time-factors of duration and acceleration. The list suffices, though, for our present purposes.

tently recurring articulatory differences of the corresponding phonetic events determine the ordering of the class of forms.

The articulatory differences must be indicated separately from the articulatory similarities within each class. We may indicate the relations among our forms thus:

I		II		III	
pill	(1·2·3)-(4)	fin	(10·15)-(3·14)	nap	(1·3)-(8·9)
till	(5·2·3)-(4)	thin	(11·15)-(3·14)	gnat	(5·3)-(8·9)
kill	(6·2·3)-(4)	sin	(12·16)-(3·14)	knack	(6·3)-(8·9)
bill	(1·8·7)-(4)	shin	(13·16)-(3·14)	nab	(1·7)-(8·9)

Thus the events "pill" are differentially related to the events "till" and events "kill" in that they do not begin with an alveolar or palato-velar fraction; the events "pill" are differentially related to the events "bill" in that they do not begin with an unaspirated or voiced fraction.

12. Two or more such classes of minimally phonologically different forms are similarly ordered, if the qualitative articulatory differences among the corresponding phonetic events are similar and in a one-to-one relation.

If we compare our classes I and III, we find that they are articulatorily similarly ordered. The consistently recurring articulatory differences of the corresponding utterance-events are similar differences for the two classes, and in a one-to-one relation. In class I, there is a form, pill, corresponding to events which begin with a fraction that is not alveolar, not palato-velar, not voiced. In class III, there is a form, nap, corresponding to events which end with a fraction that is not alveolar, not palato-velar, not voiced. Similarly for each term of the two classes. The relations within the two classes are similar, in that the relations (1·3):(5·3):(6·3):(1·7) recur in both classes. The relation 2:2:2:8, which we find in class I, must be left out of account; for the factor (unaspirated) 8 is one of the constant articulatory factors of class III. We conclude that the differentiation of aspirated and unaspirated exploded stops in phonetic events is correlated to certain sequences within the event (initial 'position' before stressed vowels), and that in these sequences the differentiation of aspirated and unaspirated stops is parallel to the differentiation of voiceless and voiced stops.

Thus although there is no similarity between classes I and II or classes II and III, between classes I and III there is a similarity of ordering. These classes are in a one-to-one relation: Given the order pill—till—kill—bill or any other order of class I, there is one and only one order of class III nap, gnat, knack, nab which satisfies the requirements of a one-to-one relation. This order must be found by trial and error, since we make no assumptions concerning phoneme-membership. (The arrangements I have given are for purposes of exposition adapted to reveal that relation at once; that is, so to say, accidental.) Thus we may say that our classes

pill	(1·3)-(2)	nap	(1·3)
till	(5·3)-(2)	gnat	(5·3)
kill	(6·3)-(2)	knack	(6·3)
bill	(1·7)-(8)	nab	(1·7)

are similarly ordered, for the phonological differences among the forms of the two classes correspond to a consistently recurring articulatory set of differences among the phonetic events, and those articulatory differences are similar and one-to-one in the two classes, as correlated with the classes of forms.

Since the classes I and III of forms are phonologically similarly ordered, the phonological differences among the terms of classes I and III are similarly ordered. Above (paragraph 9) we have defined a micro-phoneme as the term of a minimum phonological difference. Since the differences of classes I and III are similarly ordered, the micro-phonemes which are terms of these differences are similarly ordered.

13. In articulatorily similarly ordered classes of forms, the differences (i. e. ordering) of the several classes are respectively similar. The micro-phonemes, as terms of these similar and one-to-one differences, are similarly ordered in the classes. The sum of all similarly ordered terms (micro-phonemes) of similar minimum phonological differences among forms is called a macro-phoneme.

Let us consider the micro-phonemes which are terms of the phonological differences of classes I and III.

pill . . . (1·3) . . . nap
till . . . (5·3) . . . gnat
kill . . . (6·3) . . . knack
bill . . . (1·7) . . . nab

Putting it diagrammatically: We have hitherto seen in these forms only a vertical relation. We have noted differences; these differences have been determined as phonological differences. Later we have seen that these differences can be correlated to consistently recurring articulatory differences of the corresponding events. But now we have established that these differences (the orderings of the two classes) are similar and in a one-to-one relation. Now we can begin to establish horizontal relations; we may connect with a dotted horizontal line the similarly ordered terms (micro-phonemes) of the similarly ordered (vertical) classes. Thus we set up a new abstraction, and say that the micro-phoneme which is correlated to pill belongs with the micro-phoneme which is correlated to nap. We can do this, not because the articulatory complexes which correspond to the micro-phonemes are inherently indentical or positively similar, but solely because those articulatory complexes are similarly differentiated from other articulatory complexes. The initial fraction of an event "pill" is not identical with the final fraction of an event "nap". But the initial fraction of a "pill" differs from the initial fraction of a "till" in a relation which is similar to the relation wherein the final fraction of a "nap" differs from the final fraction of a "gnat". (The analogy of the middle fingers will be recalled.)

The 'p-phoneme' is therefore the sum of all those phonological differentiae which correspond to a bilabial articulation as opposed to alveolar or palatovelar, a voiceless articulation as opposed to voiced, a stop articulation as opposed to fricative. Thus we can combine the stops of "pill, nap, tapper", etc. as opposed to the stops of "till, gnat, tatter", etc.; "kill, knack, tacker", etc.; "bill, nab, tabber", etc. Any articulatory complex which is a bilabial voiceless stop corresponds to a constituent member of the 'p-phoneme' if it occurs in a phonetic sequence where it may contrast with an articulation which is bilabial, stop, but not voiceless; (labial), voiceless, but not stop; voiceless, stop, but not bilabial.

We have no right to (and we don't want to) establish any 'phonemic' relations between the stops of a "pill" and of a "spill", for the stop of a "spill" is not in a phonetic sequence where it may contrast with a not-voiceless articulation. Any constituent member of the 'p-phoneme' must correspond to an articulatory complex which is in a phonetic sequence where it is different from a complex corresponding to a constituent member of the 'b-phoneme'. The stop of a "pill" and the stop of a "spill" cannot correspond to the same macro-phoneme, for the corresponding micro-phonemes are not similarly ordered. There is a phonological difference between the forms pill and bill; there is no similar phonological difference between the forms spill and *sbill. There appears to be no alternative to considering the stops of "spill, spare, spin", etc. as corresponding to a different phoneme from the stops of "pill, pair, nap, lip, tapper", etc. The stops of "spill, spare", etc. are significantly bilabial and stop, but not significantly voiceless; the stops of "pill, nap, tapper", are significantly bilabial, stop, and voiceless.

When we speak, then, of a (macro-)phoneme, we are using an abstraction as a terminological convenience to describe the recurrence of similar phonological differentiations among the elements of a language. It cannot be too strongly emphasized that the phoneme, so defined, is meaningless as applied to any particular linguistic element: it is a negative, relational, differential abstraction; it is a unit of that sort of relation which de Saussure describes:[4] 'Dans la langue il n'y a que des différences sans termes positifs.' It follows, therefore, that it is meaningless to speak of 'the third phoneme (micro- or macro-) of the form sudden', or to speak of 'an occurrence of a phoneme'. What occurs is not a phoneme, for the phoneme is defined as the term of a recurrent differential relation. What occurs is a phonetic fraction or a differentiated articulatory complex correlated to a micro-phoneme. A phoneme, accordingly, does not occur; it 'exists' in the somewhat peculiar sense of existence that a brother, qua brother, 'exists'—as a term of a relation. Linguists who accept as important de Saussure's distinction between 'parole' and 'langue' may find it helpful to regard the differentiated articulatory complex as a fraction of 'la parole', the phoneme as a term of those relations which comprise the system of 'la langue'; of course we can admit no mentalistic assumptions as to the real existence of the phoneme in the souls or what not of the speakers of that 'langue'.

There is no denying that this definition is complicated and forbidding. But the definition of any fundamental unit is always difficult, and must be particularly difficult in the case of linguistic phenomena, where we are dealing with events in time and bodies in space, with recurrence and uniqueness of events. The only defense that may be offered for this procedure is that it appears to be characterized by a minimum of the undemonstrable. With one coherent set of assumptions and conventions, which are indispensable to all scientific linguistic study, and one sound laboratory generalization, we may apply strictly mathematical methods and deduce a logically unimpeachable definition of some entity, which we may call a (macro-)phoneme. Any errors in reasoning are accidental to the author's own deficiencies and are fortunately detectible; as between a sound and a merely simple procedure there can be no choice.

Two corollary details of procedure should be mentioned.

Few, if any, languages present what we may call an absolutely symmetrical recurrence of phonological differences, i. e. it is not always possible to match classes of micro-phonemes in a one-to-one relation. We can set up in American English five phonemes, corresponding to the front vowels [i, ɪ, e, ɛ, æ][5] in the series beet, bit, bait, bet, bat; seek, sick, sake, sec, sack; etc. But in the frame [f–t] the series is incomplete: feet, fit, fate, —, fat. The question is whether the absence of a form [*fɛt] is a fortuitous or a fundamental characteristic of the [f–t] series. To decide such questions, we may admit a procedural convention: We find, in American English, that all fundamental characteristics involving the absence of

[4] Cours de Linguistique Générale (1922) 166.

[5] Here, as elsewhere, I make traditional use of the IPA symbols in transcribing American English rather than Bloomfield's, not because I regard that traditional use as inherently better—for I consider Bloomfield's transcriptions of themselves simpler and more rational—but quite simply because phonetic transcriptions, for the reasons given elsewhere in this study, are arbitary and conventional; they partake, at least in part, of the nature of orthographies, and accordingly an established transcription is preferable to any new one which is based on the same principles. Cf. R.-M. S. Heffner, Concerning Transcription, Lang. 10.288 ff.

(presumably potential) distinctive forms can be correlated with immediately preceding or following phonetic fractions, including the omnipresent factor of stress. We have already seen, from such examples as bet, met, set, etc., that we can discover phonemic relations involving the fourth term of the series [i : ɪ : e : ɛ : æ] before voiceless alveolar stops. We test for relations with preceding voiceless labiodental fricatives, and find such series as fane : fen : fan; fade : fed : fad; phase : fez; etc. We conclude that the absence of the phonetic fractions [fɛ-] and [-ɛt] is not a fundamental characteristic of American English; we conclude that the absence of a fourth term in the series of forms feet : fit : fate : — : fat is fortuitous. The discovery of fetlock is an unnecessary support of our conclusion.

This convention must be applied with caution. For the language of some Americans, it appears to be fortuitous, for others fundamental, that the front-vowel series is always defective before voiced palato-velars in monosyllables. In cases of doubt, the burden of proof is of course upon the one who regards such an absence as fortuitous; for the language itself, as it actually is, is our final authority.

The stops of "writing, latter" furnish another kind of difficulty, which leads to almost ridiculous inconsistencies in the attempt to apply some definitions of the phoneme. These stops, in many dialects of General American English, are definitely voiced; yet the corresponding events are distinctively different from "riding, ladder". The micro-phonemes corresponding to latter and ladder must be correlated to some articulatory difference; that difference may be formulated in terms of duration: the first stop is definitely shorter than the second. We can correlate these two stops with those of "tin" and "din", if the first of these is also regularly shorter —as it appears to be from the tables presented by Fletcher.[6] In the case of "tin : din", the difference in duration of the initial phonetic fractions is by no means the most conspicuous or 'distinctive' difference. But if that difference is regularly present here, and is present (and 'distinctive') is "latter : ladder", we may regard the two classes of micro-phonemes as similarly ordered with respect to an articulatory factor, and combine the micro-phonemes corresponding to tin, latter in one macro-phoneme, those corresponding to din, ladder in another. This combining is of course not justified by any positive similarities between the stops, but only by the similarity of the relations of one factor of their articulations. If there were no such forms as riding, ladder, the stops of "writing, latter" could no more be correlated with that of "tin" than can the stop of "still". Cases of this sort, where the important articulatory difference corresponding to one class of micro-phonemes is similar to a relatively minor, apparently insignificant articulatory difference corresponding to another class of micro-phonemes, are fairly rare; but any definition of the phoneme must be prepared to meet them.

It goes without saying that an analogous procedure is to be followed in defining phrase and sentence phonemes, corresponding to stress, pitch, tempo, etc., in so far as they constitute phonetic differentiae among utterances.

VI. COMPARISONS WITH EARLIER DEFINITIONS OF THE PHONEME

Any comparison of this definition with the earlier ones reveals a difference in procedure, to be sure; it is also clear that the object of this definition is a new entity. Since this new entity may, however, be made use of in much the same way as what others have defined as a phoneme, I have taken the liberty of applying that name to the entity I define. The term 'macro-phoneme' is of course available to anyone who protests against that application.

The greatest difference between the macro-phoneme and the various 'phonemes' is that the former is an abstractional fiction, the latter are realities of some sort. The macro-phoneme is a term of recurrent relations; the 'phonemes' are a repertory of positive additive entities. The macro-phoneme is an abstraction from forms; the 'phonemes' are the constituent elements of forms, of phonetic events, or sometimes of both. It suffices to quote two definers of radically different 'phonemes': Bloomfield:[1] 'This word consists of such and such of the basic phonemes of my language'; and Trubetzkoy:[2] 'Aber ebenso wird dasselbe Wort duby als aus den Phonemen d + u + b + y bestehend wahrgenommen.' The 'phonemes' for these linguists are obviously positive additive entities; in some cases, those entities are regarded as possessing inherent potencies of utilizable distinctiveness, or as offering to the speaker a repertory of autonomous code-signals. Thus Daniel Jones speaks[3] of 'the fact that separate phonemes are capable of distinguishing words'; and Jespersen refers[4] to phonemes as 'sounds that can be used for distinctive purposes, i. e. to keep words apart which would otherwise be identical'. It is plain from Jespersen's statement, quoted earlier, on the relations of phoneme and form, that this characterization of the phoneme is a much abbreviated and inverted statement of his real interpretation. But such formulations, if not significant, are at all events dangerous, as leading all too readily to a kind of mythology in which the hypostasized 'phonemes' play their rôles, or an equally mythological view of the linguistic process according to which a speaker reaches into his store of phonemes, selects the proper number of each, arranges them tastefully, and then produces an utterance.

6 Speech and Hearing 60.

1 Modern Philology 25.217.

2 TCLP 1.39. 3 TCLP 4.77.

4 Linguistica 391.

The macro-phoneme is a fiction, defined for the purpose of describing conveniently the phonological relations among the elements of a language, its forms. The sum of such relations among the elements is the phonological system of the language. This phonological system is of course nothing objectively existent; it is not definable as a mental pattern in the minds of the speakers of the language; it is not even a 'platonic idea' which the language actualizes. It is quite simply the sum of all the phonological relations among the forms of a language, as those relations are determined by objective study. The phonological system is the phonetician's and phonologist's summarized formulation of the relations; it is not a phenomenon, nor an intuition.

There are various kinds of phonological relations in a given language. These relations may be classified into groups, corresponding to the differentiations in a given articulatory range. When we say that American English, as a phonological system, has a maximum of six front vowel and diphthong phonemes, we mean that there are, within the range of that mode of articulations which we call vowel or diphthong, at most fifteen[5] significant phonetic differentiations of utterances by differentiation in the positions and movements of the front of the tongue. By taking all the articulatory ranges within which significant differentiation occurs in the language, we can construct the maximal phonological system of the language. But in nearly all languages, that potential maximum of differentiation is not uniformly realized. There are systematic gaps, i. e. there are cases of less than maximal differentiation within a given articulatory range. These systematic gaps are just as much a part of the phonological system as are the maximal differentiations. To illustrate with the vowels and diphthongs of my dialect of American English:

bite	beet	bit	bait	bet	bat	bot	bought	boat	—	boot	bout	butte	Bert	butt
like	leak	lick	lake	—	lack	lock	Lawk	—	look	Luke	—	—	lurk	luck
pyre	pier		pair			par	pore		poor		power	pure	purr	

It is clear that the differentiation of vowels and diphthongs before [-r] are just as systematic and just as 'symmetrical' as the quite dissimilar differentiations before [-t, -k]. There is a vowel system in monosyllables before [-r] in American English, but it is not the same vowel system as before [-t, -k]. And to call either of these systems the American English vowel system is to suppress an important fact about the phonological system of the language. To force the phonemes corresponding to the vowels of our third row into some violent and arbitrary classification in terms of the first two rows is almost (if not quite) as stultifying as to try to fit French vowel-phonemes into an English system. The phonological relations which obtain in such a series of forms as pyre : pier : pair, etc., are not similar nor comparable to the relations in such a series as bite : beet : bit : bait, etc. Since a phoneme has been defined as the sum of terms of recurrent phonological relations, it follows that the phonemes which correspond to the two series are not comparable. The phonemes which correspond to the [-r]-series must be different phonemes from those corresponding to the [-t]-series. Similarly, the phoneme corresponding to the stop in "spill" is a different phoneme from the one corresponding to the stops in "pill, tapper, nap".

The relatively large number of such phonemes in a given language will doubtless appear unfortunate to some linguists. Most of their objections, I believe, can be met if the purpose of the phoneme as a terminological unit is considered. For me, the phoneme is a unit defined for a convenient description of phonological relations. Naturally, then, I need different phonemes to describe different phonological relations. For many linguists, it appears, the phoneme functions as a unit to be represented by a symbol in so-called phonetic transcriptions. It appears that the unit these linguists require cannot sufficiently take into account either phonological or phonetic facts; it would clarify the issue if these units might be called 'graphemes', 'transcribemes', or even 'letters'. For I know of no earlier phoneme-definition which does not achieve transcriptional sanctions by violence to essential phonological relations and palpable phonetic fact.

It follows that, according to this definition, there are as many different phonemes in a language as there are consecutive relations of significant phonetic differentiation (plus one) in each articulatory range. That is, if we have in American English five consecutive relations in bite : beet : bit : bait : bet : bat, there are six phonemes for these and similar relations; if we have two consecutive relations in pyre : pier : pair, there are three phonemes for these and similar relations; polysyllables with accented vowel before [-r-] will display another group of relations, which may not correspond to either of the earlier series.

[5] $(6-1) + (6-2) + (6-3) + (6-4) + (6-5)$. Thus, bite : beet, bit, bait, bet, bat; beet : bit, bait, bet, bat; bit : bait, bet, bat; bait : bet, bat; bet : bat. Some readers may prefer the formulation: If x is the maximum number of significant phonological differentiations within a given articulatory range in a language, then $2x = n(n-1)$, where n is the maximum number of phonemes in that range, and $(n-1)$ is the number of consecutive phonological relations within that range.

The number of phonemes in a given language is thus limited; that number is a sub-multiple of the number of forms of the language. Therein one must agree with those definitions of the phoneme which specify that the phonemes of a language are strictly limited in number. But that number is frequently set much lower than this definition will admit; that number is usually set in terms solely of the maximum differentiations within all articulatory ranges. (The coincidence of this circumstance with the fact that such a number of written symbols suffices for transcription purposes—if some arbitrary conventions are adopted—need not surprise us.) But if we want to define some unit for purposes of describing the phonological relations within a language, we must reconcile ourselves to having as many of these units as there are recurrent phonological relations within the language.

Jespersen, in his Monosyllabism in English,[6] estimates, on the basis of permutations and combinations of the maximal variations within all articulatory ranges, that the number of possible English monosyllables is 'rather more than 158,000'. The exact number does not concern us; it is enough to know its general order, and to know that the actual number of English monosyllables represents but a fraction of it. In what might be called 'the potential monosyllabic vocabulary of English', there are thus numerous gaps. Some of these gaps are unquestionably 'fortuitous' (cf. [*fɛt] above); but equally unquestionably some of those gaps are systematic. In so far as the latter is the case, those gaps are a part of the phonological system of English; the systematic absence of those 'potential monosyllables' is a highly important phonological relation within the language.

[6] Linguistica 390.

VII. ARTICULATORY RATHER THAN ACOUSTIC CHARACTERIZATION OF THE PHONEME

⟦Most of this brief chapter is omitted as inessential.⟧

The discovery of certain similarities[3] among the articulatory complexes, which correspond to similar terms of classes of micro-phonemes, is not surprising. Indeed, that similarity is a basic assumption (usually tacit) of most phonetic study and even of many definitions of the phoneme. For these classes of articulatory complexes represent a distribution of differentiation within a given articulatory range. Given a one-to-one correspondence of distributed differentiation within a constant range, there is a high degree of probability of an approximation of the differentiated objective phenomena. The nature of the approximation is of course for the psychologist to study, in terms of imitation and habit. But it is not certain that the factors of imitation and habit are the sole determinants of the objective articulatory phenomena. The distribution of differentiation within a given articulatory range may be a factor in itself. There is of course no automatic adjustment of the mode of articulation to an optimum of communication-efficiency; nor is there any conscious effort on the part of the speakers of a language toward such an adjustment. But the possibility of long-range partial adjustment as an important factor in phonetic change is apparent upon realistic consideration of the way in which children are trained to speak, i. e., to produce utterances which are sufficiently differentiated, and differentiated in articulatory modes which are sufficiently similar to those prevailing in their community.

[3] That is, not only are the classes beet : bit : bait : bet : bat and seek: sick: sake: sec: sack similarly differentiated, but there is considerable objective similarity between the vowels of "beet" and "seek", "bit" and "sick", etc.

VIII. SOME POSSIBLE APPLICATIONS OF AN ABSTRACTIONAL FICTITIOUS PHONEME

It should be clear for what kinds of procedure in linguistic study a unit like the (macro-)phoneme is adapted. It is a procedure very much like the 'phonology' of the Cercle Linguistique de Prague. That such a procedure is in order can scarcely be questioned; there will be few students of language who disagree seriously with Trubetzkoy's statement:[1] 'Eine vergleichende Untersuchung der phonologischen Systeme aller Sprachen der Erde ist die dringendste Aufgabe der heutigen Sprachwissenschaft.' The only limitation which the definition proposed above would impose upon such a procedure is the necessity for antecedent and concurrent phonetic (and articulatory) analysis. If the valuable and suggestive work of many members of the Cercle Linguistique de Prague has not been wholly convincing to many students of language, it is (aside from its newness) because of the subjective mentalistic definition of units and a somewhat truculent denial of the relevance of phonetic analysis.[2]

Many students of language will agree, I believe, that the tasks of the phonetician and of the phonologist are not antithetical or unrelated, but that phonological synthesis is an integral continuation of phonetic analysis. The phonetician, in so far as he is anything more than a laboratory technician, must also be a phonologist; the phonologist, in so far as he is anything more than an artist, must be a phonetician. It is the phonetician's failure to finish his job which the phonologist rightly protests against, not the part of the job he has done. In so far as a specialization of labor is necessary, it is for the phonetician to consider utterances as articulatory events, objectively measurable (and correlated to habits); it is for the phonologist to consider abstractions from utterances as terms of recurrent differentiations (and correlated to social situations).

[1] TCLP 1.41.

[2] For an excellent discussion of this point, see K. Bühler, Phonetik und Phonologie (TCLP 4.22 ff.); see also Jespersen, Linguistica 213.

The necessity for phonetic analysis as a basis for the determination of phonemes is clear. The following remarks venture to suggest some possible values of a continuation of phonetic analysis even after the phonemes have been determined.

We have seen that the relations between pairs of articulatory complexes, correlated to pairs of micro-phonemic sets,[3] though qualitatively constant (if the several micro-phonemes belong to the same macro-phonemes), may be objectively different. Thus, there is a constant qualitative relation between the stops of "tin, hat, latter" and "din, had, ladder". But the articulatory complexes which are the terms of those differences are not identical: there is even a quantitative variation in the degree of difference. There are more habitual articulatory differences between the stops of "tin" and "din" than between those of "hat" and "had", or of "latter" and "ladder". We are justified in speaking of the position of maximal articulatory differentiation between phonetic fractions correlated to phonemes; we may even in some cases arrange the articulatory differentiations in a descending scale of degree of differentiation, thus: tin : din, hat : had, latter : ladder. The scale, in this case, reaches zero degree of differentiation with such a form as still, where there is no differentiation (and no micro-phonemic class) within the articulatory range of alveolar stop: still is different only from spill and skill. This is not to say that we can 'explain' the peculiarly ambiguous (in terms of a [t-d] opposition) articulation of the stop in "still"; it is merely a rather interesting correlation. It is possible that similar correlations might be established for the degree of difference between articulatory complexes which occur in other positions, as corresponding to sets of micro-phonemes. The determination of the 'functional burdening' which would serve as the correlative to such articulatory differentiation is however not so feasible as some operations with the term might indicate. To be sure, we can readily compute the number of pairs of forms minimally different by a given pair of micro-phonemic sets; we can even approximately compute the relative frequencies of each of these forms. But the semantic utilization of these forms in relation to one another, i. e. the possibilities of ambiguity in otherwise similar contexts, is quite impossible to measure. Yet the first two factors, or even the first alone, may be regarded with all due reserves as a rough index of 'functional burdening', if we explicitly state that phonemes are meaningless, and that any selection of forms on the basis of phonemes is therefore random sampling in terms of meaning.[4] If we can find that the 'functional burdening', as roughly indicated, is greater between [t-:d-] than between [-t: -d] or [-t-: -d-], we may set up a correlation which is of considerable importance for the study of American English, and, as a tentative principle, for the study of the linguistic process in general. And in the classifying of such correlations, if they can be found, it is possible that a specifically relational unit may prove a useful terminological convenience.

The proposed terminology may also be useful in formulating diachronic relations of phonological significance. Among the events which we class as 'phonetic changes' there is a wide range of importance from the phonological point of view.[5] The results of phonetic change may or may not be a modification of the qualitative differential relations of forms in the language. If a modification of the habits of articulation occurs in all phonetic fractions corresponding to forms which stand in a certain phonemic relation to the other forms of a language, then we have a case of so-called 'absolute phonetic change'. If such a modification occurs only in phonetic fractions corresponding to forms, the relations of which constitute relations of sets of micro-phonemes (subclasses of a macro-phonemic relation), then it is a 'conditional phonetic change'. When an absolute or phonemically total phonetic change is accompanied by similarly total changes in an entire articulatory class, the product is a phonetic shift, which, despite the extent of modification of articulatory habits, does not modify the phonological system of the language, as a system of qualitative relations among forms. The first Germanic consonant shift (with the exception of *sp, *st, *sk, *pt, *kt, which may not be exceptions at all) is an example. Any pairs of forms which were qualitatively differentiated before such a shift are also qualitatively differentiated afterwards. But if the results of a phonetic change or changes are an alteration of the qualitative differentiations among forms, that is a fact of prime phonological importance. That between Middle High German and Modern German there has been a change which we describe as [ɛɪ > ae] is a phonetic fact; similarly the change [i: > ae]. But the combination of these phonetic facts is a phonological fact, for the relations of such forms as ein : mîn are now qualitatively modified: ein : mein. The results of conditional phonetic change obviously are very often of phonological importance, since they are a new differentiation or a new distribution of differentiations among the forms.

[3] Hereafter, the term 'set of micro-phonemes' means 'set of micro-phonemes which are similarly ordered in sequentially similar classes'. Thus the vowels of "beet : bit" correspond to a class of microphonemes; the vowels of "beet, feet" and of "beet, bean" correspond to sets of micro-phonemes. A set of micro-phonemes is accordingly a fraction of a macro-phoneme.

[4] It is worth noting that this assumption of the meaningless phoneme, which alone validates the claim of random sampling and thereby justifies operation with 'functional burdening', has sometimes been explicitly denied by the very linguists who speak of 'functional burdening'.

[5] Cf. B. Trnka, Some Remarks on the Phonological Structure of English, Xenia Pragensia 357 ff.

In so far as the denial of autonomy and linguistic relevance to the 'speech-sounds' as such involves a repudiation of Junggrammatiker assumptions, it is of course necessary to state a definition of phonetic change in terms of the proposed definition, so as to justify the continued use of the products of the Junggrammatiker procedure. We may define a phonetic change as a (gradual) substitution of new habits of producing differentiated articulatory complexes, correlated to sets of micro-phonemes. Then we can claim all the validity of phonetic law to which the Junggrammatiker procedure can pretend. If the sets of micro-phonemes involved are the totality of a macro-phoneme, the phonetic change is absolute. If the sets of micro-phonemes are less than the totality of a macro-phoneme, the phonetic change is conditional; and the conditions are no harder to specify than under the Junggrammatiker procedure. From the point of view of the end-product, a phonetic change is a modification either of the qualitative differentiation or of the mode of qualitative differentation among the forms of a language.

Just as it was suggested that it might be possible to find a correlation between 'functional burdening' and the degree of articulatory differentiation, so here, in the field of diachronic study, it may be suggested that there is a possibility of correlation between a kind of 'functional burdening' and apparently conditional phonetic change. The somewhat peculiar history of the linguistic and articulatory habits associated with IE *sp, *st, *sk (reduplication, throughout the various consonant shifts, in Old Germanic metrics, down to the present) may be correlated with the absence (as we conclude for other reasons) of any *sb, *sd, *sg with which they could enter into phonemic relations.

The material (though not the explanations) which the 'functionalists' like Horn adduce may be susceptible of study from this point of view. An example from American English may serve: In many dialects, the preterit tenses of certain weak verbs are not regularly marked by a final dental stop. Thus [krip : krɛp; kip : kɛp; slip : slɛp; wip : wɛp]. Other weak verbs, however, always have the final dental in the preterit: [hip : hipt; ræp : ræpt; hɛlp : hɛlpt]. To be sure, the collocation of these preterits effectively destroys any fable of an exceptionless phonetic 'treatment' of [t] after [p]. And any attempt to explain the divergence on the basis of an analogy will involve some rather spectacular arguments. But if we consider the earlier forms [krip : *krɛpt — hip : hipt], it appears that in the second instance we have a differentiation [t] : zero which corresponds to a micro-phonemic class; in the first instance, that objectively similar phonetic differentiation can be correlated only to a partially micro-phonemic class. It is not for us to say that the vowel alternation is more significant than the suffix for preterit marking of the verbs creep, keep, sleep, weep, or any such psychologistic formulation; it is enough to point out that the final alveolar stops in "crept, kept, slept, wept" were not correlated to the same set of micro-phonemes as the final stops of "heaped, wrapped, helped". This method of classification would not conflict with the definition of a phonetic change given above, and of course does not involve the introduction of mentalistic factors.[6]

The only use of the various other 'phonemes' to which the proposed macro-phoneme cannot be put is the easy establishing of sanctions for broad transcriptions. For obviously the proposed definition justifies the use of the same symbol for the initial and final stops of "top-hat" as correlated to the same phoneme, but not for the vowels of "pair" and either "pain" or "pen". It is difficult to feel too gloomy about this deficiency. Many students of language, probably, have felt acutely or obscurely that our conventional transcriptions are merely a somewhat less awkward but still conventionalized orthography, that phonetic transcription says either too much or too little. According to the proposed definition four kinds of quasi-phonetic transcription would be possible: (1) A more or less mathematical indication of the relations of micro-phonemes in terms of intra-class differentiations; (2) A more or less clinical indication of articulatory movements and positions; (3) A more or less subjective indication of the acoustic effect upon the transcriber as a kind of imperfect phonograph; (4) A more or less conventionalized indication of highly abstracted units of combined phonemes—which is about what our present transcriptions are—but in terms of clearly defined conventions. It would be eminently desirable to have a transcriber explicitly and expressly state that he intends to indicate the vowel of "pair" as [e, ej, ɛ, ɛɪ, ɛj] etc., rather than imply tacitly that it is related to the same phoneme as the vowel of either "pain" or "pen", which is to conceal rather than reveal the phonological facts. If he chooses to use an entirely different symbol, no one can object. At all events, a temporary embarassment in the codifying of transcription conventions may be a small price to pay if some dangerous assumptions and inconsistencies can be eliminated and clarity can be brought to the study of the phonological relations within languages.

[6] Cf. Modern Philology 25.225.

⟦Looking back at any such controversy after twenty years, we must expect either to be baffled or to find a misunderstanding at the bottom of it; and if we find one, then we wonder why it was not pointed out at the time. But if it had been, then there would have been a different controversy instead of this one....

American linguists were still too widely separate both in their ideological backgrounds and in their geographical locations, except for the few hours of the annual meetings of the Linguistic Society, to have been able to reach a meeting of minds easily. Seeing something in print with which one agreed throughout was apt to give rise to a presumption that all the connotations of the wording, and all the prejudices which had led the author to think in that direction, were the same for author and reader. With more intimate personal contacts, we have since learned how prevalent the hidden disagreements are likely to be, and to some extent we have learned how to understand each other by calibrating our prejudices.

For instance, it is only a few years ago that the boundary-line was clearly marked for us (by Fred Householder, I understand) between two attitudes of a linguist towards what he is doing when he sets up a description, with the labels 'God's-truth' against 'hocus-pocus'. The God's-truth assumption is that the language has a structure that is just there, waiting for the analyst to work it out; uncertainty about the facts bears witness to insufficient observation or defective procedure or both. This assumption is pretty sure to infect even such an attempt as this one to state the point objectively: one automatically says 'uncertainty' 'about' the 'facts'. The procedure based upon this assumption will naturally be a way to derive the description logically from the data; the expectation will be that logic always gets the same description from the same data. The paragon of this sort of this procedure, so far, is Bloch's A set of postulates for phonemic analysis (Lang. 24.3 [1948]).

Hocus-pocus linguistics is pejoratively described as a game played with symbols. Its practitioner may perfectly well share in the God's-truth faith that the language has an autonomous structure. But the conclusion that the structure is therefore accessible to frontal attack is for him a non-sequitur. If he happens to be a theorist on procedure, he will say that he is setting up maps or models for ('for', not 'of') seemingly coherent areas of the phenomena, testing these each against its parallel phenomena by simple inspection, altering them repeatedly and observing the improvement in fit, combining them into larger maps and testing the combinations by observing how well they seem to fit larger phenomenal territories, and so on until the description is complete enough to be acceptable for the time being.

Each fit is good when the map or model seems to predict all the observed phenomena and does not predict the opposite of any observed phenomenon. Now it usually turns out that it also predicts some phenomena that have not yet been observed. This is the great advantage of the hocus-pocus map: it leads to new discoveries. The corresponding disadvantage is that different workers may make different maps for the same phenomena; this is the 'arbitrariness' 'in' the 'description' which parallels the God's-truth 'uncertainty' 'about' the 'facts'.

Probably no human thinker can stay always on the same side of the line between the God's-truth and the hocus-pocus attitudes. One is needed to supply the motive, the other to supply the tricks of method. For it is a fact of experience that the most grimly consistent God's-truth worker frequently discovers in his symbolization something useful that was not in his raw data: he has done some hocus-pocus in spite of himself. And it is also true that the most consistently cynical hocus-pocus worker gets a good deal of his pleasure out of discovering what he feels to be the truth about his language, not all of it out of the refinement of his procedure.

For this reason everybody continually fools himself about what he is doing; he wouldn't be human if he didn't. It is here that I classify Bloomfield's faith in his phoneme feature: he wrote as if this were a necessary implication of his procedure, which it was not. In a letter from him to Twaddell (Sept. 7, 1934) I find this: 'As you describe the situation ⟦Twaddell pronounces regal and wriggle identically, apparently halfway between Joos's two pronunciations of them⟧, it would not matter whether a scheme for your dialect ⟦n.b.: not 'of' but 'for'⟧ classed the vowel of pig with that of peek or with that of pick. In either case there would be no overlapping: you would have two, not three vowel phonemes.' Compare the solution by a Bloomfield disciple below, p. 101 fn. 11.

In the winter of 1933–34 Twaddell and I and a few others frequently discussed the sad state of phonemic or broad transcription. Jones threw the final vowel sound of city into the same basket with its other vowel; Bloomfield did the same with seedy. Once either thing had been accomplished, there was no way to undo it; hence it was right. But they couldn't both be right. Or could they? No: that way lies madness. Evidently complementary distribution was not enough, and phonetic similarity was impossible to measure. At last Twaddell got his bright idea: return to de Saussure's 'Dans la langue il n'y a que des différences sans termes positifs' ⟪74⟫. The phoneme would have to be a fiction, and the phonemes would have to be defined by starting from differences. And after all, wasn't that what everybody said was the important thing about phonemes—that the difference between one and another made the difference between one form and another?

It is interesting to observe how the hocus-pocus practitioners attacked this monograph with God's-truth arguments (Lang. 11.244, 12.1; rejoinders 12.53, 12.294 [1935–36]). Bloomfield held his peace, content to have seen the issues stated so plainly. The macrophoneme was not adopted; but phonemic discussion was noticeably more cautious for a few years after.⟧

PHONETIC AND PHONEMIC CHANGE

ARCHIBALD A. HILL

Language 12.15–22—1936

The theory of phonemes has received a great deal of attention from linguists within the last few years, and the applications of the theory to descriptive linguistics have become reasonably clear, though there still remain problems in need of further study. However, there has been less interest in the theory on the part of students of the history of language, many of whom practically ignore the theory altogether; or assume, on the other hand, that the sound changes which we can prove to have taken place in the past were practically coextensive with phonemic shifts.[1] It seems, therefore, worth while to attempt a tentative examination and classification of the relations between sound change and phonemic change in the hope that the applications of the theory of phonemes to the historic study of language may be to some extent clarified.

In the first place it is clear that the shifts in the pronunciation of a whole set of phonemes, which leave the phonemes as far apart as at the start of the change, involve no shift in the phonemic pattern. This is usually clearly recognized by all scholars, and involves no particular difficulty. A simple example is the fact that most phoneticians who visit the Southern United States for the first time, or after a stay in New England, are struck by the fact that the whole Southern vowel scheme is a notch higher than that of other parts of the country. Aside from individual differences in the pattern of vowel phonemes due to other causes there are, however, no striking differences in phonemic pattern in the two dialects. Historically, also, the first consonant shift from Indo-European to Germanic did not result in extensive phonemic changes, since the three groups of IE sounds remained separate in PGmc., though on a new basis.

Allied to this principle is a second, less often noticed. Phonetic shifts can result in a change in what constitutes the significant element in a phoneme or set of phonemes. This likewise produces no change in the phonemic pattern, though, as in the type of change cited above, the individual phonemes affected are all altered. An example of this type of change is found in the history of English long and short vowels. Originally the long and short vowels of English seem to have had the same quality; thus the significant feature of the two sets must have been length; and that the difference was phonemic is proved by such OE pairs as fullīce 'fully, completely', and fūllīce 'foully, basely'. However, in the late 13th century in the North, and a little later in the Midlands,[2] a change set in in the quality of the short vowels, whereby the natural tendency toward relaxation in short sounds resulted in open quality, eventually giving rise to the distinction that exists between such modern phonemes as [u] and [ʊ]. The gradual result of this sound change has been that quality has replaced quantity as a mark of distinction between phonemes in Modern English. The phonemes remain at equal distance from each other, but the nature of the difference has changed. It is interesting that this change has indirectly contributed to a new treatment of length. Since length has become a non-distinctive feature, the way has been left open for a regrouping of long and short quantities in rigid correspondence with the phonetic situation.[3] In fact I think most of the puzzling changes in the quantity of Modern English vowels can be referred to this general tendency, rather than to elaborate 'laws' describing the treatment of individual long and short vowels in special situations, as was the method of many older grammarians.

A third type of phonetic shift which need not involve phonemic readjustment is combinative sound change. Combinative sound change does not necessarily produce a phonemic shift as long as the sound causing the change remains. The simplest example of this sort of assimilation, not resulting in phonemic difference, is to be found in the almost universal American treatment of the vowels of <u>pat</u> [pæt] and and <u>pan</u> [p æ̃n]. In spite of the nasalization of <u>pan</u>, the two vowels are still members of the same phoneme, and it usually requires training in phonetics for an American speaker to perceive the phonic difference. If, however, the two final consonants should disappear, while the nasality persisted, the two vowels [æ] and [æ̃] would then automatically become members of different phonemes.

[1] This seems to be the attitude of Bloomfield, Language, N. Y., 1933. In his chapters on Phonetic Change and on the Comparative Method he makes quite clear that in general the formulae in which historic states of language are summed up indicate historic phonemic rather than narrowly phonetic structure. He does not, however, give any detailed discussion of the exceptions to this rule, or of the relations of the two types of change.

[2] Cf. Luick, Historische Grammatik der Englischen Sprache 374–9, Tauchnitz, Leipzig, 1921.

[3] The best description of the phonetic rules governing NE vowel length is to be found in E. A. Meyer, Englische Lautdauer, Uppsala, 1903.

An almost exactly similar assimilation which does not affect the phonemic pattern occurs in the speech of Spaniards, who often nasalize the first vowel of a word like notario without recognizing any difference between it and the last vowel of the word. A further example is the velarization of the nasal consonant of Spanish cinco [θiŋko], which is still felt to be a member of the n phoneme. Another case is the French unvoicing of the final m of words like rhumatisme [ʁymatism̥].

A more complicated example of the principle that as long as the sound which causes the assimilation remains, the phonemic pattern is not affected, is found in Modern English. Thus in my own speech the Early Modern English open [o] before [r] has resulted in a long [ɔ]-like phone. Since I use this phone in all words of the [o + r] type, and since the [r] is always preserved, I make no distinction between pairs like coarse and course, morning and mourning. This open phone is therefore still a member of the [o] phoneme, though the change which produced the variant phone is of considerable antiquity. In the speech of Virginians and New Englanders who do not pronounce final and preconsonantal r, on the other hand, the loss of the sound which brought about the lowered variant of the phoneme has resulted in the setting up of a new phoneme, since foe and for now contain significantly different sounds, not phonetically controlled variants. In a phonemic transcription of such a type of speech foe and for would have to distinguished by some such symbols as [fo] and [fɔə].

The difficulty of determining whether a historic sound change represents a mere phonic shift, or is one involving phonemic difference, is sometimes considerable. Thus the OE change of 'breaking' is a case in point. OE æ was 'broken' to a diphthong, written ea, and presumably pronounced [æə], before double ll as in [*fællan] > [fæəllan]. The generally accepted cause of this breaking was the development of a glide vowel before a 'dark' variety of l in the same syllable. If the [æə] had continued to occur only before such dark sounds, it would clearly have remained only a subsidiary member of the [æ] phoneme, in spite of the different spelling. There were, however, other varieties of ll, particularly a brighter ll from WGmc. lj, before which breaking often did not take place.[4] The occurrence, however, of occasional forms like Northern sealla from WGmc. *saljan suggests that perhaps the diphthong was carried over to the bright varieties of ll as well, in which case phonemic readjustment of either the vowel or the consonant must have taken place.

Occasionally we are more fortunate in being able to determine the phonemic standing of an ancient sound change. Thus the Gothic lowering of Gmc. u represented in Gothic by the spelling au, occurs only before r, h, and hw. There is, therefore, no evidence that it was not still a member of the u phoneme, since it is obviously phonetically controlled.

Even without the loss of the sound which brings about change in the members of a phoneme placed in its neighborhood, phonemic shifts may, however, occur. Such phonemic shifts nevertheless do not result in the setting up of new phonemes. Their sole result is to bring about a redistribution of already existent phonemes in the words affected. What happens in such a case is that the combinative sound change produces a phone which is closer to a member of some other phoneme than it is to the original phoneme, with the result that attraction sets in, assimilating the aberrant phone to this new close neighbor. This is what has happened in forms like [kæpm̩] for older [kæptən]. On a larger scale it is illustrated by those people who, while still preserving final and preconsonantal r, refer the [o + r] words to the same phoneme as in law, making no distinction between war and wore. An instructive example of phoneme regrouping of this sort is cited by Grammont.[5] He points out that in the French phrase robe courte the final b of the first word is unvoiced, but remains a member of the b phoneme, since it is still a lenis. In obtenu, on the other hand, the following voiceless sound is a constant part of the environment, not a mere accident of the phrase. Here, therefore, the unvoiced b goes completely over to the p phoneme, since it loses its lenis quality.

To turn to phonetic shifts which involve shifts in the phonemic pattern. The most obvious of these is a shift in the direction of some already existent phoneme. Such a change results in the falling together of two phonemes, eliminating one from the total number. A well known example of such a falling together is that of ME [e:] as in [kwe:nə] and [ɛ:] as in [hɛ:θ] which have both given rise to NE [i:] as in queen and heath. A type resulting in an increase of the number of phonemes by means of a split in what was once one phoneme has already been discussed; that is, the splitting of a phoneme because of the loss of a sound which caused a combinative change, as in [fo], [fɔə], above.

Here it is only necessary to add that it is sometimes difficult to determine when the change-causing sound can be called lost. This is particularly true when complete assimilation takes place. Thus it was mentioned that WGmc. lj resulted in a double ll, as in WGmc. *taljan > OE tellan. Can one speak of this j as being lost if the second l is still its representative? The answer should be in the affirmative, since we have essentially one sound, though long, as the representative of the two earlier ones. Moreover it is probable that this ll was different in character (perhaps palatalized?) from the common Germanic ll, since the geminated ll did not produce breaking

[4] Sievers-Cook, Grammar of Old English 51, Ginn and Company, N. Y., 1903.

[5] Grammont, Traité de Phonétique 186–7, Delagrave, Paris, 1933.

in OE. As long, therefore, as the difference in character persisted, the two ll's constituted separate phonemes.

No less important than these purely phonetic changes are changes in the phonemic pattern resulting from dialect mixture. Thus if a given local dialect shifts a whole phoneme in a new direction (without thereby bringing about a collision with some other phoneme) no phonemic shift occurs. However, if the speakers of that dialect thereafter come in contact with another dialect, or a standard language which they imitate, phonemic changes almost certainly result. If phonemic changes occur, the result may be either the setting up of a new phoneme, or a redistribution of already existent phonemes. The only instance in which such dialect mixture does not produce phonemic changes is when a true variphone is set up, each speaker using either of the dialectically variant phones in all of the words in question. Such cases would seem to be rare. A more common state of affairs is fixation of the variants, either in different ones of the affected words, or in different senses of the same word. An interesting example of the setting up of a new phoneme by fixation of the second type is found in the speech of a subject from eastern Maine. This speaker comes from a region in which the [o] phoneme is strongly centralized, giving a phone which can be written [ɵ]. However, this particular subject belongs to a family in which local dialect has long been abandoned for Standard English. Thus coat has the [ou] phone of the Standard English phoneme. But in the special, and more homely, sense of coat of paint the local phone [ɵ] occurs. Thus there has been a phonemic split, actually in two senses of the same word.

The type of shift which results in the redistribution of already existent phonemes can be exemplified from the speech of many Virginians. The local dialect of eastern Virginia has the [a] phoneme in words of the aunt, dance type. However, the [æ] phoneme characteristic of General American occurs in the special use of aunt or auntie as a title for an old colored woman. It now seems probable that the puzzling divergences in the history of ME [a] and [u], resulting respectively in NE [a] as in father and [æ] as in rather, [ʊ] as in put and [ʌ] as in but, but with fixations in individual words, are the result of dialect mixtures of the types described above; the first resulting in redistribution of existent phonemes, the second giving rise to a new phoneme.

The case of genuine variphones is unknown to me in personal experience of dialect investigation. However, I am acquainted with speakers who vary separate phonemes in a way almost exactly similar. Thus one subject who has lived both in Virginia and the middle Atlantic states uses either [æ] or [a] phonemes in words of the aunt, dance, ask type, according to what sort of speakers he is addressing. Also the border-line cases in which some words occur with either phone, but some are limited to one or the other, is known to me from subjects in Maine. Thus one speaker can say either [stoun] or [stɵn], but always says [bout]. In such types of distribution it seems closest to the truth to say that there are two phonemes, but that some words can be pronounced with either one.

There remain fairly numerous examples of change in pronunciation where there is a phonemic shift without any general sound change. This is the type of change found in individual words, in which the change is not supported by a similar drift in other words of the same history. An example of this kind of individual change is found in the speech of some localities in Virginia where the single word say has undergone lowering in the stressed position so that it appears with the phoneme of bed. This is in contradiction to the general tendency in this region, which is to raise rather than lower vowels in stressed syllables. Another similar example is found in Maine where at least one speaker says that an ox is driven with a [gɔəd], using the phoneme of board. It is highly improbable that such an individual change, of whatever origin, should result in the setting up of a new phoneme, occurring only once in the speaker's language, since it can usually be assumed that the attraction of existent phonemes will be too strong for a single word to resist it. Only in the more or less isolated and sub-linguistic forms of interjections and similar highly colored words can phones not found in the general phonemic pattern easily maintain themselves. The origin of such individual changes as the two cited above is extremely various, and must always be explained out of a knowledge of the history of the individual word in question. Thus, though I cannot prove it, I suspect that the first change is due to the analogy of the third singular says and the preterite said. As to the second example, the explanation would more probably be found in the existence of the words gore, gored, gourd, which have somehow become blended with goad, always a word of limited application in folk speech. Thus analogy, folk-etymology, and the restoration of worn-down forms all play an important part in such individual changes.

Closely allied to the phenomena of individual phonemic attraction are certain other phenomena that result from closely similar or overlapping phones within two separate phonemes. In English, a characteristic change is the reduction of many unstressed vowels to [ə]. When any of these reduced vowels are restressed, an 'incorrect' form, i. e. not belonging to the original phoneme, may be the result. Such a form is the Louisiana [ˈpʌkɔn] for pecan. More interesting, and less widely known, however, are cases of individual attraction resulting from contiguity of two whole phonemes. Thus in many parts of New England there are raised and fronted variants of the [a] phoneme, producing a phone, [a˄], which is very close to the lower limits of the [æ] phoneme. In general the two phonemes are kept quite distinct, but in occasional words attraction between the two phonemes has produced confusion. A clear instance of this kind of confusion is found in the speech of a subject from southern Massachusetts, who pronounces the first syllable of clapboard with the [a˄] phone, which is a member of the [a] phoneme, not the [æ] phoneme.[6]

From the preceding discussion it seems possible to deduce a few general principles which govern phonemic change in its relation to phonetic change. The most important of these is that when phonetic change brings two phonemes close together, attraction may set in. This attraction may manifest itself more strongly in some words than others, thus appearing at first as a confusion between phonemes of individual words, though the two similar phonemes may elsewhere remain distinct. Later the attraction may extend to the whole group, in which case we say that 'two sounds have fallen together'. Indeed, I think it may safely be assume that no two phonemes ever fall together without passing through such a transition stage, in which the attraction manifests itself sporadically in ever increasing numbers of words.

However, attraction is not the only possibility when phonetic change brings two phonemes close to each other. A second possibility is phonemic repulsion, which results in the selection by the speaker of variants which offer less overlapping, and so tend to increase the distance between the phonemes, rather than to lessen or eradicate it. An instance of phonemic repulsion seems to have taken place in the history of British English in early modern times. We know that at one time some varieties, at least, of London English had a voiced intervocalic t, which we can assume was probably the same phone as the flapped, voiced t so common in America at present.[7]

[6] The pronunciations [kætrɪdʒ] for cartridge, and [pæsl̩] for parcel, common in New England, are not examples of the reverse confusion, but of early loss of [r] before dentals.

[7] Cf. the spellings collected by Wyld, A History of Modern Colloquial English 312–13, E. P. Dutton, N. Y., 1920.

We also know that at some time, presumably fairly recent, British English must have developed the flapped intervocalic voiced r which is characteristic of Standard British English today. These two phones are extremely close to each other, differing principally only in length. Consequently if they existed as members of separate phonemes at the same time, we should expect confusion to have arisen. Evidence of this confusion, and so of the contemporaneity of the two phones is found in porridge, the by-form from pottage. But at present British English t is unvoiced, and even slightly aspirated, medially, so that there is no longer the slightest danger of confusion with r. I know of no explanation other than habitual selection of variants farther removed from r than is the flapped t to account for this drift.

As to whether attraction or repulsion will result from the overlapping or contiguity of two phonemes, it seems to me that we must resort to the principle of dangerous as against unimportant confusion laid down by the French linguistic geographers to account for the disappearance or preservation of homonymous words. Thus it is demonstrably more important to keep consonant phonemes clear and distinct in English as it is at present organized, than it is to do the same for vowel phonemes. It is thus not strnage that confusion in consonants should be rarer than in vowels, where several ME sounds have been confused in NE.

In conclusion, the theory of phonemic attraction and repulsion, if accepted, should modify considerably our notions of how linguistic change takes place. Where the neo-grammarians held that the individual speaker was without control over sound drift, the theory of phonemes emphasizes that many more things than inexorable phonetic law can control the non-distinctive features of utterance. The selection of those phones within a given phoneme which offer least likelihood of confusion may often spring from a necessity for clearness which has too often been ruled out of court by students of language.

⟦Seldom referred to, even at the time, and almost forgotten today, this paper was actually of very great importance. By discussing phonetic realities in the familar historical field, while taking phonemics for granted, so that the distinction between the phonetic and the phonemic aspects was illustrated again and again, a hearing was gained for phonemic philosophy with readers who had shunned indoctrination by such things as Swadesh's The phonemic principle ⟪32⟫, and very likely a good many readers who had not shunned Swadesh still learned more from Hill than they had learned about phonemes before.

Bloomfield had said simply 'Phonemes or classes of phonemes may gradually change. ... Such change is sound-change.' ⟪30⟫ Change what? What is it that changes in them? How d'ye mean, they 'change'? the reader was apt to ask. Is this change a movement, and if so, then in what dimension? Do they change their color, or is it a change of affiliation? Such questioners, who had previously been content with textbook descriptions of pronunciation-shifts in the histories of particular languages, now felt that they were being offered a stone for bread. Hill showed them that a historical-drift theory on phonemic principles could make good sense.

Writing today, Hill would use a radically different transcription for English, of course; but few of his points would be lost, if any. The theory of phonemic attraction and repulsion would involve bilingualism on all scales, down to the conflict of idiolects.⟧

A NOTE ON OLD HIGH GERMAN UMLAUT

W. FREEMAN TWADDELL

Monatshefte für deutschen
Unterricht 30.177–81—1938

It is generally agreed that a group of modifications of vowels and diphthongs known collectively as umlaut occurred in connection with a following palatal element, i, ī, or j; and that the modifications begin to be represented orthographically in MHG, but not in OHG, except for the mutation of short a.

A difficulty arises from the fact that, in large measure, the i, ī, or j which 'caused' the umlauting was no longer present in MHG. We are faced with two alternative interpretations: either the umlaut occurred after the disappearance of the condition which caused it—a patent absurdity—or the umlaut occurred in OHG times but for some reason was not recorded orthographically until centuries later.

There is general agreement that the differences caused by umlaut existed in OHG, that however only the umlaut of short a was represented [as e] in the writing.[1] And there have been attempts to answer the question: Why, if the umlaut changes occurred in OHG, were they not represented until MHG, except in the case of short a? It has been suggested[2] that the phonetic differences due to umlaut were inconsiderable in OHG times, too inconsiderable to call for orthographical representation. This suggestion leaves the essential problem unsolved, for it entails as a corollary the unsupported and inherently improbable assumption that the difference became considerable only after the disappearance of the factor which had caused the original 'slight' differences. A variant of this type of answer is an explanation in terms of a delayed mediate palatalization through intervening consonants: The i, ī, or j is supposed to have palatalized the preceding consonant or consonants, which, having acquired a palatal articulation, subsequently palatalized the preceding vowel. This explanation has several serious weaknesses: It implies that the palatalization of the consonants, originally dependent upon the following i, ī, or j, became an independent phonetic characteristic (though never indicated orthographically), and survived the depalatalization or loss of the following i, ī, or j. The allegedly palatalized consonants would have to retain their palatalization long enough to palatalize the preceding vowel; and then they would have to lose their palatalization, since the phonetic history of German shows no traces of a differential treatment of palatalized and non-palatalized consonants. This is in itself a highly improbable sequence of combinatory changes. There is the further difficulty of imagining any chain of combinatory changes which involves a succession of regressive palatalizations in trahani, aruzzi, or hawi. The most serious practical objection is of course the complete lack of any evidence for such mediate palatalizations; the only reason why anyone should have thought of such a rationale was the need to explain the delay in orthographical representation of umlaut. It is, in short, an explanation with no basis in objective evidence—a purely ad hoc hypothesis. Another suggested answer[3] is the argument that the Latin alphabet did not supply the required symbols. But the MHG scribes were able to invent symbols; and they knew the same Latin alphabet as the OHG scribes, so far as the number of symbols is concerned. If the Latin alphabet was inadequate in the 9th century, it was similarly inadequate in the 13th; if new symbols were invented in the 13th, they could have been invented in the 9th.

– – – – – – – – – –

Let us consider the umlauts which are not regularly indicated in OHG, taking u as a paradigm. We note the following phonetic developments:[4]

Uxi — [yxi]
Uxxi — [uxxi]
Uxa — [uxa]

Then [y] is the phonetic form of sound-type U, when followed by -xi. [y] always represents U before -xi, and never represents any other sound-type. Hence [y] and [u] can never occur in a similar phonetic environment; they are the two complementary repre-

[1] Cf.: Behaghel, Gesch. d. d. Spr. (5) §253; Braune, Ahd. Gram. (3) §51; Paul, Mhd. Gram. (10) §40. a 1; Priebsch and Collinson, The German Language II. I B. 8; Prokosch, Outline of Germ. Hist. Gram. p. 51; Schade, Ahd. Gram. §§47, 63; Sütterlin, Nhd. Gram. I. 1. 5. a. A concise account of the history of investigation is presented by Jellinek, Die Erforschung der indogermanischen Sprachen, II. Germanisch (Streitberg, Michels, Jellinek), 1936, pp. 381–395.

[2] E.g., Braune, Paul, op. cit.

[3] E.g., Behaghel, Schade, op. cit.

[4] A capital letter is used to represent a sound-type, which is that of the stressed vowel to be considered in connection with umlaut. Thus U represents OHG u at the beginning of the divergent developments due to umlaut; x represents a consonant or consonant group which permits phonetic mutation of the preceding vowel; xx a consonant group which inhibits umlaut, temporarily or permanently; -i represents the umlaut-inducing elements i, ī, j; -a represents any other suffixal element. Vowel-symbols in square brackets indicate the actual phonetic form of a given sound-type in a given phonetic environment.

sentatives of the general sound-type U. [y] and [u] represent two aspects of U, dependent upon the phonetic environment. If the phonetic environment is orthographically indicated, the phonetic representative of U (either [y] or [u]) is automatically indicated. When the OHG scribe wrote uxi, the OHG reader had to pronounce the vowel as [y], for the written symbol in this -xi environment had to be interpreted as indicating the fronted variety of U.

It is indeed conceivable that the speaker of OHG was unaware of the phonetic difference between [y] and [u], or at most regarded them as slightly different forms of the 'same vowel', U.

In this earlier phase, the nature of the vowel and the phonetic environment were so correlated that the environment was the determining, primary factor, the independent variable; and the nature of the vowel was secondary, the dependent variable. It was the difference between -xi and -xa which determined the difference between [y] and [u].—This is the definition of the conditions of umlaut.

But when the post-tonic vowels fall together to [ə],[5] then an entirely new set of relations obtains. In this later phase, the old relationships between [y] and -xi, between [u] and -xa, can no longer exist. For both -xi and -xa have been replaced by -xə. We have accordingly arrived at a state in which our three formulae must be represented:

Uxi — [yxi] — [yxə]
Uxxi — [uxxi] — [uxxə]
Uxa — [uxa] — [uxə]

As between the first and third of these formulae, the difference [y/u], which had originally been dependent upon and secondary to the difference [-i/-a], has now become an independent and autonomous difference. In the terminology of the Cercle Linguistique de Prague, the phonetic opposition [y/u] has been 'phonologized'. The result is a new sound-type, Y. Instead of the earlier status, in which [y] and [u] were representatives of two aspects of U, dependent upon phonetic environment, [y] and [u] are now representatives of two different sound-types, Y and U, which occur independently of phonetic environment.

In this phase, then, our formulae must be interpreted as

[yxə] representing Yxə
[uxxə] representing Uxxə
[uxə] representing Uxə

The application to our problem is plain. In the earlier phase, as long as -i [that is: i, ī, j] remained distinct from other suffixal vowels, then there would be no need, indeed no occasion, to record the phonetic difference between [y] and [u]. For, in that phase, the difference between [y] and [u] was not the significant difference; it was a secondary difference, dependent upon and induced by the difference between -i and -a.

[5] Or, for that matter, to [i].

As soon as the difference between -i and -a has ceased to be significant, then (and not until then) the difference between [y] and [u] becomes a significant difference, which must be represented orthographically. What is here paradigmatically and over-simply referred to as the dephonologization of the difference -i/-a was in reality of course a series of processes: [-j] was lost or assimilated earlier than the weakening of [-i] to [-ə]; many of the [ī] suffix vowels were long maintained. There must have been a period in which the opposition [y/u] was in part independent (where [-j] had been lost) and in part dependent (where [-i] remained). The failure to record immediately the [y/u] opposition in the former cases was a natural orthographical conservatism, since such cases constituted a minority of the occurrences of [y], and were pretty completely restricted to certain morphological classes and functions,[6] with related forms still displaying [-i]: e.g., infinitive of weak verbs I and related finite forms. Further, the loss of [-j] and the weakening of [-i] occupied appreciable periods of time, and we must assume fluctuations of usage, local, individual, and probably even within the speech of one individual. Not until a considerable majority of the occurrences of [y] were definitely independent of phonetic environment was the phonologization of [y/u] sufficiently valid to call for orthographical representation.

According to this rationale of OHG umlaut, there is nothing surprising about the absence of orthographical representation of [y, ø], etc. in OHG. Indeed, the failure to represent these conditional variants of the sound-types U, O, etc. is entirely natural. To have represented them would have been an act of supererogation, of orthographical pedantry, parallel to an attempt at representing orthographically the various phonetic forms of the sound-type K in modern English or German, or of the sound-type CH in German Frauchen : rauchen.[7]

In following this line of argument, we encounter however one major difficulty, which is the reverse of the usual one. For, if we account for the failure to represent the umlauts of u, o, etc. as above, we are faced with the necessity of accounting for the fact that the umlaut of short a is represented in the OHG orthography.

In dealing with the umlaut of short a, we have to distinguish three lines of development:

Axi — [exi]
Axi — [æxi][8]
Axa — [axa]

[6] Similar to the status of ch in Frauchen/rauchen; see L. Bloomfield, German ç and x, Le maître phonétique (1930) 27 f.

[7] A similar phonological process (though with a different orthographical outcome) in Russian is described by Trubetzkoy, Archiv für vergleichende Phonetik 1.144.

[8] x represents such combinations as -ht-, etc.; cons.-vowel-cons.

As between the second and third formulae here, with [æ] and [a], we have a relation analogous to that between [y] and [u]. The difference [æ/a] is merely phonetic in the earlier phase, but is phonologized subsequently, and appears as the so-called 'secondary' umlaut.

With respect to the first formula, Axi, however, a different relation exists. The [e]-aspect of sound-type A was phonetically rather similar to a phonetic aspect [ɛ] of a different sound-type, E. Further, this [ɛ]-representative of sound-type E appeared in another phonetic environment, as in erda. This is the only phonetic environment in which sound-type E can historically be expected, because of the earlier shift of e to i before i, etc.

The phonetic similarity of [ɛ] (from E) and [e] (from A) would then have had a surprising consequence. It must be remembered that the [e] of gesti was a closer vowel than the [ɛ] of erda. The complex of sounds representing the old E and A sound-types would then have assumed this form:

[exi] from A
[ɛxa] from E
[æxi] from A
[axa] from A

Historically, three of these represented one old sound-type, one represented the other. But the speakers of OHG knew their language functionally, not historically. And functionally, there would have been a neat pairing-off, resulting in a new and symmetrical distribution of sound-types:

[exi] representing Exi
[ɛxa] representing Exa
[æxi] representing Axi
[axa] representing Axa

The preponderant OHG orthography represents such a new distribution of E and A. The functional unity of the new sound-type E is confirmed by the cases in which OHG [ɛ], occurring exceptionally before -i in new formations, was replaced by [e].[9]

- - - - - - - - - - -

Thus we arrive at a formulation for OHG in which there were two phonetic forms for each of the vowel-types, with the exception of the palatal vowels and diphthongs. But in each case these two phonetic forms are substantially complementary, dependent upon the phonetic environment; and therefore no orthographical representation is called for. Subsequently, when the environmental differentiation is eliminated, the phonetic differences are phonologized. Orthographical evidence of this is found in MHG for every vowel but e; and for e the rime-usage of the poets is conclusive evidence.

It goes without saying that the actual historical shiftings of orthographical usage were often tentative and inconsistent, with all the fumblings that a change in craft tradition can entail. This discussion is not concerned with them, nor with subsequent disturbances of umlaut-relations through operations of analogy. It is presented as a sketch of the main trends of the earlier stages of umlaut in High German, viewed as a phonetic and phonological (therefore orthographical) phenomenon.

[9] Cf. v. Bahder, Grundlagen d. nhd. Lautsystems 132 f.

⟦Nowadays we expect every discussion in historical phonology to be in harmony with 'phonemic theory' as most of us call it. More than that, we expect the phonemic arguments to come into the discussion at the start and to play the principal role right through to the end. For us this is something like the rule of 'the best evidence' in law, neglect of which casts suspicion on the strength of the case. So much is all this taken for granted today that we are apt to forget how new it all is. The foregoing paper is less than twenty years old, but it was a startling novelty when it was published—except for those who didn't know the philological tradition, who didn't know enough to be surprised, and so read it attentively and saw that this was plainly the right way to do things.

It was a fair exchange. A very large fraction of the stimulation to descriptive linguistic thinking has its origin in Germanic philology, as we see from the careers of no less than ten of the authors here, from Sapir and Bloomfield down to a co-author of the last paper in this volume; and that was true of Twaddell too. This paper begins to repay the debt.

The morpheme {-eme} does not appear in the paper. In order to leave the field free for future historians of linguistic thought, I will leave unsaid what little I know of the reasons for the omission.⟧

A PROBLEM IN PHONOLOGICAL ALTERNATION

MORRIS SWADESH and CHARLES F. VOEGELIN

Language 15.1–10—1939

One may expect to find instances of phonologic (morpho-phonemic) alternation in almost any language. In English there are changes in consonants, vowels, and stress, insertions, and elisions;[1] and many of these are conditioned only by the phonetic surroundings of the morphemes. An example is the possessive suffix, which is -əz (or -ɩz) after a sibilant, -z after a voiced non-sibilant, -s after a voiceless non-sibilant.

In the case cited, the alternation is called regular. It might be more correct to say that the phonologic[2] basis for the alternation is patent, as we may demonstrate by contrasting with this example another one involving 'irregularities'. The plural suffix, otherwise homonymous with the possessive, differs in the case of certain nouns, whose final fricative is voiced.[3] Thus, leaf : leaves contrasts with belief : beliefs (note also leave 'furlough' : plural leaves). An account of plural formation in English may consist of giving the more usual phonology as the rule and then listing the other cases as irregularities. But note the plural formation of leaf is completely consistent with that of sheaf, calf, half, knife, house, and several other nouns. There is, so to speak, regularity within this limited group of 'irregular' words. These cases cease to be irregular if one recognizes that there are two types of voiceless spirant morpho-phonemes, one that is fixed, and one that is subject to voicing on the addition of the plural suffix. If we wish, we may provide different symbols for the two types of morpho-phonemes, as, for example, *bəlif versus *liF. Different phonologic behavior requires the differentiation of the morphophonemes.

A system of special morpho-phonemic symbols would have little operational efficiency in English, because the instances of non-patent phonology are limited in number and scope. In other cases, one of which we give here in full, the use of special symbols may greatly clarify and objectify an otherwise complicated system of alternations. Before we leave the English examples, let us note that alternations are the result of phonetic history, affected also by foreign borrowings and analogical changes. The most efficient formulation of the synchronic facts is ordinarily not the same as a reconstruction of the actual historical developments, but the process of constructing morpho-phonemic formulae has some resemblance to that of historico-phonological reconstruction.[4]

We give Tübatulabal, a Uto-Aztecan language of California, as a striking illustration of what may be accomplished by recognizing the non-patent in synchronic phonology. In his published account of this language, Voegelin reported a technique of vocalic reduplication accompanied by consonantic changes, contractions, syncopes, and changes in vowel length. For these changes two or three highly productive treatments could be pointed out ('regular principles'), but there remained many less productive treatments ('irregularities'). Again, alternation of length in suffix vowels followed a highly productive treatment, but so many unproductive treatments of stem phonology were found beside this that the only feasible plan seemed to be to list the reduplicated and unreduplicated forms of each stem.[4] Swadesh, having learned the use of formulae in synchronic phonology from Sapir in his work on Nootka,[5] suggested that the morpho-phonemic alternations of Tübatulabal might be effectively treated by this method. In the beginning of our collaboration, Swadesh suggested some hypotheses based on the behavior of a number of stems mentioned in the grammar; then both col-

[1] See Palmer, A Grammar of Spoken English 7–12, Heffer, 1924; Bloomfield, The structure of learned words, A commemorative volume issued by the Institute for Research in English Teaching on the occasion of the tenth annual conference of English teachers 17–23, Tokyo, 1933.

[2] We use the term phonology to refer to alternations (synchronic phonology) or changes (historical, diachronic phonology) in sounds, rather than for the theory of the nature and permutations of the sounds. The latter we call phonemics. Those who use 'phonology' in this sense, probably in imitation of French 'phonologie', deprive themselves of a convenient means of distinguishing two fundamentally distinct subjects.

The phonemic point of view is essential to a proper understanding of the phonology, both synchronic, as will be seen in this paper, and historical, as is nicely shown in W. F. Twaddell's A Note on Old High German Umlaut, Monatshefte 30.177 ((85)), 1938.

[3] We omit mention of the irregularity that certain stems use a different formation, as oxen, men,...

[4] Voegelin, Tübatulabal Grammar, University of California Publications in American Archaeology and Ethnology 34.55. See also Voegelin, On Being Unhistorical, Am. Anthropologist 38.344; and Whorf, Notes on the Tübatulabal Language, ibid. 38.341.

[5] See Sapir-Swadesh, Nootka Texts, Linguistic Society of America, 1938, 236–9.

laborators went through Voegelin's lexical files and text material (assembled before the present theory was conceived) to find which morphemes could and which could not be explained on the basis of the first assumptions. This led to a correction and extension of the phonological theory. The theory was counted as finally developed when it accounted for all the phenomena illustrated in the assembled material. The value of the theory is not merely that it is accurate, but that it provides an overlying general pattern (regular principles) to phenomena which, otherwise, could only be presented as a series of distinct, partial, limited patterns (rules and irregularities).

The suffixation vowel

A relatively simple problem is that of the vowels used before different suffixes. Let us compare the infinitive of several stems and themes with the simple imperfective, the causative, and the benefactive.

tək 'to eat'	təkat 'he is eating'	təkinat 'he is causing him to eat'	təkanat 'he is eating for him'
ala·w 'to talk'	ala·wat	ala·winat	ala·wanat
ta·wək 'to see'	ta·wəgat	ta·wəgi·nat	ta·wəga·nat
pohol 'to get blisters'	poholat	poholi·nat	pohola·nat
in 'to do'	inət	ini·nat	ina·nat
halʔ 'to sit'	halət	hali·nat	hala·nat
o·l 'to get up'	o·lot	o·linat	o·lanat
mu·yh 'to celebrate'	mu·hyut	mu·hyinat	mu·hyanat
təkilo·k 'to pretend to eat'	təkilo·got	təkilo·ginat	təkilo·ganat
təkiwə·t 'to eat collectively or ravenously'	təkiwə·dət	təkiwə·dinat	təkiwə·danat
pələ·la 'to arrive'	pələ·lat	pələ·linat	pələ·lanat
yə·wu 'to hold'	yə·wut	yə·winat	yə·wanat

Disregarding for the present the length of the suffixation vowel we note that an i is regular in connection with the causative; this is likewise true of several other suffixes, including: -^{i}WkaÑ past habituative, -^{i}Šamā future, -^{i}wa passive, -^{i}ninəMa distributive, -^{i}wə̄də collective intensive, -^{i}baĦa 'to want to ...', -^{i}lōgo 'to pretend to'.[6] The vowel with the benefactive is consistently a; no other suffix is so characterized. The quality of the suffixation vowel for the imperfective element element may be any back vowel, a, o, u, ə (a is by far the most common; e is found in one or two cases), and is determined by the preceding morpheme. Several other suffixes agree with the imperfective -t in their behavior with regard to the suffixation vowel; thus: -H imperative, -maR· exhortative, -puWa 'to seem to ...', -laR 'going', -gima 'coming'. Furthermore, the vowel which a morpheme has before these suffixes is the same as that which it has in final position in the case of those morphemes that end in a vowel in final position. We may therefore take the vowel preceding suffixes of this group to be a part of the preceding morpheme, even though most morphemes lack the vowel in word-final. Suffixes like the causative have the peculiarity of inducing a change of the final vowel to i and the benefactive has the peculiarity of changing it to a.

Since most morphemes lose their final vowel when they stand in final position, it is simplest to mark those that retain it. We may do this by means of the symbol R, e.g. hūdāR 'for the sun to be up' (inf. hu·da).

[6] The reader is asked to disregard capital letters and other special symbols until they are explained later.

Terminal unvoicing

The stops and affricates of certain morphemes alternate between voiced and unvoiced according to whether they stand in medial or terminal position. This is illustrated for final position by ta·wəgat : ta·wək, təki-lo·go-t : təki-lo·k, təki-wə·də-t : təki-wə·t, quoted above. The same is true of initial position, as appears in reduplication, for example, a·dawə·k '(he) saw' (perfective) : ta·wək 'to see', ə·bələ·la 'he arrived' : pələ·la 'to arrive', u·buw 'he irrigated' : puw 'to irrigate'. Now, it is generally true in Tübatulabal that voiced stops and affricates occur only in intersonantic, syllable-initial position, and it is clear that we are dealing with a case of positional alternation: the substitution of voiceless for corresponding voiced takes place in those positions where voiced stops do not (one might say, cannot) occur.

There are, of course, morphemes with fixed voiceless stops, e.g., tək 'to eat' : ətəki-n 'he caused him to eat', pušk 'to blow' : upušk 'he blew'.

Modification of final clusters

Cases like mu·yh : mu·hyut may be accounted for under a rule that clusters of h plus sonorant metathesize in word-final position. Other examples are: a·na·hlət 'he is making it fast' : aʔana·lh 'he made it fast'; ponihwəy 'of the skunk' : poniwh 'the skunk'.

In cases like halʔ : halət, the morpho-phonemic formula must be based on the final form, in order to distinguish such cases from others like pohol : poholat. We set up formulae like *halʔə̄ and the rule that clusters of liquid or nasal plus ʔ lose the latter except in word-final. Other examples are: gülʔa- 'to play', MoNʔmōnʔo- 'to boil', Lohōmʔa- 'to enter'.

Vowel length

The greatest complexity is found in the matter of vowel lengths. The vowel length of suffixes is determined by the stem, or stem-suffix complex, to which they are attached. The vowel lengths of the stem frequently vary as between unreduplicated and reduplicated forms, and the vowel lengths of the suffixes may differ according to whether the stem is reduplicated or not. Let us take a number of words which illustrate different treatment of vowel lengths, giving the infinitive to show the unreduplicated form, the perfective to show the reduplicated form, except in a few cases where other forms have to be taken. The reduplication consists of repeating the stem-vowel, rather the first vowel of the stem, before the word. The examples are selected to show the nature and complexity of the phonologic problem. Long themes, either primary or involving suffixes, are expressly chosen in order to show the treatment in syllables remote from the initial. Morphophonemic formulae for the stems are given here for convenience, but have yet to be justified.

(1) ta·wəgi·-na-na·-la 'to go along causing him to see'	a·dawə·gina·nala 'he went along causing him to see'	*dawəga
(2) pələ·la 'to arrive'	ə·bələ·la	*bəlālaR
(3) təwəla·-n 'to fix it for him'	ə·dəwəlan	*dəWalə
(4) to·yla·n 'to teach him'	o·do·yla·n	*dōylāR
(5) payʔigə-la 'to go along turning'	a·bayʔigəla	*bāYʔgə
(6) puwa·-n 'to irrigate it for him'	u·buwa·n	*buwā
(7) poloŋa·-n 'to beat it for him'	opolo·ŋan	*poLoŋa
(8) poholi·-n 'to cause him to get blisters	opoholin	*poHoLa
(9) či·čwana·bə 'to accompany him'	iči·čwana·bə	*čīǯwanābəR
(10) təʔəbinugaʔadawa·-n 'to tell a myth for him'	ətəʔəbinugaʔ-adawa·n	*tōʔbinugāʔ-dawa
(11) tugaʔana-n 'to make it deep for him'	utugaʔanan	*tugāʔna
(12) togo·yʔa-n 'to decoy it for him'	otogo·yʔan	*togōyʔa
(13) puški-na·-n 'to blow it for him'	upuškina·n	*pūška
(14) kina-n 'to bring it for him'	iŋgina·n	*giNa
(15) cami·-n 'to burn it'	anǯami·n	*ǯamā
(16) kami·ǯa-n 'to catch it for him'	akami·ǯan	*kamīǯə
(17) cənənə·ʔ 'to shake it'	əcənənə·ʔ	*cəNənēʔa
(18) ta·twal 'man'	ata·twa 'group of men'	*tādwaR
(19) ha·ya·-n 'to stir it for him'	a·ha·ya·n	*hāyā
(20) šiwga-n 'he combed his hair'	i·šiwganat 'he is combing his hair for him'	*šīWga
(21) halayʔi-n 'to make him wet'	a·halayʔin	*halāYʔa
(22) hu·da 'for the sun to be up'	uhu·da	*HūdāR
(23) wi·mi·wi·mi·-n 'to cause him to zigzag'	i·wi·mi·wi·mi·n	*wīmīwīmīna
(24) mə·hli·n 'to hurt him'	ə·mə·hli·n	*māhlīna
(25) ma·ncuʔi-n 'to make him tame'	a·ma·ncuʔin	*māncūʔu
(26) ma·ygi-n 'to make him go ahead'	a·ma·ygin	*māygə
(27) wi·na-gə·m 'to come to give him a present'	i·wi·nagə·m	*wīna
(28) wə·ʔin 'to pour water'	ə·wə·ʔin	*wəʔina
(29) lu·mi·n 'to take it off'	u·lu·mi·n	*lūmīna
(30) yahna 'to believe him'	a·yahnan	*yāHnana
(31) yə·wa·-n 'to hold it for him'	a·yəwa·n	*yəʔəwūR
(32) ya·yaŋ 'to be timid'	a·yayaŋ	*yayaÑa
(33) yilaho·-la 'to go along happy'	iyilahola	*YiLaHo
(34) nəbaʔ 'to snow'	ənəbaʔ	*NəbāʔR
(35) wi·bi-n 'to make him fat'	iwi·bin	*Wībə
(36) wimšini·-n 'to make him move out of the way'	iwimšini·n	*WīMšin
(37) u·di-na·-n 'to untie it for him'	u·ʔu·dina·n	*ʔūda
(38) a·gi-na·-n 'to cause him to open his mouth for him'	aʔa·gina·n	*ʔāga
(39) aya·w 'to grow'	aʔaya·w	*Ɨayāwə
(40) əhcaw 'to help him'	əʔəhcaw	*ƗəHcawa
(41) a·na·hli-n 'to cause him to fast'	aʔana·hli·n	*Ɨanaʔahlə
(42) ə·wəni·-n 'to stop him'	ə·ʔə·wəni·n	*ʔəwənə
(43) ina-n 'to do it for him'	ina·n	*ʔiNə
(44) o·li-n 'to help him up'	o·li·n	*ʔolo
(45) i·ʔa-n 'to give him a drink'	i·ʔa·n	*ʔiʔa
(46) o·wi·-n 'to mark it'	o·ʔowi·n	*ʔoʔowā
(47) kə·ʔi-n 'to cause him to bite'	ə·gi·n	*gəʔə
(48) šu·ʔa-n 'to dry it for him'	u·ša·n	*šuʔa

We observe that stems beginning in a vowel have ʔ in the reduplication. As will be seen later, it is convenient to assume an initial ʔ to be morpho-phonemically basic in these cases. All stems then begin in a consonant. There is never more than one initial consonant.

Turning to the matter of vowel-length, we note first that the reduplication vowel is always long before a voiced stop or affricate, always short before a voiceless stop or affricate. This correlation must have some connection with a certain fact of phonemic occurrence: in those positions where either a voiced or voiceless stop may occur, only a short vowel ever precedes a voiceless stop; either a short or a long vowel may precede a voiced stop.

Other consonants, which do not have the voiced-voiceless contrast, reduplicate with long vowel for some stems, with short vowel for others. This difference in treatment of vowels established a morpho-phonemic dichotomy extending beyond that of the stops; one class includes all the basic voiced stops and some instances of each of the other phonemes, the other class includes all fixed voiceless stops and some instances of each of the other phonemes. Let us refer to the latter group as shortening consonants, the former as neutral consonants. The classification may be partly extended to the non-initial position by analogy with the stops. All consonants which are preceded, in any of the forms of the morpheme, by a long vowel are neutral. Of those non-stop consonants which are never preceded by a long vowel, some may be vowel-shortening consonants. We may symbolize shortening non-stops by a capital letter; and for the glottal stop, we use Ɂ for capital ʔ.

From examples 14–17 we observe that a nasal after the stem-vowel is included in the reduplication if the initial consonant is a basic voiced stop but not if it is fixed voiceless: iŋgin 'he brought it', anǯam 'it burnt'; but akami·č 'he caught it', əcənə·ʔ 'he shook'. The nasal is assimilated to the consonant. The vowel before the nasal + consonant is short.

Our criteria of consonantal type, though applicable only in some cases, enable us to identify some themes as containing only neutral consonants, and in such themes (1, 2, 4, 6, 15, 19, 23, 24, 26, 28, 29, 31, 37, 42, 44, 45, 46, 47, 48) we can observe the principles of vowel-length as they apply when not interfered with by secondary shortening. We find that some vowels are always long, some vowels alternate between long and short; it is perhaps simpler to speak of 'heavy' and 'light' vowels instead of fixed-long and alternating-length vowels. Except for 31 and 45–48, the actual length of light vowels can be covered by simple rules: (a) in the syllable adjacent to one containing a heavy vowel, a light vowel is always short; (b) otherwise, a sequence of light-vowel syllables alternate in length, the first being long, the next short, and so on. Heavy vowels are illustrated in to·yla·n : o·do·yla·n (4), ha·ya·n : a·ha·ya·n (19), wi·mi·wi·mi·n : i·wi·mi·wi·mi·n (23), mə·hli·n : ə·mə·hli·n (24), and others. Alternating length of light vowels is shown very well in the first example: ta·wəgi·nana·la : a·dawə·gina·nala. In 37 and 42 we see how a preceding heavy vowel affects the alternation of light vowels by preventing the first following vowel from being long: u·dina·n : u·ʔu·dina·n (stem *ʔūda); ə·wəni·n : ə·ʔə·wəni·n (stem *ʔə̄wənə). In 2 and 6 we have a following heavy vowel preventing a preceding light vowel from being long, but the reduplication, being two syllables removed, is long: pələ·la : ə·bələ·la (stem *bələ̄la); puwa·n : u·buwa·n (stem *buwā).

Examples 31, 44, 45, and 46, although they contain only neutral consonants, seem to show contradictions to the phonological theory already presented. Take example 31, yə·wa·n : ə·yəwa·n. If the base were *yə̄wāna, the reduplicated form should be *ə·yə·wa·n and it is not. If it were *yəwāna, the unreduplicated form should be *yəwa·n. Example 46 is similar. Examples 44 and 45 show no reduplication but only a change in the vowel lengths: o·lin : o·li·n; i·ʔan : i·ʔa·n. The clue to these anomalies is to be found in 47 (kə·ʔi-n : ə·gi·n) and 48 (šu·ʔa-n : u·ša·n), which show that contraction takes place under some circumstances. If o·lin is from *ʔo·lina· (stem *ʔolo), its reduplication would be *o·ʔoli·na; a contraction in the first two syllables would give us the actual form o·li·n. Similarly, i·ʔan : i·ʔa·n are from *ʔi·ʔa-na, *i·ʔiʔa·na. yə·wa·n : ə·yəwa·n can then be derived from *yə·ʔəwa·n : *ə·yəʔəwa·n < stem *yəʔəwū. Similarly, the forms of 46 are based on a stem *ʔoʔowā. The rule of contraction is that it takes place between light vowels separated only by ʔ except as between the two syllables of an unreduplicated dissyllabic stem (47, 48) and between the vowels of a certain type of extension of the stem final, illustrated in wə·ʔinat 'he is pouring water' : wə·ʔina·ʔat 'he is pouring lots of water' (stem *wəʔina). The quality of the contract vowel is that of the second of the two component vowels, as is seen in u·ša·n (< *u·šuʔa·na), and the quantity is long if one of the components is long, short if both are short. Only two of three light vowels separated by ʔ contract, as in i·ʔa·n < *i·ʔiʔa·na.

If we turn now to words containing shortening consonants, we soon see that a shortening consonant affects only the vowel before it. The phonological effect of the vowel, whether light or heavy, remains the same. In constructing our formulae a vowel, even though followed by a shortening consonant, may be identified as light or heavy according to the behavior of the adjacent vowels, and consonants may be identified as shortening if vowels are short before them under conditions where one would expect a long vowel before a neutral consonant. təki-n : ətəkin points to a stem *tə̄ka-; the heavy vowel is evidenced by the fact that the following vowel is short whether in the second or third syllable of the word. poloŋa·-n : opolo·ŋan points to a stem *poLoŋa- with all light vowels; the actual forms show secondary shortening from *po·Loŋa·n : *o·poLo·ŋan. And the remaining examples can similarly be reduced to adequate formulae.

Word-final vowels insofar as they are retained are shortened. R might thus be called a vowel-shortening consonantal morpho-phoneme. (Indeed, it might be identified with Ɪ, if we could then say that a morpheme-final Ɪ is lost entirely except in word-final position, and that in word-final position it appears only in its effect of retaining and shortening the preceding vowel.)

In addition to the foregoing theory it is necessary to recognize a special VˀV group which acts in the length theory like a single heavy vowel (see 5, 10, 11). We may set these up as V̄Ɪ and state the rule that a heavy vowel plus a syllable-final Ɪ is pronounced as VˀV, e.g., təˀəbinugaˀadawa·n < *tə̄Ɪbinugā̄Ɪdawa-. If a semivowel intervenes between the heavy vowel and the syllable-final Ɪ, as in 5, a high vowel (i or u according to the semivowel) is inserted.

Conclusion

If it has been possible, by the recognition of a non-patent phonology involving two morpho-phonemic types of consonants and two of vowels and a set of mechanical rules, to reduce the apparent irregularity of Tübatulabal phonology to system, this very fact guarantees the truth of our theory. Truly irregular alternations could not be reduced to order.

The value of a phonological theory is in direct proportion to the extent of its application, in inverse proportion to its complexity. Our theory might be called fairly complex, but it applies to a great many words. There are several hundred verb stems attested in Tübatulabal and about a score of suffixes. Not only are the suffixes quite freely added to the stems, but quite a number of different combinations of suffixes are possible. It is probably not an exaggeration to estimate that any particular stem may enter into 300 stem-suffix combinations and that some suffixes occur in 25,000 stem-suffix combinations. These, then, are measures of the value of determining the phonological formula for any given stem or suffix. In presenting the lexicon of the language, the formulae will serve as a shorthand method of indicating the facts for each lexeme.

For other languages we hope our treatment of Tübatulabal may offer some useful methodological suggestions. To linguistic theory Tübatulabal phonology is an instructive instance which can contribute to eventual generalization.

⟦In the asterisked note ⟨⟨38⟩⟩ which Chao now adds to his Non-uniqueness paper, he says 'this was written at a time when the differences between transcription and phonemicization and between phonemes and morphophonemes were not as clear as they are today'. The difference(s) between transcription and phonemicization are not under consideration here; at this point we are interested rather in the difference or differences between phonemes and morphophonemes.

Chao was certainly right to consider this worth saying. When we look back at Bloomfield's work, we are disturbed at this and that, but more than anything else Bloomfield's confusion between phonemes and morphophonemes disturbs us. Bloomfield kept himself out of trouble here, usually, by describing just one language at a time, or one area within each at a time, adjusting for the effects of the confusion. But it made his procedure an unsafe model for neophytes and made the corpus of his work an inadequate source to distill procedural theory out of.

The escape from this confusion was, naturally, itself a confused as well as an arduous journey, like that of the Israelites from Egypt. Most of it remains undocumented, consisting of endless hours of discussion and of private pondering. Thus, even if we reread all that is in print on it, it would still seem far simpler than it was; and the picture is not much further falsified by confining ourselves to two items: this paper by Swadesh and Voegelin, and the following by Bloch.

In this one we find morphophonemes abundantly illustrated, and phonemes taken for granted. Many attempts have been made to characterize the difference succinctly; one more will, it is hoped, do no harm. The native listener may be said to perceive—to somehow exploit for message-understanding ends—items in what he hears. Insofar as this process does not depend on understanding, the items are phonemic; insofar as items cannot be perceived without understanding, morphophonemics at least (perhaps more) is involved. I borrow an example from C. F. Hockett: Once he heard someone say 'She has poise' and, momentarily insufficiently attentive, innocently said 'What's a poy?' The phonemic items had been apprehended perfectly, but, through a lapse in understanding, the morphophonemic items had not.

Incidentally, these two papers beautifully show the typical American way of advancing linguistic theory: by working out specific problems and then, perhaps, drawing the methodological conclusions.⟧

PHONEMIC OVERLAPPING

BERNARD BLOCH
American Speech 16.278-84—1941

The first step in the phonemic analysis of a language or dialect is to group the infinitely varied sounds which make up the spoken utterances of the speech community into a limited number of classes called phonemes. The principles governing this classification do not concern us here;[1] but it is obvious that each phoneme, defined as a class, will include as many actual and objectively different speech sounds as there are utterances containing a member of the class.

We know that the sounds comprising a single phoneme—the allophones, to give them a convenient name—sometimes differ strikingly among themselves. Most writers on the subject have dwelt on this fact, and all readers are familiar with the stock examples offered as illustrations: the different varieties of [k] in keep cool, of [l] in leaf and feel, or of the velar spirant in German ich and ach.[2] To offset this diversity among the allophones, some writers postulate a basic resemblance which unifies the entire class, by defining the phoneme, like Daniel Jones,[3] as a 'family' of sounds clustering around a norm or, like Bloomfield,[4] as a constant feature in the sound waves.

But though writers are agreed that allophones of the same phoneme are often very different phonetically, they appear to be uniformly silent on another aspect of the phonemic interrelation of sounds. I do not know of any published work that has even posed the question—important as it is both in practice and in theory—whether phonemes may intersect: whether a given sound, that is, may belong to two or more different phonemes in the same dialect. If the question has ever occurred to writers on phonemic theory, they appear to have treated their answer to it, whatever it may be, as a tacit assumption. It is my purpose here to state explicitly what is usually tacit, and to offer arguments in support of a principle which is usually assumed.

Is the phonemic analysis of a dialect valid if it forces us to assign successive occurrences of the same sound to different phonemes? For the purposes of this discussion, we may define a sound as a recurrent particular combination of sound features (such as labial or alveolar position, stop or spirant or lateral articulation, voicing or voicelessness, aspiration or the lack of it, etc.), of which some are distinctive in the language and some not; and we may agree that two sounds are 'the same' if they represent the same particular combination of such features.[5] The intersection or overlapping of phonemes will be called partial if a given sound x occurring under one set of phonetic conditions is assigned to phoneme A, while the same x under a different set of conditions is assigned to phoneme B; it will be called complete if successive occurrences of x under the same conditions are assigned sometimes to A, sometimes to B.

Our question concerning the possibility of intersection is best answered by examining specific examples. These are all taken from varieties of Midwestern American English, since this is the only dialect for which I have worked out the phonemic analysis at first hand. I shall begin with some cases of partial intersection.

In the speech of many Americans, the [t] phoneme includes as one of its constituent sounds or allophones an alveolar flap (something like the r of London English very), which occurs intervocalically after a stressed vowel, and in this position varies freely with the familiar voiced t and with the aspirated voiceless t, as in butter, betting, kitty (contrast budded, bedding, kiddy). In the speech of some of these persons,

1 For several divergent statements of these principles see Leonard Bloomfield, Language (New York, 1933), chap. 5; Morris Swadesh, The Phonemic Principle, Lang. 10.117-29 (1934) ((32)); W. F. Twaddell, On Defining the Phoneme (Language Monograph No. 16, 1935) ((55)); N. S. Trubetzkoy, Grundzüge der Phonologie (Travaux du Cercle Linguistique de Prague No. 7, 1939).

This paper was read at the 17th annual meeting of the Linguistic Society of America, Dec. 1940. For clarification of my views on phonemic theory I am indebted especially to Professor Bloomfield, Dr. George L. Trager, and Dr. Charles F. Hockett.

2 See for example Daniel Jones, An Outline of English Phonetics, 3d ed. (Cambridge, 1932), pp. 48-49; John S. Kenyon, American Pronunciation, 6th ed. (Ann Arbor, 1935), pp. 33-35.

3 Op. cit., p. 48. Cf. also Ida C. Ward, The Phonetics of English (Cambridge, 1931), p. 60.

4 Language, pp. 78-81.

5 This statement does not, of course, solve the difficult question of phonetic identity, Since we know from laboratory evidence that no two sounds are exactly alike (and that even one sound is never uniform throughout its duration), but since on the other hand we know that the best-trained ear can distinguish only a small fraction of the objectively different sounds, there would seem to be no solution of the dilemma capable of satisfying both logic and practical necessity. A serviceable rule-of-thumb is to regard two sounds as 'the same' phonetically if an average native speaker, once his attention has been directed to them, cannot tell them apart.

the [r] phoneme includes as one of its allophones the same alveolar flap, occurring after [θ] in words like *three*, *throw*, less commonly after [ð] in dissyllabic pronunciation of words like *withering*, *gathering*. (The flap after [θ] is often partly or wholly voiceless; but the voiced variety also occurs.) In this dialect of English, then, the [t] phoneme and the [r] phoneme appear to intersect in the alveolar flap; but the intersection is only partial and never leads to uncertainty or confusion: every such flap between vowels belongs to the [t] phoneme, every flap after a dental spirant belongs to the [r] phoneme.

It is a well-known fact, emphasized especially by Menzerath,[6] that in the articulation of any sound in the stream of speech, the speaker normally anticipates part or even all of one or more following sounds. The phenomenon is of course familiar to students of historical grammar as the cause of regressive assimilation. In words like *tool*, *cool*, where the initial stop is followed by a rounded vowel, the articulation of the stop often anticipates the lip-rounding of the next sound (contrast the stops in *tin*, *keen*). These labialized stops are of course nothing but positionally determined allophones of the [t] and [k] phoneme, and their labialization is non-distinctive. The same kind of lip-rounding appears before [w] in words like *twin*, *queen*; but in a rapid and relaxed pronunciation of such words the separate phonetic fraction constituting the [w] may be considerably reduced or even lost altogether, so that this anticipatory lip-rounding of the stops remains as the only trace of its presence. (Forms of *twin*, *tweezers*, *twist*, *queen*, *quick*, *quiz*, and the like with a labialized stop immediately followed by a front vowel are not too common, but they are familiar to observers of the spoken language.) In such pronunciations, then, the lip-rounding of the stop is all by itself an allophone of the [w] phoneme, even though it appears simultaneously with the articulation of another sound, and even though in words like *tool*, *cool* the phonetically identical lip-rounding is non-distinctive, a mere positional feature of the allophones of [t] and [k]. The intersection is obvious, but again it is only partial; for the character of the following vowel always distinguishes the two values of the lip-rounding.

My third example of partial intersection, which I owe to a communication from Dr. Charles F. Hockett of the University of Michigan, is more complicated. In Hockett's dialect, and probably in that of many other Midwestern speakers, *mints*, *mince*, *dents*, *dense* all end either in [-ns] or in [-nts], *warmth* ends either in [-mθ] or in [-mpθ], *length* ends either in [-ŋθ] or in [-ŋkθ], *finds* and *fines* both end either in [-nz] or in [-ndz]. The facts can be formulated by saying that at the end of a stressed syllable after a nasal, there is free variation between a spirant and a cluster of stop plus spirant (the stop being homorganic with the nasal but voiced or voiceless like the spirant). Now, when the nasal is [n] and the spirant is [š] or [ž],* there is the same free variation between [š] and [tš], [ž] and [dž]: *bench* ends either in [-nš] or in [-ntš], *hinge* ends either in [-nž] or in [-ndž]. As Hockett observes, the clusters [ts], [dz] and the unit phonemes [tš], [dž] are phonetically quite comparable, and [tš], [dž] differ from [š], [ž] very much as [ts], [dz] differ from [s], [z]. That [tš], [dž] are unit phonemes and not, like [ts], [dz], clusters of two phonemes each, appears from their patterning elsewhere (their distribution, their occurrence before and after other consonants, etc.); yet at the end of a stressed syllable after a nasal, they behave exactly like ordinary clusters of stop plus spirant. The simplest way to describe the facts, it seems to me, is to posit partial intersection: in all positions except the one here defined, the sounds in question are phonemic units; in this one position they are clusters of two phonemes each, [t] + [š] and [d] + [ž], and alternate in free variation with the corresponding simple spirants [š] and [ž] just as other clusters do.

Similar examples could easily be added, from this and other dialects of English as well as from other languages. Partial intersection, as our illustrations show, can never lead to uncertainty in practice and may therefore be admitted in theory without violating sound phonemic method. The same cannot be said, however, of complete intersection. Examples are rare, and are always the result of an error in the analysis.

The unstressed vowels of English have long been a problem. Some writers, including Jones and Kenyon, treat the unstressed vowel of *about*, *sofa*, *condemn* as a separate phoneme, but regard the unstressed vowels of other words (as *adding*, *city*, *window*, etc.) as belonging to classes that include also stressed allophones. Other writers, notably Bloomfield, classify all unstressed vowels in terms of the vowel phonemes found in stressed syllables. A special problem is created by words that appear in two distinct forms according to the accentual conditions under which they are uttered; thus the word *at* has the vowel of *cat* in the phrase *where át*, but the second vowel of *sofa* in the phrase *at hóme*. Since the two vowels in this word always appear under different phonetic conditions and are thus in complementary distribution, it is possible to make out a fairly good case for treating both vowels as allophones of the same phoneme. But against this treatment there are two alternative objections, both involving intersection.

[6] For instance in P. Menzerath and A. de Lacerda, Koartikulation, Steuerung und Lautabgrenzung (Phonetische Studien, No. 1, Berlin & Bonn, 1933).

*For convenience in typing, this reprint uses [š] and [ž] for the IPA and near-IPA symbols found in the original publication in American Speech.

If the weak vowel of at hóme is a member of the same phoneme as the stressed vowel of where át because it alternates with the latter vowel in complementary distribution, what shall we do with the weak vowels of about, sofa, confess, and many other words, which never alternate with a stressed vowel? Those who agree with Bloomfield, as I do, that stress in English is phonemic (distinctive) and who are therefore unwilling to posit a separate phoneme to accommodate the unstressed vowel of the words just mentioned, will probably class this vowel, on the basis of phonetic similarity and pattern congruity,[7] with the stressed vowel of cut, come, rush. But if the weak vowel of abóut, atóne is thus identified with the vowel of cut, while the weak vowel of at hóme is identified with the vowel of cat, then successive occurrences of the same sound under the same phonetic conditions have been assigned to different phonemes.

The alternative objection involves intersection on an even greater scale. The same reasoning by which the weak vowel of at hóme is identified with the stressed vowel of where át leads us to identify the weak vowels of such phrases as sée them gó, théy could gó, théy will gó, nót so múch (all phonetically identical in my speech with the second vowel of sofa) with the stressed vowels of the phrases not thém, they cóuld, they wíll, not só, etc. In short, the 'neutral' vowel which appears at the end of sofa would come to function as the unstressed member of nearly all the syllabic phonemes of English; or, to put it differently, all the syllabic phonemes would intersect in their unstressed allophones.

Now it is of course true that such intersection will not seem troublesome if we know in advance which phoneme is represented in a particular occurrence of the ambiguous allophone. Knowing the stressed forms of the words at and them (as in where át, not thém), we are able to assign the identical unstressed vowels of at hóme and sée them gó unhesitatingly to their respective classes. But what if we know only the unstressed form, either because we have not heard the stressed alternant or because such an alternant happens not to exist? Suppose that we are studying a new and unfamiliar dialect of English, and that we have succeeded in pairing the stressed and the unstressed vowels of such words as at, them, could, will, so, and the like: if we now hear a phrase like óut of tówn, with the unstressed vowel of the second word perceptually the same as those which we have already identified with various stressed alternants, how are we to treat this? We must defer the phonemic analysis until we chance to hear a stressed form of the same word, which may not occur at all in the dialect we are studying, or which, if it does occur, we may fail to recognize as 'the same word.' In the case of English or any other familiar language, such an objection may seem less than academic; but it becomes practically important in working with a new language (especially one that has no written literature), and is theoretically important even for an understanding of the structure of our mother tongue. In short, a system in which successive occurrences of a given sound x under the same conditions must be assigned to different phonemes necessarily breaks down, because there can be nothing in the facts of pronunciation—the only data relevant to phonemic analysis—to tell us which kind of x we are dealing with in any particular utterance.

With this general principle stated, I proceed now to what I regard as my most seductive example of apparent intersection. I observed it first in my own speech, but have noticed it also in the speech of others. Indeed, since my pronunciation agrees rather closely, in its general pattern, with the Chicago dialect described by Bloomfield,[8] the feature may be fairly common in Midwestern English.

The pairs of words bit bid, bet bed, bat bad, but bud, bite bide, beat bead, etc., have respectively the same vowel phoneme, but exhibit a regular and fairly constant difference in the length of the vowel allophones. This difference is summarized in the well-known habit of English pronunciation, that vowels and diphthongs (and also liquids and nasals) are longer before a voiced than before a voiceless consonant. The alternation between longer and shorter allophones runs through the whole phonemic system. The vowel of pot is affected by the same automatic alternation: in the pairs pot pod, cop cob, font fond, the vowel of the first word is regularly shorter than that of the second; and there is nothing, so far, to show that a pair like pot pod is not in every way comparable to bit bid.

In my speech bomb is different from balm, bother does not rime with father, and sorry does not rime with starry: the vowel quality is the same in all these words, but in the first word of each pair the vowel is short (just as it is in pot), and in the second noticeably longer. Since the difference in length cannot be explained as an automatic alternation (like the difference in bit bid), we conclude that bomb and balm, bother and father, sorry and starry have different vowel phonemes; and we naturally indentify the vowel of bomb, bother, sorry with the phoneme

[7] On pattern congruity, see Swadesh, 'The Phonemic Principle,' and cf. his article 'The Phonemic Interpretation of Long Consonants,' Lang. 13.1–10 (1937). For the analysis of the weak vowel of sofa on the basis here mentioned, as well as for what I regard as the correct interpretation of the other unstressed vowels, see G. L. Trager and Bernard Bloch, 'The Syllabic Phonemes of English,' Lang. 17.223–46 (1941).

[8] 'The Stressed Vowels of Chicago English,' Lang. 11.97–116 (1935). The phonemic difference between the vowels of pot and balm, noted below, is attributed to the Chicago dialect (ibid., pp. 97–8); but my pronunciation of the two phonemes and their distribution in my speech both differ slightly from Bloomfield's.

of pot. The vowel of balm, father, starry appears also in alms, palm, pa, star, card. Again there is nothing, so far, to show that the phonemic organization is in any way abnormal. But now comes a hitch.

In the sentence Pa'd go (if he could), the utterance fraction pa'd must be analyzed, according to what we have just said, as containing the phoneme of balm. In the sentence The pod grows, the utterance fraction pod must be analyzed, again according to what we have said, as containing the phoneme of pot. But pod, with a vowel distinctly longer than that of pot (just as the vowel of bid is longer than that of bit), is phonetically identical with pa'd! Two occurrences of x under the same conditions have been assigned to different phonemes.

Approaching the intersection, as we have done, from different directions, and starting each time from a body of data already systematized, the conclusion seems inevitable. But the intersection here, as elsewhere, is inadmissible; for if we start from the facts of pronunciation as we meet them, there is never any clue in the utterance itself to tell us which kind of x we are dealing with. The apparent intersection of the phonemes of pot and balm reveals the fact (which otherwise could scarcely have been suspected) that the analysis we have made is faulty, even though we have proceeded on both sides of the intersection according to sound principles and usually valid methods.

If the fraction pa'd in Pa'd go is identical, under the same conditions, with the fraction pod in The pod grows, then both contain the same phoneme. We must choose between assigning the vowel of pa'd to the phoneme of pot, and assigning the vowel of pod to the phoneme of balm. Our choice will be determined by the validity of the resulting analysis.

If we say that pa'd has the phoneme of pot, bomb, bother, font, and the like, we must necessarily classify the vowels of pa, balm, father, alms, card, and so on in the same way; that is, we must deny the obvious fact that in the dialect here considered bomb and balm are different, and the pairs bother and father, sorry and starry do not rime.

We are left, then, with the other alternative. By classifying the vowel of pod—and consequently also the vowels of rob, nod, bog, fond, and the like—as members of the phoneme of balm, we destroy the neat parallelism of the pairs bit bid, bet bed, bite bide, pot pod: the words in the last pair, instead of exhibiting shorter and longer allophones of the same phoneme, have totally different phonemes. But by sacrificing this symmetry we are able to account for all the facts of pronunciation, which is surely the more important requirement. The resulting system is lopsided; but the classes it sets up are such that if we start from the actual utterances of the dialect we can never be in doubt of the class to which any particular fraction of utterance must be assigned.

⟦It was the present article by Bloch that made clear, as it never had been before, that phonemics must be kept unmixed from all that lies on the opposite side of it from phonetics: kept uninfluenced by the identities of the items of higher rank (morphemes and so on) which the phonemes 'spell', and hence free from all that their identities entail, such as their meaning and their grammar. It was a great deal to accomplish in so few pages, and few readers realized that it had been done: the ghost of the slain dragon continued to plague the community of linguists under such names as 'grammatical prerequisites to phonemic analysis' and has not been completely exorcized to this day. But if not all the readers, at least the workers who had participated in the discussions leading up to this publication (see fn. 1 above) were clear about it, and saw that it was now time to codify phonemic theory.

The task of codification was taken on by—indeed, in a way it was assigned to—the youngest of the persons spoken of, Bloomfield's disciple C. F. Hockett. The first result follows as the next paper here.

An older term for the new trend in linguistics was 'structural'. It is not idle to consider how the term 'descriptive' now came to replace it, even if not all the reasons can be identified. The Sapir way of doing things could be called structural, but the term was more often used for the stimulating new ideas that were coming out of Europe, specifically from the Cercle Linguistique de Prague. American linguistics owes a great debt to that stimulation; but in the long run those ideas were not found to add up to an adequate methodology. Trubetzkoy phonology tried to explain everything from articulatory acoustics and a minimum set of phonological laws taken as essentially valid for all languages alike, flatly contradicting the American (Boas) tradition that languages could differ from each other without limit and in unpredictable ways, and offering too much of a phonological explanation where a sober taxonomy would serve as well.

Children want explanations, and there is a child in each of us; descriptivism makes a virtue of not pampering that child. I recall being disconcerted, on first reading the Hockett article, to find that the title was to be taken literally. I would probably have been still further disconcerted if I had appreciated all the implications of the first word of that title.

As a matter of fact, within a few years Hockett in effect withdrew sections 6 and 7 of this article; see his Peiping Phonology of 1947 in this volume. And in 1955 his A Manual of Phonology did not leave the '47 position unaltered. Because of the importance of this paper to the understanding of what followed, it was necessary to persuade him to allow its reprinting.⟧

A SYSTEM OF DESCRIPTIVE PHONOLOGY

CHARLES F. HOCKETT

Language 18.3–21—1942

1. Linguistics is a classificatory science. The starting-point in such a science is to define (1) the universe of discourse and (2) the criteria which are used in making the classifications. Selection and preliminary ordering of data determine the range of analysis; the choice of criteria fixes the level of analysis. In linguistics there are various ranges, discussed in §2, and two basic levels, phonological and grammatical, each with subdivisions. The phonological level is the subject of this paper.[1]

2. The universe of discourse of any linguistic study is a set of utterances. It is necessary, therefore, to define the term 'utterance' and the limits of the various types of sets.

2.1 An utterance is an act of speech. An act of speech is an item of human behavior with certain physiological and sociological characteristics.

2.11 The physiological characteristic of an act of speech is that it occurs in a specific locus of a human body: the respiratory tract and the mouth.

2.12 Not all the events in this tract are utterances. All the behavior of a human organism is biophysical: it is subject to physical and biological analysis. Certain acts are, in addition, biosocial.[2] A biosocial act is one which (1) is determined ultimately by the life-history of the individual in a given social group, (2) functions directly or indirectly as a stimulus for the behavior of others and of the actor himself, and (3) does this in a manner similarly determined by the life-histories of the individuals involved.

Utterances are biosocial. A sneeze occurs in the same area; it may function as a stimulus for others, and it may do this in a socially determined way, but the source of the sneeze is purely physiological. Therefore a sneeze is not biosocial, and is not a speech act. On the other hand, a cough in our society, where it may be an indication of polite embarassment, or a belch in some parts of Africa, where it shows appreciation to one's host, fulfills all the requirements of biosocial behavior, takes place in the proper portion of the body (for the stomach and the esophagus form an adequate substitute for the respiratory tract in esophagal speech), and must therefore be considered an act of speech. This does not mean that such events cannot be proved to have a marginal status (§2.22).

2.2 Range varies from one linguistic investigation to another. A large random sample of the speech-acts of some one individual over a period of a few months will afford a safe basis for the description of the speech behavior of that one individual for that short period. When a number of such specific studies have been made, more or less completely, in a single community, one can generalize therefrom to describe the typical behavior of the whole community. But in any case only statistical sampling is possible, and the resulting description will always be incomplete.

A particular universe of discourse is subject to certain orderings. Those orderings which are made before the criteria of classification are applied may be termed extra-systemic. Those which result from the analysis itself are intra-systemic. Finally, some of the latter have extra-systemic implications and may be termed mixed.

2.21 The material may be ordered with respect to time. Thus if one classes together those utterances that were produced in January, and those that were produced in February or a year or ten years or a century later, the result of analysis will be to show the change in speech behavior during that time. Such treatment is termed historical. Similarly, if the material is ordered with respect to geography or social status, the resulting analysis is synchronically comparative, indicating the difference between the English of Michigan and that of Rhode Island, or between that of carpenters and that of sailors.

[1] The present paper derives from the phonemic systems of Bloomfield, Sapir, Trubetzkoy, and their followers. It owes most to Bloomfield, though rather to the methodological rigor of his work than to his phonemic theories. Apart from published material, the writer's chief stimulus has been his correspondence and discussion with George L. Trager and Bernard Bloch. He owes thanks also to Morris Swadesh for many suggestions in the past; to Mary R. Haas for specific criticism of the present paper; and above all to Bloch for advice and active assistance in giving the paper its final shape.

Many of the principles here set forth are illustrated and applied to the problem of English vowels by G. L. Trager and B. Bloch, The Syllabic Phonemes of English, Lang. 17.223–46 (1941). For a general bibliography on phonemic theory, see fn. 1 of that article [: "We have made use of the following works, among others, bearing on phonemic theory: Leonard Bloomfield, Language, ch. 5–8 (New York, 1933); id., A Set of Postulates for the Science of Language, Lang. 2.153–64 (1926) ⟨⟨26⟩⟩; Morris Swadesh, The Phonemic Principle, Lang. 10.117–29 (1934) ⟨⟨32⟩⟩; id., Lang. 11.244–50 (1935) ⟦critique of the next item⟧; W. F. Twaddell, On Defining the Phoneme, Lang. Mon. No. 16, 1935 ⟨⟨55⟩⟩; id., On Various Phonemes, Lang. 12.53–9 (1936) ⟦reply to Swadesh⟧; N. S. Trubetzkoy, Grundzüge der Phonologie, Travaux du Cercle Linguistique de Prague No. 7, 1939."].

[2] Albert P. Weiss, A Theoretical Basis of Human Behavior[2]; Columbus, 1929.

But historical and comparative study implies first the completion of descriptive analysis of each of the temporally or spatially or socially grouped ranges of material. Descriptive procedure establishes the fiction that the various utterances to be dealt with have no temporal or spatial or social order. This fiction is valid only when the time or space or social span covered by the material is relatively small; it breaks down, for instance, when we take our records of Old English as a single unordered set. If the actual course of change in speech behavior through time be pictured as a curve, then the approximation of descriptive technique to the actual situation can be represented by a tangent to the curve at a given point.

2.22 The English interjection pst does not conform to the statistically most frequent phonetic and grammatical habits. These facts, which are only revealed by analysis of the data, show the marginal character of the interjection. It is this type of evidence which puts conventionalized coughs and belches in their proper place, though as a matter of procedure the linguist may choose to predict this result and exclude such items from consideration at the very beginning.

2.23 It may turn out that a randomly selected sample of speech-acts from some individuals includes forms from two (or more) distinct languages or dialects. It is the analysis itself which shows this, since it makes clear a clustering of the material around two (or more) norms. Therefore this ordering might be termed intra-systemic. But careful examination reveals that the social situations in which one set of forms is produced are different from those in which the other set occurs. The ordering is therefore not purely intra-systemic, but mixed. These statements hold likewise for stylistic contrasts, involving such things as tempo or the difference between he arrived prematurely and he came too soon.

2.3 It will be assumed in the rest of this paper that the set of utterances to be handled descriptively is homogeneous enough to require none of the kinds of ordering just described.

3.1 Since speech acts are biophysical, they are subject to biophysical analysis and classification. The technique of doing this will here be called α-phonetics;[3] α-phonetic analysis uses physiological and acoustic procedures, with the necessary symbolic devices—charts, diagrams, and α-phonetic transcription.

3.2 An oscillograph record of the stream of speech shows it as a continuum. Articulatory analysis, on the other hand, shows it as segmented.[4] An examination of articulation reveals a concurrent sequence of motions or phases of rest of the various organs of the speech area. If a cross section be taken of the stream of speech at a given moment, each of the organs concerned is seen to have at that moment a specific functional status; for example, the lungs are pushing, the vocal cords are drawn apart, the entrance to the nasal passage is closed, the tip of the tongue is just leaving the alveolar ridge, the lips are open. A moment later the situation will be different.

3.3 Obviously, the different organs do not change from one functional status to another always at the same moment; the statuses overlap. A diagram can be made of any articulatory sequence, with horizontal lines showing the functioning of the several organs; the temporal cross section is represented by a vertical line cutting through all the horizontal lines. A change-point is any point at which any organ changes from one type of function to another. The segment between two successive change-points is an α-sound. In deciding just where to draw the line representing change-points there is some ambiguity, but it turns out that this does not matter for phonological purposes.

3.4 An α-sound is nothing more than the simultaneity of the functionings of the various organs. But for terminological reasons it is convenient to speak of these functionings as qualities, rather than as things or events; the initial sounds in peat and beat[5] share the quality of having the lips closed. All such qualities may be termed α-phonetic elements.

4. The next step is to describe the classification of all the utterances of a descriptive range into phonological equivalence classes.

4.11 Two utterances which have approximately the same elements in the same arrangement are said to be α-phonetically similar. This is, of course, a matter of degree.

4.12 Two speech acts are biosocially equivalent if they are produced under similar conditions and act similarly as biosocial stimuli. This, also, is a matter of degree.

4.2 Phonological equivalence involves, generally, the two factors of α-phonetic similarity and biosocial equivalence. The correlation is not absolute, and an examination of the limiting cases will clarify the general situation.

[3] The term 'phonetics' has two distinct meanings in current usage, unfortunately not always kept clearly apart. To avoid coining one or two completely new terms, this paper uses the expressions α-phonetics and β-phonetics for the two different meanings.

[4] Kenneth L. Pike, A Reconstruction of Phonetic Theory; University of Michigan diss., 1941 [see now Pike's book Phonetics, Ann Arbor, U. of Mich. Press 1943]. This is the purest treatment of α-phonetics known to the writer; most of the α-phonetic material here presented is taken from Pike's work.

[5] Phrases in the form 'the initial sound in beat' are to be taken as shorthand for the logically correct but cumbersome 'the first sound of an utterance consisting of the word represented in traditional orthography as beat'.

4.21 α-phonetic similarity is not measurable in the isolated case, but only in the light of careful examination of all the material. Thus the Spanish words sur and sud both mean 'south'. Furthermore, the α-phonetic difference between sur and sud is slight. Nevertheless the total set of utterances of these words constitutes two phonological equivalence classes, not one; for although in this particular pair of sets the contrast between the final consonants is biosocially irrelevant, in other pairs, say sed 'thirst' and ser 'to be', the same difference is biosocially important.

4.22 If a number of utterances of the English word meat and a number of meet be examined,[6] the following facts are revealed: (1) The α-phonetic differences between the various cases of meat and those between the various cases of meet cover the same range. No phonetician, and no native speaker of the language, could tell by listening to successive utterances of the two words which of them was involved in any particular utterance. (2) The biosocial nature of the various cases of meat is fairly constant, and so is that of the various cases of meet; but (3) the biosocial nature of the cases of meat and of meet are different. Thus it is seen that biophysical similarity does not necessarily imply biosocial equivalence. In a situation of this kind the forms constitute a single phonological equivalence class.

4.3 An utterance, by definition, begins and ends with a pause. Sometimes a consecutive portion of one utterance is phonologically identical with all of another except for the absence of pause at one or both of its ends. The term phrase may be used to subsume both utterances and such portions of utterances. It is convenient to extend the definition of phonological equivalence class so that its members are phrases instead of utterances.

4.4 In further classification on the phonological level, one transcription is used to denote ambiguously any member of a phonological equivalence class. Such an ambiguous name, which denotes an indefinite single member of a specified class, is termed in logic a variable. So the transcriptions ['sɪi̯] and /síj/ are variables.[7] Phonological analysis is not concerned with anything which differentiates the various members of an equivalence class.

5.1 An α-phonetic element which recurs in a certain position in all the members of some equivalence class is a distinctive element. To this there is one exception: an element which is constant in all the members of the range is not distinctive. Thus the peculiarities of one person's voice are eliminated, if the range includes only his utterances; if it includes more, the differences of voice quality give rise to an intra-systemic ordering which has extra-systemic significance in that it serves to identify the speaker—a mixed ordering.

A distinctive element is distinctive wherever within the range it is found, even though in some positions it is sometimes present, sometimes absent. For example, in English, aspirate release of stop consonants is a distinctive element, since it occurs always after the first consonant of put or tack or keep; at the end of those same utterances the aspiration is sometimes present, sometimes lacking. Since this variation is subphonemic, even though it involves the presence or absence of a distinctive element, it may be termed free variation.

An element which is nowhere distinctive is non-distinctive. Non-distinctive elements are always found tangled up with distinctive ones, but are no more significant linguistically than is any other concurrent action of a speaker, such as scratching the nose or gum-chewing; they are simply harder to get rid of.

5.2 By going through all of the equivalence classes of a range it is possible to list all of the distinctive elements that occur. But this is not enough, for it turns out that some things which have been treated α-phonetically as elements, and which prove to be distinctive, are constantly associated in groups of two or more, one appearing wherever the others do. Where this is true, the two or more elements clearly constitute a single unit, one of the minimum units into which the utterances of the range may be analyzed. These units are termed features; like elements, they will be treated terminologically as qualities.

The determination of features and of the positions in which they occur is the business of β-phonetics.

5.21 For the determination of features the method of contrastive pairs is useful. It is well known that in many languages minimal pairs in the traditional sense are rare. Let us suppose for a moment that in English pairs like weave : wife, fought : vat, peach : pine were plentiful, but that there were very few like fat : vat, peep : pipe. Such a situation would not hinder analysis; for it is easy to see that part of the difference between weave and wife recurs in fought : vat, another part in peach : pine.

Indeed, in English as it actually is, the α-phonetic elements which make up the contrast between fat and vat are not bound up exclusively with any other α-phonetic elements found in that pair, any more than the [v] of weave is bound up with the [ɪi̯], or the [f] of wife with the [ai̯], in the hypothetical case given above. In sip : zip the contrast is made by the same elements which make it in fat : vat, but in a different context, while in fat : sat one of the elements common to fat and vat is changed.

[6] It is assumed that all the utterances have the same prosodic features; meat? and meat! are of course phonologically different.

[7] Transcriptions used in this paper are of two kinds, which it will be necessary to keep rigorously distinct. Phonemic transcriptions are enclosed between diagonals; β-phonetic transcriptions are enclosed between square brackets (α-phonetic transcriptions do not occur). This way of distinguishing the two kinds of transcription is adopted from the article by Trager and Bloch (see fn. 1).

For this reason the term 'contrastive pair', meaning any pair between which there are differences in a context of similarity, any pair usable for the listing of features, is used here instead of the traditional term 'minimal pair'.

5.22 In some English dialects stops are either voiced and lenis (bid) or voiceless and fortis (pit). In others some stops are voiced and lenis (bid), others voiceless and fortis (pit), still others voiced and fortis (matter). In the first case voicelessness and fortisness, two separate α-phonetic distinctive elements, constitute a single feature, as do voice and lenisness; in the second case voicelessness, voice, fortisness, and lenisness are all separate features.[8]

It is perfectly possible that within a specified range, element A should be found only in connection with element B, but that element B should also be found elsewhere. In this case both elements A and B are features. Constant reciprocal association is necessary before two elements can be termed a single feature.

5.31 When all the features have been determined and listed, they are subject to several classifications. Most of these must wait until later to be introduced (§8), but one is important here.

Features which clearly follow each other in the stream of speech are segmental. Those which clearly extend over a series of several segmental groupings are suprasegmental. Thus the positions of articulation of the final two consonants in crypt are segmental, while the modes of articulation, voiceless and fortis, are suprasegmental.

5.32 A β-sound differs from an α-sound in the following two particulars: (1) Only distinctive features are concerned in the characterization of β-sounds. (2) A suprasegmental feature is treated as a β-sound in itself, and the segmental phases which it covers are regarded, without the superimposed feature, as independent β-sounds. Thus, like features, β-sounds fall into two classes, segmental and suprasegmental. For example, the final two consonants in crypt constitute five β-sounds. The three segmental ones are characterized respectively by the features of bilabial stop closure, apical stop closure, and aspiration. The stop character of the first two is not continuous from one to the other (as it is in chapbook), and so is not a suprasegmental feature. The suprasegmental β-sounds are absence of nasality and the fortis-voiceless character of the group. In addition, the entire utterance has the suprasegmental β-sound of loud stress, and this characterizes also each of the segments at the end of the utterance.[9]

5.33 Among features which are suprasegmental one can distinguish between those which are always so and those which are sometimes segmental. In beat the final consonant consists of two segmental β-sounds, [tʻ], each of which is characterized by several features; the first β-sound has apical position, stop closure, voicelessness, fortisness, and lack of nasality. So voicelessness and fortisness are not always suprasegmental, as they are in crypt. On the other hand, loud stress never accompanies a single segmental phase in English, and is therefore always suprasegmental.

6. The difference between a β-sound and a phone is that a phone is a member of a phoneme. Phones are again of two main kinds, segmental and suprasegmental; the latter class is subdivided into accentual and junctural. Whereas a β-sound may be sometimes segmental, sometimes suprasegmental, a phone is always one or the other; what is β-phonetically segmental may prove to be phonemically suprasegmental, and conversely, since this classification for phones depends on function as well as on β-phonetic character. Nor do the borders between segmental phones necessarily coincide with those between β-sounds: a single phone may include two or more adjacent β-sounds, and conversely. Phonemics is the analysis of β-phonetic material into phones, and the classification of the phones into phonemes.

6.1 A phoneme is a class of phones determined by six criteria. (1) Similarity: if A and B are members of one phoneme, they share one or more features. (2) Non-intersection: any phone which shares this feature or set of features is a member of the phoneme.[10] (3) Contrastive and complementary distribution: if A and B occur in corresponding positions in utterances of different equivalence classes, they are members of different phonemes; if A and B are in complementary distribution (i.e. if they occur in mutually exclusive positions), they may be—though they are not necessarily—members of the same phoneme. (4) Completeness: every feature characterizing each β-sound must be considered in making the classification; every β-sound must be all of or part of or more than some single phone; and every phone must be a member of a phoneme.

These first four criteria might still permit several alternative classifications. The danger of arbitrary procedure is obviated by the two other criteria.

6.11 (5) Pattern congruity: two contrasting β-segments (single β-sounds or groups of such sounds) which occur in similar β-phonetic environments are to be analyzed as having similar structures; either they are both unit phones, members of different phonemes belonging to the same functional class, or else they are similar clusters of two or more phones. This statement emphasizes the importance of struc-

[8] Example from English in the rest of this paper are from the writer's dialect, which is of the second of these two types.

[9] On the phonemic interpretation of English stress see Trager and Bloch, The Syllabic Phonemes of English, Lang. 17.226–9.

[10] On the problem of intersection see Bernard Bloch, Phonemic Overlapping, American Speech 16.278–84 (1941) ((93)).

tural parallelism: like function, like structure. But when such structural parallelism is absent, β-phonetic parallelism between two sets of β-phonetic segments may afford a basis of parallel analysis (see §7.33).

6.12 (6) Economy: if several different analyses equally satisfy the other requirements, that which establishes the smallest number of phonemes is the one to be preferred. This is a corollary of the general scientific principle that the simplest description which accounts adequately and accurately for all the facts is to be preferred.

6.2 A homeophone is a class of phones such that all members of the class are characterized by all the features that characterize any one member; obviously all the members of a homeophone will belong to the same phoneme. An allophone is a class of phones such that all are members of the same phoneme and occur in similar β-phonetic environments (the same position).

7.1 The first two criteria of phonemic analysis may be illustrated by English /p/. Every /p/ is characterized by fortis articulation, voicelessness, lack of nasality, labial position, stop closure, and some other features. /p, b/ share the features of non-nasality, labial position, and stop closure; /p, b, m/ the features of labial position and stop closure; /p, t, k/ the features of fortis articulation, non-nasality, and stop closure; but /p/ does not share all of its constant features with the members of any other phoneme.

7.2 It is not necessary to illustrate contrastive and complementary distribution, except to discuss what may be termed partial complementation.[11] Of the Spanish[12] phones /r, r̄/, only the latter occurs initially, only the former in syllable-final;[13] both are found medially between vowels or after /d, b, k, t/. In the contrasting positions the units /r/ and /r̄/ are of course phonemically distinct, and it is impossible to regard the latter as a geminate cluster of the former, since it patterns like a single consonant. In the position where there is no contrast, the type of trill is in each case more similar to [r] or to [r̄] of the contrasting positions, and the phonemic membership is determined accordingly. The simple statement of distribution made above gives the facts without any complications; any talk of neutralization or cancellation or archiphonemes[14] confuses the facts without adding anything.

7.31 In the following two examples, certain single β-sounds, such as [i·], are regarded as constituting two phones.

In Winnebago,[15] long vowels [i·, e·, a·, o·, u·] are found under the same conditions as rising and falling diphthongs such as [i̯e, i̯a, i̯o, ae̯, ai̯]. These are all contrasting units, and there are no further types, such as [ii] different from [i·] or [ie̯] different from [i̯e]. Pattern congruity requires either (1) that all the long nuclei, homogeneous and heterogeneous, be treated as separate unit phones, or (2) that each be regarded as a cluster of two short phones, thus /ii, ee, aa, oo, uu, ie, ia, io, ae, ai/. Economy demands the acceptance of the second analysis, which sets up only five vowel phonemes (plus three nasal ones not considered here), whereas the first demands about thirty.

In Kickapoo[16] there are four vowel phonemes; /i/ includes [i, j, i̯], /o/ includes [o, w, u̯], and the four long nuclei are geminate clusters. Thus [ɛ·hki·ka·powa·towɛ·ki] 'where Kickapoo is spoken' is /eehkiikaapooaatooeeki/. There is no ambiguity in the phonemic orthography: [w] does not occur before /o/, nor [j] before /i/; so that /ooii/, for example, is always [owi·] and never [o·ji].

---

11 Another problem, that of multiple complementation, has been discussed by W. F. Twaddell, On defining the phoneme 30-2 ⟪66-7⟫ and Lang. 12.54-6; but this problem is not a real one. If a phone A in a certain position is in complementary distribution with two other phones B and C, and is phonetically similar to both, either (1) both A and B, or both A and C, can be assigned to the same phoneme, or else (2) A, B, and C are members of three separate phonemes.

(1) The stop in English spin (voiceless, fortis, unaspirated) is in complementary distribution with both the stop in pin (voiceless, fortis, aspirated) and the stop in bin (voiced, lenis, unaspirated). In §7.1 we have defined /p/ ⟦i. e. chosen to define /p/⟧ as characterized by fortis articulation, voicelessness, and some other features; this definition unambiguously includes the stop in spin. ⟦See page 80 here.⟧

(2) To illustrate the other possibility we must invent an example, for no real case is known to the writer. ⟦Japanese offers several candidates; see 329-48.⟧ In a certain language, /i/ and /e/ are found in contrasting positions everywhere except before /n/; before /n/ there is a vowel phone which is exactly half-way between /i/ and /e/ and which occurs nowhere else. The latter vowel shares with /i/ and /e/ the distinctive feature of palatal articulation, but does not share the feature of intermediate tongue-height with any other phone. If these statements include all the relevant facts, then the cases of the intermediate vowel (in spite of its limited distribution) constitute a separate phoneme. Certain dialects of English in the South, where pin and pen are homonyms, may require this analysis.

12 Spanish data are from Navarro Tomás, Manual de pronunciación española[4], Madrid, 1932; George L. Trager, The Phonemes of Castillian Spanish, TCLP 8.217-22 (1939); and the writer's observations.

13 Variations of sonority may occur α-phonetically; β-phonetically these may be distinctive or not. The terms 'syllable', 'nucleus', and 'non-syllabic' are used here only on the phonemic level, to designate a grouping of phones which is useful in describing the phonemics of a particular language. Where nothing is said to the contrary, it is assumed that points of syllable-division are non-distinctive, or that they are definable in terms of the other features involved.

14 See N. S. Trubetzkoy, Grundzüge der Phonologie 206-18 (Prague, 1939).

15 Winnebago data are from Amelia Susman.

16 Kickapoo data are from the writer's notes.

7.32 In the following example, two successive segmental β-sounds are treated as constituting a single phone: [tʻ] = /t/.

In English, fortis stop types occur with and without following aspiration. The possibility that the aspiration may be a part of the following phone is eliminated by its occurrence where no phone follows, as finally in *put*, *tack*, *keep*, though here it is variable. If this aspiration is a phone in itself, either the cases of it constitute a separate phoneme, or they are members of the same phoneme which includes also the β-phonetically distinct but similar independent aspiration of *hat*. The cases of it cannot constitute a separate phoneme, since the dependent aspiration is in complementary distribution with the independent aspiration and is β-phonetically similar to it. Therefore such a form as *pin* is either /phín/ or /pín/. But the aspirated stops are, at each point of articulation, in complementary distribution with the unaspirated (except in final position, where there is free variation between the two types); and furthermore, the aspirated stops participate in clusters like other β-sounds that are clearly unit phones, not like β-sounds that are clearly clusters: [pʻ] behaves (patterns) like [p] and [b], not like [ps, bz, sp]. Therefore *pin* is /pín/, and the other aspirated stops are likewise unit phones, members of the same phonemes that include the unaspirated fortis stops.

7.33 In Old English there were ten syllable-nuclei that were β-phonetically short, ten that were long: i, e, æ, a, o, u, y, ie, ea, eo; ī, ē, ǣ, ā, ō, ū, ȳ, īe, ēa, ēo. The members of the two sets can be paired off so that the terms of each pair differ only in length and presumably in some minor qualitative ways. There seems to be no functional difference between the short and the long: both occur in stressed and in unstressed syllables, checked and unchecked, etc. But neither is there any functional classification which goes against the short–long grouping. In the absence of a functional classification to support or to deny the β-phonetic grouping, the latter may be taken as a basis for analysis; the longs may be analyzed in one way, the shorts in another. Just what the analysis is in detail is not certain; probably there are ten vowel phonemes and two accentual phonemes, shortness and length, so that every syllable nucleus is a vowel phone plus an accentual phone.

When there are both functional classifications and β-phonetic parallelism, then the former, not the latter, must be taken as the basis for analysis. Modern English [ɑ·, ɔ·] (as in *palm*, *law*) are monophthongs, like the vowels of *bet*, *bit*, *put*; but structurally they are like the diphthongs of *ride*, *bait*, *read*, and their analysis must reflect the structural fact rather than the phonetic—provided that this is possible in a manner that satisfies all the other principles of phonemic analysis.[17]

[17] It is possible: Trager and Bloch, Lang. 17.237–41.

7.4 There are four possible relations between a homeophone and an allophone if some phones are common to both.

7.41 The homeophone and the allophone may be identical: all the members of one are members of the other, and conversely. For example, Dutch [g], a member of the /k/ phoneme, occurs only before a voiced consonant in the next syllable and never varies with any other β-phonetic variety of /k/ in that position.[18]

7.42 The homeophone may include the allophone and also have members which are not in the allophone. An example is English [pʻ], the only β-phonetic type of the /p/ phoneme found in phrase-initial before a stressed vowel, but also occurring optionally in utterance-final and in some other positions.

7.43 The allophone may include the homeophone, and also have members which are not in the homeophone. In some Spanish dialects /f/ before a voiced consonant in the next syllable varies between [f] and [v]; the latter occurs only in this position.

7.44 In some cases, finally, a homeophone and an allophone may intersect but each may include phones which are not members of the other. The Spanish [f] just mentioned is an example: the allophone includes also [v], and the homeophone includes also [f] in other positions. Further, the final consonant of English *tap* may be aspirated or not, and both varieties occur elsewhere.

These last two paragraphs illustrate free variation, mentioned in §5.1.

7.5 There is sometimes, in some definable position in utterances, a *free alternation* between phones that must be assigned to different phonemes. In some dialects of Spanish, for instance, there is free alternation between /d/ and /r/ before a stressed vowel, as in *pedir* 'ask' and *parar* 'prepare'. This is different, of course, from free variation between phones of different homeophones but the same allophone.

Free alternation is a matter of phonemics because the conditions for the alternation can be given in purely phonological terms. In some other dialects of Spanish such words as *pedir* have either /d/ or /r/, but such as *parar* have always /r/. This is not free alternation, since one cannot predict on phonological grounds alone where the alternation will occur and where it will not; for this reason it is not part of phonemics, but rather of morphophonemics (a subdivision of grammar; see §10.1).

7.61 In the following example, a segmental β-sound, [h], is treated as a suprasegmental phone.

In early classical Greek,[19] there were two accen-

[18] Willem L. Graff, Language and Languages 41 (New York and London, 1932).

[19] Greek and Latin data are from E. H. Sturtevant, The Pronunciation of Greek and Latin[2]; Linguistic Society of America, 1940. The phonemic analysis of the Greek breath-types is G. L. Trager's.

tual phones which may be termed breath-types; they may be written respectively with /ʻ/ before the vowel and with zero. Syllable nuclei bearing the aspirate breath-type occurred in phrase-initial, after initial and medial /r/, after initial and medial /p, t, k, pt, kt/, and after /m, n, l, r/ when these were preceded by /p, t, k/. The phonetic influence of the aspirate breath-type on the vowel itself is not known. An initial aspirated vowel had an aspiration before it; a preceding /r/ was probably voiceless; preceding voiceless stop had aspirate release, even if /m, n, l, r/ or another voiceless stop intervened. Thus orthographic ὅστις, φώς, φλέξ, φράζω, θνῄσκω, φθάνω, ῥέω, θάῤῥος were phonemically /ʻóstis, pʻoás, plʻeks, prʻádsoa, tnʻeáiskoa, ptʻánoa, rʻéoa, tʻárrʻos/.[20]

There are two other possible analyses; one does not satisfy the criterion of pattern congruity so well, though it gives fewer phonemes, and the other, though it satisfies pattern congruity, gives several more phonemes. The first is to consider the aspiration as a separate segmental phone (which could be written /h/) wherever it occurs; this would require the recognition of such clusters as /phth/, for which there is no pattern at all. The other is to consider aspiration a separate segmental phone except where it accompanies the trill or a voiceless stop, and to set up as separate phonemes the classes of aspirated stops and trill—four additional phonemes. This is feasible because the dependent and the independent aspiration were probably β-phonetically distinct, though similar. The drawbacks to these two analyses lead one to accept instead the treatment first given above.

7.62 In the following examples a β-sound which is generally suprasegmental, or at least on the borderline, is treated as phonemically segmental.

In Winnebago there is a single consonant phoneme in each stop or spirant position, which is represented in different environments by phones with different β-phonetic features. The first member of a cluster of two obstruents (stop or spirant) is voiceless; if it is a stop it is aspirated unless followed by /h/. The second member of such a cluster, unless it is /ʔ/, is slightly voiced, unaspirated, and lenis. Thus /p, pt, h, ʔ, ph/ are [pʻ, pʻd, h, ʔ, p].[21] The crucial case is /pʔ/, β-phonetically [p'] (glottalized [p]): here two segmental phones correspond to two overlapping features.

20 The transcription of vowels represents the phonemic analysis by G. L. Trager and the writer; its correctness is irrelevant to the validity of these examples. The phonemic nature of zeta is not known.

21 Our traditional predilection for treating [p] as a unit and [pʻ] as a cluster can only lead us astray in dealing with Winnebago; for the former here patterns like a cluster, the latter like a unit phone, and the habitual voicing of the second member of clusters explains quite adequately how /pha/ is [pa]. A similar comment applies to the example immediately following.

In Takelma[22] there is a single set of stops and spirants, occurring initially, medially, and finally; clusters of two, including those with /h/ or /ʔ/ as first member, occur initially and medially, and those with /ʔ/ as first member occur finally. As first member of a cluster, a stop other than the glottal stop is aspirated (as is the latter in such a cluster in final position); as second member it is unaspirated and lenis. Thus /hp/ is [p], and /p/ is [pʻ]; /ʔp/ is [p'] initially and medially, [ʔʻpʻ] finally. Here again two overlapping features, glottalization and oral stop closure, are treated phonemically as segmental.

7.7 A suprasegmental phone has a *domain*, defined as the type of sequence of segmental phones which it covers. Thus the domain of English stresses and ancient Greek breath-types is the syllable nucleus. This does not mean that only phones of that particular group are β-phonetically affected, but that the limits of the β-phonetic influence of the suprasegmental phone can be described in each case in terms of the segmental phones involved. When the starting point of the influence, or its end point, is not so determinable, it may be called *determining*, and there must be some device in the phonemic orthography to record it.

The beginnings and endings of utterances, where there is by definition the β-phonetic feature of leaving a pause or starting one, are also characterized in some languages by special features, such as typical intonations, stresses, quantities, or other features of sonority. These same features are in some cases found within the utterances, accompanied by shorter pause or by none at all. The segmental and other suprasegmental phones adjacent to such points will be accompanied by these differences, and will not sound the same as they do elsewhere within utterances. Under such circumstances, the analytical principles will frequently demand that these accompanying features be extracted from their context and set up as independent suprasegmental phones. In other cases the same principles will lead instead to a greater differentiation of the other phones.

A suprasegmental phoneme is *junctural* if each member phone has a determining starting-point (or a determining end-point), and if either (1) every utterance begins (or ends) with a member of the phoneme, or (2) the phoneme is one of a contrastive set such that every utterance begins (or ends) with a phone which is a member of one of the phonemes of that set.

The fact that a junctural feature may be constant at the beginning or at the end of an utterance does not mean, according to the criterion of §5.1, that it is non-distinctive. For it occurs elsewhere in utterances, at points where it is not common to all the utterances of the range, and must therefore be regarded as distinctive wherever it is found.

22 Edward Sapir, Takelma (in Franz Boas, Handbook of American Indian Languages, vol. 2; Washington, 1922).

7.71 Winnebago syllabic nuclei consist of a single vowel or of a cluster of two vowels. Each nucleus occurs in two types, stressed and unstressed; the preceding consonants are also influenced by the stress, but this influence is determined, not determining. The vowels can be ranked in the order /i, u, e, o, a/; those to the right are 'stronger', those to the left 'weaker'. If a cluster of two phones has identical vowels, the distribution of stress, β-phonetically, is even; if the vowels are different, the stronger vowel—whatever the order of the two—bears the greater part of the stress. The nucleus types are thus /a, á, aa, áa/ (where /áa/ means the same as if we had written /aá/, i.e. /a͡a/), as in /hapé/ 'he waited for him', /haapé/ 'I waited for him', /hačhá/ 'he sees him', /hačháak/ 'he sees him moving about'; the domain of stress is the syllabic nucleus as a whole.

In classical Greek, on the other hand, where also the nuclei contain either one vowel or certain clusters of two or three, the domain of the accent (which α-phonetically may have been either stress or pitch, though probably it was the latter) was a single vowel. The nucleus types were /a, á, aa, áa, aá/, written α, ά, ᾱ, ᾶ, ᾱ́.

In some languages (perhaps Japanese) the situation is like that in ancient Greek except that both members of the nucleus may bear the accent, giving the nucleus types /a, á, aa, áa, aá, áá/.

7.72 The domain of an accentual phone is not necessarily nuclear. In Potawatomi[23] there are two contrasting accentual situations, which may be called fortis and lenis strength. The domain of fortis strength is a single obstruent (here /p, t, č, k, s, š/) or a cluster of two or more obstruents. The starting-point of influence is determined: it is the first obstruent of the group, preceded by the beginning of the phrase, by a vowel, or by a non-obstruent consonant. The end-point is determining, for /s·s/ and /ss·/ are different. A syllable beginning with a fortis obstruent or cluster is more strongly accented than one beginning with a lenis obstruent or cluster or with a non-obstruent consonant. In utterance-final there occur fortis non-syllabics, lenis obstruent non-syllabics, and non-obstruent non-syllabics, as well as vowels. Thus, although fortis strength has both nuclear and marginal β-phonetic effects in some positions, the fact that in phrase-final it has only marginal implications means that its domain is marginal. It is an accent, not a juncture, since it is not constant in phrase-final and since it does not belong to a contrastive set of which one member is found in every phrase-final.

7.73 There may be also accentual phones which have the entire syllable as domain; the tones of Chinese and Thai may belong here.

7.74 Junctural phones are not matters of grammatical segmentation, though a junctural situation may define phonological segments which are of grammatical significance. English examples will show the type of correlation that may exist; in the following transcriptions[24] a juncture phone that might be called 'drawl release' is indicated by a hyphen: syntax /síntàks/ : tin-tacks /tín-tàks/; mistake /mistéjk/ : Miss Tait /mîs-téjt/ : missed eight /mîst-éjt/ : misstate /mîs-stéjt/; psychological /sàjkəwláhǰikəl, sàjkəláhǰikəl/ : psycho-logical /sâjkəw-láhǰikəl/; minus /májnəs/: slyness /sláj-nəs/; conquered /káhŋkərd/ : Concord (place-name) /káhŋ-kərd/; aboard /əbórd/ : a board /ə-bórd/.

7.75 In Czech there seem to be three independent junctural phones: pause, here written with zero, since it occurs before the beginning of the phrase; loud stress, here written with a raised tick; and point of onset of stress, here written with a space. All three are found at the beginning of an utterance; the second and the third together are found at some points within utterances; and the third alone, without the loud stress, is found infrequently at points within the segment between two loud stresses. Orthographic nevíme o tom ani vy ani já 'we do not know that, neither you nor I' may be transcribed as /ˈne vjiime ˈo tom ˈanji ˈvi ˈanji ˈjaa/.[25]

7.76 Our phonetic information for Latin is defective, but it seems quite possible that the stress in early classical Latin was not an accent but part of a junctural phone. It can be located mechanically if certain borders are assumed. Grammatically these borders are clear, but without adequate material it is impossible to tell whether they were also phonological or not. In later times, however, when such words as vīgintī, trīgintā, audīt, adhūc no longer followed the penultimate rule, we may be certain that the stress was an accent, as it was in Vulgar Latin and is in those Romance languages which maintain it.

7.8 Sometimes when a β-sound contrasts with the absence of that sound, the absence is phonemically simply zero; in other cases it also is a phone, of the same structural class as the presence of the β-sound. The interpretation depends on the presence or absence of parallelism in the function of the two. The two features of shortness and length in Old English (§7.33) parallel each other in their function, and so if either is an accent, both are. In ancient Greek

[23] Potawatomi data are from the writer's notes.

[24] The phonemic transcription of English here used, including the marking of stress and juncture, follows the practice described by Trager and Bloch (fn. 17). An acute accent over a vowel symbol denotes the loud stress, a circumflex the reduced loud, a grave the medial; absence of a mark denotes the weak stress.

[25] A. Mazon, Grammaire de la langue tchèque; Paris, 1921. The cited phrase occurs in §161; stress is discussed in §6. The transcription given here is certainly erroneous on several points, but the junctural indications are probably correct. The writer has not heard Czech himself.

(§7.61) aspiration and its absence parallel each other, with differences; both are accents. Winnebago stress does not parallel the absence of stress: every utterance contains a stress, but some do not contain any unstressed nuclei; therefore the stress is an accent, its absence is not. The pitch (or stress) of classical Greek is a similar case. In Potawatomi the fortis strength has a determining end-point, but the lenis strength does not; only the former is an accent.

7.9 One of the types of segmental features which it is easy to overlook is hiatus. Hiatus is not α-phonetic zero, nor need it be non-distinctive; if it is distinctive it may be a phone, not simply the absence of a phone.

7.91 In Potawatomi the absence of a consonant in phrase-initial and certain positions within the phrase patterns like the presence of a consonant. This absence of a consonant is describable α-phonetically as consisting sometimes of hiatus, or point of sharp syllable division, sometimes of a glottal stop. Because of its patterning, this must be set up as a consonantal phone.

In German there is a similar 'absence of a consonant' which often is α-phonetically a glottal stop, but sometimes just point of onset of stress. But in German this distinctive feature turns out to be part of a junctural phone, not a segmental phone in itself.

In English the same thing exists, with the same analysis as in German; α-phonetically there is the difference that the 'absence of a consonant' is much less frequently a glottal stop, more frequently just point of onset of stress.

7.92 A good case of relevant hiatus is found in Delaware.[26] Here there is a consonantal phone which may be written /ˀ/, since there is no contrasting glottal stop, and which patterns like Delaware /h/. These two occur initially before a vowel and medially between vowels, and the latter also occurs in a medial geminate cluster. Both occur as first members of clusters when the second member is a stop. In all these positions /h/ is [h]. Initially and medially /ˀ/ is hiatus; before a stop it is a short phase of closure at the point of articulation of the stop that follows, so that /ˀp/ is [p·]. The preaspirated and long stops occur only medially, and they are the only medial non-syllabics (except /hh/) which cannot be divided into an occurrent final plus an occurrent initial. This suggests that these two sets of non-syllabics have parallel structures. It is not possible to analyze the long stops as geminates, because various real geminates occur initially and medially, doubly released in the case of stops. No other analysis than the one here given conforms to pattern congruity, except by the introduction of many more phonemes. The parallelism between /ˀ/ and /h/ is disturbed only by the presence of the cluster /hh/.

It is also quite possible that hiatus in Sanskrit, between words and within such words as títaü 'sieve' and práüga 'wagon-pole', was a phone, not the absence of a phone. This would add one consonantal phoneme, but would give only three vowels and clear patterns, instead of a larger number of vowel phonemes and obscure patterns. There are problems which must still be solved; but if Sanskrit hiatus was a phone, we may write /títaˀu, práˀuga/, vrīhi-yavāu 'rice and barley' /uriihiiauaau/, and the like.[27]

26 Observed by the writer in a class under C. F. Voegelin at the Linguistic Institute of 1939. Voegelin's orthography for Delaware is quite unambiguous and therefore perfectly satisfactory for the collection of texts, though it does not agree with the present analysis.

8.1 A feature which characterizes all the members of a phoneme is determining for that phoneme; a feature which characterizes all the members of some allophone, but not all the members of the phoneme which includes that allophone, is determined. Thus, every English /t/ is fortis, apical, a stop, and non-nasal; these features are determining. In phrase-inital position, /t/ is voiceless and aspirated; these are determined. In phrase-final position it is sometimes aspirated, sometimes unreleased; these features in this position may be called indeterminate.

8.11 A single feature may be determining for one set of phones, determined or indeterminate for others. In Spanish, for example, nasalization is determining for /m, n, ñ/, since these phones are always nasalized; determined for the /o/ of conscribir 'to conscript', since /o/ in that position is always nasalized, but not elsewhere; and indeterminate for the /a/ of mano 'hand', since /a/ in that position (between two nasal consonants) is sometimes nasalized, sometimes not.

8.12 In §7.7 the word 'determining' was used in connection with the limits of the domain of a suprasegmental phone. It had there the technical meaning here assigned to it. The starting-point of the β-phonetic influence of fortis strength in Potawatomi is not constant. In /nos·/ 'my father' the fortisness begins and ends with the same segmental phone; in /ˀesp·ən/ 'raccoon' it begins with the /s/ and ends with the /n/. But the starting-point can always be predicted in terms of the sequence of segmental phones involved, and is therefore determined. The end-point of the β-phonetic influence cannot be so predicted. But it can be predicted in terms of an assigned end-point of the domain of fortisness; this is constant by definition, and therefore determining.

8.2 The relation between determining and determined features is one of two kinds; the distinction is a practical one, concerning the method by which the various features can be most simply presented.

27 Whitney, Skt. Gr.[5] §§125b, 329f, 338e, 353a. Some rule must be establishable, of course, to tell exactly when /u/ or /r/ will be consonantal and when vocalic. If it is impossible to discover such a rule, then the proposed analysis cannot be accepted.

8.21 In certain cases a determining feature is a matter of clear-cut alternatives: Spanish /d/ is either a stop, as in phrase-initial *dar* 'give', *condenar* 'condemn', *Aldaba*, or else it is a frictionless spirant, as in *ayudar* 'assist', *sed* 'thirst'. In this case the terms of the contrast must be given, along with the circumstances under which each term is found. The determining feature is that Spanish /d/ is a lenis obstruent; the determined feature is that it is a stop in a particular position, a frictionless spirant in another position.

8.22 In other cases the determining feature is a general area, and the precise point within the area which is hit by a particular phone is determined, but the listing of all the points is difficult or impossible. Thus Spanish /k/ occurs in phrase-initial before all the vowels and before /r, l/; in phrase-medial after any vowel or certain consonants, and before any vowel or certain other consonants; and in phrase-final at least after /a/. Each of the positions defines an allophone. The members of the different allophones vary over a relatively small area of points of articulation, and the areas of the different allophones intersect. The facts are covered adequately by stating that the general position is dorsal and that the exact position varies within certain extreme limits according to the adjacent phones—more fronted next to front vowels, further back next to back vowels, neutral next to consonants.

But it is essential to include this blanket statement; the variation cannot be taken for granted. In Potawatomi, /k/ varies much like the Spanish phone just discussed, but over a much smaller range; the accommodation of the point of contact to the articulatory positions of adjacent sounds is less than it is in Spanish. In Nootka, where there are two distinct dorsal stop positions, giving /k, q/, the phone which varies is not the consonant but the vowel, very strikinly in the case of /i/.

8.3 Determining features can be classified according to the phones in which they occur. In English, bilabial articulation is a determining feature for three consonants, /p, b, m/; /p/ has fortis quality as another determining feature, which is shared by /t, č, k, f, θ, s, š/; /p/ is a stop, as are /b, t, d, č, ǰ, k, g/. Such an inventory could continue until all the determining features had been considered.

8.31 An ideal diagram of the determining features would have as many dimensions as there are such features; if the total number of dimensions is N, then any N-minus-one-dimensional cross section of the diagram will include all those phones which share a particular feature. This can be illustrated for sixteen English consonants by setting two such cross sections side by side (with diagonal brackets omitted for convenience):

p t č k	b d ǰ g
f θ s š	v ð z ž

Those in the same flat cross section have the same strength (fortis or lenis); those in the same vertical plane have the same point of contact; those in the same horizontal plane have the same manner of articulation (stop or spirant).

8.32 Phones in a single line in a diagram that is so arranged constitute the member of a **minimal contrast**—minimal in that only one determining feature is different in the set. The **context** of the contrast is the complex of determining features that are shared by the set. In a particular context—that is, in any particular straight line in the diagram—there may be any number of members of the contrast: a contrast is bipolar, tripolar, and so on. Position of articulation in English, for stops, constitutes a quadripolar contrast: /p, t, č, k/. Strength, for stops, constitutes a bipolar contrast, e.g. /p, b/.

Non-minimal contrasts are those involving more than a single determining feature. **Direct** contrasts are those between phones which share some determining feature, e.g. /p : f/; indirect contrasts those between phones which share no determining feature, e.g. /p/ and loud stress.

8.33 It is the survey of the participation of determining features in phones that classifies those features in the way suggested by such name as 'point of articulation', 'strength', 'manner of articulation', and so on. Sometimes a set of determining features belongs to a single class of this kind when from the α-phonetic point of view they seem to have no relation. This is probably true of lenis strength, fortis-aspirated strength, and glottalization for stops in Navaho.

8.34 The suborganization of phones in different contexts need not be parallel. In the diagram given above, the organization in the fortis plane and that in the lenis plane are parallel, but the organization in the stop plane and in the spirant plane is not: different points of contact are involved. Vowel articulation and consonant articulation are contrasting determining features in English; but the subdivision in the consonant cross section of the total diagram is nothing at all like that in the vocalic cross section.

8.35 If one flattens out the ideal multi-dimensional diagram of determining features and phones, so that it appears as a series of two-dimensional tables, the result is a phonologically accurate diagram which superficially resembles the more haphazard 'tables of sounds' to be found in many of the older treatises on specific languages, in Trubetzkoy's Grundzüge der Phonologie, and elsewhere.

9.1 When determining features are classified according to their participation in phones, the result is also a classification of phones according to the determining features which characterize them. This classification is a matter of β-phonetics.

9.2 The structural classification of phones and phonemes is based on the principle that two phonemes belong in a single structural class if their member phones occur in similar environments. Every possible environment forms a test.

9.21 Spanish segmental phones may serve as an example. The vowels /i, e, a, o, u/ are distinguished from the consonants in constituting the domain of the stress; /i, u/ are distinguished from the other vowels in being sometimes syllabic, sometimes not, whereas the others are always syllabic; /i/ forms a class by itself in that it does not occur unstressed after /ñ, ʎ, j/ before a vowel. Of the consonants, /r/ forms a class by itself in that it does not occur in utterance-initial; /p, t, k, b, d, g, f/ occur before /r/ in the same syllable, the other consonants do not; /p, k, b, g, f/ occur before /l/ in the same syllable; /t, k, b, d, θ, s, n, r/ occur in utterance-final. And so forth.

9.22 The structural classification of phonemes in Spanish shows very little correlation with the β-phonetic classification of the phones. Thus /p, t, k, b, d, g, f/, which form a structurally defined set, include the voiceless stops except /č/, the lenis obstruents except /j/, and one member only of the fortis spirants. The set of occurrent finals /t, k, b, d, θ, s, n, r/ includes miscellaneous members of several β-phonetic groups.

A similar situation exists in English. The β-phonetic contrast between /f/ and /v/ is minimal, while that between /f/ and /ð/ is not minimal, though direct. But the structural contrast between /f/ and /v/ is entirely comparable to that between /f/ and /ð/: /f/ participates in initial clusters, while the other two do not; /f/ occurs before /t, s/ in final clusters, /v/ and /ð/ only before /d, z/. Other structural facts show the same relation.[28]

In some languages there is a much closer connection between β-phonetic groupings and structural groupings. In Polish and German, for instance, the voiceless obstruents occur in final position, the voiced obstruents do not.[29]

10. This completes the presentation of the principles of phonology. There are three comments to be made about phonology as a whole.

10.1 The criteria for grammatical classification are (1) recognition of morpheme, word, and construction, and of the borders between them, (2) the phonemic shape of morphemes, words, and constructions, and (3) biosocial function, or meaning. The third is used in determining the first. The branch of grammar which deals with the phonemic shape of morphemes, words, and constructions, without regard to their meaning, is <u>morphophonemics</u>.

[28] See the exhaustive structural classification of English non-syllabics in Bloomfield's Language 131–4 (New York, 1933). Bloomfield establishes 38 overlapping sets defined by the occurrence of consonants singly and in clusters.

[29] G. L. Trager, La Systématique des phonèmes du polonais, Acta Linguistica 1.179–88 (1939).

It is important to recognize that the criterion of biosocial function used in grammar is not at all the same as the criterion of biosocial equivalence used in phonology. The latter involves only the observation of whether two situations are the same in general outline, whereas the former involves extensive analysis of situations. There is no circularity; no grammatical fact of any kind is used in making phonological analysis.

From these definitions it follows that phonological analysis is necessary, though not sufficient, for the completion of grammatical analysis. Grammatical work is carried on, of course, in cases where phonological information is incomplete, either slightly deficient as it is for Old English, or sadly inadequate as for ancient Egyptian. But many of the gaps and ambiguities in such grammar have their source directly in the lack of complete phonemicization, and the recognition of that fact clarifies the issue as much as it can be clarified.

10.2 It has not been proved that the phonological system presented in this paper is the correct one, or even that there is just one correct phonology. The writer has attempted to satisfy the six requirements which seem essential for a correct system, but which no other system that he knows of completely fulfills. (1) Range and criteria must be accurately and unambiguously defined. (2) There must be no mentalism. (3) The terminology must involve no logical contradictions; terms defined as variables, class names, and quality names must be consistently used in those values. (4) No material should be excluded which might prove to be of grammatical importance, and none should be included which cannot be of grammatical importance. (5) There must be no circularity; phonological analysis is assumed for grammatical analysis, and so must not assume any part of the latter. The line of demarcation between the two must be sharp. (6) The way should be left open for the introduction of any criteria whatsoever on the grammatical level, barring mentalism.

10.3 Analytical procedure is a trial-and-error process, in which the analyst makes successive approximations. He gathers phonological and grammatical material at the same time, though he may emphasize now one, now the other. He makes errors of omission and commission, and later corrects them. At certain stages he may work by 'feelings', but later he substitutes rigorous criteria. Finally the correct statement of the material emerges. In this, the organization depends on what is most efficient for the particular language concerned; if the source material is a body of written records, the very defects of the record may condition the order of presentation.

Thus neither the process of analysis, nor the presentation of the results of analysis, need resemble the general picture of phonology given in this paper. The system given here is a <u>frame of reference</u>. If the analyst operates constantly in terms of such a frame, being careful not to confuse the distinctions made in it, and using terms in logically valid ways, the resulting description is the clear-cut, efficient statement of facts which a classificatory science requires.

⟦It is doubtful whether the matter will ever command enough interest from non-linguists to attract any expert historical research worker; but if it does, there may yet be a fascinating history written on what our linguists did as their peculiar contribution to what was called 'the war effort' beginning about the time of this paper. The most visible result is a couple of dozen sets of books, with phonograph records, for learning various languages. First made for the government, these became commercial publications after the war, and their royalties are mostly being used to support linguistics today, for instance by making the publication of the present book possible. A substantial portion of these royalties is currently being used, aside from the main purpose of supporting research, for grants in support of study at the Linguistic Institute of the Linguistic Society each summer. There is a certain justice in this, for it was just such grants, made from foundation funds, which before the war sent many young students to the Institutes and thus substantially helped to build up the number of linguists who could be called on to do that wartime work.

Before the war it was still possible to wonder what all those apprentice linguists could be used for —it was still commonly said that a linguistic student had better have a Brotwissenschaft too. Still, there was not yet any threatening over-supply, or at least not enough to dampen the enthusiasm which was then as characteristic of young linguistics students as it still is. Thus Hockett's paper was by no means such an attempt to freeze doctrine as can appear in the maturity of a science. It was a stock-taking and a report which can serve to show where phonological thought stood at the time but does not show that it had halted there. To readers who were not aware of what interchange and communal development it had come out of, this paper may have seemed 'radical'—that is, private or even irresponsible. It was neither; it was, with all credit to Hockett's originality as to this or that detail, and to his skill and personal way of putting the case, simply what Bloomfieldian phonemics was pretty sure to develop into through those years of discussion. Very little of that discussion had so far been reflected in print, which accounts for the shock effect of this publication.

In the hothouse atmosphere of the wartime work, American linguistic theory was to develop far more swiftly than it had before. At first there was little time to write for professional publication, and the supply of paper was restricted too. But after the war, fully a quarter of the content of this collection was published in two years, making a picture very different from that of a decade earlier. Hockett's phonemics, for example, was noticeably different then from what it had been in 1942.

But the historical importance of the 1942 System is by no means merely an antiquarian importance, for it represents what the wartime developments had for their source and the point of reference for their departures. It is true that the source and point of reference is in certain respects better represented by Bloch and Trager's Outline of Linguistic Analysis of 1942, which is today still in such demand as to require repeated reprinting. Yet the Hockett paper is a better representative in other respects, because of a certain yeastiness which helps us to understand the way things were fermenting then: the Outline is too settled and clarified for that.

For obviating unnecessary misunderstandings it is worth while to try here to characterize at least one departure from the 1942 position: the one that has given us what might as well be called 'phonemics without the phoneme'. I may be mistaken (here as well as elsewhere), but I have the impression that the term 'phonemics' became popular in America as a token of independence from European 'phonology'. And from what little I know of the workings of the human brain, I shouldn't be surprised if it turned out that this American choice was responsible for the tendency later on to use the term 'phoneme' in spots where it was, strictly, unnecessary, perhaps even inappropriate. The drift after 1942 was in the direction of making this term gratuitous. To follow along with Hockett, although he was not alone in this, in his 1947 Peiping Phonology §7 he spoke of 'symbols for inclosure between solidi' ⟨⟨221⟩⟩, and in his 1950 Peiping Morphophonemics ⟨⟨315⟩⟩ some of these were replaced by a differently segmented set, with no statement in either place to the effect that 'phonemes' were being represented one-for-one by symbols; finally, in his 1955 A Manual of Phonology he completes an immediate-constituent analysis of Fox consonantal clusters and then comments (163): 'Now is /č/ a unit phoneme or a cluster? We have not used the term "phoneme" in our IC analysis, since we do not know where [i. e., at what stage] to introduce it.'

In the present 1942 paper, the dominance of the term 'phoneme' is a matter of course, and nothing is allowed to seem vague in immediate context with it. The vagueness in the argument appears rather in earlier paragraphs, where the segmentation into 'sounds' is not so much logically justified as taken for granted. Today it is even considered possible to defend the thesis that such segmentation can't be done strictly until after phonemic segmentation has been somehow (say distributionally) established.

There is no error here and no correction. In 1942 Hockett codified good analytic practice into theory; the later discussion pattern simply makes the theory independent of the accidents of analytic practice.⟧

MORPHEME ALTERNANTS IN LINGUISTIC ANALYSIS

ZELLIG S. HARRIS

Language 18.169-80—1942

The purpose of this paper is to suggest a technique for determining the morphemes of a language, as rigorous as the method used now for finding its phonemes. The proposed technique differs only in details of arrangement from the methods used by linguists today. However, these small differences suffice to simplify the arrangement of grammars.

THE PRESENT TREATMENT OF MORPHEMES

1.0 In essence, the present treatment uses the following criterion: Every sequence of phonemes which has meaning, and which is not composed of smaller sequences having meaning, is a morpheme.[1] Different sequences of phonemes constitute different morphemes; occurrences of the same sequence with sufficiently different meanings constitute homonyms.

In some cases, this criterion dissociates certain morphemes which we wish, because of the grammatical structure, to unite. Various methods are used at present to get around this contradiction. In cases 1-3 below, different sequences of phonemes are considered as different forms of the same morpheme. In cases 4-5, sequences of phonemes are called not morphemes but processes and the like. In case 6, a special relation is seen between different morphemes.

1.1 Tübatulabal[2] puw 'to irrigate', u·buw 'he irrigated' would have to be analyzed as containing different morphemes, since the phoneme sequence /puw/ does not occur in the second word. Similarly, pələ·la 'to arrive', ə·bələ·la 'he arrived'; for every morpheme which begins with a voiced stop after a prefix there is a similar morpheme beginning with the homorganic voiceless stop in word-initial. In spite of the phonemic difference between the members of each of these pairs, we wish to consider each pair a single morpheme, since in other cases we have a single morpheme in the position of both members of these pairs: wə·ʔin 'to pour', ə·wə·ʔin 'he poured'. We say that there is a regular alternation in the language: a voiced stop is replaced by the homorganic voiceless stop in word-initial.

Similarly, Early Hebrew[3] has ró·š 'head', ro·šó· 'his head', but máwt 'death', mo·tó· 'his death'. Since unstressed /aw/ never occurs before a consonant, we say that it is regularly replaced by /o·/.

1.2 We would also have to say that there are different morphemes in knife and knives. However, the connection between these is too obvious to be disregarded in the grammar, and the difference occurs also in several other pairs: wives, but strifes. We therefore create a morphophonemic symbol, say /F/, which represents /v/ before /-z/ 'plural' and /f/ elsewhere, and say that there is but one English morpheme /najF/. Or we give a morphophonemic formula: /f/ is replaced by /v/ before /-z/ 'plural' in the following morphemes—knive, wife, ...

The use of morphophonemic statements or symbols is however of little use in the next case, and of no use in cases 4-6.

1.3 By the criterion of §1.0, Heb. ʿi·r 'city' and ʿa·ri·m 'cities' contain different morphemes.[4] Since the difference between ʿi·r and ʿa·r- is not found between other morphemes with identical meanings, it seems awkward to state it in a morphophonemic formula: /i/ is replaced by /a/ in ʿi·r before -i·m. Some linguists have called such pairs morpholexical alternants of one morpheme.[5]

1.4 In Greek ménō 'I remain', meménēka 'I have remained', lúō 'I loose', léluka 'I have loosed', the meaning of the reduplication is the same in all cases, but the phonemic sequences vary so much that they are not commonly considered to constitute a single morpheme. Instead, reduplication is often called a morphological process, a special kind of affix, and the like.

1.5 Much the same is true of vowel changes which correlate with meaning changes. They cannot be expressed by morphophonemic formulas, since these formulas state the alternate forms of a single morpheme, whereas take and took are not the same morpheme, having different meanings. Such vowel changes are usually described as special kinds of morphological modification, though they may alternate with additive suffixes like -ed 'past time'.

1.6 There remain cases of morphemes which complement each other but are entirely dissimilar in their phonemic sequences: am, are, is, be, etc. These are considered different morphemes, but with a special mutual relation of suppletion.

[1] L. Bloomfield, Language 161 (New York, 1933).

[2] M. Swadesh and C. F. Voegelin, A problem in phonological alternation, Lang. 15.4 ((89)) (1939).

[3] Z. S. Harris, Linguistic structure of Hebrew, JAOS 61.155 (1941).

[4] Ibid. 159.

[5] L. Bloomfield, Menomini morphophonemics, TCLP 8.105 (1939).

PROPOSED TREATMENT OF MORPHEMES

2.0 It is proposed here to arrange the morphemes of a language more clearly by carrying out rigorously three linguistic procedures, the first and third of which are in common use today.

2.1 We divide each expression in the given language into the smallest sequences of phonemes which have what we consider the same meaning when they occur in other expressions, or which are left over when all other parts of the expression have been divided off. This is identical with the criterion of §1.0. The resultant minimum parts we call not morphemes, but morpheme alternants.

It is useful to generalize this definition of morpheme alternant by taking sequence to mean not only additive sequence (the addition of phonemes), but also zero (the addition of no phonemes), negative sequence (the dropping of a phoneme), and phonemic component sequence (the addition of a physiological feature of phonemes). In He cut it there is a zero morpheme meaning 'past time' after cut. In Hidatsa, we have a minus morpheme, consisting of dropping the final vowel mora, with the meaning of command:[6] cixic 'he jumped', cix 'jump!', ika·c 'he looked', ika 'look!'. In took we have two morphemes: take, and /ej/ ~ /u/ 'past time'. The latter occurs also in shook as compared to shake. It is a combination of negative and additive sequences: dropping /ej/ and adding /u/. Another negative-additive morpheme is /a/ ~ /e/ 'plural', which occurs in men as compared to man. Lastly, we have a phonemic component morpheme in to believe, to house, etc., if we wish to divide these words into belief, house, etc. plus a morpheme consisting of voicing the final consonant and having the grammatical meaning 'verb'.

As in the case of ordinary additive morphemes, zero and the others can be recognized only by comparison with other morphemes. Thus in deciding whether to recognize a minus morpheme in Hidatsa we are faced with the following choice: Consider cixic, ika·c, also kikuac 'he set a trap', kiku 'set a trap!'. If we call cix, ika, kiku single morphemes (functioning both as stems and as command), then the morphemes meaning '(he) did' would be ic, ·c, ac, etc. We would have no way of indicating which of these forms occurs after each stem except by listing all the stems. Linguistic procedure chooses the simpler arrangement: it considers the stems to be cixi, ika·, kikua, and the suffix always -c. Then the command form must be analyzed as having two morphemes, the stem plus the dropping of the last mora.[7]

Note that at this stage of the analysis every element, here called morpheme alternant, has only one sequence of phonemes: knife and knive- are two separate morpheme alternants.

2.2 From the list of morpheme alternants which results from the preceding step, we take any two or more alternants which have what we consider the same meaning (but different phonemes) and no one of which ever occurs in the same environment as the others.[8] The two or more alternants which meet these conditions are grouped together into a single morpheme unit: am, which occurs only in phrases with I, and are, which never occurs with I, are put into one morpheme unit. In many cases when we take one alternant and try to find another to group with it, we fail: e.g. in the case of walk, rain. In such cases we say that the single alternant constitutes a morpheme unit by itself. A morpheme unit is thus a group of one or more alternants which have the same meaning and complementary distribution. To make these units more similar to our present morphemes, and more serviceable for grammatical structure, we now add a further condition: In units consisting of more than one alternant, the total distribution of all the alternants (i.e. the combined range of environments in which each of them occurs) must equal the range of environments in which some unit with but a single alternant occurs. Thus the combined environments of am, are, be are included in the environments in which walk occurs: I am, they are, to be, compared with I walk, they walk, to walk. The case is different with twenty and score, even though they have the same meaning and never occur in the same environment.[9] For there is no morpheme unit in English which consists of only one alternant and which occurs in the combined distribution of twenty and score. Therefore, we consider the alternants am, are, be as being members of a single morpheme unit; but of the alternants twenty and score, each constitutes a morpheme unit by itself.

A few examples of alternants which can be grouped together into units: knife and knive-: knive- occurs only before /-z/ 'plural', knife never does; the sum of the positions in which both occur equals the range of positions in which the single alternant fork occurs.

go and wen-: wen- only before -t 'past', go never; walk occurs in both positions.

/-əz/ (only after alternants ending in /s, š, č, z, ž, ǰ/ but not after all of these), /-s/ (only after alternants ending in the other voiceless phonemes), /-z/ (only after alternants ending in the other voiced phonemes), /-ən/ (after ox), zero (after sheep), /a/ ~ /e/ (with man), etc., meaning 'plural'; the total

[6] R. H. Lowie, Z. S. Harris, and C. F. Voegelin, Hidatsa Texts, Indiana Historical Society Prehistory Research Series 1.192 fn. 38 (1939).

[7] Cf. Bloomfield, Language 217, where it is shown that the relation between masculine and feminine adjectives in French can be most simply described by regarding the feminine forms as basic.

[8] This excludes synonyms, i.e. morphemes of approximately similar meaning, which usually occur in the same positions: a fine youngster, a fine lad.

[9] As in a score of voices, but twenty voices. However, we may consider that twenty occurs in the same position as score in a twenty 'a $20 bill'.

range of environments equals that of zero 'singular', the suffix -ful, and other single-alternant morpheme units.

/-əz, -s, -z/ (all these in the same environments as above), zero (only after the /-əz, -s, -z/ alternants of 'plural'), and no more, all meaning 'possessed by' or the like.

/-əd, -t, -d/, zero (after cut, set, etc.), /ej/ ∼ /u/ (with take, etc.), and several other alternants, 'past'; no two of these occur after the same alternant, and the combined environments in which they all occur equals the distribution of -s '3rd sg. pres.'

One might ask why it is necessary to perform this step formally, instead of merely recognizing that various suffixes (e.g. -ed) have occasional variant (suppletive) forms like vowel change (e.g. /ej/ ∼ /u/), or that reduplication is an affix having special phonetic similarity to its stem. The drawback in the latter method is that it tells both the special form and the morphological status of the affixes at the same time. This makes it difficult to treat these two features separately, to discuss the special forms together with the special forms of other stems and suffixes (i.e. with the other groupings of alternants), and to discuss the morphological status on the same plane as the morphological status of affixes which do not have special forms. In the proposed method, reduplication is described as a group of morpheme alternants, grouped into a unit, between whose members a particular kind of difference exists; the status of these alternants in the morphology is irrelevant here and would be discussed in the section dealing with the relations between morpheme units.

2.3 We now have a list of morpheme units. We take each unit which consists of more than one alternant, and note the difference between its alternants. If we find another morpheme unit having an identical difference between its alternants, we can describe both units together. Thus the difference between knife and knive-, which make up one unit, is identical with the difference between wife and wive-, which make up another, and with the difference between leaf and leave-, and so on. Instead of listing both members of each unit, we now list only one representative of each unit with a general statement of the difference which applies to all of them: Each of the units knife, wife, ..., has an alternant with /v/ instead of /f/ before /-z/ 'plural'.

In cases like this we can readily see that the units in question have identical relations between their alternants. In other cases it is far more difficult to see that the difference between alternants is identical in various units. For example, in Tübatulabal there are many units whose alternants differ in length of vowel: ya·yaŋ 'to be timid', after the reduplication morpheme (which means 'past time') -yayaŋ; ta·wək 'to see', after reduplication -dawə·g-; but pələ·la 'to arrive', after reduplication -bələ·la; the reduplication vowel, too, is short before some morphemes, long before others. Swadesh and Voegelin[10] showed that a general statement can be made for all these differences in vowel length. They first investigated each morpheme unit to see whether any of its vowels had basic length or basic shortness. A vowel is here said to have basic length if it is long in all the alternants of the unit:[11] e.g. the second /ə/ in pələ·la. A vowel has basic shortness if it is short in all the alternants of the unit:[12] e.g. the second /a/ in ya·yaŋ. Vowels which do not have basic length or shortness may be called neutral. Then the general statement is: In every morpheme alternant, counting from the beginning of the word, every odd-numbered vowel which is neutral is long, and every even-numbered vowel which is neutral is short.[13] The length of the neutral vowels in each alternant of any particular unit is therefore determined by the number of vowels which precede the alternant within the same word: in ta·wək the first neutral vowel of the morpheme is the first vowel of the word, and therefore long; in a·-dawə·g- the same first neutral vowel of the morpheme is the second vowel of the word, hence short. As a result of this general statement, it is no longer necessary to list the alternants which differ in vowel length.[14] We merely indicate which vowels of each unit have basic length or shortness.

In the case of some morpheme units, the difference between the alternants is expressed in two or more general statements: e.g. the difference in consonants between ta·wək and -dawə·g- is expressed in the statement that all morphemes with voiced stops have alternants with voiceless stop when the stop is at word boundary, while the difference in vowel length was expressed above.

THE RESULTANT ANALYSIS

3.0 We can now describe the six cases of §1.1–6 as being all particular instances of one general operation.

3.1 The Tüb. alternants puw and -buw, both 'irrigate', are grouped together into one morpheme unit. For the first alternant occurs only at word initial, the second never; and the total range of positions in which both occur equals that of the single-alternant unit hu·da 'to be up (sun)'. Similarly, Heb. máwt and mo·t-´, both 'death', are grouped into one unit (compare ró·š and ro·š-´ 'head').

10 Language 15.5 ff. (1939). The formulation presented here is a restatement, in terms of morpheme alternants, of their morphophonemic analysis.

11 Or if it is always short when each of its neighboring vowels is either always long or always short.

12 Unless it is next to a basically long vowel, in which position even a neutral vowel is always short.

13 But a neutral vowel next to one with basic length is always short.

14 Certain additional general statements involving /ʔ/, etc., must be applied before the statement about vowel length.

3.2 knive and knive- satisfy the condition for composing one unit.

3.3 Heb. ʿi·r and ʿa·r- 'city' are grouped into one unit: ʿa·r- occurs only before -i·m 'plural', ʿi·r never; the combined positions of both equal the positions in which su·s 'horse' occurs.

3.4 Greek me, le, and other reduplication prefixes, meaning 'perfect aspect', are alternants of one morpheme unit: me occurs only before morphemes beginning with /m/, le only before those beginning with /l/, and so on (with other alternants before special types of morphemes); the combined range of environments of all these alternants equals the range of the e- verb prefix (augment). A similar case is that of the echo words in the languages of India. Thus, in Kota,[15] puǰ is 'tiger', puǰ-qiǰ is 'any tiger'; kaḷṇ is 'thief', kaḷṇ-qiḷṇ is 'some thief'. qiǰ, qiḷṇ, and the other echo-words have the same meaning; qiǰ occurs only after morphemes of the form CVǰ, qiḷṇ only after morphemes of the form CVḷṇ, and so on. The combined range of positions of all these echo words beginning with qi is equal to the range of any single alternant which occurs as second member in compounds and which (unlike the echo words) is not restricted to particular first members. We therefore group all these echo words into one morpheme unit with the meaning 'any, some, and the like', and say that the general form of the unit is qiX, where X is whatever follows the initial CV of the first member of the compound.

3.5 The form took is divided into take plus /ej/ ∾ /u/; /ej/ ∾ /u/ is an alternant which is grouped with /d/ and other alternants into a morpheme unit meaning 'past time', since they all satisfy the conditions for such grouping.

3.6 The forms am, are, be, i- (before /z/ '3d sg. pres.'), -as, -ere (both after w-, which is an alternant grouped with /d/ 'past time') are all grouped into one morpheme unit.

4.0 It is not enough to show that all such relations between alternants are special cases of one relation, namely that between the alternants of one morpheme unit. For there are differences between these cases, and we must see if it is possible to arrange these differences systematically as subdivisions of the operation of grouping alternants into units. It appears that we can record these differences in a simple manner if each time we group alternants into one unit we answer four questions: 1. What is the difference between the alternants of this unit? 2. In what environments does each alternant occur? 3. What similarity is there, if any, between the alternant and the environment? 4. What morpheme units have this difference between their alternants?

[15] M. B. Emeneau, An Echo-Word Motif in Dravidian Folk Tales, JAOS 58.553–70 (1938); Echo Words in Toda, New Indian Antiquary 1.109–17 (1938).

4.1 The difference between the alternants. In some morpheme units the alternants are the same except for one or two phonemes: e.g. the cases in §3.1–3. In other units there are many alternants, all (or most) having some phonemic structure in common: e.g. the reduplication alternants in §3.4 have the form Ce. In both cases we say that the alternants differ in only part of their phonemic sequence. In other units, however, such as in §3.5–6, the alternants differ entirely.

4.2 The environment in which each alternant occurs. When a morpheme unit occurs in a given context, the alternant which appears there is determined by the environment of neighboring alternants. Each alternant of that unit occurs only in the neighborhood of particular other alternants; and often, if we investigate each of the morphemes in whose neighborhood the given alternant occurs, we will find that there is a common feature to all of them.

However, we will find that it is not enough to say that there is a common feature to all the environments in which a particular alternant occurs. It is not enough to say that all the environments in which /-əz/ 'plural' occurs have a common feature, namely that they all end in a sibilant or affricate. For while it is true that every time we have /-əz/ we find before it a morpheme ending in /s, š, č, z, ž, ǰ/, e.g. fox, foxes, the statement seems to be false when we consider ox, oxen. Since ox ends in /s/ we might have expected the /-əz/ alternant to occur after it. The catch lies in this: that every time /-əz/ occurs it has a morpheme ending in a sibilant or affricate before it, but not every morpheme ending in a sibilant or affricate has the /-əz/ alternant after it. After we have counted all the morphemes before /-əz/—and all of them end in /s, š, č, z, ž, ǰ/—we have left over one or two morphemes which end in sibilants without having /-əz/ after them. We therefore say that /-əz/ occurs only after morphemes ending in /s, š, č, z, ž, ǰ/ but not after all of them. The case is different with the Hebrew alternant mawt. This alternant occurs only with main stress; that is, whenever we find mawt, we find the stress on it. The other alternant, mo·t, occurs only before the stress. Here we can turn the statement around, as we could not in the case of /-əz/. We can say that whenever the stress is on the unit mawt, the alternant which appears is mawt, and whenever the environment is stressed after the unit, the alternant which appears is mo·t. After we have counted all the unstressed occurrences, where the alternant is mo·t, we have no unstressed occurrences left over where the alternant is something else. We therefore say that mo·t occurs only in unstressed environments and in all unstressed environments. The difference between these two cases is seen again in the Menomini e,[16] which is an alternant

[16] Bloomfield, TCLP 8.105–15 no. 10–2.

of the morpheme juncture /-/. In most cases, when a Menomini morpheme follows another within one word, there is no extra sound between them, and we may mark the junction between them with a hyphen. However, every time the first morpheme ends in C and the second begins in C, we find an e between the two morphemes, appearing, we might say, in place of the hyphen. This e also occurs between certain morphemes ending in V and certain ones beginning in /w/. As in the cases of /-əz/ and mo·t, we must distinguish between the two environments: the first is any morphemes ending and beginning in C; the second is certain particular morphemes ending in V and beginning in /w/. Hence we say that the alternant e for /-/ (morpheme juncture) occurs in all environments of the form ...C-C..., and in certain environments of the form ...V-w....

A special case of environments which consist of a phonemic feature is that of junctures (boundaries of words, etc.). Some alternants occur only at word boundary and at any word boundary: e.g. Tüb. ta·wək as compared with -dawə·g-.[17]

In some morpheme units, what is common to all the environments in which a particular alternant occurs is the presence of a morpheme from a particular grammatical class. Thus, the contraction which occurs in Menomini[18] between certain morphemes ending in Vw and others beginning in /ε/, occurs between all such morphemes if the first is a verb stem and the second an inflectional suffix.

In other units, a given alternant appears only next to particular morpheme units (knive- only before /-z/ 'plural', am only with I), or only next to particular morpheme alternants (zero alternant of 'possessed by' only after the /-s, -z, -əz/ alternants of 'plural').

A special problem of morpheme division may be mentioned here. In some cases, not only does a morpheme unit have a unique alternant which occurs only when it is next to a particular second unit, but the second unit also has a unique alternant when it adjoins the first; e.g. children, if it is divided into /čild/, alternant of /čajld/ only before -ren, and -ren, alternant of /-z/ 'plural' only after child. Such situations often result from vowel contraction; e.g. Menomini morpheme units ending in /ε̄/[19] have alternants with /y/ (instead of /ε̄/) before morpheme units beginning with /o/; and units beginning with /o/ have alternants with /ā/ (instead of /o/) after units ending in /ε̄/: instead of having the sequence /... ε̄-o .../ we have /... y-ā .../. Each morpheme functions as the environment which determines the alternant of the other. In such cases it is sometimes hard to decide where to put the division between the two alternants. Thus children could alternatively be divided into /čildr/ and -en; from the point of view of grammatical arrangment each of the points of division has advantages and disadvantages. In another Menomini contraction,[20] the sequence of certain morpheme units ending in /aw/ followed by certain other units beginning in /ε/ has not /... aw-ε .../ but /... ō .../. We could say that the unit ending in /aw/ had an alternant ending in /ō/, and the one beginning in /ε/ had an alternant without the /ε/; or we could divide differently. The choice is immaterial here, and can be decided only by seeing which division would be more similar to the division of other morpheme sequences.

4.3 Similarity between the alternant and its environment. In many morpheme units there is no recognizable similarity between the alternants and the environments in which they occur; e.g. between am and I, between i- (alternant of am) and /-z/ '3d sg. pres.', between /ej/ ∼ /u/ and take. In some cases, however, there is identity in phonemic feature (partial assimilation) or in phonemes (repetition or total assimilation); e.g. /-s/ 'plural' occurs only after alternants ending in voiceless phonemes and is identically voiceless with the phoneme preceding it, while the voiced alternant /-z/ occurs only after voiced phonemes. Indentity in whole phonemes is rarer: the consonant of the Greek reduplication, and the X of the Kota qiX.

4.4 Morpheme units in which the difference occurs. Some differences between the alternants of a morpheme unit occur in all the units of that language which have the particular phoneme involved in the difference; e.g. the difference between alternants with voiced and with voiceless stops occurs in all Tübatulabal units, if they but have a voiced stop at either end. Other differences occur in many units, but not in all; e.g. the difference between alternants ending in /f/ and in /v/ occurs in wife, life, etc., but not in fife. Still other differences appear only in one unit; e.g. the differences between the alternants in §3.3, 6.

5.0 To sum up: The difference between alternants of a unit may be partial or complete. It may occur in all units which have a stated feature (e.g. a given phoneme in a certain position), or in some units having a stated feature in common, or in a unique unit (or in several units which have no stated feature in common). The range of environments which de-

[17] What is called external sandhi, therefore, differs from internal sandhi merely in that the former contains statements which have word juncture as a necessary part of their determining environments, while the latter does not. In some languages, alternants next to word juncture may differ so much from those which are not, and differences determined by word juncture may have so many features in common, that it becomes convenient to arrange all statements involving word juncture environments together. In other languages, however, where many statements apply to environments both within words and across word juncture, it is simpler not to distinguish external from internal sandhi.

[18] Bloomfield, TCLP 8.105–15 no. 18.

[19] Ibid. no. 15.

[20] Ibid. no. 18.

termine the appearance of the alternant in question may consist of all morphemes which have a stated feature, or of only some of the morphemes having that feature, or of a unique morpheme (or of several morphemes having no common feature).

It now becomes a simple matter to recognize wherein one grouping of alternants into a unit differs from another (see §4.0).

5.1 If the difference between alternants of a unit is complete, it necessarily applies only to one unit.[21] If the difference is partial, it may occur in one, some, or all units which have a stated feature.

5.2 If there is a phonemic or morphologic feature which is present only in the units in which the difference under discussion occurs (and in no other units), then we may name the feature in a general statement and there is no need to list the units in which the difference occurs: all Hebrew morphemes with /aw/ had alternants with /o·/. On the other hand, if there is a feature which is common to all the units in which the difference under discussion occurs, but which is also present in other units (in which this difference does not occur), then we may either list all the units, or else make a mark upon their common feature to distinguish these units from the other units in which the difference does not occur: see knife in §5.4.

But if the unit in which the difference occurs is unique, or if there are several units which have no common feature, then we must list all of them.

5.3 The method of describing the environments in which an alternant occurs is similar to the method of describing the units in which the difference occurs.

If whenever a certain feature is present in the environment only a given alternant (and no other one of its own unit) occurs, i.e. if the given alternant is the only one of its unit to occur when that feature is present in the environment, then we name the feature in a general statement and there is no need to list all the environments in which the given alternant occurs: Hebrew units with /aw/ always had alternants with /o·/ when the unit was unstressed. Similarly, if a certain feature is always present in the environment when a given alternant appears, but if some other alternants of the same unit also have that feature in their environment, then we may either list all the specific environments in which the given alternant appears, or else mark these environments to distinguish them from other environments which have the same feature: the /ej/ ~ /u/ alternant of -ed 'past time' appears only with morphemes having the structure CejC, but not all morphemes CejC are followed by the /ej/ ~ /u/ alternant, since rake and other morphemes of this structure are followed by the -ed alternant.

If the environment in which the alternant occurs is unique, or if there are several environments which have no common feature, then we must list all of them.

5.4 A few examples:

Early Hebrew: All units having /aw/ have alternants with /o·/ instead, when any stressed morpheme follows within the word. (Both the units and the environments to which this applies include all those which have the features stated here.)

Menomini:[22] Some units ending in /n/ have alternants ending in /s/ instead, before all morphemes beginning with /e/. (The units involved here are only some of those having the stated feature /n/. Therefore they must be listed or marked. Bloomfield writes the units which do not have the /s/ alternant with N, and those which have the /s/ alternant with n, thus distinguishing the two groups.)

Kota: The unit for 'any, some, and the like' has alternants of the form qiX after any morpheme CVX. (The unit is unique; the environment is any unit having the stated feature.)

English: Some units ending in /f/ have alternants ending in /v/ instead, before /-z/ 'plural'. (We may write all these units with F: /najF/, but /fajf/. The environment, being unique, need not be specially marked.)

The unit /čajld/ has the alternant /čild/ before -ren 'plural'.

The unit -ed 'past time' has the alternant /ej/ ~ /u/ with some units of the form CejC. (Note that here it is the environmental morphemes that have to be listed or marked.)

The unit /-z/ 'plural' has the alternant /-s/ after most morphemes which end in a voiceless phoneme, and in no other environments. (The unit is unique. The environments have to be listed or marked. However, since the cases where an alternant other than /-s/ occurs after the stated feature are relatively rare, it is simpler to list the cases where /-s/ does not occur. They may be listed in connection with the alternants with which they occur: i.e. we list the alternants of 'plural': /-əz/ after /s, š, .../, -en after ox, ..., /-s/ after the other morphemes ending in a voiceless phoneme.)

5.5 Statements made for unique alternants are best included in the dictionary rather than the grammar. Units referred to in general statements are written with one base form representing all the alternants and containing any special marks which the general statement may require. By applying to the base form all the general statements which refer to it we obtain the alternants which occur in the environments named in the general statements.

[21] E.g. the complete difference between go and wen- exists only between these two sequences of phonemes, hence (barring homonyms) only in this particular unit. However, the partial difference between knife and knive- can occur between any two sequences of phonemes that contain /f/ and /v/.

[22] Bloomfield, TCLP 8.105–15 no. 13.

CONCLUSION

Possible advantages of the method described here are:

6.1 It prescribes three explicit procedures which, if rigorously followed, will lead to a unique[23] arrangement of the phenomena described here for a particular language.

6.2 It presents regular phonology, morphophonemics, sandhi, morphological processes like vowel change, morpholexical variation, suppletion, and the like as cases of a single linguistic relation, described in §2.2. The differences between these cases are systematized in §§4 and 5.

6.3 It leaves not merely less, but a simpler morphology. This is necessarily so, because the procedure of §2.2 (especially the condition concerning the total range of environment) removes from consideration as a separate morpheme unit any alternant which has a more specialized distribution than the rest of its class and which is complementary to other over-specialized alternants. The morphology describes the relations between morpheme units, all those in a given class now having roughly the same distribution.

23 Except for sequences of unique alternants (see last paragraph of §4.2). Such cases should be indicated in a special list of alternative possibilities.

6.4 It simplifies our general picture of linguistic structure, i.e. of what relations can be discovered between the elements of linguistic expressions. For it shows that we can arrange alternants into units in exactly the same manner as we arrange sound types (positional variants) into phonemes.

7.1 Summary: The method of arranging the phonemes of a language consists of three steps: 1. dividing each phonemically written linguistic expression into the smallest parts which recur with the same meaning in different expressions, each such part to be called a morpheme alternant; 2. grouping into a distinct morpheme unit all alternants which satisfy the following conditions: (a) have the same meaning, (b) never occur in identical environments, and (c) have combined environments no greater than the environments of some single alternant in the language; 3. making general statements for all units which have identical difference between their alternants.

7.2 Every statement, general or particular, about the alternants must contain three pieces of information: (a) what is the difference between the alternants; (b) in what environments does each alternant occur; (c) in what units does the difference occur. It is seen that various groupings of alternants into units differ on these three counts.

⟦Just as Hockett undertook to codify good practice in phonological analysis and description, so now, and at about the same time, Harris worked out his codification of the next higher levels of analysis and of description. His paper gives the impression of a little more originality. It may be that the reason for this is that dissatisfaction with looser techniques had brought improved phonological methods to the surface at a time when a similar dissatisfaction in the morphological field had still only subconsciously determined what the next steps would have to be.

The step that Harris now took was a move to make morphology look more like phonology. The Bloomfield-Hockett phonology had sought simply to escape from the gooey continuity of phenomena on the phonetic level, and by skillful use of Occam's razor had shaped a phonological theory according to which an utterance was completely described just by naming its constituent phonemes and their arrangement of sequence and simultaneity, needing nothing else (nothing that is not a phoneme) to hold them together: seemingly a quite homogeneous phonology. (But see now the comment on page 138 below!)

Now morphological tradition still lacked that kind of homogeneity: besides the 'morphemes', there was still something of an essential different kind, called 'process', without which the morphemes would not be glued together into utterances but would be left loose in the analyst's hand. Sapir's vitalistic way of thinking welcomed this duality as an essential dualism in human nature. But these were other times, and Sapir's disciple Harris drove out the spirit and showed that the structure of the utterance was still all there.

Later this building-block style of description was extended systematically, especially in terms of immediate-constituency theory, into the higher levels of grammar, where we find it well elaborated by 1947.⟧

THE SEGMENTAL PHONEMES OF THE PEIPING DIALECT

LAWTON M. HARTMAN III

Language 20.28–42—1944

1. It must be emphasized at the outset that this paper is concerned with phonemics and not with transcriptions. This is not an attempt to add one more segment to that remarkable product of Natural Selection, the Wade-Giles-Gardner-Dubs System.[1] The distinction between transcriptions and orthographies has been clearly discussed by Denzel Carr in connection with the Rōmaji controversy[2] and by others in both practical and theoretical papers devoted to linguistic techniques. The point need not be elaborated here.

This investigation was begun primarily with the purpose of discovering the phonemic relationships of the so-called 'palatal series' of initial consonants in the Peiping dialect. It was soon found, however, that a resolution of this problem required a general study of the phonemic system of the dialect.[3] The problem itself is simply stated. There exists a set of palatalized initials [tś, tś', ś] which always occur before the vowels [i, y] or the corresponding semivowels. There also exist three distinctive sets of initials, respectively alveolars [ts, ts', s], cacuminals [tṣ, tṣ', ṣ], and medio-velars [k, k', x], none of which may occur in this position. Although two or more phonetically similar sounds in complementary distribution may usually be assigned to the same phoneme, this situation serves here merely to state the problem, for there are three cases of complementary distribution, each involving the same set of sounds. On the other hand, it certainly cannot be concluded immediately that the members of the palatal series correspond to three independent phonemes, since there is never contrast between this series and any of the other three. This dilemma has long proved to be annoying to students of the language. As long ago as 1814 Marshman was aware of some difficulty when he wrote, 'The character 其 khee,... which the Imperial Dictionary and all others, unite in beginning with the initial k, the inhabitants of Pekin sound as though beginning with ch. This however is no wonder: even London has its provincialisms which a good speaker would not imitate'![4] Since the palatal series has developed in the Peiping dialect from both dentals and velars in Ancient Chinese, many writers have avoided the problem by retaining the distinctions of Ancient Chinese and writing the syllables in question with both the modern [ts, ts', s] and [k, k', x]. But this leads to an impossible phonemic intersection and in any case encroaches upon the domain of transcriptions. A more serious treatment has been attempted by Henri Frei, who, nominally adopting the procedures established by Trubetzkoy, considers the initials of the palatal series to be separate phonemes: 'Une affriquée palatale: c, qui neutralise la différence entre k et ζ'[5] and so on for the others. Since the cacuminals [tṣ, tṣ', ṣ] also 'neutralize' the difference between [k, k', x] and [ts, ts', s], it is not clear why he does not go on to conclude that the palatals and cacuminals are conditioned variants of the same phonemes! Still later Tchen Ting-ming is confronted by this problem and writes, 'Ce phénomène de palatalisation a créé trois archiphonèmes .... L'affriquée palatale K résulte de la neutralisation des trois phonèmes k, c, et č devant les voyelles i et y'.[6] Since he does not define what is to be meant by the term 'phonème', much less by 'archiphonème', it must be considered that he has in no way solved the problem but has merely restated it in different terms.

2. The definition of the phoneme which has been adopted for the purposes of this paper is that which has been enunciated by Bloch and Trager as follows: 'a phoneme is a class of phonetically similar sounds, contrasting and mutually exclusive with all similar classes in the language.'[7] The results which are obtained in the following pages are determined by this definition and the procedure implied by it.

[1] Cf. Derk Bodde, JAOS 62.8, fn.1 (1942). A reference to the transcription used by H. H. Dubs, JAOS 61.215–21 (1941).

[2] Denzel Carr, Japanese Romanization Again, JAOS 61.188–90 (1941).

[3] For the results contained in this paper I am indebted to Yuen Ren Chao and George L. Trager for their help and suggestions during many hours of discussion. Without their advice on many points of theory and detail this paper could never have appeared. The material used is taken largely from phonetic descriptions of the Peiping dialect made by Professor Chao. I wish to thank also Francis W. Cleaves for his help in collecting examples of syllables ending in the phoneme /r/. I am also indebted to Bernard Bloch for numerous suggestions about terminology and other details in the preparation of the typescript.

[4] J. Marshman, Elements of Chinese Grammar 87 (Serampore, 1814).

[5] Henri Frei, Monosyllabisme et polysyllabisme dans les emprunts linguistiques, avec un inventaire des phonèmes de Pékin et de Tokio, Bulletin de la Maison Franco-Japonaise 8.1.130 ff. (1936).

[6] Tchen Ting-ming, Les phonèmes de la langue chinoise, Bulletin de la Société de Linguistique de Paris 40.109 (1939).

[7] B. Bloch and G. L. Trager, Outline of Linguistic Analysis 40 (Baltimore, 1942).

In the problem introduced above there is phonetic similarity between the sound-types of the palatal series and those of the two series of alveolars and cacuminals. There is, furthermore, complementary distribution between the sound-types of the first series and those of each of the three series of alveolars, cacuminals, and velars. No immediate solution, therefore, can be reached, but this does not imply the impossibility of a solution consistent with the stated definition of a phoneme. It means simply that the analysis is not complete and that the whole matter must be examined again later.

3. To discuss junctural and prosodic phonemes is beyond the scope of this paper. However, it may be stated tentatively that there exist two prosodic systems, namely, four prosodemes of tone: *high level* (â), *high rising* (á), *low falling* (or low falling-rising in loud-stressed syllables occurring finally: ǎ), and *high falling* (à); and three prosodemes of stress: *loud*, *secondary* (which usually precedes the loud stress in a phonemic phrase), and *weak* (which usually follows the loud or a secondary stress in a phonemic phrase, that is, cannot normally begin a phrase).[8] Syllables with the high level or the high rising tone are shorter than syllables having one of the other two tones. Syllables having weak stress do not have phonemic tone but have a pitch which is determined completely by sandhi rules and which may be interpreted in each case as part of the allophone of the tone on the preceding syllable. There are also certain changes with weak stress such as the voicing of initial consonants, etc., but these will not be taken up here.

This paper is concerned with the segmental phonemes of syllables having loud or secondary stress.

4. *Syllabic finals*. For reasons of convenience the syllable in this dialect is considered to consist of two parts, the *initial* and the *final*. The *final* is defined as that part of the syllable which extends from the first semivowel preceding the syllabic nucleus (or from the syllabic nucleus itself if there is no preceding semivowel) to the end of the syllable, the *initial* being, of course, anything else that precedes the final. This includes those case of zero initial where the final coincides with the syllable. Again for convenience the finals may be divided into two parts, those which end with an r-like sound and those which do not. The latter will be considered first. There are forty of these, phonetically distinct, and they may be grouped roughly into three classes: those having predominantly low and mid vowels respectively and a residue having chiefly high vowels:[9]

(1) [-ȧ, -jȧ, -wȧ, -ȧj, -ɑw, -jɑw, -wȧj, -jȧj];
[-an, -jɛn, -wan, -ɥan, -ɑŋ, -jɑŋ, -wɑŋ].
(2) [-ë, -jᴇ, -wɔ, -ɥᴇ, -ej, -ow, -jow, -jʊw, -wej, -wɪj];
[-ən, wən, -wën, -əŋ, wəŋ].
(3) [-z·, -ẓ·, -i, -u, -y];
[-in, -yn, -iŋ, -ʊŋ, -jʊŋ].[10]

[jɛn] This final, having a lower-mid vowel, is included with the general low vowel group in anticipation of the analysis. In groups 1 and 2 there is only one final with this structure. There is apparently free choice, therefore, in the assignment of this vowel [ɛ] to a phoneme. The choice is made as indicated, in spite of somewhat greater phonetic similarity between this vowel and those included in group 2, because of its behavior in the formation of a final having an r-like ending. Note in Table 1 below that in this respect this final function's precisely like others included here in group 1. It is thus more convenient to include this final too in group 1, especially as it preserves a characteristic feature of group 1, namely, that the vowel is fronted before [n].

[jow, jʊw] There is complementary distribution between these two finals. The lower vowel occurs in syllables having the third and fourth tones mentioned above, the higher vowel with the first two tones. The raising of this vowel varies according to circumstances and from speaker to speaker. Syllables having the first two tones are considerably shorter than those having the third and fourth tones and the tension is correspondingly greater. In rapid speech the diphthongization becomes less apparent, although it seems that a vowel perceptibly lower than the following semivowel never completely disappears. These two finals, therefore, will be considered to be phonemically identical.

[wej, wɪj] The situation here is exactly parallel to the preceding one.

---

8 These statements of stress distribution are true in general for minimal free forms occurring in isolation. They are approximations rather than complete descriptions. There is in addition a contrastive stress, while C. F. Hockett reports a fourth stress-level between loud and secondary. The whole subject needs a thorough investigation.

9 The phonetic transcription used here follows as closely as typographical circumstances will permit the system presented by Bloch and Trager, OLA, Chap. 2. Affrication is denoted by two symbols in juxtaposition, e.g. [ts] [tś], the position of articulation being indicated by a diacritic on the second element. Nasalization is indicated by the subscript [ṇ], retroflexion by the subscript [ṛ]. The symbols [z·] and [ẓ·] are admittedly makeshifts; they denote syllabic, frictionless, voiced spirants, homorganic with the preceding consonants, and having mid-central vowel timbre. The vowel denoted by [ɜ] is lower-mid central unrounded.

10 The vowels [a] and [ɑ] are respectively not as far front and back as the cardinal positions for these vowels. In actual speech the vowel [ë] tends to shift during the utterance through the whole mid vowel range, while remaining back unrounded, and this symbol serves merely to define a norm. The vowels in [jʊw] and [wɪj] are centered slightly and somewhat lower than the positions indicated. The vowels in [in], [yn], and [iŋ] are slightly lower than the cardinal position. In addition to these finals there also occurs a final [m]. It is rare in absolute final position, one example, however, being [t'ȧm], a contraction of the more usual [t'ȧ-mən] (first tone on first syllable, second syllable weak) 'they, them'. Otherwise it occurs internally and remains a problem to be investigated, its solution being related to the matter of juncture.

[wən, -wën] In the second of these two finals the vowel is quite short and is raised in the direction of the preceding semivowel from the position of [ə]. The mid vowel quality, however, is never completely absent. Note that the Wade-Giles transcription for this final is -un, which gives an approximate though quite misleading conception of the actual situation. This final never occurs as a complete syllable without a preceding consonant; the first form occurs only as a complete syllable; the two are thus in complementary distribution.

[-z·, -ẓ·] These two finals are in complementary distribution with respect to the initial. The first occurs only after [ts, ts‘, s], the second only after [tṣ, tṣ‘, ṣ, ẓ]. They never occur initially. Both are fairly tense and unrounded and are described by Karlgren as respectively ‘apico-gingivale’ and ‘apico-alvéolaire’.[11] As indicated by the notation, they are homorganic with the preceding consonant and hence the point of articulation falls outside of standard vowel classifications. This has led a number of observers to conclude that the consonants in question form syllables without vowels. As noted above, an approximate though misleading description of the situation results here from quasi-phonetic transcription habits or from incomplete observation. Actually the division of these syllables into two parts is clearly audible. They begin with consonants, which differ in no way from [ts, ts‘, s, tṣ, tṣ‘, ṣ, ẓ] obtained by induction from syllables having different finals. They end with the syllabic, voiced, frictionless continuants of these consonants, syllabic in that they carry the prosodemes. These finals are modified slightly by central vowel timbre, although the dorsum and mid-part of the tongue are not actively concerned in the articulation. The precise specification of this secondary modifcation is difficult to determine, but it appears to be principally higher-mid and central. The important point to note, therefore, is that these syllables do not consist of syllabic consonants but rather of consonants followed by what are essentially syllabic continuants of these consonants. These finals are minimal. Their principal characteristic property is syllabicity, while their qualities are conditioned by the preceding consonants.

5. From an examination of groups 1 and 2 above it is clear that five phonemes may be established immediately. These will be denoted as follows: A syllabic /a/, to which, for reasons stated above, the vowel of [-jɛn] has been assigned; two non-syllabics /j, w/ whose allophones in pre-nuclear and post-nuclear position are defined by the statement of the finals themselves; and two additional consonant phonemes /n, ŋ] whose allophones have been observed so far in final position only. A second syllabic /e/ may now be set up because of contrasts between groups 1 and 2. Note that all the various vowel qualities of group 2 are, as already shown, in complementary distribution.

There remain, however, group 3 and the semivowel [ɥ]. As noted above, the first two finals listed under this group are in complementary distribution with respect to the initial consonants. The two then are allophones of the same syllabic and this syllabic will be denoted by /i/. This is a third syllabic phoneme. There is thus a syllabic phoneme in each of the principal phonetic vowel levels: low, mid, and high. The remaining high vowel qualities which have been observed phonetically must be examined in terms of this situation. The vowel [i] occurs either as a syllabic final or as a complete syllable. It never follows a phonetically observed semivowel [j]. However, the phoneme /j/ has already been established from the total list of finals, and there exists in addition a syllabic /i/ whose allophones have as their primary characteristic only syllabicity, their phonetic qualities being determined entirely by the preceding consonant. The situation here is similar to that encountered with the alveolars and cacuminals discussed in the last section. It is possible, therefore, to interpret [i] as consisting structurally of a consonant /j/ followed by a syllabic continuant of this consonant, that is, by the phoneme /i/. This final then will be analyzed as the cluster /ji/. It must be emphasized that this analysis follows directly from the establishment of a ‘minimal’ syllabic /i/ having the properties described above. Again, by the same analysis, it is convenient to interpret [u] as the cluster /wi/.

The situation is slightly different, however, with [y] and the semivowel [ɥ]. Here there are several possibilities, one being the obvious procedure of setting up immediately a third non-syllabic and continuing as before. Consider the final [-juŋ]. Phonemically this is conveniently analyzed as /-jwiŋ/. There is thus an initial cluster /jw-/, since this final may occur as a complete syllable. It will be seen immediately that there is no necessity of setting up a third non-syllabic. This final is analyzed phonemically as /j+wiŋ/, while elsewhere /jw-/ functions as a unit and corresponds to the phonetic properties of high, front, and rounded. Thus the finals in question are interpreted as follows:
[y] = /jwi/, [yn] = /jwin/, [ɥᴇ] = /jwe/, [ɥan] = /jwan/. Note that this follows at once from the establishment of a cluster /jw-/.

The continuity in the historical development of this dialect from Ancient Chinese is clearly seen when the comparison is made in terms of a phonemic description. ⟦This republication omits a table of twelve items of comparison with Karlgren's reconstructions.[12]⟧ Note that in every case the recon-

11 B. Karlgren, Études sur la phonologie chinoise 295–97 (Leiden and Stockholm, 1915): a thorough discussion of these two finals and a summary of attempts to transcribe them.

12 The numbers refer to the class headings in B. Karlgren, Analytic dictionary of Chinese and Sino-Japanese (Paris, 1923).

structured syllable has *[jɨ̯u-], *[-ɨ̯ʷ-], *[jɨ̯ʷ-], and so on. ... This is not intended as proof of the analysis made here, for the cluster /jw-/ is obtained quite independently, but rather in anticipation of systematic phonemic studies of Ancient Chinese.

Recapitulating, there have now been established seven phonemes: three syllabics /a, e, i/, two medials /j, w/, and two consonants /n, ŋ/ whose allophones have been noted in final position. These phonemes form thirty-six finals:

/-a, -ja, -wa, -aj, -aw, -jaw, -waj, -jaj/;
/-an, -jan, -wan, -jwan, -aŋ, -jaŋ, -waŋ/.
/-e, -je, -we, -jwe, -ej, -ew, -jew, -wej/;
/-en, -wen, -eŋ, weŋ/.
/-i, -ji, -wi, -jwi/;
/-jin, -jwin, -jiŋ, -wiŋ, -jwiŋ/.

Of these, /weŋ/ is never preceded by an initial consonant.

6. The basic form of the set of finals which end with an 'r-like sound' is the syllable [ᵊr] 兒 . When this syllable occurs in isolation it has the second tone mentioned above as one of the prosodemes. It is a morpheme analogous in certain respects to 子 . As such it occurs commonly as the final element of words in the Peiping dialect. However, this formation is always accompanied by certain morphophonemic changes. One of these is the loss of syllabicity either by this or by the preceding syllable. The resulting forms are syllables whose finals are discussed in this section. The dissyllabic forms do not normally occur, the contraction being in every case automatic and determined by the pattern for this formation. The correspondence, however, is not one-to-one. Thus, for example, to the two combinations [-ȧ] + [ᵊr] and [-ȧj] + [ᵊr] there corresponds normally the single final [-ȧə̯r]. The two-syllable forms appear to be restricted to Peiping speakers of Manchu derivation, whose dialect otherwise presents no special peculiarities. There is never any question of morpheme identification, since to each 'r' form there corresponds an optional form without an 'r'. This situation is summarized in Table 1.[13] The columns correspond to the pre-nuclear medials, the rows to the remainder of the corresponding 'non-r' finals. Thus the final derived from /-jan/ will be found in the column headed by /j-/ and the row headed by /-an/. Each position in the table has two finals. The upper one is the final in syllables having first or second tone, the lower one in syllables having third or fourth tone.

It will be remembered that the only finals having high vowels are [uə̯r], [ʊnə̯rn], and [jʊnə̯rn]. Remembering, therefore, that the final [u] was analyzed phonemically as /wi/, choose from this table three pairs of finals, each with a vowel in one of the three principal vowel ranges: high, mid, and low, such that the pairs corresponding to mid and low vowels begin with

[13] Adapted from a table prepared by Prof. Chao.

TABLE 1

	—	/j-/	/w-/	/jw-/
—	[ᵊr] [ᶟr]			
/-i/	[ᵊr] [ᶟr]	[jᵊr] [jᶟr]	[uə̯r] [uə̯r]	[ɥᵊr] [ɥᶟr]
/-a/	[ȧə̯r] [ȧə̯r]	[jȧə̯r] [jȧə̯r]	[wȧə̯r] [wȧə̯r]	
/-e/	[ə·ə̯r] [ᶟr]	[jə·ə̯r] [jᶟr]	[wə·ə̯r] [wᶟr]	[ɥə·ə̯r] [ɥᶟr]
/-aj/	[ȧə̯r] [ȧə̯r]	[jȧə̯r]	[wȧə̯r] [wȧə̯r]	
/-ej/	[ᵊr] [ᶟr]		[wᵊr] [wᶟr]	
/-aw/	[ɑwə̯r] [ɑwə̯r]	[jɑwə̯r] [jɑwə̯r]		
/-ew/	[owə̯r] [owə̯r]	[jowə̯r] [jowə̯r]		
/-an/	[ȧə̯r] [ȧə̯r]	[jȧə̯r] [jȧə̯r]	[wȧə̯r] [wȧə̯r]	[ɥȧə̯r] [ɥȧə̯r]
/-en/	[ᵊr] [ᶟr]		[wᵊr] [wᶟr]	
(/-in/)		[jᵊr] [jᶟr]		[ɥᵊr] [ɥᶟr]
/-aŋ/	[ɑnə̯rn] [ɑnə̯rn]	[jɑnə̯rn] [jɑnə̯rn]	[wɑnə̯rn] [wɑnə̯rn]	
/-eŋ/	[ənə̯rn] [ənə̯rn]		[wənə̯rn] [wənə̯rn]	
(/-iŋ/)		[jənə̯rn] [jənə̯rn]	[ʊnə̯rn] [ʊnə̯rn]	[jʊnə̯rn] [jʊnə̯rn]

the semivowel [w]. Two of these selections may be made. Consider first the one without nasalization:

[uə̯r] [wᵊr] [wȧə̯r]
[uə̯r] [wᶟr] [wȧə̯r]

The second pair of finals are in complementary distribution with respect to tone, the upper one occurring with the first or second tone, the lower one with the third or fourth tone. This is also found to be the case elsewhere in the table with finals having these two vowels. Furthermore there is complementation with respect to the final consonant. When the vowel is [ə, ɜ], it is accompanied by retroflexion; elsewhere there is the final non-syllabic [ə̯r]. Therefore, [r] and [ə̯r] will be considered to be the allophones in final position of a phoneme which will be denoted by /r/. On the basis, then, of phonetic similarity between these vowels and the respective allophones of the nuclear phonemes established above, the phonemic interpretation of these finals may be made at once:

/-wir/ /-wer/ /-war/

Again, from the finals listed in the last three rows of Table 1, which are characterized by nasalization as a modification both of the vowel and the final consonant, choose three finals corresponding to those chosen above:

[ʊn̯ə̑rn] [wən̯ə̑rn] [wɑn̯ə̑rn]

It is not necessary to choose pairs since the two members of each pair are identical. It will be noted that final /n/ disappears regularly in the formation of the finals in Table 1. The existing correspondence, therefore, is sufficient for the interpretation of the nasalization as an allophone of the phoneme /ŋ/. The position of this phoneme in the final cannot be determined directly, but the nature of the derivation suggests immediately the following interpretation as a possible one:

/-an/ + /er/ : /-ar/
/-aŋ/ + /er/ : /-aŋr/

Accepting the conclusion that the nasalization is an allophone of the phoneme /ŋ/ and that its position is between the syllabic and the final /r/, the three finals above may be easily described in terms of the results obtained previously:

/-wiŋr/ /-weŋr/ /-waŋr/

Finals derived from syllables with final /-e/ have long vowels in the first and second tone. This appears to be the only case of a significant long vowel in the dialect. Contrasts may be found between these finals and those having the short vowel. For example:

歌兒 [kə·ə̑$_\mathrm{r}$] 'songs'
根兒 [kə$_\mathrm{r}$] 'roots' (of plants), etc.

Both of these examples have first tone. It may not be concluded that the first example consists of two syllables, the second syllable having weak stress, since the sandhi rules (noted above in connection with weak stress), forming a regular pattern throughout the dialect, would require that the second syllable have a fairly low pitch. Actually this does not occur in the example cited, the tone remaining high and constant throughout. Because of the way in which these finals are formed it is most convenient to consider that these long vowels are double vowels. The two examples above may then be interpreted as follows:

/kê/ + /ér/ : /kêer/ (one syllable)
/kên/ + /ér/ : /kêr/

It is not certain that this distinction is made by all speakers of the dialect. Syllables having the third or fourth tone are normally long. As seen in the table there is no corresponding contrast in these tones and the finals in question are interpreted as /-er/.

It should be remarked that in the formation of these finals there is a redistribution in the total pattern caused by the replacement of the syllabic /i/ by /e/. The syllabic /i/ is preserved only in the cluster /wi/. An apparent exception is presented by /-jwiŋr/, but, as noted above, although the cluster /jw/ exists in the final /-jwiŋ/ it does not function as a unit. Elsewhere the cluster /jwi/ is in morphophonemic alternation with /jwe/. This is interesting when considered in the light of the properties that /i/ was found to have. It is not surprising to find it replaced under certain conditions by another syllabic. Thus:

/-i/ + /er/ : /-er/
/-ji/ + /er/ : /-jer/

and so on. There are then phonemically twenty-five of these derived finals:[14]

/-ar, -jar, -war, -jwar, -awr, -jawr/,
/-aŋr, -jaŋr, -waŋr/,
/-er, -jer, -wer, -jwer, -ewr, -jewr/,
/-eŋr, -jeŋr, weŋr/,
/-wir, -wiŋr, -jwiŋr/,
/-eer, -jeer, -weer, -jweer/,

the last four found in the first and second tones only.

7. Initial consonants. In initial position the following consonants are found in the dialect:

[p]	[t]	[k]	[ts]	[tʂ]	[tś]
[p']	[t']	[k']	[ts']	[tʂ']	[tś']
[f]		[x]	[s]	[ʂ]	[ś]
				[ʐ]	
[m]	[n]				
	[l]				

The unaspirated consonants, those listed in the first row, are all voiceless lenes.

Three phonemes may be established at once, those which were introduced above in incomplete form as consonants in final position.

/n/ : [n-, -n]
/ŋ/ : [-ŋ], [n̯] with all allophones of /a, e, i/ + ... + /r/[15]
/r/ : [ʐ-], [$_\mathrm{r}$] with any allophone of /e/,
[ə̑r] after allophones of /a, i/ and /ŋ/[16]

The remaining consonants only occur initially. Minimal contrasts are common. There is furthermore nothing in the distribution to suggest that the aspirates are anything but unit consonants. The only apparent alternative would be to interpret these consonants as unaspirated consonants plus aspiration, that is, some spirant which would be in complementary distribution with [x] or [f], etc. On the other hand, it will be shown below that the corresponding aspirated and unaspirated consonants belong to the

14 Although it has never been reported heretofore, an additional final cluster /-rw/ should be mentioned for the sake of completeness. I have heard it in the pronunciation of three native Peiping speakers. It was lacking in the speech of one informant of Manchu derivation. With the three informants who distinguished it from /-wr/ it occurred after both /a/ and /e/ in syllables beginning with both the aspirated and unaspirated velar and alveolar stops. No minimal contrasts were found. An example is [tə$_\mathrm{r}$w] 'a small pocket'. The final [w] is quite lax. Information on this point is by no means complete.

15 No allophone is listed for /ŋ/ in initial position although with many speakers [γ] may occur initially in syllables containing /a/ or /e/. It is in free variation with no initial consonant and is thus analogous in this respect to the initial glottal stop in English. In Tientsin [ŋ] is heard initially in this same role. It is concluded here that this onset of the vowel is not significant and it is hence excluded.

16 The principal sound features of /r/ in final position are voice and retroflexion. This and the positional complementation are sufficient to permit the inclusion of initial [ʐ] as an allophone of the /r/ phoneme. Note that [ʐ] is usually modified by slight lateralization.

same structural sets, and hence it is more convenient to treat them as units. Thus seven additional phonemes may be set up, each having only one allophone: /p, p‘, t, t‘, f, m, l/.

8. There still remain twelve consonants to be investigated and these present the problem discussed at the beginning of the paper. Restating the problem in terms of the analysis of finals made above, there exists the following situation:

(1) [tś, tś‘, ś] occur only before /j/ and are mutually contrasting in this position. This statement includes as a special case the finals [-i] and [-y], phonemically /-ji/ and /-jwi/ respectively.

(2) [k, k‘, x, ts, ts‘, s, tṣ, tṣ‘, ṣ] are all contrasting and never occur before /j/.

(3) There is phonetic similarity between [ts], [tṣ], and [tś]; between [ts‘], [tṣ‘], and [tś‘]; and between [s], [ṣ], and [ś].

The criterion of phonetic similarity (as defined by Bloch and Trager, OLA 38-9), while not affording a solution to the problem, is sufficent to permit its reduction by excluding the velars. It will be considered, therefore, that three additional phonemes may be set up, each characterized by the statement of distribution that it does not precede /j/: /k, k‘, x/.

In order to examine the nine remaining consonants, assume for the sake of convenience that they correspond to nine unit phonemes. There is then an immedichotomy of the consonant phonemes of the dialect, namely, those which form syllables of the CV type with the syllabic /i/ and those which do not. Of the first class there are the following syllables: /tsi, ts‘i, si; tṣi, tṣ‘i, ṣi; ji, wi, ri/. In connection with the immediate problem consider further the kinds of syllables that occur when there is a pre-nuclear /j/ or /w/. An example of this pattern is the following:

/tswi, ts‘wi, swi; tṣwi, tṣ‘wi, ṣwi; jwi, rwi/;
/tśji, tś‘ji, śji/;
/tśjwi, tś‘jwi, śjwi/.

Note again that the clusters /jj/ and /ww/ do not occur. The basic pattern, therefore, involving not possible syllables but rather possible initial clusters is:

/ts-/	/tṣ-/	/r-/
/tsw-/	/tṣw-	/rw-/
/tśj-/		
/tśjw-/		

and similarly for the other corresponding sets. Considering first the cacuminals there exists the following situation.

(1) /ts, ts‘, s/ are phonetically similar to /tṣ, tṣ‘, ṣ/ respectively. There are two pairs of affricates, aspirated and unaspirated, and a pair of homorganic spirants, all of which are voiceless. Further, both sets are similar to the set /tś, tś‘, ś/.

(2) /tṣ, tṣ‘, ṣ/ are distinguished phonetically from /ts, ts‘, s/ and /tś, tś‘, ś/ by retroflexion, a characteristic sound-feature of /r/. There is thus phonetic similarity between the cacuminals and /r/.

(3) /tṣ, tṣ‘, ṣ/ form initial clusters in precisely the same way as /r/.

The consonant /r/, however, functions quite differently from /tṣ, tṣ‘, ṣ/, since it may appear in either pre-nuclear or post-nuclear position. /r/ may, therefore, be interpreted as functioning in this dialect as a semivowel. In initial position it is parallel to /j/ and there are the following pre-nuclear semivocalic clusters:

/j-/	/w-/	/r-/
/jw-/		/rw-/

Again, the palatals /tś, tś‘, ś/ are phonetically similar to /ts, ts‘, s/ and are also phonetically similar to /j/ in that they are palatalized.

The phonemic interpretation of these nine consonants, therefore, is now clear. It is most convenient to analyze the cacuminals not as unit phonemes but as clusters having /r/ as the second element. Secondly, the palatals [tś, tś‘, ś] and the alveolars [ts, ts‘, s] remain as allophones of the same phonemes, the palatalization being conditioned by the following /j/. This analysis, therefore, yields three phonemes which will be denoted by /ts, ts‘, s/.[17]

Corresponding then to the semivocalic clusters above there are the following:

/tsj-/	/tsw-/	/tsr-/
/tsjw-/		/tsrw-/

and similarly for /ts‘/ and /s/.

9. In Table 2 is contained that part of the total syllabary of the dialect which is relevant to the problem just discussed. The columns correspond to initials, the rows to finals. All syllables of the dialect which begin with these initial consonants or clusters and which do not end with /r/ are noted, the existence of the syllable being indicated by the sign +.

⟦Omission: documentation for rare syllables.⟧

Note in connection with these forms and the others listed in Table 2 that /ts/ etc. denote unit phonemes and not clusters. The situation here is similar to that encountered with the aspirates. There is no reason suggested by the pattern for further analyzing these phonemes as clusters.

An additional problem, however, is raised by the pattern indicated in Table 2. The structures (/-in/), (/-win/), and (/-iŋ/) are enclosed in parentheses to indicate that they do not exist independently as finals. They serve in the table as counters to indicate the corresponding rows which involve the actually occurring finals /-jin/, etc. It will be noted immediately that these finals /-jin/, /-jwin/, and /-jiŋ/ are

17 The result that the palatals and alveolars are allophones of the same phonemes was implicitly stated by Morris Swadesh in A Short Account of Mandarin Phonetics, Travaux du Cercle Linguistique de Prague 8.213-16 (1939), where, however, it appears to be assumed rather than proved. The length of his paper permitted only the listing of conclusions. It is guilty, however, of a number of inaccuracies, considered at least from the standpoint of Peiping phonetics.

The suggestion that the cacuminals might be analyzed as clusters with /r/ as the second member was first made by Trager in 1941.

TABLE 2

	ts	ts'	s	tsj	ts'j	sj	tsr	ts'r	sr
/-aj/	+	+	+		+		+	+	+
/-wa/							+	+	+
/-waj/							+	+	+
/waŋ/							+	+	+
/-ej/	+		+				+	+	+
/-en/	+	+	+				+	+	+
/-eŋ/	+	+	+				+	+	+
/-wej/	+	+	+				+	+	+
/-wen/	+	+	+				+	+	+
/-i/	+	+	+	+	+	+	+	+	+
(/-in/)				+	+	+			
(/-win/)				+	+	+			
(/-iŋ/)				+	+	+			
/-wiŋ/	+	+	+	+	+	+	+	+	
/-a/, /-aw/, /-an/, /-aŋ/, /-wan/, /-e/, /-ew/, /-we/, /-wi/	all occur			all occur			all occur		

in complementary distribution with corresponding forms in /e/. The complete set shows this clearly, the forms in parentheses again being those which do not occur:

/en/	(/jen/)	(/in/)	/jin/
/wen/	(/jwen/)	(/win/)	/jwin/
/eŋ/	(/jeŋ/)	(/iŋ/)	/jiŋ/
/weŋ/	(/jweŋ/)	/wiŋ/	/jwiŋ/

There is furthermore complementary distribution between /weŋ/ and /wiŋ/, the former never preceded by an initial consonant, the latter always preceded by an initial consonant.[18] Hence it would seem most attractive to interpret all of these finals as having the same vowel. Against this interpretation, however, are the phonetic qualities of the respective vowels, for in addition to complementary distribution there is a clear-cut distinction of vowel quality. This distinction corresponds precisely to the division of other, contrasting finals into those having respectively high and mid vowels, and this division led directly to the establishment of the corresponding nuclear phonemes. There is an even more compelling argument against the suggestion above. That the finals /weŋ/ and /wiŋ/ are phonemically distinct is indicated by the retention of phonetic distinction in the corresponding /r/ finals, these being respectively [wəŋərn] and [-ʊŋərn], both distinct from [-waŋərn]. [-ʊŋərn] is parallel to [-jʊŋərn] and [-uər], while [wəŋərn] has the same vowel quality as [-əŋərn], etc. It cannot, therefore, be concluded, purely on the basis of the complementation shown above, that there is only one vowel in the nine finals in question.

[18] This complementary distribution may be illusory. I have heard the pronunciation /wîŋ/ used several times by a Peiping informant for a surname. This surname has been reported universally to be /wêŋ/. Whether this syllable will be found to have more general occurrence or not, it serves nevertheless to illuminate further the phonemic difference between these two finals.

TABLE 3

a	ja	wa	(ra)		rwa
aj	jaj	waj	(raj)		(rwaj)
aw	jaw		raw		
ar	jar	war	rar	jwar	rwar
awr	jawr		rawr		
an	jan	wan	ran	jwan	rwan
aŋ	jaŋ	waŋ	raŋ		(rwaŋ)
(aŋr)	jaŋr	waŋr	raŋr		(rwaŋr)
e	je	we	re	jwe	rwe
ej		wej			rwej
ew	jew		rew		
er	jer	wer	rer	jwer	rwer
ewr	jewr		rewr		
en		wen	ren		rwen
eŋ		weŋ	reŋ		
(eŋr)	jeŋr	weŋr	reŋr		
eer	(jeer)	weer	(reer)	(jweer)	(rweer)
(i)	ji	wi	ri	jwi	rwi
		wir			(rwir)
	jin			jwin	
	jiŋ	(wiŋ)		jwiŋ	rwiŋ
		(wiŋr)		jwiŋr	rwiŋr

10. In Table 3 are listed the total set of finals for the Peiping dialect. This includes those finals containing /r/, interpreted above as a semivowel. Parentheses enclose those finals which have not been found as complete syllables. The suggested cluster /-rw/ is omitted since it has not yet been substantiated by sufficient observation, the same being true of the possible syllable /wiŋ/. All syllables of the dialect may be analyzed, therefore, as beginning with one of the fourteen initial consonants (or with none) and ending with one of these finals.

⟦Omission: documentation of rare /-r/ syllables.⟧

11. For the dialect as a whole there are nine structural sets of phonemes formed by the system of consonants. These are shown schematically in Table 4. In this table the defining conditions are to be interpreted as true everywhere to the right of vertical lines and everywhere above horizontal lines.

From a comparison of the two diagrams it is clear that /l/, /n/, /j/, and /r/ form four structural sets, each having one member. These classes demonstrate further what was concluded before, namely, that the aspirates are unit phonemes. The suitability of interpreting /r/ as a semivowel is also clear.

TABLE 4

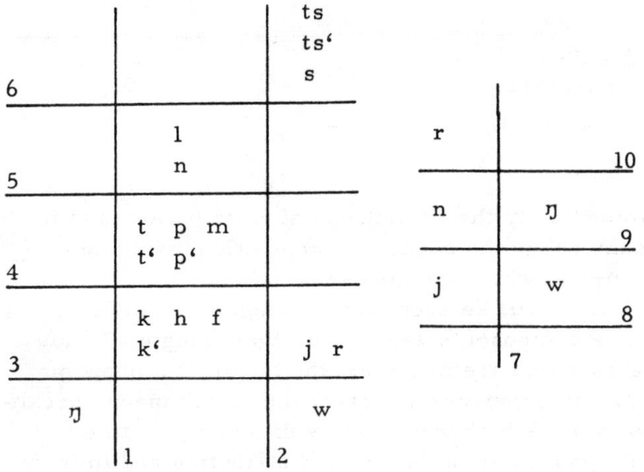

			ts ts' s
6			
		l n	
5			
		t p m t' p'	
4			
		k h f k'	j r
3			
	ŋ		w
		1	2

r		
		10
n	ŋ	
		9
j	w	
		8
	7	

Pre-nuclear classes	Post-nuclear classes
1 Occurs before /e, a/	7 Occurs before /r/
2 Occurs before /i/	8 Occurs after /e, a/
3 Occurs before /w/	9 Occurs after /i/
4 Occurs before /j/	10 Occurs after /w/
5 Occurs before /jw/	
6 Occurs before /r, rw/	

12. In conclusion it has been shown that in the Peiping dialect there are twenty-one segmental phonemes in syllables having loud or secondary stress. They are:[19]

(1) Fifteen consonants:	p	t	k	ts
	p'	t'	k'	ts'
	f		x	s
	m	n	ŋ	
		l		
(2) Three semivowels:	j	w	r	
(3) Three syllabics:	i	e	a	

It has furthermore been shown that, contrary to what is commonly assumed, the syllabic structure of this dialect is not essentially simple. Such a form as /ts'wíŋr/ 'insects' may be compared with such an English syllable as /streŋθs/ 'strengths' and should serve to dispel any illusions concerning Chinese.

19 A practical system of transcription, one which has been based upon this analysis and which has been put into actual use in class, involves the one-to-one substitution of unit symbols for the symbols based upon the phonetic analysis and presented above. Thus /p, t, k, ts/ are written b, d, g, z respectively, while /p', t', k', ts'/ are written p, t, k, c. This of course does not affect the system and serves merely to introduce a neater orthography.

⟦The reader will of course compare this paper with Hockett's Peiping Phonology ⟨⟨217⟩⟩, perhaps to its own disadvantage. More than one warning, however, will need to be borne in mind, to protect against a hasty decision on their relative merits; the safest conclusion is probably that each is superior by its own lights.

To begin with, the languages described are not precisely the same. Hartman was dealing with a style of speaking which did not force him to recognize dissyllabic microsegments, it would seem. This made it possible for him to follow tradition and base his description upon 'the syllable'. Again, he did not go as far as Hockett did in the direction of incorporating distinctions made by one speaker and others made by another speaker into a single dialect more highly differentiated than anybody's idiolect.

For another thing, he and his mentor in analytic theory, Trager, saw no harm in admitting a certain redundancy between the roles played by the terms 'syllable' and 'syllabic'. Their syllabic /i/ has no distinctive features of its own: the distinctive features, distinguishing it from /e/ and /a/, which are phonetically manifest at the point where Hartman writes /i/, are entirely predictable from the preceding semivowels and consonants (perhaps with some help from what follows, especially in the sequence /jwiŋ/). Again, its occurrence (against non-occurrence) is entirely predictable within the frame adopted, namely the single syllable: given a page of transcription, in separated syllables, from which the occurrences of /i/ had been expunged, with the gaps closed up to conceal what had been done, any reader of this paper could infallibly put them all back in again, all in the right spots, with no extras. Now to me at least it seems obvious that whatever is completely predictable and has no distinctive features of its own is no phoneme, whatever else it may be: I can find no better name for it than 'zero'. Accordingly I would say that this Chinese has two vowels, /a/ and /e/, and that not every syllable has a vowel. This, incidentally, is what Chao prefers to say—or did whenever I talked with him about it—though, with characteristic urbanity, he likes to help out his interlocutor by writing say an asterisk * at the very spot where Hartman writes /i/ and calling it things like 'star' or 'the zero vowel'.

Now such an interpretation cannot be derived directly from the Bloch and Trager definition of the term 'phoneme' quoted here at the beginning of §2. But that definition is no definition, but only a good artistic description, until its key words, especially 'similar classes', have been operationally defined.

Be that as it may, this paper is a classic example of classical phonemics, by which I mean phonemics with the phoneme. It may well be that there is no such language as the one described here; but that is more or less true of every description, including of course Hockett's, and does not affect the usefulness of such papers for our purposes unless it is far too true. Thorough mastery of this description, together with a smattering of spoken Chinese, can be used to set up a quite effective demonstration of how to do a phonemic analysis, as I know from experience.⟧

SIMULTANEOUS COMPONENTS IN PHONOLOGY

ZELLIG S. HARRIS
Language 20.181-205—1944

1.0 This paper[1] investigates the results that may be obtained when phonemes, or utterances in general, are broken down into simultaneously occurring components: as when the English phoneme /b/ is said to consist of voicing plus lip position plus stop closure, all occurring simultaneously.[2]

1.1 The analysis presented here rests on the fact that two independent breakdowns of the flow of speech into elements are physically and logically possible. One is the division of the flow of speech into successive segments; this is used throughout phonology and morphology, and gives us the standard elements (allophones or positional variants; phonemes; morphemes; words; phrases) of descriptive linguistics. The other is the division of each segment into simultaneous components, as when the single sound ['á] (high-pitched loud-stressed low mid vowel) is said to be the resultant of three components: high pitch, loud stress, and low-mid vowel articulation. It is this type of breakdown, only little used in phonemics today, that is investigated here.

1.2 This investigation will show that intonations, prosodemes and 'secondary phonemes', pitch and stress morphemes and phonemes, and suprasegmental features in general, can all be obtained as a result of the single operation of analyzing the utterances of a language into simultaneous components. It will show that the various limitations of phonemic distribution, including defective distribution of phonemes, can be compactly expressed by means of the same operation. When this operation is carried out for a whole language, it breaks all or most of the phonemes into new sub-elements (components). Each of the old phonemes will be a particular simultaneous combination of one or more of these new elements; and the total number of different components will be much smaller than the previous total number of different phonemes. It will be possible to select and symbolize the components in such a way as to show immediately the limitations of distribution, and in many cases the phonetic composition, of the phonemes in which they occur.

1.3 It will be seen that the linguistic status of these components varies with their length. Components which are precisely the length of a phoneme, i.e. which represent merely the simultaneous breakdown of each phoneme by itself, enable us to eliminate phonemes of defective distribution and to indicate the phonetic composition of each phoneme (§5.3, 4).[2a] We shall also permit some components to have the length of more than one phoneme, i.e. we shall say that such a component stretches over a sequence of phonemes. When phonemes are written with such long components, we shall be able to know the limitations of distribution of any phoneme by looking at the components of which it is composed (§5.2). Some of these long components will extend over all the phonemes of an utterance or linguistic form. These components will turn out to constitute the intonational or other contours of the language (§5.1).

In the following sections, these three groups of components which differ as to their length will be kept separate.

Present Treatment

2.0 We have then a large number of linguistic situations which, it will turn out, can all be described by means of the analysis into simultaneous components. It will be helpful if we briefly note how these situations are usually treated at present.

2.1 Pitch and Stress. There is a particular group of phonetic features which has customarily been separated from the rest of the linguistic material even though simultaneous with it. This is pitch and stress. The extraction of these features out of the flow of speech is due to the fact that they constitute morphemes by themselves, independent of the rest of the speech, with which they are simultaneous. In You. : You? : Yes. : Yes? we have four different sound-sequences, and four different meanings. These must therefore have four different phonemic compositions. This requirement would be satisfied if we had phonemic /U/ and /E/ as high-pitched vowels contrasting with low-pitched /u/ and /e/. Then we would write /yuw/, /yUw/, /yes/, /yEs/. However, the pitch features which are symbolized by /U, E/

[1] I am glad to express here my thanks to Dr. Henry Hoenigswald and the members of the linguistic seminar at the University of Pennsylvania for valuable criticism and for linguistic material. I am particularly indebted to Dr. Roman Jakobson for an interesting conversation on the phonetic breakdown and grouping of phonemes. I owe an exceptionally heavy debt to Dr. Bernard Bloch, who has helped me state many of the more difficult points.

[2] This example of phonetic components is given here only for introductory simplicity. The analysis presented below is primarily distributional rather than phonetic.

[2a] E.g. it is this technique that enables us, in languages which have a phonemic tone on each vowel (Fanti, Chinese, etc.), to extract the tones as separate phonemic elements.

have the specific meaning of interrogation. We therefore wish to consider some part of /yUw/, /yEs/ as the morphemes 'you', 'yes' and another part as the morpheme 'interrogation'. This can be done only if we consider /U, E/ to consist of two simultaneous components /u, e/ and /ˊ/. Then the phonemes /u, e/ are part of the morphemes for 'you' and 'yes'; and the phoneme /ˊ/, or rather the rising pitch which extends over the whole utterance, is the morpheme for interrogation.

In most languages that have been investigated, pitch and stress have been found to constitute the elements of special morphemes (such as phrase and sentence intonation or the English contrastive stress). These elements are pronounced simultaneously with the other morphemes of the language. It would be impossible to isolate the other morphemes without extracting the pitch and stress morphemes that occur simultaneously with them. Perhaps as a result of this, it has been customary to extract pitch and stress features even when they form part of the phonemic make-up of ordinary segmental morphemes (words and parts of words). Thus we do not usually say that a language has ten vowels, five loud and five weak, but rather that it has five vowel phonemes plus two degrees of stress.

2.2 Relations among phonemes, and the limitations of distribution of particular phonemes, are not presented in linguistics as an essential part of the individual phonemes. There exists no method which would enable us to say '/b/ is phonemic everywhere except after /s/' or '/t/ is a phoneme except after initial /k/, etc.' Instead we say that /b/ and /t/ are phonemes, and then tack on statements which correct the phonemic list by pointing out that /b/ does not occur after /s/, i.e. that there is no allophone occurring after /s/ which is assigned to /b/. If a number of phonemes have identical distributions, a single statement is devoted to them all. We say, for example, that morpheme-medial clusters in English hardly ever include both a voiceless consonant and a voiced one which has a voiceless homorganic counterpart: we get /ft/, /ks/ in after and axiom, but not /vt/, etc.[2b] If a phoneme occurs in few positions as compared with other phonemes in the language, as is the case with English /ŋ/, we say that it is defective in distribution. But the writing system which we create does not reveal these limitations. Given the phonemes of a language, a person would not know how to avoid making non-extant sequences unless he kept in mind the distribution statements.

The phonologists of the Prague Circle tried to indicate some of these limitations of distribution by saying that a phoneme which does not occur in a given position is 'neutralized' by one which does, and that an 'archiphoneme' symbol can be written to represent either phoneme in that position. Thus /b/ and /p/ are neutralized after /s/, and can then be represented by the archiphoneme /P/, which would indicate the 'common element' of both: /sPin/ instead of /spin/. This did not in itself prove to be a productive method of description. In the first place, most cases of 'neutralization' involve not merely two phonemes that directly neutralize each other. Usually several phonemes occur in a given position while several others do not, and 'neutralization' may be said to exist between the two whole classes of phonemes; thus after word-initial /s/ we find /p, t, k, f, l, w, y, m, n/ and the vowels, but not /b, d, g, v, θ, ð, š, ž, s, z, r, ŋ, h/. To select /p/ and /b/ out of the two lists and assign them to a separate archiphoneme /P/ implies some further and hitherto unformulated method of phonemic classification on phonetic grounds. And what shall we do with /θ/ or /š/ or /z/?[3]

Related to these limitations of individual phonemes are other distributional facts. In a particular language, certain positions have the greatest number of phonemic contrasts, and others have the least: in Swahili every phoneme may occur in the position after pause, but only the five vowels ever occur before pause or between consonants. There are also limitations upon clustering: in English, not more than three consonants occur in succession initially, nor more than four or five (depending on the inclusion of foreign names) medially in a morpheme. These clusters may be further limited in the order of the phonemes: /t/ occurs after /p/ and /k/ before word-juncture, but not before them. In our present descriptions, facts of this type are not automatically derivable from any other information given. They must be separately stated, and are not represented in the phonemic writing itself.

A less important point in which our present method of description is inadequate is the phonetic similarity among the allophones of various phonemes. Thus English /p, t, k/ all have identically varying allophones in identically varying positions (strongly aspirated initially, unaspirated after /s/, etc.); /k, g, ŋ/ have identical places of articulation in identical environments (fronted allophones after front vowels, etc.). These similarities are recognized in the grammar when we describe the variation in allophones of all the analogous phonemes in one statement, as we have done above. But the similarities among these phonemes are not explicit in the phonemic inventory or directly marked in the transcription.

[2b] Voiced-voiceless sequences like /rp/ in carpet are not counted here, since /r/ has no voiceless homorganic counterpart.

[3] The Prague Circle more closely approached the technique of dividing elements into simultaneous components, but purely on arbitrary phonetic grounds, when they said that the difference between two phonemes was not a vs. b, but a vs. a + x (where x is is a Merkmal denoting the extra features which differentiate b from a). See N. S. Trubetzkoy, Grundzüge der Phonologie 67 (Travaux du Cercle Linguistique de Prague 7; 1939).

2.3 Breaking an allophone into two phonemes. Whereas the two previous types of treatment have been fairly clear-cut, there is a group of linguistic facts in which the usual treatment is ambiguous: in some cases simultaneous elements are separated out and in other cases they are not, with no very clear criteria to decide whether the separation is to be performed or not.

It is customary to divide an allophone x into two successive allophones $x_1 x_2$ if we can then assign x_1 and x_2 to two otherwise recognized phonemes whose sequence is complementary to x. Thus we may break up English [č] into two successive phonemes /tš/, considering the retracted [t] as a positional variant of /t/ and the fronted [š] off-glide as a positional variant of /š/. We do this because phonemes /t/ and /š/ have already been recognized in English, but do not (except here) occur next to each other. We therefore consider the two successive parts of [č] as the allophonic values of the two phonemes /t/ and /š/ when they do occur next to each other. Certain accessory criteria influence us in deciding to consider the allophone as a combination of the allophones of two phonemes. The positions in which [č] occurs should be such in which sequences of the same type as /tš/ also occur. The new allophones, back [t] before a palatal spirant /š/, and [š] off-glide after a stop /t/, should have some phonetic similarity to other allophones of the phonemes to which they will be assigned, and should if possible have the same relation to them that analogous allophones have in analogous positions. Finally, the original allophone [č] should have some of the phonetic qualities which characterize a sequence of two phonemes in English (e.g. it should be longer than a single phoneme; or should have the tongue moving not directly from the alveolar stop to the position of the next sound, but going out of its way via the spirant off-glide).

In practice, however, this last criterion is often disregarded. Among speakers who distinguish the initials of tune and tool, many pronounce in tune a simple consonant—a palatalized post-dental blade stop with no recognizable [y] off-glide; nevertheless we consider that allophone to represent the phonemic sequence /ty/. Similarly the nasalized alveolar flap in painting, which contrasts with the alveolar nasal continuant in paining, is not considered a new phoneme occurring only after loud-stressed vowel and before zero-stressed vowel, but is assigned to the sequence /nt/.[4] Analyses of this type constitute an important departure in method, because we are here analyzing a sound segment into two simultaneous parts and assigning one part to one phoneme and the other to another. In the case of /ty/ we may say that the post-dental occlusion is the allophone of /t/ and the simultaneous palatalization is the allophone of /y/. In the case of /nt/, we may say that nasalization combined with the obstruction of the breath in the dental-alveolar area is the allophone of /n/, and the alveolar flap movement is the normal allophone of /t/ between loud and zero-stressed vowels. In each case we have avoided the introduction of a new phoneme with defective distribution, by assigning the sound to a sequence of previously recognized phonemes.

In all these cases we have an allophone broken up into components each of which we consider an allophone of phonemes which had already been recognized in other positions. As an extension of this analysis we have the occasional setting up of a new suprasegmental phoneme to account for a whole sequence of allophones which always appear together. Thus in Moroccan Arabic a new suprasegmental emphatic phoneme[5] is set up to account for the emphatic allophones. Phonetically, we have [ṣog] 'drive' (with cerebral [ṣ]); [ḍaṛ] 'house' (with cerebral [ḍ] and [ṛ]), but [dær] 'he built'; [lanba] 'lamp' (with low back [a]), but [læbs] 'dressing'. We could write this phonemically by considering [ṣ, o, ḍ, a, ṛ] to be different phonemes from [s, u, d, æ, r] respectively. But we notice that to say this would indicate a greater phonemic distinction than actually exists. In [lanba] ∿ [læbs], the difference between [a] and [æ] is phonemic; for there is nothing in the neighboring phonemes to indicate that the vowel is [a] in one word and [æ] in the other. But in [ḍaṛ] ∿ [dær] the difference between [a] and [æ] need not be considered phonemic; for [æ] never occurs next to [ḍ], and we could say that [a] is the positional variant of the [æ] phoneme next to /ḍ/ and other emphatics (i.e. cerebrals). This crux is avoided by breaking each emphatic phoneme into two simultaneous parts: a regular consonant or vowel, and an emphatic component: [ṣ] is analyzed as /s/ plus /'/, [o] as /u/ plus /'/, etc. It is then shown that when this emphatic component occurs after consonants it affects a sequence of phonemes, but when it occurs after vowels it affects only the preceding phoneme: /s'ug/ = [ṣog], /d'ær/ = [dar], /læ'nba/ = [lanba]. But it must be noted that this new phoneme is not inescapable. We could have written each of the Moroccan emphatic sounds as a new emphatic phoneme, and added a statement that in certain positions emphatic phonemes occur with each other to the exclusion of non-emphatic phonemes. However, such a statement would be at least as complicated as the equivalent statement which gives the domain of the single emphatic phoneme, and would leave us with a large number of extra and defectively distributed phonemes instead of the single emphatic /'/.

[4] Y. R. Chao gives other 'cases of one homogeneous sound represented by two or three piece symbols, each of which represented some aspect or aspects of the sound' in his article The Non-Uniqueness of Phonemic Solutions of Phonetic Systems, Bulletin of the Institute of History and Philology 4.371 (Academia Sinica; Shanghai, 1934) ((38)).

[5] Z. S. Harris, The Phonemes of Moroccan Arabic, JAOS 62.309–18 (1942).

Introduction of Simultaneous Components

3.0 The various linguistic situations mentioned in §§2.1–3 can all be compactly described by the use of simultaneous components. In order to introduce these components, all we need do is to permit the segmental elements of our linguistic description to be resolved into any number of simultaneous component sub-elements.

3.1 This is not a new operation in linguistics: it is used implicitly when pitch and stress features are extracted as separate phonemes, and it is used when we analyze English flapped [n] as /nt/. There is no particular reason to admit such analysis in these cases and to deny it in such cases as the Greek aspiration (which, like stress, occurred in most forms only once within a word) or English voicelessness (which, like the Moroccan Arabic emphatic, occurs over a sequence of phonemes). No new methods or postulates are therefore required to extend the analysis of simultaneous components into all the phonemes of a language.

3.2 It may also be noted that this operation involves us in no theoretical difficulties. It does not prevent us from having a statable physical character for our linguistic elements. The traditional phonemes indicate explicit physical events: time-stretches of sound (sound-waves), or sets of simultaneous motions of the 'vocal organs'. The new component elements also indicate explicit physical events: time-stretches of sound-waves,[5a] or motions of particular vocal organs.[6] The only difference is that phonemes are elements which can, in general, occur only after one another, while components are elements which can also occur simultaneously with each other (as well as after each other).

3.3 If we are to permit our segmental elements to be resolved into components, we must bear in mind that there are many different ways in which any elements can be broken down into sub-elements. There are a great many ways in which components—various numbers of them and variously grouped—can be arranged so that every combination of components recognized in the arrangement will yield a particular phoneme. Such expressions of phonemes in terms of components are not in themselves of value to linguistics. The advantage they offer in reduction of the number of elements may be more than offset if connecting them with the distributional and phonetic facts requires more complicated statements than are required for regular phonemes. We consider the possibility of such analysis into components only because, as will be shown below, we can select the components in a way that will enable us to give simpler statements of the facts about phonemes.

3.4 We can now say in general terms what we must do when we analyze phonemes into components. We take a list of phonemes, each with its phonetic and distributional description; we select a number of components; we select some method for combining these components simultaneously (e.g. not more than three components at a time), in such a way that each combination permitted by the method will identify a phoneme, and that the grammar becomes simpler and briefer when written in terms of the components.

Properties of the Components

4.0 Since the components are to be physical elements (§3.2), we must consider the phonetic values that they can have (§4.1). Furthermore, it will be seen that in special cases a component (or its phonetic value) may extend over more than one phoneme; and it will be important to note what happens when we get such long components (§4.2). The work that a component can do in the description of a language depends on its length. Components whose length is that of one phoneme can be used to describe the phonetic composition of phonemes (§5.4) or the dissection of a single allophone into two or more phonemes (§5.3). Components whose length is that of two or three phonemes (or thereabouts) can be used to indicate the limitations of distribution of any phoneme which contains them (§5.2). And components which can extend over long sequences of phonemes are used in the descriptions of intonational and other contours (§5.1).

4.1 Phonetic values. Since the components are to identify phonemes, or more generally speech sounds, each component must have a stated phonetic value in each environment in which it occurs. As in the case of phonemes, there is no reason to require that its phonetic value be identical in all environments. The component can therefore have different phonetic variants (allophones) in various positions, and the environmental factor which determines the particular allophone may be anything outside the component itself: other components with which it is concurrent, neighboring components or pauses, position of the component within the sequence of segments, etc.

Again as in the case of phonemes, it is not required that components have a constant phonetic value throughout their duration. A component may have a phonetic value which changes in a fixed way in respect to its end-points: e.g. falling tone, increase in nasality, voiceless beginning and voiced ending.

[5a] It is possible, by Fourier analysis, to replace periodic waves by a sum of simpler periodic waves. The original waves (e.g. sound waves) can then be considered the resultants which are obtained by adding together all their component waves.

[6] E.g. vibration of the vocal cords, giving 'voice'. This might be the phonetic value of a particular component in a particular position, whereas the phonetic value of a particular phoneme in a particular position might be, for example, voice plus closing off of the nose plus closing of the lips (English /b/). A phonetic system of this kind without the phonemic limitations is Otto Jespersen's analphabetic system, presented in his Lehrbuch der Phonetik (2d ed. Leipzig and Berlin, 1912) and elsewhere.

Finally, if we are ready to admit partial overlapping among phonemes,[7] we may agree to have different components in different environments represent the same phonetic value. So long as we do not have a component in one environment represent two phonetic values which are not freely interchangeable, or two components or component-combinations in the same environment represent the same phonetic value, we are preserving the bi-unique one-to-one correspondence of phonemic writing. (The term bi-unique implies that the one-to-one correspondence is valid whether we start from the sounds or from the symbols: for each sound one symbol, for each symbol one sound.)

4.2 Length values. Whereas the considerations of phonetic value are comparable for phonemes and for components, we find that in the matter of length there is an important restriction upon phonemes which can be lifted in the case of components. In the operations which lead to the setting up of phonemes, one of the most important steps is segmenting the flow of speech into successive unit lengths, such that every allophone or phoneme consists of exactly one of these lengths.[7a] In analyzing out the components, we make use of this segmentation, because what we break down are phonemes or allophones, not just random parts of the speech flow. However, there is no reason for us to restrict every component to the length of one phoneme. If a component is always common to a sequence of phonemes, we can say that its length is the length of the sequence. This will enable us to describe the limitations of phoneme sequences. When particular phonemes occur next to each other (e.g. English /sp/ in /spin/), while others do not (e.g. /sb/), we will say that the phonemes which occur next to each other all have some one component in common. The length of a component will therefore always be an integral number of phoneme-lengths—1, 2, 3, etc.—but need not be just one.

It follows that just as a component may have different phonetic variants in different positions, so it may have different lengths in different environments. When the Moroccan Arabic emphatic occurs after a vowel, it affects only the preceding vowel; when it occurs after a consonant, it affects a whole neighborhood, including several consonants and vowels.

Obtaining the Components

5.0 The greatest advantage from the analysis into components comes from the components with a length of two or more phonemes. These components enable us to express situations which could not be symbolized by the fixed-length phonemes. We shall investigate these components first. The first technique we shall use will yield the syntactic contours. The second will yield a way of treating the limitations of distribution of phonemes. The third will yield special cases of segmental phonemes. Finally we shall consider the components whose length is that of only one phoneme.

5.1 Automatic sequences expressed by long components. Our first operation is to extract those components which appear only in fixed patterns.

Intonations. We first consider the case where some connection among particular successive components in successive allophones is readily noticeable to us—that is, where we do not have to conduct a search to find a series of components which we can extract. Since we are assuming that no simultaneous elements have as yet been extracted, we have our language material in the form not of phonemes but of allophones, with each future phoneme, or at least each vowel, represented by many allophones:[7b] loud and middle-pitched [a], loud and high-pitched [a], very loud and middle-pitched [a], soft and low-pitched [a], etc. As a result of our past experience with languages, we may tend to scrutinize particularly the various stresses or pitches of each successive allophone in an utterance. However, we may also happen to note fixed patterns in the sequence of other features in successive allophones: e.g. a decrease in sharpness of articulatory movements from the beginning to the end of English utterances. Or we may notice a fixed pattern composed of several phonetic features of successive allophones: decrease in sharpness plus level tone during most of the utterance, followed by a falling tone at the end, in certain types of English statement.

In any case, we look for successions of phonetic features which recur in various utterances. We note that the occurrence of these features is limited: only certain sequences appear. For instance, we find the relative pitch sequence 1221130 (where 3 = highest and 0 = lowest) in I don't know where he's going. We can't tell when they're coming. etc. Among utterances with the same stress positions we do not find other pitch sequences ending in 30. For utterances with these stresses then, we tentatively count the above pitch sequence as one of the fixed patterns. We then see if we can in any way reduce the number of fixed patterns. We note that before the final 30, the slightly raised pitch 2 occurs wherever a mildly loud stress occurs; we therefore consider pitch 2 to be an allophone of pitch 1 in stressed position. Other

[7] Bernard Bloch, Phonemic Overlapping, American Speech 16.278–84 (1941) ((93)).

[7a] The lengths are not absolute (so many hundredths of a second) but relative. This means that an allophone [p], for instance, is not composed of two shorter allophones 'p-closure' and 'p-release'.

[7b] We will assume that these allophones satisfy all the criteria for phonemes—that is, that complementary allophones have been grouped together—except that allophones having different stress and pitch have been considered different sounds and hence not grouped together under one symbol. It is impossible to obtain the conventional phonemes until intonational components have been extracted from the allophones.

pitch sequences can also be considered special cases of this one: occurrences of relative high pitch 4 at one or more places in such utterances will always be accompanied by a loud contrastive stress (Wé can't tell when they're coming. 4221130), and can therefore also be considered an allophone of pitch 1. As a result of such manipulations a large number of pitch sequences ending in 30 become identical. They are all cases of one fixed sequence: as many relatively low tones as vowels (with slightly raised tones under stress and fairly high tones under contrastive stress) followed by a middling high tone on the last stressed vowel with a drop to zero (lowest) pitch on the vowels or consonants after it.

In English, a number of other sequences will not be reducible to this. For instance, there is the sequence in which every loud-stressed vowel, and every vowel or consonant after the last loud stress, has a higher pitch than the preceding one, while every zero-stressed vowel has the same pitch as the preceding loud-stressed: You're not going over to Philadelphia? 012233333456.

By investigating all these intonations, we obtain a small number of pitch-sequence patterns, occurring over whole utterances or over sections of utterances (phrases, etc.). In phonemics, if we were dealing with a fixed sequence of segmental phonemes as long as these sequences of pitch, we should have to consider it as composed of the observable successive elements; and the fact that only a very few of the possible sequences of these elements occur could only be stated as a limitation upon their distribution. Since, however, components are not restricted as to length, we can say in this case that each of these pitch sequences is a single component whose length is that of a whole utterance or phrase. This is permissible, since the successive parts of the sequence are not independent of each other (e.g. before 30, only 1's occur) and may all be considered parts of one element. And it is advantageous, since we thus avoid having to state limitations of distribution for individual phonemic tones.

The essential operation here is to put two successive sounds or sound features into one unit if they always occur together in a particular environment. This is often done in phonemics, as when we consider the aspiration after initial [p, t, k] to be not a separate phoneme but part of the allophones of /p, t, k/ in that position.[8] Similarly, in these few fixed sequences of pitch or the like, we consider the parts of each sequence to be automatically dependent upon each other, so that the whole sequence is one phonemic element.[9]

[8] This operation is used implicitly throughout phonemics to keep us from breaking sounds down into smaller and smaller segments ad infinitum. We do not consider the lip closing and the lip opening of intervocalic /p/ to be separate phonemes, because they always occur together in that position.

[9] A fuller discussion of the character of these contour components is given in fn. 22a below.

<u>Components of components.</u> If we wish to reduce the number of such dependent-sequence elements, we analyze them in turn into components on the basis of phonetic similarity (since there are no limitations of distribution among them) in the same way that this will be done for segmental phonemes. (see §5.4 below). That is, we break up the sequences into any simultaneous components which seem most convenient, and the combinations of which uniquely indentify each sequence: e.g. the direction of pitch change after the last stressed vowel, the degree of change there, etc.

<u>Stress.</u> An analogous operation is performed when we have word or morpheme junctures phonemically established and note that some feature always occurs exactly once between each two junctures, or that some phonetic feature has fixed patterns between junctures. Thus we may note that there is never more than one loud stress between word junctures in English, and that the other vowels between these junctures have medium or weak stress, usually in fixed patterns: e.g. 1030 in <u>distribution</u>, <u>independent</u>, etc. Certain facts about the stresses are thus automatic: the number of loud stresses, the occurrence of some of the weak stresses. We therefore mark as phonemic only the remaining non-automatic facts: the place of the loudest stress, and where necessary the place of any secondary stress. In a similar way, English contrastive stress (1040 in <u>distribution, not production</u>) would be discovered, since when it does occur it hardly ever appears more than once between two word junctures. This operation, however, will not discover features which do not appear in a limited number of fixed sequences, e.g. pitch in languages where all sequences occur and where the different sequences cannot be reduced into special cases of one another.

In dealing here with dependent sequences, it has been assumed that the phonetic features comprising the sequences would be readily noticed by the linguist. This is usually the case not only because pitch and stress are so frequently the features concerned, but also because it is relatively easy to notice phonetic features which show recurrent patterns in many sequences of allophones. Nevertheless, the analysis in no way depends upon a lucky finding of these phonetic features. It is possible to discover any fixed sequences methodically by the laborious process of taking each allophone (or each of a class of allophones, e.g. vowels) in many utterances and seeing in what respect the allophone after it is limited: e.g. given a low-pitched, sharply-articulated, weak-stressed vowel at the beginning of various utterances, can we find examples of every grade of pitch, sharpness, and stress in the vowel after it, or do only certain grades occur?

Segmental allophones. The net result of this operation has been not only to produce a number of phonemic sequences of phonetic features (e.g. pitch-sequence phonemes), but also to extract these same phonetic features (e.g. pitch) from the recorded flow of speech. The recurring fixed patterns helped us to notice these phonetic features and gave us the basis for extracting them as a single independent element. But by doing so we are left with the original sequence of allophones minus these features. If we now go back to the allophones, we shall find that the extraction of these dependent-sequence elements (e.g. pitch) has reduced the allophones, which had originally differed in these features, to the conventional phonemes: the variously stressed and pitched [a]'s are now identical /a/, since they no longer represent classes of actual sounds but only features of sounds—namely, all the features except stress and pitch. What we thus obtain out of our original allophones equals the conventional phonemes merely because it has been customary for linguists to extract pitch and stress features, so that our usual phonemes are even now not classes of sounds but classes of sounds minus their pitch and stress features. The original allophones with which we began here were pure classes of freely varying or complementary sounds, and when we extracted the dependent sequences, which in most cases are composed of the pitch and stress features, we obtained the conventional phonemes.

The fact that most of these fixed sequences of sound components have meanings, or correlate with morphological constructions, is a matter apart. This fact is independently recognized by including them in the list of morphemes of the language. Dependent sequences may turn out to be phonemic without being morphemes, e.g. word-stress, varying rhythms and melodies of speech.

5.2 Limitations of distribution expressed by long components. In our second operation we consider the usual type of limitation of distribution, in which a phoneme that occurs in most environments is limited by never appearing in certain positions. Here no solution is possible within the methods of segmental phonemics. The difficulty with the archiphoneme device, and with the statements about distributional relations between phonemes, is that they seek only to find a relation or common factor among the phonemes that can or cannot occur in a given environment. But there also exists a relation between the phonemes which occur in a given environment and the environment itself, namely the fact that they occur next to each other. That relation exists, for instance, between English /ŋ/ and /k/, but not between /ŋ/ and /t/. If we are willing to break phonemes up into simultaneous components, we restate relation as a factor common to /ŋ/ and /k/ but not to /t/; and we say that /ŋ/ and /k/ each contain a certain component (say, back position) and that this component spreads over the length of two phonemes when the first is nasal. /ŋt/ therefore does not occur, nor /nk/, because the component of mouth position always extends identically over both phoneme places. If we mark $\underline{\underline{n}}$ for nasal without regard to mouth position, and $\underline{\underline{s}}$ for stop without regard to mouth position, and $\overline{\quad}$ for alveolar and $\overline{\overline{\quad}}$ for velar position, then we say that the latter two marks always have 2-phoneme length when beginning with /$\underline{\underline{n}}$/.[9a] Thus /$\overline{\underline{\underline{n}}\underline{\underline{s}}}$/ = /nt/ and /$\overline{\overline{\underline{\underline{n}}\underline{\underline{s}}}}$/ = /ŋk/; there is no way to write /nk/, since $\overline{\quad}$ is so defined that it cannot be stopped after the /$\underline{\underline{n}}$/.

By the use of components which are defined so as to extend over a number of phoneme places, we thus circumvent the limitation in distribution of the phonemes. This is not merely a trick, concealing the limitations of the phonemes in the definitions of the components. For the components are generalized phonemes: they appear concurrently with each other as well as next to each other, and they may have a length of several phoneme-places as well as of one phoneme-place. And when we write with these components it is natural that various ones will have various lengths; each of them has to have some stated length, and the components symbolized by $\overline{\quad}$ and $\overline{\overline{\quad}}$ are simply among those that in some situations have 2-phoneme length.

Since we should like our new elements, the components, to have as general a distribution as possible, we try to select them in such a way that the components which occur under (or together with) a two-length component should also occur without it. Thus given English morpheme-medial /sp/ but not /sb/, we say that the component common to /s/ and /p/ is unvoicing, or fortisness, and that its length is that of the cluster in which it is present. /sp/ is then a sequence of sibilant plus stop, with overriding unvoicing. The same sequence occurs with the unvoicing absent: /zb/ in Asbury. As in the case above, /sb/ and /zp/ cannot be written in terms of components, because of our definition of the length of the unvoicing.

9a Linguistic forms which are written in components will be set between diagonals, in the same way as forms written phonemically. It is convenient to use identical brackets for these two systems, because many linguistic forms cited in this paper are written partly in phonemes, partly in components: e.g. /†sz'r/ 'tree'. We write in components only those parts of a form which are under discussion. This is permissible because phonemics is merely a special case of component analysis; the extension from phonemics into components can be carried out to any degree desired. In the analysis of Moroccan Arabic cited in fn. 5, the phonemes are of the usual kind except for the component /'/ (§2.3 above), which is included among the phonemes.—In some cases, where it is clear that a symbol indicates a component, the diagonals are omitted. The use of non-alphabetic marks like the horizontal bar (§5.2) is not in general desirable; but only such marks can depict on paper the effect of a long component that extends over more than one phoneme.

General formula. The procedure of obtaining these 2-length (and longer) components can be stated generally. If we have a sequence of two phonemes xy, we can select any number of factors which they have in common (both may be oral, both articulated in a certain position, both voiced or both voiceless, both explosive as against implosive, etc.). If one of these two phonemes does not occur with some third phoneme (say xc does not occur), we can then say that xy have significantly that component in common which c lacks. We call this component γ, and say that it has 2-phoneme length. Then x consists of this component γ plus some residue w, and y consists of the same γ plus some other residue u; thus /s/ = unvoicing plus sibilant articulation, /p/ = unvoicing plus lip and nose closing. We try to identify some other sequence of phonemes with these residues, and in particular to have the phoneme c equal the residue u, since the phoneme c is already known as lacking the component γ; in this case such a sequence would be /zb/, where /z/ = sibilant articulation, /b/ = lip and nose closing.[10]

If xy occurs then xy = γ + (wu)
xu does not occur x = γ + (w)
wu occurs y = γ + (u)

Then our new elements are w, u, and the 2-length γ, and all possible sequences of them occur. There is no longer any limitation of distribution: w and u occur alone (intervocalic /z/ and /b/) and together as wu (cluster /zb/), and each of these occurs with γ in the combinations γ + w = /s/, γ + u = /p/, γ + wu = cluster /sp/.[11] If we represent unvoicing by a small circle, we may paraphrase our general formula as follows:

Since /sp/ occurs /sp/ = ° + (zb)
/sb/ does not occur /s/ = ° + (z)
/zb/ occurs /p/ = ° + (b)

Assimilations. In Moroccan Arabic, the clusters /šš/, /žž/, /šž/ all occur, as well as the clusters /ss/ and /zz/; and there are morphemes which contain both /š/ and /ž/, or both /s/ and /z/, not contiguous to each other and in any order. But no morpheme containing /s/ or /z/ ever contains also /š/ or /ž/ anywhere within its bounds, nor does /s/ or /z/ ever occur in a morpheme with /š/ or /ž/. This complete statement of limitations[12] can be eliminated if we extract the feature † as a component and define it as having the length of a morpheme[13] and the phonetic value of retracting the tongue when in sibilant position (and as having zero phonetic value when the tongue is not in sibilant position). In doing this we can simply follow the formula above. /š...ž/ occur in one morpheme and represent our xy; /š...z/ do not occur in one morpheme and represent our xc. The factor common to /š, ž/ and absent in /z/ (our γ component) is †, a component of morpheme length. Then /ž/ (our y) consists of † (our γ) plus a residue (our u), and we identify this residue with /z/ (our c), which fits in with the fact that /š...z/ does not occur. And since /s...z/ does occur, we consider /s/ to be the residue of /š/ when the † component is extracted: /š/ = † + /s/, /ž/ = † + /z/, /šž/ = † + /sz/, etc. We now have three elements /s/, /z/, and †, each with its stated length and phonetic value, and all sequences of them occur:[14] /s/ in /iams/ 'yesterday', /zz/ in /zzit/ 'the olive', /sz/ in /†sz'r/ (= /šž'ṛ/) 'tree', /ss/ and /z/ in /†ssrzm/ (= /ššržm/) 'the window', etc.

/šš/ occurs /šš/ = † + (ss)
/šs/ does not occur /š/ = † + (s)
/ss/ occurs /s/ = (s)

Note that † has a defined phonetic value when it occurs with some phonemes (the sibilants) and zero phonetic value when it occurs with other phonemes within its length.

Frequently the γ + u and the u, i.e. the phonemes which do and which do not occur next to the γ + w, represent whole classes of phonemes. In Swahili, /t, d, k, g, s, z, l, r, n/ occur after /n/, but the other consonants /p, b, f, v, m, h, θ, ð, ɣ/ do not.

/nt/ occurs /nt/ = — + (mp)
/np/ does not occur /n/ = — + (m)
/mp/ occurs /t/ = — + (p)

We call /n/ a 2-length component having the value of a dental nasal when occurring by itself, and stated other values (mostly, retarding of the tongue) when occurring simultaneously with various other components. Hence the n-component by itself = /n/. When the n-component is simultaneous with a labial, its value is tongue retarding, so that (n+p) = /t/. Since the n-component has the length of two phonemes, it will always stretch over the p whenever n occurs before it, so that /n p/ = /n (n+p)/ = /nt/. In terms of fixed-length phonemes, the distributional statements seem paradoxical: we are saying that p occurs after /n/, but when it does, it isn't /p/ at all but /t/. This apparent paradox brings out the difference, and the profit, in speaking in terms of components. For in terms of components we have two statements: 1. t = (p+n), d = (b+n), etc.; 2. n has 2-phoneme length when over consonants. Initially, or after m or vowels, we may have the components which constitute /p/, or those which constitute /t/ (i.e. the p components plus the n component): /paka/ 'cat', /tatu/ 'three'. After /n/, the components which

10 More briefly: Given that xy occurs, we select u such that xu does not occur. Then y = γ + u (where γ has 2-phoneme length, when two phonemes are present), and x = γ + w, where w is selected so that wu occurs.

11 Note that in this example γ does not occur alone.

12 Aside from an unrelated limitation between /s/ and contiguous /z/.

13 Or of a word, except for one enclitic. That is, when † occurs, it extends from one word juncture to the next.

14 See fn. 12.

comprise /p/ may indeed occur, but they then fall under the length of the n component, and their conjunction with that component yields /t/: /amentizama/ 'he saw me'. If we take an /n/, we can say that the /p/ components may follow it (in which case the n component extends over them); or we may say that the /t/ components follow it, since the segment following /n/ will actually contain precisely the /t/ components (/p/ components plus the n component). It makes no difference which we say, since either statement describes the same situation. This type of description, which cannot differentiate between /np/ and /nt/ in Swahili, corresponds exactly to the Swahili situation where /np/ does not exist phonemically as against /nt/. When we speak in terms of components, therefore, we do not have to make statements of limitation of distribution such as that the phoneme /p/ does not occur after the phoneme /n/.

A component may have a particular length when it occurs in one environment, and another when it is in other positions. In the case of the Moroccan Arabic emphatic (§2.3), we find the following sequences: /tæ/, /ta/ (rare), /ṭa/ (the /ṭ/ being domal unaspirated), but not /ṭæ/ (except across word juncture). We say that /ṭ/ and /a/ each contain a 2-place component ' whose phonetic value in general is to pull consonants and vowels to central position. The lack of /ṭæ/ is explained by that fact that /æ/ does not contain the ' component. We call /æ/ the residue of /a/ after the ' is extracted. Then since /tæ/ does occur, we call /t/ the residue of /ṭ/ after ' is extracted. Now /a/ = ' + /æ/, /ṭ/ = ' + /t/, /ṭa/ = ' + /tæ/, and every combination occurs. We write /mæt/ 'he did', but /gæt'/ for [gaṭ] 'pliers' and /t'æb/ for [ṭab] 'he repented'. However, in this case we also have /ta/ occurring, though rarely, as in [banka] 'bank'. The only way to write it is to restrict our previous statement: ' is a 2-place component only when it appears with a consonant; on the rare occasions when it appears concurrently with a vowel (written after the vowel) it is a one-place component. Now we add /ta/ = /tæ/ + '; we write /bæ'nkæ'/ 'bank'.

/ṭa/ occurs	/ṭa/ = (t'æ)
/ṭæ/ does not occur	/ṭ/ = (t')
/tæ/ occurs	/a/ = (æ')
/ta/ occurs rarely	/ta/ = t(æ')

This situation is repeated for all the vowels and nine of the consonants, and the length of ' when placed after a consonant turns out to be several phonemes, not all continguous. However, all these additional results can be obtained merely by repeating the investigation sketched above.

The technique of using these components to express limited distribution may simplify the description of morphophonemic alternation. For example, German has (to take only one pair) contrasting /t, d/ before vowels, as in *bunte* 'colored ones', *Bunde* '(in the) group', but only /t/ before open juncture (- or #, and in certain types of clusters). The lack of the sequence /d-/ involves morphophonemic complications, since morphemes ending in /d/ before a vowel, end in /t/ before open juncture: /bunt/, /bunde/ 'group'. The /t-/ is the xy of our formula, and /d-/ is the xc which does not occur. We recognize a 2-place component having the phonetic value of unvoicing (but having zero value on certain phonemes such as /e/) which is common to /t/ and open juncture /-/ but lacking in /d/. If we write this component as ¯, we can say that open juncture equals ¯, and /t/ = /d/ + ¯. Since /e/ does not contain the ¯ component, /d/ is free to occur before it. However, since we also have /t/ before /e/, we must define ¯ as having 2-place length only when it occurs by itself (i.e. when it equals open juncture) and as having one-place length otherwise. We now have /bund¯, bunde¯/ = *bunt*, *bunte*, and /bund¯, bunde¯/ = *Bund*, *Bunde* (where the overhanging ¯ is the phonemic open juncture). The writing is still phonemic /bund¯/ 'group' and /bund¯/ 'colored' are still identical. But now we need not say that there is a morphophonemic alternation in the word for 'group'. The morpheme is /bund/ in both environments; the unvoicing heard before open juncture is not part of the morpheme /bund/ but is an automatic part of open juncture. This juncture consists of the component ¯, which is a 2-place component in this position. Note that since open juncture is phonemic, we should have to write it one way or another, if in no other way than by a space. We can equally well write this open juncture with one or more of the new components, so long as the sum of their phonetic values in that position equals the phonetic value of open juncture (and pause). In contrast with this, the morpheme 'colored' is /bund̄/, as in the inflected form /bund̄er/; when it occurs before open juncture the ¯ component of the juncture and the ¯ component of the last place in the morpheme coincide, and we have /bund¯/.

/t-/ occurs	/t-/ = ¯ + (d (+vowel))
/d-/ does not occur	/t/ = ¯ + (d)
/d/ + vowel occurs	/-/ = ¯

In view of the possibilities of a component coinciding with a 2-length component extending over the next place, this case does not eliminate the practical lexical problem: given /bund¯/ we do not know whether the morpheme is /bund/ or bund̄/. But in terms of components we need no longer say that *Bund* has two forms.

Dissimilations. In all the foregoing cases there has been a physical similarity between the phonemes that occur together, which is not shared by the phonemes that do not occur in such combinations. The matter is somewhat more difficult when it is the dissimilar phonemes that occur together while the similar ones do not.

In classical Greek, only one aspirate occurs in a stem with its affixes, except for a very few morphemes, and there is a morphophonemic alternation between aspirates and non-aspirates, as when an aspirate-initial stem is reduplicated with the homorganic non-aspirate: φύ̄ω 'I produce', pf. πέφῡκα. We analyze φ into /p/ plus a component ʿ having the length of a stem plus its affixes, and the phonetic value of aspiration after one of the voiceless stops (which one, to be stated in terms of the phonetic structure of the word) and zero after every other phoneme. It is now possible to write /ʿpépūka/, with the ʿ component written anywhere in the word, and with no need for morphophonemic statements.[15]

In Moroccan Arabic, double consonants are common (e.g. /tt/ in /fttš/ 'he searched', etc.), but no two different phonemes pronounced in the same mouth position (labial, dental, palatal, laryngal) ever occur next each other (with certain exceptions): there is no /fb, bf, td, gx, ɛh/,[16] etc. If we try to pin this limitation upon a component of one of the phonemes, say /f/ among the labials, we must recognize that component in all the other homorganic phonemes—/b/ and /m/—since the limitation applies equally to them. In order to enable the component to have any effect upon the neighborhood of the labial (so as to preclude another labial there), it must be present also in the neighboring position. We are thus faced with the need for a component which occurs in all the labials and in the place next to each labial, and which permitts only a doubling of that labial, or a non-labial, to occur, but no different labial. This can be done by a 3-length component whose phonetic value is defined as follows: in its middle length, labial (so that the component serves to distinguish, say, the labial voiced stop /b/ from the dental voiced stop /d/); in its first and third lengths, labial if the other components are identical with those of the middle length, and laryngal otherwise. If this component is simultaneous in its middle length with the components for voiced stop, it will yield /b/ in that position; and if on either side there are again the voiced-stop components alone, this component will yield with them another /b/; while if the components there are anything else, say voiceless continuant, this component, extending over them, will with them yield a corresponding laryngal voiceless continuant, /ḥ/.[17]

If, as in English, there are no double consonants, we have to say that certain components, one or another of which is present in every consonant, have 3-phoneme lengths and have some stated value in their middle length and some contrary value in their end lengths, if the other components are identical with those of the middle length.

Clustering. Further extensions of our method are necessary when we treat some of the more complicated limitations upon clusters, especially when limitations of order are present, i.e. when certain phonemes occur in one order but not in another. For example, English has morpheme-medial clusters like /rtr/, /ndw/, as in portrait, sandwich, but never clusters like /trt/, with any one of the consonants /r, l, m, n, ŋ, y, w/ in the middle. We cannot say simply that phonemes in the class of /r/ do not occur after stops, because in clusters of two consonants we have /rt, kr, lr, pt/ (curtain, secret, walrus, reptile; but no stop other than /t/ or /d/ after another stop). We require, therefore, a component extending over the length of a cluster and having the following phonetic values: in first position, general consonant value (serving incidentally to distinguish consonants from vowels; this because any consonant may occur here); in second position, continuant or /t, d/ if it follows a stop, otherwise general consonant value; in third position, continuant if it follows a stop (but if the stop is /t, d/, this value only if a continuant precedes it), otherwise, vocalic value. This value of the consonant-component permits any clusters of two except stop plus /p, b, k, g/, and then permits the third place to have continuant value (and to remain a member of the cluster) only if the preceding two are continuant and stop; otherwise the component has non-consonant value and thus changes the third position into a vowel. This statement does not allow for clusters with middle /s/, as in sexton, and omits several details which would be taken care of in the other components for the individual phonemes. However, it is included here to show that even fairly complicated clusterings can be described by single components.

Summary. The net result of this technique is the extraction of 2-length and longer components from all sequences that can be matched against non-occurring sequences (a sequence being an environment and the phoneme that occurs in it); e.g. from English /rtr/ matched against /trt/. These components do part of

15 The morphophonemic alternation of φ for π + ʿ (e.g. in ἀφ' ὧν) can also be avoided, if the ʿ component is written where it is heard. In the few cases of two aspirates within a word, a second ʿ would have to be written over the extra aspirate, and the statement of the length of ʿ would have to be adjusted accordingly. In the case of reduplication there is a real elimination of the morphophonemic statement: the stem initial in /ʿpépūka/ (or /pépʿūka/) is /p/, which is duly present in the reduplication.

16 For the phonetic values of these phonemes see op. cit. in fn. 5.

17 The laryngal value for the ends of the labial component is not essential, though it seemed most convenient for various reasons. It would also be possible to assign merely a 'non-labial' value to the ends of the labial component, leaving it to the components in the neighboring positions to decide whether they are laryngal, dental, or palatal. They cannot be labial because a 'non-labial' component extends over them.

the work of identifying and phonetically describing the phoneme over which they extend (e.g. the ʿ gives the aspiration component of Greek φ), so that only a residue of the original phoneme is required to accompany them (in this case /p/ to accompany ʿ: /ʿp/ = φ). This residue in turn can designate another phoneme which occurs without the component (/p/ = π). Meanwhile, the length of the component, covering an environment and the phoneme that occurs in it, takes care of the original limitation in distribution. In the simplest cases this may be just a special limitation between contiguous phonemes, when in a given environment only such phonemes occur as are similar in some respect to that environment: the extracted component then has a single phonetic value throughout its length (so /n̿s̿/ for English /nt/). In other cases, the phonemes which occur in an environment may be no more similar to it than those which do not; in fact, it may be precisely the phonemes similar to the environment that never occur in it: the extracted component will then have different phonetic values in different parts of its length (so the Moroccan labial component). More generally, these components can be set up to express the fact that particular phonemes occur in one order and not in another (English morpheme-medial /pt/ occurs, /tp/ does not), and that only certain types of clusters occur; in such cases the phonetic values of the components may vary according to what phonemes or components adjoin it (just as allophones of phonemes vary in value according to what phonemes adjoin them).

Where two groups of phonemes are completely separated, so that no member of one group occurs with a member of the other, the extracted component always keeps its particular length (e.g. when in Moroccan Arabic neither /š/ nor /ž/ occurs near either /s/ or /z/). Where the separation is not complete (so that Moroccan /ṭ/, for example, occurs with /a/ but not with /æ/, while /t/ occurs with both /a/ and /æ/), the extracted component must have different lengths in different positions: with /ṭ/ it has 2-phoneme length so as to exclude /æ/, but with /a/ it has one-phoneme length so as not to exclude /t/.[18] Where the limitation of distribution operates only between adjoining phonemes, their common component extends only over the sequence in question (i.e. the environment, and the phoneme which occurs in it to the exclusion of some other phoneme): so in English /ŋk/ or in Swahili consonant clusters. Where the limitation operates across unaffected phonemes, or throughout some stated limits such as a cluster or a morpheme, then the extracted component has zero value over those phonemes which happen to occur in its length but are not party to the limitation which it expresses: e.g. the Moroccan limitation on the occurrence of /š, ž/ and /s, z/ is operative throughout word limits; and the voiced-voiceless separation in English morpheme-medial clusters applies only to phonemes with voiced or voiceless homorganic counterparts and hence does not affect /r, l, m, n, ŋ, y, w/ if they occur in the same cluster (thus /ŋgz/ in *anxiety*, but /ŋkš/ in *anxious*; there is no /ŋkz/).

5.3 *Defective distribution expressed by simultaneous components.* Our third operation is to try to break up into simultaneous components any allophones which cannot be assigned to the existing phonemes and which have a very defective distribution in themselves. This is the case with the nasalized alveolar flap of *painting*, which occurs only after loud-stressed and before weak-stressed vowels. In this position it contrasts with all the consonant phonemes, so that we would be forced to recognize it as a new phoneme occurring only in this one environment.[18a] Since we cannot set up this restricted allophone as complementary to some single previously recognized phoneme, we ask if it may not be complementary to some sequence of previously recognized phonemes. We find that /nt/ is one of the very few sequences which occur between vowels under other stress conditions without also occurring after loud and before weak-stressed vowels. The nasalized flap is therefore in complementary distribution with this sequence and is analyzed into two simultaneous components, one an allophone of /n/ in this position (V́-tV) and the other an allophone of /t/.

There is, of course, a morphophonemic consideration: *painting* can be divided into two morphemes, the first of which would have a morphophonemic alternation between /nt/ and the nasalized flap if we recognized the latter as being anything but /nt/. This consideration is not important here, but might be resorted to in other cases. In any event, it is not essential to such analysis. When we break up the palatalized post-dental blade stop into simultaneous allophones of /t/ before /y/ and of /y/ after /t/ (/tyuwn/ for *tune*), we have no morphophonemic advantage, since when a morpheme ending with /t/ comes before a morpheme beginning with /y/, we get not the palatalized stop but /č/ (or /tš/) by morphophonemic alternation.

From the point of view of relations between allophones, this operation means that we extend complementary distribution to apply not only to single allophones but also to sequences of allophones. From the point of view of the physical nature of allophones, it means that we no longer require an allophone to be an observable complete sound; we extend the term to include observable components of a sound. The net result is to eliminate some potential phonemes of exceptionally limited distribution.

[18] Or we may say that with /t/, absence of that component has one-phoneme length so as not to exclude /a/ (which contains the component).

[18a] Rather than include it in one of the vowel phonemes, which would confuse all the general statements about the distribution of vowel phonemes and their allophones.

5.4 Phonetic similarity expressed by short components. In carrying out the distributional analysis, we shall have extracted components from various phonemes in whatever language we investigate. It may be profitable to continue this extraction until all phonemes have been reduced to combinations of components.

When long components have been set up for all the important distributional limitations, we proceed to analyze those phonemes which have not been broken up, or the residues of the phonemes which have been broken up. Each of these phonemes or residues may be analyzed into simultaneous components so chosen as to distinguish the phonemes phonetically one from the other in the simplest manner. 'Simplest' can be determined with the aid of a few obvious criteria: where possible we should utilize components already recognized in the previous analysis, stating that in this position (or in this combination) the component has only one-phoneme length, since it affects only the phoneme which it identifies phonetically. For example, if in a particular language we have had to recognize front, middle, and back consonants because they follow /m, n, ŋ/ respectively, whereas all vowels occur after each of these three nasals, we may nevertheless use the front, middle, and back components to differentiate vowels, with the proviso that they do not have 2-phoneme length when they occur with vowels, and hence do not preclude the occurrence of a front vowel (say /i/) after a back nasal /ŋ/.[19] This means in effect that the limitations of distribution among certain phonemes are used as a partial guide to show us what phonetic differences among the other phonemes are the relevant ones.

Another criterion is the parallelism of allophones among the different phonemes. If the allophones of English /p, t, k/ are all analogous in that they all have comparable differences of aspiration in identical environments (as [p^h, t^h, k^h] after word-juncture but [p, t, k] after /s/, etc.), we can say that a particular component γ is contained in each of them and that this γ (which may be the combination of the unvoicing and the stop components) is strongly aspirated after word-juncture, unaspirated after /s/, etc.

The physical movements of articulation may also offer certain absolute factors common to various phonemes: /p, t, k/ are generally voiceless, fortis, stopped. Since the components will in the last analysis have to identify articulatory (as well as acoustic) events, it is desirable to reflect these as closely as possible. However, as is well known, the correlation with articulatory events will rarely coincide completely with our other criteria, not even with the criterion of complementary distribution for phonemes. To take the simplest example, there are sounds in the /t/ phoneme which are not stops (in butter, etc.).

[19] In varying measures, this is the case in English (within a morpheme), Swahili, and Fanti.

Some components which are commonly extracted by linguists merely because they consist of pitch or stress features have no basis for being thus extracted except the phonetic considerations of this section. Such, for example, are the tones in languages where each vowel in a morpheme has an arbitrary phonemic pitch.[20] As far as distributional simplicity goes we could just as well state that a language has not, say, 5 vowels and 3 tones, but 15 vowel phonemes (high /í/, mid /i/, low /ì/ — all of which might differ in quality as well as pitch; high /é/, etc.). If these vowels have not already been completely broken down into components on distributional grounds, we may now extract the tones as components on grounds of phonetic simplicity.

5.5 Manipulating the components. When all the phonemes of a language are completely analyzed into components, various additional problems are met. A set of components which conveniently express certain limitations of distribution (e.g. of the voiced-unvoiced group in English as against /r, l, m, n, ŋ, y, w/) may conflict with a different analysis which results from a different limitation but which involves some of the already-analyzed phonemes of the first group (e.g. /s/ which in certain respects behaves like /r, l, m, n, ŋ, y, w/). Sometimes the only way to resolve such difficulties is to reconsider the phonemic system. This is, of course, permissible, since in grouping allophones together into phonemes there are often alternative ways of grouping within the basic phonemic criteria.[21] We choose one way for our phonemic statement, but a slightly different grouping of some of the allophones may be more convenient for the component analysis. Furthermore, we sometimes obtain an extremely complicated component analysis for the distributional limitations and clusterings of the phonemes throughout the vocabulary of the language, where a much simpler system may be possible if we eliminate from consideration certain morphemes (often borrowed ones) which have a different phonetic structure from the rest.[22] It is often possible to identify phonemically the parts of the vocabulary which we wish to exclude from consideration, and perhaps to give them a separate component analysis. For all these reasons, any attempt at a component analysis of a whole phonemic system requires considerable attention to the detailed facts of the language. No examples of such systems will therefore be presented here. It has been possible, however, to carry out the analysis for a few languages, and to obtain sets of components which had only mildly complicated phonetic values, and which required very few statements about distribution (so that practically every combination or sequence of components occurred).

[20] E.g. Fanti. See W. E. Welmers and Z. S. Harris, The Phonemes of Fanti, JAOS 62.319 (1942).

[21] Y. R. Chao, op. cit. in fn. 4.

[22] Leonard Bloomfield, The Structure of Learned Words, A Commemorative Volume Issued by the Institute for Research in English Teaching 17–23 (Tokyo, 1933).

Are the Components Usable?

6.1 *Their status in descriptive linguistics.* Having worked through specific cases of analysis into components, we may now ask: What is the status in linguistic science of the new techniques and the new elements which they produce? At present the phonemic elements of linguistic analysis are obtained by segmenting the flow of speech and calling each group of mutually substitutable segments ('free variants') an allophone. Now the components described in this paper are not complete physical events; therefore, they cannot actually be substituted for each other to see if any two of them are free variants or 'repetitions' of each other. First, therefore, we must move as before from unique sounds to allophones, which in general have the relative length of a phoneme (that is, are not composed of smaller segments which in turn are allophones of phonemes). Only then can we proceed to analyze the allophones into simultaneous components, producing a new set of elements instead of the previous allophones. The operation of complementary distribution can be performed upon the new elements as well as upon the old. Theoretically, therefore, we could break the allophones into components and then do all the complementary grouping upon the components. Actually, it is more efficient to group the complementary allophones into tentative phonemes, and to analyze these tentative phonemes into components. We can then try to group the components by complementary distribution in order to get fewer components, each having wider coverage. If certain limitations of occurrence exist for some components, we may even try to express their limitations in turn by a second extraction of components, on much the same grounds that we used in expressing phonemic limitations by components, in order to obtain the most general and least limited set of elements.

We thus obtain for the language a new set of elements, each of which occurs with fewer limitations than the original phonemes. This is so because each setting up of a component of more than one-phoneme length takes care of at least one limitation of phonemic occurrence; this is equally true of the automatic-sequence components (§5.1) which replace the highly limited distribution of phonemic pitch and stress.[22a] In some cases the components can be so selected that practically every possible combination and sequence of the components actually occurs. Any combinations and sequences that do not occur will, of course, have to be stated.

The new elements are still, like the phonemes, in bi-unique correspondence with speech events: given the writing we know uniquely what sounds to pronounce, and given the sounds we know uniquely how

---

22a We have seen that the 2- and 3-place components of §5.2 and the fixed-sequence components of §5.1 differ in effect, in that the former describe limitations of distribution and the latter describe contours. It is of interest to notice wherein these two types of long components differ structurally and wherein they are similar.

They are similar in that they are all expressions for limitations of distribution of different segments. In the case of the pitch contours, we begin with allophonic segments that contain pitch and stress features in them. We notice that there are limitations upon the distribution of these segments. For instance, after a sequence of segments in which each loud-stressed segment is higher-pitched than the preceding, we never get a low-pitched segment: after *Is your brother ?* we never get a low *going*, but only a *going which is* pitched even higher than *brother*. And in *Is your brother going?* we do not get a low pitched *ing*. We express this limitation of distribution by saying that all the segments of the utterance contain a particular component in common, and that this component has various phonetic values at various parts of its stretch: low pitch on the first low-stressed vowel, higher pitch on the next, etc. Exactly this is what we do with the 2- and 3-place components: We notice that after /s/ we never have /b/, but only /p/. We express this by saying that both successive segments have a particular component in common, and that this component has fortis value throughout its stretch.

The differences between the two types of long components are four. First, the phonetic values of the contour components are usually all pitch and stress features, which we are accustomed to consider a thing apart, while the phonetic values of the other components may seem to us to be arbitrarily extracted from the rest of the segment, as when we distinguish the closure of /b/ from its lip position.

Second, since the contour components are often constituents of simultaneous morphemes (e.g. the question intonation), we often cannot obtain the phonemes of the segmental morphemes (e.g. *your* or *brother*, without regard to intonation) until after the contour components have been extracted. Therefore we usually extract the contour components while working on sequences of allophonic segments, whereas we extract the other long components by working on sequences of phonemes.

Third, whereas the long components usually extend over a definite small number of phonemes, the contour components usually extend over a variable (and much larger) number—as many as there may be in a linguistic form or utterance of a particular type.

Fourth, we usually have many more positional variants of a contour component than of a 2- or 3-place component. The 1221130 of *I don't know where he's going.* (§5.1) and the 2230 of *Bud Clark fumbled.* are positional variants of the 230 in *He told him.* The phonemic component environment, which determines the number of 1's and the number and place of 2's in all these variants, is the simultaneous sequence of stress contours. The 2- or 3-place components usually have fewer though more complicated positional variants, as when the Swahili n component indicates tongue retarding with labial components, but velar occlusion with h (n + p = t, n + b = d, n + h = k).

to write them.[23] The components are essentially similar to phonemes in that both are distributional symbols with phonetic values. That is to say, the observed physical events are always sounds, and the criteria for classifying them into linguistic elements—whether phonemes or components—are always distributional.

The components are merely generalizations of the phonemes, extending the very development which gives us phonemes out of sounds. In writing allophones we have one distinguishable sound per symbol (hence closely abiding by the physical event); but there are many symbols and each usually has a highly restricted occurrence. In writing phonemes we often have several distinguishable sounds per symbol, usually but not always having considerable phonetic similarity (hence abiding rather less closely by the physical event); but there are fewer symbols with a wider distribution for each. In writing components we usually have more distinguishable sounds per symbol, sometimes with no common feature (hence abiding much less by the physical event); but there are fewer symbols yet, with much wider distribution for each. It follows that analysis into components completes what phonemics can only do in part: the transfer of the limitations of sounds from distributional restriction to positional variation in phonetic value. This is not an argument for the use of components: phonemics is undoubtedly the more convenient stopping point in this development, because it fits alphabetic writing; but we must recognize the fact that it is possible to go beyond it.

6.2 Practical and historical considerations. The use of components will clearly be practicable only within narrow limits. Components which enter into supra-segmental morphemes (e.g. sentence intonations) are now extracted and must be extracted in order to permit isolation of morphemes in general. Components which resolve major distributional limitations, e.g. Moroccan ʼ or ˀ, can easily be extracted and written among the segmental phonemes. Such components are especially worth extracting if many morphophonemic statements are thereby eliminated.[24] One-length components produce little saving and would not normally be extracted except for cases like vowel tones (§5.4), where the extraction is due chiefly to tradition or is desirable because the tones have morphophonemic alternations under various syntactic pitches.

Analysis into components may be of interest to linguists even where it is not used to simplify the writing system, for components may offer correlations with historical change, and may in a sense quantify the structural importance of various phonemic limitations. The connection with linguistic change derives from the fact that many phonemic limitations are produced by single historical changes[25] or by a related series of them, so that the long components may represent the effect of events in history. The structural quantification derives from the fact that some non-occurrences of phonemes are represented by long components and others merely by the non-occurrence of one component with a particular other component in a position where the first component otherwise occurs. Let us take the non-occurring */sbin/ and */stend/ in English. If the cluster-long unvoicing component is ¯, we may say that spin is /z̄b̄in/; the sequence /z̄b̄/ (= /sb/) is impossible since ¯ always extends over the whole cluster in which it occurs. On the other hand the general vowel component contained in /e/ occurs after /st/, but only with the particular quality component of /æ/ and not that of /e/: stand but not *stend. There is no long component excluding the /e/ quality component from the position after /t/ or before /n/ or between clusters, since the /e/-quality component occurs in those positions: tend, spend. Therefore all we have is the fact that while the general vowel component occurs in between /st/ and /nd/, it does not occur there with the /e/-quality component, although it does with that component elsewhere. We may then say that forms like */sbin/ are excluded from the phonetic structure as it is described by our components, while forms like */stend/ are not excluded. True, the same considerations which led us to set up a long component in the first case and not in the second could have led us directly to such a judgment concerning these two forms. But no form of expression creates new information: the only question is the availability and organization which it gives to the information. The difference in terms of components is perhaps more clear-cut than a direct discussion of each form, and in setting up the components we may have used relevant considerations which we should not have thought of in a direct discussion.[26]

23 If only the first of these were true, we should have morphophonemic writing. We may permit partial overlapping among our components, i.e. the same sound feature may be represented in different environments by different components, but that is no bar to phonemic writing.

24 This will in general happen only in cases of automatic morphophonemic alternation.

25 See now Henry Hoenigswald, Internal Reconstruction, Studies in Linguistics 1944. [Superseded by Hoenigswald's Sound Change and Linguistic Structure, Lang. 22.138 (1946) ((139–41)).]

26 Various other facts about the phonetic structure also transpire from a component analysis. One can tell, by looking at the combinations of components representing the phonemes, which phonemes ever occur next to each other and which never do (i.e. whether they have a long component in common), which phonemes replace each other in complementary environments (i.e. whether all their one-length components are identical), which phonemes have the smallest number of different phonemes next to them (i.e. the ones that contain the largest number of long components).

Summary

7. This paper has tried to show that many linguistic facts can be discovered and described by the application of a single operation: the analysis of speech into simultaneous components. Automatic sequences of phonetic features yield intonations, word stresses and the like. Defectively distributed phonemes complementary to sequences of phonemes are broken up into allophones of those sequences. Limitations of phonemic distribution, including neutralization, cluster limits, and certain automatic morphophonemic changes, are resolved by components having a length of more than one phoneme. Phonemes and residues not otherwise broken up are analyzed into components of one-phoneme length on the basis of phonetic considerations. The length of a component can vary in different positions, and can be bounded by phonemic environment or by junctures. The phonetic value of a component can vary in different positions, and can be determined by its concurrent components, or its neighboring components, or the section of the component's length. Whole phonemic systems can be replaced by component systems.

No one technique is essential, but rather the method of attack. Different devices will have to be used in different situations. For each language, it will be necessary to state what system of combination of the components is being used, what the length and phonetic value of each component is, and what limitations of occurrence remain among the components.

It has been shown that this analysis creates a new set of elements out of the original allophones or phonemes, and that these elements have the same status as phonemes and are, indeed, merely generalized phonemes. Analysis into simultaneous parts is the only operation aside from segmentation into allophones that produces usable elements for descriptive linguistics.

⟦I remember being asked more than once what Harris meant to accomplish by using components to remove limitations upon the occurrence of phonemes: why is it so important to him to remove limitations? How is description improved if it is done by introducing a complication? The answer seems to be that a worse complication is thereby removed. This is worth considering in detail for the light that it throws on the special Harris sort of contribution to theory. A phonemic analysis starts out from two kinds of concrete givens: (1) phonetic stuff, and (2) same-vs-different reactions of speakers and native listeners. The completed analysis yields a phonological model for that language. This model is purely phonological: it has nothing to do with meaning, hence nothing to do with the identities of items (morphemes, etc. [the 'etc.' refers to such things as the 'arrangements' of the morphemes, or the 'processes' through which they build utterances, or whatever is called for further by the particular higher-level model adopted later]) which the phonological elements (phonemes) spell. Again, this phonological model of the language has no longer anything to do with the physical texture of the phonetic stuff which was one of the two kinds of original givens. The independence of the phonology from meaning is easy to understand and accept; but this other independence (from phonetics) sounds like treason, and its rejection is found in some schools of phonological doctrine. But the independence of the phonological model from phonetic texture is an essential prerequisite to abstract proceeding.

Having established a phonological model for a language, one henceforth treats it as autonomous: no further regard for phonetics or for meaning is permissible while one examines the functioning of the phonological model. This allows (and forces) the examination to be abstract. The elements of the phonological model are treated as counters—as marks on paper, for instance. What can be the 'functioning' of counters like that? By 'functioning' one might mean different things depending on the linguistic level under consideration. A whole utterance, for example, fulfills a communicative function; hence it is properly said to have meaning. At the other end of the scale, an individual phoneme can do nothing more (and nothing less) than help spell an utterance. Its 'functioning' thus consists of cooperating with the other phonemes to spell it. Its way of doing this is again nothing more (and nothing less) than occurring in context with other phonemes. (If it is objected that phonemes are not properly said to 'occur', a longer paraphrase may be used involving phonetic correlates of phonemes.) The phoneme-combinations that occur may be listed; and this completes the model.

That is, a complete phonological model consists of (a) the list of phonemes, and (b) the list of their occurrent combinations. The latter, it would seem, could only be the list of all utterances. But there is a cheap substitute for this: a set of formulas saying what does (not) occur in immediate context. It is made both a cheap and an adequate substitute by setting up classes (sub-lists of the list of phonemes) to appear as terms in the formulas, and defining 'immediate context' as cheaply as the language will allow.

Now the present article is an attempt to eliminate an undesirable complication: the dualism between (a) and (b) or its substitute. Complete elimination would give a model consisting of a homogeneous list of elements combining freely (because the model has no (b) any more) to spell utterances in the language.

To achieve an elimination that is both cheap and total (or asymptotically total) it is expedient, in setting up classes to serve in co-occurrence formulas or long components, to forget phonetic homogeneity (end of first paragraph here). See Harris, Methods in Structural Linguistics (Chicago, 1951), 136–43.⟧

SOUND CHANGE AND LINGUISTIC STRUCTURE

HENRY M. HOENIGSWALD

Language 22.138–43—1946

The interplay of sound change and analogy may create patterns so typical as to make it possible to recover from them the process to which they owe their existence. Such internal reconstruction serves to supplement the comparative method. In this paper sound changes are classified with regard to their effect on structure: 1. non-phonemic change; 2. phonemic change without loss of contrast; 3. unconditioned merger with loss of contrast; 4. conditioned merger with loss of contrast; 5. secondary rearrangement induced by a primary loss of contrast; 6. borrowed contrast.

1. Pronunciation changes which leave intact existing contrasts between forms of different meaning must be very common. Most of them go unnoticed, since an uninterrupted writing-tradition naturally will not reveal meaningless fluctuations. However, comparative study in phonetic terms, or a break in the alphabetic tradition with the subsequent adoption of a new writing practice on a quasi-phonetic basis, will show up the more drastic changes. What seems to have been IE [dʻ] was changed to [d] or [ð] in Germanic. This change did not affect any of the existing contrasts (since old IE [d] remained distinct). The Roman alphabet, introduced after the change had taken place, indicates, however, its phonetic result, namely, a sound type close enough to Latin [d] to be spelled with the same letter. Many instances of sound change belong here: extensive portions of the English vowel shift, the rotation of stops in Armenian, and parts of Grimm's law (as indicated above). Since this kind of change leaves no structural traces, it could not be recovered by internal evidence from the resulting stage.

2. Of three similar sound types, [A], [B], and [X], if [A] and [B] occur in the same environment while [X] occurs in a different environment, [X] will naturally be assigned to the same phoneme, say /a/, as one of the other two—whichever is phonetically closer, say [A]. (In an extreme case, this phonetic similarity amounts to 'identity', say of [X] and [A], so that [A], distributed more widely in various environments, contrasts in part with [B], which is more restricted.) Let us now assume that the pronunciation of [A], [B], or [X] (or any two, or all three) changes in such a manner as to make [X] more similar to [B] than to [A]. This will make [X] a part of another phoneme, say /b/.

Grimm's law offers a famous example. IE voiceless stops were changed in Germanic to spirants (e.g. [t] to [θ]), and voiced stops to voiceless ones (e.g. [d] to [t]). But after voiceless consonant, only some kind of [t] occurred in IE. The latter, which was presumably not changed at all at the time of the general shift, was originally most similar to the stop of the old [t]-words; it is now most similar to that of the new [t]-words. This is customarily formulated by saying that [t] changes to [θ] except after initial [s]; that is, it suffers a conditioned sound change. This is a natural formulation in historical grammar, since written records are more nearly in terms of phonemes than of sound types. The alternation between þ and t in Goth. salbō-þ-s 'anointed' and haf-t-s 'restrained' reflects the redistribution of allophones and allows us to reconstruct one original morpheme -to-. See §3c and §4a.

3. Sound changes that wipe out contrasts between meaningfully different forms affect the linguistic structure much more drastically. It is necessary to distinguish between the primary process of phonemic merger and the secondary phonemic rearrangement of neighboring sounds which such a merger may entail. The extent of the merger and, occasionally, the fact that zero is involved, set off these processes into further sub-groups.

When all the sound types (allophones) functioning as members of one phoneme fall together with another sound type or with other sound types, the phoneme will disappear as a separate entity. The following combinations seem to be possible.

(a) All the allophones of phoneme /x/ merge with allophones of phoneme /y/, so that /axb/ > /ayb/; the contrast /axb/ : /ayb/ is wiped out. In historical grammar, these cases appear as unconditioned change. IE dh (presumably a unit phoneme /dʻ/) falls together with d in such languages as Iranian and Slavic; IE a, e, o all become Skt. a; Lat. u and ō fall together in Romance. The process leaves only inconclusive traces in the form of an occasional statistical preponderance of the surviving phoneme, as in the case of Skt. a or Mod. Gk. /i/, which comes from eleven different sources.

(b) All the allophones of phoneme /x/ disappear, i.e. they merge with zero,[1] so that the contrast

[1] Treating the disappearance of phonemes as merger with zero simplifies our statements concerning loss of contrast. Zero behaves like a phoneme of extremely wide distribution; it may be said to occur (if its alternation with a real phoneme recommends this formula) between the members of any permitted sequence of phonemes, including pauses. Two zeros occur in Gk. /ána/ 'lord!', i.e. /ána00/ vs. /ánakt-os/ 'of the lord'.

/axb/ : /a0b/ = /ab/ is obliterated. From the viewpoint of the historical record, this is unconditioned loss. IE p was thus lost in Celtic, Latin h in Vulgar Latin. This process will leave no traces in the subsequent structure.

(c) All the allophones of /x/ merge with allophones belonging to different phonemes, or some allophones of /x/ merge with allophones of one or more other phonemes and others disappear, i.e. merge with zero. Thus, some allophones of /x/ fall together with allophones of /y/, others with allophones of /z/, and still others disappear. In Sanskrit, the particular variety of IE ə which preceded y fell together with the old a, e, o (> Skt. a), while the other varieties or allophones merged with IE i. In traditional parlance this is stated more briefly as a conditioned sound change: ə before y > a, otherwise > i. As in the foregoing cases, /x/ as a separate phoneme has vanished from the language. Where a paradigm has been thus affected by the split of /x/, the subsequent stage will exhibit an alternation, say, of /y/, /z/, and zero (or any two of them). This alternation will not be compulsory in point of phonemic occurrence; for /y/ and /z/ are presumably phonemes of free distribution so far as they include cases of old /y/ and /z/ (not developed from /x/). But it will be a regular alternation, in the sense that it can be stated mechanically in terms of phonemic environment; for the conditions under which /y/, /z/, and zero, respectively, appear in the alternation, are still those which used to govern the different allophones of /x/.[2]

4. Not all losses of contrast eliminate entire phonemes.

(a) More often, a change will work in such a way that some allophones of /x/ (traditionally, 'x under certain conditions') merge with allophones of /y/ ('yields y'), while the others continue in contrast. /xa/ and /ya/ fall together as /ya/, whereas /xb/ and /yb/ remain distinct. The immediate result of this change (a common type of conditioned sound change) is a restriction upon the distribution of /x/, now barred from occurrence before /a/. In addition, the change may affect paradigms. The phoneme /y/ will make its appearance in a paradigm, replacing original /x/. In that case, it will alternate compulsorily with the restricted /x/, i.e. it will appear in those positions and only in those positions in which /x/ never occurs anywhere in the language. Reversed, this rule is one of the main tools of internal reconstruction: compulsory alternation between restricted /x/ and free /y/ in a paradigm indicates a previous conditioned sound change from /x/ to /y/ in the position from which it is now excluded. The reconstruction is often supported by the existence of parallel non-alternating paradigms showing only /y/. Mod. Ger. /d/ is restricted in comparison with /t/, in that it does not occur in syllable-final position: it is found in /štúnde/ Stunde 'hour', but not in /ʔunt/ 'and'. Moreover, /d/ and /t/ are in compulsory alternation in such paradigms as /búnde/ Bunde 'alliance [dat.]' : /búnt/ Bund 'alliance [nom.]'. A parallel paradigm involving only /t/ is furnished by /búnte/ bunte 'motley ones' : /búnt/ bunt 'motley'. From this state of affairs the merger of the syllable-final allophone of /d/ with an allophone of /t/ (or the change of syllable-final d to t) could be inferred even if it were not known from historical records.

(b) Some allophones of /x/ may merge with zero (x under some conditions is lost; 'conditioned loss'); e.g. /xa/ falls together with /a/ while /xb/ continues to contrast with /b/. Alternations resulting from this process are not fundamentally different from those discussed in the preceding paragraph: /x/ will be found to alternate with zero, the latter appearing in those positions in which /x/ never occurs, as in Gk. /mélit-os/ 'of honey' : /méli/ (i.e. /méli0/) 'honey' (all stops being excluded from word-final position), or E /a-knóledž/ acknowledge : /nóledž/ (i.e. /0nóledž/) knowledge (/k/ being excluded from initial position preceding /n/). As in the preceding case, the sound changes[3] can be recovered from an interpretation of the paradigms.

(c) Some allophones of /x/ may merge with /y/, others with /z/, still others with zero, etc., while some allophones continue phonemically distinct. This instance does not add anything new to the other cases of partial survival of /x/.

5. The effects of merger sometimes force a reinterpretation of the environment. This reinterpretation will be referred to as secondary change.

(a) Let some allophones of /x/ merge with /y/ or zero, so that /x/ becomes limited and alternates compulsorily with the more freely occurring /y/ or with zero (see §4a, b); further, let the missing portion of /x/ be filled up, entirely or in part, by a change in the pronunciation of a sound type [Z] from an outside phoneme /z/, now reassigned to /x/ on the basis of phonetic similarity (see §2). The alternation between /x/ and /y/ or zero will then cease to be compulsory, although it will remain regular. When /s/ between vowels was lost in Homeric Greek, the paradigm /génes-si/ 'generations [dat.]' : /géne-os/ [gen. sg.], i.e. /géne0-os/ showed compulsory alternation between /s/ and zero; when [t] before [i] under certain conditions changed to a sibilant which naturally became a member of the /s/ phoneme, the alternation was no longer compulsory (since e.g. */eîti/ 'he will go' had now become /eîsi/). This history can no doubt be inferred for most instances where zero is a party to a non-compulsory alternation.[4]

[2] For examples of sound alternation in paradigms, see the following paragraph.

[3] Loss of final t in Greek, of initial k before n in Modern English.

[4] See three paragraphs below.

(b) Let there be two similar sound types [Z_1] and [Z_2], such that [Z_1] occurs only in the environment of phoneme /x/ (is conditioned by /x/), while [Z_2] does not occur in that environment. The two sound types are, of course, members of a phoneme /z/. Furthermore, let /x/ (or some of its allophones) merge with /y/ or with zero. This will transform [Z_1] and [Z_2] into contrasting phonemes. In pre-Indo-Iranian, a sound [č] must have existed or developed before [e] and [i], corresponding to [k] in other positions; i.e. a phoneme */k/ had allophones [č] and [k]. When */e/, */a/, and */o/ all fell together in one phoneme, Indo-Iranian /a/, [ča] from [če] and [ka] from [ka] or [ko] came to be in contrast; in other words, /č/ and /k/ had developed from allophones of a single phoneme into members of separate phonemes through merger of the conditioning factor. English /θ/ and /ð/, once automatic variants, have become contrasting phonemes in Modern English (thigh : thy; wreath : wreathe) through loss of the conditioning factors. German [ö] and [ü] started out as allophones of /o/ and /u/ respectively, conditioned by the vowel in the following syllable; as this vowel has not remained intact and in many instances has been lost, the umlaut vowels are now distinct phonemes (e.g. Mod. Ger. /šó:n/ schon 'already' : /šö́:n/ 'beautiful').

(c) If the conditioning factor lost is a so-called juncture, a situation arises which can be characterized as the carry-over of an allophone within a paradigm into a contrasting position. In 'General Eastern' American English a longer and slightly diphthongal [æ·] before certain or all syllable-final voiced consonants corresponds to a shorter [æ] in other positions.[5] In some forms of this dialect, this distribution is still recognizable in [pǽ·d) pad, [pǽdɪŋ] padding (noun), [kǽt] cat. However, there is also [pǽ·dɪŋ] padding (verb form). This form can be explained by assuming that the verb form at one time differed from the noun by showing features of open juncture (onset of loudness on the vowel [ɪ] etc.) which was later lost, thus putting [æ] and [æ·] into a contrasting position (/æ/ vs. /æh/).

Phonemes which have developed from allophones through loss or merger of an outside conditioning factor (§5b, c), will be found to be in non-compulsory alternation provided that paradigms have been affected. Zero will not be a party to such an alternation, since it would be meaningless to assume a development at the start of which zero was an allophone of a phoneme. In addition to being non-compulsory, the alternations will be quite regular—i. e. statable, at best, in terms of morphological categories, but not of the phonemic environment.[6] Where the conditioning factor lost was open juncture, the newly contrasting phonemes are likely to occur in a characteristic distribution: their morphologically isolated occurrences will still show complementary distribution.

6. New contrasts may be created as a result of borrowing. Aside from the instances in which a foreign sound is taken over bodily and added to the list of contrasting phonemes (e.g. /f/ in Russian), loanwords may introduce a contrast between what had up to then been non-contrasting variants. In Hindustani, [ṛ^1] (a retroflex flap) and [ḍ] (a cacuminal voiced stop) are distributed almost complementarily: [ḍ] initially, after /n/, and in the geminate cluster /ḍḍ/; [ṛ^1] elsewhere. There are, however, instances of [ḍ] in other positions, all in loanwords such as /re:ḍi:o:/ 'radio'. If the foreign vocabulary can be set aside on a descriptive basis, as is to some extent possible in English, the old structure can be recovered. Note that E [f] and [v] were allophones of the same phoneme until borrowing introduced words where they occurred in contrasting positions.

7. This analysis of sound changes and their effect on the pattern of a language rests on such general linguistic assumptions as the regularity of phonetic change and the phonemic principle, and is therefore believed to be applicable to any kind of language structure. By distinguishing reversible processes (i. e. those which leave unambiguous traces behind) from ambiguous ones, it furnishes the rules of internal reconstruction, a method which supplements or (in the absence of comparative data) substitutes for comparative reconstruction. It is worth noting that unambiguous traces necessarily involve the distribution of sounds in morphological paradigms: compulsory alternations permit the reconstruction of conditional merger between phonemes; regular non-compulsory alternations (especially those (involving zero) may be traced back to the same kind of merger with an intervening secondary change; irregular alternations, if paralleled in sets, frequently point to the loss or merger of an outside factor; a peculiar distribution of paradigmatic against isolated forms will reveal loss of juncture. Rules such as these (which have been tested though not formulated[7] by generations of linguists) imply that the analogical processes and syntactical constructions whereby meaningful forms (morphemes, words, clauses) are put together, are essentially regular, i. e. statable in terms of order and selection, while alternation is brought about by sound change (and then again frequently abolished by new analogical handling of forms). What remains to be done is to classify the structural changes brought about by certain types of analogical and syntactic construction in the widest sense, including such linguistic forms as boundary markers (junctures) and intonations.

[5] G. L. Trager, American Speech, 15.255–8 (1940).

[6] Belated loss or merger of the conditioning factor may also occur in the cases treated under §3c and §4. It will not create new phonemes, but make both the free (§3c) and the compulsory alternations (§4) irregular. Paradigms like E sing: sang: sung have developed in that way.

[7] J. H. Bonfante in Word 1.132 refers to them briefly as a 'simple play of logical deduction'. Among those who have helped to clear up the details we mention E. Hermann, KZ 41.1–69; N. van Wijk, Phonologie [passim] (The Hague, 1939); A. A. Hill, Lang. 12.15–22 ((81)); L. Bloomfield, Language 369–91; R. Jakobson, TCLP 4.247–67. Some of the facts presented in this paper were dealt with by the author in SIL 2.4.78–87. The author wishes to acknowledge the suggestions and encouragement which he has had in discussing the matter with Bernard Bloch, Zellig S. Harris, George L. Trager, Rulon S. Wells, and many others.

FROM MORPHEME TO UTTERANCE

Zellig S. Harris

Language 22.161–83—1946

1.0. This paper presents a formalized procedure for describing utterances directly in terms of sequences of morphemes rather than of single morphemes.[1] It thus covers an important part of what is usually included under syntax. When applied in a particular language, the procedure yields a compact statement of what sequences of morphemes occur in the language, i.e. a formula for each utterance (sentence) structure in the language.

1.1. At present, morpheme classes are formed by placing in one class all morphemes which are substitutable for each other in utterances, as *man* replaces *child* in *The child disappeared*. The procedure outlined below consists, essentially, in extending the technique of substitution from single morphemes (e.g. *man*) to sequences of morphemes (e.g. *intense young man*). In so far as it deals with sequences, it parallels the type of analysis frequently used in syntax, so that the chief usefulness of this procedure is probably its explicitness rather than any novelty of method or result.

1.2. The reason for a procedure of the type offered here is not far to seek. One of the chief objectives of syntactic analysis is a compact description of the structure of utterances in the given language. The paucity of explicit methods in this work has made syntactic analysis a tedious and often largely intuitive task, a collection of observations whose relevance is not certain and whose interrelation is not clear. Partly as a result of this, many grammars have carried little or no syntactic description. In many of the descriptions that have been written, the lack of explicit methods has permitted the use of diverse and undefined terms and a reliance on semantic rather than formal differentiation.

If we now seek a clearer method for obtaining generalizations about the structure of utterances in a language, it should preferably deal with the simplest observables. These are the morphemes, which are uniquely identifiable and easy to follow. Constructs such as 'morphological levels' may be useful in particular cases, but there is an advantage in avoiding them if we can achieve the same results by direct manipulation of the observable morphemes. The method described in this paper will require no elements other than morphemes and sequences of morphemes,[2] and no operation other than substitution, repeated time and again.

[1] I am indebted to Rulon S. Wells for several valuable discussions of this paper, and to C. F. Voegelin and Bernard Bloch for helpful criticisms. In view of the fact that methods as mathematical as the one proposed here have not yet become accepted in linguistics, some apology is due for introducing this procedure. However, the advantage which may be gained in explicitness, and in comparability of morphologies, may offset the trouble of manipulating the symbols of this procedure. Furthermore, the proposed method does not involve new operations of analysis. It merely reduces to writing the techniques of substitution which every linguist uses as he works over his material. One works more efficiently when one thinks with pencil and paper.

[2] And, of course, phonemic constituents of suprasegmental 'morphemes' (if we wish to call them that), e.g. stress, intonations, and pauses.

The Elements

2.0. We assume, then, that we have isolated the morphemes of the language. An exact list of the morphemes is of course required for any description of the language, no matter what method is followed. It is possible to obtain somewhat different lists of morphemes, depending on certain choices made at the start:

2.1. We might say that a particular phoneme sequence which has widely divergent meanings represents more than one morpheme: homonyms such as *pair* and *pear*, or *make* in *What make is it?* and *She's on the make*. Alternatively, we may say that the sequence (/peyr/ or /meyk/) constitutes only one morpheme under any circumstances.

2.2. We may say that each morpheme can have only one phonemic form, so that for example the English plural endings /s/, /z/, /əz/ (as in *books*, *chairs*, *glasses*) constitute three morphemes, and *am*, *are* constitute two morphemes. Alternatively, we may include each of these sets in a single morpheme, if we say that different phoneme sequences constitute positional variants of one morpheme when they are complementary to each other.[3]

2.3. We could say, as is usually done, that repeated morphemes express concord, as in Latin feminine *-a* in *mēnsa parva* 'the small table' or the modern Hebrew article *ha* (and feminine *-a*) in *haiša haktana* 'the small woman'. Alternatively, we could say that in each of these cases we have not a repeated word-suffix or word-prefix, but rather a single phrase-infix consisting, in the case of the Hebrew article, of the phonemes /ha/ before every noun-morpheme (including adjectives) in a noun phrase. This would mean that instead of our being given a morpheme *ha* and having to state that it occurs only with certain syntactic selections, we are given a morpheme which we may write *ha*...*ha*... and which has no further limitations of selection, but either occurs or does not occur in a phrase, just as do the other morphemes. If the phrase contains the morpheme for 'man' and 'small', it is *iš katan* 'small man'; if it also contains the morpheme for 'the', it is *haiš hakatan*; if it also contains the morpheme for 'feminine', it is *iša ktana*; if it contains both, it is *haiša haktana*.[4]

[3] The conditions may be phonemic or morphological.

[4] In effect, such a treatment of concord takes some of the features of selection, e.g. the fact that all nouns in the Hebrew phrase agree as to the article, and puts these facts into the phonemic form of the repeated morpheme. As a result, not only the physical recurrence of a repeated phoneme, but also its special position (e.g. before every noun of the phrase), is now given when we describe that morpheme. Such treatment permits a simpler syntactic statement, because the information about the recurrence of the repeated morpheme would otherwise have to be given somewhere in the course of the syntactic description. The syntactic equations to be offered below will suffice to describe what morphemes occur together and in what order, but will not be able to describe conveniently the agreements among the morphemes in a sequence. To do so would require various devices; e.g. instead of writing NN (N for noun), we would have to write something like $^{ha}N^{ha}N$, meaning that we can have either NN or $haN\ haN$ but not $haNN$. Hence it is preferable to get as much of this information out of the way as possible before we attack the sequences. Not only the obvious cases of repeated morphemes but also more complicated types of agreement can be stated as being merely the special forms of particular morphemes. For further discussion of this treatment of repeated morphemes as single morphemes, see Lang. 21.121–7 (1945).

2.4. In the alternatives presented in §§2.2–3 above we find that in each paragraph the first method yields phonemically simple morphemes about which statements of selection remain to be made. Thus, we would have to say somewhere that the plural morpheme /s/ occurs only after morphemes ending in a voiceless consonant; that *am* occurs only after *I*; that when *parv-* is in one phrase with *mēnsa* it always has *-a* following; and that whenever *ha* occurs with one noun it will also occur with all other nouns in the phrase. The second method in each case offers phonemically more complicated morphemes which have fewer special limitations of selection as distinguished from other morphemes.

Each method clearly has its advantages and its uses. The syntactic procedure to be indicated below can be carried out regardless of the method followed in setting up the morphemes. However, as will be seen, the fewer limitations of selection we have to deal with, the simpler will be this syntactic procedure. Therefore, in the examples used in this paper it will be assumed that the morpheme list for the language concerned has been constructed by the second method, i.e. that we have included in the phonemic form and definition of the morpheme as many of its limitations as we could.

The Operation

3.0. The procedure to be indicated below consists essentially of repeated substitution: e.g. *child* for *young boy* in *Where did the — go?*. To generalize this, we take a form A in an environment $C — D$ and then substitute another form B in the place of A. If, after such substitution, we still have an expression which occurs in the language concerned, i.e. if not only CAD but also CBD occurs, we say that A and B are members of the same substitution-class, or that both A and B fill the position $C — D$, or the like.

The operation of substitution is basic in descriptive linguistics. Not only is it essential in phonemics, but it is also necessary for the initial setting up of morphemes, for the recognition of morpheme boundaries.

3.1. Morpheme Classes. The first step in our procedure is to form substitution classes of single morphemes. We list, for the language concerned, all single morphemes which replace each other in the substitution test, i.e. which occur in the same environments (have the same selection). If any of them do not occur in the same order, they are placed in a special sub-class. Thus, Moroccan Arabic *n-* 'I will' and *-t* 'I did' are mutually substitutable, although they occur at different points in the order of morphemes: *ana nmši ld'aru* 'I'll go to his house', *ana mšit ld'aru* 'I went to his house'.

3.2. In making these substitution classes of morphemes we may be faced with many problems. In some languages, relatively few morphemes occur in exactly the same environments as others: *poem* occurs in *I'm writing a whole — this time*, but *house* does not. Both morphemes, however, occur in *That's a beautiful —*. Shall we say that *poem* and *house* belong in general to the same substitution class, or that they have some environments in common and some not?

It will be seen that the method proposed in §§3.5–9 below can be used no matter how this problem is met.[5] However, in order to keep the examples of §§4–6 as simple as possible, it will be assumed here that morphemes having slightly different distributions are grouped together into one class if the distributional differences between their environments correspond to the distributional differences between the morphemes. That is, if *poem* and *house* differ distributionally only in the fact that *poem* occurs with *write* and *house* with *wire*, and in comparable differences, and if *write* and *wire* in turn differ only in that *write* occurs with *poem* and *wire* with *house*, and in comparable differences, we put *poem* in one class with *house*, and simultaneously put *write* in one class with *wire*.

3.3. Other differences of environment are less easily handled. English *cover* occurs after both *un-* and *dis-*, while *dress* occurs only after *un-*, *connect* only after *dis-*, and *take* after neither (but *connected* occurs also after *un-*). On the other hand, *cover*, *dress*, *connect*, and *take* all occur before *-ing*, and in environments like *Let's not — it just now*. Here again, shall we group these into the same morpheme class, or into four different classes? That is, should the classes to be used in our method below be set up on the basis of relation to *-ing*, or on the basis of relation to *un-*? We find that the selections which these four have in common (their occurrence before *-ing* and in *Let's not — it just now*) differentiate them from other large substitution classes, such as *India*, *child*, or *to*, *from*, which do not occur in these positions. On the other hand, the selections in which they differ do not differentiate or equate morphemes in a way that is useful in analyzing many utterances. Although *un-* occurs before some of the morphemes which occur before *-ing*, we also find *un-* before a few of the morphemes which occur not before *-ing* but in *the — man:* e.g. *just*, *true*.[6]

As in the case of §3.2, the method to be described below is applicable regardless of the definition of morpheme class that we select. If we put *cover*, *dress*, *connect*, and *take* into four different classes on the basis of relation to *un-*, we will be able to group the classes together later on the basis of their relation to *-ing*. And if we treat them as members of one class on the basis of *-ing*, we will have to note that they differ distributionally (as sub-classes) with respect to *un-*. For brevity, we will here consider them as members of one morpheme class.

3.4. In some cases of morphemes having one environment but not another in common, both the similarity and the difference are relevant for utterance structure. Thus *cover*, *note*, *find* all occur in *—ing*, *We'll — his path*, as well as

[5] If *poem* and *house* are placed in one class N, overlooking the difference in their distribution, then *write* and, say, *wire* (*I'm wiring a whole house this time*) would be placed together in a class V since the distributional difference between them corresponds to that between *poem* and *house*. We would then obtain a statement connecting N and V. If we kept *poem* and *house* in separate classes, and *write* and *wire* in separate classes, we would obtain two statements, one connecting *write* and *poem*, and another connecting *wire* and *house*. These two statements together would equal the one statement about N and V.

[6] The criterion which decides for *-ing*, and against *un-*, as the relevant environment in determining substitution classes is therefore a criterion of usefulness throughout the grammar, a configurational consideration. It will be seen below that the classes defined on the basis of *-ing* can be replaced by certain sequences of classes, which is not the case for any classes based on the *un-* environment. Special statements will have to be made later about the selection of *un-*, which in part will run across the boundaries of the classes set up on the basis of *-ing*, etc.

in —*s* ('plural'), *You can have my* —. But *think* occurs only in the first two types of environment, and *child* only in the last two.[7] In general, practically all morphemes which occur in —*ing* also occur in many environments like *We'll* — *his path*. Similarly, almost all morphemes which occur in —*s* ('plural') occur also in many environments like *You can have my* —. We will therefore recognize these two sets of positions as being diagnostic, and will say that every morpheme which occurs in several environments of one of these two sets is a member of the substitution class which is identified as occurring in that set of positions. There will be two such classes: *cover, note, find, think;* and *cover, note, find, child.* The fact that many morphemes occur in both classes is not relevant at this point, since some do not.[8]

3.5. Morpheme sequences. The chief novelty in the procedure which is offered here is the extension of substitution classes to include sequences of morphemes, not merely single morphemes. We now ask not only if A and B each occur in the environment $C — D$ but also if AE together, or FGH, also occur in that environment. If they do, then A, B, AE, FGH are all substitutable for each other. We may say that they are all members of one substitution class, which is now not merely a class of morphemes but a class of morpheme sequences. The single morphemes in the class are merely the special cases where the sequence consists of one.

Thus we note that in *Please put the book away* we can substitute for *book* not only other single morphemes like *bottle* or *brandy* but also sequences of two and more morphemes like *books, bank-book, brandy bottle, bottle of brandy, silly green get-up.* These sequences differ in various respects: in *brandy bottle* each of the component morphemes could have been substituted singly for *book*; in *books* only the first could; in *silly green get-up* no one of the morphemes could (in most utterances) have alone been substituted for *book.* These differences, however, are not relevant to the essential criterion of our present procedure, which is merely whether or not the sequences are substitutable for each other.

3.6. In the case above, and in most applications of this procedure, we have single morphemes for which the sequences can be substituted. That means that the sequences of morphemes do not yield new classes; we simply group them with various morpheme classes which we have already obtained in the usual manner described in §3.1. We may say that in any such application of our procedure, we reduce sequences to the status of single morphemes (or of environmental classes of single morphemes).

However, there may be sequences of morphemes which occur in environments where single morphemes do not occur, i.e. where they cannot be replaced by any single morpheme. Such sequences may or may not be useful as elements of the utterance structure. For example, Semitic roots plus verb patterns occur in environments in which no single morpheme occurs. They occur before verb suffixes, after verb prefixes, and in various sentence positions such as (in early Semitic) before an accusative noun (presumably with command intonation): thus, in classical Arabic, root *ftḥ* 'open' and pattern (*i*)*--a-* 'command' in *iftaḥ ilbāba* 'open the door!'. In all these environments we always find the sequence of some root plus some pattern; we never find a single morpheme here. We may consider this sequence to constitute an element in the utterance structure, calling it, say, verb stem.

3.7. Since our procedure now permits us to make any substitutions of any sequences, it may become too general to produce useful results. For example, we might take the utterance *I know John was in* and substitute *certainly* for *know John*, obtaining *I certainly was in.* This substitution conceals the fact that the morphemes of *I know John was in* can be said as two utterances instead of as one, if we make the single change of pronouncing its intonation twice, over the first two words and again over the last three, instead of once over all five. That is, it conceals the fact that *I know John was in* can be described as two sentences strung under one sentence intonation. It further conceals the fact that *certainly* may also occur in a different place in the sentence: *I was certainly in*, whereas *know John* would occur only in the one position. And it conceals the concord of *was* with *John*: for if we substituted *we* for *I*, we would still have *was* in *We know John was here*, but *were* in *We certainly were here.* All this suggests that substitution of sequences be so carried out as to satisfy all manipulations of that environment which forms the frame of the substitution.[9]

3.8. In the following sections (§§4, 5), this procedure will be carried out, in a very sketchy manner, for English and for Hidatsa, a Siouan language of North Dakota. There will of course be no attempt to approach even remotely a complete analysis for either language. The purpose of these descriptions is only to show the general lines of the procedure; countless details, as well as some of the types of utterance in each language, will be omitted.

3.9. Equations will be used to indicate substitutability. $BC = A$ will mean that the sequence consisting of a morpheme of class B followed by a morpheme of class C can be substituted for a single morpheme of class A. In cases where unclarity may arise, we shall write $B + C$ for the sequence BC. When we

[7] With variant *-ren* plus vowel change for plural *-s*.

[8] This would give us a class V including *cover, note, find, think,* and a class N including *cover, note, find, child.* It would permit individual morphemes to be members of more than one class. Alternatively, we could put *cover, note, find* into a class G, *think* into V, *child* into N. Then each morpheme could only belong to one class, and morphemes having wider distributions, or having the distributions of two classes, would find themselves in a new class. Bernard Bloch uses yet another solution in his analysis of Japanese. He would regard the noun *cover*, which occurs in positions of N, and the verb *cover*, which occurs in positions of V, as two independent morphemes whose homonymy is syntactically irrelevant. That is, he uses class membership as a necessary condition for morpheme identity. Any of these methods of classification can be followed rigorously, and may be advantageous for particular purposes. Any one of them can be used in the method discussed below without affecting the final result.

[9] Such substitutions as *certainly* for *know John* can be precluded by analyzing the utterance into immediate constituents. However, the analysis into immediate constituents requires a technique different from that used in this paper, a technique based on comparing the apparent structures of utterances and parts of utterances. In this paper, on the other hand, we seek to arrive at a description of the structure of an utterance, without having any prior way of inspecting these structures or of saying whether two utterances are equivalent in structure. Therefore, the analysis into immediate constituents is not used here, and we must state other methods of excluding such substitutions as *certainly* for *know John*.

want to say that A substitutes for B only if C follows, we shall write $AC = BC$.

English

4.1. The morpheme classes. For the purposes of the English examples, we shall set up the following classes of morphemes, on the criterion that for each class there are particular sentence positions which can be filled by any member of that class and by these alone.[10]

N: morphemes which occur before plural *-s* or its alternants, or after *the* or adjectives: *hotel, butter, gain, one,*[11] *two.*

V: before *-ed* past or its alternants; before *-ing*; after N plus *should, will, might,* etc: *go, gain, take, think, will* ('desire'), *have, do.* We may distinguish several sub-classes such as those listed below, while V without any sub-class mark will be used to indicate all the sub-classes together.

V_b: *be, appear, become, get, keep, stay,* etc. (but not *have*). These occur between N and adjectives other than V *-ing: The stuff will stay fresh.*[12]

V_c: verbs which occur between N and V *-ing: stop, try, be* in *Mac will — walking.*

V_d: the transitive verbs which occur before N: *make, buy, want* (but not *go, sleep*) in *I'll — butter.*

V_e: intransitive verbs which do not occur before N: *go, sleep.*

V_f: verbs which occur before two independent N's: *make, consider, want* (but not *buy, go*) in *I'll — this book a best seller.*

V_g: verbs (often causative in meaning) which occur before NV (a noun phrase followed by a verb phrase): *make, let, see* (but not *consider, buy, go*) in *I'd like to — newcomers try it.*

V_h: verbs which occur before N *to* V: *cause, teach, dare, want* (but not *make, go*) in *The other kids — Junior to do it.*

R: between N and V (the V lacking *-ing, -ed*); NRV occurs initially, or after a list of V including *think, guess* (*I think the boy can win it*): *will, do, shall, can, may, must, ought* (but not *to*). The *-s* of 3rd-person-singular concord does not occur with these, nor does *-ing. Should* can be considered as *shall* + *-ed*, and so on.

have, be: appearing in R positions and in some other positions. These two have the *-s, -ed,* and *-ing* occurring after them. After *have* the V is followed by *-en* (if that particular member of the class V ever has *-en*, it has it also after *have*), and after *be* by *-en* or *-ing*: *we are going, we have taken,*[13] as compared with *we did go.* When a position is discussed below in which R, *had, be* can all occur equally, the abbreviation R_a will be used to indicate all three.

A: between *the* and N, never before plural *-s*: *young, pretty, first.*

D: between *the* and A, but not between *the* and N: *rather, very, now, not.* Many of these, e.g. *now*, occur in various positions in the utterance (after V: *Don't look now*; before V: *He now wishes it weren't*; at the beginning of an utterance, with a level /,/ intonation: *Now, what's up?*). Some adverbs, e.g. *very*, do not occur in most of these positions. When we wish to indicate only the more widely-occurring ones, to the exclusion of *very* and the like, we write D_a. In more detailed analysis, many more sub-classes of D would be necessary.

T: before N, or A, or DA, but not before V (unless *-ing* or *-ed* or *-en* follow it): *a, my, some.* These may all be considered as substituting for *the* and so forming an article-class. Here we must include *all*, which, in addition to occurring in the above positions also occurs before T (*all the very good people* as well as *all very good people*); also the cardinal numbers, which occur not only in T position but also after T (*my two very uncertain suggestions* as well as *the two very new suggestions, two very new suggestions*, parallel to *the very new suggestions*).

I: before or after V, after *from, before*, but not after A or T or before plural *-s*: *it, all, some, now, here.*[14] Some morphemes in this class do not occur after *from, before,* etc., or after utterance-initial V: *he, I.* Others do not occur before V unless NV precedes them: *me.*

P: before N, T, A, D, I, and before V only if *-ing* follows: *of, from.* Several morphemes in this preposition class also occur after certain V; when they are in this position we mark them P_b: *up, off, over* (*walk off, beat up*). Some prepositions (marked P_c) sometimes alternate with zero when an N which precedes P_cN is placed after the $(P_c)N$: *to, for* in *They're giving a present to the boss, They're buying a present for the boss*, are replaced by zero in *They're giving the boss a present, They're buying the boss a present.* This does not occur with *from* as in *He's receiving a raise from the boss.*

-Nn: After N and before anything which follows N: *-let, -eer, -er, -ess,* (*playlet, engineer, Londoner, lioness*).

-Vv: After V and before anything which follows V: past *-ed*, 3rd person singular *-s* (*rowed, rows*).

-Aa: After A and before anything which follows A: *-er, -est, -ish* (*older, oldest, oldish*).

-Nv: after N and before anything which follows V:[14] *-ize, -(i)fy* (*colonize, beautify*).

-Na: *-ful, -ish, -th, -'s* (*beautiful, boyish, sixth, parent's*).

-Vn: *-ment, -ion, -er, -ing* (*atonement, abolition, writer, writing* in *Writing is just what he hates*).

[10] This does not mean that every member of the class occurs in all the positions in which any other member occurs (fn. 5). A particular morpheme may occur in several classes (fn 8). Some morphemes occur in two or more classes in the list below; cf. class-cleavage in Leonard Bloomfield, Language 204 (New York, 1933). The statement of the environments of each morpheme class given here is far from complete, and is merely sufficient to identify the class.

[11] In such expressions as *the one I saw, a good one.*

[12] If subdivisions are not recognized here they will have to be dealt with as special types of selection (§7.6).

[13] We may include *have* and *be* in R in some environments, e.g. in relation to *not*: *have not taken* parallel to *will not take* as against *don't get going.* Note that when *do, have,* or *be* have *-ing* after them they are in the position of V, not of R.

[14] There are special utterances like *the here and now*, but in general these limitations hold.

-Va: *-able*, *-ing*, *-ed*, *-en* (*likable*, ***a shining light, the cooked meal, his shaven head***).

-An: *-ness*, *-ty* (*darkness*, *cruelty*).

-Av: *-en*, *-ize*, (*darken*, *solemnize*).

-Ad: *-ly* (*really*).

Nv-: before *N*, and after anything which precedes *V*:[15] *be-*, *en-* (*bedevil*, *enshrine*).

Xd'-: before morphemes of several classes, chiefly *N* or *A*. The combination, consisting of these morphemes plus *Xd'-*, may be marked *D'*. It occurs chiefly after *V* (often with intervening *N*, etc., as in *Are you asleep?*): *a-* (*astray*, *afresh*, *asleep*, *ashore*). *D'* is used here to indicate the adverbs which occur in this post-*V* position, since it is a position in which both D_a and *A* occur. *D'* sometimes occurs after *N*: *A day ashore.*

Av-: *en-* (*enlarge*).

Na-: *pre-*, *anti-*, *pro-* (*pre-war*, *anti-war*, *pro-war*).

Ap-: *be-* (*below*, *behind*).

Xx-: before any morpheme class or sequence, and after anything which preceded that same morpheme class. The environment of the morpheme which follows is not affected by the addition of the *Xx-* morpheme, except that it now contains that addition itself: *dis-*, *re-*, *pre-* (*disorder*, *recall*, *preview*).

S: stems which occur only next to affixes, i.e. next to the 16 classes *-Nn* to *Xx-* immediately preceding. These stems cannot be assigned to any of the preceding classes *N*, *V*, *A*, *D*, etc., except by seeing if they occur with the same affixes as *N*, etc. Thus, in *society*, *social*, it would have been possible, instead of considering *soci-* as *S* (as we do here), to consider it as *A* when it occurs before *-ety* and *N* when it occurs before *-al* (compare *superiority*, *A -An* and *communal N -Na*). However, what is *nat-* in *native*? It could be either *N* or *V* before *-ive*, since *-ive* is both *-Na* and *-Va*: *massive*, *adoptive*. We therefore put all such morphemes in the class *S*. Many of the affixes in the classes above occur not only next to *A*, *N*, or *V*, but also next to *S*.

&: conjunctions between any two sequences: *and*, *but* (*I wanted to go, but couldn't make it.*) In some environments (e.g. in the example above) the member of *&* is preceded by /,/ intonation; in other environments the /,/ intonation does not occur (e.g. *war and peace* without /,/).

B: in *-NV* /,/ *NV* or in *NV* /,/ *NV*: *if*, *since*, *as*, *while* (*If you go, I won't*). The last subordinative and sometimes also the others lack the preceding /,/ intonation when they are in the middle of the utterance: *We fix it while you wait.* Some members of this class occur after *A* or *N*, etc., before *NV*, *VN* (*Little as there is of it*, —. *Man though he is*, —.) These will be marked B_a.

Finally, there remain various independent morphemes, some of which occur almost anywhere in utterances, often set off by /,/: *then*, *now*, *thus*. Others are set off either by /,/ or by quote-intonation, or have /./ by themselves: *yes*, *no*. Others usually have /!/ intonation by themselves: *hello*, *oh*.

4.2. We now consider sequences of these thirty-odd morpheme classes, to see what sequences of morphemes can be substituted for single morphemes.

Sequences of morpheme classes which are found to be substitutable in virtually all environments for some single morpheme class, will be equated to that morpheme class: $AN = N$ means that *good boy*, for example, can be substituted for *man* anywhere.[16] If we write $DA = A$ (*quite old* for *old*), then DA can be substituted for A wherever A appears, e.g. in $AN = N$ (*old fellow* for *man*, where we can substitute *quite old* for *old*, and obtain *quite old fellow* $DAN = AN = N$).[17] There is nothing to prevent us from substituting DA for A even in the equation $DA = A$. We would then obtain $DDA = A$: *really quite old* for *old*.

If, however, it proves impossible to substitute the equivalents of a symbol for that symbol in some of its occurrences, we distinguish those occurrences by giving the symbol a distinctive raised number. For instance, N *-s* $= N$: *paper* + *-s* = *paper*; and *papers* can be substituted for *paper* in most environments. However, we cannot substitute N *-s* for the first N in this very equation: we cannot substitute *papers* for the first *paper* and then add *-s* again (*papers* + *-s*), as this equation would seem to indicate. We therefore write N^1 *-s* $= N^2$ and state that wherever N^2 occurs we can substitute for it any N^1 or another N^2, while for N^1 we can only substitute any member of N^1 (never N^2). Then it becomes impossible to construct a sequence *papers* + *-s*, since *papers* is N^2 and *-s* is added only to N^1.

The procedure in assigning these raised numbers which indicate uni-directional substitutability is in essence as follows: we assign raised ^{1} to each class symbol, say X, when it first appears. Next time the X appears in an equation, we assign it the same number ^{1} if the equivalents of this X can be substituted for X^1 in every equation which has so far been written. If the new X cannot be substituted for all the preceding X^1 we number it X^2. If we later obtain an X which cannot be substituted for all the preceding X^1 or X^2, we will number it X^3, and so on. If some symbols never go above ^{1} we can dispense with the raised number for them and merely write the symbol without numbers.

On the left-hand side of the equations, each raised number will be understood to include all lower numbers (unless otherwise noted). Thus in $TN^2 = N^3$ we have not only *the men* (N^2) equalling N^3, but also *the man* (N^1). Any N^1 can be substituted for the N^2 on the left side. On the right-hand side, however, each number indicates itself alone: N^3 on the right can only substitute for another N^3, and $N^{1,2}$ for an N^1 or an N^2.

[15] For the remaining morpheme classes of this type, the analogous statement of environment will not be made, since the class mark (*-Na*, *Na-*, etc.) is sufficient indication.

[16] This is true only within the broad limits of what utterances frequently occur in the culture. There are also limitations when *man* is preceded by an adjective *A* (e.g. *young man*). There would then be two adjectives, the *A* of *good boy*, and the *A* of *young man*, which together should yield *young good boy* ($A\ A\ N = A\ N = N$). The conditions under which the two adjectives would occur next to each other in this way are mentioned in §4.32.

[17] The standard procedure being as follows: since $D\ A = A$ permits us to substitute $D\ A$ for A wherever A appears, we write $D\ A$ in place of the first A in this very equation: if $D\ A = A$, then $D\ D\ A = A$, i.e. $D\ D\ A = D\ A = A$.

4.3. Morpheme sequence equations for English now follow.

4.31. Equations involving N^1, V^1, A^1 are almost all cases of word formation, i.e. of adjoining morphemes within one loud-stress unit.

N^1 *-Nn* = N^1: e.g. for *engineer* we can substitute *engine* in *I saw the —.*

A^1 *-An* = N^1: *darkness* for *smell* in *I don't like the — here.*

V^1 *-Vn* = N^1: *abolition* for *bread* in *We demand —.* Note that *abolition* (V^1 *-Vn*) is N^1 and can be followed by *-Nn: abolitionist.*

N^1 *-Nv* = V^1: e.g. *colonize* for *conquer* in *The French Government —ed North Africa.*

Nv- N^1 = V^1: *enchant* for *scare* in *He —s them.*

A^1 *-Av* = V^1: *sharpen* for *break* in *Don't — the knife.*

Av- A^1 = V^1: *enlarge* for *print* in *Do you want to — it?*

A^1 *-Ad* = *D*: *beautifully* or *really* for *well* in *It's — finished.*

Ap- A^1 = *P*: *below* for *at* in *It fell — the dividing line.*

D_a V^1 = V^1: *cordially despise* for *like* in *I — him* (this applies if there is no /,/ or /!/ after D_a; *P N* for D_a is rare in this position).

Xd'- + any class (chiefly N^1 or A^1) = *D'*, where *D'* represents a class of words which occur almost always after *V*, though not always immediately after: *asleep* in *He is —*, *He fell —*, *He is fast —*; *ashore* in *A day ashore.*

Xx- + any class = that class: e.g. *dislike* for *like* in *He really —s it.*

S + any affix = the class indicated by the second letter in the affix mark: e.g. *S -Vn* = N^1: *nature* for *life* in *He loves —.*

all + *T* = *T*: *all my* for *some* in *We lost —books.* When *all* is not followed by *T*, it may itself be a member of *T*: *all* for *the* in *— assertions are arbitrary.*

T + *cardinal number* = *T*: *Which two* for *which* in *— really modern composers?* When cardinal numbers are not preceded by *T*, they may themselves be members of *T*: *two* for *the* in the sentence above.

As a result of these equations, we may consider affixes not as distinct elements in the sentence structure, but merely as elements altering the substitution class of the neighboring morphemes. The affix classes will no longer appear in our picture of the sentence structure (except for special cases of selection), since any structure into which they enter can also be composed of *N*, *V*, *A*, *D*, and *P* morphemes.

4.32. We next obtain equations in which A^2 is necessary, though N^1 is still adequate.

A^1 *-Aa* = A^2: e.g. *oldish* for *old* in *Aren't they a bit —?*

V^1 *-Va* = A^2: *likeable* for *oldish* in *My — uncle.* Note that the V^1 can be obtained from N^1 *-Nv*: *A heartening* (N^1 *-Nv -Va*) *thought.*

D A^2 = A^2: *completely false* for *false* in *That's a — statement.* (*D* here from *A -Ad*).

A^2 N^1 = N^1: *peculiar fellow* for *Senator* in *Isn't he a —.*[18]

A^2 A^2 N^1 = A^2 N^1: Two adjoining *A* in a particular order, which we will call the 'usual' (e.g. as between *ambitious* and *young*, *ambitious* is first in the usual order), will be stressed $\hat{A}\breve{A}$ (reduced loud, medial):[19] *ambitious young, pretty dark*, substitutable for *funny* in *She is a — girl.* If the adjectives are not in the usual order, or if they are in the usual order but with greater note given to the second *A*, or if no usual order obtains between them, or if the second *A* is composed of *D A*, the pattern is $\hat{A}$ /,/ $\hat{A}$: *pretty, dark; dark, pretty; young, ambitious; ambitious, very young* in *She is a — girl.*[20]

4.33. Equations involving N^2 and N^3 develop the noun-phrase.

N^1 *-s* = N^2: *papers* for *paper* in *I'll get my — out.*

N^2 *-Na* = A^2: e.g. *parents'* for *big* in *— day at school.*

Na- N^2 = A^2: *pro-war* for *big* in *a — industrialist.*

N^2N^2 = $N^{1,2}$: *family heirloom* substitutable for *boy* in *It's a —.* *Albert Einstein* for *Jim* in *— was here.*

Any sequence including one loud stress and one or more reduced loud (or medial) stresses = $N^{1,2}$, V^1, or $A^{1,2}$, according to which of these may be substituted for the sequence. Most of these = N^1: *blackbird* (*AN*), *by-pass* (*PN*), *get-up* (VP_b), *our third motor-boat crash* (*NNN*). Some ending in A^2 = $A^{1,2}$: *air-minded* (N^1A^2, the A^2 being a sequence of V^1 *-Va*). Others = V^1: *They by-passed it*; *They'll railroad* (N^1N^1 = V^1) *the strike leader* (N^1N^1 = N^1; N^1 from V^1 *-Vn*).

T N^2 = N^3: *the orchestra* or *these pointless, completely transparent jokes* for *butter* in *I don't like —.*

T A^2 (with no *N* following) = N^3: *The longer* or *the uncertain* in *— is what interests us more.* The *-s* 'plural' does not occur after this N^3 substitute, except in special cases.

N^3PN^4 = N^3: *This piece of junk* for *the book* in *Who brought — here?*. The occurrence of N^3 PN^3 in the position of N^3 or N^4 in the equations below is restricted by various special selections for particular *P*. Repetition is not frequent except when *P* is *of*: *This piece of junk of my mother's* = $N^3PN^3PN^3$ = N^3PN^3 = N^3 (*my mother's* is *T N -Na* = *T* A^2 = N^3).

4.34. Equations requiring V^2 to V^4 develop the verb phrase.

---

[18] We determine that it is A^2 rather than A^1 in this equation by testing whether *peculiar* (A^1) can be replaced by *older, oldish* (A^2). In constructing all these equations we may use either of two working procedures. One is to obtain a large amount of data, including many sequences which have the same environment as N^1; we may then sort out, from among these, those sequences which consist of *A* followed by *N*, and see whether the *A* is always A^1 or also sometimes A^2: e.g. we see whether among the sequences having the same environment as *senator* we have not only *peculiar fellow* but also *older fellow*. The other procedure is to set up equations as working hypotheses, on the basis of whatever data we have, and then try various substitutions for each symbol in our equations, until we discover which symbols are mutually substitutable. Thus on the basis of *He's a peculiar fellow* we may write tentatively *A* N^1 = N^1. Then we would test to see if *A* is A^1 or A^2 by seeing if we can substitute *older* for *peculiar* and still get an English utterance. The two procedures are, of course, epistemologically equivalent.

[19] See George L. Trager and Bernard Bloch, The Syllabic Phonemes of English, LANG. 17.228 (1941).

[20] When we have the stress pattern `^ the medially-stressed morpheme is in class *D*: *pretty young* is *D A* in *She's a pretty young girl to be out this time of night.* It parallels *very young* in *He's a very young fellow.* The addition of emphasis stress, and other changes in the environment, complicate these stress statements. Exact statements will be necessary, however, since various morphemes (e.g. *first*) occur in both *A* and *D*.

R_a *not* = R_a: *will not* or *have not* or *was not* for *will* or *have* or *was* in *I will go.*; *Has he gone?*; *I was going.*

R_a N *not* = R_a N: *did he not* for *did he* in *But — attempt it?*.

have V^1 *-en* = V^2: *have eaten* for *know* in *I — it.*; *I will — it.*

V_c^1 V^2 *-ing* = *have* V_c^1 *-en* V^2 *-ing* = V^2: *be eating* or *stop eating* or *have stopped eating* for *know* in *I — it now.*

$V_b^1 A^2$ = *have* V_b^1 *-en* A^2 = V_e^2: *is gone* or *has been gone* or *seems neat* or *is grayish* for *comes* in *He — now.* Note that A^2 on the left-hand side represents both *neat* (A^1) and *grayish* (A^2).

R V^1 = R = V^2: *will go* or *will* for *go* in *We — today.*

R N^4 V^2 *?* = *have* N^4 V^1 *-en ?* = *be* N^4 V^1 *-en ?* = *be* N^4 V^1 *-ing ?* = R_a N^4 *?* = N^4 V^2 *?*: *Did you talk* or *Haven't you gone* or *Are you taken* or *Are you going* or *Were you* in *— with him?*.

V^2 P_b = V^2: *walk off* (V^1) or *have walked off* (V^2) for *escape* in *We'll — before them.* The appearance of V^2 on both sides of the equation means that we can also obtain V^2 P_b P_b = V^2, etc. This occurs in *walk on over* or *fly on up* for *go* in *Let's —*. However, the selection and number of these sequences of P_b is highly restricted, and detailed equations would have to be given to indicate the selections which actually occur.

V_d^2 N^4 = V_e^2: *take it* for *go* in *I'll — now.* When V^2 includes P_b, there are certain V, P_b, and N for which the order is VNP_b (*I'll knock your opponent down.*), while for others the order is VP_bN (*I'll take over my father's estate.*). The N^4 will be identified below.

V_f^2 N^4 N^4 = V_e^2: *make Harding President* for *vote* in *We're going to —*.

V_g^1 N^4 V^3 = V^3: *make him vote* for *vote* in *We'll — your way.*

V_b^2 N^4 *to* V^3 = V^3: *force him to vote* for *vote* in *We'll — your way.*

V_d^2 N_1^4 P_c N^4 = V_d^2 N^4 N_1^4 = V_e^3: For P_c and certain N, we find both the first sequence (e.g. *I'll make a party for my husband.*), and the second (e.g. *I'll make my husband a party.*). The N_1 with the subscript is used only to identify the N in its two positions. The first sequence is identical with the usual order, as in *I'll get a nickel from my dad.*

V_d^2 N^4 V^4 (all under one sentence intonation) = V_d^2 N^4 = V_e^2: *know he is* for *know it* in *I — now.* The N^4 V^4 is thus the object of the V_d^2. The V^4 indicates a full verb phrase, e.g. *was* as well as *is* in the example above.

V^3 *to* V^3 = V^3: *try to escape* or *kill the guard to avoid getting caught* in *Let's — here.* Note that *avoid getting caught* is V_c^1 V_b^1 *-ing* V^1 *-en* = V_c^1 V_b^1 *-ing* A^2 = V_c^1 V_e^2 *-ing* = V^2.

V^3 *-Vv* = V^4: *walked* or *walked off* or *had eaten* or *tried to escape* for *walk* or *have eaten* in *I — alone.* The *-Vv* is added to the first V or R of the whole V^3 phrase.

V^4 D_a = $V^{3,4}$: *travel smoothly* for *go* in *We'll — in this place.*

V^4 P N^4 = $V^{3,4}$: *travel in this place* for *go* in *Let's — today.* For certain P N and D_a the order is V^3 D_a P N; for others it is V^3 P N D_a; compare the two examples above.

4.35. The noun phrase is completed with the introduction of N^4. N^3 N^4 V_d^4 = N^3 N^4 V_e^4 P = N^4: *The clock he fixed* or *The house he slept in* for *The clock* in *— is all right now.* The second N in the sequence usually has reduced stress, while the first N^3 and the end of the V^4 phrase (if it is not sentence-final) usually have a level tone. The sequence N^3 N^4 V^4 here is therefore distinguished formally, as well as in its environment, from the sequence N^3 N^2 V^4 = N^3 V^4 (with N^3 N^2 = N^3; since we have seen that N^2 N^2 = N^2 and this can be built up into an N^3 by completing the noun phrase before the first N^2): *The family heirloom broke.*

Since V_d^2 N^4 (*fixed it*) = V_e^2, and since V_e^2 occurs in this equation only if P follows, we see that V_d^2 N^4 (without P) is excluded from this sequence. We may have N^3 V_d^2 N^4 (*He fixed it.*), and we may have N^3 N^4 V_d^2 (*the clock he fixed*); but we never have the first N^3 and the last N^4 together in one sequence (there is no *the clock he fixed it*). We may therefore say that the first N^3 replaces the last N^4. This indicates the semantic connection between these two noun phrases, since each of them represents the object of V_d^2.

I = N^4: *it* for *the room* in *Was — very hot?* For each morpheme here we can substitute a whole noun phrase, including *I*, i.e. anything equalling N^3.

N^4 A^2 P N^4 = T A^2 N^2 V^1 *-Va* = V^3 *-ing* = N^4: *strawberries fresh from the field* or *the best drinks obtainable* or *having you* all substitutable for *hope* in *It was only — that kept me going.*

PN^4 = D_a = D': These three classes, represented by *in a moment* or *eventually* or *ashore*, all occur *We'll do these things —*. and less freely in *—, we'll do these things.* However, since style and selection features differ markedly for PN and D_a, detailed statements would be needed to specify in each equation which is more frequent.

N^3 /,/ = P N^4 /,/: *Some day*, for *in a moment*, in the utterances above. This applies only to particular N^3; detailed statements of selection or equations involving particular sub-classes of N would be necessary.

Quoted material = N^4 (with special quote-intonation); "*Not today, thanks.*" or "*wanted*" for *this* in *He said — in a loud voice.*

4.36. Subordinations and Coordinations.

A^2 B_a = N^4 B_a = B: *Little as* or *Child though* or *Since* in *— he is, I like him.*

B N^4 V^4 = P N^3 N^4 V^4 = N^4 V^3 *-ing* = V^3 *-ing* = P N^4: *If he goes home* or *In the event that he goes home* or *Everyone having left* or *Being at home* are all substitutable for *At night* in *—, he'll lock up the house.*

any class + & + same class = same class: *records and new needles* (N^2 & N^2) for *records* (N^2) in *I have — for you today.*

V^4 /,/ & V^4 = V^4: *found it but lost it again* for *found it* after *We.*

4.37. Equations involving whole utterances.

P N^4, N^4 V^4 = N^4 V^4, P N^4 = P N^4 N^4 V^4 = N^4 V^4 P N^4: *At night, it's too hard.*; *It's too hard, at night.*; *At night it's too hard.*; *It's too hard at night.* The morpheme /,/ before or after P N^4 or any of its substitutes underscores the conditional meaning.

& + any utterance = that utterance: *But John!* for *John!*; *And I know that too.* for *I know that too.* Only a few conjunctions occur frequently in this position.

$N^4\ V^4$ /,/ & $N^4\ V^4 = N^4\ V^4$: For any $N^4\ V^4$ utterance we may substitute two $N^4\ V^4$ sequences with a conjunction between them, and with reduced loud stress on the second: *I know, but I can't tell.* for *I know.*

4.4. A check of the preceding equations will show that all morpheme classes and all sequences of morphemes, except the independent ones in the last paragraph of §4.1, occur in positions where they can be replaced by N^4 or V^4. We can therefore state in terms of these classes what sequences of morphemes occur in English utterances. The great majority of English utterances are a succession of the following forms:

$N^4\ V^4$ with /./, /?/, or other intonations; with N^4 (= $PN^4 = D_a$), independent morphemes, and successive repetitions introduced by &, set off by /,/.

Independent morphemes and almost all others except affixes (classes *-Nn* to *Xx-* in §4.1), occurring singly or with affixes, with /./, /?/, /!/, and other intonations: *Yes.*; *Why?*; *No!*; *Come!*;[21] *John!*; *English.*; *Here.*

Hidatsa

5.1. A particularly brief sketch will be given for Hidatsa, which is of interest here because its structure is very different from that of English. For the most part, Hidatsa consists of morphemes which are not in themselves nouns, verbs, etc., but which combine with affixes of nominal, verbal, or other meaning.

Most morphemes of Hidatsa may be grouped into the following classes on the basis of substitutability:

S: stems, which occur with any affixes or with no affix (or zero), and next to other stems: *ika·* 'look' in *ika·c* 'he looks', *ika·s* 'watcher', *ika·ʔi·s* 'the one who always watches', *ikako·wiha·k* 'finishing to look'; *ko·wi* 'end', *ko·wic* 'it is the end', *ko·wihe·c* 'he finished'.

P: prefixes, which occur before almost any stem and with each other. There are special selections and relative order among them, as also among the suffixes: *ki-* 'suus' in *ki·ka·k* 'looking at their own'; *aru-* 'place or object, future' in *aruʔika* 'something to look at'.

Pr: a group of mutually exclusive personal prefixes: *w-* 'I', *r-* 'you', *i-* (or zero, etc.) 'he', in *wiru·hic* 'I stand up', *riru·hiʔi* 'do you stand up', *iru·hic* 'he stands up'.

Inst: about 70 stems occur in most cases only with instrumental prefixes: *-saki-* 'split' in *pasakic* 'he split with a stick', *rusakic* 'he split with the hand', *kasakic* 'he split by pounding'.

Pinst: about 6 prefixes which occur only with *Inst* stems: see above.

U: utterance-final suffixes which occur at the end of (as well as within) stretches of speech: *-c* 'it is', vowel repetition '?': *wahkuc* 'he is here' *wahkuʔu* 'is he here?'.

F: clause-final suffixes which can be substituted for *U* if the utterance continues: *-k* '-ing', *-wa* 'when' in *wuʔusiak* 'we arriving, . . .', *wuʔusiʔawa* 'when we arrived' (cp. *wuʔusi·ʔac* 'we arrived'). In the equations below, *F* will be taken to include *U*, since no statements are needed for *F* that do not apply also to *U*.

N: non-clause-final suffixes. Some of these are final in the stress-group (word) and others are not, but none of them normally occur at the end of a sequence of words such as have *U* or *F* at their end: *-s* 'naming suffix' in *wa·ʔahtu·ʔas* 'the skulls'; *-se* 'by', *-aʔa* 'several' in *a·taʔase* 'by their several houses'.

Post: a few postpositive morphemes which occur after word-final affixes (sometimes at the end of an utterance): *isa* 'again' in *wa·hacisa* 'we go again'.

Ind: a very few stems which occur with no affixes, as calls or whole utterances: *ho·* 'yes', *riskare* 'friend'.

5.2. We proceed to state what sequences of morphemes can be substituted for single morphemes of the classes named above.

$S^1\ S^1 = S^2$: *ris·i* 'dance' and *hiri* 'make' in *waʔo·ris·ihirak* 'making a dance' (*o·* is nominalizing prefix, member of *P*).

Pinst Inst = S^2: we can substitute *rusaki* 'split by hand' for *aciwi* 'follow' in *wa —c* 'I did —'.

Pr $S^2 = S^3$: *wa* 'I' + *aciwi* 'follow'; *wi* 'I' or *i* 'he' + *ru·hi* 'stand up'.

$P S^3 = S^3$: *hiru* 'bone', *aruhiru* 'skeleton'. There is considerable limitation of selection for individual members of *P* and for sub-classes.

$S^3\ S^3 = S^3$: *ika·* for *ikako·wi* in *—c* (see under *S* in §5.1). Substitution of *Pr* S^2 and $P S^3$ from the preceding equation for S^3 permits sequences like $P\ S^1\ P\ S^1 = S^3$, or $Pr\ S^1\ P\ Pr\ S^1$ as in *wahku·ciwa·wa·ha·ʔac* 'we want to get': *wah-* '1st person', *ku·ci* 'get', *wa·-* 'something' (a prefix of the second stem), *wa·-* '1st person', *he·* 'want', *-aʔa* 'severally, i.e. plural', *-c* 'verbalizer'.

$S^3\ N = S^4$: *ikahke·* 'he caused to look', substitutable for *ika·* in *wiʔika·c* 'he looked at me', *wiʔikahke·c* 'he makes me look'. Substitution from the preceding equations gives us results like this: $S^3\ S^3\ N = S^4$, $P\ S^3\ P\ S^3\ N = S^4$; see the example in the equation above, where the *-aʔa* plural applies to both stems with their prefixes. Here too there are some individual members and sub-classes of *N* which have restricted distribution.

$S^4\ S^4\ F = S^4\ F$: we can substitute *araxe·xak* 'holding' or *ika·k* 'looking' or *ika·c* 'he looked' for *ixpase araxe·xak* 'holding by the wing' (*ixpa* 'wing', *-se* 'by').[22]

$S^4\ S^4\ U = S^4\ F\ S^4\ U = S^4\ U$: *haruk kara·k re·ware·c* 'thereupon running he went, they say'[23] can be replaced in context by *re·ware·c* 'he went, they say', or by *re·c* 'he went' alone, but not by any single morpheme. Similarly, *tahe·ruk aruʔisiak hap·e·hisahic* 'If he kills him it will be bad. It will be dark.'[24] can be replaced in its context by *aruʔisiac* 'It will be bad'.

[21] *V!* can substitute for *N V* in many utterances: *Come into the house!* for *He came into the house.* Therefore *V!* can be considered as equalling *N V*, with the morphemic intonation *!* substituting syntactically for *N*. This cannot be done for *N!*, since the stretch of speech immediately following *N!* has the complete intonation of an independent minimum utterance: *John, why don't you come!* Therefore *N!* too must be taken as an independent minimum utterance.

[22] The position of this phrase in the sentence may be seen in II 5, p. 205, of R. H. Lowie, Z. Harris, and C. F. Voegelin, Hidatsa Texts (Indian Historical Society, Prehistory Research Series 1.6, May 1939), from which volume most of the Hidatsa examples given here have been taken. The analysis in §§5.1–3 is tentative.

[23] Ibid. II 31, p. 207.

[24] Ibid. I 49, p. 195.

5.3. In terms of the classes of morpheme sequences, we can now say that most utterances in Hidatsa, in the style of talking summarized here, consist of S^4 U (representing stretches of speech of any length), or S^3 N $(= S^4$ representing usually a single stress-unit, e.g. a person's name uttered by itself), or *Ind* (again a single word occurring as an utterance with its separate intonation). *Post* occurs in several positions in S U utterances, and we may say that its syntactic value within the S U formula is zero: $Post\ S\ U = S\ U\ Post = S\ U$.

Discussion

6.0. Having sketched how our procedure could be applied in two languages, we may now ask what kind of description it has given us. The following sections attempt an interpretation of the linguistic status of this analysis, and a summary of the kind of results that it yields.

6.1. Position analysis. The procedure begins by noting the environments of each morpheme and by putting in one class all those morphemes that have similar distributions. However, in many cases the complete adherence to morpheme-distribution classes would lead to a relatively large number of different classes: *hotel* would be N, *think* would be V, and *take* would be in a new class G since it has roughly the distribution of both *hotel* and *think*. In order to avoid an unnecessarily large number of classes, we say that *take* is a member of both N and V. This means that we are no longer studying the morpheme *take* or *think*. We are studying the positions, Bloomfield's 'privileges of occurrence', common to both *take* and *think*, or those common to both *take* and *hotel*.[25]

This means that we change over from correlating each morpheme with all its environments, to correlating selected environments (frames) with all the morphemes that enter them. The variables are now the positions, as is shown by the fact that the criterion for class membership is substitution. The element which occurs in a given class position may be a morpheme which occurs also in various other class positions. We merely select those positions in which many morphemes occur, and in terms of which we get the most convenient total description.[26]

6.2. Stopping point. One might ask how we can tell where to stop the analysis. This is answered by the nature of the work. All we do is to substitute one sequence for another in a given context. When we have the formula for English utterances with assertion intonation, we find that all we can substitute for it is another utterance, with the same or another intonation. When more work has been done on sentence sequences and what is called stylistics, we may find that in certain positions within a sequence of sentences only N V /./, say, ever occurs, to the exclusion of V /!/. When we have such information, we will be able to extend the substitution procedure to sentences and sequences of utterances (whether monologs or conversations).

6.3. Resultant construction formulae. The final result, for each language which can be analyzed in this manner, takes the form of one or more sequences of substitution classes ('utterance constructions', 'sentence types'). The formulae tell us that these are the sequences which occur. The final formulae therefore give us the limitations upon the freedom of occurrence of morphemes in the language, for they imply that no sequence of morphemes occurs except those which can be derived from the formula.[27]

The utterance formulae are thus rather like the formulae for the phonetic structure of a language, and even like phonemic writing: all of these are formulae showing what occurs in the language. The signs used in the utterance formulae have value: N has the values A N, T A N, T A, etc.; and each of these has specific morphemes as values. Supplying morpheme values for the signs of the formula will give us expressions in the language.

This is not quite the whole story, for there are further limitations of selection among the morphemes, so that not all the sequences provided by the formulae actually occur.[28] Individual limitations of selection cannot be described in these formulae; at best, the more important among them can be stated in special lists or in the dictionary. Limitations applying to various groups of morphemes in each class can, however, be included if we give our formulae the form of charts. The second dimension which the chart provides enables us to state selections among sub-groups in the several columns (each column representing a position, i.e. a class), by placing along one horizontal line the sequences of sub-groups that actually occur.

6.4. The procedure outlined here could be paralleled by a series of substitutions beginning with the whole utterance and working down, instead of beginning with single morphemes and working up. In that case we would have to find formal criteria for breaking the utterance down at successive stages. This is essentially the difficult problem of determining the immediate constituents of an utterance.[29] It is not clear that there exists any general method for successively determining the immediate constituents, when we begin with a whole utterance and work down. In any case, it would appear that the formation of

[25] This is also done, in essence, by Bloomfield's class cleavage (Language 204), and by his functions of form classes (ibid. 196), which in essence provide for the syntactic equivalence of words and sequences of words (phrases). Needless to say, the whole procedure described here owes much to Bloomfield's method.

[26] It may be necessary to point out that this positional analysis is strictly formal, as compared with form-and-meaning analyses like the one in Otto Jespersen's Analytic Syntax (Copenhagen, 1937).

[27] Of course, from the formula N V we derive many sequences that occur: e.g. T A N V (*The old order changeth*) since $T\ A\ N = N$, and so on.

[28] Some of these limitations can be included by giving the signs more than one alternative value depending on the value of the other signs, somewhat as phonemic letters are given various allophonic values. We could say that after N^4, English V^4 has two values: simple V^4, and V^4 N^4. The utterance sequence N V could represent both N V and N V N (see §4.4). The more limitations of selection we wish to indicate by these equations, the more raised numbers we may need. This may not always be the case; but if we wished for example to indicate which noun stems occur with which *-Nn* suffixes we would require a long list of equations, involving several numerically differentiated resultant N's, before the first N^1 $-Nn = N^1$ equation of §4.3.

[29] Bloomfield, Language ch. 13. Note also Kenneth L. Pike, Taxemes and Immediate Constituents, Lang. 19.65–82 (1943), and the method of analysis used for Japanese by Bloch, Studies in Colloquial Japanese II, Lang. 22.200–48 (1946). ((154))

substitution classes presents fewer theoretical difficulties if we begin with morphemes and work up.

IMPLICIT IN THE FORMULAE

7.0. We have seen the application and the interpretation of the procedure outlined here. This is perhaps all that is required of a procedure. However, in order to fit it into the rest of the description of a language we should find out how much of the information which we expect from syntactic description is derivable from this procedure.

7.1. SUPRASEGMENTAL FEATURES. The intonational and other suprasegmental features, as well as the pauses, are generally included in the equations. When one sequence is substitutable for another in an utterance, it is understood that the intonations, pauses, etc. of the utterance remain unchanged under the substitution. If the substitution is associated with a change in intonation, as in *Who* for *John* in — *got lost*, we state that fact. Some substitution groups may require not only particular sequences but also particular suprasegmental features; e.g. any English sequence with loud stress followed by reduced loud stress may equal N (§4.33). The domains of suprasegmental features often coincide with the sequences which we recognize in our substitution equations; e.g. /,/ and slight pause separating adverbial phrases in certain positions in English.

In general, therefore, the formulae are based not only on the sequences involved but also on the suprasegmental features of the sequences substituted and of the utterances in which they are substituted. The formulae may thus correlate with phonemic junctures which express the limits of suprasegmental features.

7.2. MORPHOLOGIC BOUNDARIES. The formulae also correlate with nonphonemic (structural) junctures, such as may be set up to mark the boundaries of intervals which serve as elements of the utterance structures.

7.3. MORPHOLOGIC RELATIONS. Many of the relations between a morpheme class and other morpheme classes, or the interval or utterance in which it occurs, can be derived from the formulae, although they are not explicitly stated there for their own sake. The formulae show what morpheme classes (or sequences) are syntactically zero, like *Xx-* prefixes and *-Aa* suffixes in English (§4.31); we can even learn from them that in English most prefixes, but relatively few suffixes, are syntactically zero.

The formulae show which morpheme classes occur by themselves in utterances, and which classes are bound not to other morpheme classes (as are most affixes) but to constructions, i.e. to sequences of classes: e.g. English *&* is limited to any class or extant class sequence; English T is bound to a following noun phrase as a sort of phrase prefix (§4.33); Hidatsa suffixes operate on the whole preceding word, whereas prefixes operate usually only on the immediately following stem (§5.2). The fact that English *-Vv* suffixes (*-ed*) are best added not to V^1 (verb morphemes) but to V^3 (verb phrases including object, etc.), shows that *-ed* may best be regarded as a suffix of the whole verb phrase. In general, a class may be considered as bound to the level indicated by the number with which it is associated; i.e. it is bound to whatever is substitutable for the symbol-and-number combination that accompanies it in the equations.

We can also learn from the formulae which morpheme classes are the heads and which are the closures of the sequences in which they appear: the closure is the class which always appears last; and the head is the class which can always substitute for the sequence, e.g. an N morpheme for an N-phrase sequence. The formulae can thus show which sequences are endocentric (e.g. $A\ N = N$) and which are exocentric (e.g. $T\ A = N$).

It goes without saying that adequate information about the morpheme classes can be derived not from sketchy examples of the equational procedure such as we have given, but from detailed analyses of all the mutually substitutable sequences of the language.

7.4. ORDER. The formulae are devised in part on the basis of the order of classes in each sequence, and can therefore be used to show it explicitly or by means of the raised numberings.

7.5. ALWAYS OR SOMETIMES. They also enable us to indicate if certain classes occur always or only sometimes in a given sequence. If we write $D\ A = A$ and $A\ N = N$, and are free to apply or not to apply the results of one equation in the other, then we can derive from these equations the fact that N, $A\ N$, and $D\ A\ N$ all occur.

7.6. SELECTION. Some of the features of selection, the restrictions on particular morphemes which occur only with particular other morphemes, are indicated in these formulae, or derivable from them. Some selection, such as that between *I* and *am* as against *he* and *is*, is included in the list of variant forms of the morphemes. Selections of concord are listed as special domains of the morpheme in question (§2.3 above).

We can also consider selections and order among sub-classes, e.g. the fact that certain Hidatsa stems are always the last stem in the word, or that *ought* alone among English preverbs usually has *to* after it. This can be expressed by the formulae if they are allowed to become more complicated in form, and especially if they are made into two-dimensional diagrams. Lastly, the formulae in themselves are statements of selection, saying for instance that $N\ V$ sequences occur, but not $N\ T$.

7.7. MEANING. The formulae can be used as a source of information on the grammatical meaning of the morpheme classes symbolized in them. To do this, it is necessary to say that morpheme classes or class sequences which replace each other in various equations, i.e. which occur in identical morpheme-class environments, have similar functions or grammatical meanings. Thus the N^3 of $N^3\ N^4\ V_d^4$ (§4.35) is shown to replace the N^4 which is otherwise found after V_d; both of these represent the object of the V_d.

7.8. COMPARABILITY OF LANGUAGE STRUCTURES. The nature and number of the morpheme classes that have to be set up for a particular language, the forms and number of the equations, and the number of levels which have to be differentiated by raised figures for some of the class symbols, all permit comparisons between the descriptions of one language and another. Such comparisons must not be made too lightly, since considerable choice remains in the setting up of equations for any language. In particular, there may be room for ingenuity in keeping the raised numbers of certain symbols—say N, V, S—at a minimum for each language; so that of two sets of equations for a language, one might reach up to N^8 while the other does not go beyond N^4. Undoubtedly, the procedures of setting up equations and assigning the raised numbers can be made more explicit and, if desired, standardized for greater convenience in structural comparative research. An analysis of this type for Moroccan Arabic comes out rather similar to the English, ending up with $N^5\ V^3$ and $N^4\ N^4$ for the former as against $N^4\ V^4$ for the latter, while the Hidatsa equations are very different, ending with $S^4\ U$. This fits in with the general similarity between Indo-European and Semitic structure as against Siouan.[30]

7.9. TESTING MORPHOLOGICAL CRUCES. In §6.1 it was seen that the values of the symbols in the equations are not morphemes but positions, indicating whatever morphemes occupy these positions (irrespective of what other positions these morphemes may occupy in other equations). Therefore, when we wish to know the analysis of a particular utterance, it is impossible merely to replace each morpheme by its class symbol (e.g. *I know it* $= N^4\ V^1\ N^4 = N^4\ V^1$) since many morphemes may be members of several classes. W. F. Twaddell has suggested[30a] that such analyses of utterances be carried out by repeated substitution tests on the basis of the equations, in what he termed 'experimental substitution at all levels'. To carry this out, we would ask what substitutions are permitted by the equations for each morpheme or morpheme sequence of our utterance, in the class environment which it has in that utterance. This is repeated until we know unambiguously to what class each occurrence of each morpheme in our utterance belongs.

We take, for example, the utterance *She made him a good husband because she made him a good wife.* We know that there is a difference in meaning between the two occurrences of *made*; and since we know this without any outside information beyond hearing the sentence, it follows that indication of the difference, in meaning and in construction, can be derived from the structure of the utterance. We proceed to analyze the utterance, going backward along the equations as far as may be necessary to reveal this difference. First, we know that the utterance is an instance of $N^4\ V^4\ \&\ N^4\ V^4 = N^4\ V^4$. At this stage the two halves of the sentence are still identical in structure. Each V^4 has the structure V^2 (*make*) N^4 (*him*) N^4 (*a good husband/wife*) $+$ *-Vv* (*-ed*). The equations show the two cases of this sequence (§4.34): $V_f^2\ N^4\ N^4 = V_e^2$ (*make Harding President*) and $V_d^2\ N^4\ N^4 = V_e^3$ (*make my husband a party*). We cannot tell which of these applies to each of our V^4, or whether both go back to the same one, because *make* is equally a member of V_d and V_f.[31] We find, however (§4.34), that $V_d^2\ N^4\ N_1^4 = V_d^2\ N_1^4\ P_e\ N^4$ (where the subscript number merely identifies the N which has different positions in the two sequences). We try now to discover whether either V^4 in our utterance has the structure $V_d^2\ N^4\ N^4$, by applying to each V^4 the substitution which is possible for $V_d^2\ N^4\ N^4$. To do this we interchange the two instances of N^4 and insert between them an instance of P_e. In the first V^4 we get a meaningless utterance which would practically never occur: *she made a good husband* (N_1) *for* (P_e) *him* (N) in place of *she made him* (N) *a good husband* (N_1). In the second V^4, however, the substitution gives us an equivalent and not unusual utterance: *she made a good wife* (N_1) *for* (P_e) *him* (N) in place of *she made him* (N) *a good wife* (N_1). Clearly, then, the second V^4 in our utterance is analyzable into $V_d^2\ N^4\ N^4 + \text{-}Vv = V_e^3 + \text{-}Vv$. Since the first V^4 can not be analyzed in this way, it can equal only the one remaining $V\ N\ N$ construction, namely $V_f^2\ N^4\ N^4 + \text{-}Vv = V_e^2 + \text{-}Vv$.[32]

We have thus found that the two halves of the original utterance are formally different in the substitutions which can be performed upon them. The whole analysis could of course have begun with morphemes. We could have assigned class symbols to each morpheme, and upon reaching the two occurrences of *made* would not have known whether to indicate each of them by V_d, V_f, or any one of several other symbols. We would then have had to decide the question by carrying out on the $N\ N$ following them the very substitutions attempted above.

EXCLUDED FROM THE FORMULAE

8.0. Having seen what syntactic facts can be derived from the formulae, we now ask which ones cannot be included in them and must be found by separate investigations and expressed in separate statements.

8.1. The great bulk of selection features, especially those that distinguish between individual morphemes, cannot be expressed except by very unwieldy formulae. Although it may be of theoretical interest to know that two-dimensional diagrams of such detailed selections are conceivable, in practice this information can only be given in lists and statements appended to the formulae.

8.2. This is true also of such relations among morphemes as the families of mutually replacing English suffixes, e.g. *-id*, *-or* in *squalid: squalor, candid: candor*, etc.[33]

8.3. The formulae also cannot in themselves indicate what meanings may be associated wth the various positions or classes.

[30] Cf. also a comparable brief analysis of Kota in LANG. 21.283–9 (1945), based on the data supplied in M. B. Emeneau, Kota Texts, Part I (Berkeley and Los Angeles, 1944).

[30a] In a private communication.

[31] All members of V_f are also members of V_d: V_d are verbs which occur before N, V_f are verbs which occur before $N\ N$ (as well as before N). Cf. §4.1.

[32] We can check this by noting that if in the first V^4 we substitute a verb which is not a member of V_f, we get a sequence which hardly ever occurs, and whose meaning is not changed by the substitution of $N^4\ P_e\ N^4$: *She bought him a good husband* would not differ in meaning (if it occurred) from *She bought a good husband for him.* But if we try another member of V_f, for instance *think*, we find again that the substitution gives a 'meaningless' (non-occurring) utterance, or in any case one with a greatly altered meaning: *She thought him a good husband* as against *She thought a good husband for him.* Verbs in V_f are therefore verbs which involve obvious change in meaning when the $N_1\ P_e\ N$ substitution is imposed upon them; verbs not in V_f do not involve any reportable change in meaning under that substitution. Therefore the *made* in *made him a good husband* functions as a member of V_f.

[33] Such families of morphemes came to my notice in Stanley Newman's and Morris Swadesh's material on English.

Thus, in Hidatsa, of two formally equivalent words (with noun suffixes) before the clause-final word (which ends in a verbalizing *F*), the first will normally indicate the subject and the second the object: *ruwac·iri istacu rux·iak* 'one of them his eye opening (when one of them opened his eye)'. Such information about the meaning of positions and constructions have to be given in separate statements accompanying the formulae.[34]

8.4. The formulae will also fail to give information about the complete distribution of any one morpheme, which may occur in various classes (§3.4), or about the frequency of morphemes or classes, or about the phonemic structure of various classes (e.g. the fact that Hidatsa *F* or various English affixes are unstressed).

9. We have seen that by extending the term substitution class from single morphemes to sequences of morphemes, we arrive at formulae equating various sequences which are substitutable for each other in all or certain utterances of the language in question. We have seen further that when the setting up of equations is continued until no new results are forthcoming, we obtain succinct statements for the sequences of morphemes which constitute the utterances of the language. The procedure of constructing these equations has here been investigated in order to see what syntactic information it gives or fails to give.

It is clear that the usefulness of this procedure will vary from language to language, the more so in view of the fact that many languages (e.g. to some extent Hidatsa) reveal comparatively little difference between the structure of all utterances and the structure of minimum utterances, and in view of the fact that some languages have great freedom in the distribution of minimum utterances within all utterances.

[34] See, for example, Edward Sapir, Language 86 ff. (New York, 1921).

⟦This classic paper stands in no need of extended comment. It should be read together with the two papers which follow it in this collection; and serious students with an abundance of time on their hands may try to re-state Bloch's Japanese Syntax in Harris formulas. Certainly that would advance their understanding both of language in general and of Japanese and of syntax in particular.

That is to say, the Harris paper will have had an educative effect upon the student, rather than adding to his stock of information or even to his armament of methods: for this effect is quite independent of whether the student adopts the Harris formulas as a permanent part of his procedure (most will not). We may even feel (justifiably, I hope) that we are getting a good deal of this educative effect merely through an attentive reading of the Harris paper.

For example, after reading this paper one will find that one has new ways (perhaps better ways than ever before) of answering these questions: What is the difference between morphology and syntax? What is a word? What is the difference between an endocentric and an exocentric construction? How long is it possible to make an English sentence? How different from each other can languages be? And so on.

And now for a little critical comment. In spite of recognizing that English intonations are meaningful and stand in construction with the other constituents of the sentence, Harris completes his discussion and sets up his formula picture of English without them. If his maneuver is to be regarded as successful, the implication is clear: a seemingly complete syntax can be set up for part of a language, the rest of the language being treated as redundant thereto even if we know that it is not.

Here we may recall the mathematician's maxim: 'Always invert!' It must be worth trying to see if it is possible to start out from intonation, juncture, and stress, and build up a complete English syntax while disregarding a substantial part of what Harris relied upon. One would, that is, use Harris-type classes of segmental morphemes only to the point where one's syntax had been made a closed structure, and forget the rest of them.

Whether such a purpose was part of the motivation or not is irrelevant: just such an anti-Harris procedure ['anti' here is logical, not polemic] is to be found in the Smith and Trager syntax work (very little published as yet: early hints in their Outline).

Now if Smith and Trager cover all of Harris's morphemes with a homogeneous syntax, along with their intonations, stresses, and junctures, that will prove that Harris was wrong; but if it turns out that they need only a fraction of the Harris stuff and can treat the rest as redundant, that will confirm my outrageous suggestion above concerning redundancy.⟧

STUDIES IN COLLOQUIAL JAPANESE II: SYNTAX

BERNARD BLOCH

Language 22.200–48—1946

This paper is the second in a series of articles dealing with various phases of colloquial Japanese grammar.[1] The dialect to be described is the present-day standard language, based on the speech of educated persons native to Tokyo. Forms and constructions peculiar to other dialects, including the literary style, are not considered.

Although the syntax of colloquial Japanese has been treated in beginners' books and special articles, it has never, so far as I know, been the subject of a systematic study. Partial descriptions of Japanese sentence structure are not wanting, for the most part scattered through books chiefly concerned with other problems; but no attempt has been made to give a clear and unified account of the syntax as a whole.[2] This paper is an effort to supply a first step toward such an account. It presents, as briefly as possible, an outline of the general structure—omitting many details, but providing categories in which all details, it is hoped, may be accommodated.

1. Sentence, Pause-Group, Word

1.1 An utterance in Japanese ends with one of four intonations:

(1) Falling, with the last syllable lower in pitch than the second-last. Meaning: conclusive ('end of sentence' or the like). Symbol /./,[3] e.g. Sóo desu ka. 'Is that so?'.

[1] The first paper in the series, dealing with inflection, appeared in JAOS 66.97–109 (1946); the third, dealing with the derivation of inflected words, will appear in JAOS, Vol. 66, No. 4 (1946). These two papers will be referred to as SCJ I and SCJ III respectively. ⟦Apparently not yet planned at the time of this paper, SCJ IV (Phonemics), Lang. 26.86–125 ((329)) (1950), deals with its topic in minutest detail and arrives at a phonological analysis which differs radically from that assumed as the basis for this paper. Fortunately, the difference does not directly affect the discussion here.⟧

My thanks are due to the American Council of Learned Societies, which granted me a fellowship in the Intensive Language Program from February to August 1942, and thereby made it possible for me to begin the study of Japanese. I am grateful also to the many Japanese informants with whom I have worked, in particular to Lincolna McKinnon, Mikiso Hane, Toshio Kono, Kentaro Ikeda, Masako Yokoyama, and Miyo Okada. Mr. Kono kindly checked the phrasing and accentuation of the examples used in the present paper.

In arriving at the final form of this article I have been greatly assisted by discussions with Rulon S. Wells, Henry M. Hoenigswald, and Elizabeth F. Gardner, and above all by the careful and illuminating criticism of Leonard Bloomfield. The more general debt which I owe to Bloomfield is obvious on every page.

[2] The only approach to such an attempt that I know of is Henry Saburoo Tatsumi's Simplified grammar table of the spoken Japanese (Tokyo, 1936). Tatsumi tries to exhibit the over-all structure of Japanese sentences on a single chart (approximately 31 by 40 inches); but his arrangement is impossibly cumbersome, and his analysis both unscientific and incomplete. The first sentence under the heading Syntax indicates the general approach: 'The usual word order in a Japanese sentence is as follows: (A) Subject, (B) Time, (C) Means of transportation, (D) Place, (E) Indirect Object, (F) Instrument, Means, Material or Agent, (G) Direct Object, (H) Complements, (I) Quotations, (J) Predicate verb or adjective, (K) Auxiliary suffixes.'

[3] But the period will be omitted when the Japanese expression is followed by a gloss.

The transcription used here is a modification of the official Japanese romanization (Kokutei Rōmazi), as set forth in SCJ I, fn. 4. The chief points in the phonemic analysis are repeated here.

A syllable contains a syllabic, alone or with one non-syllabic preceding. Syllabics are of two kinds, vocalic and consonantal. Vocalic syllabics are a, o, u, e and ya, yo, yu, ye; the second group palatalize a preceding non-syllabic, or, when forming a syllable alone, begin with a palatal glide. But ye is [i], and will be written i for simplicity. Consonantal syllabics, never initial after a pause and never preceded by a non-syllabic, are ñ and q. The former is [m] before a labial, [n] before a dental, [ŋ] before a velar, elsewhere [n] or [ŋ] in free variation. The syllabic q is voiceless and homorganic with the following non-syllabic; it occurs only in the sequences qp, qk, qt, qs, phonetically [p·, k·, t·, s·], here written pp, kk, tt, ss respectively. (The writing of pp for qp, etc., conforms to traditional romanization. In SCJ I, the writing with q was used because it makes morphophonemic statements easier.)

Thirteen consonants function as non-syllabics: h, p, k, t, s, b, g, z, m, n, r occur before all the vocalic syllabics; d occurs only before a, o, e; and w occurs only before a. Between voiceless consonants, u and i (ye) are voiceless; so also is u final after s in rapid conversation, esp. in the forms -másu and désu. Note that ty is phonetically [č], sy is [š], zy is [dž] (rarely [ž]), tu is [tsu], hu is [fu] or [ɸu] or [hu].

On intonations and pauses see §§1.1–2 in the text; on the word accent see §1.4 below. Capital letters are used in the transcription according to the rules of English orthography. In the glosses, round parentheses enclose explanatory matter, literal translations, and equivalents of Japanese words not required in the English sentence; square brackets enclose English words not corresponding to any words in the Japanese expression.

(2) Rising, with the last syllable considerably higher in pitch than the second-last. Meaning: animation or special interest. Symbol /?/, e. g. Sóo desu ka? 'Is that [really] so?' (expressing interest or surprise).

(3) High-falling, with a wide interval between the highest pitch (on the last accented syllable, or, if no syllable is accented, on the first syllable of the utterance) and the lowest (on the last syllable). Meaning: lively emotion. Symbol /!/, e. g. Sóo desu ka! 'Oh so that's it!'

(4) Level, with the last syllable slightly higher after an unaccented syllable, lower and slightly rising after an accented syllable. Meaning: suspensive ('incompleteness' or the like). Symbol /../, e. g. Sóo desu ga.. 'That may be so, but [still]...'.

Pauses within an utterance are preceded by the same four intonations, and are symbolized in the same way, except that a pause after level intonation within an utterance will be marked /,/ or /;/, as explained below. A pause after falling, rising, or high-falling intonation is generally longer than a pause after level intonation.

At the end of an utterance, each of the four intonations marks the end of a sentence. Within an utterance, only the first three (falling, rising, high-falling) mark the end of a sentence; level intonation marks the end of an element included in a sentence.

1.2 All pauses within a sentence are preceded by level intonation. Every such pause is facultative: repeated utterances of the same sentence (by the same speaker or by different speakers) will show the pause sometimes present, sometimes absent, without any change in meaning. The presence or absence of pauses within a sentence depends partly on stylistic factors (with more pauses in emphatic or affective speech), partly on the tempo and the care of utterance.

However, some facultative pauses are more constant than others, appearing more consistently in repeated instances of the same sentence. It is enough to distinguish two ranks of facultative pauses: higher (more constant), marked with a semicolon; and lower (less constant), marked with a comma. Where one or more lower-ranking pauses are followed by a higher-ranking pause, the lower-ranking pauses appear only if the higher-ranking pause is present. The sentence Kono goro wa, yoohuku o, kaú no ni wa; okane ga, takusañ; irimásu yo 'It takes a lot of money to buy a suit these days' will occur with all, some, and none of the facultative pauses actually present; but it will never occur with pauses after yoohuku o and okane ga unless there are also pauses after kaú no ni wa and takusañ.

In citing Japanese phrases and sentences, we shall mark all facultative pauses; but the reader should bear in mind that not all the pauses will be actually present in all instances of the expression. —From this point on, the term pause will be taken to include facultative pause.

Pauses do not occur within a word: every pause marks a word boundary. On the other hand, many word boundaries are never marked by pause. In our transcription we separate words by spaces, but these have no phonetic value.

1.3 An utterance, or a fraction of an utterance between two pauses (or between the beginning of speech and the first pause, or between the last pause and the end of speech), not interrupted by a pause, is a pause-group. The sentence cited above contains six pause-groups (kono goro wa] yoohuku o] kaú no ni wa] okane ga] takusañ] irimásu yo); this count is not affected by the number of pauses actually made in any particular instance of the sentence.

By definition, no pause-group consists of smaller pause-groups; but many pause-groups contain speech forms which in other sentences occur as pause-groups. Thus, the pause-groups matí kara 'from the town', ano matí 'that town', ano matí kara 'from that town' all contain a fraction matí which occurs elsewhere as a pause-group by itself, with the meaning 'town'. The form tihooséihu spoken as a pause-group (i. e. not interrupted by a facultative pause) means 'local government'; it consists of two fractions tihóo 'locality' and séihu 'government', both of which occur in other contexts as pause-groups. On the other hand, many pause-groups contain no such fraction; thus, matí 'town' contains no element that occurs as a pause-group by itself.[4] A pause-group that contains no fraction which occurs elsewhere as a pause-group by itself is a minimal pause-group; every minimal pause-group is a word.

The converse, however, does not hold: not every word occurs as a minimal pause-group. On the one hand, many Japanese words occur only as parts of non-minimal pause-groups, e. g. ano 'that' and kara 'from' in the examples already cited. On the other hand, many words, though they occur as pause-groups, do not constitute minimal pause-groups; e. g. the compound word tihooséihu 'local government'.

A complete definition of the word in Japanese must therefore go beyond the statement that every minimal pause-group is a word. In the following sections we shall state the criteria by which a word is distinguished from a phrase of two or more words (§1.4), from a bound form (§1.5), and from another word (§1.6).

1.4 Among the words identified by the criterion of minimal pause-groups, some but not all contain an accent: there are accented and unaccented words in Japanese. In an unaccented word, all the syllables

4 There is a minimal pause-group ma meaning 'space, room, interval', and another minimal pause-group ti meaning 'blood'; but neither of these is to be regarded as part of the word matí 'town'. The semantic criterion by which these three pause-groups are kept separate is the same as the one that is used to identify morphemes; cf. Leonard Bloomfield, Lang. 2.155 (1926) ((27)) and Language 161 (New York, 1933).

are spoken on approximately the same pitch, though the first syllable of such a word is usually somewhat lower than the rest; e.g. ki 'mind, spirit', mizu 'water', kodomo 'child', dekakeru 'starts out', aikawarazu 'without change'. In an accented word, one syllable or one unbroken sequence of syllables is spoken on a higher pitch than a following unaccented syllable.[5] The high-pitched syllable, if there is only one, or the last syllable of a high-pitched sequence, is the accented syllable; we mark it with an acute (á). The distribution of high pitch is as follows:

If the first or the second syllable is accented, this alone has the high pitch; e.g. kí 'tree, wood' (accented only when followed without pause by an unaccented syllable), mádo 'window', háyaku 'quickly', máiniti 'every day'; damé 'no good' (accented only when followed without pause by an unaccented syllable), anáta 'you', tatémono 'building', tabénakattaroo 'probably did not eat'.

If the third or any later syllable is accented, this and all preceding syllables except the first have the high pitch;[5a] e.g. koobá 'factory' (with high pitch setting in on the second o; accented only when followed without pause by an unaccented syllable), sayonára 'goodbye', bakugékiki 'bombing plane', atatakái 'is warm', arukimasyóo 'let's walk', okakekudasaimáse 'please sit down' (with high pitch setting in on the syllable -ka-).

The distribution of high-pitched syllables in accented words isolated by the criterion of minimal pause-groups yields a further criterion for distinguishing single words from phrases. We state this criterion in the form of three assumptions:

(1) Two high-pitched syllables or sequences separated by one or more syllables of lower pitch belong to different words. In the pause-group dóno tatémono 'which building?', the high-pitched syllables dó and té are separated by the low-pitched syllables no and ta; accordingly the pause-group contains at least two words, though the accent here does not tell us where to divide them. (The division might be dó no ta té-, dó nota té-, dóno ta té-, dó no taté-, dónota té-, or dóno taté-;[6] our choice of the last possibility as the right one is due to considerations to be discussed in §1.5).

(2) In a sequence of low-pitched syllables preceding a single high-pitched syllable, there is a word division after the second-last or the last low-pitched syllable, or after each. In the pause-group ano tatémono 'that building', the high-pitched syllable té is preceded by three low-pitched syllables; accordingly the pause-group contains at least two words.

(3) An unbroken sequence of high-pitched syllables belongs to a single word, together with the immediately preceding low-pitched syllable. In the pause-group tabetarasíi 'seems to have eaten', the first syllable ta is low-pitched, the next four (-betarasí-) are high-pitched; accordingly the pause-group is a single word, not a phrase, even though it contains a fraction tabeta- similar in form and meaning to the independent word tábeta 'ate, has eaten'.[7]

By analogy, the criterion of accent can be applied also to pause-groups or fractions of pause-groups containing no sequence of high-pitched syllables, or no high-pitched syllable at all. We assume that if the accent shows a certain combination of morphemes amx to be a single word, then another combination bny is also a single word if each member of the second combination belongs to the same morphologic class as the corresponding member of the first; and if the accent shows amx to be a phrase, then bny is a phrase also. Thus, the pause-group tabemóno 'food (lit. thing eaten)' has a high pitch on the syllables -bemó-, and is therefore a single word.

[5] Accordingly, if the accented syllable is the last or the only syllable of a word, the high pitch is perceptible only when the word is followed without pause by another word with a low-pitched first syllable. When such a word is not so followed, it loses its accent. We infer from this that no accented syllable is ever followed by another accented syllable; i.e. no word has an accent on its last or only syllable when the following word has one on its initial syllable.

In citing words with an accent on the last or only syllable, and pause-groups ending with such a word, we shall nevertheless indicate the place of the accent by an acute. Our transcription in this one respect is thus morphophonemic.

[5a] Unless one of the preceding syllables is q, i.e. the first part of a long voiceless consonant (fn. 3). Such a syllable is always neutral with respect to pitch: it is neither high nor low. Thus in the word massúgu 'straight' (more strictly maqsúgu), the syllable ma is low-pitched, q is neutral, sú is high-pitched, and gu is low-pitched; in the word mizuppói 'is watery' (more strictly mizuqpói), the neutral syllable q stands between the two high-pitched syllables zu and pó.

[6] The division dó notaté- is ruled out. The syllable ta is low-pitched, but would be high-pitched if it were the second syllable of a word with accent on the third.

[7] The accent does not rule out the possibility that the last syllable (-i) might be a separate word; but morphologic considerations lead us to regard it as a suffix. Knowing tábeta to be a separate word, we might attempt to analyze tabetá rasíi as a phrase, explaining the shift of accent (tábeta > tabetá) as a function of the environment. But since rasíi has high pitch on both the first and second syllables, it cannot be a separate word.

In emphatic speech, some formations with -rasíi have an accent on the first syllable instead of the second-last; e.g. tábetarasii, emphatic variant of tabetarasíi. But other formations have no such variant; e.g. musumerasíi 'seems to be [his] daughter'. In discussing these formations below (§1.5 and §3.12, and fnn. 21, 22) we shall disregard the emphatic variants with initial accent.

Tatémono 'building (lit. thing built)' has only one high-pitched syllable (té), and kimono 'clothing (lit. thing worn)' has none at all; but both of these are structured morphologically like tabemóno, and are therefore single words also. Conversely, since the pause-group dóno tatémono 'which building?' is a phrase, not a single word, the similarly structured pause-group ano kimono 'that clothing' is a phrase also.

1.5 In analyzing a given sentence, we first isolate the immediate constituents of the sentence as a whole, then the constituents of each constituent, and so on to the ultimate constituents—at every step choosing our constituents in such a way that the total number of different constructions will remain as small as possible. We regard the analysis of the sentence (the syntactic analysis) as complete when further analysis would reveal only constructions different in kind from all the constructions established up to that point.[8] An element that emerges from the analysis as an ultimate constituent of a sentence is typically a word.

Subject to the limitations imposed by the criterion of accent (§1.4), we follow the guiding principle[9] that no form has as its immediate constituents a phrase of two or more words on the one hand and a bound form (i. e. a constituent of words) on the other. The pause-group ano tatémono e 'to that building' has the immediate constituents ano tatémono 'that building' and e 'to'. The latter never occurs alone as a pause-group, and might therefore be a bound form (a suffix); but since the prior constituent is a phrase (§1.4), the element e is a word.

In one type of construction, the criterion of accent obliges us to abandon this last principle, and set up a phrase and a bound form as immediate constituents. The expression tomodati no, musumerasíi 'seems to be [my] friend's daughter' consists of two pause-groups. To cover this case and other expressions ending with -rasíi, we set up the immediate constituents tomodati no, musumé 'a friend's daughter' and -rasíi 'seems to be'. The prior constituent is a phrase (since no word contains a pause); but the second constituent -rasíi is shown by the accent to be part of the single word musumerasíi 'seems to be a daughter' (with high pitch on the sequence -sumerasí-), and is therefore a bound form.

1.6 To decide whether words are the same or different, we adopt the following conventions.

(1) Words that differ in both form and meaning are different. In particular, members of an inflectional paradigm with different endings and different class meanings are different; thus tabéru 'eats' and tábeta 'ate' are different words. (For the sake of brevity, however, we may choose one member of a paradigm to represent the whole set, and speak of other members as inflections of this form—for instance, of tábeta as the past indicative form of tabéru.)

(2) Words that differ in form but not (appreciably) in meaning, and are not distributed according to the phonetic or the syntactic environment, are different; thus ko and kodomo 'child', iru and óru 'is', morau and itadaku 'receives' are pairs of different words.[10]

(3) Words that are alike in form but differ in syntactic function (i. e. belong to different word classes) are different; thus the adverbs kéredomo 'nevertheless' and to 'so saying', which appear at the beginning of clauses, are different respectively from the particles kéredomo 'although' and to 'thus', which appear after other elements without intervening pause.

(4) Words that are alike in form but differ in meaning and in morphologic structure are different; thus kakéru 'hangs it' (related to kakáru 'it hangs') is different from kakéru 'can write' (derived from káku 'writes').

(5) Words that differ in form but not in meaning, and are distributed according to the phonetic or the syntactic environment, are the same; thus nán̄ 'what?' (before a dental consonant) is the same word as náni (before a non-dental consonant, a vowel, or a pause); the forms of the copula dá, na, and no 'is', which are distributed according to the syntax of the surrounding words, are all the same word.[10a]

(6) Words that are alike in form, syntactic function, and morphologic structure, but different or apparently different in meaning, may be regarded as the same or as different without affecting the description of the syntax. The decision in most cases will be a matter of individual judgment or taste. Most persons would probably regard kao 'face' and kao 'expression' as the same word, but sóotyoo 'first sergeant' and sóotyoo 'university president' as different words. Occasionally the choice may be difficult—ki means among other things 'spirit, mind, intention, will, temper, disposition, precaution, air, vapor, favor'—but it is never important.

8 Cf. Bloomfield, Language 183: 'In languages which use bound forms, the word has great structural importance because the constructions in which free forms appear in phrases differ very decidedly from the constructions in which free or bound forms appear in words. Accordingly, the grammar of these languages consists of two parts, called syntax, and morphology.'

9 I owe the formulation of this principle to Rulon S. Wells.

10 It is convenient to make an exception to this rule in the case of synonymous words which differ only by the presence or absence of the phoneme q before p, t, k, s, or of the phoneme n̄ before m, n. Thus totemo and tottemo 'quite, very', sírokute and sírokutte 'being white', amari and an̄mari 'too much' are alternants of the same word respectively.

10a Cf. Zellig S. Harris, Morpheme alternants in linguistic analysis, Lang. 18.169–80 (1942) ((109)).

2. The Major Sentence Type

2.1 A major sentence is one that ends with a certain type of clause, which we shall call a final clause. Some major sentences consist of a final clause alone; in other sentences, the final clause is preceded by one or more non-final clauses. Every final clause can be used by itself as a major sentence; but no non-final clause can be so used.[11]

A final clause (and therefore a major sentence) ends with falling, rising, or—much less commonly—high-falling intonation, and is followed by a pause. A non-final clause is followed by facultative pause with level intonation.

2.2 Every clause, whether final or non-final, ends with a predicate; the predicates of final and non-final clauses are different in form. Some clauses consist of a predicate alone; in other clauses, the predicate is preceded by one or more clause attributes. Every predicate can be used by itself as a complete clause (and every predicate of a final clause, therefore, can be used by itself as a major sentence); but no clause attribute can be so used.

A clause attribute is followed by facultative pause with level intonation, of the same kind as the pause which occurs at the end of a non-final clause. But the pause after a predicate is of higher rank than the pause after a clause attribute; and this, in turn, is of higher rank than any pause that may occur within the clause attribute.

2.3 Every major sentence thus ends with the predicate of a final clause. A sentence that ends in any other way is a minor sentence (§8).

The proportion of major to minor sentences varies with the tempo and the formality of the discourse. In extremely rapid, informal conversation, especially between close friends or under emotional stress, there may sometimes be almost as many minor sentences as major;[12] in the deliberate style appropriate to formal exposition, minor sentences are lacking altogether. It is probably safe to say that in ordinary polite conversation the ratio of major to minor sentences is about 5 to 1. The major sentence, then, is the favorite sentence type of Japanese.[13]

2.4 The immediate constituents of a major sentence containing two or more clauses are all the non-final clauses on the one hand and the final clause on the other. The prior constituent, in turn, has as many constituents as there are non-final clauses. A sentence of only one clause has only one constituent as a sentence; further analysis reveals the internal structure of the clause, not of the sentence as such.

The immediate constituents of a clause with one or more clause attributes preceding the predicate are all the clause attributes on the one hand and the predicate on the other. The prior constituent, in turn, has as many constituents as there are clause attributes. A clause containing only a predicate has only one constituent as a clause; further analysis reveals the internal structure of the predicate, not of the clause as such.

3. The Predicate

3.1 Every predicate contains an inflected word as its nucleus.[14] Some predicates consist of a nucleus alone; in other predicates, the nucleus is preceded without pause by one or more other words, or followed without pause by a word of a special class called a particle, or both so preceded and so followed. The following predicates all contain the same nucleus: itta 'went', arúite itta 'went on foot (lit. went walking)', motte itta 'took (lit. went holding)', isóide déte itta 'quickly went out (lit. went emerging hurrying)', ittá ka 'did [someone] go?', ittá kara 'because [someone] went', arúite ittá kara 'because [someone] went on foot'.

The words preceding the nucleus within a predicate are most often inflected also; but some nuclei are preceded by uninflected words, or (rarely) by words of both kinds in combination. The nucleus daróo 'may be' is preceded by an inflected word in the predicate itta daróo 'may have gone', by an uninflected word in heitai daróo 'may be a soldier', by two uninflected words in kono heitai daróo 'may be this soldier', and by one word of each kind in heitai dátta daroo 'may have been a soldier'.

A particle is a word that never begins a pause-group. Particles that follow the nucleus of a predicate in a final clause are sentence particles; those that follow the nucleus of a predicate in a non-final clause are clause particles. The two classes have no member in common.[15]

The words that compose a predicate are usually joined without pause; in particular, the nucleus is

[11] However, some non-final clauses occur at the ends of utterances as minor sentences; see §2.3, §8.2.

[12] Elinor M. Clark has counted sentence types in a large sample of recorded dialog, chosen as an extreme type of rapid, elliptical conversation. She found the following proportions: major sentences 58%, exclamations 15%, other fragments 27%. (On the distinction between exclamations and other fragments see §8.) The relatively high proportion of exclamations is probably due to the presence of a drunken man among the speakers. It is doubtful whether any sample of conversational Japanese would show a lower proportion of major sentences.

[13] Cf. Bloomfield, Language 171 ff.

[14] For the morphology of inflected words, and for terms relating to inflectional categories, reference is here made once and for all to SCJ I (see fn. 1).

[15] Some sentence particles and clause particles are homonymous with particles of other types, occurring in different environments. In accordance with the convention stated in §1.6 (No. 3), we regard such homonyms as different words.

never separated by a pause from an immediately preceding word or from the following particle. But among predicates in which the copula as nucleus is preceded by two or more words, some consist of more than a single pause-group. Thus, the predicate watakusi no, itibañ, sukí na, hoñ da '[it] is my favorite book' (with nucleus dá 'is') consists of four pause-groups.

The nucleus of a predicate, together with all preceding words within the predicate, is an inflected expression. According as the nucleus is a verb, an adjective, or the copula, the inflected expression is a verbal expression (§3.11), an adjectival expression (§3.12), or a copular expression (§3.13).

Japanese distinguishes a total of ten categories in its inflected words. The categories are listed here, together with the more inclusive terms that we shall use for brevity in referring to two or more of the categories together:

Indicative	Non-past indicative Past indicative
Presumptive	Non-past presumptive Past presumptive
Imperative	(one category only)
Hypothetical	Provisional Conditional
Participial	Alternative Gerund Infinitive

The non-past indicative form of a verb, an adjective, or the copula serves as the name form, used to refer collectively to all the members of a paradigm.

When the nucleus of an inflected expression is in a certain inflection, we speak of the whole expression as having the inflection. Thus, 'the indicative of an inflected expression' (or simply 'an indicative inflected expression') means either an inflected word in the non-past or the past indicative form (e.g. iku 'goes', itta 'went'; samúi 'is cold', sámukatta 'was cold'; dá 'is', dátta 'was') or an inflected expression whose nucleus is in this form (e.g. arúite iku 'goes on foot', arúite itta 'went on foot'; sámuku nai 'is not cold', sámuku nákatta 'was not cold'; heitai dá 'is a soldier', heitai dátta 'was a soldier'). Similarly, we speak of the indicative or some other category of a verbal, adjectival, or copular expression.

In a predicate that ends with a particle, the immediate constituents are the inflected expression on the one hand and the particle on the other. A predicate without a particle has only one constituent; further analysis reveals the internal structure of the inflected expression (preceding elements + nucleus), not of the predicate as such.

3.11 A verbal expression is a verb or a verb phrase.

Verbs are inflected for all ten of the categories listed above. Except for stylistic restrictions affecting a few verbs and verb forms, all verbs have essentially the same syntactic functions. The following examples illustrate each of the morphologic classes and subclasses of verbs:[16] tabéru 'eats', mátu 'waits', iku 'goes', kowaréru 'gets broken', kowásu 'breaks it'; tatéru 'erects, builds', ugokásu 'moves it', takasugíru 'is too expensive'; kokoroéru 'understands', utau 'sings', kokorogakeru 'intends', osiakeru 'pushes open', tabesugíru 'overeats', tositóru 'grows older', utikorosu 'beats to death', nakidasu 'bursts into tears', tabemásu = tabéru 'eats', beñkyoosuru 'studies'.

A verb phrase consists of a verb as nucleus preceded without pause by an inflected expression in a participial form. There are three types of verb phrases:[17]

(1) The verb suru 'does' or its equivalent preceded by the alternative of an inflected expression. The equivalents of suru, all having the same meaning but different connotations of politeness (see §3.3) are itasu, nasáru, simásu, itasimásu, and nasaimásu. Examples: tábetari suru 'eats and does other things, eats and so on', sámukattari suru 'is sometimes cold', heitai dáttari suru 'is a soldier and other things [by turns], is sometimes a soldier', hataraitári itasimásu '[I] work and so on', yóñde itari nasaimásu '[you] are reading and so on'.

(2) The verb náru 'becomes' (or its equivalent narimásu) or the verb gozáru 'is' (or its equivalent gozaimásu) preceded by the infinitive of an adjectival expression. Before náru (narimásu), the adjective appears in the usual form of its infinitive, ending in -ku; before gozáru (gozaimásu), an adjective appears in a special 'honorific' form of the infinitive, ending in morphophonemic -wu, which occurs in major sentences only in this position. Examples: sámuku náru 'grows cold', hósiku naku naru 'becomes undesirable (lit. not desirable)', arúite ikitaku narimásu '[I] begin to wish to go on foot (lit. become desirous of going walking)', sámuu gozaimásu 'is cold' (equivalent in meaning to the indicative adjective samúi), ohayoo gozaimásu 'good morning' (lit. 'it is early', equivalent to hayái).

(3) Any verb preceded by the gerund of a verbal expression. This is the most frequent type of verb phrase. The verbal expression which precedes the nucleus may itself be a verb or a verb phrase of any type. Examples: (a) with a verb preceding the nucleus: arúite iku 'goes on foot', tábete iru 'is eating',

[16] These classes will be named and defined in SCJ III.

[17] In addition to the three types of verb phrases enumerated here, there is a combination consisting of the verb áru 'is, there is' or its equivalent preceded by the gerund of a copula phrase; e.g. heitai de áru 'is a soldier'. Combinations of this kind are more conveniently classified as copular expressions, and will therefore be treated in §3.13.

mótte iru 'has, owns (lit. is holding)', motte iku 'takes (lit. goes holding)', tábete áru 'is eaten', tukatte simau 'uses up (lit. finishes [by] using)'; (b) with a verb phrase of type 1 preceding the nucleus: tábetari site iru 'is eating and so on', sámukattari site iru 'is (being) sometimes cold'; (c) with a verb phrase of type 2 preceding the nucleus: sámuku nátte kita 'has grown cold', kuraku nátte kuru 'starts to get dark'; (d) with a verb phrase of type 3 preceding the nucleus: arúite itte simatta 'has gone away on foot', tukatte simatte iru 'is using it up', isóide arúite káette kuru 'comes back rapidly on foot (lit. comes returning walking hurrying)'.[18]

3.12 An adjectival expression is an adjective, an adjective phrase, or an adjective group.

Adjectives are inflected for nine categories, including all the verbal categories except the imperative. All adjectives have essentially the same syntactic functions, except that not all adjectives occur as nuclei in adjective phrases. Adjectives that have this function in addition to others are nuclear adjectives; they include three groups: (a) the adjective nái 'is non-existent, is not, there is not', and its equivalent arimaséñ (§3.32); (b) negative adjectives, derived from verbs by a suffix -na-/-ana- attached to the base, or their equivalents, derived from compound verbs in -másu by a suffix -eñ (§3.32); and (c) desiderative adjectives, derived from verbs by a suffix -ta- attached to the infinitive.

The following examples illustrate each of the morphologic classes and subclasses of adjectives: nagái 'is long', samúi 'is cold', kiiroi 'is yellow'; siroppói 'is whitish', isogasíi 'is busy', hosonagái 'is long and thin'; mizuppói 'is watery', kokoroyasasíi 'is kind-hearted'. Examples of nuclear adjectives: negative: tabénai 'does not eat' (derived from tabéru 'eats'), karinai 'does not borrow' (from kariru 'borrows'), matánai 'does not wait' (from mátu 'waits'), noranai 'does not ride' (from noru 'rides'); desiderative: tabetái 'wants to eat' (derived from tabéru), karitai 'wants to borrow' (from kariru), matitái 'wants to wait' (from mátu), noritai 'wants to ride' (from noru).

An adjective phrase consists of an adjective as nucleus preceded without pause by an inflected expression in a participial form. There are four types of adjective phrases:

(1) Any nuclear adjective preceded by the gerund of a verbal expression. Examples: káite nái (káite arimaséñ) 'is not written', kákete nái 'is not hung', motte itte nái 'is not taken'; tábete itai 'wants to be eating'; arúite ikitai 'wants to go on foot'; motte kónai 'does not bring (lit. come holding)', tukatte simawanai 'does not use up'; óokiku nátte inai 'has not grown big'.

(2) The adjective nái 'is not, there is not' (or its equivalent arimaséñ) or the adjective naránai 'does not become' (or its equivalent narimaséñ) or the adjective naritái 'wants to become' preceded by the infinitive of an adjectival expression. Examples: sámuku nái (sámuku arimaséñ) 'is not cold', arúite ikitaku nái 'does not want to go on foot'; sámuku naránai 'does not get cold', túyoku naritái 'wants to grow strong'.

(3) The adjective sinai 'does not do' (or its equivalents itasanai, nasaránai, simaséñ, itasimaséñ, nasaimaséñ) or the adjective sitai 'wants to do' (or its equivalent itasitai) preceded by the alternative of an inflected expression. Examples: tábetari sinai (tábetari simaséñ) 'does not eat and so on', sámukattari sinai 'is not sometimes cold'; hataraitári sitai 'wants to work sometimes, wants to work and do other things'.

(4) The adjective nái 'is not, there is not' (or its equivalent arimaséñ) preceded by the gerund of a copula phrase (§3.13). Examples: heitai de nái (heitai de arimaséñ) 'is not a soldier', soo de nái 'is not so', kore bákari de náku 'not only this'.

An adjective group, like an adjective phrase, has a nucleus (an adjective or a bound form deriving adjectives); but the element preceding the nucleus is not an inflected expression in a participial form. There are two types of adjective groups:

(1) The adjective nái 'is not, there is not', usually in the infinitive (náku), preceded by a noun.[19] Instances are limited to a few clichés: eñryo náku 'without reserve', yoosya náku 'without mercy', kawari náku 'without change', and others.

(2) The bound form -rasíi 'seems to be or do' preceded by a noun expression, by a relational phrase,[20] or by a clause with an indicative predicate. The form -rasíi combines with a preceding single word, or with the last word of a preceding phrase, to form a complex adjective. But although the construction by which -rasíi is attached to an underlying word is morphologic, the scope of the suffix is syntactic, i.e. extends over a whole preceding phrase.[21] When the adjective group ending with

[18] The immediate constituents of this last expression are shown by the following arrangement: [<(isóide) arúite> káette] kuru.

[19] Nouns will be defined in §5.1.

[20] Noun expressions will be defined in §5.1 and §5.3–6. The noun expressions used as examples in this paragraph are limited to the simplest type: a single noun, with or without one modifier preceding. Relational phrases will be defined in §4.3.

[21] The scope of -rasíi resembles the scope of the English possessive suffix; cf. Bloomfield, Lang. 2.156 ((27)). In the phrase "the King of England's daughter", the immediate constituents are "the King of England's" and "daughter"; the immediate constituents of the prior expression are "the King of England" and "-s": the suffix, though attached to the noun "England" by a morphologic construction, has a syntactic scope which includes the whole preceding phrase. (Note that the possessive suffix sometimes appears at the end of a phrase whose last word is not a noun: "the man that went by just now's daughter"; "the man I saw's daughter".) Japanese and English are thus alike in that each has one bound form that combines with phrases in a syntactic construction.

-rasíi consists of two or more words, its immediate syntactic constituents are the whole preceding phrase on the one hand and -rasíi on the other (§1.5); in such a case, the complex adjective containing -rasíi does not appear at all among the syntactic constituents of the group or of the sentence.[22] Examples: musumerasíi 'seems to be a daughter' (prior constituent musumé 'daughter'); tomodati no, musumerasíi 'seems to be [my] friend's daughter' (prior constituent tomodati no, musumé 'a friend's daughter); watakusi norasíi 'seems to be mine' (prior constituent watakusi no 'of me'); taberurasíi 'seems to eat' (prior constituent tabéru 'eats'); takusañ, taberurasíi 'seems to eat a lot' (prior constituent takusañ, tabéru 'eats a lot'); tabetarasíi 'seems to have eaten' (prior constituent tábeta 'ate'); niñniku ka, tamanégi o, tabetarasíi 'seems to have eaten garlic or onions' (prior constituent niñniku ka, tamanégi o, tábeta 'ate garlic or onions'); samuirasíi 'seems to be cold' (prior constituent samúi 'is cold'); samukattarasíi 'seems to have been cold' (prior constituent sámukatta 'was cold').

3.13 A copular expression is the copula or a copula phrase.

The copula is inflected for eight categories, including all the adjectival categories except the infinitive. It has two equivalent paradigms with different social connotations (§3.3), one with the name form dá and one with the name form désu. The copula constitutes a copular expression by itself only in a few clichés: dá kara 'therefore (lit. because it is)', dé wa 'well then (lit. as for being)', dé mo 'nevertheless (lit. even being)'. In all other uses the copula is the nucleus of a copula phrase.

A copula phrase consists of the copula as nucleus preceded without pause by one of five different types of elements:

(1) By a noun or other type of substantive expression (to be defined in §§5, 6). Examples: heitai dá 'is a soldier'; sóo da 'is so'; watakusi no, boosi dá 'is my hat'; kádo ni, áru, ano sírokute, tiisái uti dá 'is that small white house (which is) on the corner'; nedañ ni, yotté da 'is dependent on the price'; señsoo ni, túite da 'is about the war'.

(2) By a relational phrase (to be defined in §4.3). Examples: watakusi nó da 'is mine'; Tookyoo kára da 'is from Tokyo'; Tookyoo kára no da 'is the one from Tokyo'; tomodati no, musumé no da 'is [my] friend's daughter's'; bañgóhañ o, tábete kara dátta 'it was after eating dinner'.

(3) By an indicative inflected expression. The following examples illustrate all the common combinations of an indicative form with an indicative, presumptive, or hypothetical copula; tabéru 'eats' and samúi 'is cold' represent all verbs and all adjectives respectively. With an indicative copula as nucleus: samúi desu 'is cold', samúi desita 'was cold', sámukatta desu 'was cold'; with a presumptive copula as nucleus: tabéru daroo or tabéru desyoo 'will probably eat', samúi daroo or samúi desyoo 'will probably be cold', tábeta daroo or tábeta desyoo 'probably ate', sámukatta daroo or sámukatta desyoo 'probably was cold', (heitai) dátta daroo or (heitai) dátta desyoo 'was probably a soldier'; with a hypothetical copula as nucleus: tabéru nara or tabéru naraba 'if [someone] eats', tábeta nara or tábeta naraba 'if [someone] ate', samúi nara or samúi naraba 'if it is cold'. Other examples: sámuku náru daroo 'will probably grow cold', arúite iku daroo 'will probably go on foot', túyoku naritái daroo 'probably wants to grow strong', arúite ikitaku nákatta daroo 'probably did not want to go on foot'.

(4) By an indicative inflected expression with a clause particle following. Examples: tábeta kara da 'it is because [someone] ate', tábete iru kara da 'it is because [someone] is eating', sámuku nái kara da 'it is because it is not cold'.

(5) Rarely, by a presumptive verbal expression. The only common instance is ikóo de (gerund) in the expression ikóo zya nái ka 'let's go' (lit. 'shall we not go?').[23]

[22] We treat -rasíi in this way because we wish to keep our description of the syntax as free as possible from exceptions and special cases. By recognizing that -rasíi is unique among bound forms in serving as a constituent of syntactic constructions, we escape the necessity of describing anomalous combinations —e.g. a noun modifier (§5.2) preceding an adjective, as tomodati no 'of a friend' in the expression tomodati no, musumerasíi, or kono 'this' in the expression kono kadorasíi 'seems to be this corner'.

The semantics of the construction agree with our analysis. An adjective group ending with -rasíi means 'seems to be or do x, looks like x, is x-like'; the x is the meaning of the whole noun expression or clause preceding -rasíi within the adjective group. When someone says of a girl, Tomodati no, musumerasíi, he means not merely that she seems to be a daughter, but that she seems to be a friend's daughter; when he says of her, Tamanégi o, tabetarasíi, he means not merely that she seems to have eaten, but that she seems to have eaten onions: the meaning of tomodati no or of tamanégi o is part of the x. However, the semantics of the construction are not enough to make the analysis here adopted necessary or even particularly desirable. Similar semantic relations obtain in expressions that we analyze differently. Thus the expression tamanégi o, tabetái 'I want to eat onions' (where the suffix -tai attached to the infinitive of the verb tabéru carries the desiderative meaning) might be described as having the immediate constituents tamanégi o, tábe 'eating onions' and the bound form -tai; but we find it simpler in the long run to say that the phrase tamanégi o here is not part of the predicate, but rather a clause attribute preceding the predicate tabétai 'I want to eat'.

[23] In this expression the combination de wa is optionally replaced by zya — a morphophonemic alternation found also in other contexts. Cf. SCJ I, §8.3 (JAOS 66.109).

In the expository style and in rather formal conversational style (§3.31), forms of the copula are often replaced by a combination of dé (the gerund of the copula) and the appropriate forms of the verb áru 'is, there is' or its equivalent (arimásu, gozáru or gozaimásu, irassyáru or irassyaimásu). Thus, dá is replaced by de áru, dátta by de átta, désu by de arimásu, and so on. An inflected expression that ends with a combination of this kind is a verbalized copula phrase. We include such phrases under copular expressions rather than verbal expressions (§3.11) because their internal structure is precisely the same as that of the expressions which they replace.

Before the particle ka (§3.21, §4.4), the non-past indicative of the copula, dá, is replaced by a zero alternant (i. e. drops out); e. g. Heitai ka, súihei ka, siranai 'I don't know whether he is a soldier or a sailor' (cf. Heitai dátta ka, súihei dátta ka, siranai 'I don't know whether he was a soldier or a sailor', with the past indicative of the copula before ka).

3.2 The predicates of final and of non-final clauses differ in the inflectional form of the nucleus or in the selection of the particle following the nucleus, or in both respects.

Predicates of final and non-final clauses have a nucleus in the indicative, the presumptive, the imperative, or the hypothetical form. An inflected expression whose nucleus is in a participial form (alternative, gerund, or infinitive) is not the predicate of a clause, final or non-final, but an element of a different type (a pseudo-predicate), to be discussed in §6.

3.21 A final predicate (the predicate of a final clause) is in the indicative, the presumptive, or the imperative form, with or without a following sentence particle. Sentences with an indicative final predicate have the class meaning of definiteness or certainty; e. g. Tookyoo e, itta 'He went to Tokyo'. Those with a presumptive final predicate have the class meaning of uncertainty, suggestion, or supposition; e. g. Tookyoo e, ikoo 'I guess I'll go to Tokyo' or 'Let's go to Tokyo'. Those with an imperative final predicate have the class meaning of request or command; e. g. Tookyoo e, ike 'Go to Tokyo'.

A few imperative verbs alternate optionally with uninflected words of the same meaning and syntactic function. Thus, kói 'come [here]', the imperative of the verb kúru 'comes', alternates with oide, serving as an abbreviation of oidenasái, the imperative of the honorific verb oidenasáru 'comes, goes, is' (§3.31); mí and míro 'look [here]', the imperatives of the verb míru 'looks, sees', alternate with gorañ, serving as an abbreviation of gorañnasái, the imperative of the honorific verb gorañnasáru 'looks, sees'. Words like oide and gorañ serve as final predicates either alone or as nuclei of longer expression (e. g. motte oide 'bring it', equivalent to motte kói). We shall call them verb surrogates.

The class meaning of sentence particles is a general modulation or coloring of the class meanings of the sentences to which they are attached. The denotation of a sentence is largely the same with or without a sentence particle; the sentence particle adds an indication of the speaker's attitude or purpose. The most common sentence particles are the following:

Ka, after an indicative or presumptive nucleus, marks a question. Some sentences ending with ka have, except for the particle, the form of a statement; e. g. Otóosañ wa, moo, káette imásu ka 'Has your father returned already?' (cf. Otóosañ wa, moo, káette imásu 'Your father has already returned'). Other sentences ending with ka contain an interrogative word like dáre 'who?', náni 'what?', ítu 'when?', or the like (§5.1); these do not match any corresponding statement without ka: e. g. Dáre ga, to o, tatakimásita ka 'Who knocked at the door?'. Every statement that does not end with a sentence particle can be turned into a question by adding ka; but not every question can be turned into a statement by omitting ka.[24]

Na, after a non-past indicative verbal nucleus in the plain state (§3.3), marks a negative command; e. g. tabéru na 'don't eat it', mátu na 'don't wait', té o, hureru na 'don't touch it (lit. don't touch the hand); hands off'.

Yo, after an indicative or imperative nucleus, marks an emphatic statement or command; e. g. Sóo desu yo 'It is so', Sore o, tabé yo 'Eat that'. A statement that implies a warning or an injunction very often ends with yo; e. g. Añmari, hatarakisugíru to; byooki ni, narimásu yo 'If you overwork (too much), you'll get sick'.

Zo, after an indicative nucleus, marks an emphatic statement; e. g. Kono hóñ wa, taiheñ, tumaránai zo 'This book is terribly dull'. The connotation of warning sometimes present in yo is absent here.

The particle née or ne 'nicht wahr, n'est-ce pas' has a different syntax from other particles that appear at the end of a major sentence: it is added to the sentence as a whole, not to the last inflected expression; a line dividing the immediate constituents of a sentence ending with née or ne is to be drawn just before this particle. There are two features which demand this analysis: née or ne occurs after sentence particles; and it occurs at the end of some minor sentences (§8.5). It is worth noting also that née appears more often than other particles in sentences with high-falling intonation.

In major sentences, née or ne occurs after an indicative or presumptive final predicate, and after

24 Not all questions end with ka. Some questions are distinguished from statements only by rising intonation; e.g. Moo, kité itú ñ da? 'Has he come already?'. When such a question has a presumptive copula phrase as its final predicate, the meaning of the question is often rhetorical; e. g. Nakanaka, zyoozú daroo? 'He's pretty skillful, isn't he?'.

a predicate ending with ka (see above). After a predicate that does not include a sentence particle, née or ne marks a suggestion, a softened statement, or a rhetorical question; e. g. Kyóo wa, atúi née 'It's hot today, isn't it?' or 'Isn't it hot today!', Koko wa, kírei na, tokoro desu née 'Isn't this a nice place!', Kanemotí desyoo née 'He must be rich, don't you think?'. Note also the cliché Sóo desu née 'Hm!' or 'Let me see' (lit. 'It is so, isn't it?'). After the sentence particle ka, née adds a meaning of deliberation or doubt; e. g. Dóo desyoo ka née 'I wonder how it will be' (cf. Dóo desyoo ka 'How will it be?'), Dótira ni, siyóo ka née 'I wonder which one I ought to decide on' (cf. Dótira ni, siyóo ka 'Which one shall I decide on?'). In the familiar style of conversation (§3.31), the sentence particle ka is very often followed in questions by ne; e. g. Dóko ni, oite kitá ka ne? 'Where did you (go and) put it?', Nihoñzíñ ka ne? (with zero alternant of the copula before ka, §3.13) 'Is he a Japanese?'.[25]

3.22 In a non-final predicate (the predicate of a non-final clause), the nucleus is (a) indicative and followed by a clause particle; (b) much less commonly, presumptive and followed by a clause particle; or (c) hypothetical. A non-final clause with an indicative or presumptive predicate has the class meaning of certainty or uncertainty respectively, modified by the meaning of the clause particle. A non-final clause with a hypothetical predicate has the class meaning of provision or condition (eventual or temporal); e.g. Tití ga, háyaku, káette kureba; kiite mimasyóo 'If my father comes back early, I'll ask him'; Nihoñ no, kotó nara; anó hito wa, náni mo, sirimaséñ 'If it's Japanese matters [that you're talking about], he doesn't know anything'; Sore o, tábetara; byooki ni, náru desyoo 'If you should eat that, you'd get sick'; Tookyoo e, túitara; deñwa o, kakemasu 'When I get to Tokyo, I'll telephone':

The class meaning of clause particles is to relate the clause to the following clause in meaning. The most common clause particles are the following:

Ga 'but', after an indicative or presumptive nucleus: anáta to, issyo ni, ikitái ga 'I'd like to go with you but [I can't]';[26] sóo desyoo ga 'that may be so but [I doubt it]'.

Si 'and', after an indicative or presumptive nucleus: koko wa, natú wa, suzusíi si 'the summer here is cool and [the winter is mild]'; kinóo wa, inaka no, itóko ga, kitá si 'yesterday my cousin from the country came, and [a lot of other people came too]'.

Kara 'because', after an indicative nucleus: áme ga, hútte irú kara 'since it's raining (lit. rain is falling), [I'll stay in]'; sore o, tábeta kara '[he's sick] because he ate that'.

Kéredomo 'although', after an indicative nucleus: taiheñ, tukárete ita kéredomo 'although I was terribly tired [I went out anyway]'; kono yoohuku wa, atarasíi keredomo 'although this suit is new [it's already wrinkled]'.

Made 'until', after an indicative nucleus: Tároo ga, káette kúru made '[let's wait here] until Taro gets back'; misé ga, kóñbañ, simáru made '[I've got to stay] till the store closes tonight'.

To 'whenever, when, if', after a non-past indicative nucleus: sóto ga, samúi to 'whenever it's cold outside [I stay in]'; añmari, hatarakisugíru to 'if you overwork (too much) [you'll get sick]'.

3.3 Stylistically, a predicate is either in the plain state or in the polite state. The two states of any inflected expression are synonymous, but differ in stylistic and social connotations. A predicate in the polite state has not only the denotation of the corresponding plain predicate, but in addition a flavor of courtesy lacking in the other.[27]

3.31 The use of plain and polite predicates (i. e. of predicates in the plain and the polite state) characterizes different styles or levels of discourse. It is enough here to distinguish three such levels.

The plain level is used in two styles of discourse, the informal and the expository. The informal style is that of conversation among intimate friends or among workmen engaged in a common task; it is also used by anyone in addressing a social inferior or a younger member of his own family. The expository style is used by public lecturers, teachers in the classroom, radio commentators, or anyone speaking impersonally to convey information to an audience. The two styles differ in several respects—thus, in the proportion of major sentences (§2.3), the use of sentence particles (§3.21), and the use of verbalized copula phrases (§3.13); but they agree in having all predicates in the plain state.

25 The theoretical combination dá ka ne (where dá is the plain non-past indicative of the copula) is usually replaced by one of two equivalent combinations: by ka ne, with dá omitted (i. e. replaced by a zero alternant); or by da ne, with ka omitted. The question Nihoñzíñ ka ne? cited in the text occurs also as Nihoñzíñ da ne? — In rapid speech, the sequences ka ne and da ne are replaced by the conglomerates kai and dai respectively; thus Nihoñzíñ kai? and Nihoñzíñ dai?

26 In these examples, square brackets enclose the English equivalent of a possible final clause added after the clause particle to complete the sense.

27 This flavor of courtesy is of course entirely conventional and often largely fictitious. The use of polite predicates does not necessarily imply, and is not necessarily understood to imply, any genuine respect on the speaker's part. The difference between plain and polite predicates may be compared to the difference between French tu and vous, German du and Sie.

The intermediate level is used in the normal polite style of conversation, in addressing a stranger, a casual acquaintance, or an older member of one's family. On this level, every final predicate is in the polite state. Other inflected expressions—in non-final clauses and elsewhere in the sentence—are plain or polite at the speaker's option. They may be all plain, or nearly all[28] polite; in a typical average style the polite state appears (outside of final predicates) only in non-final predicates before a clause particle—chiefly ga 'but' and kara 'because'.

The highest level is that of the honorific style, used by persons of low social rank in addressing a superior, by women also in addressing an equal, and by anyone in speaking deferentially to a person of high rank or to an equal in certain social situations—thus, when acting as host or guest. The honorific style uses a great variety of ceremonious circumlocutions and many special terms with connotations of humility and esteem; it resembles the most courteous variety of the normal polite style in having nearly all inflected expression in the polite state.

3.32 The polite state of a verbal expression contains as its nucleus a compound verb with -másu (-másita, -masyóo, etc.) as the second member; the prior member of the compound is the infinitive of the verb which appears as nucleus in the corresponding plain expression.[29] Thus, the plain verbs tabéru 'eats' and tábeta 'ate' (infinitive tábe) have the polite correspondents tabemásu and tabemásita respectively; similarly kariru 'borrows' (inf. kari) : polite karimásu, mátu 'waits' (inf. máti) : polite matimásu, noru 'rides' (inf. nori): polite norimásu, kúru 'comes' (inf. kí) : polite kimásu.

The plain and polite states of a copular expression differ in the selection of the nucleus. A plain expression contains as its nucleus a member of the so-called plain paradigm of the copula, with the name form dá 'is' (§3.13); a polite expression contains as its nucleus a member of the polite paradigm, with the name form désu. Each member of the plain paradigm is matched by a member of the polite paradigm (thus dá is matched by désu, dátta by désita, daróo by desyóo, etc.), except that the plain provisional nára[ba] has no polite correspondent.

All adjectival expressions are in the plain state. Their polite correspondents are of several kinds.

(1) An adjective that is not a negative adjective has as its polite correspondent a copula phrase with a polite copula as nucleus, preceded by the indicative of the adjective.[30] Thus the polite state of samúi 'is cold' is supplied by the phrase samúi desu; similarly sámukatta 'was cold' : polite sámukatta desu or samúi désita, samukaróo 'may or must be cold' : polite samúi desyoo, etc. One primary adjective deviates from the pattern here described: nái 'is non-existent, is not, there is not' most commonly has as its polite correspondent the form arimaséñ (see below).

(2) A negative adjective in the non-past indicative has as its polite correspondent a compound formation with -maséñ as the second member; the prior member is the infinitive of the verb which underlies the negative adjective. Thus the negative adjective tabénai 'does not eat', derived from the verb tabéru 'eats' (infinitive tábe), has the polite correspondent tabemaséñ; similarly karinai 'does not borrow' (from kariru, inf. kari) : polite karimaséñ, matánai 'does not wait' (from mátu, inf. máti) : polite matimaséñ, noranai 'does not ride' (from noru, inf. nori) : polite norimaséñ, kónai 'does not come' (from kúru, inf. kí) : polite kimaséñ. Also, as mentioned above, nái 'is not, there is not' : polite arimaséñ, with the infinitive of the verb áru 'there is' as prior member of the compound. The formation with -maséñ is not inflected. Since it has, on the whole, the same syntactic functions as a negative adjective, we call it an adjective surrogate.

(3) A negative adjective in any form except the non-past indicative has as its polite correspondent a copula phrase with a polite copula as nucleus, preceded by a formation with -maséñ of the kind already described. Thus the negative adjective tabénakatta 'did not eat' (past indicative of tabénai) has the polite correspondent tabemaséñ desita, and the negative adjective tabemái or taberumái 'probably will not eat' (non-past presumptive of tabénai) has the polite correspondent tabemaséñ desyoo; similarly karinákatta 'did not borrow' : polite karimaséñ desita, matánakatta 'did not wait' : polite matimaséñ desita, noranákatta 'did not ride' : polite norimaséñ desita. Also, nákatta 'was not, there was not' : polite arimaséñ desita.

4. Clause Attributes

4.1 Some clauses consist of a predicate alone; in other clauses, the predicate is preceded by one or more other words. Any predicate, with a few restrictions,[31] will occur both as a clause by itself and as the last part of a longer clause. The words preceding

[28] Even in very polite speech, adjectives are almost never in the polite state outside a final predicate and certain types of non-final predicates. The provisional form of the copula (nára, náraba) has no polite correspondent.

[29] For the details of the morphologic structure see SCJ III, §3.5.

[30] What is here said of adjectives applies equally to adjectives constituting adjectival expressions alone and to adjectives serving as nuclei of longer expressions.

[31] A predicate consisting of a copula plus a particle (with no other words preceding the nucleus within the predicate) is never preceded by a clause attribute.

the predicate in a clause constitute one or more clause attributes.

Clause attributes are of three types: adverbial phrases, relational phrases, and quotational phrases. The three types differ in their internal structure, as shown below; but as elements in the structure of the clause they are coordinate—i. e. play equivalent roles as attributes of the predicate.

The number of clause attributes preceding a predicate is not limited; it varies in different clauses from none to as many as nine or ten. When there are several clause attributes preceding the same predicate, they may be all adverbial phrases, or all relational phrases, or a combination of adverbial and relational phrases in any order; but a clause usually contains no more than two quotational phrases, and these commonly follow the other clause attributes.

The relative order of clause attributes is not determined by their type: an adverbial phrase, as such, can precede or follow a relational phrase. But particular adverbial and relational phrases have preferred or even compulsory positions relative to other clause attributes. The sentence Nísatu, hóñ ga, arimásu 'There are two books' (lit. 'There are books to the extent of two') contains an adverbial phrase nísatu 'two (when speaking of volumes)', a relational phrase hóñ ga 'books (as subject)', and a predicate arimásu 'there is, there are'; if the two clause attributes are transposed (Hóñ ga, nísatu, arimásu), the resulting sentence is completely equivalent to the first. On the other hand, no such transposition is possible in the sentence Nísatu, hóñ ni, káite arimásu 'It is written in two books', though it contains precisely the same types of elements: an adverbial phrase nísatu, a relational phrase hóñ ni 'in books', and a predicate káite arimásu 'is written'.[32]

In describing the internal structure of adverbial and relational phrases, we shall speak of certain elements as substantive expressions. There are two types of substantive expressions: noun expressions and pseudo-clauses. These terms will be defined in §5 and §6 respectively. Meanwhile, in citing adverbial and relational phrases which contain substantive expressions, we shall choose the simplest subvariety, a single noun; as we shall see later, most of the positions filled by a single noun in these illustrations can be filled also by other types of substantive expressions.

4.2 An adverbial phrase consists of a substantive expression or an adverb. Such a phrase has only one constituent; if it contains two or more words, they are constituents of a substantive expression, not of the adverbial phrase as such.

The following nouns illustrate common types of adverbial phrases: kyóo 'today', kotosi 'this year', íma 'now', sibáraku 'for a while', nizíkañ 'for two hours', hutatú 'two (lit. to the extent of two)', sukósi 'a little, a few', taiheñ 'terribly, very much', hóoboo 'here and there', sóo 'that way, so', ítu 'when?', ikága 'how?'.

An adverb is an uninflected word that occurs alone as a pause-group, but never stands before the copula. Adverbs are of three kinds: connective adverbs, modal adverbs, and interjectional adverbs or interjections.

A connective adverb always begins a clause. The class meaning of most connective adverbs is a reference to the preceding sentence (whether uttered by the same speaker or by someone else) or to the preceding clause in the same sentence; e. g. sosite 'then, and', áruiwa[32a] 'or', sikási 'but', kéredomo 'nevertheless', to 'so saying'. The word mósi 'if, supposing' has a class meaning different from that of most other connective adverbs: it appears only in non-final clauses with a hypothetical (usually a conditional) predicate, and serves to anticipate or emphasize the class meaning of this predicate.

A modal adverb does not always begin a clause; if there are several clause attributes, a modal adverb may occupy the first, the second, or any other position. The class meaning of most modal adverbs is 'in such-and-such a way' or 'to such-and-such an extent' or the like; e. g. nakanaka 'considerably, quite, very', tyoodo 'exactly, just', tyótto 'a moment, a bit', mótto 'more (in degree)', moo 'more (in quantity), any more, already', mata 'again'.

Interjections are distinguished from other adverbs on a statistical rather than a formal basis: an interjection is an adverb which rarely or never occurs in a major sentence. All interjections occur alone as minor sentences; some occur in no other way. Examples will be given in §8.3.

4.3 A relational phrase has two immediate constituents: an element called the relatum, and a following particle. The relatum is most commonly a noun or other type of substantive expression; but in some relational phrases the relatum is an adverb, a demonstrative (§5.21), a quotational phrase (§4.4), or another relational phrase. When the relatum is a phrase, either quotational or relational, the total phrase ends with two particles: the one that ends the inner phrase constituting the relatum, and the one that follows this relatum. Thus the relational phrase tomodati to sika 'only with a friend', contains the relatum tomodati to 'with a friend' followed by the particle sika 'only'; this in turn contains the

32 The difference is due to the difference between the particles which follow the noun hóñ in the two sentences. When a noun is followed by the particle ga, o, wa, or mo, a quantity noun (§5.1) referring to it may precede or follow as an adverbial phrase. When a noun is followed by any other particle, such an adverbial phrase always precedes.

32a The adverb áruiwa is initial in the clause (and is therefore classified as a connective adverb) except in discontinuous noun expressions of the type discussed in §5.51 below.

relatum tomodati 'friend' followed by the particle to 'with'. When the relatum is a relational phrase whose own relatum, in turn, is a still smaller relational phrase, the total phrase ends with three particles. Thus the relational phrase Tookyo kára no yori 'more than the one from Tokyo' has the relatum Tookyoo kára no 'the one from Tokyo' followed by the particle yóri 'more than'; this in turn contains the relatum Tokyoo kára 'from Tokyo' followed by the particle no 'of'; and this, finally, contains the relatum Tookyoo 'Tokyo' followed by the particle kára 'from'.[33] Successions of more than three particles are rare.

The particle that ends a relational phrase is a referent particle. It modifies or adds to the semantic content of the relatum, and in most cases also indicates the relation of the relatum to a following element—usually but not always the predicate of the clause. The most common referent particles are the following:

Ga 'emphatic subject'.[34] After a noun: Heitai ga, kureta 'The soldier gave it to me' (when the emphasis is on who gave it, not on what the soldier did); Gyuuniku ga, sukí da 'I like beef', more lit. 'Beef is pleasing' (when the emphasis is on what is pleasing, not on how I feel about beef); Eigo ga, yoméru 'I can read English', more lit. 'English is readable' (when the emphasis is on what I can read, not on whether English is readable or not).

O 'emphatic object'. After a noun: Heitai o, míta 'I saw a soldier' (when the emphasis is on what it was that I saw); Gyuuniku o, tábeta 'I ate [some] beef'; Tokei o, nusumáreta 'My watch was stolen' or 'I had my watch stolen', more lit. '[I] suffered through having [my] watch stolen'.

De 'by means of; in, on, at'. After a noun: Té de, sita 'I did it by hand'; Kisyá de kíta 'I came by train'; Koobá de, hataraite iru 'I work at the factory'.

E 'to (of motion)'. After a noun: Tookyoo e, itta 'I went to Tokyo'; Sóto e, déta 'I went outside'; Dóko e, ittá ka 'Where did he go?'.

Kára 'from; after (of place or time)'. After a noun: Sitamati kára, káetta 'I returned from downtown'; Sore kára, déta 'After that I left'; Kyóneñ kára, byooki da 'I've been sick since last year'.

Máde 'as far as, up to, until (of place or time)'. After a noun: Giñkoo máde, arúite itta 'I walked as far as the bank'; Doyóobi máde, isogasíi 'I'm busy till Saturday'; Ima máde, kirai dátta 'Up to now I've disliked it'.

Ni 'in, on, at (of place or time); to; into', and a great variety of other meanings. After a noun: Inaka ni, súñde iru 'I live in the country'; Nitiyóobi ni, sañposita 'I took a walk on Sunday'; Tookyoo ni, itta 'I went to Tokyo'; Náka ni, ireta 'I put it (into the) inside'; Kodomo ni, yatta 'I gave it to a child'; Kaimono ni, ikoo 'I'll go (for the purpose of) shopping'; Tomodati ni, átta 'I met a friend'; Zyúñsa ni, kiita 'I asked a policeman'; Byooki ni, nátta 'I got sick'; Tití ni, nite iru 'I look like my father'; Téñki ni, yoru 'It depends on the weather'. After an adverb: Issyokéñmei ni, hataraita 'I worked with all my might'. After a demonstrative: Soñna ni, beñkyoosuru to; atamá ga, ítaku náru yo 'If you study like that you'll get a headache'.

To 'with'. After a noun: Tomodati to, hanásita 'I talked with a friend'; Eikoku to, tatakátta 'We fought with [i. e. on the side of] England'; Nippóñ to, tatakátta 'We fought with [i. e. against] Japan'.

Daké 'only'. After a noun: Áni dake, iru 'Only my (older) brother is [here]'; Kusuri daké, utte iru 'They sell only drugs'; Siñbuñ daké, kaoo 'I'll only buy a newspaper'. After a relational phrase: Tookyoo e daké, itta 'I went only to Tokyo [i. e. nowhere else]'; Suzukisañ to daké, hanasánakatta 'I didn't talk with Mr. Suzuki only' or 'Mr. Suzuki was the only one I didn't talk with'; Nitiyóobi ni daké, sañposuru 'I take walks on Sunday only'.

Sika 'only, nothing but'. After a noun: Áni sika, inai 'Only my (older) brother is [here];[35] Kusuri sika, utte inai 'They sell only (nothing but) drugs'; Zíppuñ sika, kakaránai 'It takes only (no more than) ten minutes'. After a relational phrase: Tomodati to sika, hanasánakatta 'I talked only with a friend'; Nihoñgo de sika, hanasánai 'They speak nothing but Japanese'; Nitiyóobi ni sika, sañposinai 'I take walks on Sunday only'.

Bákari 'just, nothing but'. After a noun: Bíiru bákari, nóñde iru 'He drinks just (i. e. nothing but) beer'; Syokkoo bákari da 'They are just (i. e. all) mechanics'.

Yóri 'more than'. After a noun: Kore yóri, yasúi 'It's cheaper than this', lit. 'It is cheap more than this'; Eigo yóri, muzukasii 'It's more difficult than English'; Kinóo yóri, samúi 'It's colder than yesterday'. After a relational phrase: Watakusi nó yori, tiisái 'It's smaller than mine'; Tookyoo kára yori, tooi 'It's farther than from Tokyo'; Tookyoo kára no yori, osoi 'It's slower than the one from Tokyo'.

33 Relational phrases may be symbolized as follows. In the simplest type, a relatum—say a noun n—is followed by a particle p. When the relatum is itself a relational phrase, we have (n p) p. When the relatum is a relational phrase whose own relatum is a still smaller relational phrase, we have [(np) p]p. Note that in each case the immediate constituents are the final particle on the one hand and everything that precedes it on the other.

34 The grammatical subject of a Japanese predicate is the word or the expression most intimately connected with it. It is often but not always the 'actor'.

35 Note that the predicate in this sentence is the negative adjective inai. In the synonymous sentence cited above (Áni dake, iru), the predicate is the underlying verb. A relational phrase with daké followed by an affirmative predicate is equivalent to a relational phrase with sika followed by a negative predicate.

Hodo 'to the extent of, as much as'. After a noun: Kore hodo, yásuku nái 'It's not as cheap as this', lit. 'It is not cheap, to the extent of (or: as much as) this'; Eigo hodo, muzukasiku nái 'It's not as difficult as English'; Kinóo hodo, sámuku nái 'It's not as cold as yesterday'. After a relational phrase: Anáta no hodo, óokiku nái 'It's not as big as yours'; Tookyoo kára hodo, tooku nái 'It's not as far as from Tokyo'; Tookyoo kára no hodo, osoku nái 'It's not as slow as the one from Tokyo'.

Ka 'indefinite'. After a noun:[36] Ítu ka, kónai ka 'Won't you come sometime?'; Náni ka, mótte iru 'He's got something'; Dáre ka, iru 'Somebody is [here]'; After a relational phrase: Dóo ni ka, site kure 'Do it in some way'.

Nádo 'and the like, etcetera'. After a noun (usually followed by another particle): Hóñ nádo ga, sukí da 'I like books and such'; Turi nádo o, sita 'I fished and so on', lit. 'did fishing and so on'; Kitte nádo wa, utte inai 'They don't sell stamps and things of that sort'. After a relational phrase: Yamá e nádo, ikitai 'I want to go to the mountains or some such place'.

No 'of'. After a noun: Watakusi no, hóñ da 'It's my book'; Beikoku no, heitai da 'He's an American soldier'; Tomodati no, boosi da 'It's my friend's hat'. After a relational phrase: Tookyoo kára no, kisyá da 'It's the train (of) from Tokyo'; Kooeñ é no, básu da 'It's the bus (of) to the park'.

Wa 'topic'.[37] After a noun: Heitai wa, kureta 'The soldier gave it to me' (when the emphasis is on what the soldier did); Gyuuniku wa, sukí da 'I like beef' (when the emphasis is on how I feel about beef); Eigo wa, yoméru 'I can read English' (when the emphasis is on the fact that I can read it). After an adverb: matá wa 'again, or again'. After a relational phrase: Koko ní wa, nái 'There isn't any here'; Kisyá de wa, ikanákatta 'I didn't go by train'; Suzukisañ daké to wa, hanasánakatta 'Mr. Suzuki was the only one I didn't talk with'. After a quotational phrase: Nizíppuñ mo, kakáru to wa, omowánai 'I don't think it'll take as much as twenty minutes'; Byooki dá to wa, siranákatta 'He didn't say he'd come'.

Mo 'also; even'. After a noun: Tomodati mo, kíta 'My friend came too'; Zíppuñ mo, kakaránai 'It doesn't take even ten minutes'; Zíppuñ mo, kakátta 'It took all of ten minutes'. After a relational phrase: Koko ní mo, áru 'There's one here too'; Kisyá de mo, ikeru 'You can go by train too'; Kooeñ é mo, iku 'It goes to the park also'. After a quotational phrase: Isóide ikéba, ma ni, áu ka mo, sirenai 'If we hurry, maybe we'll be on time', lit. 'If we go hurrying, it cannot be known even whether we shall meet the interval'; Kono tegami wa, tomodati kara ká mo, sirenai 'This letter may be from my friend' (with zero alternant of dá before ka).

4.4 A quotational phrase has two immediate constituents: an element called the quotation, and a following particle. The quotation is a sentence or any other element: part of a sentence, a series of two or more sentences, a word, a series of words, or even part of a word or a nonsense expression.[38]

The particle that ends a quotational phrase is a quotative particle. There are only two such particles: to,[39] which follows any kind of quotation; and ka, which follows only a quotation in the form of a sentence.

Examples of to: after a sentence: Watakusi wa, tomodati ni, mátti o, kure to, itta 'I said to my friend, "Give me a match"' or 'I asked my friend to give me a match'; Áme ga, hútte iru to, omóu 'I think it's raining'; Áme ga, hútte iru ka to, kiita 'I asked, "Is it raining?"' or 'I asked if it was raining'. After a word: Sayonára to itta 'He said goodbye'; Tanaka to yuu 'He's called Tanaka'; Wa to iwanákatta 'I didn't say wa'.

Examples of ka: Dóko ni, súñde iru ka, kiita 'I asked [him] where he lived'; Aite irú ka, simátte iru ka, siranai 'I don't know whether it's open or closed'; Ano ryooríya no, tabemóno wa; oisíi ka, dóo ka, obóete inai[40] 'I don't recall whether the food at that restaurant is good or not (lit. or how it is)'.

5. Noun Expressions

5.1 Substantive expressions (§4.1) are of two kinds: noun expressions and pseudo-clauses. A noun expression is an endocentric phrase whose head is a single noun (§5.1), two or more nouns in apposition (§5.3), a series of two or more conjunct nouns joined by a conjunctive particle (§5.4, §5.5), or a compound numerical expression (§5.6). In its simplest form, a noun expression contains a single noun as head, with or without one or more modifiers preceding. (On modifiers see §5.2).

A noun is an uninflected word that occurs before the copula (§3.13); most nouns, but not all, occur also as pause-groups alone. In meaning, Japanese nouns correspond not only to English nouns but also to many English words of other classes. Seven subdivisions of Japanese nouns are distinguished by syntactic criteria; these are listed here, with examples of each.

36 The noun before ka is always an interrogative, defined in §5.1.

37 The relatum in a relational phrase with wa is unemphatic, in the sense that it does not constitute the novel or important part of a statement. Compare Heitai wa, kureta with Heitai ga, kureta above (both sentences translated 'The soldier gave it to me'): the former might be an answer to the question Heitai wa, náni o, sitá ka 'What did the soldier do?'; the latter might be an answer to the question Dáre ga, agetá ka 'Who gave it to you?'

38 Hypostatized elements in Japanese are regularly treated as prior constituents of quotational phrases. On hypostasis see Bloomfield, Language 148.

39 Note that we regard this word as different from the connective adverb to 'so saying' (§4.2), the referent particle to 'with' (§4.3), and the clause particle to 'whenever' (§3.22). There is also a conjunctive particle to 'and' (§5.41). Cf. §1.6, No. 3, and fn. 15.

40 This sentence and the preceding each contain two quotational phrases. In the second sentence, the phrase dóo ka contains the zero alternant of the copula dá; cf. §3.13 end, and fn. 25.

Pronouns, occurring before the referent particle wa, never preceded by a modifier: kore 'this one, this thing, this', sore 'that one (near by)', are 'that one (farther off)', koo 'this way, thus', soo and aa 'that way, so'.

Interrogatives, occurring before the referent particle ka, never before wa and never preceded by a modifier: dáre or dónata 'who?', dóre 'which one (of several)?', dóko 'what place?', dótira or dótti 'which direction?' or 'which one (of two)?', dóo 'what way?, how?', ikága 'how?', íkura 'how much?', íkutu 'how many?', ítu 'when?', náni or náñ 'what?', náze 'why?'. Interrogatives begin with d-, i-, or n-; all but ikága have an accent on the first syllable.

Limited Nouns, always preceded by a modifier: hóo 'direction, side, alternative', sóo 'hearsay', yóo 'appearance, likeness, manner', no or ñ 'one; fact, act', dake 'extent, limit', hodo 'extent, degree', yori 'comparison' (in effect, 'more than'), bákari 'just'. The last four of these are homonymous, aside from their accent, with referent particles of related meaning (§4.3).

Quality nouns, followed in clausal modifiers by the alternant na of the copula regardless of the following word (§5.23): sízuka 'quiet', béñri 'convenient', húbeñ 'inconvenient', kírei 'pretty, neat, clean', sukí 'pleasing', kirai 'displeasing', iyá 'hateful', sitúrei 'rude', géñki 'healthy, high-spirited', iroiro 'various', taihéñ 'grave, terrible, terribly, very much', yóo 'appearance, likeness, manner', dekisóo 'looking as if it were possible', kanasisoo 'sad-looking'. Note that yóo is listed both here and under limited nouns. Intersection between these two classes presents no formal difficulties, since the criteria by which we establish them are independent.

Quantity nouns, occurring before the referent particles ga and o only in a few rare cases, combining to form discontinuous adverbial phrases in the manner to be described in §5.43: three subclasses according to morphologic structure. Numerals: ití '1', ní '2', sañ '3', zyúu '10'; hitótu '1', hutatú '2', mittú '3', tóo '10'.[41] Numbers: itizíkañ '1 hour', níhuñ '2 minutes', sañeñ '3 yen'; issatú '1 (when speaking of volumes)', níhoñ '2 (of cylindrical objects)', sáñmai '3 (of thin flat objects)'; hitóbañ '1 night', hutáhako '2 boxfuls', mítuki '3 months', hitóri '1 person', hutarí '2 persons', mikka '3 days, the 3d day'. Indefinite quantity nouns: takusañ 'many, much', oozei 'many (of persons)', sukósi 'a few, a little', amari or añmari 'too much'.

Participial nouns, occurring rarely as heads in noun expressions, commonly as heads in pseudo-clauses (§6.21): arukinágara 'while walking', tukisídai 'as soon as [someone] arrives'.

Other nouns, not subject to any of the restrictions mentioned above: heitai 'soldier', tatémono 'building', náka 'inside', aida 'interval', kyóo 'today', íma 'now', watakusi 'I, me', anáta 'you', watakusítati 'we, us', anatagáta 'you (pl.)', koko 'this place, here'.[42]

5.2 A modifier is an element preceding a noun and forming with it an endocentric phrase with the noun as head; such a phrase fills the same syntactic positions as the noun alone. The class meaning of modifiers is limitation (identification, particularization, or description) of the meaning of the following noun. Modifiers are of three types: demonstratives, phrasal modifiers, and clausal modifiers. If a noun is preceded by two or more modifiers, not more than one will be a demonstrative, and usually not more than two will be phrasal modifiers.

5.21 A demonstrative is a word that never ends a pause-group and never occurs before the copula. The class meaning of demonstratives corresponds to that of English demonstrative and indefinite adjectives like 'this', 'that', 'every', and so on.

Some demonstratives have only the one function of serving as modifier to a following noun; e.g. kono 'this', sono 'that (near by)', ano 'that (far off)', dóno 'which?', onazi 'the same', káku 'every, each', áru 'a certain'.[43]

Other demonstratives have besides this function also the function of serving as relatum in a relational phrase with the referent particle ni. These are koñna 'this kind of, such a', soñna and añna 'that kind of, such a', and dóñna 'what kind of?' (koñna ni 'in this way, like this, thus', soñna ni and añna ni 'in that way, like that, so', dóñna ni 'in what way?, like what?, how?').

A noun expression consisting of a noun preceded by the demonstrative dóno 'which?' or dóñna 'what kind of?' has the same syntactic fuctions as an interrogative (§5.1).

41 The difference in use between the series ití—zyúu and hitótu—tóo is one of the details which fall outside the scope of this paper.

42 This classification of nouns into syntactic subdivisions is independent of the morphologic classification into such groups as complex and compound. Only participial nouns are characterized as a class by a particular morphologic structure (see §6.21). The derivation of nouns will be treated in a later article.

If it should seem strange to apply the term 'noun' to such words as yori 'more than', iroiro 'various', dekisóo 'looking as if it were possible', and arukinágara 'while walking', our justification is that these words fit the definition of nouns that we have adopted. Grammatical terms must be defined anew for every language; and the choice of particular terms (for instance 'noun') is at best a matter of convenience.

43 The last three words are homonymous with three words belonging to other word classes: the noun onazi 'the same', and the verbs káku 'writes' and áru 'is, there is'. In the expression onazi desu 'it is the same', onazi is a noun; in the nearly synonymous expression onazi kotó desu 'it is the same thing', onazi is a demonstrative.

In a sequence of two or more modifiers, a demonstrative may occupy any position. It usually stands first, unless one of the other modifiers contains a noun to which the demonstrative might be mistakenly referred. Thus ano takái, tatémono 'that tall building', ano Eikoku no, heitai 'that English soldier' (since ano here would scarcely be referred to Eikoku 'England'), but tomodati no, ano hóñ 'that book of [my] friend's', kádo ni, tátte iru, ano heitai 'that soldier standing on the corner'; cf. ano tomodati no, hóñ 'that friend's book', ano kádo ni, tátte iru, heitai 'the soldier standing on that corner'.

5.22 A phrasal modifier is a relational phrase with the referent particle no 'of'; the relatum in such a phrase is a substantive expression or a relational phrase with a different particle (never an adverb, a demonstrative, or a quotational phrase). The meaning of the particle no is to subordinate this relatum to the following noun, so that the meaning of the noun is in some way limited by that of the relatum. Examples: watakusi no, tomodati 'my friend (lit. friend of me)'; tomodati no, hóñ 'a friend's book'; koko no, kikoo 'the climate here (lit. of this place)'; heya no, náka 'inside (of) the room'; kí no, sita 'under the tree (lit. the underneath of the tree)'; kí no, teeburu 'a wooden table (lit. a table of wood)'; Eikoku no, heitai 'an English soldier (lit. a soldier of England)'; Eigo no, hóñ 'an English book (lit. a book of the English language)'; Yokohama no, kooeñ 'the park in (lit. of) Yokohama'; kisóku no, hitótu 'one of the regulations'; gakkoo no, tatémono 'school building'.

When a noun is preceded by two relational phrases, each with the referent particle no, the two phrases are sometimes independent modifiers of the same noun, sometimes one single modifier. In the expression watakusi no, Eikoku no, tomodati 'my friend in (lit. of) England', the noun tomodati 'friend' is preceded by two independent phrasal modifiers: watakusi no 'of me' and Eikoku no 'of England'. In the expression Eikoku no, tomodati no, hóñ 'an English friend's book', the noun hóñ 'book' is preceded by only one phrasal modifier: Eikoku no, tomodati no 'of the friend in England'; this modifier contains a noun tomodati which is preceded by a phrasal modifier of its own (Eikoku no). Occasionally an expression of this type is ambiguous; thus Eikoku no, heitai no, guñpuku may mean 'the uniform of an English soldier' (guñpuku 'uniform' preceded by a single modifier) or 'the British uniform for soldiers [as opposed to sailors]' (guñpuku preceded by two independent modifiers).

5.23 A clausal modifier is an inflected expression in the indicative (non-past or past), with or without one or more clause attributes preceding. It has thus the same internal structure as one type of final clause, and hence one type of major sentence. The meaning of the sequence x n (where x is a clausal modifier and n is a noun) is 'an n described or otherwise limited by the statement contained in x'.

The inflected expression that constitutes or ends a clausal modifier is the predicate of the modifier. It may be verbal, adjectival, or copular. In the normal polite style of conversation (§3.31) it is usually in the plain state.

In the following examples, each gloss is followed in parentheses by the literal meaning of the clausal modifier when used as an independent sentence: míta, heitai 'the soldier who saw it [or me, etc.]' or 'the soldier whom I saw' ('Someone saw'); kázi o, míta, heitai 'the soldier who saw the fire' ('He saw the fire'); watakusi ga, míta, heitai 'the soldier whom I saw' ('I saw'); kádo ni, tátte iru, heitai 'the soldier standing on the corner' ('He is standing on the corner'); kooeñ e, iku, básu 'the bus that goes to the park' ('It goes to the park'); kinoo, inaka kára, kisyá de, kíta, itóko '[my] cousin, who came from the country yesterday by train' ('He came from the country yesterday by train'); takái, tatémono 'a tall building' ('It is tall'); sírokute, takái, tatémono 'a tall white building' ('It is white and tall'); séñ, kyúuhyaku, zyúuneñ ni; atarásikatta, déñsya 'a streetcar that was new in 1910' ('It was new in 1910'); móto, sírokatta, boosi 'a hat that used to be white' ('It was formerly white'); señsoo no, aida, heitai dátta, otootó 'my younger brother, who was a soldier during the war' ('He was a soldier during the war'); syokkoo to site, koobá de, hataraite; sono áto de, kyúuzi dattari, déñsya no, uñtéñsyu dattari sita, tosiyóri 'an old man who worked in a factory as a mechanic and afterwards was by turns a waiter and a streetcar motorman' ('He worked in a factory in the capacity of mechanic and after that was alternately a waiter and the driver of a streetcar').[44]

Though identical in its internal structure with one type of final clause, a clausal modifier differs from a final clause in intonation, in the selection of certain referent particles, and in the selection of certain alternants in a predicate whose nucleus is the copula.

A final clause ends with falling, rising, or high-falling intonation; it is always followed by a pause (§1.1, §2.1). A clausal modifier ends with level intonation and is followed by a facultative pause.

The referent particles wa and ga that appear in an independent clause (§4.3) are replaced in a clausal modifier by no; wa is always so replaced, ga optionally. Examples: Watakusi wa, koobá de, hataraite iru 'I work in a factory' : watakusi no, hataraite iru, koobá 'the factory where I work'; Giñkoo wa, simaránai 'The bank doesn't close' : giñkoo no, simaránai, uti ni 'before the bank closes', lit. 'in the interval [while] the bank does not close'; Déñsya ga, tomaru 'The streetcar stops' : déñsya no, tomaru, tokoro or déñsya ga, tomaru, tokoro 'the place where the streetcar stops'; Ano gakkoo ní wa, tomodati ga, itta '[My] friend went to that school' : tomodati no, itta, gakkoo or tomodati ga, itta, gakkoo

44 As these examples show, a clausal modifier often corresponds to an English relative clause, either restrictive or non-restrictive.

'the school that [my] friend went [to]'. But the particle no in a clausal modifier does not always correspond to either wa or ga in an independent clause; often it corresponds to no meaning 'of' (§5.22), as in heya no, náka ni, áru, kágu 'the furniture in (lit. which is in the inside of) the room'. Where there is an instance of no meaning 'of' in a clausal modifier, the particle ga is usually not replaced by no; e. g. watakusi no, tomodati ga, itta, gakkoo 'the school that my friend went to'.

When the predicate of a clausal modifier is a copula phrase with the non-past indicative of the copula as its nucleus, this word appears sometimes as da (the form which appears also in the predicate of a final clause), sometimes as na, and sometimes as no. The selection of the alternants is determined by the surrounding words. (1) Before the noun sóo 'hearsay' (in the expression sóo da or sóo desu 'they say, I hear, etc.') the alternant is da; e. g. Byooki da, sóo desu 'They say he's sick', Taiheñ, kírei da, sóo desu 'I hear she's extremely pretty'. (2) Before the noun no 'one; act, fact, etc.' the alternant is na; e. g. Heitai ná no desu 'He's a soldier', lit. 'He is the one who is a soldier'; kekkoñsuru hí na no de 'since it's [my] wedding day'. (3) After a quality noun (§5.1) the alternant is na, regardless of the following word (but da before sóo 'hearsay'); e. g. kírei na, musumé 'a pretty girl', i. e. a girl described by the statement Kírei da 'She is pretty'; sízuka na, tokoro 'a quiet place'. (4) Elsewhere the alternant is no; e. g. tomodati no, Tároo 'my friend Taro', i. e. a person named Taro described by the statement Tomodati da 'He is a friend'; isya no, ozi 'my uncle, who is a doctor'; ozi no, isya 'the doctor, who is my uncle'.[45]

5.31 In some noun expressions, the head consists of two or more nouns joined without pause. Such nouns are said to be in apposition.

Nouns in apposition are most often personal names (a family name followed by a given name) or combinations of name and title; e. g. Suzuki Tároo 'Taro Suzuki', Kimura Masaosañ 'Mr. Masao Kimura', Tanaka táisa 'Colonel Tanaka', Yamamoto Saburoo táisyoo 'General S. Yamamoto'. In such combinations only the first noun is ever preceded by a modifier; e. g. tomodati no, Suzuki Tároo 'my friend Taro Suzuki', Nippoñ no, rikúguñ no, Tanaka táisa 'Colonel Tanaka of the Japanese Army'.

Less common are expressions like wareware Nihoñzíñ 'we Japanese', anatagáta Beikókuziñ 'you Americans'. In such combinations the second noun is sometimes preceded by a single modifier; e. g. wareware wakái Nihoñzíñ 'we young Japanese'.

The combination sono monó (lit 'that thing'), added without pause to a noun, has the meaning 'itself'; e. g. tatémono sono monó 'the building itself (as distinct, say, from the grounds or the interior furnishings)', sigoto sono monó 'the work itself'. The first noun in such a sequence is often preceded by one or more modifiers; e. g. watakusi no, hurúi, kurói, yoohuku sono monó 'my old black suit itself'.

5.32 A special case of nouns in apposition, limited to a few instances and occurring chiefly in narrative style and in emotional discourse, is the repeated noun—i. e. the same noun spoken twice, without intervening pause. Examples are mukasi mukasi 'long long ago' (in narrative; cf. mukasi 'ancient times; decade'), taiheñ taiheñ 'very very much; terribly; terrible' (cf. taiheñ 'grave, terrible, terribly; very much').

5.41 In some noun expressions, the head consists of a series of two or more nouns, each noun with or without one or more modifiers preceding, and each noun, or each except the last, followed by a conjunctive particle. Such nouns are said to be conjunct. An element that follows the series—a referent particle, the copula, or the predicate of the clause—applies equally and in the same way to each noun in the series. Thus, in the sentence Sore wa, nikúyasañ to, páñyasañ to, yaoyasañ kára, kiita 'I heard that from the butcher, the baker, and the grocer', the referent particle kára 'from' applies equally and in the same way to the three conjunct nouns nikúyasañ 'butcher', páñyasañ 'baker', and yaoyasañ 'grocer' (the conjunctive particle here is to 'and'). In meaning, this sentence is equivalent to the three statements Sore wa, nikúyasañ kára, kiita 'I heard that from the butcher', Sore wa, páñyasañ kára, kiita 'I heard that from the baker', and Sore wa, yaoyasañ kára, kiita 'I heard that from the grocer', taken together.

There are four conjunctive particles: to 'and', used when the enumerated series is complete; ya 'and', used when the enumerated series is not complete; ni 'and', equivalent in meaning to to but much less common; and ka 'or'. Only one of these particles appears in any one noun expression. Examples: Súihei to, heitai ga, hanásite ita 'A sailor and a soldier were talking';[46] Késa no, siñbuñ to;

[45] Since no, the alternant of the copula, is homonymous with the referent particle no 'of', some expressions are ambiguous. Isya no, ozi means 'my uncle, who is a doctor' if no is the copula, but 'the doctor's uncle' if no is the particle. Since the head of each expression is the noun ozi 'uncle', there is no way of distinguishing them except by meaning. To analyze a sequence A no B (where A and B are nouns), we apply the following semantic test: if the statement A da 'someone or something is A' provides a description of B, then no is the copula; if not, it is the particle.

[46] This is the meaning of the sentence if to is the conjunctive particle 'and'. If to is the referent particle 'with', the sentence means 'A soldier was talking with a sailor'. This ambiguity is resolved most directly by a semantic criterion: to is a conjunctive particle only if the sentence is equivalent in meaning to the two statements Súihei ga, hanásite ita 'A sailor was talking' and Heitai ga, hanásite ita 'A soldier was talking', taken together. That is, if A

ano tukue no, ue ni, áru, hóñ to; siróì, biñseñ to o; motte kite kudasai 'Please bring me this morning's newspaper, and the books that are on (top of) that desk, and some white stationery'; Watakusi no, itibañ, sukí na, zíki wa, háru to, áki da 'My favorite seasons are spring and fall'; Beikoku no, kusuriya dé wa; hóñ ya, zassi o, utte iru 'In American drugstores they sell books and magazines [and other things]'; Otootó ya, imootó wa; koko no, gakkoo e, itte iru 'My younger brother and sister [among others] go to a local school'; Tukí ni, murakumo; haná ni, kaze 'The moon—and clustered clouds; blossoms—and the wind';[47] Déñsya ka, básu ni, noroo 'Let's take a streetcar or a bus'; Kisyá de, hutuka ka, mikka, kakáru daroo 'By train it will probably take two or three days'.

5.42 Many sentences contain a series of two or more nouns with no particle between them, but with each noun, or each except the last, followed by a pause; the last noun is followed by a referent particle, the copula, or the predicate of the clause. In some sequences of this kind, each noun before the last constitutes an adverbial phrase (§4.2); e. g. Kinoo, taiheñ, áme ga, hútta 'It rained very hard yesterday', lit. 'Yesterday terribly rain fell'. But in other sequences, the element that follows the last noun applies equally and in the same way to each noun in the series—that is, the nouns are conjunct; e. g. Hóñ, zassi, siñbuñ o, katta 'I bought a book and a magazine and a newspaper', equivalent to the three statements Hóñ o, katta 'I bought a book', Zassi o, katta 'I bought a magazine', and Siñbuñ o, katta 'I bought a newspaper', taken together.

To cover sequences of this type, we posit a fifth conjunctive particle, phonemically zero, with the same syntactic functions as the four already mentioned. The sentence just cited might be written Hóñ 0, zassi 0, siñbuñ o, katta, with 0 (zero particle) syntactically equivalent to the particle to 'and'. Other examples: Kono heñ ní wa, yamá 0, kawá 0, mizuúmi ga, oói 'In this region are many mountains, rivers, and lakes'; Géñkañ no, migi ní wa; syosai 0, oosetuma 0, daidokoro nádo ga, áru 'To the right of the entrance hall are a study, a drawing room, a kitchen, and so on'; Nihoñ no, ómo na, simá wa; Hokkáidoo 0, Hóñsyuu 0, Sikóku 0, Kyúusyuu de áru 'The main islands of Japan are Hokkaido, Honshu, Shikoku, and Kyushu'.

5.43 In a noun expression with a series of conjunct nouns as head, any or all of the nouns can be replaced by a combination of two or three nouns in apposition. A sequence like Suzuki to, Tanaka to, Yamamoto 'S. and T. and Y.' has the same structure as Suzuki Tároo to, Tanaka Zíroo to, Yamamoto Saburoo 'T. S. and Z. T. and S. Y.' or Suzuku syóosa to, Tanaka táisa to, Yamamoto táisyoo 'Major S. and Colonel T. and General Y.'

5.51 Some noun expressions containing a series of conjunct nouns as head are discontinuous, i. e. interrupted by the intrusion of another clause attribute. Two types of discontinuous noun expressions are especially common: one type involving the adverbs mata 'again' and áruiwa 'or', the other type involving quantity nouns (§5.1).

In the sentence Nihóñ wa, tetu, sekiyu, yoomoo o, yunyuusuru 'Japan imports iron, oil, and wool', the three nouns tetu 'iron', sekiyu 'oil, petroleum', and yoomoo 'wool' are conjunct, joined by a zero conjunctive particle. The predicate yunyuusuru 'imports' is preceded by only two clause attributes: a relational phrase Nihóñ wa 'as for Japan', with a noun as relatum; and another relational phrase tetu 0, sekiyu 0, yoomoo o, with a series of three conjunct nouns as relatum. In the synonymous sentence Nihóñ wa, tetu, sekiyu, mata, yoomoo o, yunyuusuru, the adverb mata stands between two of these conjunct nouns, with the meaning 'and, and also, and again'. We analyze the latter sentence as containing the same clause attributes as the other, with the addition of an adverbial phrase mata intercalated between two parts of the second relational phrase. In the same way, the sentence Anó hito wa, ítu mo, hóñ, mata, zassi o, yóñde iru 'He's always reading books and magazines' contains a predicate yóñde iru 'is reading' preceded by four clause attributes: (1) a relational phrase anó hito wa 'as for that person', with a noun expression as relatum; (2) another relational phrase ítu mo 'always', with an interrogative noun as relatum; (3) a third relational phrase hóñ 0 ... zassi o 'books and magazines', with a discontinuous noun expression as relatum; and (4) an adverbial phrase mata 'and, and again', intercalated between two parts of the preceding.

The following case is similar. The sentence Maituki, Tookyoo, matá wa, Oosaka e, ikú no da 'I go to Tokyo or to Osaka every month' contains a predicate ikú no da 'goes' (lit. 'it is a fact that [someone] goes') preceded by three clause attributes: (1) an adverbial phrase consisting of the noun maituki 'every month'; (2) a relational phrase Tookyoo 0 ... Oosaka e, with a discontinuous noun expression as relatum; and (3) another relational phrase matá wa

---

and B are nouns, and p is a conjunctive particle, and x is the element that follows the series (a referent particle, the copula, or the predicate of the clause), then the sequence ApBpx or ApBx is equivalent to the two sequences Ax and Bx taken together, or to either Ax or Bx taken separately. For this semantic criterion it might be possible to substitute a rather complicated distributional criterion based on the selection of the nouns before and after the particle in question. It is not possible to base the identification of conjunct nouns simply on the selection of the conjunctive particle, since three of these (to, ni, and ka) are homonymous with referent particles.

[47] An epigram expressive of the impermanence of perfection, quoted from H. G. Henderson, Handbook of Japanese grammar 202 (Boston etc., 1943). On the sentence type see §8.1, fn. 51.

'or, or else, or again', with the adverb mata as relatum, intercalated between two parts of the preceding. Other examples: Sitizyúu, matá wa, nanázyuu to, ieru 'You can say either "sitizyúu" or "nanázyuu" [to mean 70]'; Kono heñ no, hyakusyóo wa; komé, matá wa, yasai o, tukútte iru 'The farmers in this neighborhood raise either rice or vegetables'.

The adverb áruiwa 'or' appears between two parts of a discontinuous noun expression most often in sentences that offer a choice of examples or illustrations; e.g. Tatóeba, Eikoku, áruiwa, Beikoku ga, miñsyukoku de áru 'For instance, England or America is a democracy' (in illustrating the term miñsyukoku 'democracy').

In short, if a noun is followed by mata or matá wa or áruiwa and by another noun, the two nouns together constitute a single discontinuous noun expression, with a zero conjunctive particle after the first. It is understood that the first noun may be preceded by still other nouns belonging to the same expression.

5.52 The other common type of discontinuous noun expression involves the use of quantity nouns. In the sentence Watakusi wa, áni ga, hitóri, áru 'I have one older brother' (lit. 'As for me, there are older brothers to the extent of one person'), the predicate áru 'there is, there are' is preceded by three clause attributes: (1) a relational phrase watakusi wa 'as for me', with a noun as relatum; (2) another relational phrase áni ga 'older brother(s)', also with a noun as relatum; and (3) an adverbial phrase consisting of the number hitóri 'one person'. In the sentence Watakusi wa, áni ga, hitóri to; ototó ga, hutari, áru 'I have one older brother and two younger brothers' (lit. 'As for me, there are older brothers to the extent of one person, and younger brothers to the extent of two persons'), the general structure is similar, but the number hitóri is here followed by the conjunctive particle to. We analyze the second sentence as follows: the predicate áru is preceded by four clause attributes: (1) a relational phrase watakusi wa; (2) another relational phrase áni ga; (3) an adverbial phrase consisting of a discontinuous noun expression hitóri to ... hutarí 'one person and ... two persons'; and (4) another relational phrase ototó ga 'younger brothers', intercalated between two parts of the preceding.

Precisely similar is the analysis of the sentence Anáta wa, otoko no, kyóodai ga, náñniñ to; oñna no, kyóodai ga, náñniñ, áru ka 'How many brothers and sisters have you got?' (lit. 'As for you, there are male siblings to the extent of how many persons, and female siblings to the extent of how many persons?'). Here the discontinuous noun expression is náñniñ to ... náñniñ 'how many persons and ... how many persons?', constituting an adverbial phrase like the expression hitóri to ... hutarí in the sentence above.

Both the sentences here cited occur also without the conjunctive particle to, with exactly the same meaning: Watakusi wa, áni ga, hitóri; ototó ga, hutari, áru and Anáta wa, otoko no, kyóodai ga, náñniñ; oñna no, kyóodai ga, náñniñ, áru ka. The parallelism with the construction already discussed leads us to posit here a discontinuous noun expression with a zero conjunctive particle in each sentence: hitóri 0 ... hutarí and náñniñ 0 ... náñniñ.[48]

In the following sentence, the discontinuous noun expression has three members: Ano misé de wa, hóñ o, nísatu to; zassi o, sáñsatu to; siñbuñ o, itímai; katta 'At that store I bought two books, three magazines, and one newspaper' (lit. 'books to the extent of two volumes and magazines to the extent of three volumes and newspapers to the extent of one sheet'). The same sentence occurs with a zero conjunctive particle in place of to.

If, then, two or more relational phrases with the same referent particle are each followed by a quantity noun, and if each of the quantity nouns, or each except the last, is followed by a conjunctive particle (to or ya or zero), the quantity nouns constitute a discontinuous noun expression functioning as an adverbial phrase.

5.6 In some noun expressions, finally, the head is a compound numerical expression. This consists of a sequence of two or more quantity nouns (§5.1) which together denote a single amount. In most sequences of this kind, all the members are numerals, or else all but the last are numerals and the last is a number; but in some sequences, some or all of the members before the last are numbers also. Examples: Niséñ, roppyakú, hatizyúu, sí no, hañbúñ wa; séñ, sáñbyaku, yóñzyuu, ní de áru 'Half of 2684 is 1342'; Watakusi wa, séñ, happyaku, kyúuzyuu, sitíneñ ni, umareta 'I was born in (the year) 1897'; Anó hito wa, maituki, hóñ ya, zassi o; nízyuu, gosatuízyoo, yómu sóo da 'They say that he (lit. that person) reads more than 25 books and magazines every month'; Sore wa, nízyuu, itíeñ, sitízyuu, góseñ mo, sita 'That cost (all of) 21 yen 75 sen'; Ríeki wa, itíwari, níbu, góriñ datta 'The profit was 12 1/2 percent', lit. 'one tenth, two hundredths, five thousandths'.

Two indefinite quantity nouns together constitute a compound numerical expression in amari, takusañ 'too many, too much'.

[48] If it were not for the parallelism, we could regard the pause-groups hitóri and hutarí in the former sentence, and the pause-groups náñniñ and náñniñ in the latter, as constituting two separate adverbial phrases. The analysis given in the text is preferable because it recognizes the semantic and structural similarity of the sentences with and without to.

6. Pseudo-Clauses

6.1 Substantive expressions which are not noun expressions are pseudo-clauses. A pseudo-clause is an endocentric phrase whose head is a pseudo-predicate. Some pseudo-clauses consist of a pseudo-predicate alone; in others, the pseudo-predicate is preceded by one or more clause attributes—adverbial phrases, relational phrases, and quotational phrases as defined in §4. A pseudo-clause has thus the same internal structure as a real clause. It differs from a real clause in only two respects: in its function and in the form of its predicate.

A real clause, as already noted (§2.4), is one of the immediate constituents (or the only constituent) of a sentence. A pseudo-clause is a sub-constituent of a clause—a constituent of a constituent. It functions only as a substantive expression; as such, it serves as an adverbial phrase, as the relatum of a relational phrase, or as the element preceding the nucleus of a copula phrase—all three of these positions being filled also by noun expressions. As one consequence of this difference, real predicates and pseudo-predicates are followed by different sets of particles: a real predicate is followed by sentence or clause particles, a pseudo-predicate by referent particles.

6.21 The pseudo-predicate is a participial noun or an inflected expression in a participial form.

A participial noun (cf. §5.1) has the syntactic features of nouns in general: it is an uninflected word that occurs before the copula; and it occurs (though rarely) as the head of a noun expression, preceded by a modifier. But it differs from all other kinds of nouns in occurring also and most commonly as the head of a pseudo-clause—i. e. as a pseudo-predicate.

In form, a participial noun consists of the infinitive of a verb or the base of an adjective, plus one of the bound morphemes -nagara and -sidai.[49] The class meanings of participial nouns differ according to the bound morpheme which they contain; but all include the meaning of action, state, or attribution, which is otherwise characteristic only of verbs and adjectives. Examples: tabenágara 'while eating' (from tabéru 'eats', infinitive tábe), arukinágara 'while walking' (from arúku 'walks', inf. arúki), sinagara 'while doing' (from suru 'does', inf. si); tabesídai 'as soon as [someone] eats' (from tabéru), tukisídai 'as soon as [someone] arrives' (from tukú 'arrives, etc.', inf. tukí), arisídai 'as soon as there is' (from áru 'there is', inf. ári).

[49] There may be other bound morphemes deriving participial nouns, but only these two are known to me. The morpheme -nagara appears also in (non-participial) nouns derived from nouns, e. g. biñboonagara 'although [someone] is poor' from bíñboo 'pauper'; -sidai appears both in nouns derived from nouns and as a noun by itself, with the meaning 'order, precedence'. But these uses of the morphemes in question we regard as different from their use in deriving participial nouns.

In each of the following sentences there is one pseudo-clause with a participial noun as head. The limits of each pseudo-clause are marked by a pair of angle-brackets; its syntactic function is indicated after a dash following the gloss.

Áni wa, <hóñ o, yominágara,> góhañ o, tábeta 'My (older) brother read a book while he ate', lit. 'ate a meal while reading a book'—adverbial phrase. <Kono miti o, arukinágara,> hanasóo ka 'Shall we talk as we walk along this street?'—adverbial phrase. <Tookyóo-eki e, tukisídai,> eñtaku o, yoñda 'As soon as I got to the Tokyo station I called a cab'—adverbial phrase.

6.22 More often, the pseudo-predicate is an inflected expression—verbal, adjectival, or copular—in a participial form, i. e. in the alternative, the gerund, or the infinitive. Note that an inflected expression in a participial form is a pseudo-predicate only when it is not followed without pause by a verb or an adjective; when it is so followed, the inflected expression is part of a longer expression (a verb phrase or an adjective phrase, §3.11, §3.12).

In each of the following sentences there is one pseudo-clause with an inflected expression in a participial form as head. The limits of each pseudo-clause are marked by a pair of angle-brackets.

With a pseudo-predicate in the alternative (functioning only as an adverbial phrase, and always followed by a verb phrase or an adjective phrase containing another alternative form before the nucleus): Hyakusyóo wa, <múgi o, máitari,> íne o, uetári suru 'The farmers sow grain and plant rice [and so on]'. <Hataraitári,> hatarakanákattari suru, kotó wa; kirai dá yo 'I hate to keep changing back and forth between working and not working'. Ano mise no, tamágo wa; <óokikattari,> tíisakattari suru ga; nedañ wa, ítu mo, onazi da 'The eggs at that store are sometimes large and sometimes small, but the price is always the same'. Señsyuu wa, <yukí dattari,> áme dattari sita 'Last week there was (lit. it was) alternately snow and rain'.

With a pseudo-predicate in the gerund (the syntactic function indicated after a dash following the gloss): <Hóteru no, syokudoo de, bañgóhañ o, tábete;> sore kara, utí e, káetta 'I ate dinner in the hotel dining room, and after that I went back home'—adverbial phrase. <Koko no, áki wa, suzúsikute;> kaze ga, yóku, huku 'The fall here is cool, and the wind blows a great deal'—adverbial phrase. <Kore wa, musuko de;> kore wa, musumé da 'This is my son and this is my daughter'—adverbial phrase. <Góhañ o, tábete> kara; súgu, sóto e, déta 'He went outside right after eating (a meal)'—relatum of a relational phrase. <Anáta ga, itté> mo; watakusi wa, ikitaku nái 'Even if you go, I don't want to (go)'—relatum of a relational phrase. Soñna kotó wa, <dáre de> mo, sitte iru 'Everybody knows that (lit. that sort of thing)'—relatum of a relational phrase. Kono hóñ wa, <Nihoñ no, nóogyoo ni, túite> da 'This book is about Japanese agriculture'—element preceding the nucleus of a copula phrase.

With a pseudo-predicate in the infinitive (the syntactic function indicated after a dash following the gloss): <Tookyoo wa, Hóñsyuu ni, ári;> Nagásaki wa, Kyúusyuu ni, áru 'Tokyo is on Honshu, and Nagasaki is on Kyushu'—adverbial phrase. <Nippóñ ni wa, kázañ ga, óoku;> oñseñ ga, sukúnaku nái 'There are many volcanoes in Japan, and not a few hot springs'—adverbial phrase. Koréra no, monó wa, <kisyá de, hakobazu;> húne de, hakobu 'These things are not transported by train, they are transported by ship'—adverbial phrase. <Háyaku,> miti o, hasítta 'He ran quickly down the street'—adverbial phrase. <Eñryo náku,> hanásite kudasai 'Please speak without reserve'—adverbial phrase. Kádo no, sakabá e; <bíiru o, nisañbai, nómi> ni, ikanái ka 'How about going (lit. Won't we go) to the bar on the corner to have (lit. to drink) two or three beers?'—relatum of a relational phrase. Tomodati wa, kóñbañ, <asobi> ni, kuru daroo 'My friend may come for a visit (lit. in order to visit) tonight'—relatum of a relational phrase. <Mizu ni, háirazu> ni; hamá de, asoñda 'Instead of going into the water, he [just] loafed on the beach'—relatum of a relational phrase.

In the honorific style and in the higher varieties of the normal polite style (§3.31), some pseudo-predicates with an alternative or a gerund nucleus are in the polite state. Thus, the alternative of the copula will sometimes appear as désitari instead of dáttari, and the gerund of such a verb as itasu '[I] do' will appear as itasimásite instead of itasite. But pseudo-predicates with an infinitive nucleus are always in the plain state.

7. Summary of the Major Sentence Type

7.1 The structure of major sentences in Japanese, discussed in §§2–6 of this paper, is summarized in the following twenty definitions. These definitions provide a concise description of the major sentence type; but it should be noted that the description is unilateral. Any actually occurring major sentence can be analyzed in terms of the categories here defined; but since the definitions do not specifically mention combinations that fail to occur, they cannot be used as a guide in the construction of new sentences.

1. A major sentence contains a final clause, with or without one or more non-final clauses preceding (§2.1).
2. A clause contains a predicate, with or without one or more clause attributes preceding (§2.2).
3. A predicate is an inflected expression in the indicative, presumptive, or imperative form with or without a following particle, or in a hypothetical form (§3.1).
4. An inflected expression is a verbal expression, an adjectival expression, or a copular expression (§3.1).
5. A verbal expression is a verb or a verb phrase (§3.11).
6. A verb phrase is a verb preceded without pause by an inflected expression in a participial form (§3.11).
7. An adjectival expression is an adjective, an adjective phrase, or an adjective group (§3.12).
8. An adjective phrase is an adjective preceded without pause by an inflected expression in a participial form (§3.12).
9. An adjective group is the adjective nái preceded without pause by a noun, or the bound form -rasíi preceded by a noun expression, a relational phrase, or a clause with an indicative predicate (§3.12).
10. A copular expression is the copula or a copula phrase (§3.12).
11. A copula phrase is the copula or its equivalent preceded without pause by a substantive expression, a relational phrase, an indicative inflected expression with or without clause particle, or (rarely) a presumptive verbal expression (§3.12).
12. A clause attribute is an adverbial phrase, a relational phrase, or a quotational phrase (§4.1).
13. An adverbial phrase is an adverb or a substantive expression (§4.2).
14. A relational phrase is a substantive expression, an adverb, a demonstrative, a quotational phrase, or another relational phrase, each with a following referent particle (§4.3).
15. A quotational phrase is a sentence or other element followed by a quotative particle (§4.4).
16. A substantive expression is a noun expression or a pseudo-clause (§4.1).
17. A noun expression is a noun, with or without one or more modifiers preceding; or a sequence of nouns in apposition, the first or the last or both with or without one or more modifiers preceding; or a series (continuous or discontinuous) of nouns or sequences of nouns in apposition, joined by a conjunctive particle, each with or without one or more modifiers preceding; or a compound numerical expression (§5.1–6).
18. A modifier is a demonstrative, or a relational phrase with the referent particle no, or a clause with an indicative predicate (§5.2).
19. A pseudo-clause contains a pseudo-predicate, with or without one or more clause attributes preceding (§6.1).
20. A pseudo-predicate is a participial noun, or an inflected expression in a participial form not followed without pause by a verb or an adjective (§6.2).

To these definitions we add two more to differentiate between final and non-final clauses:

21. The predicate of a final clause is an inflected expression in the indicative, presumptive, or imperative form, each with or without a following sentence particle (§3.21).
22. The predicate of a non-final clause is an inflected expression in the indicative or presumptive form with a following clause particle, or in a hypothetical form (§3.22).

7.2 To complete the summary, we assemble here the definitions of the seven word classes (parts of speech) whose members appear as the ultimate constituents of major sentences.

A verb is a member of an inflectional paradigm containing ten members (§3.11).

An adjective is a member of an inflectional paradigm containing nine members (§3.12).

The copula is a member of an inflectional paradigm containing eight members (§3.13).

A noun is an uninflected word that occurs before the copula (§5.1). For subclasses see §5.1; for participial nouns see also §6.21.

An adverb is an uninflected word that occurs as a pause-group alone, but does not occur before the copula (§4.2). Connective adverbs are always initial in a clause; modal adverbs are not always initial in a clause; interjections occur chiefly in minor sentences (§4.2).

A demonstrative never ends a pause-group and never occurs before the copula (§6.21).

A particle never begins a pause-group (§3.1). Sentence particles occur in final predicates (§3.21); clause particles occur in non-final predicates (§3.22); referent particles occur after noun expressions[50] to form relational phrases (§4.3); quotative particles occur after sentences to form quotational phrases (§4.4); conjunctive particles occur after each of two or more nouns, or after each except the last, to form noun expressions (§5.41).

8. Minor Sentence Types

8.1 A sentence that contains a final clause—in other words, one that ends with a final predicate—is a major sentence; all other sentences are minor. Only two types of minor sentences occur commonly in conversation: fragments and segments.[51]

8.2 A fragment is any pause-group or sequence of pause-groups that occurs in a major sentence but lacks a final predicate. Every fragment can be expanded into a major sentence by adding one or more other pause-groups, including a final predicate. According to the internal structure of the fragment, we distinguish two general types: clause fragments and phrase fragments.

A clause fragment consists of one or more non-final clauses, most often ending with level or falling intonation (with level intonation only at the end of an utterance; cf. §1.1). Examples: Áme ga, hútte imásu kara 'Because it's raining' (perhaps in answer to the question Dóo site, sóto e, demaséñ ka 'Why don't you go out?', or added as an afterthought to the statement Íma wa, sóto e, demaséñ 'I won't go out now'); Sitúrei desu ga.. 'Excuse me' (lit. 'It is rude but', a cliché used in calling someone's attention or interrupting a conversation); Ano sibai wa, totemo, kokkei da, sóo desu kara; mí ni, ikitái desu ga.. 'Since they tell me that that play is very funny, I'd like to go to see it, but...' (implying: 'but I can't').

A phrase fragment consists of one or more phrases that occur as clause attributes in major sentences (adverbial phrases, relational phrases, and quotational phrases), ending with level, falling, or rising intonation. Examples: Koñniti wa 'Hello' (lit. 'As for this day'); Anáta wa? 'What about you?'; Náñzi ni or Náñzi ni? 'At what time?'; Mádo no, sóba ni, kosikákete iru; ano hutótta, oñna no, hito ni 'To that fat woman sitting near the window' (perhaps in answer to the question Dáre ni, yarimásita ka 'To whom did you give it?'); Dokú o? 'Poison!' (perhaps in response to the statement Dokú o, nóñda 'He took poison'); Kyóo 'Today'; Gógatu no, mikka 'May 3rd'; Háyaku! 'Quickly!'; Sóo 'Yes' (lit. 'So').

Some minor sentences are a combination of a clause fragment with a phrase fragment, i. e. one or more non-final clauses followed by one or more clause attributes. Examples: Áme ga húttara; sitamati e, ikitákute mo.. 'If it rains, even though I want to go downtown [I won't]'; Sóo de wa, nái ga; sukósi, sámuku nátte.. 'It isn't that (lit. so), but it's getting a little cold and...'.

8.3 One type of adverbial phrase occurs only rarely in major sentences, but very commonly as a phrase fragment. It is convenient to have a special name for the minor sentences in which these phrases appear; we shall call them exclamations.

An exclamation is a phrase fragment consisting (a) of an interjection (see §4.2), (b) of two interjections together, (c) of a vocative expression (see below), or (d) of an interjection followed by a vocative. Typical interjections are hái 'yes', ée 'yes', iie 'no', dóozo 'please', sayonára 'goodbye', áre 'ah', kóre or kóra 'here', náni 'hm', óya 'oh', ói 'hey', ano or anoo 'well, er...', áita 'ouch', á or áa 'oh', máa 'well', sáa 'well, gee, hm', yáa 'oh; oh no; hi there'.[52] A frequent combination of two interjections is Hái, dóozo 'Yes please' (in offering something or accepting something offered).

A vocative expression is a personal name, a title, or some other designation used as a term of direct address, as when calling or speaking to someone. Vocative expressions are thus nouns, or sequences of nouns in apposition; e. g. Tároo (man's given name), Suzuki (family name), Suzuki Tároo (man's

50 Some referent particles occur also after other elements (adverbs, demonstratives, pseudo-clauses, etc.); but it is the occurrence after nouns that defines the class.

51 A third type, collocation, appears chiefly in proverbs and epigrams. This consists of two parallel parts, each containing one or more adverbial or relational phrases. Examples: Íma no, hitóhari; noti no, tóhari 'One stitch now, ten stitches later' (i. e. A stitch in time saves nine); Kane no, kiremé ga; éñ no, kireme 'The end of money, the end of love' (lit. affinity). Cf. also the epigram cited in §5.41 (fn. 47).

52 Cf. the list in J. K. Yamagiwa, Modern conversational Japanese 16-7 (New York and London, 1942), from which some of these examples are taken.

full name), Suzukisañ 'Mr. Suzuki' or 'Mrs. Suzuki' or 'Miss Suzuki', Suzukikuñ 'Mr. Suzuki', señséi 'sir' (lit. 'teacher'), kyúuzisañ 'waiter', néesañ 'miss' (lit. 'older sister'), ozíisañ 'old man' (lit. 'grandfather'). A typical combination of an interjection with a vocative expression is Yáa, Suzukisañ 'Hi there, Mr. Suzuki'.

Exclamations end most commonly with high-falling intonation. Falling intonation occurs also, and rising intonation especially in the exclamation Iie? 'No!'.

An exclamation is sometimes found embedded, as it were, in a major sentence: either at the beginning with level intonation, or between two clauses or two constituents of a clause. The following represents a common type: Sore dé wa, máa! sikata ga nái 'In that case, well, there's no help for it'. Here the interjection máa constitutes an exclamation with high-falling intonation, embedded in the longer sentence. The elements which precede and follow it are not two separate sentences; together they exhibit the normal features of the major sentence type.

8.4 A segment is a word or a sequence of words that does not occur alone as a pause-group in a major sentence (unless it be as part of a discontinuous noun expression with a zero conjunctive particle; §5.51). Thus, a noun like teisyaba 'railroad station' or a noun expression like ano sirói, tatémono 'that white building' might occur as an answer to the question Ano tatémono wa, náñ desu ka 'What is that building?' or Dóno tatémono ga, teisyaba désu ka 'Which building is the railroad station?' (more commonly answered by Teisyaba desu or Ano sirói, tatémono desu—i.e. by a major sentence with a copula phrase as final predicate). A very common segment is Ohayoo (beside the major sentence Ohayoo gozaimásu, §3.11) 'Good morning', lit. 'It is early'.

8.5 The particle née (§3.21) occurs after all types of minor sentences, with a meaning like that which it has after a major sentence: 'isn't it so?', 'don't you agree?', 'hm?', or the like. Examples: Yatótte agetái ñ desu ga née 'I'd like to hire you but [you know how it is], don't you?'; Watakusi mo, súgu kekkoñdekíreba, íi desu ga née 'I hope I can get married soon too', lit. 'If I also can get married soon it will be good but—eh?'; Watakusi wa née 'Me, eh?'; Tookyoo kara née '[It's] from Tokyo, isn't it?'; Teisyaba née '[It's] a railroad station, isn't it?'; Ano née 'Er ...'.

9. Sample Text

9.1 To illustrate the application of the system outlined in this paper, we analyze here a number of sentences in terms of the categories that we have defined. Our text is the well-known Japanese folk tale of Momotaro, in the excellent colloquial version printed by Rose-Innes.[53] The kana text is transcribed as it stands, except that two short passages have been omitted. Only the first thirty sentences of the story are used.

In every sentence, the major constituent elements —predicates and clause attributes—are marked off by prefixing, to each, one of the following symbols:

A	adverbial phrase	P′	final predicate
R	relational phrase	P″	non-final predicate
Q	quotational phrase	E	exclamation

When the same sentence contains two or more elements of the same kind, the symbols referring to them are distinguished by subscript numerals; thus A_1 and A_2 identify the first and second adverbial phrases in a given sentence. Clauses are not marked as such, since their number and the limits of each are sufficiently indicated by the number and position of the predicates.

Sentence-final intonations are marked by a period (falling), a double period (level), and a question-mark (rising); high-falling intonation does not occur in the text. The facultative pauses after level intonation are marked by commas and semicolons; the latter symbol is used only when a facultative pause of higher rank follows one or more facultative pauses of lower rank (§1.2).

The Japanese sentence is followed by a free translation (and where necessary by a more literal translation in parentheses), together with an indication of its general structure. Major sentences are described, according to the form of the final predicate and the sentence-final intonation, as statements, questions, animated questions, and commands. Minor sentences are described as fragments and exclamations.

The analysis of each sentence is given in outline form, so arranged that the analysis of a constituent element is in every case subordinated to that of the larger element in which it appears, and that every word in the sentence is mentioned in the outline once and once only. The symbols A, R, P′, etc. that appear in the sentence are repeated as the main heads of the analytic outline. Two special symbols are used: a colon, to be read everywhere as 'consisting of' or 'in the form of'; and a plus sign to separate the immediate constituents of a construction.

[53] Arthur Rose-Innes, Kana 65–85 (= Japanese reading for beginners, Vol. 1; Yokohama etc., [1923]).

1. Mukasi mukasi, áru tokoro ni, ozíisañ to, obáasañ ga, arimásita.
A R_1 R_2 P′

Long long ago, in a certain place, there lived (lit. were) an old man and an old woman.
—Statement, one clause.

A : noun expression: noun mukasi 'ancient times' repeated
R_1 : noun expression + referent particle ni 'in'
noun expression: demonstrative áru 'a certain' + noun tokoro 'place'
R_2 : noun expression + referent particle ga 'subject'
noun expression: nouns ozíisañ 'old man', obáasañ 'old woman' + conjunctive particle to 'and'
P′ : indicative verb arimásita 'there was, there were' (polite state)

2. Áru hi, ozíisañ wa, yamá e, kareeda o, hiroi ni; dekakemásita.
A R_1 R_2 R_3 P′

One day, the old man started out for the mountain to pick up dried twigs.—Statement, one clause.

A : noun expression: demonstrative áru 'a certain' + noun hi 'day'
R_1 : noun ozíisañ 'old man' + referent particle wa 'topic'
R_2 : noun yamá 'mountain' + referent particle e 'to'
R_3 : pseudo-clause + referent particle ni 'for the purpose of'
pseudo-clause: relational phrase + pseudo-predicate
relational phrase: noun kareeda 'dried twigs' + referent particle o 'object'
pseudo-predicate: infinitive verb hiroi 'pick up'
P′: indicative verb dekakemásita 'started out' (polite state)

3. Sono áto de, obáasañ mo, tenugui o, kabútte; hadasi ni, nátte; kawá e, señtaku ni, ikimásita.
R_1 R_2 A_1 A_2 R_3 R_4 P′

After that, the old woman (also) put on a kerchief and took off her shoes (lit. became barefoot) and went to the river to [do her] laundry.—Statement, one clause.

R_1 : noun expression + referent particle de 'in, at'
noun expression: demonstrative sono 'that' + noun áto 'subsequent time or place'
R_2 : noun obáasañ 'old woman' + referent particle mo 'also'
A_1 : pseudo-clause: relational phrase + pseudo-predicate
relational phrase: noun tenugui 'towel' + referent particle o 'object'
pseudo-predicate: gerund verb kabútte 'putting on the head'
A_2 : pseudo-clause: relational phrase + pseudo-predicate
relational phrase: noun hadasi 'barefoot' + referent particle ni 'to'
pseudo-predicate: gerund verb nátte 'becoming'
R_3 : noun kawá 'river' + referent particle e 'to'
R_4 : noun señtaku 'washing, laundering' + referent particle ni 'for the purpose of'
P′: indicative verb ikimásita 'went' (polite state)

4. Señtaku ga, súñde; kaeróo to, suru to; kawakami kara, óoki na, momo ga, nagárete kimasita.
A Q P″ R_1 R_2 P′

The laundry being done, when she was about to return, a large peach came floating from upstream.
—Statement, two clauses.

A : pseudo-clause: relational phrase + pseudo-predicate
relational phrase: noun señtaku 'washing' + referent particle ga 'subject'
pseudo-predicate: gerund verb súñde 'coming to an end, being finished'
Q : sentence + quotative particle to 'thus'
sentence: predicate only: presumptive verb kaeróo 'I'll return'
P″: indicative verb suru 'does, makes' + clause particle to 'whenever, when'
R_1 : noun kawakami 'upstream' + referent particle kára 'from'
R_2 : noun expression + referent particle ga 'subject'
noun expression: clausal modifier + noun momo 'peach'
clausal modifier: predicate only: indicative copula phrase
copula phrase: noun óoki 'large' (appearing only in this expression) + copula na, alternant of dá in clausal modifiers
P′: indicative verb phrase: gerund verb nagárete 'floating' + indicative verb kimásita 'came' (polite [state)

5. Náñ to yuu, óoki na, momo daróo?
P′
What kind of large peach can [this] be?—Animated question, one clause (predicate only).
P′: presumptive copula phrase: noun expression + presumptive copula daróo 'may be'
noun expression: two clausal modifiers + noun momo 'peach'
clausal modifier: quotation + predicate
quotation: noun náñ 'what?' + quotative particle to 'thus'
predicate: indicative verb yuu 'says, calls'
clausal modifier: óoki na 'large' (see sentence 4, R_2)

6. Kono tosí ni, náru made; koñna óoki na, momo wa, míta, koto ga, nái.
R_1 P″ R_2 R_3 P′
To this day (lit. Until I reach[ed] this age), I haven't seen such a large peach.—Statement, two clauses.
R_1: noun expression + referent particle ni 'to'
noun expression: demonstrative kono 'this' + noun tosí 'age, year'
P″: indicative verb náru 'becomes' + clause particle made 'until'
R_2: noun expression + referent particle wa 'topic'
noun expression: two modifiers + noun momo 'peach'
demonstrative: koñna 'this kind of, such a'
clausal modifier: óoki na 'large' (see sentence 4, R_2)
R_3: noun expression + referent particle ga 'subject'
noun expression: clausal modifier + noun kotó 'act, fact, thing'
clausal modifier: predicate only: indicative verb míta 'saw, has seen'
P′: indicative adjective nái 'there is not'

7. Tyoodo, íi.
A P′
It's exactly right (lit. good).—Statement, one clause.
A: adverb tyoodo 'exactly, just'
P′: indicative adjective íi 'is good'

8. Hirotte itte, ozíisañ no, omiyage ni, siyoo.
A R P′
I'll take it (lit. pick it up and go) and make it a present for the old man.—Statement, one clause.
A: pseudo-clause: pseudo-predicate only: gerund verb phrase
verb phrase: gerund verb hirotte 'picking up' + gerund verb itte 'going'
R: noun expression + referent particle ni 'into, as'
noun expression: phrasal modifier + noun omiyage 'souvenir, gift'
phrasal modifier: noun ozíisañ 'old man' + referent particle no 'of'
P′: presumptive verb siyoo 'I'll make'

9. To, hitorigoto o, iinagara; toróo to, simásita ga; té ga, todokimaséñ.
A Q P″ R P′
While thus speaking a soliloquy, she tried to take it, but her hand didn't (lit. doesn't) reach.
—Statement, two clauses.
A: pseudo-clause: two clause attributes + pseudo-predicate
adverbial phrase: adverb to 'so saying, thus'
relational phrase: noun hitorigoto 'soliloquy' + referent particle o 'object'
pseudo-predicate: participial noun iinagara 'while saying'
Q: sentence + quotative particle to 'thus'
sentence: predicate only: presumptive verb toróo 'I'll take'
P″: indicative verb simásita 'did, made' (polite state) + clause particle ga 'but'
R: noun té 'hand' + referent particle ga 'subject'
P′: adjective surrogate todokimaséñ 'does not reach'

10. Náni ka, boo wa, nái ka.
R_1 R_2 P′
Isn't there any stick?—Question, one clause.
R_1: noun náni 'what?' + referent particle ka 'indefinite' (together 'anything')
R_2: noun boo 'stick' + referent particle wa 'topic'
P′: indicative adjective nái 'there is not' + sentence particle ka 'question'

11. To, hóoboo, mimawasimásita ga; ainiku, náni mo, arimaséñ kara; obáasañ wa, áru kuhuu o, kañgáete;
A1 A2 P″1 A3 R1 P″2 R2 A4
tooi, mizu wa, nigái zo; tikái, mizu wa, amai zo; amai, hóo e, yotte oide to, utainagara; té o, tatakimásita.
A5 R3 P′
So saying, she looked around here and there; but since unfortunately there was nothing [at hand], the old woman, thinking of a certain stratagem, sang, "The far waters are bitter; the near waters are sweet; come to the sweet side," and at the same time clapped her hands.—Statement, three clauses.

A1 : adverb to 'so saying'
A2 : noun hóoboo 'here and there'
P″1 : indicative verb mimawasimásita 'looked around' (polite state) + clause particle ga 'but'
A3 : adverb ainiku 'unfortunately'
R1 : noun náni 'what?' + referent particle mo 'even' (together 'anything, nothing')
P″2 : adjective surrogate arimaséñ 'there is not' + clause particle kara 'because'
R2 : noun obáasañ 'old woman' + referent particle wa 'topic'
A4 : pseudo-clause: relational phrase + pseudo-predicate
relational phrase: noun expression + referent particle o 'object'
noun expression: demonstrative áru 'a certain' + noun kuhuu 'device'
pseudo-predicate: gerund verb kañgáete 'thinking [of]'
A5 : pseudo-clause: quotational phrase + pseudo-predicate
quotational phrase: three sentences + quotative particle to 'thus'
sentence: relational phrase + predicate
relational phrase: noun expression + referent particle wa 'topic'
noun expression: clausal modifier + noun mizu 'water'
clausal modifier: predicate only: indicative adjective tooi 'is far'
predicate: indicative adjective nigái 'is bitter' + sentence particle zo 'emphasis'
sentence: relational phrase + predicate
relational phrase: noun expression + referent particle wa 'topic'
noun expression: clausal modifier + noun mizu 'water'
clausal modifier: predicate only: indicative adjective tikái 'is near'
predicate: indicative adjective amai 'is sweet' + sentence particle zo 'emphasis'
sentence: relational phrase + predicate
relational phrase: noun expression + referent particle e 'to'
noun expression: clausal modifier + noun hóo 'direction, side'
clausal modifier: predicate only: indicative adjective amai 'is sweet'
predicate: imperative verb phrase: gerund verb yotte 'approaching' + verb surrogate [oide 'come'
pseudo-predicate: participial noun utainagara 'while singing'
R3 : noun té 'hand' + referent particle o 'object'
P′ : indicative verb tatakimásita 'struck, clapped' (polite state)

12. Soo, suru to; husigi ní mo, momo wa, dañdañ, nagárete kíte; obáasañ no, máe de, tomarimásita.
A1 P″ R1 R2 A2 R3 P′
Thereupon (lit. When she does so), strangely enough (lit. also strangely) the peach gradually came floating and stopped in front of the old woman.—Statement, two clauses.

A1 : noun soo 'that way, so'
P″ : indicative verb suru 'does' + clause particle to 'whenever, when'
R1 : relational phrase + referent particle mo 'also, even'
relational phrase: noun husigi 'strangeness' + referent particle ni 'in'
R2 : noun momo 'peach' + referent particle wa 'topic'
A2 : pseudo-clause: adverbial phrase + pseudo-predicate
adverbial phrase: adverb dañdañ 'step by step, gradually'
pseudo-predicate: gerund verb phrase: gerund verb nagárete 'floating' + gerund verb kíte ['coming'
R3 : noun expression + referent particle de 'in, at'
noun expression: phrasal modifier + noun máe 'front'
phrasal modifier: noun obáasañ 'old woman' + referent particle no 'of'
P′ : indicative verb tomarimásita 'stopped' (polite state)

13. Obáasañ wa, isóide, sore o, hiroiágete; señtakumono to, issyo ni, uti e, motte kaerimásita.
R1 A R2 R3 R4 P′
The old woman, quickly picking it up, carried it back to the house together with her laundry.—Statement, one clause.

R1 : noun obáasañ 'old woman' + referent particle wa 'topic'
A : pseudo-clause: two clause attributes + pseudo-predicate
adverbial phrase: pseudo-clause: pseudo-predicate only: gerund verb isóide 'hurrying'
relational phrase: noun sore 'that thing' + referent particle o 'object'
pseudo-predicate: gerund verb hiroiágete 'picking up'
R2 : noun señtakumono 'laundry, things washed' + referent particle to 'with'
R3 : noun issyo 'accompaniment' + referent particle ni 'in' (together 'together')
R4 : noun uti 'house, home' + referent particle e 'to'
P′ : indicative verb phrase: gerund verb mótte 'holding' + indicative verb kaerimásita 'returned' (polite state)

14. Soo site, háyaku, ozíisañ ga, káette kúreba, íi.
A_1 A_2 R P″ P′
Then [she said], "I wish the old man would come back soon." (lit. So doing, if the old man comes back early it will be good.)—Statement, two clauses.

A_1 : pseudo-clause: adverbial phrase + pseudo-predicate
adverbial phrase: noun soo 'that way, so'
pseudo-predicate: gerund verb site 'doing'
A_2 : pseudo-clause: pseudo-predicate only: infinitive adjective háyaku 'quickly, early'
R : noun ozíisañ 'old man' + referent particle ga 'subject'
P″: hypothetical verb phrase: gerund verb káette 'returning' + provisional verb kúreba 'if [someone] comes'
P′: indicative adjective íi 'is good, will be good'

15. To, mátte imásu to; hi ga, kureru, koro; ozíisañ wa, kareeda o, yama no, yóo ni, syotte; káette kimásita.
A_1 P″ A_2 R A_3 P′
While she was talking like this and waiting, about the time that the day was drawing to a close the old man came back, lugging a mountainous load of dried twigs. (lit. So saying, when she is waiting, [at] the time that the day darkens, the old man came back, carrying on his back dried twigs in the likeness of a mountain.)—Statement, two clauses.

A_1 : adverb to 'so saying'
P″: indicative verb phrase + clause particle to 'whenever, when'
verb phrase: gerund verb mátte 'waiting' + indicative verb imásu 'is' (polite state)
A_2 : noun expression: clausal modifier + noun koro 'approximate time'
clausal modifier: relational phrase + predicate
relational phrase: noun hi 'day' + referent particle ga 'subject'
predicate: indicative verb kureru 'grows dark'
R : noun ozíisañ 'old man' + referent particle wa 'topic'
A_3 : pseudo-clause: two relational phrases + pseudo-predicate
relational phrase: noun kareeda 'dried twigs' + referent particle o 'object'
relational phrase: noun expression + referent particle ni 'in'
noun expression: phrasal modifier + noun yóo 'likeness, manner'
phrasal modifier: noun yamá 'mountain' + referent particle no 'of'
pseudo-predicate: gerund verb syotte 'carrying on the back'
P′: indicative verb phrase: gerund verb káette 'returning' + indicative verb kimásita 'came' (polite state)

16. Kyóo no, atúi kóto.
A
What a hot day! (lit. The fact that today is hot.)—Fragment, consisting of an adverbial phrase.

A : noun expression: clausal modifier + noun kóto 'act, fact, thing' (in this use semantically equivalent to a sentence particle with exclamatory meaning)
clausal modifier: relational phrase + predicate
relational phrase: noun kyóo 'today' + referent particle no 'subject' (replacing ga in a clausal modifier)
predicate: indicative adjective atúi 'is hot'

17. Áse, bissyóri da.
A P′
I'm covered with sweat.—Statement, one clause.

A : noun áse 'sweat'
P′: indicative copula phrase: noun bissyóri 'covered, all over' + indicative copula dá 'is, am'

18. Ozíisañ no, kóe o, kiite; obáasañ wa, uti no, náka kara, isóide déte kimásita.
A R_1 R_2 P′
Hearing the old man's voice, the old woman came quickly out of (the inside of) the house.—Statement, one clause.

A : pseudo-clause: relational phrase + pseudo-predicate
relational phrase: noun expression + referent particle o 'object'
noun expression: phrasal modifier + noun kóe 'voice'
phrasal modifier: noun ozíisañ 'old man' + referent particle no 'of'
pseudo-predicate: gerund verb kiite 'hearing'
R_1 : noun obáasañ 'old woman' + referent particle wa 'topic'
R_2 : noun expression + referent particle kára 'from'
noun expression: phrasal modifier + noun náka 'inside'
phrasal modifier: noun uti 'house' + referent particle no 'of'
P′: indicative verb phrase: gerund verb phrase + indicative verb kimásita 'came' (polite state)
gerund verb phrase: gerund verb isóide 'hurrying' + gerund verb déte 'emerging'

19. Okaerinasátta ka?
P′
Have you come back?—Animated question, one clause.

P′: indicative verb okaerinasátta 'deigned to return' + sentence particle ka 'question'

20. Watasi wa, háyaku, okaerinasáreba; íi to, omótte; zúibuñ, mátte itá no désu yo.
R A_1 A_2 P′
I've been waiting a long time, wishing you'd come back early. (lit. Thinking that it will be good if you return early, I have been waiting very much.)—Emphatic statement, one clause.

R: noun watasi 'I' (used chiefly by women) + referent particle wa 'topic'
A_1: pseudo-clause: quotational phrase + pseudo-predicate
quotational phrase: sentence + quotative particle to 'thus'
sentence: non-final clause + final clause
non-final clause: adverbial phrase + predicate
adverbial phrase: pseudo-clause: pseudo-predicate only: infinitive adjective háyaku ['quickly, early')
predicate: hypothetical (provisional) verb okaerinasáreba 'if [someone] deigns to [return'
final clause: predicate only: indicative adjective íi 'is good'
pseudo-predicate: gerund verb omótte 'thinking'
A_2: adverb zúibuñ 'fairly, very, very much'
P′: indicative copula phrase + sentence particle yo 'emphasis'
copula phrase: noun expression + indicative copula désu 'is' (polite state)
noun expression: clausal modifier + noun no 'fact, act'
clausal modifier: predicate only: indicative verb phrase: gerund verb mátte 'waiting' + indicative verb ita 'was'

21. Rúsu ni, náni ka, okótta no ka?
R_1 R_2 P′
Did anything happen in [my] absence?—Animated question, one clause.

R_1: noun rúsu 'absence' + referent particle ni 'in'
R_2: noun náni 'what?' + referent particle ka 'indefinite' (together 'anything')
P′: indicative copula phrase + sentence particle ka 'question'
copula phrase: noun expression + zero alternant of indicative copula dá 'is'
noun expression: clausal modifier + noun no 'fact, act'
clausal modifier: predicate only: indicative verb okótta 'happened'

22. Iie.
E
No.—Exclamation (interjection).

23. Sóo zya, arimaséñ ga; íi, monó ga, áru no de; háyaku, ozíisañ ni, ome ni, kakétakutte..
R P″ A_1 A_2
It isn't that; but since I've got something good [here], I wanted to show it to you quickly. (lit. It is not so, but since there is a good thing, wishing to hang it quickly on his eyes for the old man...)
—Fragment, non-final clause and two following clause attributes.

R: pseudo-clause + referent particle wa 'topic'
pseudo-clause: pseudo-predicate only: gerund copula phrase: noun sóo 'that way, so' + gerund copula dé 'being', here fused with wa to yield zya
P″: adjective surrogate arimaséñ 'there is not' + clause particle ga 'but'
A_1: pseudo-clause: relational phrase + pseudo-predicate
relational phrase: noun expression + referent particle ga 'subject'
noun expression: clausal modifier + noun monó 'thing'
clausal modifier: predicate only: indicative adjective íi 'is good'
pseudo-predicate: gerund copula phrase: noun expression + gerund copula dé
noun expression: clausal modifier + noun no 'fact, act'
clausal modifier: predicate only: indicative verb áru 'there is'
A_2: pseudo-clause: three clause attributes + pseudo-predicate
adverbial phrase: pseudo-clause: pseudo-predicate only: infinitive adjective háyaku 'quickly, early'
relational phrase: noun ozíisañ 'old man' + referent particle ni 'to, for'
relational phrase: noun ome 'eyes (honorific)' + referent particle ni 'on'
pseudo-predicate: gerund adjective kakétakutte 'wanting to hang'

24. Sékkati no, obáasañ wa; así o, aratte; uti ni, agatta, bákari no, ozíisañ no, máe ni; sákki no, óoki na,
R_1 R_2 R_3
momo o; kakaete kimásita.
P′

The impetuous old woman brought the aforesaid large peach before the old man, who had just washed his feet and entered the house.—Statement, one clause.

R_1 : noun expression + referent particle wa 'topic'
noun expression: clausal modifier + noun obáasañ 'old woman'
clausal modifier: predicate only: indicate copula phrase: noun sékkati 'impetuous'
+ copula no 'is', alternant of dá in clausal modifiers
R_2 : noun expression + referent particle ni 'in'
noun expression: phrasal modifier + noun máe 'front'
phrasal modifier: noun expression + referent particle no 'of'
noun expression: clausal modifier + noun ozíisañ 'old man'
clausal modifier: predicate only: indicative copula phrase
copula phrase: noun expression + copula no 'is' (see R_1)
noun expression: clausal modifier + noun bákari 'just'
clausal modifier: two clause attributes + predicate
adverbial phrase: pseudo-clause: relational phrase + pseudo-predicate
relational phrase: noun así 'feet' + referent particle o 'object'
pseudo-predicate: gerund verb aratte 'washing'
relational phrase: noun uti 'house' + referent particle ni 'into'
predicate: indicative verb agatta 'ascended'
R_3 : noun expression + referent particle o 'object'
noun expression: two modifiers + noun momo 'peach'
phrasal modifier: noun sákki 'a little while ago' + referent particle no 'of'
clausal modifier: óoki na 'large' (see sentence 4, R_2)
P′: indicative verb phrase: gerund verb kakaete 'holding in the arms + indicative verb kimásita
['came' (polite state)

25. Tyoodo, onaka mo, suite irú kara; oyu wa, áto ni, site; sassoku, gotisoo ni, naróo.
A_1 R_1 P″ A_2 A_3 R_2 P′

I'm hungry just now, so I'll bathe later and have the food at once. (lit. Since just [now] my stomach also has grown empty, making a bath afterwards, I'll come to the feast at once.)—Statement, two
[clauses.

A_1 : adverb tyoodo 'exactly, just'
R_1 : noun onaka 'stomach' + referent particle mo 'also'
P″: indicative verb phrase + clause particle kara 'because'
verb phrase: gerund verb suite 'growing empty' + indicative verb iru 'is'
A_2 : pseudo-clause: two relational phrases + pseudo-predicate
relational phrase: noun oyu 'hot water, bath' + referent particle wa 'topic'
relational phrase: noun átu 'subsequent time' + referent particle ni 'in, at'
pseudo-predicate: gerund verb site 'doing, making'
A_3 : adverb sassoku 'at once'
R_2 : noun gotisoo 'good food, feast' + referent particle ni 'to'
P′: presumptive verb naróo 'I'll become'

26. Obáasañ, manaitá to, hootyoo o, motte oide.
E R P′

Old woman! bring the chopping board and the knife.—Command, one clause with embedded exclama-
[tion.

E : vocative expression: noun obáasañ 'old woman'
R : noun expression + referent particle o 'object'
noun expression: nouns manaitá 'chopping board', hootyoo 'knife' + conjunctive particle to 'and'
P′: imperative verb phrase: gerund verb mótte 'holding' + verb surrogate oide 'come'

27. Ozíisañ wa, momo o, manaitá no, ue ni, nosete; hutatú ni, siyoo to, simásu to;
R1 A1 Q P"
náka kára, ozíisañ, tyótto, mátte to; kawaíi, kóe ga, kikoete; momo ga, mahutatu ni, waremásita.
A2 R2 R3 P"

When the old man was about to put the peach on (top of) the chopping board and cut (lit. do) it in two, a lovely voice was heard from the inside, [saying] "Old man! Wait a moment!" and the peach split completely in two.—Statement, two clauses.

R1 : noun ozíisañ 'old man' + referent particle wa 'topic'

A1 : pseudo-clause: two relational phrases + pseudo-predicate

relational phrase: noun momo 'peach' + referent particle o 'object'

relational phrase: noun expression + referent particle ni 'in, on, onto'

noun expression: phrasal modifier + noun ue 'top'

phrasal modifier: noun manaitá 'chopping board' + referent particle no 'of'

pseudo-predicate: gerund verb nosete 'placing, putting'

Q : sentence + quotative particle to 'thus'

sentence: relational phrase + predicate

relational phrase: noun hutatú 'two' + referent particle ni 'in, into'

predicate: presumptive verb siyoo 'I'll do, I'll make'

P": indicative verb simásu 'does, makes' (polite state) + clause particle to 'when'

A2 : pseudo-clause: three clause attributes + pseudo-predicate

relational phrase: noun náka 'inside' + referent particle kára 'from'

quotational phrase: fragment + quotative particle to 'thus'

fragment: exclamation + adverbial phrase

exclamation: vocative expression: noun ozíisañ 'old man'

adverbial phrase: pseudo-clause: adverbial phrase + pseudo-predicate

adverbial phrase: adverb tyótto 'a bit, a moment'

pseudo-predicate: gerund verb mátte 'waiting'

relational phrase: noun expression + referent particle ga 'subject'

noun expression: clausal modifier + noun kóe 'voice'

clausal modifier: predicate only: indicative adjective kawaíi 'is lovely'

pseudo-predicate: gerund verb kikoete 'being audible, being heard'

R2 : noun momo 'peach' + referent particle ga 'subject'

R3 : noun mahutatu 'exactly two' + referent particle ni 'in, into'

P´: indicative verb waremásita 'split, cracked' (polite state)

28. Soo site, hutótta, kírei na, hutuu no, ko to wa; maru de, tigau, akañboo ga; tobidasimásita.
A R P´

Then a plump, pretty baby, completely different from ordinary children, jumped out.—Statement, [one clause.

A : pseudo-clause: adverbial phrase + pseudo-predicate

adverbial phrase: noun soo 'that way, so'

pseudo-predicate: gerund verb site 'doing'

R : noun expression + referent particle ga 'subject'

noun expression : three clausal modifiers + noun akañboo 'baby'

clausal modifier: predicate only: indicative verb hutótta 'has grown fat'

clausal modifier: predicate only: indicative copula phrase: noun kírei 'pretty' + indicative copula na 'is' (cf. sentence 4, R2)

clausal modifier: two relational phrases + predicate

relational phrase: relational phrase + referent particle wa 'topic'

relational phrase: noun expression + referent particle to 'with'

noun expression: phrasal modifier + noun ko 'children'

phrasal modifier: noun hutuu 'ordinary' + referent particle no 'of'

relational phrase: noun maru 'whole, complete' + referent particle de 'by'

predicate: indicative verb tigau 'differs, is different'

P": indicative verb tobidasimásita 'jumped out' (polite state)

29. Ozíisañ to, obáasañ wa; sibáraku, aita, kuti ga, husagaranai hodo, odorokimásita ga; sízyuu, kodomo ga,
R_1 A_1 A_2 P''_1 A_3 Q
hitóri, hosíi to, omótte ita tokoro désu kara; táisoo, yorokóñde; sono ko o, sodatéru, koto ni, simásita.
P''_2 A_4 R_2 P'

For a while, the old man and the old woman were so astonished that their mouths hung open; but since they had long desired a child, they were very happy and decided to bring up that one. (lit. The old man and the old woman for a while were astonished to the extent that their open mouths do not close, but since it is the occasion that they have always been thinking that one child is desirable, greatly rejoicing they decided on bringing up that child.)—Statement, three clauses.

- R_1: noun expression + referent particle wa 'topic'
  - noun expression: nouns ozíisañ 'old man', obáasañ 'old woman' + conjunctive particle to 'and'
- A_1: noun sibáraku 'a while'
- A_2: noun expression: clausal modifier + noun hodo 'extent'
  - clausal modifier: relational phrase + predicate
    - relational phrase: noun expression + referent particle ga 'subject'
      - noun expression: clausal modifier + noun kuti 'mouth'
        - clausal modifier: predicate only: indicative verb aita 'opened'
    - predicate: indicative negative adjective husagaranai 'does not close'
- P''_1: indicative verb odorokimásita 'were astonished' (polite state) + clause particle ga 'but'
- A_3: adverb sízyuu 'all the time, always, continually'
- Q: sentence + quotative particle to 'thus'
  - sentence: two clause attributes + predicate
    - relational phrase: noun kodomo 'child' + referent particle ga 'subject'
    - adverbial phrase: noun hitóri 'one person'
    - predicate: indicative adjective hosíi 'is desirable'
- P''_2: indicative copula phrase + clause particle kara 'because'
  - copula phrase: noun expression + indicative copula désu 'is' (polite state)
    - noun expression: clausal modifier + noun tokoro 'place, time, occasion'
      - clausal modifier: predicate only: indicative verb phrase: gerund verb omótte 'thinking' + indicative verb ita 'was, were'
- A_4: pseudo-clause: adverbial phrase + pseudo-predicate
  - adverbial phrase: adverb táisoo 'a great deal'
  - pseudo-predicate: gerund verb yorokóñde 'rejoicing'
- R_2: noun expression + referent particle ni 'in, on'
  - noun expression: clausal modifier + noun kotó 'act, fact, thing'
    - clausal modifier: relational phrase + predicate
      - relational phrase: noun expression + referent particle o 'object'
        - noun expression: demonstrative sono 'that' + ko 'child'
      - predicate: indicative verb sodatéru 'rears, brings up'
- P': indicative verb simásita 'did, made' (polite state)

30. Momo no, náka kara, umaretá no de; Momótaroo to yuu, na o, tukemásita.
A R P'

Since he had been born from a peach, they called him by the name Momotaro [Peach Taro]. (lit. Since he was born from the inside of a peach, they attached [to him] the name called Momotaro.) [—Statement, one clause.

- A: pseudo-clause: relational phrase + pseudo-predicate
  - relational phrase: noun expression + referent particle kára 'from'
    - noun expression: phrasal modifier + noun náka 'inside'
      - phrasal modifier: noun momo 'peach' + referent particle no 'of'
  - pseudo-predicate: gerund copula phrase: noun expression + gerund copula dé 'being'
    - noun expression: clausal modifier + noun no 'fact, act'
      - clausal modifier: predicate only: indicative verb umareta 'was born'
- R: noun expression + referent particle o 'object'
  - noun expression: clausal modifier + noun na 'name'
    - clausal modifier: quotational phrase + predicate
      - quotational phrase: noun Momótaroo + quotative particle to 'thus'
      - predicate: indicative verb yuu 'says, calls'
- P': indicative verb tukemásita 'attached' (polite state)

9.2 Twenty-seven of these sentences (all but nos. 16, 22, 23) belong to the major sentence type. They contain a total of 39 clauses, final and non-final; to these we may add the non-final clause at the beginning of sentence no. 23. Disregarding the difference between final and non-final clauses and the inclusion of an exclamation in sentence 26, we list here the occurring clause types in the order of their frequency:

ARP....	nos. 8, 11, 25, 28, 30	AAP...........	no. 11
AP......	nos. 7, 12, 15, 17	ARAP.........	no. 15
RP......	nos. 6, 9, 23, 26	RAQP.........	no. 27
RRP....	nos. 4, 6, 10, 21	RRRP.........	no. 24
ARRP	nos. 1, 18, 27, 29	ARRRP.......	no. 2
P.........	nos. 5, 14, 19	RAARP.......	no. 11
AQP....	nos. 4, 9, 29	RRARP.......	no. 12
AARP	nos. 14, 25	RARRRP....	no. 13
RAAP	nos. 20, 29	RRAARRP	no. 3

[[With phonemics under control to the point where its remaining weaknesses promised to do little harm in grammatical analysis, and a good start made on the next higher level (morphemics, morphology), it was not surprising in 1946 to see a serious attempt at a comprehensive syntax. What was surprising was to see how good it was. There were signs of weakness in it, e. g. at fn. 20 or §5.5; but it certainly did not look like an attempt that would have to be thrown away when something radically different came along later: it could obviously stand without collapsing while repairs were being made upon it. In short, this paper is a classic. It is likely to be studied again and again for generations—admitting that the generations seem to be getting shorter nowadays!

There has been time enough now for it to have been superseded—by Bloch's pupil Eleanor Harz Jorden, The syntax of modern colloquial Japanese, Language Dissertation No. 52 (1955). It is only fair to list here, very briefly, the three features in the Bloch analysis which she found it necessary to disagree with (op. cit. pp. 2–5).

(1) Bloch's use of (facultative) pause, of which she finds that 'some cannot occur', which seems to mean that Bloch's informants sometimes, perhaps unconsciously, helped him analyse the language by making unidiomatic pauses at structurally strategic points. Or perhaps he assumed analogical pauses in sentences where he had never heard any. Both things are likely to happen in high-pressure work with informants living outside their own culture. Moreover, when the analyst has less active command of the language, it is harder to find counter-examples.

(2) The new analysis gets along without any dependence on minor pauses by using the Wells theory of expansions (see the next paper here). It results that the ICs of any given clause are not necessarily 'all the clause attributes on the one hand and the predicate on the other' (Bloch §2.5), but may well be all the clause attributes but the last on the one hand, and the last of them plus the predicate on the other. An example of both structures, with different meanings, for the same sequence of words, is given by Jorden (4): Mótto usiro ni [iru 'they are further back', Mótto [usiro ni iru 'there are more in the back', apparently with facultative pauses at each [. One is tempted to say, then, that usiro ni iru is still another type of composite predicate besides those given by Bloch in §3.1.

(3) In Jorden's experience, the high pitch marked by Bloch's single ´ has a domain extending earlier than the second syllable of the same word, onto the preceding (unaccented only?) words of the phrase. (The details are not immediately clear to outsiders, because Jorden does not present her data in a form easily converted to Bloch's terms as I have tried to do here.) Therefore Bloch's word-test can only give us potential words, to be cut up, occasionally (quite often), into words ('lexemes'), by an elaboration of the method given in the last paragraph of Bloch §1.4.

This last-mentioned difference between the two experiences, no doubt, has a similar explanation to that suggested here under (1) above.

In addition to the consequences of the differences listed, Jorden's description of the syntax is far less ambitious than Bloch's. That is, it avoids giving the reader any illusion of understanding the structure of Japanese sentences such as he can easily gain from the Bloch description. Most readers very likely prefer the Bloch technique of presentation, as I do, for this or similar reasons. It gives us a strong feeling of confidence when we can begin with Bloch's sketch of the major sentence type and then gradually work our way into more complex sentences by expanding each of its constituents into more complex ones. It also helps a good deal to have handy names like the ones listed in Bloch §7.1, for which the more sober labels of Jorden's §6.4 seem like a poor substitute. But it must be admitted that the Bloch presentation risks saying more than is justified, and his labels are too easily reified. For example, one wonders what difference it would have made if the 'pseudo-predicate in the alternative' of §6.22 had been called a 'conjunct predicate' instead. That is, the reader who tries to make the material his own by reworking it is in danger of wasting his efforts on such pseudo-problems. The Jorden labels offer no such temptation. By the same token, they are far less fun.]]

IMMEDIATE CONSTITUENTS

RULON S. WELLS

Language 23.81–117—1947

We aim in this paper[1] to replace by a unified, systematic theory the heterogeneous and incomplete methods hitherto offered for determining immediate constituents (hereafter abbreviated IC, plural ICs). The unifying basis is furnished by the famous concept of patterning, applied repeatedly and in divers special forms.

I. Expansion

§1. Zellig S. Harris, in his article From Morpheme to Utterance,[2] makes explicit an operation of substituting one sequence of morphemes for another; by somewhat elaborating this operation, and defining some auxiliary terms, we arrive at a concept of expansion. This characterizes one special variety of patterning: two sequences of morphemes, insofar as one is an expansion of the other, pattern alike.

§2. Morphemes are assigned to morpheme-classes on the basis of the environments in which they occur. Each environment determines one and only one morpheme-class, namely the class of all morphemes occurring in that environment. To the morpheme-class determined by the environment ( )ly (adverbial) belong slow, near, quaint, and many other morphemes; but not dead, because the ly of deadly is not the adverbial ly; not pick, because pickly does not occur, and not unhesitating, because unhesitating is not a morpheme.[3] A morpheme A belongs to the morpheme-class determined by the environment ( )X if AX is either an utterance or occurs as part of some utterance. Thus man occurs in the environment a ( ) are, i.e. the morpheme-sequence a man are occurs; witness the utterance The sons and daughters of a man are called his children. This example shows how it can happen that a morpheme occurs in an environment only if that environment, together with the morpheme itself, occurs in a certain larger environment (the phenomenon called 'grammatical agreement'); it was selected to show also that some morpheme-classes are trivial, and in practice ignored by the grammarian. The fact is that certain morpheme-classes wholly or nearly coincide. The morpheme-class determined by the possessive singular morpheme is very nearly the same as the one determined by the plural morpheme, both classes being called 'nouns' in common parlance. It is such clusters of roughly coincident classes on which the grammarian focuses his attention. Also, some classes are included in others; e.g., all single-morpheme proper nouns are single-morpheme nouns, but not conversely.

§3. Besides morpheme-classes, the grammarian sets up classes of other expressions; we will call these sequence-classes, since every expression is a sequence of one or more morphemes. Given a sequence S, a sequence-class to which S belongs is defined as the class of all sequences whose first morpheme belongs to the same morpheme-class as the first morpheme of S, whose second morpheme belongs to the same morpheme-class as the second morpheme of S, and so on; it follows that all members of a given sequence-class contain the same number of morphemes. Given blackbird, redcoat belongs to the same sequence-class; for black belongs to the same morpheme-class as red, bird belongs to the same class as coat, and the stress-pattern, here treated

[1] The central importance of the problem of immediate constituents was driven home to me in many valuable conversations with Zellig S. Harris, who also let me read a number of his manuscripts, of which not all have yet been published. Subsequently it was my privilege to acquire a minute acquaintance with Bernard Bloch's fine and well-balanced description of Japanese. Extensive viva voce discussion yields an insight into nuances, the weighing of alternative possibilities, and the far-reaching implications of any assumption that no written account can achieve.

I am indebted to Bloch, to Elizabeth F. Gardner, and to Henry M. Hoenigswald for pointing out ways in which two earlier drafts of this paper needed revision.

The present study is part of a project sponsored by the American Council of Learned Societies, whose support I gratefully acknowledge.

[2] Lang. 22.161–83 (1946) ((142)).

[3] Farly does not occur in actual utterances. The grammarian must decide whether this non-occurrence is accidental—because farly would have no meaning, or because the meaning which it would have is expressed by some other, current expression, or because (like brownbird; cf. blackbird, bluebird) it describes an object or a situation which people never have occasion to talk about—or whether, on the other hand, farly is grammatically impossible, like pickly or kindlily. To demarcate what is grammatically impossible (ungrammatical) from what does not occur merely for some stylistic or semantic reason is a difficult problem. We do not deal with it here because it is irrelevant to the theory of ICs, which takes as its data all those utterances known to occur, and analyzes them.

In citing environments, we use a pair of parentheses to indicate the position of morphemes or morpheme-sequences that occur in a given environment. Thus, the parentheses in ( )ly, above, indicate the position of such morphemes as slow, near, quaint before the morpheme ly.

as a morpheme or morpheme-sequence (cf. §70), is identical in the two words. The two-word sequence black bird belongs to a different sequence-class, however, because the stress-pattern is different. Even when contrastive stress is applied—It's a black bird, not a red one—black bird is phonemically and morphemically the same as blackbird (§§67, 72, 75) but constructionally (§38) different; in other words, black bird and blackbird are in this environment homonymous.

A sequence belongs to more than one sequence-class whenever at least one of its component morphemes beongs to more than one morpheme-class—which is usually the case. Since city is both a common noun and a noun, city-bred belongs to at least two sequence-classes; London-bred, containing the proper noun London, belongs to one of the sequence-classes but not the other.

Let us repeat that by 'sequence' we shall understand not only a sequence of two or more morphemes, but also a sequence of a single morpheme, that is, the morpheme itself, so that all morphemes are sequences but not conversely. It follows that every morpheme-class is a sequence-class, but not every sequence-class is a morpheme-class. The purpose of this use of terms is to avoid the cumbersome phrase 'morpheme or sequence', which we should otherwise very often have to employ.

§4. Now the simple but significant fact of grammar on which we base our whole theory of ICs is this: that a sequence belonging to one sequence-class A is often substitutable for a sequence belonging to an entirely different sequence-class B. By calling the class B 'entirely different' from the class A we mean to say that A is not included in B, and B is not included in A; they have no member sequences in common, or else only a relatively few—the latter situation being called 'class-cleavage'. For instance, Tom and Dick is substitutable for they, wherever they occurs; They wanted me to come is a grammatical sentence, and so is Tom and Dick wanted me to come.[4] They did it because they wanted to is grammatical, and Tom and Dick did it because Tom and Dick wanted to is equally grammatical, being uncommon for stylistic reasons only. Similarly, The stars look small because they are far away and The stars look small because Tom and Dick are far away are both grammatical, the second sentence being uncommon (or not used) for semantic reasons only.

We may roughly express the fact under discussion by saying that sometimes two sequences occur in the same environments even though they have different internal structures. When one of the sequences is at least as long as the other (contains at least as many morphemes) and is structurally diverse from it (does not belong to all the same sequence-classes as the other), we call it an expansion of that other sequence, and the other sequence itself we call a model. If A is an expansion of B, B is a model of A. The leading idea of the theory of ICs here developed is to analyze each sequence, as far as possible, into parts which are expansions; these parts will be the constituents of the sequence. The problem is to develop this general idea into a definite code or recipe, and to work out the necessary qualifications required by the long-range implications of each analysis of a sequence into constituents.

§5. A preliminary example will give an inkling of how the method works. The king of England opened Parliament is a complete sentence, to be analyzed into its constituent parts; we ignore for the time being its features of intonation. It is an expansion of John, for John occurs as a complete sentence. But it is an expansion of John only in this special environment, the zero environment—not in such an environment as ( ) worked [John worked]. It helps the IC-analysis to show that the sequence being analyzed is an expansion, but only if it is an expansion of the same shorter sequence in all, or a large proportion, of the environments where the shorter sequence occurs. For the sequence taken as an example, The king opened, or The king waited, or John worked will serve as shorter sequences. (It is not necessary, in order for A to be an expansion of B, that A should contain all the morphemes of B and in the same order. This is only a special case of expansion, called by Bloomfield 'endocentric'. Moreover, the king of England is an endocentric expansion of a queen—insofar as a and the belong to the same morpheme-classes—just as much as of the king.)

§6. Our general principle of IC-analysis is not only to view a sequence, when possible, as an expansion of a shorter sequence, but also to break it up into parts of which some or all are themselves expansions. Thus in our example it is valuable to view The king of England opened Parliament as an expansion of John worked because the king of England is an expansion of John and opened Parliament is an expansion of worked. On this basis, we regard the ICs of The king of England opened Parliament as the king of England and opened Parliament.

The king of England is in turn subject to analysis, and John is no help here because it is a single morpheme. The king will serve; the king of England is an expansion of the king and, in turn, king of England is an expansion of king. The king of England is accordingly analyzed into the and king of England (cf. §20). The reasons for analyzing the latter into king and of England (rather than king of and England) will be given later.

As for the second half of the sentence, opened Parliament, besides the obvious analysis into opened and Parliament there is another, instantly rejected by common sense but yet requiring to be considered, into open and -ed Parliament. The choice between these two analyses is dictated not by the principle of expansions as stated and exemplified above but by

[4] The converse does not hold. For instance, they is not substitutable for Tom and Dick in the sequence I met Tom and Dick downtown.

two other principles of patterning, equally fundamental for English and very probably for other languages: the principle of choosing ICs that will be as independent of each other in their distribution as possible, and the principle that word divisions should be respected. The first of these principles is stated in §18, the second in §40 and §47.

§7. Let us call the ICs of a sentence, and the ICs of those ICs, and so on down to the morphemes, the constituents of the sentence; and conversely whatever sequence is constituted by two or more ICs let us call a constitute. Assuming that the ICs of The king of England opened Parliament are the king of England and opened Parliament, that those of the former are the and king of England and those of the latter are opened and Parliament, and that king of England is divided into king and of England, of England is divided into the morphemes of and England, and opened is divided into open and -ed—all of which facts may be thus diagrammed:* the]][king]]][of]]]][England][open]]][ed]][Parliament—then there are twelve constituents of the sentence: (1) the king of England, (2) the, (3) king of England, (4) king, (5) of England, (6) of, (7) England, (8) opened Parliament, (9) opened, (10) open, (11) -ed, (12) Parliament. And the six constitutes in the above sentence are those five of the constituents (nos. 1, 3, 5, 8, 9) that are not morphemes, plus the sentence itself. According to this analysis the sequence the king of, for instance, or England opened, is in this sentence neither a constituent nor a constitute. And in terms of this nomenclature the principle relating words to IC-analysis may be stated: every word is a constituent (unless it is a sentence by itself), and also a constitute (unless it is a single morpheme). But if opened Parliament were analyzed into open and -ed Parliament, the word opened would be neither a constituent nor a constitute.

§8. What we view as the correct analysis of The king of England opened Parliament has now been stated, but it remains to consider why other analyses of it were rejected. For an IC-analysis is never accepted or rejected on its own merits. Our procedure aims only to tell, given two or more mechanically possible dichotomies (whose number is always one less than the number of morphemes in the dichotomized sequence), how to decide in favor of one of them. Assuming that all the words in The king of England opened Parliament except opened are single morphemes (the possibility of analyzing England and Parliament into two morphemes each being neglected here as irrelevant), there are six analyses to be evaluated one against the other; the analysis into the king of England and opened Parliament has the same advantage over all the other five, and therefore it will suffice to consider exhaustively only one of these five: the analysis into the king and of England opened Parliament. A common-sense response would be to say that analysis into the king and of England opened Parliament violates the meaning. This is true, but it is possible in our exposition to leave the factor of meaning out of account until much later (Part III), meanwhile going as far as possible on formal grounds alone.

§9. Several more sophisticated arguments based on formal patterning might be advanced. One could argue that of England opened Parliament is not an IC of the whole sentence because it is a sequence that could not be found anywhere except after a noun-phrase. But while this argument is sufficient ad hoc, it is too weak to exclude other analyses which one would regard as wrong, e.g. the king of][England opened Parliament. For there is no question about England opened Parliament, and the king of can be found in such other environments as I wonder what country he's the king of.

Or again: there is an actor-action pattern in English, and whatever occurs as an actor or as an action in an actor-action sentence also occurs as a sentence by itself (i.e. accompanied by nothing but a sequence of pitch morphemes. Thus: [Who opened Parliament?] The king. [What did you say the king of England did?] Opened Parliament. This consideration certainly cuts out the king][of England opened Parliament, but it does not preclude either the king of][England opened Parliament or the king of England opened][Parliament; to deal with these one must revert either to meaning or to supplementary formal principles. And in the second place, the consideration that we have mentioned is available only at a later stage of grammatical description than we are taking for granted at this point. For the principles delineated in this paper are intended to be used not only in deciding to which of the known constructions or patterns of the language any given sentence belongs, but also as part of the means for ascertaining those very patterns themselves. If they are adequate they will suffice, for example, when applied to the data of English, to establish the existence of the general actor-action pattern itself.

§10. An argument might be based on economy or simplicity: the constituents of a sentence should be those units in terms of which the sentence is most easily described.[5] Now other sentences such as I saw the king of England alongside of I saw John,

*For typing convenience, this reprint combines brackets instead of duplicating the conventional bars and clusters:][>][for |,]]][>]]][for |||, etc.

[5] Leonard Bloomfield, Language 212 (New York, 1933); Kenneth L. Pike, Taxemes and Immediate Constituents, Lang. 19.65–82, esp. §4.19 (1943).

One particular version of simplicity which someone might propound but which must be rejected would call for the totality of analyses that requires the minimum number of sequence-classes to be defined. The proposal is sound in itself but inadequate to exclude all wrong analyses, such as the king of][England. Note that the king of must be described as a constituent in certain other occurrences, e.g. What country is he the king of?

and he opened Parliament alongside of he came, require us to treat the king of England and opened Parliament as units, but no sentence (unless, circularly, those of the very type under consideration) constrain us so to treat of England opened Parliament.

It will be noted that this argument does not exclude all wrong divisions, as for instance the king of|England opened Parliament (see above). However, perhaps we cannot expect that any one principle should be completely sufficient. Be that as it may, a more powerful and satisfactory version of this argument, and the one which we shall adopt as a fundamental principle of IC-analysis, is stated in terms of expansions, and a fuller definition of expansions is necessary than the preliminary one already given in §4.

§11. Every sentence may be divided into focus and environment. The focus is any sequence that is viewed as replaceable by other sequences; correlatively, the rest of the sentence is the environment of such a sequence. In practice it is often possible to narrow down the focus-plus-environment from a whole sentence to some shorter part of it. As a rule, that shorter part turns out to be a constituent in the technical sense. Thus, we can investigate what sequences may function as focus (may fill the blank) in the ( ) of England, without considering the wider environment of which the sequence the ( ) of England is itself the focus. In such cases there is a relevant environment smaller than the total environment. When a whole sentence is considered as focus, the environment is zero.[6]

The class of all sequences substitutable for a given focus in a given environment may be called the focus-class relative to that environment. Now every focus is a sequence (of one or more morphemes). If we analyze our sentence as The||king||| of||||England|open|||ed||Parliament so that the main break comes after England, we can explain the constituents as expansions down to the following point: the king of England is an expansion of the king (which in turn is an expansion of a proper noun, say John) because king of England is an expansion of king; opened Parliament is an expansion of a past-tense intransitive verb like worked. The whole sentence, therefore, is an expansion of John worked, which is of a fundamental sentence-type because it is not an expansion (except in a very few environments, such as the zero-environment) of anything shorter; but John worked and John works, each containing three morphemes, may be regarded as expansions of each other.[7] Thus the search for expansions leads us to the actor-action sentence-type; we do not need to take it for granted.

But if, on the other hand, we analyze our sentence as the king|of England opened Parliament, then no matter what further analysis we make, of England opened Parliament is not an expansion of anything shorter than of England worked or of England works. Thus it compares unfavorably with opened Parliament. And the other half has no compensating advantage, because the king of England can be construed as an expansion just as well as the king. Therefore the principle of expansion conclusively favors the analysis the king of England|opened Parliament. It cannot strictly be said to confirm or corroborate common sense, although it agrees with it; for it is precisely one of the reasons on which the common-sense judgment is based, although of course common sense alone would never be able to formulate it.

§12. Some implications of our procedure need to be made explicit. Expansion was defined relative to an environment. If two sequences belong to all the same sequence-classes, then each is an absolute equivalent of the other, in the sense that each occurs in all the environments where the other occurs and nowhere else. However, it is rare, if it happens at all, that one sequence is an absolute equivalent of a sequence belonging to an entirely different sequence-class. On this account our interest centers in non-absolute expansions, and the problem is to find expansions that approximate as closely as possible to being absolute.

§13. It is frequently the case that one sequence occurs wherever a certain other one occurs but not conversely. This asymmetry is typical of endocentric expansions. Wherever the expansion oldish occurs, the model old occurs also, but the converse is not true; for instance, old occurs in oldish, but oldishish is grammatically impossible. (It may be that there are also cases of the opposite sort where the expansion occurs wherever the model occurs but not conversely.) A much more frequent case, given any two sequences chosen at random, is that there are some environments in which both the first and the second occur, some in which only the first occurs, and some in which only the second occurs. Both boy and boys occur in the environments I saw the ( ) and the ( ) saw me. But only boy occurs in I saw that ( ) and the ( ) sees me, and only boys in I saw those ( ) and the ( ) see me. It is because of the former environments that there is a class of nouns, and because of the latter that this class is divided into singulars and plurals.

6 In the sequel, we shall often speak loosely of a sequence as occurring in the zero-environment when we mean that its total environment is the pitch-morpheme of the sentence. Cf. fn. 34.

7 This statement is made on the assumption that worked consists morphologically of only the two morphemes work and -ed. If, as some would consider, the proportion they work : John works = they worked : John worked is perfect, so that worked includes also a zero-alternant of the 3rd-singular morpheme -s when it has a singular subject, then John works is indeed shorter than John worked (since it lacks the past-tense morpheme -ed), and furnishes a simpler example of the fundamental sentence type.

§14. It is easy to define a focus-class embracing a large variety of sequence-classes but characterized by only a few environments; it is also easy to define one characterized by a great many environments in which all its members occur, but on the other hand poor in the number of diverse sequence-classes that it embraces. What is difficult, but far more important than either of the easy tasks, is to define focus-classes rich both in the number of environments characterizing them and at the same time in the diversity of sequence-classes that they embrace. Actor and action (or in the older terminology subject and predicate) are such focus-classes. Another (less grand) example is the focus-class of verbs and verb-phrases; subsumed under this, as a subclass, is the focus-class of third singular present verbs and endocentric phrases containing such a verb as their head. Again, the pronouns he, she, it, this, that, and one; all singular proper nouns; and all singular noun phrases beginning with the, a, this, that, any, each, every, together form a focus-class whose diversity of membership is as we have just specified and which occurs in a large number of environments —environments which are not themselves unified by all belonging to a major focus-class. The traditional parts of speech are focus-classes, not morpheme-classes or other sequence-classes.[8] Thus the class of English nouns includes compounds and derivatives as well as single morphemes. (Paradigms, including all the inflected forms of a given stem, are yet another kind of class, unless it should happen that there are one or more environments in which all the inflected forms occur. Cf. fn. 14.)

§15. An instructive formula summarizing the contrast between sequence- and focus-classes is in terms of external and internal grammar. The internal grammar of a sequence is the class of all sequence-classes to which it belongs; the external grammar is the class of all focus-classes to which it belongs. If two sequences have the same internal grammar, they must have the same external grammar, but the converse does not hold true; this is why the method of expansion is possible. If two sequences are similar in external grammar, but internally different, then by definition one of them is an expansion of the other. The contrast between internal and external grammar makes precise what is sometimes meant by the contrast between form and function.

§16. In choosing the major focus-classes that will be used in dividing any utterance into constituents, it is necessary to consider the whole system which these focus-classes, taken collectively, form with each other. This is why an analysis is not pronounced good or bad of itself, but only better or worse than some other.

§17. Judged by this criterion of over-all consequences, the analysis the king of England | opened Parliament is better than the king | of England opened Parliament, because there is a focus-class to which opened Parliament belongs, embracing more sequence-classes and occurring in more environments than any focus-class to which of England opened Parliament belongs. It is true that there are some environments, such as the king of Scotland and ( ), where the latter sequence but not the former occurs; it is also true that a focus-class to which of England opened Parliament belongs includes some sequence-classes not included in the focus-class of opened Parliament—for instance, the class to which by marriage runs a bank belongs in my cousin | by marriage runs a bank. In fact, the example makes it clear that wrong analyses into ICs tend to support each other, just as right ones do.[9] But right analyses are ultimately supported from without by the method of regarding them as expansions of shorter sequences, whereas wrong analyses lack this ultimate extraneous support. And right analyses turn out to relegate more sequences to larger focus-classes (larger both in diversity of membership and in the number of characterizing environments) than those to which wrong analyses would relegate them. Opened Parliament occurs, thus differing from of England opened Parliament, after adverbs and also in zero environment (i.e. as a sentence by itself).

§18. This is the fundamental aim of IC-analysis: to analyze each utterance and each constitute into maximally independent sequences—sequences which, consistently preserving the same meaning, fit in the greatest number of environments and belong to focus-classes with the greatest possible variety of content.

§19. Another way of stating the basic utility of expansions is that they furnish a way of proceeding from the simple to the complex, from the established to the not yet established, from that whose analysis is transparent to that whose analysis is obscure. But a difficulty is that, given a complex constitute to be analyzed, a number of different models (§4) seem to offer themselves. We turn now to the problem of how to choose between these.

§20. For instance, shall the king of England be analyzed as the | king of England or as the king | of England? Our principle directs us to analyze into constituents which are expansions; but at first sight the advantages of the alternatives appear to be about equal. King of England is an expansion of king, but the king is an expansion of John.[10] In respect of their other ICs, the | king of England is better than the king | of England, since the is a single morpheme while

[8] So are Bloomfield's 'form-classes'; cf. his Language 185 top, 190 top, 194 second paragraph, etc.

[9] We call an IC-analysis wrong when there is another possible analysis of the same sequence that is better, and right when there is none.

[10] That the king of England is itself an expansion of John is relevant in determining the king of England to be a constituent of any longer sequence in which it occurs, but not relevant in determining its own constituents.

of England is neither a morpheme nor yet an expansion. But this is too slight to figure in the decision. As before, it is necessary to see how close to equivalence is the reciprocal substitutability of king of England with king, and of the king with John. It turns out that while the relation of king of England to king is almost absolute equivalence, the environment poor ( ) —poor being here replaceable by any other non-pronominal adjective—differentiates John from the king, for there is no poor the king. Rather, and instead, there is the poor king. But if the better analysis the|king of England were for some reason excluded, the fact that the king is in some environments an expansion of John would support the king| of England in comparison with the other possibility, the king of|England; for the king of is not an expansion of anything in very many environments.

II. Further methods

§21. Having tentatively settled upon the|king of England as the best analysis of that phrase, we proceed to draw out its consequences by checking how it harmonizes with other analyses. King of England and (for example) English king belong to a focus-class in common; therefore it is desirable, unless other considerations weigh against it, to treat one of them as a constituent and a constitute if the other is so treated. The pair of analyses the|king of England and the|English king is the only pair achieving this result; no other pair does so.[11]

§22. A further step is now possible. The two sequences king of England and English king belong to a certain focus-class, and they contain a part in common, namely a noun. The former belongs to the class of sequences composed of noun plus following modifier, the latter to the class of sequences composed of noun plus preceding modifier. We define a noun modifier as whatever is either a preceding modifier or a following modifier;[12] it will be seen that the class of noun modifiers is neither a sequence-class nor a focus-class. So far from the two kinds of noun modifiers occurring in the same environment, they are, in a sense, in complementary distribution to each other.[13] We unite the two classes of modifiers (each of which is, by itself, a focus-class) into a new type of class, which we may call an associative group. The grammatical reason for doing so is that we thus create a common structure for two sequence types (modifier + noun; noun + modifier) which are included in the same focus-class. This construction obviously does not imply that the two types of modifier-and-noun phrases are completely identical in structure; it only points out one common feature—a feature which proves, as formal features often do, to correlate with modification in the semantic sense.

The constructability of associative groups does not argue for one analysis rather than another. The English, an English, many a, more than one, all the are sequences of diverse internal grammar (§15) that belong to a common focus-class; and there is a sequence-class of which some member (a, the, one) is a subsequence of each of these sequences. Therefore English, many, more than and all belong to an associative group. But this is not the reason for regarding the English, an English, many a, more than one, and all the as constituents. No IC-analysis will recognize all the focus-classes there are, nor all the associative groups; an analysis results from determining some focus-classes and some associative groups to be more important (more major) than others. And the associative groups worth defining are those that harmonize with the IC-system.

§23. Another variety of patterning argument is based on paradigms. King and kings belong to the same paradigm;[14] therefore, derivatively the king of and the kings of would be expected to relate to each other as king and kings relate to each other. Accordingly, if the king of England were analyzed the king of|England, then the kings of England should be analyzed the kings of|England, and the king of England and Scotland should be analyzed the king of|England and Scotland. But the latter analyses are to be rejected not only for reasons similar to those invalidating of England opened Parliament, but also for the additional reason that the king of and the kings of do not pattern like modifiers. More exactly expressed, the associative group 'modifiers' that we have set up could not be augmented by the focus-class of the king of, the kings of, etc., without radically altering its defining properties. Any sequence consisting of singular noun plus modifier 'patterns like' (is an expansion of) singular nouns, and any sequence consisting of plural noun plus modifier is an expansion of plural nouns. This is not true of the king of, the kings of; for the king of England and Scotland is singular, and the kings of England is plural. This same fact differentiates them from pronominal modifiers like this, these, which indeed are themselves inherently singular or plural but which grammatically agree, in respect of number, with what they modify. Thus sequences like the king of, if treated as modifiers, stand isolated in a focus-class of their own, and since there is another analysis of the king of England not suffering from this undesired consequence, the analysis the king of|England is rejected.

11 Until we admit discontinuous constituents. See Part V of this paper.

12 The circularity is only apparent. What is assumed as previously defined is the whole phrase 'preceding modifier' and the whole phrase 'following modifier'. A third type of modifier is discussed in §56.

13 Cf. Moroccan Arabic n- 'I will' and -t 'I did', in nmši 'I will go' and mšit 'I went' (Harris, op.cit. §3.1).

14 And also to a number of focus-classes in common. But it is always a coincidence when a paradigm is also a focus-class; it may be that some paradigms in some languages have no environment characteristic of all their members.

§24. Further examples will at the same time illustrate the principles already stated, and occasion the introduction of some additional principles.

Taking for granted that I will be ready should be analyzed I|will be ready, let us inquire into the further analysis of the second IC. Assuming each of the three words to be a single morpheme, the two possibilities are will|be ready and will be|ready. Each analysis recognizes important focus-classes, so that it would be hard to decide between them on this basis. Like will be pattern not only must be, could be, may be, etc., and will become, will seem, will appear, will look, etc., but also more complex sequences like will pretend to be and less complex ones like am, is, are, was, were.[15] Like be ready pattern become ready, seem ready, look ready, as well as go, wait, read a book, etc. The solution lies in comparison with certain other sequences, e.g. was ready. Even if was be regarded morphologically as be + past-tense morpheme + third-singular morpheme, the principle (§40, §47) that every word is a constitute leaves was|ready as a better analysis than any other. Now since will be is in many environments an expansion of was, the analysis will be|ready comports well with the analysis was|ready.

But why not argue, on the same basis, that since will wait must be analyzed will|wait, and be ready is in many environments an expansion of wait, the analysis of will be ready should be will|be ready?—Because in any environment where will be is not an expansion of was, it is an expansion of were; whereas in the environments where be ready is not an expansion of wait, it is not an expansion of anything. This is an instance of how paradigms play a part in determining ICs—was, were, will be all belong to the same pardigm. Paradigms are valuable in IC-analysis when they occur in pairs, standing in agreement relations with each other. Here, for example, the pairs consist of nouns and pronouns on the one hand and verbs on the other: I agrees with am, and he, she, it, etc. with is. Thanks to this feature we are able to show that is and are together are absolute equivalents of will be, so that will be|ready is an analysis superior to will|be ready.

§25. Another example: infinitives. Shall we analyze want to|go or want|to go? Want to is in some environments an expansion of can, must, will, should, etc.[16] On the other hand, to go is in some environments an expansion of a proper or collective noun; thus, both to go and food occur in the same environment ( ) is pleasant, I wanted ( ), ( ) is better than ( ), etc. There are other environments that differentiate the two—environments, that is, where one but not the other occurs; thus, only the infinitive occurs in it is pleasant ( ) [synonymous with ( ) is pleasant], I tried not ( ), I want him ( ), it's good for you ( ), while only the noun occurs in I'm waiting for ( ), this kind of ( ). The method of expansion as we have stated it so far is therefore not suited to decide between want to|go and want|to go.

§26. In the sequence to go is easy, the two ICs are to go and is easy; this is demonstrated by the considerations that establish the actor-action construction in general. Since to go is a constituent in this environment, it is desirable that it be treated as a constituent wherever it occurs with the same meaning; on this ground we choose the analysis want|to go.

§27. The principle just stated is an exceedingly important one, but it has two equally important exceptions. A continuous sequence treated as a constituent in one environment should be treated as a constituent in any other environment where it occurs, unless (1) there is some longer sequence of which it is both a part and a model (in other words, some endocentric expansion of it) and which is treated as a constituent, or (2) it bears a different meaning.[17] The fact that want to is a constituent in the sentence I go there because I want to does not entail that want to should be treated as a constituent in want to go, for to (in want to at the end of a clause) is a model for to go; therefore the analysis want|to go is compatible with the analysis of want to as a constituent when it occurs at sentence-end. Similarly, the occurrence of the king as a constituent of I|saw|the king does not entail treating it as a constituent in I|saw||the|||king of England.

This exception to the general principle is necessary, since otherwise almost every constitute would be subject to conflicting analyses. The sequences I saw the king and John of England would entail the king|of England, while he became king of England would entail the|king of England. But even with the exceptions noted above, the principle is a very powerful and valuable one, playing a somewhat analogous role to that played in Euclid's geometry by the axiom that one figure may be moved around and superimposed on another while remaining constant in shape and size.

§28. A subsidiary and related principle is that if a given sequence occurring with the same meaning in two environments is treated in both environments

[15] But a focus-class to which only one of the three sequences am, is, are belongs is characterized by more environments than one to which two or all three of them belong, because of the grammatical agreement which these words require with their subject or actor.

[16] But not, for example, in the environment he ( ) go. Here the expansion of can is wants to. Want to and wants to are paradigmatically related, like want and wants, so that if want to is treated as a constituent, it is desirable to treat wants to in the same way. And if, on other grounds, it has been decided to treat them both as constituents, then they will conjointly support the analysis of any sequence of which they are conjointly either an expansion or a model.

[17] For the purposes of stating this principle, we assume that every sequence has a meaning, though actually it is in general much more difficult to define the meaning of non-constituents—especially when they are discontinuous—than of constituents.

as a constitute (therefore also as a constituent, unless it is a complete utterance), it must in both occurrences receive the same analysis into ICs. This principle, like the preceding, is valuable in allowing us to establish a consistent system by checking and testing our analyses one against the others. Another such principle (indispensable but so obvious as to need no discussion) is that if two sequences belong to exactly the same sequence-classes (§3), they must be identically analyzed. If one of them, occurring with a certain meaning in a certain environment, is analyzed in such-and-such a way, then the other, when it occurs with the same meaning in the same environment, must be analyzed in the same way.

§29. One IC-analysis involves others; its soundness is not tested until its most far-reaching effects on the system have been explored. Ultimately, what is accepted or rejected is not the analysis of a single sentence but what we may call the IC-system of the language, an entire set or system of analyses, complete down to the ultimate constituents, of all the utterances of the language. Since every constitute is wholly composed of constituents, every proposal to regard such-and-such a sequence as a constituent entails that every other constituent of the sentence in which it occurs shall wholly include it or wholly exclude it or be wholly included in it. The analysis the king of|England opened Parliament is obviously excluded if of England is a constituent of that sentence; conversely, if the king of | England opened Parliament is the accepted analysis, it is impossible that of England should be a constituent. Hence errors, as well as right analyses, compound each other.

For this reason, we do not propose our account as a mechanical procedure by which the linguist, starting with no other data than the corpus of all the utterances of the language and a knowledge of the morphemes contained in each one, may discover the correct IC-system. For any language, the number of possible IC-systems is very large; but in practice it is easy to see that most of the possibilities are negligible. Just as when working out the phonemics, the practicing linguist will discover many shortcuts.

Because of the systematic interlocking of one IC-analysis with others, both of the same sentence and of other sentences of the language, it is not possible to demonstrate conclusively upon one or a few selected examples that, all things considered, such-and-such analyses are the best. All we can do is to delineate the proof and to show how far-reaching the consequences of any one particular IC-analysis may be.

III. Constructions

§30. In §8 we remarked that a theory of ICs could be developed up to a certain point without a consideration of meaning; that point has now been reached. We have, indeed, several times used the phrase 'with the same meaning' (§§18, 26, 27, 28), but without explaining why the proviso is necessary. Very simply, it is necessary because there are many instances of a sequence which in some occurrences has one meaning and in other occurrences has another, and which, moreover, has different analyses into ICs accordingly. An example is the sequence old men and women. In one meaning this is nearly synonymous with old men and old women; in another, with women and old men. One of the prime functions of analysis into ICs is to reveal a formal difference correlated with the semantic one. In the former meaning, the sequence is old|men and women; in the latter, old men|and|women.[18]

Again, the king of England's people has two meanings, and correspondingly two IC-analyses: (1) the| king‖of England's people means 'the king of a certain people, viz. the English'; (2) the king of England‖'s |people means 'the people of a certain king, viz. the king of England'.

§31. This sort of equivocation, if not found in every language of the globe, is certainly widespread. Its import for grammar is very great. For it means that the grammarian must include among his data something more than morphemes and their sequences. Grammatical 'order' is something more than mere sequence. To this 'something more' we propose to give the name construction.[19]

§32. The king of England's people (1) and the king of England's people (2) as defined above are the same sequence of phonemes, yet they have two different meanings. How is the difference to be accounted for, how localized? It cannot plausibly be ascribed to the morphemes taken severally; it is not like the homonymy of of 'effected by' and of 'effected upon' in the conquest of Pizarro : the conquest of Peru. Nor is it like It's father (e.g. in answer to Who is it?) and Its father (e.g. in answer to Who is the man holding that baby?), where two morpheme-sequences having the same sound belong to different sequence-classes. The only remaining factor to which the difference in meaning between (1) and (2) can be ascribed is the arrangement of the morphemes (the taxis).

It has long been recognized that the order in which morphemes are arranged is often a bearer of meaning; as John hit Bill vs. Bill hit John. But although in the pair before us, (1) and (2), the meaning-difference is ascribable to the arrangement of morphemes in some sense, it is obviously not ascribable to their order. Therefore, as stated above, order does not exhaust arrangement.

§33. Preparatory to defining constructions, we distinguish between sequences and occurrences (or instances) of sequences.[20] The sequence he writes

18 We shall justify in §54 the analysis of a noun phrase A and B into three ICs, A|and|B.

19 The reader must constantly bear in mind that our definition of this term is not the same as Bloomfield's (Language 169), although both are generalizations of what is meant in traditional grammar by such expressions as 'the ablative absolute construction'.

20 Cf. Y. R. Chao, The Logical Structure of Chinese Words, Lang. 22.5 (1946).

pages and pages contains six morphemes: he, write, -s (3rd singular), page, -s (plural), and; but eight morpheme-occurrences, since the morphemes page and -s (plural) each have two occurrences. Likewise he writes pages and pages is the same sequence as the first underlined sequence of this paragraph, but a different occurrence of that sequence. Sequences are universals; occurrences are particulars.[21]

§34. Now a construction is a class C of occurrences, subject to the following conditions: (1) there is at least one focus-class which includes all the sequences of which the members of C are occurrences; (2) all these occurrences have a certain meaning in common; and optionally (3) all these occurrences occur in a certain total environment or in all of a certain class of total environments. Note that while a sequence may occur in more than one environment, a given occurrence of a sequence occurs in just one occurrence of an environment.

We have given above a broad definition of the term construction; it admits as constructions a great many classes that are of no interest in the theory of ICs.[22] But it is easy enough simply to ignore these uninteresting cases, and thus to avoid a complicated and cumbersome definition. When the verb run occurs with the pitch morpheme of an indicative sentence /24/[23] as its total environment (i.e. as a sentence) and with the meaning of command, the construction to which it belongs is different from the construction of the same verb with the same pitch phonemes occurring as a sentence with the meaning of statement (e.g. in answer to the question Which would you rather do—walk or run?); and both of these constructions are different from the respective constructions of come in the sentences Come here, I'm coming, and I'll try to come (with whatever intonation and whatever meaning). But there are several constructions (clause, declarative sentence, imperative sentence, etc.) which include both the sequence come here occurring with the pitch morpheme of an indicative sentence as its total environment, and the single morpheme come occurring in the same environment.

Our definition of the term construction allows an occurrence to belong to more than one construction. Thus we may say that Come here (as a sentence, accompanied by the pitch morpheme of an indicative sentence) belongs at the same time to the clause construction and to the declarative or imperative sentence construction, whereas in the sequence Come here and I'll tell you it belong only to the clause construction. Similarly, in The king of England opened Parliament, the sequence the king of England belongs simultaneously to the noun-phrase construction and to the subject (actor) construction. There is no conflict in this, because the meaning of the one construction is compatible with the meaning of the other, and sometimes a part of it.

But there is conflict in the cases of old men and women and the king of England's people. An occurrence having one of the meanings does not have the other; therefore, while old men and women, meaning 'old men and old women', may belong to several constructions at once, there are some constructions to which it does not belong and to which the same sequence with the other meaning 'women and old men' does belong.

§35. We have assumed (fn. 17) that every sequence has at least one meaning; hence every one of its occurrences has the same meaning or meanings, and belongs to at least one construction. Now the meaning of the king of England is compounded of a number of lesser meanings: (1) the meanings of the several

21 Therefore, the statement 'pages and pages contains three morphemes but five morpheme-occurrences' is only a loose way of saying 'pages and pages contains three morphemes and every occurrence of pages and pages contains five morpheme-occurrences'. When we said, in §3, that two members of the same sequence-class must contain the same number of morphemes, we meant that these members, or more strictly any pair of occurrences of them, must contain the same number of morpheme-occurrences.

A sequence might be defined as a class of occurrences; then the statement 'the sequence A occurs in the environment B' could be explained as meaning 'some members of A occur in some members of B'.

22 For instance, if no condition of type (3) is imposed, every sequence-class is also a construction.

23 The four English pitch phonemes are designated by the numerals from 1 (highest pitch) to 4 (lowest pitch), following Kenneth L. Pike, The Intonation of American English (Ann Arbor, 1946). In a phonemic transcription, each pitch phoneme is written as a superior numeral before the syllabic which it accompanies; when a succession of two pitch phonemes accompanies a single syllabic, the two appropriate numerals are written before the appropriate letter. The absence of a superior numeral before one or more successive syllabics means that those syllabics bear the same pitch phoneme as the last syllabic preceding them on which a pitch is indicated; see fn. 56. But we write, for example, I won't go pronounced emphatically as /^{3}ayw^{2}ôwnt-g^{24}ów/, where the practice described above would lead to confusion with /^{3}ayw^{2}ôwnt-g^{4}ów/; see §79. It is often convenient (e.g. in §54) to write a mixture of standard orthography for the segmental phonemes and phonemic transcription for the pitch phonemes; in this mixed notation, the stress phonemes (see §§66 ff.) are sometimes indicated and sometimes not, depending on their relevance.

Pitch morphemes, like segmental morphemes, are generally identified by citing one of their alternants—the alternant of a pitch morpheme being a sequence of one or more pitch phonemes. The alternant of the pitch morpheme contained in the first pronunciation of I won't go mentioned above would be written either as /32(24)/ the parentheses indicating that the last two pitch phonemes accompany the same syllabic) or—with a deliberately ambiguous cover notation—as /324/, which indicates what pitch phonemes occur and in what order, but not how many syllabics there are in the phrase.

morphemes; (2) the meaning of the sequence the king; (3) the meaning of the sequence of England; and (4) the meaning of the sequence compounded of the king and of England. Or, alternatively, (1) the meanings of the individual morphemes; (2) the meaning of of England; (3) the meaning of the sequence compounded of king and of England; (4) the meaning of the sequence compounded of the and king of England. Clearly, since by our assumption every occurring sequence has a meaning, the meaning of every sequence of three or more morphemes can be described in terms of the meanings of any two sub-sequences into which it is divided, plus the meaning of the sequence compounded from them. The two sub-sequences need not be the ICs of the sequence.

However, the two meanings of old men and women are most readily accounted for in the following way. In the meaning 'women and old men', the sequence[24] belongs to that construction (noun or noun-phrase + and + noun or noun-phrase) which has the meaning of conjunction; the first noun-phrase belongs to the construction modifier + noun or noun-phrase. But in the meaning 'old men and old women', the sequence belongs to the construction modifier + noun or noun-phrase; the noun-phrase in turn belongs to the construction noun or noun-phrase + and + noun or noun-phrase.

The point is that although these are not the only constructions in terms of which the two meanings of old men and women could be accounted for, they are nevertheless the most efficient ones. If, for example, we switched the explanations given above and accounted for old men and women in the meaning 'women and old men' as an instance of modifier + noun or noun-phrase, we could do it, in view of our postulate that every sequence has a meaning; but the meaning would be enormously involved: the class 'modifier + noun or noun-phrase' with this meaning would be by definition a different construction from the same class with the usual meaning, and the resulting construction would be a very uncommon one, supported only by other wrong analyses. But no consistently carried out system of wrong analyses will be as efficient as a set of right analyses; indeed, it is precisely this fact which is the criterion of a right analysis.

§36. Now—and this is the relevance of constructions in the theory of ICs—the IC-analysis should reflect the construction. Consequently, when the same sequence has, in different occurences, different meanings and therefore (provided that the meaning-difference cannot be ascribed to the morphemes taken separately) different constructions, it may have different IC-analyses.[25] The IC-analysis of a sequence often reflects the semantic analysis of what the sequence means, but the meaning needs to be considered in making the analysis only when two occurrences of the same sequence (or of two sequences belonging to all the same sequence-types) have meanings incompatible with each other.

§37. Such cases exhibit homonymous constructions, analogous to homonymous morphemes. Perhaps the most current meaning of the word 'homonym' is that two morphemes (or two sequences in general) are homonyms if they are phonemically identical but different in meaning. A narrower definition is that two morphemes are homonymous if they differ in meaning alone. It follows that two morphemes cannot be homonymous in this narrower sense unless they belong to all the same morpheme-classes, for otherwise they would be grammatically as well as semantically different.[26]

§38. Homonymy of constructions is similar in that there are sequences such that two occurrences of a given sequence will contain the same morphemes, belong to all the same sequence-classes, and yet have different meanings solely because they belong to different constructions. The difference between homonymy of morphemes and homonymy of constructions is that constructions may be only partly homonymous. Two constructions are wholly homonymous if every sequence that in some occurrences belongs to the one construction, in other occurrences belongs to the other; they are partly homonymous if some but not all sequences meet this condition. The two constructions exhibited by old men and women are only partly homonymous, because old men belongs to the same construction as old|men and women, but not to the same construction as old men|and|women; whereas men and women belongs to the latter construction but not to the former.[27]

§39. As an example of wholly homonymous constructions in English, consider compounds that are stressed on the prior member. One construction whose members are of this form ÁB has the mean-

[24] More strictly, every occurrence of it has that meaning.

[25] But there is also the case where two sequences, even of three or more morphemes each, have different constructions but the same analysis into ICs; e.g. go|to||the|||store (a) as a command, and (b) in answer to the question What are you going to do? So also we treat the cases where others would recognize a solitary IC (cf. §52) and the cases of wholly homonymous constructions (fn. 30).

[26] Special cases are presented by morphemes that have more than one morpheme-alternant. Thus, the four alternants of the English 3rd-singular morpheme /-z, -s, -ez, -0/, as in reads, writes, teaches, can, are respectively homonymous with four alternants of the plural morpheme, as in dogs, cats, horses, sheep, but not with the alternants that appear in oxen, children, geese, etc. But such cases do not concern us here.

[27] There are other constructions to which both (A) old|men and women and (B) old men|and|women belong, such as the noun-phrase construction; but these constructions are not responsible for the difference in meaning between A and B, and hence do not interest us here. Both the special construction of A and the special construction of B are compatible with all the more general constructions to which both A and B belong.

ing 'a B which is identical with or has the property of being (an) A'; examples: *lady-friend*, *he-goat*, *postoffice-building*.[28] A homonymous construction has the meaning 'a B of or connected with (an) A'; examples: *birthday*, *name-plate*, *lady-killer*. Since *friend* and *killer* belong to a number of focus-classes in common, and there is a compound *lady-friend* 'friend who is a lady', there should be a grammatically possible compound *lady-killer* 'killer who is a lady', homonymous with *lady-killer* 'killer (in a metaphorical sense) of ladies'.[29] If no such compound actually occurs, this fact is without grammatical significance.[30] Similarly, in actual occurrences *old men and children* generally has the meaning 'children and old men', since one does not speak of 'old children'. An analogue in homonymy of morphemes is that although *steak* and *stake* belong to all the same morpheme classes, /əjûwsiy-stéyk/ very seldom means 'a juicy stake'; the meaning of the morpheme *stake*, and the resulting meaning of *juicy stake*, exclude it.

It remains to note that just as there is often doubt whether to relegate a number of morpheme-occurrences to one morpheme with two meanings or to two homonymous morphemes, there may also be the same practical doubt with respect to constructions.

IV. Words

§40. People of some grammatical sophistication feel that there is something 'funny' about a phrase like *the president of the bank's daughter*. We have already (§6), in anticipation of the present section, formulated the principle which is the basis for this feeling: every word should be a constituent, and *bank's*, generally regarded as a word, is certainly not a constituent here.

Three solutions of the paradox are open to the grammarian: (1) abandon or qualify the principle; (2) maintain that *bank's* is a constituent; (3) admit that *bank's* is not a constituent but maintain that, in this occurrence, it is not a word either.

We do not flatly assert that the second alternative is absurd, but we do not envisage any plausible theory of ICs which would allow it to be true.

The third alternative admits of a subdivision. On the one hand, *the president of the bank* could be regarded as a sort of compound word, so that *president-of-the-bank's*, a derivative thereof, is also a single word. *Bank's*, therefore, is only a fragment of a word, like *writer's* in *typewriter's*. This solution is embraced by Bloomfield.[31] The other recourse is to regard the possessive morpheme *'s* as a separate word. Both alternatives offend common sense. Both views, as well as alternative (1) above, presuppose a clear definition or set of criteria for the word.

§41. Since the publication of Bloomfield's Language, the best general treatment of the word known to me is Nida's.[32] Nida distinguishes two kinds of criteria for determining what the words of a given language are: phonemic and grammatical. Juncture is a common marker of word-boundaries, though perhaps there is no language where every sequence that one would want to regard as a word is marked off, in every occurrence, by the occurrence of a juncture both at its beginning and at its end. It is also common, in languages possessing junctures, that those junctures occur not only at word-boundaries but in the interior of certain words (e.g. English *night-rate* /náyt-rêyt/). In many languages certain phonemic patterns signify the presence or (more commonly) the absence of a word-boundary; for instance, Japanese has an accent phoneme whose non-automatic occurrences in any one word are at most one. It is a prevailing fact that these phonemic indices of word-boundaries are incomplete; even in a language that includes a number of such signals, not every word-boundary in every occurring sentence is signalized by means of some combination of them.

§42. It must be borne in mind that wherever we have said that not every word is marked off in such-and-such a way, we have meant that not every sequence that one would want to consider a word is so marked. The grammarian, undertaking to characterize the words of a certain language, starts with a certain common-sense working conception of what a word in that language is, based largely on his conception of what a word is in his native language and in any others that he may have studied. He sets about to formulate his criteria explicitly, to modify them in case they conflict, and to supplement them if they are insufficient to decide, for any given occurrence of any sequence, whether it is a word or not.

§43. Because of their insufficiency, the phonemic criteria of a word must be supplemented, for every or nearly every language, by criteria of the second kind remarked by Nida, the grammatical. In some languages, indeed (apparently French is an example),

[28] Assuming these and our other examples to be compounds rather than word-sequences.

[29] Unless we choose to assume that there is no such word as *lady-killer* 'killer who is a lady', and conclude therefore that in this respect *friend* and *killer* belong to different focus-classes.

[30] In this example, as in all wholly homonymous constructions that have come to my notice, the IC-analysis is the same regardless of which construction the sequence belongs to. If a given sequence is to have different analyses into ICs according to the different constructions to which it belongs, it must necessarily contain at least three morphemes.

[31] Language §11.5 end. Also by Eugene A. Nida, Morphology 149–50 (Ann Arbor, 1946); Bloch and Trager, Outline of Linguistic Analysis 67 bottom (Baltimore, 1942).

[32] Chapter 7 of his Morphology (cf. fn. 31). Also noteworthy are Bloch's characterization of the Japanese word (Studies in Colloquial Japanese II: Syntax, Lang. 22.202–6, §§1.3–6 [1946]) and Chao's characterization of the Chinese word (op.cit. our fn. 20).

phonemic criteria are quite lacking. Classical Greek and Latin, as well as the other predominantly inflecting Indo-European languages, exhibit par excellence the word as a grammatically characterized unit: the majority of their words terminate in one of a small class of endings, verbal or substantival. Moreover, in Greek and Latin the order of morphemes within a word is rigid, but the order of words relative to each other is somewhat variable. This is not to say that word order in these languages is free or indifferent. There are standard orders in prose both colloquial and literary; verse too has factors — and not only meter — that determine the arrangement of words. But the prose orders are rather different from the verse orders, while the order of morphemes within a word is identical in all styles. Whether or not two orders of the same words have different meanings, they serve to emphasize words as shiftable units; whereas order within the word (excepting compounds) is meaningless precisely because it is automatic. This justifies a contrast between morphology and syntax, a contrast fortified by the phonemic, especially the accentual properties of the grammatically characterized words.[33]

In fact, the word is most solid as a unit in those languages where phonemic and grammatical criteria reinforce each other. Bloomfield's definition of a word as a minimal free form involves both criteria: considered as a phoneme-sequence, a word occurs in a phonemic zero-environment; considered as a morpheme-sequence, it occurs in a morphemic zero-environment.[34] The corollary that a word must be pronounceable in isolation likewise contains both criteria, for an 'unpronounceable' form may be so either because of its phonemic composition (e.g. the possessive 's by itself) or because it is a bound form (e.g. -ness with weak stress). A linguist would regard five and fif (as in fifty, fifth) as alternants of the same morpheme; but from the common-sense point of view it is alternants, not morphemes as such, that are pronounceable or not. And unpronounceability of both kinds is a partial reason why the possessive 's of England's is regarded by common sense as not being a word.

§44. When the phonemic and the grammatical criteria do not confirm each other, they may sometimes be used to supplement each other. If certain sequences belonging to a particular sequence-class are phonemically marked as single separate words, then we may consider all members of this sequence-class to be words whether or not they are phonemically marked.

§45. One of the points implied in Harris's article From Morpheme to Utterance is that in describing what utterances occur in that language, the distinction between morphology and syntax may be dispensed with; that the word is not a necessary, perhaps not even a useful unit of grammar. This is not to deny that at some point in the description of a language one should state whatever correlations may obtain between phonemic and grammatical features of morpheme-sequences, nor that for some languages this statement is most efficiently cast in the form of a definition of a word. It is only to propose that in doing one part of the task of grammar, namely describing the utterances of the language in question, the division into a morphological phase and a syntactic phase of this description may be given up.

§46. We do not here offer any opinion on this proposal. The task of IC-analysis is the task not of describing what utterances occur, but of describing, after these utterances have been given, what their constituents are. In practice, the grammarian studying a language will prosecute both inquiries at once, and will have made up his mind about both before he expounds either; but this fact of procedure does not concern us. Nor do we mean, when we say that all the grammatically possible utterances of a language are presupposed as data for the IC-analysis, that only a complete characterization of them is presupposed — a characterization which may well be in terms of the constituents of those utterances. This is circularity of exposition, but it is not vicious, nor is it avoidable except by basing the grammatical description, including the IC-analysis, on a finite sample of text. The distinction between methods of discovery and methods of proof (or more generally, methods of exposition), and between the order in which certain facts are discovered and the order in which they are expounded, is familiar to logicians. In descriptive linguistics, discovery consists in finding the best scheme in terms of which to describe the facts; it is not strictly part of the exposition to show that that scheme is the best.

§47. But the word is a relevant unit in IC-analysis. Many analyses can be made without taking word-boundaries into account; but many others are left undetermined. In such cases, if a consideration of word-boundaries and the principle that every word is a constituent will decide the analysis, it seems to us reasonable to consider word-boundaries and to invoke this principle. In other words, the word is not a dispensable unit in the present theory of IC-analysis.

33 The term grammar is here used in the narrower sense, as coordinate with phonemics, rather than including it. In this narrower sense, grammar is commonly divided into morphology and syntax: the former treating the internal grammar of words (§15), the latter their external grammar and the sequences of words; but the division does not apply to languages that lack words as a distinct kind of unit. Harris (op. cit. our fn. 2) shows how it is possible to ignore the distinction between morphology and syntax even in other languages (cf. §45). The term taxemics has been suggested to me to cover the narrower sense of grammar; I have not adopted it, because it rests on Bloomfield's unclearly defined term taxeme.

34 See fn. 6 and Bloomfield, Language 168–9. Bloomfield's definition must be suitably modified if the sentence-intonations and certain stresses (§66) of such a language as English are regarded as morpheme-sequences rather than (op.cit. 163, 169) as modulation, one of the four 'ways of arranging linguistic forms'.

§48. Harris also says (178–9) ((150–1)): 'The procedure outlined here could be paralleled by a series of substitutions beginning with the whole utterance and working down, instead of beginning with single morphemes and working up. In that case we would have to find formal criteria for breaking the utterances down at successive stages. This is essentially the difficult problem of determining the immediate constituents of an utterance. It is not clear that there exists any general method for successively determining the immediate constituents, when we begin with a whole utterance and work down. In any case, it would appear that the formation of substitution classes [in our terminology, focus-classes] presents fewer theoretical difficulties if we begin with morphemes and work up.'

But the major purpose of this paper is to show that expansions and focus-classes, the very concepts developed in Harris's paper, furnish the basic apparatus necessary for a theory of ICs. And a theory of ICs is not necessarily bound to the order of 'working down'. Regardless of whether the exposition of the descriptive grammar works up or works down, the constituents of any utterance will be the same. As for the order of discovery, which is what Harris has in mind, 'working up' will systematically determine the focus-classes of a language; but we have pointed out that a complete set of IC-analyses must rest on more than the focus-classes: it must also rest (a) on the importance of each focus-class, in respect of diversity of members and in respect of the number of environments characterizing it, and (b) on the constructions.

§49. There are instances where the pattern of the language opposes treating every word as a constituent. In Japanese, the suffix -rasíi 'has the appearance of' forms compounds with nouns (kodomorasíi 'looks like a child'), noun phrases (kodomo norasíi 'looks like a child's' [cf. kodomo no 'of a child']), verbs (tabetarasíi 'appears to have eaten') and certain other sequences. Now kodomorasíi, norasíi, tabetarasíi (orthographic abbreviations for kodómórásíi, norásíi, tabétárásíi, where the acute marks a high-pitched syllable) are to be regarded as single words, because if -rasíi (i.e. -rásíi) is regarded as a separate word (1) it will be the only word in the entire language accented on both the first and the second syllables; (2) in no other case is a word with accent on the final syllable immediately followed by one with accent on the first syllable.[35] On the other hand, purely syntactical considerations favor the IC-analysis kodomo no][rasíi, etc.

Instead of proclaiming, therefore, that every word in every language must be a constituent of any sequence in which it occurs as a part, the most we may say is that every word should be so regarded unless it engenders a conflict or complication in the description of the language.

§50. In Japanese itself the principle is useful, and even enables us to treat the class of particles as a word-class.[36] Sequences such as ano hito wa 'as for that person', ano hito ni 'to that person', ano hito kara 'from that person' are undoubtedly to be analyzed ano hito][wa, ano hito][ni, ano hito][kara; this is shown very easily by the method of expansion, since ano hito 'that person' is an expansion of hito 'person', but hito wa 'as for the person', hito ni 'to the person', and hito kara 'from the person' are not expansions of anything. The phonemic criteria (in Japanese, occurrence as a minimum pause-group, and the accent) do not determine the particles wa, ni, and kara either to be words or not to be words; and since none of the other particles ever has an accent except in phonemic environments that leave its status as a word indeterminate, we derive no help from the principle that a given sequence is a word if and only if every other member of the same sequence-class is a word (see §44). But if hito wa were one word (so that ano hito][wa would be two words), the principle that every word is a constituent would be needlessly contravened; therefore we regard the particles as separate words.

V. Multiple and discontinuous constituents

§51. Up to this point we have proceeded as though every IC-analysis divides a constitute into two ICs, each a continuous sequence. We have now to consider other possibilities of analysis and the circumstances under which they may reasonably be resorted to.

First, are there sequences which are best analyzed into fewer or more than two ICs?

Second, is it ever useful to recognize constituents that are discontinuous?[37]

For example, should not the sequence men, women, and children be analyzed into three coordinate ICs: men,][women,][and children? And should not the sequence Call your friend up be analyzed into the continuous constituent your friend and the discontinuous constituent call ... up?

§52. In our system, no constitute has only one IC. (It will be recalled that single morphemes are not called constitutes.) Anything that has ICs at all, has two or more. Other systems, however, allow solitary

[35] Bloch, op.cit. [our fn. 32] §1.5 and fn. 7. Cases where one would expect this result are rare; and when they do occur (perhaps in personal names?) the prior word morphophonemically loses its accent (Bloch, op.cit. fn. 5).

[36] Bloch, op.cit. §1.5.

[37] Bloomfield recognizes the possibility of solitary constituents (Language, 218) and of multiple constituents (194, lines 10–11; 227, line 6). He is followed by Pike, Taxemes and Immediate Constituents, Lang. 19.70, line 1 and §4.1. Bloch and Trager (op.cit. [our fn. 31] 67) recognize 'usually ... two and only two immediate constituents'. The same view seems to be taken by Nida (Morphology 81; Syntax §2.5.3 et passim [Ann Arbor, 1946]). Pike further admits discontinuous constituents (op.cit. §§4.12–4).

constituents. Thus Bloch[38] describes every Japanese sentence as consisting of one or more clauses; if there is but one clause, it is the sole IC of the sentence, though it may have, as a clause, two ICs of its own. Again, in line with Bloomfield's handling of modulation, one might describe the Japanese verbal noun yasumí 'vacation' as derived from the infinitive yasúmi 'rest' by applying the taxeme of modulation (here a shift of accent). Then the infinitive would be the sole IC of the noun, though consisting, in turn, of the two ICs yasúm- (the verbal base) and -i (the infinitive ending).[39]

The system that we have set up does not ignore the facts, it only treats them in a different way: in terms of constructions. When a clause is a sentence by itself, it participates in the sentence construction as well as in the clause construction; but (like the English example come here, see §34 and fn. 25) its ICs are the same whether it participates in both constructions or only in the one. The noun yasumí, on the other hand, we would describe as containing the infinitive yasúmi plus a morpheme, or else as replacing a morpheme contained in yasúmi by some other—depending on how the accent-phoneme is handled morphologically. Whatever the details, the Japanese accent-phoneme, like any phoneme of any language, would always be assigned to some morpheme, either by itself or as part of a phoneme-sequence, and not to a 'grammatical process' of modulation (cf. fn. 34).

§53. We propose to recognize multiple (three or more) ICs only under one definite condition. Given a constitute consisting of three continuous sequences A, B, and C, then, if no reason can be found for analyzing it as AB|C rather than A|BC, or as A|BC rather than AB|C, it is to be analyzed into three correlative ICs, A|B|C. Similarly, four ICs may be recognized when no analysis into two and no analysis into three ICs is recommended, and so on.

§54. A possible example is furnished by English noun-phrases of the type A and B. A and never occurs as a constitute except before a noun (or noun-phrase) B; and B never occurs as a constitute except (a) after a noun A and (b) as a separate clause. Now the latter occurrence is not an argument for the analysis A|and B. And women occurs as an independent sentence, and its ICs there are and and women. But its focus-class is of the structure and + clause: the same basic structure as in and|I saw it myself or and|then we'll go home. Correspondingly, the basic constructional meaning of and|women is that of a clause, not of a noun-phrase. When and women occurs at the beginning of a clause, it is never a constitute: and|women were lined up hours ahead of time, not and women|were lined up etc. Thus it is perfectly clear that the sentence and women does not support the analysis men|and women. So the theory of IC-analysis developed in this paper gives no basis for choosing between men|and women and men and|women; consequently, we adopt the tripartite analysis men|and|women.

With conjunctive clauses it is different. He huffed and he puffed is undoubtedly to be analyzed he huffed |and he puffed; each of the two constituents has great freedom of combination, including occurrence as a separate sentence. When and he puffed occurs as a separate sentence it participates in the sentence construction, which of course it does not when preceded by he huffed. But there are some constructions common to it in both occurrences (the clause construction, for instance); whereas there is no single construction in which the two occurrences of and women —(a) as a separate sentence and (b) in men and women —participate.

But when there are three or more clauses connected by and, the number of ICs is the same as the number of clauses. There is no reason to analyze (A) H^{3}e h^{2}uffed (B) ^{3}and he p^{23}uffed (C) ^{3}and he bl^{2}ew the house d^{24}own (with a pause before each and) into AB|C rather than into A|BC, or conversely; therefore the three clauses are three correlative ICs of the sentence.

Should a detailed study of English reveal some here unnoticed reason for analyzing men|and women rather than men and|women, or conversely, then of course the phrase would simply cease to be an example; the proposal stating when we must recognize three or more ICs would not thereby be impugned.

§55. The same basic rationale that leads to the proposal discussed above prescribes the conditions for discontinuous constituents. Analysis of the English king into English and the ... king yields constituents of much greater independence and mobility than the analysis into the and English king. Moreover, the pattern of poor|John and English|literature would be better imitated. But if the admission of multiple and of discontinuous constituents were subject to no other restriction than yielding maximally independent constituents, IC-analysis would become a tremendously intricate affair. The possibilities requiring investigation would be enormously multiplied. A more orderly and manageable procedure is to extend the IC-system as far as possible on the basis of two continuous ICs for each constitute; and then to supplement this system and revise it where revision is called for by admitting the more complex kinds of analysis. In order to keep the revision at a minimum, we have proposed a restricting condition for multiple

38 Bloch, op.cit. §2.4. For a similar case in morphology, see Bloch, Studies in Colloquial Japanese III: Derivation of Inflected Words, JAOS 66.305, §1.3.

39 For the factual data, see Bernard Bloch and Eleanor H. Jorden, Spoken Japanese, 135, Note 5.15, and 504, Note 16.18 (New York, 1945–46). Bloch no longer insists on this way of describing the derivation.

ICs, and we propose now the following for discontinuous ICs: A discontinuous sequence is a constituent if in some environment the corresponding continuous sequence occurs as a constituent in a construction semantically harmonious with the constructions in which the given discontinuous sequence occurs. The phrase 'semantically harmonious' is left undefined, and will merely be elucidated by examples.

§56. English noun-modifiers are of three sorts: those that precede, those that follow, and those that partly precede and partly follow the noun or noun-phrase that they modify. Examples are: (1) [a] very interesting [book], only [the finest quality], too expensive [a choice], such [a method], [a] mere [boy]; (2) [a scholar] second to none, [a contract] signed by the manager, [a possession] more priceless than jewels; (3) [a] better [movie] than I expected, [the] best [friend] in the world, [an] easy [book] to read, too heavy [a box] to lift. Of the examples of type (3), all but best ... in the world satisfy the proposed condition for being discontinuous constituents: the corresponding continuous sequences all occur after a copula; thus (4) [this movie is] better than I expected, [this book is] easy to read, [this box is] too heavy to lift. And the constructional meaning of these predicates (better than I expected, etc.) is harmonious with—is in fact almost or quite the same as—the meaning which the corresponding discontinuous constituents bear in the examples under (3): in each case a certain property is meant, whether the larger construction into which it fits is that of modification (3) or of predication (4).

§57. Best ... in the world is chosen as an example of a discontinuous modifier that perhaps does not qualify as a constituent. At least it does not occur in the environment (4).[40] The nearest approximation is [as a friend, he's] the best in the world. Predicates of the type the + adjective or adjective-phrase are limited; generally the adjective (if singular) is either a comparative or superlative or else an ordinal. In these sequences, it seems that a noun is always 'understood', e.g. friend after best in he's the best in the world, or day after fifth in the fifth of January. If so, the construction of best (and a fortiori of best in the world) in he's the best is different from that of easy or easy to read in this book is easy to read, and consequently best ... in the world is not a constituent of the best friend in the world.

§58. The clause this possession|is||more priceless than jewels, analyzed as shown, justifies admitting the corresponding discontinuous constituent in a more priceless possession than jewels—provided that the constructional meanings are harmonious in the required sense. By harmonious we mean, approximately, identical except insofar as there is a necessary reason for difference. If the predicate I: more priceless than jewels is harmonious in this sense with the discontinuous modifier II: more priceless ... than jewels, then what is its relation to the continuous modifier III: [a possession] more priceless than jewels? We are committed to recognizing at least a potential difference of meaning between II and III. (1) It may be that I has two distinct senses, in one of which its constructional meaning definitely corresponds to that of II, in the other to that of III. If so, there is no problem. Or (2) it may be that I has only one sense, which definitely corresponds to that of II rather than of III, or to that of III rather than of II, insofar as the senses of III and II differ from each other. In this case, again there is no problem; it is merely a fact that the distinctive sense of II (or of III) is not expressed by an adjective phrase used in predicate rather than in modifier position. But (3) I may have a unitary sense, and yet at the same time the difference of meaning between II and III may be so tenuous that neither the distinctive meaning of II nor the distinctive meaning of III can be detected in the meaning of I. This possibility is troublesome. Perhaps an adequate definition of harmony could be devised according to which the meaning of I is harmonious with the meanings of both II and III, even though the meanings of II and of III are not harmonious with each other.

§59. Besides modifiers, there is another important type of discontinuous constituent: a clause interrupted by an intrusive phrase, as in the sentence His father, according to John, is the richest man in Scarsdale. These interrupted clauses meet the proposed test, since the intrusion can simply be dropped and then what was discontinuous becomes continuous, with practically the same constructional meaning.

§60. Verb phrases of the type verb + prepositional adverb (up, away, through, etc.) may seem to deserve being treated as constituents even when they are discontinuous; wake up your friend and wake your friend up are almost synonymous. But there are other pairs like see through your friend 'discern your friend's sham or false front' and see your friend through 'aid your friend through to the completion of his project' where a difference in meaning stands out.[41] The meaning-difference here can be accounted for in several ways. (1) Perhaps different meanings of through are involved. (2) Perhaps the construction of see through your friend does not bear the same semantic relation to that of see your friend through as the construction of wake up your friend bears to that of wake your friend up, and the difference reflects itself in the IC-analysis as follows: see||your friend|through vs. see through|your friend. In other words, perhaps see ... through is not a constituent. Or (3) the analysis may be see...through|your friend but the discontinuous constituent see...through participates in a construction that is different in mean-

40 Usages such as [Washington was] first in the hearts of his countrymen are not regular or free.

41 Note that see through him occurs, often bearing the emphatic morpheme on through; but wake up him does not, no matter how accented.

ing from that of the continuous constituent see through and not harmonious with it; the difference in the constructional meanings of see through and see...through would account for the difference in meaning between see through your friend and see your friend through.

§61. Pike (op.cit. §4.14) suggests analyzing the noun-phrase the large books, the important papers, the new pens as 'a complex endocentric phrase with head and attribute alike consisting of noncontiguous members', viz. the large...the important...the new + books...papers...pens. By our proposed criterion, books...papers...pens could be a discontinuous constituent, but the large ... the important ... the new could not. And indeed no reason is apparent why the above noun-phrase should not be analyzed as a 'coordinative endocentric' sequence (Bloomfield 195) of three ICs, each IC being a 'subordinative endocentric' sequence (ibid.).

§62. Analysis of the English king into English and the ... king satisfies our proposed condition for discontinuous constituents. If this analysis be accepted, then the analysis of the king of England needs reconsideration. For one of the arguments in favor of the|king of England was its basic conformity with the|English king. The identical argument, applied to the new analysis English + the ... king, would equally tolerate the king|of England, which after all seems to be the analysis favored by common sense. The noun-preceding modifier English and the noun-following modifier of England belong then to about the same focus-classes, as do the king (conjointly with its discontinuous counterpart the ... king) and proper names like John. The English king and poor John would then have corresponding analyses: English + the ... king, poor + John.

There is much to be said for this proposal to admit discontinuous phrases as well as (§56) discontinuous noun-modifiers. We here merely point out the possibility, and the fact that it is compatible with our suggested criterion of §55.

VI. English Juncture, Stress, and Pitch

§63. Most of our examples in this paper have been drawn from English, though not even a hint of a comprehensive IC-system for English has been given. However, one topic is so central that at least brief attention must be paid to it: the topic of the prosodic morphemes, juncture, stress, and pitch. Our treatment applies, mutatis mutandis, to a number of other languages, but we shall not point out the parallels.

The English phonemes—and, by extension of sense, the morphemes—of juncture, stress, and pitch, are called prosodic, modulational, or suprasegmental.[42] Applied to stress and pitch, these terms mean that the simple linear or one-dimensional order of segmental morphemes[43] is complicated into a two-dimensional one by the occurrence of stresses and pitches. In the sentence What is it? /hw^{3}àt-^{2}íz^{4}it/, we may consider the stress phoneme /´/ and the pitch phoneme /2/ as occurring simultaneously with the first occurrence of the vowel phoneme /i/.[44] Now since a linear series is the easiest to deal with, we may try to convert What is it? into a strictly linear series like the following: /hw3`at-2´iz4it/. But the sequence of phonemes /324/ constitutes (an alternant of) one single morpheme; by converting the two-dimensional order of phonemes to one dimension, certain morphemes (e.g. /324/) have been made phonemically discontinuous which were continuous before the conversion (cf. §88 and fn. 52). This is the difficulty: this is why one distinguishes between segmental phonemes and morphemes on the one hand, and suprasegmental ones on the other. Juncture is reckoned as suprasegmental instead of segmental, in spite of its not being simultaneous with anything else, for the grammatical reason that in its distribution and in its meaning it resembles stresses and pitches more than vowels and consonants.

We do not flatter ourselves that the following treatment will satisfy anyone. The disagreement will reflect the small amount of widespread discussion that the subject has received. Because of the exploratory nature of our proposals, we have aimed at a system which is conservative at the expense of being cumbersome, preferring this to one that is economical but liable to be scuttled by the discovery of some irreducible fact that it cannot embrace.

§64. Juncture. The validity of juncture phonemes is open to grave doubts on phonetic grounds. Linguists find themselves tempted to institute 'junctures' simply as notational devices for reducing the number of phonemes. For instance, what phonetic warrant is there for saying that night-rate differs from nitrate by /t-r/ vs. /tr/ rather than by /Tr/ or /tR/ vs. /tr/? Strictly, ought we not to say that night-rate differs phonemically from nitrate either in containing a different single t-like phoneme before the /r/ or else a different r-like phoneme after the /t/?

We assume that these questions can be answered somehow and that the English juncture phoneme can

42 Bloomfield, Language 163; George L. Trager, The Theory of Accentual Systems, Language Culture and Personality 131–45 (Sapir Memorial Volume; Menasha, Wis., 1941); Bloch and Trager, op.cit. 41. For further references see R. S. Wells, The Pitch Phonemes of English, Lang. 21.28 fn.10 (1945).

43 A morpheme is called segmental if each of its one or more morpheme-alternants consists either of one or more vowels and consonants (with or without stresses /ˆ/ or /`/), or else of nothing at all (a zero-alternant).

44 Bloomfield (Language 113) proposes to phonemicize the contrast between a name and an aim in terms of stress rather than of juncture: /ə ńeym/ vs. /ən éym/ rather than /ənéym/ vs. /ən-éym/. This is a good suggestion, but since the cases of contrast in English between ĆV and CV́ are relatively few, we retain here the more customary notation.

be salvaged.[45]

Whether pause at the beginning and at the end of an utterance may be regarded as an allophone of juncture, and whether more than one juncture should be recognized in some dialects and styles of English, are minor questions in the present discussion. Pause, and as many junctures as there are, all behave alike in IC-analysis and all have generically similar meanings.

§65. There are pairs of phrases differing phonemically only in that one contains, the other lacks, a juncture; e.g. thank you /θǽŋkyùw/ and /θǽŋk-yùw/, at your leisure /ætyurlə́žər/ and /æ̀t-yurlə́žər/. There is some discernible difference of meaning between the two members of each pair, if we understand 'meaning' in a very wide sense that includes stylistic overtones such as meticulousness of speech, etc. It is reasonable to say, therefore, that the juncture here contributes to the meaning of the whole phrase, hence that it has a meaning, and hence that it is a morpheme.

In night-rate it is less apparent that the juncture has a meaning. There is no /náytrêyt/ containing the morphemes night and rate with which night-rate is in minimal contrast. But it is a valuable principle of linguistics that every phoneme in a given utterance belongs to one and only one morpheme. So the juncture of /náyt-rêyt/ belongs either to /nayt-/ or to /reyt-/ or to a morpheme by itself. General considerations make the third way of considering it seem wisest: juncture, wherever it occurs, is a morpheme —though often with no detectable meaning.

§66. Stress. The stress symbolized /´/ is here considered to constitute a morpheme by itself, wherever it occurs, with the generic meaning of emphasis. Every sentence contains at least one occurrence of /´/, and therefore at least one occurrence of the emphatic morpheme.[46]

§67. Whereas the stress /´/ is 'skimmed off' from the segmental morphemes, the other two stress-phonemes /ˆ/ and /`/ remain as parts. This treatment gives rise to systematic sets of morpheme-alternants. In a blackbird /əblǽk-bə̂hrd/, bird occurs in the alternant /bə̂hrd/, but black occurs in the alternant /blæk/, because the /´/ belongs to a different morpheme. But in a black bird /əblæ̂k-bə́hrd/, bird occurs in the stressless alternant /bəhrd/, and black occurs in the alternant /blæ̂k/. The stress /´/ is treated differently from /ˆ/ and /`/, in spite of its phonetic relationship, because its grammatical and semantic roles are different.

§68. The alternants of each morpheme may be conveniently classified into ranks according to the stresses they contain. Those of the first rank contain /ˆ/; those of the second rank contain /`/ but not /ˆ/; those of the third rank contain no stress-phonemes. Each rank may be subdivided according to the other stress-phonemes that enter into the alternants of that rank. Thus the morpheme Balaclava has two alternants of the first rank: /bæ̂ləklæ̂və/ (as in B. helmet) and /bæ̂ləklævə/. The latter occurs in the presence of the emphatic morpheme; the phonemic result of combining these two morphemes is /bæ̂ləklǽvə/. When the morpheme-alternant that occurs in the presence of the emphatic morpheme contains two or more unstressed syllabics, there is no way of knowing, from inspection of that alternant alone, which of these the stress /´/ of the emphatic morpheme will coincide with—unless one of the syllabics occurs, when preceded or followed by particular non-syllabics, only in conjunction with /´/, /ˆ/ or /`/.[47]

§69. When a morpheme has alternants differing in their segmental phonemes, each of these may have stress-alternants. Thus clear has altogether five

[45] In order to preclude extravagances, one might adopt the requirement that every phoneme have at least one allophone consisting of an actual segment of sound, or else of a silence between or before or after such segments. This would involve assigning some segments simultaneously to more than one phoneme—e.g. assigning the first i of What is it? simultaneously to the vowel phoneme /i/, to the pitch phoneme /2/, and to the stress phoneme /´/. See R. S. Wells, op.cit. fn. 7. If we could reckon the silence at the beginning and end of an utterance as one allophone of juncture, we would be justified in positing another allophone, a zero-allophone, which occurs for example in night-rate.

[46] Except perhaps short sentences in which a normal occurrence of /´/ is replaced by an occurrence of the contrastive stress /¡/; see §70.

The system of stress-phonemes assumed in this paper is the one described by Bloch and Trager, Lang. 17.226–9 and Outline of Linguistic Analysis 47–8; but we differ from Bloch and Trager in regarding their phoneme of weak stress as simply the absence of a stress phoneme. The remaining three stress-phonemes are written as accents over vowel letters: /á/ = Bloch and Trager's 'loud stress', /â/ = 'reduced loud stress', /à/ = 'medial stress'.

I am especially indebted to Bloch for supplying the phonemic transcriptions of English in Part VI, which reflect his own dialect. To get a system of English phonemes that will apply, with modifications, to as many different dialects as possible, it has seemed wise to take as a descriptive basis a more complicated dialect like Bloch's, rather than a less complicated one like mine, which does not distinguish, for instance, between 'reduced loud' stress and 'medial' stress.

[47] Of course it is easy to design a notation that will show which syllabic potentially bears the stress, e.g. /bæ̂ləkl*æ*və/. This use of italics, like the leaving of a space between words in most phonemic transcriptions, has no phonemic status whatever; it is purely a mnemonic device equivalent to the statement that the stress /´/ (belonging to the emphatic morpheme) occurs—when it occurs at all in conjunction with a given segmental morpheme—on such-and-such a syllabic of that morpheme. Moreover, simply to cite the phonemic result of juxtaposing the segmental and the stress morpheme (e.g. /bæ̂ləklǽvə/, the result of juxtaposing /bæ̂ləklævə/ and /´/) conveys the same knowledge; and so does a comparison of alternants like /bæ̂ləklævə/ and /bæ̂ləklæ̂və/.

alternants: /klîhr, klihr, klæ̂r, klæ̀r, klær/, occurring respectively in clêar úp, it's cléar (accompanied by the emphatic morpheme), clârify thís, clàrificátion, and clárity (again accompanied by the emphatic morpheme). In general, for every alternant containing one or more occurrences of /ˆ/, there is an otherwise identical alternant in which one of these occurrences is lacking.[48] But many morphemes have no alternant containing /ˆ/; and those containing /ˋ/ do not in general alternate with otherwise identical ones lacking /ˋ/. Thus, /èyt/ as in rotate and calculate has no corresponding alternant /eyt/.[49]

§70. Contrastive stress is of two sorts: (1) the stress /ˊ/ is placed on a syllabic where /ˊ/ and /ˆ/ do not normally occur; (2) a contrastive stress phoneme /¡/, distinct from /ˊ/, either (a) replaces /ˊ/ or (b) is placed on a syllabic where /ˊ/ and /ˆ/ do not normally occur.[50] Cases (1) and (2b) involve morpheme alternants additional to the ones recognized above. Every morpheme without exception, provided that at least one of its alternants contains a syllabic, is subject to this kind of alternation; moreover, if it has more than one syllabic, /ˊ/ and /¡/ may fall on any of them.

There is often concomitant alternation within the syllabic itself. Thus, when the first syllabic of allusion is contrastively stressed (to distinguish the word, say, from illusion), the result is either /æ¡llúwžən/[51] or /ǽllûwžən/. Abstracting the contrastive and emphatic morphemes leaves /ælluwžən/ or /ællûwžən/, both different from the alternants /əlûwžən/ and /əluwžən/ normally encountered—the latter only in the presence of /ˊ/ and perhaps /¡/, yielding /əlúwžən/ and /əluw¡žən/ respectively. When contrastive stress is applied to a syllabic of a morpheme other than the one on which the ordinary emphatic morpheme /ˊ/ normally falls, we may consider either that the morpheme is used hypostatically or that it has a special complex of hypostasis and primary meaning together. In our present account, it is sufficient to deal with /ˊ/ and /¡/ as they combine with segmental morphemes in non-hypostatic uses; the simplification affects only the details, not the principles.

§71. In phonetic and phonemic fact, the emphatic and contrastive morphemes always occur simultaneously with some segmental morpheme. It is easy to treat them conventionally as being themselves segmental, so that we have only one string of morphemes to deal with—a string in which every morpheme either precedes or follows, immediately or mediately, every other morpheme. There are, indeed, two possibilities, between which the choice is indifferent: to consider that emphasis and contrast always precede, or that they always follow the morpheme with which they are phonetically and phonemically simultaneous.[52] But the conventional order of conversion must be rigidly uniform, even when it is inconvenient; otherwise we should be not merely rearranging the order of the morphemes but trying to improve upon it.

§72. The temptation is apparent in treating derivatives and compounds. Suppose that we consider emphasis and contrast as always following the modified morpheme. Then the sequence He speaks clearly /h^{3}iyspîyks-kl^{2}íhrl^{4}iy/ consists, in morphological terms, of the following sequence of morphemes (each morpheme being cited, as in fn. 52, in the alternant that actually occurs in the sequence to be described) hiy + spîyk + s + juncture + klihr + emphatic stress + liy + 324. Common sense would want to say that it is the whole word clearly, not only the morpheme clear, that is 'affected' or 'modified' or 'governed' by the morpheme of emphatic stress—in short, that the whole word is emphasized.

[48] Exceptions are morphemes like the loom in heirloom /éhr-lûwm/, which accidentally occur only in compound words.

[49] The verbs alternate /óhltərnèyt/, degenerate /dijénərèyt/, etc. might be regarded morphologically as derived from the adjective alternate /óhltərnət/, degenerate /dijénərət/, etc. by addition of a morpheme; or the adjectives might be regarded as derived from the verbs in the same way. If so, the morpheme /èyt/ has an alternant /ət/. Moreover, the nouns alternation, degeneration, etc. exhibit the alternants /êyš/ and /eyš/ of the same morpheme. But even so, the verb as a word by itself never shows an alternant /eyt/ or /ət/ or /eyš/.

[50] Bloch and Trager posit 'contrasting intonation /¡/, involving both a distortion of the normal sentence tone and an extra-loud stress' (op.cit. 52). But we may equally well view the stress, rather than the pitch, as the non-automatic feature. This allows us to group the phoneme /¡/, (now renamed 'the contrastive stress phoneme') with the phoneme /ˊ/, which it resembles (1) in always constituting a morpheme by itself, namely the contrastive morpheme, and (2) in its meaning and grammatical patterning.

[51] According to Bloch's oral statement.

[52] It would be possible to make emphasis and contrast phonemically as well as morphologically segmental, in the manner suggested in §63: what we now write as /hw^{3}àt-^{2}íz^{4}it/ would become, say, /hw3ˋat-2ˊiz4it/. Applying this procedure to all utterances would result in two types of discontinuity: (1) discontinuous morphemes and (2) discontinuous sequences. The morphemes would be discontinuous not in the sense treated by Harris (Discontinuous Morphemes, Lang. 21.121–7 [1945]), but in the sense in which the Arabic morphemes a...a...a 'past tense, 3rd person singular' and k...t...b 'write' are each discontinuous in the word kataba 'he wrote'. The sequences would be discontinuous in the sense discussed in Part V above; cf. §88. When an alternant of one morpheme phonemically intrudes into or interrupts an alternant of another morpheme, it is convenient in morphology to consider that one of the morphemes wholly precedes the other—e.g. that ktb, in the example just given, wholly precedes or wholly follows aaa. The reason is the one already mentioned: that a perfectly linear sequence of units is the easiest to deal with. Accordingly, the sequence /hw3ˋat-2ˊiz4it/ would be morphologically described, say, as follows—using plus-signs to separate single morphemes in the alternants that occur in the sentence What is it?: hwˋat + juncture + iz + ˊ + it + 324.

Again, blackbird is blæk + emphatic stress + juncture + bə̂hrd in some environments, e.g. It's a ( ); but blǽk + juncture + bə̂hrd in others, e.g. a ( ) pie. In the latter environments, it is homonymous with the two-word sequence black bird. One might want to say that blackbird, wherever it occurs, contains some morpheme that allocates the potential emphatic stress to the first morpheme of the compound rather than to the second, and that thus blackbird is everywhere distinguished from black bird. Further, one might want to implement this notion by setting up a zero-alternant of the emphatic morpheme; and this morpheme would then be present equally in (A) [It's a] blackbird and in (B) [It's a] blackbird [pie].

§73. The latter proposal can be dismissed at once, because /ˊ/ can occur simultaneously with black in (C) [It's a] blackbird [pie]. (So also can /¡/; in this environment, both /ˊ/ and /¡/ would be called instances of contrastive stress.) Therefore, in this environment, the alternant /ˊ/ and the proposed zero-alternant would contrast.[53]

This suggests a retrenchment. Instead of supposing a zero-alternant of the emphatic morpheme, suppose a morpheme with no phonemic shape, whose sole meaning or rather function is to signify whether the first or the second member of the compound potentially bears the emphatic morpheme; compare hóusebrôken and hêartbróken. Housebroken might be described morphologically as house + broken + ˊ- ; the fact that broken is itself a derivative—brok (alternant of break) + en—complicates the picture because heart + brok + en + ˊ- is an ambiguous notation. We must punctuate, perhaps, like this: (heart) + (brok + en) + ˊ-.

§74. The objections against the morphemes ˊ- and -ˊ are twofold. In the first place, as a check against extravagant and merely ingenious analyses, it is wise to observe the requirement that every morpheme have at least one alternant consisting of a phoneme or phoneme-sequence. This principle, parallel to the phonemic principle mentioned in connection with juncture, rules out zero-morphemes, that is, morphemes whose presence is known solely by their effect on other morphemes or by the presence of a certain meaning. But it sanctions a zero-alternant of a morpheme, provided the morpheme has other alternants besides. The proposed morphemes ˊ- and -ˊ would be zero-morphemes, i.e. having phonetic zero as their only alternant, and are therefore excluded by the requirement just mentioned. It might be thought that the phoneme /ˊ/ is one of their alternants, but it is not; for one phoneme, in any given occurrence, belongs to one and only one morpheme. Accordingly, if /ˊ/ is ever assigned to the morpheme ˊ- or -ˊ, it cannot in that occurrence belong to the emphatic morpheme. One last possibility is to say that each of the three morphemes ˊ-, -ˊ, and the emphatic has a zero-alternant: the zero-alternant of ˊ- and -ˊ appears when the emphatic is absent, and the zero-alternant of the emphatic appears when either ˊ- or -ˊ is present (these two morphemes being present only at the end of compound words. But /ˊ/, as the non-zero alternant of the emphatic, appears when both ˊ- and -ˊ are absent, and /ˊ/, as the non-zero alternant of ˊ- and of -ˊ, appears when the emphatic morpheme is present. By this juggling, the first objection is circumvented; ˊ- and -ˊ are then free to proceed to their doom in breaking against the second.

§75. The supposed morphemes ˊ- and -ˊ are figments. It is a fact that blackbird never occurs with stress /ˊ/ on bird, but sometimes with /ˊ/ on black. But this fact is not conveyed by any morpheme contained in blackbird, any more than the fact that blackbird is sometimes found before the plural s but never before the superlative est. It is simply a fact about the external grammar (cf. §15) of the word blackbird. If ˊ- and -ˊ be regarded not as the names of morphemes but as symbols of environments analogous to such writings as it's a ( ) and the ( )est thing I ever saw, then it is true to say that blackbird occurs in the (partial[54]) environment ˊ- but not in the environment -ˊ, just as it is true to say that blackbird occurs in the environment it's a ( ) but not in the environment the ( )est thing I ever saw. Having decided to treat the two-dimensional array of morphemes ÁB as the one-dimensional array AˊB, we must accept the result that AB becomes a discontinuous sequence A...B. However, this A...B passes our proposed test for discontinuous constituents. So we may say that the sequence black + emphatic stress + juncture + bird contains the ICs (1) black + juncture + bird and (2) emphatic stress; for elsewhere—viz. in the absence of emphasis—the sequence black + juncture + bird occurs as a continuous sequence. The problem could not be solved simply by considering the emphatic morpheme to precede rather than follow what phonetically it coincides with, since in that case the exactly analogous difficulty would be presented by those compounds that occur in the environment -ˊ, e.g. hêartbróken.

§76. It is, as we have said, a fact of the external grammar of blackbird that it occurs in the environment ˊ- but not in -ˊ; a fact, let us add now, tied up with the construction. A nearly minimal pair like hóusebrôken and hêartbróken clearly shows the meaning-difference between compounds of the structure AˊB and those of the structure ABˊ.

53 Though not minimally; for when blackbird is contrastively stressed with /ˊ/, pie appears in the alternant /pây/, unaccompanied by the emphatic morpheme. All the sentences (A), (B), and (C) contain the same pitch-morpheme, though in different alternants.

54 See §11.

The basic unsoundness of regarding ´- and -´ as morphemes is that it involves placing different occurrences of these morphemes in different relative segmental positions, even though in all the occurrences their suprasegmental phonemic position is the same. Suppose two sequences of morphemes ÁBC and D́EF, and suppose further, to free the case from complications, that each of the morphemes from A to F contains a single syllabic; and finally, suppose that ABC is a two-word sequence of the compound AB and the simple word C, while DEF is a single compound word consisting of the simple word D and the derivative word EF (night-watchman or the like). Then in terms of ´-, ÁBC would be regarded as A + B + ´- + C, but D́EF would be regarded as D + (E + F) + ´-.

For this inconsistency or lack of parallelism there is no justification. Phonemically, the proposed morpheme ´- occurs simultaneously with the first morpheme of each sequence; in converting or translating the two-dimensional phonemic order to a one-dimensional morphemic order, there is no warrant for embellishing the original order by translating it differently in extrinsically different cases. But, when this privilege is denied to ´- and -´, their main usefulness as morphemes is lost.

§77. Even a last vestige of apparent utility must be stripped away. One might grant that the emphatic morpheme must always be assigned a segmental position in the same mechanical way, and yet hold that it should be distinguished into several (or an indefinite number of) homonymous morphemes E_1, E_2, E_3 ..., each one governing a different scope. Thus ÁBC of the above example would contain the morphemes A + E_1 + B + C, in that order, and D́EF would contain D + E_2 + E + F. The morphemes E_1 and E_2 would both have /ˊ/ as their phonemic value, but E_1 would signify that the preceding and the following morpheme together make a compound word, whereas E_2 would signify that the preceding morpheme is the first member and the two following morphemes together are the second member of a compound (E_1 and E_2 etc. would have zero-alternants in the absence of the emphatic morpheme, and the emphatic morpheme would have a zero-alternant in their presence, just like ´- and -´ as formulated above.) The function of E_1, E_2, etc. would be threefold: (1) to identify compound words, (2) to show whether it is the first or the second member that potentially bears the accent, and (3) to show the scope of the emphatic morpheme when the latter is present—that is, to show how extensive a sequence is emphasized. (The scope is, in each case, the entire compound word.)

Our answer to this proposal is that it is not the business of linguistic analysis to invent morphemes that fulfill functions of this sort. These three pieces of information are conveyed by the constructions in which the morphemes A, B, C, etc. and the emphatic morpheme participate, not by some other morpheme additional to all of these. If the morphemes E_1, E_2, etc. were phonemically distinguished so that their existence and distinctness were indisputable, there would be no question and no difficulty about admitting them; but it is not a sufficient ground for positing a certain morpheme that it would be convenient to have it.

§78. Such is the line of reasoning that dissuades us from ever assigning /ˊ/ to any but the one emphatic morpheme. The fact that a certain sequence is a compound word is dealt with in our system, like the fact that this or that sequence is a word of any sort, by assigning it to a certain construction. If the sequence /blǽ̂k-bə̂hrd/ is a single word in some occurrences and a two-word sequence in others, then it belongs in the two occurrences to different constructions, and there is no need to create an invisible morpheme present in the one and lacking in the other.

§79. Pitch-morphemes and their sequences need less extensive discussion than stress because they have already been worked out in considerable detail by Kenneth L. Pike.[55] Each occurrence of a pitch-morpheme has a scope—i.e. a sequence of segmental morphemes with which it is coincident and which, in general, it semantically modifies or 'modulates'; and each pitch-morpheme has an indefinite number of alternants, varying according to the number of syllabics in their respective scopes. Another conditioning factor is the position of the emphatic morpheme. The following examples illustrate a few of the alternants of the most common pitch-morpheme, that of the indicative sentence:

(a) He bought a book. /h^{3}iybôht-əb^{24}úk/; alternant /333(24)/.
(b) He bought a book. /h^{3}iybôht-^{2}éy-b^{4}ûk/; alternant /3324/.
(c) He bought a book. /h^{3}iyb^{2}óht-^{4}əbûk/; alternant /3244/.
(d) He bought a book. /h^{2}íy-b^{4}ôht-əbûk/; alternant /2444/.

All of these alternants involve four syllabics; the cover symbol for the first three is 324, for the fourth 24 (cf. fn. 23 end). The parentheses in the first alternant indicate that the two pitch-phonemes /24/ occur on the same syllabic; this happens only when the last syllabic in the scope of a pitch-morpheme coincides with the stress /ˊ/ or /¡/.[56] In phonemic transcription and in citing alternants of pitch-morphemes (as for instance in §34), it is convenient to record only the first of a series of occurrences of the same pitch-

55 The Intonation of American English; cf. fn. 23.

56 An alternative notation would be to ascribe two occurrences of pitch-phonemes to every syllabic. Then the pitch-phonemes of (a) would be written /33333324/, which would indicate four syllabics. This is cumbersome, because each numeral in an even-numbered position would always be identical with the numeral immediately preceding it, unless it accompanies the last syllabic in the scope (the fourth, in our example) and furthermore this last syllabic bears the stress-morpheme /ˊ/ or /¡/.

phoneme—e.g. as in example (a) above, instead of writing /h^{3}iyb^{3}ôht-^{3}əb^{24}úk/—because such iterations are extremely common.

(e) H^{3}e bought a new b^{24}ook; alternant /3333(24)/.
(f) H^{3}e bought a handsome b^{24}ook; alternant /33333(24)/.
(g) H^{3}e bought an expensive b^{24}ook; alternant /333333(24)/.
(h) H^{3}e sl^{2}ipped ^{3}and f^{3}ell d^{24}own; alternant /3233(24)/.

§80. Some further alternants of the same pitch-morpheme of the indicative sentence are shown in the following examples:

The last alternant /3233(24)/ occurs instead of /3333(24)/ when there are two occurrences of the stress-phoneme /´/ in the sentence, one on the second syllable and one on the last.

§81. In this alternant /3233(24)/, the indicative-sentence pitch-morpheme is homonymous, except for its lack of pause between the two successive occurrences of the pitch-phoneme /3/, with the two-morpheme sequence consisting of the non-final pitch-morpheme (one of the pitch-morphemes orthographically symbolized by a comma) + the indicative-sentence pitch-morpheme, when these occur in the alternants /323/ and /324/ respectively. An example of this two-morpheme sequence is

(i) ^{3}If h^{2}é c^{3}ân, th^{3}èn ^{2}Í c^{4}ân.

If, as sometimes happens, this sentence is pronounced without pause between the two clauses, then it contains not two pitch-morphemes but one, exactly like (h) above. In this case, the construction alone shows that the sentence contains two clauses; but in sentence (i), the existence of two clauses is further shown—is reinforced—by the internal pause and by the pitch-morphemes that precede and follow it.[57] Such reinforcement or over-characterization is very widespread in language. Another example of it is the fact that in English yes-or-no questions the interrogation is usually signified both by the word-order and by the pitch-morpheme, though less commonly each of these occurs without the other.

§82. As the preceding discussion has implied, the scope of a pitch-morpheme is always taken to be a pause-group, a sequence of morphemes bounded at both ends, but not interrupted, by pauses.[58] In other words, every pause-group contains one and only one pitch-morpheme. Presumably, an internal pause in an utterance should be regarded as a phoneme (symbolized /#/),[59] and hence, like every other phoneme, should be assigned, in each of its occurrences, to one and only one morpheme. We may consider that pause, like juncture, belongs to a morpheme by itself. The sequence of pitch-phonemes /323/ is a separate morpheme when followed by /#/, as in sentence (i) above: /^{3}ifh^{2}íy-k^{3}ǣn # ð^{3}èn-^{2}áy-k^{4}ǣn/, and perhaps also when followed by the juncture phoneme /-/; otherwise the same sequence /323/ is part of a longer pitch-morpheme, as in sentence (h).

§83. It remains to state how juncture-, stress-, and pitch-morphemes function in IC-analysis.

One can be sure that any segmental morpheme which ends the scope of a pitch-morpheme also ends a constituent (or else the whole utterance); but it is not always true that the beginning of the scope of a pitch-morpheme similarly coincides with the beginning of a constituent (or of the utterance). If, in our orthography, we marked a parenthetical expression by placing a closing parenthesis) at the end but no corresponding opening parenthesis (at the beginning, we should have a parallel to the manner in which the beginning and end of the scope of a pitch-morpheme may be said to mark the limits of a constituent. In the sentence They served me a nice, juicy steak /ð^{3}ey-sə̀hrvdmiy-ən^{2}âys #j^{2}ûwsiy-st^{24}éyk/, the scope of the pitch-morpheme 32 is they served me a nice; but the analysis of the sentence into ICs must be into (1) the indicative-sentence pitch-morpheme 24 and (2) all the remaing morphemes of the sentence. These, in turn, divide into the 'actor' constituent they and the 'action' constituent served me a nice, juicy steak. The 'action' consists of me and the discontinuous constituent served...a nice, juicy steak; the latter, obviously, has the ICs served and a nice, juicy steak. The analysis of the remaining sequence, as it occurs in this sentence, shown by the following diagram:

ə‖nâys‖‖32‖‖‖‖ # ‖jûws‖‖‖‖iy‖‖‖2‖‖‖‖juncture‖‖steyk‖‖‖ ´

The constituent with which the pitch-morpheme is paired is not its whole scope in the sense that we have defined, but only the one word nice. The same morpheme 32 occurs a second time in the same sentence (in the alternant /2/), and is there paired with the word juicy.

[57] How to distinguish whether a given sequence of pause + A + pause + B + pause is one utterance with internal pause or two utterances, is a difficult question. Here we assume outright that the distinction is tenable.

[58] Two sequences A + B and A + pause + B may be very similar in meaning or quite indistinguishable; Bloomfield (Language §12.3) even calls the difference non-distinctive. However, for reasons stated in connection with juncture, it is unwise to say that pause—supposing that it has the status of a morpheme—exhibits a zero-alternant in the sequence A + B. The two sequences A + B and A + pause + B are close in meaning; but they are no more identical morphemically than I ate dinner there once and I ate a dinner there once. Nevertheless, facultative pause as defined by Bloch (Lang. 22.202) is useful in IC-analysis, because it is more fruitful to define words initially as minimum facultative pause-groups than as minimum free forms.

[59] Distinct from juncture, because there are environments in which both occur; e.g. after came in the sentence When he came I left.

§84. We conventionally assign to a pitch-morpheme the position immediately following the last morpheme of its scope. It must not be thought that this is merely a symbolic gesture aimed at simplifying the IC diagrams. If we wrote our symbols in one line but regarded the morphemes as nevertheless arrayed in a two-dimensional order, we should still have to deal with this order. By reducing the order of the morphemes themselves, and therewith the graphic order of their symbols, to a single dimension, we eliminate these complexities.

§85. It is the construction that reveals how many of the morphemes preceding a pitch-morpheme make up the partner with which it is paired. In the example of §83, the indicative-sentence morpheme 24 is paired with the entire remainder of the sentence, whereas the morpheme 32 (appearing as /32/ and /2/), in each of its occurrences, is paired with only a single word. We now take up another sentence. Line A gives the phonemic transcription; line B shows the sequence of morphemes as conventionally reduced to a single dimension; line C is a diagram of the analysis of the whole sentence into ICs.

(A) <u>He said so, but I doubt it.</u> /h^{3}iys^{2}éd-s^{3}ôw # b^{3}ətayd^{2}áwt^{4}it/

(B) hiy + se + ´ + d + juncture + sôw + 323 + # + bət + ay + dawt + ´ + it + 324

(C) hiy ||| se...||||||...d ||||| ´ |||| juncture |||| sôw || 323 | # | bət ||| ay |||| dawt |||||| ´ ||||| it || 324

§86. The same information about the IC-analysis of the sentence is conveyed less compactly but more explicitly by the following set of statements:

The ICs of the entire sentence are (1) hiy + se + ´ + d + juncture + sôw + 323;
(2) #;
(3) bət + ay + dawt + ´ + it + 324.
The ICs of (1) are (4) hiy + se + ´ + d + juncture + sôw; (5) 323.
The ICs of (3) are (6) bət + ay + dawt + ´ + it; (7) 324.
The ICs of (4) are (8) hiy; (9) se + ´ + d + juncture + sôw.
The ICs of (6) are (10) bət; (11) ay + dawt + ´ + it.
The ICs of (9) are (12) se + ´ + d; (13) juncture; (14) sôw.
The ICs of (11) are (15) ay; (16) dawt + ´ + it.
The ICs of (12) are (17) se ... d; (18) ´.
The ICs of (16) are (19) dawt + ´; (20) it.
The ICs of (17) are (21) se; (22) d.
The ICs of (19) are (23) dawt; (24) ´.

§87. This, then, is an exhaustive IC-analysis of the sentence <u>He said so, but I doubt it.</u> (To list the constructions in which the morphemes and the constitutes participate is a further task, not undertaken here). Needless to say, the analysis is tentative; we particularly call attention to the fact that at two different points it involves multiple constituents—in the analysis of the sentence as a whole into (1), (2), and (3), and in the analysis of the constitute (9) into (12), (13), and (14)—and once a discontinuous constituent—in the analysis of the constitute (12). An alternative possibility that especially deserves investigation is to divide the sentence as a whole into two ICs only: (1) the initial sequence ending with and including the pause #, and (2) all that follows the pause. If detailed investigation of English syntax should reveal both of these analyses to be untenable, a third possibility would be to divide the sentence into the morpheme 324 on the one hand and everything else on the other (like the example of §83).

For the treatment of juncture and pause as coordinate with the sequences that precede and follow them, compare the analysis of <u>men and women</u> into three ICs (§54).

§88. The matter of dimensions calls for one further remark. In the sentence <u>He said so, but I doubt it</u>, the pitch-morphemes 323 and 324 form a continuous suprasegmental sequence. In conventionally accommodating them in a one-dimensional segmental sequence, we lose this continuity: 323 + 324 now become 323 + ... + 324. As we have already pointed out (§84; cf. §63 and fn. 52), the difficulty is not simply notational: if we give up the two-dimensional order, we must give up its advantages as well as its defects. However, as it happens, it is no loss to let the sequence of pitch-morphemes become discontinuous; for we never wish to regard this sequence as a constitute.

If A and B are segmental sequences separated by a pause #, and S and T are pitch-morphemes having A and B as their respective scopes, then the analysis of the sentence

S T
A # B

presents no difficulties. The fundamental criterion of independence pronounces decisively in favor of AS | # | BT (or perhaps AS # || B | T), not A # B | ST.

[[Were it not that the phonology of English is outside the scope of the present volume, certain details of the English examples here would have required comment. As it is, the reader is simply warned that the theory of accent and intonation, very fluid in 1947, is still not quite solid today; specifically, the line between phonemics and morphophonemics here is not yet agreed upon... With respect to juncture, see the next article.]]

JUNCTURE IN MODERN STANDARD GERMAN

WILLIAM G. MOULTON

Language 23.212–26—1947

0. INTRODUCTORY. The following paragraphs attempt to give a partial phonemic analysis of modern standard German.[1] §1 establishes the segmental phonemes that are needed to describe utterances of only one syllable. §2 discusses the role that stress plays in German, describes the effect of stress on the segmental phonemes already established, and adds one new segmental phoneme (ž) which does not occur in monosyllabic utterances. §3 describes the inadequacies of this phonemic analysis, and shows how they may be removed either by giving phonemic status to a number of sounds which are not phonemic in monosyllabic utterances, or by assuming a segmental phoneme of open juncture. §4 gives the reasons why the present writer considers it preferable to assume a phoneme of open juncture. §5 discusses a possible second type of juncture, for which no explanation is offered.

1.0. TENTATIVE PHONEMIC ANALYSIS. We may begin a phonemic analysis of German by examining utterances of only one syllable.

1.1. SYLLABIC VOWELS. We find the following:

SHORT VOWELS: [ɪ ɛ ʌ ɔ ʊ ʏ œ],[2] as in [bɪn] 'am', [dɛn] 'for', [mʌn] 'man', [fɔn] 'from', [dʊm] 'dumb', [dʏn] 'thin', [gœnt] 'grants'.

LONG VOWELS: [i: e: a: o: u: y: ø:], as in [ši:n] 'shone', [ve:n] 'whom', [ha:n] 'rooster', [lo:n] 'pay', [t'u:n] 'do', [k'y:n] 'bold', [šø:n] 'nice'.

[1] Lacking a scientific definition of 'standard German', I have made an arbitrary one for the purposes of this paper. I have based my investigations on the speech of a single individual, a member of the upper middle class and a native of northern Germany. It is the speech of my wife, Jenni Karding Moulton, to whom thanks are due for her infinite patience as an informant. She was born in Flensburg, Schleswig-Holstein, but moved at an early age to Berlin, where she lived until 1938. She is one of those rather numerous middle- or upper-middle-class northern Germans who are almost totally ignorant of any Low German local dialect, having spoken only the local variety of High German from earliest childhood. Her knowledge of Low German is limited to a few jokes, songs, and poems. As an informant for 'standard German', such a speaker from the Low German dialect area is perhaps preferable to one from the High German dialect area. Speakers from the latter area usually grow up speaking the local dialect; their 'standard German' is usually just a more or less extensive modification of the local dialect.

A few peculiarities of the informant's dialect should be mentioned. She is a /ˈfunt/ *Pfund* 'pound' speaker; I have standardized this to /ˈpfunt/, etc. Where standard German demands long vowel plus /ren/, her speech shows either /rn/ or /ern/, in free variation: thus *führen* 'lead' is either /ˈfü:rn/ or/ˈfü:ern/; I have standardized this to /ˈfü:ren/, etc. Unvoiced /g/ is of course nearly always /x/: /ˈtra:gen/ 'carry', but /ˈtre:xt/ 'carries', /ˈtru:x/ 'carried', etc. Long vowels are often shortened before unvoiced /b d g/: /ˈgra:ben/ 'dig', but /dasˈgrap/ 'the grave'; /ˈra:deln/ '(to) bicycle', but /dasˈrat/ 'bicycle'; /imˈtsu:ge/ 'on the train', but /de:rˈtsux/ 'the train'.

W. Freeman Twaddell was kind enough to read an earlier draft of this article. I am indebted to him for a number of suggestions and corrections.

[2] [ʌ] is a higher-low central unrounded vowel. Note that the [ʌ] of [štʌt] 'city' is both shorter and higher than the [a:] of [šta:t] 'state'.

On the basis of these data, we may set up two sets of vowel phonemes: short /i e a o u ü ö/; and long /i: e: a: o: u: ü: ö:/. The long vowels may, if we wish, be further analyzed as consisting of short vowel plus /:/; and we may then state that /:/ lengthens and 'decentralizes' short vowels, i.e. causes high and mid vowels to be higher, low vowels to be lower, front vowels to be farther front, and back vowels to be farther back.[3]

1.2. NON-SYLLABIC VOWELS. We find the following:

AFTER SHORT VOWELS: [j w], as in [bʌjn] 'leg', [nɔjn] 'nine', [bʌwm] 'tree'.[4]

AFTER LONG VOWELS: [r],[5] as in [he:r] 'army', [vi:r] 'we'.

BEFORE LONG AND SHORT VOWELS: [j w], as in [ja:] 'yes', [pfwi:] 'phooey'.[6]

In analyzing the phonetic structure of German, we find that the clusters [ʌj ɔj ʌw] occur generally in the same surroundings as long and short vowels; we may therefore describe them as compound vowel phonemes—diphthongs. Since [j w] occur in complementary distribution with [ɪ ʊ], we may analyze them as allophones of /i u/. The syllabicity of /i u/ may be described as follows: except in the diphthongs (where they are always non-syllabic), they are syllabic before consonants, non-syllabic before vowels.

[r] occurs only after long vowels, as in the examples above, and is in complementary distribution with [ɣ], which occurs only after short vowels, as in [hɛɣ] 'Mr.', [vɪɣ] 'confused'. We may therefore analyze [r] and [ɣ] as allophones of a single phoneme /r/.

1.3. CONSONANTS. In utterances of only one syllable, we find the following consonants before and/or after vowels and diphthongs. Those followed by a hyphen occur only before vowels and diphthongs; those preceded by a hyphen occur only after vowels and diphthongs; and those unmarked occur in both positions.

VOICELESS STOPS, strongly aspirated: [p'- t'- k'-], as in [p'ʌs] 'passport', [t'ʌjl] 'part', [k'ʌjl] 'wedge'.

VOICELESS STOPS, unaspirated: [p t k ʔ-], as in [špa:s] 'fun', [štʌjl] 'steep', [ska:t] 'Skat' (a card game), [ʔʌjns] 'one'.

VOICELESS STOPS, weakly aspirated or unaspirated, in free variation: [-p -t -k], as in [di:p] 'thief', [hu:t] 'hat', [ɣɔk] 'skirt'.

VOICED STOPS: [b- d- g-], as in [bʌjn] 'leg', [dʌn] 'then', [gu:t] 'good'.

VOICELESS SPIRANTS: [f s š -ç -x h-], as in [fɪš] 'fish', [se:f] 'safe-deposit box', [šʊs] 'shot', [ʔɪç] 'I', [ʔʌx] 'oh', [ho:l] 'hollow'.

VOICED SPIRANTS: [v- z- ɣ], as in [vʌjn] 'wine', [zo:n] 'son', [ɣʌjn] 'pure'.

NASALS (voiced): [m n -ŋ], as in [me:l] 'flour', [nʌjn] 'no', [jʊŋ(k)] 'young'.

LATERAL (voiced): [l], as in [lʌwt] 'loud', [fɔl] 'full'.

[3] My informant has an eighth long vowel, roughly [ɛ:], which is used as the name of the letter *ä*, and as a mock-formal pronunciation for words in which [e:] is spelled *ä*. Thus, *spät* 'late' is normally [špe:t]; but a mock-formal pronunciation is [špɛ:t]. This may, if we wish, be analyzed as a marginal phoneme /ä:/.

[4] Plus [ʊj] in the one word [pfʊj] 'phooey'.

[5] Non-syllabic [r], syllabic [r̩], is a lower-mid unrounded vowel, halfway between central and back. (Limitations of the type font have led to the choice of this symbol.)

[6] Also, if we consider utterances of more than one syllable, in [ˈli:njə] 'line', [t'wʌˈlɛtə] 'toilet', [ˈjʌnwa:r] (beside [ˈjʌnu:a:r]) 'January', [zi:twʌˈtsjo:n] (beside [zi:tu:ʌˈtsjo:n]) 'situation', etc.

1.31. The voiceless stops [p t k] are strongly aspirated only in initial position before vowels or before [l n γ v] plus vowel: [p'ʌs] 'passport', [p'la:n] 'plan', [p'γʌjs] 'price'; [t'ʌjl] 'part', [t'γɔj] 'faithful'; [k'ʌjl] 'wedge', [k'lʌjn] 'small', [k'ni:] 'knee', [k'γʌjs] 'circle', [k've:r] 'crosswise'.[7] Initially before other sounds they are unaspirated: [pfʊnt] 'pound', [pšɔγ] 'Pschorr' (name of a brand of beer), [tse:n] 'ten'; there are no examples for [k]. Following any sound they are unaspirated: [špa:s] 'fun', [gɪps] 'plaster of Paris'; [štʌjl] 'steep', [zʌts] 'sentence'; [ska:t] 'Skat' (a card game), [zɛks] 'six'; but in final position they are weakly aspirated or unaspirated, in free variation: [di:p] 'thief', [hʌlp] 'half'; [hu:t] 'hat', [hʌnt] 'hand'; [γɔk] 'skirt', [mʌγk] 'mark'. (In the following paragraphs, the term 'aspiration' will refer only to strong aspiration.)

This distribution allows us to posit the phonemes /p t k/, with strongly aspirated, weakly aspirated, and unaspirated allophones in complementary distribution or free variation, as described above.

1.32. The voiceless spirants [ç] and [x] are in complementary distribution with each other: [x] occurs only after central and back vowels and semivowels: [bʌx] 'brook', [na:x] 'towards', [nɔx] 'still', [ho:x] 'high', [bγʊx] 'breach', [bu:x] 'book', [ʔʌwx] 'also'; [ç] occurs only after front vowels and semivowels, and after consonants: [mɪç] 'me', [p'ɛç] 'hard luck', [k'γi:çt] 'crawls', [ne:çst] 'next', [hø:çst] 'highest', [γʌjç] 'rich', [ʔɔjç] 'you', [ʔɛlç] 'elk', [mœnç] 'monk', [dʊγç] 'through'. We may therefore analyze [ç] and [x] as allophones of a single phoneme /x/.

1.33. The voiced spirant [γ] has already been analyzed as an allophone of a phoneme /r/ (§1.2). This /r/ occurs only immediately before and immediately after vowels. Before vowels it appears as [γ]: [γo:] 'raw', [štγo:] 'straw'; after short vowels it appears as [γ]: [hɛγ] 'Mr.', [ʔɪγt] 'errs'; after long vowels it appears as [r]: [he:r] 'army', [fy:rt] 'leads'.

1.34. The glottal consonants [ʔ] and [h] occur only initially, immediately before vowels. Since the vowels themselves never occur initially, we might analyze either [ʔ] or [h] as part of the allophone which any vowel shows in initial position. As long as we confine our investigation to utterances of only one syllable, however, the choice as to whether [ʔ] or [h] should be so analyzed is quite arbitrary; we may therefore postpone the matter for later consideration (in §3.2).

1.4. Segmental phonemes. The above analysis, based on utterances of only one syllable, allows us to posit the following segmental phonemes for German:

Vowel phonemes:

Short:	i	e	a	o	u	ü	ö	
Long:	i:	e:	a:	o:	u:	ü:	ö:	(ä:)
Diphthongs:	ai	oi	au	(ui)				

Consonant phonemes:

	Labial	Alveolar	Palatal	Velar	Glottal
Stops:	p b	t d		k g	ʔ
Spirants:	f v	s z	š	x r	h
Nasals:	m	n		ŋ	
Lateral:		l			

1.5. Stress. All utterances of only one syllable are spoken with two degrees of stress. Normally they begin with what we may call loud stress. This sets in with the first phoneme of the utterance and continues through the syllabic vowel. Then it drops quickly, so that the remainder of the utterance is spoken with what we may call weak stress. For example, the first two phonemes of /fiš/ 'fish' bear loud stress, while the third bears weak stress: [FIš]; contrast the louder /š/ and softer /f/ of /šif/ = [ŠIf] 'ship'. In the case of long vowels, the decrease in loudness occurs before the end of the vowel: /ze:/ = [ZE:] 'sea', /nu:n/ = [NU:n] 'now'; in the case of diphthongs, it occurs before the semivowel: /tau/ = [TAw] 'rope', /noin/ = [NOjn] 'nine'. This means that, as far as the distribution of stress is concerned, [:], like [j] and [w], functions as a non-syllabic.

Contrasting with loud stress is a greater degree of loudness, which we may call overloud stress. This likewise sets in with the first phoneme, and continues through the syllabic vowel; the rest of the utterance is again spoken with weak stress. If we place a double tick above the line at the point where overloud stress begins (always at the beginning), we get such contrasts as the following: with loud stress /rexts/ = [REXts] 'Go to the right'; with overloud stress /"rexts/ = [*RE*xts] 'Turn right quickly!', or 'Go right, not left!' This gives us two meaningfully distinctive degrees of stress.[8]

2.0. Completing the tentative analysis. We may now complete this tentative analysis by examining utterances of more than one syllable.

2.1. Distinctive degrees of stress. We find, first, that there is more than one meaningfully distinctive degree of normal loudness. For example, the phoneme sequence /ʔainflus/, spoken with the normal minimum of stress on the first syllable and with the normal maximum of stress on the second syllable, has one meaning: /ʔain'flus/ 'a river'. If the stress on the first syllable is increased, but still kept below that of the second, we get another meaning: /ˌʔain'flus/ 'one river'. If the stress on the first syllable is greater than that on the second (though this still remains relatively strong), we get a third meaning: /'ʔainˌflus/ 'influence'. Finally, in any of these meanings the first or the second syllable may bear overloud stress: /"ʔain'flus/ 'A river (not THE river)', or 'ONE river (not TWO)'; /"ʔainˌflus/ 'INfluence (not /"ʔausˌflus/ 'EFfluence')'; /ʔain"flus/ 'a RIVER (not a LAKE)'; etc.[9]

[7] Aspiration is here used as a cover-term to include voiceless vowels, voiceless [l], voiceless [n], voiceless [γ] (= [x]), and voiceless [v] (= [f]). Strictly speaking, we find the following combinations (where [k] stands for [p], [t], or [k], [a] stands for any vowel, and voiceless sounds are indicated by superior letters): [k'a] = [k^{a}a]; [k'la] = [k^{l}la]; [k'na] = [k^{n}na]; [k'γa] = [k^{γ}γa]; [k'va] = [k^{v}va].

[8] Pitch is also meaningfully distinctive in German, but I have not fully investigated it.

[9] It will be noted that the three degrees of stress which I have called 'normal' are used to distinguish morphemes: /ʔain/ 'a', /ˌʔain/ 'one', /'ʔain-/ 'in'; whereas the abnormal (overloud) degree of stress is used to distinguish whole utterances.

This gives us four meaningfully distinctive degrees of stress.[10] The loudest degree—above the normal maximum—may still be called OVERLOUD STRESS (''). The loudest normal degree may be called LOUD STRESS ('); the next loudest MEDIAL STRESS (ˌ); and the weakest WEAK STRESS (unmarked). It will be convenient to refer to overloud, loud, and medial stress as STRONG STRESS, in contrast with weak stress; and to use the term STRESSED to refer to phonemes bearing strong stress, and UNSTRESSED to refer to phonemes bearing weak stress.

2.2. ONSET OF STRESS. It should be emphasized that the assumption of four degrees of stress is a shorthand method of saying that each phoneme has four different allophones which differ in degree of loudness. We might symbolize these four allophones of /a/ by writing [a ᴀ A *A*]. Furthermore, it will be recalled (from §1.5) that the loudness of any syllable starts with its first phoneme, continues through the syllabic vowel, and then drops to weak stress. Thus we get the following contrasts (writing the glottal stop with a *q* to show the different degrees of stress): /ˀain'flus/ = [qajnFLUs] 'a river'; /ˌˀain'flus/ = [ǫᴀjnFLUs] 'one river'; /'ˀainˌflus/ = [QAjnꜰʟᴜs] 'influence'; /''ˀain'flus/ = [*QA*jnFLUs] 'ONE river'; etc.

2.21. ONSET OF STRONG STRESS. The stress phonemes which we symbolize /'' ' ˌ/ thus represent not only degrees of stress, but also the places where these degrees of stress begin. That the contrast in degree of stress is phonemic has been demonstrated in §2.1. That the place where strong stress begins is also phonemic may be demonstrated by the following example. The phoneme sequence /kauflaks/ consists, by definition, of two syllables, since /a/ is always syllabic and /u/ is non-syllabic after /a/. When we hear this utterance, the first syllable bears medial stress, the second syllable loud stress. If we consider that only degrees of stress are phonemic, we might mark them by placing accents over the two syllabics: /kàufláks/. But we have not yet analyzed all the meaningfully distinctive features. If the loud stress of the second syllable begins with the /f/, we get one meaning: /ˌkau'flaks/ = [ᴋᴀwFLAks] 'Chew flax'; if it begins with the /l/, we get another meaning: /ˌkauf'laks/ = [ᴋᴀwfLAks] 'Buy salmon'. Acoustically, this contrast is produced by the difference in the loudness of the /f/; phonemically, it is produced by the difference in the place where loud stress begins. We may therefore redefine slightly the phonemes which we symbolize by /'' ' ˌ/, as follows: /'/ is not just 'loud stress', but 'loud stress from this point through the next syllabic'; and similarly with /''/ and /ˌ/.

Other utterances showing a contrast in the place of onset of strong stress are: /'tauˌfriš/ = [TAwꜰʀɪš] 'fresh as dew', but /'taufˌrext/ = [TAwfʀᴇxt] 'baptismal law'; /di:'sla:ven/ = [di:SLA:ven] 'the Slavs', but /bis'london/ = [bisLOndon] 'as far as London'; /ˌdu:'šmutsiger/ = [ᴅᴜ:ŠMUtsiger] 'You dirty fellow!', but /ˌdu:š'mutsiger/ = [ᴅᴜ:šMUtsiger] 'Give Mutziger a shower!'; /'brautˌšlaier/ = [BRAwtšʟᴀjer] 'bridal veil', but /'doitšˌlant/ = [DOjtšʟᴀnt] 'Germany'.

2.22. ONSET OF WEAK STRESS. The weak degree of stress which we leave unmarked is best interpreted phonemically as absence of strong stress; i.e. it is not, in itself, meaningfully distinctive. Similarly, the place where onset of weak stress begins is not meaningfully distinctive. The reason for this is that all the consonants preceding any weak-stressed vowel (whether they belong to the same syllable as the vowel or not) are themselves weakly stressed, and hence do not differ acoustically in loudness. For example, one might expect that the /s/ of *in Slavonien* 'in Slavonia' would differ in loudness from that of *ins Lateinische* 'into Latin', since the morphological boundaries in these two utterances occur in different places. This is not, however, the case. The former utterance is /ˀinsla'vo:nien/ = [qinslaVO:njen]; the latter is /ˀinsla'tainiše/ = [qinslaTAjniše]; the segment [qinsla] is acoustically identical in both cases.[11]

2.3. UNSTRESSED VOWELS. Our previous analysis of vowels, since it dealt only with monosyllabic utterances, showed only the loud (and overloud) stressed allophones of vowels. When we examine utterances of more than one syllable, we find that all the vowel phonemes—short, long, and diphthongal—occur in other degrees of stress with the same phonetic values, except that length decreases along with stress. This is particularly true of the long vowels. Contrast, for example, the [o:] of /na'tsio:n/ 'nation' with the [o·] or [o] (but not [ɔ]!) of /natsio:'na:l/ 'national'. In unstressed position, therefore, the contrast between what we may still call short and long vowels is more one of quality than of quantity.

In addition to these differences in quantity, we find the following qualitatively new syllabics in unstressed position: [ə l̥ m̥ n̥ r̥], as in ['bɪtə] 'please', ['mɪtl̥] 'means', ['ˀa:tm̥] 'breath', ['bɪtn̥] 'ask', ['bɪtr̥] 'bitter'.

2.31. UNSTRESSED [ə] is in complementary distribution with stressed [ɛ] (except as noted below). For example, the word for 'it' appears stressed as ['ˀɛs], but unstressed as [əs] (or [s]): [ˌˀɛsɪst'hi:r] 'It's here', but [ˌvo:'ˀɪstəs] 'Where is it?' The only exception to this complementary distribution concerns a few words of foreign origin, in which unstressed [ɛ] serves as a more formal variant of [ə]. For example, beside the more formal [t'ɛ'no:r] 'tenor' and

[10] The number of absolute degrees of stress is theoretically infinite. An even weaker degree than what I have called 'normal minimum' is easily distinguished: [ˀn̥'flus]. But it is not meaningfully distinctive, since the meaning is still 'a river'.

[11] The material in §§2.21–2 might be re-stated in terms of syllable division; i.e. instead of speaking of 'onset of stress', we might speak of 'syllable release'. In /ˌkau'flaks/ the second syllable is released by the /f/; this distinguishes it from /ˌkauf'laks/, in which the second syllable is released by the /l/. This would mean that the place of release of a strongly stressed syllable is phonemic; and we could re-define the loud stress phonemes as follows: /'/ is not just 'loud stress', but 'place of release of a loud stressed syllable'; and similarly with /''/ and /ˌ/.

The reason I do not choose to speak of syllable division is that I am often unable to determine the place of release of an unstressed syllable. In the case of such an utterance as /ˀinber'li:n/ 'in Berlin', I am reasonably certain that the second syllable is released by the /b/; but I suspect that this is only because I know that the cluster /nb/ occurs neither at the beginning nor at the end of an utterance. But in the utterances /ˀinsla'vo:nien/ and /ˀinsla'tainiše/, I am unable to determine whether the second syllable is released by the /s/ or by the /l/. (The cluster /ns/ occurs at the end of an utterance, as in /'gans/ 'goose'; and the cluster /sl/ occurs at the beginning of an utterance, as in /sla'vo:nien/ 'Slavonia'.) It may well be that there is a physiological difference in the articulation of the segment /ˀinsla/ in these two utterances; I wish I had the training in the use of laboratory instruments to find this out. But there is no audible difference; and any physiological difference can therefore not be phonemic.

[tʻɛ'γʌsə] 'terrace', with [ɛ], we find, in free variation, the less formal [tʻə'no:r] and [tʻə'γʌsə], with [ə]. Since the contrast between unstressed [ɛ] and [ə] is never meaningfully distinctive, we may analyze [ə] as an allophone of /e/.

2.32. The syllabicity of [l̩ m̩ n̩ r̩] is not automatically determined by their surroundings, since we have such contrasts as ['γʌjn] 'pure', but ['γʌjn̩] 'rows'. Hence the syllabicity must be phonemic. Rather than posit a phoneme of syllabicity, it seems preferable to analyze this syllabicity as an allophone of unstressed /e/, i.e. to analyze [l̩ m̩ n̩ r̩] as /el em en er/. This analysis is supported by such slow speech forms as ['γʌjən], in free variation with ['γʌjn̩].

2.33. The phoneme /r/ must, as a result of the analysis of [r̩] as /er/, be redefined (cf. §1.33). When followed by a vowel, /r/ appears as [γ]: /'ro:/ = ['γo:] 'raw', /'fü:re/ = ['fy:γə] '(I) lead', /'bitere/ = ['bɪtəγə] 'bitter ones'. When not followed by a vowel, /r/ appears (1) after long vowels as [r]: /'he:r/ = ['he:r] 'army', /'fü:rt/ = ['fy:rt] 'leads'; (2) with unstressed /e/ as [r̩]: /'biter/ = ['bɪtr̩] 'bitter', /'šaitert/ = ['šʌjtr̩t] 'fails'; (3) after other short vowels as [γ]: /'her/ = ['hɛγ] 'Mr.', /'ʔirt/ = ['ʔɪγt] 'errs'.

2.4. The phoneme /x/. In utterances of only one syllable, /x/ occurs only after vowels, or after vowel plus /l n r/ (see §1.32). In utterances of more than one syllable, we find /x/ occurring initially before vowels, where it shows its palatal allophone [ç]: /'xi:na:/ 'China', /xe:'mi:/ 'chemistry'. The complementary distribution of [x] and [ç] remains unchanged, however: [x] occurs after central and back vowels and semivowels, [ç] in all other positions.

2.5. New segmental phonemes. An examination of utterances of more than one syllable also reveals a number of new segmental phonemes.

2.51. Voiced palatal [ž] occurs in such words as /'lo:že/ 'loge', /ga'ra:že/ 'garage'. In the speech of my informant it also occurs at the beginning of an utterance, as in /že'ni:ren/ 'embarrass', /žur'na:l/ 'journal'; many other speakers, especially those of lower social status, say /še'ni:ren/, /šur'na:l/.

2.52. Nasalized vowels occur in such words as [ba'sæ̃] 'washbowl', [γɛsto'γã] 'restaurant', [bal'kʻɔ̃] 'balcony', and [pʻaγ'fœ̃] (beside commoner /par'fü:m/) 'perfume'. In the speech of many persons of the same social status as the informant, these nasalized vowels are formal alternants of [ɛŋ ʌŋ ɔŋ œŋ] respectively; in the speech of persons of lower social status, these less formal alternants are used almost exclusively. Hence, even though we may analyze the formal nasalized vowels as /eŋ aŋ oŋ öŋ/, it is clear that we are dealing with marginal phonemes. Since we know that words containing these nasalized vowels are borrowed from French, we may classify them as foreign phonemes, and exclude them from further investigation. They do not affect the results of the present study in any way.[12]

3.0. Inadequacies of the tentative analysis. The phonemic analysis of German made in §1, as amended in §2, is inadequate in a number of respects. We may now examine these inadequacies, one by one.

3.1. Aspiration of voiceless stops. The voiceless stops /p t k/ are aspirated only when they occur before vowels, or before /l n r v/ plus vowel, as follows (letting /a/ stand for any vowel): /pa pla pna pra ta tra ka kla kna kra kva/. The following investigation is therefore limited to establishing when aspiration occurs in these surroundings. As a working hypothesis, we may assume that /p t k/ are normally unaspirated, and investigate only the factors which seem to produce aspiration.

3.11. Stressed /p t k/ are aspirated when they occur immediately after onset of strong stress. We may contrast stressed and aspirated /p t k/ in this position with unstressed and unaspirated /p t k/ immediately before onset of stress, as follows (with aspiration written in):

Aspirated /pʻ tʻ kʻ/	Unaspirated /p t k/
'su:ˌpʻlatler 'clog dance'	'šu:pˌla:de 'drawer'
'ši:ˌpʻrais 'skiing prize'	'li:pˌraits 'charm'
'ʔanˌtʻra:t 'fell into line'	'lantˌra:t 'head administrative official of a *Kreis*'
'bauˌkʻlots 'building block'	'štraikˌlo:n 'strike pay'
'šu:ˌkʻnopf 'shoe button'	'špukˌnapf 'spittoon'
'ze:ˌkʻraŋk 'seasick'	'šte:kˌraif 'stirrup'
'ʔainˌkʻvetšen 'squeeze in'	'taŋkˌvart 'gas station attendant'

It should be noted that stressed /p t k/ are aspirated only immediately after onset of strong stress; they are not aspirated if strong stress begins on a preceding phoneme. This accounts for such contrasts as the following (with aspiration written in):

Aspirated /pʻ tʻ kʻ/	Unaspirated /p t k/
'laušˌpʻosten 'listening post'	'šauˌšpi:l 'spectacle'
'fišˌpʻlate 'fish plate'	'tauˌšplais 'rope splice'
'taušˌpʻrais 'trade-in price'	'tsvi:ˌšpra:xe 'dialogue'
des'tʻe:ters 'of the doer'	ʔe'ste:tiš 'esthetic'
'flaišˌtʻopf 'flesh-pot'	'blaiˌštift 'pencil'
'vunšˌtʻraum 'wishful thinking'	'rainˌštro:m 'Rhine stream'
das'kʻitseln 'the tickling'	di:'skitse 'the sketch'
das'kʻlait 'the dress'	di:'skla:ven 'the slaves'
des'kʻrüpels 'of the cripple'	di:'skru:pel 'the scruples'

3.12. Unstressed /p t k/ after a pause are always aspirated. This is most apparent at the beginning of an utterance. Examples (with aspiration written in): /pʻa'ro:le/ 'password', /pʻla'ne:t/ 'planet', /pʻnoi'ma:tiš/ 'pneumatic', /pʻro:'bi:ren/ 'try out'; /tʻa'blet/ 'tray', /tʻra'gö:die/ 'tragedy'; /kʻo'lone/ 'column', /kʻla'vi:r/ 'piano', /kʻre:'di:t/ 'credit', /kʻvali:'te:t/ 'quality'. Aspiration also occurs after the brief pauses which may occur within utterances. Examples (with a space written to indicate pause): /'vas kʻain'bi:r pʻro:'bi:renzi:esˌma:l/ 'What? No beer? Just try it!'; or, in slow speech: /ʔixˌʔantvorte tʻe'rase/ 'I answer "terrace"' (contrast: /ʔixˌʔantvortete 'rase/ 'I answered "race"').

3.13. Unstressed /p t k/ not preceded by a pause sometimes show aspira-

[12] Also excluded are such isolated sound sequences (also foreign borrowings) as [a:j] in [de:'tʻa:j] 'detail', [wɪ] in ['wɪski] 'whiskey', etc.

tion and sometimes do not, in apparently identical surroundings. For example, we find [kʻ] in /ˌdi:zeskʻabi:ˈnet/ ‘this cabinet’, but [k] in /ˌdi:zeskanˈda:le/ ‘these scandals’. Furthermore, it is clear that the presence or absence of aspiration is meaningfully distinctive. Even when they are spoken without pause, we still get a contrast between the utterances /ʔixˌʔantvortetʻeˈrase/ ‘I answer “terrace” ’, with [tʻ], and /ʔixˌʔantvorteteˈrase/ ‘I answered “race” ’, with [t]. Obviously, then, aspiration must be made part of our phonemic analysis.

3.14. Two PHONEMIC ANALYSES OF ASPIRATION are possible. The most obvious analysis would be to posit a phoneme of aspiration: /ʻ/. But there is another way of interpreting the data. We may state, first, that /p t k/, regardless of stress, are always aspirated after a pause. There remain the cases where /p t k/ are aspirated when not preceded by a pause. Such contrasts as /ˈtʻail/ ‘part’ and /tʻaˈblet/ ‘tray’, with [tʻ], versus /ˈštail/ ‘steep’, /štaˈbi:l/ ‘stable’, /ˈbite/ ‘please’, and /ˈhu:t/ ‘hat’, with [t], suggest the formulation: /p t k/ are aspirated after a pause, but unaspirated after any segmental phoneme. (This was our analysis of aspiration in §1.31.) We might then interpret such contrasts as /ˈlantˌra:t/ but /ˈʔanˌtʻra:t/, or /ʔixˌʔantvorteteˈrase/ but /ʔixˌʔantvortetʻeˈrase/ by saying: there are places within an utterance where /p t k/ behave as if they were preceded by a pause, i.e. show the allophones [pʻ tʻ kʻ].

If we accept this interpretation, it remains for us to give a phonemic analysis of it. We may do this by assuming a segmental phoneme—to be symbolized, say, with a plus sign—after which /p t k/ are always aspirated. This segmental phoneme /+/ has the following allophones: at the beginning or end of an utterance it appears as a pause of indeterminate duration: /+ˈtail+/, /+taˈblet+/; within an utterance it appears either as a pause of brief duration or, in free variation with this, as zero: /+ˈʔan+ˌtra:t+/, /+ʔixˌʔantvorte+teˈrase+/.

When the allophone of /+/ is pause, we may describe it phonetically as inactivity of the vocal organs; acoustically it is silence. It is not necessary to describe the length of this pause, since there is no meaningful contrast between pauses of different duration.

The assumption of a zero allophone for /+/ needs clarification; I believe that such clarification may be given by citing a parallel example from Japanese. In Japanese,[13] the phoneme /y/ shows two allophones: at the beginning of an utterance and after syllabics it appears as [j]: /yaoya/ = [jaɔja] ‘grocer’; after consonants it shows a zero allophone, but its presence is indicated by the palatalization of any preceding consonant: /syuu/ = [šu:] ‘week’, /tya/ = [ča] ‘tea’; contrast /suu/ = [su:] ‘smoke (a cigarette, etc.)’, /tá/ = [tá] ‘rice field’. This enables us to make the following statements concerning /s/ and /t/ (and other consonants): they show the allophones [š] and [č] before /y/, but the allophones [s] and [t] before all other phonemes.

The phoneme /+/ which we may assume for German behaves similarly: at the beginning or end of an utterance it shows an allophone of pause: /+ˈtail+/, /+taˈblet+/; within an utterance it may show a zero allophone, but its presence is indicated by the aspiration of a following /p t k/: /+ˈʔan+ˌtra:t+/, /+ʔixˌʔantvorte+teˈrase+/ (contrast /+ˈlantˌra:t+/, /+ʔixˌʔantvorteteˈrase+/). This enables us to make the following statement concerning /p t k/: they show the allophones [pʻ tʻ kʻ] after /+/, but [p t k] after all other phonemes.

Just what name we may wish to give to the phoneme /+/ is relatively unimportant. The important thing is that we are able to define it phonetically, state the occurrence of its allophones, and describe the allophones of other phonemes before and after it. In the remainder of this paper I shall refer to it as OPEN JUNCTURE.

On the evidence of the voiceless stops alone, one would hardly assume a phoneme of open juncture; a phoneme of aspiration would be preferable. The following paragraphs (§3.2 and §3.3) are therefore written on the assumption that no decision has been made as to whether /+/ or /ʻ/ should be set up as a phoneme.

3.2. THE GLOTTAL STOP. It has already been noted (in §1.34) that /ʔ/ and /h/ occupy a unique position among the consonant phonemes. Both of them occur only before vowels and, in monosyllabic utterances, only in initial position. Furthermore, both of them always have the same stress as the following vowel: we get such sequences as /di:ˈʔeke/ ‘the corner’ and /di:ˈheke/ ‘the hedge’, but never any such sequences as */di:ʔˈeke/ or */di:hˈeke/. All of this suggests that one or the other of them might be analyzed as part of the allophone which any vowel shows under certain conditions. This is further suggested by the occurrence of the vowels themselves. Vowels never occur initially in an utterance. Within an utterance, stressed vowels occur only after stressed consonants or unstressed vowels, but never after unstressed consonants or stressed vowels. That is (letting V and C symbolize any stressed vowel and consonant, and v and c any unstressed vowel and consonant), we find the sequence ˈCV (as in the /ˈrai/ of /beˈrainigen/ ‘purify’), but never the sequence cˈV; and we find the sequence vˈV (where v is a long vowel, as in the /i:ˈo:/ of /špi:ˈo:n/ ‘spy’), but never the sequence VˈV.

Both /ʔ/ and /h/ are also ‘unstable’ phonemes, i.e. there are many utterances, alike in meaning, which sometimes show /ʔ/ or /h/, and sometimes (especially in informal, rapid speech) do not. Of the two, however, /ʔ/ is far more unstable that /h/. The latter is lost only sporadically in such rapid speech forms as /ˈba:no:f/ ‘railroad station’, beside slower /ˈba:nˌho:f/; or in informal /ˌkomenzi:ˈrunter/ ‘Come down’, beside more formal /ˌkomenzi:heˈrunter/. The glottal stop is lost even more frequently in informal, rapid speech (cf. the word /ˈʔes/ ‘it’ in §2.31). In addition, there are whole morphological classes which always show loss of /ʔ/. For example, when such words as /ˈʔauf/ ‘up, on’ and /ˈʔaus/ ‘out’ are compounded with /ˈhin/ ‘to there’, /ˈhe:r/ ‘to here’, /da:r-/

[13] Cf. Bernard Bloch, Studies in Colloquial Japanese I: Inflection, JAOS 66.98 footnote 4 (1946). I am indebted to Bloch for the suggestion that /+/ be analyzed as a segmental phoneme with allophones consisting of pause and zero.

[This is a correct interpretation of the statement in JAOS 66.98; but there is a better way to explain the analysis of [šu:] as /syuu/ and of [ča] as /tya/: the sound [š] is simultaneously an allophone of /s/ and an allophone of /y/; the sound [č] is simultaneously an allophone of /t/ and an allophone of /y/. In general, a sound belongs to as many phonemes as it contains distinctive features—here voiceless sibilance and palatalization in [š], voiceless dental occlusion and palatalization in [č]. (The order /sy/ rather than /ys/, etc., is established on the basis of patterning: thus there is /ky/ but no /yk/, etc.)—BB] (compounding form of /'da:/ 'there'), and /vo:r-/ (compounding form of /'vo:/ 'where'), the glottal stop is always lost: /hi'nauf/, /he'raus/, /da:'rauf/, /vo:'raus/, etc. Since /ʔ/ is more unstable than /h/, we may set up the hypothesis that [ʔ] is not a separate phoneme, but merely part of the allophone which any vowel shows under certain conditions; and we may try to establish what these conditions are.

3.21. Stressed vowels always show the glottalized allophone when they immediately follow onset of strong stress, unless they are immediately preceded by an unstressed long vowel. Only if we analyze [ʔa] as an allophone of /a/, etc., do we find stressed vowels occurring (1) after a pause: /'ʔale/ 'everybody'; (2) after stressed vowels and diphthongs: /'bauˌʔart/ 'type of construction'; (3) after unstressed short vowels: /be'ʔamter/ 'official', /te'ʔa:ter/ 'theater'; and (4) after unstressed consonants: /fer'ʔainigen/ 'unite' (contrast /be'rainigen/ 'purify'), /'šu:lˌʔamt/ 'school bureau' (contrast /'šu:ˌlats/ 'shoe tongue'). When the stressed vowel is immediately preceded by an unstressed long vowel, the glottal stop sometimes appears and sometimes does not: /te:'a:ter/ 'theater' (more formal than /te'ʔa:ter/); /ru:'i:nen/ or /ru:'ʔi:nen/ 'ruins'; /špi:'o:ne/ 'spies', but /di:'ʔo:per/ 'the opera'.

3.22. Unstressed vowels after a pause, whether at the beginning of an utterance or within an utterance, always show the glottal stop allophone: /ʔa'lain/ 'alone', /ʔe:'ga:l/ 'all the same', /ʔer'lauben/ 'allow', /ʔain'flus/ or /ʔen'flus/ 'a river', /'ʔax ʔesist'hi:r/ 'Oh! It's here'.

3.23. Unstressed vowels not preceded by a pause rarely show the glottalized allophone. For example, the utterances meaning '(to) know the farmer' and '(to) recognize the building' are usually homonymous: /de:n'bauerˌkenen/. But that the glottal stop can be meaningfully distinctive is indicated by the fact that, to make a contrast between these two meanings, my informant says: /de:n''bauerˌkenen/ '(to) know the farmer', but /de:n''bauʔerˌkenen/ '(to) recognize the building'. The same thing is true of other utterances of this type: /''ʔarbaiterˌzu:xen/ '(to) look for workers', but /''ʔarbaitʔerˌzu:xen/ '(to) request work'. (When such a contrast is made, a pause sometimes occurs before the glottal stop: /de:n''bau ʔerˌkenen/, /''ʔarbait ʔerˌzu:xen/.)

3.24. Two phonemic analyses of the glottal stop are possible. The most obvious analysis would again be to posit a segmental phoneme: /ʔ/ (though it would be a remarkably unstable phoneme). But there is, again also, another way of interpreting the data. We may begin by stating that all vowels, regardless of stress, show the glottalized allophone after a pause. Such contrasts as /'ʔeke/ 'corner' and /ʔer'zats/ 'substitute', with [ʔe], versus /'heke/ 'hedge', /fer'zu:x/ 'attempt', /kli:'ent/ 'client', /'ha:ben/ 'have', and /'ze:en/ 'see', with [e], suggest the formulation: vowels show an allophone with glottal stop only after a pause. We may then analyze such examples as /'bauˌʔart/, /'šu:l ˌʔamt/, and /de:n''bauʔerˌkenen/, where the glottal stop is not preceded by a pause, by again assuming a phoneme of open juncture. This phoneme has the same allophones as described in §3.14: at the beginning or end of an utterance it appears as a pause of indeterminate duration: /+'ale+/, /+a'lain+/, /+e:'ga:l +/; within an utterance it shows a zero allophone or, occasionally and in free variation, a brief pause: /+'bau+ˌart+/, /+be+'amter+/, /+fer+'ainigen+/, /+'šu:l+ˌamt+/, /+ru:+'i:nen+/ (or /+ru:'i:nen+/), /+de:n''bau+er+ˌkenen+/, /+''arbait+erˌzu:xen+/, etc. By assuming this phoneme, we are enabled to make the statement: vowels show an allophone with glottal stop after /+/, but without glottal stop after all other segmental phonemes.

3.3. The phoneme /x/. Our analysis states (in §1.32 and §2.4) that /x/ shows the allophone [x] after central and back vowels and semivowels, but [ç] after all other segmental phonemes and after a pause. There are, however, cases where [ç] also occurs after central and back vowels and semivowels, and the distinction between [x] and [ç] is meaningfully distinctive. Examples (with [ç] written in): /'ku:xen/ 'cake', but /'ku:çen/ 'little cow' (given as a nursery word); /'šta:xen/ 'stung', but /ma'ma:çen/ 'little mama'; /'brauxen/ 'need', but /'frauçen/ 'dog's mistress'. The above examples illustrate unstressed [x] and [ç]; examples of stressed [x] and [ç] are: /ra'xi:tis/ 'rickets', /ma'xandel/ 'juniper brandy'; but /da:ˌçi:na:(zo:'gro:sˌʔist)/ 'since China (is so large)', /vo:'çe:miker(ˌʔarbaiten)/ 'where chemists (work)'.

Our previous analysis of /x/ (in §2.4) stated that /x/ appears as [x] after central and back vowels and semivowels, but as [ç] in all other positions. If we accept a segmental phoneme of open juncture, we can amend this statement to read: /x/ appears as [x] after central and back vowels and semivowels, but as [ç] after all other segmental phonemes (including, of course, /+/). The phoneme /+/ has the same allophones as described in §3.14: at the beginning or end of an utterance it appears as a pause of indeterminate duration: /+'xi:na:+/ 'China', /+xe:'mi:+/ 'chemistry'; within an utterance it shows a zero allophone or, occasionally and in free variation, a brief pause: /+'ku:+xen+/, /+'frau+xen+/, /+da:+ˌxi:na:zo:'gro:s+ˌist+/, etc.

4.0. Final analysis. The preceding section describes the inadequacies of our phonemic analysis of German, and indicates the two alternative ways of removing these inadequacies. In making a final analysis we must choose between these two alternatives.

4.1. New phonemes. One alternative is to accept /ʔ/ as a phoneme, and to add /'/ and /ç/ as new phonemes. This alternative has the advantage of keeping our analysis on familiar ground; it has the disadvantage of requiring us to accept as phonemes three sounds which certainly would not be analyzed as phonemic in utterances of one syllable.

4.2. Open juncture. The other alternative is to assume a segmental phoneme of open juncture. This phoneme has two allophones: at the beginning or end of an utterance it appears as a pause of indeterminate duration; within an utterance it appears as a brief pause or, in free variation, as zero. We may assume this phoneme wherever we find a pause (of whatever duration) and, in addition, wherever we find (1) aspirated /p t k/; (2) a glottal stop; and (3) the sound [ç] following (phonetically) a central or back vowel or semivowel. By assuming this phoneme, we are enabled to make the statements: (1) /p t k/ are aspirated after /+/, but unaspirated after all other phonemes; (2) vowels show an allophone with glottal stop after /+/, but an allophone without glottal stop after all other phonemes; and (3) /x/ shows the allophone [x] after central and back vowels and semivowels, but [ç] after all other phonemes (including /+/).

This second alternative has the advantage of economy: we can get along with two fewer segmental phonemes. (We add /+/, but subtract /'/, /ʔ/, and /ç/.) The importance of this is not, however, in the numerical reduction in the number of phonemes, but rather in the grouping together under one heading of a number of phonetic details. Just as it is preferable to accept four phonemic distinctions of stress rather than to assume various series of four phonemes differing in loudness (like the [a ᴀ A *A*] mentioned in §2.2), so it is preferable to bring together under one heading the behavior of /p t k/, vowels, and /x/ when they are preceded by a pause, and their identical but superficially abnormal behavior when they are not preceded (acoustically) by a pause. This alternative is all the more preferable because it agrees with our analysis of the segmental phonemes in utterances of one syllable. The present writer therefore prefers it to the first alternative.

4.3. Occurrence of /+/ within utterances. An examination of the frequency with which /+/ occurs within an utterance, of the places where it occurs, and of the distribution of its allophones, gives further reasons for preferring it to the other alternative.

4.31. The frequency of /+/ within an utterance is determined largely by the speed with which the utterance is spoken. In extremely slow speech it may appear between every two words of an utterance: /+ˌvan+ˌfe:rt+ˌe:r +tsu:'rük+/ 'When is he going back?' (said, for example, in a long-distance telephone call with a poor connection; at normal speed there are no open junctures within this utterance: /+vanˌfe:rte:rtsu:'rük+/). The assumption of a phoneme /+/ thus allows us to analyze one of the phonetic features characteristic of slow speech.

4.32. The places where /+/ occurs usually coincide with syntactic and morphological boundaries. The only exceptions are a few words (all of foreign origin) in which open juncture and onset of strong stress precede a voiceless stop or a vowel: /+pa+'pi:r+/ 'paper', /+la+'terne+/ 'lantern', /+as+'ke:ze+/ 'asceticism', /+te+'a:ter+/ 'theater', /+ru:+'i:nen+/ 'ruins', etc.

Aside from these few exceptions, /+/ occurs only at a syntactic or morphological boundary. It often occurs (as a brief pause) between sentences: /+ˌdasistsu:'gro:s+ˌne:menzi:'di:s+/ 'That's too big. Take this one'; between the constituents of a compound sentence: /+ˌputsdi:rdi:'tse:ne+ˌkemdaine 'ha:re+untˌvašdaine'hende+/ 'Brush your teeth, comb your hair, and wash your hands'; before and after subordinate clauses: /+alse:r'fertixˌva:r+ˌgiŋe:r 'vek+/ 'When he was through, he went away'; and before and after appositives: /+de:r'iüŋere+'hans+ˌbli:p'hi:r+/ 'The younger one, Hans, stayed here'. Such syntactic boundaries do not allow us to predict the occurrence of /+/; but the assumption of a phoneme /+/ allows us to analyze one of the phonetic features characteristic of such syntactic boundaries.

Open juncture always occurs before stressed /p t k/, before stressed vowels, and before stressed or unstressed /x/ where these phonemes occur at the beginning of a morpheme. Before unstressed /p t k/ or unstressed vowels at the beginning of a morpheme, /+/ often does not cocur. Contrast, for example, the [t'] of ['mo:nˌt'ᴀx], as in /+e:rˌfe:rt'mo:n+ˌtax+/ 'He's going Monday', with the [t] of [ˌmo:ntᴀx], as in /+e:rˌfe:rtˌmo:ntax'morgen+/ 'He's going Monday morning'. Such morphological boundaries do not allow us to predict the occurrence of /+/; but, again, the assumption of a phoneme /+/ allows us to analyze one of the phonetic features characteristic of such morphological boundaries.[14]

4.33. The distribution of the allophones of /+/ is determined both by the speed of the utterance and by syntactic and morphological criteria. In normally rapid speech the brief pause allophone occurs commonly only at the syntactic boundaries mentioned above; the zero allophone occurs primarily at the morphological boundaries mentioned above. In extremely slow speech the brief pause allophone may occur also between words which are not separated by a syntactic boundary; but only the zero allophone occurs at morphological boundaries within words (usually only between the constituents of compound words).

5. Half-open juncture? The above description of open juncture was developed from the original interpretation (in §3.14) that there are places within an utterance where certain phonemes behave as if they were preceded by a pause, rather than by another phoneme. At such points we have posited a phoneme of open juncture. If we now examine the behavior of phonemes before these points, we find that they behave in the same way as before a pause: /h b d g v z ž/ never occur before /+/, and /r/ shows the allophone [ɣ] only after short vowels. This statement merely justifies our assumption of a phoneme /+/. It amounts to saying that other phonemes behave before the zero allophone of /+/ in the same way as before the pause allophone of /+/.

There are, however, points within an utterance (again coinciding with morphological boundaries) where one phoneme behaves as if it were followed by a pause, but the following phoneme does not behave as if it were preceded by a pause. We find this only in the sequence /r/ plus unstressed vowel. It was stated (in §2.33) that /r/ shows the allophone [ɣ] before vowels. This statement holds for such an utterance as /+ixˌfü:re'tsvantsix+/ = [ʔɪçˌfy:ɣə'tsvᴀntsɪç] 'I lead twenty'. But in identical surroundings we find /r/ showing the allophone [r], which we have described as occuring only (after long vowels) before conson-

[14] The fact that /+/ occurs almost exclusively at syntactic and morphological boundaries raises the question: Should we accept syntactic and morphological boundaries as part of our phonemic analysis if, by so doing, we can limit the scope of—or even avoid assuming—open juncture?

For a number of reasons I believe that this should not be done. First—and this is a purely methodological reason—I believe that the phonemes of a language should be analyzed without reference to syntax or morphology (as I have tried to do in this paper). Secondly, we could not do so successfully even if we tried, because of the cases (noted above) in which open juncture does not coincide with a syntactic or morphological boundary. Finally, it would seem that the phonetic marking of morphological and syntactic boundaries is more clearly described precisely by the assumption of open juncture.

ants or /+/: /+ˌfi:run'tsvantsix+/ = [ˌfi:rʊn'tsvʌntsɪç] 'twenty-four'. (In the speech of my informant, /r/ behaves this way at the end of any word or constituent of a compound word.)

In such an utterance we cannot assume /+/, since the vowel /u/ does not show an allophone with glottal stop. It would seem that we must either assume two different phonemes /γ/ and /r/; or that we must posit a second phoneme of juncture (half-open juncture?), though the present writer is unable to give a satisfactory description of it. It is to be hoped that further investigations will shed light on this problem.

⟦The following addenda were supplied in 1955⟧

In the above analysis, especially in §2.31, [ɛ] and [ə] are interpreted as allophones of a single phoneme /e/. It now seems to me preferable to analyze them as separate phonemes: [ɛ] = /e/, and [ə] = /ə/. Two types of reasoning may be adduced. On the one hand, there seem to be a very few actual contrasts between the two. Thus 'amen' is always /'a:men/ (with [ɛ]), but 'names' is always /'na:mən/ (with [ə]). More important is the fact that /e/ and /ə/ differ distributionally from one another: /e/ occurs either stressed or unstressed, but never before /+/; /ə/ occurs freely before /+/, but never stressed. This leads us into a three-way structural classification of the syllabic nuclei of German: (1) occurring freely before /+/, but only unstressed, is the single phoneme /ə/; (2) occurring either stressed or unstressed, but never before /+/, are the seven short vowels /i e a o u ü ö/; and (3) occurring either stressed or unstressed, and freely before /+/, are the seven long vowels /i: e: a: o: u: ü: ö:/ and the three diphthongs /ai au oi/. The alternations mentioned in §2.31 (stressed ['ɛs] beside unstressed [əs], or more formal [t'ɛ'no:r] beside less formal [t'ə'no:r]) still remain, but they are now morphophonemic rather than allophonic. (Note. I know of only two forms which violate the statement that short vowels never occur before /+/: the interjections /+'na+/ and /+'tia+/.)

For two discussions of German [ç] and [x] which appeared after the above article was published, see Werner F. Leopold, German ch, Lang. 24.179–80 ⟦see below⟧ (written in reply to the above article); and Gerhard Dietrich, '[ç] und [x] im Deutschen—ein Phonem oder zwei?', Zeitschrift für Phonetik 7.28–37 (1953) (written without knowledge of the above article). Both of the above scholars favor introducing morphological considerations into phonemic analysis. For a well reasoned and vigorous defense of this practice (with reference, among other things, to my footnote 14) see Kenneth L. Pike, 'Grammatical prerequisites to phonemic analysis', Word 3.155–72 (1947); and 'More on grammatical prerequisites', Word 8.106–21 (1952).

GERMAN CH

WERNER F. LEOPOLD

Language 24.179–80—1948

On the occasion of W. G. Moulton's brilliant phonemic analysis of standard German ⟦above⟧, I wish to raise certain questions with regard to the sounds written ch.

In §§4.1f., Moulton states the alternatives of accepting /ç/ as a phoneme, or of assuming a segmental phoneme of open juncture. He decides in favor of the second alternative.

He gives examples in §3.3 which show that there are cases in which 'the distinction between [x] and [ç] is meaningfully distinctive.' These examples could easily be multiplied. Tauchen [ç] 'small rope' is contrasted with Tauchen [x] 'diving', Pfauchen [ç] 'little peacock' with Fauchen 'spitting' (of cats). Photochemie [ç] contains the same sequence as the place-name Cochem [x].

Moulton's reason for not accepting [ç] as a separate phoneme, in spite of these facts, is that it does not occur as a separate phoneme in monosyllabic utterances (§4.1). The preliminary analysis on the basis of monosyllables is an acceptable method; but is it justifiable to make final decisions on this basis if the examination of polysyllabic utterances discloses discrepant facts?

Open juncture is a valid phonemic category because a pause is an observable phonetic fact. According to Moulton, open juncture appears within an utterance 'as a brief pause or, in free variation, as zero' (§4.2). The assumption of zero phonemes (and morphemes) is a trick of analysis which is useful where it serves to simplify the analysis without obscuring linguistic facts. In the case under consideration, however, it does obscure linguistic facts. To say that /x/ shows the allophone [ç] after open juncture in its zero form, means that there is no observable sign of open juncture. It amounts to saying that we must assume open juncture when /x/ shows the allophone [ç]. This is a vicious circle.

Some native observers claim that, in their form of German, open juncture is actually present before [ç]. I take this to mean that an observable pause is present. My own North-German form of speech has no observable pause before the diminutive suffix -chen or in Photochemie or in similar cases, and I have other native observers on my side. I am glad that Moulton, who describes a practically identical form of North-German speech, agrees that the pause can be zero.

I claim that the facts preclude the possibility of accepting Moulton's open-juncture alternative and that /ç/ must be recognized as a separate phoneme on the basis of Moulton's phonemic analysis. Considerations concerning the length of the vowel preceding ch, or the quality of the vowel following it, do not affect the problem, and Moulton does not bring them up. We are concerned with the question whether or not the phonetic form of ch depends entirely on quality of the preceding phoneme. Besides, in the case of Northern German Tauchen, for example, there are no such differences.

If we allow considerations of word-formation to be added to the rules about the pronunciation of ch, the matter becomes clear. Actually Moulton does so; his zero allophone of open juncture amounts to recognition of a boundary in word-formation. But he does not admit it, because of his conviction that a phonemic analysis should be based on phonetic facts alone (see his note 14). Bloomfield, Maître Phonétique 3.8.27 f. (1930), also states this conviction explicitly: 'the definition of a phoneme is properly made in purely phonetic terms'; but he proceeds to take word-formation into account nevertheless, seeking refuge in the phrase 'same situation', to which he gives a non-phonetic extension. His further observations concerning phonetic differences in the syllable beginning with ch, besides being irrelevant, are not correct. There is no difference in stress in the two versions of Tauchen, and no significant difference in the quality of the last vowel; the pronunciation of suffix -chen with a full vowel is an artificial pronunciation and not, as he takes it, 'the best' pronunciation. His phonetic remarks are an unsuccessful attempt to give a phonetic twist to facts which belong to word-formation.

Apparently, this is where the crux of the matter lies. Is it permissible to introduce considerations of word-formation into phonemic disquisitions? If so, the alternative of assuming two allophones of ch is tenable. If not, it becomes necessary to return to the separation of /ç/ and /x/ into two phonemes, for which Moulton leaves the door open.

There is no question that this approach is preferable for practical and pedagogical purposes; for instance, the use of [x] alone in the German transcriptions of Kenyon and Knott's Pronouncing Dictionary of American English, which otherwise gives phonetic, not phonemic transcriptions, is not justifiable. More important, however, is the theoretical problem of the bases for phonemic decisions. Word-formation should probably be taken into account,[1] since it is obviously taken into account by German speakers when they decide whether to pronounce [ç] or [x]. But the matter is apparently not completely clear, since Bloomfield and Moulton try to avoid doing so. I invite discussion of this basic question. We must either introduce matters of word-formation (compounding, suffixation) frankly into phonemic statements, or we must retain /ç/ and /x/ as two separate phonemes.

If we choose the former alternative, we must devise means of indicating the morphemic boundary in the phonemic transcription. This could be done easily by using a hyphen, which would distinguish /tau-xen/ from /tauxen/, /ku-xen/ from /kuxen/, /foto-xeˈmi/ from /koxem/. This slight correction would set matters right; but it involves an important decision on the bases of phonemic deliberations.

[1] Trubetzkoy does so; cf. his Anleitung zu phonologischen Beschreibungen 31 (Brno, 1935), on 'Morphemgrenze'. Moulton sees the possibility (in note 14), but decides against it.

⟦The semantics of the word 'juncture' is confusing and fateful. Originally signifying merely the where that belongs to two successive segmental items in immediate succession on their own structural level, its denotations and connotations have vastly shifted and ramified and have suffered accretions from the outside, e. g. from teleological theories of speech as in Leopold's 'when they decide' here, or from a wish to simplify description as in Harris's usage.

As a label for where, the word was of little use. Phenomena have therefore been getting appropriated to it right along from the time when it first became popular (during the war, apparently), unfortunately too often without adequate attention to the meanings it had already picked up.

As long as the aforesaid 'two items' are in immediate succession on their own [phonological] level the juncture phenomena either have to be on another level or get assigned to another type on the same.

While determining vowel and consonant phonemes Moulton accordingly assigned juncture phenomena to the next lower (allophonic-phonetic) level. Leopold, as I understand him, would instead have assigned them to the next higher (grammatical) levels. But Moulton was operating under the principle I spoke of in my comment on page 96 above.

Finally one must assign juncture to a phonemic status: otherwise it is nothing. By hypothesis it can't be segmental: no room there. Hence we are forced to the Hockett solution ⟨⟨100⟩⟩: it is suprasegmental.⟧

PEIPING PHONOLOGY

CHARLES F. HOCKETT
Journal of the American Oriental
Society 67.253–67—1947

The phonetics and phonology of Peiping Chinese[1] have been extensively studied.[2] The justification for yet another discussion is the approach, which is in some respects new. A detailed presentation of this approach would be out of place here, but brief mention of its major points will render the body of the paper more readily intelligible:[3]

1 Study of Chinese was begun in connection with the preparation of teaching materials for members of the Armed Forces, as part of the Program of the Language Section, Education Branch, Information and Education Division, ASF. The present paper was drafted during the tenure of a Grant-in-Aid from the Intensive Language Program, ACLS, Spring-Summer 1946. Of the dozen or more Chinese with whom the writer has worked, special mention is due to Mr. Chaoying Fang, his collaborator, transcribing informant, and (save in the technical phases of phonology) co-analyst for several years. A number of colleagues read an earlier version of this paper, and many constructive criticisms were received (not always acted on), especially from Yuenren Chao, Robert A. Hall, Jr., Zellig S. Harris, George L. Trager, and W. Freeman Twaddell. To all the individuals and agencies just mentioned, and to numerous others, the writer is deeply indebted.

2 Each of the alphabetizations of Chinese (Wade, Wade-Giles, Latinxua, Chinese National Romanization, Yale, and the usual Cyrillization) reflects a more or less sophisticated phonological analysis. The following is partial list of discussions not ancillary to the devising of an alphabetization (those the writer was not able to consult in preparing this report are in brackets):

[Y. R. Chao, Singing in Chinese, Le Maître Phonétique, 3.39.9–10 (1924).]

Lawton M. Hartman 3rd, The segmental phonemes of the Peiping dialect, Lang. 20.28–42 (1944) ((116)).

[Daniel Jones, Chinese Tones, Le Maître Phonétique 28.95–6 (1913).]

B. Karlgren, A Mandarin phonetic reader in the Pekinese dialect, Arch. d'Études Orientales 13.23; Upsala, 1917.

Jos. Mullie, The structural principles of the Chinese language, Anthropos Linguistische Bibliothek vols. 5, 6; Peiping 1932, 37.

Morris Swadesh, A condensed account of Mandarin phonetics, TCLP 8.213–6 (1939).

[L. T. Wang, Recherches expérimentales sur les tons du Pekinois, Arch. Néer. Phon. Exp. 13.1–40 (1937), 14.1–48 (1938).]

[——, Whispering in Chinese, Le Maître Phonétique 3.40.4 (1935).]

3 See also the writer's earlier discussion, A system of descriptive phonology, Lang. 18.3–21 (1942) ((97)) (except §§6–7, now superseded).

(1) Any articulatory event which occurs in a certain position in some utterances of a language, but not in all, is distinctive. Any feature which characterizes all the utterances of the language is non-distinctive. Likewise, a feature which does not regularly occur at least in all repetitions of one particular utterance, is non-distinctive. This is a somewhat wider definition of "distinctive" than has been customary. For example, in English the difference between the aspirated t of till and the unaspirated t of still has usually been termed non-distinctive (or "non-phonemic"); we cannot so classify it, since whenever one says still the aspiration is absent, and whenever one says till the aspiration is present. Any such feature must be accounted for in our phonological description. It is true, as Bloomfield points out,[4] that in our examination of a language we may miss some such features, because of the accidents of our training; such difficulties are encountered in many branches of science; we do the best we can.

(2) Within the total mass of distinctive material in a language, we find a relatively small set of determining features, characterized as follows: (a) if two articulatory events (or what might be described in purely phonetic terms as two articulatory events), A and B, are so distributed that A occurs only and always in conjunction with B, they constitute a single determining feature; (b) two articulatory events, A and B, so distributed that A occurs only when B occurs, but that B occurs also without A, are two determining features; (c) if A occurs both with and without B, and vice versa, A and B are two determining features. But an articulatory event A is not a determining feature at all, nor part of one, if its occurrence is predictable in terms of the occurrence and arrangement of those events which are determining features; for example, if A is found with B, with C, and with D, but nowhere else, and neither B, C, nor D is found without A, then A is not a determining feature. Distinctive features which are not determining are determined features. Often one may divide the total stock of distinctive features into determining and determined, and itemize the determining features, in more than one way; such differences of statement are stylistic, in no way reflecting facts about the language being described.[5]

4 Leonard Bloomfield, Language (New York, 1933), 84 and elsewhere.

5 [This footnote is on the next page.]

(3) In the examination of the raw data, we avoid the (usually unstated) linearity-assumption to which our tradition of linear orthography renders us susceptible. Two features, that is, may occur successively (dental closure and labial closure in hatpin), or simultaneously (labial and velar closure in some African languages), or in various overlapping sequences. Bundles of simultaneous or immediately adjacent features are given no priority, save precisely for the purpose of deriving an essentially linear notation; this purpose is phonologically irrelevant, though such a notation is useful, if not unavoidable, in making phonological statements.

(4) We ignore all considerations of grammatical structure, including such matters as morpheme or word borders. The purpose of this is to avoid circularity: if phonology is dependent on grammatical analysis, then phonology is just so much the less useful as a tool in grammatical analysis. Suppose, for example, that following the procedure here recommended we find in a particular language a type of open juncture, and then, when grammatical examination has been carried to the point of identification of words (= minimum free forms), discover that word-boundary coincides always, or usually, with this type of open juncture. Such a correlation is of importance; in some languages it does not exist. But if we had merely assumed that word-boundaries are phonologically relevant, the discovery of the juncture, and thus of the correlation between open juncture and word-boundary, would have been impossible.

(5) Phonological description thus consists of: (a) a list of the determining features (with alternative statements if alternatives exist); (b) a statement of the arrangements in which determining features occur in utterances; (c) a statement of the circumstances under which each determined feature occurs. This itemization is logical; the actual arrangement of one's statements will of course depend on the specific problem.

The body of this paper will serve as an example in extenso of the principles just listed.

[5] An analogy may be helpful. In stating the law of gravitation, one says that the force of attraction between two bodies varies, among other things, inversely as the square of the distance between them. It would be just as accurate to say, "inversely as the 1.99997 power of the distance between them," or "inversely as the 2.00003 power of the distance between them;" our techniques of measurement do not allow of sufficient precision to judge between these alternatives. In such a case we choose, for simplicity's sake, the nearest "round number," keeping clearly before us the degree of relative accuracy thereby attained. The analogy breaks down, however, in that, as yet, we do not know how to decide which of two phonological descriptions is the "rounder." Apparently the only legitimate use of the criterion of economy in science is in matters of this kind: where applicable, it gives us neater statements, but not necessarily more accurate ones.

We describe a dialect with a maximum number of phonemic distinctions.[6] Simpler patterns, perhaps more common in Peiping, are more easily dealt with in terms of the complex type than vice versa.

1. Segmentation. A Chinese utterance has two simultaneous components: a register-contour, and a sequence of one or more macrosegments.[7]

A macrosegment is bounded by macrojunctures, and has two simultaneous components: an intonation and a sequence of one or more mesosegments.

A mesosegment is bounded by mesojunctures, and has two simultaneous components: a stress-contour and a sequence of one or more microsegments.

A microsegment is bounded by microjunctures, and has as its simultaneous components a stress, a tone, and a residual structure (of vowels and consonants).[8]

2. Junctures. All the junctures to which names are assigned above are open. We find no need to postulate also a close juncture; in terms of the present system, close juncture is the absence of all open junctures.

Microjuncture is a zero-point of sonority,[8a] a clear and unambiguous point of syllable division; symbol / / (space).

Mesojuncture is a slight pause. It occurs only in combination with microjuncture, and the combination is symbolized /, /.

Macrojuncture is a pause, often no longer than mesojuncture, but sometimes long enough for a breath to be taken. The constant distinction is that macrojuncture falls at the juxtaposition of two intonations, whereas mesojuncture without macrojuncture falls within a single intonation. Macrojuncture occurs only in combination with the two less open types; symbol for the combination of the three /;/, except that at the end of an utterance we write /./ or /?/ (the choice dependent on intonation) instead of /;/.

3. Register-contours and Intonations. The analysi of these features is as yet incomplete; we try to suppl categories enough to take care of the maximum nur

[6] Essentially that of Chaoying Fang (b. Tientsin, educated Peiping) and Victor Ch'üan (b. Paris, educated Peiping); where these differ, the more complex type is chosen.

[7] This systematic, though somewhat unwieldy, terminology is introduced here primarily because it seems inadvisable to extend the meaning of the term syllable so as to cover segments which, in tl traditional meaning, may be "dissyllabic" (i.e., ha two peaks of sonority); see §8.1.

[8] Residual structure is what has heretofore bee called linear or segmental structure. The latter terms are unsatisfactory because the structure referred to (in Chinese, at least) is not linear. "Residual" is also not too fortunate, but it will serve until a better expression has been found.

[8a] Paul Benedict (private conversation).

ber of distinctive features of the kind that may be discovered.

By "register" is meant the range of pitch at any particular place in an utterance, within which the ups and downs of pitch which constitute intonations and tones take place. The most typical, and best identified, of the register-contours is found in utterances of at least four or five macrosegments' length: wide at first, narrower and with a lower average pitch in the interior, and wider again, but still somewhat lower than at the beginning, in the terminal macrosegment.[9]

However, this and other register-contours may be, not independent features, but rather automatic resultants of the sequence of intonations on successive macrosegments, and of the number of macrosegments in the utterance.

The clearest thing about intonations is their scope: there is usually little doubt as to where a particular intonation begins and ends. The exact nature and number of intonations is less clear. For the last macrosegment of an utterance, we indicate by terminal /./ a lowering of pitch from the nuclear stress (§4) to the end, and by /?/ the absence of such a fall in pitch; thus, in short utterances: /ˈtuei^4 me?/ 'Is that right?': /ˈtuei^4 le./ 'That's right.' Under /?/ we are probably lumping together several phonemically distinct types; possibly several are covered by /./.

A third clearly recognizable intonation, for which no symbol is here provided, consists of a squeezing of the pitch-range into a narrow band at median level, with only slight variations of stress (probably no nuclear stress) and relatively rapid articulation. This occurs, for example, in short introductory phrases before a direct quotation: /tha^1 ˈsrue^1; ˈhau^3./ 'He said "OK".'

4. Stress-contours and Stresses. The stress-contour of a mesosegment consists of varying degrees of prominence (produced largely by volume, but partly by length and speed) of its constituent microsegments. The position within the mesosegment of the microsegment of greatest prominence is not predictable, nor, given the position of this, are the degrees of prominence of the remaining microsegments. Therefore the degree of stress of each component microsegment has to be recognized as phonemically primary, and the stress-contour of the mesosegment is an automatic resultant thereof.

The most prominent microsegment in a mesosegment bears loud stress (/ˈ/ before the microsegment). The remaining microsegments bear quiet stress (/ˌ/), or else no stress at all (unmarked; "zero stress" if that terminology is preferred).

In addition, in macrosegments bearing certain intonations (e.g., /./), it is necessary to specify one of the loud stresses in the macrosegment as the nuclear stress, the stressed element at which the intonation turns. The nuclear stress is often, but not always, the last loud stress in the macrosegment. Since its location is not predictable, nuclear stress must be recognized as phonemically distinct from loud stress. No separate symbol is here provided, however, because none of the forms cited require distinctive marking of the nuclear stress in contrast to loud stresses.

Finally, in some cases one finds an extra-loud contrastive stress (/ˈˈ/) instead of a loud stress; further intonational analysis may eliminate this as a separate stress-level.

5. Tones. The tones are contrasting contours of pitch, volume, glottalization, and length. There are six tones; we number five of them, indicating them by superscript numerals after the microsegment; the sixth is indicated by the absence of such marking, and a microsegment bearing it is referred to in the discussion as "toneless."[10]

Toneless microsegments are staccato; microsegments with a tone are legato. Staccato microsegments have an observable pitch ("high," "low," etc.), but only legato microsegments have a discernible pitch-contour ("level," "rising," "falling").

Pitch: /^{1}/ and /^{3}/ are usually level, and have contrasting pitches as their distinguishing features: /^{1}/ is high, /^{3}/ low. /^{2}/, /^{4}/, and /^{5}/ have contrasting pitch-contours as their distinguishing features: /^{2}/ and /^{5}/ are rising, /^{4}/ falling. The rise for /^{2}/ begins and ends somewhat higher than that for /^{5}/.

Volume: With loud stress (or nuclear or contrastive stress), /^{1}/ and /^{2}/ are crescendo, /^{3}/, /^{4}/, and /^{5}/ diminuendo. With quiet stress this contrast is sometimes audible; with no stress, never.

Glottalization: With loud stress, /^{3}/ and /^{5}/ often have glottal friction during the lowest-pitched phase of the contour.

Length: With loud stress, /^{3}/ is longest, /^{4}/ half-long, and the other three relatively short.

/^{1}/ and /^{3}/, though usually level, are on occasion not level. When /^{1}/ is accompanied by loud stress and followed by /;/ (possibly by /,/), there is sometimes a slight fall in pitch at the end; this variant is in some circles considered "elegant."[11] When /^{3}/ is accompanied by contrastive stress, it starts relatively high, but immediately dips to extra low; when /^{3}/ bears any loud stress and is followed by /;/, there is usually a terminal rise. The combination of these occasional features on a single microsegment with third tone cited in isolation is the source of the customary description of the third tone as "dipping."

9 George A. Kennedy (private conversation).

10 The numbering /^{1}/ through /^{4}/ is as in Wade-Giles Romanization; /^{5}/ is the so-called "raised-third" tone (usually not considered phonemically distinct from the second tone).

11 Yuenren Chao (private correspondence).

With quiet stress or no stress, certain tonal distinctions are lost or facultatively lost. /^{5}/ is often not distinguishable in these circumstances from /^{2}/. In posttonic position in the mesosegment, with no stress, /^{1}/ and /^{2}/ are in free alternation. In the transcription we maintain the distinctions despite their optional loss (morphophonemically, on the basis of lexical identifications).

The pitch-range within which the contour constituting a tone is placed depends, of course, on the position of the microsegment relative to intonations and register-contours. It is also affected by the stress-level: with higher stresses the range is wider, with lower stresses narrower. The dynamic range for the crescendo or diminuendo contour of a tone is similarly affected by stress-level: greater range with higher stress, less with lower (none with no stress). For unstressed microsegments, with or without tone, the pitch-range is also conditioned by the terminal pitch of a preceding stressed microsegment in the same mesosegment, if any, and the initial pitch of a following stressed microsegment within the mesosegment, if any.

This last factor operates as follows: initially in a mesosegment, an unstressed microsegment tends towards mid or lower mid pitch. Finally in a mesosegment, such a microsegment has lower mid pitch if /^{1}/, /^{2}/, or /^{5}/ precedes, higher mid pitch after /^{3}/, and low pitch after /^{4}/. Flanked on both sides by stressed microsegments, within a single mesosegment, the pitch of the unstressed microsegment is a compromise between the terminal pitch of the preceding and the initial pitch of the following.

The phonemic status of the contrast between the first four tones can be demonstrated abundantly by lexical citation of free forms one microsegment in length, e. g.: /chru^{1}/ 'to exit' : /chru^{2}/ 'divided into'; /pau^{2}/ 'thin' : /pau^{3}/ 'to go bail for'; /cieu^{3}/ 'nine, wine' : /cieu^{4}/ 'thereupon'. The fifth tone does not appear on such elements, but can be demonstrated in free forms of two microsegments' length; our examples contrast it with the second and third tones, which are most similar: /'ta^{5} pan^{4}/ 'make-up,' /'ma^{5} fan^{4}/ 'annoying' : /'sr^{2} heu^{4}/ 'time,' /'i^{2} khuai^{4}/ 'one (dollar)' : /'mai^{3} mai^{4}/ 'business,' /'u^{3} khuai^{4}/ 'five (dollars).'[12] In all these examples, the second microsegments are facultatively toneless (see below).

Toneless microsegments cannot be demonstrated by direct lexical citation at all. There is a distinction, however, between the utterances /'hau^{3}./ 'OK' in answer to a question, and /'hau./ 'Yes, go on' said quietly over the telephone as an indication to the other party that one is following what is being said; the latter utterance has the intonation indicated by /. /, but no tone. In longer utterances, toneless microsegments are common. Certain forms, such as the particle /te/ (mark of attribution), /le/ (completive aspect), /cre/ (continuative aspect), /me, ne/ (question), are always toneless, even when stressed: /,ue^{3} "te, 'pheng^{2} ieu^{3}. / 'I said "my friend" using the attributive particle, not without the particle.' For some of these particles there are formal citation forms, /ti^{4}/ for /te/, /liau^{3}/ for /le/, with differing phonemic structures, based, as it happens, on the shape of the morphemically distinct elements that are written with the same characters; this does not affect the present discussion. Many elements other than the particles listed above, for example, the second microsegments in the two-microsegment free forms cited in the last paragraph above, are regularly without stress, and optionally retain or lose their tones.

6. Residual Structure: Determining Features. Under constant conditions of register, intonation, stress, tone, and placement in utterance, macrosegment, and mesosegment, microsegments contrast on the basis of the occurrence or non-occurrence, and the arrangement, of the following fifteen determining features:[13]

- p bilabial position
- t apico-alveolar position
- k dorso-velar position
- c tongue-front position with sibilance or with affricate release
- f labiodental position
- q glottal position (for which k is substitutable, though not vice versa)
- S unaspirated complete closure without nasalization
- F fricative spirant contact
- N nasalization, with stop closure or approximation thereto
- l lateral frictionless continuant
- i high-front tongue position
- u lip rounding
- r tongue retroflexion
- e mid tongue height
- a low tongue height

12 /'ma^{5} fan^{4}/ is written with a sequence of two characters, read individually as /ma^{2}/ and /fan^{2}/; this has afforded the basis of a protest against the present treatment. If the writer's hearing has not been at fault, then either (a) the morphemic identification reflected by the orthographic convention is incorrect, or (b) the morphophonemics of tone must be considered more complex than has been customary. More probably (a) is the case: Chinese characters serve about as well as an indication of morphemic identities as the letters in English orthography serve as an indication of phonemic identities.

13 There are probably a number of alternative possibilities here; we may mention one. Instead of writing /c/, we could write /ts/; given a slightly different definition of t, we would define /s/ as simultaneous t and F, and make the necessary minor modifications of wording in ensuing sections. This would eliminate c as a separate determining feature. The difference seems trivial.

The total stock of determining features in the language, therefore, consists of the register contours (?), intonations, junctures, stresses, tones, and the fifteen features just enumerated. Every linguistically relevant event in the speaking of Chinese is either one of these features arranged in a particular way relative to others, or a mechanically determined and predictable product of a particular arrangement of these features.

7. Residual Structure: Notation and Terminology. Some of the features listed above occur only in simultaneous bundles. Since it is inconvenient to transcribe other than linearly, we derive the symbols for inclosure between solidi from the symbols defined above in such a way as to eliminate the need for non-linear notation:

$$/\text{p t k c}/ = \frac{\text{p t k c}}{\text{S S S S}},$$

$$/\text{f s h}/ = \frac{\text{f c q}}{\text{F F F}},$$

$$/\text{m n ng}/ = \frac{\text{p t k}}{\text{N N N}};$$

and, for the others, simply

/l i u r e a/ = l i u r e a.

The digraph "ng" saves a type-face, and leads to no ambiguity since "g" is not otherwise used.

"#" is used, when needed, for zero.

The following cover terms are used: /a e/ are vowels; /i u r/ are semivowels; /c s/ are semiconsonants; /p t k f h m n ng l/ are full consonants. Both the semiconsonants, and all but one of the full consonants, are simultaneous clusters; it is convenient to classify the successive cluster /ch/ also as a semiconsonant, and the successive clusters /ph th kh/ also as full consonants.

8. Residual Structure: Arrangements. The above definitions of the symbols for use between solidi are statements of phonemic structure: the definition of /p/, for example, at the same time states that the simultaneous bundle of p and S occurs as one arrangement of distinctive features in utterances.

Statements of arrangement still to be made are made in terms of the elements and simultaneous bundles described above, on the convenient assumption that all the remaining arrangements are linear successions of these elements or simultaneous bundles; later on we indicate at what points this assumption is false.

8.1 Types of Microsegments. Microsegments are monosyllabic, containing a single peak of sonority, or disyllabic, containing two peaks, the first much more prominent than the second. The latter type is much the rarer, and (probably) does not occur toneless.

8.2 Monosyllabic Microsegments. For the description of these we recognize four successive positions for elements, symbolized as [1], [2], etc. Elements in position [1] are initials; the remainder is a final.[14]

8.21 Initials. These fall into the following classes: /#/; /c ch s/; /n l/; /t th/; /p ph m/; /f/; /k kh h/; /ng/; /cr chr sr/; /r/.[15]

TABLE OF FINALS

Group 1.									
#									
e	ei	en	eng	eu	em	er	eir	engr	eur
a	ai	an	ang	au	am	ar	air	angr	aur
Group 2.									
u			ung			ur		ungr	
ue	uei	uen	ueng		uem	uer	ueir	(uengr)	
ua	uai	uan	uang			uar	uair	uangr	
Group 3.									
i		in	ing		im				
ie				ieu		ier	ieir	iengr	ieur
ia	iai	ian	iang	iau		iar	iair	iangr	iaur
Group 4.									
iu		iun	iung			iur		(iungr)	
iue						(iuer)			
		iuan					iuair		

8.22 Finals. In position [2] occur /# u i iu/; in [3], /# e a/; in [4], /# i n ng u m r ir ngr ur/. The finals are listed in the Table. In the top row of each group, [3] is /#/; in the middle row, /e/; in the bottom row, /a/. The finals of a single group have the same element in [2]; those in a single column have the same element in [4]. The three parenthesized finals are morphologically to be expected but are not attested.

The following points, though implicit in the Table, are not obvious:

(1) /u/ does not occur in both [2] and [4] of a final. The same is true of /i/ in those finals which do not contain /r/, save for /iai/, which is rare and perhaps only literary.[16]

(2) [4] elements other than /#/ occur only with positions [2] and [3] not both empty.

(3) /r/ as [4] does not occur with /#/ as [3] and /i/ as [2].

14 Almost all earlier treatments of Chinese syllables (= our monosyllabic microsegments) make use of this initial-final division. The convenience of the device, however, seems not to reflect anything of a fundamental nature about the structure of the language (to the contrary: Bloomfield, Language, 182).

15 An alternative is to eliminate the initial classes /cr chr sr/ and /r/, and to add two further groups of finals, one with /ru/ and one with /r/ in position [2].

16 /,tuan^4 'iai^2/ 'precipice' has an alternative form with /ia^2/; /chiai^3/ (Hartman, 39 ((122)), has the alternative pronunciation /khai^3/.

8.23 Combinations of Initial and Final. For combinations of an initial and a final which does not contain /r/, we say that the combination occurs if (1) there exists a morpheme consisting of such a shape (plus a tone), or part of which consists thereof (e.g., if the first microsegment of a two-microsegment morpheme has the required shape), or if, there being no such morpheme, (2) there is clear evidence that the shape in question, with some tone, is pronounceable as a nonsense-element. Such a combination is termed literary if the required pronunciation is assigned to a character in character-dictionaries, but the element does not occur in ordinary colloquial speech (and thus not at all in the speech of many individuals). For combinations of an initial and a final which does contain /r/, we say that the combination occurs if (1) there exists a morpheme or group of morphemes of the required shape, or if (2) the existence of such is morphologically to be expected, even if it has not been heard.[17]

Finals with /m/ as [4] are ignored until (12) below.

(1) Final /#/ occurs only with initials /c ch s, cr chr sr, r/.

(2) Initial /#/ occurs with all finals except /ung ungr/. /ung^{1}/ has been heard as an alternative pronunciation of the surname usually pronounced /ueng^{1}/, but this is probably a non-Peiping or even non-Mandarin feature.[18]

(3) Finals /ueng uengr/ occur only with initial /#/. /ueng/ and /ung/, likewise /uengr and /ungr/, may thus be in complementary distribution. /iai/ seems to occur only with the initials /# ch/; both are literary.

(4) Initials /c ch s/ do not occur with finals /ua uai uang uar uangr/; nor do the combinations /chei, chen, sen, seng, sengr/ occur.*

(5) Initials /n l/ do not occur with finals /uei ua uai uar uangr iun iung iungr iuer iuair/.* The only* case of /len/ is in a recently given personal name, where the use of a "non-occurrent" microsegment was premeditated;[19] but the name is pronounced without difficulty by native speakers. /niue, liue, liuan/ occur only in literary context; /ne/ occurs only toneless; /nuang/ is questionable; /nen, neu, nuen, luang, nia, niuan/* are not attested.

Finals of group 4 do not occur with any of the initials yet to be discussed, save for a peculiar occurrence of /iu/ (and possibly /iur/) after /k/: /ˌchiue^{3} ˈkiu^{4}/ is the form assumed in a variety of "Pig-Latin" by ordinary /ˈchiu^{4}/ 'to go.'[20]

(6) Initials /t th/ do not occur with finals /ua uai uang uar uangr in ia iang iar iangr/.* There are no cases of /thei, thieu/;* /thuen/ is literary. Dictionaries based on characters give no pronunciations involving /ten, then/, but these occur at least in /ten^{4}/ 'to pull on with sudden tugs' and /ˈtung^{4} then/ 'to be not at rest.'

(7) Initials /p ph m/ do not occur with finals /ieu ieur ia iang iar iangr/,* and probably not with final /er/, nor with any of the finals of group 2 except /u ur ue uer/. There are no cases of /phe, peu/; /pheu/ is literary; /pe, me/ occur only toneless.

Finals of group 3 do not occur with any of the initials yet to be discussed.

(8) Initial /f/ does not occur with the finals /e er ai au aur/, nor with any of the finals of group 2 except /u ur ue uer/.

(9) Initials /k kh h cr chr sr/ occur with all finals not excluded by statements in the foregoing, except that there are no cases of /chrei, srung/;* /chrua/ is literary.

(10) Initial /r/ does not occur with finals /ei a ai ar ua uai uang uar uangr/.*

(11) Initial /ng/ occurs only with final /e/, toneless (§10).

(12) Finals with /m/ in position [4] are rare, and apparently confined to relatively fast speech (§8.3). /em/ occurs with initials /sr cr c/; /am/ with /t th c/; /uem/ with /#/; /im/ with /n/. The following examples are exhaustive or almost so: /srem^{2}, cem^{3}, nem^{4}/ ~ /sreme^{2}, ceme^{3}, neme^{4}/ 'what, how, thus'; /crem^{4}, cem^{4}/ ~ /creme^{4}, ceme^{4}/ 'thus'; /ˈtam^{4} cr^{3}/ ~ /ˈta^{4} me ˌcr^{3}/ 'thumb'; /tham^{1}, cam^{2}/ ~ /ˈtha^{1} men, ˈcan^{2} men/ 'they, we'; /uem^{3}/ ~ /ˈue^{3} men/ 'we'; /nim^{3}/ ~ /ˈni^{3} men/ 'you (pl.).'

Since more finals containing /r/ are recognized in this analysis than is customary, examples are given here of all except the three parenthesized in the Table: /er^{4}/ ~ /air^{4}/ 'two'; /ˌai^{1} ˈmeir^{2}/ 'go from door to door'; /hengr^{2}/ 'horizontal stroke' (in writing characters); /ˌpi^{3} ˈtheur^{2}/ 'pen point'; /par^{3}/ 'handful, bunch'; /ˌsiau^{3} ˈhair^{2}/ 'child'; /pangr^{1}/ 'group'; /phaur^{4}/ 'bulb'; /ˌsiau^{3} ˈsrur^{1}/ 'small book'; /khungr^{4}/ 'free time'; /ˌsiau^{3} ˈsruer^{1}/ 'novel'; /khueir^{3}/ 'spool'; /ˌsiau^{3} ˈsruar^{1}/ 'small brush'; /uair^{2}/ 'to amuse oneself with'; /khuangr^{1}/ 'basket'; /ier^{4}/ 'leaf'; /tieir^{3}/ 'bottom' (as of a cup); /piengr^{3}/ 'cake'; /chieur^{2}/ 'ball'; /iar^{2}/ ~ /iangr^{1}/ 'sprout, seedling'; /iair^{4}/ 'swallow' (bird); /tiaur^{4}/ 'melody'; /ˌsiau^{5} ˈiur^{3}/ 'shower, light fall of rain'; /ˌhua^{1} ˈiuair^{2}/ 'flower garden'.

---

17 Most elements with a retroflex final are bimorphemic, consisting of a first constituent without retroflexion in its final and a second constituent of retroflexion added according to a fairly complex pattern. The first constituents fall into certain grammatical classes; if an element of such a class exists having a certain phonemic shape, one may legitimately expect the existence of the corresponding bimorphemic form with retroflexion, whether one has heard it or not.

18 Hartman, op. cit., fn. 18, reports this presumably from a Peiping speaker.

19 Information from Chaoying Fang.

*⟦See the Addenda ⟨⟨228⟩⟩, where these starred lists and statements are modified, especially by including onomatopoetic formations.⟧

20 Victor Ch'üan (fn. 6) speaks this jargon; Yuenren Chao, Eight varieties of secret language [in Chinese], Bull. of Inst. of Hist. and Philol., Acad. Sinica, 2.3.312.

8.3 Disyllabic Microsegments. In these there are five positions for elements: [1], [2], and [3] as for monosyllabic microsegments, save that [2] and [3] are not both empty; [4´] one of the set /p t k c m n ng f s h l/ (not all of these have been observed, but the nature of the alternation between two-microsegment sequence and single disyllabic microsegment [see below] is such as to suggest that the list is correct); [5] /e i u r/. The limitations of sequence in the first three positions are as for monosyllabic microsegments; if [5] is /i u r/, the same limitations apply to positions [4´]-[5] as to [1]-[2] in all microsegments.

Most disyllabic microsegments occur only in fast speech, being replaced at slower speeds by sequences of two monosyllabic microsegments, the first of which is stressed and has the tone of the disyllabic alternant, the second of which is unstressed and toneless or optionally toneless: /pusr^{2}/ ~ /'pu^{2} sr^{4}/ 'isn't'; /siesi^{4}/ ~ /'sie^{4} sie/ 'thanks'; possibly /tulu^{1}/ ~ /'tu^{1} lu/ 'cluster' (as of grapes).[21]

A few disyllabic microsegments occur in either rapid speech or normal-speed speech, but in the latter case are paralleled by groups of two monosyllabic microsegments. All the cases citable have, also, in fast speech only, still shorter alternants consisting of a single monosyllabic microsegment: /crem^{4}, cem^{4}/ ~ /creme^{4}, ceme^{4}/ ~ /'cre^{4} me/ 'thus, this way'; /nem^{4}/ ~ /neme^{4}, name^{4}/ ~ /'na^{4} me/ 'thus, that way'.

There are two disyllabic microsegments which have the shorter alternant just mentioned, in rapid speech, but no two-microsegment replacement except as a highly artifical reading-pronunciation: /srem^{2}/ ~ /sreme^{2}/ ~ (reading-pronunciations) /'sren^{2} ma^{4}, 'sren^{2} mue^{4}, 'sr^{2} ma^{4}, 'sr^{2} mue^{4}/ 'what'; /cem^{3}/ ~ /ceme^{3}/ ~ (reading-pronunciations) /'cen^{3} ma^{4}, 'cen^{3} mue^{4}/ 'how'.

9. Residual Structure: Determined Features. The statements of arrangement just made were based on the assumption that features or bundles of features represented in the transcription by single letters (or the digraph "ng") occur only in linear sequence (§8, beginning). As we proceed with the presentation of determined features, we also indicate at what points that assumption was false.

9.1 Features Dependent on Placement.

9.11 Release and Onset. Consonants initial in a microsegment have distinctive release; final in a microsegment, distinctive onset; medial in a disyllabic microsegment (position [4´]), both.

→ /l/ is now completely described. Examples: /lau^{3}/ 'always', /tulu^{1}/ (?) 'cluster'.[22]

[21] Yuenren Chao discussed such fast-speech forms in a talk to the Yale Linguistics Club c. 1943.

[22] Beginning here, we mark with an arrow each paragraph which concludes the discussion of one or more vowels and consonants.

→ /m/ is completely described on the addition of the following: the simultaneous occurrence of determining features p and N involves, as a determined feature, complete closure, the alternant possibility covered by the definition of N (approximation) being eliminated. Examples: /ma^{3}/ 'horse', /tham^{1}/ 'they', /sreme^{2}/ 'what'.

9.12 Voicing and Voicelessness. Microsegments are voiced throughout unless they begin with /p t k c ph th kh ch f s h a/. Microsegments beginning with one of these are voiced except for an initial voiceless phase (the phase indicated by the symbols listed), except as follows: Initial /p t k c/ are usually voiced in an unstressed microsegment, rarely elsewhere. /a/ in initial position often has a glottal stop onset (constituting an initial voiceless phase); this is rarer in unstressed microsegments.

→ /p t k ph th kh f h/ are now completely described. Examples: /pau^{4}/ 'newspaper', /'la^{3} pa/ 'trumpet'; /ta^{4}/ 'large', /'ue^{3} te/ 'my'; /kau^{1}/ 'high', /'i^{2} ke/ 'one'; /phau^{3}/ 'run'; /than^{2}/ 'converse'; /khai^{1}/ 'open'; /fan^{4}/ 'food'; /he^{1}/ 'drink'.

9.13 Peaks of Sonority. By definition, one peak of sonority occurs in each monosyllabic microsegment, two in each disyllabic microsegment.

If a monosyllabic microsegment contains a vowel, there is a peak of sonority simultaneous with the vowel. If it contains no vowel, but contains a semivowel /i u/ or the cluster /iu/ in position [2], there is a peak of sonority simultaneous with the /i/ or /u/ or with the second phase of the cluster /iu/. If it contains no vowel and no semivowel /i u/, the peak of sonority is simultaneous with the last phase of the microsegment, whatever it may be (e.g., with the /r/ of /sr^{4}/ 'is', with the terminal vocalic phase [§9.2] of /s^{4}/ 'four').

The major peak of sonority in a disyllabic microsegment is simultaneous with a vowel or semivowel in position [3] or [2], as the case may be. The minor peak is simultaneous with the element /e i u r/ in position [5].

9.2 The Semiconsonants. /c/ or /s/ as the only residual constituent of a microsegment has two successive phases. Phase one is, in each case, consonantal (simultaneous bundle of c and S, or of c and F), with the added determined feature of lowering of the central part of the tongue, raising of the dorsal part, and often some tension of the throat muscles. The second phase is vocalic, identical for /c/ and /s/, and composed entirely of determined features: an unrounded high back vowel, with tongue as for the consonantal phase and the throat muscles still tense. Examples: /c^{4}/ 'word', /s^{4}/ 'four'.

When the only residual constituent of a microsegment is /ch/, /c/ has the two phases just described, but the /h/ falls between them, after the consonantal phase of /c/ and before the vocalic phase; the determined features of tongue-position and throat tension are maintained during the /h/: /ch^4/ 'time, occurrence'.

In all other circumstances, /c s/ have only a single phase. When this phase is not simultaneous with palatalization or retroflexion (§9.3), the tongue position is as described above.

→ /c ch s/ are now completely described.

9.3 /i u r/ not in Position [4]. We take up separately /i u iu/ in position [2] and /r/ in position [1] or in the [1]-clusters /cr chr sr/.

9.31 /i/. In the arrangement symbolized /CiV/ ("C" = consonant, "V" = vowel), our assumption of linearity is false. The /i/ begins at the beginning of the microsegment, as palatalization of the consonant,* and continues after the consonant as a high-front-unrounded glide. The palatalization of the consonant is clearest in the case of /c ch s/; these consonants with palatalization are articulated with the tip of the tongue behind the lower teeth, the frontal surface of the tongue in contact with the upper teeth and the alveolar ridge to produce the closure or friction. Examples: /siang^3/ 'think', /chiau^2/ 'bridge', /pian^1/ 'side'.

In the arrangement /Ci/ (no vowel), /i/ begins with the consonant as palatalization (as above*), continues after the consonant optionally as high-front-unrounded glide, then in all cases as high-front-unrounded vowel simultaneous with the peak of sonority. If /n/ follows, the glide phase is usually present, and the vocalic phase is lower than otherwise. Examples: /si^1/ 'west', /sing^1/ 'star', /sin^1/ 'new', /phin^1/ 'to spell out'.

In the arrangement /iV/ (no initial consonant), /i/ is a high-front-unrounded glide (and our assumption of linearity is correct): /iang^2/ 'ocean', /ian^1/ 'smoke'.

In the arrangement /i/ (no initial consonant and no vowel), /i/ begins as a high-front-unrounded glide and continues as a high-front-unrounded vowel simultaneous with the peak of sonority. The vowel is slightly lower if /n/ follows than otherwise. /i^1/ 'one', /in^1/ 'sound', /ing^1/ 'should'.

9.32 /u/. All cases of /u/, save when /i/ overlaps (§9.33), add high-back tongue position as a determined feature.

In the arrangements /(C)uV/, /u/ is a high-back-rounded glide: /uan^3/ 'bowl', /kuan^1/ 'officer'.

In the arrangement /Cu/, /u/ is a high-back-rounded vowel: /phu^4/ 'store', /tung^1/ 'east'.

In the arrangement /u/, /u/ begins as a high-back-rounded glide and continues as a high-back-rounded vowel: /u^3/ 'five', /ur^1/ '(small) room'.

9.33 /iu/. (1) When /ng/ follows immediately, /i/ has the varieties described in §9.32 for the arrangements /CiV/ and /iV/, and the /u/ is a high-back-rounded vowel: /siung^1/ 'fierce', /iung^4/ 'use'.

(2) When /ng/ does not follow immediately, four cases must be distinguished as for /i/ alone:

In the arrangement /CiuV/, /i/ begins with the consonant as palatalization thereof,* /u/ begins after the consonant, the /i/ continuing, the two together constituting a high-front-rounded glide: /chiuan^2/ 'together'.

In the arrangement /Ciu/, /i/ begins with the consonant as palatalization thereof,* /u/ begins after the consonant, the /i/ continuing, the combination constituting (a) if /n/ follows, a high-front-rounded glide followed by a slightly lower high-front-rounded vowel; (b) otherwise, just a high-front-rounded vowel: /ciun^1/ 'army', /chiu^4/ 'to go'.

In the arrangement /iuV/, /i/ begins first, as high-front-unrounded glide; then the /u/ begins, the /i/ continuing, the combination forming a high-front-rounded glide: /iuan^4/ 'court', /iue^4/ 'month'.

In the arrangement /iu/, /i/ begins first, as high-front-unrounded glide; then the /u/ begins as the /i/ continues, the combination constituting (a) if /n/ follows, a high-front-rounded glide followed by a slightly lower high-front-rounded vowel; (b) otherwise, just a high-front-rounded vowel: /iun^4/ 'to ship', /iu^3/ 'rain'.

9.34 /r/. In the arrangements /CrV/ and /Cru/, /r/ begins and ends with the consonant, as retroflexion thereof. The consonants /c ch s/ with simultaneous /r/ have as position of articulation, therefore, the tongue retracted and lifted to the roof of the mouth, so that the tip is behind the alveolar ridge, the contact being between an area of the tongue including tip and blade and the roof of the mouth behind the alveolar ridge. Examples: /chru^1/ 'exit', /srau^3/ 'few'.

In the arrangement /Cr/ (with no vowel or following /u/), /r/ begins with the consonant as retroflexion thereof (as above), and continues after the consonant as retroflex vowel simultaneous with the peak of sonority. The tongue position for the vowel is identical with the position described above for /c ch s/ with simultaneous /r/. Examples: /cr^3/ 'point', /chr^1/ 'eat', /sr^4/ 'is'.

In the arrangements /rV/ and /ru/, /r/ is a retroflex glide, often with some friction: /re^4/ 'hot', /ru^4/ 'enter'.

In the arrangement /r/ (no consonant and nothing following), /r/ begins as a fricative retroflex glide and continues as retroflex vowel simultaneous with the peak of sonority: /r^4/ 'day, sun' (bound form).

9.4 Position [4]. /m/ has already been covered in this position and elsewhere (§9.11). The remaining elements in position [4] are discussed in the order /i u n ng r ir ngr ur/.

/i/ is a glide towards (not necessarily to) the high front tongue position: /hai^3/ 'sea', /kei^3/ 'give'.

/u/ is a glide towards (not necessarily to) the high back tongue position with concomitant increasing lip rounding: /hau^3/ 'OK', /keu^3/ 'dog'.

/n/ is motion of the tongue to or towards the apico-alveolar position, with concomitant nasaliza-

*⟦But in /Ci.../ with C = /t th n l/, the consonant is not palatalized; see details in the Addenda.⟧

tion. If the following microsegment in the same mesosegment begins with /i/, the apico-dental closure is often not completed; in this case the nasalization begins with the peak of sonority or even immediately after an initial consonant, if any: thus in /ˈman^{4} i ˌtian/ 'a little slower'. If the following microsegment in the same mesosegment begins with /p ph m/, the closure of the lips for that consonant is often made simultaneously with the final /n/ of the preceding microsegment; similarly for the dorsovelar closure for an initial /k kh h/ of a following microsegment. Because the features constituting /n/ are still present, this is not a morphophonemic replacement of /n/ by /m/ and /ng/. Thus: /ˌchian^{1} ˈpi^{3}/ 'pencil', /ˈnuan^{3} he/ 'warm'.[22a]

/ng/ in this position involves no determined features: /ˌpang^{1} ˈmang^{2}/ 'to give help'.

/r/ is a glide to the retroflex position, frictionless, the tongue approaching the roof of the mouth less closely than for /r/ in other positions: /far^{2}/ 'method', /ier^{4}/ 'leaf', /her^{2}/ 'small box', /uer^{1}/ 'nest'.

/ir/: the /i/ and /r/ are simultaneous, constituting a glide to palatalized retroflex position: the front and central portions of the tongue are raised, and the tip slightly curled: /tiair^{3}/ 'a little', /tieir^{3}/ 'bottom'.

/ngr/: the nasalization begins with the peak of sonority, or even immediately after an initial consonant, if any. After the peak of sonority there are, simultaneously, a glide of the front part of the tongue to the retroflex position (as with /r/ alone in [4]), and motion of the dorsal part of the tongue towards, but not to, contact with the velum; the nasalization increases throughout. Examples: /hengr^{2}/ 'horizontal stroke', /piengr^{3}/ 'cake'.

/ur/ is a combination of /u/ and /r/, each as described above for position [4]; the two glides come in any arrangement relative to each other—/u/ first, /r/ first, simultaneous, or overlapping with either starting first: /phaur^{4}/ 'bulb'.[23]

→ /i u r/ are now completely described;[24] /n ng/ are completely described once we add that, save as specified above, /n ng/ involve closure, not approximation. There remain to be treated only the vowels, /e a/.

[22a] Perhaps rigor would require that we say, rather, that in such cases one has simultaneously /n/ and /m/, or /n/ and /ng/—that is if simultaneous p and N constitute /m/, and simultaneous t and N constitute /n/, perhaps simultaneous p, t, and N must be interpreted as simultaneous /n/ and /m/. But the p or k in such cases is a long component, stretching back across microjuncture from the following microsegment.

[23] Hartman, op. cit., fn. 14, suggests a possible contrast of terminal /ru/ and /ur/ postvocalically, but I have not heard any.

[24] Except for phases simultaneous with /e/ or /a/, discussed in §9.5.

9.5 Vowels. Microsegments with otherwise identical residual structure (as here analyzed) often occur in triads, in which a prominent feature of the contrasts between them is the height of the tongue at the peak of sonority. Thus: /i^{1} : ie^{1} : ia^{1}/ 'one : coconut : to press down', /u^{3} : ue^{3} : ua^{3}/ 'five : I : tile', /c^{3} : ce^{2} : ca^{2}/ 'purple : duty : variegated'. Sometimes there are only two terms: /in^{1} : ian^{1}/ 'sound : smoke', /tuen^{4} : tuan^{4}/ 'ton : segment'. And sometimes there is only one: /iung^{4}/ 'use'.

Vowel-sounds at the peaks of sonority of such microsegments differ in more than tongue-height: that of /ie^{1}/ is front, that of /ue^{3}/ is back and rounded. The vowel-sound at a peak of sonority in some cases has several simultaneous components. For high vowel-sounds, the only components are parts of determining features written with symbols other than /e a/; thus in /i^{1}/ 'one', /u^{3}/ 'five', /chr^{1}/ 'eat', /c^{4}/ 'word', /iu^{3}/ 'rain', and the like (§9.2–3). In other cases, such components are often present, but there is in addition the component of mid or low tongue-height, symbolized by /e a/. For example, the mid-front-unrounded vowel-sound of /ie^{1}/ has two components: the front position is part of /i/, the mid tongue-height is the /e/; the mid-back-rounded vowel-sound of /ue^{3}/ has three components: the roundedness is part of /u/, the mid tongue-height is the /e/, and the back position is a determined feature occurrent whenever this concatenation of determining features is found.

In what follows statements of the kind just made are greatly abbreviated: when nothing is said to the contrary, /e/ (plus whatever other simultaneous components may be involved) is to be taken as having its "normal" value, mid-back-unrounded; /a/, similarly, its "normal" value low-central-unrounded.

9.51 Triads. Three-way contrasts occur in the following frames ("C" = consonant, #, or a cluster /cr chr sr/; "V" = /# e a/): /CV#, CuV#, CuVr, CuVng, CuVngr, CiV#/.

/CV#/: /e/ has its normal value or, optionally, is a glide downwards and forwards from a fairly high back position, the peak of sonority near the beginning of the glide. /cre^{1} : cra^{1}/ 'to cover up : to jab'.

/CuV#, CuVr/: /e/ is rounded (otherwise "normal"), often with a glide after the peak of sonority towards mid-central-unrounded. /a/ is sometimes slightly retracted and rounded. /ue^{1} : ua^{1}/ 'nest : to vomit', /ˌsiau^{3} ˈuer^{1} : ˌsiau^{3} ˈuar^{4}/ 'small nest : small stockings'.

/CuVng, CuVngr/: /a/ is often a bit retracted and rounded: /ueng^{1} : uang^{2}/ (surnames), /khuangr^{1}/ 'basket'.

/CiV#/: /e/ is mid-front-unrounded, often with a centering glide after the peak of sonority; /a/ is sometimes slightly fronted: /ie̜^{1} : ia^{1}/ 'coconut : duck'.

9.52 Pairs. Two-way contrasts occur as follows:

9.521 /e/ versus /a/, in frames /CVr, CVi, CVir, CVn, CVng, CVngr, CVur, CVm, CuVi, CuVir, CuVn, CiVngr, CiVu, CiVur, CiVr, CiVir.

/CVr/: as in frame /CV#/: /chrar^1 : ˌsiau^3 ˈchrer^1/ 'X-mark : small cart'.

/CVi/: /e/ is mid-front-unrounded; /a/ slightly fronted and raised: /kei^3 : kai^3/ 'to give : to alter'.

/CVir, CVn/: /e/ higher-mid-central-unrounded, even more fronted in the specific frames /rVn, rVir/; /a/ is slightly fronted and raised: /keir^1 : kair^1/ 'root : dried stuff', /cren^4 : cran^4/ 'to give relief : to stand', /ren^2/ 'people'.

/CVng, CVngr/: /a/ is often a bit retracted: /reng^1 : rang^3/ 'to throw : to call out', /fengr^1 : fangr^2/ 'small envelope : small house'.

/CVu, CVur/: both /e/ and /a/ are optionally rounded, /e/ usually so; /a/ is optionally a bit retracted: /keu^3 : kau^3/ 'dog : pick (tool)', /teur^1 : taur^1/ 'pocket : small knife'.

/CVm/: /e/ is slightly fronted: /srem^2 : tham^1/ 'what : they'.

/CuVi/: with /k kh h cr chr sr r #/ in position [1], /e/ is higher-mid-central-unrounded; with anything else in [1], higher-mid-back-rounded: /kuei^1 : ˈkuai^1 ta/ 'to pertain to : to pat with a flat instrument', /tuei^4/ 'correct'.

/CuVir/: both /e/ and /a/ are fronted and raised: /tueir^1 : tuair^4/ 'pile, heap : segment'.

/CuVn/: with # as [1], /e/ is slightly fronted; otherwise, /e/ is raised, almost to a (lax) high-back position, and rounded. /a/ is slightly fronted and raised. /tuen^4 : tuan^4/ 'pause : segment'.

/CiVngr/: /e/ is higher-mid-central-unrounded: /piengr^3 : iangr^4/ 'cake : manner'.

/CiVu, CiVur/: with tones /1 2/, /e/ is raised and optionally rounded; with tones /3 4 5/, not raised but optionally rounded; toneless, between these two. /a/, with tones /1 2/ and with /c ch s/ is position [1], is markedly raised and retracted, usually with rounding. /ieu^1 : iau^1/ 'to swing : waist', /siau^1/ 'flute', /chieur^2 : chiaur^2/ 'ball : bridge'.

/CiVr/: as in frame /CiV#/: /ier^4 : iar^2/ 'leaf : seedling'.

/CiVir/: both /e/ and /a/ are fronted and raised: /tieir^3 : tiair^3/ 'bottom : a little'.

9.522 /#/ versus /e/, in frames /CiuV#, CiuVr/: as in frames /CiV#/ or /CiVr/: /ciue^2/ 'to dig', /ˌsiau^5 ˈsiuer^3/ (?) 'light fall of snow'.

9.523 /#/ versus /a/, in frames /CiVn, CiVng, CiuVn/.

/CiVn/: /a/ is raised and fronted radically, almost a lower-mid-front-unrounded vowel-sound: /tian^3/ 'a bit'.

/CiVng/: /siang^4/ 'towards'.

/CiuVn/: /a/ varies between its normal value, and low-front-unrounded: /iuan^3/ 'far away'.

9.53 Unpaired Items. In the following frames there are no contrasts: with /#/: /CiVm, CiuVng, CiuVngr/; with /e/: /CuVm/; with /a/: /CiuVir/.

/CuVm/: /e/ is rounded: /uem^3/ 'we'.

/CiuVir/: /a/ is slightly fronted and raised: /ˌhua^1 ˈiuair^2/ 'flower garden'.

9.54 Unstressed and Disyllabic Microsegments. Unstressed monosyllabic microsegments are in general the same in their residual characteristics as those bearing stress. However, final /e/ in an unstressed monosyllabic microsegment, and /e/ in position [5] of disyllabic microsegments, are centered and lowered, and alternate freely with a slightly raised variety of /a/. In unstressed monosyllabic microsegments, though not in position [5] of disyllabic microsegments, there is a morphophonemically distinct /a/ (slightly raised) which does not alternate with /e/. The transcription is on this score morphophonemic: /ˈceme^3 ne?/ 'What?!'; but /ˈkuai^1 ta/ 'to pat with a flat instrument'.

In position [3] of a disyllabic microsegment, /e/ has the same quality that it has with the same elements in position [1] and [2], and /n/ in position [4], in a monosyllabic microsegment: /sreme^2 : ceme^3/ 'what : how'.

→ /a e/ are now completely described.

9.55 Alternative Treatments. Our analysis above selects in a few cases one rather than the other of two apparently equally acceptable choices, the reasons for our choice being irrelevant to the phonological facts:

In the frame /CiVn/, the vowel quality interpreted as /a/ has higher tongue-position than any other vowel quality so interpreted; there is no contrasting /e/ in this frame, and the vowel quality in question could also be interpreted as /e/; e.g., /tien^3/ 'a little', instead of /tian^3/. This alternative choice is reflected in the Wade Romanization.

In the frames /CuVi, CuVir, CiVu, CiVur/, and in frame /CuVn/ when C is not zero, only /e/ and /a/ occur. The vowel qualities interpreted as /e/ are quite high, and could also be interpreted as zero; thus /kui^4/ for our /kuei^4/ 'expensive', /khuir^3/ for /khueir^3/ 'spool', /iu^2/ for /ieu^2/ 'oil', /chiur^2/ for /chieur^2/ 'ball', and /tun^4/ for /tuen^4/ 'pause'. /uen^4/ 'to ask' would not be altered, for in this case the vowel quality is clearly in the mid tongue-height range. Since the symbolism /iu/ would thus become ambiguous for our present /iu/ (as in /iu^3/ 'rain') and /ieu/, another orthographic convention would have to be introduced: simultaneous or overlapping /i/ (i) and /u/ (u) would have to be written with a single symbol, say /y/, giving /iu^3/ 'to have', /y^3/ 'rain'.[25]

Had the alternative choices been made in these cases, the arrangement of our descriptive statements would have been modified slightly; neither this nor the necessity for introducing /y/ militates against this treatment.

[25] This alternative was suggested by Morris Swadesh (private conversation).

10. Limitations on Sequence of Microsegments. A microsegment with initial /ng/ occurs only in macrosegment-final, preceded in the same mesosegment by a microsegment ending in /ng/: /ˌlau³ ˈuang² nge?/ 'O friend Wang!'

Within a macrosegment: the third tone does not occur on two successive microsegments; neither does the fifth tone; the fifth tone does not fall on the terminal microsegment; a mesosegment with an initial pretonic toneless and stressless microsegment does not occur initially.

11. Comparison with Hartman's Analysis. The formulation just completed above of Peiping phonology is based on and supported by the writer's own observations; but both observation and formulation were guided by the work of predecessors. In the late thirties George L. Trager, working with George A. Kennedy, developed the theories of: three basic vowels (high, mid, low); the biphonemic status (/iu/ in our notation) of high-front-rounded vowels or glides; and the analysis of retroflex initials /sr cr chr/ into non-retroflex initials /s c ch/ and a retroflex semivowel /r/. The results were not published by either Trager or Kennedy; Hartman later took up the investigation, carried it further, and published.[26] The present analysis is also, so to speak, in the same "tradition"; but there are differences, and these differences are worth discussion.

(1) Hartman posits three vowels, /a e/ and high /i/; he writes the semivowels as /j w r/. To each syllable one of these vowels is assigned.[27] Monosyllabic microsegments which here are taken as having no vowel at all are by Hartman taken to contain the high vowel. Thus he writes /njwi/ for our /niu/, and so on.

It turns out, upon inspection, that if Hartman's high vowel is omitted, the remaining set of symbols with which such a microsegment is written, together with the fact that they constitute a single microsegment, defines unambiguously both the location of the peak of sonority and the vowel-quality which occurs there. It is therefore redundant to indicate, with a separate symbol, the location and high-vowel nature of the peak of sonority in such microsegments.

Of paramount importance in the statement just made are the words "together with the fact that they constitute a single microsegment." Hartman assumes this fact, not discussing (save in one footnote) phenomena in sequences larger than a single monosyllabic microsegment. Until such phenomena have been observed, however, we cannot know for sure whether Hartman's "syllable," the structure of which is his topic, is a unit defined phonologically by the fact that it has a peak of sonority, or by the fact that a phonemically relevant syllable-juncture occurs between each two successive syllables. If the former should turn out to be the case, then the presence of a peak of sonority is necessarily a primary factor (a determining feature, in our terminology); but if the latter is the case, then at least so long as we confine our attention to monosyllabic microsegments (as Hartman did), the presence of a peak of sonority is not a primary factor, but a resultant of the arrangement of other factors. Furthermore, if the former is the case, we cannot legitimately discuss segmental structure in terms of "syllables," but must instead take as our larger units, within which certain arrangements of features occur, whatever unit happens to be marked off by successive occurrences of the closest phonemic variety of open juncture—perhaps, for example, whole phrases.

Within Hartman's range of discussion, therefore, with arrangement of material within what we here call monosyllabic microsegments as the topic, the high vowel, the "syllabicity" vowel with no other distinguishing characteristic of its own, is clearly a resultant rather than a determining feature in its own right. In the present discussion we have explicitly introduced the determining feature (microjuncture) which enables us to discuss arrangement of material within microsegments, and are led a fortiori to exclude the high vowel as a separate entity. However, we also see that there are disyllabic microsegments, not discussed by Hartman, the structure of which must also be accounted for in our complete analysis. It might have turned out, quite easily, that in this special and rare type of microsegment the high vowel would be necessary; and, if that had been the case, it would of course have had to be used throughout. Since disyllabic microsegments are hard to observe, further familiarity with allegro speech may still necessitate a return from the two-vowel system to Hartman's, but at the present writing this does not seem likely.

(2) Hartman reports a smaller variety of finals containing /r/ than are recognized herein. Thus he recognizes the contrast here transcribed as /eir/ versus /er/, providing the microsegment bears first or second tone, but not with any of the other tones, and no comparable distinction between /air/ and /ar/. This, of course, may well be the situation for some speakers.

Hartman's analysis of /eir/ and /er/ takes the first as /er/, the second as /eer/, with the mid vowel doubled; this is based on a reputed difference in length of the vocalic phase of the final, which he takes, instead of the qualitative difference, as primary. This could be extended to the cases he does not distinguish: /eer, er; aer, ar/, respectively, with all tones, instead of my /er, eir; ar, air/. There is perhaps little basis for choice; I hear distinct palatalization in the second of each pair, and have interpreted accordingly.

[26] See fn. 2 above.

[27] Hartman's "syllable" = our "monosyllabic microsegment"; Hartman, like his predecessors, does not discover disyllabic microsegments, and does not examine too closely the problem of establishing syllables as phonologically relevant units to start with.

(3) Hartman, §7, says "there is ... nothing in the distribution to suggest that the aspirates [/ph th ch kh/] are anything but unit consonants." Here our phonemic working assumptions differ; Hartman is analyzing occurrent material into phonemes; I analyze into determining (and determined) features; Hartman uses distributional facts as the basis for phonemic conclusions, I find the determining features and then state the distributions. The aspiration of /ph th ch kh/ sounds like the independent aspiration /h/; so I take it to be the same thing.

(4) Hartman does not, in his paper, recognize tone /^{5}/ ("raised third") as phonemically distinct; but it was Hartman who, after publication of his paper, discovered cases of minimal contrast which establish /^{5}/ as different from both /^{2}/ and /^{3}/.

Addenda: Since this report was submitted several facts have come to light (mainly through the courtesy of Yuenren Chao) which bear on the discussion.

(1) (To §8.23) The following monosyllabic microsegments, excluded in the text, are attested: /sen, seng, sengr, liun, nen, neu, tiang, tiangr, thei, pia, phia, chrei, rua/. /len/ occurs elsewhere than in the name referred to (§8.23, (5)). Many of the above additions are from onomatopoetic forms.

(2) (To §§9.31, 9.33) In the sequence /Ci.../, if /C/ is /t th n l/ the consonant is not palatalized; rather, the /i/ is a rather low high-front glide or vowel, not overlapping the consonant.

(3) There are a number of interjections having vocalic structure not subsumable under the system here set up. In addition, there is a minimum contrast between /ˌieu^2 ˈcing^3/ 'oil wells' and what we would here transcribe identically in the meaning 'there are wells,' where the first syllable of the latter might also bear tone /^{5}/. /ieu^2/ in the first of this pair has a relatively high back rounded vowel; in the second of the pair, a considerably lower vowel (identical with that of /ieu^3/ or /ieu^4/). In the light of this phenomenon there is serious doubt as to whether the two-vowel system, or its three-vowel predecessor, can be maintained. Perhaps it can, if we accept the modification suggested in §9.55.

⟦On page 108 I spoke of the later trend towards what I called 'phonemics without the phoneme', and now this paper appears as its first exemplification here; others will follow. Some credit is due, at least, (and Hockett among others has given it) to stimulation from the Trubetzkoy-Jakobson theory of distinctive features, but it would also be possible to call this an autonomous American development. Its autonomy is evident in both negative and positive ways.

Negatively, there is for example the refusal to take the distinctive features as universals, exactly nine polar sets of them being extant—or is it ten?—for all the world's languages to use, and the same distinctive oppositions being found in disparate parts of the phonology, e.g. 'acute-versus-grave' alike in the stop-system and the vowel-system; instead, the distinctive features are established ad hoc for each language or even dialect. (The Trager theory of the 'over-all pattern', identical for all the dialects of a language, could be derived from these distinctive features; but as a matter of historical fact seems to have developed independently of them.) Again, any resolution of distinctive-feature sets into binary components is treated as a game, not a discovery of ultimate truth.

Negative or positive would both be good interpretations of the American rejection of the limitation to segmental elements and corresponding insistence on the importance (or even primacy) of the 'suprasegmental' frame in which the segmental elements are found to occur in all languages. Related to this is the readiness to recognize dynamic segmentals such as semivowels, against the Jakobson way of treating e. g. English /w/ as simply an /u/ vowel.

In short, there is an air of independence in it all.

The positive trend of the American development, which makes it look like an autonomous sequel to earlier American phonemics, is the one which I have characterized ⦅108⦆ as 'making the theory independent of the accidents of analytic practice'. The practicing analyst, in the American sense, is the one who has a language previously quite unknown to him to work on and has to do everything from the ground up. (He is likely to sympathize with those who complain that European phonologists avoid the spade-work and just shuffle other people's data, even when he knows that the accusation is not true.) For him, analysis begins with his own phonetic transcribing. This is segmental because his marks on paper have to be countable. Hence, when (if ever) he becomes a sophisticated theorist, he views his segmented transcription with dark suspicion. The segmentation needs justifying. In his Boas tradition (languages can differ without limit as to either extent or direction), no universal theory of segments can be called upon to settle the moot points. Only the particular language can yield proper criteria. Where these fail, segmentation is arbitrary. There have to be enough units to picture the significant differences among utterances: this is the crosswise dimension, 'at right angles' to the time-flow of speech, and it is in this dimension that one makes discoveries which increase the number of phonemic symbols. To reduce their number, one looks for distributional criteria in the other, the time-flow dimension. In Chinese, these criteria fail with at least one question still unresolved.

To make sure that the description has been freed from segmental prejudice, it is expedient to redo it as if one had started out from the other end. Hence the first paragraph on this page.

The word 'phoneme' can be and often is avoided, but the adjective 'phonemic' still labels distinctive differences; then the orphaned noun 'phonemics' is attached to it, and the adverb 'phonemically' is kept.⟧

PROBLEMS OF MORPHEMIC ANALYSIS

CHARLES F. HOCKETT
Language 23.321–43—1947

I. Introductory

1. This paper develops further the theory of morphemic analysis presented by Zellig S. Harris in 1942.[1] Morphemic analysis is the operation by which the analyst isolates minimum meaningful elements in the utterances of a language, and decides which occurrences of such elements shall be regarded as occurrences of 'the same' element.

This operation does not constitute all of grammatical analysis: when it is completed, there remains the task of describing the arrangements in which the minimum meaningful elements occur, and—where the same elements are observed to occur in more than one arrangement with a difference in meaning—the features other than morphemes (the 'tagmemes') that are involved. For this latter phase, I have proposed the term 'tactics'.[2]

The fact that John hit Bill and Bill hit John have different meanings,[3] or that old men and women is sometimes approximately the same as 'old men and old women', sometimes rather comparable to 'women and old men',[4] proves that features other than morphemes have to be recognized—unless, of course, we wish to redefine 'morpheme' to cover features of this type too. There is other evidence: a graduate student in a hurry to prepare himself for a French reading exam, or a scholar deciphering a dead language written in a non-phonetic or semi-phonetic orthography, may achieve good control of the tactics and semantics of the language, but remain in almost total ignorance of anything submorphemic. To do this he needs some mnemonically satisfactory device for keeping morphemes apart. The device probably consists of speech sounds;[4a] but these may be purely private. Thus a western sinologist may know Confucius backwards and yet stumble in passing the time of day with any speaker of a modern Chinese dialect.

Although, then, morphemics and tactics are both necessarily involved in grammar, we nevertheless have considerable range of choice in drawing the line between them.[5] Faced with a language of a certain degree of complexity, we may prefer to describe it with simple morphemics and complicated tactics, or conversely, or somewhere in between. The language is not disturbed by our choice; its complexities remain whether itemized in one part or another of our description. But the resulting descriptions may vary a great deal in the clarity with which they depict the situation. Presumably we should try to obtain that distribution of data between morphemics and tactics which produces the greatest clarity. In this paper we assume, without steadfast conviction, that this end is achieved by the simplest possible tactics, whatever submorphemic complications may be necessitated.

2. The same assumption was apparently involved in Harris's formulation of 1942. Yet Harris realized that this cannot stand as the only assumption. We must have, also, a set of principles on the basis of which we identify, or refuse to identify, different stretches of speech as morphemically the same. The great value of Harris's paper lies in this: that although he does not add any individual method of morphemic identification to those currently used, he demonstrates how all the superficially diverse methods can be regarded as cases of one general procedure. This general procedure we outline herewith, with such minor modifications of terminology as will be useful to us:

Step 1. The utterances of a language are examined.[6] Recurrent partials with constant meaning (ran away in John ran away and Bill ran away) are discovered; recurrent partials not composed of smaller ones (-way) are alternants or morphs.[7] So are any partials not recurrent but left over when all recurrent ones are accounted for. The citable case most nearly approaching this is the cran- of cranberry, which does indeed recur, but always with berry following. By definition, a morph has the same phonemic shape in all its occurrences. Because we

[1] Zellig S. Harris, Morpheme Alternants in Linguistic Analysis, Lang. 18.169–80 (1942) ((109)).

[2] Review of Eugene A. Nida, Morphology: the Descriptive Analysis of Words, Lang. 23.273–85 (1947).

[3] Leonard Bloomfield, Language §10.4 (New York, 1933).

[4] Rulon S. Wells, Immediate Constituents, Lang. 23.81–117, esp. 93 ff. (§§30 ff.) (1947).

It would be possible to say that this ambiguity of old men and women was grammatically irrelevant; but features of order of the type involved in John hit Bill versus Bill hit John cannot be ignored. This being so, Bloomfield's term 'tagmeme' for a feature of meaningful arrangement is useful.

[4a] This is a reasonable assumption because of man's million years or so of natural selection, in which ability in aural memory and oral mimicry has been a factor making for survival.

[5] Cf. Zellig S. Harris, From Morpheme to Utterance, Lang. 22.161–83, esp. 162–3 (§2) (1946) ((142–3)).

[6] Obviously not all of them, but a sampling which we hope will be statistically valid. By working with successively larger samplings, and by predicting on the basis of each what else will occur, we approach, at least asymptotically, a complete description.

[7] A convenient term, because it (1) eliminates the lengthy expressions 'morpheme alternant' and 'morpheme unit', and (2) suggests a valid analogy (allo)phone : phoneme = morph : morpheme.

operate with whole utterances, morphs are not always composed of continuous uninterrupted stretches of phonemes,[8] but they are always composed of phonemes. Every utterance is composed entirely of morphs. The division of a stretch of speech between one morph and another, even if the two are simultaneous, overlapping, or staggered, we shall call a cut.

Step 2. Two or more morphs are grouped into a morpheme if they '(a) have the same meaning, (b) never occur in identical environments, and (c) have combined environments no greater than the environments of some single alternant in the language',[9] e.g -en in oxen, /z/ in cows, and various others, all meaning 'noun plural', with combined environments, or range, paralleling the range of zero with meaning 'noun singular'.[10]

Step 3. The differences in the phonemic shape of alternants of morphemes are organized and stated; this constitutes morphophonemics. Morphophonemic statements may involve morphophonemes—that is, the symbols used for phonemes, plus supplementary ones, with special definitions as to phonemic value under varying circumstances—or they may not; often lists are more convenient, and sometimes they are unavoidable. But regardless of the methods used in describing them, such alternations are morphophonemic.

3. In several ways a rigorous adherence to Harris's system as here stated is troublesome.

(1) Sometimes we are confronted with a set of alternants with apparently identical meaning which are almost, but not quite, in complementary distribution. So with the two alternants meaning 'noun plural' in hoofs and hooves, or laths with /θ/ and with /ð/. These would forbid the tactically desirable conclusion that there is but one noun-plural morpheme in English.

(2) Sometimes a set of alternants with identical meaning and completely in complementary distribution have to be kept apart because we can find no single alternant whose range parallels that of the given group. In Latin, for instance, there is no case-number combination represented after all noun stems by the same suffix; therefore we may not legitimately (by Harris's criteria) speak of a single 'nominative-singular' morpheme, or a single morpheme for any other case-number meaning.

(3) Sometimes a stretch of speech may be cut at either of two places, so as to produce equally satisfactory—and equally unsatisfactory—morphs. In Menomini, when an element ending (otherwise) in a consonant precedes, in the same word, an element beginning (otherwise) in a consonant, an /e/ appears between them. Do we cut before or after this /e/? Either cut will do; either choice is arbitrary. Harris proposes that we cut in both places, and regard /e/ as an alternant of /-/ 'morpheme juncture'.[11] In this proposal he does not adhere to his own rules, for morpheme juncture has no meaning, and is not a morpheme; yet any Algonquianist will say that his solution is correct, and the problem is to readjust the rules so that the interpretation does not violate them.

(4) Since there is no way in which French /o/ 'to the (masc.)' can be cut, we must take it as a single morph. But the tactical survey suggests rather that it be taken as two successive morphemes, à 'to' plus le 'the (masc.)'. There is at present no way in which the latter conclusion can be reached without doing violence to our criteria.

(5) As we perform step 1 of Harris's procedure, only morphs of overt phonemic content turn up. It is suggested that the definition of morph be extended to cover also the following: minus-features, such as that which added to French bonne 'good (fem.)' produces bon 'good (masc.)'; replacement features, as man : men; zero features, as in sheep (sg.) : sheep (pl.); and combinations of these, such as the difference between child and children. This is a difficult maneuver, however desirable; Harris (within the scope of his paper) tells us neither under what conditions it is called for nor how to perform it.

The items just listed are not criticisms, but points on which improvement is clearly possible within Harris's general framework. The first two difficulties are easily handled; the remaining three are more serious, but respond to a single modification in plan of attack.

Many of the problems of morphemic identification met with in dealing with any language are trivial. Before turning to the full-scale discussion of the five difficulties listed above (in Parts III and IV below), we attempt to show how the more trivial problems can be solved quickly and easily, in a fashion that sheds light on the more intricate questions to which one must eventually turn.[12]

[8] The possibilities are investigated by Harris, Discontinuous Morphemes, Lang. 21.121-7 (1945)—but the added complication of this is avoided in the examples of the present paper.

[9] Harris, Morpheme Alternants §7.1.

[10] The zero element with meaning 'noun singular' is one of Harris's parallels (Morpheme Alternants §2.2). Such a morpheme has very dubious status, having no alternant of other than zero shape (see fn. 37 and reference cited there). Harris lists also the parallel -ful; given the modification of criteria proposed in §13 of this paper, one could add also 's 'genitive'.

[11] Harris, Morpheme Alternants §4.2.

[12] We propose to say both 'the morph x occurs in such-and-such an utterance', and 'the morpheme x occurs in such-and-such an utterance'. By our definition, a morpheme is a class of morphs, so that the latter type of expression, without further qualification, is logically invalid. We render it valid by stating that an expression of the form 'the morpheme x' shall be taken in some cases as a class-name, in other cases as a variable indicating the appropriate though unspecified member of the class, depending on what the context requires. No ambiguity results; this is customary usage in linguistics; but it is a point on which more care is needed than is usual.

II. Preliminary Normalization

4. Let us assume that we have before us a display of a large number of utterances of a language, in a phonemic notation. As we begin the search for recurrent partials, we may discover that a phonemic notation other than the one we have used—for there are always several mutually convertible possibilities—would simplify the task.

In Yawelmani,[13] for example, the point of syllable division is phonemic. One way to write Yawelmani is to use a hyphen for syllable juncture; then the phonemic content of syllables can be indicated with a relatively small number of vowel and consonant letters. If our display of utterances is in this notation, we find such obviously related forms as /gˀadsˀ/ 'obsidian' : /gˀadsˀ-ni/ 'obsidian (dative)' : /gˀa-dsˀa/ 'obsidian (accusative)'. The second form contains a stretch identical with the first, plus /-ni/ 'dative'; the third form contains, before /a/ 'accusative', a stretch identical with the first part of the other two save for an inserted hyphen. If we are to identify the non-identical stretches /gˀadsˀ/ and /gˀa-dsˀ/ as being morphemically the same (whether one morpheme or more is another matter), and make similar identifications in other cases where the presence or absence of a hyphen is the phonemically differentiating factor, then we must handle this evanescent hyphen in our morphophonemic statements.

Yawelmani can also be written phonemically without the hyphen. If we want to write it so, we must use unit symbols for certain consonants which otherwise might be interpreted either as belonging wholly to a single syllable or as being divided between two: for example, /Vgˀ V/ would be an ambiguous notation for both /V-gˀ V/ and /Vg-ˀ V/; but if we replace /gˀ/ in a single syllable by /k'/, the ambiguity is removed.[13a] With all such changes as are necessary, we reach a notation which does not write the point of syllable division with a separate symbol, but which nevertheless indicates it unambiguously: when a single consonant symbol stands between two vowel symbols, a point of syllable division falls before the consonant symbol; when two consonant symbols stand between two vowel symbols, a point of syllable division falls between them.

In this notation, the forms given above appear as /k'ac'/ : /k'ac'ni/ : /k'ac'a/. The partial /k'ac'/ appears to be identical in all three forms. Phonemically, of course, it is not; but the only phonemic difference has been relegated to a status of notational predictability, and can be ignored in our further manipulations. There are so many intricate problems in Yawelmani morphemics that any advantage of this kind that we can obtain is greatly to be desired.[14]

5. A notation is phonemic if it indicates, in every position, only those phonemic contrasts which occur in that position, but indicates all of them. Once one has found the morphemically most desirable phonemic notation, one can often handle certain additional simple morphemic problems by modifying it in such a way that, in addition to indicating unambiguously all the phonemic contrasts occurring in a position, it also indicates in certain positions contrasts which are not there phonemic.

If our display is of Navaho utterances,[15] we notice, sooner or later, that vowel symbols do not occur before pause (P). The sequence /VhP/ (with V for any vowel symbol) does occur. When we examine the display for recurrent partials, we find certain stretches with constant meaning that end in /Vh/ both before P and elsewhere, others that end in /Vh/ before P but without the /h/ elsewhere. Thus /bìtàhP/ 'among them' : /bìtàh níhP/ 'among them, he says', but /dò·dàhP/ 'not' : /dò· dà níhP/ 'he says no'. The morphemic identification of /dò·dàh/ (P) and /dò·dà/ (no P) is elementary, as are other such cases. So we modify our notation throughout the display, by erasing certain pre-pause h's—namely, those at the end of stretches that occur medially with the same meaning but without the /h/. In our notes we enter the memorandum: both V and Vh before pause represent phonemic /Vh/. Thereafter, save when reading off our transcription with Navaho speech sounds, we ignore the memorandum; the new /dò·dà/ now has the same shape, to the eye, before P and elsewhere.[16]

Or suppose that we are dealing with Latin. We find pairs like ars : artis, noks : noktis, urps : urbis,

13 Stanley S. Newman, The Yokuts Language of California (New York, 1944). The phonemicity of the point of syllable division is my conclusion from the evidence he gives.

13a In this notation the letter k and the apostrophe ' are meant to constitute one symbol together. Similarly c and ' below.

14 The second notation is that used by Newman. It may be wondered why anyone would be led to investigate the potentialities of our first notation, the one that we decided to reject. But in Southern Athabascan (see citations in fn. 15) an entirely similar problem arises, and Hoijer chooses an orthography comparable to our first Yokuts orthography, not to our second. The complexity of morphophonemic statement which results is considerable, and could be rendered measurably easier if a phonemic notation were used in which syllable division is marked indirectly instead of overtly.

15 Harry Hoijer, Navaho Phonology, University of New Mexico Publications in Anthropology I (Albuquerque, 1945); a similar phenomenon in Chiricahua Apache: Harry Hoijer, Chiricahua Apache, Linguistic Structures of Native America 55–84 (New York, 1946).

16 Hoijer's working notation incorporates this normalization, though he calls the contrast between 'constant' pre-pause h and the evanescent type phonemic instead of morphophonemic. A similar normalization leads to the writing, within word borders, of phonemes both of the s-series and of the š-series, although, at least in rapid speech, only those of a single series occur within the stretch bounded by word junctures; see Zellig S. Harris, Navaho Phonology and Hoijer's Analysis, IJAL 11.239–48 (1945).

re·ks : re·gis, niks : niwis. The semantic and morphemic difference between ars and artis recurs with other pairs, but the difference in phonemic shape between the members of a pair is not so constant from one pair to another. Whatever may be our ultimate morphemic conclusions (e.g. that artis is ars plus something, or that ars and artis are both art plus something), they will be more easily reached if we can make the difference in shape to the eye parallel the morphemic difference.

This can be done. From phonemics we know that the sequences rts, kts, rbs, gs, gws do not occur before word juncture,[17] and that gw does not occur intervocalically. We may therefore rewrite the forms with precisely these non-occurrent sequences: arts : artis, nokts : noktis, urbs : urbis, re·gs : re·gis, nigws : nigwis. We note that in the modified orthography, rts and rs (before word juncture) are both representations of phonemic /rs/, and so on.[18] In the new notation, the second form of each pair differs from the first only in the presence of an i before the final consonant.

6. Sometimes it helps to perform this type of normalizing operation more than once.

In Potawatomi, a first normalization introduces, at certain points within utterances, a mark (say a space) indicating *potential pause*. Then we examine the stretches between successive points of potential pause to see which ones recur in various positions (relative to actual pause, or to adjacent stretches of varying structure) with the same meaning and the same or almost the same phonemic shape. Neither preceded nor followed by (actual) pause, we find kak 'porcupine', k·we 'woman', muk· 'beaver', k·uk· 'bucket'. Preceded but not followed by pause, we find rather kak, kwe, muk·, kuk·. Followed but not preceded by pause, the forms with the same meanings are kak, k·we, muk, k·uk. Both preceded and followed by pauses, the forms are kak, kwe, muk, kuk.

Now observation shows that the phonemes /p·/, /t·/, /č·/, /k·/ occur neither directly after nor directly before pause. Therefore we normalize all such forms as those itemized above, in all positions in which they occur, to kak, k·we, muk·, k·uk·, with the necessary memorandum that when either preceded or followed by pause, both k and k·, both p and p·, etc., represent phonemic /k/, /p/, etc.

This same normalization also accounts for all other alternations turning on the presence or absence of pause. When we have retranscribed our entire display of forms, we look further, and discover such pairs as nkutšuwe 'he wins a race' : nnuktušwe 'I win a race', kwtumočke 'he's fishing' : nkwutmočke 'I'm fishing', pmos·e 'he's walking' : npums·e 'I'm walking', msunʔukun 'paper' : nmusnuʔkun 'my paper'. If we want to, we can begin at this level to cut our forms up into smaller recurrent partials. Clearly n means 'I, my'; the remainder of the first form, nuktušwe, presumably means 'win a race', but is not the same morph as nkutšuwe '(he) win(s) a race', because of the difference in phonemic shape. For that matter, each of these may be more than one morph. Whatever comes of this, our morphophonemic statements are going to have to be complicated at every stage by an alternation of the positions in which vowels appear.

So instead of continuing our comparison and cutting, we can try first to make a further notational normalization that will take care of the alternating vowels, or many of them. We do this by rewriting the original forms, writing a vowel in *both* forms of a pair whenever it appears in *either* form, and in a few other places for good measure: nUkUtUšUwe : nUnUkUtUšUwe, kwUtUmočUke : nUkwUtUmočUke, pUmOs·e : nUpUmOs·e, mUsUnUʔUkUn : nUmUsUnUʔUkUn. Our memorandum this time states how these graphs are to be interpreted, not directly into a phonemic notation, but into the supraphonemic notation achieved by the previously applied normalizations: the first and each alternate one of a series of capitalized vowel symbols counts as zero, unless it precedes a final consonant.[19]

The second form of each pair now consists, to the eye, of nU (presumably 'I, my') followed by something that is identical with the first form of the pair. All the remaining problems of morphemic isolation and identification are rendered simpler.

7. There is no real drawback to counter the advantages of this kind of preliminary notational normalization, but there is a caution which must be observed. Our notational changes make morphs of differing phonemic shape look alike—indeed, that is why we make them. But the ultimate problem of the grouping of such morphs into morphemes is one which must be solved in a manner consistent with our handling of less patent cases—that is, on the basis of Harris's criteria (Step 2, §2) or of some other set. Performed as we have here suggested, notational regularizing is not apt to obscure more desirable morphemic identifications; but in extensive work with any specific language, one needs to check back over such preliminary operations from time to time to make sure.

17 Though it is not clear what word juncture is in Latin; it may be a non-phonemic matter introduced by a previous notational normalization.

18 Full phonemic information is still given, since such a graph as rts before word juncture stands *always* for phonemic /rs/, never anything alse. In *the new* notation we have multiple writings for certain phonemic sequences, but only one phonemic sequence for each writing.

19 We are forced to use capitals or some other device for evanescent vowels, because other vowels, phonemically the same, are not evanescent. This fact marks these alternations as *non-automatic*. Where no extra symbols are needed—where the symbols already used phonemically are merely extended to positions in which they do not phonemically occur—the alternations are *automatic*.

III. Revision of the Grouping-Requirements

8. In step 2 (§2) are stated Harris's three *grouping-requirements*—the three conditions which must be met by two or more morphs if they are to be regarded as belonging to the same morpheme. Some of the troubles itemized in §3 result from the particular way in which these grouping-requirements are formulated. The first of them, involving meaning,[20] is obviously the most difficult to handle. We attempt no revision of it here, and any choices dependent on it under the Harris procedure will remain in the present scheme. The second and third requirements are purely distributional, and more easily subject to analysis and modification.

Preliminary to our proposal for a modification of the second grouping-requirement we define *non-contrastive distribution*. Two elements of the same kind (i.e. both allophones, both morphs, or the like) are in non-contrastive distribution if either (1) they are in complementary distribution, or (2) they are in partial complementation, and in those environments in which both occur, they are in free alternation. By free alternation is meant (a) that one cannot predict, save perhaps statistically, which form will occur in a particular instance, and (b) that the occurrence of one, rather than of the other, does not produce an utterance different in meaning.

In phonemic analysis, non-contrastive distribution is often used as a criterion permitting the grouping of two or more allophones into a single phoneme. Thus the unaspirated [t] of *stick* and the aspirated [tʻ] of *tick* are both found at utterance-final and in certain other positions: *He's in the skit* may end with [t] or with [tʻ]. But this utterance is 'the same' utterance whether the aspiration is present or not; similarly with any other pair differentiated only in this respect. The occurrence of both allophones in certain environments does not deter us from classing both in the same phoneme, /t/.

We propose, then, to revise the second grouping-requirement from 'never occur in identical environments'—which is another way of saying 'are in complementary distribution'—to read 'are in non-contrastive distribution'.[21]

The examples which follow (§§9–11) will demonstrate both the way in which this change increases the efficiency of our analysis, and also a danger inherent in it.

9. In Modern West Armenian[22] a number of morphs occur with meaning 'genitive singular': /o/ and /0/ with one stem of preceding noun, /van/, /u/, /an/, and /i/ with other stems. The environments in which these occur can be differentiated in terms of the nouns which immediately precede, and such nouns fall into a series of classes (of purely morphophonemic importance) by virtue of the morph or morphs of this meaning which follow them. One occurs only with /o/ and the oblique stem: /asdəvaʒ/ 'God' : /asduʒ.o/ 'of God'. Some occur only with /0/ and the oblique stem: /kuyr/ 'sister' : /kəroč/ 'of sister, sister's'. Some occur only with /i/ and the singular stem; this is the most common pattern: /atoř/ 'chair' : /atoř.i/. Most of those which occur with /van/ and the singular stem, for example /irigun/ 'evening' : /irig.van/, are also observed to occur with /i/: /irigun.i/. The same is true for most of those which occur with /u/ or with /an/: /meg/ 'one' : /meg.u/ or /meg.i/; /axčig/ 'girl' : /axčəg.an/ or /axčig.i/.

The morphs meaning 'genitive singular' are thus not in complementary distribution, and by the original form of the second grouping-requirement could not be combined into a single morpheme. However, there is no observable difference in meaning between, say, /axčəgan/ and /axčigi/; nor is the speaker's choice of one or the other of these on any particular occasion predictable, save perhaps statistically. Therefore, within the limits of semantic judgment available to us at present, the various morphs in question are indeed in non-contrastive distribution, and by the modified second grouping-requirement—providing the third grouping-requirement is also met—are classifiable as a single morpheme.

10. In Peiping Chinese there are, as the elementary texts usually put it, two words for 'two': èr and lyǎng. The latter graph, by a preliminary normalization that need not concern us here, subsumes two distinct forms, lyǎng and lyáng. Unit numerals (those for 'one' through 'nine') occur in Chinese in the following positions: before a measure; after a group numeral ('ten' etc.); before a group numeral; after an ordinal demonstrative (dì 'the ...th'); preceded and followed by unit numerals (in counting 'one, two, three,...'). Sān 'three' appears in all these positions with a single phonemic shape. Èr occurs in the second, third, fourth, and fifth positions, lyǎng in the first and third. In the third position, before a group numeral, only èr occurs before shŕ 'ten', but either may occur before bǎi 'hundred', chyān 'thousand', and wàn 'ten thousand' and its multiples. The choice here is free. Èr also occurs in position one, to the exclusion of lyǎng, before the measure lyǎng 'tael, ounce'; and before a few other measures either èr

[20] In a manuscript not yet published, Harris demonstrates how, at least in theory, this criterion can be eliminated, thus appealing to semantic considerations at only one step of the whole process of descriptive analysis: the step at which one must decide whether two *utterances*, as historic events, are 'the same' or not (Bloomfield's fundamental assumption of linguistics, Language §5.3, §9.5). The first grouping-criterion (same meaning) thus becomes a practical shortcut; as such it is used here.

[21] In Yokuts Structure and Newman's Grammar, IJAL 10.196–211 (1944), Harris makes explicit use (§6) of the second grouping-requirement as modified, but without theoretical discussion.

[22] Information and forms were kindly supplied by Gordon H. Fairbanks. It does not matter for the present discussion whether the stem differences are submorphemic within the stem or are part of the suffix. Some other complications, which do not alter the picture materially, are omitted here. In the cited genitive forms, a dot separates stem from ending.

or lyǎng may be found, with no difference in meaning.

This statement of distribution is not quite exhaustive, but a completely exhaustive one reveals the same facts. Clearly, èr and lyǎng cannot be regarded as a single morpheme under the old form of the second grouping-requirement, but can under the new form.

The case of èr and lyǎng is unique in Chinese; most other sets of morphs differing in phonemic shape but classed nevertheless as belonging to single morphemes have at least some phonemic feature in common. If this factor is to deter us in grouping èr and lyǎng together, then some additional grouping-requirement, not mentioned by Harris, and apparently quite difficult to formulate in a strict fashion, must be involved. We mention this possibility because we feel the Chinese example 'instinctively' to be somewhat different in nature from the Armenian.

11. As indicated in §3 (1), Harris's example of English noun-plural morphs will not hold by a strict application of his criteria, because of such pairs as hoofs : hooves. One of the more interesting of such pairs is brothers : brethren. Cases like hoofs : hooves present no difficulty under the modified second grouping-requirement because the morphs involved (hoof and hoove-, /s/ and /z/) are in non-contrastive distribution: hoofs and hooves do not differ in meaning. This is not true of brothers and brethren.

There are several possible ways of handling the problem. One way, which fits both versions of the second grouping-requirement but seems not too pleasing, is to group the /z/ of brothers, along with most other morphs meaning 'noun plural', into a single morpheme, but to exclude from this morpheme the morph found in brethren, both because it is not in free alternation with /z/ in this environment and because it has a different meaning: 'plural, with semantic specialization, producing a form of address for fellow lodge- or church-members of the male sex'.

Another solution is to postulate two distinct, though homophonous, morphemes brother: $brother_1$ 'male child of same parents', and $brother_2$ 'fellow lodge- or church-member of the male sex'. The plural of $brother_1$ is brothers; that of $brother_2$ is either brothers or brethren, in free alternation. The morphs meaning 'plural of noun' in these two cases, together with others of the same meaning, are now in non-contrastive distribution, and can be grouped into a single morpheme.

This breakdown of brother into two homophonous morphs, in order to achieve a greater differentiation of the environments in which various morphs meaning 'noun plural' occur, may seem artificial; but if one starts with the plural forms and then works to the singular, it seems less so. For brethren occurs in larger environments in which brothers also occurs, whereas brothers occurs in some larger environments in which brethren does not occur, e. g. I want you to meet my ( ), John and Bill. If one groups the cases in which both may occur, and contrasts the non-linguistic environment of these cases with that of the cases in which only brothers occurs, the semantic difference is fairly clear. Extension by analogy to the singular forms then seems justified. The source of difficulty here, as often, lies of course in the complexity of manipulating any type of semantic criterion.

12. The proposed revision of the second grouping-requirement leads rather clearly to simpler tactics; but it raises a problem for which I have no answer.

There is a generally accepted working assumption in descriptive analysis to the effect that while there may be homophonous morphemes, there are no exactly synonymous ones.[23] No matter how subtle the difference in meaning may be between, say, twenty and score,[24] the difference in phonemic shape implies non-identity morphemically. Now the revised version of the second grouping-requirement implies that we will violate this working assumption when the evidence leads us to believe that the violation is desirable. But I can make no statement as to the formal conditions under which the principle should be suspended. In every case of not quite complete complementation, we have to examine the positions in which more than one morph of the set appears, and decide whether in these positions they are in free alternation or not. In every case, this decision seems to turn on semantic considerations. If this is true, then for a long time to come such decisions are going to be partly a matter of individual taste. This need not deter us; for in any such case we need only suspend judgment, state both or all the alternative analyses, and indicate that our choice of one for further analytical purposes is only tentative.

13. The modification of Harris's third grouping-requirement that we propose is somewhat simpler; cf. §3 (2). Instead of requiring that the morphs to be grouped 'have combined environments no greater than the environment of some single alternant in the language', we require that they have a total range which is not unique. The range of a morpheme is the class of all environments in which the member morphs of that morpheme occur. Our revised requirement still stipulates that a morpheme obtained by grouping several morphs together shall have a range identical with (or paralleling) that of some other morpheme, but no longer requires that the second morpheme (the test morpheme) shall consist of a single morph.

The tactical advantage to be gained by either form of the requirement is that we thereby avoid the need to list separately the ranges of individual morphemes; we prefer to handle them in terms of classes having identical or closely parallel ranges. With either form

23 Bloomfield, Language §9.5.

24 Harris, Morpheme Alternants §2.2.

of the requirement, there may remain morphemes containing only a single morph, which have unique ranges; but this we cannot handle in the present connection.[25] For those morphs which perhaps can be grouped into complex morphemes, the tactical advantage is worthwhile.

The revised form of the requirement enables us to gain this tactical advantage in cases where it is impossible under the older form. Latin case-endings are a clear example. Since no single case-number category is represented after all noun stems by the same morph, it is impossible under the old form of the requirement to group all the morphs of any single case-number combination into a single morpheme. Under the new requirement, we may do so for one case-number combination, providing we also do so for at least one other case-number combination; the natural conclusion is to do so for every such combination. The set of eight or ten case-number morphemes can now be handled tactically as a class: they occur after noun stems; and a noun stem occurs before a case-number morpheme.

IV. Morph and Morpheme

14. We now attempt to remove the source of the remaining difficulties mentioned in §3 (3–5). This we do by a single rather fundamental alteration of the relationship between morph and morpheme.

Both before and after this alteration, an utterance consists wholly of morphs: every bit of phonemic material in an utterance is part of one morph or another. Before the alteration, every morph belongs to one and only one morpheme, so that there are as many morphemes in an utterance as there are morphs. After the alteration, the number of morphs in an utterance and the number of morphemes therein may not be identical: some of the morphs, and hence some bits of phonemic material, of some utterances, are morphemically irrelevant. How this change is brought about, and with what utility, will be demonstrated presently. In making it, we must conform to a principle which Harris does not state but which he adheres to rigorously: the principle of total accountability. Every morph, and every bit of phonemic material, must be determined by (i.e. predictable from) the morphemes and the tagmemes (if any) of which the utterance is composed.[26]

25 In his unpublished material [see now his Methods in Structural Linguistics 202 (Univ. of Chicago Press, 1951)] Harris shows how this can be handled. His example is English /tuw/ (to, two, too), which in the absence of semantic criteria first appears as a single morph.

26 No defect of many older grammars of less-well-known languages is more marked than the confusion, or at best fuzziness, which results from a neglect of the principle of total accountability. Of course we do not condemn their writers for being 'men of their times rather than of ours'; for one thing, this doctrine could hardly be stated explicitly until the phonemic principle had been discovered.

Two morphemic analyses of an utterance are tactically equivalent if they give the structure of the utterance in terms of the same morphemes and tagmemes—whatever the differences in the handling of submorphemic matters. For example, according to one analysis, Fox[27] poonimeewa 'he stops talking to him' consists of the morphs pooni 'cease', m 'act by speech on an animate object', and certain succeeding elements which do not concern us. A different analysis breaks the form into poon and im, with the same meanings. These two analyses are tactically equivalent. By the first one, the morpheme 'cease' has form poon before morphs beginning with a vowel, form pooni before those beginning with a consonant, and the morpheme 'act by speech on an animate object' has everywhere form m. By the second analysis, 'cease' has everywhere form poon, and the second morpheme has the two forms m and im, depending on what precedes. In either case, the sequence of morphemes involved can be indicated as {poon} + {m}; it is only below the tactical level that there is any difference.

If, on the other hand, we divide the given form into poon 'cease', i, and m 'act by speech etc.', and consider each of these a morpheme as well as a morph, the analysis will not be tactically equivalent to the first two. For in this case the sequence of morphemes must be indicated as {poon} + {i} + {m} —there are more morphemes in the word than by the first two analyses. It is easy to see also why this analysis is tactically inferior to the first two: the statement as to the occurrence of the morpheme i—to which no meaning can be assigned—will have to operate in terms of submorphemic (phonemic) properties of environments, whereas on the tactical level we should like to be able to state environments of occurrence and non-occurrence of classes of morphemes in terms of other classes of morphemes, without regard to submorphemic matters.

But can we find any valid basis for preferring the first of the above alternative treatments to the second, or vice versa? Clearly, there can be no tactical reason for choosing any one of two or more tactically equivalent analyses. If any reason at all is discoverable, it will be within the submorphemic realm: a matter of patterning, or perhaps simply of greater convenience. And although convenience is a legitimate basis for a choice, we must recognize such a criterion as different in kind from others, and as more open to disagreement. A more convenient analysis tells us nothing more about a language than a less convenient one that is otherwise equivalent; but what it does tell it tells more clearly.

27 I choose Fox rather than Menomini because the examples are a bit easier to cite; the same principles apply. The Fox forms are from Leonard Bloomfield, Notes on the Fox Language, IJAL 3.219–32, 4.181–226 (1924–7), and from the same writer's Algonquian, Linguistic Structures of Native America 85–129 (New York, 1946).

15. The alteration by which the number of morphemes in an utterance fails in some cases to coincide with the number of morphs consists of recognizing two special kinds of morphs: empty morphs, which have no meaning and belong to no morpheme; and portmanteau morphs, which belong simultaneously to two (or, theoretically, more) morphemes, and have simultaneously the meanings of both.

If for some submorphemic reason (patterning or convenience), the breakup of Fox poonimeewa into poon + i + m (+) is to be preferred to either of the two alternative procedures outlined in §14, this breakup can be made tactically equivalent to the latter two, rather than to the analysis which requires the occurrence of i to be taken care of on a tactical level, by calling i an empty morph. Total accountability is maintained because we say, on the submorphemic level, that when a morph ending in a consonant is followed in the same word by one beginning with a consonant, the empty morph i appears between them.

The simplest example of a portmanteau morph is French /o/ 'to the (masc.)' (§3). If this be taken as a single morpheme, tactical difficulties ensue. What other morpheme has a range of positions of occurrence parallel to the range of this one? On the other hand, since /o/ is a single phoneme, it is hardly possible to make a cut and produce two morphs. But if we interpret it as a portmanteau morph, the representative of the morpheme sequence {à le}, we not only eliminate a forlorn morpheme, but round out the distribution of {à} and of {le}, both otherwise somewhat defective. For à 'to' parallels to a great extent the distribution of sur 'on', après 'after', and other morphs, but—unless the proposed interpretation is accepted—does not occur in one important position where the others occur: before le 'the (masc.)' when the following noun begins with a consonant. Similarly, the suggested treatment of /o/ makes the parallelism between le and la 'the (fem.)' much neater. The case is so clear-cut that there is nothing remarkable in the fact that au has been traditionally so interpreted.

It is to be noted that our morphemic expansion of /o/ to {à le} involves not only the morphemes {à} and {le}, but also a specific order thereof: /o/ is not morphemically {le à}. This specific order, like the morphemes themselves, is given not by the portmanteau as such, but by its distribution and that of the morphs to which we propose to relate it. Choice of the order {à le} leads to the parallelism indicated above; choice of the reverse order leads to nothing at all.

16. The simple examples just given speak, it is believed, for the naturalness of this approach; but as yet we have given no formal statement of the conditions under which an empty morph or a portmanteau morph is to be set up.

Because of the possible importance of submorphemic patterning, it will be necessary to consider the typical phonemic shapes, or canonical forms, of morphs. It is a well-recognized fact that in any particular language, if we examine and classify those cases of morphs which do not patently involve the questions here being raised, we find that many different morphs have much the same general phonemic shape.[28] Fijian affords an elementary example.[29] A large number of morphs have the shape $\#C_1V_1C_2V_2(C_3)$, where # is word juncture, the C's indicate any consonant (or none), the V's any vowel, and C_3 is lacking when word juncture or a consonant follows: koro 'village' (C_3 = zero), sala 'path', dina 'true, truth', selev 'cut, knife', ðabet 'go up', kaðiv 'call, announce'. A second, much smaller, group have the shape $\#C_1V_1C_2V_2C_3V_3(C_4)$: taŋane 'man, male', yalewa 'woman, female'. A third group have the shape V or V_1CV_2: a 'transitive with common object', as in ðabeta 'go up (a hill)', raiða 'to see (a child, etc.)'; i 'transitive with proper object', as in raiði 'to see (John, me, etc.)'; aka 'transitive indirective', as in ðabetaka 'carry (someone) upwards'. Lastly, there is a group of structure #CV#, occasionally $\#C_1V_1C_2V_2\#$: na 'the (common)', as in na koro 'the village'; ni 'of the (common)', as in na yaða ni koro 'the name of the village'; i 'that connected with the act of', as in na i sele 'the knife'; ko 'the (proper)', as in ko viti 'Fiji' or ko ðei 'who?'.

In some languages the variety of canonical forms is far greater than in Fijian, but in every language the total number—however assessed, for there is some choice in the process of abstraction from specific phonemes to symbols like C and V—is relatively small. In English many morphs have the shape of a single syllable with # preceding[30] (girl, act); others consist of a single consonant, or of a single syllable with initial vowel, with no preceding # (-s, -ing, -ed, -or). In both Fijian and English, and probably generally, some canonical forms can be expressed as the 'sum' of certain smaller ones: Fijian #CVCVCV(C) as #CVCV(C) plus V; the English type of author as the type of act (or watch) plus the type of -or (or -ing). Moreover, in these cases the 'sums' occur as sequences of several morphs (actor) as well as in single morphs (author). Those canonical forms which cannot be so expressed may conveniently be called minimum.

28 A point discussed in detail by Benjamin L. Whorf in various unpublished material, and orally.

29 C. Maxwell Churchward, A New Fijian Grammar (1941).

30 This avoids the risky complications which result from calling word-juncture a morpheme, as Rulon S. Wells does in his Immediate Constituents §64 (see fn. 4). The semantic contrast between Thank you with word juncture and the same without it means that word juncture is morphemic, but in such cases it might just as well be concluded—I think, a little better so—that absence of word juncture is the morpheme.

17. If in analyzing the morphemics of a language we make a preliminary classification of canonical forms, based only on those morphs whose status is perfectly clear, this classification can serve as a guide in handling the less obvious cases.

Multiplicity of analytical choice turns on two things: the location and number of cuts to be made in certain utterances; and the classification of the resultant morphs as ordinary, empty, or portmanteau. When faced with alternatives, we base our decision, wherever possible, on the relative desirability of the resulting tactics. It is on this account that the treatment of French /o/ 'to the (masc.)' as a single morpheme, or of Fox connective i as a morpheme, is rejected. When this factor cannot play a part, we turn next to morphophonemic simplicity. Morphemes of constant phonemic shape are simplest; when we cannot find these, we look next for sets of morphemes showing similar alternations in phonemic shape, since then we can describe the alternations of many different morphemes at once. When this also is not decisive, we turn to canonical forms, and prefer that analysis which produces morphs most closely conforming to the canonical forms already established—if possible, to minimum canonical forms. It may be that the second and third of these considerations should be assigned the other order of priority; apparently they are not often in conflict.

When we are confronted with three tactically equivalent alternatives for Fox poonimeewa (pooni|m, poon|im, and poon|i|m with i as an empty morph), we need only proceed to the second consideration to reach an answer. If we make either the first or the second choice, one of the morphemes involved will have two alternants (poon and pooni, or else im and m). If we make the third, both poon and m become morphemes of constant phonemic shape. If this were not enough, the third criterion would show us that failure to set up i as an empty morph would force us to recognize some morphs, beginning or ending in i, of canonical forms not otherwise required (though not in the case of the elements in the particular word poonimeewa), whereas the decision to set up the i by itself produces only morphs of shapes necessary anyway.

Likewise in the French case: tactical considerations rule out a monomorphemic interpretation of /o/, but do not decide whether we must take it as a single (portmanteau) morph or may cut it further. Now by a criterion mentioned in §2 under Step 1, a morph must have overt phonemic content. In order to cut /o/ into two morphs, we must break up the phoneme /o/ into two components, say mid-back tongue position and lip-rounding. Neither of these components fits into any otherwise necessary canonical form of morphs in French (though in some other languages some morphs do have a shape definable in components rather than in phonemes). On the other hand, /o/ taken as a single morph fits into a canonical form, represented by such clear cases as /o/ 'water', /e/ 'and', /u/ 'or', /a/ 'to'. The vote is clearly for the interpretation as a portmanteau morph.

In the succeeding sections of Part IV we give further examples in which these same principles call for the recognition of empty or portmanteau morphs.

18. In Nootka[31] a word consists—submorphemically, as we shall show—of a stem plus one or more suffixes. (This statement is circular: a stem is a morpheme which begins with word-juncture, a suffix one which does not; but it will suffice for orientation.) Certain suffixes, which we may call *location suffixes*, occur both after ordinary stems and after a stem hina-, hin-, hiṫa-,[32] which Sapir and Swadesh label an *empty stem*.

Thus ƛ̓iḥ- 'red' + -(q)o·(ʕ) = ƛ̓iḥo·ʕ 'red on the face'; sixʷ- 'sores, pox' + the same suffix = sixo·ʕ 'having sores on the face'; but hina- + the same suffix = hino·ʕ 'on the face, being on the face'. Similarly, ƛ̓iḥ- 'red' + -(ʔ)akso(ʕ) = ƛ̓iḥaksoʕ 'red at the lips'; hap- 'hair, fur' + the same suffix = hapaksoʕ 'having a moustache'; but hina- + the same suffix = hinaksoʕ 'at the lips or mouth, being at the lips or mouth'. Finally, maƛ- 'tied' + -aḥo·p 'cause momentarily to be in front' = maƛaḥo·p 'ties in front'; but hina- + the same suffix = hinaḥo·p 'places in front'.

The empty stem has no meaning. Our tactics are just as well suited, and our morphophonemics are not complicated, by interpreting each form of the empty stem as an empty morph. The remaining stems constitute a class of morphs which begin with ≠. Suffixes other than the location suffixes constitute a class of morphs which do not begin with ≠. When a location suffix is preceded by a stem, neither ≠ nor any other phonemic material intervenes. When a location suffix is not preceded by a stem, it is preceded instead by the appropriate (predictable) form ≠hina-, ≠hin-, ≠hita-, which in any case is meaningless and tactically irrelevant. The principle of total accountability is not violated; and the empty morphs conform to canonical forms. The alternative of taking ≠hina- etc. as a stem (a morpheme) is undesirable because of the meaninglessness of this element. The alternative of taking hinaḥo·p as an alternant going with -aḥo·p, and similarly for every other such combination, produces a greater complication of canonical forms.

31 Edward Sapir and Morris Swadesh, Nootka Texts (Philadelphia, 1939), esp. Part III, The Primary Structural Elements of Nootka; Morris Swadesh, Nootka Internal Syntax [sic], IJAL 9.77–102 (1936–8). The specific examples were generously supplied by Swadesh.

32 The alternation among these three shapes of the element will not concern us; it is covered by statements on a lower level of morphophonemic treatment.

19. In most of the central Algonquian languages occurs a phenomenon which we shall here illustrate with Potawatomi examples. Nouns appear in both unallocated and allocated forms: wUkUma 'chief' : nUtOkUmam 'my chief' or kUtOkUmamwa 'your (pl.) chief'. Some nouns, however, appear only in allocated forms; so nos· 'my father', kos· 'your (sg.) father'. A noun in an allocated form contains a personal prefix before the noun stem, and after the noun stem one or more of several suffixes (including, in the allocation is plural, a personal suffix) and various inflectional endings. Some of these nouns which occur in both unallocated and allocated forms contain, after the noun stem in an allocated form, a morph m, Um, im, om; so, for example, the forms for 'my chief' and 'your chief' above. Other such nouns appear sometimes with a morph of this shape, sometimes without it, but with no semantic contrast —the presence and absence of the morph are in free alternation. Still others, including all nouns which appear only in allocated forms, never occur with the m element.

The m elements are more satisfactorily regarded as morphs than as parts of the preceding morphs, particularly since the choice among the various forms of the m element depends on the environment in much the same way as does the choice among the alternants of the morpheme {k} 'locative' and (though with less similarity) among the various alternants of a number of other suffix morphemes. But the m elements are meaningless, even where forms appear both with and without one of them, and it is tactically convenient to eliminate them from the picture before tactical discussion begins. So we take them to be empty morphs.

20. The English interjections written conventionally as hm!, eh?, and the like, consist phonemically of an intonation-sequence, a stress, and a segmental 'carrier' for these features. In my dialect, this segmental component may have any vocalic quality (whether this occurs elsewhere or not), or any oral closure or closures, but it must be nasalized. Such a segmental structure is atypical in its wide range of nondistinctive variation, but the articulatory feature involved distinctively—nasalization—is one which does recur in more typical segmental structure, for example as that which distinguishes /m/ from /b/, /n/ from /d/.

If we compare the utterance hm (intonation 32)[33] with yes(32) and with hm(24), we see that the meaning of hm(32) is that of yes(32) minus the meaning of the intonationless abstraction yes; between hm(32) and hm(24) there is no semantic similarity. Hm itself, then, apart from the intonation which it serves to carry, has no meaning at all.

[33] Following Pike (The Intonation of American English; Ann Arbor, 1946), and Wells (Immediate Constituents §79) in the assignment of figures, and numbering the four levels from top down.

We may conclude that the hm part of such interjections is an empty morph. The intonational morphs which accompany it are also found spread through such morphs or morph-sequences as yes, I know, maybe, he didn't come, and so on. Accountability is maintained: if an utterance consists morphemically of an intonational morpheme alone, the empty morph hm will be present; otherwise hm is absent.

The tactical implications are interesting: the only free morphemes of English, in Bloomfield's sense of 'free', are intonational morphemes, and the only monomorphemic utterances of the language are those consisting of such a morpheme.

21. In certain Spanish verb forms there appears, between the stem and the endings, an element often called a conjugation vowel: the á, é, and í of amar 'to love', beber 'to drink', vivir 'to live'; the áb, í, and í of amábamos 'we loved', bebíamos 'we drank', vivíamos 'we lived', etc. Which vowel (or in one case vowel plus consonant) appears, depends on the stem and on the ending: the infinitive ending r, for example, requires á after a stem of the first conjugation, é after one of the second, and í after one of the third. The three conjugations are classes of stems, in fact, based precisely on this feature of behavior.

The conjugation vowels have no meaning. The meaning of amar is that of the two component morphemes, stem am 'love' and the infinitive ending, whether we treat the latter as ár in this case, alternating with ér and ír elsewhere, or simply as r. The latter alternative relegates the á, and all other such conjugation vowels, to the status of empty morphs.

Not all the post-stem vowels which occur in Spanish verbs have this status. The a of amas 'thou lovest', for example, is the only thing which distinguishes this form from ames 'that thou love' (subjunctive). Here the a is no empty morph, but an ordinary morph with meaning 'present indicative'. In one possible analysis of Spanish verbs, which would perhaps be the simplest from the morphophonemic standpoint, distinctions such as that between a 'present indicative' and the meaningless á of amar are not made. But this somewhat greater morphophonemic ease is outweighed by more complicated tactics.

22. Our first additional example of a portmanteau morph comes from Yokuts.[34] In the Yawelmani dia-

[34] See fn. 11. The capital letters at the beginning of cited suffixes are components of the vowels in the part of the word which precedes the specific phonemes of the suffix. Thus the stem me·k'i 'swallow' contains two consonants and parts of two vowels: after the first consonant, the vowel components high-front and long, and after the second consonant, the vowel components high-front and short. When this stem occurs with the suffix FRit 'passive aorist', the component F merges with the first group of vowel components in the stem to give e·, and the component R merges with the second group of vowel

lect there are about a dozen morphemes which occur after a verb stem and before a finite or gerundial suffix. One of these is WZa·la· (with alternants WZla·, FRla·, WW'e·, WLe·, FZWZla·, ila·, la·, WSla·, variously apportioned among different types of preceding element, but in non-contrastive distribution) 'cause someone to x': tisa·la·hin '(he) caused (it) to come out, (he) took (it) out', with stem tisi 'come out' and finite suffix hin 'aorist'. Another is WAda· (with variants da·, R = reduplication) 'x often or repeatedly': sodoxdoʔ 'will throw him repeatedly', with stem sodox 'throw' and final suffix ʔ 'future'.

In some cases two of these elements occur in succession, within the position of occurrence stated above. Indeed, the alternant R of the morpheme 'x repeatedly' occurs followed by the alternant FZWZla· of the morpheme 'cause to x': muhmuhlat 'was made to dive repeatedly', with stem muhu 'dive' and final suffix t 'passive aorist'. But other alternants of the morpheme 'x repeatedly' do not occur before any alternant of the morpheme 'cause to x'. No semantic gap results, however, for there is an element WE·lsa· ∿ WE·sa· of the same positional class, meaning 'cause to x repeatedly': nine·lsa·hin 'got him to keep still several times', with stem nine· 'keep still, become quiet', and final suffix hin 'aorist'.

It is far from convenient, within the morphophonemic economy of Yokuts, to cut WE·lsa· ∿ WE·sa· into smaller morphs; each alternant subsumed by this notation is best taken as a single morph. The distribution and meaning lead one to interpret each of these morphs as a portmanteau representative of the sequence of two morphemes 'x repeatedly' + 'cause to x'.

23. In finite forms of the Spanish verb the tense-mode is usually indicated by one morph, and the person-number by another, in that order: amáb|a|mos 'we loved', ama|ré|is 'you (pl.) will love'. In a few cases, it is difficult or impossible to separate the element meaning a tense-mode from that meaning a person-number; in these cases, we may regard the undivided endings (after any conjugation vowel that may occur) as portmanteau morphs: o 'present indicative + first person singular', as in amo 'I love', é (with verbs of the first conjugation) ∿ í (with those of the second and third conjugations) 'preterit indicative + first person singular', and ó (first conj.) ∿ ió (second and third conj.) 'preterit indicative + third person singular'. This treatment, combined with the empty-morph interpretation of conjugation vowels, reduces all finite Spanish verb forms to a uniform structure: stem + tense-mode morpheme + person-number morpheme.[35]

24. In Fijian there is a construction consisting of any of certain particles followed by a noun or pronoun: na sala 'the path', na ðava '(the) what?', ni koro 'of-the village', ko viti '(the) Fiji', vei au 'to me'. One of the particles is vei 'to, with, of', as in the last example above and in vei keda 'with, to, of us', vei Joni 'with, to John'. One of the pronouns is koya 'he, she', as in ko koya '(the) he, she', nei koya 'of him, of her'. But the specific combination of vei and koya seems not to occur.[36] Where semantically it would be expected, one finds, instead, the portmanteau morph vuaa 'with, to, of him or her', as in au na vosa vuaa na ŋone 'I future speak-to-him the child' = 'I shall speak to the child'.

25. We may best approach a consideration of the fifth difficulty of §3 by examining some English cases. On the tactical level, it is certainly desirable to consider men as consisting of the morpheme man plus the morpheme s 'plural'. When cutting utterances containing men into morphs, we will not be led to men into smaller pieces; it fits a canonical form and if broken further the smaller fragments do not. So one solution, and certainly the most obvious one, is to regard men as a single portmanteau morph, representing the morpheme sequence {man} + {s}.

It is true that there is a phonemic similarity between man and men—the identity of initial and final consonants—which we do not want to lose sight of. This places men in a different category from French /o/, Yokuts WE·(l)sa·, Spanish o, or Fijian vuaa, for in the latter cases the resemblance of the portmanteau to other alternants of either of the constituent morphemes is negligible. Even if men were an isolated case in English, this resemblance would be worthy of mention. But it is, of course, far from isolated; we have also mouse : mice, foot : feet, woman : women (if woman is a single morpheme), slide : slid, sing : sang, and many others.

The portmanteau interpretation of such bimorphemic forms need not obscure the phonemic resemblance of which we are speaking. In our morphophonemics we have to mention all portmanteaus. By assembling, in one section of our description, all portmanteaus which have this feature of partial phonetic identity with one of the constituent morphemes, and by organizing them into groups on the basis of the specific phonemic difference, we give ample attention to the matter.

Some may nevertheless prefer to reinterpret portmanteaus as bimorphic as well as bimorphemic, even though to do so one must extend the definition

components in the stem to give zero; the resulting form is me·k'it 'was swallowed'. With a different set of components contributed by the suffix WAʔan 'durative present', the resulting form is mik'a·ʔan 'is swallowing'. For the details of this, see Zellig S. Harris, Yokuts Structure and Newman's Grammar, IJAL 10.196–211 (1944).

[35] The 'irregular' verbs present more complex cases of both portmanteau and empty morphs, but are tactically quite the same, save where one or another form is missing.

[36] Churchward is not entirely clear on the matter: he says (op.cit. I.24.3) that vei koya is 'unusual'. If it does indeed occur, then the interpretation proposed is wrong; rather vei koya is like English with it and vuaa like therewith.

of 'morph' to cover elements of other than overt phonemic content. If this is considered desirable, then in the notion of portmanteau we have at least achieved a more rigorous way of extending the coverage of the term 'morph' in such a manner, as follows:

In our initial cutting of utterances, we obtain only morphs of overt phonemic content. Further examination, along the lines detailed in this paper so far, reveals the possibility that certain of our morphs are portmanteaus; but for our present purpose we may call them rather tentative portmanteaus. We then examine each tentative portmanteau and compare its phonemic shape with that of the other alternants of the constituent morphemes. If we find that the tentative portmanteau has some phonemes (or components) in common with one of the non-portmanteau alternants of one of the constituent morphemes, we may set up the entire non-portmanteau alternant as one constituent morph of the form which has tentatively been regarded as a portmanteau, and the alternation from this shape to that of the tentative portmanteau as the other constituent morph. Alternatively, we may set up the tentative portmanteau, as a whole, as an alternant of that constituent morpheme which it resembles phonemically, and set up a zero morph as an alternant of the other constituent morpheme.[37] For example, our initial cutting produces men, which does not look like more than one morph. The sequence man plus s does not occur. Men fills the tactical place which one might expect to be filled by the sequence man plus s. Men is therefore morphemically {man} + {s}. But—so runs the argument that would set up alternation morphs—men and man resemble each other in phonemic shape, both containing m-n. So men is not a portmanteau. One morph in men is man. The other is the alternation a∿e. Or—arguing now for a zero morph—men is not a portmanteau, but consists of an alternant men of {man} plus an alternant /0/ of {s}.

If a language contains only a few isolated instances of this kind, probably everyone would agree to reject the last steps of the above argument and return to the portmanteau interpretation, relying on the organization of one's morphophonemic statements to put the matter of partial phonemic resemblance into clear relief. But if the language contains a sufficient number of such cases that one is warranted in setting up a canonical form for morphs like a ∿ e, or like /0/, then some may prefer the extension.

Somewhat similar considerations apply to French bon 'good (masc.)' and to English sheep (pl.). In the course of examination, the portmanteau interpretation is that which first presents itself; from it we may proceed to the recognition of morphs of other than overt phonemic content if we find factors comparable to those in the case of men. It is to be emphasized that when portmanteaus are eliminated in this way, the new definition of 'morph' is no longer that with which we began; perhaps, therefore, it would be advisable to distinguish terminologically between, say, 'primary morphs' (those of overt phonemic content) and 'extended morphs' (including primary ones and morphs of the zero, replacement, or subtraction types).

English children, however, remains recalcitrant. Obviously it is morphemically {child} + {s}; so that whatever submorphemic interpretation we chose, the tactical picture is clear. The first part of children resembles child, and the last part is identical with one of the alternants of {s}, namely the -en of oxen. The alternative analyses are (1) child|ren, (2) childr|en, (3) child|r|en, (4) child + vowel change and -ren, and (5) no cut, i.e. portmanteau. The first gives a morph /čild/, the difference between which and child recurs in other contexts, e.g. slide : slid, bite : bit; but then the morph -ren is unique. The second gives a morph -en which recurs; but then the difference between /čildr/ and child is unique. The third has the merits of each of the first two, without the defects, but involves an empty morph r, which is not observed to recur and therefore requires a special statement for this occurrence. The fourth produces a morph (vowel change and -ren) which fits no canonical form, unless the vowel-change-plus-en of bitten, hidden, and others is grouped with it from the point of view of shape. Apparently this is one of the cases in which all our preferential criteria (§14) fail, and nothing remains but a resort to convenience.[38]

[37] This second alternative is that proposed by Bernard Bloch, English Verb Inflection, Lang. 23.399-418 (1947). Bloch rejects all alternation or subtraction morphs, and interprets all tentative portmanteaus as an alternant of one of the constituent morphemes plus a zero alternant of the other. One special criterion is introduced for dealing with zero alternants: no morpheme is postulated which has only a zero alternant.

[38] The unsolved case of children is discussed in detail for a reason. There is no merit in an analytical procedure which 'eliminates' all but one of a set of alternative analyses simply by fiat—by saying that when such-and-such types of alternative present themselves we shall accept the one which has certain characteristics and reject the others. Our aim is to achieve the most accurate and clearest picture possible of the workings of a language, on all levels—phonemic, morphemic, and tactical; in some cases this is attained not by giving a single treatment, but precisely by indicating the alternatives. For in some cases a range of choice is determined not by our approach, but by the nature of the language; and when this is so, the existence of a range of choice in a particular portion of the language is one of the facts about the language that ought to be portrayed in our description. In one sense, any method of description which conforms to the principle of total accountability is correct; if we nevertheless discuss the relative merits of one procedure or another within this fundamental framework, the purpose is to attain greater mutual intelligibility among the writers of grammars and, in terms thereof, more accurate pictures of the languages we describe.

V. Conclusions

26. We now summarize the procedure of morphemic analysis worked out in the course of our discussion, and end with an example from English which illustrates several of the points that have been made. Our summary of the procedure is given in steps, as in §2; but in actually working with a particular language one has to skip back and forth, operating by trial and error.

Step 1. We assemble the utterances of the language before us, recorded in some phonemic notation. If preliminary examination reveals that a different (also phonemic) notation would make the task simpler, we retranscribe them all. If further preliminary examination shows that some normalization of notation, maintaining all phonemic distinctions but adding thereto, would further simplify the task, we retranscribe again, and perhaps again. As we proceed to other steps, we check back from time to time to be sure we have not involved ourselves in contradictions.

Step 2. The utterances are now examined in the notation finally chosen. Recurrent partials with constant meaning are discovered; those not composed of smaller ones are morphs. So are any partials not recurrent but left over when all recurrent ones are accounted for; therefore every bit of phonemic material belongs to one morph or another.[39] By definition, a morph has the same phonemic shape in all its occurrences; and (at this stage) every morph has an overt phonemic shape, but a morph is not necessarily composed of a continuous uninterrupted stretch of phonemes. The line between two contiguous morphs is a cut.

Step 3. Omitting doubtful cases, morphs are classed on the basis of shape and the canonical forms are tentatively determined.

Step 4. Two or more morphs are grouped into a single morpheme if they fit the following grouping-requirements: (a) they have the same meaning; (b) they are in non-contrastive distribution; (c) the range of the resultant morpheme is not unique. Some morphs, however, may be assigned to no morpheme at all, and some may be assigned simultaneously to two (or more) morphemes. An empty morph, assigned to no morpheme,[40] must have no meaning, and must be predictable in terms of non-empty morphs. A portmanteau morph must have the meanings of two or more morphemes simultaneously, and must be in non-contrastive distribution with the combination of any alternant of one of the member morphemes and any alternant of the other (usually because no such combination occurs).

Step 5. Where there are alternative possibilities, choice is based on (a) tactical simplicity, (b) morphophonemic simplicity, and (c) conformity to canonical forms, in this order of priority.

Step 6. The differences in the phonemic shape of morphs as alternants of morphemes are organized and stated; this (in some cases already partly accomplished in Step 1) constitutes morphophonemics. In particular, portmanteaus are compared with the other alternants of the morphemes involved, and if resemblances in phonemic shape and the number of cases warrant it, morphs of other than over phonemic content are recognized, some of the portmanteaus being thus eliminated.

27. Our final example is the system of personal pronouns in English (including who, whom, whose).

At least in certain dialects, the morphs I and me (and similarly we and us, he and him, etc.) are in non-contrastive distribution; in some dialects, indeed, the complementation is probably complete. We may suspect that if it were not for the Latinizing school tradition, the complementation would be complete for most speakers: I initially except in isolation, me directly after a verb or a preposition and in isolation. Actual exceptions to this are either on the Latin pattern (It's I, or Who's there?—I, instead of Me), or are overcorrections (between you and I). For many speakers whose usage of I and me does not put them in complete complementation, there is no contrast between, for example, It's I and It's me. In other dialects and styles, on the other hand, the forms are in contrast: literary English, schoolteachers' on-duty English, and certain whimsical styles.[41] The remainder of this discussion applies only to a dialect in which the distribution is non-contrastive.

My and mine (and similarly our and ours, your and yours, etc.) are in complete complementation: my occurs when a noun follows without pause, mine otherwise.

If the above statements are to hold, we must split the occurrences of her into those which parallel those of his and those which parallel those of him; the former, her_1, is morphemically identical with with hers, while her_2 is morphemically identical with she.

Paralleling John in John came, Bill saw John, John's book, the book is John's, and virtually every other utterance containing the morpheme John, we have I came, Bill saw me, my book, The book is mine, etc. John's is two morphs and two morphemes; we conclude that my and mine are two morphemes each, though each is only a single morph.

[39] We say 'phonemic' for simplicity's sake; if our notation has been normalized, then more accurately this should read 'every bit of orthographic material'.

[40] All the empty morphs in a language are in complementary distribution and have the same meaning (none). They could, if there were any advantage in it, be grouped into a single empty morpheme—but one which had the unique characteristic of being tactically irrelevant.

[41] For example, that style in which one says 'me, myself, and I' as if the reference were to three people. This is not unrelated to a style which obviously has to be excluded, both here in the discussion of English pronouns and in any other discussion of morpheme alternants: the style of the discussion itself, in which such forms as me and I contrast because they are are used as names of particular morphs.

We conclude, therefore, that the English personal pronouns have the following morphemic structure:

{I} I, me	{she} she, her_2
{I} + {s} my, mine	{she} + {s} her_1, hers
{we} we, us	{it} it
{we} + {s} our, ours	{it} + {s} its
{you} you	{they} they, them
{you} + {s} your, yours	{they} + {s} their, theirs
{he} he, him	{who} who, whom
{he} + {s} his	{who} + {s} whose

The forms it, its, and whose are the same morphically and morphemically; the others illustrate one or more of the grouping-requirements that we have discussed. Together, the twenty-six forms are analyzed into only nine different morphemes.[42]

The tactical implications are considerable. Except for the category of number, the pronouns are now exactly like any proper noun in their tactics, and can be classed as a subdivision of proper nouns. There is no longer any justification for speaking of case in English; for the distinction between subjective and objective 'cases' (under whatever name) disappears as soon as I and me, etc., are shown to belong to the same morpheme. A form with added -'s is not a case-form either, but simply a form with added -'s: the -'s is simply another morpheme, with a statable range of positions in which it occurs.

42 We might go further, interpreting we, us as {I} + pluralizing {s}, with a similar treatment for the other plural pronouns. We are deterred from this step not because plural you is identical with singular you (since after all sheep and other nouns manifest this property), but because {he} + {s}, {she} + {s}, and {it} + {s} would all add up to they, them.

⟦This re-codification of morphemic analysis, five years after Harris ⟨(109)⟩, in part represents what most workers including Harris had come to agree on, in part is original and presents notions that did not all find favor, though all of them did stimulate the professional readers to clarify their own thinking. Hockett himself, characteristically, treated the new ideas just as if someone else had propounded them; for instance, in his Peiping Morphophonemics of 1950 ⟨(317)⟩ he cheerfully left unused the notion of 'empty morphs' and instead spoke of morphemically irrelevant phonemic material. This sort of behavior is, as a matter of fact, quite usual among American linguistic theorists and has caused unsympathetic critics to speak of irresponsible zig-zagging. Rather than stigmatize it thus, I should prefer to call it a protection of one's own flexibility and would maintain that a free indulgence in, or even cultivation of, this habit has been one of the most favorable traits in the growth of descriptive linguistics among us. The opposite would have required replacement, not reinforcement, of the front-line fighters; and the new men would have been less effective replacements if they had felt it expedient to withhold theses that they might someday have to alter or replace.

This paper was composed at the same time as the following one by Bloch. They were both read at the same summer meeting of the Linguistic Society. And both authors considered it best to publish them with no adjustment to each other—for similar reasons.⟧

ENGLISH VERB INFLECTION

BERNARD BLOCH
Language 23.399–418—1947

1. Introductory

1.1 The inflection of verbs in present-day colloquial English[1] has been described in many works—most clearly and exhaustively, perhaps, by Sweet, Palmer, Curme, Fries, Jespersen, and Hockett.[2] In view of the number and fullness of these descriptions, no new treatment can hope to add any facts hitherto overlooked: at most, a new treatment may be able to arrange the known facts more systematically than has been done before, or in a way that will be more useful to other linguists.

In all previous works, the inflection of English verbs is described in terms of the processes by which various inflected forms are derived from underlying bases. Thus, the preterit waited is said to be derived from wait by the addition of a suffix, took from take by vowel change, built from build by consonant change, sold from sell by vowel change and suffixation together, went from go by suppletion, put from put by zero change, and so on. Statements of this kind, referring to processes of derivation, are useful for showing the relation of any inflected form to its base; but they have at least one serious shortcoming: they cannot be readily used for the description of specific forms, viewed as words in their own right.

1.2 To describe the structure of a language as a whole, the linguist must be able to describe also the structure of any single sentence or part of a sentence that occurs in the language. He does this in terms of constructions—essentially, in terms of morphemes and their order.[3] Any sentence, phrase, or complex word can be described as consisting of such-and-such morphemes in such-and-such an order; each morpheme has a meaning, and so also has the order in which they occur (the 'constructional meaning').

For the purposes of this paper we adopt Bloomfield's definition of a morpheme, which has been accepted by nearly all descriptive linguists. A morpheme, according to Bloomfield, is 'a linguistic form which bears no partial phonetic-semantic resemblance to any other form'; a linguistic form is 'any combination of phonemes ... which has a meaning'.[4]

To illustrate: the preterit form waited—considered simply as a word, without the morphemes of stress and pitch that would accompany it in a real utterance—can be described as follows. It consists of two morphemes, /weyt/ and /ed/,[5] occurring in that order. The meaning of the first morpheme is a par-

[1] The dialect here studied is a somewhat generalized northeastern variety of standard American English. For the methodological groundwork of this paper see Zellig S. Harris, Morpheme alternants in linguistic analysis, Lang. 18.169–80 (1942) ((109)); Rulon S. Wells, Immediate constituents, Lang. 23.81–117 (1947) ((186)); and C. F. Voegelin, A problem in morpheme alternants and their distribution, Lang. 23.245–54 (1947). Compare now also Charles F. Hockett, Problems of morphemic analysis, Lang. 23.321–43 (1947) ((229)). Though my views in general agree with Hockett's, it will be observed that his treatment of certain problems of English inflection (especially in §24 of his paper) differs markedly from the one here proposed.

I have profited from discussions with R. S. Wells, W. F. Twaddell, and Martin Joos.

[2] Henry Sweet, A new English grammar logical and historical 1.391–428 = §§1283–493 (Oxford, 1892); Harold E. Palmer, A grammar of spoken English on a strictly phonetic basis 88–122 = §§199–270 (Cambridge, 1930); George O. Curme, A grammar of the English language, II. Parts of speech and accidence 241 ff., esp. 269–96 = §60, 304–19 = §63 (Boston etc., 1935); Charles Carpenter Fries, American English grammar 59–71 (New York and London, 1940); Otto Jespersen, A modern English grammar on historical principles, VI. Morphology 28–83 = Chaps. 4–5 (Copenhagen, 1942); Charles F. Hockett, English verb inflection, SIL, Vol. 1, No. 2 (1942). For an entertaining travesty of American English verb inflection see H. L. Mencken, The American Language[4] 427–47 (New York, 1936).

[3] Wells, Lang. 23.93–8.

[4] Leonard Bloomfield, Language 161 and 138 (New York, 1933).

[5] The phonemic transcriptions in this paper necessarily reflect my own speech, except that a few distinctions not commonly made in other dialects of English have been disregarded. On the transcription of vowels and diphthongs see George L. Trager and Bernard Bloch, The syllabic phonemes of English, Lang. 17.223–46 (1941), and cf. Lang. 19.189 fn. 15 (1943). The following stressed syllabics occur in the dialect here transcribed: /i/ in pit, /e/ in pet, /æ/ in pat, /a/ in pot, /ʌ/ in cut, /o/ in coffin, /u/ in put, /ə/ in just (adverb); /iy/ in beat, /ey/ in bait, /ay/ in bite, /oy/ in boil, /uy/ in ruin (monosyllabic); /aw/ in bout, /ow/ in boat, /uw/ in boot; /ih/ in theater, /eh/ in yeah, /æh/ in mad, /ah/ in calm, /oh/ in law, /əh/ in er (hesitation form); /ir/ in here, /er/ in there, /ar/ in part, /or/ in port, /ur/ in sure, /ər/ in curt; /ihr/ in beer, /ehr/ in bare, /ahr/ in bar, /ohr/ in bore, /uhr/ in boor, /əhr/ in burr. Pitch will not be marked in this paper; stress will be marked only in transcriptions of whole utterances. A space between words has no phonetic or phonemic significance.

Needless to say, the treatment of verb inflection offered here does not depend on the system of transcription. The cited forms could be written just as well according to any other system, so long as it recognized the existing phonemic distinctions in American English.

ticular action that we need not specifically describe here; that of the second is 'past time' or the like. The constructional meaning of the order in which the two morphemes occur is approximately 'perform a certain action at a certain time'.

How shall we describe, now, the preterit form took? Its relation to the uninflected form take is irrelevant, because we are concerned here simply with the structure of this one word, not with its derivation. Either took is one morpheme, or it is two morphemes; the possibility of its being more than two may be neglected as improbable. If it is one morpheme, it is either the same morpheme as take, or a different morpheme: as a morpheme, it cannot be partly the same and partly different. If it is the same morpheme as take, its meaning must be the same also; but of course we know that took and take are not synonymous. If took is a single morpheme different from take, then there can be no morphological connection between them—just as there is none between took and talk; but since the semantic and syntactic relation of took to take is exactly the same as that of waited to wait, we do not like to give up the possibility of connecting them in a morphological system. Finally, if took consists of two morphemes, what are they? Perhaps they are (1) /teyk/ and (2) vowel change; but if a morpheme is ultimately a combination of phonemes, then it is clear that vowel change, a process, is not a morpheme. Perhaps, instead, the two morphemes in took are (1) /t...k/ and (2) /u/; but then what about take? Does take then consist of the two morphemes /t...k/ and /ey/? If so, it differs in a fundamental respect from a verb like wait, which consists of only a single morpheme; and we must classify English verbal bases into two morphological groups according to the number of their morphemes. Or perhaps take is only one morpheme, and the two morphemes in took are (1) /teyk/ and (2) /– ey + u/;[6] but again the second of these entities fits no definition of a morpheme that linguists are commonly agreed upon.

The difficulty is even greater with an 'unchanged' preterit like put (He put it there yesterday). How can we phrase a description of this word that will be different from a description of put, the corresponding base form?

1.3 The treatment of inflection to be given here is intended to make possible a clear and unambiguous description of all verb forms. By analyzing every inflected form as a combination of morphemes in a particular order, and by avoiding all reference to the process by which the form is derived, we shall be able to systematize the facts of English verb inflection in a way that will be not only more useful to the descriptive linguist than the treatments hitherto published, but also more uniform and in the long run simpler.

[6] Read: minus /ey/ plus /u/. Cf. Zellig S. Harris, Lang. 21.121 and fn. 3 (1945).

2. Categories and Assumptions

2.1 A verbal base, in English, is used without any suffix in several different functions: as an infinitive (I can't wait; I don't want to wait), as an imperative (Wait a minute), as a finite present with a subject in the 1st or 2d person singular or in the plural ⟦or as A. A. Hill puts it, 'with a genderless subject'⟧ (I wait here every day; If you wait for him; They wait in line for it), and in some other ways. In other functions, the verbal base appears with a following inflectional suffix:[7] as a finite present with a subject in the 3d singular ⟦'a gender subject'⟧ (He waits here every day), as a finite preterit (I waited for him), as a participle (I've waited long enough), and as a gerund (I'm still waiting; perhaps also Waiting is tiresome).

We shall speak of 3d singular, preterit, participle, and gerund as the four inflectional categories of English verbs; and we shall speak of every verb form that is used in one of these four functions as an inflected form.[8]

2.2 To prepare the ground for further discussion, we shall briefly examine a number of typical verb forms. Comparing the 3d-singular forms passes, waits, and lives /pæhs-ez, weyt-s, liv-z/,[9] we note that the inflectional suffix appears in three different phonemic shapes /ez, s, z/, whose choice depends on the last phoneme in the base. If we now add the 3d-singular form need (He need not go) and interpret this like the others as consisting of a base plus an inflectional suffix, we find that the suffix has yet another phonemic shape, namely zero, and that the occurrence of this shape cannot be predicted from the last phoneme in the base but only from the base itself; i. e. the choice of zero instead of /z/ depends on the fact that the base here is need and not some other base, such as lead.

Again, the preterit forms waited, passed, and lived /weyt-ed, pæhs-t, liv-d/ reveal three phonemic shapes of the preterit suffix. In general, the choice among them depends on the last phoneme in the base; but a form like dwelt /dwel-t/ instead of the expected /dwel-d/ shows that the alternation among the three shapes is not wholly determined by this criterion.

[7] We shall pay no attention in this paper to derivational suffixes (like the -er in waiter, the -ful in wakeful, or the -th in growth), except for a brief mention in §4.5. On the difference between inflection and derivation see Bloch and Trager, Outline of linguistic analysis 54–5 = §4.3 (Baltimore, 1942).

[8] The verb be has inflected forms not included among these four categories. Since this verb presents a special and vexing problem, we shall postpone all reference to it until §5. Inflected verb forms used only with a subject in the 2d person singular (archaic forms like waitest, preterit waitedst, and Quaker forms like [thee] waits) are not regarded in this paper as part of present-day standard American English.

[9] Hyphens in the phonemic transcription throughout this paper indicate morphological boundaries, not phonemic junctures.

The preterit form put (He put it there yesterday) contains an additional shape of the same suffix, namely zero again.

Not only the inflectional suffixes but bases also may have more than one phonemic shape. If we compare the preterit forms cried and fled /kray-d, fle-d/ with the corresponding uninflected forms, we find that the base cry /kray/ remains unchanged before the suffix /d/, whereas the base flee /fliy/ appears before this suffix in the special shape /fle/. In just the same way, the base take /teyk/ appears before the same suffix in the special shape /tuk/—the only difference being that after this particular base the preterit suffix has the phonemic shape zero, as it has also after the base put.

2.3 We are now ready to state the special assumptions that underlie our treatment of English verb inflection. (1) Every verb form functioning as a 3d-singular finite present, as a finite preterit, as a participle, or as a gerund consists of a base and an inflectional suffix. (2) Different phonemic shapes of a given base appearing before different suffixes, and different phonemic shapes of a given suffix appearing after different bases, are morpheme alternants of the same morpheme.[10] (3) One of the alternants of a given morpheme may be zero; but no morpheme has zero as its only alternant. (4) Different morphemes may have one or more alternants (including zero) in common. (5) Phonemically different forms that occur in the same environment, and are not in completely free variation with each other, are morphemically different.

3. Inflectional Suffixes

3.1 We list here the four morphemes that appear as inflectional suffixes after verbal bases, together with their morpheme alternants. Alternants whose choice depends on the last preceding phoneme (automatic alternants) are connected by a curve (∿); alternants whose choice depends not on a phonemic feature but on the base itself (non-automatic alternants) are separated by a semicolon. The four suffix morphemes are designated by underlined numerals.

Suffix 1 (3d singular): /ez/ after sibilant ∿ /s/ after voiceless non-sibilant ∿ /z/ elsewhere; /0/ (zero).

Suffix 2 (preterit): /ed/ after apical stop ∿ /d/ after voiced sound other than apical stop; /t/; /0/.

Suffix 3 (participle): /ed/ after apical stop ∿ /d/ after voiced sound other than apical stop; /t/; /n/ after syllabic[11] ∿ /ən/ elsewhere; /0/.

Suffix 4 (gerund): /iŋ/.

3.2 Certain alternants of different suffix morphemes are associated, in the sense that if a given base is followed by one of them, it will be followed also by the other; thus the /t/ alternant of suffix 2 occurs only after bases that are followed also by the /t/ alternant of suffix 3, and conversely. On the other hand, certain alternants of different suffix morphemes are mutually exclusive, in the sense that they never appear after the same base; thus no base that is followed by the zero alternant of suffix 1 is followed also by the zero alternant of suffix 2 or 3.

Among verbs inflected for all four categories we have listed, we find that the alternants of the four suffix morphemes appear in seven different combinations. (Automatic alternants are not differentiated in this count.) These combinations provide a basis for grouping such verbs into seven inflectional classes (A to G). To these we must add two more (H and I) to accommodate verbs that are not inflected for all four of the categories. Some verbs have no participle or gerund; other verbs lack not only these forms but a preterit also.

The following list shows the nine inflectional classes of English verbs, based on the combinations of suffix alternants that accompany their bases. To simplify the listing, the automatic alternants /ez ∿ s ∿ z/ are represented by /z/, the alternants /ed ∿ d/ by /d/, and the alternants /n ∿ ən/ by /n/. One example is given for each class.

Class	Suffix 1	Suffix 2	Suffix 3	Suffix 4	Example
A	z	d	d	iŋ	live
B	z	t	t	iŋ	pass
C	z	0	n	iŋ	fall
D	z	0	0	iŋ	put
E	z	d	n	iŋ	show
F	z	0	d	iŋ	dive
G	0	d	d	iŋ	need
H	0	d			can
I	0				must

3.3 In traditional terminology, verbs in classes A and B are weak verbs; those in classes C and D are strong verbs; those in classes E, F, and G are mixed or anomalous verbs; and those in classes H and I are auxiliaries.

Auxiliaries are not only defective in their morphology, but syntactically peculiar as well. The uninflected form (can, shall, must, may, etc.) is used as a finite present with a subject in the 1st or 2d person singular or in the plural (cf. §2.1), but not as an infinitive or as an imperative.

[10] On morpheme alternants and morpheme units see Harris, Lang. 18.170–3 ((110–111)); and cf. Hockett, Lang. 23.341–2 ((241)).

[11] A syllabic is a vowel alone or a vowel plus /y, w, h, r, hr/; cf. fn. 5.

4. Verbal Bases

4.1 Turning now from the suffix morphemes to the base morphemes, we observe that some verbs (wait, live, beat, show, etc.) have a base with only one phonemic shape—in other words, with only one morpheme alternant.[12] Other verbs (flee, take, fall, bite, etc.) have a base with two different morpheme alternants: one that appears when the base is used alone and before certain of the inflectional suffixes, another that appears before certain other suffixes. And some verbs (sing, fly, drive, do, etc.) have a base with three different morpheme alternants.

This divergence among the base morphemes allows us to divide them into seven base groups according to the number of their morpheme alternants and the particular suffix morphemes before which the alternants occur. When a given base has two alternants or more, they are designated as 'first alternant', 'second alternant', and so on: the first alternant being the one that appears when the base is used alone, and the others being numbered arbitrarily.

Base group 1. Single alternant. (Example: wait.)
Base group 2. Second alternant before suffix 2. (Example: take.)
Base group 3. Second alternant before suffixes 2 and 3. (Example: break.)
Base group 4. Second alternant before suffixes 1, 2, and 3. (Example: say.)
Base group 5. Second alternant before suffix 2; third alternant before suffix 3. (Example: sing.)
Base group 6. Second alternant before suffix 2; third alternant before suffixes 1 and 3. (Only example: do.)
Base group 7. Second alternant before suffixes 2 and 3; third alternant before suffix 1; fourth alternant before suffix 4. (For the only example see §6.1 s.v. have.)

4.2 In citing a verbal base (in the lexicon or elsewhere) we must give all its morpheme alternants, listed in the order determined by the tabulation in §4.1. If we do this, it is obvious that the complete inflection of the verb can then be defined simply by noting the inflectional class and the base group to which it belongs. The following illustrations will make this clear:

wait (A1) /weyt/	take (C2) /teyk; tuk/
build (B3) /bild; bil/	put (D1) /put/
beat (C1) /biyt/	sing (D5) /siŋ; sæŋ; sʌŋ/

The indication A1 after wait means that the suffix morphemes appear after this base in the alternants /s, ed, ed, iŋ/, and that the base appears before all these suffixes in the single form /weyt/; the complete inflection of this verb is accordingly /weyt-s, weyt-ed, weyt-ed, weyt-iŋ/. The indication B3 after build means that the suffix morphemes appear in the alternants /z, t, t, iŋ/, and that the base has two alternants of its own: one, /bild/, appearing before the suffixes /z/ and /iŋ/, the other, /bil/, appearing before /t/ and /t/. The indication C1 after beat means that the suffix morphemes appear as /s, 0, ən, iŋ/, and that the base is uniformly /biyt/ before these suffixes. In the same way, the indications C2, D1, and D5 after take, put, and sing respectively, mean that the complete inflection of these verbs is /teyk-s, tuk-0, teyk-ən, teyk-iŋ; put-s, put-0, put-0, put-iŋ; siŋ-z, sæŋ-0, sʌŋ-0, siŋ-iŋ/.

The twofold classification of a verb according to its inflection class and its base group (indicated by a double symbol such as A1, B3, C2) we shall call its conjugation type.

4.3 The overwhelming majority of English verbs belong to one of two conjugation types: to B1 if the base ends in a voiceless consonant except /t/, otherwise to A1. Such verbs are regular; all others are irregular.

A considerable number of verbs belong to both a regular and an irregular conjugation type. Thus, burn belongs to both A1 and B1 (with inflected forms /bəhrn-z, -d, -d, -iŋ/ and /bəhrn-z, -t, -t, -iŋ/ respectively; fit belongs to both A1 and D1 (with inflected forms /fit-s, -ed, -ed, -iŋ/ and /fit-s, -0, -0, -iŋ/ respectively); heave belongs to both A1 and D3 (with inflected forms /hiyv-z, -d, -d, -iŋ/ and /hiyv-z, howv-0, howv-0, hiyv-iŋ/ respectively). There are also verbs that belong to two or more different irregular conjugation types. Thus, spit belongs to D1 and D3 (with inflected forms /spit-s, -0, -0, -iŋ/ and /spit-s, spæt-0, spæt-0, spit-iŋ/ respectively); tread belongs to C3 and D3 (with inflected forms /tred-z, trad-0, trad-ən, tred-iŋ/ and /tred-z, trad-0, trad-0, tred-iŋ/ respectively); and shrink belongs to four different types—C3, C5, D3, and D5 (with inflected forms /šriŋk-s, šrʌŋk-0, šrʌŋk-ən, šriŋk-iŋ/, /šriŋk-s, šræŋk-0, šrʌŋk-ən, šriŋk-iŋ/, /šriŋk-s, šrʌŋk-0, šrʌŋk-0, šriŋk-iŋ/, and /šriŋk-s, šræŋk-0, šrʌŋk-0, šriŋk-iŋ/ respectively).

[12] Strictly considered, every verbal base has at least two alternants differing in stress; see Wells, Lang. 23.108–14 ((202–5)) = §§66–78. Thus, wait has the following alternants: (1) /weyt/, without inherent stress, when the base is accompanied in an utterance by the emphatic stress morpheme /´/, e.g. Wait a minute /wéyt ə mînit/; (2) /wêyt/, with reduced-loud stress, when the base is not accompanied by the emphatic stress morpheme, e.g. Let's wait here /lèt s wêyt hír/; (3) /wèyt/ with medial stress, again when the base is not accompanied by the emphatic stress morpheme, e.g. Let's not wait up /lèt s nât wèyt ʌ́p/. (The first of these alternants would appear also if the base were pronounced without any phonemic stress; but this would scarcely happen with a word like wait.) In our discussion, we shall disregard all stress differences among morpheme alternants.

Some verbs exhibit a difference in meaning according to their conjugation type; thus, *shine* is transitive in A1 (I shined my shoes) but intransitive in D3 (The sun shone). Other verbs have the same or approximately the same denotation, but slightly different stylistic and social connotations: the participle *shown* (E1) is for many speakers more elegant than the participle *showed* (A1). Still other verbs are apparently identical in both meaning and connotation regardless of their conjugation type, so that the different inflected forms (e. g. *burned* and *burnt*) occur interchangeably in all situations—i. e. in completely free variation. According to our assumptions (§2.3), if a verb that belongs to a given conjugation type differs in meaning or connotation, however slightly, from a verb with a phonemically identical base that belongs to another type, the verbs are different morphemes: the *shine* whose preterit is *shined* is a different verb from the *shine* whose preterit is *shone*; and by the same argument the *show* whose participle is *shown* is a different verb from the *show* whose participle is *showed*.[13]

Since in practice it is often difficult to decide whether a given phonemic shape that belongs to two or more conjugation types is one verbal base or more than one, we shall not attempt the distinction. Hereafter, we shall use an asterisk to identify all bases that either (1) belong to both a regular and an irregular type, or (2) belong to an irregular type and are homonymous (in at least their first morpheme alternant) with a base belonging to a regular type.

4.4 A number of bases have morpheme alternants whose appearance is controlled not by an inflectional suffix but by some other following element. Chief among such elements is the unstressed morpheme *n't* — /nt/ after a syllabic, /ənt/ elsewhere — that occurs after eleven of the uninflected bases and after some of the corresponding inflected forms.[14] The following verb forms appear before this morpheme unchanged:[15]

can, pret. /kud/: /kud-ənt/.
dare, /dehr/: /dehr-nt/.
do, 3d sg. /dʌz/, pret. /did/ : /dʌz-ənt, did-ənt/.
have, uninflected /hæv/, 3d sg. /hæz/, pret. /hæd/ : /hæv-ənt, hæz-ənt, hæd-ənt/.
may, /mey/: /mey-nt/.
might, /mayt/: /mayt-ənt/.
ought, /oht/: /oht-ənt/.
need, /niyd/: /niyd-ənt/.
shall, pret. /šud/: /šud-ənt/.
will, pret. /wud/: /wud-ənt/.

Certain other bases (and homonymous 3d-singular forms including the zero alternant of suffix *1*) appear before the morpheme *n't* in an alternant that occurs nowhere else:

can, /kæn/: /kæh-nt/.
do, uninflected /duw/ : /dow-nt/.
must, /mʌst/: /mʌs-ənt/.
shall, /šæl/: /šæh-nt/.
will, /wil/: /wow-nt/.

4.5 There are also bases that appear in a special alternant shape before certain derivational suffixes. Thus, the base of the verb *see* has the alternants /siy/ and /soh/ before the inflectional morphemes, but the alternant /say/ before /t/ in the derivative noun *sight* /say-t/; the base of the verb *sing* has the alternants /siŋ/, /sæŋ/, and /sʌŋ/ before the inflectional morphemes, but the alternant /sohŋ/ before a zero derivational suffix in the noun *song*.[16]

Finally, some bases have special sandhi alternants when followed in the same phrase by a word with an initial consonant, especially one that is homorganic or identical with the last consonant of the base in its fuller form. This is especially true of bases ending with /t/ or /d/ after another consonant. Thus, the verb form *last*, normally /læhst/, may appear as /læhs/ in the phrase How long will it last today? or the like; the verb forms *find* and *found*, normally /faynd/ and /fawnd/, may lack the final /d/ in the phrases Did you find time to do it? and I found two dollars. The use of such sandhi alternants is optional: the same person will speak sometimes the shorter form, sometimes the longer in the same context. In the remainder of this paper we shall ignore them entirely.

5. The Verb *be*

5.1 The base of the verb *be* has a greater number of morpheme alternants than any other. As the first alternant—the one that appears when the base is used without any inflectional suffix—we may set up the shape /biy/; but this has a more limited use than the first alternant of other verbs except the auxiliaries (§2.1, §3.3). It occurs freely as an infinitive

[13] The argument: Phonemically different forms that occur in the same environment, and are not in completely free variation with each other, are morphemically different (§2.3). In the two participles *shown* /šow-n/ and *showed* /šow-d/, the phonemically different elements /n/ and /d/ both follow the base /šow/. They are not in free variation, since the two forms have different connotations of elegance and hence are not interchangeable. Therefore, either /n/ and /d/ are different morphemes, or the environment in which they occur is after all not the same for both. Since we wish to identify /n/ and /d/ as alternants of the same morpheme (suffix *3*), we assume that the /šow/ that precedes /n/ is morphemically different from the /šow/ that precedes /d/. In other words, we choose to set up two different but homonymous morphemes /šow/, and to refer to them—rather than to the suffix alternants—the stylistic or connotative difference between the inflected forms *shown* and *showed*.

[14] The form *n't* is best regarded as a separate morpheme, not as an alternant of the full form *not*. The two forms contrast, at least stylistically and in their connotations, in such phrases as I cannot go : I can't go.

[15] Any form in this list not otherwise identified is both the uninflected form of the verb and the homonymous 3d-singular form with zero suffix.

[16] It goes without saying that historical considerations play no part in a structural description. The actual historical relation between *sing* and *song* is irrelevant here; all that is relevant is their morphological relation in the structure of present-day English.

(I can't be there; I don't want to be there) and as an imperative (Be quiet); but as a finite present it occurs only after if, lest, etc., and only in rather formal style (If they be still there; If such there be). In the latter use, /biy/ occurs also with a 3d-singular subject (If it be not presumptuous; Lest it be objected that...), thus differing again from other verbal bases. Moreover, /biy/ is unique in its optative and concessive uses (God be praised; The public be damned; Be it never so humble; Be that as it may).[17]

5.2 The inflected forms of the verb be in the four usual inflectional categories are as follows: 3d singular is (base alternant /i/, suffix alternant /z/); preterit was and were (base alternants /wʌz/ and /wəhr/ in complementary distribution,[18] suffix alternant zero); participle been (base alternant /bi/,[19] suffix alternant /n/); gerund being (base alternant /biy/, suffix alternant /iŋ/).

But there are still other inflected forms of be that belong to none of these four categories. This constitutes the most striking idiosyncrasy of the verb: that its inflection distinguishes categories not recognized by the morphology of any other verb. We find, first, the forms am and are /æm, ahr/. These might be regarded as uninflected forms, in complementary distribution with the alternant /biy/; for the three words together have the same distribution as the uninflected form of such a verb as wait. The objection to this view is that the alternant /biy/ occurs, as already mentioned, in clauses with if (§5.1), contrasting in this position with /æm/ and /ahr/ (If I be not mistaken : If I am not mistaken; If you be he : If you are he). If the contrast is valid, we must set up a new inflectional category for am and are, perhaps to be called general present (i. e. non-3d-singular present). But in that case am and are include an inflectional suffix; and this cannot be zero, since we have assumed (§2.3) that no morpheme has zero as its only alternant. Any solution of the problem is inescapably ad hoc; we propose to regard the alternants of the base here as /æ/ and /ah/ in complementary distribution, and to posit a suffix morpheme with two alternants /m/ and /r/, the choice between them being regulated by the shape of the base alternant: /m/ after /æ/, /r/ after /ah/.

Complementary distribution and identity of meaning have allowed us to treat the two preterit forms was and were as both containing the zero alternant of suffix 2. But there is another form were which is not preterit and which contrast with was: the form that appears in conditional clauses after if with a subject in the 1st or 3d person singular (If I were rude, I'd apologize; If he were here, he'd see it; contrast If I was rude, I apologize; If he was here, he saw it). This were must be an inflected form different from the preterit were; its category we may call (with Hockett) the unreal. Again we analyze the form ad hoc: base alternant /wəh/, suffix morpheme /r/.[20]

5.3 Our analysis results in the following array of forms for the verb be: uninflected /biy/; 3d singular /i-z/; preterit /wʌz-0/ and /wəhr-0/ in complementary distribution; participle /bi-n/; gerund /biy-iŋ/; general present /æ-m/ and /ah-r/ in complementary distribution; unreal /wəh-r/. The base morpheme has eight alternants: /biy, i, wʌz, wəhr, bi, æ, ah, wəh/; and the six inflectional morphemes appear in the following alternants: 1 /z/, 2 /0/, 3 /n/, 4 /iŋ/, 5 /m/ and /r/ in complementary distribution, 6 /r/. This multiplicity of forms calls for an addition both to our list of inflectional classes (§3.2) and to our list of base groups (§4.1). Accordingly, we set up (again ad hoc) class J and base group 8 to accommodate the verb be. The former has been defined already in the list of suffix alternants just given; the latter is defined as follows:

Base group 8. Second alternant before suffix 1; third and fourth alternants before suffix 2; fifth alternant before suffix 3; sixth and seventh alternants before suffix 5; eight alternant before suffix 6.

5.4 Three of the inflected forms of be (but not the uninflected form) appear unchanged before the morpheme n't (§4.4). These are 3d singular /iz/, preterit /wʌz/ and /wəhr/, general present /ahr/ but not /æm/ : /iz-ənt, wʌz-ənt, wəhr-nt, ahr-nt/. In the substandard form ain't /ey-nt/, the /ey/ is a ninth alternant of the base, here followed by the zero alternants of suffixes 1 and 5.

6. List of Irregular Bases

6.1 The following list shows the bases of irregular verbs as they might appear in the lexicon. The list is thought to be complete, including all irregular verbs current in standard colloquial English, together with a few that are no longer used in conversation but are still occasionally spoken in a formal or literary style. Completely obsolete forms and all clearly substandard forms are omitted.

17 The optative use of be is paralleled by other verbs in a few formulas: God have mercy; God forbid; Perish the thought. The concessive use of other verbs than be is limited to such archaic locutions as Try they never so hard.

18 The alternant /wʌz/ occurs only with a subject in the 1st or 3d person singular; the alternant /wəhr/ occurs with all other subjects.

19 Or /biy/ in British English, identical with the alternant that appears in the uninflected form.

20 Since be has more inflected forms than any other verb, we might have begun our discussion with it instead of saving it for the end. In that case we should have said that all other verbs (except the auxiliaries) have the same inflectional categories as be, but that only be formally distinguishes the general present from the uninflected form or the unreal from the preterit. This is essentially what Hockett did in his rigorously systematic treatment of English verbs (op. cit. in fn. 2). The treatment here adopted seems preferable because it results in a simpler statement.

Verbs are alphabetized according to the conventional spelling of their uninflected forms. Each entry includes a symbol denoting the conjugation type of the verb, and a phonemic transcription of the base alternants that appear before the inflectional suffixes. If there is also a special alternant of the base appearing before the morpheme n't (§4.4), this is added after the symbol N; but alternants that appear only before derivational suffixes (like the /say/ in sight) and all sandhi alternants (§4.5) are omitted. Verbs that belong also to a regular conjugation type (A1) are marked with an asterisk. Verbs that belong to more than one irregular conjugation type are entered separately for each type: beat, bite, cleave, get, have, hide, spit, spring, stink, stride, tread, wake, are entered twice each; bid and shrink are entered four times each.

Compound verbs containing an irregular verb as the second member (e. g. broadcast) and derivative verbs formed with a prefix from an irregular verb (e. g. be-come) are not entered. Where a given base does not occur without a prefix (e. g. be-gin), the full form of the verb is given, but the prefix is disregarded in alphabetizing and in citing the base alternants.

Comments on individual verbs are included where they seem necessary.[21]

be J8 /biy, i, wʌz, wəhr, bi, æ, ah, wəh/. The only member of class J and of base group 8. In some dialects the alternant /bi/ is lacking; in others, it is /be/.
bear C3 /behr, bohr/.
beat C1 /biyt/.
beat D1 /biyt/.
bend B3 /bend, ben/.
*bet D1 /bet/.
better I1 /betər/. The only dissyllabic base. Used as a verb in colloquial speech without any form of had: I better; You better go (cf. I must; You must go). When had or 'd is present (I'd better; You'd better go), the word is not a verb but an adverb like rather.
bid C1 /bid/. Also outbid, underbid, overbid; not forbid.
bid C2 /bid, bæhd/. Also forbid.
bid D1 /bid/. See bid C1.
bid D2 /bid, bæhd/. See bid C2.
*bide D3 /bayd, bowd/.
bind D3 /baynd, bawnd/.
bite C3 /bayt, bit/.
bite D3 /bayt, bit/.
bleed D3 /bliyd, bled/.
blow C2 /blow, bluw/.
break C3 /breyk, browk/.
breed D3 /briyd, bred/.
bring B3 /briŋ, broh/.
build B3 /bild, bil/.
*burn B1 /bəhrn/.
burst D1 /bəhrst/.
buy B3 /bay, boh/.
can H2 /kæn, ku/; N /kæh/. Not homonymous with /kæhn/ 'tin'.
cast D1 /kæhst/.
catch B3 /kæc, koh/.
choose C3 /cuwz, cowz/.
*cleave 'split' B3 /kliyv, klef/.
*cleave 'split, adhere' C3 /kliyv, klowv/.
cling D3 /kliŋ, klʌŋ/.
come D2 /kʌm, keym/.
cost D1 /kohst/.
*crow F2 /krow, kruw/.
creep B3 /kriyp, krep/.
cut D1 /kʌt/.
*dare G1 /dehr/.
deal B3 /diyl, del/.
dig D3 /dig, dʌg/.
*dive F2 /dayv, dowv/.
do E6 /duw, di, dʌ/; N /dow/. The only member of base group 6.
draw C2 /droh, druw/.
*dream B3 /driym, drem/. In the pronunciation [drempt], the [p] is predictable and hence not phonemically distinctive.
drink D5 /driŋk, dræŋk, drʌŋk/.
drive C5 /drayv, drowv, driv/.
dwell B1 /dwel/.
eat C2 /iyt, eyt/. In standard British English, base alternants /iyt, et/.
fall C2 /fohl, fel/.
feed D3 /fiyd, fed/.
feel B3 /fiyl, fel/.
fight D3 /fayt, foht/.
find D3 /faynd, fawnd/.
*fit D1 /fit/.
flee A3 /fliy, fle/.
fling D3 /fliŋ, flʌŋ/. There is a jocular preterit /flæŋ/, one of a number of non-standard 'strong' preterits occasionally heard in facetious utterance.
fly C5 /flay, fluw, flow/.
freeze C3 /friyz, frowz/.
get C3 /get, gat/. Also beget, forget.
get D3 /get, gat/. Not beget, forget.
begin D5 /gin, gæn, gʌn/.
*gird B3 /gəhrd, gər/.
give C2 /giv, geyv/.
go C5 /gow, went, goh/. The classical instance of 'suppletive' inflection. In went, the /t/ could also be regarded as an alternant of suffix 2; but this interpretation would require the creation of a new inflectional class for this verb alone, with suffix alternants /z, t, n, iŋ/. By regarding went as consisting of a base alternant /went/ and the zero alternant of suffix 2, we escape this necessity. —The phonemic dissimilarity between /gow/ and /went/ is no bar to grouping them together as alternants of the same morpheme; for we have not assumed (in §2.3) that morpheme alternants must resemble each other phonemically.
grind D3 /graynd, grawnd/.
grow C2 /grow, gruw/.
*hang D3 /hæŋ, hʌŋ/.
have 'possess, etc.' A4 /hæv, hæ/.
have 'be obliged' G7 /hæf, hæ, hæs, hæv/. The only member of base group 7. In colloquial speech, this verb has the following forms: uninflected /hæf/ (I have to leave), 3d singular /hæs-0/ (He has to leave), preterit /hæ-d/ (I had to leave), participle /hæ-d/ (I've had to leave), gerund /hæv-iŋ/ (I'm having to leave tomorrow). The form /hæs/ is analyzed as including the zero alternant of suffix 1; another possible analysis would be into the base alternant /hæ/ and the suffix alternant /s/; but this would be the only case of /s/ after a voiced sound, and would make it impossible to regard the alternation of /ez ∼ s ∼ z/ as automatic.
hear A3 /hihr, həhr/.
*heave D3 /hiyv, howv/.
*hew E1 /hyuw/.
hide C3 /hayd, hid/.
hide D3 /hayd, hid/.
hit D1 /hit/.
hold D3 /howld, held/.
hurt D1 /hərt/.
keep B3 /kiyp, kep/.
*kneel B3 /niyl, nel/.
*knit D1 /nit/.
know C2 /now, nuw/. In some dialects the second alternant is /nyuw/ or /niw/.
lead D3 /liyd, led/.
*lean B3 /liyn, len/.
*leap B3 /liyp, lep/.
*learn B1 /ləhrn/.
leave B3 /liyv, lef/.
lend B3 /lend, len/.
let D1 /let/.
*light D3 /layt, lit/.

[21] One verb not listed in this section requires a word of comment. Beware is used as an infinitive and as an imperative (I told him to beware; Beware of the dog); inflected forms (bewares, bewared, bewaring) are either not used at all in present-day English or at best extremely rare. We may tentatively assign beware to conjugation type A1 as a regular verb whose inflected forms happen to be not in use.

lose B3 /luwz, lohs/.
make A3 /meyk, mey/.
may I1 /mey/. See might.
mean B3 /miyn, men/.
meet D3 /miyt, met/.
might I1 /mayt/. Historically but no longer in colloquial usage the preterit of may.
must I1 /mʌst/; N /mʌs/.
*need G1 /niyd/.
ought I1 /oht/.
*pen B1 /pen/.
*plead D3 /pliyd, pled/.
*prove E1 /pruwv/.
put D1 /put/.
*quit D1 /kwit/.
read D3 /riyd, red/.
*bereave B3 /riyv, ref/.
rend B3 /rend, ren/.
*rid D1 /rid/.
ride C5 /rayd, rowd, rid/.
*ring D5 /riŋ, ræŋ, rʌŋ/. Regular in the meaning 'encircle'.
rise C5 /rayz, rowz, riz/.
run D2 /rʌn, ræhn/.
forsake C2 /seyk, suk/.
say A4 /sey, se/.
see C2 /siy, soh/.
*beseech B3 /siyc, soh/.
seek B3 /siyk, soh/.
sell A3 /sel, sowl/.
send B3 /send, sen/.
set D1 /set/.
*sew E1 /sow/. Same as *sow.
shake C2 /šeyk, šuk/.
shall H2 /šæl, šu/; N /šæh/. Though may and might (qq.v.) have become different verbs in colloquial usage, should can still be viewed as the preterit of shall. Those who deny this possibility would set up two independent verbs: shall I1 /šæl/, N /šæh/; should I1 /šud/.
*shear C3 /šihr, šohr/.
shed D1 /šed/.
*shine D3 /šayn, šown/. In standard British English the base alternants are /šayn, šon/.
*shoe A3 /šuw, ša/.
shoot C3 /šuwt, šat/.
*show E1 /šow/.
shrink C3 /šriŋk, šrʌŋk/.
shrink C5 /šriŋk, šræŋk, šrʌŋk/.
shrink D3 /šriŋk, šrʌŋk/.
shrink D5 /šriŋk, šræŋk, šrʌŋk/.
*shrive C5 /šrayv, šrowv, šriv/.
shut D1 /šʌt/.
sing D5 /siŋ, sæŋ, sʌŋ/.
sink D5 /siŋk, sæŋk, sʌŋk/.
sit D3 /sit, sæt/.
slay C2 /sley, sluw/.
sleep B3 /sliyp, slep/.
slide D3 /slayd, slid/.
sling D3 /sliŋ, slʌŋ/.
slink D3 /sliŋk, slʌŋk/.
*slit D1 /slit/.
*smell B1 /smel/.
smite C5 /smayt, smowt, smit/.
*sow E1 /sow/. Same as *sew.
speak C3 /spiyk, spowk/.
*speed D3 /spiyd, sped/.
*spell B1 /spel/.
spend B3 /spend, spen/.
*spill B1 /spil/.
spin D3 /spin, spʌn/.
*spit D1 /spit/. Regular 'impale'.
spit D3 /spit, spæt/.
split D1 /split/.
*spoil B1 /spoyl/.
spread D1 /spred/.
spring D3 /spriŋ, sprʌŋ/.
spring D5 /spriŋ, spræŋ, sprʌŋ/.
stand A3 /stæhnd, stu/.
*stave D3 /steyv, stowv/.
steal C3 /stiyl, stowl/.
stick D3 /stik, stʌk/.
sting D3 /stiŋ, stʌŋ/.
stink D3 /stiŋk, stʌŋk/.
stink D5 /stiŋk, stæŋk, stʌŋk/.
*strew E1 /struw/.
stride C5 /strayd, strowd, strid/.
stride D3 /strayd, strowd/.
strike D3 /strayk, strʌk/.
*string D3 /striŋ, strʌŋ/.
*strive C5 /strayv, strowv, striv/.
swear C3 /swehr, swohr/.
*sweat D1 /swet/.
sweep B3 /swiyp, swep/.
*swell C3 /swel, swowl/.
swim D5 /swim, swæm, swʌm/.
take C2 /teyk, tuk/.
teach B3 /tiyc, toh/.
tear C3 /tehr, tohr/.
tell A3 /tel, towl/.
think B3 /θiŋk, θoh/.
*thrive C5 /θrayv, θrowv, θriv/.
throw C2 /θrow, θruw/.
thrust D1 /θrʌst/.
tread C3 /tred, trad/.
tread D3 /tred, trad/.
used I1 /yuws/. Though spelled with -d, this acts in colloquial speech like a finite present, not a preterit—the past-time meaning in this verb can be regarded as inherent in the base itself.
*wake C3 /weyk, wowk/.
*wake D3 /weyk, wowk/.
wear C3 /wehr, wohr/.
*weave C3 /wiyv, wowv/.
*wed D1 /wed/.
weep B3 /wiyp, wep/.
*wet D1 /wet/.
*will H2 /wil, wu/; N /wow/. On would as the preterit of will, cf. shall. Regular 'effect by the will' or the like.
win D3 /win, wʌn/.
wind D3 /waynd, wawnd/.
*wreak B3 /riyk, roh/. Wrought seems to be semantically closer to wreak than to work; and the relation wreak: wrought has a parallel in seek: sought, whereas work: wrought would be unique. Except in very formal discourse and in a few clichés, this verb is now obsolete. The adjective wrought (in wrought iron and the like) is of course not a form of the verb.
wring D3 /riŋ, rʌŋ/.
write C5 /rayt, rowt, rit/.

6.2 The foregoing list contains 200 entries, representing 182 orthographically different words. The number of verbs in each inflectional class, base group, and conjugation type is shown in the table below. The letters across the top denote inflectional classes; the numerals from 1 to 8 at the left denote base groups.

	A	B	C	D	E	F	G	H	I	J	Total
1		8	2	26	6	–	2	–	6	–	50
2	–	–	14	3	–	2	–	3	–	–	22
3	7	31	20	44	–	–	–	–	–	–	102
4	2	–	–	–	–	–	–	–	–	–	2
5	–	–	12	9	–	–	–	–	–	–	21
6	–	–	–	–	1	–	–	–	–	–	1
7	–	–	–	–	–	–	1	–	–	–	1
8	–	–	–	–	–	–	–	–	–	1	1
Totals	9	39	48	82	7	2	3	3	6	1	200

[The inadvertent omission of the verb lie (lay, lain) has resulted in certain statistical and other errors, especially in the section on morphophonemics. The following entry should be inserted in the above list:
lie C3 /lay, ley/ ⟦addendum supplied in 1957⟧]

6.3 We now show in full the membership of each of the twenty conjugation types to which irregular verbs belong. The ten inflectional classes (A to J) are again defined by the suffix alternants that appear after the verbal base; within each class, the bases that belong to it are grouped according to their conjugation types. Since the morpheme alternants of the bases have already been given (§6.1), bases are cited here only in the conventional spelling of the uninflected form.

An asterisk, as before, marks bases that belong also to a regular conjugation type; a plus sign marks bases that belong to more than one irregular type.

Class A. Suffix alternants: 1 /z/, 2 /d/, 3 /d/, 4 /iŋ/.

Type A3: flee, hear, make, sell, *shoe, stand, tell.

Type A4: have+, say.

Class B. Suffix alternants: 1 /z/, 2 /t/, 3 /t/, 4 /iŋ/.

Type B1: *burn, dwell, *learn, *pen, *smell, *spell, *spill, *spoil. Bases end with /n/ or /l/. Except for dwell, all verbs belong also to A1.

Type B3: bend, bring, build, buy, catch, *cleave+, creep, deal, *dream, feel, *gird, keep, *kneel, *lean, *leap, leave, lend, lose, mean, *bereave, rend, *beseech, seek, send, sleep, spend, sweep, teach, think, weep, *wreak.

Class C. Suffix alternants: 1 /z/, 2 /0/, 3 /n/, 4 /iŋ/.

Type C1: beat+, bid+.

Type C2: bid+, blow, draw, eat, fall, give, grow, know, forsake, see, shake, slay, take, throw.

Type C3: bear, bite+, break, choose, *cleave+, freeze, get+, hide+, *shear, shoot, shrink+, speak, steal, swear, *swell, tear, tread+, *wake+, wear, *weave.

Type C5: drive, fly, go, ride, rise, shrink+, stride+, *strive, smite, *shrive, *thrive, write.

Class D. Suffix alternants: 1 /z/, 2 /0/, 3 /0/, 4 /iŋ/.

Type D1: beat+, *bet, bid+, burst, cast, cost, cut, *fit, hit, hurt, *knit, let, put, *quit, *rid, set, shed, shut, *slit, *spit+, split, spread, *sweat, thrust, *wed, *wet. All bases end in /t/ or /d/.

Type D2: bid+, come, run.

Type D3: *bide, bind, bite+, bleed, breed, cling, dig, feed, fight, find, fling, get+, grind, *hang, *heave, hide+, hold, lead, *light, meet, *plead, read, *shine, shrink+, sit, slide, sling, slink, *speed, spin, *spit+, spring+, *stave, stick, sting, stink+, stride+, strike, *string, tread+, wake+, win, wind, wring. By far the largest conjugation type of irregular verbs.

Type D5: drink, begin, *ring, shrink+, sing, sink, spring+, stink+, swim. Except for swim, bases end with /ŋ/ or /ŋk/; without exception, they end with a nasal or a nasal + /k/.

Class E. Suffix alternants: 1 /z/, 2 /d/, 3 /n/, 4 /iŋ/.

Type E1: *hew, *prove, *sew, *show, *sow, *strew. All bases belong also to A1. Sew and sow differ only in meaning (and spelling), but perhaps not more widely than different senses of certain verbs listed only once.

Type E6: do.

Class F. Suffix alternants: 1 /z/, 2 /0/, 3 /d/, 4 /iŋ/.

Type F2: *crow, *dive. Both bases belong also to A1.

Class G. Suffix alternants: 1 /0/, 2 /d/, 3 /d/, 4 /iŋ/.

Type G1: *dare, *need. Both bases belong also to A1.

Type G7: have+ 'be obliged'.

Class H. Suffix alternants: 1 /0/, 2 /d/.

Type H2: can, shall, *will.

Class I. Suffix alternant: 1 /0/.

Type I1: better, may, might, must, ought, used.

Class J. Suffix alternants: 1 /z/, 2 /0/, 3 /n/, 4 /iŋ/, 5 /m, r/, 6 /r/. Type J8: be.

7. Morphophonemics

7.1 Morphophonemics is the study of the alternation between corresponding phonemes in alternant shapes of the same morpheme. When the morpheme alternants of a language, or of some form-class in a language, have been listed in full, a statement of the morphophonemics will serve as a convenient index to the listing. Since the base alternants of English irregular verbs have been listed in §6.1, the present section is an index to that one.

We shall group together here all bases that exhibit the same phonemic difference among their alternants, regardless of the inflectional classes to which they belong. There is no necessary connection between any morphophonemic set and any inflectional class. Some of the sets to be listed include verbs of several different classes; for instance, the alternation /iy/ ∼ /e/ is found in bases of class A, class B, and class D. Other sets include verbs of only one class, but not all the verbs that belong there; for instance, the alternation /ay/ ∼ /aw/ is found only in bases of class D, but by no means in all the bases of that class. No set is coextensive in its membership with any class.

In listing the alternations between phonemes, we shall regard every syllabic as a unit, whether it consists of a vowel alone or of a vowel and a following semivowel /y, w, h, r, hr/. Thus, we shall express the difference between eat /iyt/ and ate /eyt/ as /iy/ ∼ /ey/, not simply as /i/ ∼ /e/, and the difference between bind /baynd/ and bound /bawnd/ as /ay/ ∼ /aw/, not simply as /y/ ∼ /w/.

Verbs of base group group 1, whose bases have only a single alternant, naturally do not appear in the listing.

7.2 There are ten types of morphophonemic alternation between base alternants of English irregular verbs. The first four types are found in bases with two alternants, the next three in bases with three alternants, and the rest in bases with more than three alternants. The types may be characterized as follows:[22]

Type I. Alternation between two different syllabics ($V_1 \sim V_2$).

Type II. Alternation between a syllabic with one or two following non-syllabics and a different syllabic without a following non-syllabic (V_1C or $V_1CC \sim V_2$).

Type III. Alternation between a syllabic with a following non-syllabic and a different syllabic with a different following non-syllabic ($V_1C_1 \sim V_2C_2$).

Type IV. Alternation between the presence and the absence of a non-syllabic ($C \sim 0$).

[22] The following symbols are used to characterize the several types of alternation: V = syllabic (not merely vowel), C = non-syllabic consonant, 0 = zero (i. e. absence of a phoneme), V_1 and V_2 = different syllabics. The symbol ∼ everywhere means 'in alternation with'.

Type V. Alternation among three different syllabics ($V_1 \sim V_2 \sim V_3$).

Type VI. Alternation between a syllabic with a following non-syllabic and two different syllabics without a following non-syllabic ($V_1C \sim V_2 \sim V_3$).

Type VII. Suppletion: alternation among three phonemic shapes that have no phoneme in common.

Type VIII. Alternation among four different syllabics ($V_1 \sim V_2 \sim V_3 \sim V_4$).

Type IX. Alternation among three different non-syllabics and the absence of a non-syllabic ($C_1 \sim 0 \sim C_2 \sim C_3$).

Type X. Suppletion: alternation among eight phonemic shapes that have no phoneme in common.

Type I

/ay/ ∿ /i/ bite, hide, light, slide.
/iy/ ∿ /e/ bleed, breed, creep, deal, dream, feed, feel, flee, keep, kneel, lead, lean, leap, mean, meet, plead, read, sleep, speed, sweep, weep.
/ey/ ∿ /e/ say.
/ow/ ∿ /e/ hold.
/oh/ ∿ /e/ fall.
/i/ ∿ /æ/ sit, spit.
/e/ ∿ /a/ get, tread.
/uw/ ∿ /a/ shoe, shoot.
/i/ ∿ /ʌ/ cling, dig, fling, shrink, sling, slink, spin, spring, stick, sting, stink, string, win, wring.
/æ/ ∿ /ʌ/ hang.
/ay/ ∿ /ʌ/ strike.
/ey/ ∿ /u/ forsake, shake, take.
/i/ ∿ /ey/ give.
/ʌ/ ∿ /ey/ come.
/iy/ ∿ /ey/ eat.
/ay/ ∿ /aw/ bind, find, grind, wind.
/e/ ∿ /ow/ sell, swell, tell.
/iy/ ∿ /ow/ cleave, freeze, heave, speak, steal, weave.
/ey/ ∿ /ow/ break, stave, wake.
/ay/ ∿ /ow/ bide, dive, shine, stride.
/uw/ ∿ /ow/ choose.
/ey/ ∿ /uw/ slay.
/ow/ ∿ /uw/ blow, crow, grow, know, throw.
/oh/ ∿ /uw/ draw.
/i/ ∿ /æh/ bid.
/ʌ/ ∿ /æh/ run.
/iy/ ∿ /oh/ see.
/ay/ ∿ /oh/ buy, fight.
/ihr/ ∿ /əhr/ hear.
/ihr/ ∿ /ohr/ shear.
/ehr/ ∿ /ohr/ bear, swear, tear, wear.

Type II

/iyk/ ∿ /oh/ seek, wreak.
/iyc/ ∿ /oh/ beseech, teach.
/æc/ ∿ /oh/ catch.
/iŋ/ ∿ /oh/ bring.
/iŋk/ ∿ /oh/ think.
/æhnd/ ∿ /u/ stand.
/əhrd/ ∿ /ər/ gird.

Type III

/iyv/ ∿ /ef/ cleave, leave, bereave.
/uwz/ ∿ /ohs/ lose.

Type IV

/d/ ∿ 0 bend,build, lend, rend, send, spend.
/t/ ∿ 0 must.
/k/ ∿ 0 make.
/v/ ∿ 0 have 'possess'.

Type V

/i/ ∿ /æ/ ∿ /ʌ/ drink, begin, ring, shrink, sing, sink, spring, stink, swim.
/ay/ ∿ /ow/ ∿ /i/ drive, ride, rise, shrive, smite, stride, strive, thrive, write.
/ay/ ∿ /uw/ ∿ /ow/ fly.

Type VI

/æn/ ∿ /u/ ∿ /æh/ can.
/æl/ ∿ /u/ ∿ /æh/ shall.
/il/ ∿ /u/ ∿ /ow/ will.

Type VII

/gow/ ∿ /went/ ∿ /goh/ go.

Type VIII

/uw/ ∿ /i/ ∿ /ʌ/ ∿ /ow/ do.

Type IX

/f/ ∿ 0 ∿ /s/ ∿ /v/ have 'be obliged'.

Type X

/biy/ ∿ /i/ ∿ /wəz/ ∿ /wəhr/ ∿ /bi/ ∿ /æ/ ∿ /ah/ ∿ /wəh/ be.

8. Atonic Verbs

8.1 We have not quite finished. In the sentence I have seen it /ày hǽv sîyn it/, the verb have /hæv/ is accompanied by the emphatic stress morpheme /´/ (cf. fn. 12). In the sentence I've seen it /ày v sɪ́yn it/, where the stress morpheme accompanies the participle seen, the verb have appears as /v/. This difference between the two phonemic shapes of the finite verb might be attributed to the different locations of the stress—a view that would add to the number of morpheme alternants of have and of some other bases, but would not essentially complicate the system. Unfortunately, this obvious and convenient explanation will not work. The alternant /hæv/ also occurs without the stress morpheme /´/, as in I have seen it /ày hæv sɪ́yn it/,[23] which contrasts at least in style and connotation with I've seen it /ày v sɪ́yn it/. Phonemically different forms that occur in the same environment, and are not in completely free variation with each other, are morphemically different (§2.3); therefore /hæv/ and /v/, so far as they differ in their social connotation, are not merely alternants of the same morpheme, but different morphemes.

[23] We have already agreed to disregard the difference between such alternants as /hæ̂v, hæ̀v, hæv/—a difference in stress alone (fn. 12). But even if we discriminate such alternants, the situation will not be affected; for the completely unstressed alternant /hæv/ is common and perfectly natural in the cited context.

A similar contrast exists between some of the inflected forms of the verb /hæv/ and those of the verb /v/; 3d singular /hæz/ in He has left : /z/ in He's left; preterit /hæd/ in He had left : /d/ in He'd left. But no such contrast is possible between different participles or gerunds: the verb /v/ simply lacks these categories. Now the form /hæz/ obviously consists of the base alternant /hæ/ and the suffix alternant /z/; /hæd/ consists of /hæ/ and the suffix alternant /d/. In parallel fashion, the verb forms /z/ in He's left and /d/ in He'd left are analyzed as consisting of a base alternant and the suffixes /z/ and /d/ respectively. The base alternant, accordingly, is zero. In the light of our assumptions (§2.3) and of our treatment of suffix morphemes (§3.1), there is no theoretical objection to such a view: if /0/ can be admitted as a morpheme alternant of /ez ∿ s ∿ z/ (suffix *1*), it can equally well be admitted as a morpheme alternant of such a base as /v/.

The verb form /s/ in Jack's left is of course an automatic alternant of the /z/ in He's left: the base alternant in both forms is zero, and the choice of the suffix alternant, as already noted (§3.1), depends on the preceding phoneme.

8.2 But *have* is not yet fully disposed of. We can say not only I have seen it /ày hæv síyn it/ and I've seen it /ày v síyn it/, both with the emphatic stress morpheme on *seen*, but also /ày həv síyn it/ and /ày əv síyn it/—with forms of *have* that are phonetically intermediate between the 'full form' /hæv/ and the 'completely reduced form' /v/. To what morphemes do these intermediate pronunciations belong? Reluctant as we may be to allow the multiplication of elements, we cannot escape the conclusion that the verb forms /həv/ and /əv/ belong to none of the morphemes mentioned so far. Since they occur in the same environments as /hæv/ and /v/, and differ from them—though perhaps only minutely—in their social flavor, they are morphemically different from both.

In the same way, the inflected forms /həz/ and /əz/, /həd/ and /əd/, as in He has left and He had left, are to be analyzed as consisting of the base alternants /hə/ and /ə/ respectively and the suffix alternants already mentioned.

Accordingly, we set up four verbal bases of related meaning but different connotation: one with morpheme alternants /hæv/ and /hæ/; one with morpheme alternants /həv/ and /hə/; one with morpheme alternants /əv/ and /ə/; and one with morpheme alternants /v/ and /0/. The first of these belongs to conjugation type A4; the other three, forming their 3d-singular and preterit forms with /z/ and /d/ respectively but lacking a participle and a gerund, belong to none of the types that have been established.

8.3 It is a syntactic peculiarity of the verbs /həv/, /əv/, and /v/ that they are never, like other verbs, accompanied by the emphatic stress morpheme /ˊ/. For this reason we may call them *atonic verbs*.

The number of atonic verbs is at least eleven. In addition to the verbs /həv/, /əv/, and /v/, we find the following:

Be, with morpheme alternants /bi/ uninflected, /0/ before suffixes *1* and *5*; /wəz/ and /wər/ in complementary distribution before suffix *2*; /wə/ before suffix *6*. Inflected forms: 3d singular /0-z/ and /0-s/, preterit /wəz-0/ and /wər-0/, general present /0-m/ and /0-r/, unreal /wə-r/; participle and gerund lacking.

Be, with morpheme alternants as above except for /ə / instead of /0/ before suffix *5*. Inflected forms: as above except for general present /ə-m/ and /ə-r/.

Can, with morpheme alternants /kən/ and /kəŋ/ in complementary distribution[24] uninflected and before suffix *1*, /kə/ before suffix *2*. Inflected forms: 3d singular /kən-0/ and /kəŋ-0/, preterit /kə-d/; other categories lacking, as in the verb /kæn/.

Do, with unique morpheme alternant /də/. Inflected forms: 3d singular /də-z/; other categories lacking.

Shall, with morpheme alternants /šəl/ uninflected and before suffix *1*, /šə/ before suffix *2*. Inflected forms: 3d singular /šəl-0/, preterit /šə-d/; other categories lacking, as in the verb /šæl/.[25]

Will, with morpheme alternants /wəl/ uninflected and before suffix *1*, /wə/ before suffix *2*. Inflected forms: 3d singular /wəl-0/, preterit /wə-d/; other categories lacking, as in the verb /wil/.

Will, with morpheme alternants /əl/ uninflected and before suffix *1*, /ə/ before suffix *2*. Inflected forms: 3d singular /əl-0/, preterit /ə-d/; other categories lacking, as in the verb /wil/.

Will, with morpheme alternants /l/ uninflected and before suffix *1*, /0/ before suffix *2*. Inflected forms: 3d singular /l-0/, preterit /0-d/; other categories lacking, as in the verb /wil/.

8.4 The most efficient way of describing these atonic forms is to set them up as a major subclass of English verbs, coordinate with a subclass of tonic verbs that will include all the rest.[26] The inflectional classes and base groups that were established in the first part of this paper apply to tonic verbs only; for atonic verbs we must add a separate classification:

[24] /kəŋ/ before /k/ or /g/ (I can come; I can go), /kən/ elsewhere.

[25] Some speakers use also a preterit form /št/, as in I should think so /ày št θíŋk sə̂w/. For such dialects we must set up another verb *shall*, with morpheme alternants /šəl/ uninflected and before suffix *1*, /š/ before suffix *2*.

[26] For pedagogical purposes, this description of atonic verbs—and of tonic verbs too, for that matter—would certainly be over-meticulous and ineffective. To the student learning to speak English, busy at his primary task of memorizing model sentences, it would be unhelpful at best, if not actively confusing. But the intent of this paper is not pedagogical.

Class	Suffix 1	Suffix 2	Suffix 5	Suffix 6
A′	z	d		
B′	0	d		
C′	z			
D′	z	0	m; r	r

Base group 1′. Single alternant.
Base group 2′. Second alternant before suffix 2.
Base group 3′. Second alternant before suffixes 1 and 2.
Base group 4′. Second alternant before suffixes 1 and 5; third and fourth alternants before suffix 2; fifth alternant before suffix 6.
Base group 5′. Second alternant before suffix 1; third and fourth alternants before suffix 2; fifth alternant before suffix 5; sixth alternant before suffix 6.

Accordingly, we list our eleven atonic verbs as follows:

be D′4′ /bi, 0, wəz, wər, wə/.
be D′5′ /bi, 0, wəz, wər, ə, wə/.
can B′2′ /kən ∿ kəŋ, kə/.
do C′1′ /də/.
have A′3′ /həv, hə/.
have A′3′ /əv, ə/.
have A′3′ /v, 0/.
shall B′2′ /šəl, šə/.
will B′2′ /wəl, wə/.
will B′2′ /əl, ə/.
will B′2′ /l, 0/.

⟦The foregoing paper by Bloch and the following one by Nida, taken together, could easily lead us into far more extensive discussion than I can find room for. I content myself with a few hints; interested readers will find others in the texts.

This is no one-dimensional opposition between an A and its not-A. There is, rather, something like a dramatic encounter. I don't want this to be taken in the sense of a polemic or personal conflict between the two writers; I intend it to refer rather to ideas and to modes of thought. These are, between the two sides, as multiply different as could be imagined, or more so. Further, as if to make the whole thing all but inaccessible to discussion, there is even a total difference in the kind of participation or involvement in the encounter.

In principle, Bloch's procedure is to adopt a set of axioms and then to develop the consequences of the set à outrance. (In another capacity, that of the interested bystander, he may express something like dismay at this or that outré result; but that has just exactly nothing to do with his main business.) This paper, as published, does not group all the axioms first and then present the development in strictly logical sequence. But the difference between that and what he actually does is merely literary. His interspersed arrangement is intended to hold the reader's interest, which it adequately does. (This, incidentally, is one of the leading characteristics of Bloch's papers. In its own right, it is a great merit. But it can result in his being misapprehended by any reader of a different cast of mind.)

The ultimate justification for such a proceeding would have to be an understanding that other writers are expected to adopt other sets of axioms, and to develop their private sets with equal ruthlessness. As such publications accumulate, practical descriptions (cf. fn. 26 above) may be expected to improve gradually, as their makers (any one of whom may be one of those theorists, acting now in another capacity) gradually learn from the various theoretical papers (their own and others) how to avoid inconsistency while working to satisfy other requirements, such as pedagogical effectiveness or easy reading. There is an assumption concealed here, to the effect that a division of functions of this sort is at least one of the better ways to procure progress in theoretical and practical work both. I don't mean that Bloch and the others who behave like this do so in consequence of having adopted this assumption as one of their axioms; rather, I suppose they do it because it feels right to each of them, and my 'assumption' is just a postulate that I think I might well use if I were to construct A Set of Postulates for the Scientific Study of Linguistic Thought. Anyhow, I am inclined to feel that this assumption is sound; but I leave to others the task of trying to show that Nida did wrong to depart from it. I don't feel that he did wrong in doing so; he was simply being himself, which is the only way to make one's own contribution.

Bloch as reader of Nida's paper, in turn, couldn't help but sort out the one from the other. From one of the sorts of things he found there, he got what he had in mind, I suppose, when he recently said to me that after reading Nida's paper he would do some things differently if he were to rewrite the English verb paper. What these would be, I must not try to guess. Whether, if he were to do another pedagogical book on Japanese, he would, after reading Nida's paper, do some things differently, is a separate question.⟧

THE IDENTIFICATION OF MORPHEMES

EUGENE A. NIDA

Language 24.414-41—1948

1. Recent developments and publications[1] concerning the analysis and classification of morphemes have been of great importance: they have provided a variety of new approaches to old problems, refined the statements of relationships, demonstrated the applicability of the method to a number of languages, emphasized the importance of distributional criteria, and pointed out a number of unsolved or perhaps only partially solved problems. All this has been a genuine gain. Nevertheless, a close examination of some of these developments is rather disturbing, and certain rather basic objections can be raised. For one thing, the term morpheme has come to be used by Hockett, and to a somewhat lesser extent by others, as a designation for forms which are related almost wholly in terms of distribution. I do not wish to deny the significance of tactics in linguistic structure; but when the primary criterion for the choosing of alternative possibilities is stated by Hockett as being 'tactical simplicity',[2] I am inclined to doubt the validity of quite so much stress being laid upon distributional characteristics, especially when such a choice leads to the conclusions which Hockett has described. In both Bloch's and Hockett's recent papers on morphemic problems there is a conspicuous tendency to make covert distinctions more important than overt ones, though the treatment is quite different as regards detail.

I am in complete agreement with the desire to attain simplicity of statement and to reveal the whole structure of a language in terms of such statements; but it is possible that too much emphasis on structural simplicity, both of statement and language structure, can give a false impression of simplicity and can actually misrepresent some of the pertinent facts. The objections which this paper raises are not directed against any lack of logic in the presentations cited. Bloch and Hockett have been thoroughly consistent in following to the end the implications of their basic premises. Any disagreement with their treatments is not a criticism of their handling of the data as such, but is directed rather at the fundamental principles upon which all of us as descriptive linguists have been working. Some linguists have become increasingly aware of certain of the peripheral but methodologically fundamental problems of our descriptive science, and we are genuinely indebted to Hockett, Bloch, Harris, Wells, Voegelin, and others for pointing out the ramifications of our principles. It would seem, however, that if the principles upon which we operate lead us to the conclusions adopted in the recent articles by Bloch and Hockett, there should be some refining of statement, or perhaps complete change in statement. Even Bloch does not seem particularly pleased about some of his conclusions. He says, (Lang. 23.417 ((253))), 'Reluctant as we may be to allow the multiplication of elements, we cannot escape the conclusion...'

We shall attempt to treat in §2 some of the specific problems raised by Bloch's and Hockett's papers. These will constitute a background for the development of certain principles of analysis and classification, considered in §3. A fourth section will describe the types of morphemes.

2. We shall not attempt to treat systematically all the types of problems introduced by Bloch and Hockett, nor try to give any overall criticism. Rather, we shall restrict ourselves to considering a few examples of where their systems would seem to break down, or where there appear to be other factors which must be considered.

2.1 Bloch points out (Lang. 23.406 ((247))) that in accordance with his system the stem morphemes of shown /šown/ and showed /šowd/ must be considered as different morphemes. Since he considers that the suffixal morphemes /-n/ and /-d/ are most conveniently treated as alternants of the same morpheme and hence do not differ in meaning, and since the total forms shown and showed are not in free variation, the difference in meaning must be attributed to a difference in the stems. Bloch states the problem as follows:

Since we wish to identify /n/ and /d/ as alternants of the same morpheme, we assumed that the /šow/ that precedes /n/ is morphemically different from the /šow/ that precedes /d/. In other words, we we choose to set up two different but homonymous morphemes /šow/, and to refer to them—rather than to the suffix alternants—the stylistic or connotative difference between the inflected forms shown and showed.

[1] Zellig S. Harris, Morpheme alternants in linguistic analysis, Lang. 18.169-80 (1942) ((109)); id., Discontinuous morphemes, Lang. 21.121-7 (1945); id., From morpheme to utterance, Lang. 22.161-83 (1946) ((142)); Rulon S. Wells, Immediate constituents, Lang. 23. 81-117 (1947) ((186)); C. F. Voegelin, A problem in morpheme alternants and their distribution, Lang. 23.245-54 (1947); Charles F. Hockett, Problems in morphemic analysis, Lang. 23.321-43 (1947) ((229)); Bernard Bloch, English verb inflection, Lang. 23. 399-418 (1947) ((243)).

[2] Op. cit. 342 ((241)).

This type of procedure results in attributing a distinction in meaning to formally identical items, rather than to items which are formally different. This also means assigning a meaning-difference to certain covert elements rather than to overt distinctions. It would seem that the difference in connotation between these forms when they are not in complete free variation is precisely the type of difference which exists in the range of distribution of the suffixes /-n/ and /-d/. A procedure to treat this type of problem will concern us in §3.4.

2.2 Bloch employs a similar treatment in the analysis of sang, the past tense of sing (Lang. 23.407 ((247))). The past tense form /sæŋ/ is treated as an alternant of /siŋ/. The meaning-difference is considered as expressed by a zero suffix. By this procedure an overt distinction—the replacement of /i/ by /æ/[3]—is treated as meaningless, while the covert distinction becomes the meaning-carrier. I do not deny the significance of zero in such a form, nor the importance of the pattern which leads one to recognize a zero; but it appears to me as strikingly contradictory to treat overt distinctions as meaningless and covert distinctions as meaningful. Undoubtedly the unsophisticated speaker of the language has no such reaction, and though I do not argue for following the judgment of such a person, I do insist that we should not disguise features which, as as far as the native speaker is concerned, bear all the evidence of being meaningful and distinctive. If we do so, we have given entirely too high a priority to the arrangements of items (i.e. the tactics).

2.3 A further problem is introduced by Bloch in his treatment of were (Lang. 23.408 ((248))). The two forms was and were are treated as morpheme alternants, both occurring with zero alternant of the past tense suffix. The were which occurs in conditional clauses of an 'unreal' type is considered to consist of an alternant /wə-/[4] (an alternant of /biy/) plus the suffix /-r/. Bloch insists that this conditional were is different in meaning from the past-tense were and contrasts with it in distribution. As evidence he cites the following: If I were rude, I'd apologize; If he were here, he'd see it; and If I was rude, I apologize; If he was here, he saw it. It is true that within the if clause there is contrast of occurrence with identical constituents, but one should not overlook the fact that within the apodoses there is a contrastive use of 'd apologize and 'd see vs. apologize and saw. Hence, it can be stated that was and were are still in complementary distribution on the basis of the forms occurring elsewhere in the sentence. The so-called two forms of were, the past tense and the unreal, do bear a certain phonetic-semantic resemblance to each other (following Bloomfield's definition)[5] to which the treatment by Bloch does not appear to give full recognition. The methodological problem is that the past-tense forms was and were, which are formally different, become morphemically identical, while two identical forms, past-tense were and unreal were, become morphemically different.

What seems to be basic in Bloch's development of this situation is that were occurs with different meanings in different situations. Note, however, that in the clause If they were there, we have no idea whether this is an unreal or a simple past tense. It is the choice of the apodosis that provides the clue. If the apodosis is they would do it, we conclude that the were is unreal, but if the apodosis is they did it, then we know that were is a simple past-tense form. We should not be surprised to find forms with different meanings in different syntactic combinations, e.g. run in they run away and they run him away. The meaning in the intransitive and transitive constructions is quite different, and this contrast is paralleled by a difference in distribution of occurrence. Hence, we conclude that both run's are the same morpheme.

2.4 Hockett states that 'some bits of phonemic material, of some utterances, are morphemically irrelevant'.[6] The problem involved is the familiar one: the determination whether a structural unit which has no definable meaning in terms of a bio-social context is a morpheme, or whether such a unit is to be assigned to some other element, instead of being given independent status. Hockett considers, for example, that the stem vowels in the Spanish verb are 'empty morphs.' As empty morphs, they do not belong to any morpheme. That is to say, the vowels a, e, and i of amar 'to love', beber 'to drink', and vivir 'to live' are meaningless and hence are not morphemes.

It is perfectly true that these stem formatives cannot be given a meaning which corresponds to anything in the practical world. Their meaning, if they have any, must be stated purely in terms of grammatical situations. But the inability of the linguist to assign a non-linguistic meaning to a form is not, it seems, a sufficient basis for regarding such a structural unit as not constituting a morpheme. Otherwise, one may be faced with an amazing assortment of empty morphs which Hockett would speak of as morphemically irrelevant. On the other hand, it is rather difficult to see just how the infinitive suffix -r, which Hockett describes as a morpheme, is to be regarded as having more than grammatical meaning, i.e. meaning in terms of distributional situations. It is possible that such a line of distinction could be drawn; but the establishment of empty morphs on the

3 [The use of the word 'replacement' evades the objection raised in Lang. 23.400 ((244)).—BB]

4 The phonemic writing of English is here adapted to conform to my own speech, in order that all citations of English in this article may be consistent.

5 Leonard Bloomfield, Language 161 (New York, 1933).

6 Op. cit. 331 ((235)).

basis of so-called meaning-deficiency would certainly produce quite a change in the traditional treatment of primary derivatives. For example, the -er in such words as spider, hammer, otter, badger, ladder, auger (there are more than 100 nouns in English with this suffixal formative) would be ruled out as being morphemically irrelevant—unless, perhaps, some way could be found to construe this -er as an affix similar to the Spanish infinitive ending. In any case, the meaning is essentially one which is derived from the distribution of the form in the language.

Rather than postulate structural units whose position and distribution must be described (if the description of the language is complete), but which are supposedly morphemically irrelevant, it would seem to me much safer, as well as structurally more valid, to follow Bloomfield in contending that 'every complex form is made up entirely of morphemes'.[7]

2.5 In treating so-called portmanteau items (Lang. 23.333 ff. ((236 ff.))), Hockett has introduced an interesting solution to matters which have caused complication for some time. Hockett's treatment of a form such as men differs considerably in outward form from Bloch's, but is essentially the same. Hockett would not say that men is a morphemic alternant of man plus a zero alternant of the plural suffix, but rather that men is one morph, which belongs simultaneously to two morphemes, namely {man} and {-s}. Except for the type of statement, such a description does not differ appreciably from Bloch's. It is only that Hockett's appears to employ zero less frequently.

In handling inflexional endings like the -o in Spanish amo 'I love' (Lang. 23.338 ((239))), Hockett says that this is a morph which belongs to two morphemes: a tense-mode morpheme and a person-number morpheme. In this instance, however, he does not provide any overt form for the separate morphemes. Only the morph has overt form; the morphemes are merely structural parallelisms as indicated by such related paradigmatic forms as amábamos 'we loved' and amaréis 'you (pl.) will love', in which the tense-mode morpheme precedes the person-number morpheme. In the instance of French au 'to the' occurring in place of the analogically demonstrable but non-occurring à le, there is more basis for speaking of a single morph belonging to two morphemes, since these morphemes may be identified as occurring elsewhere in the language. But in the case of Spanish -o, Hockett's morphemes are only statements of sequence evidenced at other points in the paradigmatic series; there are no overt forms to which this particular morph may be referred.

2.6 The complications which arise from the portmanteau concept are extreme. For example, Hockett combines she /šiy/ and her (object form) /hər/ as two morphs in complementary distribution, and assigns them both to the morpheme {she}. Just why the subject rather than the object form should have been chosen as the basic form of the morpheme, we are not told. It is possible that the responsibility lies in an unconscious recognition of the series: he, him; they, them; who, whom. In Hockett's system the parallel development of these three sets of forms is not considered significant, even though the final /-m/'s do bear a strong phonetic-semantic resemblance to each other. Hockett considers that complementary distribution is all that fundamentally counts. But the implications of this method seem to be greater than he may have anticipated. For example, consider what could be done on that basis with number distinctions in English. Not only would it be possible to combine all the plural affixes of nouns in one morpheme (a step which we should all agree to), but one could say that these are in complementary distribution with the partly homophonous third-singular suffix of verbs. A single morpheme could then be set up with the meaning 'number distinctiveness' and with the additional distributional characteristic that if an alternant occurs after the noun it does not occur after the verb, and vice versa, e.g. /ðə boyz rən/ the boys run vs. /ðə boy rənz/ the boy runs. By slight extensions it might be possible to construct a descriptive system by which practically all the features of concord, government, and cross-reference could be treated on a submorphemic level. If this were done, we should only have succeeded in changing the meaning of the word 'morpheme' to apply to certain distributionally related forms.

If distribution should be taken as the all-important factor, we could invade the traditional lexical area with new statements of relationships. We could say that -ology is a morphemic alternant of science, since they are in complementary distribution in such series as biology : life-science, geology : earth-science. (The bound form -ology and the free form science would never occur in identical environments.) Since the meanings of the two forms are closely related (we admittedly have no scale for measuring degrees of difference), we should have no objection to relating this series, except perhaps Hockett's caveat that 'the total range should not be unique' (Lang. 23.331 ((234))).

2.7 The recent attempts to refine morphological methodology have, nevertheless, been exceedingly valuable and important; for some phases of Bloomfield's treatment have caused difficulty, primarily because of the apparent confusion as to the status of some types of changes. The distinction between processes and morphemes is not always clear, and it is sometimes hard to know when a change is to be considered as independently meaningful and hence as constituting a morpheme. The refinements of methodology which are suggested in this paper do not attempt to contradict Bloomfield's basic analysis, but rather to refine the statements and point out the specific areas of difficulty, with suggestions of how such problems can and should be treated.

[7] Op. cit. 162.

3. The analysis of morphemes proposed here[8] takes as a basic definition Bloomfield's statements:[9] 'a linguistic form which bears no partial phonetic-semantic resemblance to any other form, is a... morpheme', and 'any combination of phonemes... which has a meaning, is a linguistic form.' It should be noted that this definition is essentially a negative one, in that it prescribes limits to the morpheme by setting it off from other morphemes, rather than by defining the nature and relationship of its own parts. Its lack of phonetic-semantic resemblance to other morphemes is the essential characteristic, not necessarily its possession of an exact phonetic-semantic identity in all of its occurrences. It is by virtue of such a negative definition of the morpheme that we can include as members of one morpheme structural units which are not identical in form. For example, we admit as morphemic alternants such a series as /-əz ∿ -z ∿ -s/, plural formatives with nouns (e.g. in roses, cows, sticks). The distribution of these alternants may be phonologically defined. We also speak of /-ən/ in oxen as an alternant of the plural suffix, but in this instance we recognize that the distribution cannot be defined in terms of phonological criteria, but rather that the distribution of /-ən/ can only be described by identifying the morpheme ox. The essential difference between these two types of alternants has been recognized by everyone; in his recent article, Bloch makes a special point of distinguishing the two types of alternants (Lang. 23.402 ((244 f.))). There is not, however, complete agreement on the degree of difference which can be admitted in morphemic alternants, nor on the types of distribution which are significant in determining patterns of morphemic alternation. For that reason, we need more precise clarification of our procedure.

Before treating such details of method, it should be pointed out that Bloomfield's definition, which we are adopting here as basic, provides not only for sub-morphemic distinctions of phonetic form but also for sub-morphemic distinctions of semantic value. This will be more evident as we consider Principles 4 and 6 below. A definition which contrasts one phonetic-semantic entity with all other entities in the language still permits the sub-morphemic distinctions of phonetic form and semantic areas within the basic distinctiveness which sets off such a form from other possibly related forms. An understanding of this essentially negative character of the underlying definition is necessary for a proper evaluation and analysis of the following principles.

These principles of analysis are not here numbered by any system of priority, nor necessarily by any system of logical delimitation of the field. Rather, they are arranged as a sort of related series of working postulates, beginning with the more general and readily accepted and advancing toward the more specific and complex.

3.01 Principle 1. Forms which possess a common semantic distinctiveness[10] and an identical form in all their occurrences constitute a single morpheme.

With this principle no one can disagree, for it means that such a suffix as /-ər/ in dancer, walker, runner, worker, swimmer, etc., constitutes a morpheme, since it has a single form (i.e. consists of the same phonemes in the same order), and since in each instance it possesses a common semantic distinctiveness, which may be defined as 'agentive' with respect to the underlying verb form. Note, however, that this first principle of analytical procedure is not a definition of a morpheme; rather, within the scope of the basic definition, such a principle of identification holds true.

3.02 Principle 2. Forms which possess a common semantic distinctiveness but which differ in phonemic form (i.e. constituency or shape) constitute a single morpheme provided that the distribution of formal differences can be phonologically defined.

Principle 2 provides for the identification of phonologically defined alternants as members of the same morpheme. For example, the distribution of the English plural formatives /-əz/, /-z/, and /-s/ may be described as phonologically defined: /-əz/ occurs after sibilant phonemes, /-z/ after voiced non-sibilant phonemes, and /-s/ after voiceless non-sibilant phonemes. Such a distribution is phonologically definable, and, as such, is meaningless (see Principle 6). This morphemic series may be symbolized as /-əz ∿ -z ∿ -s/.[11]

Such phonologically defined alternation is not restricted to affixes. For example, the atonic indefinite article in English has in some dialects the forms /æn/ and /ə/. The first occurs before vowels: /æn æpəl, æn orinǰ/.[12] The second occurs before consonants: /ə mæn, ə fiš/. Accordingly these morphemic alternants may be related as /æn ∿ ə/.[13]

[8] I am indebted to my colleagues Kenneth L. Pike and William L. Wonderly for many helpful suggestions made during the development of the system described here.

[9] Op. cit. 161 and 138.

[10] For a definition of 'common semantic distinctiveness' see Principle 3, fn. 15.

[11] In this paper the symbol ∿ is used only to designate phonologically defined alternation. The symbol ∞ is used to relate alternants whose distribution is defined morphologically (see Principle 3).

[12] The space left in writing between proclitics and nouns is not morphemic.

[13] Morphemic alternants can conveniently be called allomorphs. Accordingly, allomorphs are related to morphemes as allophones are related to phonemes. In the process of analyzing a language there might be occasion to use the term morph to designate a a structural unit which has not as yet been assigned to any morpheme; but in the description of a language (as distinct from the procedure of analyzing it) every structural element except features of arrangement is either a morpheme or part of a morpheme. Hence every element is also an allomorph or part of an allomorph.

In the reduplicative formations of the Greek perfect there occur forms which exhibit a considerable variety of phonemic content. Compare the following: /leluka, bebouleuka, gegrap^{h}a, dedoika, tet^{h}eika, keklɛ·ka, memɛ·na/ from stems meaning 'loose, consider, write, give, place, call, rage' respectively. Despite the phonological differences in the forms /le ∿ be ∿ ge ∿ de ∿ te ∿ ke ∿ me/, it is easy enough to predict the form by saying that the initial consonant is identical with the initial consonant of the stem, except that the consonant of the reduplicated element is unaspirated even if the initial consonant of the stem is aspirated (Grassman's law). This type of morpheme we may set up as /C_1e/ by defining C_1 as any consonant which is first in the underlying form, with the restriction that in potential sequences of aspirated consonants the first becomes unaspirated.[14]

In the above illustrations the difference of form is primarily one of phonemic constituency. It is also possible that the same phonemes may occur in related forms, but in a different order. If, for example, a suffix -an is found to occur after consonant-final stems and -na after vowel-final stems, these two related forms can be combined into the same morpheme—provided, of course, that they possess a common semantic distinctiveness. Differences of form may therefore be treated as affecting either the constituency of phonemes or their arrangement. This type of arrangement we may speak of as the phonological shape of the form.

3.03 Principle 3. Forms which possess a common semantic distinctiveness,[15] but which differ in their phonemic form in such a way that the distribution of the forms cannot be phonologically defined, constitute a single morpheme if the forms are in complementary distribution, subject to the following restrictions:

(1) Forms that occur in complementary distribution may occur in tactically identical environments or in tactically different environments.[16] Complementary distribution in tactically different environments constitutes a basis for combining different forms into one morpheme only on the following condition: that some other morpheme—belonging to the same distribution-class, and having either a single phonemic shape or phonologically defined alternant shapes—occurs in all the tactically different environments where the forms in question are found.

(2) In determining the morphemic status of forms, tactically identical environments take precedence over tactically different environments.

(3) In determining the morphemic status of forms, the immediate tactical environment takes precedence over the larger (non-immediate) environment.

(4) Different forms that contrast in identical distributional environments may nevertheless be assigned to the same morpheme, if the difference in meaning between them is identical with the difference in meaning derived from the distribution of the related forms.[17]

By the application of Principle 3 we are able to combine such forms as /-əz ∿ -z ∿ -s/ in axes, hills, lips with the /-ən/ of oxen, even though the distribution of the alternants cannot be stated in terms of phonological environments. Only the identification of the morpheme (or morphemes) with which the suffixal elements form a construction can suffice to tell us which collocations occur. Since the morphemes must be identified, we may say that the distribution is morphologically defined. A zero alternant also occurs in this construction, e.g. in sheep, trout, elk, salmon. Principle 3 permits us to combine into a single morpheme at least three such alternants, and since the alternation is morphologically defined we may symbolize the series as /(-əz ∿ -z ∿ -s) ∞ -ən ∞ 0/.

[14] In a descriptive grammar of Classical Greek such a statement concerning the potential sequences of aspirates would be included in the morphophonemic section, and would apply to all situations described in later sections where such sequences might arise.

[15] To say that forms possess 'a common semantic distinctiveness' does not mean that all the occurrences of these forms must have an identical meaning, but rather that they possess some semantic feature in common which remains constant in all their meanings and which sets them apart from all other forms in the language. The phrase 'a common semantic distinctiveness' is essentially a negative formulation: it implies merely that the forms which possess that distinctiveness are in semantic contrast with other forms. It is this definition by exclusion that makes it possible to deal with certain sub-morphemic semantic differences, which will be treated under Principles 5-7.

[16] It is necessary to distinguish between 'immediate' and 'non-immediate' tactical environments, and between 'identical' and 'different' tactical environments. The distinctions overlap. In the expressions this man and that boy, the forms this and that occur in identical immediate tactical environments. In the sentence This man hit that boy, the immediate tactical environments of this and that are identical, but the non-immediate tactical environments are different. In the expressions for this man and by that boy, both the immediate and the non-immediate tactical environments of this and that are identical; but in the sentence That boy worked for this man, the forms this and that again occur in different non-immediate tactical environments. In the sentences They left me and They left late, the non-immediate tactical environments of me and late are identical (both occur in subject-predicate constructions), but their immediate tactical environments are different: me occurs in a verb-goal construction, late occurs in a construction of verb plus temporal attributive. For any one occurrence of a morpheme there is usually only one immediate tactical environment; but the number of its non-immediate tactical environments is limited only by the number of sets within sets of immediate constituents in which that morpheme is included. Hence immediateness of tactical environment is determined by the analysis into immediate constituents.

[17] Restriction 5 is covered by a separate principle (§3.07).

These three alternants of the plural morpheme contrast completely in phonological form; they are what Bloomfield calls 'suppletive alternants' (Language 215). Often, however, the morphologically defined alternants bear a strong phonetic resemblance to the underlying form. Compare, for example, the following sets: wife /wayf/ : wives /wayvz/; path /pæθ/: paths /pæðz/; house /haws/: houses /hawzəz/. The bound stems which occur in the plural formations resemble the singular except for a change from a voiceless to a voiced phoneme. This series of alternant forms cannot be phonologically defined, since there are other, phonologically similar forms which do not exhibit the same alternants, e. g. in cliffs, myths, classes. It is needless to attempt to symbolize the exact degree of phonological difference between related forms; the definable basis of distribution is more important. For example, the atonic forms of the indefinite article an /æn/ and a /ə/ have no phoneme in common, but the alternants occur in phonologically definable environments; the stem forms /wayf/ and /wayv-/ are only slightly different in phonological form, but the distribution of the alternants must be defined in terms of morphemes.

The application of Principle 3 is not particularly difficult as long as there is but one immediate tactical environment, i. e. one construction. When, however, the complementation occurs in more than one tactical environment, i.e. in more than one construction or set of constructions, the problems are much more complex. For example, the forms I and me generally occur in complementation:[18] I occurs in preverbal subject position, me in postverbal object position and after prepositions.

The situation in all languages known to me is so complicated by a number of other factors that it seems preferable, for the initial statement of the principles here described, to construct an artificial set of forms, and on the basis of these to point out the methodological implications in actual languages.

Let us suppose that we encounter the following set of pronouns:

	Subjective	Objective
1st person	na	fi
2d person	so	ka
3d person animate	ri	po

If these pronouns occur in complete complementation (e. g. the subjective set preceding verbs and the objective following verbs), we should perhaps be inclined to consider the related forms as morphemic alternants, or allomorphs. There would, however, be a basic objection to such an analysis: we could not know whether the tactical arrangement of order was itself structurally meaningful, since there are two contrastive features relating these forms to the verb, one of order and one of form. It would thus be impossible for us to describe the related forms in these two series as allomorphs unless we were able to demonstrate that a morpheme of the same class possessing only one allomorph or phonologically defined allomorphs could exist in the same environments and that hence the meaningful relationship of the parts could be indicated solely by the tactical arrangement. Thus, for the sake of developing our procedure, let us assume that we find a 3d-person-inanimate pronoun with the form go occurring in both subject and object relationships and in the same tactical environments as the subjective and objective pronominal forms. This circumstance would provide evidence of the grammatical significance of the tactical arrangement.

The situation in English is somewhat parallel. The forms I, we, she stand in complementary distribution (except for fluctuations considered under Principle 7) with me, us, and her respectively. There is also one pronoun you, which occurs in all the tactical environments of the formally contrastive set. If these were the only forms, we could combine the forms I ∞ me, we ∞ us, and she ∞ her as allomorphs in accordance with the second restriction on distribution stated under Principle 3. The situation would be completely analogous to the hypothetical pattern just described. But the situation in English is complicated by the fact that three pronouns have other types of contrasts, namely he : him, they : them, who : whom.

The forms him, them, and whom bear a partial phonetic-semantic resemblance to each other, and we are thus obliged to regard -m as a morpheme (even though its distribution is very limited). On the basis of this pattern, it is possible (and perhaps obligatory) to postulate a zero objective suffix for the other pronominal forms. But if this is the case, we must follow the application of Principle 4, which requires the recognition of overt differences in such situations as being morphemically significant, hence morphemes.[19]

In elucidating the second and third restrictions I shall use another hypothetical illustration. Let us assume that nouns occur in the subject case-form with the suffix -ma and in the object case-form with the suffix -li,[20] and that the distribution is precisely the same as in the previous hypothetical example, namely that subject forms always precede the verb and object forms always follow it. As in the previous problem, we cannot know whether the meaningful

18 This complementation holds good except for such phrases as It's me : It's I, for you and me : for you and I, which are treated as special problems under Principle 7.

19 The relations between I : me, we : us, she : her is not the same as the relation between any set of six completely unrelated morphemes in the language. Rather, me, us, and her constitute a type of replacive morpheme (see §4.32).

20 These hypothetical illustrations are intentionally extreme, since they are designed to point up the theoretical limits of the restriction.

element is the form of the nouns or their position in the construction. Nevertheless, we regard the suffixes -ma and -li as morphemes, since they contrast in the identical and immediate tactical environment in which they occur, namely as suffixes to nouns. The significance of restrictions 2 and 3 is simply that a contrast in an identical or immediate tactical environment cannot be controverted by complementation in non-identical or non-immediate tactical environments.

In practice this principle of distributional environments means that in such a language as German we may establish the morphemic value of the case endings quite apart from such differences of meaning as in dem Tempel 'in the temple' and in den Tempel 'into the temple'. If there were no prepositions which occurred with both dative and accusative case-forms, and if, in all situations in which the dative and accusative case-forms were attributive to verbs, there existed a similar complete complementation, we should still consider the dative -m as a morpheme in contrast to the accusative -n, because in the identical and immediate tactical environments there is a contrast, namely den : dem 'the', ihn : ihm 'him', meinen : meinem 'my'.

To illustrate the implications of these principles, I turn to a Huichol problem.[21] The second singular pronominal reference is indicated by the following forms: a- preceding nouns in a possessive construction (aki 'your house'), pe- preceding verbs as subject of an intransitive (peptikuye 'you are sick'), and -ma- as object of a transitive verb (pəmatsireiya 'he sees you'). On the basis of such data alone, it is impossible to determine whether the forms a-, pe-, and -ma- should be considered a single morpheme. It may be that this difference of form is essential to the defining of the relationships of constituent parts of the constructions. The three relationships may be stated as follows: (1) 'A (the prefix a-) possesses B', (2) 'A (the prefix pe-) is the actor of the action B', and (3) 'A (the prefix -ma-) is the goal of the action B'. If all the pronominal elements exhibited similar sets of formally different forms, we should be forced to conclude that for the defining of the various relationships not only a difference in tactics (tactical environment) is necessary, but also a difference in the form of the pronominal elements. This, however, is not the case. The first person pronominal element ne- occurs in all positions, and the differences of meaning are attributable purely to the tactics, e.g. neki 'my house', neptikuye 'I am sick', and pənetsireiya 'he sees me'. Accordingly, we conclude from the patterns of the two series that there are two morphemes: ne- first person singular pronoun, and a- ∞ pe- ∞ -ma- second person singular pronoun.

It is possible, however, to take an exactly opposite position. Bloomfield says (224), 'The existence of even a single over-differentiated paradigm implies homonymy in the regular paradigms'. In analyzing the structure of a language such a principle can be helpful. For example, we usually say that in the imperative expression Run away! the form of the verb is 'infinitive' because we find a distinctive infinitive form in the over-differentiated verb to be, e.g. Be good!.[22] A strict application of this principle of over-differentiation, however, means that the structural analysis is 'tied' to the most diverse series, and in practice this would involve the recognition and description of a tremendous amount of homonymy. Though the logic of Bloomfield's statement cannot be denied, I have not followed it because it seems to violate the basic functional operation of the language. Productive patterns, analogical constructions and the structurally principal forms and combinations of forms do not appear to be based on the most diverse paradigmatic set or sets. It is possible that the best solution to this dichotomy of form vs. distribution lies somewhere between the poles which I set up; but the defining of such a mid-point is extremely difficult, if not impossible. I have, however, introduced one important restriction to the autonomy of distribution: namely, that before complementary distribution in different tactical environments is valid for uniting different forms into the same morpheme, it must be demonstrated that at least one homophonous set of forms belonging to the same distribution-class occurs in all such positions.

This restriction on different tactical environments also becomes meaningful in limiting the types of semantically related forms which one may combine into the same morpheme. For example, in English the nominal prefix ex- in ex-president, ex-chairman, ex-official indicates past time. Similarly the morpheme /-əd ∾ -d ∾ -t/ indicates past time with verbs: accepted, turned, walked. These morphemes are in complementary distribution in that they occur in different constructions.[23] If it were not for the first restriction on Principle 3, they could be combined as alternants of the same morpheme. But in this instance, there is no set of identical forms which may occur as prefixes to nouns and suffixes to verbs and which in both positions define a tense relationship. This is the situation in Makushi,[24] a

[21] I am indebted to John McIntosh of the Summer Institute of Linguistics for this illustrative material.

[22] Note, however, that Bloch (Lang. 23.401 ((244))) does not use this type of analysis, but combines all formally identical items.

[23] There is admittedly a certain difference in meaning between ex- and the past-tense morpheme of verbs. But since our science does not provide us with an adequate measuring-rod for handling such differences, and since our basic definition of the morpheme is primarily negative and admits of sub-morphemic distinctions, my main reason for refusing to combine ex- in one morpheme with /-əd ∾ -d ∾ -t/ is distributional.

[24] For the Makushi data I am indebted to Neill Hawkins, a research fellow of the University of Oklahoma and the Summer Institute of Linguistics.

language spoken on the borders of Brazil and British Guiana. In Makushi the regular past-tense suffix is -pï: wïiya 'he kills', wïpïiya 'he killed'. This same -pï occurs as a derivative suffix with noun expressions: to the phrase aʔnay ipu 'ear of corn' (aʔnay 'corn' and ipu 'its foot') one can add the suffix -pï to produce aʔnay-ipupï 'corn cob'—that is to say, an ear of corn in the past tense. It is true that Makushi lacks other tense formatives with the same distribution, but this occurrence of -pï could establish a pattern which would permit the combining of forms exhibiting the same distribution even though they differ in shape in such a way that the occurrence of the alternants could not be phonologically defined.

In describing and identifying morphemic alternants (allomorphs) it is frequently convenient to distinguish two types: basic and non-basic. This distinction may include phonologically defined allomorphs or morphologically defined allomorphs or both. In the series /-əz ∿ -z ∿ -s/, whose distribution is phonologically definable, it is possible to select one alternant as basic and the others as phonologically 'derived'. There are three types of criteria, in the following order of importance: (1) parallel structure, (2) general patterns of morphophonemic change, and (3) limitation of distribution.

The selection of a basic alternant or allomorph of the set /-əz ∿ -z ∿ -s/ may depend on the parallel structure in such atonic forms as /-iz ∿ -z ∿ -s/ for is (Bess's gone : Bill's gone : Dick's gone) and /-əz ∿ -z ∿ -s/ for has (Bess's done it : Bill's done it : Dick's done it). In these instances the fuller forms /-iz/ and /-əz/ are obviously closer to the full word.

The second criterion, involving phonological change, is directly supplementary to the first. By referring to general patterns of morphophonemic change we can explain the loss of a vowel more easily than the development of a vowel, although in some languages developed vowels might be frequent in certain phonological sequences. In the English forms just cited, the choice of /-z/ as a basic form would not permit us to predict the vowel of the longer form, while the choice of the fuller form permits us to make a completely regular statement for all the changes that occur. In general, there a number of phonological principles which may guide our choice, e. g. assimilation, palatalization, reduction of clusters, Verner's phenomenon. The choice of a basic form from which we may derive the alternants by frequently observed phonological developments (or sets of correlations—speaking on a purely synchronic level) constitutes a much sounder principle of procedure than to assume for a language all sorts of rare or unique patterns of phonological change or alternation.

The third criterion is based on patterns of limitation in the distribution of forms. Thus, if one allomorph of a morpheme occurs after all but three morphemes of a certain class, and another allomorph occurs only after those three, we should accept as basic the allomorph with the wider distribution. It is the observable structural patterns of a particular language, not its general phonological tendencies or the mere statistics of occurrence, that constitute the chief criterion for any given analysis. Accordingly, in English there is no difficulty in establishing the alternant /-əz/ as basic.[25] Following Harris, Hockett, and Bloch, we can symbolize the whole morpheme (including all its allomorphs) as {-əz}.

To determine the basic alternant among allomorphs whose distribution is morphologically defined, the productiveness of a given type of formation is of prime importance as a guide in applying our third criterion. Two types of synchronic data are significant in comparing the productivity of different formations: their relative frequency of occurrence and their relative regularity. The two are of course interrelated. Allomorphs that occur in a larger number of combinations and in a larger number of actual utterances are likely to illustrate the productive patterns; but regularity of formation is important also. If two alternants have approximately the same frequency of occurrence, but if one of them combines usually with forms that exhibit considerable modification of their underlying forms, while the other combines with unmodified forms, the latter is likely to illustrate the more productive pattern, and—other things being equal—should be chosen as the basic alternant.

3.04 Principle 4. An overt formal difference among related forms (forms containing recurrent partials or occurring in complementary distribution) constitutes a morpheme, if in any of these forms this difference, together with a zero tactical difference, is the only significant feature for establishing a minimal unit of phonetic-semantic distinctiveness.

Principle 4 means that in the case of /sæŋ/, where the only differences to contrast it with /siŋ/ are a covert zero alternant of {-əd} and the overt replacement of /i/ by /æ/, we shall consider the overt replacement of the vowels as constituting a morpheme (see §2.2). Zero features are covert features, but minus features (or subtractives, as I prefer to call them) are not covert. A minus feature is overt; compare for instance the French feminine form platte /plat/ 'flat' with the masculine plat /pla/, which may be described as derived from the feminine by subtraction.[26]

[25] This type of pattern furnishes a reason for choosing /-əd/ as the basic alternant in the series /-əd ∿ -d ∿ -t/, the past-tense morpheme of English verbs. Compare also the parallel atonic alternants of would and had.

[26] Bloomfield, op. cit. 217.

Principle 4 does not rule out the significance of zero, though it is hard to determine how extensive a pattern must be to demand the introduction of zero. Such problems are too much a matter of proportion, balance, symmetry, pattern congruence, and the like —features closely allied to one's esthetic feeling. It is for this reason that different linguists describe the same structure somewhat differently.[27] But though Principle 4 does not rule out zero, it does mean that overt formal differences have at least equal status with zero. It will mean, for example, that we cannot say that song /soŋ/ is an alternant of sing /siŋ/ with the addition of a zero derivative suffix, as Bloch does (Lang. 23.407 ((247))). In the first place, the nominalizing suffixes in English do not constitute a complementary distributional set. There are such series as receiver, receipt, receptor, reception and creator, creation, creature. Since I adopt Hockett's general principle that zero must not constitute the only allomoprh of a morpheme (Lang. 23.340 ((240))), I am obliged to assign the zero of song to some morpheme with at least one overt allomorph (if, indeed, there is a zero derivative affix), but there is no morpheme or set of allomorphs to which such a zero can be assigned. In this instance, a derivative zero allomorph proves untenable. If one wishes to describe the form-meaning relationship between sing and song as pertinent to the language (they certainly exhibit partial phonetic-semantic resemblance), the structurally significant feature is the replacement of the vowel, not the addition of zero.

On the basis of Principle 4, in such related words as breed : bred, feed : fed, meet : met, plead : pled, the replacement of /iy/ by /e/ is meaningful. This establishes the replacement /e ← iy/ (read '/e/ replaces /iy/') as a morpheme. The same replacement occurs in the related words leave : left /liyv, left/. Having established the replacement /e ← iy/ as a morpheme at one point, we cannot deny its status as a morpheme just because the usual suffix /t/ is overt. The past-tense formation of left thus includes two morphemes in addition to the stem. This occurrences of two morphemes with the structural value of one morpheme in other situations should not unduly disturb us, since the situation occurs in a number of other languages. In Greek, for example, some perfects occur both with reduplication of the initial consonant plus /e/ and with a suffix /-k-/, e.g. /leluk-/ 'have loosed'; but others have only the reduplication, e.g. /leloip-/ 'have left'.[28]

In the English past tense form /left/ there is another change which distinguishes it from its underlying form /liyv/, namely the change of /v/ to /f/. Why is not this change of consonant just as meaningful as the change of vowel? Precisely because it does not occur as the only modification (with the exception of zero) in a related series. But in describing the related forms strive and strife such a difference of consonant does constitute the 'meaning-carrier' of the semantic difference; and so, in the series strive : strife, thieve : thief, grieve : grief, the replacement of /v/ by /f/ constitutes a morpheme.[29] It would be possible, it is true, to analyze the replacement in left somewhat differently. We could, for example, describe the difference between /liyv/ and /lef-/ as /ef ← iyv/. Such a change would be paralleled by the one in /luwz/ lose and /los-/ los(t). On the other hand, an examination of the forms in which such replacements occur shows us that wherever a consonant other than postvocalic /y/ or /w/ is replaced or lost, an overt form of the morpheme {-əd} also occurs. This means that only the replacement of a syllabic[30] is independently meaningful (i. e. serves as the only overt difference between forms); differences of consonantal phonemes may be treated as meaningless, since wherever they occur, an overt alternant of {-əd} occurs also.

One other problem confronts us in treating the replacement of syllabics in English. The replacement /o ← uw/ occurs only in the form /lost/. Since this specific replacement is not independently meaningful, as is the replacement /e ← iy/ (e. g. in bred, led, fed, met), it would be possible to treat it as 'conditioned' by the occurrence of the morpheme {-əd}. But if English past-tense formations are considered as structurally related, the pressure of the pattern would seem to be sufficient to permit the classification of changes by types: (1) the replacement of syllabics as morphemic, and (2) the replacement of consonants as sub-morphemic.

On the basis of Principle 4 we treat noun plurals in English such as men, feet, mice, teeth as occurring with 'replacives' (i.e. replacements which are

27 Any science of classification becomes involved in the same difficulty. Thus, taxonomists in the fields of botany and zoology are faced with the same problem of determining the degree and the nature of structural likeness or difference which are to be regarded as significant in establishing classes and subclasses.

28 The change of vowel here need not be taken as a morpheme, since it is not independently meaningful (does not occur as the only difference between related forms, or as the only difference aside from a zero difference). The element /le...k-/ could be taken as a single discontinuous morpheme (cf. Harris, Lang. 21.121–7), except for the fact that one of the two parts occurs without the other. See §4.2.

29 The so-called direction of derivation (strive derived from strife, or strife derived from strive) depends on factors which are not discussed here. See §4.32.

30 In this use of the term syllabic I follow Bloch (Lang. 23.414 ((251))), who says, 'we shall regard every syllabic as a unit, whether it consists of a vowel alone or of a vowel and a semivowel.' In my own English, only the postvocalic semivowels /y/ and /w/ combine with vowels to constitute single syllabics.

morphemic). Whether we are to say that both a replacive morpheme and a zero alternant of the plural suffix occur in these words depends on how much significance we attach to that part of the structural design which provides the basis for zero.

Following the same procedure we treat was /wəz/ and were /wər/ as morphemically different from be /biy/, rather than as morpheme alternants with the past-tense zero suffix, as Bloch does (Lang. 23.416 ((252))). The morphemic difference is not, however, simply that /wəz/ is one morpheme and /wər/ is another morpheme. These forms /wəz/ and /wər/ contain a recurrent partial, namely /wə-/; the contrast between /-z/ and /-r/ may be said to be meaningful, in that they occur in certain patterns of concord. The morpheme /-z/ occurs in 'realis' expressions containing first- and third-person singular subject constituents; the morpheme /-r/ occurs in all other situations. The meanings of /-z/ and /-r/ are thus essentially grammatical (see §3.6). This problem and the one involved in the treatment of were in such expressions as If John were here, he would help can be more easily understood if we examine contrasts occurring in the present-tense forms of English.

We establish the morphemic value of the suffix {-əz} in tries /trayz/ by such contrasts as try : tries /tray : trayz/ in boys try /boyz tray/ vs. John tries /Jan trayz/ and the like; and we establish the contrast as morphemic on the basis of the immediate tactical environment, namely /trayz/ vs. /tray/ (Principle 5, restrictions 2 and 3). Otherwise, we might regard such a suffix as meaningless, on the ground that it is conditioned by the class (singular vs. plural) of the subject expression (see §3.3).

Having once established that /trayz/ occurs after third-person singular subject expressions and /tray/ occurs after all other subject expressions, we are not to be surprised to find that this contrast is not always valid; thus, try /tray/ occurs after a third-person singular subject expression in I move John try it. On the basis of our principles of procedure[31] we regard this try as identical with the try that normally occurs after all persons except the third. We have established a morpheme on the basis of a contrast in one environment, and such a contrast is valid; but we must now go farther in our description of the distribution, so as to take in all environments. The fact that try occurs with only certain persons in one type of environment but with all persons in another environment, does not negate its original contrast with tries.

We now return to a more complex problem. On the basis of contrast in simple 'realis' contexts we distinguish between /-z/ and /-r/ in the forms was and were. In the 'irrealis' context (which demands the occurrence of some potential form such as would in the principal clause), the form were occurs with all persons, and was is absent altogether. But the distributional difference in the larger environment does not invalidate the original contrast. Nor does the difference in the meaning of were in the two situations impair the analysis, since we are prepared to recognize subordinate semantic differences within the basic semantic contrastiveness, and the differences of meaning here can be related directly to the difference in environment (see §3.6 and §3.7).

3.05 Principle 5. The meaning of any form is definable in terms of the feature or features common to the situations in which the form occurs.

This means that signification is statable only in terms of environment. Certain forms are definable (or identifiable) as symbols for objects in the invironment of the practical world, e. g. animal, house, brick, moon, policeman. Other forms, such as joy, peace, love, blue, good, only identify features which exist as parts of other things. Still other forms have substantially what we may call 'grammatical meaning', e. g. {-əz} as the third singular suffix in verbs, /-m/ as the object suffix in him, them, and whom, and the /-ər/ in hammer, ladder, spider, otter, badger, water. 'Grammatical' or 'linguistic meaning' depends on the occurrence of a form in significant situations defined only or at least primarily in terms of the linguistic environment. Many forms—especially stems—are significant in biosocial environments; but every form has linguistic meaning as well, since every form occurs in some linguistic environment.

The linguistic meaning of a morpheme can be defined in terms of several criteria: (1) the types of construction in which it occurs, (2) its frequency of occurrence, and (3) its productiveness in new combinations. The first of these are linguistically the most meaningful.

We can give part of the meaning of boy by identifying the referent (or the referent-types) for which this morpheme occurs as a symbol; but another part of the meaning of boy is the distribution of the morpheme in particular linguistic situations. The linguistic meaning of boy includes such facts as the following: boy occurs as the subject of a sentence, the object of a verb, and the second member in a prepositional phrase; it combines with derivative formatives such as -ish (boyish); and it occurs in an exclamatory phrase Oh boy!. If we disregard entirely the biosocial distinction in the meanings of boy and girl, we can still say that the linguistic meanings of these two words differ in that boy occurs in a type of exclamatory phrase from which girl is excluded. Bloomfield (op. cit. 164) recognizes that distribution is meaningful by saying: 'Selection of forms contributes a factor of meaning'. (Bloomfield's 'selection' is identical with what I here call distribution.)

[31] On the basis of Bloomfield's principle of overdifferentiation (see §3.03), we might consider the second try a different morpheme, since in the verb to be the regular third-person form is is but after a principal verb such as move the form instead is be.

The very frequency of occurrence of a form also contributes a feature of linguistic meaning; for it is important on the one hand in establishing patterns of analogy, and on the other in preserving the form against levelling influence. Irregular forms of frequently occurring words (e.g. the forms of the verb to be in English) resist levelling analogies which extend to other verbs of less frequent occurrence.

The productiveness or non-productiveness of a formation is similarly a meaningful morphemic feature. As descriptive linguists we are sometimes inclined to overlook such a dynamic aspect of the language. We assume that a form is a fixed feature and that its distribution is fully defined or definable. We tend to imply that productiveness is only a diachronic fact, but it may be a synchronic reality as well.[32] In syntax it is essential to recognize that the limits of the distribution of many constructions cannot be fixed, as far as the possible collocations of morphemes are concerned; for otherwise a speaker would only be able to repeat verbatim the phrases which he had previously heard. If we recognize this openness of class membership in the constituency of many syntactic constructions, we must be prepared to recognize a similar phenomenon in morphology. When we say that the distribution of a form is open (at least in terms of certain types of environment), we say simply that the form is productive—that is, it occurs with a class of forms whose membership we cannot accurately delimit. This is a synchronic fact, and also part of the distributional meaningfulness of the form in question.

3.06 Principle 6. Morpheme alternants whose distribution is not phonologically definable exhibit sub-morphemic differences of meaning.

I have already anticipated this principle in the discussion of sub-morphemic phonetic and semantic distinctions (§3). Note also Bloomfield's assumption (op. cit. 145) that there are 'no actual synonyms'—no items that are different form but absolutely identical in meaning. If it is true that 'selection of forms contributes a factor of meaning', then the different selection (i.e. distribution) of allomorphs implies that they have different meanings.

One obvious sphere in which this principle holds true is the description of productive patterns, formations which cannot be said to have a rigidly limited distribution (§3.5). Compare the allomorphs of the plural suffix, /-əz ∿ -z ∿ -s/ vs. /-ən/: the former set is productive, the latter is not. This productiveness is a distributional characteristic, and as such is meaningful.

It is often extremely hard to define the differences of meaning between allomorphs, since it depends solely on a difference of distribution. But our inability to correlate this difference with biosocial contrasts does not invalidate the principle (especially Principle 5, which underlies Principle 6), nor the basic assumption that we adopt as a premise for all descriptive analysis: that there are no actual synonyms.

3.07 Principle 7. Related forms which occur in the same environment, but which could otherwise be regarded as allomorphs, can still be so regarded if (a) there is no apparent difference of meaning between them, or (b) the difference of meaning is derivable from the distribution of the related forms. Condition (a) is known as free variation.

This principle is designed to treat instances of 'overlap', i.e. forms which are in complementary distribution except at certain points where there is a contrast resulting from fluctuation of forms. Because of difficulties with such fluctuation of forms, Bloch has treated the show in shown and the show in showed as two distinct morphemes, since he had already combined /-n/ and /-d/ as morphemic alternants (Lang. 23.406 ((247))). This type of analysis has already been discussed in §2.1.

On the basis of Principle 7, we can say that the participial suffixes /-n/ and /-d/ are nevertheless allomorphs, each having its sub-morphemic distinction of meaning derived from its own distribution. Where they both occur with the underlying form /šow/, they are no longer in complementary distribution, and there is a difference of meaning; but the difference of meaning is precisely that which depends on the distribution of the two allomorphs. The allomorph /-d/ is productive: its potential distribution is not arbitrarily fixed like that of /-n/. Both allomorphs may occur in the same person's speech, but /-d/ occurs in more colloquial socio-linguistic environments. On the other hand, /-n/ has a fixed distribution, but within this fixed range of occurrence the /-n/ may be said to have greater 'socio-linguistic acceptability'. These facts are synchronic as well as diachronic; they apply to the present functioning of the language.[33]

The descriptive linguist is always faced with the problem of fluctuations of forms. The series roof : roofs : rooves and hoof : hoofs : hooves is illustrative. The suffixes conform to the regular pattern of alternation; if there is any difference in meaning, it must be associated with the stems roof- vs. roov- and hoof- vs. hoov-. Some speakers of English may

32 Any body of material sufficiently extensive to serve adequately as a basis for descriptive analysis must include fluctuations of forms, which are symptomatic of different degrees of acceptability. Synchronic contrasts of this kind are closely allied to contrasts of productivity vs. non-productivity.

33 I admit readily that the viewpoint here expressed is different from the traditional descriptive approach; but we are forced to treat fluctuations of forms in some way within the framework of our descriptive statements. It does not seem to me wise to go to the extremes proposed by Bloch within the rigid confines of his method.

contend that these forms are in completely free variation, and they may be right. Yet on the assumption that there are no actual synonyms, we should still say that a difference of meaning exists between roofs and rooves, hoofs and hooves — though it may be very slight, and though it may affect only the connotations of the various forms.[34] The semantic difference between roofs and rooves, hoofs and hooves derives from the different distributions of unchanging noun-final /f/ and of noun-final /f/ replaced in the plural by /v/. The former is the productive type. The latter is non-productive, with a strictly limited distribution; within that range, it has greater socio-linguistic acceptability in some social groups but is considered pedantic in others.

A more complicated problem is presented by the series /hæv, həv, əv, v/ have. Bloch's treatment considers these related forms as four different morphemes. Common sense reacts to this type of analysis as being incorrect; but in terms of the conventional handling of morphemic problems, Bloch's analysis is probably inevitable.[35] The differences of meaning that exist between the various forms of the series /hæv, həv, əv, v/ are essentially connotative and reflect usage in various types of discourse, which may be described as being increasingly colloquial. That is to say, /hæv/ occurs in more 'elegant' socio-linguistic context than the form /v/, and the other forms stand somewhere between. But we must not assume that these forms are the only distinguishing characteristics of such contexts. There are supplementary differences of lexical choice, as well as many types of phonological reduction and change which mark the various 'levels' of discourse. Compare /səm mowr, səmowr/ some more; /did yuw, didyə, diǰə/ did you. There are still other features, not normally included in a phonemic statement but meaningful in the characterization of socio-linguistic context: preciseness of articulation, speed of utterance, 'voice color' (serious, happy, non-committal, etc.). The forms /hæv, həv, əv, v/ occur in environments that are connotatively distinct; and from the difference in their distribution they acquire a certain difference in meaning. When they are then contrasted in an identical environment, they exhibit the connotative differences which are characteristic of the general surroundings where they are usually found. Since, then, their difference of meanings does not violate the negatively defined phonetic-semantic distinctiveness, we may say that this series constitutes a set of allomorphs with submorphemic phonetic-semantic distinctions, symbolized as /hæv ∞ həv ∞ əv ∞ v/.[36]

Principle 7 has not been developed solely for the purpose of helping us to describe some of the awkward things about a language. It is, rather, a common-sense statement of situations with which we deal constantly, and which we must describe in such a way as not to violate the very evident relationships to which we intuitively react. We cannot afford to make fluctuations of form and overlapping of patterns the pivotal points of any system. We must fit them into the system, rather than tailoring the system to fit them.[37]

Principle 7 introduces a feature of analysis into the morphology and syntax which does not apply to phonemics. In phonemics, a difference of form in any part of an utterance, accompanied by a difference of meaning for the whole, justifies the isolation of the formal difference as meaningfully pertinent, and hence as a distinct formal unit. This is not true of the analysis of morphemes, which are themselves meaningful units. In phonemics we admit conditioned and free variation only when the meaning of the whole remains constant. In morphology we must admit submorphemic difference of both form and meaning within the phonetic-semantic distinctiveness of a single morpheme (its non-resemblance to other forms).

3.08 Principle 8. Homophonous forms possessing more than one distinct area of meaning and belonging to correspondingly different distributional classes[38]

34 When two fluctuating forms are shifting their status—when the originally more frequent form is growing less frequent and the other is climbing up —there is undoubtedly a point at which the two are equally in use. At such a point one might insist that free variation actually exists between the forms. But the semantic difference between them derives from the whole pattern of the language; and even though the forms may have the same frequency statistically, they can and will nevertheless be different in meaning, if this is measured by their distribution in terms of the language as a whole.

35 One might also consider that the terms in this series exhibit sufficient semantic-phonetic resemblance to each other to justify a different treatment. One might take /hæv/ as the basic form, and regard the other forms as consisting of the morpheme /hæv/ plus various morphemes of replacement (/ə ← æ/) or loss (/-h/ or /-hæ/). Then the form /əv/ would consist of three morphemes: /hæv/ plus /ə ← æ/ plus /-h/. Such an analysis, however, not only would be awkward but would seem to be untenable in the absence of parallel formations.

36 The occurrence of particular allomorphs here is not determined solely by phonological criteria, nor does the characteristic distribution depend on purely phonetic features. The distribution involves both phonological and morphological criteria, and the alternation between allomorphs is accordinly symbolized by ∞.

37 The fluctuation between It's I and It's me is covered by this principle, but the form me is related to the overt series him, them, whom. See §3.03.

38 The expression 'distributional classes' is used to avoid the possible ambiguity of the term 'form-classes'. The latter is now applied to two fundamentally different sets of forms: not only to distributional classes in the present sense, but also sometimes to classes of forms with a particular phonological structure (e.g. CVCV as against CV, or high-low tone as against low-high). Classes of the second kind may or may not be distributionally pertinent. There is often a correlation between the two kinds of classification, but it is nevertheless important to distinguish them.

consist of as many morphemes as there are parallel semantic and distributional classes.

Principle 8 means that we assign the verb read /riyd/ and the noun reed /riyd/ to two different morphemes. They cover two distinct areas of meaning[39] and belong to two different distribution classes, respectively verbs and nouns. This principle is accepted by practically all linguists and requires no further elaboration.

3.09 Principle 9. Homophonous forms are semantically related when they identify regularly associated aspects of the same object, process, or state.

This principle is intended to define the term 'semantically related'. The morphemic status of semantically related forms will be treated under Principles 10 and 11. Any attempt to classify semantic relationships is extremely difficult; but there are certain relationships between words which we all recognize to a greater or lesser degree. For example, we note a similarity in run as a verb and the homophonous run as a noun. Both forms identify regularly associated aspects of what may be a single process. In the phrases they run and their run, even the relationship of actor to action may be substantially the same, though we normally describe the latter phrase as expressing a possessor-possessed relationship. In the phrase the run in her stocking the word run may be said to identify the result of a process. In the phrases they fish and the fish the homophonous forms are related as process and characteristically associated object. This is not true in the phrase to pare the pear, for a pear is not an object regularly associated with the process of paring; nor is the process of paring regularly associated with pairing. Accordingly, although the homophones run and run, fish and fish, are semantically related, the homophones pair, pare, and pear are not.

The meaningful relationship between homophonous forms may be one of form and function. The term horn which designates a particular shape and/or substance (the horn of an animal or by extension of appearance the horns of the moon) is related to horn meaning a musical instrument, because the two meanings may be combined in a single object, for instance a ram's horn used as an instrument. Some speakers of English may not recognize such a relationship; for them, such homophonous forms would be completely unrelated. In this matter, we are obliged to introduce some subjectivism; for in describing the functioning of a language we must consider the relationships which words possess for the native speakers.

There are many possible semantic relationships between homophonous forms. The following very limited series will give some idea of the range. (Note that the order of meanings in this list has no reference to the order of derivation.)

39 Criteria for distinguishing 'related' and 'distinct' are given in the next section.

(1) Form and function: horn of an animal and horn as an instrument
(2) Process and result: to run and a run in her stocking
(3) Process and associated object: to fish and the fish
(4) State and cause: foul (adjective) and to foul the job
(5) Process and agent: to man the ship and a man
(6) Process and instrument: to spear and a spear
(7) Object and associated characteristic: it is a pill and he is a pill
(8) Form and process: a cross and to cross

There are a number of historically related homophones which are probably unrelated in present-day speech. The noun board (A) meaning a particular material and the noun board (B) in the expression room and board are historically related, but today they are probably not associated by any speakers with the same object, process, or state. It is also possible that speakers do not regularly associate either A or B with another historically related form board (C) in the expression board of directors. In the verb expression to board up the house the form board is undoubtedly related to A, and it is even possible that in to board a ship the speaker may make some association with A, but we cannot be certain. It is precisely this dependence upon subjective factors which makes the situation so complex. Nevertheless, despite the inadequate tools which we possess for treating such problems, the answer to the difficulty of identifying morphemes must be found at least partially in the native speaker's response to the meaningful units in his speech.

3.10 Principle 10. Homophonous forms which are semantically related and which occur in correspondingly different distributional environments constitute a single morpheme with multiple distribution-class memberships.

The expressions (1) a run in her stocking, (2) they run away, and (3) they run the office refer to related areas of meaning. The first denotes a condition resulting from a process; the second denotes a process in which the grammatical subject performs the action directly; and the third denotes a process in which the grammatical subject causes an action. The meanings here are not identical, but the subdivision into related areas corresponds to different distributional environments. The first environment is definable as one in which nouns occur; the second, as one in which verbs without objects (i. e. intransitives) occur; and the third, as one in which verbs with objects occur. We may combine the homophonous forms in a single morpheme because the related meanings are paralleled by different distributions.

The distributional differences may be less conspicuous. The sentences it is a pill and he is a pill are structurally identical; but there is a slight difference in the environment: in the first sentence the subject is it, in the second it is he. The differences of meaning in the two occurrences of pill parallel this difference of distribution.

Relating transitive and intransitive verbs or combining various meanings of a single noun by complementary distribution does not involve any departure from the usual method; but combining noun and verb forms in the same morpheme seems more radical. Nevertheless, we must either do this or be faced by two clumsy alternatives. First, we might attempt to derive one of the forms from the other. We might set up man, fish, and angle as basic nouns and derive verbs from these by a zero affix. But zero should be a zero alternant of something, and there is no parallel series in English (see §3.04). Similarly, we might set up run, swim, and dive as basic verbs and derive nouns by a zero affix, but the same objection would hold. Furthermore, a division into basic nouns and basic verbs would be questionable on any purely descriptive basis.

The second alternative would be to consider the homophonous forms entirely different morphemes. The difficulty with such a procedure is first that it involves considerable repetition and second that it violates our basic definition of a morpheme as a form which does not exhibit partial phonetic-semantic resemblance to any other form. This definition would obviously not hold if we regarded the homophonous forms of run as more than one morpheme.

Accordingly, we are left with the conclusion that the simplest and best treatment of such homophones occurring in different distributional environments is to consider them single morphemes, but with different class memberships. In dealing with noun and verb classes in English we could list (1) forms which occur both as nouns and as verbs: man, fish, walk, run, swim, jump, mother, father, sun, moon, star, spring; (2) forms which occur as nouns only: boy, girl, grass, elephant, bee; (3) forms which occur as verbs only: be, seem, see, come.

3.11 Principle 11. Homophonous forms which are semantically related but which do not occur in correspondingly different distributional environments constitute as many morphemes as there are meaning-distribution classes.

Suppose that someone insists upon relating board (A) 'construction material' with board (B) 'food' (see §3.09). These two forms occur in the same grammatical environment, e. g. the board we got was terrible; without other information it is impossible to know whether meaning A or meaning B is intended here. The two forms are thus not in complementary distribution, though in other situations they often are. For example, board (A) occurs only with a determiner, e. g. a board, the board, some board, etc.; but board (B) occurs both with and without a determiner, e. g. board is five dollars a week, this board is expensive at any price. Whether, then, we consider these homophonous forms related in meaning or not, they constitute different morphemes because they are not in complementary distribution.

In treating the semantically related forms horn (A) 'animal's horn' and horn (B) 'instrument', we may again treat them as two morphemes. Form A occurs both as a noun and as a verb, e. g. the animal's horn and he horned in; form B occurs only as a noun, e. g. the man's horn. The sub-morphemic semantic difference under A is paralleled by a distributional difference and hence the noun and the verb are subsumed under the same morpheme. Horn (A), however, contrasts in its distribution with horn (B); and so we describe these forms with related meaning as constituting two different morphemes.[40]

3.12 Principle 12. The allomorphs of two (or possibly more) morphemes may be partially or completely coexistent, provided one of the allomorphs is not zero.

Instances in which juxtaposed morphemes fuse and thus reduce their phonemic size are not uncommon. Thus, the expression /did yə/ may reduce to /diǰə/, the sequence /dy/ being replaced by /ǰ/. This /ǰ/ is part of both morphemes. For convenience we usually speak of the alternants /did ∞ diǰ-/ and the alternants /yə ∞ ə/, but this does not describe the situation accurately. We might use an underline to mark phonemes which are 'possessed' simultaneously by two allomorphs: /did ∞ diǰ-/ and /yə ∞ -ǰə/.

Allomorphs that coincide either partially or wholly are numerous in some languages. In Yipounou (a Bantu language of the Gabon), the first-person object is denoted by a nasal, /n-/ or /m-/ according to the first phoneme of the stem; but before a stem with initial /r/, the nasal is 'lost' and the /r/ is replaced by /t/. A form consisting of the morphemes /ama/ + /n/ + /ronda/ appears as /amatonda/ 'she loved me'. In describing this form we usually say that the prefix /n- ∿ m-/ occurs in a zero alternant and the stem /-ronda/ occurs in the alternant /-tonda/; but this does not do justice to the facts. Rather, the stem morpheme /-ronda/ occurs in the alternant /-tonda/, and at the same time the prefix morpheme /n- ∿ m-/ occurs in the alternant /t-/: the underlinings indicate that the two morphemes coincide.

In French, the morphemes à 'to' and le 'the (m.)' occur in the fused form au /o/.[41] This is simply an extension of the process already noted: here the two allomorphs coincide completely. We say that the allomorph of à is /o-/ and the allomorph of le is /-o/, and further that the distribution of these allomorphs is so restricted that each occurs only with the other, the tactical order of the morphemes being à + le.

[40] I admit that my classification is to some extent open to criticism, since I here classify in two or more morphemes certain forms which are identical in shape and related in meaning, but which do not occur in complementary distribution. It is true that such forms exhibit partial phonetic-semantic resemblances to each other. If I adopt the formal criterion of distribution as basic, it is because we have no technique as yet which will enable us to define the various degrees of semantic difference.

[41] Cf. Hockett's discussion, Lang. 23.333 ((236)).

The final stipulation of Principle 12, that one of the allomorphs is not zero, is added to obviate the contradictory situation which arises in Hockett's treatment of she and her as allomorphs of the single morpheme {she} (Lang. 23.343 ((241))). Hockett's solution is simply another device to render a covert zero element meaningful, while setting aside the overt difference between related forms. By insisting in Principle 12 that allomorphs be overt, I only confirm what has already been discussed under Principle 4.

3.13 Principle 13. A single morpheme may be tactically equivalent to two or more morphemic categories.

In the Greek verb /lu·ɔ·/ 'I loose' the form /-ɔ·/ covers a wide area of meaning: it identifies the tense, mode, number, person, and voice of the combined form. In the form /lu·sontai/ 'they will loose for themselves' these categories are all overtly indicated: /s/ future tense, /o/ indicative mode, /n/ plural number, /t/ third person, and /ai/ middle or passive voice. Such forms, in which all five categories are separately indicated, are rare, and the combination of all these categories into a single form such as /-ɔ·/ is not uncommon. This situation in Greek is different from the one in French au /o/. In the Greek /-ɔ·/ we are not able to identify specific morphemes which would have coexisting allomorphs of the shape /-ɔ·/, for in too many instances such allomorphs would be relatable to zero. It is the particular characteristic of 'inflectional' languages that single morphemes are tactically equivalent to a number of categories, which may be fully and overtly expressed in some forms but only partially in others.[42]

4. Having discussed the principles which govern the identification of morphemes, we turn to an analysis of the types of morphemes. A classification of such types may be based upon (1) the types of phonemes which comprise the morphemes, (2) the positional relationship of the parts of the morphemes, and (3) the positional relationship of the morphemes to other morphemes.[43]

4.1 Morphemes may be classified as consisting of (1) segmental phonemes, (2) suprasegmental phonemes, and (3) both kinds together.[44]

4.11 Morphemes consisting of segmental phonemes are very common. The /-θ/ of growth, the /-t/ of lost, the replacive /æ ← i/ of sang, the /riy-/ of receive are a few examples.

4.12 Morphemes consisting entirely of suprasegmental phonemes are less common. One relatively common variety, however, is intonational pattern. The meaningful units of such patterns constitute morphemes. Thus, in English, the different glides following the last primary stress in a phrase are in meaningful contrast,[45] and are therefore morphemes.

We sometimes find that the so-called morphological tones accompanying particular segmental sequences constitute morphemes in their own right. In Ngbaka (a 'Sudanic' language of the northwest Congo) simple verbs have no inherent tone; rather, they occur with four different accompanying tone patterns: (1) low, denoting continuous action, (2) mid, denoting completive action, (3) high, denoting imperative, and (4) low-to-high, denoting future. Regardless of the length of the stem, the tone patterns are constant; cf. the two verbs sa 'to call' and yolo 'to stand': (1) sà, yòlò; (2) sā, yōlō; (3) sá, yóló; (4) sǎ, yòló. In this three-register tone language, the tones of verbs have independent status as morphemes, since there is no basic tonal form of any verb to which the four modifications can be related.

4.13 Finally, there are morphemes consisting of both segmental and suprasegmental phonemes. The English morpheme /bɔ́y/ consists of three segmental phonemes plus the suprasegmental phoneme of stress.[46] In Ngbaka, nouns have inherent tone: lí 'face', lī 'name', lì 'water'.

Note that Ngbaka morphemes have two 'canonical' forms:[47] some include an inherent tone, like the nouns just cited; others are toneless, like the verbs cited above. There are other examples of such breaks within the basic structure of a language. In Semitic languages there are three types of morphemes:[48] (1) radicals of the type CCC, e.g. Hebrew /šbr/ 'break'; (2) patterns of vowels, or of vowels plus length, or of vowels plus a consonantal affix, e. g. --u- 'active', -a-i·- 'object with a particular quality', -a-·a- 'transitive intensive', n-a-i- 'middle'; (3) sequences of vowels and consonants, e. g. mí· 'who?', -tím 'you (masc. pl.)', baltí· 'without'. Again, the accentual system of classical Greek shows a structural break: in verbs the position of the accent is determined by the phonological structure of the form; but in other parts of speech it is not thus conditioned.

42 Hockett treats a similar problem in his discussion of tense-mode and person-number elements in Spanish verbs, Lang. 23.338 ((239)).

43 This paper makes no attempt to treat the significance of various classes of structure, such as derivational vs. inflectional formations, criteria for class determination, the relative order in descriptive statements, and the relation of constituent elements to the sets of immediate constituents. For these subjects see my book Morphology (Ann Arbor, 1946).

44 Juncture is intentionally excluded from this classification. Junctures are to be treated on the same level as order, which is the other formal feature of arrangement.

45 See Kenneth L. Pike, The intonation of American English (Ann Arbor, 1945).

46 In some positions within the intonational pattern the phoneme of full stress may be reduced.

47 The term 'canonical form' is Hockett's; see Lang. 23.333-4 ((236)).

48 Zellig S. Harris, Linguistic Structure of Hebrew, JAOS 61.143-67 (1941).

The segmental and the suprasegmental phonemes which compose a morpheme need not occur simultaneously (see §4.2). In Turu (a Bantu language of Tanganyika), the subjunctive ends in -è, but in addition the verb as a whole has a characteristic subjunctive tone pattern: the stem syllable is high, all succeeding syllables are low. Here a tonal pattern and a particular suffix combine to make a single functional unit.

Non-simultaneous components of morphemes also exist in English. The suffix /-itiy/ in such words as ability, facility, banality, regularity, similarity, and generosity always occurs with presuffixal stress. This position of the stress may be regarded as a part of the nominalizing morpheme. It is thus no longer a 'property' of the underlying form, but rather of the suffix.

4.2 Morphemes may be classified by the positional relationship of their constituent parts into continuous and discontinuous. Morphemes of which the constituent phonemes (segmental and suprasegmental) are adjacent or simultaneous constitute the usual type. Indeed, the very fact of separation generally leads one to believe that the parts constitute separate morphemes unless (1) the units can be demonstrated to be separated by replacive or infixal forms, or (2) the units never occur without each other. In a form such as /sæŋ/ the phonemes /s...ŋ/ constitute a discontinuous morpheme. In the Hebrew examples cited in §4.13 the phonemes of the radical CCC are usually discontinuous. In all true instances of infixation the two parts of the morpheme in which the infix appears together make up a discontinuous morpheme, e.g. the sequence vi...c in Latin vincō (with infix -n-).

Sometimes we find separable units which occur only with one another. In Kissi (a 'Sudanic' language of French Guinea) there are two interrogative particles yɛ̀ and nɛ̄. In any interrogative expression the first of these occurs immediately after the verb and the second occurs in sentence-final position, e.g. vɛ̀ yá gbɛ́ngbɛ́lá yɛ̀ ndū sísà nɛ̄, literally 'how I see interrogative-particle him now interrogative-particle'. The forms yɛ̀ and nɛ̄ constitute a discontinuous morpheme yɛ̀ ... nɛ̄.[49]

4.3 Morphemes may be classified, finally, by their position with respect to other morphemes as (1) additive, (2) replacive, (3) additive and replacive, and (4) subtractive.

4.31 Additive linear morphemes are stems and affixes. The affixes may be prefixes, infixes, or suffixes. Such morphemes are so common in so many languages that no illustrations are needed. Additive supralinear morphemes (consisting solely of suprasegmental phonemes) are intonational units and tonal morphemes.

[49] The situation with respect to French ne ... pas is not analogous. The element ne occurs without pas (in ne ... rien, ne ... point, ne ... que, etc.), and pas occurs without ne (in pas du tout, pourquoi pas, etc.).

Additive morphemes of this last variety are not common, but the Ngbaka data (§4.12) are not unique. In Kissi, polysyllabic verb stems have no independent basic tone, but are accompanied by four sets of tone patterns indicating mode-aspect and number-person categories. With plural subject, the typical verb baŋa 'redeem' has the following tones: bàŋá completive, bàŋà incompletive, báŋà negative, and bāŋā interrogative. The tones on the verbs are in no way associated with basic morphological classes of verbs, and hence are genuine additive morphemes.

4.32 Replacive morphemes, like additive morphemes, may consist of segmental or of suprasegmental phonemes; we have already noted a number of examples (§3.04, §4.11). A rather rare type of replacement is represented by the English series bath : bathe, sheath : sheathe, wreath : wreathe, teeth : teethe, safe : save, strife : strive, thief : thieve, grief : grieve, half : halve, shelf : shelve, serf : serve, advice : advise, house /haws/ : house /hawz/, etc. In each pair, the noun has a voiceless continuant, the verb a voiced continuant. If we agree to derive the verbs from the nouns,[50] we set up three specific replacive elements: /ð ← θ/, /v ← f/, and /z ← s/; but since these three elements exhibit a phonetic-semantic resemblance to each other, and since their occurrence is phonologically conditioned, we combine them into a single replacive morpheme.

In Shilluk (a Nilotic language of the Anglo-Egyptian Sudan), there are four principal ways of forming plural nouns from singular bases in phrase-final position: by syllabic replacives, by lengthening of the stem vowel (a type of additive morpheme), by the suffixation of -i, and by tonal replacives. No one of these types is sufficiently predominant to be called the basic alternant; and there are even certain combinations of two of the types in one formation. The tonal replacives occur in a definite pattern; compare the following singulars and plurals: wāt 'house' : pl. wàt, ógāṭ (where o- is a prefix) 'cloth' : pl. ógàṭ, yíṭ 'ear' : pl. yīṭ, tík 'chin' : pl. tīk, tɔ́ŋ 'spear' : pl. tɔ̄ŋ. The plural stems differ from the singular through the replacement of a mid tone by a low tone, or of a high tone by a mid tone: in either case, the replacement of a higher tone by a lower one. Both types of replacement may be combined in a single morpheme.

In Mongbandi (another 'Sudanic' language of the northwest Congo), verbs have basic tonal patterns. Verb stems, both monosyllabic and dissyllabic, belong to various form-classes according to the fundamental tone that accompanies them with a singular subject and in the completive aspect. With a plural subject these form-classes are not distinguished: all monosyllabic verbs in the completive aspect have a high tone, all dissyllabic verbs have mid-high tone.

[50] The direction of derivation depends primarily on semantic criteria; but there are parallel formal patterns to guide the choice.

Accordingly, the morpheme that means plural number and completive aspect consists of the replacement of the basic tone (whatever it may be) by a high or a mid-high tone.

The shift of stress in related nouns and verbs in English (impact, import, insult, insert, discourse, rebel, protest, etc.) is also a type of replacive. The morpheme in this instance is /V́...V ← V...V́/, where V stands for any syllabic. The stress of the underlying verb is not here regarded as a morpheme by itself; what is morphemic is rather the replacement of a stress on the second syllable by a stress on the first.

4.33 Morphemes may also consist of a combination of additive and replacive elements. As examples I may refer to the morphemes cited in §4.13, which are composed of segmental and suprasegmental phonemes not simultaneous in their occurrence. Thus, the Turu final -è (an additive element) occurs in combination with a particular tonal pattern on the preceding syllables (a replacive element).

4.34 Subtractive morphemes are illustrated by the masculine forms of certain French adjectives.[51] In the series plat /pla/ : platte /plat/ 'flat', laid /lɛ/ : laide /lɛd/ 'ugly', long /lɔ̃/ : longue /lɔ̃g/ 'long', soûl /su/ : soûle /sul/ 'drunk', the subtractive element (the final consonant of the feminine forms) has different phonological shapes—/t, d, g, l/; but at least it is always final. Accordingly, in spite of the diverse phonemic make-up of the various allomorphs, we may still combine them all into one morpheme on the basis of their semantic distinctiveness and the phonological determination of their distribution.

[51] Bloomfield, op. cit. 217. William L. Wonderly has proposed in discussion that these French forms might be most economically handled as morphophonemic. Cf. George L. Trager, The verb morphology of spoken French, Lang. 20.131–41 (1940).

⟦If there can be any such thing as 'common sense' in descriptive linguistics, Nida's work is where we may expect to find it, because he carries a responsibility both to perform and to guide work that is adequate to practical purposes and will also stand up under theoretical criticism. Because I lack experience to match his, I must content myself here with referring to the general comments appended to Bloch's paper, p. 254.⟧

COMPONENTIAL ANALYSIS OF A HEBREW PARADIGM

ZELLIG S. HARRIS
Language 24.87–91—1948

The linguistic structure of an utterance is presumed to be fully stated by a list of the morphemes which constitute it, and by their order. The difference between two utterances is expressed by the difference in morphemic constituency between them. Frequently, however, we find that there is a set of morphemes in a language, such that each morpheme in the set is identified by its contrast with all the others in the set. Such morphemes are often arranged in paradigms, and the various crisscrossing relationships among the morphemes of the paradigm are often called categories. Thus there are such Latin morphemes as -us, -um, -ī, -ōs which are defined by their membership in a paradigm, and which are considered as expressing, within the paradigm, such categories as case and number.

The presence of these categories is not a happy situation for structural linguistics, which is most useful if it can define everything in terms of some stock of elements (phonemes, morphemes) which are all on a par with each other. It is therefore of interest to note that the categories represented in a paradigm can be set up by means of the very methods which are used to set up the more traditional morphemes. Just as the morphemes the and a can be isolated by comparing, say, You've lost the job with You've lost a job, so also the categories of singular and plural can be isolated by comparing certain utterances, even in a language in which these appear not as distinct morphemes but as categories in a paradigm. One important difference between isolating the traditional morphemes and isolating these categories is that the categories are not readily identifiable as consisting of any particular phonemes in the utterances. Another is that it is usually necessary to consider not a simply localized substitution, like the for a in You've lost ( ) job, but a more diffuse substitution, on the order of -ose are ...-s for -is is ...0 in Th( ) my book( ): Those are my books as compared with This is my book. We will therefore call these morphemically analyzed categories components.[1]

In order to see how this componential representation of paradigmatic categories can be carried out, we consider the morphemes for 'I', 'you', etc. in Modern Hebrew.

If we consider the following 17 utterances, and many sets of utterances of the same type, we would set up a class (C) of 17 morphemes -ti 'I did', a- 'I will', y...u 'they will', etc.[2]

lo	limádti	oto	davar.	I did	not teach him a thing.
"	limádta	"	"	you (m.) did	" " " " "
"	limadt	"	"	you (f.) did	" " " " "
"	limed	"	"	he did	" " " " "
"	limda	"	"	she did	" " " " "
"	limádnu	"	"	we did	" " " " "
"	limadtem	"	"	you (m. pl.) did	" " " " "
"	limadten	"	"	you (f. pl.) did	" " " " "
"	limdu	"	"	they did	" " " " "
"	alamed	"	"	I will	" " " " "
"	tlamed	"	"	you (m.) or she will	" " " " "
"	tlamdi	"	"	you (f.) will	" " " " "
"	ylamed	"	"	he will	" " " " "
"	nlamed	"	"	we will	" " " " "
"	tlamdu	"	"	you (m. pl.) will	" " " " "
"	tlamédna	"	"	you (f. pl.) or they (f. pl.) will	" " " " "
"	ylamdu	"	"	they (m.) will	" " " " "

[1] It can be shown that they are identical in analytic status with all other morphemic 'long components', which can be set up for morphology in much the same way that phonemic long components are set up for phonology. Cf. Lang. 20.181–205 (1944) ((124)).

[2] If a vowel adjoins limed with no intervening juncture (i. e. within the same word) a preceding vowel is replaced by zero (limdu). Aside from that, if any phonemes (except the unstressed na) adjoin limed with no intervening juncture, the vowel of limed which is nearest to them is replaced by a. The forms are cited here in phonemic transcription, so that such segments as the ə between two initial consonants are not shown. ⟦Here limed is used as base form to achieve simplicity of morphophonemic statement.⟧

Every member of the class V (katav 'write', ba 'come', and other verbs) occurs with every one of these C morphemes. At this stage of the analysis, the 17 morphemes isolated by comparing the utterances listed above would constitute a separate class of morphemes, restricted in their use to occur only with members of the class V.

However, we find additional environments in which some members of C occur while others do not. The first nine occur in lo limad( ) oto davar etmol '( ) didn't teach him a thing yesterday', but not in lo ( )lamed( ) oto davar maxar '( ) won't teach him a thing tomorrow'; the last eight occur in the latter but not in the former.[3] We therefore extract a component T common to the first nine and to their differentiating environments, and another component I common to the last eight and their differentiating environments. The residues of the nine T morphemes may be identified with the residues of the eight I morphemes if we find a convenient way of matching pairs of these residues.

This pairing may be carried out on the basis of the particular members of the N class[4] with which each member of C occurs.

with	there occur only	
	+ T	+ I
ani 'I'	-ti 'I did'	a- 'I will'
ata 'you (m.)'	-ta 'you (m.) did'	t- 'you (m.) will'
at 'you (f.)'	-t 'you (f.) did'	t...i 'you (f.) will'
hu 'he'	-0 (zero) 'he did'	y- 'he will'
hi 'she'	-a 'she did'	t- 'she will'
anáxnu 'we'	-nu 'we did'	n- 'we will'
atem 'you (m. pl.)'	-tem 'you (m. pl.) did'	t...u 'you (m. pl.) will'
hem 'they (m.)'	-u 'they (m.) did'	y...u 'they (m.) will'
hen 'they (f.)'	-u 'they (f.) did'	t...na 'they (f.) will'
aten 'you (f. pl.)'	-ten 'you (f. pl.) did'	t...na 'you (f. pl.) will'

We can therefore identify the residue (X) of -ti with the residue (X) of a-, and so on: X + T = -ti, X + I = a-; Y + T = -ta, Y + I = t-; etc.

In the environment ani vəhu ( ) oto bəyáxad 'I and he ( ) him together', the only members of C which occur are in limádnu and nlamed. In ata vəhem ( ) oto bəyáxad 'you (m.) and they (m.) ( ) him together', only limadtem and tlamdu occur, and in at vəhen ( ) only limadten and tlamédna. In hu vəhi ( ) oto bəyáxad 'He and she ( ) him together', only limdu and ylamdu occur, and in hi vəišti ( ) 'she and my wife ( )' only limdu and tlamédna occur. If we consider only the presence of və 'and' in N və N, we find that only the last five of the ten morphemic residues occur in N və N ( ). We may therefore extract a P component from these five and from their environment N və N, and may seek a basis for identifying the residues of these five with some of the remaining five morphemes.

The basis for pairing the residues of these two new subclasses—of those morphemes which contain P and those which do not—may be found in a more detailed consideration of the occurrence of our ten residues with particular members of class N. The residue of -nu/n- 'we' occurs not only with anáxnu 'we' but also with any N və N where one of the two N is ani 'I' or anáxnu 'we' and the other N is any other member of the N class: ani vəhi limádnu oto 'I and she taught him', anáxnu vəhamore haxadaš nlamed otxa 'We and the new teacher will teach you'. No other one of our ten morphemes occurs in these environments. Analogously, the residue of -tem/t...u 'you (m. pl.)' is the only one that occurs with any N və N where one N is ata or atem and the other is any member of N (including these two) except ani and anáxnu: e. g. ata vəhu tlamdu oto 'you (m.) and he will teach him'. Similarly, only -ten/t...na 'you (f. pl.)' occurs with N və N where one N is at or aten and the other is at, aten, hi, hen or any member of N containing the F component to be defined below: e. g. at vəaxoti tavóna 'You and my sister will come'. The residue of -u/y...u 'they (m.)' is the only one that occurs with any N və N where neither N is ani, anáxnu, ata, at, or atem, and where not more than one N includes F: hu vəhi ydabru ito 'He and she will talk with him', habanai vəozro sidru et ze 'The builder and his helper arranged it'. Similarly, only -u/t...na 'they (f.)' occurs with N və N where each N is either hi or hen or an N including F: hi vəhabaxura tdabérna 'She and the girl will talk'.

Of the five morphemes containing P, then, only the first (-nu/n-) occurs with ani in either N position of N və N; we therefore pair it with the -ti/a- morpheme which also occurs with ani. Only the second ever occurs with ata or atem in each N position; we therefore pair it with the -ta/t- morpheme which occurs with ata. An analogous restric-

[3] E. g. lo limádnu oto davar etmol 'We didn't teach him a thing yesterday', lo alamed oto davar maxar 'I won't teach him a thing tomorrow'.

[4] Where N indicates a class of noun morphemes containing ani 'I', hu 'he', hamore haxadaš 'the new teacher', etc.

tion to at leads to the pairing of -ten/t...na with -t/t...i. The third morphemic residue occurs only with hu, hi, hem, hen or the members of N not listed here, in either N position:[5] we pair it with the morpheme 0/y- which occurs with hu. Analogously, we pair -u/t...na with -a/t- on the basis of hi. We can express these matchings by five morphemic components: 1 contained in -ti/a- and -nu/n-, 2 contained in -ta/t- and -tem/t...u, A contained in -t/t...i and -ten/t...na, 3 contained in 0/y- and -n/y...u, B contained in -a/t- and -u/t...na.

If we consider the limitations of occurrence of these morphemes or their segments in respect to the -a 'feminine' morpheme, we find that N occurring with A or B always has the -a morpheme, whereas N occurring with 2 or 3 does not.[6] The restriction upon B as against 3 is clear: habaxura sidra et ze 'The girl arranged it', habaxura vəhaxavera šela tsadérna et ze 'The girl and her friend (f.) will arrange it'; as against habaxur sider et ze 'The fellow arranged it', habaxur vəhaxavera šelo ysadru et ze 'The fellow and his friend (f.) will arrange it'. No N with the -a 'feminine' morpheme substitutes for habaxur in the last two utterances, nor can baxur substitute for baxura or xavera in the first two.[7] We may therefore say that the -a/t- and -u/t...na residues, hi 'she' and hen 'they (f.)', and -a 'feminine' all contain a component F which is absent in 0/y-, -u/y...u, hu 'he', and hem 'they (m.)'.

The same component F can be extracted from A as against 2. Just as hi contains F, so does at 'you (f.)': hi baxura haguna 'She's a decent girl', at baxura haguna 'You (f.) are a decent girl', ata baxur hagun 'You (m.) are a decent fellow'. Since A occurs with at but not with ata, we extract the F component from A also.

Further consideration shows a limitation of occurrence of 2 and 3 in respect to at and hi, as well as to ata and hu, respectively. Before 3, hi or hen sometimes constitutes one member of N və N (see fn. 5), whereas at does not. Similarly, ata vəat 'You (m.) and you (f.)' occurs before 2, but ata vəani 'You and I' does not. Hence the component 2 may be extracted from at, aten, and the A morphemes which occur with these, and 3 may be extracted from hi, hen, and the B morphemes which occur with them.

Component A is thus replaceable by the combination of components 2 and F; and B by the combination of components 3 and F.

We now have a set of components in terms of which each member of C may be identified and differentiated from each other one, without residue:

morpheme	represented by components
-ti 'I did'	1 T
-ta 'you (m.) did'	2 T
-t 'you (f.) did'	2 F T
-0 'he did'	3 T
-a 'she did'	3 F T
-nu 'we did'	1 P T
-tem 'you (m. pl.) did'	2 P T
-ten 'you (f. pl.) did'	2 F P T
-u 'they (m.) did'	3 P T
-u 'they (f.) did'	3 F P T
a- 'I will'	1 I
t- 'you (m.) will'	2 I
t...i 'you (f.) will'	2 F I
y- 'he will'	3 I
t- 'she will'	3 F I
n- 'we will'	1 P I
t...u 'you (m. pl.) will'	2 P I
t...na 'you (f. pl.) will'	2 F P I
y...u 'they (m.) will'	3 P I
t...na 'they (f.) will'	3 F P I

5 But only one of the two N positions can be occupied by any one of the group hi, hen, and N plus -a 'feminine'. Before -u/t...na, both N positions are occupied by morphemes of this group.

6 And N occurring with 1 sometimes has the -a and sometimes does not.

7 N + -a may substitute for N without -a, e.g. habaxur in such environments as N və N (habaxur vəaxi sidru et ze 'The fellow and my brother arranged it'); or in the N of VN = V (limádti et habaxur 'I taught the fellow', limádti et habaxura 'I taught the girl'); or in the second N of N še PN = N (ze hamakom šel habaxur 'That's the fellow's place', ze hamakom šel habaxura 'That's the girl's place'); etc.

⟦At first sight it may seem that the end result is no more and no less than what was already implied in the glosses. But it is characteristic of our rigorous modern methods to place no reliance upon glosses: at most, they give hints regarding what may perhaps be established by distributional analysis. And in this case they could have led us astray, for instance if a sentence had been included which called for an 'it' in English: Hebrew has only two genders, like French.

No component, or a zero component if you like, is assigned to 'masculine' or the lack of 'feminine'. Similarly, the 1, the genderless person, could have been represented by no component or another zero, and one of T and I (probably T) likewise, as far as we can see from these data, with equivalent effects. Possibly the tradition of Semitic grammar guided the author here: our proposal would have assigned nothing but zeros to the 'I did' form, and the usual base form is rather the 'he did' form (limed, etc.), which, incidentally, is customarily glossed, when cited as base form, with the English base form, e.g. katav 'write' (lit. 'he wrote').

Here, as often, Harris depends on careful reading: no jumping to conclusions is likely to be profitable.⟧

NUCLEAR STRUCTURES IN LINGUISTICS

RICHARD S. PITTMAN

Language 24.287–92—1948

1. The expression 'nuclear structures' has become, in our day, a term to conjure with; but the concept is not new in lingustics. It is mentioned or implied in contemporary discussions under the terms 'immediate constituents', 'rank', and 'endocentric phrases'; in the older literature it is referred to as 'modification', 'attribution', or 'subordination'.[1] An assumption of different ranks is implicit in such word-pairs as stem—affix, head—attribute, noun—adjective, substantive—modifier, verb—adverb, principal—subordinate.

The purpose of this paper is not to offer a new concept for linguistic theory, but rather to codify the criteria which probably serve as the basis for most judgments of relative rank that have been tacitly invoked in lingustic analysis.[2]

2. We begin with the assumption that the principle of immediate constituents is valid.[3] This principle might be described as a sort of gravitational attraction between certain morphemes or groups of morphemes, but not between others. As an analyst observes it when undertaking the description of a given language, he might call it 'concomitance' or 'affinity', or simply the tendency of a given class of sequences to occur only with certain other selected classes of sequences. Thus, some sort of 'essential affinity' is observed to exist between red and -ish but not between red and -ing, between very and fast but not between very and runs.

The usefulness of this principle consists in the very considerable simplification of analysis which it affords. If one does not accept the IC[4] hypothesis, one is almost compelled to regard every morpheme in an utterance as pertinent to the description of every other morpheme. But a good analysis in terms of ICs usually reduces the total possible environmental factors of a given morpheme or sequence of morphemes to one: in other words, it states that the only pertinent environment of a given IC is its concomitant (the other IC).[5] Thus, in the sentence I would like to have gone, the IC principle strips down the pertinent environment of would to the single morpheme like, and that of have to gone.[6] This means that a proper analysis of the ICs of any expression should be rewarded by a very appreciable saving of labor, since it eliminates the non-pertinent parts of an utterance at each level of description.

3. It is not the intention of this paper, however, to examine the techniques for determining ICs. Whatever method a linguist follows, his final result will in all probability assume several degrees of rank. To certain constituents he is likely to assign a principal or 'central' status; these he may label roots, stems, bases, themes, heads, nouns, verbs, main clauses, etc. To other constituents he is likely to assign a subordinate or 'lateral' status; these he may call affixes, enclitics, formatives, attributes, modifiers, subordinate clauses, etc. It would be possible to term the central constituents 'nuclei'[7] and the lateral ones 'satellites'.

These terms are of course not meant to imply that there must be anything inherently principal or subordinate about all the morphemes or groups of morphemes. They merely affirm that in most expressions the linguistic structure is such as to make this distinction and this relationship a very convenient one for the systematizer.[8]

[1] Cf. Leonard Bloomfield, Language 161, 209 f. (New York, 1933); Otto Jespersen, The philosophy of grammar 97–107 (New York, 1924). Needless to say, my development owes a great deal to these sources.

[2] The first stimulus for this paper was received while I was attending the Linguistic Institute at the University of Michigan in the summer of 1945, holding a scholarship from the American Council of Learned Societies. An earlier version of the paper was read at a meeting of the Linguistic Society of America, 30 December 1947. I am indebted to Zellig S. Harris for help in preparing the published draft.

[3] Cf. especially Bloomfield, op. cit.; Kenneth L. Pike, Taxemes and immediate constituents, Lang. 19.65–82 (1943); Pike, Analysis of a Mixteco text, IJAL 10.113–38 (1944), esp. 120 ff.; Eugene A. Nida, Syntax 44–61 (Glendale, Calif., 1946); Rulon S. Wells, Immediate constituents, Lang. 23.81–117 (1947) ((186)). I am especially indebted to Pike and Nida for instruction in the principles of immediate constituents.

[4] This useful abbreviation for immediate constituent (plural ICs) is taken from Wells, op. cit.

[5] Of course there are always exceptions, for instance factors of intonation, concord, and substitution (pronouns). The last two might be handled by the method suggested in Zellig S. Harris, Discontinuous morphemes, Lang. 21.121–7 (1945), and the first by the method suggested in the same writer's Simultaneous components in phonology, Lang. 20.181–205 (1944) ((124)).

[6] On have gone see Harris, Discontinuous morphemes (fn. 5 above).

[7] Pike appears to have been among the first to use the term 'nucleus' in this sense. See his Analysis of a Mixteco text (fn. 3 above).

[8] The equations in Zellig S. Harris, From morpheme to utterance, Lang. 22.161–83 (1946) ((142)), though not using the term IC, are based on the 'nuclear hypothesis'. His highest surviving numbered formulas represent the basic nuclei. The eliminated formulas at each level represent the satellites.

4. But what, precisely, is the advantage of labeling one constituent central and another lateral? Probably the principal gain is that since we conventionally describe the largest classes first, and smaller classes (or satellites) in terms of their relation to nuclei, the central—lateral classification gives us a desirable working basis for our description. It shows us the essential nuclei at all levels, so that in the descriptive arrangement the satellites may then be simply grouped with their respective nuclei. Just as an astronomer finds it simpler to describe the moon's relation to the earth than its relation to the sun, so a linguist, in analyzing the sentence *Eat your bread*, finds it simpler to describe the relation of *your* to *bread* than its relation to *eat*.

5. This dichotomy into nuclei and satellites poses the question which is the primary concern of this paper: What procedures are followed in deciding that this is a nucleus and that a satellite, this a stem or head and that an affix or attribute? Most linguists seem to make the classification intuitively. The following is an attempt to suggest some of the assumptions that may underly this intuition.

Ten premises are proposed as probably constituting the basis for most of the distinctions of rank that linguists make. In illustrating the premises, the sequence AB represents any two immediate constituents of an expression in any given language. Theoretically, it does not matter whether these are regarded as morphemes, words, or phrases; actually, however, the more morphemes there are in an IC, the more complicated it would be for illustrative purposes. For this reason, most of the illustrations will contain only single words and morphemes. An arrow points from satellite to nucleus: *my*→*hat*. A subscript numeral after a letter indicates that the letter represents an entire form-class rather than a single form; thus, A_1 (*man*) = the form-class to which *man* belongs, i. e. the class of nouns. It is assumed in the illustrations that the ICs have already been determined: the problem which will occupy us is their relative rank.

Premise 1. Independence.[9] If one of two ICs occurs alone but the other does not, the former is usually considered to be central and its concomitant lateral. Thus, we probably consider affixes as subordinate to stems because stems, in many languages, occur alone, whereas affixes usually do not. In English, a morpheme of the class of *talk* may occur without the suffix *-ing*, but not conversely. In Spanish, a word of the class of *perro* may occur without the morpheme *su*, but not conversely. This premise might also be referred to as 'dispensability': the more dispensable of two ICs is usually regarded as the satellite.

Premise 2. Class size. If one of two ICs belongs to a larger form-class (i. e. a class with more members) than the other, it is usually considered to be central and its concomitant lateral. If A_1 of the sequence A_1B_2 represents a class of fifty members and B_2 a class of five members, it is probable that A will be labelled central and B lateral. This premise is fairly apparent in the relative sizes of the English adverb and verb classes, pronouns and verbs, affixes and stems, e. g. *go*←*away*, *short*←*en*; cf. Fr. *je*→*mange*.

Premise 3. Versatility (range). If one of two ICs has a potential range of occurrence with more different classes of concomitants than the other, it is usually considered central and its concomitant lateral. If A of the sequence AB occurs with five different classes of concomitants, while B occurs with only two, it is probable that A will be interpreted as a nucleus and B as a satellite. An example is the relationship of English nouns and adjectives. Their relative independence and class size might be debatable, but there seems to be little doubt that nouns occur in a much greater variety of environments than adjectives. Other illustrations: *come*←*down*, *in*→*side*, Fr. *deux*→*ans*.

Premise 4. Endocentricity.[10] If a constitute[11] belongs to the same class as one of its immediate constituents, that constituent is usually interpreted as a nucleus and its concomitant as a satellite. If the sequence AB belongs to Class 1 and the constituent B also belongs to Class 1, B will probably be regarded as a nucleus. Most endocentric expressions come under this premise. Examples: *can*→*read*, *big*→*dog*, Sp. *yo*→*voy*.

Premise 5. Class frequency.[12] If one of two classes of ICs occurs oftener than the other, it is likely to be considered central and its concomitant lateral. If A_1 of the sequence A_1B_2 occurs 100 times to 10 occurrences of B_2, class A_1 will probably be regarded as central. In testing this premise in English, one would check to see if nouns occur more often than adjectives, verbs more often than adverbs, stems more often than affixes, independent clauses more often than dependent clauses. Of course, if the premises of independence and versatility are valid, this one would seem to be a necessary corollary, since more independent and versatile classes would be expected to occur more often than those which are less so.

[9] Premises 1, 2, and 9 have been suggested, in slightly different form, by Hockett, and Premise 4 by Bloch, in Charles F. Hockett's review of Nida's Morphology, Lang. 23.273-85 (1947), esp. 282-3. Several of these premises were used by Kenneth L. Pike and Eunice V. Pike, Immediate constituents of Mazateco syllables, IJAL 13.78-91 (1947).

[10] Many linguists might accept this as the only valid form of rank, excluding all exocentric constructions. But rank is nevertheless implied by the description of an exocentric form like *love-ly* as consisting of stem plus affix.

[11] A constitute is an expression that consists of two (or more) ICs; see Wells, op. cit.

[12] Martin Joos, Statistical patterns in Gothic phonology, Lang. 18.33-8 (1942), distinguishes between text frequency and list frequency. I am referring here to text frequency.

Premise 6. Individual frequency. In seeming contradition to the premise of class frequency, it may be possible to state that an individual constituent which occurs more often than its concomitant is likely to be considered lateral and its concomitant central. If A of the sequence AB is observed to occur more often in the language than its concomitant B, it is very possible that A will be interpreted as lateral and B as central. This, of course, is readily apparent in a language such as Nahuatl, where stems do not occur without affixes, and where hence certain affixes must occur very much more often than any member of the stem classes, e. g. the prefix ni- and the suffix -tl have much higher frequencies than any of the stems with which they occur.

Exceptions to this premise will immediately become apparent; but there seems to be enough evidence to justify its inclusion. For example, a high percentage of the words which were eliminated from Van der Beke's, Morgan's, and Buchanan's word counts (for French, German, and Spanish respectively)[13] because of frequencies too high to be worth counting, were words which would generally be considered lateral types.

Premise 7. Prosody. In some languages, factors of syllable length, stress, pitch, or intonation may influence determinations of rank. In Nahuatl, for example, a stress on the word kiénika 'how' leads one to describe it as kieni<ka, stem plus enclitic.

Premise 8. Length. If nothing is known about two ICs except their length (i. e. the number of phonemes contained in them), it is very likely that the longer will be classified as nuclear and the shorter as a satellite.[14] If a linguist were asked to make a guess at two Nahuatl terms about which he knew nothing, e. g. i-kal and nehnemi-s, he would, in all probability, surmise that the i- and the -s were lateral elements (affixes). This premise may sound like linguistic heresy, yet there can be little doubt that the really 'fast' linguists who 'get the hang' of a language in record time use all sorts of undefined mental shortcuts, including this one, in probing linguistic structures. It is also worth while to compare this premise with the premise of individual frequency, and to recall at this point Zipf's hypothesis that 'as the relative frequency of a word [or morpheme] increases, it tends to decrease in magnitude.'[15] It would seem that there may indeed be a detectable correlation between length, frequency, and rank.

Premise 9. Meaning. Many linguists might deny any valid correlation between meaning and rank; and yet, given the sequences no-ča: 'my house' and kin-kʷa 'them he-eats', and no further information about them, they would very probably be willing to hazard a guess that ča: 'house' and kʷa 'he-eats' are nuclei and that the other elements are prefixes. Substantival and verbal concepts are very strongly associated in the minds of most of us with linguistic nuclei.

Premise 10. Pattern. This premise operates here, of course, as in all other phases of linguistic analysis: unfamiliar elements are interpreted on the analogy of those which are familiar. Cran- is listed as lateral to berry because black, for instance, is lateral to berry.

6. Having alleged that the foregoing premises probably form the basis for many or most of the judgments which linguists make regarding rank, one might ask, Are these criteria valid?

Doubtless they represent varying degrees of validity, depending on the language in question and on the linguist handling them. The first four seem to be especially useful. The others probably represent 'reinforcing' criteria rather than primary determinants. The difficulty with the ninth is, of course, the universal problem of the definitive classification of meanings and the interference of the linguist's own background. Perhaps it is safe to say that where the premises are unanimous in favoring a given ranking, few linguists would object. Where there is considerable contradition between the criteria, there will be hesitancy and disagreement with regard to rank.

7. This, however, is not too disturbing, since it is not claimed that a graded relationship exists between all the constituents of any language. The most immediately apparent exceptions are compounds and coordinate constructions in which, instead of one nucleus and one satellite, there may be two (or more) nuclei of the same class, e. g. It's going to rain, I'm going home. But even these may tend, at times, to be interpreted as having a graded structure. English compound constructions like mailman, post office, goldbug, etc., while ostensibly having two co-equal nuclei, are actually often analyzed as satellite-nucleus constitutes instead. Many other variations are also possible, such as satellite-nucleus-satellite (un-truth-ful), nucleus-satellite-satellite (whisper-ing-s), nucleus-nucleus-satellite (cat-fish-es), etc. A close IC analysis of such forms, however, often results in breaking them into separate layers.

It is also possible, of course, for a single constituent to be simultaneously a nucleus and a satellite. Thus, in the phrase very good idea, good is simulta-

[13] George E. Van der Beke, French word book (Publications of the American and Canadian Committees on Modern Languages, Vol. 15; New York, 1929); Bayard Q. Morgan, German frequency word book (PACCML, Vol. 9; New York, 1928); Milton A. Buchanan, A graded Spanish word book (PACCML, Vol. 3; Toronto, 1927).

[14] This is probably much less likely in syntax than in morphology.

[15] George K. Zipf, Relative frequency as a determinant of phonetic change, Harvard Studies in Classical Philology 40.1–95 (1929); The psycho-biology of language (Boston, 1935). Martin Joos, in his review of the latter work, Lang. 12.196–210 (1936), though rejecting Zipf's causal relationship between frequency and length, nevertheless appears to admit the correlation as a 'functional interrelation'.

neously a nucleus for the satellite very and a satellite to the nucleus idea.

Perhaps the hardest cases to handle are those where each IC represents a different class, but the classes are approximately equal in size, versatility, frequency, etc. English subject-predicate constructions are of this type. It is hardly possibly to call them coordinate, and yet to rank either subject or predicate as subordinate to the other might incur considerable controversy. It might be convenient to terms such forms 'collateral' classes, meaning classes which are approximately equal, judged by our premises, but not identical.

8. Although the primary implication of these premises has been conceived as applying to grammar, it seems that they may also be profitably applied to phonemic and syllabic structures. The chief illustration of this treatment is the article by Kenneth L. Pike and Eunice V. Pike on Mazateco syllables, already cited (fn. 9).

⟦This admirable paper has been much misunderstood: hasty readers have thought that Pittman was advocating or proposing what he was simply describing; which is not to say that he was rejecting the consensus. If enough more papers like this had been published, I wouldn't have needed to say so much in my comments scattered through this book, for my purpose has mostly been the same as Pittman's, plus a historical one.⟧

A NOTE ON 'STRUCTURE'

CHARLES F. HOCKETT

International Journal of American Linguistics 14.269-71—1948

In the course of his critical review,* Preston makes the following assertion: 'Structure is a series of statements. The structure of a given language or language corpus does not exist until it is stated.' At first reading, this statement is ridiculous. Upon deeper consideration, taken in conjunction with the statements which follow it in Preston's discussion, it is not ridiculous; yet it begs a question of fundamental importance, or, perhaps better, implies an answer to that question which seems to me misleading.

Linguistics—specifically, descriptive or structural linguistics—can be regarded as a game or as a science. As a game, the necessary equipment is a body of utterances from some language or dialect, or, indeed, a body of pseudo-utterances coined by a nimble mind for the purpose (as Nida, who does not take linguistics to be a game, makes up Papawapam problems for the training of his students). The rules of the game are any rules you prefer, with one limitation. The object of the game is to compare and analyze the utterances of the corpus and arrive at a redescription of them as composed of smaller recurrent (or occasionally non-recurrent) parts. The limitation on rules—that is, the one rule that all devotees of the game agree on pretty well—is that all the utterances of the corpus must be taken into account; as a matter of fact, even on this some players like to hedge, as when it is considered desirable to remove recent loan-words before describing phonology.

As a game, it matters not a whit what relation there may exist between the 'structure' produced by the player as he manipulates his toy, and anything that a native speaker of the language might say, either in or about his language, save for those very utterances of his which comprise the corpus.

No one can quarrel with games as games. In this particular case, extensive experimentation with the game, as a game, can be of use over and above its entertainment value, precisely as the proliferation of pure mathematics, which is in essence a game, is of tremendously great value for the 'practical' application of mathematics in physics, biology, and perhaps someday in social science. This practical value, however, is not susceptible of being described unless we stand away from game-linguistics and consider the science of the same name, as a science.

*Review of C. H. de Goeje, Études linguistiques caribes II (Amsterdam, 1946), by W. D. Preston, IJAL 14.131 (1948).

This Preston does not do; I hope there is no injustice involved in stating that he seems almost to reject such a consideration as irrelevant.

The task of the structural linguist, as a scientist, is, as Preston implies, essentially one of classification. The purpose, however, is not simply to account for all the utterances which comprise his corpus at a given time; a simple alphabetical list would do that. Rather, the analysis of the linguistic *scientist* is to be of such a nature that the linguist can account also for utterances which are *not* in his corpus at a given time. That is, as a result of his examination he must be able to predict what *other* utterances the speakers of the language might produce, and, ideally, the circumstances under which those other utterances might be produced.[1]

The analytical process thus parallels what goes on in the nervous system of a language learner, particularly, perhaps, that of a child learning his first language. The child hears, and eventually produces, various whole utterances. Sooner or later, the child produces utterances he has not previously heard from someone else. At first these newly coined utterances may be rejected by those about him; but by a process of trial and error, supplemented by the constant acquisition of new whole utterances from those who already speak the language, the child eventually reaches the point of no longer making 'mistakes'. *Lapses* there may still be—that is, utterances which the speaker himself, sometimes, follows by remarks of the general nature of 'Oh, I meant to say such-and-such,' or else by simple partial repetition with the lapse eliminated. But by the time the child has achieved linguistic adulthood, his speech no longer contains *errors*; for he has become an authority on the language, a person whose ways of speaking *determine* what is and what is not an error.

The child's coining of an utterance he has not heard is, of course, a kind of prediction: 'If I make such-and-such noises, those about me will react in a certain way.' (We do not imply that any such 'thought' passes through the 'mind' of the child.) The parallel between this and the process of analysis performed by the linguist is close. When the child is just beginning, his coinage of utterances is often ineffective;

[1] Attempts to include prediction of the circumstances (except in terms of preceding utterances) constitute semantic analysis. Structural analysis can be scientific without being semantic.

when the linguist's corpus is small, his predictions are inaccurate. As the child continues to learn, or as the corpus grows and analysis is modified, prediction becomes more and more accurate. In theory, at least, with a large enough corpus there would no longer be any discernible discrepancy between utterances the linguist predicted and those sooner or later observed.

The essential difference between the process in the child and the procedure of the linguist is this: the linguist has to make his analysis overtly, in communicable form, in the shape of a set of statements which can be understood by any properly trained person, who in turn can predict utterances not yet observed with the same degree of accuracy as can the original analyst. The child's 'analysis' consists, on the other hand, of a mass of varying synaptic potentials in his central nervous system.[2] The child in time comes to *behave* the language; the linguist must come to *state* it.

The player of linguistics as a game has no criterion by which to judge the relative merits of one analysis versus another. This gives him a freedom for experimentation which is valuable—but not for any reason, as we have said, statable within the economy of the game as a game. The worker in linguistics as a science (and he may be wrapped in the same skin as the game addict) has such a criterion: accuracy of prediction beyond one's corpus, and communicability of the basis for such prediction to others.

In the light of the above discussion, the relevance and the absurdity of Preston's statement quoted in the first paragraph are both clear. The structure of a language may be regarded as the end-product of a game; in this sense structure is created by the person who plays the game. But every speaker of a language plays just such a game, the end-product being a state of affairs in his nervous system rather than a set of statements. The linguistic scientist must regard the structure of the language as consisting precisely of this state of affairs. His purpose in analyzing a language is not to create structure, but to determine the structure actually created by the speakers of the language. For the scientist, then, 'linguistic structure' refers to something existing quite independently of the activities of the analyst: a language is what it is, it has the structure it has, whether studied and analyzed by a linguist or not.

There is no reason why we should not use the term 'structure' in both of the senses just given. They can be kept apart when necessary; in most linguistic discussions one is apt to be referring to both senses at the same time anyway. What does need to be avoided is useless argument as to whether linguistic structure is 'objective' or 'subjective', or the like; the purpose of this note is to help ward off such time-wasting discussion.

[2] Preston might reject reference to the nervous system of a speaker as he rejects de Goeje's reference to the 'mind' of the speaker. For our purpose predictability is the factor of importance; it would not matter whether the internal state which correlates with speech were in the central nervous system, the soul, or the small intestine. But when we speak as scientists, we have the right and duty to accept the findings of other fields of science: psychology refers such matters to the nervous system, not to any other physical or non-physical component of a human being.

⟦The above Note does not say something that I have heard Hockett say and which I believe he has printed somewhere where I can't find it at the moment (but see also the first sentence of §10.2 on page 107 here). This is the way I reconstruct it: Depending on such things as the analyst's axioms and what he had for breakfast, he will eventually arrive at this or that one of an indefinite number of seemingly different descriptions of the same set of data. 'Arriving' here means perfecting the description to the point where it predicts adequately; and 'adequately' is a matter of taste and custom: for instance, if prediction fails only once in twenty hours of further observation, and then only in such a way as to call for adjustment, not abandonment of the whole pattern of description, the description may fairly be called adequate. Now we find that those various descriptions are 'mechanically interconvertible' in general. This is a matter of experience; but I believe it could also be derived by logic. It is assumed that all workers present at the same interview will agree as to whether the informant classes a given pair of utterances as 'same' or 'different'. Then it can, I believe, be shown that say two phonemic analyses which are both adequate to the informant's data will be interconvertible by rule without remanding moot points back to the informant for new testimony. Example: the difference between Hockett 1947 and Hockett 1950 as to Peiping Chinese: c > z, ch > c, etc. ⦅315⦆. What saves this from being a trivial shift in transcription practice is that h is also 'a phoneme' as we usually say, and here the shift-rule is h > h. And the shifting will work by rule both ways: c < z, etc., with no details lost.

Now 'the structure' of the language is defined as *the invariant* (mathematician's term) implicit in all the mechanically interconvertible descriptions: it is that which remains intact under those conversions. Some have said that that invariant is an empty fiction, because no one has ever displayed it except in the shape of this or that single description. But that is in turn an irrelevant objection, as shown by the Gödel theorem that the internal consistency of a set of propositions can't be demonstrated within the set.

See now also the comments on page 80 above.⟧

IMPLICATIONS OF BLOOMFIELD'S ALGONQUIAN STUDIES

CHARLES F. HOCKETT

Language 24.117-31—1948

It is generally known[1] that one of Leonard Bloomfield's life works is the descriptive and comparative study of Algonquian.[2] It is also generally conceded that his work in this field is of considerable importance.[3] But most of those who are quite willing to admit this do so on indirect evidence: since Bloomfield's other work proves him a sound scholar, his Algonquian studies must be sound too. Algonquian, after all, is an out-of-the-way language family, and few have concerned themselves with it. In view, particularly, of Bloomfield's endeavors in this field, this neglect is unfortunate. To the writer the following points seem beyond dispute: (1) careful study of Algonquian as Bloomfield has described it can be a fascinating, enlightening, and rewarding experience even for established comparatists and historical linguists; (2) for the newcomer to linguistics, a reading of Bloomfield's Algonquian works is one of the finest indoctrinations into the best of linguistic method.

In a sense, any body of data on any group of languages can serve in both these roles. But if, for example, the would-be linguist attempts to learn the elementary principles of comparative method in terms of Indo-European, or even of Germanic or Romance, the external difficulties are great: the material is widely scattered and bulky, some of it is old and hard to interpret, some of it is excellent but some is extremely bad. On the other hand, even though the Algonquian languages are 'exotic' (whatever that may mean), they are phonetically simple, not too widely divergent from the familiar Indo-European languages in structure—remarkably similar, in some ways, to older Germanic—and Bloomfield's treatment is compact, uniform in approach, and uniformly excellent.[4]

Most of the lessons which can be learned from Bloomfield's Algonquian are apparent to anyone who reads, with suitable diligence, his Sketch.[5] There are, in addition, a few important points which are not apparent from that paper alone, nor even necessarily from that paper together with his other writings in this field, save to someone who has had some independent first-hand contact with the extant Algonquian languages and with earlier efforts, mainly by missionaries, to describe this or that language of

[1] Many of the non-Algonquian references given in the footnotes of this paper were found with the assistance of Robert A. Hall Jr. For my understanding of the 'almost mystical' version of the drift theory (see §8), I am indebted to Gordon H. Fairbanks (who is not a proponent of this version of the theory). All of my colleagues at Cornell have participated in instructive discussion of this paper, and to all of them I express my thanks.

[2] Bloomfield's publications on Algonquian are listed here, approximately in order of publication. They will be referred to hereafter as 'Ref. 1' and so on, except that the third and twelfth items will be termed, respectively, the Sound System and the Sketch. The latter includes a bibliography of Algonquian which is complete save for a few items which have appeared since 1941.

(1) Review of The Owl Sacred Pack of the Fox Indians, by Truman Michelson, AJP 43.276-81 (1922).
(2) The Menomini Language, Proceedings of the Twenty-first International Congress of Americanists 336-43 (The Hague, 1924).
(3) On the Sound System of Central Algonquian, Lang. 1.130-56 (1925).
(4) The Word-Stems of Central Algonquian, Festschrift Meinhof 393-402 (Hamburg, 1927).
(5) Notes on the Fox Language, IJAL 3.219-32 (1924), 4.181-219 (1927).
(6) A Note on Sound Change, Lang. 5.99-100 (1928).
(7) The Plains Cree Language, Proceedings of the Twenty-second International Congress of Americanists 427-31 (Rome, 1928).
(8) Menomini Texts, Publications of the American Ethnological Society, Vol. 12 (New York, 1928).
(9) Sacred Stories of the Sweet Grass Cree, Bulletin 60, National Museum of Canada (Ottawa, 1930).
(10) Plains Cree Texts, Publications of the American Ethnological Society, Vol. 16 (New York, 1934).
(11) Proto-Algonquian -iit- 'Fellow', Lang. 17.292-7 (1941).
(12) Algonquian, in Linguistic Structures of Native America 85-129 (Viking Fund Publications in Anthropology, Number 6; New York, 1946).

[3] 'A remarkable contribution', says Sturtevant of Bloomfield's Sketch, Lang. 23.314 (1947).

[4] Bloomfield has noted the resemblance to older Germanic several times in conversation but not, so far as I know, in print; in Ref. 5, 4.191, the comparison is rather with Indo-European as a whole. Needless to say, the attempts of Rider T. Sherwin, The Viking and the Red Man (4 vols. to date; New York, 1940-46), to establish a genetic connection between Algonquian and Germanic are entirely misguided.

[5] See fn. 2.

the group. It is our purpose here to list those principles and procedures of historical and comparative linguistics which seem to emerge with especial clarity and force from Bloomfield's Algonquian studies. It is the writer's hope that this listing and discussion will serve to focus more attention on the work dealt with, and to be of some assistance to the person who does undertake the study recommended.[6]

We shall discuss the following points:

(1) Description and history
(2) The evaluation of written records'
(3) The use of phonemic notation
(4) Preliminary internal reconstruction
(5) Assumptions about directions of linguistic change
(6) The assumption of regular phonemic change
(7) The Wörter-und-Sachen technique
(8) Drift
(9) The significance of starred forms
(10) Negative lessons

On each of these there has been, and is, disagreement among those who occupy professional posts in which they purport to deal with language. On each point (save the last) Bloomfield's Algonquian material unambiguously indicates one answer, to the exclusion of the various alternatives that have been proposed.

1. Description and History. There are still extremists who say that descriptive linguistics is balderdash,[7] and a few, equally extreme, who scorn the comparative method in historical linguistics as irrelevant antiquarianism and, at best, guess work.[8] Some of the disagreement is genuine, but some stems simply from the insufficient complexity of our terminology for different types of linguistic operation. In order to see the genuine issue we must clear away the terminological obscurities.

A synchronic analysis describes the speech habits of an individual or a relatively homogeneous group at a particular time.[9] It ignores what interpersonal differences may be known, and makes no mention of changes in habits that take place during the period from which the evidence dates. A contrastive study compares the speech habits of different individuals or groups and tallies the similarities and differences —regardless of the relative position of the speakers or groups in space or time.[10] A diachronic analysis states the changes in speech habits in a single community from one point in time to a later period. Occasionally one can observe marked personal differences even in a small community, or clear instances of change of habit during a very short span of time; when such observations are included in a monograph which is mainly synchronic, that does not necessitate any change in the definition of 'synchronic', but simply means that the content of the monograph is not purely synchronic. This comment should not be interpreted as an objection to the practice, which is often valuable.[11]

In the gathering of information, for synchronic, contrastive, or diachronic, purposes, there are several different methods. The contact method consists in first-hand observation of the speakers. The philological method consists in the interpretation of written records. The comparative method extrapolates backwards from the earliest evidence available (or the earliest used) from two or more dialects or languages which seem to be related. Between these methods there is no sharp line of demarcation. The field worker, though he uses the contact method, later studies his own notes and in so doing involves himself in a kind of philological method; another linguist may read the notes, or the completed report, of the first, and so places himself in a position somewhat analogous to that of the interpreter of written records which date from earlier generations. The close intertwining of the philological and comparative methods is obvious.[12]

The extraneous sources of argument about 'description' and 'history' stem from the ambiguity in the use of those two terms (or of others used in place of them). 'Description' sometimes refers to synchronic analysis; sometimes to contact method. 'History' sometimes means diachronic analysis,

6 The principles itemized in this paper are by no means intended to constitute a complete canon of historical or comparative linguistics. The choice is based on the nature of the Algonquian material, not on a general analysis of linguistic method.

7 Classical Philology 38.210–11 (1943), 39.218–22 (1944); also the implications of the review in Lang. 16.216–31 (1940).

8 Acta Linguistica 2.1–22 (1940–1); IJAL 10.192–3 (1944); and see Robert A. Hall Jr., Bàrtoli's 'Neolinguistica', Lang. 22.273–83 (1946).

9 The terms 'synchronic' and 'diachronic' date at least from Ferdinand de Saussure, Cours de Linguistique Générale (Lausanne, 1916).

10 'Contrastive' is Whorf's proposal (I cannot find the reference), made because the more natural term 'comparative' is already pre-empted for a different technical use. [[I can't find the reference either.]]

11 Good illustrations of the value of mixed synchronic and diachronic discussion are Ref. 4, 401—which includes also some extremely penetrating remarks on the relation between the synchronic and diachronic points of view—and Bloomfield's paper Literate and Illiterate Speech, American Speech 2.432–9 (1927).

12 This three-by-three categorization of types of linguistic activity is more general in its application than here indicated: it applies, as a matter of fact, to all the subject-matter of cultural anthropology, of which linguistics is logically a subdivision. This is clearly indicated in Sapir, Time Perspective in Aboriginal American Culture (Ottawa, 1916) [now more accessible in Selected Writings of Edward Sapir..., ed. David G. Mandelbaum, Univ. of California Press, 1949]. There are doubtless some types of fruitful and valid investigation, of language or of culture as a whole, not subsumed in the classification.

sometimes philological or comparative method or both. With the more narrowly defined terms, the logical interrelationships are easy to see:[13]

(a) Synchronic analysis may be based on any of the three methods, or on combinations of them. Synchronic analysis of a language no longer spoken, obviously, cannot involve the contact method; that of a language for which there are no direct records has to be based on the comparative method. In this sense, 'description' is not logically prior to 'history'.

(b) Either diachronic or contrastive analysis involves prior synchronic analysis. In this sense, 'description' is logically prior to 'history'.

(c) The comparative method has to involve comparison of something. The data to which the comparative method is applied consist of bodies of synchronic descriptions of related languages. The assumptions which underlie the comparative method are distilled from diachronic analyses of bodies of synchronic material, all of which are based, in turn, on a method other than the comparative method.[14]

These interrelations are complex. The virtue of Bloomfield's Algonquian studies on this score is that the interrelations not only are perfectly clear to Bloomfield, but are made equally clear to his reader. His Sketch, for example, is at one and the same time all of the following: (1) a brief synchronic outline grammar of four Algonquian languages still extant;[15] (2) a brief synchronic outline grammar of their parent; (3) a contrastive analysis of the four modern languages and the parent language; (4) an outline of the diachronic analysis of the continuum from the parent to each of the modern languages; and (5) a demonstration of the application of the comparative method to the modern data for the reconstruction of the parent language. The Sketch does not take up these problems one by one, but rather gives a composite picture. A single careful reading produces an accurate and realistic general impression of Algonquian structure. A subsequent reading with special attention to any one of the facets listed above can give more detailed information. In such successive readings, one is never at a loss to know the range of application of each individual statement: it applies just to F, or just to the development of F from PA, or just to PA, or to all the languages, and so on.

Bloomfield's Sketch, then, is a model useful to anyone who faces the task of organizing information about a family of languages into an arrangement that makes synchronic, diachronic, and contrastive sense.

2. The Evaluation of Written Records. The documentary material on which Bloomfield bases his Algonquian analysis is of several types: (1) his own field records of M and C, made with full benefit of phonemic theory; (2) F records from William Jones, a native speaker of F who was trained under Boas and Michelson in phonetics, but not in phonemics;[16] (3) O records from the same person; (4) earlier records by missionaries and traders, without benefit of either phonetics or phonemics, and with English or French as native language, but with the advantage of long residence with the Indians and constant practical use of the languages. Since Bloomfield's first publications, others trained under him or within his sphere of influence have recorded F and O,[17] and Bloomfield himself has recorded O. We thus have a check on the accuracy of older reports, except for the negligible extent to which speech patterns may have changed between missionary times and the present.

Jones's F materials are overloaded with superfluous diacritics, indicating evanescent distinctions or subphonemic differences, but in general no phonemic contrast is omitted. O materials from the same observer have the same unnecessary indication of minutiae, but in addition obscure certain phonemic contrasts which are of considerable comparative importance—for example, the contrast between sk and šk. Certainly there is a relationship between these facts and Jones's background. F does not have the contrast sk : šk; it is not surprising that as a native speaker of F, Jones missed the contrast when

[13] The methodological points or 'principles' drawn from the discussion are lettered serially through the paper, from (a) to (p).

[14] That is, we derive our notions of linguistic change in the first instance from the history of those languages, such as English, French, and German, for which there is documentary evidence over a considerable span of time. We then make a comparative analysis of some group of languages whose common ancestor is known to us independently—for example, Romance—assuming the kinds of linguistic change discovered by the first operation, and comparing our reconstruction with the documentary evidence for the parent. Since our inverted predictions in such cases have a considerable degree of accuracy, we feel confident of at least statistically accurate results when the same comparative method is applied to a group of languages for whose parent there is no other evidence. It is true that linguistic science in the 19th century did not follow this course in its chronological development; but this does not invalidate the logical statement. Until the logical interrelationships had clearly emerged, the statements of historical linguistics were somewhat more tentative than afterwards.

[15] That is, Fox (F), Cree (C), Menomini (M), and Ojibwa (O). The abbreviations indicated will be used in the rest of this paper, together with 'PA' for Proto-Algonquian, the reconstructed parent (but see §10).

[16] For references see the Sketch. Later contributions by Michelson use approximately the same notation. It is not clear whether this notation was a joint product of Jones and Michelson, or was worked out by one and passed on to the other.

[17] F: at least J M. Cowan, Carl F. Voegelin, and the present writer; O: the latter two, J. A. Geary (other dialects), F. T. Siebert Jr., and—in the summers when O was the language studied in the field-methods course at the Linguistic Institute—a good many others.

listening to the rather similar O. His phonetic training, without phonemics, led to the overly minute recording of what he had happened to be trained to hear; his native control of F prevented omission of contrasts that were relevant there.[18]

As might be expected, the missionary records are much less satisfactory. Some of them consistently fail to indicate such important features as vowel length; some of them write subphonemic distinctions heard at one time or another, because those distinctions were present phonemically in French or in English; sometimes certain contrasts are recorded irregularly. As a result of the last, when one desires to check on some feature of a particular word, one often finds that the missionary recording is unreliable on that point.[19]

We may distil from this the following methodological observations:

(d) The extent to which one can use written records made by an untrained person can only be determined by direct observation of the language by a trained person. For a language no longer spoken, this is of course impossible.

(e) When a direct check is impossible, records made by a native speaker are more trustworthy than those made by a foreigner; those made by a person with some training (as Jones's training in phonetics to the exclusion of phonemics) are more trustworthy than those from a person with no training at all; obviously, records from a person with long practical contact, other things being equal, are more trustworthy than those from a casual passer-by.

3. The Use of Phonemic Notation. If one compares Bloomfield's Sketch with a recent paper by Geary[20] one difference is striking. All forms cited in Bloomfield's paper are phonemicized, and the choice of symbols for each language is such as to render the switch from one language to another as easy as possible for the reader. Geary could not validly do this; for his object was to cull from all sources, including the missionary records, forms which are evidence for a particular PA consonant cluster; of necessity he cites each form from an older record in the graphic shape in which it was found. Anyone can read Bloomfield; only an Algonquianist can really read Geary.

Further scrutiny of these two papers, and of some of the older records, shows that the close relationship of the Algonquian languages is immediately apparent from the missionary records; but it would be almost impossible to attempt the reconstruction of PA on the basis of the missionary records alone. On the other hand, once something is known of the structure of PA many of the missionary records can be used, though sometimes with uncertainty, to find additional cases of this or that correspondence.

This further supports points (d) and (e), and suggests the following:

(f) Written records are a means to an end, and there is no justification for holding them in high esteem, or even in reverence (as is sometimes the case) except as indirect evidence for what one is trying to discover.[21]

(g) When his only evidence consists of written records, the analyst should attempt a phonemic interpretation of the material. He can achieve accuracy in his synchronic description, in his diachronic deductions, and in his use of the material for comparative purposes, only to the extent that the phonemic interpretation of the written records is feasible without ambiguity.[22] Furthermore, he should make his phonemic interpretation clearly recognizable to his readers, by including for every form cited, explicitly or by implication, a possible phonemicization.[23] Failure to do the former impairs his own results; failure to do the latter hampers his readers.

Some of the undue esteem in which written records are held has probably been supported by the following additional principle, which is not deducible from Bloomfield's Sketch, but does appear in some of his earlier writings and quite clearly in Geary's paper:

(h) When the interpretation of written records cannot be completely free from ambiguity, the graphic shape actually occurrent in the source should be included along with the attempted phonemicization—or, when more convenient, a transliteration of the original graphic shape. The reader is then in the best possible position to re-examine the evidence and draw his own conclusions.

[18] It would be tempting to generalize as follows. If a native speaker of a language is trained in phonetics in such a way that he will hear, in any language, at least all those contrasts which are distinctive for his own speech, and will have the symbols easily at hand to record them, he will, in recording his own language, sometimes include subphonemic contrasts, but will never omit contrasts that count. But this statement is far from obviously true. Suggestions of this kind were made by Sapir in Sound Patterns in Language, Lang. 1.37–51 (1925) ((19)), and more elaborately in La réalité psychologique des phonèmes, Journal de Psychologie 30.247–65 (1933) [see now Selected Writings..., op. cit. in fn. 12 here, for the original English of this], but Twaddell's discussion, On Defining the Phoneme 8–16 ((56–9)) (LSA Monograph 16 [1935]), raises serious doubts.

[19] Some such cases are discussed in J. A. Geary, Proto-Algonquian çk: Further Examples, Lang. 17.304–10 (1941).

[20] See fn. 19.

[21] Lang. 22.256 (1946); French Review 17.168–70 (1944).

[22] Disagreements about methods of phonemicization are another matter. If 'phonemic solutions' are non-unique, as seems likely to me at the present moment, any alternative one will do. There is a gain in clarity and simplicity if each of a set of languages to be compared is phonemicized by the same principles, but if this is not done reconstruction is still perfectly feasible. Against phonemics of any kind: Archivio Glottologico Italiano 31.159 (1940)—one instance of many.

[23] Bloomfield, Language §5.10 (New York, 1933).

4. Preliminary Internal Reconstruction. The statement made above that in Bloomfield's Sketch all forms are phonemicized now has to be modified. His notation for O, and possibly for M and F, deviates from the phonemic 'ideal' in being somewhat more than phonemic.

In Southern O occur three varieties of vowels: long /ii ee aa oo/, short /i a o/, and ultra-short /ə u/. Within the limits of a word, the distribution of short and ultra-short vowels is almost, but not quite, predictable in terms of environment. Since the predictability is not complete, the distinction is phonemic: one must write /i a o/ and /ə u/ as they are heard. Bloomfield does not do so: he writes only ii ee aa oo and i a o, e.g. mittik instead of məttik 'tree'. For most Southern O dialects, one cannot tell whether the vowel in the first syllable—an ultra-short one—is /i/ or /a/, and phonemically one would have to use a special symbol /ə/; the same symbol would have to be used in a completely phonemic transcription of what Bloomfield transcribes as akkikk 'kettle', rather than the initial a of that form. O itself, and the diachronic analysis of the continuum from PA to O, are treated by Bloomfield in terms of this normalized notation. Can this procedure be justified?

The answer is yes. Bloomfield's notation is based on the preliminary internal reconstruction[24] of an O dialect-type that must have preceded the current dialects by only a relatively short period of time. The reconstruction is internal, not based on comparison of dialects, since the earlier stage can be postulated with validity on the basis of the data for any one dialect. If one compares phonemic /məttik/ 'tree' with /naməittəkoom/ 'my tree', and /əkkikk/ 'kettle' with /nəntakkəkkoom/ 'my kettle', one observes that /ə/ alternates (under statable conditions of word-rhythm) with both /i/ and /a/. There are a few cases in which no larger form can be found of the right rhythmic pattern to determine whether the alternation is with /i/ or with /a/, and in most of the dialects there are a few cases in which ultra-short vowels have disappeared altogether. Even in a synchronic description of O, however, the restoration of /i/ and /a/ rather than /ə/ in all such cases, with statements on the reduction of short vowels in words of each rhythmic pattern, is a necessary step for efficient treatment. One's working notation then becomes morphophonemic rather than purely phonemic; from the graphs /mittik/, /nimittikoom/, /akkikk/, /nintakkikkoom/, and the statements, one can infer the actual phonemic shape with very little difficulty.

In other words, what Bloomfield does in the case of O is to use a morphophonemically regularized notation instead of a straight phonemic transcription.

24 H. M. Hoenigswald, Internal Reconstruction, SIL 2.78–87 (1944); Sound Change and Linguistic Structure, Lang. 22.138–43 (1946) ((139)).

There is evidence of such regularization in M and F too. F forms are given with intervocalic /w/ and /y/, which are morphophonemically correct and which must have been phonemically correct in a slightly earlier stage, rather than with the curious alternation and evanescence that those morphophonemes now exhibit.[25] M is cited with five short and five long vowels, though Bloomfield himself has said that in actual pronunciation the three-way distinction of /i/ : /e/ : /ɛ/ is partly obscured.[26]

We deduce the following principle:

(i) Before comparative analysis is undertaken, each body of synchronic data should be examined carefully to see whether there are not internal clues, mainly morphophonemic, to the structure of the language at a slightly earlier stage. When there are, any possible internal reconstruction should be undertaken, since it will dispose of later innovations in each language, getting them out of the way for a clearer view of the deeper time-perspective of external comparison.

5. Assumptions about Directions of Linguistic Change. Bloomfield's description of Proto-Algonquian reveals it as a language of approximately the same degree of complexity as any one of the modern languages. Each of the modern languages has retained some of the features of the parent, lost some, and developed some new ones. F has the vocalic system of PA; C and O have one vowel fewer than PA; M has two more. The number of individual consonants in PA (excluding first members of clusters, §9) is greater than in any of the modern languages; it seems highly probable, however, that θ and s, and similarly t and č, which stand in close morphophonemic relation in PA, were at a slightly earlier stage allophones of single phonemes—perhaps, indeed, this was true even in PA times. The larger number of consonants in PA, then, was a temporary matter, the result of certain phonemic and analogic changes, and the number was later reduced in each line of development. The modal systems of verbs in the daughter languages correlate exactly only in a few cases. One suspects that some of the modes present in PA have split in some of the modern languages, and have been lost in others; certainly the

25 Obvious from Jones's texts; observed by the present writer in the Kickapoo and Sauk dialects of Fox.

26 Ref. 8, xiv: 'The texts are here recorded as they struck my ear. Analysis shows that this record (and therefore, if I heard aright, the actual pronunciation) largely obscures the distinction between three short front-vowel phonemes, which here appear as i and e.' Since Bloomfield became a fluent speaker of Menomini (a fact which he does not admit, but which is fairly obvious from his discussions), his recording is probably accurate. Nowadays we would cast his statement in the terminology of morphophonemics rather than phonemics, but the fact stated would not be altered.

total number of modes in PA did not exceed the rather large number in present-day F.[27]

(j) In undertaking a reconstruction, there is no justification for any of the following a-priori assumptions: (1) that the parent language was simpler than the descendants; (2) that it was more complex than the descendants; or (3) that it manifested about the same degree of complexity as the descendants.

The first of these a-priori assumptions is the old theory of the 'primitiveness' of 'early' language, and of contemporary languages spoken by 'simple' peoples.[28] The second is the inversion of the first brought about primarily by Jespersen's discussion.[29] More concrete suggestions, akin to one or the other, are also found.[30] All such theories derive from a hope which a hundred years ago was legitimate: that comparative linguistics might in time push our perspective on the history of language appreciably nearer the beginnings of human speech. Now that we realize how old human speech is, and what a scratch on the surface of that depth is our deepest reconstruction, the hope must be abandoned.

Bloomfield's PA reconstruction speaks not only against assumptions (1) and (2), but against any a-priori assumption of this kind whatsoever. In his paper of 1925 (Ref. 3), Bloomfield postulated two more vowels and one more consonant for PA than are included in the Sketch. Since then he has discovered the analogical bases, in certain of the individual languages, for the complications that had earlier led him to assume these additional phonemes. The first, more complex system was not set up because Bloomfield thought than an older language 'should be' more complex; nor did he later simplify the picture through any conviction that an older language 'should not be' more complex. In each case the assumed degree of complexity was simply an inference from the facts known about the modern languages.

27 Sketch §33.

28 Max Müller's myth of speakers with vocabularies of only a few hundred words is related. W. von Humboldt, Die Verschiedenheit des menschlichen Sprachbaues §19, gives three stages in the history of language: 'growth' before IE, a 'state of perfection' in IE, and 'decay' since then; for other early references see Lang. 12.101 (1936) and Italica 18.145–54 (1941). Later survivals of these older notions: the subject of review in Lang. 11.154–60 (1935); Emérita 3.257–76 (1935), esp. 272, 274–5; Alf Sommerfelt, La langue et la société (Oslo, 1938).

29 Otto Jespersen, Progress in Language (London, 1894); cf. also his Efficiency in Linguistic Change (Copenhagen, 1941), and the review in Lang. 17.350–3 (1941). Bernhard Karlgren, in reconstructing ancient and archaic Chinese, posits extremely complex phonological structure for those stages of Chinese, and seems (though without explicit reference) to justify this greater complexity for the older stage in terms of Jespersen's theory; see his Philology and Ancient China, esp. 16–18 (Oslo, 1926).

30 See more recent references in fn. 28.

6. The Assumption of Regular Phonemic Change. One story in the slow development of our understanding of PA is worth telling in detail, even though it is already perhaps the most generally known phase of Algonquian linguistics.

In his Sound System (Ref. 3) Bloomfield postulated the PA cluster çk (F O šk, C M hk) on very slim evidence. There was only one stem, meaning 'red', to be found which showed just this correspondence in the extant languages, and each of those languages had the cluster in question also as a reflex of one or more other PA clusters. Yet there seemed to be no analogical basis in any of the languages whereby a reconstruction could be made with a better attested PA cluster, and borrowing seemed unlikely in view of the meaning of the stem. There were a few other sets of apparently related words showing unique correspondences of clusters—'spoon' has F C hk, O kk, as though from PA hk, but M has sk instead of the hk which would arise from the latter. But these other cases are in morphologically isolated words, whereas the PA stem 'red' underlies many derivatives in every language.

A year or so later, it was discovered that Swampy Cree, a dialect from which records had not earlier been available, had in words containing this stem not hk but htk, a cluster not found in Swampy Cree as the reflex of any other PA cluster so far set up. Here was not merely an exceptional correspondence between usual clusters, but an extant dialect in which the postulated PA cluster is kept separate from all others. Bloomfield published a note giving this as evidence for the productivity of the assumption of regular phonemic change.[31] Sapir cited the case, together with a similar one from his own Athabascan work, in an article on the comparative method as one of the methods of social science.[32]

But the story did not end there. New investigators discovered that Jones had consistently misheard the O forms: the O words with this stem have sk, not šk, and this sk is not found as a reflex of any other PA cluster.[33] Swampy Cree no longer stood as the only extant dialect to keep PA çk separate; O was now known to do so too. Geary examined the missionary sources and discovered a number of other cases of the same correspondence, so that the stem for 'red' was no longer isolated—even though PA çk still seemed to be relatively rare. In his Sketch, Bloomfield includes a footnote: 'The fuss and trouble behind my note in Language [see above]...would have been avoided if I had listened to O, which plainly distinguishes sk (<PA çk) from šk (<PA šk); instead, I depended on printed records which failed to show the distinction.'[34]

31 Ref. 6.

32 Edward Sapir, The Concept of Phonetic Law as Tested in Primitive Languages by Leonard Bloomfield, Methods in Social Science 297–306 (ed. Stuart A. Rice; Chicago, 1931). Also Bloomfield, Language §20.8 (end).

33 See fn. 17, and Geary, loc.cit. 34 Sketch, fn. 10.

It should be clear that the wording of Bloomfield's note detracts in no way from the importance of the sequence of events outlined above as evidence for the productivity of the assumption we are discussing. After the publication of the Sound System, events might conceivably have taken a different turn. Instead of discovering additional cases of the same correspondence, Jones's error, and the special reflex in Swampy Cree, Algonquianists might have found an analogical basis or an opportunity for borrowing whereby PA çk could be eliminated. This turn of events would also have proved the fruitfulness of the assumption.

For what we mean in this case by 'productivity' or 'fruitfulness' is just what Bloomfield states in his book Language (§20.5): residual forms, not accounted for at a particular stage in the history of the reconstruction of a particular parent language either by well-attested sound change or by analogical formations or borrowing, or accounted for by postulated changes for which there is very little evidence—such residual forms stimulate further investigation. As a basis for further investigation, the linguist sets up hypotheses to explain what might have been the past history of certain forms. Many such hypotheses remain unproved, because additional investigation reveals no additional evidence; others are disproved by new evidence that is uncovered. But some of them are proved right. Slowly but surely the stock of residual forms is reduced, though it may never be exhausted. The contrary fundamental assumption—that sound changes proceed at random—produces nothing at all, because there are never any problems: given any form that won't fit the sound changes so far observed, one simply assums a sporadic change of a different sort.

(k) We must assume regularity of phonemic change.

7. The Wörter-und-Sachen Technique.[35] Bloomfield reconstructs PA paaškesikani 'gun' and eškoteewaapoowi 'whisky', both on the basis of perfectly normal correspondences between whole words in the extant languages. The items named by these terms, of course, are post-Columbian. The forms are compound; Bloomfield says in a footnote to the first that 'here, as in some other examples, the meaning is modern, but the habit of formation is old.'[36]

If only this is to be ascribed to pre-Columbian times, then each of the modern languages concerned has coined new terms for the new items of material culture, using identical (cognate) morphemes according to identical patterns of formation, in such a way that the phonemic correspondences between the whole words are perfect. But it might also be that the terms themselves date from PA times, and that since the introduction of whisky and guns by Europeans the semantic shifts have been parallel in the various languages. Or, as European influence spread, the forms may have been invented by the speakers of one language and then borrowed by loan-translation into the other languages.[37]

It does not matter, for our present purpose, which of these alternatives is true. The fact that from well-attested modern forms one can reconstruct PA forms with meanings that were obviously impossible for PA is a clear indication of danger in the Wörter-und-Sachen technique. We deduce the following composite principle:

(l) Attempts to infer the culture of the speakers of a reconstructed parent language wholly from the forms and meanings of the daughter languages are always dangerous. The danger is less, though probably still considerable, if the forms compared are morphologically simple than if they are compounds.

8. Drift. There are two versions of the theory of drift. One is almost mystical: in a particular linguistic continuum the same sound shifts may happen over and over again; there is something in the genius of the language which leads to these sound shifts rather than to others.[38] The other is realistic, and fairly simple: when a speech community has split, inherited speech habits are for a while fairly similar, and may lead to the independent analogical development of forms which look like inherited cognates. If at a later date the descendant languages are compared with a view to reconstruction of the parent, some such pseudo-cognates may be falsely ascribed to the parent language.[39] The Algonquian words for 'gun' and 'whisky', in all probability, are illustrations of this, though we cannot be absolutely sure.

(m) Any individual reconstructed form is suspect because of the possible influence of drift (in the second sense). In comparative linguistics one may achieve only statistical accuracy.

9. The Significance of Starred Forms. There have been two theories of reconstructed forms.[40] The so-

35 Bloomfield, Language §18.14, and his references.

36 Sketch, fn. 13.

37 The English expression fire-water may be a loan-translation from Algonquian; if the former is older, then one or more Algonquian languages may have loan-translated the English.

38 E. Prokosch, A Comparative Germanic Grammar, esp. 34 ff. (Philadelphia, 1939).

39 The discussion in Sapir's Language, chapters 7–8 (New York, 1921), is sufficiently broad to justify (apparently) either interpretation; for the realistic theory, see 184–5 in particular.

40 Cogently discussed by C. D. Buck, Some Questions of Practice in the Notation of Reconstructed IE Forms, Lang. 2.99–107 (1926). Buck says (102): the purpose of reconstructions 'is not to furnish a picture of the parent speech for its own sake, but as a background of the historical relations.' This is in part an answer to the charge of 'irrelevant antiquarianism' sometimes levelled at the comparative method; even so, we should say that 'a picture of the parent speech for its own sake', to the degree attainable, is also a legitimate aim.

called 'realistic' theory holds that in reconstructing the phonemic pattern of a parent language, one should try to arrive at a set of phonemes bearing a relation to each other of the kind that is known to exist in languages more directly observed. The 'formula' theory, on the other hand, holds that reconstructions are simply short notations representing sets of correspondences.

Bloomfield's Algonquian reconstructions show clearly the circumstances under which the first practice is possible, and those under which the second is necessary. The vowel system postulated for PA is certainly phonemically realistic, being identical with that of one modern language, F. The fundamental consonant system is also: p t č (possibly an allophone of t) k s θ š (possibly an allophone of θ) h l m n w y (the last two possibly allophones respectively of o and i). Of these, l m n (w y) were in all probability voiced; the others may have been voiced or voiceless, or perhaps were sometimes one and sometimes the other, without phonemic distinction.[41] θ may have been a voiceless lateral rather than an interdental spirant, or, again, perhaps both, depending on dialect or on environment.[42] The phonetic details are naturally obscure; it is the phonemic pattern which we claim to be 'realistic'.[43] The only type of doubt which could be raised as to the status of these elements as the actual phonemes of PA would be purely logistic: if, for example, every daughter language had, independently, changed PA m to n and PA n to m, no one could be the wiser. One could even claim that such a change would be subphonemic; in any case such possibilities need not disturb us.

When it comes to medial clusters, the situation is different. Medial clusters consist of two members; the second is always clearly identifiable as one of the ordinary consonants; but the multiplicity of correspondences requires the postulation of a somewhat larger number of purely arbitrary elements as prior members.[44] Thirty-one different medial clusters are attested; no one of them has identical reflexes in all four of the modern languages.[45]

In this case all one can do is to choose for the prior members a set of symbols which will have, if possible, some mnemonic value; e.g. PA mp nt nč nk ns nš nθ nl for clusters which in O have a nasal as first element, especially since such clusters in O occur only as reflexes of this set in PA.

Similarly, instead of writing çk for the PA cluster which gives F šk, C M hk, O sk, one could write sk, which is not otherwise used. It may well be that the PA clusters customarily written mp, nt, etc. actually had a nasal as first element. It may also be that PA çk was phonemically sk, the first element being phonemically identical with the independently occurring PA s. But the use of these notations for mnemonic reasons is not evidence for such a phonemic interpretation: one may attain a spurious appearance of realism, but the actual phonemic nature of the first members of the clusters is still as obscure as before.

That the number of medial clusters in PA was larger than the number in any descendant language is surprising only to one who is not familiar with aspects of Algonquian linguistics other than phonology. In most of the modern languages there is a sandhi habit whereby an element ending in a consonant, when due to be followed in the same word by one beginning with a consonant, is separated therefrom by a non-morphemic i.[46] This habit existed in PA times, but was then apparently rather new. The new habit prevented the re-formation of many clusters that had formerly existed; but compounds surviving from an earlier stage retained the more complex consonantism. The trend towards simplification of the cluster system was a characteristic of PA which continued in the various separate dialects after their split, but the details varied from one dialect to another. Some of the pre-PA compounds are reconstructible from the modern languages, giving an essential clue to the statements just made; most, however, remain obscure.[47]

Thus it is quite possible that Algonquian research may in time produce evidence that will make the interpretation of the prior members of PA consonant clusters less purely algebraic. Only a deeper time-perspective, achieved by more detailed comparisons with Algonquian languages not of the Central Algonquian type, can do this. In the meantime, to underscore the point, 'realism' in this phase of the reconstruction of PA can only be spurious.

(n) Reconstruction should be phonemically realistic whenever possible.

(o) When realistic reconstruction is not possible, arbitrary indices of correspondences must be used. The fact that they are arbitrary, and the reasons which necessitate this arbitrariness, should be clearly stated. This practice will prevent a spurious impression of realism on the reader, and will obviate futile speculation on his part as to what the arbitrarily symbolized elements may 'really' have been.

41 Sketch, §6.

42 Loc. cit.

43 In several recent papers (Lang. 20.84–6 [1944], 23.34–42 [1947]), Herbert Penzl has demonstrated, in connection with problems of early English, the difference between phonemic realism and what might be meant by phonetic realism.

44 Sketch, §7.

45 Since the phonemic systems of the modern languages are different, 'identical' must be interpreted relatively: since F and O š and k are elements in differing sets of contrasts, F šk and O šk are not in any absolute sense 'identical'.

46 Sketch, §16.

47 Sketch, §17.

10. Negative Lessons. This paper could not serve its purpose fully without mentioning a few points on which, in the present writer's opinion, Bloomfield's Sketch can be misleading.

(1) Bloomfield labels his reconstructed prototype 'Proto-Algonquian'. It is based mainly on the comparison of F, C, M, and O; eastern Algonquian and the three groups of Plains languages are not often brought into the picture. Indeed, it would be difficult to include more mention of them in the present state of our knowledge. In feeling that the PA reconstructed in his Sketch will take care of the Plains languages, Bloomfield gives Michelson's work in the comparative analysis of the latter languages more credit than it deserves.[48] The course of wisdom for the reader of Bloomfield's Sketch is to replace 'PA' everywhere by 'PCA', standing for 'Proto-Central-Algonquian', and to withhold judgment on the status of the eastern and Plains languages until a good deal more of descriptive and comparative work has been done.

(2) Bloomfield says, 'before syllabic vowels, PA i, o are nonsyllabic; we write y, w.'[49] The phonemic status of y and w is another point on which judgment is best reserved. Bloomfield's notation (with all four symbols i o y w) is good; his statement seems hasty.

(3) Bloomfield cites Penobscot forms from Siebert, following Siebert's orthography except that accent marks are omitted. This conceals the fact that a number of the eastern languages of the family have an accentual system, more or less complex but definitely phonemic; these accentual systems have to be taken care of in the reconstruction of anything that can be called Proto-Algonquian. Exact citation of Siebert's forms, including the accent marks (perhaps with a footnote), would have been more in line with the general principles on which Bloomfield's work is based.

Point (3) turns on the discussion of §2 and §3 in this paper. Point (2) is connected with the content of §9. From point (1) we derive our last principle:

(p) A parent language reconstructed from the comparison of a certain set of daughter languages can be regarded as the parent only of the languages so used. Information from languages not previously used may change the reconstruction, deepen the time-perspective with a new reconstruction of an earlier stage, or demonstrate that the reconstruction already made is capable of handling the new data also.[50]

Conclusion. The sixteen principles which have been listed in the course of our discussion are not new or startling; indeed, by this time each of them ought to be so generally agreed upon that any mention of them, save in the most elementary textbooks of linguistics, would be ridiculous. We have unhappily not yet reached such uniformity of opinion about fundamentals. Yet if, for any one of the sixteen, Bloomfield's Algonquian evidence stood alone—if there were no comparative Germanic, comparative Romance, comparative Indo-European, comparative Semitic, and so on—that isolated support for the principle would still be persuasively solid.

48 Sketch, §2, referring to T. Michelson, Phonetic Shifts in Algonquian Languages, IJAL 8.131–71 (1935). The implication here is not that Michelson's study is not 'brilliant', as Bloomfield terms it, but that the synchronic information on Plains Algonquian available to Michelson was unsatisfactory.

49 Sketch, §4.

50 Thus Potawatomi is probably historically analyzable on the basis of Bloomfield's P(C)A without modification thereof (C. F. Hockett, The Position of Potawatomi in Central Algonkian, Papers of the Michigan Academy of Sciences, Arts, and Letters 28.537–42 [1942]); but Delaware is probably not (C. F. Voegelin, Proto-Algonquian Consonant Clusters in Delaware, Lang. 17.143–7 [1941]).

THE PREHISTORIC GERMANIC SHORT SYLLABICS

W. FREEMAN TWADDELL
Language 24.139–51—1948

Our reconstruction of a proto-language is theoretical and partial; but the language itself was necessarily real and whole. As a real language, it shared with all real languages the characteristic of non-uniformity. Some of its speakers spoke differently from others; they spoke differently from their linguistic predecessors and successors. And at any time, in any dialect, the phonemes of a real language display variations in different phonetic environments. In short, the language which our reconstructions adumbrate had linguistic change; it had isoglosses; and it had allophones.

The normal purpose of reconstruction is to establish a single formula which can be regarded as a starting point for subsequent evolutions. This purpose involves necessarily an emphasis on maximum simplicity and an intentional neglect of non-uniformities. A reconstructed Proto-Germanic form, for example, is designed to display with a minimum of complication the relations of Gothic, Norse, Old English, Old Saxon, and Old High German to each other, and to provide a plausible formula from which the historical forms in the historical languages can all be derived, by definite and consistent changes. A successful reconstruction transcends the several changes; it antedates dialect differences which appear in the sequel-languages; and it is a phonemic formula, not a phonetic description.

The fruitfulness of such reconstructions is attested by a century of scholarship; the punctuation (*) is established, and the terms Proto-, Ur-, Primitive are firmly attached to formulae which are timeless, non-dialectal, and non-phonetic.

This paper is an essay in a different type of reconstruction. Here an attempt is made to examine an unrecorded language as though it were real; to describe changes, isoglosses, and allophones in one portion of the structure of that unrecorded language. The language will be given the colorless and noncommittal name of Prehistoric Germanic. The portion of the structure is that which can be called the short syllabics of stressed syllables, here written /i, e, a, o, u/.[1]

The earliest set of short syllabics which it is profitable to attribute to Prehistoric Germanic can be written thus: /i, e, a, u/. This system is a starting point for a specifically Germanic structural history. We can regard these phonemes as independent of IE accentual conditions; they are not allophones determined by this or that condition of IE stress or pitch. Indeed, in a fairly early stage of Prehistoric Germanic, a stress accent is regularly associated with the root syllables; and the syllabics that we are concerned with are those of stressed syllables in Prehistoric Germanic.

Of the phonetic character of these phonemes it can be said that /i/ and /u/ were relatively high, /a/ relatively low, and /e/ relatively mid. The phonemes /i/ and /e/ were relatively front or lip-spread; /u/ was relatively back or lip-rounded; /a/ was central or lip-neutral. Distributionally, we note that /i/ occurred only (or almost only) before obstruent consonants (stops and spirants), while /e/, /a/, and /u/ occurred before obstruents and resonants (nasals and /l, r/).

From the phonetic point of view, the system was somewhat asymmetrical. It had a phonetic contrast between front and back, or lip-spread and lip-rounded: /i/ vs. /u/. The /e/ phoneme shared frontness or lip-spreading with /i/; the /a/ phoneme was neutral with respect to this contrast, being central or lip-neutral. The system also had a contrast between high and low tongue position: /i/ and /u/ are high, /a/ is low. In the category front or lip-spread and not low, there were two phonemes: /i/ and /e/; we must describe /i/ as high and /e/ as mid. There was no such contrast in the category back or lip-rounded and not low. In that category there was only one phoneme, /u/.

This asymmetry is of course nothing impossible or unnatural. Real languages frequently show asymmetry at one or another point in their phonemic systems, and so may a reconstructed language. But symmetry is commoner than asymmetry, and structural changes from asymmetry to symmetry are

[1] The sound changes discussed in this study are described in the handbooks, in detail and with examples. Reference can be made to Kluge, Urgermanisch[3] 106 ff., 120 ff.; Hirt, Handbuch des Urgermanischen 1.30 ff.; Prokosch, A comparative Germanic grammar 93 ff., 100 ff., 112 ff. Historical surveys of the important investigations can be found in Streitberg-Michels-Jellinek, Germanisch 1.357 ff. (= Die Erforschung der idg. Sprachen II), and in L. E. van Wijk's De klinkers der oergermaanse stamsyllaben in hun onderling verband (Utrecht proefschrift, 1936). H. M. Hoenigswald, Sound change and linguistic structure, Lang. 22.138 ff. (1946) ((139)), gives a comprehensive theoretical survey of the relations between phonetic changes and the restructuring of allophones and phonemes.

commoner than the reverse. One would therefore not be surprised to see structural developments in the direction of symmetry.

There seem to be three theoretically possible simple developments toward symmetry:

1. The /a/ phoneme might become a back or lip-rounded vowel, remaining low. Then the /e/ phoneme might become a low vowel, remaining front or lip-spread. The result would be a simple symmetrical system, with two contrasts: high vs. low, front (lip-spread) vs. back (lip-rounded).

	Front Spread	Back Rounded
High	i	u
Low	e [æ]	a [ɔ]

This theoretically possible development did not occur.

2. The /i/ and /e/ phonemes might coalesce, perhaps completely, perhaps as allophones. The result would be a fairly simple system, with one main contrast: high vs. low, and a minor contrast between the two high phonemes: front (lip-spread) vs. back (lip-rounded).

	Front Spread	Central Neutral	Back Rounded
High	i		u
Low		a	

This development did occur, in varying degrees and through various rearrangements of allophones, in some Prehistoric Germanic dialects.

3. The /u/ phoneme might undergo fission into two phonemes, through the development of allophones and the subsequent promotion of these allophones to phonemes. This would result in a symmetrical system, with a triple contrast of high vs. mid vs. low, and a double contrast in high and mid vowels of front (lip-spread) vs. back (lip-rounded).

	Front Spread	Central Neutral	Back Rounded
High	i		u
Mid	e		o
Low		a	

This development also occurred in some Prehistoric Germanic dialects.

The distribution of the four phonemes /i, e, a, u/ of early Prehistoric Germanic is also asymmetrical in at least one important respect. All four phonemes occurred regularly before obstruent consonants. But before the resonant consonants, only /e/, /a/, and /u/ occurred regularly; /i/ before resonants was at best very rare, if indeed the combination ever occurred. The /i/ phoneme was thus distributionally defective, in that it occurred only before obstruents, whereas its 'neighbor' /e/ occurred before both obstruents and resonants. The way is accordingly open for the /e/ phoneme to develop [i]-like allophones before resonants, since the /i/ phoneme is defective in not occurring there.

These phonetic and distributional asymmetries have implications. Phonetically, the phoneme /u/ obviously permits a wide range of variation in pronunciation. It is the only vowel phoneme of the system which was back or lip-rounded. Any pronunciation, from [u] to [ɔ], would be possible as a free variant or allophone of the /u/ phoneme. This consideration makes it seem rather futile for so many investigators to have argued the possibility that IE syllabic /m, n, r, l/ became Proto-Germanic [om, on, or, ol] rather than [um, un, ur, ul]. It makes not the slightest difference, from the structural point of view, since in either pronunciation the vowel would have been an allophone of the same phoneme, capable of precisely the same phonemic and allophonic distributions in subsequent structural changes.

Phonetically and distributionally, the phonemes /i/ and /e/ may be suspected of subsequent instability. Phonetically, they were the only short vowels involved in a high-vs.-mid contrast; together, they shared a range of phonetic variation comparable to that which was available to the /u/ phoneme alone. Distributionally, they were partially in direct contrast (both occurred before obstruents), partially in complementary distribution (/e/ occurred before resonants, /i/ did not). In one other respect, /i/ and /e/ were in complementary distribution: historically, no words in late Indo-European had /i/ in two successive syllables, nor did /i/ occur before /j/ of a following syllable. Historically, /e/ occurred before /i/ or /j/ of a following syllable. Analogies and inter-dialect borrowing probably created some exceptions to this historical state of affairs, but apparently not many in early Prehistoric Germanic.

We shall accordingly not be surprised to find the first new allophones of Prehistoric Germanic developing in the /i/ and /e/ phonemes.

Preh. Gmc. /e/ developed relatively high allophones before certain resonants (nasal followed by consonant) and before syllables with /i/ or /j/. These high allophones proved to be structurally important. As we have just seen, /i/ did not occur in these positions. The new allophones of /e/ were, therefore, in complementary distribution to all allophones of /i/, and to all other allophones of /e/. A redistribution of these high /e/ allophones took place, in that they functioned as allophones of /i/. Examples: Gk. estí, Lat. est : Gmc. ist 'is'; Lat. medius : OE midd, OHG mitti 'middle'; Lat. uentus : OE wind, OHG uuint 'wind'; Lat. of-fend-imentum : OE bindan, OHG bintan 'bind'. But Lat. edere : OE etan 'eat'; Lat. decem : OHG zehan 'ten'; Lat. pecu(s) : OS fehu 'cattle'.

The combined picture of /i/ and /e/ allophones looked like this:

before resonant alone		[e]
before nasal + consonant	[i]	
before /r, l/ + consonant		[e]
before obstruent + /i, j/	[i]	
before obstruent + /u, a/	[i]	[e]

Only in the position before obstruent + /u, a/ did the phonemes /i/ and /e/ contrast with one another. In the other positions, each was in complementary distribution with the other. Were /i/ and /e/ on the way to becoming a single phoneme? This question, the most perplexing in the history of the Prehistoric Germanic short syllabics, will occupy us soon.

Meanwhile, we must note that /u/, the one back (or lip-rounded) high vowel, was developing allophones under comparable conditions. Before nasal + consonant, and before syllables with high vowels (/i/ and /u/), a higher allophone was developed. No possibility of redistribution existed here, of course, since /u/ was the only phoneme in the high back (or lip-rounded) classification. Before low vowels in the following syllable, a lower allophone was developed; this lower [o] sound remained an allophone of the /u/ phoneme.

Now to return to the front (or lip-spread) syllabics /i/ and /e/. Did /i/ and /e/ become one phoneme? E. Prokosch[2] answers with caution and evident embarrassment: 'This seems to indicate that Gmc. i and e were practically one "phoneme".' 'Practically one phoneme' certainly seems to be an odd expression; but it is excusable in the complicated situation of Middle Prehistoric Germanic /i/ and /e/.

These phonemes /i/ and /e/ were partly in direct contrast with one another (before obstruent + /u, a/), partly in complementary distribution (under other phonetic circumstances). To understand the development of allophones and the redistribution of allophones here, let us look forward to the several Germanic languages, rather than back to an earlier structural phase.

We must first distinguish two major dialects of Prehistoric Germanic in terms of developments from the situation sketched above: Pre-Gothic on the one hand, all the remaining dialects on the other.

In Pre-Gothic the situation was fairly simple. Gothic, as recorded in the late 4th century, points fairly clearly to an earlier, Pre-Gothic structure, in which there were only three short-syllabic phonemes, which we can write /i, a, u/. Both /i/ and /u/ had a clearly marked allophonic structure, and the two phonemes /i/ and /u/ were almost entirely parallel. The determinant of the allophonic distribution of /i/ and /u/ in stressed syllables was the consonant which followed. Before most consonants, a high allophone appeared: [i] or [u]. Before /h/, before [r], or when no consonant followed (open internal juncture, e.g. in the reduplicating syllable of certain past tense verbs), a low allophone appeared: [e] or [o]. (In unstressed syllables, the higher allophone appeared.) The Pre-Gothic structure was thus simple and symmetrical:

```
    [i]      [u]
  i              u
    [e]      [o]
         a
```

In Pre-Gothic, the /h, r, -/ determinant overrode earlier Preh. Gmc. allophone determinants. Specifically, the change of /e/ to /i/ before /i, j/ in the next syllable was completely superseded, if the syllabic in question was followed by /h, r, -/. Examples: the accusative singular of 'shepherd' [herdi], or the dative singular [herdja].

By the late 4th century, when Gothic was recorded, we can detect signs of a breakdown in this distribution. There are cases in which [i] as well as [e] occurred before /h, r/, and other cases in which [e] as well as [i] occurred before other consonants. In other words, the primacy of /h, r, -/ as allophone determinants was infringed by one or more new determinants, perhaps patterns of pitch or a more complex stress pattern, certainly reinforced by vocabulary borrowings from Greek and Latin, where a five-phoneme short-vowel system had /i/ and /e/ as distinct phonemes, as well as /u/ and /o/. The very fact that Bishop Wulfila made it possible for us to distinguish the high and mid allophones by writing them differently is an indication that these allophones could be promoted to phonemes.[3]

But this was a specifically Gothic development, and, as such, later than the Preh. Gmc. structure that here concerns us. We can confidently set up a three-vowel system for the Pre-Gothic dialect of Prehistoric Germanic, with following /h, r, -/ as the determinant of low allophones of stressed /i/ and /u/.

In the other dialects of Prehistoric Germanic, the developments were less simple. All the North Germanic and West Germanic languages, by the time they were recorded, point toward a previous stage with a five-phoneme short-syllabic system:

```
  i        u
  e        o
       a
```

The most striking element of this diagram is of course the presence of /o/ as a phoneme distinct from /u/. Obviously, a distinct phoneme /o/ could develop only through three stages: (1) An earlier phoneme (/u/ in this case) developed an allophone [o].

[2] A comparative Germanic grammar 109. Cf. A. Meillet, Caractères généraux des langues germaniques[3] 61 (Paris, 1926): 'Tout se passe donc à peu de chose près comme s'il y avait en germanique commun une voyelle unique, qui deviendrait i ou e suivant les cas.'

[3] Cf. W. G. Moulton, The phonemes of Gothic, Lang. 24.76 ff. (1948).

(2) The determining conditions of the distribution [o] vs. [u] were superseded by new conditions, in which [o] contrasted directly with [u]. (3) [o] was promoted from allophonic to phonemic status.

Our first task, then, is to reconstruct the stage in which [o] and [u] were allophones of the same phoneme, a back (or lip-rounded) relatively high vowel phoneme. This is easy. Despite subsequent disturbances by analogies and by new allophones, we can state with assurance that in these dialects [u] and [o] had been allophones of the same phoneme. The determinants were these:

in monosyllables:	[u]	
before high vowels:	[u]	
before low vowels:		[o]
(except) before nasal + cons.:	[u]	

Examples: Gmc. *furi : OHG furi 'before'; Gmc. *fura : OHG fora 'before'; Gmc. *wurða : OHG uuort 'word'; Gmc. *juha : OHG joh 'yoke'; Gmc. *sunus : OE sunu 'son'; Gmc. *hunða : OHG hund 'hundred'.

This development of a low allophone [o] was a phonetic change, a change in pronunciation, which involved no structural disturbances. Like most phonetic changes, it presumably started in one community and spread: the isogloss expanded. In this case, the isogloss expanded to the extent of all the Preh. Gmc. dialects except Pre-Gothic. (Perhaps even Pre-Gothic was affected; we have no way of telling. For as long as [u] and [o] were allophones of one phoneme, the /h, r, -/ determinant would create new allophonic distributions which would wholly obliterate any older allophones.)

Let us pause at this stage and study the overall structure of the short-syllabic system in these (non-Gothic) dialects of Prehistoric Germanic. For the moment, let us consider allophones only:

before nasal + consonant:	[i]		[a]		[u]
before /i, j/ in following syllable:	[i]		[a]		[u]
before /u/ in following syllable:	[i]	[e]	[a]		[u]
before low vowel in following syl.:	[i]	[e]	[a]	[o]	

The speakers of these dialects had three different phonemes before nasal + consonant: /i, a, u/. They had the same three before /i, j/ in the following syllable. In these phonetic circumstances, they had a two-contrast system of syllabics: high vs. low; front (lip-spread) vs. back (lip-rounded).

Before /u/ or a low vowel in the following syllable, these dialects had a more complex short-syllabic system: front (lip-spread) /i, e/ vs. back (lip-rounded) [u] and [o]. In the front (lip-spread) category there was a triple contrast of high vs. mid vs. low: /i, e, a/. But in the back (lip-rounded) category there was only a double contrast: before /u/, high vs. low: [u], /a/; before low vowels, mid vs. low: [o], /a/.

The critical asymmetry was the situation as between /i/ and /e/ before /u/ and before low vowel in the following syllable.

We have seen how Pre-Gothic achieved symmetry. It was by an allophonic development of [i, e] and [u, o], determined by the following consonant (the /h, r, -/ determinant). This development affected the two originally distinct phonemes /i/ and /e/ as precisely parallel to the one phoneme /u/.

This complete parallelism in the Pre-Gothic treatment of /i, e/ and /u/, and the partial parallelism is the other dialects, has attracted Germanists for the past century and a quarter. For a half century after Jakob Grimm's first attack on this problem, it was agreed that the two developments were parallel. Then discoveries of the Proto-IE vowel system revealed certain major difficulties. There have been several attempts to reassert parallelism;[4] but Germanists since the 1870s have had to accept the asymmetry.

The tantalizing feature of the situation is that we can see signs of developments toward symmetry.

Where is the critical difficulty? Obviously in the existence of two distinct phonemes /i/ and /e/, while [u] and [o] are merely allophones of one phoneme. Did /i/ and /e/ contrast phonemically in all phonetic circumstances? By no means. Before nasal + consonant there was no contrast between /i/ and /e/; before /i, j/ of the following syllable there was no contrast: under these conditions there was only /i/ in the one series, parallel to [u] in the other.

No: the critical asymmetry existed only before /u/ or low vowel of the following syllable. Here there were both /i/ and /e/, while in the other series the [u] allophone occurred before /u/, the [o] allophone before low vowels.

If the phonemes /i/ and /e/ had developed new allophones under these conditions, a very slight rearrangement would have created complete parallelism. If /e/ had developed a higher allophone before /u/, and if /i/ had developed a lower allophone before low vowels, the parallelism would have been there. And precisely these developments did occur—but only in some cases in some dialects.

There were cases of [e] > [i] before /u/, chiefly in OHG and OSaxon. Examples: Gmc. *fehu : OSax. fehu, OHG fihu 'cattle'; Gmc. *seƀun : OHG sibun 'seven'; Gmc. *meðu : OHG metu, mitu 'mead'.

There were cases of [i] > [e] before low vowel, fairly numerous cases, in all the non-Gothic dialects, but most strongly represented in OHG: Gmc. *wira : OE, OSax., OHG wer 'man'; Gmc. *kwika : OE cwicu, OIcel. kuikr, OHG quec 'alive'; Gmc. *libēn : OE libban, OHG leben 'live'; Gmc. *nista : OE, OHG nest 'nest'; Gmc. *likkōn : OSax. liccon, OHG leccon 'lick'; Gmc. *niþan : OIcel. neþan, OHG nidana 'from below'; Gmc. *biðanar : OIcel. beþenn, OHG (gi)bitan 'waited' (ppl.).

[4] For example Otto Bremer's powerful article, Die germanische Brechung, IF 26.148 ff.

But these developments were not complete. At no time, in any North or West Germanic language accessible to us, can we postulate a complete coalescence of the /i/ and /e/ phonemes.

The picture is obviously too complex to admit either of the two simple answers: either that /i/ and /e/ became allophones of one phoneme, or that /i/ and /e/ were entirely distinct phonemes. Prokosch's characterization 'practically one phoneme' is symptomatic of the ambiguous relationship.

We cannot say that /i/ and /e/ were allophones of the same phoneme, because they both occurred, in contrast with each other, in certain phonetic circumstances. And yet the distribution of /i/ and /e/ was complementary in too many respects to justify treating them as two normal distinct phonemes.

A key to an understanding of this situation is supplied by H. Collitz in an article called Early Germanic Vocalism (1918).[5] The view that Collitz here elaborates was first put forward by him in an article called Das Analogiegesetz der westgermanischen Ablautsreihen (1905).[6] Not that Collitz's suggestion, as he made it, is acceptable (he proposed successive phonetic changes, of varying degrees of completeness); it has been either explicitly denied or ignored by most recent writers. Collitz of course was unable to operate with phonemes and allophones. And the apparatus of linguistic geography, available in 1918, apparently did not appeal to him. He accordingly tried to work solely with the classic linguistic methology of successive phonetic changes and analogies; and that methodology is simply too rigid and crude for this problem. In the description that follows, Collitz's thesis is treated as an aperçu, and developed in terms of modern structural linguistics and linguistic geography.

The Middle Preh. Gmc. period presents a picture of three different phonemic arrangements of the sounds [i] and [e], and [u] and [o]. One of these arrangements, the Pre-Gothic, was symmetrical: it combined [i] and [e] as allophones of one phoneme, [u] and [o] as allophones of another. A second arrangement was potentially symmetrical: here /e/ developed a high allophone [ɪ] before /u/, which was potentially assignable to the /i/ phoneme; and /i/ developed a low allophone [ᴇ] before low vowels, which was potentially assignable to the /e/ phoneme:

/i/ [i] — [ᴇ] before low vowel
/u/ [u] before high vowel — [u] bef. nasal + cons. — [o] before low vowel
/e/ [ɪ] before /u/ — [e]
/a/

In so far as these [ᴇ] and [ɪ] allophones were redistributed, all the [i] and [e] sounds would be in complementary distribution. We should then have had [i] before nasal + consonant, and before high vowel, [e] before low vowel except when nasal and consonant intervened.

This development did not proceed to completion in any Prehistoric Germanic dialect we can reconstruct. And we have no right to invent, for our convenience, a lost dialect in which it did occur. We must be content with the facts as we find them, and say that in some Preh. Gmc. dialects these allophones developed, but that the rearrangement by new assignment to phonemes did not occur.

The third arrangement was simply the old distribution, in which /i/ and /e/ were in contrast before /u/ and before low vowels, except where nasal + consonant intervened. This third arrangement implies, of course, that no new allophones of /i/ and /e/ were developed. This arrangement may have been associated with certain changes in the vowel of unstressed syllables: an early weakening of some unstressed vowels to [ə], or their complete disappearance. If so, the absence of high-low allophones of /i/ and /e/ was a necessary consequence. Also, the old allophones of /u/, [u] and [o], would be promoted to phonemic status. For as soon as there was no contrast between high and low vowels in unaccented following syllables, the sounds [u] and [o] would contrast with one another, and be separate phonemes:

/i/ /u/
/e/ /o/
/a/

The three arrangements would then have had the following repertories of short-syllabic phonemes other than /a/:

I	II	III
/i/ [i] usually	/i/ [i] nasal cons.	/i/ [i] nasal cons.
/i/ [e] /h, r, -/	/i/ [i] /i, j/	/i/ [i] /i, j/
	/i/ [ᴇ] low vowel	/i/ [i] /ə, -/
	/e/ [ɪ] /u/	/e/ [e] /u/
	/e/ [e] low vowel	/e/ [e] /ə, -/
/u/ [u] usually	/u/ [u] nasal cons.	/u/ [u] nasal cons., /ə, -/
/u/ [o] /h, r, -/	/u/ [u] high vowel	/u/ [u] high vowel
	/u/ [o] low vowel	/o/ [o] /ə, -/

Here was a situation familiar to students of dialect geography: three different allophonic structures within a linguistic region. And no student of dialect geography is surprised at what happened. The isoglosses shifted, expanded and contracted, irregularly, word by word, form-class by form-class.

[5] MLN 33.321 ff. (1918).

[6] MLN 20.65 ff. (1905). Also Segimer, JEGP 6.279 ff. (1907).

The Pre-Gothic structure (type I) was the most compact and relatively invulnerable to influence from other structural types. Unaffected itself, this structural arrangement did influence other dialects. Pre-Norse developed low allophones of /i/ and /u/ before /h/; these allophones were reassigned to /e/ and /o/ and shared in the later developments of the /e/ and /o/ phonemes (A. Heusler, Altisländisches Elementarbuch[2] §86). The same development occurred in Pre-Norse before /ʀ/ (op.cit. §83). This is striking: the /ʀ/ which determined low allophones of /i/ and /u/ was the new /ʀ/, developed from /z/, not the old /r/ which was historically cognate with Gothic /r/. This is clearly not a case of borrowed vocabulary; it unmistakably was the spread of a phonetic characteristic. In Pre-OHG there were cases which show /i/ developing a low allophone before /r/, with subsequent reassignment of this allophone to the /e/ phoneme (G. Baesecke, Einführung in das Althochdeutsche 29).

The second structure was the one in which /e/ developed a high allophone [ɪ] before /u/, and /i/ developed a low allophone [ᴇ] before low vowels. This structural type could spread, and did. Isoglosses of [i]>[e] spread, word by word, through all the non-Gothic dialects. Norse, Old English, Old Saxon, Old High German all show a number of words with /e/ where there had been an old /i/ before a low vowel.

We are dealing here with the mutual influences of neighboring dialects, those of the second and third structural types above.

In dialects of the second type, there were high [ɪ] allophones of /e/ before /u/, and there were low [ᴇ] allophones of /i/ before a low vowel. In these dialects, the new allophones represented changes in pronunciation, not in phonemic structure. The new allophone [ᴇ], though [e]-like, was still an allophone of the /i/ phoneme.

But the neighboring dialect of the third structural type had developed no such low allophone of /i/. It presumably had lost many of its low unstressed vowels, by reduction to [ə] or by complete loss. In this third type of dialect, /i/ and /e/ were of course distinct phonemes, and there were no low [e]-like allophones of /i/.

Now, a dialect of type III borrowed a word (say /sila/) from a type II dialect. Structurally, phonemically, this word had /i/ before low vowel. In the type II dialect, it had the phonetic form of the low allophone of /i/: [sᴇla]. To speakers of a type III dialect, this phonetic form represent /selə/, and would be borrowed as such.

Conversely, a type II dialect borrowed a word from a type III dialect. Such a word as /rimə/ would have the phonetic form [i] before /ə/: [rimə]. In a type II dialect, [ə] was a non-native sound; it would be assigned either as a variant of a low vowel, or as in free variation with no vowel at all: zero. If [ə] were assigned as a variant of a low vowel, then the borrowed word would develop the usual low [ᴇ] allophone of /i/ of type II dialects: [rᴇma] /rima/. But if [ə] were assigned as a variant of no vowel at all, then the /i/ of the borrowed word would appear as the normal high allophone of /i/: /rim/ [rim].

The picture presented here is one of flux, of shifting isoglosses. Given enough time, with stability of the determining conditions, we should expect some kind of settling down throughout the dialects of the second and third types. This might have taken place in either direction, either the complete independence of /i/ and /e/, or a reassignment of their allophones so that they were in complementary distribution, and thus one phoneme.

Neither happened; for the determining conditions did not remain stable. The unstressed vowels of final syllables became reduced to [ə] or were lost. One final result of this loss of the high-low contrast in following syllables was to promote [u] and [o] to phonemic status in the back or lip-rounded series.

No such simple resolution occurred in the front or lip-spread series. Here there had been two phonemes—partly in complementary distribution, to be sure, but still two phonemes. As the high-low contrast of unstressed final vowels was lost, the distinction between /i/ and /e/ was preserved, and no coalescence took place. The words which had earlier had the form /i/ [ᴇ] before low vowel were randomly assigned to either /i/ or /e/, lexical and grammatical analogies playing a deciding role. The details are in the handbooks.

Further, a major new development sets in. A new determinant of allophonic distribution arises, the last of the Preh. Gmc. structural evolutions.

Prehistoric Germanic, in this fairly late stage, was divided by a major structural isogloss, so far as the short stressed syllabics were concerned. One type (Pre-Gothic) was a three-phoneme system: /i/ [i, e]; /a/; /u/ [u, o]; the following consonant determined the allophones. The other type, Pre-Norse and Pre-West-Germanic, was a five-phoneme system: /i/, /e/, /a/, /o/, /u/.

The five-phoneme system had come into existence when the old distinction between following low and high vowels was lost or blurred by the reduction of such following vowels to [ə] or zero. This reduction took place at different times in the various dialects, with the several vowels, and after different types of root syllables.

This step-by-step loss of the high-low allophones left some confusion in grammatical forms. A given noun might have [u] in some cases, [o] in others, depending upon the original following vowel. Once the complete phonemic distinctness of /u/ and /o/ had been established, this confusion was usually leveled out analogically, by the spread of one phoneme or the other. The result was that a given word, by and large, had a particular phoneme throughout all its inflectional forms.

Then something happened to introduce a new type of allophonic structure. Before /i/, /ī/, or /j/ of a following unstressed syllable, special allophones of /u/, /o/, and /a/ developed (Umlaut). These /i, ī, j/ determinants were in part old endings. But some important new tendencies in Preh. Gmc. word formation introduced a decisive number of new /i, ī, j/ in unstressed syllables. One may note such unstressed syllables as īn, isk, ig, līk, as adjective suffixes. These were not all new Germanic suffixes, but they were wide-spread and productive in Prehistoric Germanic; they were freely combinable with a wide range of word stems. Very important also is the wide spread of the jan suffix for verbs.

At first, the combination of one of these /i, ī, j/ suffixes probably produced merely the ordinary high allophone: [u] instead of [o], or [i] instead of [e]. But when these /i, ī, j/ suffixes were in their period of flourishing free combinability, the syllabics /u/ and /o/, /i/ and /e/, were distinct and separate phonemes. Accordingly, these suffixes with /i, ī, j/ determined [i]-like allophones of the preceding stressed vowel.

The reader has certainly noticed earlier in this paper the expressions front or lip-spread vowels and back or lip-rounded vowels. The standard description is simply front and back. I have used the more cumbersome expression in preparation for this point of structural development.

For now the development of allophones before /i, ī, j/ requires the description of /u/ and /o/ as primarily lip-rounded vowels. The contrast between the high vowels /i/ and /u/ was primarily between spread-lip and rounded-lip articulations. The phonemes /i/ and /e/ were primarily spread-lip, secondarily front.

Before /i, ī, j/, the rounded-lip syllabics /u/ and /o/ developed front allophones. These front allophones retained the lip-rounding which was the phonemic characteristic of /u/ and /o/, combining with it the front-tongue articulation which was present in /i, ī, j/: probably phonemic in the case of /j/, secondary and non-phonemic in the case of /i, ī/.

The result was that the /u/ phoneme had two allophones: a rounded-lip, high, back allophone [u], and a rounded-lip, high, front allophone [y]. The back allophone was the usual one; the front allophone occurred before /i, ī, j/. Similarly, /o/ had two allophones: usually a rounded-lip, mid, back allophone [o], but before /i, ī, j/ a rounded-lip, mid, front allophone [ø].

The low /a/ developed a front, raised allophone [æ] before /i, ī, j/.

The mid and high lip-spread (front) /i/ and /e/ were practically immune. There are a few instances of /i/ before /i, ī, j/ as compared to /e/ before other vowels: OHG erda 'earth' : irdīn 'of earth'. But there is no way of distinguishing early and late changes here.

The product of this development was still a five-phoneme system: /i, e, a, o, u/. Three of these phonemes had front allophones: /a/ [æ]; /o/ [ø]; /u/ [y]. The five phonemes are to be identified phonetically as follows:

/i/ high, lip-spread (front)
/e/ mid, lip-spread (front)
/a/ low (front allophone [æ] before /i, ī, j/)
/o/ mid, lip-rounded (back [o] usually; front allophone [ø] before /i, ī, j/)
/u/ high, lip-rounded (back [u] usually; front allophone [y] before /i, ī, j/)

	Spread		Rounded
High	[i]		[y, u]
Mid	[e]		[ø, o]
Low		[æ, a]	

This was the final form of the short-syllabic system of Prehistoric Germanic of the Pre-Norse and the Pre-West-Germanic dialects. The later development of this system, the varying phonemicizations of umlaut, differed in significant details in Old Norse, Old English, Old Saxon, and Old High German. The principal trends in the several dialects can only be sketched in large strokes here, from the structural point of view. The specific phonetic changes are described in the handbooks.

Old Norse. Fronted allophones of /u/, /o/, and especially /a/ developed in other phonetic circumstances, in addition to the position before /i, ī, j/: e.g. before /ʀ/, before /g, k/. The fronted allophone of /a/, in Norse as in West Germanic, was liable to reassignment as an allophone of /e/. The reason is a very old fact of distribution: the old shift of /e/ to /i/ before /i, j/ in early Preh. Gmc. times. This shift had left /e/ defective in the position before /i, j/; the [æ] or [ɛ] allophone of /a/ complemented the other allophones of /e/.

The remaining allophones of /a/ developed into two phonetic forms: [a] usually, but a back allophone before /u/. This back allophone [ǫ] became a separate phoneme when unstressed /u/ in final syllables was lost.

The allophones [y] and [ø] became phonemes when /i, ī, j/ were reduced to [ə] or lost in many classes of forms. The phonemic structure of stressed short syllabics was thus changed without any change in pronunciation. Norse then had high, mid, and low vowels as before. But the double distinction (spread-lip vs. rounded-lip) was replaced by a triple distinction (front spread /i, e/ vs. front rounded /y, ø/ vs. back rounded /u, o/).

Before /w/, the front spread syllabics /i, e/ developed phonetic forms which were partially lip-rounded or (if they remained lip-spread) had a retracted tongue position. These allophones were reassigned to /y, ø/ when /w/ was lost in some form classes.

Old English. In many classes of forms, the /i, ī, j/ was lost or reduced to [ə]. The distinction spread vs. rounded is replaced by a threefold distinction: front spread, front rounded, back rounded. Then this system was simplified by the coalescence of [æ] with the /e/ phoneme, /ø/ with the /e/ phoneme, and (last) /y/ with the /i/ phoneme.

The new allophones which developed in some dialects of Old English (before /l, r, h/; after palatal consonants; after /w/; before back vowels) were chiefly diphthongs; they belong to the purely English phase of linguistic history.

Old Saxon and Old High German. The fronted allophone of /a/ was early reassigned to the /e/ phoneme. The rounded /u/ and /o/ remained phonemically intact, each with its fronted and back allophones: [u, y] and [o, ø]. With the reduction or loss of /i, ī, j/, the fronted rounded allophones were promoted to phonemes.[7] In some dialects this led to a triple distinction: front spread /i, e/ vs. front rounded /y, ø/ vs. back rounded /u, o/. In other dialects (as in English), the two front classes merged, leaving a distinction of front (spread) vs. back (rounded). Compared to Norse and English, German developed relatively few new allophones until a restructuring of the syllable led to major quantitative reassignments.

Thus one phase of linguistic change. Only a small fraction of the words of a Germanic language display a short syllabic which has been unchanged since its Proto-IE protǫtype. Great shifts, even transformations, have taken place, phonetic and structural modifications have occurred step by step; quite specifically step by step, as one foot advances, then becomes the base of support while the other advances. Through any one change, either pronunciation or structure remains stable. A pronunciation changes by the development of allophones, while the phonemic structure is maintained; the differences in pronunciation are slight (that is, allophonic). Then the pronunciation stays constant, while the determinant is changed or loses importance, perhaps for the very reason that the allophones themselves now share in the distinction. The pronunciation is maintained, and the differences are those of structure (assignment of a given pronunciation to different phonemes) and hence unobtrusive. At all stages, there are only slight differences in pronunciation between older and younger generation, or between neighbors who transact business with one another. Throughout linguistic changes, linguistic communication remains effective. To return to a truism, the members of a linguistic community can talk to each other.

7 Twaddell, A note on OHG umlaut, Monatshefte für deutschen Unterricht 30.177 ff. (1938) ((85)).

THE PRINCIPAL STEP IN COMPARATIVE GRAMMAR

HENRY M. HOENIGSWALD
Language 26.357-64—1950

[Reconstruction by the comparative method (as distinct from internal reconstruction based on alternations between phonemes in a paradigm) is essentially a problem in phonemics, in which the place of allophones is taken by sets of sound correspondences that are partially alike (share one component) and in complementary distribution. The principle is illustrated by the IE dental and labial stops as reconstructed from Sanskrit and Germanic, by IE *s in Greek and Latin, and by the IE aspirates in Italic.]

Theorists of comparative grammar have concerned themselves a great deal with the reality of our reconstructions: whether they are phonetically concrete and fixed in time and space, or merely formulas for observed correspondences, lacking chronological depth. The question is, of course, important. But surprisingly little has been done about a much humbler task, namely that of rigorously describing the procedure used in reconstruction. The reason is no doubt that the matter has been considered too humble even to require formulation. The great tradition in comparative linguistics is teaching by example: if the examples are taken from languages with which the student is familiar because he is also a student of texts, they can be relied upon to build up a sound feeling for the workings of the comparative method. There is much to be said for this pedagogical approach, and even more against mere discussion of methodology as contrasted with the development of new methods implicit in the treatment of concrete new problems as they arise. On the other hand, generalizations are essential, both in discussing our science with investigators from other fields and, within our own domain, in weighing the merits of alternative reconstructions. Characteristically, some of the best efforts to put reconstructive procedures into words are found in polemic writings, where criteria are needed to prove oneself right and one's opponent wrong.

We assume that when two or more languages are compared (in the technical sense) the initial hypothesis, namely that of genetic relationship, has been made, and lists of corresponding morphemes or longer forms have been drawn up. We also assume that the task of weeding out material which is not directly inherited has somehow been accomplished. Some of the procedures used to this end are well known. Thus, in discarding analogical new formations one follows, roughly, a hierarchy of trustworthiness in which phonemes in morphologically isolated forms come first; then phonemes in paradigms where they alternate with other phonemes (because many alternations result from conditioned sound change); and finally phonemes in regular paradigms (because the regularity may be due to leveling). Or, to guard against the effects of secondary developments in daughter languages, we may refer to Meillet's rule that in reconstructing the vocabulary of a proto-language we need the testimony of three, rather than two, independent witnesses.[1] For many other purposes, however, reconstruction from more than two witnesses may well be viewed as a mere extension of the fundamental operation involving only two.

[1] Introduction à l'étude comparative des langues indo-européennes[5] 340 (Paris, 1922).

From the material thus restricted, we abstract sets of correspondences. Considering, for instance, (Vedic) Sanskrit and Germanic, we find a great many sets; among them are the following:[2]

	1	2	3	4	5	6	7	8	9	10	11	12
Sanskrit:	t	t	t	d	d	dh	p	p	p	b	b	bh
Germanic:	t	d	þ	d	t	d	p	b	f	b	p	b

Examples: 1 ásti : ist 'is'; 2 pitár- : fadar 'father'; 3 bhrā́tar- : broþar 'brother'; 4 dehī́- 'wall' : deigan 'knead'; 5 véda : wait 'I know'; 6 mádhya- : midjis 'middle'; 7 spáç- 'watcher' : OHG spehōn 'look out'; 8 lip- '(stick,) smear' : bi-leiban '(stick,) stay'; 9 see 2; 10 bódhati 'awakes, is attentive' : ana-biudan 'bid, charge with'; 11 rámbate 'hangs down' : MG lampen 'droop'; 12 see 3.

[2] Germanic forms quoted are Gothic unless otherwise identified; with respect to the crucial features, the dialects used agree among themselves and with proto-Germanic. The list is in no way exhaustive: it does not include Skt. t = Gmc. s (in clusters from IE t before t) or any reflex of the IE voiceless aspirates; nor does it include sets that involve Gothic specifically, such as where Gmc. b has been unvoiced to f in Gothic.

The components of the various sets are phonemes, obtained by descriptive analysis of phonetic records in the case of living languages or by interpretation of written sources in the case of dead languages. Since alphabet records are often in effect phonemic, we are mostly in the dark about subphonemic differences in earlier stages of a language. In the light of the discussion below, such knowledge, where we have it, may be helpful, though perhaps never crucial. For instance, it is helpful to know that the allophones of Gmc. b were spirants in the positions where set 8 occurs.

The sets are now classified according to the relations that exist between them. There are two criteria. First, certain sets are partially alike in that they share either their Sanskrit component (e.g. 2 and 3) or their Germanic component (e.g. 2 and 4). Second, certain sets are so distributed with respect to the sets which precede and follow them in the etymologies considered that they occur only in mutually exclusive environments (e.g. 2 after Skt. unaccented vowel and Gmc. vowel, 3 after Skt. accented vowel and Gmc. vowel or after pause in both languages, but not conversely), while other sets are found to be in contrast with each other in at least one environment (e.g. 3 and 9: both, say, after pause and before r, as in tráyas : þreis 'three', pra- 'fore' : fra- prefix).

The following sets are partially alike:

1	2	3										share Skt. t
			4	5								share Skt. d
						7	8	9				share Skt. p
									10	11		share Skt. b
	2		4		6							share Gmc. d
							8		10		12	share Gmc. b
1				5								share Gmc. t
						7				11		share Gmc. p

Only some of these partially like sets, however, are taken to be continuations of one and the same phoneme of the proto-language. Thus, 4 and 6 are thought to derive from one IE phoneme, written *dh, which remained a single phoneme (d) in Germanic, but split in Sanskrit, by conditioned sound change, into two phonemes (d if the following syllable begins with an aspirate, otherwise dh). On the other hand, 2 and 6, though they share Gmc. d, are interpreted as representing two different IE phonemes, written *t and *dh, of which the first was affected in Germanic by a conditioned sound change in such a way that some of its occurrences merged with the second. In other words, although sets 2, 4, and 6 all share Gmc. d and are different only in their Skt. members, the difference between 4 and 6 is taken to be a recent development while the difference between 2 and 6 is taken to be original. (The relation between 2 and 4 will be dealt with later.)

What is it that enables us to infer these particular historical events? Clearly it is the manner in which the sets are distributed in our comparative material. Set 4 (Skt. d = Gmc. d) occurs when the next syllable begins with Skt. h = Gmc. g, Skt. dh = Gmc. d, or a few other sets; set 6 (Skt. dh = Gmc. d) does not occur in these environments. Set 2 (Skt. t = Gmc. d) occurs only after Skt. unaccented vowel = Gmc. vowel with or without certain consonants intervening; set 6 occurs in this environment also, as well as in others.[3]

These examples illustrate a fundamental assumption of comparative grammar: partially like sets occurring in mutually exclusive environments are taken to be continuations of one and the same phoneme of the proto-language.[4] The assumption has one important corollary: if, after the reconstruction has been made, we describe the relations between the phonemes of the proto-language and those of only one of the two or more daughter languages (ignoring the rest), our statements constitute the historical phonology of this language in terms of sound changes. Examples can be found in the preceding paragraphs.

Possible applications of our assumption may, however, be in conflict. Let us examine the entire table of partially like sets (given above) for the distribution of the sets in various environments. Sets 4 and 5, as well as 10 and 11, are in contrast; for in the few surroundings where 4 and 10 are found (before h = g, dh = d, and a few other sets in the following syllable), 5 and 11 occur also. The same is true, as has been shown, for sets 2 and 6, and equally for sets 8 and 12, whose distribution is parallel to that of 2 and 6. No contrast can be established between any other partially like sets: they are all more or less obviously in complementary distribution. This leaves the following choices. Set 1 may be grouped together with 3 (and possibly 2; see the next statement), which would amount to reconstructing a single source for all the occurrences of Skt. 5; but also with 5, which is one of the sources of Gmc. t. Set 2 may be grouped with 1 and 3 (all sharing Skt. t), but also with 4, though not with 6 (both Skt. d). Set 3 is grouped with 1 and perhaps 2 (see above). Set 4 cannot, as we have seen, be grouped with 5 (Skt. d), hence it can only be grouped with 6 or perhaps 2 (Gmc. d). Set 5 can only belong with 1 (Gmc. t), provided 1 is not rather linked with 3 (and 2), in which case 5 would stand alone. Set 6 goes with 4, but not with 2. The relationships among sets 7–12 are parallel to those among sets 1–6; in what follows sets 7–12 will not be specially noted.

[3] Of course, IE was not reconstructed from Vedic Sanskrit and Germanic alone. Actually, scholars made use of the fact that the other major IE languages are apt to show one and the same phoneme in 4 and 6 (not Greek, which has, roughly, t t t t d th from 1 to 6; see note 6 below) but two different ones in 2 and 6. Still, such multilateral comparison may be viewed as a system of bilateral ones. This is important since it becomes increasingly clear (and not only for Romance; see R. A. Hall Jr., Lang. 26. 24 ((313))) that some of the well-known difficulties about the setting up of family relations between languages disappear as soon as these relationships are interpreted in terms of successive bifurcation rather than simultaneous, multiple split.

[4] In terms of surrounding sets. Instances where two partially like sets differ in language A, but the environments appear as mutually exclusive only because they are different in language B, are the particular triumphs of the comparative method. Sets 2 and 3 differ only in Germanic, under conditions that are revealed only in Vedic Sanskrit (and, if we compare Germanic with other IE languages, only where the IE accent has left direct traces, as in Greek); hence the startling effect of Verner's discovery.

The principal criterion to decide among these choices is economy. If we were not concerned with economy, we could be content with reconstructing as many phonemes for the proto-language as there are sets of corresponding phonemes in the daughter languages—a frequently criticized flaw in poor comparative work. Examining the possibilities, we find that two different choices will each result in three reconstructed phonemes for sets 1–6 (and three more for 7–12); no choice will yield fewer than three, and several others will yield more. The two possibilities of grouping sets as reflexes of only three phonemes in the proto-language are these: either 1 and 5, 2 and 3, 4 and 6; or else 5 by itself, 1 and 2 and 3, 4 and 6. In other words, the only question still unsolved is whether set 1 (t = ṭ) should be derived from the common source of 2 (t = d) and 3 (t = þ), or from the source of 5 (d = t), i.e. from *t or from *d. We note that set 1 occurs only after s = s, p = f, etc. (set 7 probably only after s = s).

It may sometimes be irrelevant to decide the status of such a set as 1. In some instances of ambiguity, both possible reconstructions may be equally effective. However, for set 1 (though not for 7) we can go a step further. It is true that 1 (t = t) nowhere contrasts with 2 and 3, or with 5, since 2, 3, and 5 do not occur in the same environments as 1 (say after s = s). But it is also true that 5 (d = t) occurs in at least one environment where 2 and 3 do not: after y = s, as in Skt. meda- 'fat': MG Mast 'fattening'. (Here Skt. y is seen in the second element in long e.) Upon further examination the set y = s is in turn found to occur only in positions from which s = s is barred; there is an equation st = st (ásti: ist) and an equation yd = st (meda-: Mast), but there is no sd = st and no yt = st. Consequently the choice between the two possible assignments of set 1 (t = t) will affect also the status of the set y = s. As soon as set 1 is grouped with 5, i.e. derived from *d, the sets s = s and y = s must be said to contrast with each other before *d of the proto-language, and we must reconstruct something like *sd for ásti: ist and *zd for meda-: Mast. But if set 1 is grouped with 2 and 3, i.e. derived from *t, we need to reconstruct only *st and *sd. The former grouping requires the reconstruction of a new IE phoneme *z, of very limited distribution; the latter grouping requires only such IE phonemes as have been reconstructed already on the basis of other evidence, and at the same time gives them a more complete distribution (both *t and *d now occur after *s).[5]

Thus, considerations of economy have again decided the dilemma. On the strength of the general parallelism between the dentals and the labials, set 7 (p = p) will now be grouped with 8 and 9 rather than with 11.

To sum up, we have obtained the following reconstructions and sound laws: IE *t for sets 1, 2, and 3; IE *dh for sets 4 and 6; IE *d for set 5; IE *p for sets 7, 8, and 9; IE *bh for sets 10 and 12; IE *b for set 11; Verner's law for sets 2 and 8; Grassmann's law for sets 4 and 10; and the treatment of *t and *p after a Gmc. spirant for sets 1 and 7. Incidentally we have also decided against the reconstruction of IE *z.

The next application of our basic assumption points up some limitations of a strictly bilateral comparative procedure. In the comparison of Latin and Greek we observe, among others, the following sets of correspondences:

	13	14	15	16
Latin:	s	s	r	r
Greek:	s	h	0	r

Examples: 13 genus: génos 'family'; 14 sequ-: hep- 'follow'; 15 generum: genéōn 'of families'; 16 ferō: phérō 'I bear'.

Sets 13 and 14, as well as sets 15 and 16, are partially alike in sharing their Latin component. As for distribution, set 16 is in contrast with the other three: set 14 occurs after pause before a vowel, 15 occurs between vowels, 13 occurs in other environments; 16 occurs in all these surroundings (vowel prothesis aside). Distributionally, sets 13 and 14 can of course be derived from a single phoneme of the proto-language, say IE *s, with a conditioned sound change in Greek. But set 15 cannot be connected with sets 13 and 14 by distribution alone, since the criterion of partial likeness is absent: set 15 shares no component with the other two.[6] The realization that set 15 is also a reflex of IE *s is reached by other means or on the basis of other data.

Aside from a presumption which arises from the defective distribution of the Greek phoneme h (it is barred from precisely those positions where 0 appears in our sets, i.e. between vowels), and aside

[5] In this case, then, the criterion of mutually exclusive environments solely in terms of surrounding sets must be to some extent implemented by saying that if the structure of the environments has been reinterpreted through reconstruction or phonemicization, the distribution of the set in question must be reexamined in terms of the newly described environments. The general theory involved here is an interesting problem in itself. (Brugmann's *zd is unnecessary in any case.)

[6] This peculiar result is of course due to the fact that IE *s has been reassigned to different entities (Lat. r, Gk. 0) under what happen to be identical conditions. In a comparison between Greek and Sanskrit, the set Gk. t = Skt. d, corresponding to set 4 above, would be in a similar relation with th = dh (corresponding to set 6) as is 15 with regard to 13 + 14, reflecting the two independent dissimilations of aspirates in the two languages (see above, note 3). In the case of 15, we have reason to assume that IE *s between vowels was h at one time in Proto-Greek before it was lost entirely. If we had to reconstruct IE from that stage, we would find ourselves in a somewhat better position: 13 and 14 (sharing Lat. s), and 14 and 15 (sharing early Greek h) are partially alike, though 13 and 15 are not.

also from certain additional evidence which, in effect, merely adds further sets to the ones already listed (and which is here ignored for the sake of the argument), set 15 can be referred to IE *s only by two methods: (a) by recourse to material from other IE languages, or (b) by internal reconstruction, in Greek and Latin separately, on the basis of the morphophonemic behavior of the set in question. Thus, in Latin, the r of set 15 (but not the r of 16) is found to alternate with the s of 13, as in gener(um) ∿ genus, ger(it) 'he conducts' ∿ ges(tus) 'conducted'; in Greek, the θ of set 15 alternates similarly with the s of 13, as in génos ∿ gené(ōn)—i.e. genéθ(ōn).

By the same kind of internal reconstruction, the derivation of Gmc. t (of set 1) and þ (of set 3) from the same phoneme of the proto-language finds support in the alternating forms of the past participial morpheme: (haf)t(s) ∿ (salbo)þ(s). Such considerations are entirely valid in themselves, but they have nothing to do with the comparative method.

Where the distribution of sets is simple to state, the application of comparative procedure can be condensed into a two-dimensional arrangement. This is here illustrated by a comparison of parts of the Latin and the Osco-Umbrian consonant system. The reconstructed phonemes based on this material may be regarded either as proto-Italic or as (provisionally) Indo-European, according as one accepts or rejects the assumption of a historical proto-Italic unity.

The Osco-Umbrian phonemes in question are here ordered on the horizontal axis, the Latin phonemes on the vertical axis:

OU:	b	d	f	v	Lat.:
					b
					d
					f
					v

An entry at the intersection, say, of the Osco-Umbrian b column and the Latin v row will mean that a set OU b = Lat. v has been abstracted from the material compared (as in U berus [abl. pl.]: Lat. verū 'spear'). If the entry at this point reads 'I', it will mean that the set occurs initially, 'M' that it occurs medially, 'IM' that it occurs both initially and medially. These two symbols and their combination happen to be sufficient for a simplified presentation of the problem.

We have eight sets, denoted by the symbols I, IM, and M in the following table:

OU:	b	d	f	v	Lat:
	IM		M		b
		IM	M		d
			I		f
	IM		M	IM	v

Entries in the same vertical column are alike in their Osco-Umbrian component; entries in the same horizontal row are alike in their Latin component. Distribution among mutually exclusive environments is shown in the OU f column: the set OU f = Lat. f must be grouped with f = b, or with f = d, or with f = v; the choice is probably irrelevant. We can arbitrarily group this set with f = b on the basis of greater phonetic plausibility. The sets f = d and f = v remain, then, as representatives of defectively distributed phonemes occurring only in medial position. Each of the other entries reflects a separate phoneme of the proto-language. Choosing the traditional alphabetic symbols, we reconstruct as follows:

OU:	b	d	f	v	Lat:
	*b		*-f-		b
		*d	*-þ-		d
			*f-		f
	*g^{w}		*-x^{w}-	*w	v

Here *f- stands for the phoneme *f in initial position, *-f- for the same phoneme in medial position.

This is as far as the comparative method itself will take us, on the basis of Osco-Umbrian and Latin alone. It does not tell us, for instance, that the set f = f < *f- is the reflex of four originally contrasting IE phonemes (*bh-, *dh-, *g^{w}h-, and *s before r), of which three parallel the medial entries in the Osco-Umbrian f column; nor that the set f = b < *-f- similarly represents a merging of several sources (IE *-bh-, *-dh- in some environments, and *-s- before r). These additional facts are perhaps suggested, though not clearly shown, by certain limitations upon the distribution of the reconstructed phonemes: *þ only medial, and not in the particular environments where IE *dh > Lat. b rather than d; *s before most consonants but not before *r; and *x^{w} only medial. The same facts can also be recovered by internal reconstruction on the basis of such alternations as Lat. con-dere 'found' (with d) ∿ fēcī 'I made' (with f), representing an IE morpheme *dhē/dhə with and without a prefix. But such facts cannot be revealed by simply applying the comparative method to the sounds of the Italic dialects.

If the formulation here proposed for the principal procedure in comparative reconstruction sounds unfamiliar to historical linguists (who have nevertheless consistently used the procedure), it clearly reminds us of certain formulations in descriptive phonology. Phonemes have been defined as classes of sounds which are phonetically similar and not in contrast—i.e., chiefly, in complementary distribution.[7] The second criterion is matched in historical work, while the first is paralleled, not too incongruously, by the criterion of partial likeness. Phonemic problems that arise from lack of symmetry in the distribution of sound segments have led investigators to look for additional criteria of patterning to decide between alternative arrangements; such a criterion was used in the reconstruction for set 7 (Skt. p = Gmc. p)

[7] E. g. B. Bloch and G. L. Trager, Outline of Linguistic Analysis (Baltimore, 1942).

above. Economy is an avowed goal of phonemic analysis (however controversial the means of achieving it may be); it is the same in comparative work. The sets of correspondences play the role of positional allophones. In short, when we use the reconstructive method of the nineteenth-century scholars we are in fact describing the phonemic system of the proto-language—on the basis, to be sure, not of a minutely diversified phonetic record but of the results of phonetic changes preserved in the daughter languages.

It is trivial to say that only the assumption of regular sound change makes reconstruction possible, and unnecessary to inquire into the implications of that assumption. But if the question be asked why the results of sound change should behave like allophones, we answer that it is through positional allophones that sound changes take place. This is usually expressed by saying that a sound change is conditioned by the phonemic environment. If Early Latin s between vowels becomes r (i.e. falls together with the old r phoneme), we have no difficulty in picturing the change as a reassignment of the particular allophone of s that appeared between vowels—something like [z], as we have reason to believe. Comparison of two related languages reveals such allophones of the parent language as happened subsequently to change their phonemic status in certain ways.

The phonemic principle was implicit in the neogrammarian assumption of regular sound change; formal syntactic definitions of meaning were implicit in Paul's statement of semantic change. The fundamental unity of diachronic and synchronic thinking is beyond doubt.[8] But it is useful, and somewhat surprising, to realize how directly and how concretely that unity is reflected in scholarly practice, once it has been described in detail.

[8] Some doubt it. J. Lohmann, in an otherwise very valuable discussion of Steinitz' reconstruction of the Finno-Ugric vowel system on the basis of phonemic interpretation, declares (DLZ 70.201) that here 'Trubetzkoy's phonologie' has undergone its first (!) historical test, and adds that if it proves successful, all our earlier reconstructions, including the traditional work in Indo-European, will be worthless: a sorry misunderstanding of the continuity of linguistics and of the reviewer's own position.

THE RECONSTRUCTION OF PROTO-ROMANCE*

ROBERT A. HALL, JR.

Language 26.6–27—1950

1. Comparative Reconstruction: Desirability and Possibility

Leonard Bloomfield, in his book Language,[1] makes the statement:

> Students of the Romance languages reconstruct a Primitive Romance ("Vulgar Latin") form before they turn to the written records of Latin, and they interpret these records in the light of the reconstructed form.

Two later writers, discussing the reconstruction of earlier stages of related languages, have made relevant statements in this connection. Bruno Migliorini says:[2]

> Ci manca e ci mancherà sempre il metodo di ricostruire ciò che è il carattere fondamentale di una lingua: la sua consistenza in sistema, in un dato tempo e in un dato luogo.

George L. Trager, on the other hand, makes the programmatic declaration:[3]

> It seems to me that historical linguists must now restate their tasks much more precisely. When we have really good descriptive grammars of all existing French dialects, we can reconstruct Proto-Francian, Proto-Burgundian, Proto-Norman-Picard, etc. Then we can reconstruct Proto-French; then, with a similarly acquired statement of Proto-Provençal, we can formulate Proto-Gallo-Romanic; next, with similar accurately developed reconstructions of Proto-Ibero-Romanic, Proto-Italian, etc., we can work out Proto-Romanic as a whole.

These three statements stand in a historical relation to each other. Bloomfield's represents the aim of comparative reconstruction held by many Romance scholars of the epoch of Meyer-Lübke; Migliorini's, the disillusionment of post-Meyer-Lübkean scholars with that aim; and Trager's, the goal of some present-day workers, to return to comparative reconstruction and to revivify it with an infusion of descriptive (synchronic) analysis. Meyer-Lübke and his immediate followers attempted to apply the comparative method, as developed in the 19th century and particularly by the Junggrammatiker[4] of the 1870's, to the reconstruction of the common ancestral form of the Romance languages. This method, which requires the scholar to work backward in time, proved difficult of application and exposition, and even Meyer-Lübke, in such finished products as the Grammatik der romanischen Sprachen,[5] or his historical grammars of individual languages,[6] resorted to the procedure of presenting his material as developing forward in time, from Latin and 'Vulgar Latin' to the Romance languages. Later and lesser comparatists in the Romance field tended toward the errors which often resulted from a misunderstanding of Neo-Grammarian procedure: abuse of 'starred' forms and neglect of historical factors other than those of phonetic change, analogical new-formation, and learned borrowing. The comparative method and the Neo-Grammarian hypothesis of regular sound change came to be identified—in the Romance field especially through the influence of Croce, Vossler, and their 'idealistic' followers[7]—with a positivistic approach which was no longer the

*Parts of this paper were read before meetings of the Linguistic Society at Rochester in 1946, the Cornell Linguistic Club in 1948, and the Modern Language Association at New York in 1948. I am indebted for suggestions to many colleagues and critics, including Professors F. B. Agard, C. F. Hockett, Y. Malkiel, W. G. Moulton, L. Pumpelly, and L. Spitzer—not all of whom agree with my fundamental thesis and none of whom are responsible for any errors the paper may contain in its present form.

1 Language 302 (New York, 1933).

2 Linguistica 104 (Firenze, 1946). On this point, cf. also the reviews by T. A. Sebeok (American Speech 22.137–8 [1947]) and the present writer (Lang. 22.259–61 [1946]).

3 Studies in Philology 43.463 (1946).

4 I use this term to refer specifically to Brugmann, Leskien, and the other Indo-Europeanists of the 1870's, 80's, and 90's who first developed the explicit formulation of the principles of comparative reconstruction. For that group of scholars—far more extensive in number and in time—who have accepted the basic postulate of regular sound-change, I would suggest using the term 'regularist'; my Terminological Notes, Studies in Linguistics 7.60–2 (1949).

5 Leipzig, 1890–1900.

6 E. g. Italienische Grammatik (Leipzig, 1890); Historische Grammatik der französischen Sprache (Heidelberg, 1908–21).

7 Cf. the present writer's discussions of the 'idealistic' approach and its effects on linguistics, in Italica 20.239–43 (1938); Lang. 17.263–9 (1941); Italica 23.30–4 (1946); Lang. 22.273–83 (1946); and SIL 6.27–35 (1948).

mode. Modern Romance scholars, with few exceptions, have abandoned even the effort to reconstruct Proto-Romance,[8] and present work in the Romance field follows, in general, the technique of Hugo Schuchardt (who, as is well known, stood aside from the Neo-Grammarian movement and made little use of comparative reconstruction): detailed examination of Classical and Late Latin material and of modern Romance material, bridging the gap between them with as few assumptions as possible concerning intermediate stages. Most present-day Romanists distrust hypothetical reconstructions attained by working backwards from later-attested material, as exemplified in Migliorini's remark.[9] Only a few scholars at present—in general, with training in both historical and descriptive technique—envisage, as does Trager in the passage cited, the reconstruction of Proto-Romance as a worthy goal, and not only for Proto-Romance alone, but also for all the intermediate stages between Proto-Romance and the present time.

Yet, even though current fashions in Romance linguistics are unfavorable to it, such an integral re-application of the comparative method as Trager proposes—of course accompanied by as thorough as possible a synchronic analysis and description of each stage—is very much needed at present. Its use is not only possible but highly desirable, to correct certain serious misconceptions now widespread, concerning the relation of Romance and Latin, and the relation of the Romance languages to each other. One of these misconceptions is even reflected in Bloomfield's statement, where 'Vulgar Latin' is equated with Proto-Romance. This terminological identification is a result of the customary conception of Romance linguistic history as having been unilinear in its development: Old Latin > Classical Latin > Vulgar (Imperial) Latin > the first stages of differentiation among the Romance dialects > the later languages. The normal procedure of manuals of historical grammar[10] is to trace Romance sounds and forms over a portion of this assumed development, usually from Classical Latin to the earliest attested stage of the language concerned. This works well enough for the languages usually studied: Italian, French and Provençal, and the Iberian languages, since 'Vulgar Latin' as usually set up is essentially equivalent to the ancestral form of these languages, i.e. the intermediate stage of Proto-Italo-Western Romance. But it will not work for Eastern (Balkan) Romance or for Southern Romance (Sardinian, Sicilian, Calabrian, Lucanian), which are in general conveniently neglected, or passed over with the remark that they show divergent developments from 'Vulgar Latin'. Departures from this customary procedure, such as efforts to trace Romance developments to features found in Old Latin but not in Classical Latin (thus skipping one or more of the traditional stages), often provoke irate tertiary responses, as in d'Ovidio's use of the term 'rancido' for Old Latin when he was arguing[11] against Förster's suggestion of OLat. -nunt as an ancestor for the Italian 3 pl. verbal ending -no.[12] We can avoid this type of confusion only by re-applying the comparative method and seeing what it has to tell us about the relation of the Romance languages.

2. Procedure: Reconstruction of Intermediate and Ultimate Stages

A thoroughgoing and complete application of the comparative method to the Romance languages would have to follow essentially the steps that Trager proposes. A first approximation thereto would involve the comparison of the earliest attested stages of each language, with consideration of relevant modern dialectal material where the latter would shed light on aspects of the reconstructed ancestral language not evident from consideration of the earliest attested dialects;[13] the end results of the two procedures would, I believe, be approximately equivalent.

[8] Cf. such criticisms of the comparative method as those of Bàrtoli, Introduzione alla Neolinguistica (Genève, 1925; Biblioteca dell'Archivum Romanicum II.12); B. A. Terracini, ¿Qué es la Lingüística? (Tucumán, 1942).

It must be emphasized that our reconstruction does not lead us to set up a completely 'unified' or 'unitary' Proto-Romance, as is often assumed (cf. most recently Y. Malkiel, StP 46.512 [1949]). We do not have to suppose absolute uniformity for proto-languages, any more than for any actually observed language (cf. B. Bloch, Lang. 24.194 fn. 1 [1948]). Our Proto-Romance was undoubtedly a composite of several dialects of the Latin spoken at the end of the Republican period.

[9] Cf. also Y. Malkiel, Lang. 21.149 (1945).

[10] E. g. Meyer-Lübke's Grammatik der romanischen Sprachen; Bourciez's Eléments de linguistique romane[4] (Paris, 1946); Grandgent's Introduction to Vulgar Latin (Boston, 1907); and the historical grammars of individual languages, e. g., for Italian: Meyer-Lübke's Italienische Grammatik and its various Italian reworkings; Grandgent's From Latin to Italian (Cambrige, 1927); and Pei's The Italian Language (New York, 1941).

[11] ZRPh. 23.313–20 (1898).

[12] ZRPh. 22.521–5 (1898).

[13] For instance, the evidence afforded by Upper Aragonese dialects for preservation of intervocalic unvoiced stops, or by Asturian (Cabranes) dialect for preservation of the distinction between final -u and -o (cf. Y. Malkiel, Lang. 23.63 [1947], reviewing Josefa María Canellada, El bable de Cabranes [Madrid, 1944; RFE Anejo 31]); the similar evidence afforded by Upper Bearnese for preservation of intervocalic unvoiced stops (cf. the discussion in Part 2 of this article) and their ascription to Proto-Gallo-Romance; or the evidence afforded by Central and South Italian dialects (in the so-called 'metafonesi centro-meridionale') for the distinction between final -u and -o, which we must, therefore, likewise ascribe to Proto-Italo-Romance.

The reconstruction must be done by working backward and reconstructing the immediate ancestral forms of those languages which are most closely related (e. g. Portuguese, Spanish, Catalan, and Mozarabic; North and South French; etc.). It would be unjustified, for instance, to start off by comparing less closely related dialects in preference to more closely related ones, whenever the latter were available; although the picture of the ultimate ancestral language would perforce be the same, the intermediate stages of development would be seriously misrepresented by such a procedure. 'Close relation', in this connection, means of course 'sharing linguistic features' or 'bounded by the same isoglosses', not only or mainly 'juxtaposed geographically', since dialects going back to different intermediate stages can be found in close proximity to each other, as are, say, Neapolitan-Campanian, Lucanian, and the area which Lausberg calls the 'outpost' (Vorposten) of Eastern Romance in Lucania.[14]

A concrete example of how this type of intermediate reconstruction can be done and what it gives us can be seen in the phonological system of Proto-Gallo-Romance. We shall set this up first on the basis of a comparison between Old South French (Provençal) and Old North French, later modifying our reconstruction of PGRom. on the basis of (1) internal re-analysis and (2) the evidence of other dialects. For the vowels, there are twelve basic sets of correspondences, given here with a provisional symbol assigned to each:[15]

	PGRom.	OSFr.	ONFr.	
1.	i	i	i	OSFr. vída vida 'life' : ONFr. víðə viḍe
2.	E	e	éi	OSFr. téla tela 'cloth' : ONFr. téilə teile
3.	e	e	e	OSFr. éntre entre 'between' : ONFr. éntrə entre
4.	Ɛ	ɛ	iɛ́	OSFr. kɛ́ra quera 'that he seek' : ONFr. kiɛ́rəθ quiereṭ
5.	ɛ	ɛ	ɛ	OSFr. tɛ́rra terra 'earth' : ONFr. tɛ́rə tere
6.	A	a	æ[16]	OSFr. ála ala 'wing' : ONFr. ǽlə ele
7.	a	a	a	OSFr. kánta canta 'he sings' : ONFr. čántəθ chanteṭ
8.	Ɔ	ɔ	ɔ	OSFr., ONFr. mɔ́rt mort 'death'
9.	ɔ	ɔ	uɔ́ > uɛ́	OSFr. bɔ́na bona 'good' : ONFr. buɔ́na buona > buɛ́nə buene
10.	o	o	o	OSFr., ONFr. fórn forn 'oven'
11.	O	o	óu	OSFr. góla gola 'throat' : ONFr. góulə goule
12.	u	u	u	OSFr. núza nuza 'naked' : ONFr. núðə nude

All other correspondences between vowel phonemes can be stated in terms of these twelve, as divergent developments conditioned by phonetic surroundings or as developments of combinations of these twelve elements, e. g.:

12a.	e	e	ə	after certain consonants or clusters; e. g. OSFr. ǧúǧe jutge 'judge' : ONFr. ǧúǧə juge
12b.	au̯	au̯	ɔ	OSFr. áur aur 'gold' : ONFr. ɔ́r or

Similarly for the consonant phonemes, we find that there are thirty-five further correspondences, which at first we would set up as follows:

13.	p	p	p	OSFr. pɛ́ire peire 'stone' : ONFr. piɛ́ð̌rə pieḍre
14.	t	t	t	OSFr., ONFr. tánt tant 'so much'; OSFr. méta meta 'that he put' : ONFr métəθ meteṭ
15.	k	k	k	OSFr., ONFr. kórt cort 'short'; ONFr., OSFr. sék sec 'dry'
16.	b	b	b	OSFr. bátre batre 'to beat' : ONFr. bátrə batre; OSFr. ábas abas 'abbot' (nom. sg.) : ONFr. ábəs abes
17.	d	d	d	OSFr., ONFr. dúr dur 'hard'; OSFr. fréida freida 'cold' : ONFr. fréidə freide
18.	g	g	g	OSFr. góta gota 'drop' : ONFr. gótə gote
19.	f	f	f	OSFr. fáire faire 'to do' : ONFr. fáirə faire
20.	v	v	v	OSFr. víva viva 'alive' : ONFr. vívə vive
21.	s	s	s	OSFr. séda seda 'silk' : ONFr. séiðə seiḍe; OSFr. fɔ́sa fosa 'ditch' : ONFr. fɔ́sə fose
22.	c	c	c	OSFr., ONFr. cínk cinc 'five'; OSFr. fáca faza 'that he do' : ONFr. fácəθ faceṭ
23.	ʒ	ʒ	ʒ	OSFr. dóʒe doze 'twelve' : ONFr. dóʒə doze
24.	ǧ	ǧ	ǧ	OSFr. ǧúǧe jutge 'judge' : ONFr. ǧúǧə juge

[14] Die Mundarten Südlukaniens (Halle, 1939; ZRPh. Beiheft 90), especially pp. 84–6.

[15] Examples are given first in phonemic transcription (easily identifiable as such by the phonemic stress mark in each form: see example 48), then in the conventional orthography of the language, with English glosses enclosed in quotes. The ONFr. conventional orthography is the normalized style used, for instance, by Schwan-Behrens-Bloch (Grammaire de l'ancien français^4 [Leipzig, 1932]) and by Jenkins in his edition of the Chanson de Roland (revised ed., Boston, 1929). The transcription is based on that of the IPA, except that c stands for [t^s], ʒ for [d^z], and a prime after a consonant letter indicates palatalization.

[16] The symbol suggested by me (StP 43.579 [1947]) for the phonemic entity in ONFr. which normally corresponds to /á/ of OSFr. and the other Romance languages, which assonated only with itself in the earliest stage of literary Old French (including the earlier stratum of the Roland), and which was later merged with /ɛ/ and spelled e. The exact phonetic nature of this phoneme is irrelevant, whether it was [æ] (as seems to me most likely, at least for the first stage of its development), [ɛ·], [e·], or what not.

25.	m	m	m	OSFr. amár amar 'love' : ONFr. amǽr amer
26.	n	n	n	OSFr. nɔ́č, nuɛ́č noch, nuech 'night' : ONFr. núit nuit;
				OSFr. menár menar 'to lead' : ONFr. mənǽr mener
27.	l	l	l	OSFr. lavár lavar 'to wash' : ONFr. lavǽr laver; OSFr. ála ala 'wing' :
				ONFr. ǽlə ele; OSFr. fɔ́la fola 'mad' : ONFr. fɔ́lə fole
28.	r	r	r	OSFr. rábia rabia 'rage' : ONFr. ráǧə rage; OSFr. árdre ardre 'to burn' : [ONFr. árdrə ardre
29.	h	—	h	OSFr. ápča apcha 'axe' : ONFr. háčə hache
30.	w	g	gu̯	OSFr. gardár g(u)ardar 'to guard' : ONFr. guardǽr guarder
31.	p′	pč	č	OSFr. sápča sapcha 'that he know' : ONFr. sáčəθ sacheṭ; cf. also example 29
32.	t′	č	i̯t	OSFr. fáč fach 'done' : ONFr. fáit fait
33.	b′	bi̯	ǧ	OSFr. kambiár 'cambiar 'to change' : ONFr. čanǧiǽr changier
34.	v′	vi̯	ǧ	OSFr. abreviár abreuiar 'to shorten' : ONFr. abreǧiǽr abregier
35.	s′	š, i̯s[17]	i̯s	OSFr. bašár baisár baissar 'to lower' : ONFr. baisiǽr baissier
36.	z′	ž, i̯z[17]	i̯z	OSFr. bažár baizár baisar 'to kiss' : ONFr. baiziǽr baisier
37.	c′	c	i̯s	OSFr. palác palatz 'palace' : ONFr. paláis palais
38.	ʒ′	z, i̯z[17]	i̯z	OSFr. po(i)zón po(i)zon 'poison' : ONFr. poizón poison;
				OSFr. plazér 'to please' : ONFr. plaizír plaisir
39.	m′	mi̯, mǧ[17]	nǧ	OSFr. komiáṭ komǧát comjat 'leave' : ONFr. konǧiǽθ congieṭ
40.	n′	n′	n′	OSFr., ONFr. bán′ banh, bain 'bath'; OSFr. sen′ór senhor 'lord' : ONFr. sen′óur [seignour
41.	l′	l′	l′	OSFr. fíl′a filha 'daughter' : ONFr. fíl′ə fille;
				OSFr. trabál′ trabalh 'work' : ONFr. travál′ travail
42.	r′	i̯r, r[18]	i̯r	OSFr. váira vaira 'many-colored, bright' : ONFr. váirə vaire;
				OSFr. kuɛ́r cuer 'leather' : ONFr. kúir cuir

In addition to those listed above, there are five other correspondences of consonants occurring only intervocalically, which must, at first, be assigned separate symbols:

43.	β	b	v	OSFr. kobrír cobrir 'to cover' : ONFr. kovrír covrir
44.	ð	d	ð	OSFr. -áda -ada ending of past part. (f. sg.) : ONFr. -ǽðə -eḍe
45.	ð	z	ð	OSFr. lauzár lauzar 'to praise' : ONFr. lɔðǽr loḍer
46.	z	z	z	OSFr. pauzár pauzar 'to put' : ONFr. pozǽr poser
47.	γ	g	i̯	OSFr. pagán pagan 'pagan' : ONFr. paiiǽn paiien

Other correspondences between consonants can all be interpreted as conditioned developments of one of the PGRom. phonemes tentatively assumed above, or as resulting from clusters of two or more consonants:

47a.	k (bef. a)	k	č	OSFr. kantár cantar 'to sing' : ONFr. čantǽr chanter
47b.	ðr	i̯r	ðr	OSFr. páire paire 'father' : ONFr. pǽðrə peḍre

We must further assume at least one phoneme of stress:

48.	′	′	′	OSFr. kánta canta 'he sings' : ONFr. čántəθ chanteṭ;
				OSFr. kantác cantatz 'you sing' : ONFr. čantǽc chantez

Thus far we have set up twelve basic correspondences in vowels, thirty-five in consonants, and one in stress. Now these might conceivably represent the same number of phonemes in the parent language: forty-seven segmental phonemes is not an excessive number to posit for a language without transcending the limits of realism. But our task is not ended with the setting up of these forty-eight correspondences; after all, what we have obtained here is only a first approximation, and we must now proceed to examine our stock of 'phonemes', just as we would our initial results in studying a language at first hand, and reanalyze and re-phonemicize, seeking to observe the distribution of elements within the parent language and, if possible, to reduce the number of unit phonemes that we posit.[19]

[17] Dialectal differentiation within OSFr.

[18] With /r/ occurring in word-final position and involving diphthongization of a preceding /ɛ/ or /ɔ/.

[19] For further discussion of this procedure of reanalysis and rephonemicization, cf. Zellig S. Harris, Methods in Structural Linguistics §9 (Chicago 1951).

When we look over the material we have assembled, we notice, first of all, a marked limitation on the occurrence of those vowel correspondences which we have symbolized with capital letters (i.e. nos. 2, 4, 6, 8, 11; henceforth referred to, for brevity's sake, as 'capital-letter vowels'). They occur only under stress; and they occur in both free and checked syllables, but the checked syllables in which they occur are almost exclusively limited to word-final position. That is, we find a great many correspondences of the type OSFr. ála ala 'wing' : ONFr. ǽlə ele < PGRom. Ála, and also of the type OSFr. tál tal 'such' : ONFr. tǽl tel < PGRom. tÁl, but almost none of the type which we may represent by a hypothetical OSFr. *másta : ONFr. *mǽstə, for which we would have to set up a PGRom. *mÁsta. The corresponding 'small-letter vowels' (nos. 3, 5, 7, 9, 10) and the high vowels /i u/ (nos. 1 and 12) are much freer in their occurrence; we find them in both stressed and unstressed, both free and checked syllables, but quite freely in non-word-final position, as in OSFr. kánta canta 'he sings' : ONFr. čántəθ chanteṭ, and OSFr. kantár cantar 'to sing' : ONFr. čantǽr chanter.

This limitation on occurrence suggests that the capital-letter vowels which we first set up for PG-Rom. may at one time have been positional variants of the corresponding small-letter vowels, whose occurrence was conditioned by certain factors which were later lost.[20] Let us assume, provisionally, that the capital-letter vowels were at first limited to free stressed syllables, and that the checked syllables in which they would seem to occur according to the evidence of ONFr and OSFr. were, in PGRom. times, not checked but free, because of some vowel which earlier followed the final consonant but which was later reduced to zero. This following vowel we may provisionally symbolize by the cover-symbol /ə/, simply meaning 'some as yet unidentified following vowel', without prejudice to any later reinterpretation we may make of it. Our previous reconstruction of PGRom. Ála 'wing' we now replace by ála; of tÁl 'such', by tálə; and, if we had need of reconstructing a PGRom. *mÁsta, we would replace it by *másəta. By this device we reduce our inventory of PGRom. vowel phonemes from twelve to eight or possibly seven; five of the basic correspondences are now seen to be reflexes, very possibly, not of independent vowel phonemes in PGRom., but of conditioned developments of other vowels when stressed and in a free syllable.

But this new theory immediately comes into conflict with a further fact: that the small-letter vowels occur in free syllables in ONFr. and OSFr., as in OSFr. bátre batre 'to beat' : ONFr. bátrə batre < PGRom. bátre; OSFr. kápa capa 'cape' : ONFr. čápə chape < PGRom. kápa. How can we square this fact with our new theory? When we look further and observe the other instances of small-letter vowels occurring in free syllables in ONFr. and OSFr., we notice that we find them only before certain consonants that are intervocalic or that stand between vowel and /r/ + vowel (as in the examples given). We could obviate our difficulty if we assumed that these consonants had some characteristic that caused them, though intervocalic, to check the preceding syllable—e. g. that they were ambisyllabic in PGRom. This means that there would have been a contrast in PGRom. between ambisyllabic and non-ambisyllabic intervocalic consonants, which phonetically would most probably have been a contrast between long and short, double and single.[21] Hence, if we set up PG-Rom. báttre instead of our earlier bátre, or káppa instead of kápa, and, similarly, a double consonant phoneme after each instance of a small-letter vowel in an apparently free syllable in PGRom., we find our difficulty removed. Nor is this a wholly abstract or unrealistic procedure, so far as our OSFr. and ONFr. evidence is concerned, for we must set up a PGRom. double consonant anyhow at least in the case of /rr/, as in the correspondence OSFr. térra terra 'earth' : ONFr. térə tere < PGRom. térra.

Once we have set up double consonants for PGRom., we find that certain consonant correspondences which we set up originally, noting that they occur only between vowels or between a vowel and /r/ + vowel (nos. 43–7), now appear to be in complementary distribution with single consonants elsewhere: /β/ with /b/, /z/ with /s/, /γ/ with /g/. Hence we are justified in replacing such a first approximation as PG-Rom. koβrír 'to cover' with kobrír, since our first approximation of PGRom. ábas 'abbot' (cf. no. 6) is now reinterpreted as ábbas. But we are still in a quandary as to what we originally set up as /ð/ and /δ/, since both are in complementary distribution with /d/ elsewhere. On the evidence of OSFr. and ONFr. alone, we simply cannot decide the problem, and must leave it unsolved; according to the evidence with which we have been working so far, there were too many allophones in partial complementary distribution in PGRom., and we cannot tell what their earlier status was. Was their occurrence determined by some other factors now lost and not recoverable by deduction? Do they represent a dialectal differentiation within PGRom.? Or do they represent two phonemes which were earlier quite distinct?

Here the modern dialects give us an answer. In Béarn, in the upper mountain valleys, there are dialects which clearly indicate that, not only for the dental series, but also for the labials and gutturals, there were single unvoiced stop consonants as well as voiced stop consonants in PGRom.[22] Consider the following tables of correspondences, the first set showing PGRom. /p t k/ and the second set showing PGRom. /b d g/:

Bearnese	OSFr.	ONFr.	PGRom.
sápo 'sap'	sába	sǽvə	sápa
espáto 'sword-like part of plow'	espáda 'sword'	espǽðə 'sword'	espáta
pleká 'to fold'	plegár	pleiiǽr	plekárə
hábo 'bean'	fába	fǽvə	fába
sudá 'to sweat'	suzár	suðǽr	sudárə
ligá 'to bind'	ligár	liiǽr	ligárə

[20] For the significance of such limitations on occurrence and their implications for earlier stages of the language, cf. H. M. Hoenigswald, Internal Reconstruction, SIL 2.78–87 (1944), and Sound Change and Linguistic Structure, Lang. 22.138–43 (1946) ⟪139⟫; and for a discussion of the relation between phonemic change and the loss of factors which condition positional variants, cf. most recently W. F. Twaddell, Lang. 24.151 (1948) ⟪296–7⟫.

[21] Cf. M. Swadesh, The Phonemic Interpretation of Long Consonants, Lang. 13.1–10 (1937).

[22] Cf. the materials gathered by W. D. Elcock, De quelques affinités phonétiques entre le béarnais et l'aragonais (Paris, 1938), especially the sections entitled Versant béarnais in Chapters 1–3 and the Conclusion in Chapter 4. The examples given here are from Elcock and the ALF.

These correspondences survive only scatteringly in Bearnese, and in a very restricted region; but they are sufficient, and the evidence (including absence of false reconstructions, i.e. hyper-urbanisms) is enough to show that they are relics of an earlier state of affairs, not later developments.[23] The evidence of Bearnese thus helps to remove a further doubt, and to assign PGRom. [ð̌] to the /t/ phoneme and [ð] to the /d/ phoneme, and also to distinguish between single intervocalic /p/ and /b/, /k/ and /g/ for PGRom.

Furthermore, it is obvious that for PGRom. we may retain the symbols used for correspondences nos. 31–42, but must interpret them phonemically as consisting of consonants plus a phonemic feature of palatalization, similar to the situation in modern Russian,[24] Marshallese,[25] and other languages. We are thus enabled to reduce our stock of PGRom. phonemes to the following:

Vowels			Consonants		
i		u	p	t	k
e		o	b	d	g
ɛ	(ə)	ɔ	f	s	
	a		v		
				c	
				ǯ	ǧ
			m	n	
				l	
			w	r	h

plus phonemes of palatalization and stress. Further reduction might be possible: we might suspect, for instance, that /ǧ/ was in complementary distribution with /i/ in hiatus, and thus eliminate one further phoneme.

The modern dialects are also of help in giving evidence for the occurrence in PGRom. of a greater variety of final vowels than we might deduce from the OSFr. and ONFr. evidence alone; cf. the final /i/ attested by such forms as otri, autri 'others' in the departments of Haute-Loire and Puy-de-Dôme (ALF map 76), and final /o/ or /u/ for, say, the types kútu kúto 'elbow' and pénsu pénso 'I think' in SE France and Switzerland (ALF maps 330, 996).

Now if we were limited to the evidence of ONFr., OSFr., and the present-day dialects of Gallo-Romance, without benefit of the other Romance languages or of Latin, our reconstruction as first made and later amended and simplified would probably still be the occasion for fierce debates. There might be a disagreement among scholars as to the validity of the identification of capital-letter vowels with small-letter vowels, of our postulation of double intervocalic consonants, or of a separate series of single unvoiced intervocalic stops /p t k/ for PGRom., similar to the disagreement now existing over the so-called 'laryngeals' of Hittite and the Indo-European languages.[26] Critics of the reconstructed Proto-Gallo-Romance might condemn it in the name of one special doctrine or another, or of some a-priori consideration.[27]

Fortunately, we are not in this position. Our next step, once having reconstructed PGRom., is to examine it in the light of the related Romance languages, when we have followed the same procedure and have reconstructed Proto-Ibero-Romance, Proto-Italo-Romance, Proto-Eastern (Balkan) Romance, and Proto-Southern Romance. What we find usually confirms our reconstruction of PGRom., and enables us to proceed farther back in our reconstruction to a still earlier stage. We need not go here into such detail for these intermediate stages as we have for PGRom.; suffice it to say that when we have reconstructions for these other groups as we already have for PGRom., we are able to reconstruct the further preceding intermediate stages and to arrive eventually at a reconstruction of PRom. itself. Naturally, at each stage, we apply the procedures of descriptive linguistics to our results, examining them, reanalyzing and reinterpreting them. In this way, we establish Proto-Western Romance by comparison of Proto-Gallo-Romance and Proto-Ibero-Romance, affording light especially on the earlier status of vowels (definite elimination of our cover-symbol /ə/, occurrence of final vowels) and of consonant clusters such as /kt/ and /ks/, which developed in PGRom. to /t´/ and /s´/, but in PIbRom. to /xt/ and /xs/. The inclusion of Proto-Italo-Romance again deepens our time perspective and enables us to set up Proto-Italo-Western Romance, approximately equivalent to the conventional 'Vulgar Latin'. PItRom. furnishes conclusive proof of the correctness of the consonant system (with unvoiced and voiced stops, double and single consonants) which we assumed for PGRom. and must also assume for PIbRom., and gives evidence for further distinctions in the consonant system, e.g. /č/ vs. /c/, as in PItWRom. bráčču 'arm' > PItRom. bráčču : PWRom. bráccu, but PItWRom. póccu 'well' > PItRom. and PWRom. póccu. On the other hand, the extensive system of palatalized consonants which we had to set up for PGRom. is seen to have developed from earlier clusters of /i̯/ + cons. or cons. + /i̯/, merged with other combinations such as /k/ + cons. or cons. + /k/.

23 Cf. Elcock, op. cit. 121–2.

24 Cf. G. L. Trager, The Phonemes of Russian, Lang. 10.334–44 (1934).

25 Cf. Denzel R. Carr, Notes on Marshallese Consonant Phonemes, Lang. 21.268–9 (1945).

26 Cf. E. H. Sturtevant, The Indo-Hittite Laryngeals (Baltimore, 1942), and An Introduction to Linguistic Science 158–63 (New Haven, 1947) and references given in fn. 7, p. 160, particularly the criticisms of Pedersen and Bonfante.

27 Cf. the present writer's discussion of such objections in Lang. 22.273–83 (1946).

A still further deepening of perspective comes when we bring Eastern Romance (Balkan and the 'outpost' in Lucania) into the picture, giving us Proto-Continental Romance, in which we find evidence for new consonant clusters (e. g. /p/ + cons., as in PBRom. sɛ́pte 'seven' : PItWRom. sɛ́tte < P-ContRom. sɛ́pte) and a distinction among back vowels which we did not hitherto suspect, between two types of high vowels (cf. the table below). Finally the inclusion of Southern Romance (Sardinian, Lucanian, Sicilian) shows us an analogous distinction among front vowels. Thus, we eventually arrive at nine sets of basic vowel correspondences, for which we at first postulate nine vowel phonemes in the parent (Proto-Romance) language:[28]

PRom. phoneme	PSRom.	PERom.	PItWRom.
u˄	kúlu 'arse'	kúlu	kúlu
u˅	gútta 'drop'	gútta	gótta
o˄	nódu 'knot'	nódu	nódu
o˅	mórte 'death'	mɔ́rte	mɔ́rte
a	kárru 'cart'	kárru	kárru
e˅	tɛ́rra 'earth'	tɛ́rra	tɛ́rra
e˄	éska 'bait'	éska	éska
i˅	píske 'fish'	péske	pésče
i˄	víta 'life'	víta	víta

Furthermore, we are justified in making a deduction concerning the phonetic character of the new phonemes for which we have here set up the symbols /u˅/ and /i˅/. Inasmuch as they gave /u i/ in some languages and /o e/ in others, we may consider that their phonetic character must have been intermediate between [u i] and [o e], i. e. lax [ʊ ɪ]. Theoretical considerations of phonetic patterning strengthen this assumption, in that the lax [ʊ ɪ] stand to the tense [u i] in exactly the same relation as do the lax [ɔ ɛ] to the tense [o e].

Then a further analysis of the vowel system thus obtained shows that it can be reduced from nine separate vowels to five vowels plus a phonemic feature which—so far as our Romance material shows—consists of the contrast between close and open, and which applies to four out of the five vowels of Proto-Romance. We can extract this feature and, if we choose, can symbolize it by /˄/ written after the close vowel, leaving the open vowel unmarked.[29]

[28] In this table and in following discussions of PRom. vowel phonemes, the symbol ˄ indicates relatively high and tense tongue position, and ˅ indicates relatively low and lax position; a raised dot · following a vowel symbol indicates length.

[29] We could, of course, operating on an abstract plane, equally well decide to extract lowness of tongue position as a separate phonemic feature and symbolize it by /˅/, leaving the high vowels unmarked. Our decision to extract height of tongue position and leave low vowels unmarked is admittedly determined by ulterior considerations, namely the ease of equating PRom. /˄/ with Latin /·/.

Further internal reconstruction might then lead us to suspect that the same contrast applied at one time to all five vowels; and careful consideration of its relation to stress in free and checked syllables might also lead us tc suspect (though we might not be able to prove it in detail) that stress was at one time correlated in some way with syllable length, and that our feature symbolized by /˄/ was perhaps earlier one of length rather than closeness of vowel.

Similarly, among the consonants the occurrence of /k/ in Sardinian and Vegliote corresponding to /č/ in Italo-Western Romance—as in PRom. déke 'ten' > PSRom. déke (> OSard. déke > Mod.Sard. dége), PB-Rom. déke (> Alb., Vegl. dík), but PItWRom. déče—would give us a clue to the earlier status of that /č/ as an allophone of /k/ before front vowels, including /i̯/. The passage of [č] to independent phonemic status took place when a following [i̯] before a back vowel became merged with it and the resultant [č] thus came to contrast with [k] before back vowels, as in PItWRom. bráčču 'arm' from an earlier brákki̯u, contrasting in PItWRom. with (say) kúlu 'arse'. Similar considerations hold for PItWRom. /i̯/, which turns out to have come from a merger of PRom. /g/ before front vowel, with PRom. (initial or intervocalic) /i̯/; and for PItWRom. /c/ and /ǯ/, resulting from fusion of earlier /ti̯/ and /di̯/ respectively, as in PItWRom. póccu 'well' < PRom. púti̯u, and PItWRom. ɔ́rǯu 'barley' < PRom. ɔ́rdi̯u.

A further point is in order here. What should be done in the case of such correspondences as that shown in no. 29 under the Proto-Gallo-Romance consonant system, in which we find ONFr. /h/ corresponding to zero in OSFr., and, on further examination, in other Romance languages as well? We might, of course, carry our reconstruction of /h/ all the way back to PRom., but, as comparatists have long since realized, we should be wary of assigning to the parent speech a phoneme or other feature attested only in a single language. In this instance, almost all the words in which /h/ occurs are limited to the Italo-Western Romance group. We might be justified in carrying it back at least to that intermediate stage; but, with almost all these words absent from Eastern and from Southern Romance, we have doubts about its validity for Proto-Romance. If we use our knowledge of the neighboring Germanic languages, we immediately observe cognate words in Germanic, and the obvious thing is to assume borrowing not earlier than the 'Vulgar Latin' (PItW-Rom.) stage. Even if we did not have such knowledge, we would still have our doubts, and might suspect that these words showing initial /h/ had been borrowed into PItWRom. from some language having that phoneme, and that the phoneme had been lost everywhere except in ONFr. Similar considerations would keep us from assigning the phoneme /w/ of Germanic loan-words (as we know them to be) to PRom.

The phonemic system we finally set up for Proto-Romance is, therefore:

Vowels			Consonants		
i		u	p	t	k
e		o	b	d	g
	a		f	s	
			m	n	
i̯		u̯		l	
				r	

plus the phonemic features of vowel height /˷/ and stress, and the occurrence of double consonants.

The same technique, applied to the morphological system and the syntax (phrase and clause structure) of the Romance languages, would give us a good picture of the essentials of Proto-Romance as a linguistic system. We would see a system of nominal inflection with at least two numbers, two genders, and five cases (nominative, accusative, genitive, dative, and vocative), and verbal inflection with three persons, two numbers, two stems, and at least three tenses and various non-finite forms built on each stem. A large number of the formant elements of Romance derivation can be similarly reconstructed, including prefixes, suffixes, and compound types. Comparative syntax would show us a PRom. system of endocentric and exocentric phrase-types and the existence of the major clause having a verb or equivalent phrase as its essential element, accompanied or not by a subject. This system as reconstructed and outlined here is of course nothing novel to Romance scholars; the all-important point is that we would arrive at it by methods of purely comparative reconstruction.

When we now turn to our records of Latin, we find our inferences—inverted predictions, backwards rather than forwards in time, as to what we may expect to discover concerning the past—largely corroborated. We find our reconstruction of phonemics very close to the facts as we know them for Latin; Classical Latin gives us evidence for certain further phonemic features (such as the existence of a phoneme /h/—not connected with the /h/ occurring in Germanic loan-words—and the occurrence of /m/ in word-final position) which we could not infer from any of the Romance material, and gives us a basis for a better understanding of some Romance phenomena such as the relation of vowel quality, quantity, and stress, and the loss of phonemic contrast between /a/ and /a·/. Yet Classical Latin differs in various respects from Proto-Romance, and is clearly not its direct ancestor. Thus, Romance shows a use of the relative kú˷iu -a 'whose' as an adjective which was not accepted as a normal feature of Classical Latin, where cuius was an invariable; and we have to go back to Plautine Latin to find cuius -a -um normally inflected as an adjective. Clearly, Romance is here continuing an Old Latin feature which was lost in Classical Latin. Similarly, Classical Latin gave to the word báro˷ baró˷ne 'strong man', which in Romance has meliorative meaning, a pejorative turn in the sense of 'lout, oaf', which has continued only in the Italian words bàro and baróne 'knave, rascal'; Classical Latin baro·n- cannot be considered as the direct ancestor of the Romance words built on this stem and meaning 'man, husband, nobleman'.[30] From these and similar instances, we must conclude that Classical Latin and Proto-Romance were not 'mother' and 'daughter', but rather 'sister' languages (very closely related and easily mutually intelligible), by comparison of which we are enabled to reconstruct a slightly earlier stage which we may label simply Latin.

It is perfectly true that if we had no knowledge of Latin, we should be unable to place Proto-Romance in space or in time, as Migliorini says in the passage quoted in our first paragraph. As it is, by comparison of what we know—other than by inference based on Romance sources—of Latin, we can place Proto-Romance reasonably well in time. We must place it far enough forward in time to include the simplification of /ei/ to /i·/ (ca. 150 B.C.), of /ae/ to /e/ (1st cent. A.D.) and of /n/ before /s/ to (at least) nāsalization (1st cent. B.C.), and the loss of /h/ (ca. Catullus' time or earlier). On the other hand, we must place it far enough back in time to precede the merger of /e·/ and /i/, /o·/ and /u/ (1st–2nd cent. A.D.) and the establishment of a new series of palatal phonemes through merger of the palatal allophones of /k g/ before front vowels with the developments of /ki̯/ and /i̯/ respectively. On the whole, the period of the late Republic and the early Empire (Augustan era) is indicated as the best time at which to set Proto-Romance. Certain possible survivals of features attested in earlier Latin (e.g. Plautine cuius -a -um 'whose' as an adjective in Ibero-Romance; Plautine -nunt 3 pl. of verbs in Italian ˊ-no) would indicate that the beginning of our period should perhaps be put as far back as 250–200 B.C.; this is confirmed by considerations of settlement history, earlier emphasized by Gröber and recently revived by Bonfante.[31]

3. Methodological Considerations

There are some who think that the procedure we have advocated here, the comparative reconstruction of Proto-Romance, is useless or even harmful:[32]

> For what concerns Vulgar Latin, the application of the comparative method has proved not merely largely unnecessary, but partly harmful. There is an unbroken stream of Latin-Romance written material that permits us to observe the changes that took place without having to reconstruct them by the comparative method, which was the only one applicable in the case of the other groups mentioned [Indo-European, Germanic, Celtic, Slavic]. Eyewitnesses are far more cogent than circumstantial evidence, in linguistics as at law.

30 Cf. the present writer's discussion of this word, SIL 5.65–8 (1947).

31 L'origine des langues romanes, Renaissance 1.573–88 (1943).

32 M. A. Pei, Symposium 1:3.118 (1947).

We suggest, on the contrary, that comparative reconstruction, as applied to Proto-Romance, is useful and beneficial, both for Romance linguistics and for linguistics in general. We shall discuss, in the following paragraphs, certain methodological considerations relating (a) to the comparative method as such; (b) to the relationships of the Romance languages; and (c) to future work in Romance linguistics.

A. The Comparative Method, as developed in Indo-European and Finno-Ugric linguistics in the 19th century, and later applied to other fields such as Malayo-Polynesian, Algonquian, Athabaskan, Uto-Aztecan, Bantu, etc., is a means whereby we are enabled to reconstruct the essential traits of a linguistic system from which divergent languages have developed by later differentiation. The comparative method rests, indeed, on two basic assumptions: one, that phonetic change is regular;[33] the other, that where we find obviously related but different forms, they are to be considered as having developed from an earlier common source unless evidence to the contrary can be adduced.[34] Both of these are assumptions, not exceptionless iron 'laws': there are many exceptions, but wherever exceptions are found, our assumptions are productive in that they lead to further examination and re-formulation of the facts.[35]

Romance occupies a crucial position in this respect, in that it offers one of the few instances in which we have quite full material for the 'daughter' languages, and also very full data for a language which, though not exactly the parent language, was extremely close to it. On the other hand, we do not have adequate data on the actual parent language itself (Proto-Romance) nor for the intermediate stages between Proto-Romance and the earliest documents in specifically Romance speech. Such written material as is available from the Late Latin period is so confused and untrustworthy that it would be unrealistic to interpret it literalistically and consider it a faithful reflection of popular speech.[36] These gaps must be filled in by reconstruction. Now when we reconstruct such Proto-Romance forms as u̯í-ta 'life', béne 'well', dormí-re 'to sleep', etc., we find that they correspond point for point to well-attested Latin words such as vīta, bene, dormīre and so on; the instances of such correspondences can be numbered in the thousands. Hence we are justified in concluding that the method which we have followed in the reconstruction of Proto-Romance is accurate, and that we have a right to go further and extrapolate from known Romance data to the establishment of hypothetical Proto-Romance forms. For instance—to keep to elementary, well-known material—Romance gives us no basis at all for assuming a cluster /ns/,[36a] or final /m/ in polysyllables, or initial /h/ in any words except those borrowed from Germanic (cf. above). We must reconstruct PRom. ómine 'man', píske 'fish', mé-sa 'table' and the like, even where Classical Latin wrote (and at one time spoke) hominem, piscem, mēnsam. We must reconstruct PRom. méle 'honey', féle 'gall', sále 'salt', even where Classical Latin offers us only mel, fel, sal; and we must take the word of our reconstruction as being basically more correct for PRom. than the Classical Latin. Sometimes we find direct confirmation of our reconstructions (positive or negative), as in Latin graphs like cosul for consul, or in Late Latin salem for sal. More often, the confirmation is indirect, as in Catullus' poem on Arrius and his misplaced aitches, or in classical prosody (which elides final syllables ending in m); and in the same category of indirect confirmation come the fluctuations in spelling and grammar which we find in inscriptions and other documents which reflect popular speech to a certain extent. If, for instance, we find in an inscription[37] sepulchrum istu 'this tomb' in one line, and sepulchru istum in the next, we do not assume that each vagary of spelling represents directly a corresponding vagary of speech (which is unrealistic in the light of all we know of human spelling behavior); instead,

33 Cf. the discussion in Bloomfield's Language, Chapter 20.

34 Cf. Bloomfield, Language §18.2.

35 Cf. the penetrating and illuminating discussion of the comparative method and of the assumption of regular phonetic change by C. F. Hockett, Implications of Bloomfield's Algonquian studies, Lang. 24.117–31 (1948), especially 125–7 ((286–7)).

36 H. F. Muller, The Chronology of Vulgar Latin (Halle, 1929; ZRPh. Beiheft 78); H. F. Muller and P. Taylor, A Chrestomathy of Vulgar Latin (New York, 1932); H. F. Muller, L'Epoque mérovingienne (New York, 1945), and cf. the review of the latter book by A. H. Krappe, Philological Quarterly 26.92–5 (1947).

36a In this connection, the Romance words belonging to the family of It. pensare, Fr. penser, Sp. pensar 'to think' seem at first to contradict this statement, and to give evidence for a cluster /ns/. The answer is that the evidence thus afforded is valid only for Italo-Western Romance. In Roumanian and Sardinian, only forms without /n/, meaning 'weigh' or 'press, worry', are present; cf. Meyer-Lübke, REW^3 §6391. For Proto-Romance, therefore, we have the right to set up only /pe-sáre/ 'to weigh, press down'; the learnèd word /pe-nsáre/ is to be ascribed only to the PItWRom. stage. Naturally, as soon as /pe-nsáre/ was introduced from Classical Latin, it brought the cluster /ns/ back again, but evidently only into that part of Romance speech which was continued in Italy and the West. A similar argument applies in the case of the Greek loan-word kámptein 'bend, turn, double around, bow down' > Lat. campsāre > It. cansare 'set aside, avoid' and Sp. cansar 'weary', and other Romance words showing the cluster /ns/. (Cf. Lang. 14.205–6 and 19.154–6.) Late Latin spellings such as thensaurus for thesaurus show simply that there was a dialectal difference at the time, and do not necessarily prove that we must assume the cluster /ns/ for PRom.

37 In an inscription of the Christian era from Rome, reprinted in Muller and Taylor, A Chrestomathy of Vulgar Latin 108, without further indication of source.

we draw on our knowledge of the Romance languages and of reconstructed Proto-Romance, to interpret both of these spellings as standing for /sepúlkru ístu/ (or perhaps /sepólkro ésto/), and istu(m) as meaning 'this'.

But there are certain qualifications we must make immediately. One is that comparative reconstruction is of course limited to the available material and the deductions we can make therefrom. For this reason, every scrap of reliable evidence which we can find is of value, and even unreliable evidence needs to be taken into account and sifted for its bearing on the problem in hand.[38] The existing Romance languages and dialects give no evidence for a contrast between /a/ and /a˜/ in Proto-Romance, although we might suspect on grounds of internal evidence that such a contrast had been present earlier; but if we had trustworthy material from some now lost Romance dialect which showed this contrast or developments thereof, we would be enabled to push our reconstruction still further back and to set up with certainty a pre-Proto-Romance contrast of /a/ vs. /a˜/ or /a·/. To a large extent, of course, Classical Latin fulfills this function, and enables us to state as certainties what would otherwise remain plausible but not absolutely certain hypotheses.

It also goes without saying that comparative reconstruction must be accompanied by descriptive reanalysis at every stage. If this is not done, we run the risk of needlessly multiplying the non-essential and non-significant features we set up for each stage of our reconstruction; when this potential of error is raised to several powers in successive stages of comparison, we may obtain an extremely over-complicated picture. Occasionally, scholars have made such unrealistic suggestions as setting up a special phoneme to cover one individual discrepant etymological correspondence, as Bovet did in hypothesizing a phoneme which he labeled /Δ/ and an etymon symbolized by /ambΔáre/ for Fr. aller, It. andare, etc.[39] It is only to this type of exaggeration that we may legitimately apply such strictures as the following:[40]

> ... the traditional neogrammatical procedure of piling up everything in the reconstructed mother tongue, which becomes a sort of monstrous accumulation of all possible words, forms, sounds, and declensions of every kind ...

But we can see from the foregoing discussion that this description is not applicable to intelligent reconstruction, practiced with all the resources of descriptive analysis and with all care given to eliminating the effects of possible borrowings, analogical reshapings and other intefering factors. When thus performed, the example of Proto-Romance shows us that comparative reconstruction comes close enough to the 'real thing' to be regarded as quite trustworthy.

Taken in this way, and with full realization of all the factors involved, our procedure with Proto-Romance proves also the validity of the 'family-tree' type of reconstruction. Many recent writers have questioned the 'family-tree' principle in historical linguistics, and have declared it incompatible with the fact that linguistic changes spread.[41] Actually, however, there is no contradiction between 'Stammbaumtheorie' and 'Wellentheorie':[42] the 'family tree' is a schematic description of the occurrence of changes, the 'wave theory' covers the description of their spread. There are, of course, continual splittings-off of new dialects in any language, which often become overlaid again (wholly or partially) by the introduction of features from other dialects, or which themselves spread and overlay other dialectal developments. Our family-tree must be as detailed as we can make it, to give as close a picture as possible, by successive approximations, of the ever-changing reality, the differentiation of a language into multifarious dialects and of their later relationships (replacement, merger).

The method of comparative reconstruction and its schematic representation in the 'family tree' gives us a statement of linguistic relationships as such, by their main dividing isoglosses and in the order of their origin. In connection with these relationships, the geographical position of the languages concerned is a matter which it is often useful to know, but never essential. Sardinian, for instance, would be a

38 For this reason, old documents and relic forms in modern speech acquire a value, in this connection, seemingly quite disproportionate to their usefulness in other connections (literary or esthetic, or even in characterizing modern dialects). The scholar reconstructing a proto-language must, of necessity, be something of an anticuario verbal (as one Aragonese termed Elcock; cf. Elcock, op. cit. 19). Opponents of the comparative method have made a reproach of this fact, and have characterized comparatists and Neo-Grammarians as 'seekers after dead fossils' and the like; cf. M. G. Bàrtoli, Introduzione alla Neolinguistica; B. A. Terracini, ¿Qué es la Lingüística? 34; G. Bonfante, Lang. 23.360, 367 (1947). There is, of course, as much justification for 'fossil-seeking' in this connection as there is in any other historical study, such as geology or comparative anatomy. Far from being out of touch with the process of growth and change in biological or social life, the good 'fossil-seeker' derives an understanding of life from his work.

39 Cf. E. Bovet, Ancora il problem andare, in Scritti varî di filologia (A Ernesto Monaci) 243–62 (Roma, 1901); and the criticisms of his procedure by E. Gorra, Rassegna bibliografica della letteratura italiana 10.103 (1902), and by C. Salvioni, Archivio glottologico italiano 16.209–10.

40 G. Bonfante, Lang. 23.374 (1947).

41 E. g. Bàrtoli, Terracini, Bonfante.

42 As pointed out most recently by A. Goetze, Lang. 17.168 (1941); cf. also the well-balanced discussion of the relation between comparative method and linguistic geography by Bloomfield, Language, Chapters 18–20.

Figure A

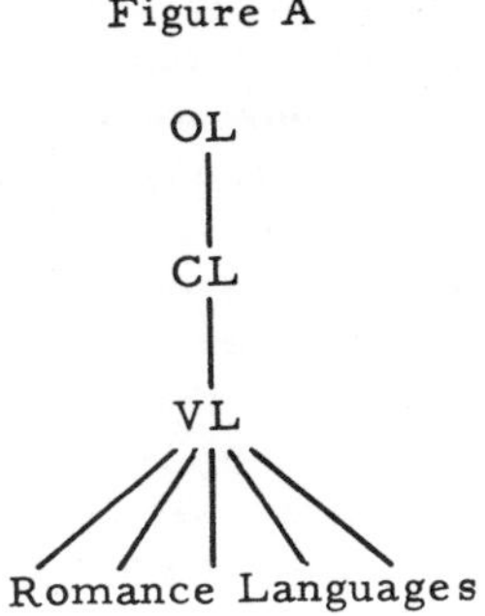

Figure B

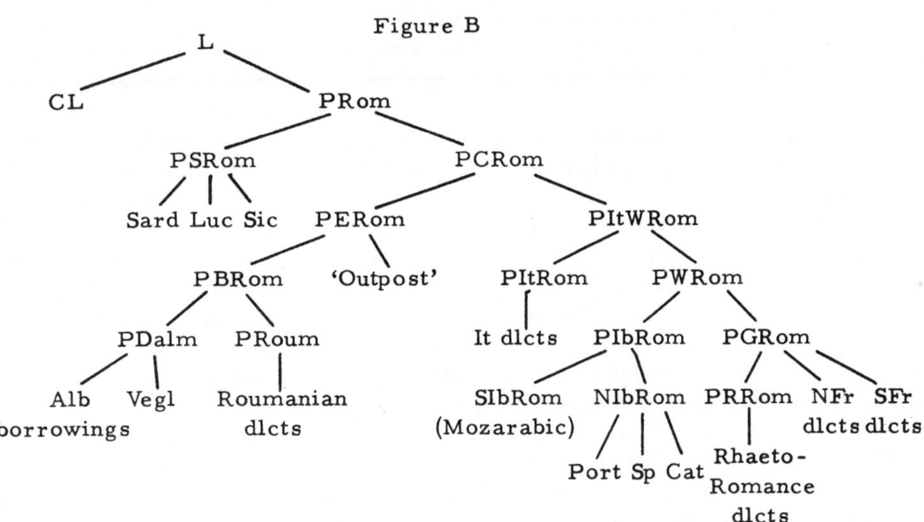

valuable witness to certain features of Proto-Romance (distinction between /i/ and /e˄/, 'hard' /k/ and /g/ before front vowels), whether its speakers lived in Sardinia, South America, or Timbuctoo.[43]

B. The Relationship of the Romance Languages. It is customary to represent the Romance languages as developing in a unilinear fashion, from Old Latin through Classical Latin to 'Vulgar Latin', and then differentiating into the various branches, as shown in Figure A. But when we apply the comparative method, we get a decidedly different picture of the relationship of these languages to each other, as shown in Figure B. For each of the later stages of dialectal differentiation, marked on Figure B as 'Roumanian dlcts' (i. e. dialects), 'It dialects', etc., further branches would have to be set up for which there is not room here.

We must recognize that, as suggested in Part 2 of this paper, the time of Proto-Romance unity must be pushed back far enough to include the features (nine-vowel system = five vowels plus contrast between tense and lax; 'hard' /k/ and /g/ before front vowels) for which Eastern and Southern Romance (especially Sardinian) give evidence. The earliest group to split off, through not sharing in the merger of /i˘/ and /e˄/, involved Sardinian, Lucanian, and Sicilian;[44] the next to split off, through not sharing in the parallel merger of /u˘/ and /o˄/, was Eastern, particularly Balkan, Romance. For the intermediate stage that was the parent of both Balkan Romance and the other Romance languages of the European continent we may provisionally adopt the name Proto-Continental Romance; and for the intermediate stage that was the parent of the Romance languages not included in the Southern or the Eastern groups, the term Proto-Italo-Western Romance. In this stage we find the merger of /ki̯/ with /k/ before front vowels into /č/, of /i̯/ with /g/ before front vowels into /ǧ/, and the seven-vowel system /i e ɛ a ɔ o u/ customarily ascribed to Vulgar Latin. (It is not surprising that such a vowel system is customarily set up for VL, since the latter is usually established on the basis of Italo-, Gallo-, and Ibero-Romance.) If we wish to keep and use the term 'Vulgar Latin', it would be well to restrict it to the sense of Proto-Italo-Western Romance as here defined.[45] Proto-Italo-Romance was then differentiated from Proto-Western Romance (the ancestral form of Gallo- and Ibero-Romance) by the assimilation of certain consonant clusters in PItRom. (/pt ps kt ks/ etc.) and by the development of a series of palatalized consonants in PWRom. (cf. Part 2 above). Later differentiations took place within each group, such as the sonorization of intervocalic unvoiced consonants in certain dialects of Gallo-Romance and of Ibero-Romance (later spreading to almost the entire Western Romance territory), the diphthongization or raising of vowels in stressed free syllable in Francien and Tuscan, etc., giving rise to the sub-varieties of each major division.

43 It is through exaggeration of the factors of geographical position that M. G. Bàrtoli and his followers have been led into setting up ad-hoc rules (norme) by which all the evidence is judged. Cf. Bàrtoli's unsuccessful attempts to explain important exceptions to his rules, such as the conservative character of Sardinian (Introduzione alla Neolinguistica) or of Italian in the center of the Romance-speaking territory (Per la storia della lingua d'Italia, AGlB 21.72–94 [1927]).

44 Cf. H. Lausberg, Die Mundarten Südlukaniens; and M. L. Wagner's works on Sardinian, especially his Historische Lautlehre des Sardischen (Halle, 1941; ZRPh. Beiheft 93) and Flessione nominale e verbale del sardo antico e moderno, Italia Dialettale 14.93–170 (1938) and 15.1–29 (1939).

45 Certainly it is not conducive to clarity to use the term 'Vulgar Latin' to apply indiscriminately to all material written in Latin since Classical times, since the degree to which popular speech is reflected in such documents varies greatly and is anything but trustworthy. 'Late Latin' is a much better term for this type of material, since it implies no judgment as to the accuracy with which the writing reflects everyday usage.

Even this proposed reorganization of the scheme of relationships among the Romance languages is sketchy, and will do only for a tentative grouping. Some dialectal divisions that undoubtedly once existed in the time of the Empire must have been lost in later centuries, and it is perhaps to the effects of such lost dialectal divisions that we should ascribe a number of apparently inexplicable divergent developments in modern Romance, such as the anomalous l- of Italian luglio 'July' < PRom. i̯ú^liu, and the equally anomalous initial /ǧ/ of Italian giglio 'lily' < PRom. lí^liu.[46] In any case, our picture of the intermediate stages of dialectal differentiation in Romance should be made as detailed as possible, with all the means at our disposal.

C. Future Work in Romance Linguistics should represent a carrying forward of all the constructive traditions established in the last century since the time of Diez, without exclusion of any type of approach on a-priori grounds. It should include, therefore, the synchronic analysis of as many modern and medieval Romance linguistic systems as possible; the comparative reconstruction of Proto-Romance and intermediate stages of Romance dialectal development; and the interpretation of historical and geographical data in the light of the results thus obtained—with, of course, resultant further illumination of our previous analyses and reconstructions.

We must emphasize especially that synchronic analysis, comparative reconstruction, and the direct study of historical data such as documents and texts are by no means mutually exclusive. They are but different angles from which the same material—human speech and its history—can be approached, and all are equally essential.[47] To emphasize any one of these approaches at the expense of any other is harmful, in that it gives a false perspective. The latter half of the 19th century may have erred in over-emphasizing comparative reconstruction at the expense of other aspects of research; but the first half of the 20th century has erred far more in its almost complete neglect of comparative work in Romance. It must be the task of the second half of our century to restore a proper balance between comparativism and philology, to heal the unfortunate breach that has arisen between them, and to integrate into Romance linguistics the more recently developed techniques of structural analysis.

Furthermore, workers in Romance linguistics are especially favored, as we have pointed out, in having material available at both ends of the period they study. For this reason, scholars in other fields often look to them for methodological guidance; Romance should be the ideal proving ground for lingustic method, and especially for testing the principles and procedures of comparative reconstruction, which is so essential in other fields where the parent speech is completely undocumented. But workers in Romance have all too often felt that the availability of material at both ends of their period frees them from the necessity of comparative reconstruction, and have turned their attention elsewhere. Hence a gap has developed between Romance and other fields of linguistics, to the regret of thoughtful scholars.[48] It is incumbent on Romance scholars to analyze and interpret their exceptionally full stock of linguistic material, using all the methods of study at their disposal, working both backward and forward in time. Only thus will Romance linguistics be enabled to do what others expect of it: to serve not only as an end in itself but as a model and a training-ground for workers in all fields of historical linguistics.

46 That is to say, we might assume that in a certain dialect of PRom., initial /l/ and /i̯/ were merged, either in /l/ or in /i̯/ or in a third development (such as /l'/), so that PRom. lí^li̯u and i̯ú^li̯u came to be identical in their initial sound. Then at a later stage, these two forms were subjected to 'false regression', with *i̯í^liu and *lú^liu arising as overcorrected forms and surviving in Italian. Cf. J. Babad, ZRPh. 19.270 (1895); also C. H. Grandgent, From Latin to Italian 70; Meyer-Lübke (tr. Bàrtoli and Braun), Grammatica storica della lingua italiana e dei dialetti toscani 91-2 (Torino, 1931); Pei, The Italian Language 50-1 (New York, 1941)—all of which either leave the problem unsolved or assume some kind of dissimilatory process.

47 Cf. the discussion of the relation between philology, field method, and reconstruction, by C. F. Hockett, Lang. 24.118 ff. (1948) ((282 f.)).

48 Cf., for instance, L. H. Gray, Foundations of Language 460 (New York, 1939).

PEIPING MORPHOPHONEMICS[1]

CHARLES F. HOCKETT

Language 26.63–85—1950

Morphophonemics, as the term is used here, subsumes every phase of the phonemic shape of morphemes: the typical shapes of alternants, the types of alternation, and the various environmental factors (phonological or grammatical) which elicit one alternant or another of those morphemes which appear in more than one shape. This usage is broader than some which have recently been described, for instance by Bloch and by Wells.[2]

Every language has morphemes, and so every language has morphophonemics. In the conceivable limiting case, the morphophonemic section of a description would list the typical shapes, and then would consist of a single statement: each morpheme appears, wherever found, in one and only one phonemic shape. Probably no such language exists. Chinese has been thought to approximate this state, and indeed it does, if we compare it with Yokuts or Navaho, or even with Spanish or Japanese. Nevertheless, the Chinese of Peiping has a respectable number of morphemes which appear in more than a single shape. In this paper we survey and classify the alternations involved; in some cases it is necessary to give relevant portions of the morphemic and tactical analysis.

[1] This paper continues the discussion of the structure of Peiping Chinese begun in Peiping Phonology (cited hereafter PP), JAOS 67.253–67 (1947) ((217)). The approach is essentially that developed by Zellig S. Harris, with the minor modifications outlined in the writer's Problems of Morphemic Analysis (cited PMA), Lang. 23.321–43 (1947) ((229)). The terminology of these two papers is here used without new definition.

In the course of the investigation letters of inquiry were addressed to Yuenren Chao and to Fang-kuei Li, both of whom graciously answered in considerable detail. For their advice—which, it must be confessed, has not in all instances been followed—I wish to express my sincere thanks.

[2] Bernard Bloch, Lang. 23.414 ((251)): 'Morphophonemics is the study of the alternation between corresponding phonemes in alternant shapes of the same morpheme.' This implies a limitation of the term to cover only alternations, rather than shapes and alternations, and, furthermore, to subsume only alternations between shapes that are more or less comparable phonemically (knife and knive-s), so that one can pick out which phoneme of one shape corresponds to which in another shape. We want also to cover such cases as go and wen-t. Also Rulon S. Wells, Lang. 25.100 (fn. 5): '[the differences between alternant shapes of morphemes are] only a part of a more general class of facts, the facts about the phonemic shapes of morphs in general in the language in question.' Wells limits the term 'morphophonemics' to the narrower class of facts.

0. Notation. As a point of departure we must have a phonemic analysis, and a notation that accurately reflects it. Any analysis which takes care of all the relevant facts will do, since we can revise it if need arises. For the most part, these prerequisites are supplied by the discussion in PP. Even to start with, however, we shall find it convenient to revise the notation of that paper in a few respects; also, unfortunately, there are some errors of fact incorporated into PP which must be dealt with before we can proceed.

The modifications of notation are these:

(1) Slant lines will be used only when needed for clarity.

(2) Microjuncture (PP §2) will be transcribed with /#/ instead of with a space during the first part of the discussion, to direct attention to its occurrence in certain places. The other junctural symbols, /,/ and /;/, defined in PP to stand respectively for simultaneous microjuncture and mesojuncture and for simultaneous microjuncture, mesojuncture, and macrojuncture, are to be interpreted here as mesojuncture and as that plus macrojuncture, without the simultaneous microjuncture in either case.

(3) Nuclear stress (discussed in PP §4 but not supplied with a symbol) will be written /˘/.

(4) The symbols /p ph t th c ch k kh/ of PP will be replaced by /b p d t z c g k/ respectively.

The discussion in PP was in error in the following respects:

(1) As indicated in addendum (3) of PP, simultaneous /i/ and /u/ must be written with a unit symbol (here /y/), because the graph /iu/ must be used for those two elements in succession. /iu/ stands in contrast with /ieu/ at least with tone /2/ and quiet or zero stress: #ˌiu²#ˈzing³ 'oil well' : #ˌieu²#ˈzing³ 'there are wells'. As a matter of fact, even apart from cases such as this (involving the type of tonal sandhi discussed in §6 below), the sequences /iu/ and /ieu/ seem to constitute two distinct points in the phonological pattern. There are speakers who will say consistently #iu² for 'oil', but who will fluctuate between that and #ieu² for 'postal', or even consistently use the latter form. The contrast carries very little functional burden, true enough; but it is there. It is possible that /ui/ and /uei/ must be similarly distinguished, but this is not yet clear, and no effort is made to do so in this paper.

(2) The choice between /ien/ and /ian/, mentioned in PP §9.55, is not so arbitrary as is implied there. There are speakers who say #bien¹ 'side' (and, with the retroflex suffix, #ˈbieir¹#srang⁴ 'on the edge'),

but #dian^3 'bit' (#i^4#ˈdiair^3 'a little').[3] It may be that for such speakers the choice of /ien/ or /ian/ correlates with tone—the former with tones /1/ and /2/, the latter otherwise—but even if so it seems preferable to keep the two apart.

(3) The statement in PP §10 precluding a sequence of two microsegments both with tone /3/, or both with tone /5/, within a single macrosegment ought rather to bar these sequences within a mesosegment. Furthermore, one does indeed find a sequence of two /3/'s within a single mesosegment, providing that the first microsegment carries contrastive stress: one may say either #″biau^3#ˌhau^3 or #″biau^5#ˌhau^3 'watches are better'. Phonetically, the first microsegment in such a sequence has the terminal rise in pitch characteristic of tone /3/ preceding a pause.

With the above revisions, the analysis and notation of PP will serve us as we begin our present investigation. Two classes of phonemically relevant phenomena are intentionally omitted. The first is tempo, the discussion of which is postponed to §9. The other is intonation, which merits some discussion here.[4]

Our chief reason for leaving out intonation is ignorance of details, and yet even if the intonational picture were clear a good case could be made for setting it aside. One does not expect to find, in Chinese or English, any morphemes composed partly of intonation phonemes and partly of phonemes of other kinds. One expects rather that intonation phonemes will cluster into intonation morphemes, produced simultaneously with the stream of non-intonational morphemes. If this is true, then the eventual analysis of intonation will not call for major reformulation of the results achieved here. In English and Chinese—and perhaps in all languages—a speaker transmits two messages simultaneously, one intonational and one composed of vowels, consonants, and the like.[5] Both messages reach the same destination; the intonations constitute, as it were, a running commentary on the rest, without which, in some cases, the latter is unintelligible.

1. The Problem. We begin with a display of several typical utterances:

a) #ue^3#de#ˈsie^2, #ˌtai^4#ˇsiau^3#le; #ni^2#ˌgei^5#ue^3#ˇzrang^4#i#ˌzrang^4.
'My shoes are too small; stretch them for me.'

b) #ˈbu^4#srang#de, #ˌnei^4#kuai#ˌiu^2#ˇdian^3#z; #iung^4#ˌning^2#meng^2#ˈzr^1#z, #i^4#ˌca^1#zieu^4#ˇmei^2#le.
'If you put lemon juice on the cloth, that grease spot will come out.'

c) #tam^1#bu^2#ˇhuei^4, #ˌhua^4#ˈhuar^4. 'They don't know how to draw pictures.'

d) #ˈsye^4, #ˌcung^2#ˈsrang^1#keu^3, #ˇliu^2#cru#ˌlai. 'Blood flowed from the wound.'

Our morphemic analysis must account for all the phonemic content of these utterances (or any others)—the junctures and stresses as well as the vowels, consonants, and tones. However, this accounting may be fairly complex if we find it desirable, for the sake of simpler tactics, to make it so. That is, we may, if we wish, regard one and the same group of phonemes as morphemic under some conditions, nonmorphemic under others, or as comprising alternants of different morphemes under different conditions, providing that the various conditions involved can be stated in terms of the morphemes we recognize, their phonemic shape, and their arrangements.

The requirement of total accountability turns out to be most easily and realistically met if we recognize three main types (canonical forms) of morphemes: (1) junctural, (2) accentual, and (3) segmental—composed phonemically, for the most part, of juncture phonemes in the first case, stresses in the second, and vowels, consonants, and tones in the third. We shall take up these types in the given order; in due time the third type will be further subdivided.

2. Juncture Morphemes. We deal first with the junctural phenomena symbolized /,/ and /;/; microjuncture can best be handled in another connection.

Our morphemic accounting is extremely simple. We recognize /,/ as one and the same morpheme wherever it occurs, and /;/ as another. These two, formally and semantically, are morphemes of a special variety which we may call structural signals:[6]

[3] I had missed this point completely during over six years of work with Chinese, until finally it was called to my attention by Henry C. Fenn Jr.

[4] Considerable information on intonation is given in Yuenren Chao, Mandarin Primer (Cambridge, 1948).

[5] There may be other messages as well—tone-quality variations indicating emotional attitudes or identity of speaker or the like. Such matters, however, either stand outside the realm of language, or else have not yet received the kind of study which would reveal their linguistic nature. Kenneth L. Pike is fond of discussing them; see in particular The Intonation of American English, Ch. 7 (Ann Arbor, 1946).

[6] The notion of structural signals was proposed by David L. Olmsted, specifically for the 'conjugation vowels' of Spanish and Portuguese. Instead of treating these as empty morphs (PMA §21), we may take them as morphemes, the meaning of which is something submorphemic in the structure of the language: a particular conjugation vowel tells us 'the verb stem just spoken belongs to such-and-such a morphophonemic class in its inflection'. Structural signals are then like Bloomfield's substitutes in that their meaning is definable within the structure of language, rather than in terms of the practical world; indeed, while this is by definition true of structural signals, there is some doubt as to whether it really holds for the forms Bloomfield calls 'substitutes'.

their meaning is the grouping, of morphemes of other types, which their occurrences serve to establish. For instance, in sample sentence (a), the /;/ divides the string of other morphemes into two portions, which are the immediate constituents of the whole; the occurrence of /,/ in the first of these two portions marks the structure of that portion as likewise bipartite. The position of each structural signal tells us which of the morphemes of other types go together as a constituent, but the structural signals themselves stand outside the hierarchical structure of immediate constituents. Of course not every set of immediate constituents, occurring in sequence to form a constitute, is marked in this way; but when the marking is there, the structure is as indicated.

We may argue for the realism of this interpretation by a demonstration of the effect of longer pauses (of uncertain phonemic status) in English. Bloomfield points out that an ordinary English utterance such as 'two plus three times five plus four' is ambiguous: it may represent forty-five, twenty-one, twenty-nine, or several other numbers.[7] In writing, we keep these apart by graphic indications of scope: $(2+3)\cdot(5+4)$, $2+(3\cdot 5)+4$, $[(2+3)\cdot 5]+4$, and so on. Using pauses as we speak, these can be differentiated fairly well as follows: two plus three (pause) times (pause) five plus four; two (pause) plus three times five (pause) plus four; two plus three (pause) times five (longer pause) plus four. The pauses thus serve as markers of scope, as indicators of what goes with what. The forms grouped and separated by the Chinese structural signals are not necessarily mathematical (indeed, they are mathematical only if some of the morphemes involved happen to have mathematical meanings), but their role is quite similar. Although it would not be easy, a sufficiently exhaustive search would reveal Chinese utterances differing only in the location of structural signals, and with different meanings as a result of the different groupings of constituents.

3. Accentual Morphemes. The morphemic status of the phonemes of stress is considerably more complicated than that of the junctures. Any occurrence of a given stress phoneme is either a morpheme, or else is morphemically irrelevant (and predictable from the surrounding morphemic material);[8] we shall not recognize any occurrence of any stress phoneme as part of a morpheme which includes also vowels, consonants, or tones. But for our discussion of the stresses we must anticipate a distinction to be made later among segmental morphemes: most of the latter are tonic, in that they occur on occasion with stress /ˇ/, /ˈ/, or /ˌ/; a few, however, are atonic, occurring with zero stress or with /"/ but not with any intermediate level. In the case of segmental morphemes longer than a single microsegment, the tonic-atonic contrast applies to the various portions one microsegment long.

Contrastive stress (") is morphemic wherever it occurs. In sample utterance (d), we could place /"/ on any of the segmental morphemes (each, in this case, one microsegment long) except possibly the last, obtaining the following meanings: 'blood flowed from the wound', 'blood flowed from the wound', 'blood flowed from the wound', 'blood flowed from the opening of the wound', 'blood flowed from the wound', and 'blood flowed out from the wound'.

Loud stress (ˈ) is a morpheme when it is followed in the same mesosegment by a quiet stress (ˌ). Thus #ˌziau^4#ˈcai^4 'order food (in a restaurant)' and #ˌziau^4#ˈcai^4#le 'ordered food' do not contain a morphemic loud stress, but #ˈziau^4#ˌcai^4 'order food' does contain one.

Nuclear stress is a morpheme if it falls in a nonterminal mesosegment. Utterance (d) thus contains no morphemic nuclear stress; but if we interchange the loud stress of #ˈsrang^1 'wound' and the nuclear stress of #ˇliu^2 'flow', we add one morpheme to those in the utterance, and change the meaning by adding a slight emphasis to 'out of the wound'.

Zero stress is nonmorphemic when it occurs with an atonic morpheme or morpheme-part. Thus in sentence (a), the zero stress accompanying segments #de (attributive particle) and #le (completive particle) is not morphemic. We also regard zero stress as nonmorphemic when it occurs with certain tonic morphemes in certain fixed tactical positions, where the accompanying stress level is limited to zero and contrastive. For example, when #i^1 'one, a, an', a tonic morpheme, occurs directly after an active verb and before a measure, as in the last part of utterance (a), #ˇzrang^4#i#ˌzrang^4 'stretch a bit', it either bears no stress, as in this case, or contrastive stress, and the former we regard as morphemically irrelevant.

Except in cases of this kind, zero stress is morphemic. In fact, we recognize two morphemes of this shape. One has the meaning 'de-emphasis', contrasting semantically with the other stress morphemes so far itemized. The first segmental morpheme of utterance (a) (#ue^3 'I', a tonic morpheme) is accompanied by this morpheme. The other is a marker of one kind of compound, and occurs on the second of two successive tonic morphemes. #mei^3 'beautiful' and #gue^2 'country', both tonic morphemes, can stand together (though the particular combination is rare) as #ˌmei^3#ˈgue^2 'beautiful country'; this contrasts with #ˈmei^3#gue^2, where the compound-marking morpheme just mentioned is also present, and which means 'America'.

7 Leonard Bloomfield, Linguistic Aspects of Science (International Encyclopedia of Unified Science 1.4; Chicago, 1939).

8 In this paper, instead of using the term 'empty morph' (see PMA), we simply classify certain phonemic material as nonmorphemic or as morphemically irrelevant.

With these interpretations of zero, loud, nuclear, and contrastive stress, quiet stress becomes everywhere nonmorphemic. We have, then, five accentual morphemes: /"/ 'strong emphasis'; /˘/ in other than a terminal mesosegment 'emphasis on the meaning of the segmental morphemes of the mesosegment'; /ˈ/ if a quiet stress follows in the same mesosegment 'emphasis on the meaning of the segmental morpheme covered' (but less emphasis than with /"/); and two morphemes of zero stress shape, 'de-emphasis' and 'compound-marker'.

Our decision to treat /ˈ/ and /˘/ as morphemic only in certain positions is based on the following considerations. An utterance which has /˘/ within the last mesosegment of each macrosegment, and /ˈ/ not followed by /ˌ/ within any mesosegment, is, so to speak, the most 'colorless' way of saying anything. The speaker can emphasize the content of the terminal mesosegments only by using contrastive stress, or by arranging the segmental morphemes in some different way; he can emphasize the meaning of a segmental morpheme which bears loud stress in the 'colorless' form, similarly, only by raising the stress level to contrastive or by rephrasing. But, with few exceptions, occurrence of loud or nuclear stress in other than these 'colorless' positions does serve to emphasize the segmental material so marked. In the exceptions, we have an analytical choice. In the segmental construction consisting of single-microsegment verb plus #i^{1} 'one, a, an' plus measure R_m (see §12), the verb regularly receives /ˈ/ and the measure /ˌ/; we can again cite as an example the form #ˈzrang^{4}#i #ˌzrang^{4} 'stretch a bit'. In the segmental construction consisting of verb plus negative element #bu^{4} plus the same verb, e.g. #ˈiau^{4}#bu#ˌiau^{4} 'want or not want?', /ˈ/ regularly falls on the first occurrence of the verb, /ˌ/ on the second. In such cases we can either say that the stress pattern, being regular and predictable, is nonmorphemic, or we can say that the morpheme of 'displaced' primary stress is regularly present as part of the construction.

We have now to pose and answer two questions. (1) Is it feasible to modify our notation in the direction of writing only the morphemically relevant stresses? (2) If this is feasible, can we revise our phonemic analysis so as to render the changed notation phonemic instead of morphophonemic?

If we accept every displaced /ˈ/ and /˘/ as morphemic (thus accepting the second analytical alternative in the cases mentioned just above), we can modify our notation so as to write non-zero stresses only where they are morphemic. We cannot manage to write only the morphemic zero stresses without leading to ambiguity. Suppose we leave quiet stress unmarked; indicate zero stress by a preposed dot /·/ instead of with no mark; and indicate morphemic loud, nuclear, and contrastive stress with /ˈ/, /˘/, and /"/. With these conventions, our four sample utterances will appear:

a) #·ue^{3}#·de#sie^{2}, #tai^{4}#siau^{3}#·le; #·ni^{2}#gei^{5}#·ue^{3}#ˈzrang^{4}#·i#zrang^{4}.

b) #bu^{4}#·srang#·de, #nei^{4}#·kuai^{4}#iu^{2}#dian^{3}#·z; #·iung^{4}#ning^{2}#·meng^{2}#zr^{1}#·z, #·i^{4}#ca^{1}#·zieu^{4}#mei^{2}#·le.

c) #·tam^{1}#·bu^{2}#˘huei^{4}, #hua^{4}#huar^{4}.

d) #sye^{4}, #cung^{2}#srang^{1}#·keu^{3}, #ˈliu^{2}#·cru#lai.

In the first macrosegment of (a), we know that the nuclear stress falls within the second mesosegment, because no mark is present to indicate its displacement. We know furthermore that it falls on #siau^{3}, since that is the last microsegment not marked with /·/ for zero stress, and there is again, within the mesosegment, no mark of displacement. In the first mesosegment, there is necessarily a non-zero stress on #sie^{2}, and since the nuclear stress of the whole macrosegment does not fall within this mesosegment, that non-zero stress must be loud. The second macrosegment of the utterance contains but one mesosegment, and so the nuclear stress will fall wherever the loud stress does, and will in fact be identical with it.[9] The loud stress is marked; the other non-zero-stressed microsegments by definition bear quiet stress.

The reader who must interpret this notation into Chinese speech sounds has to remember more complex rules than with the earlier transcription; but for purposes of further grammatical discussion, the revised notation is clearly more convenient, whether or not we can also make out a case for the phonemic, rather than morphophonemic, status of the revision.

But such a case can be made out, thus answering our second question affirmatively. For the revised notation still indicates unambiguously, and without reference to either morpheme boundaries or morpheme identities, the phonemically relevant material and its arrangement. The underlying phonemic analysis would be as follows. We recognize the contrast between zero and non-zero stress, and call the former a phoneme. We then examine the sequences of non-zero stresses in mesosegments. If a contrastive stress is present, all the microsegments which neither bear the contrastive stress nor the zero stress are approximately equal as to level; we recognize the contrastive stress as a phoneme and can thus indicate all the levels which contrast in such circumstances. We are left with mesosegments which

[9] See PP §4. The differentiation of loud and nuclear stress is meaningful only when a macrosegment includes more than one mesosegment. It is terminologically convenient to say that when a macrosegment includes but one mesosegment, loud and nuclear stress coincide.

contain no contrastive stress. If the one, two, or more non-zero stresses within a mesosegment form throughout a non-diminuendo series, we take this to be the normal state of affairs and recognize no new phonemes. But if anywhere in such a series a diminuendo sets in, the loudest point constitutes a phoneme to be written /ˈ/. Similarly, within the macrosegment, we examine the sequence of loudest stresses of each constituent mesosegment. If a contrastive stress (or more than one) is present, the phonemes already recognized take care of the situation. If not, and the sequence constitutes a non-diminuendo series throughout, we once again take that to be the normal situation and recognize no new phonemes. But if somewhere in the series a diminuendo sets in, the point at which it begins constitutes a phoneme to be written /˘/.

We have been led to this rephonemicization through grammatical considerations; but once discovered the new analysis is established purely on phonological grounds.[10]

Although the new analysis and notation are tactically preferable to the old, there will be points in the remainder of our morphophonemic discussion where the older analysis is more useful. We shall retain the new notation, and where it does not matter whether a particular microsegment bears a particular stress phonemically or automatically by the new analysis, we shall refer to zero, quiet, loud, nuclear, and contrastive stress *levels*.[11]

4. Classification of Segmental Morphemes. The early western students of Chinese, and the Chinese themselves until quite recently, perceiving the language through a haze of characters, saw utterances as rows of bricks, of uniform size and shape, each a single syllable and a single 'word', immutable, subject to no influence (or almost none) from the preceding and following bricks. Now that we have set intonation aside, have provided for the opener junctures, and have lifted off and dealt with the stresses, the material that still confronts us begins to resemble more closely this earlier picture. We have now only microsegments to deal with—composed of vowels, consonants, and tones, and held apart (or cemented together?) by microjunctures. But we must proceed cautiously; our fundamental precaution will be to speak of *morphs* for the present instead of morphemes, reverting to the latter term only as morphs are classed together, or kept separate, in the course of the analysis.

The constant occurrence of microjunctures has been underscored by representing them, so far, with a positive mark /#/ rather than merely by a blank spot on the page, because they must indeed be accounted for; we cannot simply count on their turning up 'naturally'. How shall we take care of them morphemically?

One alternative would be to treat them, like /,/ and /;/, as structural signals. We could regard microjuncture initially and finally in the mesosegment as automatic, and say that when a microjuncture occurs medially in a mesosegment, it marks a boundary between successive segmental morphs. The trouble is that this is not always the case. Some medial microjunctures separate microsegments which are parts of a single morph: #bue^{1}#·li 'glass', #ning^{2} #·meng^{2} 'lemon'. We should have to accept some medial microjunctures as structural signals of the kind indicated, but regard others as simply parts of segmental morphs. Such a solution is of course possible, but a better answer should be sought.

A second alternative would be to treat all microjunctures, medial in the mesosegment as well as initial and final, as automatic, save for those few referred to above which occur within, and as part of, a segmental morph. We could then say that when two segmental morphs stand in succession within a mesosegment, microjuncture automatically occurs between them. But this also is not universally true: #huar^{4} 'picture' is two segmental morphs, not one, and no medial microjuncture separates them. We should therefore have to specify the circumstances under which two successive segmental morphs are separated by microjuncture, and the circumstances under which they are not. This too is of course possible.

But a third alternative seems to combine the merits and avoid the defects of both of the above. This is to regard *all* microjunctures as parts of segmental morphs.[12] If we do this, then segmental morphs are of the following canonical forms as regards length:

I. Morphs beginning with a microjuncture but containing none internally: #sie^{2} 'shoe', #siau^{3} 'small', #gei^{3} and #gei^{5} (two different morphs) 'give; for', #zrang^{4} 'stretch', #·de (attributive particle), #·le (completive particle), #·z (nominal suffix), and many more.

[10] This is a statement of historical fact. Since the discovery of the possible rephonemicization obviously came about before this paper was ready for publication, it would have been possible to introduce it before, rather than after, the discussion of morphophonemics. But it seemed worthwhile to retain the ordering of matters as above, as a fairly elaborate demonstration of the way in which grammatical considerations can serve as *clues* for phonological analysis without implying that the latter is *logically* built on the former; there are still no grammatical 'prerequisites' for phonemic analysis.

Compare the similar view expressed by Bloch, Lang. 26.92–3 and fn. 16 ((332)), and the argument by which he supports it in §9 of his paper ((347–8)).

[11] With the present discussion of stress may profitably be compared that in Yuenren Chao, op.cit. 26, and that in John de Francis, Beginning Chinese 5–6 (New Haven, 1946). De Francis devises a notation for stress very much like our revised notation.

[12] Compare the handling of /#/ in Fijian (PMA §16) and Nootka (PMA §18), and contrast the handling of English /#/ by Rulon S. Wells in Immediate Constituents, Lang. 23.107–8, §64 (1947) ((201–2)).

II. Morphs beginning with microjuncture, and containing one or more internally: #bue^{1}#·li 'glass', #ning^{2}#·meng^{2} and #ning^{2}#·meng (two different morphs) 'lemon', #sran^{1}#·hu 'coral', #dung^{1}#·si 'thing'.

III. Morphs containing no microjunctures: the /r/ of #huar^{4} 'picture' or #huar^{1} 'flower' (the preceding sequence in each case constitutes a morph of type I); the /me/ of #sreme^{2} 'what' or #zeme^{3} 'how'; the /m/ of #tam^{1} 'they'. Most, but not quite all, microsegments ending in the phoneme /r/ contain a morph of this type; all ending in /m/ do; almost all dissyllabic microsegments do.

IV. In one and only one case, it seems advisable to recognize a *zero* morph—one having no phonemic shape at all. This is classed as segmental because of its morphemic assignment (see §9).

V. Similarly, in just one case we recognize a *negative* morph—one consisting of less than no phonemic material at all, a significant absence (§14). Here also we call the morph segmental because of its morphemic assignment and the tactical class of the morpheme to which it belongs.

Whether a segmental morph is preceded by microjuncture or not now becomes a meaningless question, since the microjuncture is part of the morph itself. Whether a segmental morph is followed by microjuncture or not now depends entirely on the structure of the following segmental morph, or the following structural signal or end-of-utterance.

Intersecting the classification by length is that mentioned briefly in §3 into tonic and atonic. Type I segmental morphs are, as wholes, tonic or atonic; those listed above with /·/ (for zero stress) are of the latter category, and occur only as indicated or with contrastive stress, while the others may occur with any stress level. Type II segmental morphs have one constituent microsegment, usually the first, which is tonic in this sense, while the other constituent microsegments (marked /·/ in the examples above) are atonic. The contrast does not apply to type III morphs, which are always less than a microsegment, nor of course to types IV and V.

Having chosen this interpretation for microjuncture, our symbol /#/ can henceforth safely be omitted. So long as a tone-mark or a stress-mark is present between the vowel-and-consonant letters of two successive microsegments, we will not henceforth insert any mark to indicate the location of a microjuncture; in the few cases where neither such mark is present, we retain the sign /#/. In citing morphs of type III, which involve no initial microjuncture, the absence thereof will be indicated by a preposed hyphen; thus /-r/, /-me/, /-m/.

5. Morpheme Shapes. Our working assumption for segmental morphs will be that *morphs of different shapes are morphemically different until proved otherwise*. As the classification into morphemes is made, it will be possible to group morphemes into the canonical forms (of length and tonicity) given above for morphs; expressions of the shape 'type III morpheme' will therefore appear in due course. This does not imply, as might seem to be the case, that morphs of different canonical shapes are never taken to constitute alternants of the same morpheme, although this is in general true. But the few exceptions (§9) do not require the setting up of additional canonical types for morphemes.

6. General Tonal Alternation. The four type I morphs hen^{3}, hen^{5}, hen^{2}, and hen^{1} all mean 'quite, very'. They occur in a distribution which is partly complementary. Factors in the environment limiting the privileges of occurrence of the four forms are the level of stress on the morph itself, and the tone of the following microsegment, if any, within the same mesosegment.

With contrastive stress, both hen^{3} and hen^{5} occur before a microsegment with tone /3/, but only hen^{3} otherwise. Thus ″hen^{3}hau^{3} or ″hen^{5}hau^{3} '*very* good', but only ″hen^{3}gau^{1}, '*very* tall'.

With stress-level /˘/ or /ˈ/, only hen^{5} occurs before a microsegment with tone /3/, and only hen^{3} otherwise. Thus ˈhen^{5}hau^{3} 'quite good', but ˈhen^{3}gau^{1} 'quite tall'.

With stress-level /ˌ/, both hen^{5} and hen^{2} occur before /3/, both hen^{3} and hen^{2} before /5/, otherwise only hen^{3}. Thus hen^{5}hau^{3} 'quite good', hen^{2}ma^{5}·fan or hen^{3}ma^{5}·fan 'quite annoying', but hen^{3}gau^{1} 'quite tall'.

With zero stress, both hen^{2} and hen^{1} occur before /3/, any of the three hen^{3}, hen^{2}, or hen^{1} (though more often one of the latter two) before /5/, but only hen^{3} otherwise. Thus bu^{4}·hen^{2}hau^{3} or bu^{4}·hen^{1}hau^{3} 'not very good', bu^{4}·hen^{3}ma^{5}·fan, bu^{4}·hen^{2}ma^{5}·fan, or bu^{4}·hen^{1}ma^{5}·fan 'not very annoying', but bu^{4}·hen^{3}gau^{1} 'not very tall'.

In the position defined above in which more than one of these morphs occur, the choice is non-contrastive. The distribution of the four morphs parallels the distribution of the single morph tai^{4} 'too, excessively'. We can therefore take the four tonally different forms as alternants of a single morpheme.

We might still not choose to do so if this set were isolated. But there is supporting evidence. In the first place, a microsegment with tone /3/ does not occur (unless it bears contrastive stress) before another in the same mesosegment also bearing tone /3/. Furthermore, almost every type I tonic morph bearing tone /3/ is matched, as is hen^{3}, by three others, respectively with tones /5/, /2/, and /1/, with the distribution we have found above. In fact, even if a microsegment happens to be bimorphic instead of constituting a single morph, the same alternations hold: thus uem^{3}, uem^{5}, uem^{2}, and uem^{1} 'we, us' have the same distribution as do the four forms discussed, though each is two morphs (type I tonic plus type III). Therefore we choose, in every such case, to treat the members of the set as alternants of a single morpheme or morpheme sequence.

We may normalize our notation in accordance with this decision by writing, in each case, just one of the four forms, and allowing the environment to be the indication of which shape is called for or, in the cases of free alternation, which choices can be made without affecting the morphemic structure. It is not possible, for this purpose, to generalize the form with tone /5/, /2/, or /1/, since in each case there are other morphs with the tone in question which do not participate in alternating sets of four.[13] But we can generalize the form with tone /3/ without ambiguity. This revision of notation is morphophonemic, not phonemic, and cannot be matched by a revision of the phonemic analysis, since we shall now be writing one and the same tone sometimes one way, sometimes another, depending on morpheme identity. That is, what we hear as hai^{2}hau^3 'still good' will be so written, but what we hear on occasion as hen^{2}hau^3 'quite good' will be written rather hen^{3}hau^3; when we hear such a /2–3/ sequence we know whether to write /2/ or /3/ on the first microsegment only if we know what shape the morpheme takes in other environments.

Only one of our four sample utterances is affected by this revision. Sentence (a) now appears as:

·ue^3·de#sie^2, tai^{4}siau^3·le;
·ni^{3}gei^3·ue^3'zrang^4·i#zrang^4.

7. Specific Tonal Alternation. There are a few specific morphemes which appear in shapes differing only in tone, depending on tonal environment, but which can be described only by listing—not by a covering statement, as in §6.

(1) The forms i^1, i^2, and i^4 'a, an; one' are distributed as follows: before mesojuncture, i^1; before a microsegment bearing tone /4/, i^2; otherwise i^4. Thus li^3·bai^{4}i^1 'Monday', i^{2}kuai^4 'a hunk', but i^{4}tian^1 (some speakers i^{4}tien^1) 'a day', i^{4}nian^2 (i^{4}nien^2) 'a year', i^{4}bei^3 'a cupful'. If the following microsegment is toneless, the shape of this morpheme depends on the tone which the following microsegment would have if it had one (see §8 below for alternation between presence and absence of a tone); thus i^2·ge 'a, one', where the second type I tonic morph, when not accompanied by a morpheme of absence of stress, is ge^4.

(2) The forms ba^1, ba^2 'eight', and ci^1, ci^2 'seven', are somewhat similar to the foregoing in their distribution: the form with /1/ appears in all environments; the form with /2/ appears only when the following microsegment has (or, like ge^4, in other positions would have) tone /4/. In the latter positions, then, both members of each pair occur, but without contrast. Thus ba^{1}tian^1 'eight days', ba^{1}nian^2 'eight years', ba^{1}bei^3 'eight cupfuls', but either ba^{1}kuai^4 or ba^{2}kuai^4 'eight hunks' and either ba^1·ge or ba^2·ge 'eight'; similarly with 'seven'.

due^1 'how, how much, so' is said to alternate similarly with due^2.

(3) The forms bu^1, bu^2, and bu^4 'not, don't, doesn't' match the distribution of i^1 in all details except that before mesojuncture one finds either bu^1 or bu^4, more often the latter.

In each of these cases we recognize a single morpheme with several alternants. Here no notational normalization is possible if we are to retain freedom from ambiguity when working from notation to phonemes. In a practical orthography, of course, one could select one or another of the forms in each case and write it everywhere, counting on the reader's familiarity with the morphemes involved (rather than just his ability to follow rules—phonemic and automatic morphophonemic definitions— in translating marks into sounds) to lead to the choice of the right form for each context.

8. Alternations Conditioned by Stress. The two accentual morphemes that consist phonemically of zero stress have different effects on the segmental morphemes that they accompany.

If we add the morpheme of de-emphasis to the first segmental morpheme of gen^{1}bie^2·de 'with others' and cung^{2}ner^4 'from there', we get freely alternating pairs of forms: ·gen^{1}bie^2·de and ·gen^{2}bie^2·de in the first case, ·cung^{1}ner^4 and ·cung^{2}ner^4 in the second. In each case the alternate shape with tone /1/ is rather more common. We take the form which appears when no /·/ is present as basic, and normalize the notation accordingly.

This is the source of the alternation between shapes with tones /1/ and /2/ of morphemes which basically have tone /3/ (§6).

If we add the morpheme of compound-marking to a segmental morpheme having any tone whatever, we get freely alternating sets of forms: free alternation between the basic tone and no tone at all if the basic tone is /3/ or /4/, free alternation between /1/, /2/, and no tone at all if the basic tone is /1/ or /2/. Thus one has fei^1·cru^1, fei^1·cru^2, and fei^1·cru 'fly out'; zrung^1·gue^2, zrung^1·gue^1, and zrung^1·gue 'China'; sue^5·i^3 and sue^5·i 'therefore'; sr^2·heu^4 and sr^2·heu 'time'. We can without ambiguity write everywhere fei^1·cru^1, zrung^1·gue^2, sue^5·i^3, and sr^2·heu^4. Here, as with the morpheme of de-emphasis above, replacement of basic /2/ by /1/ is somewhat commoner than replacement of basic /1/ by /2/; but replacement by no tone at all is commonest.[14]

An atonic part of a segmental morpheme of type II either is subject to the same variation, e. g. ning^2·meng^2, ning^2·meng^1, and ning^2·meng 'lemon', in which case we can write one of the forms with a

[13] Some speakers have no such independent occurrences of /5/. For them, the distinction between [3] and [5] is subphonemic, and the statements of alternation made here can be simplified.

[14] This may depend partly on which tone the morpheme has basically. Loss of tone /3/ seems to be relatively rarer than loss of the other tones.

tone on the second microsegment, or else never appears with a tone, as sran^1·hu 'coral'. In the case of 'lemon', it would not matter whether we generalized the form with tone /1/ or that with tone /2/; we have hit on the latter purely because the character usually used for the second microsegment carries tone /2/ in other contexts.

When zero stress occurs nonmorphemically on a tonic morpheme in a specified tactical position (§3), the tone seems to be regularly lost. Thus, in addition to the three alternants of i^1 'a, an; one' and of bu^1 'not' listed in §7, one also has toneless i and bu in ˈkan^4·i#kan^4 'take a look', ˈman^4·i#diair^3 'a little slower', and ˈiau^4·bu#iau^4 'want or not'.

9. Alternations Conditioned by Tempo. Like other people, the Chinese speak at varying rates. Certain features of segmental and junctural structure differ when 'the same' utterance is spoken fast or slow. We wish to codify these differences and regard them as determined by the speed of speech, rather than as constituting, individually, morphemically different structures. One way to do this is to set up varying rates of speech as themselves morphemic; but since what we call morphemes are composed, in one way or another, of phonemes, this necessitates also setting up varying rates of speech on the phonological level as phonemic.

It turns out to be sufficient to recognize two tempo phonemes: fast and slow. Any utterance begins with one of these two, which continues, simultaneous with the flow of other phonemes, either through the entire utterance or to some medial macrojuncture (or, possibly, mesojuncture), where it may be replaced by the other. That is, every piece of an utterance falls within a domain of one of the two tempo phonemes. Each tempo phoneme constitutes a single morpheme. Alternatively, of course, we could regard one of the tempo phonemes as morphemic, the other as not—presumably we would take the fast phoneme as nonmorphemic, since fast speech is more common—but the difference between these views seems slight. Meanings can be assigned, even if a bit vaguely, to the two tempo morphemes: the fast one means 'this speech is natural and conversational'; the slow one means 'this is careful emphatic speech for extra clarity'.

Now since, phonetically, there are an infinite number of possible rates of speech, the problem arises, as we consider successively faster stretches of speech, how to tell just when the 'slow' phoneme ceases to operate and the 'fast' one comes into play. It turns out, as will be shown, that this question answers itself whenever it is relevant.

In the discussion that follows, we specify the presence of the fast or the slow phoneme in each case, but supply no special notations for them.

One type of alternation conditioned by tempo is illustrated by the following:

Slow	Fast	
bu^2·sr^4	busr^2	'isn't'
sie^4·sie^4	siesi^4	'thanks'
da^4·me#zr^3	dam^4#zr^3	'thumb'
pi^4·gu, pi^4·hu	pigu^4, pihu^4	'buttocks'[15]

The slow form is in each case two microsegments, of which the second may bear a tone; the first is stressed, the second unstressed. The fast form is in each case a single microsegment, dissyllabic or monosyllabic; its tone is the same as that of the first microsegment of the two-microsegment slow form. In addition, there is a terminal /e/ in the slow alternant of the second and third examples, missing in the fast alternant.

This type of alternation takes place most often with certain forms, but from time to time one hears it with others which in slow speech have essentially the structure of the slow alternants listed above.

A second, though closely related, type of alternation is illustrated by the following (the examples are exhaustive or almost so):

Slow (or fast before /, /)	Fast (otherwise)	
ue^3·men^2	uem^3	'we'
ni^3·men^2	nim^3	'you (pl.)'
ta^1·men^2	tam^1	'they'
zan^2·men^2	zam^2	'we (inclusive)'
due^1·me, dueme^1	duem^1	'how, how much, so'
sreme^2	srem^2	'what'
zeme^3	zem^3	'how'
neme^4	nem^4	'so, that way'
zeme^4, zreme^4	zem^4, zrem^4	'so, this way'

Here some of the slow alternants are single microsegments, though dissyllabic; the -men or -me terminal in the slow alternant is replaced by bare -m in the fast alternant.

In forms of the two types cited above we see morphs of different canonical forms grouped into single morphemes: sr^4 and -sr, sie^4 and -si, and so forth, the first alternant in each case a type I tonic morph, the second a type III morph. In all such cases, we class the morpheme as type I tonic, rather than setting up a special canonical form; for apparently <u>any</u> type I morpheme in the proper setting might be replaced in this way by a type III alternant in fast speech, and the phenomenon has simply been easier to observe in the cases listed.

[15] In PP it was stated that consonants medial in dissyllabic microsegments are voiced. The fast alternant pihu^4 had not been heard when PP was written. If the PP statement holds, the /h/ in this form should be a voiced velar spirant—and so it is. In a small way, this illustrates how one can make an extrapolation beyond one's data, and how verification of this by later observation can test the validity of the analysis. On such matters, see IJAL 14.269–71 (1948) ⟨⟨279⟩⟩. ⟦See now also the editorial comment on page 80 of the present volume, especially at the end of the first column and the following sentences.⟧

A third alternation dependent on tempo involves the only zero morph which we find it necessary to recognize. Between an active verb and a measure, the form i¹ 'a, an', with nonmorphemic zero stress, appears phonemically in slow speech, but is replaced by zero in fast speech. Thus (slow) ˈkan⁴·i#kan⁴ 'take a look' but (fast) ˈkan⁴·kan⁴. (The zero stress on the measure, in the fast alternant, is also automatic.) Since, except for the difference in meaning between the two speeds, the two forms have identical meaning, and since the position for the zero alternant of i¹ is well defined, we regard the fast-speech form, with no phonemically present /i/, as morphemically identical with the slow-speech form in which it appears overtly.

We can now define the speed at which the slow morpheme (and phoneme) is inoperative and the fast morpheme (and phoneme) takes effect. Any rate of speech which is fast enough to involve the alternants labelled 'fast' in the above discussion is structurally fast; any rate of speech which is slow enough to involve the alternants labelled 'slow' in the above is structurally slow. This means that some fast speech, structurally speaking, is phonetically slower than some structurally slow speech. So long as an utterance contains at least one of the forms listed, or some other form in which microjuncture can be present or absent, this does not matter; we have a way of telling whether the fast phoneme and morpheme or the slow ones are involved. In utterances that contain no such form, we cannot tell whether the speech is structurally fast or slow. Perhaps in this case we should say that the utterance involves neither the fast phoneme nor the slow phoneme; in this case our original statement that every segment of every utterance is in the scope of one of the two would have to be modified.[16]

[16] Admittedly this treatment is circular. Not until after the analysis had been devised did it occur to me, however, that the circularity may be vicious in that we may be introducing a grammatical criterion for the phonemic analysis. If we are, then the treatment certainly has to be rejected. But we can still save the essential procedure of regarding the 'fast speech' forms as consisting of the 'slow speech' morphemes plus an additional morphemic constituent (or vice versa). We simply recognize the same segmental morphemes in each matching pair, but extract from one set (say the fast forms) an additional morphemic long component not present in the other set, without trying to identify which part of the phonemic material of each fast form constitutes this component. Speech of speech then reverts to nonphonemic status. The procedure is expounded in Zellig S. Harris, Componential Analysis of a Hebrew Paradigm, Lang. 24.87–91 (1948) ((272)). It might be useful also for the problem solved otherwise in Bernard Bloch, English Verb Inflection, Lang. 23.416–8, §8 (1947) ((252–4)).

Bloch has offered the following two highly relevant comments on this section. (1) If we set up tempo phonemes at all, one is enough; it can be present in certain stretches, absent in others. (2) The semantically preferable solution is certainly to set up only one tempo morpheme, the slow one, with the meaning 'deliberateness, emphasis, etc.'

10. The Final Particle Ce. We find a set of elements, terminal in utterances, with the shapes ·e, ·a, ·ie, ·ia, ·ye, ·ya, ·ue, ·ua, ·ne, ·na, ·nge, ·nga, ·re, and ·ra. The alternations between the shapes with /e/ and those with /a/ is entirely free (PP §9.54) and can be predicted by assuming the shapes with /e/ as basic.[17] The alternation between the various consonants and semivowels is determined by the shape of the preceding microsegment: shape ·ne after microsegment-final /n/, ·nge after /ng/, ·re after /r/, ·ie after /i/, ·ue after /u/, ·ye after /y/. If the preceding microsegment ends in a vowel, there is free alternation between shapes ·e and ·ie, the latter predominating. The forms carry various meanings, depending on context, but the variations in meaning do not correlate with the differences of shape, even where there is shape alternation in a single environment. We therefore take them all as alternants of a single morpheme ·Ce.

This morpheme then falls into a small class of sentence-final particles, including also ·me (interrogative for 'yes-no') and ·be (peremptory or suggestive).

Certain occurrences of utterance-final ·ne or ·na are not cases of the morpheme ·Ce, but rather instances of a different particle, of shape ·ne or ·na

[17] A confusing note is introduced by the relative frequency of forms with /e/ and forms with /a/ in such cases as this. The particles ·Ce, ·me, and ·be all have /a/ much more frequently than /e/; the particle ·ne, and terminal vowels of dissyllabic microsegments of the right shape, all have /e/ more commonly than /a/. Yet we cannot set the former morphemes up with basic /a/ instead of /e/, since there are some (e. g. guai¹·da 'pat, spank lightly') which always have /a/. If relative frequency is a criterion, then we must recognize three distinct morphophonemic types.

Chao (op. cit.) eliminates the alternation in initial consonantism by a different phonemicization. This particle is recognized as one of the few forms with initial vowel. Elsewhere where our phonemic analysis recognizes an initial vowel (e. g. ai⁴ 'to love, like' or en⁴ 'to press down'), Chao sets up a consonant, phonetically sometimes glottal stop, sometimes weak voiced velar spirant (almost high back unrounded semivowel). The initial consonant of this particle is then simply the final consonant of the preceding microsegment, ambisyllabic when between two vowels. Chao's analysis also eliminates microjuncture, the occurrence of which is rendered automatic and nonphonemic. The difficulty with Chao's analysis is that it does not provide for forms like sreme² and zeme³, where one has an intervocalic consonant with syllabification quite different from that between the second and third syllables of lau³fang²·nge 'Hey, Old Fang!' To take care of all the facts, microjuncture has to be introduced, together with the distinction between syllables and microsegments; and this implies the greater morphophonemic complexity of the particle here under discussion.

in all positions, with the meaning of hesitation, indecision of choice between alternatives, or continuing action. This particle is not final, but prefinal, since it occurs also with ·me or ·be after it; but when no final particle follows, and the preceding microsegment ends in /n/, it is sometimes difficult to decide which morpheme is present.

11. The Suffixes /-r/. Most forms with a terminal /r/ match similar forms without /r/ and with a somewhat similar meaning. The shapes before /-r/ are sometimes identical with the matching shapes without /-r/, and sometimes not.

The shapes are identical with and without /-r/ if the microsegment ends with /a e u y ei ai eu au eng ang ung iung/: fa^2 : far^2 'method'; ue^1 : uer^1 'nest'; ie^4 : ier^4 'leaf'; and so on.

If the preceding microsegment, without /-r/, ends in /ing/, this is replaced by /ieng/ before /r/: bing^3 : biengr^3 'cake'.

If the preceding microsegment ends otherwise in /en an yn in/ or in /i/ not preceded by a vowel, before /-r/ the final /n/ is lost, a syllabic /i/ is replaced by /ie/, and an /i/ is inserted before the /-r/: uen^1 : ueir^1 'essay'; zin^1 'this' : zieir^1 'today'; di^3 : dieir^3 'bottom'; bien^1 (for some speakers) or bian^1 (for others) : bieir^1 or biair^1 'side, edge'.

If the preceding microsegment has the segmental shape /r cr zr sr c z s/, /ei/ is added before the /-r/: z^4 : zeir^4 'word'.

When the shape before /-r/ is different from the shape without /-r/, it is of course quite irrelevant where we cut between the two morphs. In the above statements we have assumed the suffix morpheme throughout to consist simply of the /r/, all that precedes constituting an alternant of the other morpheme involved. We could just as well set up the suffix as sometimes /-r/, sometimes /-ir/.

/-r/ is one of a small class of nominal suffixes, including also ·z as in fang^2·z 'house'. There are, however, certain tactical problems. A very small number of verbs end in the phoneme /r/, particularly uair^2 'to play (with)'. This form resembles a morpheme uan^2 with similar meaning, and the difference in shape is in accordance with the statements made above for the nominal suffix /-r/. We may choose among three procedures: (1) assume a single suffix /-r/, usually occurring in nouns but rarely also in verbs; (2) assume two different suffixes /-r/, homophonous and with identical morphophonemic effect, one nominal and one verbal; (3) assume that verbs like uair^2, very few in number anyway, are simply monomorphemic, as are, for example, er^4 or air^4 'two' and er^2 'son, child'. Alternatives (2) and (3) keep the tactical picture clear; alternative (1) does not. Alternative (3) obscures the similarity between verbs ending in /r/ and morphemes not ending in /r/ that parallel them and are similar in meaning. Alternative (2) seems slightly artificial. Even so, if no further alternative is available, the second choice seems perhaps the best.

A different case of suffixed /-r/ will be discussed below in §12 (4). The morphophonemics are the same, but the tactical position is so clearly different and the meaning is so distinct that there is no problem involved in setting up another homophonous morpheme.

There are a few cases of the nominal suffix /-r/ where the morphophonemics are not in accord with the statements given above. Thus 'flower' is sometimes huar^1, expected with underlying hua^1, but for some speakers it is more often huair^1. These irregular forms can be handled only by listing.[18]

12. Chameleons. In several cases it is tactically convenient to regard a segmental morph which matches, with statable differences, the phonemic shape of some nearby morph, as an occurrence of a reduplicative or 'chameleon' morpheme rather than as a second occurrence of the morpheme whose shape it matches. We recognize four such chameleons; possibly one should also establish others.

(1) R_d (R for 'reduplication', d for 'demonstrative') occurs before a measure, rarely before a noun, and has the meaning 'distributive plural'.[19] The segmental shape and tone of R_d are those of the following measure. R_d fits into a class of morphemes which we call demonstratives, including zrei^4 'this', nei^4 'that', nei^3 or nai^3 'which', and mei^3 'every'; mei^3 and R_d have very similar meanings. Examples: ˈzrei^4·tian^1 'this day', ˈnei^4·tian^1 'that day', ˈnai^3·tian^1 'which day', ˈmei^3·tian^1 'every day', and with R_d, ˈtian^1·tian^1 'every day, daily'; zrei^4·ge#ren^2 'this man', and with R_d, ge^4·ge#ren^2 'each man, every man'; similarly ˈnian^2·nian^2 'every year, yearly'; ˈzian^4·zian^4 'item by item, section by section (as of a document)'; directly before a noun: ˈren^2·ren^2 'everyone, everybody'.

(2) ·R_n ('n' for 'noun') occurs after certain bound nominal morphemes, producing a free form; the meanings are generally kinship terms or items of childhood culture. ·R_n assumes the segmental shape of the preceding bound morpheme, but is atonic and toneless. ·R_n is one of a small class of nominal suffixes, including also ·z, -r, and ·teu^2—differential glosses for which are almost impossible. Examples: ba^4·ba 'papa', ma^1·ma 'mama', ge^1·ge 'older brother', di^4·di 'younger brother', zie^3·zie 'older sister', mei^4·mei 'younger sister', gue^1·gue (or gue^1·guer, with /-r/ added too) 'large green cricket', cy^1·cyr 'cricket (another kind)'; wa^2·wa 'doll'.

18 Some speakers have far less differentiation phonemically in microsegments with terminal /r/; for their speech the morphophonemic patterns are actually a bit more complex.

19 Other demonstratives also occur most usually before a measure, but sometimes directly before a noun with no intervening measure: zrei^4·ge#sr^2·heu^4 or zrei^{4}sr^2·heu^4 'this time'.

(3) R_m ('m' for 'measure') occurs after certain monosyllabic verbs, with intervening i^1 'a, an' (in its zero form if not overtly present); it means, essentially, 'for a short while, a bit, a while'. R_m has the segmental and tonal shape of the verb. R_m falls into a small class of measures which typically occupy this position; like some but not all of the others, it occurs only with the numeral i^1 'one'. Others of the class are c^4 'time, occasion', bian^4 'number of times through' (some action that involves performing a string of smaller actions in a prescribed sequence, as in singing a song), huei^2 'occurrences, times'. Examples of R_m: ˈkan^4·i#kan^4 'take a look, examine for a minute'; ˈtan^2·i#tan^2 'converse for a while, chat'; ˈting^1·i#ting^1 'listen a bit, take a listen'; ˈsiang^3·le·i#siang^3 'thought for a minute'. If the mesosegment ends with R_m, the verb, as indicated, bears a displaced loud stress; if more material follows, the stress is often not displaced, thus tan^2·i#tan^{2}huar^4 'carry on for a bit speech = have a chat'.

(4) R_a ('a' for 'adverb') occurs before almost any monosyllabic stative verb, with meaning 'intensive, much so, greatly'. R_a has the segmental and tonal structure of the following stative verb. The stative verb itself, however, in position after R_a, has tone /1/ regardless of its tone in other contexts. R_a falls into the class of adverbs, and into a subclass thereof which occur before stative verbs: hen^3 'quite, very', tai^4 'too much so', zren^1 'truly', zuei^4 'most', and others. The sequence beginning with R_a normally has an /-r/ suffix added to the stative verb; this is a different /-r/ suffix, though with the same morphophonemics, from those of §11. The combination is limited to occurrence with following particle ·de, a limitation not generally found with other combinations of adverb plus stative verb. Examples: hei^{1}heir^1·de 'extremely black'; bau^{2}baur^1·de 'very thin'; hau^{3}haur^1·de 'extremely good'; man^{4}mair^1·de 'very slowly'.

Since one also hears hau^{3}hau^1·de, the /-r/ suffix must be taken as a separate morpheme, rather than as a separate part of R_a itself.

Some stative verbs consisting of two microsegments are bimorphemic, the separate morphemes standing in the relation 'A and B'. With these, R_a takes the shape of a microsegment before each of the constituent morphemes of the compound stative verb, and the stress pattern and tonal relations are different: rung^2·i^4 'easy' : rung^2·rung^{2}i^{4}i^4·de 'very easy indeed'; ming^2·bai^2 'clear' : ming^2·ming^{2}bai^2 bai^2·de 'very clear(ly) indeed'.

In each of these four cases we have the problem of deciding which of the two similarly shaped morphs in a context is the chameleon, which is the background to which the chameleon has adapted itself. (If there were no such problem, the term 'chameleon' would of course be inappropriate.) We decide on the basis of similar structures not involving chameleons. Since ge^4·ge 'every' is like zrei^4·ge 'this', we call the first syllable of the former the chameleon; similarly in the other cases, as indicated by the analogies given for each.[20]

There are several other types of 'repeating' or partial repeating which we might choose to provide for with chameleons. The decision not to do so at present is tentative; the main difficulty is a lack of sufficient evidence. Some of these cases we itemize herewith.

(a) Certain verbs of greater than one microsegment length (normally two in slow speech) are habitually uttered twice. Thus one may merely say sie^4·sie^4 'thanks', but often enough thanks consist of the utterance /˜sie^4·sie, sie^4·sie./. 'Let's take a stroll' may be /·uem^{3}ˈliu^1·da#liu^1·da·be./; the verb liu^1·da occurs more often doubled than single. The alternative to chameleon treatment is to analyze such constructions as the same sequence of segmental morphemes spoken twice—as implied by the phrasing of the descriptions just given.

Different both from the construction of verb plus R_m, and from the construction just described in which a verb is spoken twice, is the apparently doubled occurrence of kai^1 'to open' in such a sentence as ba^{3}men^2, kai^1·kai^1 'open the door'. Both occurrences of kai^1 are occurrences of the same morpheme, but the construction is not that of doubling; rather the first occurrence is comparable to the occurrence of the same morpheme in kai^{1}wan^2 'to open completely', and the second occurrence is comparable to the occurrence of the same morpheme in da^3·kai^1 'strike open', la^1·kai^1 'pull open', tuei^1·kai^1 'push open', and many others. This construction is the <u>resultative</u> construction of two verbs, in which the first specifies the manner in which the action is brought about and the second specifies the resulting action. It just happens that kai^1 'open' occurs both as first member and as second member in this construction, in either case with various accompanying members, and it just happens that one possible case of the construction has kai^1 as both first and second member. The apparent reduplication is therefore quite accidental.

(b) A number of two-microsegment free forms, with stress on the first, the second toneless, of obscure morphemic status (quite possibly single morphemes of type II) are matched by four-microsegment free forms as follows: ga^1·da 'knot (in string or wood), bump (on skin)' : ga^1·li#ga^{1}da^1·de 'rough, bumpy (of a surface)'; hu^2·tu 'muddled' :

[20] Chao (op. cit.) handles some of these forms as instances of the 'grammatical process' of reduplication, though noting (39, fn. 7) the possibility of the chameleon treatment. But the Romanization he uses in his course implies the chameleon solution, since 'x' is used for 'preceding syllable repeated', and 'vx' for 'the two preceding syllables repeated' (333, 332).

hu^{2}·li#hu^{2}tu^{2} 'fuzzy-wuzzy';[21] with some distortion ga^{1}·la 'corner, angle' (cf. ga^{1}·la#bar^{4} or ge^{1}·le#bar^{4} 'knee') : zi^{1}·li#ga^{1}lar^{2} 'in every nook and cranny'. One could set up a chameleon consisting of preposed duplication of the shape of the underlying form, but with the substitution of the microsegment ·li for the second microsegment of the underlying form; the last instance cited would still call for special treatment.

(c) There are a number of two-microsegment free forms in which the second microsegment begins with /l/ or with /s/, and is otherwise like the first: ba^{1}·la 'scar, pockmark'; hu^{2}·lu 'to brush or stroke with the hand'; hu^{2}·lu 'gourd'; gu^{1}·lu 'to roll something along'; gu^{2}·lu 'wheel'; ha^{1}·la 'rancid'; tu^{2}·lu 'to drag on (floor); to lose one's grip'; du^{1}·lu 'bunch of (keys), cluster of (grapes)'; with /s/, due^{1}·sue 'to shake, quiver, shiver, tremble'; ma^{1}·sa 'to smooth out with the hand, rub, massage'; and others. We could set up postposed chameleons for these two sets. In some cases the underlying forms occur elsewhere, or can at least be suspected of being identical with similarly shaped morphs in other environments; in some cases, however, setting up the form as bimorphemic would necessitate recognizing unique constituents.

In (c), and perhaps in (b), we may have reached that difficult borderline represented in English by sets of words like crash, bash, smash; flip, flap, flop.

13. Suppletive Alternations. There are a number of cases in which morphs (or sets of morphs already grouped together by the various criteria discussed above) of different shapes seem to be in noncontrastive distribution and identical in meaning, tempting us to class them in single morphemes. The forms er^{4} and air^{4} 'two' are probably free alternants wherever both are found in the speech of a single individual. The case of these versus liang^{3} 'two' was described briefly in PMA §10. Similarly, in addition to crang^{3} 'a spell of' there is a form crang^{2} with identical meaning, occurring freely in any environment in which any alternant of crang^{3} would be called for. Both bue^{2} and bau^{2} mean 'thin (in dimension), weak (of human relationships)', and the two are superficially in free alternation. 'Blood' is variously sie^{3}, sye^{3}, and sye^{4}.

In such cases as these, there is no systematically recurrent phonemic difference between the alternants, and the distribution is never complementary, always involving at least some cases of apparent free alternation in a single environment. Without devices for measuring the reactions of speakers of a language to the forms they hear, far more accurate than any now available, we can never be sure that the stylistic connotations of the differing forms are not considerable, however easy it may be to supply all the members of a set with a single English gloss to cover their most obvious meaning. In the case of 'blood', there is clear evidence that such stylistic differences exist: sye^{3} is rather literary, sie^{3} and sye^{4} are more colloquial. The course of wisdom is undoubtedly to keep the members of such sets apart. I would now do this even with er^{4} and liang^{3} 'two', contrary to PMA §10.[22]

14. Minus Morphemes. The ordinary forms for 'two' and 'three' are respectively liang^{3} and san^{1}. There are also, however, two forms lia^{3} and sa^{1} which seem to have (save for stylistic differences) the same meanings. By the decision we have just reached (§13), lia^{3} and liang^{3} cannot be taken as morphemically identical, nor can sa^{1} and san^{1}. In order to determine the status of the shorter forms, we must examine their distribution.

Numerals occur before measures (as well as in some other positions), and a group of numeral plus measure may occur before a noun: liang^{3}·ge 'two' : liang^{3}·ge#ren^{2} 'two people'. The forms lia^{3} and sa^{1} do not occur before a measure, but rather directly before a noun; and in other positions where a numeral-plus-measure combination might occur, we find just lia^{3} or sa^{1}: lia^{3}·ren^{2} 'two people'; lia^{3}sreu^{3} 'two hands'; lia^{3}er^{3}·deu 'two ears, both ears'; lia^{3}ian^{3}·zing 'two eyes, both eyes'; lia^{3}meir^{2} 'two (paired) doors'; uem^{3}lia^{3} or uem^{3}lia^{3}·ren^{2} 'we two'; sa^{1}·ren^{2} 'three people'; uem^{3}sa^{1} or uem^{3}sa^{1}·ren^{2} 'we three'.

21 Chao, op. cit. 41.

22 In the case of alternations from one speaker to another, or within a single speaker's dialect but of the same general nature as those which for the most part are from one speaker to another—e.g. tien^{1} versus tian^{1} for 'day', or iu^{2} versus ieu^{2} for 'postal' (see §0)—the same principle ought in theory to apply. If in practice we do not apply it, it is because of the great difficulty in making sufficiently precise observations. We are here at the thin edge between synchronic and diachronic linguistics. If a single speaker says sometimes iu^{2} and somes ieu^{2} for 'postal', it is ultimately because he has picked up both forms from others, and there has presumably been some first individual to acquire and use both. The two forms then differ at least in the subtle connotations they have due to the specific life-history circumstances accompanying the acquisition of each. ⟦Each of us learns his language from his community, readily admitting that he falls short by learning less than the community teaches him; what is seldom recognized is that he also learns more than what he is taught by over-valuing fluctuations in the presentation of the models to him. Thus a student of mine thought that there were two English words spelled ego, respectively /íygòw/ and /égow/, with different meanings which he fluently explained to me; on prolonged cross-questioning it turned out that he had learned the word exactly twice, from two persons whom he was able to name... We each of us have our quota of similarly acquired private distinctions, which we do not know to be private and hence automatically offer as models to all around us. Most of them fail to prosper; occasionally one of them prospers and establishes a doublet-pair like sleek and slick.⟧ To make a blanket statement of this kind is easy; to try to cover all such cases in a description of a language or dialect is totally impossible.

Since the positions occupied by lia^{3} and sa^{1} are positions open also to a combination of numeral plus measure, we may suspect that these two forms also should be interpreted as a numeral plus a measure.

lia^{3} is then structurally two morphemes, respectively liang^{3} and this measure, and sa^{1} similarly. To interpret them in this way, we must recognize one morpheme which appears only in the shape of this truncation of the 'preceding' morpheme, since no measure of overt phonemic shape occurs with which we can identify this one. The similarity in shape of liang^{3} and lia^{3}, of san^{1} and sa^{1}, and the parallelism of difference in shape (absence of final consonant in each case) apparently force us to this conclusion. If it be disallowed, then the only alternative is to take lia^{3} and sa^{1} as single morphemes, thus ignoring their resemblance in shape and meaning to liang^{3} and san^{1}, and complicating the tactics since the morphemes lia^{3} and sa^{1} would then have to constitute a tactical class of their own.

15. Small-Scale Resemblances. We have almost completed our survey; the remaining cases of possible morphemic identity are in general quite problematical. This may of course reflect a defect in method, or in the breadth of the information on which the discussion is based. But it is also possible that there is something in the nature of the language —or perhaps in the nature of all languages—to produce the dilemmas: perhaps morphemic analysis must always choose between being neat but not quite complete, or else more nearly complete but not quite neat.

Without prejudice to our ultimate decisions, we shall tentatively call the forms about to be discussed 'morphemes'.

Atonic morphemes of type I, and type II morphemes, are not of minimal canonical forms. If we compare fang^{2}·z 'house' and ming^{2}·z 'name', or bue^{1}·li 'glass' and sing^{2}·li 'baggage', we see why this is so. The ·z of 'house' is a type I atonic morpheme; but the ·z of 'name' is a type I tonic morpheme z^{4} 'character, word' accompanied by the compound-marking zero-stress morpheme. Thus the atonic morpheme is seen to resemble in its phonemic shape such a combination of two morphemes. 'Glass' is a single morpheme of type II, but it resembles 'baggage' in shape, though the latter consists of two successive type I tonic morphemes, with the compound-marking zero-stress morpheme accompanying the second; so 'glass' looks like such a trimorphemic form. With every form that we suspect of being a single morpheme of a nonminimal canonical form, the problem therefore arises whether further analysis may not be possible and desirable.

Thus 'glass' and liu^{2}·li 'glaze' have similar meanings and end similarly. Instead of taking each to be a single type II morpheme, we might segregate the recurrent ·li as a morpheme in itself. This would require us to recognize bue^{1} and liu^{2} as unique constituents, and it is this that deters us; but since there are some indisputable cases of unique constituents in the language, perhaps it should not.

The other major area of ambiguity is in sets of morphemes resembling each other somewhat in sound and in meaning. In a few cases it is very clear that analysis must go further. There is a set of forms involving microsegment-initial /n/ and tone /4/ with a distal-demonstrative sense: na^{4} 'that (abstract); therefore' : nei^{4} 'that (concrete)' : neme^{4} 'so, in that case, that kind of' : ner^{4} 'there'. There is another set involving initial /n/ and tone /3/, with interrogative-indefinite sense: na^{3} 'whence, how come, in what way' : nei^{3} or nai^{3} 'which (concrete)' : neme^{3} (rare) 'how, in what case' : nar^{3} 'where'. There is a third such set, with initial /zr/ or /z/ and tone /4/, with proximal-demonstrative sense: zrei^{4} 'this (concrete)' : zeme^{4} (rarely zreme^{4}) 'so, in this case, this kind of' : zrer^{4} 'here'. And there are two isolated forms, both interrogative, one with initial /z/ and tone /3/: zeme 'how, how come'; and one with initial /sr/ and tone /2/: sreme^{2} 'what'. Except for this last form, it is clear that the difference between tone /4/ and tone /3/ accompanies the semantic difference between non-interrogative and interrogative-indefinite. With tone /4/, it is equally clear that the difference between initial /n/ and initial /zr/ or /z/ parallels the semantic difference between distal and proximal. Other partial similarities in sound and meaning can easily be spotted—for example, the terminal /r/ with a locative sense.[23]

If we find it more convenient to regard these forms as single morphs, we must at least take them to be portmanteaus, and not completely arbitrary ones, since as has been demonstrated we can identify within their phonemic structure portions which correlate with portions of the whole meanings.

[23] Probably tactical considerations must lead us to take neme^{4}, neme^{3}, zeme^{4} or zreme^{4}, zeme^{3}, and sreme^{2} as bimorphemic, an alternant of a demonstrative (itself perhaps subject to further analysis as sketched in the text) plus a measure -me, and ner^{4}, nar^{3} and zrer^{4} similarly as an alternant of a demonstrative plus a measure -r. But these forms have somewhat special tactical statuses, and the answers are not clear.

The measure -r, if we so analyze, is a different morpheme from the noun-suffix -r and the other morphemes of that shape discussed in earlier sections. Historically it is probably to be related to the type I tonic (bound) morpheme li^{3} 'in, inside': earlier na^{4}·li^{3}, na^{3}·li^{3} and zre^{4}·li^{3}, with loss of the microjuncture in rapid speech and accompanying loss of the terminal /i/, then with the /l/ changed to /r/ 'because' /l/ is not habitual in microsegment-final position. But the two-microsegment forms have been reintroduced, analogically or from writing or in both ways, and now stand beside the one-microsegment forms, as more elevated and literary alternants, so that the -r of the short forms can no longer be identified morphemically with any element occurring elsewhere.

Other cases are far less clear. There are many sets such as the following: zrung^{1} (bound form) 'middle; China' : zrung^{4} 'in the center, in the bull's-eye, square' (da^{3}zrung^{4} 'to hit the bull's-eye, to succeed in an examination'); zrang^{3} 'to grow, to spread' : crang^{2} 'long' : zrang^{4} 'wide, spread out' (as of water in flood time); dau^{3} 'to turn upside down or on one side; to fail (of a business)' : dau^{4} 'to be inverted, turned upside down; to drive (a car) backwards'; hau^{3} 'OK' : hau^{4} 'to like to (do something)'. In each case there are obviously similarities of phonemic shape and of meaning. Actually, sets such as crang^{3} and crang^{2} 'spell of' (§13). where it is hard to find any semantic difference at all, are simply limiting cases of this phenomenon of partial resemblance. At the other extreme one has forms so different in form or in meaning, or both, that the problem of possible morphemic relationship simply does not arise.

One common solution to the problem presented by such sets is to follow the identifications given by the characters with which the forms are traditionally written. Since Chinese characters constitute essentially a morphemic writing system, they also represent a centuries-old, slowly but constantly evolving folk-analysis of the language. In this characterization, the term 'folk' is not to be read with a sneer; *all* morphemic analysis is in a sense folk-analysis, and one might suspect that the identifications thus arrived at would be as valid as any the modern analyst might discover. If one does this, then one says that zrang^{3} 'to grow' and crang^{2} 'long', for example, are related forms, and one devises the necessary morphophonemic machinery to handle the relationship. On the other hand, one does not identify zrang^{3} 'to grow' and a homophonous and grammatically identical zrang^{3} 'to rise and spread (as water in flood time)', because these are written with two different characters. And when one discovers that this procedure would require an interpretation of dung^{1}·si 'thing' as consisting of dung^{1} 'east' plus si^{1} 'west' plus compound-marking zero stress—leaving the burden of the semantic difference to be borne entirely by the last-named constituent—then certainly one must reach the conclusion that the characters are helpful, if at all, only as clues, not as answers.

When that conclusion is reached, it appears that the same caution is advisable in the cases treated here as for those treated in §13, where there was no discernible difference in meaning and grammatical function accompanying the difference in phonemic shape. That is, since there is no *systematic* parallelism between the differences in meaning and the differences in shape from one set to another, we had better leave each form of such a set intact, a separate and distinct morpheme.[24]

24 Chao (op. cit. 40) reaches essentially the same conclusion: 'Although [the examples he gives] are pairs of cognate words (and often written with the same characters), they should, for practical purposes, be learned as separate words.' 'Cognate', of course, is a historical term, not a descriptive one.

STUDIES IN COLLOQUIAL JAPANESE IV

PHONEMICS

Bernard Bloch

Language 26.86–125—1950

0. Introductory. In earlier papers of this series,[1] Japanese forms are cited in a transcription that purports to be phonemic; the system that underlies the transcription is briefly outlined in the footnotes.[2] On closer examination that system proves to be untenable. Instead of being purely phonemic, it is heavily influenced by unformulated morphophonemic considerations, and even, to some extent, by the traditional representation of Japanese in roman letters.[3] There is room, then, for a new and more careful study of Japanese phonemics, based solely on the sounds that occur in Japanese utterances and on their distribution. Such a study is the object of the present paper.[4] The dialect to be investigated is the modern standard colloquial, defined as the speech of educated persons native to Tokyo.

0.1. The presence of recent loanwords in Japanese, as in many other languages, complicates the analysis; but there is no purely descriptive test by which they can be identified, and no valid excuse for excluding them—so far as the analyst can recognize them through his accidental knowledge of other languages—from the total vocabulary. The view set forth by Fries and Pike,[5] that loanwords may constitute a separate phonemic system coexisting with one or more other systems in the same dialect, is unacceptable. What we are able to discern as the phonemic system of a dialect is necessarily single, not multiple: the total network of relationships among all the sounds that occur in the dialect; and the analyst's task is to describe the system in a way that is correspondingly single, in a coherent set of general statements which will enable him to predict the phonetic shape of utterances that have not yet occurred.[6] All the details that make up a language have an equal claim to be used as evidence for the system; whatever occurs in the utterances of those who speak the language is for that reason a part of the total structure.[7] The question how to treat loanwords can have only one answer: treat them as words.

---

[1] This paper is the fourth in a series of articles under the general title Studies in Colloquial Japanese (abbr. SCJ). The earlier papers in the series are I. Inflection, JAOS 66.97–109; II. Syntax, Lg. 22.200–48; III. Derivation of inflected words, JAOS 66.304–15 (all 1946). For an acknowledgment of the help that I received from the American Council of Learned Societies, from several Japanese informants, and from my colleagues, see SCJ I, fn. 1 (JAOS 66.97), or SCJ II, fn. 1 (Lg. 22.200). ((154))

[2] In SCJ I, JAOS 66.98 fn. 4; in SCJ II, Lg. 22.200-1 fn. 3, 203–4 (§1.4). ((154))

[3] It was the neat and systematic National Romanization (Kokutei Rōmaži), promulgated by a decree of the Japanese cabinet in 1937, that especially influenced my transcription, rather than the so-called Hepburn Romanization of 1885. Yet the latter—unsystematic and cumbersome as it seems to be—is the one that turns out to be closer to a phonemic notation. (On these two systems of romanization see Denzel Carr in JAOS 59.99–102 [1939] and Edwin O. Reischauer in JAOS 60.82–9 [1940].)

So far as I know, all other attempts by American linguists to work out the phonemic structure of Japanese are open to the same objections as mine. I have seen unpublished analyses by George A. Kennedy (ca. 1942) and A. M. Halpern (ca. 1944), as well as the published account in Joseph K. Yamagiwa, Modern conversational Japanese 1–9 (New York and London, 1942). All these, like my own earlier version, overlook phonemic contrasts and rely heavily on morphophonemic data. But since their main purpose was pedagogical (again like that of my own earlier version), their morphophonemic tinge is a merit rather than a reproach.

[4] In writing this paper I have had the benefit of several suggestions by Rulon S. Wells and Eleanor Harz Jorden. Masako Yokoyama has kindly checked the examples for me. Most of the examples are drawn from my own files; but where these did not contain illustrations of particular sequences, I consulted Kenkyusha's New Japanese–English dictionary (Tokyo, 1938). All examples taken from this source were submitted to qualified informants before being transcribed.

Several accounts of Japanese pronunciation have been published in English, but none that approaches the subject from a structural (phonemic) point of view, or that presents more than crude phonetic data, undigested and naive. The most useful (or least useless) of the works that have so far appeared in English is Masatoshi Gensen Mori, The pronunciation of Japanese (Tokyo, 1929); others are listed by Borton, Elisséeff, and Reischauer in A selected list of books and articles on Japan 74–5 (Washington, 1940). Mori's treatment is detailed and exhaustive, in the best tradition of the London school of phonetics; but it remains always on the lowest phonetic level. The sounds of Japanese, for Mori (as for practically all the other scholars who have described them), are mere noises, without structural organization or any sort of interrelations except in their physical properties.

[5] Charles C. Fries and Kenneth L. Pike, Coexistent phonemic systems, Lg. 25.29–50 (1949). The crucial illustration in this article is taken from Mazateco, an Indian language of Mexico. In Mazateco words of native origin there are two dental stops: after [n] only [d], elsewhere only [t]. This situation by itself would call for a single phoneme with two allophones. But there is also a word [siento] *hundred*, a loan from Spanish, with [t] after [n]. Fries and Pike regard this [t] as belonging not only to a different phoneme but to a different phonemic system from that which includes the [t]s and [d]s of native words. But the presence of [siento] necessarily affects the treatment of all dental stops in the language: it contributes no less than other utterance-fractions to the total analysis. The cultural evidence adduced by Fries and Pike against this view, that monolingual speakers of Mazateco learn to read the [nd] of native words more easily in the spelling 'nt' than in the spelling 'nd', whatever its ultimate explanation may be, is not a cogent reason for setting aside the phonetic and distributional data.

Certain other cases of so-called coexistence are easily accounted for by traditional methods. Thus whispered utterances are utterances without pitch phonemes, singing is a non-linguistic use of linguistic material. Differences in tempo and style must probably be treated as differences in dialect, at least until a more fruitful approach can be worked out. For a phonemic interpretation of tempo differences see now Charles F. Hockett, Peiping morphophonemics §9, Lg. 26.74–7 (1950). ((315))

[6] See the admirable short statement by Charles F. Hockett, A note on 'structure', IJAL 14.269–71 (1948). ((279))

[7] This does not mean that every noise made by a speaker in speaking must be accommodated in the phonemic system. Sounds that occur in a completely unrestricted set of environments (before and after all other sound types without exception), such as hiccups, coughs, and sniffles, can be excluded from the relevant material at once. Sounds that never combine with other sound types in an utterance, such as the alveolar 'click of commiseration' in English and the polite indrawn hiss in Japanese, can be similarly excluded, or else treated as an organically separate part of the system (though not as part of an independent system coexisting with the main one). Note that the sounds here listed for exclusion are identified by their distribution.

Yet this answer does not wholly settle the problem of loanwords in Japanese, especially of those recently taken from English. Speakers of standard Japanese agree, within a fairly narrow range of personal variation, on the pronunciation of nearly all the words they use—except precisely these. In their treatment of English loans the variation from speaker to speaker is considerable. Some, who speak no English, confine themselves in these loans to sound types and combinations that occur also in longer-established words; others, with some command of English, use sound types and combinations not found elsewhere in their speech; still others are intermediate in the degree to which they assimilate English words to the rest of their vocabulary. It is clear that these different idiolects (personal dialects) cannot all be analyzed in the same way: phonemic distinctions that exist in one are absent from another; sounds that occur in one man's speech as allophones of a single phoneme belong to separate phonemes in the speech of his neighbor. In short, standard colloquial Japanese is not one dialect but several, which differ from each other, greatly or little, in their treatment of English loans.

A complete solution would be to describe separately each of the several dialects of standard Japanese; this paper will attempt only a partial solution. Only two dialects will be described: that in which English loanwords have been fully assimilated to the pronunciation of other words; and that at the other extreme (spoken chiefly by persons with a good command of English), in which these loanwords are characterized by a maximum number of special sound types and combinations. The two dialects will be referred to as the CONSERVATIVE and the INNOVATING respectively. In each dialect, the style to be described is that of normal conversation, ranging in tempo from moderately fast to moderately slow, but excluding the extremes of tempo at both ends of the scale. (The conservative dialect is treated in §§1–7, the innovating dialect in §8.)

0.2. Definitions of a few basic terms will clarify the description.[8]

A PHRASE is an utterance or part of an utterance bounded by successive pauses (interruptions of speech activity, regardless of length).[9] A phrase may be preceded or followed, or both preceded and followed, by other phrases in the same utterance, with pauses intervening; but no phrase contains a pause within itself.

A QUALITY is any aurally distinguishable single component of the total auditory impression made by some part of a phrase—a particular vowel color, the effect of a particular consonantal position or movement or manner of articulation, palatalization, oral or nasal resonance, voice or voicelessness, a particular level of loudness or pitch, and so on. Qualities are identified by ear; but in linguistic works they are traditionally defined in terms of their assumed production by the vocal organs.

A PHONE is any continuous fraction of a phrase that is heard as coextensive with a given quality; very often a phone is defined by several qualities at once, beginning and ending together. Phones are of two kinds: a SEGMENT is a minimum phone, one that contains no smaller phone; a SPAN is a phone composed of two or more segments that have a quality or a combination of qualities in common. The order of phones in a phrase is successive, simultaneous, or overlapping: segments occur only in succession; but spans, which are coextensive with qualities common to a train of several segments, occur simultaneously with the segments that compose the train, and may overlap with other spans. Every phone is a unique event. The segmentation of a phrase into phones is accomplished by ear; but in linguistic works, again, it is traditionally described in terms of the assumed movements and positions of the vocal organs.

Successive qualities are THE SAME if no difference can be heard between them; otherwise they are DIFFERENT. Two or more phones are THE SAME if they contain the same qualities and no others; otherwise they are DIFFERENT. Sameness and difference are thus determined impressionistically by ear.[10]

Two or more phones are PHONETICALLY SIMILAR if they contain a quality or a combination of qualities that is absent from all other phones in the utterances of the same dialect. (It follows that if two or more phones are the same they must be phonetically similar, but not conversely.) Under this definition phonetic similarity has an absolute, not a relative meaning.

The ENVIRONMENT of a phone is the discontinuous sequence of phones that precede and follow it in the phrase (or, if it is initial or final, the sequence of phones that follow or precede it). For most purposes the relevant environment of a phone consists only of the immediately preceding and the immediately following phone. Environments of two or more phones are THE SAME if they consist wholly of the same phones in the same order. Phones occurring in the same environment are said to have the environment IN COMMON.

If different phones have none of their environments in common, they are IN COMPLEMENTARY DISTRIBUTION; if they have in common only a phonetically or phonemically definable set of environments, they are IN OVERLAPPING DISTRIBUTION; if one phone shares all the environments of another, they are IN FREE VARIATION.[11] Different phones that are in complementary or overlapping distribution or in free variation are NON-CONTRASTIVE.

[8] These definitions are restated, with additions and with a pervading shift of emphasis, from my article A set of postulates for phonemic analysis, Lg. 24.3–46 (1948); they were presented, in a preliminary version, before a meeting of the Linguistic Society in New York, 30 December 1948. The restatement is intended to meet the objections of Martin Joos, Acoustic phonetics 8 fn. 9 and 120 fn. 85 (Language Monograph No. 23, 1948), by establishing the theory of phonemic analysis on an auditory instead of an articulatory basis.

[9] In SCJ II, Lg. 22.202 ff., this unit is called a pause-group, in order to avoid confusion with the use of the term 'phrase' for syntactic units. ((155))

It might be argued that PAUSE, the interruption of speech activity, should be distinguished from mere SILENCE, the absence of speech activity that precedes and follows a whole utterance; the two could be distinguished by assigning to pause an arbitrary upper limit of duration—say ten seconds. Such a distinction would complicate the definition of a phrase, and would appear to serve no particular purpose; but any reader who favors it can safely make for himself the small adjustments that would result from its adoption. All the pauses marked in this paper (except in §7) occur internally in utterances.

[10] Whenever two or more phones are mentioned in these definitions, it is understood that they are phones occurring in utterances of a single dialect.

[11] This statement is meant to cover both the situation where two phones P and Q have all their environments in common, and the more usual situation where P shares all the environments of Q but occurs also in environments where Q does not occur.

If different phones have some but not all of their environments in common, and if their common environments do not form a phonetically or phonemically definable set, they are IN CONTRAST. Two classes of phones are in contrast if every member of one class is in contrast with some member of the other.

A PHONEME is a class of non-contrastive and phonetically similar phones. Together, the phonemes of a dialect accommodate all the phones that occur in the utterances of the dialect; and every phoneme, as a class, is in contrast with at least one other phoneme in at least some of the positions where its members occur. Each phoneme is defined by the quality or combination of qualities present in all its members and absent from all other phones of the dialect; and every phone that contains such a quality or combination belongs to the phoneme which is defined by it. A phone that contains two or more such qualities or combinations accordingly belongs to two or more phonemes at once.

Not all the qualities that are common to the members of a phoneme are necessarily relevant in defining the phoneme. If a give phone *P* contains two qualities or combinations of qualities *a* and *x* (whether it contains other qualities or not), such that *x* occurs in other phones unaccompanied by *a* but *a* does not occur in any phone without *x*, the quality or combination *x* is DETERMINED in the phone *P*, and is not properly part of the definition of the phoneme to which *P* belongs.

A quality or combination of qualities that occurs in some but not in all members of a phoneme, and does not by itself define any other phoneme, is CONDITIONED by the environments in which it occurs.

A quality or combination of qualities that is neither determined nor conditioned is DISTINCTIVE.[12]

An ALLOPHONE is a subclass of a phoneme, composed of phones that are the same. In this paper the term 'phone' will be used ambiguously in two senses: strictly, to designate a unique event; and loosely, to designate a class of phones that are the same. In the latter meaning, the term 'phone' is a shorter equivalent of 'allophone'. The context in each case will make it clear which meaning is intended.

A PHONETIC TRANSCRIPTION is a record either of a single utterance by one speaker (PHONIC transcription) or of a class of utterances composed of the same phones in the same order (ALLOPHONIC transcription). A PHONEMIC TRANSCRIPTION is a record of a class of utterances whose constituent phones belong respectively to the same phonemes in the same order.

1. Syllables. The most striking general feature of Japanese pronunciation is its staccato rhythm. The auditory impression of any phrase is of a rapid pattering succession of more-or-less sharply defined fractions, all of about the same length. In any one utterance, or indeed in any one conversation or style of discourse, the perceived relative duration of successive phrases can be adequately compared in terms of these fractions: two phrases containing the same number of fractions are heard as equal in duration; a phrase containing twice or three times as many fractions as another is heard as lasting just twice or three times as long. The phrases [to-ko-ro][13] *place* and [ha-ko-bu] *carries* contain three fractions each; [no-*r*i-mo-no] *vehicle* and [to-*k*i-do-*k*i] *sometimes* contain four fractions each; [so-no-ko-do-mo-no-*k*i-mo-no] *that child's clothing* and [yo-ko-ha-ma-no-*m*i-na-to-de] *in the Yokohama harbor* contain nine each.

In the examples given so far, each fraction consists of a single consonantal segment and a vowel; but fractions of other types occur also. Some fractions consist of two consonantal segments and a vowel, as in [ma-tši] *town,* [*k*ʏa-ku] *guest,* [*n*yo-dži-tsu-*n*i] *true to life*; some consist of one or two consonantal segments and a voiceless vowel, as in [sᴜ-su-mu] *advances,* [*k*ɪ-ta] *came,* [ha-tsᴜ-ši-mo] *first frost of the year*; some consist of a vowel alone, as in [o-mo-u] *thinks,* [i-e] *house,* [a-o-i] *blue*; some consist of a long nasal consonant alone, as in [hõ-ŋ·] *book,* [kõ-n·-do] *this time,* [kõ-m·-bã-n·] *tonight*; and some consist of one or two long voiceless consonants alone, as in [s·-te-ru] *throws away,* [i-p·-pa-i] *full,* [ts·-tši] *soil.* All these fractions are heard as having the same time value; the perceived relative duration of successive phrases depends only on the number of fractions that they contain, not on their type.

Because the affricates [ts, tš, dž] occur in the same positions and with the same time value as [t, k, s], and other single segments, they will be regarded as unitary consonants, not as sequences of two consonants. But combinations

In this paper the term 'free variation' is used in a wider sense than is customary. Different phones are said to be in free variation not only if they share environments in the speech of a single person but also if they share environments in the speech of two or more persons who speak the same dialect. Thus, when bilabial and labiodental spirants are said to be in free variation (fn. 13), this means either that both types are used indifferently by the same person, or that each is the only type of labial spirant used by one of two different persons. For the purposes of this article the distinction between the two kinds of free variation is irrelevant.

[12] The term 'quality' is used in this paper as the auditory correlate of what I called aspects and components in my article on postulates (cited in fn. 8 above).

[13] Phonetic transcriptions in this paper, enclosed in square brackets, are allophonic; they have been simplified as much as possible, so as to avoid the use of too many special characters. The hyphen that appears in the transcriptions of §1 is merely a graphic device for showing the number of equivalent fractions in a phrase; it has no phonetic or phonemic significance. For the meaning of the phonetic terms in the following descriptions see Bloch and Trager, Outline of linguistic analysis, ch. 2 (Baltimore, 1942).

Consonant symbols for the most part have their traditional values. [p, b, m] are bilabial, but [f] is bilabial or labiodental in free variation; [t, d, n] are dental, [ts] is dental or denti-alveolar, [s, z, r, l] are alveolar; [tš, š, dž, ž] are prepalatal; [k, g, ŋ] are mediovelar. [y] is a voiced prevelar semivowel, [ʏ] is the corresponding voiceless sound. Italic letters denote palatalized sounds. The term 'palatalized' is here used to include on the one hand labial, dental, and glottal sounds pronounced with simultaneous raising of the tongue toward the hard palate ('palatalized' in the usual sense), and on the other hand prevelar sounds, pronounced with contact between the tongue and the forward part of the soft palate.

A raised dot after a consonant indicates that the sound has the time value of a full syllable.

Vowel symbols depart in some respects from their traditional meanings. [i] is high front; [e] is mean-mid front, like the vowel in English *bet,* not upper-mid; [a] is low back (slightly advanced toward central position), not low front; [o] is mean-mid back, approximately like the vowel of German *Gott,* not upper-mid; [u] is high back, often somewhat advanced toward central position, unrounded or weakly rounded. Capital letters [ɪ, ᴀ, O, ᴜ] denote voiceless vowels.

Glosses are printed in italics, without quotation marks. A gloss is meant only to identify the cited form, not to provide an exhaustive account of its meaning.

with [ʏ] or [y] as the second member will not be so regarded, since the two parts are not homorganic (not formed by the same vocal organ).

An apparent exception to the regular train of equal fractions is the presence of long vowels, with or without preceding consonants, as in [*k*i·-ta] *heard*, [te·-bu-ru] *table*, [o-ba·-sã-n·] *grandmother*, [šo·-sa] *major*, [*g*yu·-*n*yu·] *cow's milk*. In duration, each long vowel is equal to two fractions of the ordinary kind: [*k*i·-ta] is a match for [to-ko-ro], [*g*yu·-*n*yu·] for [no-*r*i-mo-no]. It is especially significant that a long vowel has the same duration as a sequence of two unlike vowels: [ko·] *thus* is a match for [ka-o] *face*, [*k*i·-ta] for [ka-i-ta] *wrote*. For these reasons, long vowels will be treated as sequences of two fractions (two like vowels) each, and will be written with double symbols: [*k*i-i-ta, te-e-bu-ru, o-ba-a-sa-n·, šo-o-sa, *g*yu-u-*n*yu-u].

All these fractions, of whatever type, will henceforth be called SYLLABLES.[14]

2. Qualities. What we hear in listening to the utterances of a speaker is a flow of interwoven, continually changing qualities. These qualities are the irreducible atoms from which all higher units in a phonemic description of the speaker's dialect must be formed. Whether the analyst prefers a description in terms of components[15] or one in terms of phonemes, his data consist ultimately of the qualities that he has heard in the stream of speech, and of nothing else. In the grouping of qualities to define phonemes, there may sometimes be a choice between alternative possibilities: a phone that contains two or more qualities may be regarded as belonging to a single phoneme defined by all the qualities together, or as belonging simultaneously to two or more phonemes defined respectively by the several qualities (or by smaller combinations within the total number); and in deciding a choice of this kind there is no theoretical objection to using morphological or even syntactic arguments.[16] If different phonemic descriptions of a dialect account with equal accuracy and completeness for all the qualities that occur in the dialect, and invoke no other criteria, there is nothing to choose between them on the phonemic level; at most, one of them may lend itself more conveniently than the others to morphological and syntactic statements.[17] But no phonemic description is valid if it fails to account, explicitly or implicitly, for any of the qualities in a dialect, or if these qualities are not the sole basis on which it is built.

2.1. In addition to the four distinctive levels of pitch to be described in §3.1, Japanese utterances are heard as containing sixteen qualities, which occur in 67 different combinations. These qualities will be defined in terms of their assumed production by the vocal organs; but it must be borne in mind that they are isolated and identified wholly by ear. The articulatory terminology is used only because a usable auditory terminology has not yet been developed.[17a]

In the following list, the first six qualities (denoted by capital letters) are referred to different places of articulation; the next seven (denoted by numerals) are referred to different kinds of articulation or degrees of aperture. This means that such an entity as labial closure (present in [p, b, m], etc.) is taken to be composed of two separate qualities, labialness and closure.[18]

---

[14] The number of syllables in a phrase is therefore not found by counting peaks of sonority or chest pulses, but only by counting the temporally equal fractions contained in it, or by comparing its duration with that of another phrase in which the number of such fractions is known. In short, the Japanese syllable is a unit of duration. Such a unit is often called a mora; but the term 'syllable' is better established in descriptions of Japanese.

It is worth noting, as a cultural correlate of the linguistic structure, that a speaker of Japanese is just as ready as a speaker of English to state the number of syllables in any phrase, though neither one, without special training, can state the number of segments. Since the two speakers count different kinds of units, they will not always agree on the number of syllables in a given phonetic continuum. In the English word *asks*, pronounced with a long vowel and distinctly released consonants, a Japanese will hear five syllables; in the Japanese word [*g*yuu*n*yuu], a speaker of English will hear only two. (The Japanese speaker's 'feeling' for the number of syllables in a phrase is no doubt partly due to his knowledge of how the phrase is written in the native syllabary; but the syllabary, in turn, must reflect the speakers' naive structural analysis of their language.)

[15] For a theoretical discussion see Zellig S. Harris, Simultaneous components in phonology, Lg. 20.181–205 (1944)* For one type of application see Charles F. Hockett, Componential analysis of Sierra Popoluca, IJAL 13.259–67 (1947), and Peiping phonology, JAOS 67.253–67 (1947). ((217)) *((124))

[16] Morphological and syntactic criteria must not be used to influence the basic analysis leading to the discovery of distinctive qualities and their distribution; but they are often helpful in deciding how to group these qualities, once they have been discovered, into combinations defining phonemes. Cf. Charles F. Hockett, Problems in morphemic analysis §§4–7, Lg. 23.324–7 (1947)((231–2)); Peiping morphophonemics §3, Lg. 26.69–70 and fn. 10 (1950)((319)).

An illustration from English. The phones [f] and [v], [θ] and [ð], [s] and [z] are of course phonemically different. Traditionally, each of them is assigned to a single phoneme contrasting as a unit with all the others; but this interpretation proves to be awkward in dealing with certain morphological relations. In such pairs as *belief* : *believe*, *safe* : *save*, *wreath* : *wreathe*, *use* (noun) : *use* (verb), it would be convenient to regard the verb as consisting of two morphemes: one that appears by itself as a noun or an adjective, the other a verb-deriving suffix; but if /v, ð, z/ are unitary phonemes, there is no phoneme present in these verbs that could be taken as a suffix. An alternative and equally accurate interpretation of the phones [v, ð, z] would be to regard the quality of voice (at least when accompanied by the quality of constriction) as defining a separate phoneme /V/, so that each of the phones [v, ð, z] would belong simultaneously to two phonemes: to /f, θ, s/ respectively, and to /V/. This treatment, like the traditional one, is based solely on the qualities observed in English utterances; but by providing a phoneme /V/ to serve as a verb-deriving suffix, it greatly simplifies the exposition of the morphology.

[17] In any case, such descriptions are always mechanically convertible into one another, and are therefore scientifically equivalent.

[17a] For an interesting but not (I think) wholly successful attempt to use an auditory terminology see R. Jakobson and J. Lotz, Notes on the French phonemic pattern, Word 5.151–8 (1949). In this article the phonemes of French are defined in terms of six auditory oppositions or contrasts: vowel/consonant, nasal/oral, saturated/diluted, grave/acute, tense/lax, and continuous/intercepted. The following statement (151) is especially to be noted: 'Our basic assumption is that every language operates with a strictly limited number of underlying ultimate distinctions which form a set of binary oppositions. These opposite features occur either solely as terms of a single relation (*pure* opposition) or they can occur together as complexes.'

[18] That such a division into qualities of position and qualities of articulation is in accord with acoustic reality has been demonstrated in the laboratory, most plainly in work with the acoustic spectrograph. See Martin Joos, Acoustic phonetics (Language Monograph No. 23, 1948), esp. ch. 4.

L	labial position	3	constriction
D	dental or alveolar position	4	flap movement
P	prepalatal position	5	small aperture
F	prevelar (front) position	6	medium aperture
B	mediovelar (back) position	7	wide aperture
G	glottal position	N	nasalization
1	closure	V	voicing
2	affrication[18a]	Q	syllabic quantity

A number of combinations require special comment:

L1: bilabial stop; L3: bilabial or labiodental spirant, without distinction; L5: weak lip-rounding.

D1: dental stop; D2: dental or denti-alveolar affricate; D3: dental or alveolar spirant, always with groove-shaped aperture (i.e. sibilant); D4: alveolar flap. A variety of flap movement in which there is a lateral opening at the moment of contact (resulting in 'flapped *l*') is denoted by the symbol D4a.

P1, P2, P3: stop, affricate, and spirant produced with contact between the blade or front of the tongue and the forward part of the hard palate.

F1, F3: stop and spirant produced with contact between the back of the tongue and the forward part of the soft palate; F5: high front vowel and semivowel, or palatalization when simultaneous with labial or dental articulation; F6: mid front vowel.

B1: stop produced with contact between the back of the tongue and the middle part of the soft palate; B5: high back vowel and semivowel; B6, B7: mid and low back vowels.

G1: glottal stop; G3: strongly pulsed voiceless onset of a following vowel or semivowel, slightly fricative ('*h*').

2.2. N, V, Q are qualities of a different kind from the rest. Each of these is one term of a dichotomy that divides the entire body of phones into halves of comparable magnitude: every phone in Japanese contains one of the two opposite qualities in each dichotomy, but in each dichotomy only one term is provided with a symbol. Accordingly, the absence of any of the three symbols N, V, Q implies the presence of the corresponding opposite: absence of N implies oral resonance; absence of V implies voicelessness; absence of Q implies the lack of syllabic time value (quantity).

A segment that contains the quality Q is described as long; a segment that lacks this quality is described as short. A long segment is one that constitutes a syllable by itself; a short segment is one that does not. The number of syllables in any phrase, therefore, is equal to the number of long segments that occur in it. As applied to consonants, the terms 'long' and 'short' have the meanings generally attached to them in phonetic works; but as applied to vowels they have special meanings different from their usual ones. A short vowel, in this paper, is a segment with vowel qualities but without syllabic time value—in other words, a semivowel; a long vowel is a segment with vowel qualities and with syllabic time value—in other words, what is elsewhere usually called a short vowel. (What is elsewhere called a long vowel, i.e. a vowel of greater-than-average duration, is here called a double vowel; cf. §1.)

3. Pitch. The phones defined in Japanese by qualities of relative pitch vary in length from one segment to a dozen or more. In the phrase [aoi] *blue*, each of the three vowels is on a separate pitch level: [a] is low, [o] is higher mid, [i] is low again; in the phrase [*k*imonoŋayoŋoreta] *the clothes got dirty*, the initial [*k*] has no quality of relative pitch, the segment [i] is low, the span [monoŋayoŋore] (comprising twelve segments) is lower mid, the [t] again has no pitch quality, and the final [a] is low.

Continual reference to the fact that voiceless phones have no pitch qualities will henceforth be obviated by adopting the following conventions. If two voiced phones with the same pitch are separated by one or more voiceless segments, the whole sequence (including the voiceless interrupting element) is regarded as a single span, defined by a single occurrence of a pitch quality. If two voiced phones with different pitches are separated by one or more voiceless segments, the latter are regarded as belonging to the following voiced phone and forming with it a single span defined by the pitch quality of its terminal part. Similarly an initial voiceless segment is regarded as part of the first span in the phrase defined by pitch.

3.1. For a complete account of the observable pitch variations in Japanese, four phonemically different levels are necessary and sufficient. Not all utterances contain all four levels; indeed, the highest level is relatively rare, and the lowest is rare except on the first and the last syllable of a phrase. But even when only one or two of the levels are heard in a given phrase, it is usually not hard to identify them.

The four pitch phonemes of Japanese will be designated by numerals as follows:

/1/ highest pitch: the highest level reached in normal conversation; near the upper limit of the speaker's voice range

/2/ higher mid pitch: near the middle of the speaker's voice range; slightly lower on the last syllable of a phrase than elsewhere

/3/ lower mid pitch: about three tones below /2/; slightly higher on the last syllable of a phrase than elsewhere

/4/ lowest pitch: near the lower limit of the speaker's voice range; slightly lower on the first syllable of a phrase than on a medial syllable, and lower still on the last syllable—here often well below the normal speaking-range

The members of these pitch phonemes, as of any phonemes, are phones: continuous fractions of utterance heard as coextensive with various audible qualities—in this case various levels of pitch. In other words, each of the four pitch phonemes includes as members (allophones) all the sequences of vowels or consonants or both—from one to a dozen or more—that are heard as having a particular pitch. In the phrase [*k*imonoŋayoŋoreta], the segment [*k*] belongs to some consonant phoneme, [i] to some vowel phoneme, [m] again to some consonant

[18a] The reason for treating affrication as a single quality rather than a succession of two qualities (closure plus constriction) has been stated in §1.

phoneme, and so on: each segment belongs to some phoneme by virtue of the qualities present in it as a segment; but beyond this, the span [*k*i] belongs to pitch phoneme /4/, the span [monoŋayoŋore] belongs to pitch phoneme /3/, and the span [ta] belongs to /4/ again. In the phrase [aoi], each of the three vowels belongs to some vowel phoneme; and in addition, each one belongs also to some pitch phoneme: [a] to /4/, [o] to /2/, [i] to /4/ again. This illustrates the statement in §0.3 that a phone which contains two phoneme-defining qualities or combinations belongs to both phonemes at once.

In citing short phrases pronounced with statement intonation (as in §3.2 and §4.1), it is enough to distinguish members of pitch phoneme /2/ by writing an acute accent on the vowel letter of each syllable with higher mid pitch (and on the letters denoting the long nasals when they have this pitch). Unmarked initial and final syllables belong to pitch phoneme /4/; unmarked medial syllables belong to pitch phoneme /3/.[19] In citing longer utterances pronounced with more varied intonations (as in §7), it will be necessary to adopt other graphic devices.

Variations in loudness are of course also observable in Japanese utterances; but these turn out to be predictable in terms of pitch phonemes. In general, greater loudness correlates with higher pitch: syllables with pitch /1/ are usually louder than those with /2/, syllables with /3/ are usually still softer, and those with /4/ are least loud. When two or more syllables in succession have pitch /2/, the last syllable in the sequence is louder than the rest.

3.2. Although minimally different pairs are not necessary to prove that a given phonetic difference is distinctive in a particular language, they illustrate such differences more strikingly than other examples. Accordingly, a number of phrases are presented here which differ only in pitch.

The sequence [soodes·ka] contains five syllables. With pitch /2/ on the first, /3/ on the next two, and /4/ on the last, it means *Is that so?*; with /2/ and /3/ as before but with two pitches, /3/ and /1/, on the last syllable, it means *Is that really so?* (expressing great interest or surprise); and with /1/ on the first syllable, /3/ on the next two, and either /4/ or /31/ on the last, it means *Oh so that's it!*[20]

In each of the following pairs, the second member contains pitch /2/, contrasting with /3/ or /4/ in the first member: [atsᴜsa, átsᴜsa] *thickness, heat*; [bãn·, bấn·] *night, inning*; [hawa, háwa] *as for the leaf, as for the tooth* (but [ha] both *leaf* and *tooth*); [its·ka, íts·ka] *five days, some time*; [kaeru, káeru] *changes, returns*; [kama, káma] *iron pot, sickle*; [kau, káu] *buys, raises* (*animals*); [*k*iru, *k*íru] *wears, cuts*; [oku, óku] *puts, hundred million*; [sakãn·, sákãn·] *plasterer, field officer*; [yome, yóme] *bride, read it!*; [atsui, atsúi] *thick, hot*; [hanawa, hanáwa] *as for the nose, as for the flower* (but [hana] both *nose* and *flower*); [mikata, mikáta] *allies, way of looking*; [omoi, omói] *heavy, a thought*; [š·tawa, š·táwa] *as for the place beneath, as for the tongue*.

In each of the following pairs, both members contain pitch /2/, but differently placed: [hášide, hašíde] *with chopsticks, at the bridge*; [kámiwa, kamíwa] *as for God, as for the paper* (or *hair*); [súmide, sumíde] *in the corner, with India ink*.

4. Phones. The following list includes every type of phone observed as a regularly recurring unit[21] in utterances of the dialect to be described, except spans defined by qualities of pitch. Some of these types are limited in their use, being rare or even non-occurrent in the speech of some persons; but all the types here listed are found in the utterances of at least some speakers of the dialect.[22]

4.1. Each paragraph in the list contains the following: a phonetic symbol to designate the phone, or rather the class of perceptually identical phones (= allophone); a phonetic description in physiological (articulatory) terms, intended to convey the auditory effect of the phone; in parentheses, a record of the qualities present in the phone, represented by the symbols explained in §2.1; a full statement of the environments in which the phone occurs, in terms of immediately preceding and following phones; a reference, where necessary, to other phones with which the phone is in free variation; and a number of examples in phonetic (allophonic) transcription, showing the phone in various typical environments. Not all the environments in which every phone occurs are illustrated. In a few cases, the list of immediately preceding and following phones includes one or more environments in which the phone has not actually been observed, but which are inferred, from the distribution of other phones, to be at least theoretically possible.

The pause that occurs (by definition) at the beginning and end of every phrase is listed as a phone because its presence internally in an utterance cannot be predicted from anything else in the utterance. Note the following utterances, which differ only by the presence or absence of an internal pause: [mádooaketenemáš·ta] *I went to bed with the window open* : [mádooakete ⌗ nemáš·ta] *I opened the window and went to bed.* Pause may be regarded as a kind of zero phone, characterized by a complete lack of qualities.[23]

[⌗] pause (no qualities): before [i, e, a, o, u, ts·, tš·, s·, š·, f·, *x*·, m·, n·], and all short consonants except [?, ŋ, *ŋ*, ž, ɤ]; after [i, e, a, o, u, ?, ts·, tš·, s·, š·, n·, *n*·,

[19] Some of the forms cited in this paper with no pitch higher than /3/ are paralleled by otherwise identical synonymous forms with pitch /2/ on all syllables but the first, when followed without pause by one or more syllables with lower pitch. Thus the word for *room* is cited in §4.1 as [heya] (with pitch /4/ on both syllables), but occurs with pitch /2/ on the last syllable in the phrase [heyáwa] *as for the room*.

[20] This example is restated from SCJ II, Lg. 22.200-1, §1.1 ((154–5)).

[21] The expression 'regularly recurring unit' is meant to exclude the sound types mentioned in fn. 7.

[22] In the strictest sense of the word 'dialect' (as defined, for instance, in Lg. 24.8, §3.2), the phones listed below represent a mixture of slightly different dialects. But they can just as well be regarded as representing a kind of average among idiolects too similar to merit individual treatment.

[23] Although pause is here called a zero phone, it is not zero in the sense of having no extension in time. Pauses occur, and have duration, like other phones. They are zero only in being characterized by the total absence of qualities rather than by the presence of one or more.

ŋ·, ŋ̇·].[24] Examples: [# isu #] *chair,* [# éki #] *station,* [# áme #] *rain,* [# oka #] *hill,* [# úso #] *lie,* [# ts·tsúmu #] *wraps,* [# tš·kára #] *strength,* [# s·teru #] *throws away,* [# š·kata #] *way of doing something,* [# f·tóru #] *grows fat,* [# x·tóts· #] *one,* [# m·ma #] *horse* (beside [# uma #]), [# n· #] *yeah,* [# hatš· #] *eight* (in rapid speech), [# arimas· #] *there is,* [# pãn· #] or [# pãŋ· #] *bread,* [# bĩn· #] or [# bĩŋ· #] *bottle.* Hereafter the presence of a pause will be taken for granted at the beginning and end of every cited phrase, and the symbol [#] will no longer be written there.

[p] short voiceless bilabial stop (L1): before [e, a, o, u, ᴀ, O, ᴜ]; after [#, i, e, a, o, u, ɪ, ᴀ, O, ᴜ, p·, m·]; slightly aspirated except after [p·]. Examples: [pẽn·] *pen,* [pãn·] *bread,* [põm·pu] *pump,* [pᴀkurito] *in one gulp,* [pOkét·to] *pocket,* [ip·pai] *full,* [ip·pᴜku] *one sip.*

[p·] long voiceless bilabial stop (L1 Q): before [p]; after [i, e, a, o, u, ɪ, ᴀ, O, ᴜ]; unreleased. Examples: [ip·pai] *full,* [tep·poo] *gun,* [kap·pa] or [kᴀp·pa] *raincoat,* [kop·pu] or [kOp·pu] *glass tumbler,* [up·pũn·] *resentment,* [kɪp·pu] *ticket,* [sᴜp·pái] *sour.*

[*p*] short voiceless bilabial stop, palatalized (L1 F5): before [i, ɪ, ʏ]; after [#, i, e, a, o, u, ɪ, ᴀ, O, ᴜ, *p·*, *m·*]; slightly aspirated except after [*p·*]. Examples: [*pĩn·*] *pin,* [ip·*piki*] or [ip·*pɪki*] *one (animal),* [*p*ʏuuto] *whizzing,* [*kĩm·pĩn·*] *gold and other valuables.*

[*p·*] long voiceless bilabial stop, palatalized (L1 Q F5): before [*p*]; after [i, e, a, o, u, ɪ, ᴀ, O, ᴜ]; unreleased. Examples: [ip·*piki*] *one (animal),* [hap·*píki*] *eight (animals),* [hap·*p*ʏaku] *eight hundred.*

[t] short voiceless dental stop (D1): before [e, a, o, ᴀ, O]; after [#, i, e, a, o, u, ɪ, ᴀ, O, ᴜ, t·, ts·, tš·, s·, š·, f·, *x*·, n·]; slightly aspirated except after [t·]. Examples: [te] *hand,* [ta] *rice field,* [to] *door,* [tᴀkái] *high,* [tOkoro] *place,* [íta] *board,* [geta] *wooden clogs,* [hata] *flag,* [botan·] *button,* [buta] *pig,* [*k*ɪta] *came,* [kᴜtábíréru] *gets tired,* [it·tóo] *one (horse),* [máts·to] *if one waits,* [katš·toosu] *wins through,* [s·teru] *throws away,* [š·ta] *tongue,* [f·tats·] *two,* [*x*·tóts·] *one,* [hõn·too] *truth.*

[t·] long voiceless dental stop (D1 Q): before [t, ts, s]; after [i, e, a, o, u, ɪ, ᴀ, O, ᴜ]; unreleased. Examples: [ít·too] *one (horse),* [mát·te] *waiting,* [*k*ɪtto] *surely,* [kᴜt·taku] *trouble,* [it·tsuu] *one (document),* [otót·sãn·] *dad* (only example of [t·s]).

[*t*] short voiceless dental stop, palatalized (D1 F5): before [y]; after [#]. Only example: [*t*yuũn·de] *since one says that* (beside [tšuũn·de] and [toyuunode]).

[*t·*] long voiceless dental stop, palatalized (D1 Q F5): before [tš]; after [i, e, a, o, u, ɪ, ᴀ, O, ᴜ]; unreleased. Examples: [i*t*·tšaku] *one (suit),* [má*t*·tši] *match,* [pɪ*t*·tšaa] *pitcher* (in baseball).

[k] short voiceless mediovelar stop (B1): before [e, a, o, u, ᴀ, O, ᴜ]; after [#, i, e, a, o, u, ɪ, ᴀ, O, ᴜ, k·, ts·, tš·, s·, š·, f·, *x*·, ŋ·]; slightly aspirated except after [k·]. Examples: [ke] *hair,* [báka] *fool,* [ikóo] *let's go,* [roku] *six,* [kᴀkéru] *hangs it,* [kOkóro] *heart,* [kᴜtsu] *shoe,* [kék·koo] *splendid,* [hats·ka] *twenty days,* [matš·kara] *from the town,* [s·kóši] *a little,* [š·kata] *way of doing something,* [f·kuro] *bag,* [*x*·kúi] *low,* [sãŋ·káŋetsu] *three months.*

[k·] long voiceless mediovelar stop (B1 Q): before [k]; after [i, e, a, o, u, ɪ, ᴀ, O, ᴜ]; unreleased. Examples: [ík·ko] *one (piece),* [kek·koo] *splendid,* [pɪk·koro] *piccolo.*

[*k*] short voiceless prevelar stop (F1): before [i, ɪ, ʏ]; after [#, i, e, a, o, u, ɪ, ᴀ, O, ᴜ, *k*·, ts·, tš·, s·, š·, f·, *x*·, ŋ̇·]; slightly aspirated except after [*k*·]. Examples: [*k*i] *tree,* [*k*ɪta] *came,* [*k*ʏúu] *nine,* [ip·pi*k*i] or [ip·pɪ*k*i] *one (animal),* [ha*k*·*k*íri] *clearly,* [kutš·*k*i] *decayed wood,* [uís·*k*ii] *whisky,* [f·*k*imáš·ta] *blew,* [níx·*k*i] two *(animals),* [gẽŋ̇·*k*i] *health.*

[*k*·] long voiceless prevelar stop (F1 Q): before [*k*]; after [i, e, a, o, u, ɪ, ᴀ, O, ᴜ]; unreleased. Examples: [ha*k*·*k*íri] *clearly,* [i*k*·*k*ʏuu] *one class.*

[ʔ] short glottal stop (G1): before [#]; after [i, e, a, o, u]. Examples: [toʔ] *so saying,* [tšeʔ] *ugh!,* [kóraʔ] *hey!*[25]

[ts] short voiceless dental or denti-alveolar affricate (D2): before [u, ᴜ]; after [#, i, e, a, o, u, ɪ, ᴜ, t·, ts·, tš·, s·, š·, f·, *x*·, n·]; unaspirated. Examples: [tsuri] *fishing,* [átsᴜsa] *heat,* [kᴜtsu] *shoe,* [it·tsuu] *one (document),* [ts·tsúmu] *wraps,* [tš·tsúdžo] *good order,* [š·tsúrei] *rudeness,* [f·tsuuno] *regular,* [*x*·tsudži] *sheep,* [sãn·tsuu] *three (documents).*

[ts·] long voiceless dental or denti-alveolar affricate (D2 Q): before [#, t, k, ts, tš], after [#, i, e, a, o, u]; released but unaspirated. Examples: [ts·tsúmu] *wraps,* [máts·to] *if one waits,* [hats·ka] *twenty days,* [ts·tši] *soil,* [*x*·tóts·] *one.*

[tš] short voiceless prepalatal affricate (P2): before [i, e, a, o, u, ɪ, ᴜ]; after [#, i, e, a, o, u, ɪ, ᴜ, *t*·, ts·, tš·, s·, š·, f·, *x*·, *n*·]; unaspirated. Examples: [tši] *blood,* [tšék·ku] *bank check,* [tšeʔ] *ugh!,* [kᴜtši] *mouth,* [tšɪsei] *topography,* [i*t*·tšaku] *one (suit),* [ts·tši] *soil,* [tš·tši] *father,* [s·tšíimu] *steam,* [š·tši] *seven,* [f·tšidži] *governor of an urban prefecture,* [*x*·tšoo] *flying bird,* [bãn·tši] *house number.*

[tš·] long voiceless prepalatal affricate (P2 Q): before [#, t, k, ts, tš]; after [#, i, e, a, o, u]; released but unaspirated. Examples: [tš·kára] *strength,* [katš·toosu] *wins through,* [tš·tsúdžo] *good order,* [tš·tši] *father,* [hatš·] *eight* (in rapid speech).

[s] short voiceless alveolar (groove) spirant (D3): before [e, a, o, u, ᴜ]; after [#, i, e, a, o, u, ɪ, ᴜ, *t*·, s·, n·, *n*·]. Examples: [sẽn·soo] *war,* [sᴜsumu] *advances,* [*k*ɪsóona] *seeming to come,* [otót·sãn·] *dad* (only example of [t·s]), [mas·súŋu] *straight,* [bĩn·sẽn·] *writing-paper.*

[s·] long voiceless alveolar (groove) spirant (D3 Q): before [#, t, k, ts, tš, s]; after [#, i, e, a, o, u, ɪ, ᴜ]; unreleased before [s]. Examples: [arimas·] *there is,* [s·teru] *throws away,* [sóodes·ka] *is that so?,* [s·tšíimu] *steam,* [mas·súŋu] *straight,* [*k*ɪs·soo] *good news,* [kᴜs·setsᴜsuru] *refracts.*

[š] short voiceless prepalatal (groove) spirant (P3): before [i, a, o, u, ɪ, ᴜ]; after [#, i, e, a, o, u, ɪ, ᴜ, š·, *n*·]. Examples: [šašĩn·] *photograph,* [šɪsei] *municipal government,* [šᴜsei] *alcohol,* [*k*ɪša] *train,* [zaš·ši] *magazine,* [ãn·šĩn·] *peace of mind.*

[š·] long voiceless prepalatal (groove) spirant (P3 Q): before [#, t, k, *k*, ts, tš, š]; after [#, i, e, a, o, u, ɪ, ᴜ]; unreleased before [š]. Examples: [s·koš·] *a little*

[24] In these statements of distribution, the nasalized vowels are not separately enumerated. In general, any phone that occurs before or after an oral vowel occurs also before or after the corresponding nasalized vowel. (But nasalization of vowels is indicated in the transcription of the examples.)

[25] The distribution of this phone is unique in type: it occurs only before pause, and only in a few expressions (mostly interjectional).

(in rapid speech), [š·kata] *way of doing something*, [š·*k*imono] *carpet*, [arímáš·ta] *there was*, [š·tsúrei] *rudeness*, [š·tši] *seven*, [zaš·ši] *magazine*, [keš·šɪte] *never*, [kúš·šõn·] or [kʊš·šõn·] *cushion*.

[f] short voiceless bilabial or labiodental spirant (L3): before [u, ʊ]; after [#, i, e, a, o, u, ɪ, ʊ, n·]. Every phrase containing [f] is paralleled (though rarely) by an otherwise identical synonymous phrase containing [h] instead. Examples: [furúi] *old*, [fúufu] *married couple*, [fʊsuma] *light opaque sliding door*, [ifu] *dread*, [sófu] *grandfather*, [kɪfu] *contribution*, [sãń·fúrãń·šís·ko] *San Francisco*.

[f·] long voiceless bilabial or labiodental spirant (L3 Q): before [t, k, ts, tš, f]; after [#, i, e, a, o, u]. Examples: [f·tóru] *grows fat*, [gof·kuya] *drygoods store*, [f·tsuuno] *regular*, [f·tšidži] *governor of an urban prefecture*, [nif·ku] *two sips*, [kaŋ́·ŋóf·fʊtari] or [kaŋ́·ŋófʊf·tari] *two nurses*.

[*x*] short voiceless prevelar spirant (F3): before [i, a, o, u, ɪ]; after [#, i, e, a, o, u, ɪ, ʊ, *ŋ*·]. Every phrase containing [*x*] is paralleled by an otherwise identical synonymous phrase containing [*hy*] instead, or [*h*] before [i, ɪ]. Examples: [*x*ima] *leisure*, [*x*aku] *hundred*, [*x*oobãn·] *fame*, [*x*uuto] *with a zip*, [*x*ífu] or [*x*ɪfu] *skin*, [koó*x*íi] *coffee*, [sẽ́*ŋ*·*x*aku] *one thousand one hundred*.

[*x*·] long voiceless prevelar spirant (F3 Q): before [t, k, *k*, ts, tš]; after [#, i, e, a, o, u]. Examples: [*x*·to] *person*, [*x*·kúi] *low*, [*x*·tsudži] *sheep*, [*x*·tšoo] *flying bird*, [ní*x*·*k*i] *two (animals)*.

[h] short voiceless glottal spirant, i.e. a strongly pulsed and slightly fricative voiceless onset of a following vowel or semivowel (G3): before [e, a, o, u, ʊ]; after [#, i, e, a, o, u, n·, ŋ·]. Every phrase containing [h] before [u] or [ʊ] is paralleled by an otherwise identical synonymous phrase containing [f] instead; the sequences [hu, hʊ] are less common than [fu, fʊ], and in the speech of many persons do not occur at all. Examples: [hébi] *snake*, [ha] *leaf*, [hṍn·] *book*, [hurúi] *old* (beside [furúi]), [góhãn·] *cooked rice*, [f·táhako] *two boxfuls*, [džúusãn·hã́n·] or [džúusãŋ·hã́ŋ·] *thirteen and a half*.

[*h*] short voiceless glottal spirant (as above), palatalized (G3 F5): before [i, ɪ, y]; after [#, e, a, o, u, *ŋ*·]. For the alternation between [*h*] or [*hy*] and [*x*] see the paragraph on [*x*]. Examples: [*h*ima] *leisure*, [*hy*aku] *hundred*, [*hy*oobãn·] *fame*, [*hy*uuto] *with a zip*, [*h*ífu] or [*h*ɪfu] *skin*, [koó*h*íi] *coffee*, [sẽ́*ŋ*·*hy*aku] *one thousand one hundred*.

[b] short voiced bilabial stop (L1 V): before [e, a, o, u]; after [#, i, e, a, o, u, m·]. Examples: [kabe] *wall*, [kooba] *factory*, [booši] *hat*, [buta] *pig*, [kṍm·bãn·] *tonight*.

[*b*] short voiced bilabial stop, palatalized (L1 V F5): before [i, y]; after [#, i, e, a, o, u, *m*·]. Examples: [*b*ĩ́n·] *bottle*, [*b*yoo*k*i] *illness*, [hé*b*i] *snake*, [sã́*m*·*b*yaku] *three hundred*.

[d] short voiced dental stop (D1 V): before [e, a, o]; after [#, i, e, a, o, u, n·]. Examples: [fude] *writing brush*, [dóko] *where?*, [*h*idari] *left (side)*, [kṍn·do] *this time*.

[g] short voiced mediovelar stop (B1 V): before [e, a, o, u]; after [#, i, e, a, o, u, ŋ·]. Some phrases containing [g] not preceded by [#] are paralleled by otherwise identical synonymous phrases containing [ŋ] instead. Examples: [ge*k*idžoo] *theater*, [gak·koo] *school*, [góhãn·] *cooked rice*, [dónogurai] *about how much?*, [agaru] *rises*, [mago] *grandchild*, [sonogo] *after that*, [sã́ŋ·gẽn·] *three (buildings)*.

[*g*] short voiced prevelar stop (F1 V): before [i, y]; after [#, i, e, a, o, u, *ŋ*·]. Some phrases containing [*g*] not preceded by [#] are paralleled by otherwise identical synonymous phrases containing [*ŋ*] instead. Examples: [*g*ĩ́n·] *silver*, [*g*yuu*n*yuu] *cow's milk*, [*n*yuu*g*yuu] *milch cow*, [ka*g*i] *key*, [áru*g*ĩ*ŋ*·koo] *a certain bank*, [*k*ĩ́*ŋ*·*g*ĩn·] *gold and silver*, [*n*ĩ*ŋ*·*g*yoo] *doll*.

[dž] short voiced prepalatal affricate (P2 V): before [i, e, a, o, u]; after [#, i, e, a, o, u, *n*·]. Some phrases containing [dž] not preceded by [#] are paralleled (though rarely) by otherwise identical synonymous phrases containing [ž] instead. Examples: [džišĩn·] *earthquake*, [džerii] *jelly*, [džari] *gravel*, [džotšuu] *maid servant*, [džúu] *ten*, [*k*ídži] *newspaper article*, [kádži] *conflagration*, [sã́*n*·džuu] *thirty*.

[z] short voiced alveolar (groove) spirant (D3 V): before [e, a, o, u]; after [#, i, e, a, o, u, n·]. Examples: [zaš·ši] *magazine*, [kaze] *wind*, [kázoku] *family*, [mizu] *water*, [bãn·zai] *hurrah*.[26]

[ž] short voiced prepalatal (groove) spirant (P3 V): before [i a o u]; after [i, e, a, o, u, *n*·]. Most phrases containing [ž] are paralleled by otherwise identical synonymous phrases containing [dž] instead; [ž] is less common than [dž], and in the speech of many persons does not occur at all. Examples: [mižíkái] *short*, [*n*ížuu] *twenty*, [sã́*n*·žuu] *thirty*.

[r] short voiced alveolar flap (D4 V): before [e, a, o, u]; after [#, i, e, a, o, u, n·]. Some phrases containing [r] before [e] or [o] are paralleled (though rarely) by otherwise identical synonymous phrases containing [l] instead. Examples: [roku] *six*, [kore] *this*, [hara] *belly*, [iru] *he is*, [sẽ́n·ro*p*·*p*ʏaku] *one thousand six hundred*.

[l] short voiced alveolar lateral flap (D4a V): before [e, o]; after [#, i, e, a, o, u]. Every phrase containing [l] is paralleled by an otherwise identical synonymous phrase containing [r] instead; [l] is far less common than [r], and in the speech of many persons does not occur at all. Examples: [loku] *six*, [kole] *this*.

[*r*] short voiced alveolar flap, palatalized (D4 F5): before [i, y]; after [#, i, e, a, o, u, *n*·]. Examples: [*r*iku] *land*, [ari*m*as·] *there is*, [*k*í*r*i] *gimlet*, [*r*yokoo] *journey*, [bẽ́*n*·*r*ina] *convenient*.

[m] short voiced nasalized bilabial stop (L1 V N): before [e, a, o, u]; after [#, i, e, a, o, u, m·]. Examples: [mame] *beans*, [momo] *peach*, [*g*ímu] *duty*, [ãm·mari] *too much*.

[m·] long voiced nasalized bilabial stop (L1 V N Q): before [p, b, m]; after [#, ĩ, ẽ, ã, õ, ũ]. Examples: [m·ma] *horse* (beside [uma]), [gũm·pʊku] *uniform*, [kṍm·bãn·] *tonight*, [ãm·mari] *too much*.

[*m*] short voiced nasalized bilabial stop, palatalized (L1 V N F5): before [i, y]; after [#, i, e, a, o, u, *m*·]. Examples: [*m*i*m*i] *ear*, [*m*yóo*n*itši] *tomorrow*, [ka*m*i] *paper*, [kṍ*m*·*m*yóo*n*itši] *today and tomorrow*.

[*m*·] long voiced nasalized bilabial stop, palatalized (L1 V N Q F5): before [*p*, *b*, *m*]; after [#, ĩ, ẽ, ã, õ, ũ]. Examples: [sã́*m*·*b*yaku] *three hundred*, [kṍ*m*·*m*yóo*n*itši] *today and tomorrow*, [*m*́·*m*i] *sea* (beside [ú*m*i]).

[26] A very few speakers of standard Japanese (but many speakers of other dialects) use a short voiced dental or denti-alveolar affricate [dz] beside or instead of [z], most commonly before [u], as in [*m*idzu] *water*. In view of its rareness, this phone has been excluded (perhaps arbitrarily) from consideration in the present paper.

[n] short voiced nasalized dental stop (D1 V N): before [e, a, o, u]; after [#, i, e, a, o, u, n·]. Examples: [neru] *goes to bed,* [hana] *nose,* [óno] *ax,* [inu] *dog,* [kãn·na] *carpenter's plane.*

[n·] long voiced nasalized dental stop (D1 V N Q): before [#, ẽ, ã, õ, ũ, t, ts, s, h, d, z, r, n]; after [#, ĩ, ẽ, ã, õ, ũ]. Examples: [n·] *yeah,* [íp·pũn·] *one minute,* [*n*ihṍn·ẽ] *to Japan,* [hãn·ãi] *philanthropy,* [pẽ́n·õ] *pen* (as goal), [hõn·too] *truth,* [sã́n·tsuu] *three (volumes),* [sẽn·soo] *war,* [džúusãn·hã́n·] *thirteen and a half,* [kṍn·do] *this time,* [bãn·zai] *hurrah,* [sẽ́n·rop·pʏaku] *one thousand six hundred,* [kãn·na] *carpenter's plane.*

[*n*] short voiced nasalized dental stop, palatalized (D1 V N F5): before [i, y]; after [#, i, e, a, o, u, *n*·]. Examples: [*n*iku] *meat,* [gyuunyuu] *cow's milk,* [kṍ*n*·nitši] *today.*

[*n*·] long voiced nasalized dental stop, palatalized (D1 V N Q F5): before [#, ĩ, y, tš, š, *h*, dž, ž, *r*, *n*]; after [ĩ, ẽ, ã, õ, ũ]. Examples: [*b*ĩ́*n*·] *bottle,* [tẽ*n*·ĩ*n*·] *salesman,* [hã́*n*·ĩ] *extent,* [hṍ*n*·ya] *book-seller,* [bã*n*·tši] *house number,* [sẽ*n*·šuu] *last week,* [sã́*n*·džuu] or [sã́*n*·žuu] *thirty,* [bẽ́*n*·*r*ina] *convenient,* [kṍ*n*·nitši] *today.*

[ŋ] short voiced nasalized mediovelar stop (B1 V N): before [e, a, o, u]; after [i, e, a, o, u, ŋ·]. Every phrase containing [ŋ] is paralleled by an otherwise identical synonymous phrase containing [g] instead. Examples: [káŋe] *shadow,* [aŋaru] *rises,* [maŋo] *grandchild,* [mas·súŋu] *straight,* [sã́ŋ·ŋẽn·] *three (buildings).*

[ŋ·] long voiced nasalized mediovelar stop (B1 V N Q): before [#, ẽ, ã, õ, ũ, k, h, g, ŋ, w]; after [ĩ, ẽ, ã, õ, ũ]. Every phrase containing [ŋ·] before a vowel or [#] is paralleled by an otherwise identical synonymous phrase containing a voiced frictionless nasalized mediovelar spirant instead of the nasalized stop; but this sound, which is everywhere in free variation with [ŋ·], is not separately listed. Examples: [íp·pũŋ·] *one minute,* [*n*ihṍŋ·ẽ] *to Japan,* [hãŋ·ãi] *philanthropy,* [pẽ́ŋ·õ] *pen* (as verbal goal), [sãŋ́·káŋetsu] *three months,* [džúusãŋ·hã́ŋ·] *thirteen and a half,* [sã́ŋ·gẽn·] or [sã́ŋ·gẽŋ·] or [sã́ŋ·ŋẽn·] or [sã́ŋ·ŋẽŋ·] *three (buildings),* [hṍŋ·wa] *as for the book.*

[*ŋ*] short voiced nasalized prevelar stop (F1 V N): before [i, y]; after [i, e, a, o, u, *ŋ*·]. Every phrase containing [*ŋ*] is paralleled by an otherwise identical synonymous phrase containing [*g*] instead. Examples: [ka*ŋ*i] *key,* [nyuu*ŋ*yuu] *milch cow,* [*k*ĩ́*ŋ*·*ŋ*ĩn·] *gold and silver,* [*n*ĩ*ŋ*·*ŋ*yoo] *doll.*

[*ŋ*·] long voiced nasalized prevelar stop (F1 V N Q): before [#, ĩ, y, *k*, *h*, *x*, *x*·, *g*, *ŋ*]; after [ĩ, ẽ, ã, õ, ũ]. Every phrase containing [*ŋ*·] before a vowel or [#] is paralleled by an otherwise identical synonymous phrase containing a voiced frictionless nasalized prevelar spirant instead of the nasalized stop; but this sound, which is everywhere in free variation with [*ŋ*·], is not separately listed. Examples: [*b*ĩ́*ŋ*·] *bottle,* [tẽ*ŋ*·ĩ*ŋ*·] *salesman,* [hã́*ŋ*·ĩ] *extent,* [hṍ*ŋ*·ya] *book-seller,* [gẽ́*ŋ*·*k*i] *health,* [mã́n·nẽ́*ŋ*·*x*·tsu] *fountain pen,* [*k*ĩ́*ŋ*·*g*ĩn·] or [*k*ĩ́*ŋ*·*g*ĩ*ŋ*·] or [*k*ĩ́*ŋ*·*ŋ*ĩn·] or [*k*ĩ́*ŋ*·*ŋ*ĩ*ŋ*·] *gold and silver,* [*n*ĩ*ŋ*·gyoo] or [*n*ĩ*ŋ*·*ŋ*yoo] *doll.*

[ʏ] short voiceless prevelar (front) vowel, i.e. semivowel (F5): before [a, o, u]; after [*p*, *k*]. Examples: [hap·*p*ʏaku] *eight hundred,* [*p*ʏuuto] *whizzing,* [*k*ʏaku] *guest,* [*k*ʏóo] *today,* [*k*ʏúu] *nine.*

[y] short voiced prevelar (front) vowel, i.e. semivowel (F5 V): before [a, o, u]; after [#, i, e, a, o, u, *t*, *h*, *b*, *g*, *r*, *m*, *n*, *n*·, *ŋ*, *ŋ*·]. Examples: [yá*ŋ*i] *goat,* [yoko] *side,* [yuka] *floor,* [omiyaŋe] *souvenir,* [heya] *room,* [ayamaru] *apologizes,* [oyu] *hot water,* [fuyu] *winter,* [*t*yuũn·de] *since one says that* (only example of [*ty*]), [*h*yaku] *hundred,* [byoo*k*i] *illness,* [gyuunyuu] *cow's milk,* [ryokoo] *journey,* [myóo*n*itši] *tomorrow,* [hṍ*n*·ya] or [hṍ*ŋ*·ya] *book-seller,* [nyuu*ŋ*yuu] *milch cow.*

[w] short voiced mediovelar (back) vowel, i.e. semivowel, weakly labialized (B5 V L5): before [a]; after [#, i, e, a, o, u, ŋ·]. Examples: [warúi] *bad,* [iwanai] *doesn't say,* [sewa] *assistance,* [kawa] *river,* [kowásu] *breaks it,* [kuwa] *hoe,* [hṍŋ·wa] *as for the book.*

[ɪ] long[27] voiceless prevelar (front) high vowel (F5 Q): after [tš, š, *x*, *h*] and before [s, š, f] or any long voiceless consonant; or after [*p*, *k*] and before any voiceless consonant, long or short. Every phrase containing [ɪ] is paralleled, especially in slow or careful speech, by an otherwise identical synonymous phrase containing [i] instead. Examples: [hatšɪsẽ́*n*·tši] *eight centimeters,* [hatšɪfúrãn·] *eight francs,* [uts·kúšɪsa] *beauty,* [šɪš·šoku] *unemployment,* [*x*ɪsomeru] or [*h*ɪsomeru] *conceals,* [šɪk·kẽn·] *judgment,* [šɪt·ta] *knew,* [*p*ɪtša*p*ɪtša] *splash,* [*k*ɪša] *train,* [de*k*ɪta] *was possible,* [*k*ɪt·to] *surely,* [*k*ɪp·pu] *ticket.*[28]

[ᴀ] long voiceless mediovelar (back) low vowel (B7 Q): after [p, t, k] and before [p, p·, *p*, *p*·, t, t·, *t*, *t*·, k, k·, *k*, *k*·];[29] in rapid speech only. Every phrase containing [ᴀ] is paralleled by an otherwise identical synonymous phrase containing [a] instead; [ᴀ] is less common than [a]. Examples: [pᴀkurito] *in one gulp,* [tᴀkái] *high,* [kᴀkéru] *hangs it,* [kᴀp·pa] *raincoat,* [kᴀt·te] *kitchen,* [tᴀ*k*·*k*ʏuu] *pingpong.*

[O] long voiceless mediovelar (back) mid vowel, weakly rounded (B6 Q L5): after [p, t, k] and before [p, p·, *p*, *p*·, t, t·, *t*, *t*·, k, k·, *k*, *k*·];[30] in rapid speech only. Every phrase containing [O] is paralleled by an otherwise identical synonymous phrase containing [o] instead; [O] is less common than [o]. Examples: [pOkét·to] *pocket,* [tOkoro] *place,* [kOkóro] *heart,* [kOt·tši] *this direction,* [kOp·pu] *glass tumbler.*

[ᴜ] long voiceless mediovelar (back) high vowel, weakly rounded (B5 Q L5): after [ts, tš, s, š, f, h] and before [s, š, f, *x*, h] or any long voiceless consonant; or after [p, k] and before any voiceless consonant, long or short. Every phrase containing [ᴜ] is paralleled, especially in slow or careful speech, by an otherwise identical synonymous phrase containing [u] instead. Examples: [átsᴜsa] *heat,* [sᴜsumu] *advances,* [šᴜsai] *supervision,* [fᴜsuma] or [hᴜsuma] *light opaque sliding door,* [hatsᴜšimo] *first frost of the year,* [sᴜp·pái] *sour,* [fᴜt·tei] *scarcity,* [ip·pᴜku] *one sip,* [kᴜtsu] *shoe,* [kᴜsa] *grass.*

[i] long voiced prevelar (front) high vowel (F5 V Q): before pause, all voiced vowels, and all consonants except the long nasals and [*t*, ʏ]; after pause, all voiced

[27] The reader should bear in mind that 'long' has a special meaning in this paper, as already noted in §2.2. A 'long' vowel is a vowel of ordinary duration, constituting a syllable alone or in combination with one or two preceding 'short' consonants.

[28] No instances of voiceless [ᴇ] have been observed, but the sound type may nevertheless occur in the dialect, perhaps with a distribution similar to that of voiceless [ᴀ].

[29] According to this statement voiceless [ᴀ] occurs only between voiceless stops; but it perhaps occurs also between voiceless consonants of other types, though I have no record of such instances.

[30] Voiceless [O] is here described as having the same distribution as voiceless [ᴀ]. Like [ᴀ] (see fn. 27), it may occur also between other voiceless consonants.

vowels, and [*p*, *k*, tš, š, *x*, *h*, *b*, *g*, dž, ž, *r*, *m*, *n*, *ŋ*]. For the alternation between [i] and [ɪ] see the paragraph on [ɪ]. Examples of [i] before and after vowels: [*k*iita] *heard*, [ie] *house*, [iie], *no*, [miaŋeru] *looks up*, [šio] *salt*, [šiutši] *attitude*, [eisei] *sanitation*, [hái] *yes*, [kói] *come!*, [núide] *taking off* (*clothes*); other examples above.

[ĩ] long voiced prevelar (front) vowel, nasalized (F5 V Q N): before [*m*·, *n*·, *ŋ*·] and after the same phones as [i]; or before the same phones as [i] and after [*n*·, *ŋ*·]; or between long nasals. Examples: [*k*ĩm·*p*ĩn·] *money and goods*, [*b*ĩ*ŋ*·] *bottle*, [tẽn·ĩn·] or [tẽ*ŋ*·ĩ*ŋ*·] *salesman*. When [ĩ] follows a long nasal, there is often a very brief nasalized glide sound [ʸ] between the two phones.

[e] long voiced prevelar (front) mid vowel (F6 V Q): before pause, all voiced vowels, and all consonants except the long nasals and [*t*, ʏ]; after pause, all voiced vowels, and all short non-palatalized consonants except [ts, š, f, ž, y, w]. Examples of [e] before and after vowels: [eisei] *sanitation*, [teeburu] *table*, [deát·ta] *encountered*, [koméo] *rice* (as verbal goal), [meuma] *mare*, [ie] *house*, [máe] *front*, [kóe] *voice*, [ue] *top*; other examples above. Some phrases containing [ee] are paralleled by otherwise identical synonymous phrases containing [ei] instead; and conversely.

[ẽ] long voiced prevelar (front) mid vowel, nasalized (F6 V Q N): before [m·, *m*·, n·, *n*·, ŋ·, *ŋ*·] and after the same phones as [e]; or before the same phones as [e] and after [n·, *n*·, ŋ·, *ŋ*·]; or between long nasals. Examples: [sẽm·mẽ*ŋ*·*k*i] *sink* (for water), [pẽn·] or [pẽŋ·] *pen*, [tẽn·ĩn·] *salesman*, [sãn·ẽn·] or [sãŋ·ẽŋ·] *three yen*. When [ẽ] follows a long nasal, there is often a very brief nasalized glide sound [ʸ] between the two phones.

[a] long voiced mediovelar (back) low vowel (B7 V Q): before pause, all voiced vowels, and all consonants except the long nasals and [*t*, ʏ]; after pause, all voiced vowels, and all short non-palatalized consonants except [ts, f]. For the alternation between [a] and [ʌ] see the paragraph on [ʌ]. Examples of [a] before and after vowels: [hái] *yes*, [máe] *front*, [obáasãn·] *grandmother*, [kao] *face*, [kau] *buys*, [miaŋeru] *looks up*, [deát·ta] *encountered*, [oaši] *cash*, [buai] *percentage*; other examples above.

[ã] long voiced mediovelar (back) low vowel, nasalized (B7 V Q N): before [m·, *m*·, n·, *n*·, ŋ·, *ŋ*·] and after the same phones as [a]; or before the same phones as [a] and after [n·, *n*·, ŋ·, *ŋ*·]; or between long nasals. Examples: [hãm·bũn·] *half*, [pãn·] or [pãŋ·] *bread*, [hãn·ĩ] or [hã*ŋ*·ĩ] *extent*.

[o] long voiced mediovelar (back) mid vowel, weakly rounded (B6 V Q L5): before pause, all voiced vowels, and all consonants except the long nasals and [*t*, ʏ]; after pause, all voiced vowels, and all short non-palatalized consonants except [ts, f, w]. For the alternation between [o] and [O] see the paragraph on [O]. Examples of [o] before and after vowels: [kói] *come!*, [kóe] *voice*, [oaši] *cash*, [hóoboo] *here and there*, [omóu] *thinks*, [šio] *salt*, [koméo] *rice* (as verbal goal), [kao] *face*, [uo] *fish*; other examples above.

[õ] long voiced mediovelar (back) mid vowel, weakly rounded, nasalized (B6 V Q L5 N): before [m·, *m*·, n·, *n*·, ŋ·, *ŋ*·] and after the same phones as [o]; or before the same phones as [o] and after [n·, *n*·, ŋ·, *ŋ*·]; or between long nasals. Examples: [kõm·bãn·] *tonight*, [hõn·] or [hõŋ·] *book*, [kõn·šuu] *this week*, [kãn·õn·] or [kãŋ·õŋ·] *gratitude*. When [õ] follows a long nasal, there is often a very brief nasalized glide sound [ʷ] between the two phones.

[u] long voiced mediovelar (back) high vowel, weakly rounded (B5 V Q L5): before pause, all voiced vowels, and all consonants except the long nasals and [*t*, ʏ]; after pause, all voiced vowels, and all short non-palatalized consonants except [t, d, w]. For the alternation between [u] and [ʊ] see the paragraph on [ʊ]. Examples of [u] before and after vowels: [núide] *taking off* (*clothes*), [ue] *top*, [buai] *percentage*, [uo] *fish*, [*g*yuunyuu] *cow's milk*, [šiutši] *attitude*, [meuma] *mare*, [kau] *buys*, [omóu] *thinks*; other examples above.

[ũ] long voiced mediovelar (back) high vowel, weakly rounded, nasalized (B5 V Q L5 N): before [m·, *m*·, n·, *n*·, ŋ·, *ŋ*·] and after the same phones as [u]; or before the same phones as [u] and after [n·, *n*·, ŋ·, *ŋ*·]; or between long nasals. Examples: [ip·pũn·] or [ip·pũŋ·] *one minute*, [gũm·pʊku] *uniform*.

4.2. In general, the auditory effect of a sequence of two or more segments can be inferred from the description of the individual segments in the foregoing list. Except as implied or expressly stated in the list itself, there are no assimilations or intervening glide sounds.[31] But the effect of consecutive vowels requires a brief comment.[32]

(1) Two different consecutive vowels are pronounced without interruption but without fusion; each vowel is part or all of a separate syllable. Examples already given are [ie, *m*iaŋeru, šio, šiutši, eisei, deát·ta, kọméo, meuma, hái, máe, kao, kau, kói, kóe, oaši, omóu, núide, ue, uo].

(2) Three or more consecutive vowels, including no sequence of two like vowels, are similarly pronounced without interruption but without fusion; each vowel, again, is part or all of a separate syllable. Examples: [deáu] *encounters*, [aói] *blue*, [šiai] *game*, [buai] *percentage*, [*n*iou] *smells*.

(3) Two like vowels in succession are pronounced as a phonetically overlong[33] vowel, equal in duration to two vowels of normal length (§1). But if the second vowel in such a combination is followed by a long nasal, or if it is higher in pitch than the immediately following syllable, there is a diminution in loudness between the two vowels (sometimes accompanied by a slight glottal constriction) and a renewed pulse of expiration on the second.[34] Examples: [*k*iita] *heard*,

[31] Compare the statement concerning nasalized [ĩ, ẽ, õ] in §4.1. What are sometimes described as assimilations—phones partaking of the character of certain neighboring phones—are here treated as distinct phones, with distributions of their own.

[32] In this comment no distinction is made between oral and nasalized vowels. But note that in a succession of two or more vowels preceded or followed by a long nasal, only the one vowel contiguous to the nasal is nasalized.

[33] The term 'overlong' is used here with the meaning usually attached to 'long' (i.e. perceptibly greater in duration than other syllabic vowels) in order to avoid confusion with the special use of 'long' in this paper (cf. fn. 27).

[34] The diminution in loudness (accompanied by glottal constriction) between certain consecutive vowels in rapid or moderately slow speech is not a phoneme of 'open juncture' or the like, but an automatic phenomenon, predictable in terms of the phonetic environment. A similar diminution in loudness, equally predictable, occurs in rather slow speech between a long nasal and an immediately following vowel.

In very slow or very careful speech (excluded from the scope of this paper), such diminutions in loudness between consecutive vowels are not limited to the environments described [*n*íisãn·] *older brother,* [tšiísái] *small,* [ée] *yes,* [teeburu] *table,* [kareeda] *dried twigs,* [aayat·te] *like that,* [obáasãn·] *grandmother,* [depáato] *department store,* [koo] *thus,* [hóoboo] *here and there,* [dóozo] *please,* [gyuunyuu] *cow's milk,* [nuu] *sews,* [kúu*k*i] *air;* but with a diminution of loudness between the two vowels [*g*iĩn·] *council member,* [goõn·] *Chinese pronunciation* (of a written character), [*m*izúúmi] *lake.*

(4) If a succession of three or more vowels includes a sequence of two like vowels, the latter is pronounced as a phonetically overlong vowel; the unlike vowel precedes or follows without interruption but without fusion. Examples: [kooatsu] *high voltage,* [tooi] *distant,* [kaoo] *let's buy it,* [kooióo] *let's say it this way,* [fuooku) *fork.*

(5) Three like vowels in succession are pronounced either as a prolonged vowel equal in duration to three vowels of normal length, or as a normal vowel followed by a phonetically overlong vowel of the same color, with a diminution of loudness between them and a renewed pulse on the second part. But if the last of three consecutive like vowels is followed by a long nasal, the sequence is pronounced instead as an overlong vowel plus a vowel of normal length, again with a diminution of loudness between them. Examples: [kooosuru] *acts in unison,* [koootsu] *gradation,* [no*m*íìi] *easy to drink;* but with a diminution of loudness before the third vowel [kooõn·] *great obligation,* [gooõn·] *signal.*[35]

5. Contrast. The list in §4.1 comprises 68 phones; these are shown (except for the zero phone, pause) in a phonetic arrangement in Table 1. As appears from the statement of their distribution, not all the phones are in contrast with each other. Some are in complementary distribution, some in free variation, some in overlapping distribution. The following sets and pairs of non-contrasting phones share one or more qualities (indicated in parentheses).

5.1. Phones in complementary distribution:

[p, p·, *p*, *p*·] (L1).

[t, t·, *t*, *t*·] (D1).

[k, k·, *k*, *k*·] (F/B1). Since F means prevelar (front) and B means mediovelar (back), the notation F/B means velar in general, without specifying the part of the velum against which the contact is made.

[p·, *p*·, t·, *t*·, k·, *k*·] (1 Q). Note that these phones appear also in the preceding three sets: the long voiceless stops are in complementary distribution with each other and with the corresponding short stops. The latter—[p, *p*], [t, *t*], [k, *k*]—are of course in contrast with each other.

	labial	labial, palatalized	dental or alveolar	dental, palatalized	prepalatal	prevelar (front)	mediovelar (back)	glottal	glottal, palatalized
short voiceless stops	p	*p*	t	*t*		*k*	k	ʔ	
long voiceless stops	p·	*p*·	t·	*t*·		*k*·	k·		
short voiced stops	b	*b*	d			*g*	g		
short voiceless affricates			ts		tš				
long voiceless affricates			ts·		tš·				
short voiced affricates					dž				
short voiceless spirants	f		s		š	*x*		h	*h*
long voiceless spirants	f·		s·		š·	*x*·			
short voiced spirants			z		ž				
short voiced nasals	m	*m*	n	*n*		*ŋ*	ŋ		
long voiced nasals	m·	*m*·	n·	*n*·		*ŋ*·	ŋ·		
short voiced flaps			r,l	*r*					
short voiceless semivowels						Y			
short voiced semivowels						y	w		
(long) voiceless high vowels						I	U		
(long) voiced high vowels						i,ī	u,ū		
(long) voiceless mid vowels							O		
(long) voiced mid vowels						e,ē	o,ō		
(long) vóiceless low vowels							A		
(long) voiced low vowels							a,ā		

TABLE 1. THE PHONES OF THE CONSERVATIVE DIALECT

[ʔ, p], [ʔ, t], [ʔ, k] (1). That is, the glottal stop is in complementary distribution with all the other stops; but these are in contrast with each other. Since the quality common to these pairs (1) is present also in other phones, and since the assignment of [ʔ] to the same phoneme with [p] or [t] or [k] would be wholly arbitrary, it is necessary to posit a separate phoneme for [ʔ] in spite of its complementation with other phones.

[ts, ts·] (D2).

[tš, tš·] (P2).

[s, s·] (D3).

[š, š·] (P3).

[f, f·] (L3).

[*x*, *x*·] (F3).

[h, *h*] (G3).

[b, *b*] (L1 V).

in the text. In that style of speech, [koo] *child* (as verbal goal) and [kareeda] *dried twigs* are often distinguished from [koo] *thus* and [kareeda] (beside [kareida]) *it is splendid* by a diminution in loudness between the two vowels, again with glottal constriction. (The diminution occurs only at morpheme boundaries.) In a description of extra-slow or extra-careful speech, it would therefore not be possible to account for the diminution in loudness as an automatic function of the environment; the diminution would have to be referred to a separate phoneme. In view of the glottal constriction that accompanies it, it would be most suitably accommodated in the same phoneme as the phrase-final glottal stop. (I owe this suggestion to Samuel E. Martin.)

[35] Successions of four or more like vowels are extremely rare. An example is [oóóo] *let's cover it* (presumptive form of the verb [oou] *covers*), which is pronounced as two phonetically overlong vowels with a diminution of loudness between them. It is possible to construct even longer sequences: [ooo óo] *let's cover the tail* (as of a half-buried fox). Such an oddity is of course not intelligible to Japanese speakers at first hearing; but when it has been explained to them, they can both understand and repeat it.

[g, *g*] (F/B1 V). For the notation F/B see above on [k] etc.

[r, *r*] (D4 V).

[m, m·, *m*, *m*·] (L1 V N).

[n, *n*] (D1 V N).

[ŋ, *ŋ*] (F/B1 V N).

[m·, *m*·, n·, *n*·] (L/D1 V N Q). The notation L/D (labial or dental) can be interpreted as meaning non-velar. Theoretical justification of such a quality is not required, since no use will be made of it in what follows.

[m·, *m*·, ŋ·, *ŋ*·] (L/F/B1 V N Q). The notation L/F/B (labial or prevelar or mediovelar) can be interpreted as meaning non-dental; this quality also will not be used in what follows. Note that the phones [m·] and [*m*·] are in complementary distribution with each other and with each of the three pairs [m, *m*], [n·, *n*·], and [ŋ·, ŋ·]; but short [m, *m*] are in contrast with the other two pairs.

[ʏ, y] (F5).

[i, ĩ] (F5 V Q).

[e, ẽ] (F6 V Q).

[a, ã] (B7 V Q).

[o, õ] (B6 V Q L5).

[u, ũ] (B5 V Q L5).

5.2. Phones in free variation:

[f, h] (L/G3). All the environments of [f] are shared by [h]; but [h] has environments not shared by [f]. The notation L/G (labial or glottal) can be interpreted as meaning not dental or prepalatal or velar—in a word, non-lingual. Although the quality L/G is disjunctive (involving alternatives and the exclusion of one or more intermediate qualities), it can be justified on the principle—adopted ad hoc—that the recognition of a disjunctive quality is valid in phonemics provided the set of intermediate qualities excluded by the disjunction is not itself disjunctive. The set of qualities D, P, F, and B (dental, prepalatal, prevelar, and mediovelar), intermediate in position between L and G, is not disjunctive because all its members are subdivisions of one class, the lingual.

[r, l] (D4 V). All the environments of [l] are shared by [r], but [r] has environments not shared by [l].

[ɪ, i] (F5 Q). All the environments of [ɪ] are shared by [i], but [i] has environments not shared by [ɪ]. As noted in §5.1, [i] (and hence [ɪ] also) is in complementary distribution with [ĩ]. Similar comments apply to the three pairs that follow.

[ʌ, a] (B7 Q).

[O, o] (B6 Q L5).

[ʊ, u] (B5 Q L5).

5.3. Phones in overlapping distribution:

[*x*, *h*] (F/G3). According to the ad-hoc principle adopted for [f, h], the notation F/G (prevelar or glottal) designates a disjunction that cannot be legitimately used as a criterion in phonemic analysis. Note that [*h*] is non-contrastive with [h] and [*x*], [h] is non-contrastive with [*h*] and [f], but [*x*] and [f] are in contrast with each other.

[n·, *n*·, ŋ·, *ŋ*·] (D/F/B1 V N Q). The first two of these phones, as already shown, are in complementary distribution; similarly the last two. It is the two pairs of phones, [n·, *n*·] and [ŋ·, *ŋ*·], that are in overlapping distribution. Both pairs occur before pause, all vowels, and [h, y]; but only [n·, *n*·] occur before dental and alveolar consonants, and only [ŋ·, *ŋ*·] occur before velar consonants. In their common environments, the pairs [n·, ŋ·] and [*n*·, *ŋ*·] occur interchangeably. The notation D/F/B (dental or prevelar or mediovelar) is a valid disjunction, since it includes all lingual nasals, excluding only the labial; but it will not be necessary to make use of it in the final classification.

5.4. In three pairs of phones—[g, ŋ], [*g*, *ŋ*], [dž, ž]—the members are in partially free variation with each other, but must nevertheless be kept apart. Nearly all phrases containing [ŋ], [*ŋ*], and [ž] are paralleled, especially in slow or careful speech, by otherwise identical synonymous phrases containing respectively [g], [*g*], and [dž] instead. But there are many phrases containing the latter three phones that are not paralleled by phrases containing the former; and these phrases are not marked by any phonetic or phonemic peculiarities. Both phones occur in [aŋaru, agaru] *rises*, [maŋo, mago] *grandchild*, [mas·súŋu, mas·súgu] *straight*; [ka*ŋ*i, ka*g*i] *key*, [*n*yuu*ŋ*yuu, *n*yuu*g*yuu] *milch cow*, [*n*ĩ*ŋ*·*ŋ*yoo, *n*ĩ*ŋ*·*g*yoo] *doll*; [mižíkái, *m*idžíkái] *short*, [*n*ížuu, *n*ídžuu] *twenty*, [sā́n·žuu, sā́n·džuu] *thirty*. But there is no such alternation in [sonogo] *after that*, [dónogurai] *about how much?*, [árugak·koo] *a certain school*; [konogyuunyuu] *this (cow's) milk*, [nihõn·nogíkai] *the Japanese Diet*, [árugĩŋ·koo] *a certain bank*; [*k*ídži] *newspaper article*, [óo*k*ina-džišĩn·] *a great earthquake*, [utšinodžotšuu] *our maid servant*. Since the alternations between [g, *g*, dž] and [ŋ, *ŋ*, ž] respectively are limited to certain phrases only, and since their common environments do not form a phonetically or phonemically definable set, the three pairs of phones must be treated separately in the phonemic analysis.

5.5. Different phones that are not in complementary or overlapping distribution or in free variation belong to different phonemes. In formulating the relations among such phones, it is not necessary to show that each one is in contrast with all the others. If two phones have no qualities in common, or share only such qualities as are present also in other phones, they cannot be grouped in the same phoneme in any case: thus [t] and [y], with qualities D1 and F5 V respectively, will belong to different phonemes whether it is possible to prove contrast between them or not; pairs like [toko] *bed* : [yoko] *side* add nothing to the evidence. It will be enough, therefore, to show contrast between phonetically similar phones or groups of phones, which might otherwise be thought to belong to the same phoneme.

In the following list, phones that have already been established as non-contrastive are grouped together. A contrast between any members of two such groupings is taken to prove contrast between the groupings as a whole.

[p, p·, *p*, *p*·]: in contrast with [t, t·, *t*, *t*·], as in [pḗŋ·*k*i] *paint*, [tḗŋ·*k*i] *weather*; with [k, k·, *k*, *k*·], as in [pḗn·] *pen*, [kḗn·] *prefecture*; with [f, f·], as in [puro] *proletarian*, [furo] *bath*; with [b, *b*], as in [pā̃n·] *bread*, [bā̃n·] *inning*.

[t, t·, *t*, *t*·]: in contrast with [p, p·, *p*, *p*·], as in [tḗŋ·*k*i, pḗŋ·*k*i]; with [k, k·, *k*, *k*·], as in [ta] *rice field*, [ka] *mosquito*; with [ts, ts·], as in [mát·te] *waiting*, [máts·to] *if one waits*; with [s, s·], as in [otót·sān·] *dad*, [tos·sa] *instant*; with [d], as in [tóo] *ten*, [dóo] *copper*.

[k, k·, *k*, *k*·]: in contrast with [p, p·, *p*, *p*·], as in [kḗn·, pḗn·]; with [t, t·, *t*, *t*·], as in [ka, ta]; with [*x*, *x*·, *h*], as in [*k*iru] *puts on (clothes)*, [*x*iru] or [*h*iru] *daytime*; with [g, *g*], as in [ko] *child*, [go] *five*.

[ts, ts·]: in contrast with [t, t·, *t*, *t*·], as in [máts·to, mát·te]; with [tš, tš·], as in [máts·to] *if one waits*, [matš·to] *town and (country, etc.)*; with [s, s·], as in [ts·tsúmu] *wraps*, [sʊsumu] *advances*.

[tš, tš·]: in contrast with [ts, ts·], as in [matš·to, máts·to]; with [š, š·], as in [tši] *blood*, [ši] *four*; with [dž], as in [katši] *victory*, [kádži] *conflagration*.

[s, s·]: in contrast with [t, t·, *t*, *t*·], as in [tos·sa, otót·sān·]; with [ts, ts·], as in [sʊsumu, ts·tsúmu]; with [š, š·], as in [suu] *smokes (a cigarette)*, [šuu] *week*; with [z], as in [séi] *stature*, [zéi] *tax*.

[š, š·]: in contrast with [tš, tš·], as in [ši, tši]; with [s, s·], as in [šuu, suu]; with [ž], as in [naši] *pear*, [onaži] *same*.

[f, f·]: in contrast with [p, p·, *p*, *p*·], as in [furo, puro]; with [s, s·], as in [*n*ífū̃n·] *two minutes*, [nisū̃n·] *two inches*; with [*x*, *x*·, *h*], as in [f·tóru] *grows fat*, [*x*·tótsu] *one*.

[*x*, *x*·, *h*]: in contrast with [k, k·, *k*, *k*·], as in [*x*iru ~ *h*iru, *k*iru]; with [š, š·], as in [*x*·to] *person*, [š·ta] *tongue*; with [f, f·], as in [*x*·tótsu, f·tóru].

[h, *h*]: in contrast with [k, k·, *k*, *k*·], as in [ha] *leaf*, [ka] *mosquito*; with [s, s·], as in [hako] *box*, [sake] *rice wine*.

[b, *b*]: in contrast with [p, p·, *p*, *p*·], as in [bā̃n·, pā̃n·]; with [d], as in [bóku] *I*, [dóko] *where?*; with [m, *m*], as in [boo] *stick*, [moo] *already*.

[d]: in contrast with [t, t·, *t*, *t*·], as in [dóo, tóo]; with [b, *b*], as in [dóko, bóku]; with [g, *g*], as in [déta] *went out*, [geta] *wooden clogs*; with [n, *n*], as in [déta], [neta] *went to sleep*.

[g, *g*]: in contrast with [k, k·, *k*, *k*·], as in [go, ko]; with [d], as in [geta, déta]; with [ŋ, *ŋ*], as in [árugak·koo] *a certain school*, [háruŋakúru] *spring comes*.

[dž]: in contrast with [tš, tš·], as in [kádži, katši]; with [d], as in [džerii] *jelly*, [déru] *goes out*; with [ž], as in [óo*k*inadžišĩ*n*·] *a great earthquake*, [onaži] *same*.

[z]: in contrast with [s, s·], as in [zéi, séi]; with [ž], as in [sḗn·zo] *ancestor*, [sē̃n·žoo] (beside [sē̃n·džoo]) *battlefield*.

[ž]: in contrast with [š, š·], as in [onaži, naši]; with [dž], as in [onaži, óo*k*inadžišĩ*n*·]; with [z], as in [sē̃n·žoo, sḗn·zo].

[r, l, *r*]: in contrast with [d]: [róo] *prison*, [dóo] *copper*.

[m, *m*]: in contrast with [b, *b*], as in [moo, boo]; with [n, *n*], as in [make] *defeat*, [naku] *cries*; with [m·, *m*·, n·, *n*·, ŋ·, *ŋ*·], as in [kama] *iron pot*, [kā̃n·ō̃n·] or [kā̃ŋ·ō̃ŋ·] *gratitude*.

[n, *n*]: in contrast with [d], as in [neta, déta]; with [m, *m*], as in [naku, make]; with [ŋ, *ŋ*], as in [kane] *metal*, [káŋe] *shadow*; with [m·, *m*·, n·, *n*·, ŋ·, *ŋ*·], as in [ka*n*i] *crab*, [hā̃*n*·ĩ] *extent*.

[ŋ, *ŋ*]: in contrast with [g, *g*], as in [háruŋakúru, árugak·koo]; with [n, *n*], as in [káŋe, kane]; with [m·, *m*·, n·, *n*·, ŋ·, *ŋ*·], as in [maŋo] *grandchild*, [kā̃ŋ·ō̃ŋ·] *gratitude*.

[m·, *m*·, n·, *n*·, ŋ·, *ŋ*·]: in contrast with [m, *m*], as in [kā̃n·ō̃n· ~ kā̃ŋ·ō̃ŋ·, kama]; with [n, *n*], as in [hā̃*n*·ĩ, ka*n*i]; with [ŋ, *ŋ*], as in [kā̃ŋ·ō̃ŋ·, maŋo].

[ʏ, y]: in contrast with [w], as in [yaku] *ignites*, [waku] *boils*; with [ɪ, i, ĩ], as in [*k*ʏoku] *office*, [*k*iots·kéru] *pays attention*.

[w]: in contrast with [ʏ, y], as in [waku, yaku]; with [ʊ, u, ũ], as in [kawanai] *doesn't buy*, [kauabura] *oil that one buys*.

[ɪ, i, ĩ]: in contrast with [ʏ, y], as in [*k*iots·kéru, *k*ʏoku]; with [e, ẽ], as in [ike] *go!*, [é*k*i] *station*; with [ʊ, u, ũ], as in [itái] *painful*, [utau] *sings*.

[e, ẽ]: in contrast with [ɪ, i, ĩ], as in [é*k*i, ike]; with [ᴀ, a, ã], as in [é*k*i], [á*k*i] *autumn*; with [O, o, õ], as in [é*k*i], [ó*k*ɪta] *woke up*.

[ᴀ, a, ã]: in contrast with [e, ẽ], as in [á*k*i, é*k*i]; with [O, o, õ], as in [akai] *red*, [oka] *hill*.

[O, o, õ]: in contrast with [ᴀ, a, ã], as in [oka, akai]; with [ʊ, u, ũ], as in [otšíru] *falls*, [utši] *home*; with [e, ẽ], as in [ó*k*ɪta, é*k*i].

[ʊ, u, ũ]: in contrast with [w], as in [kauabura, kawanai]; with [O, o, õ], as in [utši, otšíru]; with [ɪ, i, ĩ], as in [utau, itái].

6. Phonemes. The phonetic and distributional evidence makes it an easy matter to group the sixty-eight phones into phonemes. For all but two of the groupings it is enough to proceed on the double basis of non-contrastive distribution and phonetic similarity. In the two instances where these criteria fail to decide between alternative groupings, a simple appeal to patterning gives the answer.

6.1. As noted in §5.1, the long voiceless stops [p·, *p*·, t·, *t*·, k·, *k*·] are in complementary distribution with each other and with the corresponding short stops [p, *p*, t, *t*, k, *k*]; but the latter (grouped in three pairs of non-contrasting phones) are mutually in contrast. Two groupings of the long stops are possible. (1) They can be separated from the corresponding short stops and grouped all together in a single phoneme, say /q/, with a total distribution as follows: before [p, *p*, t, k, *k*, ts, tš, s], after [i, e, a, o, u, ɪ, ᴀ, O, ʊ]. (2) The three pairs of long stops—[p·, *p*·], [t·, *t*·], [k·, *k*·]—can be assigned respectively to the same phonemes as the corresponding three pairs of short stops, with total distributions as follows: /p/ before [i, e, a, o, u, ɪ, ᴀ, O, ʊ, p, *p*, ʏ], after [#, i, e, a, o, u, ɪ, ᴀ, O, ʊ, p·, *p*·, m·, *m*·]; /t/ before [e, a, o, ᴀ, O, t, ts, tš, s, y], after [#, i, e, a, o, u, ɪ, ᴀ, O, ʊ, t·, ts,· tš·, s·, š·, f·, *x*·, n·]; /k/ before [i, e, a, o, u, ɪ, ᴀ, O, ʊ, k, *k*, ʏ], after [#, i, e, a, o, u, ɪ, ᴀ, O, ʊ, k·, *k*·, ts·, tš·, s·, š·, f·, *x*·, ŋ·, *ŋ*·].

The distribution of the proposed phoneme /q/ would be unique in type: no other phoneme is limited to positions between a vowel and a consonant. On the other hand, the distributions of the three phonemes /p, t, k/ (each including both short and long stops as members) are precisely parallel in type to the distributions of several other phonemes—especially, as one might expect, of those which include as members the several voiceless affricates and spirants. (The total distributions of these latter phonemes are obtained by adding together the distributions of [ts] and [ts·], [tš] and [tš·], [s] and [s·], [š] and [š·], etc., as shown in §4.1 and restated in §6.2.)

If, in spite of its unique distribution, the phoneme /q/ made the over-all description of Japanese phonemics more compact or more economical—that is, if the recognition of /q/ resulted in fewer and more general statements—it would be legitimate to disregard the facts of patterning and accept the first of the two groupings proposed above. But the adoption of /q/ would not have such a result. The members of /q/ would be in contrast with all the remaining long voiceless consonants, as these are in contrast with each other. The phoneme /q/ could not include the phones [ts·, tš·, s·, š·, f·, *x*·]; each of these is clearly to be grouped in a single phoneme with the corresponding short consonant. The effect of adopting /q/ would be to make the descriptive statements more numerous and less general.

The argument from patterning, then, is not offset by any counterargument from economy. It is the second of the two possible groupings that must be accepted: the three pairs of long stops must be assigned respectively to the same phonemes as the corresponding three pairs of short stops.

The other case where phonetic similarity and lack of contrast are not enough to decide the phonemic grouping is that of the nasals. The three pairs of short nasals—[m, *m*], [n, *n*], [ŋ, *ŋ*]—are in contrast with each other; but the six long nasals are mutually non-contrastive. Furthermore, the short and long bilabial nasals are in complementary distribution; but the short dental and velar nasals are in contrast with the corresponding long phones. These facts lead at once to the establishment of four phonemes: /m/, including [m, *m*] as members; /n/, including [n, *n*]; /ŋ/, including [ŋ, *ŋ*]; and /ñ/, including [n·, *n*·, ŋ·, *ŋ*·]. The problem is where to place [m·, *m*·], since these phones are in complementary distribution with the members of both /m/ and /ñ/.

Total distributions are as follows: /n/ before [i, e, a, o, u, y], after [#, i, e, a, o, u, n·, *n*·]; /ŋ/ before [i, e, a, o, u, y], after [i, e, a, o, u, ŋ·, *ŋ*·]; /m/ without [m·, *m*·] before [i, e, a, o, u, y], after [#, i, e, a, o, u, m·, *m*·]; /m/ with [m·, *m*·] before [i, e, a, o, u, p, *p*, b, *b*, m, *m*, y], after [#, i, e, a, o, u, m·, *m*·]; /ñ/ without [m·, *m*·] before [#, ĩ, ẽ, ã, õ, ũ, t, k, *k*, ts, tš, s, š, *x*, *x*·, h, *h*, d, g, *g*, dž, z, ž, r, *r*, n, *n*, ŋ, *ŋ*, y, w], after [#, ĩ, ẽ, ã, õ, ũ]; /ñ/ with [m·, *m*·] before [#, ĩ, ẽ, ã, õ, ũ, p, *p*, t, k, *k*, ts, tš, s, š, *x*, *x*·, h, *h*, b, *b*, d, g, *g*, dž, z, ž, r, *r*, m, *m*, n, *n*, ŋ, *ŋ*, y, w], after [#, ĩ, ẽ, ã, õ, ũ].

It is obvious that the distribution of /m/ with the phones [m·, *m*·] included is radically different in type (with respect to the phones before which its members occur) from the distributions of /n/ and /ŋ/, to which—in view of the phonetic parallelism—one would expect it to be similar. The distribution of /ñ/ is unique in type whether the phoneme includes [m·, *m*·] or not; but so also is its membership, which consists wholly of long consonants. Accordingly, though uniqueness of distribution type was used as an argument against the recognition of a phoneme /q/ and in favor of an alternative grouping, the argument has no force when applied to the phoneme /ñ/, since there is no possibility of grouping [n·, *n*·, ŋ·, *ŋ*·] with the corresponding short nasals.

Again the conclusion is unambiguous: the long bilabial nasals [m·, *m*·] are to be grouped with the other long nasals in a phoneme /ñ/.

6.2. The conservative dialect of standard Japanese has twenty-nine phonemes, in addition to the four pitch phonemes already described: five vowels, one long nasal, ten voiceless consonants, ten voiced consonants, two semivowels, and pause. In the list below, each phoneme symbol is followed by one or more phonetic symbols (in square brackets) denoting the allophones of the phoneme, and by an indication of the qualities which define it. Determined qualities of each phoneme are added in parentheses.[36]

i	[ɪ, i, ĩ]	F5 Q
e	[e, ẽ]	F6 (Q V)
a	[ʌ, a, ã]	7 (Q B)
o	[O, o, õ]	B6 (Q L5)
u	[ʊ, u, ũ]	B5 Q (L5)
ñ	[m·, *m*·, n·, *n*·, ŋ·, *ŋ*·]	N Q (1 V)
p	[p, p·, *p*, *p*·]	L1
t	[t, t·, *t*, *t*·]	D1
k	[k, k·, *k*, *k*·]	F/B1
ʔ	[ʔ]	G1
c	[ts, ts·]	D2
č	[tš, tš·]	P2
s	[s, s·]	D3
š	[š, š·]	P3
x	[*x*, *x*·]	F3
h	[f, f·, h, *h*]	L/G3
b	[b, *b*]	L1 V
d	[d]	D1 V
g	[g, *g*]	F/B1 V
j	[dž]	P2 V
z	[z]	D3 V
ž	[ž]	P3 V
r	[r, l, *r*]	4 (D V)
m	[m, *m*]	L N (1 V)
n	[n, *n*]	D N (1 V)
ŋ	[ŋ, *ŋ*]	F/B N (1 V)
y	[ʏ, y]	F5
w	[w]	B5 (V L5)
#	[#]	None

The following paragraphs give a formal definition of each phoneme, together with the distribution of its allophones, restated from §4.1 in phonemic terms.

/i/ the class of long (syllabic) high front vowels: [ɪ] after /č, š, x, h/ and before /s, š, h, pp, tt, tc, tč, kk/, or after /p, k/ and before /p, t, k, c, č, s, š, x, h/, in free variation with [i]; [ĩ] before or after /ñ/; [i] elsewhere.

/e/ the class of mid front vowels: [ẽ] before or after /ñ/; [e] elsewhere.

[36] The convention explained in §2.2 concerning the use of the symbols N, V, Q must be modified for the purposes of this list. Here the absence of any of the three symbols N, V, Q implies the presence of the corresponding opposite quality as a necessary part of the definition of a phoneme only if the remaining qualities occur in the list accompanied by the omitted symbol. Thus, in the definition of the phoneme /p/, namely L1, the absence of the symbol V implies the presence of voicelessness as a distinctive (non-determined and non-conditioned) quality because the combination L1 V occurs as the definition of /b/; but in the definition of /y/, namely F5, the absence of V implies nothing, since there is no combination F5 V defining any other phoneme. In short, the absence of N, V, or Q in this list is distinctive only if the combination from which it is absent is otherwise identical with an occurring combination in which it is present.

/a/ the class of low vowels: [ʌ] in rapid speech before /p, t, k/ and after /p, t, k/, in free variation with [a]; [ã] before or after /ñ/; [a] elsewhere.

/o/ the class of mid back vowels: [O] in rapid speech before /p, t, k/ and after /p, t, k/, in free variation with [o]; [õ] before or after /ñ/; [o] elsewhere.

/u/ the class of long (syllabic) high back vowels: [ʊ] after /c, č, s, š, h/ and before /s, š, x, h, pp, tt, tc, tč, kk/, or after /p, k/ and before /p, t, k, c, č, s, š, x, h/, in free variation with [u]; [ũ] before or after /ñ/; [u] elsewhere.

/ñ/ the class of long (syllabic) nasals: [m·] before /p, b, m/ not followed by /i, y/; [*m*·] before /pi, py, bi, by, mi, my/; [n·] before /t, c, s, d, z/, and /r, n/ not followed by /i, y/; [*n*·] before /č, š, j, ž, ri, ry, ni, ny/; [ŋ·] before /w/, and /k, g, ŋ/ not followed by /i, y/; [*ŋ*·] before /x, ki, ky, gi, gy, ŋi, ŋy/; [n·] or [ŋ·] before /e, a, o, u/, /h/ not followed by /i, y/, and /⋕/ when not preceded by /i/; [*n*·] or [*ŋ*·] before /i, y, hi, hy/, and /⋕/ when preceded by /i/.

/p/ the class of voiceless labial stops: [p] before vowels except /i/; [p·] before /p/ not followed by /i, y/; [*p*] before /i, y/; [*p*·] before /pi, py/.

/t/ the class of voiceless dental stops: [t] before /e, a, o/; [t·] before /t, c, s/; [*t*] before /y/; [*t*·] before /č/.

/k/ the class of voiceless velar stops: [k] before vowels except /i/; [k·] before /k/ not followed by /i, y/; [*k*] before /i, y/; [*k*·] before /ki, ky/.

/ʔ/ the class of glottal stops: [ʔ] before pause. (Cf. fn. 32.)

/c/ the class of voiceless dental or denti-alveolar affricates: [ts] before /u/; [ts·] before pause and /t, k, c, č/.

/č/ the class of voiceless prepalatal affricates: [tš] before vowels; [tš·] before pause and /t, k, c, č/.

/s/ the class of voiceless alveolar spirants: [s] before vowels except /i/; [s·] before pause and /t, k, c, č, s/.

/š/ the class of voiceless prepalatal spirants: [š] before vowels except /e/; [š·] before pause and /t, k, c, č, š/.

/x/ the class of prevelar spirants: [*x*] before vowels except /e/; [*x*·] before /t, k, c, č/.

/h/ the class of non-lingual spirants: [f] before /u/, in free variation with [h]; [f·] before /t, k, c, č, h/; [h] before vowels except /i/; [*h*] before /i, y/.

/b/ the class of voiced labial stops: [b] before /e, a, o, u/; [*b*] before /i, y/.

/d/ the class of voiced dental stops: [d] before /e, a, o/.

/g/ the class of voiced velar stops: [g] before /e, a, o, u/; [*g*] before /i, y/.

/j/ the class of voiced prepalatal affricates: [dž] before vowels.

/z/ the class of voiced alveolar spirants: [z] before vowels except /i/.

/ž/ the class of voiced prepalatal spirants: [ž] before vowels except /e/, in free alternation with /j/.

/r/ the class of flaps: [r] before /e, a, o, u/; [l] before /e, o/, in free variation with [r]; [*r*] before /i, y/.

/m/ the class of short (non-syllabic) labial nasals: [m] before /e, a, o, u/; [*m*] before /i, y/.

/n/ the class of short (non-syllabic) dental nasals: [n] before /e, a, o, u/; [*n*] before /i, y/.

/ŋ/ the class of short (non-syllabic) velar nasals: [ŋ] before /e, a, o, u/; /*ŋ*/ before /i, y/.

/y/ the class of short (non-syllabic) high front vowels, i.e. semivowels: [ʏ] after /p, k/ and before /a, o, u/; /y/ elsewhere.

/w/ the class of short (non-syllabic) high back vowels, i.e. semivowels: [w] before /a/.

/⋕/ the class of pauses: [⋕] before all phonemes except /ʔ, ŋ, ž/, after /i, e, a, o, u, ñ, ʔ, c, č, s, š/.

6.3. The total distribution of these twenty-nine phonemes, with respect to the phonemes that immediately precede and follow them in phrases, is shown in Table 2. Each horizontal row shows all the two-phoneme combinations in which a given phoneme appears as the prior member; each vertical column shows all the combinations in which a given phoneme appears as the second member. Hence each row contains all the phonemes that follow a given phoneme, and each column contains all the phonemes that precede it.

Phonemes are listed in this table in a descending order according to their freedom of distribution. The following tabulation shows for each phoneme the number of phonemes that precede it (Prec.), the number of those that follow it (Foll.), and the total number of combinations in which it appears.

Phoneme	Prec.	Foll.	Totals	Phoneme	Prec.	Foll.	Totals
a	27	29	56	h	7	10	17
o	26	29	55	p	8	7	15
u	25	29	54	x	7	8	15
e	22	29	51	b	7	6	13
i	21	29	50	g	7	6	13
⋕	11	25	36	r	7	6	13
ñ	6	27	33	m	7	6	13
č	14	10	24	n	7	6	13
t	14	8	22	ŋ	6	6	12
k	14	7	21	j	7	5	12
c	14	6	20	z	7	4	11
y	17	3	20	d	7	3	10
s	9	10	19	ž	5	4	9
š	8	10	18	w	7	1	8
				ʔ	5	1	6

The text in §7 contains only slightly more than 2000 phonemes; it is too small a sample to yield significant statistical information. But a tabulation of the frequencies with which the several phonemes occur in this text may be useful as a model for the more extensive investigation of relative frequency that must some day be undertaken.

Phoneme frequencies in the text range from 296 for /a/ to 2 for /x/; two phonemes, /p/ and /ž/, do not occur at all. In the tabulation, relative frequencies

(R) are expressed in terms of occurrences per 10,000 phonemes (i.e. the actual percentage multiplied by 100). The columns I, M, and F show for each phoneme the percentage of its occurrences in initial, medial, and final position respectively.[37] The figures for /#/ refer to positions in the utterance as a whole; the figures for all other phonemes refer to positions in the phrase: 'initial' means preceded by /#/, 'final' means followed by /#/, 'medial' means neither preceded nor followed by /#/. Numerals in the first column designate pitch phonemes.

	R	I	M	F		R	I	M	F
a	1333	2.4	83.1	14.5	ñ	139	0.0	93.6	6.4
o	1081	8.3	84.2	7.5	d	130	3.4	96.6	0.0
3	774	0.6	76.2	23.2	ŋ	130	0.0	100.0	0.0
i	734	2.4	92.0	5.6	h	94	52.4	47.6	0.0
2	729	21.5	62.3	16.2	b	94	0.0	100.0	0.0
t	617	5.8	94.2	0.0	w	94	4.8	95.2	0.0
#	581	23.2	53.6	23.2	y	72	6.3	93.7	0.0
4	559	52.4	22.6	25.0	j	59	0.0	100.0	0.0
e	464	0.0	70.0	30.0	č	54	25.0	75.0	0.0
k	418	9.9	91.1	0.0	1	27	16.6	16.6	66.8
m	351	6.4	93.6	0.0	c	22	0.0	100.0	0.0
n	347	7.8	92.2	0.0	z	22	20.0	80.0	0.0
u	297	6.0	92.4	1.6	ʔ	13	0.0	0.0	100.0
r	265	1.7	98.3	0.0	g	13	0.0	100.0	0.0
s	252	17.8	82.2	0.0	x	9	0.0	100.0	0.0
š	189	4.8	95.2	0.0	p	0	—	—	—
					ž	0	—	—	—

6.4. In spite of the striking auditory effect produced by the equal duration of Japanese syllables (§1), syllabic structure seems to have only a very minor place, if any, in the phonemic structure as a whole. Subject to the limitations of occurrence shown in Table 2, phonemes occur[38] in utterances simply as phonemes,

[37] Some light is thrown on the relative INITIAL frequency of certain phonemes by the number of dictionary entries beginning with various letters (interpreted phonemically). Such a count, in which every dictionary word figures once, regardless of its frequency in speech, is of course different in kind from the running count tabulated above. (On the difference between list frequency and text frequency see Martin Joos, Lg. 18.33 [1942].) The following figures denote the number of PAGES occupied by words with various initial phonemes in Kenkyusha's New Japanese–English dictionary (total 2263 pp.).

k	416	n	105	d	68	x	41
h	225	i	102	b	62	u	39
t	185	y	101	g	60	z	25
s	168	j	76	r	55	e	24
š	148	o	76	č	50	w	17
m	139	a	72	c	41	p	7

The 41 pages shown for /x/ are included among the 225 shown for /h/; that is, there are 41 pages of words that begin with /x/ or /h/ in free alternation.

[38] On the logical error involved in saying that phonemes occur, and on the way in which the expression can be justified, see Lg. 24.36, §53.3 and fn. 30.

	a	o	u	e	i	#	ñ	č	t	k	c	y	s	š	h	p	x	b	g	r	m	n	ŋ	j	z	d	ž	w	ʔ
a	aa	ao	au	ae	ai	a#	añ	ač	at	ak	ac	ay	as	aš	ah	ap	ax	ab	ag	ar	am	an	aŋ	aj	az	ad	až	aw	aʔ
o	oa	oo	ou	oe	oi	o#	oñ	oč	ot	ok	oc	oy	os	oš	oh	op	ox	ob	og	or	om	on	oŋ	oj	oz	od	ož	ow	oʔ
u	ua	uo	uu	ue	ui	u#	uñ	uč	ut	uk	uc	uy	us	uš	uh	up	ux	ub	ug	ur	um	un	uŋ	uj	uz	ud	už	uw	uʔ
e	ea	eo	eu	ee	ei	e#	eñ	eč	et	ek	ec	ey	es	eš	eh	ep	ex	eb	eg	er	em	en	eŋ	ej	ez	ed	ež	ew	eʔ
i	ia	io	iu	ie	ii	i#	iñ	ič	it	ik	ic	iy	is	iš	ih	ip	ix	ib	ig	ir	im	in	iŋ	ij	iz	id	iž	iw	iʔ
#	#a	#o	#u	#e	#i		#ñ	#č	#t	#k	#c	#y	#s	#š	#h	#p	#x	#b	#g	#r	#m	#n		#j	#z	#d		#w	
ñ	ña	ño	ñu	ñe	ñi	ñ#		ñč	ñt	ñk	ñc	ñy	ñs	ñš	ñh	ñp	ñx	ñb	ñg	ñr	ñm	ñn	ñŋ	ñj	ñz	ñd	ñž	ñw	
č	ča	čo	ču	če	či	č#		čč	čt	čk	čc																		
t	ta	to		te				tč	tt		tc	ty	ts																
k	ka	ko	ku	ke	ki					kk		ky																	
c			cu			c#		cč	ct	ck	cc																		
y	ya	yo	yu																										
s	sa	so	su	se		s#		sč	st	sk	sc		ss																
š	ša	šo	šu		ši	š#		šč	št	šk	šc			šš															
h	ha	ho	hu	he	hi			hč	ht	hk	hc	hy																	
p	pa	po	pu	pe	pi							py				pp													
x	xa	xo	xu		xi			xč	xt	xk	xc																		
b	ba	bo	bu	be	bi							by																	
g	ga	go	gu	ge	gi							gy																	
r	ra	ro	ru	re	ri							ry																	
m	ma	mo	mu	me	mi							my																	
n	na	no	nu	ne	ni							ny																	
ŋ	ŋa	ŋo	ŋu	ŋe	ŋi							ŋy																	
j	ja	jo	ju	je	ji																								
z	za	zo	zu	ze																									
d	da	do		de																									
ž	ža	žo	žu		ži																								
w	wa																												
ʔ						ʔ#																							

TABLE 2. DISTRIBUTION OF PHONEMES IN THE CONSERVATIVE DIALECT

one after another, without being obviously grouped in any larger structural units except the spans defined by phonemes of pitch.[39] Some phonemes (as /i, ñ/) have only 'long' members, and hence constitute a phonetic syllable wherever they appear; some phonemes (as /b, n/) have only 'short' members, and hence never constitute a phonetic syllable; and some phonemes (as /t, s/) have 'long' members in certain environments, 'short' members in others.

Nevertheless, it is useful to state the correlation between phonetic syllables and phoneme sequences. Each of the following single phonemes and phoneme sequences constitutes one phonetic syllable:

Group 1: /i, e, a, o, u, ñ/, when preceded by a member of the same group or by pause

Group 2: /p, t, k, c, č, s, š, x, h/, when not followed by a member of Group 1

Group 3: /i, e, a, o, u/ together with one immediately preceding phoneme, provided the latter is not pause or a member of Group 1 and is not /y/ preceded in turn by a consonant

Group 4: /a, o, u/ together with two immediately preceding phonemes, provided the first is not pause or a member of Group 1, and the second is /y/

The pause phoneme is not included in any syllable. Pitch phonemes have no effect on the number of syllables in a phrase.

Though syllables appear to have little structural importance, they furnish a convenient basis for statements about the distribution of phonemes. In any syllable that contains more than one phoneme, the order of phonemes is unalterable and therefore non-distinctive: /ka/ and /kya/ are actually occurring syllables, but /ak, yak, kay, aky, ayk, yka/ are not (though all these except the last two are actually occurring sequences). It is therefore enough to enumerate the phonemes contained in a syllable, without making any statement about their order.[40] The total distribution of phonemes can be described by listing the syllables that occur and by stating the limitations on their occurrence in terms of preceding and following syllables. The units involved in such a description (syllables instead of phonemes) will be more numerous than in the treatment adopted above, but the statements about them will be fewer.[41] The following formulation may be compared with §6.3.

Syllables are grouped in five types, designated *V*, ˀ, *N*, *K*, *S*:

Type *V*: the syllable ends with or consists of a vowel; total 119: see Table 3.

Type ˀ: the syllable ends with a glottal stop; exact number not known; see §4.1.

Type *N*: the syllable consists of a long nasal consonant; total 1: /ñ/.

Type *K*: the syllable consists of a voiceless stop; total 3: /p, t, k/.

Type *S*: the syllable consists of a voiceless affricate or spirant; total 6: /c, č, s, š, x, h/.

[39] The impression that there is some structural unity in a sequence like /ka/ but not in /ak/ rests in part on the phonetic prominence of syllables, as noted in §1, and in part also on the traditional Japanese orthography, in which /ka/ but not /ak/ is written with a single character.

[40] Cf. Joos, Acoustic phonetics 80, §3.38.

[41] Each row and each column in Table 2 is a statement, though not explicitly verbalized.

i	pi		ki		či		ši	xi	hi	bi		gi	ji		ži	ri	mi	ni	ŋi	
e	pe	te	ke		če	se			he	be	de	ge	je	ze		re	me	ne	ŋe	
a	pa	ta	ka		ča	sa	ša	xa	ha	ba	da	ga	ja	za	ža	ra	ma	na	ŋa	wa
o	po	to	ko		čo	so	šo	xo	ho	bo	do	go	jo	zo	žo	ro	mo	no	ŋo	
u	pu		ku	cu	ču	su	šu	xu	hu	bu		gu	ju	zu	žu	ru	mu	nu	ŋu	
ya	pya		kya						hya	bya		gya				rya	mya	nya	ŋya	
yo	pyo		kyo						hyo	byo		gyo				ryo	myo	nyo	ŋyo	
yu	pyu	tyu	kyu						hyu	byu		gyu				ryu	myu	nyu	ŋyu	

TABLE 3. SYLLABLES OF TYPE V

The distribution of these syllable types is shown in Table 4. In this table, *V** denotes a syllable of type *V* that begins with a voiceless stop (the same stop that constitutes the preceding syllable of type *K*); *V*** denotes a syllable of type *V* that begins with a voiceless consonant of any kind. The distribution of syllables of type *S* is indicated only in general terms; for the details see Table 2.

	after /#/	after *V*	after *N*	after *K*	after *S*
before /#/	*V N*	*V* ˀ *N S*	*V*	*V**	*V***
before *V*	*V N*	*V N K S*	*V*	*V**	*V***
before ˀ	*V*	*V*	*V* (?)	*V** (?)	*V*** (?)
before *N*, *K*, *S*	*V*	*V*	*V*	*V**	*V***

TABLE 4. DISTRIBUTION OF SYLLABLE TYPES

7. Text. The following text is written in a strictly phonemic transcription; all morphophonemic, morphemic, and merely orthographical considerations are disregarded. The four pitch phonemes are indicated by inferior numerals from 1 (highest) to 4 (lowest); each numeral applies to the whole sequence of one or more phonemes that follows it, until canceled by another numeral or by the pause phoneme. Two numerals written together (as 31) denote a succession of two pitch phonemes coinciding with a single vowel. The pause phoneme is here written with a space instead of the symbol /#/; the substitution is only graphic, intended to make the reading of the text easier. Every space—before and after an utterance as well as internal—can be replaced by the overt symbol. Separate utterances (sentences) are numbered.[42]

(1) $_4$mu$_3$kašimuka$_2$ši $_2$a$_3$rutokoro$_2$ni $_4$o$_2$ji$_3$isañto $_4$o$_2$ba$_3$asañŋa $_4$a$_2$rima$_4$šta

(2) $_2$a$_3$ru$_2$hi $_4$o$_2$ji$_3$isañwa $_4$ya$_2$ma$_3$ekareedaohiroini $_4$de$_2$kakema$_4$šta

(3) $_4$so$_3$no$_2$a$_3$to$_2$de $_4$o$_2$ba$_3$asañ$_2$mo $_4$te$_3$nuŋuioka$_2$bu$_3$tte $_4$ha$_3$dašini$_2$na$_3$tte $_4$ka$_2$wa$_3$eseñtakunii$_2$kima$_4$šta

(4) $_4$se$_3$ñtakuŋa$_2$su$_3$ñ$_2$de $_4$ka$_2$ero$_3$otosuru$_2$to $_4$ka$_3$wakamikara $_2$o$_3$okinamomoŋa $_4$na$_2$ŋa$_3$retekima$_4$šta

(5) $_1$na$_3$ñtoyuu $_2$o$_3$okinamomoda$_2$ro$_4$o

[42] The text is a new version of the passage transcribed (on the basis of a different analysis) in SCJ II, Lg. 22.238–48 ((177–84)). Particulars concerning its provenience, as well as an English translation, will be found in that place.

(6) $_4$ko$_3$noto$_2$ši$_3$ni$_2$na$_3$ruma$_2$de $_4$ko$_3$ñna$_1$o$_3$okinamomowa $_2$mi$_3$takotoŋa$_2$na$_4$i

(7) $_4$čo$_3$odo$_2$i$_4$i

(8) $_4$hi$_3$rottei$_2$tte $_4$o$_2$ji$_3$isañnoomiyageniši yo$_4$o

(9) $_2$to$_3$xtorigotooiinaŋa$_2$ra $_4$to$_2$ro$_3$otoši$_2$ma$_3$šta$_2$ŋa $_2$te$_3$ŋato$_2$dokimase$_4$ñ

(10) $_2$na$_3$nikaboowa$_2$na$_3$i$_{31}$ka

(11) $_2$to? $_2$ho$_3$oboomi$_2$mawašima$_3$šta$_2$ŋa $_4$a$_3$iniku $_2$na$_3$nimoa$_2$rimase$_3$ñka$_2$ra $_4$o$_2$ba$_3$asañ$_2$wa $_2$a$_3$rukuhuuoka$_2$ñŋa$_3$ete $_4$to$_3$oimizuwani$_2$ŋa$_3$i$_4$zo $_2$čka$_3$imizuwaamai$_4$zo $_4$a$_3$mai$_2$ho$_3$oeyotteoide$_2$to $_4$u$_3$tainaŋa$_2$ra $_2$te$_3$ota$_2$takima$_4$šta

(12) $_4$so$_3$osuruto $_4$hu$_3$šiŋi$_2$ni$_3$mo $_4$mo$_3$mowadañdañna$_2$ŋa$_3$reteki$_2$te $_4$o$_2$ba$_3$asañno$_2$ma$_3$edeto$_2$marima$_4$šta

(13) $_4$o$_2$ba$_3$asañwa $_4$i$_2$so$_3$ide$_4$so$_3$reohi$_2$roia$_3$ŋe$_2$te $_4$se$_3$ñtakumonotoiššoni $_4$u$_3$čie$_4$mo$_3$tteka$_2$erima$_4$šta

(14) $_4$so$_3$ošte $_2$ha$_3$yakuo$_2$ji$_3$isañŋa$_2$ka$_3$ettekureba$_2$i$_4$i

(15) $_2$to? $_2$ma$_3$ttei$_2$ma$_3$sto $_4$hi$_3$ŋakurerukoro $_4$o$_2$ji$_3$isañwa $_4$ka$_3$reedaoyamano$_2$yo$_3$onišo$_2$tte $_2$ka$_3$ettekima$_4$šta

(16) $_2$kyo$_3$onoa$_2$cu$_3$iko$_4$to

(17) $_2$a$_3$sebi$_2$ššo$_3$ri$_4$da

(18) $_4$o$_2$ji$_3$isañno$_2$ko$_3$eo$_4$ki$_3$i$_2$te $_4$u$_3$čino$_2$na$_3$kakara $_4$i$_2$so$_3$ide$_2$de$_3$tekima$_4$šta

(19) $_4$o$_2$kaerinasa$_3$tta$_{31}$ka

(20) $_4$wa$_3$tašiwa $_2$ha$_3$yakuo$_2$kaerinasa$_3$reba$_2$i$_3$itoo$_2$mo$_3$tte $_2$zu$_3$ibuñ$_2$ma$_3$ttei$_2$ta$_3$nodesu$_4$yo

(21) $_2$ru$_3$suni $_2$na$_3$nikao$_2$ko$_3$ttano$_{31}$ka

(22) $_4$i$_3$i$_1$e

(23) $_2$so$_3$oja$_4$a$_2$rimase$_3$ñ$_2$ŋa $_2$i$_3$imonoŋa$_2$a$_3$runo$_2$de $_2$ha$_3$yaku$_4$o$_2$ji$_3$isañni$_4$o$_3$menika$_2$ke$_3$takutte

(24) $_2$se$_3$kkačino$_4$o$_2$ba$_3$asañwa $_4$a$_2$ši$_3$oaratte $_4$u$_3$činiaŋatta$_2$ba$_3$karino$_4$o$_2$ji$_3$isañno$_2$ma$_3$eni $_2$sa$_3$kkino$_2$o$_3$okinamomoo$_4$ka$_3$kaeteki$_2$ma$_4$šta

(25) $_4$čo$_3$odo$_4$o$_3$nakamo$_4$su$_3$itei$_2$ru$_3$kara $_4$o$_3$yuwa$_2$a$_3$tonište $_4$sa$_3$ssoku$_4$go$_3$čisoonina$_2$ro$_4$o

(26) $_4$o$_2$ba$_3$asa$_4$ñ $_4$ma$_2$naita$_3$to$_4$ho$_3$očooo$_4$mo$_3$tteoi$_4$de

(27) $_4$o$_2$ji$_3$isañwa $_4$mo$_3$moo$_4$ma$_2$naita$_3$noueni$_4$no$_3$sete $_2$htacu$_3$nišiyootoši$_2$ma$_3$sto $_2$na$_3$kakara $_4$o$_2$ji$_3$isa$_4$ñ $_2$čo$_3$tto$_2$ma$_3$tte$_2$to? $_4$ka$_2$wai$_3$i$_2$ko$_3$eŋakikoe$_2$te $_4$mo$_3$moŋa$_4$ma$_3$htacuni$_4$wa$_2$rema$_4$šta

(28) $_4$so$_3$ošte $_2$hto$_3$tta$_2$ki$_3$reina $_3$hcuunokotowa$_4$ma$_3$rudečiŋau$_4$a$_3$kañbooŋa$_4$to$_2$bidašima$_4$šta

(29) $_4$o$_2$ji$_3$isañto$_4$o$_2$ba$_3$asañwa $_4$ši$_2$ba$_3$raku$_4$a$_3$itakučiŋa$_4$hu$_3$saŋaranaihodo $_4$o$_2$dorokima$_3$štaŋa $_2$ši$_3$juu$_4$ko$_3$domoŋa$_2$xto$_3$ri$_4$ho$_2$ši$_3$itoo$_2$mo$_3$tteitatokoro$_2$de$_3$skara $_2$ta$_3$isoo$_4$yo$_2$roko$_3$ñde $_4$so$_3$nokooso$_2$date$_3$rukotoniši$_2$ma$_4$šta

(30) $_4$mo$_3$mono$_2$na$_3$kakara$_4$u$_2$mareta$_3$node $_4$mo$_2$mo$_3$tarootoyuunao$_2$ckema$_4$šta

8. The innovating dialect of standard colloquial Japanese, like any form of speech, is worth describing in full, without reference to other varieties of the language; but since it coincides at most points with the conservative dialect, a full description would be largely a repetition of what has already been said, with only a few departures and additions. It will be more convenient, therefore, to describe the innovating dialect wholly in terms of its differences from the conservative. Where no difference is specified, the two dialects are to be understood as having the same features.[43]

The innovating dialect differs from the conservative in three ways: (1) certain of its phonemes have a wider distribution, entering into combinations that are foreign to the conservative dialect; (2) it exhibits a phonemic distinction between two sound types which in the conservative dialect are allophones of a single phoneme; and (3) it contains one sound type, constituting a new phoneme, which is not present in the conservative dialect at all. As a result of these differences, the innovating dialect has two more phonemes than the conservative (thirty-one instead of twenty-nine, in addition to phonemes of pitch), and is characterized by a somewhat greater freedom of distribution.

Phonemes of the innovating dialect will be enclosed between double diagonals, thus //a//. Letters shown between single diagonals represent phonemes of the conservative dialect.

8.1. The conservative phoneme /t/ has an allophone [t] before /e, a, o/, and an allophone [*t*] before /y/ (as well as other allophones in other positions); it does not occur before /i/. The innovating phoneme //t// has the same allophones; but here [*t*] occurs not only before //y// but also before //i//, as in [va*nit*i] *vanity case*, [yuu*t*iri*t*ii] *utility*, [s·kee*t*iŋ·ŋu] *skating*, i.e. //vaniti, yuutiritii, skeetiñŋu//.[44]

The conservative phoneme /d/ has a single allophone [d], occurring before /e, a, o/. The innovating phoneme //d// has in addition the allophone [*d*], occurring before //i//, as in [*k*ʏa*d*ii] *caddy* (in golf), [hãn·*dik*ʏap·pu] *handicap*, [*d*iizeru] *Diesel engine*, i.e. //kyadii, hañdikyappu, diizeru//.[45]

The conservative phonemes /b, d, g/ have only short allophones. The innovating phonemes //b, d, g// have also long allophones, which occur before certain voiced consonants. [b·] and [g·] occur before [b] and [g] respectively, [d·] occurs before [d] and [dž], as in [mob·bu] *mob*, [béd·do] *bed*, [piramid·do] *pyramid*, [ed·džiŋ·ŋu] *edging*, [kared·dži] *college*, [hóg·gu] *hog* (in engineering), i.e. //mobbu, béddo, piramiddo, edjiñŋu, karedji, hóggu//.[46]

The conservative phoneme /w/ occurs only before /a/. The innovating phoneme //w// occurs also before //i, e, o//, as in [weetaa] *waiter*, [wĩŋ·ŋu] *wing* (*of an airplane*), [woomĩŋ·ŋuap·pu] *warming up* (in baseball), i.e. //weetaa, wiñŋu, woomiñŋuappu//.[47]

8.2. The conservative phoneme /h/ has an allophone [h] before /e, a, o, u/,

[43] The material of this section was discussed from the diachronic point of view in a paper presented before a meeting of the Linguistic Society in Chicago, 30 December 1946. The same point of view is implicit in Sanki Ichikawa, The pronunciation of English loan-words in Japanese, A grammatical miscellany offered to Otto Jespersen on his seventieth birthday 179–90 (Copenhagen, 1930). Ichikawa has gathered a wealth of material, but makes no attempt to arrive at a phonemic or other structural interpretation.

[44] /baniči, yuučiričii, skeetoiñŋu/ in the conservative dialect.

[45] /kyaji, hañjikyappu, jiizeru/ in the conservative dialect.

[46] Theoretically /mobu, bédo, piramido, ejiñŋu, kareji, hógu/ in the conservative dialect; but these forms seem not to occur.

[47] /ueetaa, uiñŋu, uoomiñŋuappu/ in the conservative dialect.

and an allophone [f] before /u/ which is in free variation with [h] (as well as other allophones in other positions). The same sound types are present in the innovating dialect, but here they are in contrast with each other: [f] occurs not only before //u// (where it is still in free variation with [h]) but also before //e, a, o//; and there is a palatalized labiodental spirant [ƒ] that occurs before //i, y//. Accordingly the phones [h] and [f, ƒ] in the innovating dialect must be assigned to separate phonemes: the phoneme //h// (qualities G3) has the allophones [h] and [*h*]; the phoneme //f// (qualities L3) has the allophones [f, ƒ], and [f·]. Examples: //firumu, figyua, feea, fauru, kafeteria, fairu, fañburu, fooku, foñto, fyuuzu, maffu// *film*, *figure* (in skating), *fair* (*ball*), *foul* (*ball*), *cafeteria*, *file* (for letters), *fumble*, *fork*, *font* (in printing), *fuse*, *muff*.[48]

8.3. The phone [v], a short voiced labiodental spirant (with qualities L3 V), occurs only in the innovating dialect, where it constitutes a separate phoneme. Examples: //verañda, vañpu, vaniti, vaioriñ, voodoviru, ravu// *veranda*, *vamp* (*movie siren*), *vanity case*, *violin*, *vaudeville*, *love* (in the movies or in tennis).[49]

8.4. The distribution of the thirty-one phonemes of the innovating dialect (exclusive of pitch phonemes) is shown in Table 5. The arrangement here follows the same plan as in Table 2. The order in which phonemes are listed is again determined by their relative freedom of distribution, as indicated by the following tabulation; compare the similar tabulation in §6.3.

Phoneme	Prec.	Foll.	Totals	Phoneme	Prec.	Foll.	Totals
a	29	31	60	p	8	7	15
o	29	31	60	x	7	8	15
u	27	31	58	b	8	7	15
i	26	31	57	g	8	7	15
e	25	31	56	d	8	6	14
#	11	27	38	h	7	6	13
ñ	6	29	35	r	7	6	13
č	14	10	24	m	7	6	13
t	14	9	23	n	7	6	13
y	19	3	22	v	7	6	13
k	14	7	21	j	8	5	13
c	14	6	20	ŋ	6	6	12
f	8	11	19	z	7	4	11
s	9	10	19	w	7	4	11
š	8	10	18	ž	6	4	10
				ʔ	5	1	6

9. A note on orthography. Only one kind of written record, according to Bloomfield,[50] is scientifically relevant: 'a record in terms of phonemes, ignoring

	a	o	u	i	e	#	ñ	č	t	y	k	c	f	s	š	p	x	b	g	d	h	r	m	n	v	j	ŋ	z	w	ž	ʔ
a	aa	ao	au	ai	ae	a#	añ	ač	at	ay	ak	ac	af	as	aš	ap	ax	ab	ag	ad	ah	ar	am	an	av	aj	aŋ	az	aw	až	aʔ
o	oa	oo	ou	oi	oe	o#	oñ	oč	ot	oy	ok	oc	of	os	oš	op	ox	ob	og	od	oh	or	om	on	ov	oj	oŋ	oz	ow	ož	oʔ
u	ua	uo	uu	ui	ue	u#	uñ	uč	ut	uy	uk	uc	uf	us	uš	up	ux	ub	ug	ud	uh	ur	um	un	uv	uj	uŋ	uz	uw	už	uʔ
i	ia	io	iu	ii	ie	i#	iñ	ič	it	iy	ik	ic	if	is	iš	ip	ix	ib	ig	id	ih	ir	im	in	iv	ij	iŋ	iz	iw	iž	iʔ
e	ea	eo	eu	ei	ee	e#	eñ	eč	et	ey	ek	ec	ef	es	eš	ep	ex	eb	eg	ed	eh	er	em	en	ev	ej	eŋ	ez	ew	ež	eʔ
#	#a	#o	#u	#i	#e		#ñ	#č	#t	#y	#k	#c	#f	#s	#š	#p	#x	#b	#g	#d	#h	#r	#m	#n	#v	#j		#z	#w		
ñ	ña	ño	ñu	ñi	ñe	ñ#		ñč	ñt	ñy	ñk	ñc	ñf	ñs	ñš	ñp	ñx	ñb	ñg	ñd	ñh	ñr	ñm	ñn	ñv	ñj	ñŋ	ñz	ñw	ñž	
č	ča	čo	ču	či	če	č#		čč	čt		čk	čc																			
t	ta	to		ti	te			tč	tt	ty		tc		ts																	
y	ya	yo	yu																												
k	ka	ko	ku	ki	ke					ky	kk																				
c			cu			c#		cč	ct		ck	cc																			
f	fa	fo	fu	fi	fe			fč	ft	fy	fk	fc	ff																		
s	sa	so	su		se	s#		sč	st		sk	sc		ss																	
š	ša	šo	šu	ši		š#		šč	št		šk	šc			šš																
p	pa	po	pu	pi	pe					py						pp															
x	xa	xo	xu	xi				xč	xt		xk	xc																			
b	ba	bo	bu	bi	be					by								bb													
g	ga	go	gu	gi	ge					gy									gg												
d	da	do		di	de															dd						dj					
h	ha	ho	hu	hi	he					hy																					
r	ra	ro	ru	ri	re					ry																					
m	ma	mo	mu	mi	me					my																					
n	na	no	nu	ni	ne					ny																					
v	va	vo	vu	vi	ve					vy																					
j	ja	jo	ju	ji	je																										
ŋ	ŋa	ŋo	ŋu	ŋi	ŋe					ŋy																					
z	za	zo	zu		ze																										
w	wa	wo		wi	we																										
ž	ža	žo	žu	ži																											
ʔ						ʔ#																									

TABLE 5. DISTRIBUTION OF PHONEMES IN THE INNOVATING DIALECT

[48] /hirumu/ or /huirumu/, /heea/ or /hueea/, /hairu/ or /huairu/, /hooku/ or /huooku/, etc., in the conservative dialect.

[49] /berañda, bañpu, baniči, baioriñ, boodobiru, rabu/ in the conservative dialect.

[50] Leonard Bloomfield, Language 85 (New York, 1933).

all features that are not distinctive in the language'—and ignoring also, if the record is to be strictly phonemic, all features that are distinctive but not immediately observable in the stream of speech, such as morpheme boundaries, word structure, and morphophonemic relations.[51] Such a record is the only safe and adequate basis for further investigations of linguistic structure; the analyst who attempts to study the morphemes or the grammatical constructions of a language in terms of a transcription that is either less or more than phonemic—a raw phonetic transcription on the one hand, or on the other a transcription that tacitly relies on non-phonetic evidence—will either be lost in a confusion of irrelevant details or overlook significant correlations between the phonemic structure and the structure of other linguistic levels. This does not mean (though it has now and then been misunderstood[52]) that the analyst should shut his eyes to all morphemic and grammatical facts until he has completely worked out the phonemics of a new language. Facts of all kinds come to his attention from the very beginning of his first interview with an informant, and should be filed away as they appear, even if some of them cannot be immediately accommodated in a larger system. But though the analyst acquires bits of information about the language piecemeal and in a random order, he cannot fully organize what he has learned about morphemes until he has codified the phonemes, or what he has learned about grammatical constructions until he has codified the morphemes. Finally, when he comes to write down his description of the language so that others may see the structure that he has discovered, he must group the many facts to be presented (since he cannot present them all at once) into separate compartments or levels, each one organically distinct from the others; and here the requirements of good method and good style demand that the statements made on any given level be as independent as possible of those made at other levels—in particular, that they assume as known only what has been said earlier, nothing that is to be said later.

However, it does not follow that a rigorously phonemic transcription must be retained throughout all the levels of a descriptive treatment, or that forms cited near the end of the work in the exposition of syntax must be written in the same way as those cited in the exposition of morphemics near the beginning. Once the transcription has been used in the study of morphemes (in particular, of morphophonemic alternations), it may be legitimately modified, elaborated, or normalized on the basis of new facts now first made fully available to the reader. A normalized notation, still firmly based on the phonemic analysis but incorporating the most common or the most important morphophonemic relations —especially those that are automatic[53]—and such grammatical features as word boundaries and pitch morphemes, approaches the character of a practical orthography. It is usually far better adapted to the discussion of morphology and syntax than a wholly unmodified transcription; when used for the writing of connected texts it reveals more of the linguistic structure; and those who already know the language find it easier to read.

It is also legitimate, in the interests of a neat-looking and easily printed orthography, to represent single phonemes by combinations of letters, even of letters that denote other phonemes in the same language, provided such a representation introduces no ambiguity. Thus it is possible to represent the Japanese phoneme /š/ by the letters *sy*, since the phonemes /s/ and /y/ do not occur in sequence.

The transcription of Japanese used in the first three papers of this series (§0), though it is not strictly phonemic, can be justified as a normalized orthography.[54] The phonemes of the conservative dialect—the only dialect treated in the earlier papers—are represented in part by the same letters as in the present paper, in part by special morphophonemic symbols or combinations. The departures from a purely phonemic representation are shown in the following list.

/p/ before /p/ . . . . *q*
/t/ before /t, c, č/[55] . . . . . *q*
/k/ before /k/ . . . . *q*
/c/ before /u/ . . . . *t*
/c/ before /t, k, c, č/ . . . . *tu*
/č/ before /i/ . . . . *t*
/č/ before /e, a, o, u/ . . . . *ty*
/č/ before /t, k, c, č/ . . . . . *ti*
/s/ before /t, k, c, č/ . . . . . *su*
/s/ before /s/ . . . . *q*
/š/ before /i/ . . . . *s*
/š/ before /a, o, u/ . . . . . . *sy*
/š/ before /t, k, c, č/ . . . . . . *si*
/š/ before /š/ . . . . *q*
/x/ before /i/ . . . . *h*
/x/ before /a, o, u/ . . . . *hy*
/x/ before /t, k, c, č/ . . . . . . *hi*
/h/ before /t, k, c, č, h/ . . . . *hu*
/j/ before /i/ . . . . *z*
/j/ before /e, a, o, u/ . . . . . . *zy*
/ž/ before /i/ . . . . *z*
/ž/ before /a, o, u/ . . . . *zy*
/ŋ/ everywhere . . . . *g*

Pause is indicated by any of four marks of punctuation, which at the same time denote the pitch of the phrase-final syllable: a period means pitch /4/, a question mark /31/, an exclamation point /1/, and a comma /3/ or /43/ if the preceding syllable has pitch /1/ or /2/, otherwise /3/ or /2/ in free alternation.[56] An acute accent denotes pitch /2/ on the syllable marked and on every preceding syllable within the word, except the first. (Word boundaries are shown by spaces.) An unmarked initial syllable has pitch /4/, other non-final syllables have /3/.

In this orthography certain phonemic distinctions are ignored—for instance between /t/ and /c/ and /č/, between /x/ and /h/, between /j/ and /ž/, between /ŋ/ and /g/. But the phonemes that are thus graphically confounded are all in free or in morphophonemic alternation with each other: in the context in which the orthography was used, the distinctions between them are unimportant.

[51] The reshaping of a phonemic transcription on the basis of morphological and other criteria, mentioned in §2 and fn. 16—what Hockett calls preliminary normalization of the orthography—does not, or at any rate need not, affect its purely phonemic character.

[52] Cf. Kenneth L. Pike, Grammatical prerequisites to phonemic analysis, Word 3.155–72 (1947).

[53] As defined by Rulon S. Wells, Automatic alternation, Lg. 25.99–116 (1949).

[54] Even though the normalization was not intended, and is now justified a posteriori.

[55] But /t/ before /s/ is *t*.

[56] These descriptions of the four pitch morphemes, denoted in the orthography by marks of punctuation, do not wholly agree with the statement in SCJ II, Lg. 22.200–1 ((154 f.)). They are based on the description given by Eleanor H. Jorden in her doctoral dissertation, The syntax of modern colloquial Japanese (Yale University, 1949).

DESCRIPTION OF LANGUAGE DESIGN

MARTIN JOOS

Journal of the Acoustical
Society of America 22.701–8—1950

Physicists describe speech with continuous mathematics, such as Fourier analysis or the autocorrelation functions. Linguists describe language instead, using a discontinuous or discrete mathematics called 'linguistics'. The nature of this odd calculus is outlined and justified here. It treats speech communication as having a telegraphic structure. (Non-linguists normally fail to orient themselves in this field because they treat speech as analogous to telephony.) The telegraph-code structure of language is examined from top to bottom, and at each of its several levels of complexity (compared to the two levels of Morse code) its structure is shown to be defined by possibilities and impossibilities of combination among the units of that level. Above the highest level we find, instead of such absolute restrictions, conditional probabilities of occurrence: this is the semantic field, outside linguistics, where sociologists can work. Below the lowest level we find, instead of such absolute restrictions, conditional probabilities of phonetic quality: this is the phonetic field, outside linguistics, where physicists can work. Thus linguistics is peculiar among mathematical systems in that it abuts upon reality in two places instead of one. This statement is equivalent to defining a language as a symbolic system; that is, as a code.

The word 'design' may be interpreted in at least two senses without violating engineering usage. First, there is the work of the engineer who is designing something, for example a telephone system. Second, there is the finished something, such as that same telephone system, considered now as something to be analysed and described. Our description of it, then, can also be called its 'design'. It is in this last sense that the word 'design' has to be understood when we are talking about the design of language and how it is analysed for description.

Engineers never have occasion to analyse a gadget the way linguists do a language. The nearest thing to it might be this sort of episode: A supplier had been asked to furnish a band-pass filter, single T section, with rather modest cut-off requirements. Instead of the expected classical constant-k filter—two series arms, one parallel arm, total three coils and three capacitors—he furnished a filter with three coils and four capacitors connected in an unexpected way. The writer was asked to analyse the design and report whether it was worth adopting for future routine construction of band-pass filters. It turned out that the odd design had two advantages: one of the coils could be a large stock-size coil used without trimming, and the design gave any desired impedance-transformation without a transformer. But—and here is the crucial point—it did not seem possible to arrive at these conclusions without taking into consideration the designer's intentions; and the experience seemed to show that a 'why' question has an answer only when intention is in the picture—when the presence of intention is given, so to speak, as a boundary-condition.

Linguists have described numerous languages, and have observed language design-changes through the centuries. But although quite a body of 'how' knowledge concerning these matters has been built up, we have so far nothing but a number of unconfirmable guesses concerning the 'why'. Hence most of us are now pretty sure about one thing: there is nothing conscious, nothing deliberate, about language-design. (Naturally we don't mean to study Basic English or Esperanto until we have first built up the theory of natural language-design.) Accordingly we do not present the design of any language as the result of intentions—we do not answer 'why' questions about the design of a language.

Having thus limited our problem, we proceed with greater confidence to look for answers to the 'how' questions of language-design. In other words, we try to describe precisely; we do not try to explain. Anything in our description that sounds like explanation is simply loose talk—deliberately loose, perhaps, for the sake of persuasion by analogy—and is not to be considered part of current linguistic theory.

We can allow other people—telephone engineers or sociologists, for example—to speak artistically, imprecisely, about language. But as linguists we lay upon ourselves the condition that we must speak precisely about language or not at all. We can do that, of course, only under two conditions, of which the first has already been hinted at. First, we must limit our field, leaving outside it certain things to be treated precisely by engineers or by sociologists, while we speak of them more or less artistically. Second, within our field we must adopt a technique of precise treatment, which is by definition a mathematics. We must make our 'linguistics' a kind of mathematics, within which inconsistency is by definition impossible. True, miscalculations may occur through inadvertence. And different workers describing the same language may arrive at conflicting statements because they have started out from different sets of axioms. But in principle every possible statement of ours must be either true or false —nothing half-way.

Have linguists succeeded in setting up such a mathematical style for describing language designs? Well, not quite; but our science is still young. In its mathematical phase it is just a quarter of a century old, for we date it from Bloomfield's 'A set of postulates for the science of language' (in the journal Language, 1926 ((26))). And even physics has not yet entirely resolved the conflict between quantum theory and the wave theory of light. But of all the sciences and near-sciences which deal with human behavior, linguistics is the only one which is in a fair way to becoming completely mathematical, and the other social scientists are already beginning to imitate the strict methods of the linguists.

Presenting only 'how' statements without regard to 'why', we of course have no assurance that we are 'right' in any sense that would satisfy a theologian. And we feel that our descriptive statements fit actual speech-behavior, but we have no right to claim that they are 'correct' in the sense that they fit the neural events in the brains of the speaker and listener. Such arrogant modesty is not peculiar to linguists; it is simply the normal attitude of mathematicians confronting the real world. The mathematical description for reality has been most illuminatingly called a 'map'. Now when one holds a map (in the ordinary sense) in one's hands, one may say, "I feel that this is a map of the countryside around me here," but there is no way to prove logically that it is not instead a map of a piece of Australia or perhaps of some imaginary Treasure Island. Undeterred by the impossibility of logical justification, explorers use maps, scientists use mathematics, and linguists use the descriptive technique called 'linguistics'. All three have the same attitude toward the map. One proceeds across the terrain and simultaneously traces a line across the map; one notes discrepancies between one's reading of the map and the sense impressions from the real world, until the discrepancies seem to form a pattern themselves; then one corrects the map and starts all over again. All this is intuitive behavior, and logically unjustifiable. Nor does it need justification. The place for logic is inside the map, not between the map and the real world.

Ordinary mathematical techniques fall mostly into two classes, the continuous (e.g.the infinitesimal calculus) and the discrete or discontinuous (e.g.finite group theory). Now it will turn out that the mathematics called 'linguistics' belongs in the second class. It does not even make any compromise with continuity as statistics does, or infinite-group theory. Linguistics is a quantum mechanics in the most extreme sense. All continuity, all possibilities of infinitesimal gradation, are shoved outside of linguistics in one direction or the other. There are in fact two such directions, in which we can and resolutely do expel continuity: semantics and phonetics.

Every language has 'meaningful' molecules called 'morphemes', sub-assemblies which roughly correspond to subdivisions of the real world outside language. The word <u>nose</u>, for example, consists of one such morpheme; the word <u>noses</u> consists of two, the second having as its real-world correspondent the conventional category of numerousness, one of our customary subdivisions or categorizations of the real world. Now consider these facts. The English word <u>nose</u> may refer to a part (how much?) of an airplane. With a lipstick draw a loop on your own face to enclose your nose and nothing else; another person will say that you have enclosed either too much or too little. Say in English: "The councillors all put their glasses on their noses" and then get the sentence translated into German; for English <u>noses</u> you will get the singular noun-form <u>Nase</u>, not the plural <u>Nasen</u>. The German knows that numerous councillors have equally numerous noses, and he has a word for 'noses', but in this sentence he uses his word for 'nose' instead. In linguistic terminology we simply say that the form <u>Nase</u> belongs to the category which we have called 'singular'. We chose that name the way the physicist chose the name 'work', because in German the category most often refers to lack of numerousness in the things referred to; but this is not a logical reason, it is only a motivation out of convenience. High-school Physics teachers often have good reason to regret the choice of the term 'work' for force times distance, and in expounding linguistic theory we often have the same reason for regretting the choice of terms 'singular' and 'plural'. The trained listener, the listening linguist in this case, is not deceived; he knows that in calling <u>Nase</u> 'singular' we have not said whether one nose or more than one nose was involved.

We keep on and say a few thousand things like this, but as long as we are talking about German or English we never place a noun-form in a third category side by side with 'singular' and 'plural', say a category which is neither singular nor plural, or is both, or is ambiguous as to number. The listening linguist, noting the absence of this other kind of statement, sooner or later decides that in German or in English every noun-form is either singular or else plural—tertium non datur. This may be called the tyranny of linguistic categories. It is found in every language. It is not a question of 'correctness' in the popular sense of the word, for every kind of speech, elegant or sub-standard, has its own categorical tyrannies. For example, in the writer's dialect the form <u>whom</u> can't follow a pause: it is permissible to say "To whom did you give it?" or "Who did you give it to?" but not "Whom did you give it to?" In situations where the normal language-design is not quite adequate, such as in the composition of a paper like this, we get amusing difficulties, such as finding it necessary to say either 'one nose or more than one nose was involved' or else 'one nose or several noses were involved.' The difficulty is just as severe if we say 'one sheep or more-than-one/several sheep was/were involved.' That is, it is the category that tyrannizes over us, not the form, and not the meaning either; and even a word like sheep must be, each time that it is used, either singular or else plural. We might like to replace was/were with a verb-form which was, like the Irishman's trousers, singular at the top and plural at the bottom, but we haven't got any such category in English. In fact, in every known language there is a limit to the kinds and numbers of its categories, a limit which may seem very low compared to the elaborations which philosophers and poets indulge in. Then when an unusual message is to be transmitted, the categories are never split or supplemented, but are instead used in unusual combinations. The listener's total reaction may or may not be as expected, but his detail reactions are predictable at least to this extent: For every form-class represented in the utterance ('noun' is one form-class, 'verb' is another) there are a certain number of dimensions of categorization (in the English noun there are two: possessive-vs.-common, and singular-vs.-plural); and now, for every dimension thus introduced into the utterance, the listener will react to exactly one of the categories in that dimension—he will not react to more than one, or to none, whether the utterance is ambiguous or not. The reader can check this fact easily. Without looking back to the sentence about the councillors, let him ask himself whether it referred to present time or to past time. He will find that he has made up his mind one way or the other; and yet, on checking the wording, he will find that he was not told. The English categorization, past-vs.-present, forced him to decide, even though the decision had to be made at random. Each language does this within the range of its own categories, which will not be the same range as in our language. In Chinese, for example, the translation lacks both the past-vs.-present dimension and the singular-vs.-plural dimension; these 'meanings' can be indicated on occasion, but when they are not, the Chinese listener leaves the question open—he says he is not even aware that it is a question.

The linguistic categories, then, are absolutes which admit of no compromise. They correspond roughly to favorite categorizations in the real world, and it is widely held that every community subdivides the phenomena in the real world according to the categories of its language, rather than the reverse. But the correspondence between the discrete categories of the language and the continuous phenomena of the real world is not and cannot be precise. Our reaction, as linguists, to this situation, is very simple: all phenomena, whether popularly regarded as linguistic (such as the tone of anger in an utterance) or not, which we find we cannot describe precisely with a finite number of absolute categories, we classify as non-linguistic elements of the real world and expel them from linguistic science. Let sociologists and others do what they like with such things—we may wish them luck in their efforts to describe them precisely in their own terminology, but no matter whether they describe them with discrete categories or not, for us they remain vague, protean, fluctuating phenomena—in a word, they represent that 'continuity' which we refuse to tolerate in our own science.

Have we ever had any choice? Could we have chosen to use a continuous rather than a discrete mathematics for describing language-design? Our experience with the analysis of a few hundred of the world's several thousand languages makes us very sure that we must answer negatively. We can, with some effort, begin to imagine a quasi-language used on some other planet by creatures unlike ourselves, in which a quasi-word [kul] (identical with the way I have just now pronounced English cool) signifies a temperature of +10° centigrade, and another one, [kold], signifies -10°, while any intermediate temperature worth mentioning is precisely signified by an intermediate pronunciation, with a vowel between [u] and [o] at just the right proportionate distance from them both (phonetically a reasonable thing to say: [o] and [u] are phonetically neighbors, and continuous gradation of quality from one towards the other is a commonplace) and just the right strength of [d] (from zero strength, or lack of [d], at one end of that segment of temperature scale, up to that full strength which I used just now at the other end of it) to measure and signify just the temperature meant. But neither this sort of thing, nor indeed any other gradation or continuity in either form or meaning, has ever been found in any language on this planet. True, the sounds (and thus all the forms) occurring in the use of the language are variable by continuous gradation, and so are not only temperatures but all things and phenomena spoken of. But in the design of the language we never find a trace of those facts! Messages are communicated in the language, both in speech and in writing, as if the forms (words, etc.) were invariants and as if the referents (things, etc.) were also invariants: that is, the only way the forms and meanings of a language are ever used is the way an accountant uses 'dollars' or 'shillings'—not the way a numismatist or even an economist uses them.

The accountant banishes two kinds of continuity from his debits-and-credits mathematics: the continuous variation in 'state' of a coin that interests a numismatist, and the continuous variation in 'real value' that interests an economist. Linguists do the same in describing language: from their linguistic calculus they banish the continuous variation in phonetic 'state' of the utterance, and the continuous variation in semantic 'real value' thereof. Now is this the right way to discuss language? Is it somehow adequate to the way languages work? Or is it instead a falsification, a Procrustean mistreatment? Let us consider the phonological half of it first.

Here we have 'phonemics' inside of linguistic science; and 'phonetics', which is not so very different from and may even be considered a division of the physicist's 'acoustics', in the realm of overt speech-behavior, which is not the realm of linguistics but belongs to the real world outside of linguistics. When a physicist analyses speech he finds a continuum of articulatory activity, of sound, and of events in the ear—at least until, working both ways from the sound, he comes to the all-or-none discharging of single nerve-fibers—and for describing any or all of this he uses a continuous mathematics, such as Fourier analysis or the auto-correlation function. On the other hand, linguists have found it appropriate always to describe every language so far studied as having, and every act of speech as corresponding to, combinations of an astonishingly small number of smallest signalling units called 'phonemes' which recur identically insofar as they can be said to occur at all. Thus the word hotel can't be spoken the same way twice, from the physicist's viewpoint, no matter whether the same person or different persons should utter it; and yet from the linguist's viewpoint it always has in the middle a phoneme /t/ which is identically the same every time. And it is not considered the same through neglect of unimportant variations in reality; rather, it is identical by definition, simply because it is a linguistic atom, a category, and these are either identically the same or absolutely different.

Here, then, linguistics insists upon being atomistic. Is this the right and only thing for a linguist to do? Telephone engineers have been known to protest at this point and say something like this: "When you were discussing linguistic discreteness and non-linguistic continuity in the semantic field you had me where you wanted me, for how should an engineer know anything about semantics? But now you are talking about sound, and here I am perfectly at home; I have even made extensive and precise observations upon normal speakers and listeners: for instance, I have gathered statistics about the variations in vowel qualities. Your mathematically identical phonemes are a delusion; what you've got are statistical norms, clusterings around averages which you take as norms and then arbitrarily make into absolutes. We are both talking about phonetics; and when you admit that I can prove continuity, you can't claim to prove discreteness.

"Let us agree to neglect the least important features of speech sound, so that at any moment we can describe it sufficiently well with n measurements, a point in n-dimensional continuous space, n being not only finite but a fairly small number, say six. Now the quality of the sound becomes a point which moves continuously in this 6-space, sometimes faster and sometimes slower, so that it spends more or less time in different regions, or visits a certain region more or less often. In the long run, then, we get a probability-density for the presence of the moving point anywhere in the 6-space. This probability-density varies continuously all over the space. Now wherever you can find a local maximum of probability-density, a place where the probability-density does not increase for short distances in any direction away from the place in question, I will let you call that place a 'phoneme'; and I expect, just as you do, that there will be not only a finite but a fairly small number of such points, say less than a hundred. Thus you see that there is no need to use a discrete mathematics to get a finite number of phonemes out of the phonetic continuum."

We could answer that our name for that would be, not 'phoneme', but 'allophone', and allophones belong to phonetics while phonemes belong to linguistics. But that would be evading the issue. The engineer's argument is a formidable one, and deserves to be met squarely. According to our view concerning the relationship between any mathematical map and the real phenomena to which it corresponds, it is not possible to argue logically in this field; therefore we have to argue by means of analogy. Fortunately a suitable analogy lies ready to hand.

Let us consider telegraphy, using Morse or Baudot coding. The units are the mark and the space; it doesn't matter whether the 'space' is an electrical impulse of opposite polarity to the 'mark', or an electrically neutral period. A Morse dash could be considered as three integrally sequent marks, and a letter-space as three spaces; then the units differ in only one dimension. Or the dash and the letter-space may be considered as independent signals; then there are four signals, differing from each other in two dimensions, namely electrical intensity (or polarity) and duration. Thus there are at least two ways of describing the Morse code, both discrete and both correct, each by its own axioms. They differ in their grammar, though. The first way requires the grammatical rule that each occurrence of mark after space (or of space after mark) is always followed by exactly two more of the same or else by one or three of the other. The second way requires the rule that either mark is followed by a space, and either space by a mark. This sort of interrelation between a set of axioms and a set of grammatical rules is a commonplace in linguistics. But now let us continue with telegraphy.

A Morse S is mark-space-mark-space-mark. A Baudot Y is mark-space-mark-space-mark—shall we say "also"? That depends; we can settle it later. At the far end of a long line, the marks and spaces are slurred together into a continuous smooth fluctuation so that on first inspection it may be far from easy to tell what the original signals must have been. Then a regenerative repeater is used to square up the marks and spaces so that they can be read or will operate an ordinary teletypewriter. But if the line is very long, not much noise will be needed to cause occasional errors in the repeater's operation. A regenerative repeater for Baudot signals will in general not handle Morse signals, nor vice versa. (We begin to see why we had better not say "also" as proposed at the beginning of this paragraph.)

Now let us find a telephone engineer who knows nothing about telegraphy, and give him the output of a long telegraph line. What does he do with it? He does Fourier analysis and auto-correlation and perhaps something else—at any rate, at first he works on it with continuous mathematics, for the material is obviously continuous. But as long as he does that, he can make no sense out of it. In desperation he next differentiates the output voltage, so that he has two data for every instant, the voltage and its first time-derivative. Now for each five milliseconds he averages each of these, and plots the two averages as a single point on a sheet of graph-paper. When he has put a few thousand points on his paper, he sees a continuous variation of point-density, with a number of local maxima—perhaps a few dozen of them. To each maximum he assigns a label, a letter or a number, arbitrarily. Now he interprets his original data, his voltage and derivative data, in terms of these labels: every time the line-output and its derivative come close to one of those maximum-density points, he will write down the label of that point, so that finally he has replaced the original data by a string of those labels. Now he can turn this result over to a cryptanalyst, who will be able to read the original plain-language text out of it—not quite completely on first reading, but probably he will be able to reconstruct a good text if he knows the language well. Ridiculous? Not at all. This is exactly what our telephone engineer wanted to do with phonetics and phonemics.

Now we also know what that same telephone engineer will do after we tell him of the existence of telegraph codes employing molecular signals made up of atomic units, each unit being identically one or another of a very small number of atoms. He will not use Fourier analysis or any other continuous mathematics at first. Rather, he will start out by looking for wave-trains that look nearly alike, their slight differences being explicable, as he can easily see, either as the effects of noise or as the effects of context. He will see many occurrences of a three-peaked wave-train, no two occurrences precisely alike. But when the first peak is rather low, then there will be a long hollow before it; when there is no hollow, the first peak is as high as the second or a bit higher. This is a context-effect. Once most of the context-effects have been spotted, the remaining variations will be ascribed to noise. In this fashion he will learn to identify the three-peaked wave for Morse S or Baudot Y, and also all the other common molecular signals.

Next he will set up the hypothesis that there are just n atomic signalling units, and that not only the inter-molecular context-effects but also the intra-molecular smoothings can be accounted for by low-pass filtering. Here he can use continuous mathematics for a while, and the result will be that this hypothesis works best if n equals two. Now it won't take him long to reconstruct the entire telegraphic code; quite easily if it is Baudot, not so easily or swiftly if it is Morse, but in either case with absolute certainty.

Finally he will describe the design of the telegraphic code, and he will describe it in terms of absolutely identical square-wave signalling atoms, even though he has never observed anything that could be called absolute identity, and even though he knows that square waves are impossible. And when he has thus finished his job, he will be able to convince his colleagues, the other telephone engineers who knew nothing about telegraphy, that this is the right way to do it. Convince them by logic? Not a chance. Nothing but the superior elegance of his results will speak for the rightness of his method, but that will be enough.

Linguists find themselves so successful in describing languages in this fashion that they have elevated their descriptive technique to the rank of a theory about the nature of language. They say, in effect, that the design of any language is essentially telegraphic—that the language has the structure of a telegraph-code, using molecular signals made up of invariant atoms, and differing e.g. from the Morse code principally in two ways: the codes called 'languages' have numerous layers of complexity instead of only two, and in each layer there are severe limitations upon the combinations permitted. This much, we find, all languages have in common. But the particular code is different from one language or dialect to another, as the Baudot and Morse codes differ. Those two telegraphic codes share, on the phenomenal level, this molecular signal among others: mark-space-mark-space-mark. Now suppose we find this signal in the output of one telegraph line, and find it again in the output of another telegraph line; are they the same or are they not the same? That depends. If they are both Morse or both Baudot, then they are identically the same signal, no matter whether or not they are distorted by different noises or different line characteristics, or are sent at different speeds, or by a well-adjusted or a badly-adjusted transmitter. If one is Morse and the other is Baudot, then they are not in the least the same signal, even when their oscillograms come out the same within the limits of instrumental error.

This is obvious to any telegraph engineer. But in the linguistic field it did not seem obvious or even credible to a certain engineer who said to the writer: "Surely you can tell when two men pronounce the word father alike!" The answer had to be: "On the data you have given me, the question has no meaning. First I have to find out whether they rhyme father with bother. If they both do, or neither does, then I must find out whether both of them or neither of them pronounces cot the same as he pronounces caught. Then I have a few more questions of the same sort, with which I explore their contrasts for some distance around the word father in all directions. If I always get the same answer from both of them, then I say, 'Yes, they pronounce father alike,' meaning 'identically the same,' even if they sound quite different when they say the word. But if, during this exploration, I find a discrepancy between their systems of phonemic contrasts before I have gone very far from the word father itself, then I shall have to say, 'No, they pronounce it differently,' meaning 'their pronunciations are incommensurable,' even if they sound so much alike that no difference can be heard." This statement was met with amazed incredulity, and a request to state honestly whether anybody else held similar views. It is to be feared that the answer to this request was not accepted at face value. The trouble was, of course, that no bridge had been built between the engineer's knowledge of telegraphy and the language experience of linguists.

Now let us go on with the design of language. We have dealt with the phonemes individually, and shown that the most important thing about them is that they are either absolutely the same or absolutely different. And yet, in another sense it is to be expected that two of them can be partly the same and partly different. This can be possible in this way. If it is possible to put phoneme /A/ into three categories x, y, and z (as the word noses simultaneously belongs to the three categories 'noun', 'common rather than possessive', and 'plural'), and to put phoneme /B/ into three categories v, w, and z (as the word were belongs to the three categories 'verb', 'past', and 'plural'), then /A/ and /B/ can be said to be similar, but of course only in the sense that they are partly identical: similarity can't be gradual, but only quantized, as in this instance, where /A/ and /B/ are identical to the extent of z and otherwise absolutely different, hence are called 'similar'. This is another way of stating the discrete nature of the descriptive method called 'linguistics': similarity is described as fractional identity. We naturally use quantized identity, wherever we can find it, to describe what we find in a language; and what has been described in that fashion has been rigorously described.

The Morse code uses two signalling units, 'mark' and 'space', differing in one dimension; or it can be considered as using four units, 'dot', 'dash', 'space', and 'letter-space' different in two dimensions, namely electrical intensity (or polarity) and duration. On the other hand, every known language uses more than a dozen (and less than a hundred) phonemes, different from each other in at least four, more probably at least five, dimensions. Spanish, for example, seems to have at least nine dimensions in its phonemic system (which some phonologists will reckon as fewer by the trick of identifying some dimension found in one area of the phonology with a dimension found only in another area) and English is known to have more than Spanish.

These are so many that a complete catalog would be confusing, but a sample may be helpful. One of the Spanish dimensions is 'vowel-vs.-consonant'. Among the five Spanish vowels, two more dimensions are clearly evident. In one dimension, the five are categorized as 'high, mid, low'; in the other, as 'front, central, back'. /i/ and /u/ are high; /e/ and /o/ are mid; /a/ is low. /i/ and /e/ are front; /u/ and /o/ are back; /a/ is neither, so it is called central. The six category-names were borrowed from phonetics into phonemics, just as the word 'work' was borrowed by physics, and as we borrowed 'plural' from other fields of discussion, where it was a synonym for 'numerous': in linguistics it is not! In phonetics, 'high, mid, low, front, central, back' refer to tongue-position in the mouth; in phonemics, of course, we have to strip away those denotations of the words, which have now become distracting connotations. Instead, the phonemic categories get whatever denotations may be useful in the further description of the language. The phonetic term 'labial' means 'articulated with a lip or lips'. The phonemic term 'labial' means different things for describing different languages. In describing the Oneida language it would be a meaningless term. In describing English, it means 'forbidden after /aw/' (where /aw/ means what we spell ou in such words as council)—that is, after /aw/ without any sort of break (such as the /+/ break in cowboy) we never have any of the phonemes /p, b, f, v, m, k, g/ and perhaps certain others; now the first five of these are said to be forbidden after /aw/ because they are labials, and other reasons are found for the others that never occur after /aw/. Thus the term 'labial' is not used in phonemics (though it might still be spoken or written casually) unless to make statements about what occurs, or, because it has not yet been found to occur, is taken to be impossible. Such statements are the characteristic statements of descriptive linguistics; and among them, the statements of non-occurrence are, oddly, of the greatest importance, as will appear again below.

A telegraphic 'mark' does not signal anything by itself. In principle, it takes an assembly of marks and spaces to make up a signal. Then the one-dot Morse E is a sort of accident, what mathematicians call a 'trivial' or 'degenerate' case; it is a molecule of only one atom, like a helium molecule.

The same is true of phonemes. Linguistic signalling is done, not with phonemes, but with morphemes, like either morpheme of the word noses. It is only when the coding has been built up at least to the morpheme level that it is permissible to talk of 'meaning'. The morphemes, when viewed from the phonemic level, are assemblies; viewed from levels of higher complexity, the morphemes appear as unanalysable units; viewed from the outside, the morphemes are sub-assemblies in engineering terminology. They combine into larger sub-assemblies, and these again and again into more and more massive ones, until a complete utterance has been built up, through a number of stages of assembly. In the English sentence about the councillors, at least seven stages of assembly can be found, at least seven layers of complexity in the coding of a fairly simple message. We shall discuss them only summarily.

If we start with the complete utterance and break it down by stages until we arrive at the phonemes, a pattern of analysis emerges which has interesting peculiarities. As a whole it belongs to the category 'sentence'; nothing less than all of it is classified thus; this classification is plainly marked by details of rhythm and intonation which the spelling does not indicate but which are essential structural details of English. Parts of it belong to different classes, as we shall see in detail; and the classes found early in the analysis are partly the same and partly not the same classes as those found later.

First analysis: cut it into the councillors and all put their glasses on their noses. The first part is a 'noun-phrase' because it fits into the sentence in the same way as a plain 'noun' might, such as the word councillors; its further analysis will of course agree with this, for example it contains the word the and a 'noun', and such combinations generally make up noun-phrases. It is an 'actor-expression', we might say "by default" (as so often in English) because of the absence of any other candidate for the job, while the rest of the sentence, the 'action-expression', can use one and will cause anything to be so classified which is not marked as having a different value: this one is rather marked as probably being an 'actor-expression' by the fact that it is a 'noun-phrase' and stands first (a position which signifies 'actor' in this language and certain others, not including German!), and its classification as an 'actor-expression' is not forbidden by any such mark as the s of man's. Hence it is 'common' rather than 'possessive', although it is not marked as such, as the words man and men are: the apostrophe of councillor's or of councillors' belongs to the spelling, not to the language. Therefore the final s here marks it as belonging to the 'plural' category; this is at least not forbidden by the form put, while puts would refuse to fit it; therefore, when we later analyse the 'action-expression' we shall classify put as 'plural'—whereupon it will be seen that put is not marked as either 'present' or 'past', while puts would have been marked as 'present'. It is marked as 'definite' by the presence of the in it; being 'definite', it will fit a 'plural' 'action-expression' containing the word all used as it is here, which at least some 'indefinite' 'actor-expressions' will not fit, for instance some councillors. In summary, this the councillors is a 'common definite plural noun-phrase' functioning as an 'actor-expression'; it will not do simply to call it a 'common definite plural noun-phrase actor-expression' because then 'common' would be made redundant by 'actor-expression'. On the other hand, 'actor-expression' is not made redundant by 'common', for 'common rather than possessive' will fit other categories besides 'actor-expression', as in I met the councillors. It is precisely such asymmetries, found everywhere in language, which makes our analysis possible and keeps our arguments from being circular. The reader may check through this paragraph for other asymmetries and see how they were taken advantage of.

Second analysis: cut the councillors into the and councillors. The reader can set up the discussion himself on the model of the preceding paragraph.

Third analysis: cut councillors into councillor and s. Now councillor looks like a word, but in this sentence it is not a word; we can call it a 'stem' here; to it is added the 'morpheme' s. Discussion of this would use up our space unprofitably.

Fourth analysis: cut councillor into council and or. Either one of these is a morpheme. The first of them looks like the one-morpheme word council, but here it isn't; a 'morpheme' is all we can call it. It belongs to that category of morphemes which is defined by the fact that each of them will combine with the morpheme or; and it belongs to other categories similarly defined by possibilities of combination: for example, it will combine with certain s morphemes, to make the possessive singular council's or the plural councils or councils'. It will be noted that these criteria of classification are essentially of the same sort as those used in our first analysis, but now the categories are different.

Fifth analysis: we may or may not choose to break council into two syllables, but it appears that we can never get any profit out of doing so in our language, so we cut it at once into seven phonemes—by an odd accident, the same as the number of letters in the spelling—by a single act of analysis.

Now we have arrived at the phoneme level, and no further analysis is called for by the kind of procedure we have been following. We can classify the phonemes into different categories of vowels and consonants, as was indicated above for Spanish and English. Then we could, if we chose, treat these intersecting categories as component parts, and this work, known as componential analysis or analysis into distinctive features, is done by some linguists. But although this procedure helps in settling arguments about the adequate phonemic analysis of a language, it doesn't often shed any light on the higher organization of the language. Hence we may as well stop here and say that we have reached the lowest level of analysis when we have split council into seven phonemes. Here it was called the fifth analysis; to get to the bottom of the second half of the same sentence would have required going to a seventh analysis. This is the reason why we prefer to start numbering from the bottom, and to speak rather of successive syntheses, from phonemes up to the complete utterance, reaching different heights in different parts of it.

Within an English morpheme some sequences of phonemes are forbidden. For example, what is commonly spelled ou (as in council) is never followed immediately by any of /p, b, f, v, m/. We have seen that analogous restrictions apply at every level of analysis up to the complete utterance. Above the level of the phonemic system, these restrictions define for us the 'grammar' of the language, and all without reference to what is popularly thought of as the 'meaning', namely the popular categorizations of continuous reality such as 'nose' or 'numerous', just as we find it expedient to define the phonemic system independently of the phonetician's categorizations of continuous speech (although borrowing some of his terms). Typically, the elements of a grammar are stated as possibilities and impossibilities of occurrence, especially the latter, for example the English elementary grammatical fact that this is not followed by men without at least a comma between: this men is not English, but This, men, is what I want is. (Statements of what can occur are more difficult.) And these possibilities and impossibilities are all a posteriori: they are based on observation only, not on logic, and thus not on meaning.

Could we perhaps do something further with 'meaning' inside linguistics? Yes, but only on condition that we distinguish sharply between the inside and the outside. Let the sociologists keep the outside or practical meaning; then we can undertake to describe the pure linguistic meaning. We can do it thus:

Among permissible combinations of morphemes, some are commoner than others. Thus there are conditional probabilities of occurrence of each morpheme in context with others. The conditional probability of a forbidden occurrence is of course zero and drops out of the picture. If we ever found a conditional probability of one, we should decide that we had made a miscalculation, and that what we thought was composed of two morphemes was really unanalysably one morpheme (perhaps a discontinuous one).

Now the linguist's 'meaning' of a morpheme is by definition the set of conditional probabilities of its occurrence in context with all other morphemes—of course without inquiry into the outside, practical, or sociologist's meaning of any of them. Of course we have no zero probabilities in the set, and in practice we should neglect all very small probabilities. So far we have done almost nothing with pure linguistic 'meaning' as so defined, for the obvious reason that its mathematics is of the continuous sort, which we are not accustomed to handling—continuous by statistical derivation from discreteness, but still unmanageable under our working habits. Still, a beginning has been made on a structural semantics by one linguist. He replaces all small conditional probabilities by zero, and all large ones by one, so as to get a discrete mathematics again, in which he can work with synonymy that is absolute by definition. (He makes no such claims for his procedure, incidentally: he calls it 'discourse analysis' and applies it to single texts.) This work is very recent, and is the most exciting thing that has happened in linguistics for quite a few years; in spite of its theoretical flaw as a semantic analysis, it has produced some very elegant and illuminating results.

We can close with a general characterization of linguistics and language. Most well-known mathematical maps are connected with the real world by a single intuitive bridge; linguistics is connected with reality by two of them, so that a language makes a correspondence between a real noise and a real thing or the like (between an utterance and its referents). This defines language as symbolic. Overt acts of speech alter reality in that changes in listener's behavior correspond to them. This defines speech as communication. The technique is organized, patterned, as disclosed by linguistic science. This defines language as systematic. Altogether, then, we have defined a language as a symbolic communication system, or in one word, as a 'code'.

[[The author of the foregoing paper is a notorious dilettante in a number of vaguely related fields, and has been known to boast of never having published twice on the same topic or a closely similar one. Through a series of accidents he was enabled to set up a book on the application of sound spectrography to linguistics. This resulted in his being invited to contribute a paper on the same subject to the Speech Communication Conference held at the Massachusetts Institute of Technology, May 31–June 3, 1950. He was incautious enough to attempt the repetition, naturally with mediocre results. Then when he was called upon to send in his paper for the Proceedings (twenty-four papers published as noted in the heading, p. 349), he reverted to his usual practice and prepared a new one. In the absolute sense, however, there is exactly nothing new in this paper, new as it may have been to its audience. It has been included here in response to insistent demand, but of course revised in spots, with the emphasis on distribution slightly reduced.]]

DIRECTIONS IN MODERN LINGUISTICS[1]

EINAR HAUGEN

Language 27.211–22—1951

1.0 Linguistic science is today in every sense of the word an international science. Few disciplines can lay better claim to this term than ours, in view of its universally and specifically human subject matter, as well as its bearing on the interrelationship and communication of nations. Even within our generation a vast expansion of linguistic study has taken place when compared with the preceding one. It is characteristic that around 1930 contributions to phoneme theory were being made by men as widely scattered as Trubetzkoy in Austria and Yuen Ren Chao in China. This was already a forward step over the much narrower field of Rask and Grimm, but we have seen a still more intense effort in the last two decades. From the occasional contributions of isolated professors we have in our own country proceeded to a concerted and eager program of linguistic research sponsored by a whole group of scholars working together in a vigorous and well-knit Linguistic Society.

1.1 Once we have granted that American linguistics is today in a more flourishing state than at any time since the founding of the Republic, we must go on to say that this is not the whole story. The very growth of an independent group of linguists has promoted a kind of scientific isolation, with even a hint of arrogance, which can only be deplored by those who, like myself, believe that our science should continue to be international.[2] American linguists are finding it increasingly difficult to read European writings in our field; younger linguists are neglecting the older writers, so that we are in some degree losing contact both with the tradition of linguistic science and with its present-day representatives in the rest of the world. Rarely does one see a reference in American writings on linguistic theory to the works of de Saussure, Trubetzkoy, or other European writers, although they were the thinkers who gave us the instruments with which we work. I yield to no one in my admiration for Bloomfield and Sapir; but I regard it as a kind of provincialism to suppose that all sound linguistics began with them.

1.2 Some of the disinterest of American linguists can be traced back to the rapid growth of a new linguistic terminology in this country among those who call themselves descriptive linguists. Those who have acquired this terminology are often unwilling to make the effort to translate other terminologies into their own language. They assume that those who use different terms are either talking nonsense or are confused in their thinking. This criticism applies equally, of course, to those European scholars who overlook the contributions of Americans.[3] It will be the purpose of this paper to take up for discussion some aspects of this movement toward a refinement of linguistic method and terminology which has been the most provocative development in American linguistics in recent years. As an observer rather than a participator in the movement I may be able to give a certain perspective which other linguists will welcome. Even if I should fail to enlighten, I hope I may succeed in awakening discussion. Primarily I am interested in contributing to that goal which one school of philosophy has called the Unity of Science.

2.0 The past decade has seen the appearance of two or three articles and books each year devoted to the techniques of linguistic analysis.[4] At first the

1 Delivered as the Presidential Address at the meeting of the Linguistic Society in Chicago, 29 December 1950. The present form of the paper owes much to discussion with colleagues at the University of Wisconsin.

2 Cf. SIL 8.8 (1950), where the label 'unscientific' is applied to 'much of the European structural studies'; ibid. 8.100: 'the usual kind of European philosophizing on the basis of insufficient evidence'.

3 As honorable exceptions note Eli Fischer-Jørgensen, Travaux du Cercle linguistique de Copenhague 5.214–34 (1949); and W. E. Collinson, Lingua 1.306–32 (1948). The latter's survey of American contributions to metalinguistic discussion is outstanding.

4 Some of the more important are: Bloch and Trager, Outline of linguistic analysis (Baltimore, 1942); Harris, Morpheme alternants in linguistic analysis, Lang. 18.169–80 (1942) ((109)); Pike, Taxemes and immediate constituents, Lang. 19.65–82 (1943); Harris, Discontinuous morphemes, Lang. 21.121–7 (1945); Chao, The logical structure of Chinese words Lang. 22.4–13 (1946); Harris, From morpheme to utterance, Lang. 22.161–83 (1946) ((142)); Bloch, Studies in colloquial Japanese, JAOS 66.97–109 (1946), Lang. 22.200–48 (1946) ((154)), JAOS 66.304–15 (1946), Lang. 26.86–125 (1950) ((329)); Wells, Immediate constituents, Lang. 23.81–117 (1947) ((186)); Voegelin, A problem in morpheme alternants and their distribution, Lang. 23.245–54 (1947); Pike, Grammatical prerequisites to phonemic analysis, Word 3.155–72 (1947); Hockett, Problems of morphemic analysis, Lang. 23.321–43 (1947) ((229)); Bloch, English verb inflection, Lang. 23.399–418 (1947) ((243)); Pike, Phonemics (Ann Arbor, 1947); Bloch, A set of postulates for phonemic analysis, Lang. 24.3–47 (1948); Harris, Componential analysis of a Hebrew paradigm, Lang. 24.87–91 (1948) ((272)); Voegelin, Distinctive features and meaning equivalence, Lang. 24.132–5 (1948); Nida, The analysis of grammatical constituents, Lang. 24.168–77 (1948); Pittman, Nuclear structures in linguistics, Lang. 24.287–92 (1948) ((275)); Nida, The identification of morphemes, Lang. 24.414–41 (1948) ((255)); Wells, Automatic alternation, Lang. 24.99–116 (1949); Nida, Morphology, 2d ed. (Ann Arbor, 1949); Joos, Description of language design, Journal of the Acoustical Society of America 22.701–9 (1950) ((349)).

emphasis was on phonemic techniques, but this has shifted to the wider fields of morphemics and syntax. New terms have been created whose purpose is to make research techniques explicit, so that we may talk not merely about language, but also about how to talk about language. Among logicians it has become standard practice to refer to such a terminology as a metalanguage, which is defined as 'a language which is used to make assertions about another language'.[5] I cannot find that American linguists have used this term, but it seems a useful one and I should propose its adoption. The discussion of linguistic research techniques is not a linguistics as we have known it, but rather a metalinguistics.[6] It is merely unfortunate that Trager already has proposed the term metalinguistics for a field which has generally become known as semantics.[7] This usage should be rejected in view of the quite different meaning given the word by the related discipline of logic. If semantics should be an undesirable term, there is always 'ethno-linguistics' or perhaps 'socio-linguistics'. In the present paper I shall find it convenient to apply the term metalinguistics to the kind of research that has brought forth such new terms as phone, morph, substitution, constitute, focus class, and tactics. These words are part of a new metalanguage created by American linguists, which is quite baffling to those students of language who know only the terms of our traditional schools of grammar.

2.1 One would not suspect it from reading recent writings by American metalinguists, but it should be pointed out that a similar movement has been going on in Europe over the past dozen years. I am referring to the recent publications of Louis Hjelmslev and a group of scholars associated with him in the Linguistic Circle of Copenhagen. Hjelmslev made up the term glossematics to describe his theory, but he has in reality created a new metalanguage. Unfortunately his chief exposition of the theory has so far [1951] been printed in Danish only; it appeared in 1943 under the title Omkring sprogteoriens grundlæggelse (Concerning the foundations of linguistic theory).[8] The real difficulty is not in the Danish, however, which is readily accessible to anyone who knows German; the problem facing the reader is the abstractness with which the theory is formulated and the comparative lack of illustrative material to make clear its bearing. Some of us find it hard going because we do not have an adequate training in mathematic or symbolic logic to follow so closely reasoned an argument. More recently a volume of so-called 'structural studies' based in part on Hjelmslev's theories has appeared as Volume 5 of the Travaux du Cercle linguistique de Copenhague.[9] Since all of these appear either in French or English and represent more or less concrete applications of the theory, they will undoubtedly engage the attention of more linguists than the previous writings by Hjelmslev himself.

2.2 It is not my purpose to present an analysis of Hjelmslev's theory nor an evaluation of its associated procedures. I merely wish to point out that in Europe a new metalanguage is being shaped which is at least as different from that of our school grammars as is the American metalanguage. The two are as mutually incomprehensible as French and English, and we shall soon need a bimetalingual lexicon to translate from one to the other. We are reaching a point where the metalanguage of linguistics is falling apart into metadialects, jeopardizing the unity of our science. Even among American metalinguists we note the rise of what may be called meta-idiolects, which make it confusing to follow recent discussion. Whatever differences of emphasis and approach there may be between the American and European schools, it is my conclusion after making an effort to assimilate the leading features of each, that they are talking about the same thing, and struggling toward the same goal.

2.3 In principle they are both attempting to give a mathematical formulation to linguistic statements. Harris has described his syntactic analysis as 'mathematical'; Hjelmslev declares his purpose to be the creation of a 'linguistic algebra'.[10] Harris expressly points out that his analysis is purely formal; Hjelmslev describes his theory as being based on 'an exclusively formal system of postulates'.[11] Both are trying to get away from the haphazard empirical terminology of traditional linguistics and establish a metalanguage which will be available in the synchronic description of every language. But their vocabulary seems to have little beyond the word phoneme in common. Both groups employ a principle of analysis which might be called

[5] Cf. D. D. Runes, Dictionary of philosophy, 4th ed. (New York, 1942); Charles Morris, Signs, language, and behavior 179 (New York, 1946); R. Carnap, Introduction to semantics 4 (Cambridge, Mass., 1942); id., Philosophy and logical syntax (London, 1935).

[6] Cf. C. H. Borgström's use of 'meta-research' in this sense, Acta linguistica 5.1–14 (1945–49). L. Hjelmslev uses 'metasprog' in his work Omkring sprogteoriens grundlæggelse (see fn. 8).

[7] George L. Trager, The field of linguistics 2 (Norman, Okla., 1949).

[8] Copenhagen, 1943; hereafter abbreviated OSG. [Now available in English (tr. Francis J. Whitfield) as Prolegomena to a theory of language, Indiana University Publications in anthropology and linguistics, Memoir 7 (Baltimore, 1953).]

[9] Recherches structurales 1949: Interventions dans le débat glossématique (Copenhague, 1949). ⟦Reviewed by Wells, Lang. 27.554–70 (1951).⟧

[10] Harris, Lang. 22.161 ⟨⟨142⟩⟩; Hjelmslev, OSG 72. Cf. Joos, op. cit. 22.702 ⟨⟨349⟩⟩: 'We must make our "linguistics" a kind of mathematics, within which inconsistency is by definition impossible.'

[11] Harris, Lang. 22.177 ⟨⟨150⟩⟩ fn. 26; Hjelmslev, OSG 9. Cf. Nida, Lang. 24.437 fn. 40 ⟨⟨268⟩⟩.

the bipartite division: they divide the utterance into two (or occasionally more) parts, and then divide each of these until they have reached its ultimate constituents.[12] Hjelmslev calls this the deductive method; Wells calls it an Immediate Constituent analysis. What Wells calls a constitute, Hjelmslev calls a class; what Wells calls a constituent, Hjelmslev calls a derivate.[13] What Wells calls a focus class, Hjelmslev calls a paradigm; what Wells calls a sequence class, Hjelmslev calls a chain. The technique which both groups use to determine the constituents of any given constitute turns out to be one which I shall here call replacement. By trying to replace any part of an utterance with other linguistic material it is possible to determine whether the utterance is divisible and how best to divide it. This technique is called substitution by Harris and those who have followed him;[14] Hjelmslev calls it the commutation test, and makes it fundamental to his whole theory.[15] Perhaps the most important common feature is the application of this basic technique to all kinds of linguistic material, at every level of the language, from the complete utterance down to the phone.[16]

2.4 It is quite possible that I shall be challenged in my comparison of the two because of the weight given by Hjelmslev to meaning, while most American metalinguists do their utmost to shun this aspect of language. Actually, it could rather easily be shown that the difference here, too, is largely one of terminology. Hjelmslev sets up a fourfold division of the linguistic universe. At one end is the real world of experience, which he calls the content; upon this is imposed a pattern, which he calls the content form. In intimate liaison with this form is the expression form, which has imposed its patterns on the expression, or the real world of sound. Aside from the rather outmoded terms content and expression, form and substance, this says almost exactly the same as the mathematical-engineering analysis made of language by Martin Joos in his recent article on the description of language design.[17] Joos distinguishes between the reality of meaning on the one hand and the reality of sound on the other, both of which are susceptible to expression in terms of a continuous mathematics. Between these stands language, with a semantic and a phonetic form, which is susceptible to expression only in a discontinuous mathematics. Barring the mathematical terminology, the analysis is the same; he writes that 'most well-known mathematical maps are connected with the real world by a single intuitive bridge; linguistics is connected with reality by two of them, so that language makes a real noise correspond to a real thing or the like. This defines language as symbolic.'

2.5 A useful task for someone with full mastery of both metalanguages would be an analysis of the Hjelmslev system which would be at once a translation into American terms and a critique of its effectiveness. The Hjelmslev metalanguage seems at first blush to be more unified and logical than the American one. But it is unlikely to be accepted in full over here because of its tendency to use terms in senses that conflict with established usage. To call a relationship a 'function', or a set of entities appearing in the same environment a 'paradigm', seems more calculated to confuse than to enlighten. But the whole development of which Hjelmslev is one of several representatives is extremely interesting, and I shall now turn from my comparison of the two metalanguages to a consideration of the advantages and the limitations for the ordinary linguist of the mathematical approach to linguistics represented by these writers. It will be my thesis that any linguistic entity can be described from two points of view, one internal to the language described and one external to it; further, that traditional linguistics has sought objectivity by adopting an external standard to which the language may be referred, while present-day linguistics seeks to find internal, relational standards; and finally, that while the internal or distributional standards may lead to useful discoveries concerning the internal organization or structure of the language, linguistics cannot, unless it wishes to become entirely circular or mathematical, afford to reject the use of external standards to give its relational data concrete validity in the real world.

3.0 There are two sets of facts which can and usually have been adduced in the description of any given linguistic item. If we are given the vowel [a] to describe, we can describe it as similar to Italian a; or we can say that it is close to 'cardinal' a; or we can state its typical physiological method of production as a low central vowel; or we can identify its

[12] Hjelmslev, OSG; Wells, Lang. 23.92 ((192 f.)). Harris originally assumed a segmentation, and then worked his way up to more inclusive classes 'from morpheme to utterance' (Lang. 22.178 ((150))); Wells showed how an analysis in terms of immediate constituents could be worked from the whole down, and pointed out that it matters little in which direction one works (Lang, 23.101 ((198))). Hjelmslev grants the same when he defines 'induction' (working up) and 'deduction' (working down) as functions of one another; his insistence on the priority of deduction is based on the sound observation that the linguist must start with the unanalyzed whole text.

[13] Wells, Lang. 23.84 ((188)); Hjelmslev, OSG 30.

[14] Harris, Lang. 22.161 ff. ((142 ff.)).

[15] OSG 67.

[16] Cf. Hjelmslev, OSG 59: 'For an understanding of the structure of language it is of the greatest significance to make it clear that this principle shall be extended to apply also to all the other invariants of the language, regardless of their degree or place in the system.' Harris writes of his morpheme analysis, Lang. 18.179 ((115)): 'it shows that we can arrange alternants into units in exactly the same manner as we arrange sound types (positional variants) into phonemes.'

[17] Journal of the Acoustical Society of America 22.701–8 (1950) ((349)).

acoustic properties with the help of a spectrograph. In any case we are describing it in terms that relate it to something in the external world; such identification can today reach any desired degree of accuracy within the limits of observational error. The more refined our standard, the greater the number of sound classes we can establish. Any two instances of sound that fall within the same categories of external space and time can be regarded as 'phonetically similar'. The determination thus arrived at may be referred to as the identity of the item concerned. It is characteristic of the new mathematical approach that the emphasis has been shifted from identity to distribution. The distribution of English [a] includes the fact that it is always a syllabic, that it can be followed or preceded by one, two, or three consonants or by none, and that it contrasts in stressed syllables with all the other vowels. This is perhaps the chief discovery made by modern linguistics: that it is possible to find relationships between linguistic items by studying their distribution. But here we are confined entirely within the given language being studied. We are no longer concerned with external standards, only with the kind of environments in which the item is found, and a comparison of those environments with the environments of other items. Even traditional linguists usually stated the environments of at least some linguistic items, especially of morphemes entering into syntactical arrangements; but the emphasis on this facet as basic to linguistic study is entirely due to the structural schools of linguistics from de Saussure on.[18]

3.1 Morphological items have a double identity, phonetic as well as semantic. Their phonetic identity can handily be described in terms of the description already made of the sounds. But their semantic identity has traditionally been established by external standards of reference. Apples have been described by reference to an actual apple or a picture of the same; a word class like that of nouns has been described by reference to such terms as 'object', though many nouns obviously do not name objects. Here, too, the trend is now toward an emphasis on distribution or function. A noun is classified by its possibilities of combination, which means its distribution in relation to other forms in the utterance. Nouns are not now the names of things, but a class of forms which occur with certain other forms. This cleavage between the traditional emphasis on identity, whether of sound or meaning, and the newer emphasis on distribution, thus seems to run through all fields of linguistic description. Distribution is the key to phonemics as distinct from phonetics, and to morphemics as distinct from semantics. It is the common factor in the mathematical approach to linguistic description.

3.2 The method which the metalinguists recognize as fundamental in their analysis, namely replacement, is primarily directed at the discovery of distribution.[19] In some ways this technique is analogous to the natural scientist's controlled experiment. Just as the latter varies a single factor while keeping the rest constant, so the linguist studies the possibilities of variation in utterances. Whenever he can, he finds utterances differing by only a single factor; if he has a native speaker available, he manufactures such utterances by asking for repetition of the same utterance with replacement of a single factor. The fact that such repetition is possible gives the linguist a great advantage over other social scientists, whose situations can rarely be duplicated at will.

3.3 As generally practiced, replacement means the actual substitution of one overt element for another, as when p and b are contrasted in pit and bit, or John and the king of England are used alternately in the sentence The king of England opened Parliament. By such a test it is possible to isolate any linguistic element and discover its potential environments. Following a usage of Wells, we shall call the element being isolated a focus and the rest of the utterance its environment. One can either keep the focus constant and change the environment, or change the focus in a constant environment. A special type of replacement, which is not mentioned in the literature, but which would seem to be most useful, is the replacement by zero, which I shall here call excision. As applied to a sentence which Wells has analyzed at some length, The king of England opened Parliament, it leads to an analysis of the king of England into two constituents, the king and of England, and the rejection of the other possible analysis into the and king of England.[20] This is because one can say The king opened Parliament, but not King of England opened Parliament. Of the two constituents the king and of England, the latter is dispensable, the former is not. This takes us a step further, and classifies them into respectively nucleus and satellite, to adopt the terms used by Pike and Pittman.[21] The distinction is an essential part of a distributional analysis, for the only part of the environment that is relevant to the phrase of England is clearly its nucleus the king. A different kind of relevance is discovered when we study the relation between the king of England and opened Parliament. These two foci are not nucleus and

18 Nida distinguishes between identification and distribution of morphemes in somewhat the same way as here suggested; cf. Morphology 78.

19 Bloomfield called it 'altering the word'; Trubetzkoy, Grundzüge der Phonologie 31–2 (TCLP 7; Prague, 1939), spoke of certain sounds as being 'vertauschbar'; the term 'substitution' was apparently first used in America by Morris Swadesh, The phonemic principle, Lang. 10.124 (1934) ⟨⟨35⟩⟩.

20 Lang. 23.83–4 ⟨⟨187–8⟩⟩; cf. Pittman's Premise 1 ⟨⟨276⟩⟩, which is here made the only principle for determining a satellite.

21 Lang. 24.287–92 ⟨⟨275⟩⟩.

satellite, but two nuclei; since neither one is more dispensable than the other, they may be called twin nuclei. In a sentence like Jack and Jill went down the hill, we also have two nuclei in the focus Jack and Jill. Since either one is dispensable, but not both, we may call them coordinate nuclei. The same analysis can be applied, on the phonological level, to a pair of words like sit and seat. Sit and seat can be cut down to it and eat, showing that the initial consonant is a satellite to the rest of the syllable; but the final consonants are not parallel, for the t of seat can be cut away while the t of sit cannot. This establishes the t of sit as a twin nucleus with the vowel; it is another way of saying that the vowel of sit is a checked rather than a free vowel. It may be remarked in passing that the three possible relationships here derived from a distributional analysis, namely nucleus-satellite, twin nuclei, and coordinate nuclei, correspond exactly to the basic functions in Hjelmslev's metalanguage which he calls determination (a presupposes b, but not vice versa), interdependence (a and b presuppose one another), and constellation (a and b occur together without presupposing one another).[22] This little sample of distributional analysis has shown that the distribution of a focus is not a statement of all its possible environments, but only of those that prove to be relevant when a test of replacement is made. We shall here call such a set of relevant environments the frame of a given focus, defined as its immediate satellites and related nuclei.

3.4 Distributional analysis is not completed with the establishment of the foci and their frames. The next step is the organization of the foci into larger classes so that the structure of the language may appear. Pure distributional analysis would involve only a comparison of frames; but there is a previous step for which our procedure so far has not prepared us: we wish to identify those foci which are 'the same'. Here phonetic and semantic criteria of identity are needed if we are to know what we are talking about. It is all very well to say that t in latter and d in ladder are in contrast; but unless we know what t and d are in some kind of phonetic terms, we cannot identify them with anything else, not even the t and d in kitty and kiddy. Having isolated the focus -er in sooner, we need to know something of its meaning to decide whether it should be grouped with the -er in later or that in runner. The comparison of frames involves comparable problems, as we see from the difficulties encountered by Bloch in defining distributional environments.[23] His general principle is that if two different foci have identical frames, they are in free variation; if they have some frames in common, they are in contrast; if they have no frames in common, they are in complementary distribution.

22 OSG 23.

23 Lang. 24.22-6; 26.89 ((330)).

But problems of identity cut across this scheme at several points. By 'identical frames' he has to mean not merely the phonetic environment, but also the morphological environment, since free variation involves the potential appearance of every variety of sound in every occurrence of a word. To check this is utterly impossible, and we are here faced with an unfeasible bit of theory. It also appears that some foci which have frames in common are really in free variation in those frames; so he has to set up a special category of overlapping distribution. Finally, he finds that those which have no frames in common are sometimes prevented from being identified by their phonetic nature, e.g. the initial and final sounds in hang. At every step it is necessary to appeal simultaneously to identity and distribution to establish the kind of classes which phonemicists wish to establish. I am not questioning the value of such classes. But I think it should be clearly realized that they are not one-dimensional constructs, but definitely established in two dimensions of criteria.

3.5 The double standard is obvious in Bloch's definition of the phoneme as a 'class of non-contrastive and phonetically similar phones'.[24] Hockett similarly groups morphs into a single morpheme if they 'are in non-contrastive distribution' and mean the same.[25] The need of thus setting up two essentially incommensurable criteria for these units has troubled the metalinguists and led to various efforts to eliminate the criterion of identity. For phonemics this means the elimination of phonetics, which was a solution advocated by some members of the Prague school. Hjelmslev asks for a 'linguistics whose theory of expression is not a phonetics and whose theory of content is not a semantics'.[26] Attempts have been made to define sound classes purely in terms of distribution, e.g. in Hans Vogt's study of the structure of Norwegian monosyllables.[27] The results are interesting, but they show chiefly that phonetic identity and distributional function do not coincide. A definition of vowel versus consonant in terms of syllabic distribution is similar to that derived from a phonetic analysis, but not identical with it; the difference appears when we consider the n in button, which is a consonant phonetically but functions as a syllabic. The English affricates ch and j have generally been regarded as double sounds by phoneticians; but phonemicists have vacillated back and forth between one and two, because the introduction of a distributional criterion has tempted them to consider the sounds single: it could then be said that there were only three consonants after English vowels in such words as bunched and bulged. Even so, there are words like jinxed, sixths, texts which elude the rule. It seems

24 Lang. 26.90 ((331)).

25 Lang. 23.328 ((233)).

26 OSG 71.

27 Norsk tidsskrift for sprogvidenskap 16.1-29 (1939).

to be characteristic of distributional classes that they are notoriously ragged around the edges.[28] Practically every statement of distribution sooner or later turns up small groups of words, even individual words, which violate the rule and bring disturbance in the system. One might investigate English for years, assuming it was a language previously unrecorded, before discovering that b could occur after m in final position, since the two words which illustrate it are iamb and dithyramb, and these are not likely to occur even in quite a few million words of running text. Total distributions are difficult to derive, being dependent on a very large sampling of the language, while the identity of the major sound types can be spotted in a few hours of recording. Most of the disagreements concerning phonemic analysis involve the problem of reconciling the facts of distribution and identity. The difficulty of nailing a distributional analysis down to anything concrete has been evident in the constant change of conclusions concerning given language systems by practicing analysts.[29]

3.6 In morphemics the desire to eliminate the double standard in favor of a single criterion of distribution has been equally evident. So far it has led only to theoretical definitions without practical feasibility.[30] The minimizing of meaning as a factor in linguistic description was at first a healthy reaction against the misuse of meaning in establishing linguistic categories, but has now become almost a fetish with some linguists. It is curious to see how those who eliminate meaning have brought it back under the covert guise of distribution. Among the distributions of a form are reckoned its possibilities of combination with other forms. Thus window might presumably be distinguished from door without reference to any actual situation if we had enough sentences in which they were used. By a technique of replacement we could find out, as in the game of twenty questions, which of various possibilities was intended. But it is important to note that only a native can make such replacements; and by definition a native knows the meanings of the forms he uses. Joos in his previously cited article gives a purely distributional definition of meaning as 'the set of conditional probabilities of the occurrence [of a morpheme] in context with all other morphemes'. Now it would seem that only a lifetime of experience can enable us to establish statistically the conditional probability of occurrence of even a single morpheme. But the native to whom we appeal for information about the meaning of a word has learned to use it in substantially the same distribution as other speakers of his language. What he gives us as its meaning is essentially a replacement, i.e. a synonym or a circumlocution which has approximately the same distribution in the language. But he can do so only because he has a constant to which he may refer the question, namely his nonlinguistic experience. In using his definitions, we are thus not merely adopting a short-cut of analysis, as is alleged by the metalinguists, but we are basing ourselves on the necessary foundation of language, its symbolic value. We have all had the experience of misunderstanding certain utterances because we were ignorant of crucial facts in the social situation which did not appear from the form of the utterances. Harris has analyzed the structure of the sentence She made him a good husband because she made him a good wife.[31] He contends that the meaning is clear because of the structural fact that the him in the second clause can be replaced by the expression for him. But one could just as well say, and with greater probability of being right, that it is clear because we know that a man cannot be a wife.

3.7 This constant effort to divorce distributional analysis from the determinations of identity is indicative of the essentially mathematical nature of distributional criteria. The technique of replacement is based on assumptions of identity which distribution alone cannot supply. Neither focus nor frame has anything but a relational value. For practical purposes we assume that the focus remains constant while we change the frame. But it is obvious that this is only a convenient fiction. In the case of phonology it has been shown by spectrographic analysis that each phone is affected by its environment: focus and frame are both variables in a common function. It is not until the relationship is tied to an external constant that we have a positive identification of linguistic description. This is apparent in phonemic analysis, where we have no criterion for identifying phones until we have determined their environment, and no way of determining the environment until we have identified the phones. Since morpheme boundaries are part of the environment, there appears to be no good way of entirely isolating phonemic and morphemic analysis. Leopold has shown that in German one either has to analyze such words as Frauchen and Kuhchen into two morphemes first or else leave the palatal and velar spirants of ich and ach as separate phonemes.[32] Pike's contention that morphological criteria must be admitted into phonemic analysis seems to be inescapable unless one can

28 Note that Wells describes classes established by distributional analysis as only 'roughly coincident classes' (Lang. 23.82 ((186))), while Harris leaves it to the linguist to decide which ones he shall use in order to get 'the most convenient total description' (Lang. 22.177 ((150))).

29 Trager analyzed American English in 1940 as having six vowels, in 1947 as having nine (Lang. 23.141); Swadesh analyzed American English diphthongs in 1935 as single phonemes, in 1947 as double (Lang. 23.137); Hockett analyzed the Chinese aspirated stops in 1944 as single consonants (in Spoken Chinese: Basic course), in 1947 as clusters with h (JAOS 67.258 ((221)); Bloch's phonemic analysis of Japanese in 1946 had several features, including a phoneme q, which he discarded in 1950 (Lang. 26.112 ((342))).

30 Cf. Hockett, Lang. 23.327 ((233)) fn. 20.

31 Lang. 22.180 ((152)).

32 Lang. 24.179 ((216)).

find external, objective criteria which will tie either the phonemes or the morphemes to some specific reality.[33] In his analysis of immediate constituents, Wells grants that a certain circularity is involved: a characterization of all the utterances of a language is presupposed for an analysis which is made in terms of the constituents of those utterances.[34] It has been a constant charge brought against the metalinguists that their procedures have seemed circular. They have often appeared to adopt arbitrary and unsupported principles of analysis, more characterized by esthetic than by scientific validity, contributing more to elegance than to learning. Perhaps we may recognize now that this is inherent in the adoption of distributional criteria. The resulting circularity is probably no more a fault in linguistics than it is in mathematics. Mathematics is also circular in that it does not depend for its validity on the existence of any particular kind of reality.

4.0 The metalinguists have shown their impatience with criteria of identity by seeking to exclude from the field of linguistics those disciplines which primarily concerned themselves with these. Hjelmslev writes of 'the hitherto presumed linguistics' which is not, like his, based on criteria internal to the language being described.[35] Trager refers to phonetics as 'prelinguistics'; only the 'analysis of language systems' will he admit to the field of linguistics proper.[36] Already Bloomfield excluded semantics as an essentially non-linguistic activity. The present paper has tried to show that distributional analysis must go hand in hand with phonetic and semantic identification in any total description of language. It follows that I cannot accept the doctrine of the metalinguists that only relations (or functions in Hjelmslev's term) are relevant.[37] The contributions of the metalinguists are important, even crucial, but they occupy somewhat the role of mathematics in a science like physics. There is a growing cleavage between the mathematical linguists, or metalinguists, and the physical linguists, whom I should call just plain linguists. A linguist must not only be a student of formal linguistic relationships, but also something of a physical scientist on the phonetic side, and something of a sociologist on the semantic side. It has been suggested by Joos that phonetics should be handed over to the physicists and semantics to the sociologists.[38] I cannot see any evidence that he himself plans to follow this advice, and I have tried to show that it is a-priori impossible. We must rely on these sciences for data of various kinds, and the actual tying up of linguistic relationships to concrete sense data is still an essential part of our science. The others cannot tell us which aspects of sound and meaning are relevant to our symbols, nor why our symbols should be relevant in various contexts. The metalinguist and the physical linguist will need to continue their cooperation if the linguistic systems are to be established without circularity and given unidirectional validity in a real world.

4.1 In conclusion I wish to return to my original topic of metalinguistic unity. Hockett has described the purpose of metalinguistic discussion to be the attainment of 'greater mutual intelligibility among the writers of grammars, and in terms thereof, more accurate pictures of the languages we describe'.[39] This is a valuable goal, but for the time being, at least, the tendency toward economy of description has resulted in making many descriptions quite unreadable for other linguists. Present-day descriptions bristle like a page of symbolic logic and lack entirely the leisurely, even charming quality of the traditional grammars. I would not go back to those grammars, but only suggest that economy may not always be a virtue; in some cases it results from poverty, and in any case it must be replaced by an expansion into real sounds and real meanings whenever it is put to any practical use. I do not believe that the present metalinguistic discussion will finally settle the advantage of one type of linguistic analysis over another. The kind of analysis that is 'best' is determined by extra-linguistic goals. But in giving us a metalanguage with which to talk about various kinds of analysis, and in thereby enabling us to point out where the analysts of the past have differed or fallen by the wayside, the metalinguists have done us a real service. If only they would get together and work out a really usable esperanto for metalinguistic purposes, instead of promoting the present Babel![40]

4.2 Whatever the metalanguage used, the goal of our investigation is the structure of the language used by actual speakers.[41] Whatever we may mean by structure, the one thing we can be sure of is that it is no more like the language itself than a botanist's description of an apple is like an apple. You can't eat the botanist's description and you can't talk the linguist's description. But once the apple or the language comes before your eye, a good description will make it possible to identify it, and even to predict some few of its major sensory features.

[33] Word 3.155–72 (1947). [34] Lang. 23.81 ((186)).

[35] OSG 7. [36] The field of linguistics 4.

[37] It is interesting to note that even a Hjelmslev disciple like Eli Fischer-Jørgensen is, in the final instance, driven back on phonetic similarity ('la parenté phonique); cf. Travaux du Cercle linguistique de Copenhague 5.227.

[38] Op. cit. 22.708 ((356)).

[39] Lang. 23.341 ((240)) fn. 38.

[40] It will appear from the foregoing that I agree with the criticisms of the Hjelmslev theory advanced by Carl Hj. Borgström, The technique of linguistic description, Acta linguistica 5.1–14 (1945–49), and A problem of methods in linguistic science: The meaning of its technical terms, Norsk tidsskrift for sprogvidenskap 14.191–228 (1947).

[41] Cf. Hockett, A note on 'structure', IJAL 14.269–71 (1948) ((279)).

KOREAN PHONEMICS

SAMUEL E. MARTIN

Language 27.519–33—1951

1. The phonemes of Korean are here analyzed in three ways: in terms of articulatory components, of auditory qualities, and of distinctive oppositions.[1] A detailed phonetic description is provided in §2 and §2.1. The language analyzed is standard colloquial Korean, ideally represented by educated speakers native to Seoul. Like many standard languages, standard Korean consists of not one but many dialects.[2] This analysis attempts to include all linguistic patterns other than those which seem to be partially assimilated borrowings from English.

1.1. Sixteen distinctive articulatory components are found: two pitch components, five vowel components, and nine consonant components. These components (represented by upper-case letters, except for pitch) occur in four types of sequence: coextensive, overlapping, successive, and interrupted. Five criteria of phoneme classification are used; the results of these are extended to the auditory and oppositional analyses in §3 and §4. With the exception of the pitch components, which receive a separate analysis, (1) a coextensive sequence of components or component clusters[3] is considered ONE PHONEME; (2) an overlapping or successive sequence is considered MORE THAN ONE PHONEME; and (3) an interrupted sequence is considered to include the phoneme of PAUSE /#/.[4] An exception to the use of these criteria is the treatment of a coextensive sequence which occurs in free variation with an overlapping sequence: if (4) the free variation of such a sequence is limited to certain environments, the sequence is considered one phoneme; if (5) it is not so limited, the sequence is considered two phonemes. (Examples are /ia/ and /wi/; see §1.31.)

1.2. The pitch components are RAISING (↑) and LOWERING (↓). In a syllable bounded on at least one side by pause, the component consists of a rise (or fall) of pitch within the syllable; in other positions, the component represents the pitch level of the syllable relative to the preceding syllable. (On syllables see §2.1.) When both components occur together within a sequence bounded by pause, the pitch range is widened. Some examples (the component symbol is here arbitrarily inserted in the phonemic writing BEFORE the syllable in which the component begins): /#nu↑ka#wa↑sqəm↓ni↓kqa#/ 'Who came?'; /#nu↑ka#wa↑sqəmni↑kqa#/ 'Did someone come?'; /#pak↑sənsɛŋi↓sici↑o#/

[1] This paper was begun as a research project in a graduate seminar at the University of California. To Mary R. Haas I owe special gratitude for developing my interest in descriptive linguistics. I have benefited from discussions of this paper with Bernard Bloch, Elinor Clark Horne, and especially Rulon S. Wells.

[2] Cf. B. Bloch, Lg. 26.87–8 (1950). I have heard the speech of three informants from Seoul: Miss Young Sook Chang, Mrs. Blanche C. Lim, and Mrs. Sang Soon Yun; and of two informants from Phyongyang: Mr. Frank Lee and Mr. Eung Pal Yun; as well as that of Miss Pauline Kim, of a Korean family living in China. (Since this article was written I have heard the speech of two more informants from Seoul: Mr. Sung Un Chang and Mr. Peter H. Lee.)

I have benefited from the studies made by Elinor Clark Horne, Introduction to spoken Korean, 2 vols. (New Haven, 1950–1), and by Fred Lukoff, Spoken Korean, 2 vols. (New York, 1947), as well as from unpublished studies by Rulon S. Wells.

A partial bibliography of other secondary sources consulted: Cosənə Hakhwe [Korean Language Society], Cosənə phyocunmal moəm [Outline of standard Korean language] (Seoul, 1939). Id., Cosən mal khən sacən [Unabridged Korean dictionary], Vol. 1, (Seoul, 1947). Id., Vol. 2 (Seoul, 1949), through Korean letter *m*. P. A. Eckardt, Koreanische Konversations-Grammatik (Heidelberg, 1923). H. H. Figulla, Prolegomena zu einer Grammatik der koreanischen Sprache, Berlin-Universität Mitteilung des Seminars für orientalische Sprachen 38.101–21 (1935). J. S. Gale, A Korean–English dictionary (Seoul, 1897). Id., Korean grammatical forms (Seoul, 1894). Sun-Gi Gim (= Sunki Kim), Korean, Le maître phonétique III.15.21–2 (1937). M. Haguenauer, Système de transcription de l'alphabet coréen, Journal asiatique 222.145–61 (1933). Hisən I (= Hisən Li), Cosənəhak nonkoŋ [Articles on Korean linguistic research] (Seoul, 1947). Kəŋno I (= Kəklo Li), Silhəm tohɛ cosənə əmsəŋ hak [A study of Korean phonetics, with diagrams] (Seoul, 1947). Yuncɛ I (= Yuncɛ Li), Phyocun cosən mal sacən [Dictionary of standard Korean] (Seoul, 1947); Insub Jung, Romanization of Korean, Actes du 4e congrès international de linguistes 210 (Copenhagen, 1936). A. A. Kholodovich, O latinizacii korejskogo pis'ma, Sovetskoje Jazykoznanije 1.147 ff. (1935). Pyəŋce Kim, Hankəl machəm pəp hɛsəl [An exposition of Korean orthographic rules] (Seoul, 1946). G. M. McCune and E. O. Reischauer, The romanization of the Korean language, Transactions of the Korean Branch of the Royal Asiatic Society (Seoul, 1939). Sinpei Ogura, The outline of the Korean dialects, Memoirs of the Research Department, Tôyô Bunko 12 (1940). Id., Tyoosengo-hoogen no kenkyuu [Research on Korean dialects], 2 vols. (Tokyo, 1944). Id., Tyoosengogaku-si [A history of Korean language study] (Seoul, 1921). E. W. Pae, Conversational Korean (Washington, D. C., 1944). K. D. Park, Oral Korean for beginners (Honolulu, 1945). E. D. Polivanov, Glasnye korejskogo jazyka (Petrograd, 1916). G. J. Ramstedt, A Korean grammar, Mémoires de la Société Finno-ougrienne 82 (Helsinki, 1939). James Scott, A Corean manual[2] (Seoul, 1893). H. W. Sunoo, A standard colloquial Korean text book for university students (Seattle, 1944). Tyoosengo-Daiziten [Unabridged Korean–Japanese dictionary] (Seoul, 1920). H. G. Underwood, An introduction to the Korean spoken language[2] (Seoul, 1914).

The romanization systems appearing in these works are many and diverse; the most consistent are those in the manuals of Horne and Lukoff. All of the systems are somewhat influenced, as for teaching purposes they should be, by morphophonemic considerations.

I am indebted to Thomas A. Sebeok for calling my attention to a lengthy bibliography of works mostly pertaining to Korean historical linguistics; this appears in a review of Ramstedt's grammar by Andrej Rudnev, Finnisch-Ugrische Forschungen, Anzeiger 27.55–68 (1941).

[3] A component cluster is itself a coextensive sequence of components which is under consideration with respect to its sequential relation with still other components.

[4] In other words, pause is defined as a phoneme uniquely characterized by the absence of distinctive components and perceived as the interruption of a componential sequence. Many instances which other analysts might consider 'open juncture' are thus included as occurrences of the pause phoneme. For example, the expression meaning 'both' (literally 'two all') is pronounced sometimes as /#tul#ta#/ and sometimes as /#tulta#/; it is also pronounced as /#tultqa#/. The occurrence or non-occurrence of pause in a given utterance or set of utterances—like the occurrence of any other phoneme—is a problem of morphophonemic description. Some analysts seem to perceive pause only when the sequential interruption is accompanied by some pitch change, usually described as 'intonational'; this is encouraged by the frequent interrelation of pause and pitch phonemes on the morphophonemic level (where the analysis of intonations is usually appropriate). On pause as a phoneme, cf. Bloch, Lg. 26.97 fn. 23.*On individual variation in pause perception, cf. J M. Cowan and B. Bloch, An experimental study of pause in English grammar, American speech 23.89–99 (1948). *((334))

'You're Mr. Pak, aren't you?'; / ⋕ co ↑ sənsa ↑ lam ⋕ chin ↑ kuhansala ↑ mi ⋕ sə-↑ u ↑ le ⋕ i ↑ sqəm ↓ ni ↓ ta ⋕ / 'I have a Korean friend in Seoul'. The possibility that these components may constitute phonemes (pitch levels or contours) has not been investigated; it is convenient to proceed directly from the components themselves to the intonation morphs. This is a part of the morphophonemic analysis, to be presented in a separate paper.

1.3. There are five vowel components:

high tongue position	I	front tongue position	Y
mid tongue position	E	lip rounding	W
low tongue position	A		

1.31. The vowel components occur in the following coextensive sequences. (Coextensive sequence of components is indicated by simple juxtaposition, and overlapping or successive sequence by a hyphen.)

	IY	I	IW
WEY	EY	E	EW
	AY	A	

For some speakers, the coextensive sequence WEY is in free variation with the successive sequence W-EY; for other speakers the two are in contrast.

Successive sequences of vowel components are:

W-IY				Y-IW
W-EY	W-E	Y-EY	Y-E	Y-EW
W-AY	W-A	Y-AY	Y-A	

Note that neither W-I nor Y-I occurs.

The phonemes formed by these sequences are eleven in number. (The symbols are chosen for convenience. A phonetic description is given in §2 and §2.1.) There are nine vowel phonemes:

	/i/	/ə/	/u/
/ö/	/e/	/ɔ/	/o/
	/ɛ/	/a/	

and two semivowel phonemes occurring before vowels as follows:

/wi/				/yu/
/we/	/wɔ/	/ye/	/yɔ/	/yo/
/wɛ/	/wa/	/yɛ/	/ya/	

For many speakers, the phoneme /ö/ does not exist, corresponding to some (in fact most) of the occurrences of the sequence /we/. For most of these speakers, the successive sequence W-EY is everywhere in free variation with the coextensive sequence WEY. For speakers who distinguish /ö/ from /we/, the two contrast in such examples as these: / ⋕ we ↑ eniili ↑ o ⋕ / 'What's the matter?', / ⋕ ö ↑ öncqoke ⋕ i ↑ sqəm ↓ ni ↓ ta ⋕ / 'It's to the left'.

For most speakers the successive sequence W-IY occurs everywhere in free variation with the coextensive sequence WIY. These two cases—WEY for some speakers in free variation with W-EY = /we/; WIY for most speakers in free variation with W-IY = /wi/—are examples of the fifth criterion of phoneme classification mentioned in §1.1.

The components Y and W of coextensive vowel sequences are in free variation with overlapping components when followed by another vowel; e.g. IY-A or IY-YA. Because of the limited environment (preceding another vowel), these sequences are not considered to include occurrences of the phonemes /y/ and /w/; the intercalated semivowels are simply ignored as free variants of the phonemic sequences /ia, ua/, and the like. This is covered by the fourth criterion in §1.1. An example is in the phrase / ⋕ mi ↑ a ↑ nham ↓ ni ↓ ta ⋕ / 'I'm sorry'. The morphophonemic implications are outside the province of the phonemic analysis.

The syllabicity of the vowels proper /i, e, ö, ɛ, ə, ɔ, a, u, o/ and the non-syllabicity of the semivowels /y, w/ is considered a conditioned, non-distinctive feature.

Examples of vowels and semivowel-vowel sequences:

pi 'rain'		swi 'soon'
ince 'now'	yemul 'gift'	kqwênta 'binds'
		kqö 'wits'
pɛ 'ship'	yɛ̂ki 'story'	wɛ 'why?'
nəl 'always'		
tɔ 'more'	pyɔl 'star'	ilwɔn 'one Won'
paŋ 'room'	yaŋmal 'socks'	wansoŋ 'completion'
mul 'water'	yuli 'glass'	
onəl 'today'	yoli 'cuisine'	

1.32. Long vowels occur in contrast with short vowels, and are treated as dyads of like vowels, by analogy with dyads of unlike vowels, which occur freely. For some speakers there are few contrasts of long and short vowels; for others there are many. In view of the variation, it is convenient to indicate those vowel lengths which are variable for a given utterance by a circumflex accent (as /yɛ̂ki/ in the list above). This notation is not completely morphophonemic, since only utterance variants—not morpheme alternants—are fully subsumed; the notation may be considered at least partly diaphonic (subsuming dialect variants). It is a morphophonemic fact that variable vowel length usually occurs only within the boundaries of a morph; vowels which are long for all speakers usually include a morph boundary.

Examples of common contrasts for each vowel follow:

Short for all speakers	Long for some speakers
il 'one'	îl 'work'
ince 'now'	cêtô 'system'
tɛk 'your house'	tɛ̂hak 'university'
ənhɛŋ 'bank'	ə̂msik 'food'
səm 'rice-straw sack'	sə̂m 'island'
pam 'night'	pâm 'chestnut'
nun 'eye'	nûn 'snow'
son 'hand'	tôn 'money'

1.4. There are nine consonant components:

Labial closure	P	Heavy aspiration	H
Dental closure	T	Glottal tension	Q
Alveolar or prepalatal affrication	C	Nasality (velic opening)	N
Sibilance (grooved friction)	S	Lateral opening	L
Velar closure	K		

1.41. The components H and Q are listed as consonant components; yet each of these overlaps both a preceding consonant and a following vowel (making the vowel respectively breathy or unusually tense). Since these components always occur in overlapping sequence, they are considered separate phonemes (the second criterion in §1.1).

1.42. The consonant components occur in nineteen coextensive and successive sequences, represented by the resulting phonemes and phoneme sequences in Table 1. (Two letters indicate a sequence of two phonemes.) The phoneme of pause, which has no components, is included in the table.

	P	T	C	S	K	—
—	p	t	c	s	k	#
H	ph	th	ch		kh	h
Q	pq	tq	cq	sq	kq	
N	m	n			ŋ	
L		l				

Table 1

In the environments /mw, mu, mo/, the nasal component sometimes ends slightly before the lip closure is replaced by lip rounding, resulting in a momentary voiced stop: [mᵇ]. Since this stop is in free variation with zero in a limited environment, the fourth criteron of §1.1 is applicable: [mᵇ] and [m] are free variants of /m/ before /w, u, o/. Examples: /mû/ 'turnip', /mwɔ/ or /mwɔt/ or /muɔt/ 'what', /mom/ 'body'. In a similar way, the phoneme /n/ is occasionally [nᵈ] before a front vowel; examples: taninta 'goes back and forth', nê 'yes'.

Some examples of consonants, and of consonant sequences in initial position after pause:

pap 'cooked rice'	namu 'tree'	koki 'meat'
pha 'onion'	cosɔn 'Korea'	kho 'nose'
pqalli 'fast'	chôn 'village'	kqot 'flower'
mal 'horse'	cqochəm 'pursuit'	paŋ 'room'
tâ 'all'	san 'mountain'	hɛ 'sun'
thanta 'rides'	sqal 'uncooked rice'	salam 'person'
tqaŋ 'land'		

2. Before proceeding to the two other types of analysis, I provide some phonetic details about the phonemes and a statement of their occurrences.

The phonemes /u, o, w/ are characterized by considerable lip protrusion and rounding, which begins simultaneously with a preceding consonant.[5] In a similar fashion, the front position for the phoneme /y/ is also frequently assumed simultaneously with a preceding consonant. This anticipatory overlap of components W and Y calls for criteria 2 and 4 in §1.1; compare the treatment of the lagging overlap of Y and W in §1.31.

The back unrounded vowels /ə, ɔ, a/ are slightly centralized, respectively high, mid, and low; when short, /ə, ɔ/ are slightly lower than the corresponding cardinal vowels.[6] With some speakers, the vowel /ɔ/ has the following allophones when short: lower-mid back unrounded if the syllable is closed by a consonant; lower-mid back, slightly rounded (but without protrusion) if the syllable is open; an unrounded [o] when long. When preceded by the phoneme /y/, the allophone of /ɔ/ is considerably centralized, approaching [ə];[7] for many words, there are variants with /yɔ/ in one dialect corresponding to /ye/ or /e/ in another.

There is often some velarization with the phoneme /h/. The phoneme /q/ is characterized by glottal tension, beginning with a preceding consonant and continuing through the following vowel, producing a tense articulation throughout, in marked contrast with the usual lax articulation.[8]

The phonemes /m, n, ŋ, l/ are tenser than most other consonants, but lack the glottal tension characteristic of /q/.

Voicing is a conditioned quality.[9] Vowels are typically (e.g. in isolation) voiced, but often lose their voicing between voiceless consonants, or in the vicinity of /h/ or /s/. The nasals and the lateral are usually voiced, but occasionally lose at least a part of their voicing in the same environment.

The phonemes /p, t, c, s, k/ are typically voiceless, and lax except before /q/.[10] Between typically voiced phonemes, these consonants are sometimes voiced in rapid speech, but in somewhat slower speech the voicing is absent or

[5] To the contrary, with respect to /u/, Haguenauer 148: 'prononcé presque sans arrondir les lèvres'. This seems more like a description of /ə/.

[6] Somewhat loosely, the color of /ə/ and /ɔ/ may be described as unrounded [u] and unrounded [o] respectively.

[7] Cf. Haguenauer 150: 'Quant à *yɔ*, dans certains cas ... il donne à l'oreille l'impression d'un *yə*.'

[8] The phonetic nature of /pq, tq, cq, sq, kq/ has been variously interpreted. Haguenauer (159 ff.) calls them 'quasi-geminées' and Polivanov considers them 'long' (La perception des sons d'une langue étrangère, TCLP 4.82 [1931]). On the other hand, the Korean phonetician Jung calls the sounds 'implosives' and the late eminent Japanese Koreanist Ogura writes them preglottalized (McCune 29 ff.). All observers seem to agree on the tenseness of the articulation, but differ in their evaluation of its nature and significance. Ramstedt (5–6) points out that the tenseness continues throughout the syllable, even raising the perceived pitch of the vowel. It is true that these sounds are of longer duration than a single consonant phoneme; so are /ph, th, ch, kh/. Although the sounds are not so heavily glottalized as many American Indian consonants, I hear distinct glottal tension. The interpretation as geminate consonants is perhaps influenced by the automatic alternations frequent in the morphophonemic structure.

[9] Cf. J. Lotz, Journal of the Acoustical Society of America 22.716 (1950).

[10] On the lax nature of these phonemes preceding /h/, cf. Haguenauer 159: 'Les aspirées du coréen sont en général sonores et plus douces qu'en chinois.' (The Peking aspirates are generally considered tense. So are the voiceless aspirates of most Chinese dialects which have hitherto been reported.)

very weak. When following a pause and not followed by /h/ or /q/, allophones of these phonemes are slightly aspirated, with the aspiration formed locally at the point of articulation, in contrast with the distinctly glottal aspiration represented by /h/. Between typically voiced phonemes, the phoneme /h/ is frequently voiced.

For many speakers, the phoneme /c/ is prepalatal when not followed by a back unrounded vowel /ə, ɔ, a/; for some speakers, this phoneme is prepalatal in all environments, for a few it is usually alveolar. The phoneme /s/ is palatalized by many speakers, especially before a front vowel. The sequences /cy/ and /sy/ do not occur.[11]

Syllable-final consonants are typically unreleased. Postvocalic syllable-initial /l/ is flapped, but otherwise formed in the same lateral manner as unreleased syllable-final /l/: the under-side of the tongue tip touches the alveolar ridge (and the upper teeth), with an opening on each side.

2.1. Stress is apparently not phonemic in Korean;[12] if there is, contrary to my view, a phoneme of stress, it belongs with the pitch components to the intonation system. There is a clear-cut syllable onset; but this may be described as conditioned, since the syllable can be defined and described wholly in terms of the phoneme sequences which compose it.[13] Table 2 illustrates the syllable structure:

#	m, n		y	i	p	#
	s	q, —		e (ö)	t	
	p, t, c, k		w	ε	k	—
—	l, m, n, ŋ, —	h, —	—	ə	m	
				ɔ	n	
				a	ŋ	
				u	l	
				o	—	

TABLE 2

[11] The phoneme /c/ is considered an affricate by most writers; Jung, however, evidently thinks it is a palatal plosive (McCune 25)—unless, like Gim, he is using the IPA symbol for a palatal plosive to represent an affricate in a 'broad' transcription. Haguenauer (258–8) describes the consonant as follows: 'le dos de la langue touche le bas des dents de la mâchoire supérieure pendant que l'apex est placé derrière les dents d'en bas. Il paraît bien y avoir occlusion synchronique du praedorsum. ... certains sujets placent la point de la langue à la base de la région alvéolaire de la mâchoire supérieure ...' He describes /s/ (156) as 'une fricative douce qui est prononcée la langue reposant à plat et sans tension; l'apex est en arrière de la face interne des incisives inférieures. L'expiration est moyenne; la bouche n'est qu'entr'ouverte.'

[12] For contrary findings, cf. E. D. Polivanov, Zur Frage der Betonungsfunktion, TCLP 6.80 ff. (1938): 'Und schliesslich hat im Koreanischen ein Wort innerhalb des Satzes Endbetonung, doch im Satzschluss sowie in isolierter Aussprache Anfangsbetonung.' This was paraphrased by N. S. Trubetskoy, Grundzüge der Phonologie, TCLP 7.246 (1939): 'Nach E. D. Polivanov soll im Koreanischen jedes Wort die Schlussilbe betonen, und nur das letzte Wort im Satze betont die Anfangsilbe.' This would seem to present a phonological criterion for defining the word. Unfortunately, my own data do not confirm Polivanov's findings, and accordingly my criteria for words must be primarily non-phonological.

[13] On phonetic and phonemic syllables, cf. JAOS 64.151–5 (1944), and SIL 3.46–50 (1945).

Any occurrent syllable can be found in Table 2, each phoneme fitting into the appropriate vertical column. Within a given sequence, consonants are joined to a following vowel whenever possible; in the utterance /#koŋ↑chεki↑isqəmni↑kqa#/ 'Do you have a notebook?', the syllables are /koŋ, chε, ki, i, sqəm, ni, kqa/. It is for this reason that /ŋ/ is put in the same box with /l, m, n, —/ in the chart, even though no morphs are observed to begin with /ŋ/.

Certain distributional limitations within the syllable are not apparent in the chart: not all sequences which can be plotted on the chart actually occur. The phoneme /y/ does not occur in syllables beginning with /t, c, s/ or including the vowel /i/; the semivowel /w/ does not occur before the vowels /ə, u, o/. The sequences /ny, ni/ and the phonemes /l, ŋ/ do not occur after pause. The positions of the phoneme of pause in the chart illustrate syllable environments (for further limitations see §2.3); it is probably best to consider the phoneme of pause as belonging to no syllable (cf. Bloch, Lg. 24.118).

2.2. Of more interest to morphophonemics, but of some relevance also to phonemics, is the list in Table 3 of occurrences of consonants and consonant clusters in morph-initial position before vowels. Occurrences of /ö/ are treated as equivalent to /we/; occurrences of the actual sequence /we/ beside /ö/ are distinguished by italicizing the vowel: /w*e*/. Symbols in the first column (headed CV) represent the vowels which directly follow the consonant or consonant cluster shown at the left; those in the second column (headed CyV) represent the vowels which follow the indicated consonant or cluster plus /y/; those in the third column (headed CwV) represent the vowels which follow the indicated consonant or cluster plus /w/.

	CV	CyV	CwV
p-	i e ε ɔ a u o	ɔ a	e
ph-	i e ε ɔ a u o	ɔ a o	
pq-	i e ε ɔ a u o	a o	e
t-	i e ε ə ɔ a u o		i *e* ε ɔ a
th-	i e ε ə ɔ a u o		i e ε
tq-	i e ε ə ɔ a u o		i e ε a
c-	i e ε ə ɔ a u o		i *e* ε a
ch-	i e ε ə ɔ a u o		i *e* a
cq-	i e ε ə ɔ a u o		e a
k-	i e ε ə ɔ a u o	ε ɔ a u o	i e ε ɔ a
kh-	e ə ɔ a u o	ɔ a u	i *e* ε a
kq-	i e ε ə ɔ a u o	ε ɔ a u	i e ε ɔ a
s-	i e ε ə ɔ a u o		i *e* ε ɔ
sq-	i e ε ə ɔ a o		i e ε
m-	i e ε ɔ a u o	ɔ a o	i *e* ɔ
n-	i e ε ə ɔ a u o	ɔ u o	i *e* ɔ a
h-	i e ε ə ɔ a u o	a u o	i e ε ɔ a
l-	i e ε ə ɔ a u o	ɔ a u o	e

TABLE 3

All the sequences in Table 3 occur after pause, except those beginning with /l, ny, ni/.

The list is perhaps not quite complete (especially if recent borrowings are to be included), so that not all blanks can be regarded as significant. The non-occurrence of /y/ after /t, c, s/ has already been noted. The non-occurrence of /ə/ after labials is parallel to its non-occurrence after /w/. Within a morph, there are occasional occurrences of /ə/ after a labial, e.g. in /kipqəta/ 'is happy', alongside a common (and expected) dialect variant /kipquta/ (the morph boundary is before the phoneme /t/).

2.3. When two syllables occur in uninterrupted succession, a limited number of consonant clusters occur. These are illustrated in Table 4. The horizontal line across the top shows the end of the prior syllable; the vertical line at the left shows the beginning of the following syllable. At a point of intersection, the symbol x indicates that the expected sequence occurs. A dyad in parentheses shows that the expected sequence does not occur, but is automatically replaced (when morphophonemically expected) by the given dyad.[14] In the last horizontal line, and in the fifth line from the end, the place of the hyphen indicates that a syllable begins with the consonant or cluster whenever possible; since this is just a reminder of a sub-phonemic phenomenon (embodied in the definition of the syllable as an automatically determined sequence of phonemes), no parentheses are used.

	-p	-t	-k	-m	-n	-ŋ	-l	—[15]
p-	(pq)	(pq)	x	x	x	x	x	x
ph-	(ph)	(ph)	x	x	x	x	x	x
pq-	(pq)	(pq)	x	x	x	x	x	x
t-	x	(tq)	x	x	x	x	x	x
th-	x	(th)	x	x	x	x	x	x
tq-	x	(tq)	x	x	x	x	x	x
c-	x	(cq)	x	x	x	x	x	x
ch-	x	(ch)	x	x	x	x	x	x
cq-	x	(cq)	x	x	x	x	x	x
s-	x	(sq)	x	x	x	x	x	x
sq-	x	(sq)	x	x	x	x	x	x
k-	x	(kq)	(kq)	x	x	x	x	x
kh-	x	(kh)	(kh)	x	x	x	x	x
kq-	x	(kq)	(kq)	x	x	x	x	x
h-	ph-	th-	kh-	mh-	nh-	ŋh-	lh-	x
m-	(mm)	(nm)	(ŋm)	x	x	x	x	x
n-	(mn)	(nn)	(ŋn)	x	x	x	(ll)	x
l-	(mn)	(nn)	(ŋn)	(mn)	(nn)	(ŋn)	x	x
—[16]	p-	t-	k-	m-	n-	ŋ-	l-	x

TABLE 4

[14] These are the principal cases of fully automatic alternation in the morphophonemic structure. (Other cases involve similar reductions of consonant clusters which do not occur phonemically). By fully automatic, I mean what Wells calls 'narrow static alternation', Lg. 25.107 (1949). The somewhat more complicated alternations of /l/ and /ny, ni/ are also cases of narrow static alternation after pause but not in other environments (e.g. word-initial within an utterance), which exhibit what Wells calls 'wide static alternation' (105–6). The difference is basically whether the automatic character is phonemically determined ('narrow alternation') or grammatically conditioned ('wide alternation').

[15] I.e. a syllable ending with a vowel.

[16] I.e. a syllable beginning with a vowel or with /y/ or /w/.

Examples of consonant clusters:

pt	haptoŋ 'merger'	nc	sincaŋ 'elongation, extension'
pth	kəpthal 'pillage'	nch	anchi 'not existing'
ptq	naptqêm 'solder, pewter'	ncq	sincqa 'let's wear (on feet)'
pc	sipcaka 'cross'	ns	sunsa 'policeman'
pch	chəpchəphi 'repeatedly, row on row'	nsq	sinsqəmnita 'wears (on feet)'
pcq	ipcqilen 'squeamish, fastidious'	nk	sinko 'hardships'
ps	sipsam 'thirteen'	nkh	ankho 'not existing'
psq	ipsqiləm 'dispute, wrangle'	nkq	sinkqo 'wearing (on feet)'
pk	sipku 'nineteen'	nh	sînhô 'signal'
pkh	cəpkhal 'pocket-knife'	nm	sinmun 'newspaper'
pkq	cipkqaci 'as far as the house'	nn	punno 'anger'
kp	kakpyəli 'especially'	ŋp	koŋpu 'study'
kph	mokphyo 'target, goal'	ŋph	saŋphûm 'goods, commodities'
kpq	pqakpqakhan 'tight'	ŋpq	pqəŋpqəŋhan 'annoying, distressing'
kt	siktaŋ 'dining room'	ŋt	koŋtək 'charity'
kth	mokyokthaŋ 'bathroom'	ŋth	saŋthê 'condition, state'
ktq	tqoktqoki 'clearly'	ŋtq	koŋtqək 'good luck, windfall'
kc	kakcu 'footnote'	ŋc	koŋcak 'construction'
kch	kakchu 'pyramid'	ŋch	saŋchi 'lettuce'
kcq	cqokcqoki 'in pieces'	ŋcq	cqɛŋcqɛŋhan 'brilliant'
ks	yuksip 'sixty'	ŋs	koŋsik 'formality'
ksq	sqiksqikhan 'brave, strong'	ŋsq	sqaŋsqaŋi 'in pairs; two by two'
mp	tampi 'badger'	ŋk	saŋkoŋ 'commerce and industry'
mph	tamphan 'negotiation, discussion'	ŋkh	saŋkhwe 'exhilaration'
mpq	tampquki 'in full'	ŋkq	kqaŋkqɛŋi 'fiddle'
mt	tamtaŋ 'charge, custody'	ŋh	koŋhwa 'republic'
mth	samthɛki 'dirt-carrier'	ŋm	koŋmû 'official business'
mtq	namtqən 'which had remained'	ŋn	myəŋnyən 'next year'
mc	namca 'man'	lp	kyəlpiŋ 'freezing'
mch	simchwî 'fascination, infatuation'	lph	kyəlphip 'scarcity'
mcq	namcqi 'remaining'	lpq	pqulpquli 'severally, respectively'
ms	simsin 'mind'	lt	talta 'is sweet'
msq	namsqəmnita 'remains'	lth	kyəlthu 'duel, combat'
mk	kâmkak 'sense, sensation'	ltq	paltqal 'progress'
mkh	samkhinta 'swallows'	lc	kôlca 'let's hang up'
mkq	namkqo 'remaining'	lch	silche 'substance, entity'
mh	tamhwa 'conversation'	lcq	kyəlcqəŋ 'decision'
mm	nammɛ 'brothers and sisters'	ls	chilsip 'seventy'
mn	namnyə 'men and women'	lsq	kyəlsqan 'settlement of accounts'
np	sînpûn 'social position'	lk	əlkul 'face'
nph	cinphûm 'curio'	lkh	kyəlkho 'absolutely'
npq	pqənpqənhan 'brazen, shameless'	lkq	îlkqun 'worker, coolie'
nt	cîntôŋ 'vibration'	lh	səlhwa 'story, narration'
nth	cînthwê 'advance or retreat'	lm	səlmyəŋ 'explanation'
ntq	sintqən 'which had worn (on feet)'	ll	səllip 'establishment'

3. Instead of speaking in terms of articulatory components, it is possible to analyze the phonemes in terms of AUDITORY QUALITIES. The terminology and the technique for such analysis are at best rudimentary, but the following attempt is made to illustrate the possibilities. (The pitch components are omitted from the analysis.)

It is assumed that there are nine distinctive auditory qualities in Korean, each of which is either present or absent in the occurrence of any phoneme. These qualities and their organization into the phonemic system are illustrated in Table 5. Where no symbol appears, the quality is absent from the phoneme written at the head of the column.

	p	t	c	s	k	m	n	ŋ	h	q	l	y	w	i	e	ö	ɛ	ə	ɔ	a	u	o
Nasal						x	x	x														
Front		x	x	x			x				x	x		x	x	x	x					
High														x				x			x	
Mid[17]															x	x			x			x
Low																	x			x		
Labial	x					x							x			x					x	x
Tense						x	x	x		x	x											
Contactual	x	x	x		x	x	x	x			x											
Fricative			x	x					x													

TABLE 5

Other qualities (such as back, voiced, syllabic, lateral) are considered conditioned.

The principal difficulty in the auditory analysis is the treatment of /l/; short of setting up a distinctive quality of lateralness peculiar to the phoneme /l/, it is necessary in order to account for the difference between /t/ and /l/, to broaden the definition of tenseness to include that of the lateral and the nasals as well as the special glottal tension of /q/. This may seem inconsistent, in view of the overlapping nature of the phoneme /q/ itself, unless the criteria for handling different types of sequence (§1.1) are regarded as logically prior to the complete analysis of qualities.

4. Some analysts have attempted to deal with auditory qualities in terms of DISTINCTIVE OPPOSITIONS.[18] These linguists assume that a limited number of binary oppositions underlie the phonemic system: each phoneme is characterized by either or both of the opposing qualities, though not every opposition is necessarily represented in every phoneme.[19] Leaving aside the question of the validity of the binary principle, I note that the technique of binary analysis, as it has been applied so far, seems to overextend its binary character in admitting both members of an opposing pair to be present in one phoneme. This device has at least the virtue of reducing the number of qualities which it is necessary to posit, in a way that makes Occam's razor seem dull indeed.[20]

To explore the possibilities of such a technique, I present here a binary analysis of the Korean phonemes (Table 6). Six distinctive oppositions are assumed: nasal/oral; front/back; high/low; labial/non-labial; tense/lax; contactual/fluid. In each pair, the first member is regarded as positive, on the basis of less frequent occurrence within the system,[21] and the second member as negative. In Table 6, the presence of a positive quality in a given phoneme is indicated by a plus sign. The presence of a negative member is not indicated overtly, but is implied by the absence of any mark.[22] When both members of an opposition are present in the same phoneme, the fact is indicated by the sign ±.

OPPOSITIONS	p	t	c	s	k	m	n	ŋ	h	q	l	y	w	i	e	ö	ɛ	ə	ɔ	a	u	o
nasal (vs. oral)						+	+	+														
front (vs. back)		+	+	+			+				+	+		+	+	+	+			±		
high (vs. low)														+	±	±		+	±		+	±
labial (vs. non-labial)	+					+							+			+					+	+
tense (vs. lax)						±	±	±		+	±											
contactual (vs. fluid)	+	+	±		+	±	±	±			±											

TABLE 6

The difficulty of the phoneme /l/ (§3) is somewhat less obtrusive in the binary analysis, since a difference between /m, n, ŋ, l/ and /q/ in the type of tenseness can here be indicated by taking advantage of the device referred to above: namely, by assuming the simultaneous occurrence of both members of an opposition. It is a question whether /p, m/ should not include the quality of frontness, since the absence of this quality presumably implies backness; and also whether highness should not be marked plus for all the consonants. Such questions re-

[17] It would be possible to eliminate the quality Mid by regarding the mid quality of /e, ö, ɔ, o/ as absence of both high and low qualities (just as the quality Back is treated as absence of front quality). This would define the phoneme /ɔ/ as having no distinctive qualities at all. While such a view is possible, it seems wiser to reserve the definition by total absence of qualities for the phoneme of pause /#/.

[18] Cf. R. Jakobson and J. Lotz, Notes on the French phonemic pattern, Word 5.151–8 (1949); R. Jakobson, On the identification of phonemic entities, Travaux du Cercle linguistique de Copenhague 5.205–13 (1949). For clarity, where Jakobson and Lotz use the terms 'higher and lower saturation' I speak of 'back and front'; where they use the terms 'gravity and acuteness' I speak of 'low and high'.

[19] Cf. J. Lotz, Journal of the Acoustic Society of America 22.715–6 (1950): 'Thus it seems that speech in its distinctive aspect is built up entirely of features in accordance with a binary principle.'

[20] Ibid.: '... in such a case we have to introduce either a complex middle term or allow trinary oppositions.' As a matter of fact, Jakobson and Lotz seem to admit still another contrast, that of applicability of a specific opposition to a particular phoneme. This may then be conceived as a double-level binary contrast: for a given phoneme, a specific opposition either occurs (i.e. is applicable) or does not occur; if it occurs, either (1) both members occur together, or (2) a secondary level of contrast is involved, that of the polarity of the two members. In other words, occurrence of either member or both members of the opposition is itself opposed to non-occurrence, and the differentiation within the opposition is relegated to a secondary level. I suspect this concept of the opposition theory may be in conflict with unstated assumptions on the part of some who support the theory.

[21] This principle of economy in the selection of positive entities is implied but usually not explicitly stated in analyses of phonemic systems.

[22] This represents a departure from the technique applied to French by Jakobson and Lotz (see fn. 18). Whereas, in their treatment, certain oppositions are not represented in certain phonemes at all (so that the number of distinctive features is not necessarily the same for all phonemes), I here assume that every one of the six oppositions is represented in every Korean phoneme, by its positive or its negative member, or by both together.

volve around the definition of the auditory qualities which our terms represent—a problem that remains to be adequately explored. One further difficulty is that the phoneme of pause /#/ cannot be included in the table, since the absence of all positive qualities implies the presence of all negative qualities—and the definition 'oral, back, low, non-labial, lax, and fluid' is considered appropriate to the phoneme /h/.

5. It is interesting to compare the results of the three different types of componential analysis by investigating the internal organization of each componential system.

In the system of articulatory components, coextensive sequence is limited to two mutually exclusive groups: I, E, A, Y, W, defining the class of vowel phonemes; and P, T, C, S, K, N, L, defining the class of consonant phonemes. The components H and Q are always in overlapping sequence, defining a class of quasi-consonant phonemes. As for the syllabicity of I, E, and A, and the non-syllabicity of Y and W, when these components occur in other coextensive sequences—i.e. in the phonemes /ə, ɔ, a, y, w/—this is taken to be conditioned, so that the class of semivowels is not defined above the phonetic level. The components N and L are the only non-pitch components which always occur in coextensive sequence, defining the subclass of sonorant consonants and its negative counterpart, the subclass of non-sonorant consonants.

In the system of auditory components, the qualities High, Mid, and Low and the qualities Nasal, Tense, Contactual, and Fricative form two mutually exclusive groups, respectively defining vowel and consonant phonemes. The qualities Front and Labial are ambivalent, forming two structural groups which cut across the vowels and consonants.

In the system of distinctive oppositions, only the quality High defines the class of vowel phonemes. Otherwise, the internal structure is superficially similar to that of the auditory analysis.

It is possible to set up groups of phonemes according to their complexity, as determined by the number of coexistent qualities present within each phoneme. Table 7 compares the articulatory and auditory analyses on this basis.

Number of Positive Qualities	In Articulatory Analysis	In Auditory Analysis
0	#	#
1	p t c s k h q	k h q y w ə ɔ a
	y w ə ɔ a	
2	m n ŋ l	p t s
	i e ɛ u o	i e ɛ u o
3	ö	c ŋ l ö
4		m n

TABLE 7

This kind of tabulation would be less meaningful for the system of distinctive oppositions, since here the negative qualities are structurally just as important as the positive. The raw quantitative data for this system are given in Table 8.

Polarity	p	t	c	s	k	m	n	ŋ	h	q	l	y	w	i	e	ö	ɛ	ə	ɔ	a	u	o
+	2	2	1	1	1	2	2	1	0	1	1	1	1	2	1	2	1	1	0	0	2	1
±	0	0	1	0	0	2	2	2	0	0	2	0	0	0	1	1	0	0	1	1	0	1
−	4	4	4	5	5	2	2	3	6	5	3	5	5	4	4	3	5	5	5	5	4	4

TABLE 8

From the data shown in Table 8, several different kinds of structural arrangements are possible; I present three of them here. Table 9 groups the phonemes into three simple quantitative classes; Table 10 groups them into two classes based on combinations of polarity; Table 11 groups them into two classes based on a reduction of polarities.

Polarity	Oppositions	Phonemes
+	0	h ɔ a
	1	c s k ŋ q l y w e ɛ ə o
	2	p t m n i ö u
±	0	p t s k h q y w i ɛ ə u
	1	c e ö ɔ a o
	2	m n ŋ l
−	2	m n
	3	ŋ l ö
	4	p t c i e u o
	5	s k q y w ɛ ə ɔ a
	6	h

TABLE 9

Throughout these lists, there are five constant sets of phonemes which always occur together in like categories: (1) s k q y w ɛ ə; (2) p t i u; (3) c e o; (4) m n; (5) ɔ a. These five sets include eighteen phonemes; the other four (h, l, ŋ, ö) are variable in their groupings.

Polarity	Oppositions	Phonemes
+ and ±	0	h
	1	s k q y w ɛ ə ɔ a
	2	p t c i e u o
	3	ö l ŋ
	4	m n
− and ±	4	p t m n i ö u
	5	c s k ŋ q l y w e ɛ ə o
	6	h ɔ a

TABLE 10

Polarity	**Oppositions**	**Phonemes**
+ minus ±	−1	ŋ l ɔ a
	0	c m n h e o
	1	s k q y w ö ɛ ə
	2	p t i u
− minus ±	0	m n
	1	ŋ l
	2	ö
	3	c e o
	4	p t i ɔ a u
	5	s k q y w ɛ ə
	6	h

Table 11

6. As a result of the comparisons made in the preceding section, it is possible to give objective reasons for preferring one of these three methods of analysis to the others. In many respects, the groups resulting from the articulatory analysis, as shown in Table 7, seem the most satisfactory. Although part of my preference may be based on a long-standing bias in favor of traditional phonetic classes, there is evidence from both the morphophonemic structure and the historical development of the phonemes that the groups resulting from the articulatory analysis are potentially more useful than the others. There are, however, some points favoring the other two analyses; the structural groups formed by the ambivalent qualities Front and Labial, cutting across vowels and consonants alike, have some useful correlations and seem to be handy categories. The mathematics of the polarity groups seems disappointingly irrelevant, but this might be a fault of the specific analysis undertaken, or of the quantitative approach in grouping, rather than of the oppositional technique itself. There is some relevance in the constant sets mentioned at the end of §5; the variability of the four phonemes /h, l, ŋ, ö/ is perhaps merely an indication that the specific oppositions chosen in §4 are inadequate.

⟦This completes our sampling of 'phonemics without the phoneme'—for although Martin uses the term, he could have replaced it with Hockett's 'symbols for inclosure between solidi' without altering his treatment of Korean in the least; see my comment ⟪228⟫. The place occupied by Bloch in this picture is easy to determine from his paper on Japanese ⟪329⟫, so clearly written that the task can be left to readers interested enough to try it. I had no room there, and thus escaped the temptation to paint the lily.

Referring again to my earlier comments ⟪228⟫, we are reminded of the paper which Martin refers to first in his fn. 18. This was at one time chosen for inclusion in this volume, but had to be dropped out for extrinsic reasons; it should be sought out for careful reading by anyone whose interest is caught by Martin's last pages. Its absence here does not, however, spoil our picture of descriptive linguistics.⟧

THE MEDIEVAL SIBILANTS

MARTIN JOOS

Language 28.222-31—1952

Modern West European languages (and their offshoots such as American English) generally have just one voiceless fortis sibilant phoneme /s/, whatever else there may be, such as /z, š, θ, c/. But in every considerable area at least two quite different [s] phones are in use, (pre)dorsal [s̱] and apical [ṣ]. The commoner variety is the dorsal [s̱]. In its articulation the tongue-tip is idle (in persons with a 'normal bite,' as the dentists say, the tip touches the lower incisors or gums or both), and the sibilant squeeze is made against the upper alveolar ridge by the upper surface of the tongue. The apical [ṣ] is nowhere truly rare, but it is the less common variety in the principal areas, except that it is standard in Castilian Spanish. The apical articulation has the tongue-tip raised, and the tip itself makes the sibilant squeeze.[1]

Thus apical [ṣ] articulation leaves a resonance chamber under the tongue-tip and behind the lower incisors; but dorsal [s̱] has this same space filled up by the tongue. Therefore the [ṣ] has a lower resonance and sounds rather 'blunt', somewhat like [š], while the [s̱] has a higher resonance[2] and sounds relatively 'sharp'. The emphasis here is on the word relatively: because of personal differences, especially in the placement of the teeth, one speaker's [ṣ] may sound enough like another's [s̱] so that we cannot tell which it is in isolation; and we may find a small child learning to produce one by imitating the other—in a given area, that is, where there is only one /s/ phoneme. But if the same person produces them both on request, we can hear the difference as soon as the listening-conditions are good enough to distinguish any [s] from [θ] or [š].[3]

It follows that a language could have /s̱/ and /ṣ/ as two phonemes. Then the difference would always be 'heard' by native speakers, with the customary reservation applicable to all cases of small acoustic differences (as between /f/ and /θ/ in English), namely that in listening to a stranger or under bad listening-conditions it would normally be the morpheme that was identified first (from the morphemic context and from the perception of either-/s̱/-or-/ṣ/) with subsequent identification (if called for) of the particular sibilant phoneme from the morpheme identity.[4] From what little we know of the dynamics

[1] Bernard Bloch and George L. Trager, in Tables for a system of phonetic description (New Haven, 1940), used [s] for the dorsal variety and called it 'laminal', and presented a new symbol for the apical sibilant. But because in this paper we must avoid a prejudicial implication that one is the norm and the other an aberration, the two are here represented by an ad-hoc use of underlined and dotted [s] symbols, where the line may be thought of as a diagram of the tongue surface and the dot as diagramming the tip of the tongue. This makes plain [s] or /s/ available for use as a cover-symbol for either or both.

[2] The writer's [s] hiss is about a musical fourth higher in pitch when he produces the dorsal sibilant that is normal in his native English than when he produces the carefully drilled apical sibilant of his Castilian Spanish; from the latter down to the pitch of his [š] (also apical, as it is for most Americans but by no means nearly all) is a slightly greater musical interval, about a fifth.

[3] For a keen ear or kinesthetic perception, there may be more discernible varieties than these two, filling in the gap between them; but these seem to be relatively rare, and usually an [s] can be unhesitatingly assigned to one of the two extreme articulations. About one third of the writer's phonetics students use apical articulation for [s, z] in *hiss* and *his*; nearly two thirds use dorsal articulation; about one in twenty is atypical. For Europeans our data are scanty; see fn. 23.

[4] In any language that has only one /s/ phoneme, the difference between dorsal and apical [s] has by definition some entirely different status. It is never 'heard' in the sense that the word has here; and yet there are various possibilities, of which two will be mentioned by way of illustration. In Japanese only the apical variety occurs before /u/ and (if we write nothing where some descriptions have /u/) before consonant or pause, as in desu ga /desuŋa/ 'though it is', desu ka /deska/ 'is it?'. Elsewhere in Japanese, e.g. before /a/, the dorsal and apical [s] are both current and appear to be distributed pretty much as in English. In English the freedom is complete: there is no absolute limitation, no structural restriction; each English speaker does what he pleases, so to speak, in every context. And yet most of us use one of the two extreme varieties wherever it is possible, in a sense of 'possible' that is personal to each speaker, the other one rarely or never. The writer, for example, has only the dorsal variety otherwise than before the apico-alveolar consonants; but before /l/ he has only the apical variety, and before /t,n/ he has either, in free and capricious variation; and although /t, n/ are otherwise always apical, in /st, sn/ they are dorsal whenever the sibilant is. Other speakers have quite different distributions, and theoretically any distribution at all is possible, but the one just described may be among the commonest. Descriptivists who use the term 'allophone' sparingly will then say, with Trager and Smith (An outline of English structure 34), 'the phonemes /f, θ, s, š/ have one allophone each.'

of phonetic change, however, we may guess that a phonemic opposition of /s̱/ and /ș/ would not very long resist heavy social pressure such as is present in situations of dialect mixture. It is, then, to be regarded as a pure accident, but not a very strange one, if we do not happen to know of a language that has /s̱/ and /ș/ as two phonemes.[5] This paper will discuss (hypothetically, because the languages are dead now) two neighboring languages of that sort, and show how the opposition between /s̱/ and /ș/, stable for a considerable time, at last broke down in each language in a period of rapidly increasing inter-dialect communication. The precise phonetics of dead languages can of course never be demonstrated in any absolute sense, as the phonemics often can be. But our phonetic hypotheses can have various degrees of likelihood, depending on their contents. In this case the situation is rather favorable to precise conclusions, both phonetic and phonemic. For instance, the hypothetical apical [ș] can be related to a necessarily apical consonant, the lingually trilled [r]; and the relatively retracted tongue position of [ș] compared to [s̱] can be related to retracted allophones of context vowels as the antecedents of new vowel phonemes in the modern language.

Over a century ago, rime studies firmly established the fact that High German, for half a dozen centuries at least down through the classical Middle High German period (MHG, ca. 1200 A.D.), had two voiceless spirant phonemes, both sibilant as far as we can tell, now written s and z in our editions, aside from the affricate /c/ [ts] also written z (or tz) and the /š/ [š] sch. One of the numerous minimal pairs for the two [s] phonemes was wîz 'white' and wîs 'manner'. They contrasted also when long (geminate) between vowels, as in wizzen 'know' and wissen 'knew'. The sibilant z is supposed not to have occurred initially, where s was common both before vowels and before consonants and the affricate z was common before vowels and w. Next to a consonant, where s was common and /c/ occurred after /l, r, n/ as in wurz 'wort', the sibilant z was sporadic; one accepted instance was hirz (from Old High German hiruz) 'hart', with no known rimes—not even wirs 'worse'. A somewhat modified discussion, which had best be postponed as long as possible, is called for by occurrences of single z and s between vowels, as in wîzen 'reproach' and wîsen 'direct', because the s there was presumably lenis toward the end of the period. In the other two regular positions of contrast (final, and geminate between vowels) both s and the sibilant z may safely be taken to have been fortis.

Ever since that discovery, Germanists have been trying, with varying plausibility, to say something reasonable about the phonetics of this phonological situation which is so very queer to us today. Some have called MHG s a lenis [š], the sch being fortis [š], both always voiceless as all MHG obstruents were. Others have said that the two sibilants z and s differed only in being fortis and lenis respectively. Both these choices would make MHG s the only lenis that could be final or geminate, an unacceptable notion.[6] Karstien avoided that particular difficulty by calling sibilant z 'an s-like sound' and calling s 'a sound similar to š' which he identified with Polish ś.[7] Those who call z 's-like' or 'a kind of lisped s' evidently attach no great importance to the fact that no modern dialect regularly (i.e. aside from Hirsch 'hart'; see above) has anything but a normal European [s] for MHG spirant z. And we know of no other language having three phonemes /s, ś, š/ without having either phonemic palatalization or a separate palatal series of consonants (cf. Polish and Sanskrit).[8] Finally, taking both Karstien's values together would improvidently leave MHG without any proper [s] at all, making it almost unique among the languages of the world and proving nothing but the desperate discomfort that everyone feels when the evidence says that s was [s] and z was also [s] and yet they were different phonemes.[9]

Among Germanists, then, we find exaggeration of the phonetic difference between two MHG sibilant phonemes. In the usual descriptions of the con-

[5] For phonologists like Roman Jakobson and John Lotz, however, this is no accident. They would point out that few languages have anywhere a distinctive feature that could serve to separate dorsal and apical [s] into two phonemes. At present such phonological arguments seem to be very strong if not absolutely decisive, and they will not be avoided in this paper. Being based on experience with many languages, they have the authority of good statistics; but in single instances they may be upset.

One language that has both these sibilant phonemes (beside /š/!) is Basque. Jean Larrasquet, Le basque de la Basse-Soule orientale (Paris, 1939), clearly describes the dorsal [š] and the dorsal sibilant, but calls the apical sibilant 'cacuminal'.

[6] That one spirant out of many obstruents should have such a unique phonological status is at least highly improbable.

[7] Carl Karstien, Historische deutsche Grammatik (Heidelberg, 1939). Karstien is cited here as a responsible exponent of standard doctrine, differing from others principally in his relative willingness to speak out on difficult points. The spirant z is characterized without argument on page 125, the s on page 138 with a reference to Behaghel for the literature. But Behaghel's sources show only that s was employed for foreign [š] sounds in early times, when sch did not yet have the [š] value because it represented an earlier stage on the road from /sk/. The compromise identification of s with Polish ś appears to be Karstien's invention; it does not demonstrate a very firm grasp of Polish phonetics.

[8] Another argument from general phonological theory; cf. fn. 5.

[9] Where MHG s is not /s/ or /z/ today, it is /š/. That is as far as the evidence goes to show that it was always [ś] or always [š] in MHG, and that is not far enough.

temporary Old French, on the other hand, we find no recognition of a phonetic difference between soft c [s] and s [s] after the former had become established in place of older /c/ [ts]; instead we find the amazing statement that [s] from Gallo-Roman ss lengthened the vowel before it in Middle French, while the identical [s] from c had no such effect.[10]

When earlier OF /c/ [ts] (c or final z) was replaced by a plain sibilant, a process which seems to have taken place gradually during parts of the 12th and 13th centuries, the standard doctrine is that the stop component simply dropped out and left a sibilant identical with older /s/ (s or intervocalic ss). Now such a change would be a phonologically uncompensated disappearance of a phonemic opposition. That is possible (as when *Mary*, *merry*, *marry* fell together in some varieties of American English), but it is less probable than a compensated disappearance such as will be described presently; and there is no reason for the phonemic change to be simultaneous with the first phonetic change (indeed that would be impossible under a strict definition of the terms), since what we usually find (as in the history of Germanic umlaut) is that the pronunciation changes first and the phonemic reclassification comes later, perhaps centuries later. Here the most probable event was a phonetic shift of the /c/ [ts] to some sort of [s] which we may temporarily write /ç/, without implying any alteration in the phonemic opposition to the old and surviving /s/ [s];[11] that is, we are entitled to assume, as the most probable first phonetic change, a shift from a contrast between affricate and spirant to a contrast between two different spirants, without alteration of the phonemic structure, yielding a stage of the language with two sibilant phonemes (among the voiceless sounds) just as in MHG.

There is direct phonetic evidence for the difference between OF /ç/ and /s/, in the form of English loanwords from French. The French /ç/ words have /s/ in English today (e.g. *face*);[12] but only part of the French /s/ words now have /s/ in English (e.g. *base*), while the others have /š/, for example *cash*, *push*, and the extensive family *finish*, *vanish*, etc. This is just what we should expect if late OF and Middle French had two sibilant phonemes here, namely dorsal /s̳/ (= /ç/ from older /c/) and apical /ṣ/ (= surviving /s/), while Middle English had only one /s/, whose most usual variety was [s̳] as it is today, so that in borrowing French [ṣ] words there was generally a sound-substitution, either a replacement in one direction by English /s/ [s̳] (usually, but [ṣ] among minority speakers who could match instead of substituting), or else roughly the same distance in the other direction by English /š/. Here we are arguing from Middle English to French sounds, that is (relatively speaking) from the known to the unknown, for there is hardly any uncertainty about Middle English sibilants. But in comparing OF with MHG there is roughly the same uncertainty on both sides, unless we consider the OF case as proved at this point without waiting for the further evidence that will be presented below, so that for the present we have only an agreement and no proof. What we find, with relatively few counter-examples, is that OF soft c and s were borrowed as MHG spirant z and s respectively, as in these two examples: MHG *buzzel* (Parzival 190.13) from OF *boucel* (Perceval 3106),[13] and OF *coussin*, MHG *küssen*, modern German *Kissen*, English *cushion*.[14]

This would seem to be an instance of 'area linguistics': in a continuous area including MHG and OF there were two voiceless fortis sibilant phonemes, namely a dorsal /s̳/ spelled c or z and an apical /ṣ/ spelled s.[15] Frankish community or Franco-German comity in cultural traits is an important

[10] Mildred K. Pope, From Latin to modern French 207 (Manchester, 1934). While this book presents hardly any theoretical innovations, it appears to overlook nothing whatever in its 600 very full pages, and is organized with extraordinary thoroughness and clarity.

[11] The symbol /ç/, borrowed from French orthography (not from any phonetic alphabet), and the cover-symbols /s/ and [s] of fn. 1, are used at this point to avoid prejudicing the argument by anticipating data introduced later.

[12] Except when palatalization supervened much later than the borrowing, as in *spacious*.

[13] It is of course conceivable that *buzzel* had MHG /c/ [ts], which was occasionally spelled zz instead of tz; but the same would be true of any single MHG example, and it is only the accumulation of examples that established the normal correspondence between the two languages. This word was the name of a wine vessel, a cask or jug, taken over from the French original by the German paraphraser because (presumably) he was not sure of its meaning. For the vowel quantity see fn. 14. English *bushel* is another word, normal OF *boissel*, Anglo-Norman *bousselle*.

[14] At this time the MHG single s between vowels was presumably lenis, so that a fortis [s] there had to be geminate unless spelled with z; also, a vowel had to be short before a geminate. Therefore, this *küssen* says nothing about the quantity of either ou or ss in OF, but only says that OF voiceless ss was matched by fortis [s] in MHG; it is agreed (on other grounds) that OF ss [s] was not long, but was merely written double to distinguish it from voiced s [z] between vowels. The MHG ü shows umlaut as is to be expected from the fact that the word was in the language long enough before so that it had i in its second syllable, later blunted to e [ə] with umlauting, i.e. phonemicization of the [ü] allophone of /u/ as /ü/. This made the word identical with MHG *küssen* 'kissing', as shown by the pun in Walther's 'si hât ein küssen, daz ist rôt' (54.7). Today standard German has *Kissen* from an unrounding dialect, the sort of thing that can easily happen to a word that is not anchored to any u word as *küssen* is to *Kuss*.

[15] The area certainly did not extend into English, nor apparently outside OF and MHG in any other direction, being sealed off to the eastward especially by the quite different sibilant systems of the Slavic languages. The somewhat similar Castilian Spanish situation belongs to a later period.

factor in medieval history which is too well known to need further discussion here; there is nothing surprising in finding it manifested in the 13th-century phonology of French and German. Indeed, the congruence of earlier OF /c/ with OHG /c/ (both [ts] from earlier stops which had different sequels in other areas) was presumably another example.

In the later history of each language, the /s̲/ behaved in one way and the /ṣ/ in another; the two sibilants partly converged, partly diverged still further, with considerable parallelism between the two languages. In German it would all be quite simple but for the artificialities (mostly spelling-pronunciations) of the modern standard. MHG /s̲/ remained stable and is represented by /s/ today except sporadically, and at least one example of sporadic treatment is diagnostically significant: in *hirz* (see the fourth paragraph of this paper) the /s̲/ was assimilated to the apical trill /r/ and became /ṣ/, after which the word, no longer unique, was treated like any other MHG /rṣ/ word and gave *Hirsch*, like *Kirsche* from *kirse*; the modern /rs/ before /t/ is an aberration of the standard pronunciation and has no basis in High German dialects, which have e.g. /vuršt/ beside the standard /vurst/ for *Wurst* 'sausage'. Otherwise the /ṣ/ gave modern /s/ finally, in /ks/ from /hṣ/ (e.g. *wachsen* /vaksen/ from *wahsen* /wahṣen/ 'grow'), and in gemination (/ṣṣ/ to /s/ with the universal shortening of geminates, but still spelled ss, e.g. /küsen/ from /küṣṣen/ with traditional spelling *küssen*); before a consonant /ṣ/ gave /š/ (falling together with old /š/ sch) initially in the modern standard (e.g. /štajn/ *Stein* from /ṣtejn/ *stein*, and /šlext/ *schlecht* from /ṣleht/ *sleht*), but in dialects both initially and internally;[16] before vowels (except in /rš/ from /rṣ/ and in /ks/ from /hṣ/) it gave /z/.[17]

In French also the /s̲/ was stable and gave modern /s/. But the /ṣ/ of OF was just as unstable as in German and not entirely dissimilarly: before a consonant it also diverged still farther from the /s̲/ (but towards zero instead of towards /š/) and also finally along with all other obstruents; elsewhere it converged with the /s̲/. The details call for step-by-step presentation, so that the highly interesting compensations can be brought out clearly.

We begin with the next-earlier stage of OF, which had among its voiceless consonants an affricate /c/ [ts̲][18] and a sibilant /s/ [ṣ]. Before the latter, vowels had a retracted allophone, by assimilation to the retracted tongue-position of [ṣ]: /basə/ [bɑṣə] *basse* 'low, base (fem.)' with the same /a/ phoneme as /facə/ [fats̲ə] *face* 'face'. The retracted allophones of other vowels before /s/ [ṣ] were of course opener (front vowels) or closer (back vowels) than their allophones elsewhere, according to the pattern of the vowel triangle, leading ultimately to modern *fraîche* with a lower-mid front vowel from an earlier higher-mid one, and to *hôte* with a higher-mid back vowel from an earlier lower-mid one.[19]

Now at roughly the same time in the 12th and 13th century, two phonetic changes took place:[20] /c/ [ts̲] became /s̲/ [s̲] (written /ç/ [ç] above), and /s/ [ṣ] (now to be written /ṣ/) gradually faded out before a consonant. Wolfram von Eschenbach, writing MHG in the first decade of the 13th century, rendered OF *forest* as *foreist* (riming with *volleist*) in his earlier work, but as *foreht* (riming with *sleht*, see above) a few years later—not that OF was necessarily changing so fast as to require both renderings within one decade, but rather because his own French was becoming more elegant.

Thus the weakening of /ṣ/ after a vowel before a consonant went by way of [h], as in some varieties of American Spanish today. This [h] now gradually became murmurous (voiced h), and ultimately fully voiced and frictionless. As the sibilant squeeze

16 There is a possibility that re-examination will find the MHG sibilant contrast surviving in Low Allemanic dialects where the three words *isst*, *ist*, and *fischt* have been somewhat unreliably reported to be all different in their sibilants. (Oral communication from the late Edwin C. Roedder.)

17 It is generally held that MHG single s was lenis between vowels already in the 13th century, perhaps even initially before a vowel; but note that there was no single fortis s for it to contrast with in either of these positions, and hence no separate /z/ phoneme. This could only be established later, through at least two shifts: merging of ss with zz, and shortening of all geminates. The modern standard opposes /z/ and /s/ only when a long vowel or diphthong precedes and a vowel follows, as in *reisen* and *reissen*—extremely light functional burdening.

18 This [t] is not underlined here, but was probably dorsal too; the difference is not worth inquiring into, since it could not have had any consequences.

19 The highest vowels /i, ü/ maintained their status as extreme vowels; and if they were ever retracted, then that divergence from /i, ü/ elsewhere was cancelled out before it had any consequences. It is practically certain that they were compensatorily lengthened when a following [s] vanished before consonant, along with the other vowels discussed below, and then also analogically lengthened before preserved ss like the other vowels; but because we have no evidence on their retracted qualities (if any), they can add nothing to the argument and are therefore omitted from the discussion. Fortunately, for the same reasons, they could not weaken the argument either.

20 The approximate simultaneity of the two gradual phonetic drifts is not involved in the argument. It is hard to see how there could have been any significant connection between them, since /c/ did not occur before a consonant, the only position where /s/ changed so early. At most it might be suggested that the apical articulation of s was not ancient, and the contrast between the two sibilant articulations developed at this very time by way of maintaining at least some phonetic difference. But it is easier to suppose that the phonetic contrast between dorsal and apical was ancient—not that it matters to us in the present problem. [continued on the next page]

relaxed and was replaced first by throat friction and then by no friction at all, the tongue, being no longer constrained to make an alveolar articulation, was free to prolong the articulation of the preceding vowel. In other words, ever since the earliest stages of this change—the drift of /ṣ/ through a slackened sibilant and [h] towards no friction at all but with a better and better approximation to normal voicing—the resonances of this segment were always as like those of the preceding vowel as the remaining frictional articulation would allow. Thus early 12th-century paste /paṣtə/ [pɑṣtə]—with /a/ as [ɑ] instead of [a] because of the retracted [ṣ]—changed phonetically to [pɑhtə] with [ɑ]-colored [h]; this [h] then became voiced with that same vocalic color; and finally its friction was lost, leaving behind another [ɑ] in the same syllable, or in other words a prolongation of the original [ɑ], so that then the word was [pɑ:tə]. This is an instance of what has long been called 'compensatory lengthening'; but it must be regretfully recorded that historical linguists have often posited a compensatory lengthening without being able to set up a step-by-step narrative of how it could have come about. The above is a paradigm of what must always be done to make a compensatory lengthening a valid assumption.

The phonemic structure of the result is another matter entirely. At every stage up to the last, as long as there was any friction the phoneme /ṣ/ was still there; the [h], voiceless and later voiced, was the appropriate allophone of /ṣ/ in this context.* But in the ultimate frictionless stage, the [:] could no longer be classified as an allophone of /ṣ/; it had to be assigned to the vowel system instead. So now a shift had been accomplished from /AṣC/ to /Â:C/, where /A/ represents any low or mid vowel phoneme (and perhaps, at least for a short time, any vowel phoneme at all: see fn. 19), and /Â:/ represents a new retracted and lengthened vowel phoneme independent of the /A/ retained in other words where it had not been followed by /ṣC/. This was the first appearance of long vowels in Old French.

The phonological situation resulting from the replacement of preconsonantal [ṣ] by [:] did not promise to be stable, for the [Â:] class of segments was doubly or redundantly contrasted to the [A] class: once by the vowel quality [^] and again by the length [:]. This redundancy was now removed—quite promptly, we may suppose—by the analogical lengthening of vowels before preserved [ṣ].

Once [ṣ] before a consonant had been replaced by [:], some typical Old French words were face [fatṣə] or [faṣə], pate [patə] 'paw', paste [pɑ:tə], basse [bɑṣə]. The [ɑ] of basse was in complementary distribution both with the [a] of pate and with the [ɑ:] of paste; it had the shortness of one and the quality of the other. For the immediate future of the basse words there were then three possibilities: (1) still another new phoneme, short /ɑ/; (2) abandonment of the quality contrast to the pate vowel, giving [baṣə]; (3) abandonment of the quantity contrast to the paste vowel, giving either (3a) [pɑtə] and [bɑsə] or (3b) [pɑ:tə] and [bɑ:sə]. The first solution would have needlessly increased the number of vowel phonemes; it was not adopted. Solutions 2 and 3a would have run counter to the phonetic drift, which was kept going in the usual way: that is, the dialects and idiolects of higher prestige were more advanced in this direction, and their speakers carried the drift farther along so as to maintain the prestige-marking difference against their pursuers. The vanity factor is needed to explain why phonetic drifts tend to continue in the same direction; the 'inertia' sometimes invoked is a label and not an argument.

After a period of confusion, in which the other word face (from Latin faciam) was replaced by fasse, solution 3b was generally adopted: the [ɑ] of basse was assigned to the phoneme of paste and acquired the appropriate length. That is, the persistence of the lengthening drift meant that the distinctive feature of the /Â:/ class of phonemes was now their quality and not their length: basse was classified according to its quality rather than according to its traditional shortness, and length was made everywhere dependent upon retracted quality. Our list now reads: face /faṣə/ [faṣə] 'face', pate /patə/ [patə] 'paw', paste /pɑtə/ [pɑ:tə], basse /bɑṣə/ [bɑ:sə]. The retracted vowels (phonetically also long) could appear before various consonants essentially excluding only /ṣ/, while the non-retracted vowels (phonetically also short) could appear before various consonants essentially excluding only /ṣ/. Conversely, the two /s/ phonemes, alone in this respect among the consonants, each excluded one of those two categories of vowels before it. Thus this area of the phonology had

There was also an early OF /č/ [tš], and there were voiced partners for /c/ and /č/, making altogether four affricates which now lost their stop component phonetically. Further, there was a /z/ beside the /s/; but there was no opposition between /z/ and /s/ before consonants, where the phonetic change took place that we are now examining: one occurred before a voiced consonant and the other before a voiceless consonant. The /z/ before a consonant faded out, it seems, at the same time as /s/ before a consonant, and similarly by way of voiced h. Its very first weakening was to a [z] so weakly squeezed as to seem like a weakened [d] (as when Southern American English business becomes [bɪdnɪs]), so that it could be written d and gave modern English meddle beside French mêler from mesler. The effects of its disappearance upon the vowel system were identical with the effects of the loss of /s/, and there were the same analogies before preserved /z/, so that including the history and sequels of /z/ here would add nothing to the discussion. Similarly, what is here said of older /c/ is equally valid, mutatis mutandis, for its voiced counterpart. As for /č/ and its voiced counterpart, they are outside this picture, unless we suppose that they lost their stop component because there was room for a new /š/ and /ž/ after preserved /s, z/ had become dorsal at last.

*But see the note appended to this republication.

not been fully stabilized, although the analogical lengthening did represent a certain improvement which we can register by henceforth writing /Â/ instead of the redundant /Â:/. By full stabilization we would have to mean the attainment of a pattern involving no such capricious defects of distribution as those just stated. It seems that no language ever settles down to such a state: in the long run, as fast as asymmetries are eliminated, others creep in. This particular asymmetry could be eliminated, so that any vowel could occur with any sibilant, either by merging /Â/ with /A/ or by merging /ṣ/ with /s̱/. Eventually the latter merger took place (see below), but by that time related asymmetries came in which we can no more than hint at here: to go on and treat them too would involve us in still others, and so on through a complete history of French.

Once the analogical phonetic lengthening had been accomplished, and a clean sweep had been made of all words like basse, it was possible at any time to reinterpret [ɑ:] as /a:/ and make length instead of quality the distinctive feature. This is the pattern that underlies the presumed lengthening effect, upon a preceding vowel, of /s/ from Gallo-Roman /ss/, 'in Middle French' according to current doctrine (much later than when it actually happened), a thing which has hitherto been utterly mysterious because the other Middle French vowel-lengthening consonants were all voiced and because the supposedly identical /s/ from Gallo-Roman /c/ had no such effect. For when Middle French voiced fricatives, palatal lateral and nasal, and /r/ (all followed by vowel), did at last phonetically lengthen preceding vowels, the long and retracted vowel phonemes were ready to receive the new recruits, and the lengthening was accompanied by the appropriate quality change. Citing our examples in modern spelling, we find pauvre then changing from a short open to a long close mid-back vowel, père changing from a short close to a long open mid-front vowel, and âge changing from a short front to a long back low vowel, while rose did not need to change because it already had the long and retracted (close mid-back) vowel of grosse, as would have appeared in the discussion if we had treated earlier OF /z/ along with /s/ (see fn. 20). Since these vowel-lengthening consonants were phonetically quite diverse, aside from all being voiced continuants, we suppose that their effect was primarily a lengthening, so that the quality changes were analogical in that they were occasioned by assigning the lengthened vowels to the established category of long and retracted vowel phonemes. At this time, then, the distinctive feature of the latter was their length, and the retracted qualities (opener in front vowels, closer in back vowels) were secondary.

In contemporary French (ca. 1900, as transcribed by Paul Passy) it is again the quality that is the distinctive feature, and the length is governed by a new rule or set of rules continuing some of the Middle French lengths and adding new ones. The quality as the modern distinctive feature helps us to determine the earlier vowel allophones, since their qualities have been phonemically frozen and preserved for our inspection—except that we are still in the dark about /i/ and /ü/. Presumably these, if they were ever split between the /Â/ and the /A/ class, were merged when /s̱/ and /ṣ/ were merged (see below), under a principle related to the principle of differentiation (Lang. 18.142 [1942]).

In still more recent years we find these vowel-quality oppositions breaking down, seemingly without compensation; but it is too early to see what the upshot of this latest drift will be. Conceivably phonemic length could emerge again as it did before, one more half-cycle of the alternation between phonemic length and phonemic quality which has dominated the development of the French vowel system for a thousand years.

We return now to the sibilants themselves. Earlier OF had both /c/ and /s/ initially before a vowel, intervocalically, and finally after vowel; but before a consonant only /s/ occurred, and after a consonant only /c/ was regular, the still earlier /s/ having fused with a preceding /t/ into /c/ and having been replaced by /c/ after other consonants. With the establishment of the new group of vowel phonemes, the /Â/ category, the opposition between /s̱/ and /ṣ/ became redundant after vowels—the only position where they both could occur except initially. With this lighter functional burdening of the contrast between [s̱] and [ṣ], it is not surprising that one of them became unstable. This was the one which was less distinctly sibilant, less different from the /š/ (from earlier /č/), namely the [ṣ], just as in German. The /ṣ/ phoneme was replaced by zero or by /s̱/ (which we must now relable /s/): at some time much later than its vanishing before consonant, it was replaced by zero at the end of the word[21] (it was probably the first to vanish in the sweeping Middle French loss of final obstruents), and by /s/ elsewhere. We can see that /ṣ/ could have fallen together with /s̱/ into a new /s/ phoneme well before the time of the Middle French vowel lengthening, since its (analogical) lengthening effect was already accomplished in OF; and it is altogether likely that, dialectally at least, there was only one /s/ as early as the 14th century or even earlier. But we can also see that /s̱/ and /ṣ/ left different impressions for a time upon Middle English and MHG, and they may have remained distinct, at least dialectally, into the 16th century: Meigret said he could hear a difference, the /s/ spelled c sounding 'sharper' to his ear than the one spelled ss.[22]

21 We speak as if word-final sounds were followed by pause, because the sandhi-data seem neither to add to the argument nor to detract from it.

22 Communicated in conversation by G. R. Shipman from his unpublished materials. Meigret was a spelling-reformer who tried not to be deceived by orthographic tradition.

We have no evidence that Franco-German comity was the cause of the near simultaneity in the dropping of /ş/ from the phoneme inventory of both languages; but if it was, then presumably the French began it and the Germans imitated them, because in German, as far as we can see, the loss of /ş/ from the list was quite uncompensated, in contrast to the rather thorough compensation in French. At any rate, the conditions for the directions of shift of the /ş/ were about as similar in the two languages as their differences in structure would allow: /ş/ merged with /s̱/ between vowels, and it became less like /s̱/ (going to zero in one language and to /š/ in the other) before consonant, in both French and German. Their falling together between vowels, a phonetically very prominent position in which distinctions among fortis consonants seldom disappear in any language, is something that demands explanation. We can find the explanation only in the redundancy and phonological compensation in French; within German we cannot find it.

Once the dorsal /s̱/ and the apical /ş/ had fallen together into a single /s/ phoneme, each speaker was henceforth free to use either variety, or to use both and distribute them as he might choose—where the word 'choose' can naturally be used only in a Pickwickian sense; see fn. 4. We might speculate that intensified communication, in late medieval and modern times, within the large area of French and High German speakers, would cause the stable medieval phoneme /s̱/ to be succeeded by a statistical predominance of [s̱] as the favorite variety of [s] today, and phoneticians have in fact stated that [s̱] is today even more usual in French and German than it is in English;[23] but our present linguistic procedures cannot attack such a problem, since its mathematics would have to be continuous, instead of discrete and categorical like phonemics.

[23] Wilhelm Viëtor, Elemente der Phonetik des Deutschen, Englischen und Französischen (Leipzig, 1915), quotes numerous authorities and concludes that the sibilants [s, z] are apical in English and usually in North German, but predominantly dorsal in South [High] German and French. The statement for English is certainly too categorical. Incidentally, Viëtor quotes numerous statements about older German and French sibilants, among which views similar to those in this paper are casually included (and rejected), for example that of Wilmanns for MHG.

⟦This paper was composed to be read at the meeting of the Linguistic Society at the end of 1951. The first impulse came from something I had read twenty years before in a history of English by H. C. Wyld—something about French loanwords, I believe. Whatever it was, it kept bothering me repeatedly, each time with accretions from things I had learned of in the meantime, until after ten years I found myself telling my students of MHG that z spelled a dorsal sibilant and s an apical one without quite knowing how I knew it. Then in 1951 I was asked to review Walshe's revision of Wright's MHG Primer, and I got so annoyed at the 'a kind of lisped s' for the z sibilant that I set out to collect the data and formulate the arguments.

When I prepared my paper I knew of no modern language with two genuine [s] phonemes, but André Martinet came to me after the reading and told me about the Basque case (fn. 5). I looked up Basque in the library and got a few test words, including two numerals in sequence ('5' and either '4' or '6' as I remember it); and just when I was telling myself to be sure and run down a Basque speaker to hear them from, a student with a Basque name turned up in a German class of mine, and when I got him to count in Basque, sure enough there were the dorsal and apical sibilants, although he didn't know that the two had different official spellings, being illiterate in his family language. That told me that Larrasquet was off the track with his 'cacuminal' label and that Martinet had put me on to the real thing. It also caused me to class Martinet among the dozens if not hundreds of casual sources not requiring footnote acknowledgement. His response to this mistake was to use my line of argument for French, with all due and polite acknowledgement, in the chapter on sibilants in his Economie des changements phonétiques, even making it seem that he had picked up the whole thing from me, although I have every sort of reason to believe that he had worked it all out independently before 1951: I had gotten into print first, and that was that. This way of doing things is also an advantage to the readers: by adopting an already-published line of argument as long as it does not conflict with one's own ideas, even though it differs in ways that can be left unmentioned, one obviates confusion and makes a valuable contribution to scientific solidarity.

The starred (*) note after fn. 20 refers to this: In 1952 I had not realized that OF probably had one other phoneme, the /h/ 'aspirated h' which today is only a ghost of a phoneme, a morphophoneme which forbids liaison, to which the [h] from /ş/ before consonant then certainly belonged; and further, I had not yet learned to properly value the Trager theory of postvocalic /h/. This, then, is another example of Franco-German comity: French, like English and (?) MHG, has postvocalic /h/ in the phonetic guise of length, this time with retraction as a counterpart of the modern English centering. The reader can work out the details by rewriting the next seven paragraphs of my paper: it will turn out, for instance, that there was not alternation of phonemic length and phonemic quality, but alternating preponderance of length and of retraction as the distinctive feature of the postvocalic /h/, and the modern breakdown can be related to the new and uncertain status of 'aspirated h'.

I believe that I owe this new insight to Trager's somehow indirectly conveying to me a suggestion that my paper could be improved in that direction.⟧

THE METHOD OF DESCRIPTIVE MORPHOLOGY

FLOYD G. LOUNSBURY
Oneida Verb Morphology
Yale University Publications
In Anthropology No. 48—1953

In morphological analysis the two principal operations are the establishment of the basic formal units and the analysis of formal structure in terms of these units. These two aspects of analysis are currently known as morphemics and tactics respectively.

1.1. THE ESTABLISHMENT OF UNITS

Morphemics, in turn, also involves two operations. The first of these is the breaking up of forms into their minimal meaningful parts, while the second is the identification of semantically equivalent parts of this order. These two operations are known as segmentation and grouping.

Two general approaches to these problems may be recognized in the history of modern linguistics. One of these, the older of the two, has sometimes been known as the morphophonemic approach, because of the so-called 'morphophonemes' (see section 1.1.2) which are sometimes employed instead of ordinary phonemes in the identification of morphemes. This usage is confusing, however, for the term has other more common meanings in contemporary descriptive linguistics (Hockett, 1947: 342 ((241)), 1950:63 ((315)); Bloch, 1947:414 ((251)); Wells 1949:99–100). We shall call it, instead, the method of internal reconstruction, for whether the orientation be historical or avowedly synchronic, it is usually based on an operation which is similar to that of reconstruction from internal evidence. The other approach, which is the newer of the two, is the method of morpheme alternants.

We consider first the possible procedures under the method of morpheme alternants and then the method of internal reconstruction. Finally, we select a procedure which seems best suited to the task at hand.

1.1.1. The method of morpheme alternants

Following the method of morpheme alternants one divides or 'cuts' forms of actual utterances into minimal segments, or sequences of phonemes, to which it is possible to assign meanings. ('Sequence' is to be understood as including cases of one or of no phonemes, as well as of more than one, and also as including both continuous and discontinuous types.)[1] Such phoneme sequences or form-segments are known in current usage as morphs. Phonemically different morphs which have the same meaning (or the same range of different meanings sharing a common feature), and which are in complementary distribution, are said to constitute a class called a morpheme and are known as morpheme alternants, or allomorphs, of that morpheme.[2] The common meaning of the allomorphs is defined as the meaning of the morpheme.

The place to make a cut between two morphs may be obvious or obscure, and the business of segmenting may be correspondingly easy or difficult according as the data permit of but one manner of interpretation or of several. In agglutinating languages the matter is obvious and simple; it is settled immediately by the very nature of the data. A cut between two morphs can be made only in one place; a morpheme in such a language has in general but a single allomorph. In languages of the fusional type[3] this is not characteristically the case; the place to make the cut may often be decided upon only with difficulty and to some extent arbitrarily, and morphemes in general have many allomorphs. The Iroquoian languages are of this type.

The basic technique employed in segmenting forms is that of varying some part of the total meaning of a form while holding the remainder constant, and noting the correlated variable segments of the resulting forms as opposed to the constant portions of those forms. Repeated applications of the technique lead to irreducible segments of the forms. In agglutinating languages this simple technique of isolating constant from variable is sufficient and yields clear-cut segments which account for the totality of any form. In a fusional language if one seeks to arrive at constant segments in such a manner, conflicts arise in the placing of the cuts. One comparison of forms suggests one placement, while another comparison suggests another. Often, in fact, no constant segment can be isolated at all which corresponds to a given constant meaning. Situations of this kind often permit of more than one solution according to different manners of selecting and grouping environments. The locations of the cuts are not always uniquely determined.

[1] Cf. Harris's discussion of discontinuous morphemes (Harris, 1945).

[2] Cf. Hockett (1947) and Harris (1942). Hockett replaces the condition of complementary distribution by that of 'non-contrastive' distribution, so as to allow for grouping into a single morpheme such morphs as are in free variation in certain environments and in complementation otherwise. Here, however, we have avoided admitting allomorphs to be in free variation or in any distribution that involves it. It is too difficult to be sure of complete sameness of meaning.

[3] 'Agglutinating' and 'fusional' are used here in the senses in which Sapir used the terms (Sapir, 1921, Chap. VI).

It is agreed that an analysis of a linguistic form into segments must account for all the phonemes in that form.[4] In the manner of accounting for all the phonemes, different policies may be adopted. There are four possibilities. (α) One may decide that every phoneme shall belong to an allomorph of one and only one morpheme. Segmentation is carried as far as possible, and such morphemes (present in meaning) as have not been accounted for in the resulting segments are said to be represented by zero allomorphs. This is the convention followed by Bloch in his treatment of English verb inflection (Bloch, 1947). (β) One might instead proceed on a different policy, one which might be stated in the form: every phoneme shall belong to an allomorph of at least one morpheme. This allows for the possibility of a phoneme belonging either to an allomorph of only one morpheme or simultaneously to allomorphs of two (or more) different morphemes; i.e., it allows of overlapping morphs. A special case of such overlapping morphs is that in which they overlap completely. Such coincident morphs have been called portmanteau morphs by Hockett (1947:333 ⟨⟨236⟩⟩).[5] Another special case of overlapping morphs is that in which the whole of one coincides with a part of another. Morphs in this relationship we call included morphs and including morphs, respectively. (γ) Another possibility is the following: every phoneme shall belong to an allomorph of not more than one phoneme. As with (α) this does not allow of overlapping morphs or of portmanteau morphs in the analysis of a form. But it allows of empty morphs (Hockett, 1947:333 ⟨⟨236⟩⟩), which (α) and (β) do not; i.e., some phonemes are isolated as morphs which do not belong to any morpheme. This is often a convenience, as it cuts down the number of different allomorphs which must be carried for various given morphemes. Taken care of in this way are phonemes which have often been described (in a different methodology) as 'inorganic elements', 'meaningless elements', 'epenthetic phonemes', etc. (δ) The final alternative policy is one which allows of all the possibilities, viz., that a phoneme may be part of a morph which belongs to zero or to one or to more than one morpheme. Under this rule we have leeway to make use of empty morphs and overlapping or portmanteau morphs as well as of the ordinary ones and zero morphs.

According to the policy adopted, different solutions of the same data are possible. We may speak of α-morphs, β-morphs, etc., according as they result from the application of policy α, or of policy β, etc. The choice of treatment accorded to any set of linguistic forms must be dictated by the nature of the case in hand, by the criterion of simplicity of final total solution, and by the particular purpose for which the analysis is being made (e.g., descriptive, historical, pedagogical, etc.).

1.1.2. The method of internal reconstruction

This method by-passes the problem of segmenting actual forms of a language of our type. In effect it sets up a fictitious agglutinating analog, such that a one-way transformation from the analog to the actual utterances is possible, and it segments that instead. This is a much easier job of segmentation—as easy as segmenting the forms of an actually agglutinating language. Forms of the analog are sometimes called morphophonemic forms (as contrasted with phonemic forms, which are actually occurring forms of the language). The relation of actual forms to those of the analog is expressed in transformation formulas called morphophonemic rules.[6] Different morphophonemic rules often have different domains of applicability within forms. The domain of applicability must be specified for each morphophonemic rule. Some linguists put this in a separate qualifying statement in connection with the rule. Others have built it into the orthography used in representing forms of the analog (Bloomfield, 1939; Hockett, 1948). In the latter case, separate morphophoneme symbols are set up to distinguish orthographically the instances where a given rule applies from those where it does not.

Three different conceptions of morphophonemic forms can be discerned in linguistic works. Some writers have explicitly ascribed to their morphophonemic units only the status of fictions devised by themselves for the facilitation of description. Such a treatment is Bloomfield's in his Menomini morphophonemics (1939) or Hockett's in his Potawatomi (1948). Others appear to have regarded them rather as 'ideal' morphemes, and true units of the language, which, however, when put together into constructions have changes wrought upon them so that they and their combinations are 'actualized' or 'realized' in an altered form. This attitude is implicit in many of the contributions to the Handbook of American Indian languages (Boas, ed., 1911, 1922, 1933). With this type of conceptualization, instead of morphophonemic rules we have 'phonological processes', as in the works of many of Sapir's students, or 'euphonic laws', as in some of Boas' works. Still others explicitly or implicitly consider their units to be historical prototypes of morphemes, and then we have 'phonetic laws' rather than morphophonemic rules

[4] Hockett's principle of 'total accountability' (Hockett, 1947:332 ⟨⟨235⟩⟩).

[5] Hockett, in discussing 'cuts' (1947:322⟨⟨230⟩⟩), mentioned the possibility of overlapping morphs, but in the section 'Morph and Morpheme' (1947:331 ff. ⟨⟨235 ff.⟩⟩) they are not included except for the special case of portmanteaus.

[6] Sometimes a complete application of this technique may not be possible and there is left over a residue of irregularities of unique types which cannot be accounted for by morphophonemic rules of this kind. Such are Bloomfield's 'morpholexical alternants' (Bloomfield, 1939).

or phonological processes. Such a treatment is Barbeau's analysis in his Classification of Iroquoian radicals (1915), where one of the purposes is historical and where internal evidence is made use of for this purpose. Some works show a mixing of the latter two points of view.

1.1.3. The relation of morphophonemic forms to historical forms

Morphophonemic constructs cannot be said to represent a previous state of the language. Although strictly agglutinating languages doubtless have existed (the Cuzco dialect of Quechua is nearly such a one) there are no grounds for supposing that every language has descended from such a forebear simply because it is possible to construct an agglutinating morphophonemic analog to it. But that the morphophonemic transformation formulas set up often correspond to actual historical sound changes of some variety cannot be doubted. Such an assumption is the basis for historical reconstruction from internal evidence.[7] The reason for the invalidity in considering morphophonemic constructs as historical forms lies in the fact that the morphophonemic rules correspond to historical changes of different types, which occurred during widely different periods of the history of the language. Some correspond to sound changes that have affected the phonetic pattern of the language as a whole and are of the type known as phonetic laws. Others correspond to analogical changes that never of themselves altered the phonetic pattern at large, but which were confined to specific morpheme combinations. Some represent changes (of either variety) which are relatively recent in history, whereas others represent changes which are, in comparison, extremely ancient. The net result of these circumstances is the differential applicability of the morphophonemic rules which can be set up. Some are of general applicability in going from morphophonemic construct to actual forms of a language and describe the so-called 'automatic' type of morphophonemic alternation. They express the manner of accommodation of morphemes and their combinations to the phonemic pattern of the language. Thus, the rules

(1) hCh > Ch (where C is any consonant), and

(2) $C_1C_2h > C_1C_2$ (C_1 and C_2 = any consonants),

and the rules

(3) VC?X > VCe?X (where C is any consonant, V any vowel, and X is word boundary or a consonant), and

(4) $V_1C?V_2 > V_1CV_2?V_2$ (where C is any consonant, and V_1 and V_2 are any two vowels, same or different),

in Oneida are of the automatic or general type for that language and are necessary conditions for the existence of its phonemic cluster pattern (see section 3.2). On the other hand, the rules

(5) a + i > ʌ, and

(6) (w)a(?) + wa > u,

and the rules

(7) ? + w >ʾh, and

(8) ? + y > ?

apply only to the domains of the pre-pronominal and pronominal prefixes and are not necessitated by the phonemic pattern of the language. The historical correspondences to these eight morphophonemic rules are various. Comparative evidence shows that the first four of these correspond to phonetic laws, though the changes were not all contemporaneous. The first two are among the changes which distinguish Oneida from Mohawk; the third and fourth are among those which distinguish Oneida and Mohawk from some of the other Northern Iroquoian languages. Comparative evidence from the extant or documented Iroquoian languages sheds no light on rules (5) and (6). If these rules correspond to real historical changes (and we assume that they do), then those changes are more ancient than the differentiation of the languages of the Iroquoian family. Their antiquity may be assumed to account for the limited domain of applicability of the morphophonemic rules to which they correspond: they would have ceased to be operative by the time later layers of formation developed. As for rule (7), comparative evidence confirms what internal evidence suggests, that it corresponds to an analogical change of very specific localization in the morphology. Rule (8) is open to more than one historical interpretation.

1.1.4. Validity of the methods

One may raise the question as to which of the methods outlined above is the more realistic procedure. It may be argued that the method of morpheme alternants is the more realistic procedure, since it deals with the segmentation of actual utterances rather than with constructs once removed from reality. This may indeed be considered a point in its favor. But opposing this is an equally legitimate contention that the resulting very discrete localizations of meaning associated with some of the procedures under the method of morpheme alternants are, or may be, highly unrealistic. We may approach the matter through an example, viz., the possible analyses of the Oneida prefix u- under the method of morpheme alternants.

The prefix u- occurs only with a certain class of bases (a-stems). E.g., compare:

katkáthos 'I see it' wa?katkátho? 'I saw it'

watkáthos 'she sees it' utkátho? 'she saw it'

Associated with its occurrence are the meanings which we designate as 'past tense' and 'third person singular feminine'. The procedure of α- or γ-morphemics requires one of the following two solutions:

'past tense' = u-, '3 sg F' = zero morph; or

'past tense' = zero morph, '3 sg F' = u-.

The procedure of β- or δ-morphemics allows of the solution:

[7] Cf. Hoenigswald (1944, 1946).

'past tense' = u-, '3 sg F' = u-,

and one would mark the two listings of u- in some way, e.g. [u]-, to show that as morphs they are one, constitute an identity, and are non-additive. (The solution according to the method of internal reconstruction would be 'past tense' = WAʔ-, '3 sg F' = WA-; WAʔ + WA > u.) It may be argued that β-/δ-morphemics gives the more realistic localization of meaning in this case; for it remains a fact that it is the occurrence of the morph u- with which both meanings are associated, since the occurrence of a zero morph cannot otherwise be perceived than through the occurrence of the morph which implicates it.[8]

1.1.5. Choice of a method

The method of morpheme alternants is chosen here, and of the possible alternatives under this method, that which has been referred to as δ-morphemics is to be followed. This allows us to deal always with actual phonemic forms, and it permits more realistic localizations of meaning.

The following rules will govern segmentation. (1) A zero morph is never set up when the meaning to be assigned would be implicated by the selection of a particular allomorph of some one other morpheme. In such cases a portmanteau or included morph is set up instead. (2) An empty morph is set up only when a given phoneme or phoneme sequence would otherwise have to be taken as identical fractions of the allomorphs of two or more different morphemes. (3) Use of the principle of overlapping morphs is restricted to the special cases where the whole of one coincides with the whole or with a part of another, i.e., it is restricted to portmanteau and included morphs. The more general case of partially overlapping morphs, which the procedure of δ-morphemics permits, is not utilized because of practical difficulties of notation. The employment of portmanteau and included morphs is sufficient to avoid zero morphs implicated solely by the selection of a particular allomorph of another morpheme.

1.2. THE ANALYSIS OF STRUCTURE

The grammatical structure of a language may be described in terms of its morphemes and their rules of combination. The latter include rules of order, of selection, and of derivation. This study deals not with the whole of grammatical structure but with only a single level within it, the morphology of the verb. This limitation simplifies somewhat the formulation of a method for describing structure, since the processes of deriving higher levels of structure are eliminated from consideration.

1.2.1. Morphemes

A morpheme, in the method of morpheme alternants, was defined above as a class of phonemically different minimal meaningful segments, or morphs, which are in complementary distribution and have the same meaning (or the same range of different meanings sharing a common feature). These are the allomorphs of the morpheme. In the method of

8 We have used the word 'implicate' in accordance with C. W. Morris's usage in his Foundations of a Theory of Signs (1938). He defines three types of sign-relations (or as we might call them, three types of meaning): signs 'implicate' other signs, 'designate' or 'denote' their referents, and 'express' their interpretants. These correspond to the syntactic, the semantic, and the pragmatic dimensions of sign-functioning or semiosis.

Referring to the possible solutions of the Oneida prefix u- which are given above, we say in the α-/γ-solution that the morph u- is an allomorph of one morpheme such as implies the presence of, or implicates, a zero allomorph of the other morpheme. (It implicates also a certain class of bases, viz., the a-stems.) In the β-/δ-solution, on the other hand, we have a sign which is a sign simultaneously of two designata. As long as we must depend upon semantics, i.e., upon sign-to-designatum relations, at certain crucial points in linguistic theory, it seems well to avoid situations like the α-/γ-solution whenever possible and to be as specific as possible in the localization of meanings.

The problem is not thus easily disposed of, however. Implication of this type happens not only to zero morphs; the occurrence of any non-final morph in an utterance implicates in some manner another morph or morpheme or class of morphemes. This is a logical consequence of structure in language. One way of viewing it is as follows: at the point of initiation of an utterance there is linguistically no limitation on the 'direction' that the utterance may take, except that it remain within the universe of forms of the given language. After the occurrence of the first morph there has already been a great reduction in the possible 'moves' from that point on: a class of forms smaller than the total universe of forms of the language is already implicated. So, after the occurrence of each additional morph, the range of future possibilities is successively greatly narrowed, and the end can often be guessed, or may even be uniquely determined, before the final morph of a word, or word of a sentence, has been reached. From this point of view the problem of localization of meaning is more complex. In Oneida, in utterance-final forms of words, a final morpheme or two of a word is sometimes represented by a zero morph. There are cases where even the verb root is zero in utterance-final forms. Such words are takná·jih. 'give me the kettle', jíten. 'let's go (you and I)', jítow. 'let's go (we, plural inclusive)'. (Compare the non-final forms: takná·jyu, jítne, jítwe, verb roots -u 'give' and -e 'go'. The -i- of takná·jih. and the -e- and -o- of jíten. and jítow. are automatic empty morphs, phonologically determined, and in no way dependent upon the verb roots -u and -e.) Whatever type of analysis we employ, we have zero morphs, i.e., nothing, for these verb roots in the utterance-final forms. We may ask what then is the locus in the forms, or for the hearer, of the meanings 'give' and 'go' in these examples? The answer is that it is in the cumulative implication of the other morphs. It remains a fact that the linguist's allocation of a meaning corresponds to only a part of the native hearer's source of derivation of a meaning, and the correspondence is considerably less close for fusional languages than for agglutinating languages.

internal reconstruction a morpheme is a minimal meaningful segment of the constructed agglutinating analog to actual linguistic forms. In both cases they are constructs. In general it is important to remember this, though in working with a strictly agglutinating language, where a construct (of either kind) always or nearly always coincides with a single segment of actual linguistic forms, the point tends to lose its significance. The allomorphs of a morpheme of the first variety, or the modified actualizations of a morpheme of the second variety, may be designated the phonemic forms of the morpheme.

A morpheme is said to occur when one of its phonemic forms occurs. Statements describing the occurrences of morphemes constitute the portion of a grammar called tactics (Hockett, 1947:321 ((229)). This includes both of the conventional divisions of grammar known as morphology and syntax. Tactics is not concerned with the phonemic forms of morphemes, whether they are constant or variable. Only the fact that some one of the phonemic forms occurs for a given morpheme is important; the question of 'which one' is not relevant. Such matters are regarded as sub-morphemic; the morphemic structure of forms can be described apart from their phonemic forms.

1.2.2. Order

A linguistic form may contain meaningful features that are not accounted for by the morphemes present. These are meaningful features of order (Bloomfield, 1933: 162-3).

In many utterances a given morpheme occurs more than once. Also, the relative order of occurrence of two given morphemes is sometimes different in different utterances, and sometimes this difference in order is meaningful. Within words, however, these two states of affairs are found much less frequently than in larger utterances such as phrases and sentences. It is possible, in fact, in the analysis of morphology, to proceed initially as if any given morpheme occurred only once, and as if the order of occurrence were fixed and therefore meaningless. That is, the method chosen may be one which is adapted to these conditions, and the few exceptions to these conditions may be given special treatment. It is, of course, desirable to have as general a method as possible, but it is also appropriate to recognize special cases within it. Thus, for the analysis of Iroquoian verb morphology we can choose a method which is a simple special case subsumable under a more general and complex method adapted to the analysis of grammar as a whole, to syntax as well as morphology. The basic method is that of the positional analysis of mutually substitutable morphemes. It is a special case of the more general method of positional analysis of mutually substitutable sequences of morphemes.

As a preliminary definition of a position class we may say that it is a class of morphemes which are mutually exclusive and which, when they occur, always occur in the same relative order with respect to other morphemes.[9] But there are two types of situations sometimes found in morphology which render this definition insufficiently flexible for general use. One of them is that sometimes different allomorphs of the same morpheme occur in different positions with respect to other morphemes. In Iroquoian this is infrequent, but it does happen. One way out of this difficulty would be to redefine the morpheme so that even if two morphs were in complementary distribution and had the same meaning, they would still not be considered members of the same morpheme unless they occurred in the same relative order with respect to other morphemes. The question is whether meaningless differences of order should be treated in the same manner as significant phonemic differences between allomorphs, or whether, in view of the usefulness of order as a dimension of analysis, differences of order might be put on a par with differences of meaning for distinguishing morphemes. A system can be developed on either basis; but current practise is to disregard differences of order unless they have contrastive value. Nevertheless, we should like to use sequential order as our chief dimension of analysis in this study, both because it is a convenient one in dealing with morphology, and because it furnishes an important tool in comparative morphology. A satisfactory way out, one which allows us to stay within our present system but still make use of position classes based upon order, is to define sub-classes of allomorphs within the morpheme on the basis of order, and to incorporate these into our definition of position class. So we define a morpheme partial as a sub-class consisting of the allomorphs of a morpheme which occur in the same relative order with respect to other morphemes or morpheme partials. And we can then redefine position class as a class

[9] It is to be noted that our position class is not the same as Harris's position class (1946, 1947). In our definitions position is always the relative order in which a morpheme occurs; in Harris's, position is a selected environment of other morphemes with which a morpheme may occur. Our classes will be order classes; his are substitution classes in which order is a subordinate consideration. When structures described in terms of the two different types of classes are put in the form of geometrical charts, certain differences become readily apparent. His chart represents certain features of selection in a convenient manner, which ours can represent only clumsily. On the other hand, our type of chart is better adapted for displaying features of order, while his sometimes necessitates violating order, a shortcoming which he comments on in his Delaware restatement (1947: 186, fn. 23). Our reason for emphasizing order rather than selection, and for developing a correspondingly different method, becomes apparent at the close of the section headed Selection.

of morphemes or morpheme partials which are mutually exclusive and which, when they occur, always occur in the same relative order with respect to other morphemes or morpheme partials.

The other of the two situations referred to is that in some cases a morph may be discontinuous (i.e., composed of a discontinuous sequence of phonemes) and hence cannot be confined within a single position with respect to other morphemes or morpheme partials but must of necessity occupy more than one position. To meet such cases we may define a morph fraction as any of the continuous or unbroken parts of a discontinuous morph, and similarly an allomorph fraction as any of the continuous or unbroken parts of a discontinuous allomorph of a morpheme. Then we can extend the application of the term morpheme partial and define it as a sub-class within a morpheme, consisting of allomorphs or allomorph fractions which occur in the same relative order with respect to other morphemes or morpheme partials. A new definition of position class is not necessary at this point, since the redefinition of morpheme partial is sufficient to accommodate the analysis of discontinuous allomorphs.

1.2.3. Derivation

The conditions of single occurrence and fixed order of morphemes within words are so prevalent in the polysynthetic languages known to the writer that they are tentatively assumed to have general validity. When they are found to be violated, it is assumed that the form involves more than one level of construction, and that a derived polymorphemic unit is present, which substitutes for a single morpheme within the pattern. This assumption receives substantiation when the semantics is examined, for in all such cases which have come to light, semantic specialization has been found.

Hence we may distinguish between purely linear constructions on a single level, and constructions in depth, involving successive levels, one within the other. The former or linear type is highly elaborated in Iroquoian morphology. For lack of a more suitable term we may extend the application of an older term and call it inflection. The second type, involving constructions within constructions, is confined to two positions in the Iroquoian morphological pattern. It may properly be called derivation.

The more general method must be one which can handle derivations as well as linear constructions. It may still be a method of position classes based upon order. The position class, however, must be redefined so as to include not only morphemes or morpheme partials, but also sequences of morphemes which, as units, satisfy the same conditions as are required of single morphemes.[10] A complete development of this method is not necessary for our present purpose. What has already been said is sufficient to indicate the treatment of such types of derivation as may occur.

1.2.4. Selection.

Besides order of morphemes and manner of derivation of complex units in morphology, it is necessary to give the rules of selection which govern the combination of units. A positional chart of morphemes, for example, tells us only that if or when a certain combination of morphemes occurs, the morphemes will be in such and such a relative order, but it does not help in predicting what combinations of morphemes will occur unless indications of selection, as well as of order, are included with the chart.

The term selection is used to refer to phenomena on two different levels. On the submorphemic level one speaks of the selection of alternants, or allomorphs, of a morpheme, where the choice is governed by the phonemic or morphemic environments in which they occur. On the morphemic level one also speaks of selection, but here it refers to limitations upon combination of morphemes one with another. We shall be concerned with selection on both levels, but in general they will be treated separately.

Two kinds of selection may be recognized among morphemes: exclusions and linkages. Of exclusions, two types may be distinguished: those between morphemes belonging to the same position class, and those between members of different position classes. Linkages are of necessity between members of different classes. Further special types of linkage are mentioned below.

Morphemes occurring in different positions in the verb structure may be mutually exclusive because of incompatible meanings or for less 'logical' reasons. Thus, in Oneida the cislocative morpheme t- 'hither', of position class 6, is mutually exclusive with the translocative morpheme y- 'yonder', of position class 2. Similarly, the aorist tense morpheme partials w- and -a-, which are of position classes 3 and 7 respectively, are mutually exclusive with the future tense morpheme ʌ- of position class 5. These are examples of mutually incompatible meanings and of exclusions between members of different position classes.

On the other hand, mutual exclusions between members of the same position class are not necessarily or even typically cases of contradictory or logically exclusive meanings. Thus, the cislocative morpheme t- 'hither', of class 6, and the iterative morpheme s- 'again, re-, back', also of class 6, are mutually exclusive not because of incompatible meanings (note that the translocative, class 2, occurs freely with the iterative), but only because the structure of the verb is such that they happen to occupy the same position with respect to other morphemes and combine with them in the same way, and

[10] This is Harris's method (Harris, 1946) except for the priority here given to order of occurrence.

in a way which does not allow their combining with each other.

The simplest type of linkage is that of a morpheme with a morpheme, i.e., such that if one morpheme occurs another must also. A one-way linkage of this type is such that if morpheme A occurs then morpheme B must also occur, but that the converse is not true, i.e., morpheme B may occur without morpheme A. Two-way linkages between single morphemes might be considered a possibility, but the only examples we have of two-way linkages are those between morpheme partials which are better considered as fractions of discontinuous morphs. Other possible types of linkage are those of a morpheme to a class, of a class to a class, etc. Further contrasting types are internal and external linkages. For example, in the latter case a morpheme in a word may be linked in occurrence with another morpheme (or with any one of a class of morphemes) elsewhere in the phrase or sentence but outside of the given word.

We have chosen the positional chart as our device for representing as concisely as possible the features of order in the verb morphology. Features of selection are in general less conveniently represented. Cases of exclusions between members of adjacent position classes are represented very simply in the geometry of the chart. For representing other exclusions and linkages a system of indexing may be used, or the information can be given separately.

Comparative evidence shows that in Iroquoian morphology, at least, features of selection have been much more mutable and variable than features of order. The latter, in fact, have been immutable except for the cases of obsolescence and coalescence of positions, which are reducible to changes in features of selection; and cases of innovation through reinterpretation of segments of older morphemes brought about by severe phonological change and analogical creation. Coincident with these facts are the ease and clarity with which features of order may be represented and the relatively unsatisfactory portrayal of features of selection. Many features of selection, such as those connected with individual members of the noun-root and verb-root positions in the morphology, cannot be portrayed in our morphological charts but must be relegated to a separate lexicon. These coincidences may be advantageous or disadvantageous, depending on one's problem. Since structural features of order appear to be more enduring than those of selection, phonemic shape, and meanings of morphemes,[11] they furnish a convenient framework for description and comparison.

[11]Compare Sapir's opinions in Chapter IX of his Language (1921).

BIBLIOGRAPHY

⟦Page 111 of the original publication, omitting items not cited above. When reference is made above to the whole of an item, there is no cross-reference page-number in ⟪ ⟫ to show that it appears in this volume; such cross-references are inserted only when needed to locate an exact page in the present republication.⟧

Barbeau, C. M., 1915: Classification of Iroquoian Radicals with Subjective Pronominal Prefixes (Canada Department of Mines, Geological Survey, Memoir 46, Ottawa).

Bloch, Bernard, 1947: English verb inflection (Lang. 23.399–418) ⟪243⟫.

Bloomfield, Leonard, 1933: Language (New York).

———, 1939: Menomini morphophonemics (TCLP 8.105–15).

Boas, Franz (ed.), 1911: Handbook of American Indian Languages, vol. 1 (Bureau of American Ethnology, Bulletin 40, pt. 1, Washington).

———, 1922: [the same] vol. 2 (the same, pt. 2).

———, 1933: [the same] vol. 3 (New York).

———, 1940: [the same] vol. 4, pt. 1 (New York). ⟦this 1940 item, not used above, listed here for clarity⟧

Harris, Zellig S., 1942: Morpheme alternants in linguistic analysis (Lang. 18.169–80) ⟪109⟫.

———, 1945: Discontinuous morphemes (Lang. 21.121–7).

———, 1946: From morpheme to utterance (Lang. 22.161–83) ⟪142⟫.

———, 1947: Structural restatements (IJAL, 13.47–58, 13.175–86).

Hockett, Charles F., 1947: Problems of morphemic analysis (Lang. 23.321–43) ⟪229⟫.

———, 1948: Potawatami (IJAL 14.1–10, 14.63–73, 14.139–49, 14.213–25).

———, 1950: Peiping morphophonemics (Lang. 26.63–85) ⟪315⟫.

Hoenigswald, Henry M., 1944: Internal reconstruction (SIL 2.78–87).

———, 1946: Sound change and linguistic structure (Lang. 22.138–43) ⟪139⟫.

Morris, Charles W., 1938: Foundation of a Theory of Signs (International Encyclopedia of Unified Science, vol. 1, no. 2, Chicago).

Sapir, Edward, 1921: Language: An Introduction to the Study of Speech (New York).

Wells, Rulon S., 1949: Automatic alternation (Lang. 25.99–116).

TWO MODELS OF GRAMMATICAL DESCRIPTION

CHARLES F. HOCKETT
Word 10.210-31—1954

1.1 By a 'model of grammatical description' is meant a frame of reference within which an analyst approaches the grammatical phase of a language and states the results of his investigations. In one sense, there are as many models as there are different descriptions ('grammars' in the sense of monographs). But in another, and very important, sense, most grammatical descriptions seem to cluster about a relatively small number of relatively distinct models; it is with these archetypical frames of reference that we are concerned here.

The bulk of the present paper was written between 1949 and 1951; at that time, the writer was under the erroneous impression that there were principally just two archetypes to be dealt with. If we confine our attention to monographs produced in the United States in the past half-century, this impression is not grossly inaccurate. One of the 'two models' which is well represented within those spatial and temporal limits is what we shall call item and process, or IP for short; the other we shall call item and arrangement, or IA. In most of what follows we shall have occasion to mention only these two.

But that limitation constitutes a defect in the paper—a defect which was recognized by the writer in 1951, and because of which the paper was long held unpublished. Quite apart from minor variants of IP or IA, or models that might be invented tomorrow, there is one model which is clearly distinct from either IA or IP, and which is older and more respectable than either. This is the word and paradigm (WP) model, the traditional framework for the discussion of Latin, Greek, Sanskrit, and a good many more modern familiar languages. It will not do to shrug this frame of reference off with the comment that it is obviously insufficiently general, incapable of organizing efficiently the facts of a language like Chinese. As yet we have no completely adequate model: WP deserves the same consideration here given to IP and IA. The writer offers his apologies for not having worked such consideration of WP into the present paper. However, lack of time prevented this, and the discussion as it stands may nevertheless be of some value.

1.2 As between IP and IA, the former is older. The key term in IP is 'process', as is evident from the following characterization by Harris (1944, p. 199):[1] "The difference between two partially similar forms is frequently described... as a process which yields one form out of the other. Thus, when bases or themes have several vocalic forms, the various forms are said to be the result of vowel-change processes operating upon the base or theme. The difference between a base and a base-plus-suffix is described as a result of the process of suffixation. This is a traditional manner of speaking, especially in American Indian grammar. It has, of course, nothing to do with historical change or process through time: it is merely process through the configuration, moving from one to another or larger part of the pattern."

Rigorous work with historical linguistics, as everyone knows, preceded almost all rigorous descriptive work; the carry-over of 'process' terminology from historical discussion is natural enough. In this country Boas (1911, pp. 27 f.) established IP, and Sapir (1921, esp. ch. 4) elaborated it; the descriptive chapters of Sapir's Language are cast entirely in this mold. Grammars written largely under Sapir's aegis, such as Newman's Yokuts (1944; the specific aim of Harris's remarks quoted above), still stand as examples of IP in action.

1.3 As a further example of IP, consider the following paragraph from Haas's shorter treatment of Tunica (1946):

> The Tunica language is mildly synthetic in structure. In its technique of synthesis it is for the most part agglutinative, but it also employs a limited amount of fusion. The morphological processes used are juxtaposition, affixation (prefixation, infixation, and suffixation), reduplication, and suppletion. Of these, prefixation and suffixation, particularly the latter, are exploited to a greater extent than are the other processes.

There is no question about the meaningfulness of this characterization. Whether it is particularly relevant, either to a description of Tunica or to a proper placing of Tunica in the gamut of linguistic types, and whether, relevant or not, it is effectively phrased, are other matters.

1.4 The younger model, IA, has been formulated at least in part because of a feeling of dissatisfaction with the 'moving-part' or 'historical' analogy implicit in IP. At the very least, these analogies seem to imply the necessity of making certain decisions in a possibly arbitrary way. Critics of IP would prefer to circumvent such decisions altogether.

For example (cf. Hockett 1947a, pp. 282-3), if it be said that the English past-tense form baked is

[1] Reference is made by author and year of publication to the bibliography at the end of the article.

'formed' from bake by a 'process' of 'suffixation', then no matter what disclaimer of historicity is made, it is impossible not to conclude that some kind of priority is being assigned to bake, as against either baked or the suffix. And if this priority is not historical, what is it?[2] Supporters of IP have not answered that question satisfactorily.

Another objection which might be raised to IP as exemplified in the above quotation from Haas is that the wording tends toward personalization and teleology. The Tunica language 'uses' or 'employs' various techniques; it 'exploits' some of these more than others. The use of the term 'the Tunica language' as a subject with such verbs is personalization; the use of such verbs seems to imply teleology—the language has a purpose to accomplish, and it makes use of such-and-such means to the end. If any entity 'uses' the techniques, it is the speakers, not the language. This objection is pointless unless it can be shown that such a way of speaking leads its users into errors of fact. So long as it is merely a 'way of speaking', easier than some other way because English is an Indo-European language, we cannot object.

1.5 The essence of IA is to talk simply of things and the arrangements in which those things occur (Harris 1944, section 5, esp. end of page 203; Bloch 1947, introductory remarks; Harris 1945b; Harris 1942). One assumes that any utterance in a given language consists wholly of a certain number of minimum grammatically relevant elements, called morphemes, in a certain arrangement relative to each other. The structure of the utterance is specified by stating the morphemes and the arrangement. The pattern of the language is described if we list the morphemes and the arrangements in which they occur relative to each other in utterances—appending statements to cover the phonemic shapes which appear in any occurrent combination.[3]

The matter is not quite so simple as that. Some of the complexities will concern us later. Here it must be noted that there is some indeterminacy even in the apparently trivial matter of deciding what to subsume as 'item' and what to call 'arrangement'. In English, intonation phonemes can be taken as comprising parts of morphemes just as do vowels and consonants. There is then a set of morphemes composed entirely of intonation phonemes, and such intonation morphemes occur, not before or after other kinds of morphemes, but simultaneously with them. In Come here!, the segmental form and the /(2)31/ intonation morpheme occur at the same time. But this is not the only way to handle the matter. An alternative is to consider pitch as a second dimension in which (segmental) forms can be arranged, there being four possible positions along this dimension, in contrast to the infinite number along the time axis. For purposes of demonstration, we could then write

```
(4)
(3)          h
(2) come      e
(1)            re
```

—where the numbers specify the pitch-levels. There would then be no intonation morphemes, but rather a two-dimensional space in which other types of morphemes are arranged relative to each other.[4] The four stress levels of English could be handled in the same way, giving three dimensions of arrangement. Bloomfield (1933, p. 163) chooses this alternative when he speaks of taxemes of 'modulation'.

IA is present implicitly, though not with complete clarity, in Bloomfield's chapters on grammar; where traces of IP survive, he is sometimes a bit apologetic (1933, p. 213 top; cf. **Wells**, 1949, p. 102). It is certainly Bloomfield's systematization which has served as the main point of departure for the train of investigators who have been trying to develop IA—Harris and his students, Bloch, Wells, lately Nida, and others (see bibliography passim under these names, Nida only in 1948, 1949. Nida 1946 is cast essentially in IP). There are few full grammatical descriptions which illustrate IA in its purest form; Bloch's discussions of Japanese are probably the closest (1946; even more—work done under Bloch's direction—Gardner 1950, Yokoyama 1950).

1.6 There is partial translatability between IP and IA, but the results of translation are apt to seem somewhat strange. By way of demonstration, here is the passage from Haas's Tunica, recast in IA:

[2] The possible criteria are examined by Pittman, 1948. But Pittman's discussion is cast in IA, and affords no obvious support for the IP approach.

[3] Floyd Lounsbury has suggested (private conversation) that we can profitably speak of the 'structure' of a word or utterance but of the 'pattern' of a language. This suggestion is followed here. (The contrast, of course, parallels one of those designated by the terms 'parole' and 'langue'.)

[4] The problem of dimensionality is confusing. Recognizing intonation morphemes, we have to accept simultaneity as one arrangement of morphemes relative to each other. This, in turn, suggests that there is a second dimension of arrangement in addition to time; but there are no contrasts between different 'arrangements' in this second dimension—the term 'superfix' is no more apt than 'subfix', and (the bad Latin) 'simulfix' might be even better. A dimension in which arrangements are not in contrast is rather thin. Lounsbury has suggested (private conversation) that it is better to speak of just one dimension, with simultaneity as one possible arrangement within it. If we treat intonations (or stresses) as features of arrangement instead of as morphemes, then clearly we have more than the one dimension time; but in this case, although two items can occur at different times on the same intonation level, two items cannot occur at the same time on different intonation levels. There is still something rather queer about the added dimensions.

The average number of morphemes per word in Tunica stands about midway between the highest and lowest averages known from various languages. The morphemes within a single word are for the most part relatively invariant in shape, but there are some cases of more alternations. Tunica morphemes fall into several position-classes: stems, prefixes, infixes, and suffixes; at least one affix [we are not told which kind or how many] is morphophonemically a chameleon. A single word may contain more than one stem. Suffixes are more numerous, both as a class and as regards the average number per word, than prefixes, and the latter in turn more numerous than infixes. In a few cases, morphophonemic alternations are between totally dissimilar forms.

The original, in all seeming, imparts relevant information about Tunica. The translation given above has little or no such impact—at least on this reader; it has the appearance, rather, of an assembly of prosaic facts, which have no particular reason for being given in the sequence in which they are here found, or, indeed, even for being given all at one place.

If this be true, then there must be more difference between the IP and the IA models than has yet been touched on; there must be major differences as to what features of a language are regarded as worthy of prominent mention and what features are prosaic —even if necessarily included somewhere in a reasonably complete description.

This last comment is offered not as a forerunner of greater elaboration to follow, but in lieu thereof. There are differences between IP and IA which will have to be ignored within the fairly formal framework that will shortly be built, and it would be wrong to ignore them altogether.

1.7 It seems to me that the current general preference for IA rather than IP—and such a prejudice is certainly observable—stems at least in part not from any great excess of merit of IA over IP, but rather from the following: (1) We like, nowadays, to be as formal as possible. (2) IA has been formalized, and IP has not. It is unfair to compare a formalized IA with an informal IP and conclude that the former is better just because it is formalized. If it could be shown that IA is capable of formalization but that IP is not, that would be another matter. But in what follows, I hope to demonstrate that no such claim can be made.

To do this, it is of course necessary to devise a formalized version of IP. This will be almost our last step. It will be preceded by: a general outline of IA, in broad enough terms to cover most, if not all, of its current varieties; a survey of some of the problems implicit in IA (in two parts: tactical and morphophonemic); an excursion into certain elementary notions of mathematics, seeking analogs for IA and other possibly useful analogs. Our formal version of IP will be derived from such an analog. We will then be in the position to assess the relative merits and defects of IA and IP.

II. ITEM AND ARRANGEMENT

2.0 The following outline of IA might be called 'semiformal'—not so formal as to qualify as 'postulates', but succinct rather than discursive. The model is familiar, so all but the most essential examples are eschewed.

2.1 A linguistic form is either *simple* or *composite*.[5]

2.2 A simple form is a *morpheme*.

2.3 A composite form consists of two or more *immediate constituents* standing in a *construction* and forming a *constitute*. Constituents and construction recur in other composite forms (save for an occasional unique constituent). Each IC (=immediate constituent) occupies a certain *position* in the construction; each is the *partner* of the other(s).[6]

2.4 Occasionally it is convenient to regard a morpheme not as participating in any construction, but rather as a *marker* of the construction in which nearby forms stand.

Any such concession necessitates a statement of the conditions under which the interpretation is to be accepted. Three such statements of conditions occur to me, the first being the trivial (but not unimportant) one of excluding the interpretation altogether.

The second is to allow the interpretation only where the marker indicates the boundary between partners in a construction, and nothing more. By this, the Peiping Chinese junctural morphemes /;/ and /,/ are allowable as markers, since in such an utterance as /ue^3 lai^2, ni^3 zieu^4 cy^4./ 'When I come, you go right away', the /,/ tells us that the segmental sequence before it and that after it are partners in a construction—that is, that this division of the whole sequence, rather than any other, is the correct one—but it does not tell us what construction is involved (Hockett 1950, section 2).

This limitation, however, would not allow us to interpret *men and women* as a bipartite construction with marker *and*, since *and* quite obviously gives us more information than the maximum amount specified. A set of conditions which would allow the interpretation in this case would have to be along the following lines: there is a form ABC consisting of three smaller forms, where (1) one of the smaller forms, say B (it would not have to be the one in the middle) is a single morpheme; (2) the remaining two, A and C, are structurally similar to each other (in some appropriate sense) but not to B; (3) there is no evidence forcing either an interpretation as

5 The term 'linguistic form' is here to be regarded as being defined by the other terms at least as much as they are by it. The outline assumes, without explicit statement, a certain amount of our linguistic common sense.

6 The only new term is 'partner', which I venture to suggest to fill a hole in our terminology in which I have stumbled more than once.

A[BC or as AB[C.[7]

Even more liberal sets of conditions might be formulated. Our reason for including the present discussion will appear in the sequel.

2.5 The tactical pattern of a language is completely covered by a set of statements of the following form (or by any set of statements which can be transformed mechanically into this form):[8]

(1) A list of the constructions.

(2) Under each construction as heading,

(2.1) Enumeration of the positions in that construction.

(2.2) Specification of any marker for that construction.

(2.3) For each position,

(2.31) A list of the morphemes which occur there, and

(2.32) A list of the constructions, composite forms belonging to which occur there.

2.6 A morpheme may appear in more than a single phonemic shape. A single shape of a morpheme is a morph; the various morphs which are the shapes or representations of one and the same morpheme are its allomorphs.

2.7 The alternations in shape of a morpheme are predictable in terms of the environments in which it occurs (plus, of course, the morphophonemic statements which one makes).

This necessitates a definition of 'environment': the environment of a morpheme-occurrence is the setting of that occurrence, insofar as that setting can be described in purely structural (i. e., nonsemantic) terms. Narrower definitions are possible; ours is intentionally wide.

2.8 All the phonemic material in an utterance is accountable for in terms of the morphemes which compose the utterance and the arrangement in which they occur relative to each other (plus, once again, one's morphophonemic statements).

2.9 Subject to the conditions just stated (2.6–8), it is possible to allow such devices as the following where they prove convenient:

(1) We may recognize phonemic zero as a possible morph shape. This requires carefully formulated supplementary criteria. At least two apparently consistent limitations have been proposed:

(1.1) A morpheme does not appear everywhere as zero (Bloch, 1947, section 2.3 (3)).

(1.2) A morpheme may appear everywhere as zero, providing it is a member of a tactically relevant class (under some suitable definition), other members of which are not (or not always) represented by zero (Nida 1948, 1949; the criterion is there by implication, though not overtly stated).

(2) We may recognize a morph which belongs to no morpheme (Hockett 1947b, p. 333 ⟨⟨236⟩⟩). Or, instead of this, we may simply classify some of the phonemic material in some utterances as nonmorphemic (Hockett 1950, fn. 8).

(3) We may recognize a morph which belongs simultaneously to two (or more) morphemes in a fixed arrangement (whether partners in a construction or not). If the morphemes involved appear, in other environments, in separable shapes, then the morph in question is a portmanteau representation of the morpheme-group (Hockett 1947b, p. 333 ⟨⟨236⟩⟩). If the morphemes involved appear only in such portmanteau representations, the usual terminology is a little different: the representations themselves are called 'morphemes', and the separate entities represented are called 'morphemic components' (Harris 1948, more extensively in 1951). This more usual, but deviant, terminology will not be used in the present discussion.

(4) We may allow a particular phoneme or sequence of phonemes to belong at one and the same time both to a morph which includes some preceding phonemes (and represents one morpheme) and to a morph which includes some following phonemes (and represents another morpheme)—linked morphs, the shared phoneme(s) being a link (Wells 1949, fn. 29, with credit to Lounsbury). Trivially different is the case in which one of the morphs, instead of both, contains phonemic material which is not part of the other.

2.10 The statement of shapes, alternations, and conditions of alternation describes the morphophonemic pattern of the language.

2.11 Morphophonemic and tactical pattern taken together constitute grammatical pattern. This, paired with phonological pattern, completes the synchronic pattern of a language. The cleavage between phonology and grammar is thought by some (including myself) to be more fundamental than that, within grammar, between morphophonemics and tactics, even though, for some purposes, other stratifications are possible. For example, it is sometimes convenient to class morphophonemic and phonological facts together, say as 'mechanics', in collective contrast to tactics (Hockett 1948, p. 185). Or, if the distinction between automatic and non-automatic morphophonemics is made (we have not taken the trouble to work it into

[7] This incorporates Wells's specification of the conditions under which one resorts to a tripartite instead of a bipartite construction (Wells 1947, pp. 103 f. ⟨⟨199⟩⟩).

[8] Many different arrangements of descriptive statements are convertible into this form. In particular there is the contrast between beginning with the most inclusive constructions and working down the scale (large-to-small), which is perhaps the traditional way at least for syntax (exemplified, e. g., by the arrangement of the grammatical chapters in Bloomfield 1933), and beginning with the least inclusive constructions and working up the scale (small-to-large), the procedure proposed by Harris, 1946. These two ways have in common—despite Harris's disclaimer in section 3.7 and fn. 8—the recognition of IC or hierarchical structure, though Harris's procedure discovers that structure step by step, whereas the alternative seems to imply discovering it in advance.

the above outline), it also makes a good deal of sense to class automatic morphophonemic facts with phonology, non-automatic with tactics; I have no labels to propose for the resulting two divisions (this is the stratification which seems to be implied by certain of Sapir's discussions: 1933, 1930). In any case, there are indeed problems about the exact location of the lines of demarcation between levels, but we need not concern ourselves with them here because the formal version of IP to be presented later will solve them neither more nor less than does IA.

III. TACTICAL DIFFICULTIES WITH IA

3.0 A grammatical description built according to the plan outlined in II sets forth principles by which one can generate any number of utterances in the language; in this sense, it is operationally comparable to the structure of that portion of a human being which enables him to produce utterances in a language; i.e., to speak. It is also comparable to a cookbook. From the lists in the tactical description, choose any set of compatible ingredients. Put them together, two by two or few by few (ICs), until all have been tentatively assembled; then treat in accordance with the morphophonemic statements (in cooking, 'cream', 'blend', 'broil', etc.); remove traces of these operations (clean and put away the cooking utensils); and one has an utterance in the language. In cooking, a difference in the sequence in which ingredients are put together can make a difference in the end-product; if this were not so, manufacturers of processed foods would not announce, as they sometimes do on packages, both ingredients and proportions. But there can also be differences of sequence in cooking operations which make no discernible difference in the end-product. For the moment this second fact is of primary relevance for the analogy. There is, in linguistics, no guarantee that different sequences of operations, performed on the same ultimate constituents, may not produce the same, or what is ostensibly the same, end-product.

In fact, we can specify the conditions under which this will be the case. The conditions involve the constructions recognized in the tactical description and the forms listed under the various positions for the various constructions. Let there be four constructions, C_1, C_2, C_3, and C_4 (some of which may be the same). Let there be three forms F_1, F_2, and F_3. Suppose that F_1 and F_2 occur in that order in C_1; F_2 and F_3 in that order in C_2. Suppose that forms conforming to C_1 (hence F_1F_2) occur in the first position of C_3, and that F_3 occurs in the second position of C_3. Finally, suppose that forms conforming to C_2 (hence F_2F_3) occur in the second position of C_4, and that F_1 occurs in the first position of C_4. Under just these conditions, the composite form $F_1F_2F_3$ will be a case in point.

We may illustrate with English. C_1 and C_4 are the construction of adjective-attribute and nominal-head. F_1 is old, F_2 is men. C_2 and C_3 are the marked construction X and Y; F_3 is women. Consequently we may build the composite form old men and women by either of two procedural sequences: putting old and men together by C_1, and then joining the result to women by C_2; or putting men and women together by C_2, and then putting old together with the result of C_2 in accordance with C_1.[9]

The converse of the cookbook nature of a grammatical description is that, when presented with an utterance in a language whose pattern has been determined, the analyst should be able to state its structure. Now it is clear that in any such case as that of old men and women, the analyst will be able to determine the ultimate constituents and the (linear) order of these constituents, but he will not necessarily be able to tell the order of association, the IC-structure or hierarchical structure, of the utterance. The fact that his description supplies more than a single procedural sequence which will build the composite form implies that when presented with the whole form the analyst cannot determine which procedural sequence was involved in its production.

We therefore have to make a decision. It was mentioned above that a grammatical description is an operational parallel to part of a speaker's internal apparatus. If we believe that this parallel extends to the matter of order of association, so that ambiguities in the description are matched (at least in some cases) by distinct internal chains of activity which produce identical linear sequences of morphemes, then we can regard the matter of hierarchical structure as an integral part of the structure of utterances even in ambiguous cases. But if we do not so believe, or if we feel that such a conclusion ought not to influence our development of analytical techniques, then we are forced to conclude that hierarchical structure is at most a convenient shorthand for description—not anything essential about the grammar of a language, but simply a way to make our description of a whole language less cumbersome—an intrusive artifact, like the dye on a bacteriologist's slide. For, obviously, it would be possible (save for lack of time) to specify all arrangements of ultimate constituents in utterances without resort to any intermediate groupings.

9 Wells 1947, p. 93 ((193)). Since normal English orthography leaves out certain grammatically relevant features of utterances (e.g., intonations), any single English notation, such as 'old men and women', subsumes ambiguously a family of linguistic forms. Some members of this family are marked clearly as having one IC structure; some are marked equally clearly as having the other. But, at least for my own speech, there are also members of the family that are not marked in either way. In the context, it is of course one of the latter with which we are dealing; here, and in similar situations later, the reader must assume that this is the case.

The IA picture is therefore potentially somewhat more complex than our original emphasis on the two notions ('item' and 'arrangement') would imply. There are more potentially independent factors than those two. Specifically, there are (1) forms, (2) [linear] order, (3) constructions, and (4) IC or hierarchical structure. We must investigate the status of these factors relative to each other. Are they all 'primitives' in the system, or are some derivable from others?

The independence of forms and order is clear almost without demonstration. Such a trivial example as John hit Bill versus John hit Dick demonstrates the independence of form from order; the former versus Bill hit John demonstrates the independence of order from form, since these two could be said to differ only as to order of ultimate constituents. But the status of constructions and of hierarchical structure needs further discussion.

3.1 Beginning with hierarchical structure, let us consider again Wells's case of hierarchical ambiguity, this time embedded in a longer utterance: The old men and women stayed at home. It is quite possible that if I say this to an audience, some hearers may conclude that I have referred to old males and all females, others may believe that I have spoken of all old people of both sexes; still others may believe that I am consciously being ambiguous (as I am!) or may simply be unable to decide the matter.

Wells adopts a very simple solution. He assumes that old men and women has one or the other hierarchical structure depending on the meaning. Since there are cases in which the hearer cannot tell what the meaning is, this must revert to a consideration of something like 'speaker's intention', which means that the step mentioned earlier is indeed being taken. Before we resort to such a drastic measure, let us look for further evidence.

We might apply the same technique by which we separate homophonous morphemes. Old men and women can be substituted for, say, old people, in one large set of environments (for example, old people belong at home and old men and women belong at home are both good English sentences); it can be substituted for women and old men in another, partly different, set of environments (The women and old men stayed at home while the young men went to war; The old men and women ...). But old people and women and old men are not so freely interchangeable. It is by just this procedure that we would, in the first instance, separate The sun's rays meet and The sons raise meat. Having separated either pair of homophones, we can seek for correlated internal structural differences. In the latter pair, the differences lie in the ultimate constituents; in the former, the only difference is in the hierarchical organization.

But there is a deeper consideration. The hearer, confronted with The old men and women stayed at home, is in much the same position as the observer who sees a picture of a hollow cube and can, almost at will, see first one corner and then another as closer to him. There is a third way to see the picture: as an assemblage of straight lines on a flat surface, without depth. This third way is difficult without the special training which artists, whose task it is to produce such visual representations, have to get. The ordinary individual, looking at the three figures A, B, and C, can easily enough see that B is different from both A and C, but he will also see B now as more like A, now as more like C. Since most of our visual experience is with depth perception, we 'read' depth into many two-dimensional portrayals.

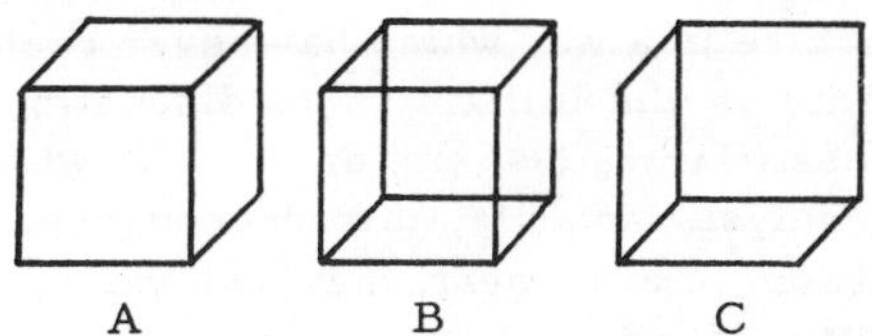

B, then, is ambiguous. An ambiguity cannot exist in the abstract; it must be between things. The alternatives in the visual case are not A and C; they are B's being like A or C respectively. 'Being like A' and 'being like C' are two distinct and mutually exclusive matters: B cannot at one and the same time be taken both as like A and as like C.

The same argument holds for hierarchical ambiguity: Our B is The old men and women stayed at home. For A and C, we can select respectively The women and old men stayed at home and The old men and old women stayed at home. B's 'being like' A is one hierarchical structure; B's 'being like' C is another. A hierarchical structure is a class of forms which are alike in a certain way; so is a construction. A single sequence of morphemes cannot be like two mutually exclusive other sequences at one and the same moment for a single hearer, but in some cases it may fluctuate between the two directions of likeness. Interpreting old men and women as merely a linear sequence of morphemes is highly unnatural; the linguist, for his special purposes, may have to develop the ability to do so, just as the artist has to develop the ability to see things without depth in order to represent them in such a way that others will report the presence of depth.

Our conclusion, then, is that hierarchical structure is a 'primitive' just as are forms and order. The demonstration turns necessarily on two considerations: (1) there must be many utterances in which the hierarchical structure in unambiguous, to afford a frame of reference; (2) there must be also at least a few in which the hierarchical structure is ambiguous, since otherwise the hierarchical structure would in every case be determined by forms and order, and hence not a 'primitive'.

3.2 One recently proposed type of morphemic analysis turns on the 'primitive' status of hierarchical structure in a way which has never been made clear. This is the utilization of discontinuous morphemes (Harris 1945a). For those to whom this type of analysis appeals, this dependence, to be demonstrated in a moment, may add weight to the desirability of recognizing IC-structure as a 'primitive'. But since there is no situation in which the analyst is actually forced to use discontinuous-morpheme analysis, its dependence on IC-structure cannot count in any sense as evidence for the status of the latter.

Consider the following two Latin sentences: (a) pater bonus filium amat; (b) pater bonum filium amat. The latter, though unusual, was certainly possible; it is easier to handle than more complex and more realistic examples that could be found.

According to the more customary procedure—rejecting discontinuous morphemes—the ultimate constituents of (a) include two occurrences of a morpheme that we may call {nominative} and one occurrence of {accusative}, while those of (b) include one of {nominative} and two of {accusative}.[10] The distribution of the two occurrences of {nominative} in (a) marks pater and bonus as going together as partners in a construction, while the distribution of the two occurrences of {accusative} in (b) mark bonum and filium in the same way. The hierarchical structure in each case is partly marked by the nature and location of these morpheme-occurrences. There is no need, in these examples, for hierarchical structure to be an independent primitive.

Using discontinuous morphemes, the results are different. The ultimate constituents of (a) in this case include <u>one</u> occurrence each of {nominative} and of {accusative}—and in (b) there will be found, also, just one occurrence of each of these morphemes. In (a), the one occurrence of {nominative} is an occurrence in discontinuous form, the separated representations coming at the ends of two successive words; in (b) similarly for the {accusative} morpheme.

Now when discontinuous morphemes are recognized, it is necessary not only for the particular shape of each representation of such a morpheme, but also for the number of representations involved in any one occurrence and the precise location of those representations, to be predictable on the morphophonemic level. It is not enough that we be able to predict that if the stem patr- and the nominative morpheme co-occur, the total form will be pater; we must also be able to predict that if the stem-sequence patr-... bon-... and {nominative} co-occur the total form will be pater bonus. Now assume that we have the partial patr-... bon-... fili-... amat and one occurrence each of {nominative} and {accusative}. There is absolutely no way of knowing that the total form will be pater bonus filium amat, or pater bonum filium amat, or possibly something else, unless among the environmentally relevant facts it is given that patr- and bon- are partners, rather than bon- and fili-. The distribution of representations of discontinuous morphemes is not predictable in Latin unless hierarchical structure is allowed to count as part of morphophonemically relevant environment. When we make use of discontinuous morphemes, then Latin sentences (a) and (b), despite overt phonemic differences, are structurally the same as the two English phrases of shape <u>old men and women</u>.

The requirement of 2.7 was intentionally phrased broadly enough to allow this. However, it has not been customary to count IC-structure as relevant environment, and it may that the necessary added complication will be enough to turn some against the whole notion of discontinuous morphemes.

3.3 Next in line is the status of constructions.

Given verb-stem <u>bake</u> and the past-tense morpheme, with instructions that they are to go together, the only thing one can do is to put them together as <u>baked</u>. There is no problem of hierarchical structure since each constituent is ultimate. Linear order is determined.

Given <u>John</u> and <u>saw</u> to be put together, the result can be either <u>John saw</u> or <u>saw John</u> (either of which, partnered by an intonation, might occur as an utterance). Here there is a choice of procedure. If to <u>John</u> and <u>saw</u> we add a specification as to linear order, then there is no longer any choice between constructions: only <u>John saw</u>, which is the actor-action construction, is possible with one order specification, and only <u>saw John</u> (action-goal construction) is possible with the other. But instead of approaching the matter in this way, we can equally well regard the order as determined by the construction: <u>John</u>, <u>saw</u>, and subject-predicate construction result necessarily in one linear order, the same forms and action-goal construction result necessarily in the other. Whichever course we follow, it is clear that we are confronted with one more variable than the maximum number which can be regarded as independent: forms to be partners, order, and construction cannot in such a case all be independent of each other.

The nearest example to complete independence of these three matters that I have so far discovered is in Chinese. Given crau^3 'to fry' and fan^4 'rice', and the specification that the first is to precede the second, there is still a choice of construction—though it does not manifest itself in any overt way within the sequence itself. One possible construction is verb-object, giving crau^3 fan^4 'to fry rice, fry rice'; the other is attribute-head, giving crau^3 fan^4 'fried rice'. These are really different: the first is also the construction of cr^1 fan^4 'to eat rice, eat rice',

[10] These morphemes, treated as discontinuous or not, are what Harris has called morphemic components, a fact which does not disturb the present argument (see 2.9 (3) of this paper).

unambiguously verb-object; the second is also the construction of hau³ fan⁴ 'good rice', which is unambiguously attribute-head.

From here on our argument about old men and women applies pari passu to crau³ fan⁴, and need not be repeated in detail. There are, of course, some larger contexts in which crau³ fan⁴ is marked unambiguously as one or the other construction, just as there are larger environments in which the hierarchical structure of old men and women is not ambiguous. But there are also larger contexts in which the ambiguity remains. The construction, then, cannot be derived from the forms and the order. The reverse is possible: given forms and construction, the order can be regarded as determined—it just so happens that either of two constructions, with the same two constituents, results in the same order.

The conclusion to which we are forced is that, at least in some cases in some languages, choice of construction is a primitive.

3.4 If a particular version of IA allows the recognition of marked constructions, then the question as to the primitive or derived status of constructions becomes trivial: at least such constructions as have markers must have primitive status. Consider John and Bill, a bipartite construction with marker and. This form contrasts with Bill and John only as to order, with John and Mary (or Tom and Mary) only as to form, and with John or Bill only as to construction—since or is the marker of a different construction. In this case, all three factors are independent. It immediately follows that in old men and women all four factors are independent, since in addition to the X and Y construction there is also the matter of hierarchical structure, already demonstrably independent of the other factors.

3.5 So the four factors, the status of which we set out to survey, all have to be recognized as potentially independent, and therefore as primitives. If there is a possible exception, it is, surprisingly enough, linear order—one of the two factors (the other being forms) which would seem so obviously primary. The only situation discussed above in which linear order had to be accepted as independent of all other factors was in the case of marked constructions like John and Bill, and it is possible to proscribe marked constructions altogether.

The survey also shows, however, that in the bulk of cases not all of this machinery is needed. In most cases, a determination of two or three of the factors leaves no choice for the remainder. It is this fact which gives rise to the most embarrassing tactical trouble inherent in IA: machinery which has to be in our workshop for use in certain marginal cases tends to obtrude itself where it isn't wanted.

Thus Bloch writes as follows (1947, p. 400 ((243))): "the preterit form waited ... can be described as follows. It consists of two morphemes, /weyt/ and /ed/, occurring in that order. The meaning of the first morpheme is a particular action that we need not specifically define here; that of the second is 'past time' or the like. The constructional meaning of the order in which the two morphemes occur is approximately 'perform a certain action at a certain time'." Bloch has cut down on the total amount of machinery by identifying 'construction' and 'order' (which, as we have seen, is in general questionable). But, still, entities are multiplied beyond necessity. Given the morphemes /weyt/ and /ed/ to be put together, actually nothing further need be said at all on the tactical level. There is no possible linear order save that of /weyt/ first and /ed/ second. Nor—if we separate order and construction—is there any choice of construction. Semantically, it is quite pointless to break down the meaning of the whole form waited into three parts: structurally, there are two and only two independent variables, and the only valid procedure is to assign, as the meaning of the second variable, everything which differentiates the meaning of waited from that of wait.

IV. MORPHOPHONEMIC TROUBLES WITH IA

4.1 Most morphophonemic problems find simple answers in IA, for there is available a wide variety of morphophonemic techniques all well within the bounds of the IA model. However, there is a refractory residue, troublesome not because no solution can be found, but either because a multiplicity of solutions present themselves, no one seeming much better than another, or because the intuitively best solution is clearly in violation of the fundamental orientation of IA. This residue includes such cases as took, put (past tense), children, French bon and bonne, Chinese lia³ and liang³ 'two'. We need deal in detail only with one of these, and took will do.

4.2 The following morphophonemic solutions have been proposed (or might be proposed) for took (we here follow, in the main, Bloch 1947, pp. 400-1 ((244))):

(1) took is a single morpheme, so that there is no morphophonemic problem.

(2) took is a portmanteau representation of the two-morpheme sequence take and /ed/.

(3) took is an allomorph of the morpheme which appears elsewhere as take, plus a zero allomorph of /ed/.

(4) took is a discontinuous allomorph /t...k/ of take, and an infixed allomorph /u/ of /ed/.

(5) took is take plus a replacive morph /u/←/ey/ (read '/u/ replaces /ey/').

Let us consider these one by one.

(1) is unacceptable because it controverts the tactical parallelism between took and baked and many other obviously composite forms.

(2) is the most general solution, since it avoids, in a sense, the problem of identification of partial similarity in shape. But this very avoidance is arbitrary: took and take are partly similar in phonemic shape just as are baked and bake, and similar in meaning also in the same way; the fact should not be obscured.

(3) is arbitrary because it assigns to something that isn't there phonemically—something that is 'there' only in the fact that it calls for a phonemically distinct allomorph of the accompanying morpheme—a meaning which would more naturally be assigned to some location within the overt form took. The same solution for the past tense put (or the plural sheep) is even more strained since there is not even this phonemic effect on the accompanying morpheme. Within the same special rules that allow (3), it would also be possible to propose that took be interpreted as an allomorph of /ed/ accompanied by a zero allomorph of take. I see no reason why (3) should be considered any more or less seriously than this alternative. (3), in effect, gains nothing at all over (2).

(4) is in some ways the most attractive (with some manipulation, this proposed solution can be derived from Nida's discussions in 1948, 1949; his 'replacive' terminology tends to obscure the matter). It meets the objections so far raised to the other alternatives, as well as that which will shortly be raised to (5). The most serious criticism so far offered is that we might be led to interpret take, also, as an allomorph /t...k/ plus an infixed allomorph /ey/; this is not justified because take, like bake, rake, catch, and so on, acts tactically like a single morpheme. This is not a very serious criticism, since we need not be so submissive to the proposed analogy. Within the IA framework, (4) is probably the best answer.

(5) is not valid within IA. It calls an 'allomorph' something which is not in conformity with the general definition of the term. A morph is composed wholly of phonemic material or (as the limiting case) of no phonemic material at all. A 'replacive', like '/u/ ← /ey/', is not by any stretch of the imagination composed of phonemic material.

The same comment applies to 'subtractives', which happen not to apply in the case of take. It is tactically convenient to regard French bon as more complex than bonne, Chinese lia3 'two' as more complex than liang3 'two'.[11] Bon is then, it is proposed, to be taken as bonne plus a 'subtractive' morph consisting of loss of final consonant (and nasalization of the vowel); lia3 is to be taken as liang3 plus a terminal 'subtractive'. A subtraction is no more composed of phonemic material than is a replacement.

4.3 Why is so much emphasis placed on this? Could we not modify our definition of 'morph' in such a way as to allow subtractives and replacives in those circumstances where they seem so clearly convenient? Of course we can do so. But such action seems to be equivalent—perhaps rather unexpectedly—to removing the keystone of the whole IA arch; the model begins to collapse. All the criteria which have been so laboriously established as a basis for the selection of one morphophonemic treatment or another have to be supplemented by new clauses. Even the tactical picture tends to be modified. When we pick up the pieces and try to fit them together again—without restoring the keystone—we find that we are no longer dealing with anything that looks like IA; we have a new model on our hands. After a short intermission this new model will be put on exhibit.

V. MATHEMATICAL INTERLUDE

5.1 Mathematics is a good place to turn to for analogs of structures, since mathematicians and mathematical logicians have as their business the construction of structures of the greatest variety and generality. For our purposes, we shall only have to venture into the most elementary phases of their activity (see the more elementary and readable portions of Quine 1940, Birkhoff and MacLane 1944).

A good many mathematical systems are characterizable wholly or primarily as consisting of a set of elements for which certain relations are defined. One such system has as elements all the positive integers, and as one elementary relation, the relation of 'greater than': two is greater than one, five is greater than two, and so on. A relation ties together pairs of elements, or, in some cases (for example, the relation 'is between ... and ...'), more than two elements. A relation is also quite satisfactorily definable as a class of ordered pairs (or of ordered n-ads with n greater than 2) of elements. In this sense, the number-pairs (3, 2), (5, 1), (2, 1) are said to be members of the relation 'greater than', while the number-pair (1, 3) or (1, 1) is not. The two approaches to relations are equivalent: we can begin with some property such as 'greater than' and observe that some pairs of numbers bear this relation, or we can begin with any set of ordered pairs of numbers—selected, it may be, quite randomly—and define a relation simply by listing the ordered pairs that belong to it.

Now it is easy to show that a construction, in the linguistic sense (within IA), is a relation (this proposal has not been made in print, to my knowledge; Wells has incorporated it in an as yet unpublished report on linguistics and semantics). The constituents of a constitute are elements; they are in a particular arrangement (linear order). A construction, then, is a class of ordered n-ads of constituents, whereupon a construction is a relation.

There is one point at which this characterization seems (wrongly) to fall down. Two and three are numbers; 'three is greater than two' is not a number, nor is (3, 2) a number. Black and cat are forms; and black cat is a form too. It makes sense to say that black cat participates, as a whole, as an element in larger constructions; it certainly does not make sense to say that (3, 2) is greater than something or

[11] This comment on 'subtractives' and 'replacives' is given by Bloch in fn. 3 of Nida 1948. The error discussed here crops up also in Hockett 1947b, pp. 339–40 ⟪239–40⟫; Hockett 1950, pp. 82–3 ⟪326–7⟫; Harris 1942, pp. 170–1 ⟪110⟫.

less than something. This apparent discrepancy is due to the perhaps overly simple nature of the particular mathematical system we have chosen. It is hardly possible to say that (3, 2) can be greater than some number, but it is perfectly possible to define—in the arbitrary way mentioned above—a relation which has as members not only ordered pairs of numbers such as (3, 2) and (3, 1) but also ordered pairs of elements one or both of which are in turn ordered pairs of numbers—such as ((3, 2), 1) or (3, (2, 1)), or even ((3, 2), (3, 1)). Most such invented relations would be trivial and uninteresting, but some might be fruitful, and all are perfectly acceptable logically. So there is nothing to keep us from recognizing a relation in linguistics which has as members both such ordered pairs as black cat and also such as big I black cat.

5.2 Another great class of mathematical systems are characterizable as consisting of a set of elements for which certain operations are defined. One such system has, as did our exemplification of a system with relations, the positive integers as its elements, and has, as one elementary operation, that of addition. Addition applies in the first instance to pairs of positive integers, and is therefore a binary operation: two plus two is four, three plus four is seven, and so on. Addition has certain further properties. For instance, it is commutative: we get the same result adding two and three whether we start with the two or with the three. There are operations which are not commutative; e.g., subtraction defined over the same set of elements, since five minus seven is not only not the same as seven minus five, but actually meaningless. Addition is also associative: $(2+3)+6$ and $2+(3+6)$ add up to the same total. By virtue of this property, parentheses can be dropped, and the operation takes on the appearance of not being binary at all, but of applying to any number of terms, two or more. Fundamentally, however, it is convenient to regard addition as binary.

It can be shown that operations are reducible to relations, so far as their logical status is concerned. Thus the binary operation of addition, by which $2+3=5$, can also be interpreted as a ternary relation holding between the ordered triad of numbers (2, 3, 5) and between any ordered triad of numbers (a, b, c) for which it is true that $a+b=c$. In general, any n-ary operation is logically reducible to an appropriate (n+1)-ary relation.

Psychologically, however, this replacement leaves something out. Relations seem static, whereas operations seem dynamic—seem to generate something which we perhaps did not know was there. One use of mathematical systems is in computing; that is, in discovering implications that are not known, or not obvious, to the computer until the computation has been performed. Computing makes use of systems involving operations, not those characterized purely by relations, underscoring the importance of the dynamic or generative nature of operations. Logical identifications are always achieved by leaving something out; the mathematical logician is willing to leave out this psychological difference between relations and operations, but the ordinary mathematician is not. For our purposes, we shall follow the inclination of the ordinary mathematician.

5.3 There are two features of operations which may render them useful to us in linguistics, in place of relations—despite the logical substitutability which has been demonstrated.

One of these is the fact that the result of applying an operation to a pair (or set) of elements, or to a single element, is also an element. 'Two is greater than one', whatever it may be, is certainly not the same kind of element as are 'two' and 'one'. But two plus three is the same kind of element as are two and three; indeed, it is specifically that element, another name for which is 'five'. So if we say that black and cat are joined by an operation, instead of by a relation, we shall be more comfortable about calling black cat a form too.

The other is the fact that there are singulary operations, but no singulary relations. We see this from the logical substitutability of operations and relations. An n-ary operation is equivalent to an (n+1)-ary relation, so that the obvious existence of binary relations guarantees equally obvious singulary operations; but if there were singulary relations there would have to be nullary operations, and the one is as meaningless as the other.[12]

An example of a singulary operation in mathematics is 'reciprocal of' or 'negative of'. The latter is undefined for positive integers, but is defined for the set of all integers, positive, negative, and zero: the negative of three is minus three; the negative of minus four is four; the negative of zero is zero. For that matter, given a binary operation, any number of singulary operations can be devised. If addition is a binary operation, the addition of two to, addition of three to, and so on, are all singulary operations.

The utility of a singulary operation for linguistic analysis can be demonstrated with a form like waited where, as we saw in 3.5, it is pointless to isolate more than two factors. It may be advantageous to interpret waited as the result of a singulary operation applied to wait, at least in that this gives us just two separate factors.

5.4 If 'relation' is our closest analog to 'construction', then certainly the linguistic analog to 'operation' is 'process'. A grammatical model constructed in terms of this analogy ought to differ from IA just as operations differ from relations: it should be dynamic instead of static. It was pointed out in 1.2-4 that this was one of the chief characteristics of the older unformalized IP model, and we shall see that it is retained in the formal version about to be presented.

[12] Since a relation is a class of ordered n-ads, the singulary analog is a class of ordered monads; i.e., simply a class. What a nullary operation would be still escapes me entirely.

VI. ITEM AND PROCESS

6.0 The statements which follow parallel, as much as possible, those of II, and are abbreviated where reference to II can easily serve to fill them in; examples are left for VII.

6.1 A linguistic form is either simple or derived.

6.2 A simple form is a root.[13]

6.3 A derived form consists of one or more underlying forms to which a process has been applied. The underlying forms and the process all recur (save for occasional uniquenesses) in other forms. The underlying form or forms is (or are) the immediate constituent(s) of the derived form, which is also called a constitute; each underlying form is said to occupy a given position; each, if there are more than one, is the partner of the rest.

6.4 Some of the phonemic material in a derived form may be, not part of any underlying form, but rather a representation or marker of the process. (Such markers are not roots.)

As in the parallel statement for IA (2.4), this necessitates a statement of conditions; we defer this to VII.

6.5 The tactical pattern of a language is completely covered by a set of statements of the following form:

(1) A list of the processes.

(2) Under each process as heading,

(2.1) Enumeration of the position or positions involved.

(2.2) For each position,

(2.21) A list of the roots which occur in that position, and

(2.22) A list of the processes which produce forms which occur in that position.

There is no analog to statement (2.2) of section 2.5.

6.6 A root may appear in more than a single phonemic shape. A single shape of a root is a root-alternant.

A process may have more than one representation. A single representation of a process is a marker. A marker consists of the difference between the phonemic shape of a derived form and the phonemic shape(s) of the underlying form or forms. That is, a marker may consist of phonemic material in some specific position relative to the phonemic material which is identical with that of the underlying form, or it may consist of something present in the derived form in place of something else present in the underlying form, etc.

6.7 The alternations in shape of roots, and the choice in a particular instance of one or another marker of a process, are predictable in terms of the environments in which they occur (plus, of course, one's morphophonemic statements).

'Environment' is definable as in 2.7.

6.8 All the phonemic material in an utterance is accountable for in terms of the roots which occur in the utterance and the processes to which they have been subjected.

6.9 Empty root-alternants, portmanteau root-alternants, and links are definable and allowable as in IA, should there be any need for them. Zero alternant roots and zero markers of processes are likewise allowable, under similar limitations.

6.10 The statement of shapes, alternations, and conditions of alternation describes the morphophonemic pattern of the language; further considerations remain as in IA (2.11).

VII. COMPARISONS

7.1 First we give examples of IP treatment.

(1) Baked is a derived form, with a single immediate constituent bake, which happens to be a root, subjected to a singulary process which we can simply label past-tense formation. This process has various markers; when applied to bake, the marker is a /t/ which follows the phonemes of the underlying form.

(2) Took is tactically like baked, with underlying form take. The morphophonemic difference is that here the singulary process in question has a marker consisting of replacement of the stem vowel /ey/ of the underlying form by /u/.

(3) John and saw, subjected to the binary process of predication, give John saw, necessarily with that order, and with zero marker unless the order be taken as a marker. The same forms, subjected to the binary process of resolution, give saw John, again with order determined and zero marker. As with IA, we could alternatively take the order as primary and the process as determined. In support of the first alternative, we can present comparable cases in mathematics. If we are concerned with positive integers only, then the operation of subtraction, if it is to apply to seven and three, necessarily requires the order 7 − 3, since 3 − 7 is undefined.

(4) Chinese crau³ and fan⁴, subjected to either the binary process of resolution or the binary process of modification, give crau³ fan⁴, respectively 'fry rice' and 'fried rice'. The difference in positions of occurrence in larger forms, and the difference in meaning, correlate with the difference in process.

(5) John and Bill is (perhaps) the underlying forms John and Bill, subjected to the process of addition, for which the only marker is and. Bill and John is a different derived form, involving the same underlying forms and the same process, but a different order—order in this case being separable from process. Note that this process, here called 'addition', does not have the properties of the mathematical operation of the same name; grammatical addition

[13] The choice of terminology is difficult here; I do not recommend continued use of 'root' and terms stemming from it. 'Morpheme' would be preferable, but is avoided here in order better to contrast the two models.

is not commutative. Indeed, probably no grammatical processes will be found to be commutative.[14]

7.2 Our IP model differs, at least superficially, from anything to be found in the writings of Sapir.

This is partly because we have tried to incorporate into the more formalized version of IP some of the results of recent investigations carried on within the IA framework. Mainly this means the contrast between tactics and morphophonemics, which does not emerge at all clearly either in Sapir's writings or in Bloomfield's 1933 discussion. It would be a loss of ground to expunge this contrast during the reconstruction of IP.

But its retention leads us to use the term 'process' in a way different from Sapir's use. For Sapir, such matters as vowel-change, suffixation, reduplication, and the like, were 'processes'. For us 'vowel-change' refers to one possible canonical form of marker, a canonical form represented both in men, from man, and in took, from take, though the markers in men and took represent tactically different processes in our sense of the word; the marker in took and the marker in baked, representing the same process in our sense, are of different canonical forms and thus would be different 'processes' in the Sapir sense. Nida's (1946) earlier contrast (derived closely from Sapir) between 'phonological process' and 'morphological process' approaches closely our contrast between canonical forms of markers, on the one hand, and tactically relevant processes on the other.

All this would be easier to say, and at the same time perhaps less necessary, had we abandoned the term 'process' and simply imported 'operation' from mathematics, or had we used such a pair of terms as 'processeme' (tactical) and 'alloprocess' (morphophonemic), as a direct splitting-up of Sapir's more nebulous notion of 'process' in the light of recent developments.

7.3 The examples of 7.1 show that, by and large, grammatical descriptions cast in IP will run parallel to those cast in IA. There will be slight differences in terminology, and the wording certainly gives a 'dynamic' rather than a 'static' feel to the statements. Apart from these matters, the main differences will be marginal—though perhaps crucial.

IP obviates the major tactical and the major morphophonemic difficulty of IA. We are not confronted with superfluous machinery in the case of baked or took: the process involved is singulary, so that the only factors are the respective underlying forms and the process. The morphophonemic difficulty which IA gets into with took is obviated, since the whole frame of reference is one in which the difference between took and take is just as acceptable as that between baked and bake.

On the other hand, IP makes for certain difficulties avoided by IA.

In the first place, a 'pure' IA approach (which bars the interpretation of any morphemes as markers of constructions) is clearly much more homogeneous than either a less pure IA, or IP. This homogeneity is not as simple as has been thought: 'items', true enough, are either morphemes or sequences of morphemes, but still one has to contend with the independent status of order, constructions, and hierarchical structure. Even so, there is a clear difference between taking some phonemic material as 'root' (= item) and some as 'marker' of processes, as IP requires, and the simple procedure of taking all phonemic material as either morphemic or else morphemically irrelevant and morphophonemically predictable.

The problem of priority, evaded by IA, comes back into the picture. How are we to tell under what conditions to interpret a derived form as involving two or more underlying forms and a binary or higher-order process, and under what conditions to interpret it as involving a single underlying form and a singulary process? In one sense, of course, this is an extension to the case of two versus one of a problem found in IA: when do we recognize three ICs rather than two, or, in general, n rather than $n-1$?

The answer probably lies partly in the cases which are solved more easily by IP than by IA. Baked and took are interpreted in terms of a singulary process because to do otherwise leads to tactical and semantic trouble in both cases, and to morphophonemic trouble in the second. Obviously cases will be found more difficult than these, and a full elaboration of the necessary criteria is not to be expected overnight. In this very connection, IP is sure to encounter its refractory residue, different in content from, but similar in implications to, that of IA.

7.4 Another contrast between IA and IP turns on the number of constructions one has to recognize for a language under IA, versus the number of processes necessary for the same language under IP. The criterion of economy seems never to be invoked in IA so far as the number of morphemes is concerned: there are in any case a great many morphemes, and

[14] The inventors of mathematics, as speaking humans, distill mathematical notions out of the raw-material of everyday language. Their notions are derived by leaving something out of the nearest everyday-language analogs. A linguist analyzing English must assume that two plus three and three plus two are different forms. The mathematician chooses to ignore everything which differentiates the meanings of these two forms, and by so doing, he renders his 'addition' commutative. It may seem strange that we who are concerned with the total complexity of language should turn to mathematics for help, considering the ultimate source of mathematics. But the circle is not in fact closed: the mathematician derives his notions by abstraction from language, whereas we are deriving, not language itself, but a way of handling language, from mathematics.

a few more or less hardly matters. But economy enters the picture in reducing the number of classes of morphemes, or the number of major form-classes, or constructions, as much as possible. This is why, when confronted with the doublet plurals brothers and brethren, we are willing either to recognize two homonymous stem-morphemes brother requiring different allomorphs of the noun-plural morpheme (Hockett 1947b, p. 330), or, if need be, to recognize that the plural element in brethren is, after all, a different morpheme from that in brothers (Ibid., and Nida 1948, p. 415, by implication). It hardly occurs to us to suspect that the constituents are the same but the construction different.

The same tendency also manifests itself in the effort sometimes made to reduce, if not the total number of constructions, at least the total number of construction-types—that is, classes of constructions which manifest some similarity of behavior. Thus in Chinese there is no way in which one can call hau3 fan4 'good food' (stative verb followed by noun) and ie3 lai2 'also come' (adverb followed by verb) instances of a single construction; their privileges of occurrence in larger stretches of speech are quite different. But one can say that the two constructions exemplified by these forms are, in their turn, instances of a single construction-type, sharing the features of endocentricity and of head second rather than first. Without much bother, one can establish a classification of all the constructions in Chinese into eight construction-types. To do so is esthetically satisfying, probably just because of the psychological impact of the criterion of economy; in addition, it affords a useful basis for the organization of tactical statements about Chinese.

Perhaps it does not matter, but if we follow IP we are going to have to sacrifice some of this partly covert drive towards one form of 'economy'. The number of processes in a language, under IP, will probably in general be greater than the number of constructions in the same language under IA. For brothers and brethren, the interpretation of two homophonous underlying forms is still open to us, but loses much of its attractiveness. There is only one alternative: a single underlying form (brother) with two different singulary processes. And while the singulary process involved in brothers (normal noun-plural formation) is one which recurs widely, that in brethren, since it contrasts with that in brothers, is presumably also different from the one in boys, men, taxes, and so on; it is as forlorn as a process as the first IC (under either IA or IP) of cranberry is forlorn as an item. Uniquenesses under IP, in other words, may be unique constituents or unique processes. The only possible way to appease our parsimoniousness is to devise process-types on the cross-model analogy of construction-types.

7.5 Whether a grammatical description of a language is satisfactory or not depends in part of the use we want to make of it. Quite apart from esthetic or stylistic considerations, which can and do vary from one reader of grammars to another, and setting aside such matters as application to language pedagogy, there remains a number of properties which a grammatical description must have if it is to satisfy us for any scientific purpose. These properties have already been hinted at (particularly in 3.0). A grammatical description must be a guidebook for the analysis of material in the language—both material examined by the analyst before the description was formulated, and material observed after that. Lexically the coverage need not be complete, since new morphemes can turn up as one continues to record the language. Otherwise it must be prescriptive, not of course in the Fidditch sense, but in the sense that by following the statements one must be able to generate any number of utterances in the language, above and beyond those observed in advance by the analyst—new utterances most, if not all, of which will pass the test of casual acceptance by a native speaker.

If these are criteria for the evaluation of a grammatical description, what we need for the evaluation of models is a set of appropriately related metacriteria. The following list is perhaps not complete, and I am hesitant about the fifth, but no set would be complete which did not include the first four:

(1) A model must be general: it must be applicable to any language, not just to languages of certain types.

(2) A model must be specific: when applied to a given language, the results must be determined wholly by the nature of the model and the nature of the language, not at all by the whim of the analyst. It is not lack of specificity if the model requires us to subsume certain facts more than once, from different angles; it would be a lack of specificity if the model allowed us to take our choice in such cases, instead of forcing one choice or other or their joint option.

(3) A model must be inclusive: when applied to a given language, the results must cover all the observed data and, by implication, at least a very high percentage of all the not-yet-observed data. This is the analog of the 'guidebook' criterion (not metacriterion) mentioned earlier.

(4) A model must be productive: when applied to a given language, the results must make possible the creation of an indefinite number of valid new utterances. This is the analog of the 'prescriptive' criterion for descriptions.

(5) A model must be efficient: its application to any given language should achieve the necessary results with a minimum of machinery.

If we were confronted with two models, one of which fulfilled all the above requirements while the other did not, choice would be easy. If we were confronted with two, both of which fulfilled all the requirements, we would have to conclude that they differed only stylistically. Neither of these situations, of course, is at present the case. Neither any existing version of IA nor any existing version of IP meets all the metacriteria. Insofar as such matters can be felt quantitatively, it seems to me that IP, as constructed here, comes at least as close to satisfying the requirements as IA does, though perhaps no closer. In other words, what we have is two main types of model, neither completely satisfactory. Our course in this case is also clear. We must have more experimentation, as much with one model as with the other—and with the devising of further models too, for that matter—looking towards an eventual reintegration into a single more nearly satisfactory model, but not forcing that reintegration until we are ready for it.

BIBLIOGRAPHY

Birkhoff, Garrett, and Saunders MacLane, 1944: A survey of modern algebra. New York.

Bloch, Bernard, 1946: Studies in colloquial Japanese: I Inflection, JAOS 66.97–109; II Syntax, Lang. 22.200–48 ⟨⟨154⟩⟩; III Derivation of inflected words, JAOS 66.304–15.

———, 1947: English verb inflection. Lang. 23.399–418 ⟨⟨243⟩⟩.

Bloomfield, Leonard, 1933: Language. New York.

Boas, Franz, 1911: Introduction. Handbook of American Indian Languages, part 1, 1–83. Washington.

Gardner, Elizabeth F., 1950: The inflections of modern literary Japanese. Lang. Dissertation No. 46.

Haas, Mary, 1946: A grammatical sketch of Tunica. LSNA 337–66. VFPA 6. New York.

Harris, Zellig S., 1942: Morpheme alternants in linguistic analysis. Lang. 18.169–80 ⟨⟨109⟩⟩.

———, 1944: Yokuts structure and Newman's grammar. IJAL 10.196–211.

———, 1945a: Discontinuous morphemes. Lang. 21.121–7.

———, 1945b: review of M. B. Emeneau, Kota Texts; Part I. Lang. 21.283–9.

———, 1946: From morpheme to utterance. Lang. 22.161–83 ⟨⟨142⟩⟩.

———, 1948: Componential analysis of a Hebrew paradigm. Lang. 24.87–91 ⟨⟨272⟩⟩.

———, 1951: Methods in Structural Linguistics. Chicago.

Hockett, C. F., 1947a: review of E. A. Nida, Morphology[1]. Lang. 23.274–85.

———, 1947b: Problems of morphemic analysis. Lang. 23.321–43 ⟨⟨229⟩⟩.

———, 1948: review of LSNA. Lang. 24.183–8.

———, 1950: Peiping morphophonemics. Lang. 26.63–85 ⟨⟨315⟩⟩.

Newman, Stanley S., 1944: Yokuts language of California. VFPA 2, New York.

Nida, E. A., 1946: Morphology, the descriptive analysis of words[1]. Ann Arbor.

———, 1948: The identification of morphemes. Lang. 24.414–41 ⟨⟨255⟩⟩.

———, 1949: Morphology: the descriptive analysis of words[2]. Ann Arbor.

Pittman, R. S., 1948: Nuclear structures in linguistics. Lang. 24.287–92 ⟨⟨275⟩⟩.

Quine, W. V., 1940: Mathematical Logic. New York.

Sapir, Edward, 1921: Language. New York.

———, 1930: The Southern Paiute language. Proceedings, American Academy of Arts and Sciences 65:1 (1–296), 2 (297–536), 3 (537–730).

———, 1933: The psychological reality of phonemes. Journal de psychologie normale et pathologique 30.247–65; reprinted in D. G. Mandelbaum, editor, SWES (Berkeley and Los Angeles, 1949), 46–60.

Wells, R. S., 1947: Immediate constituents. Lang. 23.81–117 ⟨⟨186⟩⟩.

———, 1949: Automatic alternation. Lang. 25.99–116.

Yokoyama, M., 1950: The inflections of 8th-century Japanese. Lang. Dissertation No. 45.

⟦The Chinese examples were originally given in two different spellings; here they are normalized to the pattern used in Hockett's Peiping morphophonemics ⟨⟨315⟩⟩, which he had already used for the first ⟨⟨388⟩⟩.⟧

THE PHONEMIC INTERPRETATION OF SEMIVOWELS IN SPANISH

J. DONALD BOWEN
ROBERT P. STOCKWELL

Language 31.236–40—1955

The traditional interpretation of [y] and [w] in Spanish forms like bien 'well' and bueno 'good' has been to assign them to the phonemes /i/ and /u/.[1] The semivowel allophone of each of these vowel phonemes is stated to occur in the following positions:[2] SV, VSV, CSV, VSC, VS; examples (from Chavarría-Aguilar): huerta, Tehuantepec, puerta, jaula, hoy. All analysts, however, agree that there are still other allophones that cannot be assigned to /i/ and /u/, but must be assigned to a phoneme /y/ (variously transcribed as /j, y, ž/), though with the exception of King they do not describe any allophones that must be assigned to /w/ and therefore set up no such phoneme. The assignment of [y] and [w] to /i/ and /u/ therefore achieves at best only the economy that results from having no /w/ in the phoneme inventory. Other possible advantages, such as those of pattern congruity, will be examined hereafter by comparison with the analysis to be suggested here.

We suggest that the allophones [y] and [w] that have been traditionally assigned to /i/ and /u/ should be assigned respectively to the phoneme /y/ which hitherto has included only stop and spirant allophones, and to a phoneme /w/ which includes also the stop and spirant allophones hitherto assigned to /gu/. The technique of minimal contrast will not answer the question whether bien is /byén/ or /bién/, whether bueno is /bwéno/ or /buéno/. All the arguments on both sides are specifically pattern arguments, since the phonetic data seem to be quite clear.[3]

[1] See George L. Trager, The phonemes of Castilian Spanish, TCLP 8.217–22 (1939); Harold V. King, Outline of Mexican Spanish phonology, SIL 10.51–62 (1952); O. L. Chavarría-Aguilar, The phonemes of Costa Rican Spanish, Lang. 27.248–53 (1951); I. Silva-Fuenzalida, Estudio fonológico del español de Chile (Santiago, 1953).

[2] S means semivowel, C consonant, V vowel. An acute accent indicates strong stress; a breve in phonemic transcription /˘/ indicates weak stress, in phonetic transcription [˘] an extra-short vowel. [y] before a vowel is an on-glide from high-front tongue position; [y̌] is the same combined with palatal friction; [w] before a vowel is an on-glide from high-back tongue position with lips rounded; [w̌] is the same with velar friction. The same symbols after a vowel denote off-glides toward high-front or high-back position.

[3] Our data derive from observation. Over a period of two years we have carefully observed some thirty native speakers of Spanish, from many parts of Latin America, who have worked with us in teaching the language at the Foreign Service Institute. Previously we had contacts with hundreds of Spanish-speakers, though under conditions less admirably suited to study.

The allophone which all analysts agree in assigning to a phoneme other than /i/ is the tense voiced prepalatal spirant of /kabáyo/ 'horse' and /yó/ 'I'. A minimal pair is the following:

(a) /yábísto/ [yáb̆ísto] or [y̌áb̆ísto] or [[d]y̌áb̆ísto] ya visto 'I already dress'

(b) /iábísto/ [ĭáb̆íşto] y ha visto 'and he has seen'

The alternation among the three initials in (a) occurs within idiolects, within whole dialects, and between dialects. A nearly minimal pair for /w/ and /u/ is the following:

(c) /wáka/ [wáka] or [w̌áka] or [[g]w̌áka] huaca 'Indian grave'

(d) /uóka/ [ŭóka] u oca 'or goose'

The alternation among the initials in (c) is parallel to that in (a).

The stop and spirant allophones in (a) and (c) establish two phonemes /y/ and /w/ in utterance-initial position, contrasting with /i/ and /u/. The same interpretation is possible in intervocalic position:

(e) /ayá/ [ayá] or [ay̌á] allá 'there'

(f) /áwa/ [áwa] or [áw̌a] agua 'water'

Again it is the presence of palatal friction in [ay̌á] and of labiovelar friction in [áw̌a] that compels the assignment to /y/ and /w/, even though there is no contrast here with /i/ and /u/. The contrast, once it has been established (in initial position), is part of the structure of the language, and must be recognized even in positions where it is not minimal. The fact that the stop and spirant allophones of /y/ and /w/ are less frequent and less fortis intervocalically than initially is a fact to be stated in the description of these phonemes; it is not an argument against their existence.

Conceivably an analyst might think it economical to assume open transition in (b): /i+ábísto/, making this the contrasting feature as compared with (a): /iábísto/. But normal transition between vowels in Spanish has exactly the phonetic characteristics which appear in (b); hence there can be no /+/ in this example (though there is good evidence for positing /+/ elsewhere in the structure). In normal transition, two unstressed vowels are [V̆V], as in these forms:

(g) [ĕa] /beatitúd/ beatitud 'beatitude'
[ăe] /maestríta/ maestrita 'little teacher'

(h) [ĕo] /leonés/ leonés 'Leonese'
[ŏe] /poetísa/ poetisa 'poetess'

(i) [ăo] /aoríta/ ahorita 'right away'
[ŏa] /toayíta/ toallita 'little towel'

Each vowel in the cluster makes a separate syllable,[4] but the first is shorter than the second, and can be reduced to nonsyllabic status. In that case /e/ becomes /y/, /o/ becomes /w/, and /a/ becomes zero. Thus the six forms just cited are in any dialect sometimes (and in some dialects always) of the following shapes: /byatitúd, mestríta; lyonés, pwetísa; oríta, twayíta/.

Like others who have examined the data, we should be most reluctant to describe <u>beatitud</u> and the rest as /be+atitúd/ etc. But if such a description is inappropriate for <u>beatitud</u>, it is equally inappropriate for <u>y ha visto</u>; and if /+/ is not used in such cases, then the contrasts between /i/ and /y/, /u/ and /w/ are numerous. The phonemes /y/ and /w/ may therefore be regarded as established; only the question of their distribution remains.

But first a bit of corroborative evidence from substandard dialects. There is a well known substandard process traditionally described as replacement of /b/ by /g/; in this process words like bueno and abuelo become 'güeno' and 'agüelo'—so spelled by writers attempting to show dialectal variation. In our analysis, the process is simply a loss of /b/, not a replacement:[5] /bwéno/ and /abwélo/ become /wéno/ and /awélo/, the /w/ appearing, as elsewhere in the same environment, in its stop or spirant allophone. On the other hand, the replacement description of alternation between /b/ and /g/ shows no parallels, no patterning, anywhere else in the structure.

Nonsyllabic high front [y] and high back [w] occur in the following environments with normal transition:

(j)	SV:	yo 'I'	huerta 'vegetable garden'
(k)	VSV:	allá 'there'	agua 'water'
(l)	CSV:	bien 'well'	bueno 'good'
(m)	VSC:	baile 'dance'	auto 'car'
(n)	VS:	hoy 'today'	Grau—personal name

The semivowels [y] and [w] in (j) are assigned to the phonemes /y/ and /w/ by analogy with examples (a–d) above; the semivowels in (k) are assigned to these phonemes by analogy with examples (e–f). It is our position that [y] and [w] in (l–n) are also properly assigned to /y/ and /w/ on the basis of phonetic similarity, pattern regularity, and morphophonemic simplicity.

The phonetic features of [y] and of [w] in (l), (m), and (n) do not include, of course, the spirant quality of certain allophones; but the on-glide after a consonant in (l) is comparable in every detail to the nonspirantal allophones that appear initially before vowels in (a), (c), and (j). The off-glides in (m) and (n) are mirror-images of the on-glides in (j) and (l), and are in complementary distribution with them.

In the configurational patterning of Spanish, by this analysis, /y/ and /w/ belong with /b d g r/. Each has, in a general definition, two principal allophone types: a stop (under which we include the affricates [ᵈy̌] or [ɟ], [ᵍw̌], and [ᵈr]) after juncture, after nasals, and sometimes after laterals; and a spirant elsewhere. This general definition needs refinement in some details—thus, /d/ is [d] after /l/ in all dialects and after /s/ in some; but it is accurate enough to show the patterning. The phonemes /b d g/ differ from /y w r/ in that their allophones are distributed obligatorily for speakers of all dialects, while allophones of the latter set are freer variants and in some occurrences carry connotations of substandard speech.

In the sequential patterning of Spanish, by this analysis, /y/ and /w/ belong with /r/ and /l/, as shown by the formulae for consonant clusters initial in the syllable:

Two consonants:
stop or /f/ or /r/ + /l, r/, except /t d r/ not before /l/
consonant + /y, w/, except /č w/ not before /y/

Three consonants:
stop or /f/ or /r/ + /l, r/ + /y, w/, with exceptions as above

Using the symbol R to represent /l/ or /r/, we can sum up all syllable-initial clusters in three formulae: CR, CS, CRS.

The sequential patterning of vowels and consonants appears more regular by this analysis, in that phonetic events of the same order (palatal glides and labiovelar glides) are assigned to parallel classes. As a result, the phoneme /y/ is placed in contrast not with /gu/ but with /w/.

The vocalic system of Spanish, then, includes both simple nuclei (single vowels) and complex nuclei (combinations of vowel plus /y/ or /w/). An utterance contains as many syllables as it has nuclei of either kind. The following nuclei occur:

Simple nuclei	Complex nuclei	
i	—	iw
e	ey	ew
a	ay	aw
o	oy	—*
u	uy	—

*On this gap, see p. 404 below, fn. 9.

[4] While we do not know where all the syllable boundaries are, we are convinced that a Spanish utterance has as many syllables as it has vowels. Thus, /pwérta/ puerta 'door' has two syllables, since no native speaker that we have encountered, when asked to pronounce this as slowly as possible, can reduce it below [pwérrr # tá #]—indicating that the pu- of the spelling denotes a cluster that acts as a unit; whereas /poéta/ poeta 'poet' has three syllables, at least for some speakers who pronounce it slowly as [pó # é # tá #]. We suspect, purely from observation of what native speakers of many languages do with utterances which they are asked to pronounce as slowly as possible, that a syllable is a real unit, definable as the smallest segment of utterance which an untrained native speaker can pronounce in isolation in response to the request, 'Say it as slowly as you can.'

[5] The history of Spanish has many examples of such loss; for instance the loss of /b/ in the development of the imperfect endings -ía, -íamos, -ían.

When two alternative analyses are both adequate to handle the phonemic data, the choice in favor of one or the other may be decided by the resulting morphophonemic simplicity, a corroborative argument on another level. This criterion, as the following discussion will show, appears to favor the interpretation advanced here.

When the last phoneme in the stem of a verb is a consonant, the 3d-person suffixes of the preterit can be analyzed as /-ió, -iéron/, as in comió and comieron; but when this last phoneme is a vowel, the suffixes are clearly /-yó, -yéron/, as evidenced by the spirant allophones of /y/ in /leyó, kreyéron/. By assigning the frictionless allophones [y, w] to the same phonemes /y, w/, we eliminate the need for positing suffixes of the shape /-ió, -iéron/: these are now also /-yó, -yéron/. No statement of morphophonemic alternation between suffixes of different shape is required; we simply write /komyó, komyéron/ and /leyó, leyéron/. The same gain in simplicity is found elsewhere in the morphology, as in the present participle of -ir and -er verbs.

The sequence VSC as in example (m) is particularly significant when we try to decide the phonemic status of dialectally different pronunciation. In most dialects the forms oigo 'I hear' and prohibo 'I prohibit' contrast as [óyγo] /óygo/ vs. [prŏíƀo] /proíbo/. But in some areas, for instance Costa Rica, many speakers say [próyƀo] /próybo/. These differences can be comfortably handled by the traditional phonemic treatment: /óigo, proíbo, próibo/. But now observe the prior nuclei of these forms when the stress follows: oigamos [oyγámos] /oygámos/ vs. prohibir [proiƀír] /proibír/; and add the fact that in Costa Rica, prohibir is /proybír/. These differences cannot be handled by the traditional phonemic analysis; the nuclei in question will all turn out to be written alike. Short of accepting the view put forth in this paper, the difference between oigamos and prohibir can be symbolized in only two ways, both ad hoc: (1) by positing a third level of stress in /prŏìbír/ but not in /ŏigámos/, or (2) by assuming a juncture in /pro+ibír/. The weakness of these solutions need not be argued.

The spirant allophones of /y/ and /w/ occur only in syllable-initial position. We therefore posit a juncture (open transition) after a word-final /y/ or /w/ when the next form begins with a vowel: /ay+úna/ hay una 'there is one' vs. /ayúna/ ayuna 'he is fasting', with spirantal /y/ only in the latter form. When the nature of the open transition in Spanish has been more fully examined, we predict that the features regularly ascribed to it will be found to occur in this position also. The contrast could of course be handled just as well by marking the point of syllable onset. (The traditional analysis would presumably oppose /aiúna/ to /ayúna/—a device which is adequate here but not elsewhere.)

To sum up: the problem of the Spanish semivowels has no perfectly clear and unarguable solution. We have given our reasons for preferring to assign the frictionless allophones [y] and [w] to the phonemes /y/ and /w/. The solution that we offer is the only one that will fit all the facts, and we believe that it has certain conveniences and consistencies desirable in a structural description.

A NOTE ON SPANISH SEMIVOWELS

SOL SAPORTA

Language 32.287-90—1956

In a recent article[1] Bowen and Stockwell discuss the analysis of semivowels in Spanish; in contrast to most other discussions of the problem[2] the authors suggest that the allophones [y] and [w] in forms like bien 'well' and bueno 'good', 'that have been traditionally assigned to /i/ and /u/ should be assigned respectively to ... /y/ ... and ... /w/'. Their criteria are 'phonetic similarity, pattern regularity, and morphophonemic simplicity'. The present note attempts to demonstrate that such a position is untenable, or at least creates more problems than it solves.

The phonetic data are essentially as presented in the cited article, and need not be repeated here. The disagreement arises from the statements that 'the technique of minimal contrast will not answer the question whether bien is /byén/ or /bién/, whether bueno is /bwéno/ or /buéno/. All the arguments on both sides are specifically pattern arguments'. Although it is quite true that there are no minimal pairs involving the cited forms, further investigation of the data reveals the following nearly minimal pairs, where /i/ and /y/ contrast in the frame C...V:

(1) /abyékto/ [aƀy̌ékto] abyecto 'abject': /...byé.../
/abiérto/ [aƀyérto] abierto 'opened': /...bié.../
(2) /inyeksión/ [iny̌eksyón] inyección 'injection': /...nye.../
/niébe/ [nyéƀe] nieve 'snow': /...nié.../
(3) /desyélo/ [dezy̌élo] deshielo 'I unfreeze': /...syé.../
/desiérto/ [desyérto] desierto 'desert': /...sié.../

The contrasts between the examples in (1) and (2) can be accounted for most economically by stating that [y̌] and [y] contrast, the former being assigned to /y/ and the latter to /i/.[3] In the examples included in (3), one could theoretically state that [y̌] and [y] were both members of /i/, and contrast the [z] and the [s], establishing two phonemes /z/ and /s/. The fact, however, that [z] and [s] are in complementary distribution elsewhere seems to be added evidence that in (3) the contrast is between [y̌] and [y] (and furthermore, that /y/ belongs to the class of phonemes which are preceded by the voiced allophone [z] of /s/).

The result, then, is that bien [byén] must be analyzed as /bién/, parallel to abierto [aƀyérto] /abiérto/. The corresponding off-glides in baile [bái̯le] 'dance' and hoy [ói̯] 'today' are assigned to the same phoneme, so that these forms are analyzed as /báile/ and /ói/. In short, in at least some idiolects, phones with palatal friction are assigned to /y/, those without are assigned to /i/.[4]

The distribution of /y/ and /i/ can be schematized as follows, temporarily disregarding the position of stress:

	/y/	/i/
#...V	yo 'I'	y ha visto 'and he has seen'
#...C	—	hijo 'son'
#...#	—	y 'and'
C...V	deshielo 'I unfreeze'	desierto 'desert'
C...C	—	cine 'movie'
C...#	—	comí 'I ate'
V...V	leyes 'laws'	leía 'I was reading'
V...C	—	baile 'dance'
V...#	—	ley 'law'

According to this scheme, /y/ and /i/ contrast before vowels, with only /i/ occurring before con-

[1] J. Donald Bowen and Robert P. Stockwell, The phonemic interpretation of semivowels in Spanish, Lang. 31.236-40 (1955).

[2] In addition to the treatments listed in fn. 1 of the cited article, the problem has been dealt with by the following: Emilio Alarcos Llorach, Fonología española[2] 129-35, 137-40 (Madrid, 1954); George L. Trager, The phonemic treatment of semivowels, Lang. 18.220-3 (1942); Charles F. Hockett, Manual of phonology 54-5, 81 (Indiana University publications in anthropology and linguistics, Memoir 11; 1955). For statements similar to that of Bowen and Stockwell, see B. Pottier's review of E. Alarcos Llorach, op. cit. (1st ed. 1950), Romance philology 5.263 (1952), and Washington Vásquez, El fonema /s/ en el español del Uruguay, Revista de la Facultad de Humanidades y Ciencias 10.87-94 (1953), with the same solution as the one proposed by Bowen and Stockwell, but with no discussion.

[3] An alternative solution is possible, involving the distribution of allophones in terms of syllable position: /i/ is [y̌] in syllable-initial position, but [y] in syllable-medial and final position. Abyecto is /ab-iékto/, abierto is /a-biérto/. But since Bowen and Stockwell admit that they 'do not know where all the syllable boundaries are' (237 fn. 4), presumably they could not use them as criteria.

[4] In part the problem stems from the attempt to devise a single phonemic transcription that will represent many different varieties of Spanish at the same time. In that case, one might revise the wording in the text to read, 'phones with potential palatal friction', where 'potential' means roughly 'in other speakers' pronunciation of the same morpheme'. Such a procedure is open to question, however; cf. Bernard Bloch's statement, A set of postulates for phonemic analysis, Lang. 24.9 (1948), that 'phonological analysis of a given idiolect does not reveal the phonological system of any idiolect belonging to a different dialect.'

sonants and before pause.[5]

One word about patterning: the assignment of certain classes of phones to either /y/ or /i/ has been purely on the basis of phonetic similarity and contrastive distribution. It turns out that the sequences in which the phonemes combine pattern symmetrically; but patterning has not been a criterion in the analysis. It is not clear how pattern congruity can be both a criterion and a result in linguistic analysis, without circularity. If we build symmetry into our methodology, we can be neither surprised nor pleased when it turns up in our analysis. Where possible, it seems preferable to exclude it from our criteria; then, if the analysis reveals that the material is patterned, as it so often is, so much the better.

A similar analysis serves to establish the onglide in bueno as /u/ and not /w/; observe the following contrasting pairs in the environment C...V:

(4) /deswesár/ [dezw̌esár] deshuesar 'to bone': /...swe.../

/desuéyo/ [deswéyo] desuello 'skinning': /...sué.../

/suéko/ [swéko] sueco 'Swede': /sué.../

(5) /sónwébos/ [sóŋw̌éƀos] son huevos 'they are eggs': /...nwé.../

/sónuébos/ [sónwéƀos] son nuevos 'they are new': /...nué.../[6]

Again, phones with friction are assigned to /w/, those without to /u/; bueno is like nuevo, and must be analyzed as /buéno/.

Bowen and Stockwell's claim for morphophonemic simplicity also seems unfortunate. It is quite true that the analysis of certain morphemes, e.g. -ió, -ieron, is simplified, so that comió and leyó have the same allomorph /-yó/. However, precisely the reverse situation exists in other morphemes, so that this suggestion would complicate the morphophonemics. For example, by their analysis, the morpheme {raíz} 'root' would have two allomorphs: /rraís/ in the form raíz 'root', and /rrays/ in the diminutive raicilla. At best, their suggestion simplifies the analysis of some common inflectional morphemes, while complicating the analysis of other morphemes.

Regarding the statements of consonant clusters, the solution proposed by Bowen and Stockwell does not appreciably regularize the patterning. Their analysis results in a class of phonemes /y w r l/ which always appear second in initial clusters. There is no reason to maintain that this solution is any more 'patterned' than the one in which only /r/ or /l/ forms the second member of an initial cluster. Their formulas for initial clusters—CR, CS, CRS—are reduced to CR with the disappearance of S.

There remains the interesting problem posed by the authors, of the contrast between the prior nuclei ... when the stress follows: oigamos ... vs. ... prohibir. These differences cannot be handled by the traditional phonemic analysis; the nuclei in question will ... turn out to be written alike.' This difficulty apparently results from the authors' decision to write only primary stress and not to indicate weak stress in their phonemic transcription. One could account for the difference by indicating all the stresses: oigamos /ŏigámŏs/ and prohibir /prŏĭbír/. The phonemic transcription /oi/ with no stresses indicated is certainly ambiguous: in Spanish, /o/ may represent either stressed /ó/ or unstressed /ŏ/; /i/ may represent stressed /í/, unstressed /ĭ/, or nonsyllabic /i/.[7] Consequently the transcription /oi/ could refer to any one of six phonetic sequences, at least five of which actually occur in most Spanish dialects. (In most dialects, there is no contrast between (d) and (e); the sequences hoy bailó 'today he danced', and cantó y bailó 'he sang and danced' both have /ói/.)

(a) /ŏi/ oigamos '(that) we may hear'
(b) /ŏĭ/ prohibir 'to prohibit'
(c) /ŏí/ oí 'I heard'
(d) /ói/ hoy 'today'
(e) /óĭ/ cantó y bailó 'he sang and danced'
(f) /óí/ cantó himnos 'he sang hymns'[8]

The traditional statement regarding complex syllabic nuclei seems quite adequate: any (stressed or unstressed) vowel may be flanked by /i/ or /u/ to form a diphthong (except that /í/ may be flanked only by /u/, and /ú/ may be flanked only by /i/).[9] In addition, the triphthong /uei/ occurs in a form such as buey 'ox' /buéi/, and in dialects which use the second plural form, the triphthongs /iái, iéi, uái/ occur in forms like cambiáis 'you change', cambiéis '(that) you may change', and averiguáis 'you ascertain'.[10]

[5] Alarcos Llorach, following the Prague tradition, suggests that /y/ and /i/ be considered members of the archiphoneme /I/; the two are neutralized in certain (morphologically determined) positions. He would write ley and leyes /léI/ and /léIes/.

[6] For this pair there are several alternative analyses, of varying (lack of) merit. One can (a) posit a contrast between /nn/ and /n/; (b) introduce /+/ in one or both of the examples; (c) assign both [w̌] and [w] to /u/ and contrast /n/ with /ŋ/ (elsewhere members of one phoneme); (d) indicate syllable onset, as in fn. 3; or (e) analyze [w̌] as a cluster /gu/.

[7] One could equally well transcribe unstressed /i/ in prohibir and nonsyllabic /i̯/ in oigamos: /proibír, oi̯gámos/. But see Hockett 54–5 for the position that 'no such contrast exists'. It is not clear how he would provide for the difference.

[8] One could maintain that (f) should be transcribed with /+/. But see Hockett's statement (55) that 'there is no convincing evidence for an internal open juncture in Spanish'.

[9] Bowen and Stockwell do not list /ow/ (written /ou/ in this note) among their syllabic nuclei. It occurs in admittedly rare forms such as bou 'fishing with a net dragged by two boats' and the proper name Bousoño.

[10] In these dialects, incidentally, the Bowen-Stockwell analysis would yield a final cluster /-ys/ in these forms. Except in recent loanwords (such as golf), Spanish has no final clusters.

A FURTHER NOTE ON SPANISH SEMIVOWELS

J. DONALD BOWEN
ROBERT P. STOCKWELL
Language 32.290-2—1956

In the foregoing article, Saporta raises problems which we suggest can be resolved in the following ways.

(1) How do we handle contrasts like abyecto vs. abierto? These are near-minimal forms, to be cited as examples in a discussion of internal open juncture. The contrast is /ab+yékto/ vs. /abyérto/, where /+/ means open juncture. Hockett's statement, cited in fn. 8, that 'there is no convincing evidence for an internal open juncture in Spanish', should not be accepted uncritically: we think there is abundant evidence. The distribution in normal speech of [b] and [ƀ], of [d] and [đ], of [g] and [g̵], of [n] and [ŋ], of [s] and [z] and [h] cannot be satisfactorily described, we believe, without either a phoneme of open juncture or an appeal to 'free variation' too loose for our taste—unless one is willing to add half a dozen new segmental phonemes to the inventory. We have listed here only the most unequivocal distributional data; we could have added /y, w/ and the satisfactory prediction of the phonetically medial allophone of weak stress. To quote Hockett again, however, 'juncture phonemes achieve their power precisely because of their phonetic heterogeneity' (171). We agree with his methodological principle, but we do not think that he followed it very closely in his discussion of Spanish.

(2) How can pattern congruity be used as an analytical tool, since it should be the <u>result</u> of analysis? Pattern congruity is not a circular argument: the analyst compares two convertible analyses and chooses between them according to which one shows the greater pattern congruity. For example, the traditional analysis of the phones [y] and [w] is /y/ and /gu/ ∾ /u/; in our analytical frame, these phones are simply /y/ and /w/. Aside from the fact that the criterion of phonetic similarity suggests a similar treatment for similar phones in analogous distributions, pattern congruity favors /y/ and /w/. Both solutions can account for this contrast in the phonetic data, but one of them shows greater pattern congruity and is therefore preferable.

(3) Is our solution actually simpler morphophonemically? Our solution introduces morphophonemic complexity into the description of certain stem alternants like /rraís/ ∾ /rrays-/ (which in several dialects are just /rráys/ ∾ /rrays-/), but removes it from twelve inflectional morphs or morpheme combinations /-yéndo, -yó, -yéron, -yéra, -yéramos, -yéran, -yése, -yésemos, -yésen, -yére, -yéremos, -yéren/ and from all bases with stem-final /-Vy/, such as /rréy/—an enormously more productive simplification.

(4) Why not solve prohibir by differentiating between /i/ unstressed and /i/ nonsyllabic, i. e. by writing the weak stress? We mark weak-stressed vowels by the explicit convention of leaving them unmarked. If one interprets our /y/ (all allophones except the fricative ones) as /i/, of course one must mark unstressed vowels, leaving only nonsyllabic /i/ and /u/ unmarked. The result will be that unmarked /i/ and /u/ are simply another way of writing /y/ and /w/. Since, as we have pointed out, /y/ and /w/ already exist in the inventory, the assignment of the semivowel allophones to them (making these allophones predictable without the necessity of marking weak stress) saves a good deal of trouble and has the other advantages already mentioned.

(5) How do we justify the positing of a final cluster, when 'final clusters do not occur in Spanish'? In what sense do they not occur?—only in the sense that everyone who has made this particular observation has assumed that only /-V/ or /-VC/ is possible finally, since the [i̯] of -áis was assigned to /i/. If we were advocating the traditional view, and Saporta were defending the assignment of [i̯] to /y/, he could maintain that final clusters do occur in Spanish, and we could be accused of denying them. It would make just as much sense, and would be no more circular.

(6) What is our reaction to the archiphoneme /I/? Saporta merely cites this without agreement or disagreement; but lest anyone should think it a satisfactory compromise, we must point out that Alarcos Llorach is badly confused as to levels. Since the neutralization takes place 'in certain (morphologically determined) positions' (fn. 5), the suggestion is a morphophonemic one, inappropriate to a discussion of the present problem, which involves phonemic identifications. If the archiphoneme approach is justified at all, it is because of its handling of neutralizations which are phonologically determined.

Finally, we wish to thank Saporta for adding /ow/ to our list of syllabic nuclei. The result is greater pattern congruity.

SPANISH JUNCTURE AND INTONATION

ROBERT P. STOCKWELL
J. DONALD BOWEN
I. SILVA-FUENZALIDA
Language 32.641–65—1956

[Spanish intonational structure is described in terms of three terminal junctures, three pitch phonemes, and three stress phonemes, with other intonation-like phenomena described as of a different order of structuring, the VOCALIZATIONS. Internal open juncture is described as a segmental phoneme marked by a variety of distributional evidence in the allophones of the vocalic and consonantal segments.]

0. INTRODUCTION

0.0. When this study was begun, it was expected that the contours which other investigators had repeatedly noted[1] would in fact turn out to be morphemes composed of isolable contour units: pitch phonemes and juncture phonemes.[2] It was also expected that there would be intonation-like phenomena which were not part of the microlinguistic intonational system. Among these are phenomena which may variously be labelled VOCAL DIFFERENTIATORS, VOCAL IDENTIFIERS, and VOCAL QUALIFIERS, all summarized as VOCALIZATIONS;[3] in general they can be isolated as separate systems which support the microlinguistic system itself, as do gestures. There are at least three criteria which serve to isolate them as separate though supporting systems: (1) they may be added to or imposed upon any given utterance: they do not replace any part of the microlinguistic intonational system; (2) they may all be entirely absent from an utterance, whereas a specifiable minimum of the microlinguistic intonational features must be present in any utterance; (3) they are not discrete in the same way that microlinguistic features are: they are not organizable into unit isolates which cluster into sets and patterns. Examples of the vocalizations will be cited subsequently

[1] T. Navarro-Tomás, *Manual de pronunciación española*[4] (Madrid, 1932), and, most important, *Manual de entonación española*[2] (New York, 1948). From the latter, other studies, none so extensive, have been largely derived, and have been similarly impressionistically phonetic rather than structural.

[2] See J. Donald Bowen, A comparison of the intonation patterns of English and Spanish, *Hispania* 34.30–5 (1956).

[3] See Henry Lee Smith Jr., review of *Intonation of conversational English* (*educated Southern British*), by Wiktor Jassem, in *Lg.* 31.150–3 (1955); *Linguistic science and the teaching of English* (Cambridge, 1956); The communication situation, Department of State lecture outline (1954); also Uriel Weinreich, Stress and word structure in Yiddish , *The field of Yiddish* 15 (New York, 1954). The most complete treatment of vocalizations published so far will appear in Scientific linguistics and psychiatry, by Robert E. Pittenger and Henry Lee Smith Jr., in mimeograph but unpublished at this writing (and subject to title change), to appear in the journal *Psychiatry*.

in this paper. A third expectation was that the intonational system might well resemble, in the components of its structure, others of the Indo-European family of languages which have been analyzed, such as English. It was not expected that the same patterns would be found, but rather that the same kinds of patterning were likely to appear.

0.1. In the actual process of analysis one cannot first lift off the vocalizations and leave the intonational system bare for analysis. In many real utterances, one or more of the vocal qualifiers, if not the differentiators or identifiers, are present, with the result that the analyst has constantly to determine what is additive and therefore separately structured, and what is contrastive within the intonational structure itself. Once a fair corpus has been examined, however, and the minimal counters of the intonational system have been established, one has a frame of reference which makes it possible to reduce any given further corpus to its UNCOLORED shape: uncolored, that is, by vocal qualifiers or other supra-intonational features.

0.2. In the description which follows, we will treat first the intonational system itself. All supporting vocalizations will already have been removed from the examples. When we have established the necessary frame of reference for the intonational system, we will show how and where the vocalizations support the system.

0.3. When an analyst approaches a language that is new to him with the intention of discovering its phonological structure, he must assume the following: (1) that the language has phonemes; (2) that the phonemes are at least segmental and suprasegmental; and (3) that the segmental phonemes are at least vowels and consonants. Operationally it is traditional to discover a good deal about the segmental material before discovering much about the rest, and it is a well-established tradition to present the segmental structure before the rest in a description. It is true, however, that the first features which must be partially delimited are the terminal junctures, and such delimitation is implicit in the description of segments as having 'initial allophones', 'final allophones', 'pre-pause allophones', etc. Pitch contours and loudness elements are likewise partially delimitable with no more known about the segments than was initially assumed. These delimitations are only partial, of course, since the total phonological structure is an interlocking set of dependences which cannot be said to lean in one direction only. It does appear, however, that the full description of some levels of the phonological organization cannot be arrived at until other levels are very fully described; in this sense they are hierarchically arrangeable. The hierarchy is not a linear arrangement with (say) segments at one end and junctures at the other. It is rather a circle which whirls in only one direction, or a line that curves back to meet itself.

0.31. Pitch phonemes, juncture phonemes, and stress phonemes are, in an intonational language which has them all, apparently arranged in this kind of fixed hierarchy of interdependence. The hierarchy need not be the same in one such language as in another. In English, terminal juncture and plus juncture are the first elements of the circle of organization after the segmental phonemes, because their allophones are statable in terms of the tempo of preceding segments.

Tempo is used to mean 'ratio of unit segments to units of time'; for example, a certain number of phonemes per decisecond. It is not the same as individual RATE of speech, since tempo is statable as a variable within any given rate: slowing down from the average rate, speeding up from the average rate, of any given speaker. That the terminal junctures in English are such tempo phenomena is clearly audible, /#/ being the greatest slowing down, approximately two average phoneme lengths (a still inexact figure, stated informally by Martin Joos on the basis of incomplete spectrographic measurements), /||/ being about one-half phoneme length less slowing down (accompanied by pitch rise), and /|/ slowing down about one average phoneme length. Plus juncture also represents a slowing down, but with a critical difference: the slowing down before terminal juncture is at least one average phoneme length and occurs throughout the segments that follow the last strong stress (either primary or secondary); the slowing down of plus juncture is often less than five centiseconds or within the smear-span of the human ear. Being within the smear-span, it will not be heard as what it is, but rather in terms of its effects on the immediately preceding segments. Stress is next in the sequence after junctures; it must be analyzed before and apart from the pitches because the allophones of the latter are statable only in terms of stress and juncture. The pitches then appear last before closing the circle of organization. The assumption that one of the four English stresses can be reduced to allophonic status on the basis of its co-occurrence with some point in the pitch contour is in our opinion untenable because the allophones of the pitches themselves are stated in terms of the differences in stress. The circular organization comes whole at the segments again, since their allophones are statable only partially with respect to segmental position and must be delimited also in relation to the suprasegmental elements. The sequence in English, then, is segments to juncture to stress to pitch and back to segments. This arrangement seems to us to be inherent in the particular kinds of interdependences found in English.[4]

0.32. In Spanish, on the other hand, the ordering shows two fundamental differences: (1) internal open juncture is a type of segmental phoneme, and (2) the allophones of pitch phonemes are not statable in terms of the stress phonemes: on the contrary, the allophones of the stresses are statable only in terms of the pitches, and the pitches in terms of terminal junctures and arrangement. The hierarchical sequence in Spanish, therefore, is segments to terminal juncture to pitch to stress and back to segments.

0.4. The analysis which follows is organized partially in accord with the above order of dependences, which we consider to be inherent in the language structure. The analysis of the vowels and consonants is not our objective, however; we state them first in order to facilitate the transcription of other data. The segmental phonemes are /p t k b d g f (*θ*) s č x m n ñ l ĺ r y w i e a o u/. The multiple trill sometimes assigned to a unit phoneme /r̄/ is treated here as a cluster /rr/, largely for morphophonemic reasons: **quereré* becomes *querré*, final [r̄] in *señor* alternates with [r] in *señor está*, etc.

1. Plus Juncture

1.0. A phoneme of internal open juncture (plus) is discovered operationally by the classification of contrastive segmental data that occur at many morpheme boundaries. The data classified in this way are then descriptively restated in terms of the distribution of the allophones of the segments with respect to each other, and two kinds of transition between phonemes are established: normal transition and open transition. The contrast between the two is differentially meaningful and is therefore phonemic. It is most economically handled as a contrast between presence and absence of a single phoneme, plus juncture. This plus juncture has no physical reality beyond a distributional one. It is not a physical feature of tempo as it seems to be in English. In one sense it is no more than a convenient transcriptional device, but like other segmental phonemes it brings together a set of phonetically different but functionally identical data. It clusters with other segmental phonemes, and the distribution of some allophones of other segmental phonemes are accounted for with respect to such clusters. In English the terminal junctures and the plus juncture are mutually exclusive, i.e. they do not cluster; only one or the other occurs at any point. In Spanish, since plus juncture is a segment, the terminal junctures may occur after it as after other segments. The data that support these conclusions are complex; they are presented in representative samples in the following sections.

1.1. The contrastive segmental material is of several types.

1.11. In some dialects[5] (Caribbean and Central American areas, central Spain, and others) [n] and [ŋ] contrast intervocalically:

[eŋágwas] *en aguas* 'in waters'
vs. [enágwas] *enaguas* 'petticoats'
[eŋóxo] *en ojo* 'in (the) eye'
vs. [enóxo] *enojo* 'anger'
[eŋéros] *en Eros* 'in Cupid'
vs. [enéros] *eneros* 'Januaries'

1.12. In some dialects (Caribbean and Central American areas, north- and

[4] For more discussion relevant to this point in English, see George L. Trager and Henry Lee Smith Jr., *An outline of English structure* (Norman, Okla., 1951; 2d printing, Washington, 1956); also Charles F. Hockett, *A manual of phonology* 45 ff. and 65 ff. (Baltimore, 1955).

[5] Concerning dialects our information is based largely on firsthand observation, and necessarily incomplete. Prior to this writing, we have worked closely for three years with native speakers of Spanish from the following areas: central and northern Spain, urban Mexico, urban Guatemala, urban Costa Rica, urban Venezuela, upland Colombia, upland Ecuador, west-coast Peru, urban Chile. In addition, two of us have, within the past two years, visited every Spanish-speaking capital in the western hemisphere, though in each place for only a week or so. One of the secondary purposes of these visits was to gather dialect information. Silva-Fuenzalida is a native of Santiago, Chile, and has done extensive field work throughout Chile. Among the informants who have aided us immeasurably in collecting data, and to whom we are deeply grateful, are Hugo Montero, Guillermo Segreda, María Kothe, Rodrigo Gurdián, Victor Sánchez, Piedad Becerra, Oscar Salazar, Ernesto Williams, Hugo Pineda, Rosalinda Pineda, Blanca Russell, Enrique Forlong, Juanita Jenkins, Jesús Ríos, Yolanda Lastra, Dolores Oviedo, Mónica Da Rosa, Victoria Angulo, and Antonio Linares.

west-coast lowland South American areas, Canary Islands, and others) [s], [h], and [x] contrast intervocalically:

[ahábah] *haz habas* 'make beans'
vs. [asábah] *asabas* 'you roasted'
vs. [axábah] *ajabas* 'you crumpled'
[mahórkah] *más horcas* 'more gallows'
vs. [masórkah] *mazorcas* 'ears of corn'
vs. [maxórkah] *majorcas* 'ears of corn'
[maharéteh] *más aretes* 'more earrings'
vs. [maxaréteh] *majaretes* 'corn puddings'
[máháh] *más as* 'more ace'
vs. [másah] *masas* 'doughs'
vs. [máxah] *majas* 'you pound'

1.13. In some dialects, probably in all, the point of stress onset in certain clusters is significant:

[sub.lunár] *sublunar* 'sublunar'
vs. [su.blimár] *sublimar* 'sublimate'

1.14. In all dialects the allophones of /b/ ([b] and [b]), of /d/ ([ð] and [d]), and of /g/ ([g] and [g]) fall short of perfect complementation in terms of surrounding segmental phonemes only:

[muybyén] vs. [muybyén] *muy bien* 'very well'
[ézdĕakí] vs. [ézðĕakí] *es de aquí* 'he's from here'
[edáðo] vs. [eðáðo] *he dado* 'I've given'
[éstegálgo] vs. [éstegálgo] *este galgo* 'this greyhound'

1.15. In all or nearly all dialects the first of two contiguous unstressed vowels may or may not be modified by shortening and/or raising or zeroing. Within the utterance partials that correspond to 'words' in the writing system (sequences of letters with spaces that mark boundaries), modification of the first of two contiguous unstressed vowels in one of these three ways is universal in normal colloquial speech:

[lĕonésa] /leonésa/
or [lyonésa] /lyonésa/ *leonesa* 'of León'
[pŏetísa] /poetísa/
or [pwetísa] /pwetísa/ *poetisa* 'poetess'
[ăoríta] /aoríta/
or [oríta] /oríta/ *ahorita* 'right away'[6]

The same three modifications occur in an unstressed vowel contiguous with a following stressed vowel:

[lĕón] /león/ or [lyón] /lyón/ *león* 'lion'
[pŏéta] /poéta/ or [pwéta] /pwéta/ *poeta* 'poet'
[ăóra] /aóra/ or [óra] /óra/ *ahora* 'now'

But when such vowel clusters appear across 'word' boundaries, these modifications may or may not occur, giving four phonetic possibilities of contrast—VV, V̆V, SV, (Ø)V:

[noés] vs. [nŏés] vs. [nwés] *no es* 'it is not'
[laóra] vs. [lăóra] vs. [lóra] *la hora* 'the hour'
[deúrna] vs. [dĕúrna] vs. [dyúrna] *de urna* 'of urn'

The variant forms [nwés] and [dyúrna] do not contrast, respectively, with *nuez* 'nut' and *diurna* 'diurnal'.

1.16. We are not certain that these are all the different types of phonetic data that should be taken into account. There appears to be, for instance, a contrast between the relatively low, lax [ɛ] heard in *perrito* and the relatively high, tense [e] heard in *de rico*:

[pɛrríto] 'little dog' vs. [derríko] 'of (a) rich one'

As of the present we have been unable to classify this and similar data well enough to include them here, except to assert that they exist and must eventually be brought into the full description of the distribution of the phenomena of open transition.

1.2. If there were no other data, those listed above in §§1.11–16 would be sufficient, in our opinion, to assign plus juncture /+/ (transcribed here by a space) to these contrasts:

/en ágwas/	[eŋágwas]	vs. /enágwas/	[enágwas]
/en óxo/	[eŋóxo]	vs. /enóxo/	[enóxo]
/en éros/	[eŋéros]	vs. /enéros/	[enéros]
/as ábas/	[ahábah]	vs. /asábas/	[asábah]
		vs. /axábas/	[axábah]
/mas órkas/	[mahórkah]	vs. /masórkas/	[masórkah]
		vs. /maxórkas/	[maxórkah]
/mas arétes/	[maharéteh]	vs. /maxarétes/	[maxaréteh]
/más ás/	[máháh]	vs. /másas/	[másah]
		vs. /máxas/	[máxah]
/sub lunár/	[sub.lunár]	vs. /sublimár/	[su.blimár]
/muy byén/	[muybyén]	vs. /muybyén/	[muybyén]
/és deakí/	[ézdĕakí]	vs. /ésdeakí/	[ézðĕakí]
/e dádo/	[edáðo]	vs. /edádo/	[eðáðo]
/éste gálgo/	[éstegálgo]	vs. /éstegálgo/	[éstegálgo]
/no és/	[noés]	vs. /noés/	[nŏés]
/la óra/	[laóra]	vs. /laóra/	[lăóra]
/de úrna/	[deúrna]	vs. /deúrna/	[dĕúrna]
/de rríko/	[derríko]	vs. /perríto/	[pɛrríto]

1.3. If plus juncture is not assigned to these contrasts (and others like them), a choice must be made between alternative solutions such as the following.

1.31. Set up several additional segmental phonemes to account for the consonantal contrasts—*/ŋ/, */h/, */b/, */ð/, */g/—and possibly one additional vowel */ɛ/; describe vowel length as phonemic in order to account for the contiguous-vowel contrasts; and make point of syllable division phonemic (i.e. always marked, not statable in terms of the segmental sequence).

1.32. Set up only two additional phonemes—*/ŋ/ and */h/—and ascribe the other alternations to free variation at this level, presumably controlled by stylistic choice.

[6] The phonemic interpretation of semivowels in Spanish, *Lg.* 31.236–40 (1955).((400))

1.33. It seems to us that both of these solutions are to be avoided. The second solution is easily eliminated because it is equivalent to saying that the variation cannot be described systematically even when it can be. Since FREE VARIATION is in our opinion impossible to define in a manner that allows for rigorous identification of the varying elements without the use of more than the minimum of differential meaning ordinarily used for phonemic analysis, and since furthermore it is a criterion which frustrates inquiry into the smaller details of the pattern, we prefer not to use it except in instances where there is clear indication that what appears to be free on the phonemic level is statable as conditioned on a metaphonic or stylistic level. The first solution, however, is not so easily eliminated. Part of it is, because of the redundancy of the several suggestions offered: if the point of syllable division is treated as phonemically significant (by whatever convention—either by marking the point of stress onset if the analyst is convinced that his hearing is up to such a refinement, or simply by spacing between sequences of phonemes to indicate the syllabic groups, defined either distributionally or vocoidally or otherwise), then */ŋ/ and */h/ are redundant, since the contrasts like [enáǥwas] vs. [eŋáǥwas] could be transcribed /e ná gwas/ vs. /en á gwas/, and those like [asáƀah] vs. [aháƀah] could be transcribed /a sá bas/ vs. /as á bas/. It might even be possible to eliminate the */ƀ/, */ð/, and */ǥ/ by careful decisions about where the syllables could be said to divide: [edáðo] vs. [eðáðo] could be interpreted as /e dád o/ vs. /ed ád o/, though such an interpretation would run into a problem with [ezděakí] vs. [ezðĕakí], since few phoneticians would accept /es de.../ vs. /esd e.../ as respectable transcriptions; for whereas there may be doubt about which syllable a single intervocalic consonant goes with, there can hardly be doubt about the division into syllables of a sequence like *es de*. It would, of course, be possible to throw the alternation between voiced stop and spirant into the limbo of free variation, but their patterning is in general too regular for most phonemicists to accept such a conclusion. Since our data show no indication of the presence of tempo phenomena occurring with the stop allophones that might allow for describing them in terms of a higher rank of juncture, it does not seem likely that they are a different order of problem; they must therefore be accounted for on the purely distributional segmental level. No amount of ingenuity in assigning syllable divisions will account for the vowel-length contrasts that appear in examples like [noés] vs. [nŏés], so that while some or all of the consonantal contrasts might be accounted for by syllable division as easily as by plus juncture, the problem of vowel length would remain. Finally, to interpret point of syllable division as phonemic would require that all such points be marked whether any potential contrast existed or not, a highly redundant and wearisome procedure necessitating many arbitrary decisions. In short, the first solution or any modification of it that attempts to account for all the data without plus juncture is to be avoided because it would be excessively complex.

1.4. On the basis of the evidence presented so far, plus juncture in Spanish appears in a distribution that cannot be defined or identified entirely in terms of the allophonic shape of the phonemes which precede it, nor entirely in terms of those which follow it. It appears to have effects in both directions. Thus in dialects which have [z] as an allophone of /s/, [z] occurs in normal transition before certain voiced consonants: /mísmo/ [mízmo] *mismo* 'same', /áslo/ [ázlo] *hazlo* 'do it', /ásno/ [ázno] *asno* 'ass, stupid person'. However, the phonemes /s/ and /d/ in sequence occur in two phonetic shapes: [-zd-] and [-zð-], as in [dézde] and [dézðe] *desde* 'since'. Both forms can occur in a single idiolect or dialect. Since, as pointed out above, [ð] is the allophone of /d/ which is expected in normal transition, we take it that [dézde] is phonemically /dés de/, in spite of the fact that [z] is the allophone of /s/ which occurs before the /+d/. This leaves /désde/ as the phonemic interpretation of [dézðe]. The same interpretations hold for [-zƀ-] vs. [-zb-] and [-zǥ-] vs. [-zg-]:

	/dés de/	[dézde]
vs.	/désde/	[dézðe] *desde* 'since'
	/es byúdo/	[ezbyúðo]
vs.	/esbyúdo/	[ezƀyúðo] *es viudo* 'he's a widower'
	/es gáto/	[ezgáto]
vs.	/esgáto/	[ezǥáto] *es gato* 'it's a cat'

1.41. Such a distribution creates problems. What, for instance, is the phonemic interpretation of [ésbyúðo], which surely occurs in oratorical style? If it is /és byúdo/, then the only element present to differentiate it from /es byúdo/ is the stress on /és/ (unless a higher-level juncture is present, which is quite possible). This, however, may well be enough, though the statement would be complex: /́s+b́/ is phonetically [́sb́] but /-s+b́/ is [-zb́]. At any rate, we would not object to recognizing free variation in an instance of this sort, where there is fair assurance that the variation will actually be statable on a stylistic level[7] (oratorical or emphatic style). Another solution would be to recognize two kinds of internal open juncture: one that signaled a transition involving an utterance-final allophone on its left, an utterance-initial allophone on its right: [-sb-] as in the emphatic /és byúdo/; and a second that signaled a transition involving an utterance-initial allophone on its right but either an unmarked or not-utterance-final allophone on its left: [-zb-] as in /es byúdo/ or [-zd-] as in /dés de/.

1.42. For the moment, at least, we assign the variety of data to one internal open juncture, which is not so ambivalent as it at first appeared to be: if there is conflicting testimony on the two sides of it as to whether it is present or not, the evidence of the far side is accepted as weightier than the evidence on the near side. A revision of the statement about the distribution of [z] is then required: it occurs before voiced consonants or before plus juncture followed by voiced consonants. This means that the kind of voicing assimilation represented in the [z] allophone of /s/ occurs across juncture. Such a description would appear suspiciously ad hoc to scholars accustomed to the fact that junctures regularly break or modify assimilatory sequences, for example in German and English, if it were not possible to adduce a further, and in our opinion decisive parallel: that none of the other Spanish junctures (the terminals) break assimilatory sequences, either of voicing or of point of articulation. Two examples, will serve, one allophonic, the other morphophonemic.

[7] It is, of course, recognized that no one has, to our knowledge, actually described the **conditioning** on this higher level.

1.42.1. In all dialects [ŋ] is the allophone of /n/ that occurs before the velar consonants /k/, /g/, and /x/. It also occurs before /+w/, as in /sán wiče/ [sáŋwiče] *sándwich.* In many dialects, [ŋ] is unattested in any position except in these distributions.[8] The pertinent data follow:[9]

/múybyén↓/ [múyƀyén #] *muy bien* 'very well'
/múybyén|grásyas↓/ [múyƀyéŋ = grásyas #] ...*gracias* 'thanks'
/múybyén↓grásyas↓/ [múyƀyéŋ # grásyas #]
/múybyén↓ grásyas↓/ [múyƀyén # ...grásyas #]

In this series it appears that only [...] breaks the assimilation of /n/ to its velar allophone.[10] As will appear in section 2 below, the phonetic phenomena represented by [=] and [#] are phonemically in contrast, assigned to the terminal junctures /|/ and /↓/.

1.42.2. In all dialects the only nasal phoneme morphophonemically permitted before the labial consonants /p/, /b/, and /f/ is /m/. The following series of data illustrates the same kind of assimilatory sequence as that illustrated above, except now on the morphophonemic level:

/múybyén↓/ [múyƀyén #]
/múybyém|bámos↓/ [múyƀyém = bámos #] ...*vamos* 'let's go'
/múybyém↓bámos↓/ [múyƀyém # bámos #]
/múybyén↓ bámos↓/ [múyƀyén # ...bámos #]

Again only [...] breaks the assimilation. What, then, is the phonemic status of [...]? We assign it a space in the phonemic transcription. This is also the way in which we transcribe /+/. The use of a space for both details is not fortuitous, as one more series of data will show:

/bwéno↓/ [bwéno #] *bueno* 'good'
/bámos↓/ [bámos #] *vamos* 'let's go'
/bwéno|bámos↓/ [bwéno = ƀámos #]
/bwéno↓bámos↓/ [bwéno # ƀámos #]
/bwéno↓ bámos↓/ [bwéno # ...bámos #]

1.42.3. That is, THE VOICED STOPS APPEAR IN THEIR SPIRANT ALLOPHONES AFTER VOWELS UNLESS A PLUS JUNCTURE INTERVENES. In short, plus juncture breaks regressive assimilation of any sort but does not effect progressive assimilation of any sort.[11] [...], which means silence of any duration up to initiation of a new utterance, is equivalent to plus juncture in this respect. The terminal junctures, yet to be described, do not break ANY assimilatory patterns by themselves; plus juncture breaks only the regressive ones by itself; and only a terminal and a plus together can break assimilation in both directions. That is, just as plus juncture functions like a segment rather than a suprasegment in the way it clusters with consonantal or vocalic segments, so it clusters with the terminal junctures, with the result that it breaks assimilation on both sides of it.

1.42.4. By analogy with the terms SEMIVOWEL and SEMICONSONANT, referring to a group of sounds that function sometimes as consonants and at other times as vowels, it might be useful to coin a term like SEMIJUNCTURE to refer to these transitional phenomena in Spanish that we are assigning to plus juncture: in its clustering with segments it functions like a segment; in its other functions it is more like the junctures which are familiar in English and German. But in view of the fact that the terminals alone do not break segmental assimilation, whenever that assimilation IS broken the conclusion seems to us inescapable that in absolute utterance-final position two junctural components are present: a plus juncture, and one of the three terminals. Utterance-internally, there are three possibilities for breaking normal transition: internal open juncture /+/ alone, terminal juncture alone, or terminal juncture in addition to internal open juncture.

1.5. We are now ready to examine further data whose patterning depends on the presence or absence of plus juncture. We take it that the data so far discussed established /+/ as a phoneme that has specific distributional characteristics with respect to the phonemes which precede it (nonassimilatory allophones [ŋ] and [h] appear before it, but assimilatory allophones are unaffected by it) and with respect to the phonemes which follow it (the voiced stops are not assimilated toward the preceding segmental element, i.e. do not appear as continuants of any variety). We have taken the position elsewhere[12] that the [y] and [w] glides of *bien, bueno, rey, Grau* should be assigned phonemically to /y/ and /w/ along with the fricatives [y̌], [ž], [j], and [w̌] that have traditionally been assigned to /y/ and /w/. At that time we suggested (240)+that since the spirant allophones of /y/ and /w/ occur only in syllable-initial position, it would be necessary to posit internal open juncture for contrasts like *hay una* 'there is one' vs. *ayuna* 'he is fasting', the contrast being in the juncture: /ay úna/ vs. /ayúna/. Three other Spanish scholars[13] have written us to inquire how we would handle such contrasts as the following:

[8] See Silva-Fuenzalida's analysis of the distribution of the allophones of /n/ in *Estudio fonológico del español de Chile* (Santiago, 1953).

[9] The symbol [#] means retardation of tempo with drop in pitch level, accompanied by gradual ceasing of phonation if followed by [...]. Neither phonemic nor phonetic pitch levels are indicated, since they are not pertinent to the examples, and only two levels of stress are indicated, strong by acute accent, weak unmarked, even though there are more than two levels (discussed below). Three dots mean a pause of some length (indeterminate: long enough that a second speaker knows that he may now speak without having 'interrupted' the first speaker). [=] means retardation of tempo with no change in pitch level, accompanied by abrupt ceasing of phonation if followed by [...].

[10] Even in Chilean, where final [ŋ] is otherwise unattested.

[11] Progressive assimilation as here used means that the first of two phones becomes more like the second; regressive assimilation means that the second of two phones becomes more like the first.

[12] The phonemic interpretation of semivowels in Spanish.* Since part of the utility of an analysis which includes plus juncture in Spanish depends on the validity of the interpretations in the earlier article, we insert here a further bit of evidence favoring that analysis which we had previously overlooked. There are contrasts which completely eliminate the argument that the nonsyllabicity of /i/ and /u/ is predictable next to other vowels; these contrasts are furthermore, for what it may be worth, indicated in the traditional orthography. Thus /piáda/ *pïada* 'chirping' vs. /pyále/ *piale* 'cast of the lasso'; /piadór/ *pïador* 'chirper' vs. /pyanóla/ *pianola* 'pianola'; /duéto/ *düeto* 'duet' vs. /dwélo/ *duelo* 'duel'; /duérno/ *düerno* 'double sheet' vs. /dwéño/ *dueño* 'owner'. *((401)) +((402))

[13] Sol Saporta of Indiana University, Frederick B. Agard of Cornell University, and Harold V. King of the Centro Cultural Costarricense-Norteamericano. As this article was being prepared in final draft, we learned that Saporta was publishing in this journal further discussion of the matter. He was kind enough to send us a copy of that discussion, and we have added some of his examples without modifying our analysis of the problem.

desierto 'desert'	vs. *deshielo* 'I unfreeze'
abierto 'opened'	vs. *abyecto* 'abject'
hiniesta 'Spanish broom'	vs. *inyecta* 'injects'
unieron 'they united'	vs. *un yerno* 'a son-in-law'
la siega 'the harvest'	vs. *las yeguas* 'the mares'
la suerte 'the luck'	vs. *las huertas* 'the orchards'
lo nuevo 'the new (thing)'	vs. *con huevos* 'with eggs'
desuello 'skinning'	vs. *deshueso* 'I remove the bones from'
radiador 'radiator'	vs. *adyacente* 'adjacent'

1.51. With reference to the pair *desierto–deshielo*, the problem of assuming internal open juncture in the latter form was brought specifically to our attention in this way: 'If the latter form has a juncture /des yélo/, then you have [z] as the allophone of /s/ before /+/, but [s] as the allophone before pause.' Clearly this would require a rapid reversal of position if /+/ had been described in terms of pre-pause allophones, as it usually is, and reasonably can be, for English. But in Spanish, /+/ has its unique distribution, and its effects (i.e. its distribution with respect to contiguous segmental elements) are very unlike the effects that it has in English. With respect to pattern, one may say that the fricative allophones of /y/ and /w/ are to the glide allophones as the stop allophones of /b/, /d/, and /g/ are to the fricative allophones. That is, the difference between them is that of degree of closure: [y̌] is more closed than [y], just as [b] is more closed than [ƀ]. The pattern of occurrence after /+/ is that only the more closed allophone is permitted. Furthermore, as in the example *sublunar–sublimar*, /+/ may occur to change the normal-transition point of syllable division. It then appears that these examples which have been cited involving /y/ and /w/ are closely parallel to those previously cited:

/desyérto/ [desyérto]	vs. /des yélo/ [dezy̌élo]
/abyérto/ [aƀyérto]	vs. /ab yékto/ [aƀy̌ékto]
/inyésta/ [inyésta]	vs. /in yékta/ [iny̌ékta]
/unyéron/ [unyéron]	vs. /un yérno/ [uny̌érno]
/lasyéga/ [lasyéga]	vs. /las yégwas/ [lazy̌égwas]
/laswérte/ [laswérte]	vs. /las wértas/ [lazw̌értas]
/lonwébo/ [lonwéƀo]	vs. /kon wébos/ [koŋw̌éƀos]
/deswéyo/ [deswéy̌o]	vs. /des wéso/ [dezw̌éso]
/rradyadór/ [r̄aðyaðór]	vs. /ad yasénte/ [aðy̌asénte]

The parallel elements are three: (1) /+/ does not prevent assimilation of the phoneme that precedes it; (2) /+/ closes the phoneme that follows it; (3) /+/ is the point of syllable division: when it does not occur, the syllable divides before permitted initial clusters. The end result of this parallelism is that the problem raised about [z] before /+y/ or /+w/ simply disappears: it would only be a problem if it were not [z].

1.52. We should call special attention to the contrast between *hay una* and *ayuna*: it appears that a large number of plus junctures are hereby introduced into the language because of words like *soy*, *estoy*, *voy*, *doy*, *ley*, *rey*. Our observation is, however, that this plus, like many others (e.g. between vowels) may in some styles or dialects drop in or out morphophonemically, so that a sequence like *hay una* is either [ayúna] or [ay̌úna], i.e. either /ay úna/ or /ayúna/, though beyond all doubt it is more often [ayúna]; and *ayuna* also has either shape and one more: [aǰúna] /a yúna/. When the pronunciation of either item is [ay̌úna], there is no /+/. When the pronunciation is [ayúna], there is /+/, again in either item.[14]

1.6. Up to this point we have stated our reasons for the assignment of plus juncture to one member of paired contrasts of four types: (1) those involving utterance-final allophones of a nonassimilatory type whenever these allophones appear in distributions that would otherwise contrast with nonfinal allophones of the same phoneme: [h] vs. [s], [ŋ] vs. [n]; (2) those involving sequences of contiguous vowels: [VV] vs. [V̌V]: this is in fact a subclass of the utterance-final allophone group that includes [h] and [ŋ], since [V] occurs finally but [V̌] occurs only in normal transition with a following [V]; (3) those involving utterance-initial allophones whenever these allophones appear in distributions that would otherwise contrast with noninitial allophones of the same phoneme, such as [b] vs. [ƀ], [d] vs. [ð], [g] vs. [ɡ], [y̌] vs. [y], [w̌] vs. [w]: this type is in effect a breaking of regressive assimilation without the breaking of progressive assimilation in the same environment; and (4) those involving nonpredictable syllable division. The list omits the problem of the tense and lax allophones of /e/, since we cannot describe the distribution exhaustively, and it leaves for discussion until section 4 the question of the possible relative distribution of plus juncture and medial stress.

2. TERMINAL JUNCTURE

2.0. In addition to the transition phenomena subsumed under plus juncture in the preceding discussion, there are other kinds of transition phenomena which are identified by Spanish speakers as places where various kinds of pause occur. These pauses are phonetically the effect of retardation in the tempo of utterance. There is also an effect on the pitch of the immediately preceding syllable. In footnote 9 the phonetic symbol [⋇] was defined as meaning retardation of tempo with drop in pitch level, accompanied by gradual ceasing of phonation if

[14] This is a point on which we do not wish to seem more vulnerable than we are. We recognize that this very matter will cause advocates of the alternative analysis (/aiúna/ for *hay una* vs. /ayúna/ for *ayuna*) to be more firmly convinced of the validity of their position than any other unresolved area of disagreement. We must point out that the language really is not very neat at this point, and that both solutions are about equally vulnerable. The vulnerability of our solution we have already acknowledged—it forces plus juncture into places where we would rather not have it, as in the nonfricative pronunciation of the palatal in *ayuna*. The vulnerability of the alternative solution is well stated in a letter from Harold V. King, dated 7 March 1956, which we quote with his permission: 'There is one thing which I think will continue to bother me about this for a long time. As of now, I think forms like *bien* contain an occurrence of the phoneme /i/. And this allophone of /i/ contrasts with /y/. However, those speakers who have a non-fricative /y/ (like many Josefinos and most Bogotanos) sound to me as if they are making the same noise in *mayor* that they make in *hielo*. In other words, my difficulty is that some occurrences of /y/ sound practically the same as some occurrences of /i/. The main thing that makes them different is that among many other speakers a fricative *y* is much more frequent in *mayor* than in *hielo*.'

followed by [...]. [...] means pause of indeterminate length. This set of phonetic phenomena we assign to the terminal juncture /↓/, which we label TERMINAL FALL. It can occur at any pitch level and contrasts with two other sets of phonetic data. The first of these other sets is transcribed phonetically with [||], defined to mean retardation of tempo with sharp rise in pitch level, accompanied by abrupt ceasing of phonation if followed by [...]. [||] is assigned phonemically to /↑/, which we label TERMINAL RISE. It can occur at any pitch level and contrasts with /↓/ and with one other set of phonetic data. This third set is indicated phonetically by the symbol [=], defined to mean retardation of tempo with no change in pitch level, accompanied by abrupt ceasing of phonation if followed by [...]. [=] is assigned phonemically to /|/, which we label TERMINAL LEVEL. There is some difficulty in stating through how much of the preceding utterance the retardation occurs, but in our observation it does not appear to go back beyond the last strong stress. A sound spectrograph has not been available to us for the precise measurement of this detail.

2.1. From the above definitions it would appear that all three involve retardation of tempo and are differentiated phonetically in two respects: (1) their effect on the pitch level, and (2) the degree of abruptness with which phonation ceases when pause follows, /↓/ having gradual cessation, /↑/ and /|/ abrupt cessation. If these observations are accurate, one might legitimately assign the pitch rise to pitch phonemes and make the degree of abruptness of cessation the contrasting feature, thus reducing the terminal junctures to two: abrupt vs. gradual. These could be symbolized as /|/ and /–/. The terminal possibilities within the two systems would be interconvertible as follows:

A. 3 TERMINALS		B. 2 TERMINALS
/^{3}↓/	=	/^{32}–/
/^{2}↓/	=	/^{21}–/
/^{1}↓/	=	/^{10}–/
/^{3}↑/	=	/^{34}|/
/^{2}↑/	=	/^{23}|/
/^{1}↑/	=	/^{12}|/
/^{3}|/	=	/^{3}|/
/^{2}|/	=	/^{2}|/
/^{1}|/	=	/^{1}|/

2.2 On what ground is a choice between the two systems to be made? To examine the question, assume that there are three contrasting levels of pitch on syllables that do not immediately precede one of these junctures, for example at the beginning of an utterance of two or more syllables. (Data of this type will be discussed in section 3.) By the criterion of completeness both systems are satisfactory: they handle all the data. By that of consistency, again they are about equally satisfactory, though B is somewhat better than A in that all pitch phenomena are restricted to interpretation by pitch phonemes, whereas in A some pitch phenomena are said to belong to pitch phonemes while other quite similar phenomena are assigned to the terminal junctures. But by the criterion of simplicity, A is decidedly superior to B, since B requires five pitch phonemes, two of which are restricted to occurrence with terminal junctures, while A requires only three pitch phonemes, all of which can be modified upward or downward as a result of occurrence with /↑/ or /↓/. That is, A is the interpretation which allows for greatest freedom of occurrence (widest distribution) of all the phonemes of each type. Another disadvantage of the B solution is that it introduces asymmetry into the shape of intonation morphemes: all those ending in the /↓/ or /↑/ of the A solution have, in the B conversion, one pitch phoneme more than those ending in /|/. For these reasons, then, we adopt A.

2.3. Following are minimal or near-minimal pairs of utterances transcribed phonemically, including the pitch phonemes (though only the last one before each juncture is pertinent at this point), which, uttered in such a way as to have the particular meanings assigned them, contain these three terminal junctures.

1 2 2 11
/akíbyénemaría↓/ *Aquí viene María.* 'Here comes Mary.'

1 2 2 1 1 11
/akíbyéne|maría↓/ *Aquí viene, María.* 'Here he comes, Mary.'

1 2 2 22
/akíbyénemaría↑/ *¿Aquí viene María?* '(Did you say) Here comes Mary?'

1 2 2 11
/akíbyénemaría|/ *Aquí viene María.* 'Here comes Mary (again, darn it).'

2 22 2 1 1
/bámosabér|képása↓/ *Vamos a ver qué pasa.* 'Let's see what's going on.'

2 1 1 2 2 1 1
/bámos↓ abérképása↓/ *¡Vamos! A ver qué pasa.* 'Let's go! What's the trouble, anyway?'

2 11 2 1 1
/bámosabér↓ képása↓/ *Vamos a ver. ¿Qué pasa?* 'Let's see. What's the trouble?'

2 22 2 2 2
/bámosabér|képása↑/ *¿Vamos a ver qué pasa?* 'Shall we go see what's the matter?'

1 2 2 2 2 1 1
/laseñóra↑ nóestáenkása↓/ *¿La señora? No está en casa.* 'The lady? She's not in.'

1 2 2 2 2 1 1
/laseñóra|nóestáenkása↓/ *La señora no está en casa.* 'The lady's not in.'

1 2 2 21 1 2 1 1
/laseñóra↑ nó↓ estáenkása↓/ *¿La señora? No. Está en casa.* 'The lady? No. She's at home.'

1 2 2 2 2 2 2
/laseñóra|nóestáenkása↑/ *¿La señora no está en casa?* 'The lady isn't at home?'

1 2 11 1 2 1 1
/laseñóranó↓ estáenkása↓/ *La señora no. Está en casa.* 'Not the lady. She's at home.'

2.4. The following concluding observations are made about the three terminal junctures. (1) They do not break assimilation, either allophonic or morphophonemic (see §1.42.3 above). (2) They do break contours: that is, given the six impressionistic contour possibilities of falling, rising, level, rising-falling, falling-rising, and rising-falling-rising, between any two such contours a terminal juncture is present. Indeed, the contour-breaking function is more obvious than tempo retardation when terminal junctures occur in any distribution except between two level contours of the type of /^{222}|/ or /^{111}↓/.

3. Pitch

3.0. There are only four distributional positions in which it is possible for any pair of utterances to contrast with respect to pitch level: (1) immediately after silence or terminal juncture, i.e. simultaneous with the first syllable of the PHRASE, using the term at this level to mean 'utterance-partial between two terminal junctures or between silence and terminal juncture'; (2) immediately before terminal juncture; (3) at any strong-stressed syllable within the phrase; (4) at a weak-stressed syllable that immediately precedes the last strong-stressed syllable before a terminal juncture.[15] In each of these positions in uncolored utterances there are three levels of contrasting pitch. These are assigned to three pitch phonemes: low /¹/, mid /²/, and high /³/. Each has allophones distributed complementarily with respect to (1) silence and the terminal junctures and (2) the other pitch phonemes which occur before and after within the same phrase or contour.

3.1. The lowest allophones of each pitch phoneme occur before /↓/. The next lowest appear after silence (i.e. after [...]). The mid-ranges of each pitch phoneme occur within the span of utterance that is not contiguous with either terminal juncture or silence. The highest allophones occur before /↑/.

3.2. Between the points at which a pitch phoneme may occur (i.e. the points at which significantly contrasting levels of pitch are encountered), there may be several syllables in a smooth contour that spans, with respect to relative pitch, the entire continuous range from one of these points to the next. This range is assigned to the pitch phoneme which begins the span; that is, a pitch phoneme occupies the segmental area from the point of its initiation up to the point where the next pitch phoneme is initiated. This holds for all distributions except one: the next-last pitch phoneme before a terminal juncture occupies only the area of its actual phonetic occurrence. The subsequent range between it and the final pitch phoneme is assigned to the final one. Thus, in example (a), where the pitch falls rather evenly from the mid beginning to the low ending, pitch phoneme /²/ occupies the first syllable /dí/, pitch phoneme /¹/ occupies all the rest; in example (b), where the first four syllables are low and the last falls

2 1 1 21
(a) /dígamelo↓/; (b) /semeolbidó↓/

from mid to low, pitch phoneme /¹/ occupies the first four syllables, while pitch phonemes /²/ and /¹/ together occupy the last. In the latter example, both the pitch on which the syllable /dó/ begins and the pitch on which it ends are significant (this being a final stressed syllable); here it is impossible to say at what point the final pitch begins except that it begins after the next-last pitch has occurred. This is the only distribution in which the line between the spans of occurrence of each pitch phoneme cannot be drawn cleanly.

3.3. Examples of the occurrence and distribution of the pitch phonemes follow.[16]

[15] It is assumed that strong stress can be identified even though its allophones have not been described. Note that the allophones of the pitch which occurs at this point are not described in terms of the stress; only the location of them.

[16] Open juncture is assumed not to occur in the utterances here transcribed, though it may or may not in any one of them.

1 2 1
/laseñóra↓/ *la señora* 'the lady'
1 2 2 1 2 1
/lakása|delaseñóra↓/ *la casa de la señora* 'the lady's house'
1 2 2
/laseñóra↑/ *¿la señora?* 'the lady?'
1 2 2 2 2 2
/laseñóra|delakása↑/ *¿la señora de la casa?* 'the lady of the house?'
1 2 2
/laseñóra↓/ *la señora* 'the lady' (Mexican)
1 2 21
/laseñórakí↓/ *la señora aquí* 'the lady here'
1 2 31
/laseñórakí↓/ *la señora aquí* 'the lady HERE'
2 1 1
/démeótro↓/ *déme otro* 'give me another'
3 1 1
/démeótro↓/ *déme otro* 'GIVE me another'
2 3 22
/además|/ *además* 'besides ...'

4. Stress

4.0. With the phonemes of juncture and pitch identified and described as to the distribution of their allophones, it is finally possible to describe the phonemes of stress. It will be seen that though they are the first of the nonsegmental elements usually identified, in terms of the language structure they cannot be adequately described without the other elements, since the distribution of the allophones of the phonemic stresses is otherwise not statable. We offer in advance an apology for the fact that we must describe the history of how we arrived at our position (that Spanish has three phonemic stresses), since with nearly all other Hispanists we had previously seen no need for more than two stresses to account for all the facts. We still 'feel' that two stresses ought to be enough for this language, but there are conflicts in the data which we cannot, as yet, resolve with fewer than three. In pedagogy we still use only two, assigning the medial stress to a marginal position in the structure as carrying an exceedingly low functional load. We will gladly accept a description that can predict it without mixing levels, without using free variation in a way that we cannot accept, and without ignoring any of the data that we will cite. Until such a description is proposed, we will have to be satisfied with a third stress.

4.1. The phonemic stresses of Spanish are three: strong /ʹ/, medial /ˋ/, and weak (unmarked).[17] Phonetically, however, there are four clearly distin-

[17] We would like to lay once, and we hope for all, the ghost of the descriptive approach which would say that weak stress is not a phoneme—it is only the absence of strong stress, so that there is only one stress phoneme in Spanish, which contrasts with the absence of stress. We hold that it is important to recognize an essential difference between segmental phonemes and suprasegmental phonemes: a segmental phoneme may contrast with its own absence: *cat* vs. *at*; but no utterance can be made without pitch or stress or, we believe, juncture phenomena being acoustically present. Since they are acoustically present, they either differentiate utterances or they do not. If they do not, the conditions that govern their occurrence and distribution must be stated. If they do, there cannot be fewer than TWO of each type that is significant, since they lack the possibility of being absent from an utterance altogether like a segmental phoneme.

guishable levels: weak [˘], medial [`], strong [^], and strongest [´]. Weak is assigned to phonemic WEAK, medial to phonemic MEDIAL, strong and strongest to phonemic STRONG. Many scholars, including ourselves, have attempted to predict the distribution of weak and medial. One attempt was made by Trager,[18] working from the data of T. Navarro Tomás. We were certain that his rules would not work consistently, because the beginning point of predictability for a sequence is not only silence but also any of the four junctures. The two faults of his description seemed to us to be (1) that he dealt only with stress in morphemic words, which he would be the first today to call a mixing of levels, and (2) that he did not consider the occurrence of the medial stress in its relation to juncture. He also correlated, we believe erroneously, higher pitch with louder stress, when in fact the two systems must be separated.

4.11. Working from data of the type used by Trager, we found certain phonetic observations in need of refinement. (1) We heard no medial stress on the final syllable[19] of items like /rrápido/ *rápido* 'fast', /dígamelo/ *dígamelo* 'tell me (it)', /teléfono/ *teléfono* 'telephone', /simpátiko/ *simpático* 'nice', /digámoselo/ *digámoselo* 'let's tell him (it)', /konosyéndose/ *conociéndose* 'knowing one another', /despidyéndomelo/ *despidiéndomelo* 'telling him goodbye for me', /komunikándome/ *comunicándome* 'letting me know': on the contrary, there is often reduction of the last one, two, or three weak-stressed syllables to whisper, especially the last syllable.[20] (2) In items like /rrasyonalidádes/ *racionalidades* 'rationalities', /komunikasyónes/ *comunicaciones* 'communications', /xeneralisasyón/ *generalización* 'generalization', where Trager's description would place TWO medial stresses before the primary (on syllables 1 and 3), we heard medials only on the first syllable.

4.12. The result of these disagreements seemed to be that if our hearing of medial stress was correct, it was the allophone of weak stress that appeared in one distribution: on the first syllable of a morphemic word whose strong stress appeared no earlier than the third syllable. This statement, as made, mixed levels and should have been revisable as follows: the medial allophone of weak stress appears on any syllable immediately following a juncture if that syllable does not itself have strong stress and is separated by at least one or more syllables from a following strong stress. This revision, we thought, left two problems: (1) would it be possible to avoid setting up a juncture of the internal type by phonemicizing the medial stress? (2) how are syllables identified in Spanish? To the first question the answer appeared to be that the juncture was needed to handle a variety of other data in the language (section 1 above). Once it had been established on distributional grounds by the other data, if the occurrence of medial stress could be correlated with it, a phoneme of medial stress would be redundant. To the second question the answer was, and is, that there are as many syllables as there are vowels (we analyze the semivowels [i̯] and [u̯] as /y/ and /w/[21]). A third question we did not ask until much later: would there be a conflict between segmental evidence and suprasegmental evidence as to the presence of the juncture? To this question we will return below.

4.13. The two allophones of weak stress, then, seemed to be distributed complementarily with respect to the occurrence of a following primary stress and a preceding internal open juncture and/or any higher-ranking juncture of the terminal order. Examples of the following type seemed quite convincing:

2 2 1 2 1 1
/bíbo|enlakása internasyonál↓/*Vivo en la casa internacional.*[22] 'I live in the International House.'

2 2 1 1
/dóndebá trabaxár↓/*¿Dónde va a trabajar?*[23] 'Where are you going to work?'

1 2 1 1
/paradóndebá↓/*¿Para dónde va?*[24] 'Where are you headed for?'

1 2 2 1 2 1
/mandé|un telegráma↓/*Mandé un telegrama.*[25] 'I sent a telegram.'

Like internal open junctures in other languages, it appeared that some or all of these junctures that CONDITIONED the medial allophone could drop out (i.e. the utterances were made sometimes without them, sometimes with them), though some of them were more stable than others. When no medial stress was heard and no other features of internal open juncture were present, then, regardless of morpheme boundaries, the juncture was assumed to be absent.

4.14. We returned now to the question whether there might be a conflict between segmental evidence and suprasegmental evidence as to the presence of the juncture. There was. We now believe the conflict to be irreconcilable, as shown by this unarguable piece of data:

[lozƀàtayónes] *los batallones* 'the batallions'

Between [z] and [ƀ] there is no segmental evidence of plus juncture. On the contrary, every signal of normal transition is present. But there is a phonetically medial stress on [ƀa]. That it is not a weaker allophone of the strong stress which coincides with the highest pitch is demonstrable by placing it in a larger frame:

[lozƀàtayônezƀyénen] *Los batallones vienen.* 'The batallions are coming.'

That the difference in intensity or loudness is not a function of vowel sonority is clear from the fact that the vowel of the next syllable [ta] should presumably be of identical sonority and therefore intensity, but is not. That it is not conditioned by its position two syllables back from the strong stress on [yó] is demonstrable by contrast with [tràƀaxađór] where by such a rule the medial stress ought to

[18] George L. Trager, The phonemes of Castillian Spanish, *Travaux du Cercle linguistique de Prague* 8.217–22 (1939).

[19] Unless, that is, a full primary stress is actually present. This is often the case, especially with enclitic pronouns: /dígamelo/ can be /dígameló/, and usually is so in a formal style of speaking; in certain dialects, such as that of Montevideo or Santiago de Chile, this style seems to be generalized to completely colloquial usage.

[20] Parenthetically, our English-speaking students need constantly to be corrected for their tendency to put medial stress on the final syllable if it is at two or more removes from the primary, and English speakers tend to hear extra loudness here where we hold that none is present.

[21] The phonemic interpretation of semivowels in Spanish. ((400))

[22] Medial stresses on /en/ and /in-/; we thought that [oè] and [aì] occurred in our original data without shortening of the first vowel, corroborating the position of plus as determined by medial stress.

[23] Medial stress on /tra-/.

[24] Medial stress on /pa-/.

[25] Medial stress on /te-/.

occur on [ƀa]. There is, in our opinion, only one resolution: the medial stress is a phoneme. We have not yet encountered a minimal contrast. It is predictable in more than three-quarters of its occurrences by the previously described correlation with juncture. It certainly was allophonic at some fairly recent period in the history of the language. Its functional load is exceedingly light. But for the moment we cannot escape the conclusion that it is a phoneme.

4.15. Having arrived at this conclusion, we proceeded to re-examine data that had previously given trouble. It has already been mentioned (§1.15) that sequences of vowels in normal transition show certain regular alternations: /VV/ [V̆V] ~ /SV/ [SV] ~ /V/ [V]. The item *ahorita* /aoríta/ had two reduced shapes which we could transcribe phonemically without being able to explain how, historically, both kinds of reduction could have occurred: /oríta/ and /awríta/. With a medial stress in the language, it becomes clear that the reductions go back to forms differentiated by the presence or absence of medial stress on what was the first syllable:

/àoríta/ becomes */àwríta/ becomes /awríta/
/aoríta/ becomes /oríta/

That is, in a sequence of two vowels of which the first is stressed (either strong or medial), it is the second vowel that is reduced, with the results indicated. Other examples, once the pattern is clear, are easily encountered:

/àorrár/ alternates with /awrrár/ *ahorrar* 'to save'
/àumádo/ alternates with /awmádo/ *ahumado* 'smoked'
/àixár/ alternates with /ayxár/ *ahijar* 'to adopt'

4.16. One further result of this discovery is that we must retract a published assertion:[26] 'Short of accepting the view [that [i̯] is /y/ and [u̯] is /w/] ... the difference between *oigamos* and *prohibir* can be symbolized in only two ways, both ad hoc: (1) by positing a third level of stress ... The weakness of [this] solution need not be argued.' Although no one argued it, someone should have. (It does not modify our position, however, regarding the distribution of /y/ and /w/.)

4.17. It is pertinent to note that when, for special oratorical or other stylistic effect, a speaker of Spanish wants to emphasize a multisyllabic item at more than one point, he regularly replaces a medial stress by a strong one: /tràbaxár/ appears as /trábaxár/ or even /trábáxár/, but not */trabáxár/. This stylistic device of replacing a medial stress by strong stress is especially common if the syllable involved happens to be analyzable on the morphological level as a prefix: /dèskomposisyón/ *descomposición* 'decomposition' appears as /déskomposisyón/.

4.18. It is clear that the failure to predict the occurrence of medial stress will introduce a certain amount of morphophonemic complexity into the description of Spanish. An item like *responsabilidad* appears freely with either of two shapes: /rrèsponsabilidád/ and /rrespònsabilidád/, and either medial may be heightened to strong.

4.19. On the other hand it may become much easier to describe the boundaries of minimal free forms by observing the distribution of plus juncture and medial stress. All of the implications are not clear to us at this time, and we leave them for further study.

4.2. The prediction of the distribution of strong and strongest is in terms of terminal juncture and pitch level. Between two terminal junctures, or between silence and a terminal juncture, one phonetically strongest stress must occur; in addition, at least two phonetically strong stresses may occur, and perhaps more.[27] If two or more phonemically strong stresses occur, the phonetically strongest is always the last of them unless there is a high pitch on a strong stress within the boundaries, in which case the strongest will coincide with the first high pitch on a strong stress and need not be last. In a series of phonemic phrases, each but the last terminated by /|/, the strongest stress in the last phonemic phrase is the strongest of all. Phonetically strong and phonetically strongest are therefore allophones of a single stress phoneme /ʹ/, strongest when last before a terminal juncture or simultaneous with a high pitch /³/, but strong elsewhere. Examples of this distribution follow:

2 1 1
/páblomèlodyó↓/ *Pablo me lo dió.*[28] 'Paul gave it to me.'

2 3 1
/bwénosdías↓/ *Buenos días.*[29] 'Good morning.'

1 2 2 1 2 2 2 1 1
/estámos|ènlotél|nórteamerikáno↓/ *Estamos en el Hotel Norteamericano.*[30] 'We're in the North-American Hotel.'

1 3 1 1
/peropàradóndebá↓/ *Pero ¿para dónde va?*[31] 'But WHERE're you headed?'

1 3 3 1 1
/peropàradónde|bá↓/ *Pero ¿para dónde va?*[32] 'But WHERE're you HEADED?'

1 3 3 3 1 1 1
/perokébasér|enlasyudád↓/ *Pero ¿Qué va a hacer en la ciudad?*[33] 'But what in the world are you going to do in the city?'

5. Intonation Patterns and Superfixes

5.1. Our analysis indicates that a phonemic description of Spanish requires, besides 24 segmental phonemes, the following inventory:

1 internal open juncture:	/+/
3 terminal junctures:	/|/, /↑/, /↓/
3 pitches:	/¹/, /²/, /³/
3 stresses:	/ʹ/, /ˋ/, /˘/

[26] The phonemic interpretation of semivowels in Spanish 240. ((402))

[27] In our data up to this time we find no utterances with more than three phonemically strong stresses between the boundaries above stated. When we try to expand the utterances so constructed, a terminal juncture is invariably inserted to break the material into two phonemic phrases, each containing three strong stresses or fewer. We are, however, not yet sure that this is structurally mandatory; in fact, we doubt that it is.

[28] /dyó/ strongest even though on /¹/.

[29] /dí-/ strongest.

[30] /ká-/ strongest, again even though on /¹/.

[31] /dón-/ strongest, though not last, because coincident with /³/.

[32] /bá/ strongest, though on /¹/, because last phrase.

[33] /ké/ strongest in the first phrase, being coincident with the first /³/, but /-dád/ stronger still because last phrase.

5.2. A sequence of pitches up to and including a terminal juncture will be referred to as an INTONATION PATTERN. Whether or not such a sequence of supra-segmental elements is a morph remains to be demonstrated on the morphological level of analysis. It is convenient to refer to the segmental material within the boundaries of one intonation pattern as a PHONEMIC PHRASE. A sequence of stresses, including plus junctures, up to but not including a terminal juncture, will be referred to as a SUPERFIX. Again it remains to be demonstrated whether a superfix is a morph.

6. Shift

6.0. When utterances are elicited from an informant, certain intonation patterns regularly recur. These are citation patterns. They can be re-elicited from any number of informants with almost perfect consistency. They are also heard in normal discourse, but no sampling or statistical work of any sort has been done to indicate whether such patterns are the most frequent ones or not. It is true, however, that where they are observed in normal discourse they can be shown by questioning to carry no additional component of differential meaning beyond that which is assignable to the segmental morphemes alone. Such patterns may, for convenience, be labelled NORMAL. The term is seriously misleading in that it implies that the pattern is more frequent, but it has gained currency even among those who object to it, because some term is needed for a point of reference, by contrast with which other intonation-patterns show a variety of differential meanings. Such a situation exists on this level simply because no utterance can be made in an intonational language without some intonation pattern. It is possible to have a contrast between a segmental morpheme and its absence, but not between an intonation pattern and its absence: only between one intonation pattern and another.

6.1. Any intonation pattern that contrasts with the normal pattern is the result of SHIFT. Like NORMAL PATTERN, SHIFT is poor terminology because it implies process description when in fact the process is not observable: only the units, of whatever rank, and their arrangements are observable. For lack of a more nearly adequate terminological frame of reference, we will describe briefly the kinds of shift phenomena that have been observed in Spanish in the only way open to us at this time: as a process of change from the normal pattern.

6.2. Shift is of four types in Spanish.

6.21. Raising of normal /²/ to /³/:

2 1 1 /kébrúto↓/ 'How stupid!'	becomes	3 1 1 /kébrúto↓/ 'How STUPID!'	*¡Qué bruto!*
2 1 1 /ótrakósa↓/ 'Another thing.'	becomes	3 1 1 /ótrakósa↓/ 'And ANOTHER thing!'	*Otra cosa.*
(the same)	becomes	2 3 1 /ótrakósa↓/ 'That's quite another matter.'	(the same)

6.22. Intensifying medial or weak stress to strong stress, with correlated pitch and/or phrase changes:

2 1 /syéntese↓/ 'Sit down.'	becomes	3 1 /syéntesé↓/ 'SIT DOWN!'	*¡Siéntese!*
(the same)	becomes	3 1 11 /syénte|sé↓/ 'SIT DOWN!!'	(the same)
1 2 1 /bastárdos↓/ 'Bastards.'	becomes	2 2 1 /bástárdos↓/ ('Those) BAstards!'	*¡Bastardos!*
2 22 1 21 /nósabía|nimànexár↓/ 'He didn't even know how to drive.'	becomes	2 22 1 3 31 /nósabía|nimánexár↓/ 'He didn't even know HOW TO DRIVE!'	*No sabía ni manejar.*

6.23. Occurrence of pitch /³/ on a weak-stressed syllable preceding final /′/ in the phrase:

2 1 1 /béngakonmígo↓/ 'Come with me.'	becomes	2 3 1 1 /béngakonmígo↓/ (coaxing) 'Just come with me.'	*Venga conmigo.*
2 1 1 /nómedíga↓/ 'You don't say!'	becomes	2 3 1 1 /nómedíga↓/ 'You DON'T say!'	*No me diga.*
1 2 1 1 1 /mañána|ómbre↓/ 'Tomorrow, chum.'	becomes	3 2 1 1 1 /mañána|ómbre↓/ (bored, slightly irritated) 'Tomorrow, chum.'	*Mañana, hombre.*

6.24. Shortening of normal phrase-length by insertion of /\|/:

1 2 1 1 /losestádosunídos↓/ 'The United States.'	becomes	1 2 2 1 2 1 /losestádos|unídos↓/ (more deliberate)	*Los Estados Unidos.*
2 1 1 /béngakonmígo↓/ 'Come with me.'	becomes	2 2 1 2 1 /bénga|konmígo↓/ 'Come with ME.'	*Venga conmigo.*

7. Vocalizations

7.0. The general criteria for separating the vocalizations were stated in the introduction of this discussion. The most highly structured of these supra-intonational systems are the vocal qualifiers.

7.1. The VOCAL QUALIFIERS are extensions of elements that are discretely structured within the microlinguistic system. It would seem probable that these extensions are always paired, since they may occur in two directions away from the norm. Several may occur simultaneously, but never more than one of a pair. The following pairs occur in Spanish.

7.11. OVERLOUDNESS VS. OVERSOFTNESS.

Examples of overloudness:

2 1 1
/nómeinsúlte↓/ *¡No me insulte!* 'Don't insult me!' (spoken in anger)

2 11 1 2 1
/bengaká↓ apúrese↓/ *¡Venga acá! ¡Apúrese!* 'Come here! Make it snappy!' (command with annoyance)

1 21 1 2 2 2
/maríа↓ preparólakomída↑/ *¡María! ¿Preparó la comida?* 'Mary! Is dinner ready?' (to an inferior, at a distance)

Examples of oversoftness:

1 2 2 3 1 1
/debéras↑ kyéntelodíxo↓/ *¿De veras? ¿Quién te lo dijo?* 'Really? Who told you?' (secretive, but very much interested)

2 22 1 2 22 1 2 2
/míreseñór↓ podríablár|konelxéfe↑/ *Mire, señor, ¿podría hablar con el jefe?* 'Sir, could I ... perhaps ... see the manager?' (timid)

7.12. OVERHIGH VS. OVERLOW.

Examples of overhigh:

31 31 1 33 1 11
/sí↓ sí↓ ustéd|señór↓/ *Sí, sí, usted, señor.* 'Yeah, yeah, YOU!'

2 3 1 1 1 2 3 1
/kébrúto↓ péro|kébrúto↓/ *¡Qué bruto! Pero, ¡qué bruto!* 'How stupid! How stupid can you get!'

Examples of overlow:

1 11
/abér↓/ *¡A ver!* 'We'll see (about that).'

7.13. OVERFAST VS. OVERSLOW.

Examples of overfast:

1 2 1 1
/kwidádokonelkárro↓/ *¡Cuidado con el carro!* 'Look out for the car!' (warning of imminent danger)

2 1 1
/póngaselakamísa↓/ *¡Póngase la camisa!* 'Put on your shirt!' (as to a child, in irritation)

Examples of overslow:

2 2 2 1 1
/bíba|lapátrya↓/ *¡Viva la patria!* 'Long live the fatherland!' (for dramatic effect)

2 1 1 1 1 1 1
/bénga|miniñíto|bwéno↓/ *Venga, mi niñito bueno.* 'Come here, my little man.' (affectionately, as a priest speaking to a timid child)

7.14. OVERTENSE (rasp) VS. OVERLAX (openness).

Examples of overtense:

3 1 1 1 1
/kláro|pwésómbre↓/ *¡Claro! pues hombre.* 'Natch, man!'

2 1
/myérkoles↓/ *¡Miércoles!* 'Damn!'

Examples of overlax:

2 1 1 2 2 1 1
/nómedíga↓ nópwédesér↓/ *No me diga. No puede ser.* 'Really! It just can't be.' (shocked disbelief)

2 1 1
/kébá↓/ *¡Qué va!* 'Nonsense!' (incredible idea)

2 1 2 1 1 2 2 1 1 1 1
/á|sí↓ konmúčogústo|señóra↓/ *Ah, sí. Con mucho gusto, señora.* 'Oh yes. I'll be VERY pleased, ma'am.' (ingratiatingly polite)

7.15. DRAWLING VS. CLIPPING. By contrast with overslow and overfast, these are restricted to a single syllable; overslow and overfast are phenomena of TEMPO; these are phenomena of LENGTH or DURATION, still different from overall RATE of speech.

Examples of drawling (marked by italics):

2 1 1 11
/d*é*xemelo|nom*á*s↓/ *Déjemelo, no más.* 'Oh, well, just LEAVE it with me.'

2 2 1 2 1
/k*ó*mo|seleok*ú*rre↓/ *¡Cómo se le occurre!* 'HOW can you think THAT!'

Examples of clipping (marked by italics):

21 21
/s*í*↓/ /n*ó*↓/ *Sí. No.* 'Yep.' 'Nope.' (as on a telephone to signal that you are still listening)

7.16. SPREADING VS. SQUEEZING of the distance between pitch phonemes.

Examples of spreading:

3 2 3 2 2 3 1
/tánto|gústo|debérlo↓/ *¡Tanto gusto de verlo!* 'I'm so happy to see you!' (ingratiating)

3 1 1 3 1 1 3 1
/óla|mikerído|amígo↓/ *¡Hola, mi querido amigo!* 'Ah! My good friend!' (exaggerated politeness)

Examples of squeezing:

2 32 2 22
/kédeséa|señór|/ *¿Qué desea, señor ...?* 'Yes, sir ...' (uninterested clerk speaking)

7.17. OVERVOICING VS. DEVOICING (whisper).

Examples of overvoicing:

2 2 1 1 11
/démeótrotrágo|pués↓/ *Déme otro trago, pues.* 'Just gimme another drink.' (inebriated speaker)

Examples of devoicing:

2 11 1 1 1
/kétál|miàmorsíto↓/ *¿Qué tal? mi amorcito.* 'How goes it, baby?' (intimate whispering)

7.18. Frequently two or more of the vocal qualifiers occur simultaneously; certain combinations occur more frequently than others, e.g. overloud with overhigh, overslow with overlax, overloud with spreading, overloud with overtense, oversoft with drawl, overfast with clipping.

7.2. A second large class of supra-intonational features comprises the VOCAL DIFFERENTIATORS, features that are not extensions of elements microlinguistically structured and not paired. They usually extend over the entire utterance.

7.21. CRYING is usually accompanied by vocal qualifiers of stretching and drawling.

7.22. BREAKING is of three types: laughing or giggling, rhetorical with emotion, and quavering or tremolo, which is in effect incipient breaking.

7.23. CHANTING, as in a political rally (3 2 3 2 3 2 /má|tá|ló↓/ *¡Má-ta-lo!* 'Kill that bum!'), is necessarily accompanied by several varieties of shift and a number of vocal qualifiers, but the special rhythmic effect is more than the sum of the parts.

7.24. NASALIZATION over the whole utterance may occur in Spanish as a kind of irritated mockery or it may be a feature of a given speaker's entire speech.

7.25. FALSETTO occurs in mockery of a woman's speech by a man, and also in extreme irritation.

7.3. There is a residue class of features, normally discrete, which seem to have no place in the rest of the structure. These may be assigned to the class of VOCAL IDENTIFIERS.

7.31. The question signal that often appears after statements seems to belong in this class. We have observed at least four forms of it, and suspect that there are others: [é↑], [ę́↑], [ḿ↑], [ǫ́↑]. Some speakers interject it into the normal stream of utterance in the same way that English speakers will often interject *Huh?*, as though asking for confirmation when there is nothing to confirm.

7.32. The glottal stop appears before word-initial vowels, after word-final vowel nuclei, and simultaneous with stops in utterances where there is strong emphasis and where several vocal qualifiers are present, such as overloud, overtense, and overhigh.

7.4. A complete transcription of any stretch of utterance must symbolize both the phonemically relevant data and the vocalizations. We suggest abbreviations for the latter, to be placed at each end of the stretch during which they are present: LD overloud, SO oversoft, HI overhigh, LO overlow, FA overfast, SL overslow, TE overtense, LA overlax, DR drawling, CL clipping, SP spreading, SQ squeezing, OV overvoicing, DV devoicing, CR crying, BR breaking, CH chanting, NA nasalization, FO falsetto. The question signal and the glottal stop are to be symbolized conventionally. Three short stretches of utterance containing a variety of vocalizations are transcribed here by way of concluding this discussion:

3 11
LD TE DR ʔés DR tosí↓ TE LD — *¡Esto sí!* 'THIS is it!'

33 33 3 2 2 3 1
LD TE áyʔ | kéʔ | kósa | tan rrára↓ TE LD
¡Ay, qué cosa tan rara! 'Good Lord, what a strange turn of events!'

1 3 1 1 1
LD TE HI esʔpéreme | ómbre↓ HI TE LD
¡Espéreme, hombre! 'WAIT for me, man!'

⟦In 1950 I said ⟨(351)⟩ 'all phenomena ... which we find we cannot describe precisely with a finite number of absolute categories, we classify as non-linguistic elements of the real world and expel them from linguistic science.' Now it is appropriate to append the converse of that statement, more or less thus: 'As soon as we succeed in describing precisely, with a finite number of absolute categories, any coherent mass of speech-phenomena, we have incorporated that description into linguistic science.'

It would be possible either to let this stand so or to modify it by a certain kind of limitation which I wish to present first in figurative language: The new territory has not been annexed to linguistics, but has instead merely been associated with it as an autonomous commonwealth, unless it has been brought under the government prevailing in the old territory. What I am referring to is the fact that every item in a sentence is in construction with every other item, either directly or mediately (directly: morpheme to morpheme in a two-morpheme construction such as 'this man', phoneme to phoneme as /s/ to /t/ in the morpheme {stop}, etc.; mediately, as /s/ to /n/ in 'this man', or {the} to {nose} in 'The councillors all put their glasses on their noses'); that is to say, the hierarchic immediate-constituent structure of every sentence ultimately links each item of whatever rank in it with each other item of whatever rank. Now if we adopt this sort of limitation, we should say that intonation, certainly, has been incorporated into the grammar of the language, and thus into linguistics, through such work as that reprinted above; but that the vocalizations have not. A sentence minus its intonation is not a sentence; but subtracting all the vocalizations still leaves a sentence. The intonation is in construction with the residue of the sentence, with exclusion-relations thereto like those found all through grammar; the vocalizations are 'added to or imposed upon' the sentence; indeed, according to the above paper, they may be thus added to 'any given utterance' ⟨(406)⟩, which means that there is no relation of the sorts that are characterized by exclusion and are therefore to be called grammatical ⟨(354)⟩.

I do not propose this notion as a mere quibble, even though it has for me a certain charm as such. Rather, I attach great importance to the fact that the vocalizations seem to be the next area we come to in extending the coverage of linguistic science in the way spoken of in my first paragraph above, so that if this area cannot be truly incorporated within the science as so far defined we have learned that our science has indeed reached its ultimate limit here.⟧

COMMENTS ON CERTAIN TECHNICAL TERMS

Though the entries here will serve to some extent as an index, it should be remembered that that is not their purpose and that no serious attempt was made to achieve exhaustive coverage. Figures before : are abbreviated dates, those after : are page-numbers; 57 (for 1957, but regardless of actual date of writing, mostly in 1956) labels the editor's comments; and to obviate misunderstanding the references to the ideas of de Saussure from the first paper are not marked 47 but are marked with page-numbers in the usual ⦅⦆.

ACCENTUAL and junctural are the two kinds of suprasegmental phone 42:100

ACCOUNTABILITY > total accountability 47:235

ALLOMORPH: implicit in 47:229 fn 7, current since 48:258 fn 13, replacing 'morpheme alternant' (42:109) for convenience: 53:379ff etc.

ALLOPHONES: 'sounds comprising a single phoneme' 41:93; current usage is broad, despite 42:101, even replacing 'phone', so that Harris could even say 'breaking an allophone into two phonemes' 44:126

ALTERNANCE was de Saussure's term ⦅6⦆ for

ALTERNATION in morphology; this latter term is used instead of 'variation' in phonology as a more dignified term e.g. as needed in 42:102

ANALYTIC PROCEDURE in the practical sense is 'a trial-and-error process' 42:107, 57:108, 57:228

ARBITRARY: de Saussure ⦅5⦆ and echoes since

ARCHIPHONEME: European (Prague School &c) term usually rejected in America as obfuscation 42:101, 56:405

CANONICAL FORM of morphemes 47:236

CHANGE is a term used mostly for phonological differences between successive epochs of a language; under de Saussure's principles ⦅9, 12⦆ change is mysterious; defined 26:30, discussed 36:81ff

CHANGE-POINTS in articulation 42:98

CLASS: term from (mathematical) logic frequently used since 34:40 throughout linguistics

COMMON SEMANTIC DISTINCTIVENESS 48:259

COMMUTATION: term used in 'glossematics' 51:359

COMPARATIVE linguistics, method, reconstruction 48:281ff, 48:290ff, 50:303ff

COMPLEMENTARY DISTRIBUTION (no hint of this in de Saussure ⦅4⦆) has been a key term in phonemic theory since 34:35, thus 42:100, 50:330

COMPONENTS: this term interchanges with 'categories' or 'classes' as the point of view shifts: if item A belongs to classes x, y, and z, and item B belongs to classes v, w, and x, then A and B can be said to share the component x, and e.g. A is said to be composed of x and other components (here: y and z); inverting this derivation is felt by many to be fallacious; 44:124ff, 48:272ff, 51:364ff

CONDITIONED phonetic qualities 50:331

CONGRUITY > pattern congruity

CONSTELLATION: glossematic term 51:361

CONSTITUENT, CONSTITUTE 47:188

CONSTRUCTION 47:193, 54:388ff, 57:418

CONTINUOUS reality vs linguistic discreteness: de Saussure ⦅1⦆ and ever since, e.g. 50:350ff

CONTRASTIVE 42:100, 106

CORRESPONDENCES, sets of, in comparative work 50:298, 50:305

DESCRIPTIVE: a term too easily misunderstood by outsiders, used in linguistics (as in 'd. botany' or 'd. geometry') to denote the stating of all that matters and no more; preferred in American usage to the safer term 'structural' 57:96

DETERMINATION: glossematic term 51:361

DETERMINED and DETERMINING phonetic features —42:103, 105, reworded definition 47:217, different (narrower) definition 50:331 (cf. 'conditioned')

DIACHRONIC (de Saussure term) 48:282f

DIAPHONE: supradialectal phonemic class 34:39

DISCONTINUOUS MORPHEMES 54:392

DISTINCTIVE 'making a difference' has long been a key term in phonemic theory, but definitions vary —42:99, reworded 47:217, otherwise 50:331 and 51:364; if a child says [t'ap] for top but [tap] for stop, Hockett would say that he has at least one of the distinctive features of adult [stap] stop and would recognize non-aspiration as a distinctive feature of the adult word, while others would say that the non-aspiration here is non-distinctive, being determined or conditioned

DISTRIBUTION 34:33, vs identity 51:360

DOMAIN 42:103

DRIFT 48:287, cf. 57:84

EMPTY MORPH 47:236, 48:256, 57:242, 53:379ff

EXPANSION and MODEL 47:187

FEATURES 35:61ff, 42:99, 57:80

FOCUS and ENVIRONMENT 47:189

FRAME OF REFERENCE 42:107—often said today

FREE (alternation, variation) 34:33, 42:99, 102, &c

FUNCTION as a glossematic term 51:359

FUNCTION 26:29, 35:60, 57:138

GLOSSEMATICS 51:358

GOD'S-TRUTH 57:80

HIERARCHICAL STRUCTURE is a primitive 54:390f

HISTORICAL PHONOLOGY 50:299

HOCUS-POCUS 57:80

ICs = IMMEDIATE CONSTITUENTS 47:186ff
INTERNAL RECONSTRUCTION 46:139 48:285 53:380
INTERDEPENDENCE: glossematic term 51:361
INTERSECTION (= overlapping in one sense) 41:93ff
INVARIANT 57:280
JUNCTURAL PHONES 42:100, 103
JUNCTURE 57:216: because reference today is apt to be to junctural phones or phonemes, Hall has proposed saying 'disjuncture' instead, and some have said 'zero juncture' for 'close transition'; cf. 47:201f, 47:212, 47:218, 56:406ff
LANGUAGE 26:26f
LANGUE vs PAROLE 57:18, de Saussure ((2, 9–11))
LONG COMPONENTS 44:127–34
MACRO-PHONEME 35:73, 57:80
MARKER 54:393–6–8
MATHEMATICS and mathematical (or symbolic) logic have powerfully influenced American linguistics: at least Bloomfield, Chao, Hockett, Harris, Wells, Joos and probably several others here represented have been either accomplished in the field or relatively advanced students, and have so modeled descriptive linguistics in that image that it has been called 'a mathematics' 50:349ff
MERGING, MERGER 46:139ff
METALINGUISTICS=METALANGUAGE? 51:358
MICRO-PHONEME 35:73, cf. 57:80
MINIMAL 'least in bulk, least that is found' ('minimum' 26:27ff), 35:69ff; 'minimal pairs' like hit vs sit are so named for showing a minimal phonetic difference (here [h] vs [s]) or phonemic contrast (/h/ vs /s/) and are thus crucial, but because not always available are substituted for by non-minimal 'contrastive pairs' like vision vs fission as evidence for /ž/ vs /š/ 42:100
MINUS (subtractive) MORPHEMES 50:326f, 54:394
MODEL and EXPANSION 47:187
MORPH: term invented by Hockett 47:230, 53:379
MORPHEME: old sense (e.g. de Saussure) ((5)); early American sense 42:109f; current sense 47:230 (equivalent to 'morpheme unit' 42:110); morpheme alternants (42:110) now often called allomorphs 47:229; morphemics or morphemic analysis defined 47:229, 53:379, surveyed 48:255ff
MORPHOPHONEMES are not often mentioned nowadays for fear of seeming to ascribe reality to an ancillary notion; cf. 39:88, 53:379
MORPHOPHONEMICS is the usual term for all the phonemic aspects of morphemic discussion which must be covered before the morphemes can safely be discussed abstractly, or to emphasize that any phonemic discussion must be protected against morphemic (or semantic) intrusion (57:92); definitions 42:107, 47:230, 47:251, 50:315 & fn. 2; but 'morphophonemic (writing, &c)' can still mean 'using (&c) morphophonemes' 44:137 fn. 23
NEUTRALIZATION (cf. 'archiphonemes') 42:101
NON-CONTRASTIVE 47:233, 50:330
NON-INTERSECTION (cf. 'intersection') 42:100
NORMAL TRANSITION ('close' tr.) 55:400
NUCLEAR, NUCLEUS 48:275; nowadays 'nucleus' is usually short for 'syllabic nucleus'
OPEN JUNCTURE 56:405 is the classical term for the phonemic element now usually called 'juncture' (q.v.); it implies the phonetic features of...
OPEN TRANSITION (cf. 'normal transition'), i.e. a peculiar way of uttering two successive phones so that they don't quite seem to follow in the closest possible succession 55:400ff
OPPOSITION: de Saussure's term ((7)) for the way items are linguistically different if they are, i.e. in that the speakers oppose them to each other; not often used today, but 'distinctive o.' 51:364
OVERLAPPING 41:93ff, an unsafe word for 'intersecting' (belonging to two classes at once); also, 'simultaneous (partly or wholly)' 53:380
PAROLE (cf. 'langue') denotes usage, not system
PARADIGM: glossematic term 51:359
PARADIGM in traditional sense 54:386
PARTNER in construction 54:388 fn. 6, 396
PATTERN (especially of the language, vs 'structure' of the utterance 54:387 fn. 3) was de Saussure's 'structure', namely all that is true of a language because of the oppositions in it, much favored by workers who delight in symmetries and parallelisms, so that they speak of 'pattern arguments' 55:400 and value 'patterning' 55:401; Bloomfield 26:29 alludes approvingly to the Sapir term but builds nothing upon it; for Sapir 25:19ff, as for de Saussure, the pattern of oppositions was the ultimate reality; oppositions converge into his 'points in the pattern' 25:21, 24; being often spoken of, these 'pattern-points' become real for some today, so that if two dialects share an 'over-all pattern' (57:228) they are also said to share all the pattern-points thereof even though one dialect is not yet known to have used one of the points, as for instance when my wife's English is said to imply (or even possess) an /ɔ/ phoneme although she has no /ɔ/ words (she has caught = cot /kat/)
PATTERN CONGRUITY has never been defined with any precision to my knowledge but is intuitively clear enough to serve in practice (none the less for being circular 35:66) as a criterion for a good total (phonological) description 34:35 42:100 56:405
PHONE 'sound considered as item in utterance' 34:38, is a better word than 'sound' only if phonemics is in question 42:100; not used by everyone today, it tends to signify 'sound as allophone' 50:330f
PHONEME: read all the phonological articles! — such de Saussure statements ((2)) as tend to characterize phonemes have had far less permanent influence than the two remarks that their number (in a particular language) is sharply definite ((4)) and that they are constituted by their relations: for them, to be is to be related ((6f)); of these, the first seems more useful today